Long Island's Prominent Families in the Town of East Hampton: Their Estates and Their Country Homes

Raymond Edward and Judith Ader Spinzia

VirtualBookworm

College Station, Texas

2020

"Long Island's Prominent Families in the Town of East Hampton: Their Estates and Their Country Homes" by Raymond E. and Judith A. Spinzia. ISBN 978-1-951985-62-2.

Library of Congress Control Number: 2020920157

Published 2020 by Virtualbookworm.com Publishing Inc., P.O. Box 9949, College Station, TX 77842, US.
© 2020, Raymond E. and Judith A. Spinzia. All rights reserved. No part of this publication may be reproduced, stored in a retrieval system, or transmitted in any form or by any means, electronic, mechanical, recording or otherwise, without the prior written permission of Raymond E. and Judith A. Spinzia.

Also by Raymond E. and Judith A. Spinzia

Long Island: A Guide to New York's Suffolk and Nassau Counties
(*with* Kathryn Spinzia Rayne)

Long Island's Prominent North Shore Families:
Their Estates and Their Country Homes, Volumes I and II

Long Island's Prominent South Shore Families:
Their Estates and Their Country Homes
in the Towns of Babylon and Islip

Long Island's Prominent Families
in the Town of Hempstead:
Their Estates and Their Country Homes

Long Island's Prominent Families
in the Town of Southampton:
Their Estates and Their Country Homes

Absence of Photographs

The original manuscript included 684 photographs. Requests to obtain permission to reproduce photographs from organizations and individuals were, with just four exceptions, unanswered. As a result, we have been forced to publish this book, the sixth volume in the *Long Island's Prominent Families: Their Estates and Their Country Homes* series, without photographs.

We apologize to our readers. Obviously the value of the book would have been greatly enhanced by the inclusion of photographs.

The original, unpublished manuscript with photographs will become part of the "Raymond Edward and Judith Ader Spinzia Long Island Estates and Tiffany Collection." It will eventually be archived with the research materials from all of our books and placed on deposit in C. W. Post College of Long Island University, Special Collections, for the use of researchers in the future.

The authors are sincerely indebted to the following for their assistance:

Steve Boerner, Librarian/Archivist, The East Hampton Library, East Hampton, NY

George William Fisher, Photographic Project Manager, Nassau County Village Restoration, Department of Parks, Recreation, and Museums, Old Bethpage Village Restoration, Old Bethpage, NY

Miles Jaffe, AIA, architect

Gary Lawrance, AIA, architect

Michael Moran, Michael Moran Photography, Inc.

Bruce Dean Nagel, Bruce D. Nagel & Partners Architects

Raymond Edward and Judith Ader Spinzia

Even though an individual may not have used Sr., Jr., I, II, etc., they have been added to the surnames in an attempt to designate relationships and alleviate confusion. In some instances, birth dates have been calculated using the age at the time of death as given in *The New York Times* obituary. In addition, years of birth may not be totally accurate as some people became progressively younger in subsequent census records.

The exact street address of some houses could not be determined due to the diminution of the estates by subdivision. In these cases, the road on which a major portion of the estate bordered has been recorded as the address. It should also be noted that some of the subsequent owners may not have lived in the estate's main house but rather in a service building that had been converted into a residence. To aid in tracing the estate properties, these owners have been included in the hope that this will prove useful to future researchers.

Families that rented cottages for the summer were traditionally a part of the social fabric of the Town of East Hampton, and for that matter to that of the whole East End. This has been verified by their inclusion in the various Social Registers consulted. It is possible that they rented for the season or for several seasons which is a phenomenon in the Hamptons that is not seen to the same degree in other estate areas of the Island. Especially in the summer the Social Register then, as it does today, functioned as a telephone directory and as a way of locating people for social functions and business connections. There has always been the concept of the residents and the "summer people" which has contributed to an amorphous and fluctuating society uncommon to the other estate areas. We have included these people even though we could not always confirm street addresses. Although some will say that they were just visiting, we strongly believe that they contributed to the area's fabric of social interaction.

The Spinzias

Table of Contents

Absence of Photographs iv

Acknowledgments iv

Factors Applicable to Usage v

Surname Entries A – Z 1

Appendices:

    Architects 651

    Civic Activists 670

    Estate Names 681

    Landscape Architects 691

    Maiden Names 697

    Occupations 733

    Rehabilitative Secondary Uses of Surviving Estate Houses . . . 754

    Statesmen and Diplomats Who Resided in East Hampton . . . 755

    Village Locations of Estates 758

    Biographical Sources Consulted 768

    Maps Consulted for Estate Locations 769

About the Authors 770

People disappear into the shadows of the past . . .

Abbe, James Edward, Jr. (1912-1999)

Occupation(s):	professional photographer
	merchant - president, James Abbe Gallery, Oyster Bay and East Hampton (antiques)
	educator - taught photography, Pratt Institute, Brooklyn
Marriage(s):	M/1 ____
	M/2 – 1946-1999 – Kathryn McLaughlin (1919-2014)
	- professional photographer
	writer - co-authored, with her sister Frances,
	Stars of the Twenties Observed by James Abbe, 1974;
	Twins on Twins, 1980;
	Twin Lives in Photography, 2011
	Civic Activism: clerk, Jericho Friends Meeting, Jericho, NY;
	trustee, Friends Academy, Locust Valley, NY
Address:	654 Old Montauk Highway, Montauk
Name of estate:	*Abbey Cottage*
Year of construction:	1940s
Style of architecture:	Beach Cottage
Architect(s):	
Landscape architect(s)	
House extant:	no; demolished 2014*
Historical notes:	

   The two-bedroom, one-bath, 600-square-foot house was built by James Edward Abbe, Jr. from salvaged wood taken from an East Hampton Dominy house and paneling from old sailing ships.
   He was the son of James Edward and Phyllis Edwards Abbe, Sr.
   Kathryn McLaughlin Abbe was the daughter of Francis and Kathryn McLaughlin of Brooklyn and Wallingford, CT.
   James Edward and Kathryn McLaughlin Abbe, Jr.'s son Thomas resides in Brookville. Their son Eli married Jessica Fredella Arner, the daughter of Leonard Arner, and resides in Palo Alto, CA. Their daughter Lucinda married Alan J. Willes and resides in WY.
   *Television personality Bill O'Reilly purchased the house and demolished it.

Abbott, Henry Hurlbut (1870-1930)

Occupation(s):	attorney - a founder and partner, Breed, Abbott, and Morgan
Civic Activism:	vice president, Maidstone Club, East Hampton
Marriage(s):	1896-1929 – Florence Louise Call (1873-1929)

- writer -   *The Poems of Florence Call Abbott*, 1929; poetry published in periodicals

   Civic Activism: vice president, Winifred Wheeler Day Nursery; president, Free Library of East Hampton; suffragist*

Address:	Georgica Road [Briar Patch Road], East Hampton
Name of estate:	*Briar Patch*
Year of construction:	1921
Style of architecture:	
Architect(s):	
Landscape architect(s)	
House extant: unconfirmed	
Historical notes:	

    The house, originally named *Briar Patch*, was built by Henry Hurlbut Abbott on property he purchased in 1920. [*The Brooklyn Daily Eagle* December 13, 1920, p. 12.]

    The *Long Island Society Register, 1929* lists Henry H. and Florence Call Abbott as residing at *Briar Patch* on Georgica Road, East Hampton.

    He was the son of James Hamlin and Elizabeth Andrews Abbott of Chicago, IL.

    Florence Louise Call Abbott was the daughter of Henry E. and Emma Jane Lewis Call.

    Henry Hurlbut and Florence Louise Call Abbott's son Paul, who married Elise Everitt and, later, Virginia Bruce Loney, resided at *Wehold* in Southampton and *Cloverfields* in Lloyd Harbor. [*See* Spinzia, *Long Island's Prominent Families in the Town of Southampton* and *Long Island's Prominent North Shore Families, vol. I* – Abbott entries.] Their daughter Jane married George du Pont Pratt, Jr., the son of George du Pont and Helen Deming Sherman Pratt, Sr. of *Killenworth* in Glen Cove. [*See* Spinzia, *Long Island's Prominent North Shore Families, vol. II*– Pratt entry.]

    The estate was purchased in 1930 by Dr. Shepard Krech, Sr., who built a new house on the property which he called *Briar Path*. [*The Brooklyn Daily Eagle* April 5, 1931, p. 22.]

    *For other Long Islanders involved in the suffrage movement *see* Raymond E. Spinzia, "Winning the Franchise: Long Island Activists in the Fight for Woman's Suffrage and Their Opponents, Long Island's Anti-Suffragists." wwwspinzialongislandestates.com.

Adair, Dr. Frank Earl (1887-1981)

Occupation(s):	physician -	cancer surgeon, Memorial Hospital, NY (later, Sloan–Kettering Institute for Cancer Research)*;
	educator -	assistant professor, clinical surgery, Cornell University, Medical School, NYC
	writer -	numerous articles in medical journals; wrote chapter in *Textbook of Surgery*; wrote chapter in *Treatment of Cancer*; editor, *Cancer*, 1931

Civic Activism: president, American Society for Control of Cancer;
president, American Cancer Society;
chairman, cancer committee, American College of Surgeons;
founder, Adair Fund for Cancer Research;
president, Clinical Medical Association, 1925

Marriage(s): M/1 – 1922-div. – Dorothy Wilde
M/2 – 1935-1965 – Marion Hopkinson (1906-1965)
- entertainers and associated professions -
radio voice of Mrs. Franklin Delano Roosevelt on "March of Time"
Civic Activism:
president and chairman of board, Manhattan and The Bronx United Hospital Fund;
vice-chairman, social service committee, Memorial Hospital, NYC;
member, social service committee, New York Eye and Ear Infirmary, NYC;
director, Knickerbocker Greys (military youth organization);
vice-president and director, George Junior Republic, Freeville, NY;
trustee, Manhattan School of Music, NYC;
president, Adair Fund for Cancer Research;
president, American Cancer Society

Address: Georgica Road and Crossings, East Hampton
Name of estate: *Sherwood*
Year of construction: 1903
Style of architecture: Shingle
Architect(s): John Custis Lawrence designed the house (for S. F. Johnson)
Peter Cook, 1992 alterations (for Shafran)
Landscape architect(s):
Builder: George A. Eldredge
House extant: yes
Historical notes:

    The thirty-three-room, thirteen-bedroom, and nine-bath house, originally named *Onadune*, was built by Servetus Fisher Johnson. It was later owned by his daughter Edith and son-in-law Edward de Clifford Chisholm, who continued to call it *Onadune*, and was purchased in 1940 by Adair who called it *Sherwood*.
    He was the son of Dr. Samuel Graham and Mrs. Ella Patterson Adair of Beverly, OH.
    Dorothy Wilde Adair was the daughter of George M. Wilde. She had previously been married to Earl Joseph Moon.
    Marion Hopkinson Adair was the daughter of Ernest and Elizabeth Barnes Hopkinson of New York City. Marion had previously been married to John Brooks.
    Dr. Frank Earl and Mrs. Marion Hopkinson Adair's son Robert, a bachelor, died in 1968. Their son Michael married Joanne Ruth Bowers, the daughter of Philip J. Bowers II, who resided at *The Bowerie* in Pottersville, NJ.
    *During his career Adair performed over 17,000 operations. [*The New York Times* January 5, 1982, p. D19.]
    In 1992 the house was purchased by Irving Shafan.
    Alterations were made to the house in 1907 and 1992.

Adams, Charles Henry (1824-1902)

Occupation(s):	attorney
	industrialist - president and owner, Watervliet Kitting Mill, Cohoes, NY; president and owner, Egberts Woolen Mills
	politician - first mayor, Cohoes, NY, 1870-1872; member, New York State Assembly, 1858; member, New York State Senate, 1872-1873; member, United States Congress, 1875-1877
	financier - president, Bank of Cohoes, Cohoes, NY
Civic Activism:	trustee and president, Cohoes Water Board; a founder and director, Maidstone Club, East Hampton
Marriage(s):	M/1 – 1853-1866 – Elizabeth Platt (1830-1866)
	M/2 – 1877-1902 – Judith Crittenden Coleman (1845-1929)
Address:	30 Lee Avenue, East Hampton
Name of estate:	
Year of construction:	1891
Style of architecture:	Queen Anne
Architect(s):	William B. Tuthill designed house (for C. H. Adams)*
	Aymar Embury II designed 1930s alterations (for Mairs)
Landscape architect(s):	
Builder:	Conrad & Shott, 1931 addition (for Mairs)
House extant:	yes

Historical notes:

   The house was built by Charles Henry Adams.

   He was the son of Henry Adams and a descendant of Presidents John Adams and John Quincy Adams.

   Elizabeth Platt Adams was the daughter of William Barnes and Sarah C. Cookingham Platt of Rhinebeck, NY.

   Charles Henry and Elizabeth Platt Adams' daughter Sarah was an infant at the time of her death. Their daughter Mary married Robert Johnston. Their son William married Katherine Elseffer, the daughter of Jacob W. and Delia Eliza Bonesteel Elseffer.

   Judith Crittenden Coleman Adams was the daughter of Chapman and Ann Mary Butler Crittenden Coleman, Sr.

   Charles Henry and Judith Crittenden Adams' daughter Judith married Edmund Converse, Jr., the son of Edmund and Jessie M. Green Converse, Sr. of Manhattan.

   *Tuthill also designed Manhattan's Carnegie Hall.

   The house was later owned by Dr. James M. Hodson. In 1920 it was purchased by Olney Blanchard Mairs, Sr. [*The East Hampton Star* September 12, 1930, p. 7.]

   The house was for sale in 2011. The asking price was $25.75 million.

Adams, John Cranford (1903-1986)

Occupation(s):	educator - associate professor of English, Cornell University, Ithaca, NY, 1943-1944;
	president, Hofstra College (now, Hofstra University), Hempstead, NY, 1944-1964
	writer - *Globe Playhouse: Its Design and Construction*
Civic Activism:	member, New York State Examinations Board, 1945-1952;
	member, joint committee on educational television, American Council on Education, 1953-1957;
	second vice-council, American Council on Education, 1957-1958;
	trustee, Metropolitan Educational Television Association, 1954-1986;
	commissioner, Institutions for Higher Education, Middle States Association, 1956-1986;
	member, Commission on Non-Tax Supported Colleges and Universities of the State of New York, 1957-1986;
	trustee, Abilities Inc.;
	trustee, American Red Cross;
	member, advisory council, Nassau County Planning Committee Association;
	member, advisory board, United States Merchant Marine Academy, Kings Point;
	trustee, Modern Language Association, 1955-1986;
	president, secretary and treasurer, Association of Colleges and Universities of the State of New York;
	trustee, Metropolitan Educational Association;
	member, advisory board, East Hampton Free Library
Marriage(s):	1929-1986 – Alice deBois Murray (1904-1995)
Address:	128 Egypt Lane, East Hampton
Name of estate:	
Year of construction:	1958
Style of architecture:	
Architect(s):	Aymar Embury designed the house (for J. C. Adams)
Landscape architect(s):	
House extant:	unconfirmed
Historical notes:	

    The house was built by John Cranford Adams. [*The East Hampton Star* July 16, 1959, p. 16, and March 9, 1961, p. 8.]
    He was the son of John Davis and Mary Pickavant Cranford Adams of Memphis, NY.
    Alice deBois Murray Adams was the daughter of Charles R. Murray of Glasgow, Scotland.
    John Cranford and Alice deBois Murray Adams' daughter Joan married Norcross Shelton, Jr. of Dunkirk, NY. Their son Charles married Lucy Porritt Green, the daughter of Valentine John Green of Darien, CT.
    In 1963 the house was purchased by Virginia Pulleyn Kingsley. [*The East Hampton Star* November 28, 1963, p. 4.] In 1970 Kingsley sold it to John K. Lundberg. [*The East Hampton Star* May 28, 1970, p. 4.]

Agnew, Dr. Cornelius Rea, Sr. (1830-1888)

Occupation(s):	physician - surgeon, Eye and Ear Infirmary of New York, NYC; New York State Surgeon General, 1858; Surgeon General, New York Militia, 1858
	educator - professor, diseases of eye and ear, College of Physicians and Surgeons, 1869-1888
	writer - *A Contribution to the Surgery of Divergent Squint; Trephing the Cornea to Remove a Foreign Body; Canthoplasty As a Remedy in Certain Diseases of the Eye*
Civic Activism:	a founder, United States Sanitary Commission;
	one of four founders, Union League Club, NYC;
	medical director, New York State Volunteer Hospital during the Civil War;
	a founder, Brooklyn Eye and Ear Hospital, 1868;
	a founder, Manhattan Eye and Ear Hospital, 1869;
	manager, New York State Hospital for the Insane, Poughkeepsie, NY;
	trustee and president, New York City School Board;
	trustee, Columbia University, NYC;
	president, New York State Medical Society;
	secretary, Sanitary Reform Association, NYC
Marriage(s):	1856-1888 – Mary Nash (1830-1918)
	- Civic Activism: member, New York City Board of Education
Address:	De Forest Road, Montauk
Name of estate:	
Year of construction:	1883
Style of architecture:	Beach Cottage
Architect(s):	McKim, Mead & White designed the house
Landscape architect(s):	Frederick Law Olmsted designed the site plan
Builder:	Mead and Taft

House extant: yes
Historical notes:

    The house is one of the Montauk Association's "Seven Sisters." It was owned by Dr. Cornelius Rea Agnew, Sr. He was the son of William and Elizabeth Thomson Agnew of Manhattan.
    Mary Nash Agnew was the daughter of Lora Nash of New York City.
    Dr. Cornelius Rea and Mrs. Mary Nash Agnew, Sr.'s daughter Anne married Samuel Sloan Auchincloss, Sr., the son of Edgar Sterling and Maria Sloan Auchincloss and resided at *Whale Acres* in Lawrence. [*See* Spinzia, *Long Island's Prominent Families in the Town of Hempstead* – Auchincloss entry.] Their daughter Katherine married Allen Butler Talcott. Their son Cornelius Rea Agnew, Jr. married Blanche Bean, the daughter of Curtis Coe Bean and resided in Manhattan.
    The house was later owned by Arthur Brisbane; L. W. Miller; Grant Adams; Erik Eastman; and, then, by Hazanne Smith, who restored the house after it was damaged by a fire in 1992.

Akin, Robert Macomber, Jr. (1904-1989)

Occupation(s):	industrialist - president and chairman of board, Hudson International Conductors (high temperature conductor manufacturing firm) (merged into Phelps Dodge Corp, 1989)
Civic Activism:	chairman of board, National Security Industrial Association; president, Naval War College Foundation; a founder, Phelps Memorial Hospital, North Tarrytown, NY; vice-president, Sleepy Hollow Country Club, Scarborough, NY
Marriage(s):	Elizabeth Denton (1904-1994)
Address:	44 Foxboro Road, Montauk
Name of estate:	*Hilltop House*
Year of construction:	1927
Style of architecture:	Colonial Revival
Architect(s):	Arthur B. Wood designed the house (for Fisher)
Landscape architect(s):	
House extant:	yes
Historical notes:	

The six-bedroom, six-and-a-half-bath, 8,000-square-foot house was built by Carl Graham Fisher, Sr. It was subsequently owned by Akin, who named it *Hilltop House*.

The Blue Book of The Hamptons, 1973 lists Robert M. and Elizabeth Denton Akin, Jr. as residing at *Hilltop House* in Montauk Point [Montauk].

He was the son of Robert Macomber and Charlotte Gertrude Gardner Akin, Sr. of Ossining, NY.

Robert Macomber and Elizabeth Denton Akin, Jr.'s son William married Carol Sorenson and resided in Montauk. Their son Robert Macomber Akin III, the noted race car driver, married Susan Ellen Lloyd and resided in Sleepy Hollow, NY.

In 2015 the house and 7.6 acres were for sale. The asking price was $10.5 million.

Albee, Edward Franklin, III (1928-2016)

Occupation(s):	writer - playwright*:

        The Zoo Story, 1958;
        The Death of Bessie Smith, 1959;
        The Sandbox, 1959;
        Fam and Yam, 1959;
        The American Dream, 1960;
        Who's Afraid of Virginia Woolf?, 1961-1962;
        The Ballad of the Sad Cafe, 1963;
        Tiny Alice, 1964;
        Malcolm, 1965;
        A Delicate Balance, 1966;
        Breakfast at Tiffany's, 1966;
        Everything in the Garden, 1967;
        Box and *Quotations from Chairman Mao Tse-Tung*, 1968;
        All Over, 1971;
        Seascape, 1974;
        Listening, 1975;
        Counting the Ways, 1976;
        The Lady from Dubuque, 1977-1979;
        Lolita, 1981;
        The Man Who Had Three Arms, 1981;
        Finding the Sun, 1983;
        Marriage Play, 1986-1987;
        Three Tall Women, 1990-1991;
        The Lorca Play, 1992;
        Fragments, 1993;
        The Play About the Baby, 1996;
        Occupant, 2001;
        The Goat or Who is Sylvia?, 2002;
        Knock! Knock! Who's There!?, 2003;
        Peter & Jerry, 2004 (retitled *At Home At the Zoo*, 2009);
        Me Myself and I, 2007;
essayist, *Stretching My Mind: Essays, 1960-2005*, 2005

Civic Activism:	founder and president, Edward F. Albee Foundation (maintains The William Flanagan Memorial Creative Persons Center—"The Barn"—a seasonal colony for writers, artists, and composers in Montauk)
Marriage(s):	bachelor
Address:	Old Montauk Highway, Montauk
Name of estate:	
Year of construction:	
Style of architecture:	Contemporary
Architect(s):	
Landscape architect(s):	
Builder:	
House extant:	yes
Historical notes:	

  Edward Franklin Albee III purchased the house in 1961 for $40,000.
  He is the adopted son of Reed A. and Frances Cotter Albee of Larchmont, NY.
  *Albee received the Pulitzer Prize for drama for *A Delicate Balance*, *Seascape*, and *Three Tall Women*. *Who's Afraid of Virginia Woolf?* was selected by the Pulitzer Prize drama jury but their selection was overruled by the advisory committee.
  In 1985 Albee was inducted into the American Theatre Hall of Fame.
  After Albee's death, ownership of his Montauk house was transferred to the Edward F. Albee Foundation.
  The 2,970-square-foot, four-bed, three-full-and-two-half-bath house and 2.8 acres were for sale in 2018. The asking price was $20 million.
  In 2019 it was purchased by Ralph Lauren.

Alcott, Clarence Frank (1886-1957)

Occupation(s):	financier - member, Luce, Banks, and Weeks (stock brokerage firm)
Civic Activism:	secretary and vice president, Maidstone Club, East Hampton
Marriage(s):	1908-1957 – Lucie Arrington Burke (1885-1961)
Address:	Lily Pond Lane, East Hampton
Name of estate:	
Year of construction:	1915
Style of architecture:	Cotswold
Architect(s):	Harrie T. Lindeberg designed the house (for Alcott)
Landscape architect(s):	
Builder:	Frank B. Smith
House extant: yes	
Historical notes:	

The house was built by Clarence Frank Alcott.

The *Long Island Society Register, 1929* lists Clarence and Lucie A. Burke Alcott as residing on Lily Pond Lane, East Hampton.

Lucie Arrington Burke Alcott was the daughter of Frank Gaius and Joanna Belzora Arrington Burke, Sr. of New York. Lucie's brother Oscar, who resided in East Hampton, married Edna Marston, Helen Margaret Kelly, Cicely Mary Hilger, and Margaret Stone.

Clarence Frank and Lucie Arrington Burke Alcott's daughter Lucie married Dr. James Craig Joyner, the son of Patrick Henry Joyner of Princeton, NC, and resided in East Hampton. Their daughter Jane married Jay Holmes, the son of Dr. Christian R. and Mrs. Bettie Fleishman Holmes, Sr. of *The Chimneys* in Sands Point and resided at *Shady Brook Farm* in Poughquag, NY, and East Hampton. Jane later married Dudley DeVore Roberts, Jr. with whom she continued to reside in East Hampton. [*See* Spinzia, *Long Island's Prominent North Shore Families, vol. I* – Holmes entry.]

Aldrich, Malcolm Pratt, Sr. (1900-1986)

Occupation(s):	capitalist - director, Southern Pacific Railroad
	financier - president and chairman of board, Commonwealth Fund (philanthropic foundation);
	director, Equitable Life Assurance Society of the United States;
	director, New York Trust Co.
	statesman - special assistant to Secretary of the Navy for Air, 1942-1945
Civic Activism:	trustee, American Museum;
	trustee, Metropolitan Museum of Art, NYC
Marriage(s):	1925-1986 – Ella Fisher Buffington (1900-1992)
Address:	66 James Lane, East Hampton
Name of estate:	*Pondside*
Year of construction:	
Style of architecture:	Shingle
Architect(s):	
Landscape architect(s):	
House extant: yes	
Historical notes:	

The *Social Register Summer, 1950* lists Malcolm P. and Ella Buffington Aldrich [Sr.] as residing at *Pondside* on James Lane, East Hampton. *The Blue Book of The Hamptons, 1965* lists the address as 66 James Lane, East Hampton.

He was the son of Stanley A. and Jane S. Pratt Aldrich of Fall River, MA.

Ella Fisher Buffington Aldrich was the daughter of James Buffington, Sr. of Fall River, MA.

Malcolm Pratt and Ella Fisher Buffington Aldrich, Sr.'s daughter Joan married John Howard Barnes Knowlton, the son of Clifford Freeman Knowlton, and resided in Waterford, CT. Their daughter Shirley married Gordon Woodward Daiger, the son of John Matthias Daiger of Washington, DC, and resided in Winter Park, FL. Their son Malcolm Pratt Aldrich, Jr. married Nancy Adams, the daughter of John T. Adams, and resided in NYC.

Aldrich, Spencer Wyman (1882-1948)

Occupation(s):	financier - stockbroker
Marriage(s):	M/1 – 1911 – Imogen Gaither (b. 1889) M/2 – Lillian B. Turk (d. 1972)
Address:	12 Dunemere Lane, East Hampton
Name of estate:	
Year of construction:	
Style of architecture:	
Architect(s):	
Landscape architect(s):	
House extant:	unconfirmed
Historical notes:	

   Spencer Wyman Aldrich was the son of Spencer and Harriet Holley Dall Aldrich of *Windermere* in Bay Shore. [*See* Spinzia, *Long Island's Prominent South Shore Families* – Aldrich entry.] His sister Louise married William Christen Meissner and resided in Garden City. [*See* Spinzia, *Long Island's Prominent Families in Hempstead* – Meissner entry.] His sister Mary married Charles Malcolm Fraser. His sister Helen married Talcott Hunt Clark. His sister Maude married Stanley Matthews.
   Imogen Gaither Aldrich was the daughter of George Riggs and Frances Imogen Granger Gaither, Sr. of Baltimore, MD.
   The *Social Register Summer, 1937* lists Spencer Wyman and Lillian B. Turk Aldrich as residing on Dunemere Lane, East Hampton.
   She was the daughter of Charles and Harriet Nelson Turk. Lillian had previously been married to Ralph Waldo MacKewan.

Alexander, Edward Renick, Sr. (1878-1964)

Occupation(s):	attorney - patent law
Marriage(s):	1908-1939 – Elise Alexandrine Hoban (1881-1939)
Address:	18 Further Lane, East Hampton
Name of estate:	*Sterling–Haven*
Year of construction:	1928
Style of architecture:	Mediterranean
Architect(s):	John Custis Lawrence designed the house (for Cody)
Landscape architect(s):	
Builder:	Edward M. Gay
House extant:	yes
Historical notes:	

   The twenty-room house, originally named *Fairways*, was built by Frederick Cody. In 1940 Alexander purchased the house from Cody for $35,000 and renamed it *Sterling–Haven*. [*The New York Times* February 11, 1940, p. 147.]
   The *Social Register, 1945* lists Edward R. Alexander [Sr.] as residing at *Sterling–Haven* in East Hampton.
   Elise Alexandrine Hoban Alexander was the daughter of James and Elise Angelique Piquette Hoban of Washington, DC, and the great-granddaughter of James Hoban, the architect and builder of the *White House* in Washington, DC.
   Edward Renick and Elise Alexandrine Hoban Alexander, Sr.'s daughter Sylvia married Robert Leslie Conkling, the son of Robert Duer Conkling of Teaneck, NJ, and resided in Larchmont, NY. Their daughter Elise married John Mein Carter, the son of James Newman Carter of Philadelphia, PA. Their son James resided in Water Mill. Their daughter Louise resided in Washington, DC. Their son Edward Renick Alexander, Jr. married Frances Henderson, the daughter of Charles L. Henderson of Brooklyn, NY, and resided in NYC.

Alker, Ernestine Josephine Sierck (1889-1970)

Civic Activism:	a founder and president, Welsh Terrier Club of America; president, Ladies Kennel Association
Marriage(s):	1912-1938 – Edward Paul Alker (1887-1938)

    - industrialist - vice-president, Pennsylvania Cement Co. (became Pennsylvania–Dixie Cement Corp.); director and sales manager, Pennsylvania–Dixie Cement Corp.

    financier - co-founder and president, First National Bank of Little Neck (merged into Bank of Manhattan); director, Bank of Great Neck

Address: 96 Egypt Lane, East Hampton
Name of estate:
Year of construction:
Style of architecture: Shingle
Architect(s):
Landscape architect(s):
House extant: yes
Historical notes:

The Blue Book of The Hamptons, 1958 lists Mrs. Edward P. Alker as residing at 96 Egypt Lane in East Hampton. She was the daughter of Carsten William and Ottille Stiastny Sierck of Hoboken, NJ.

Edward Paul Alker was the son of Alphonse Henry and Florence Augusta Ward Alker of *Idlewilde* in Kings Point.

[For information about Edward's Kings Point residence *Cedar Pond Farm* and that of his parents *Idlewilde*, see Spinzia, *Long Island's North Shore Prominent Families, vol. I* – Alker entries.]

The Alkers did not have children.

Altschul, Arthur Goodhart, Jr. (b. 1964)

Occupation(s):	financier - a founder and managing member, Diaz & Altschul Group, LLC;
	a founder and managing member, Diaz & Altschul Management, LLC;
	member, equity and fixed income departments, Goldman, Sachs and Co.;
	a founder, The Maximus Fund;
	member, equity research department, Morgan Stanley and Co.;
	chairman of board, Overbrook Management Corp.;
	director, General American Investors Co., Inc.;
	director, Delta Opportunity Fund
	industrialist - co-founder and chairman of board, Koltan Pharmaceuticals, Inc.;
	director, Medicis Pharmaceutical Corp.;
	senior director of Corporate Affairs, Sugen, Inc. (drug discovery firm);
	director, Diversified National Products, Inc. (now, Gourmet Mushrooms, Inc.);
	director, ValiGen N.V. (biotechnology firm)
	capitalist - chairman of board, Soliloquy (provides information via targeted online dialogs);
	chairman of board, Medrium, Inc. (provides medical billing and practice management services to physicians and hospitals)
Civic Activism:	director, The Overlook Foundation;
	trustee, Neurosciences Research Foundation;
	trustee, National Public Radio Foundation;
	director, Child Mind Institute;
	member, New York Council for the Humanities
Marriage(s):	2013 – Rula Jebreal (b. 1973)
	- physiotherapist
	- journalist - interviewer on AnnZero (Italian political television program); commentator, MSNBC
	writer - *Miral*, 2003 (novel; made into a motion picture for which Rula wrote the screenplay);
	The Bride of Aswan, 2007 (novel);
	Rejected
Address:	77 Cross Highway, East Hampton
Name of estate:	
Year of construction:	1982
Style of architecture:	Modern
Architect(s):	Norman Jaffe designed the house (for P. Cohen)
Landscape architect(s)	
House extant: yes	
Historical notes:	

The five-bedroom, five-bath, 7,000-square-foot house was built by Peter Anthony Cohen. Altschul purchased the house in 2002 and restored it to its original appearance.

He is the son of Arthur Goodhart and Siri von Reis Altschul, Sr. of Center Island.

Rula Jebreal Altschul was born in Haifa, Israel, to Sufi Othman and Zaka Jebreal. She had previously been married to Davide Rivalta.

The Altschuls do not have children.

In 2019 the house was listed for sale. The asking price was $6.495 million.

Amador, Paul A. (b. 1954)

Occupation(s):	financier - banker
Marriage(s):	bachelor
Address:	19 Northwest Landing Road, East Hampton
Name of estate:	
Year of construction:	1968
Style of architecture:	Modern
Architect(s):	Charles Gwathmey designed the house (for Sedacca)
Landscape architect(s)	
Builder:	Jon Caramagna
House extant:	yes
Historical notes:	

The 1,200-square-foot, three-bedroom, three-bath house was built by Joseph M. Sedacca. In 1993 he sold the house to Amador for $245,000.

In 2015 Amador listed the house for sale. The asking price was $2.495 million. In 2019 it was again listed for sale. The asking price was $2.395 million.

Ambrose, Jessica Lyman Mansell (b. 1960)

Occupation(s):	entertainers and associate professions - freelance disk jockey
Marriage(s):	1991 – Colin Trippe Ambrose (b. 1958) - advertising executive - director of advertising, *Top Shelf* magazine, Ridgefield, CT restaurateur - owner, Estia's Back Porch Café, Darien, CT; owner, The Little Kitchen, Sag Harbor; chef and partner, The Old Stove Pub, Sagaponack
Address:	100 Dunemere Lane, East Hampton
Name of estate:	
Year of construction:	
Style of architecture:	Modified Neo-Federal
Architect(s):	
Landscape architect(s)	
House extant:	yes
Historical notes:	

The house was previously owned by Jessica's parents Frank Luther and Edmona Elmore Lyman Mansell.

Jessica had previously been married to William Drew Briner, the son of William S. Briner of Tahoe City, CA.

Colin Trippe Ambrose is the son of Harry T. and Margie Ambrose of Glencoe, IL.

In 2010 Jessica sold the 4,500-square-foot, five-bedroom, four-bath house to George Robert Stephanopoulos for $3.5 million.

In 2012 Stephanopoulos sold it for $5.13 million.

By 2003 the Ambroses were residing at *Whit's End*, 20 Dunemere Lane, East Hampton.

Ammon, Robert Theodore (1949-2001)
aka Ted Ammon

Occupation(s):	attorney -	member, Norton, Rose, Botterell, and Roche, Great Britain; member, Lord, Day, and Lord, NYC; member, Mayer, Brown, and Platt, NYC
	financier -	partner, Kohlberg, Kravis, Roberts, 1990-1992; established several venture capitalist holding companies
	publisher -	founder, Big Flower Press, 1992 (later, Vertis Holding Inc.); chief executive officer and chairman of board, Vertis Holding Inc.

Civic Activism: chairman of board, Jazz at Lincoln Center, NYC;
established Ammon Foundation;
trustee, Bucknell University, Lewisburg, PA;
established scholarship fund, Bucknell University, Lewisburg, PA;
trustee, Municipal Art Society;
chairman of board, YMCA of Greater New York;
established R. Theodore Ammon Archives and Music Library, Lincoln Center, NYC

Marriage(s): M/1 – 1973-div. – Randee Elaine Day (b. 1948)
- shipping - director, Seabury Transportation Holdings, LLC; director, DHT Maritime, Inc.
- financier - head of Maritime Investment Banking, Seabury Transportation Holdings, LLC; a founder, chief executive officer, and president, Day and Partners, LLC; founder, Delmar Group, LLC (venture capitalist firm); head of marine transportation and finance, J. P. Morgan Chase & Co.

M/2 – 1986-2001 – Generosa Rand LaGaye (1956-2003)

Address: 59 Middle Lane, East Hampton
Name of estate:
Year of construction: 1995
Style of architecture: English Country
Architect(s):
Landscape architect(s):
House extant: yes
Historical notes:

    Robert Theodore Ammon was the son of Robert and Bettylee Ammon of East Aurora, NY.
    Randee Elaine Day Ammon was the daughter of Leroy James and Elaine Beverly Jansson Day of California. She subsequently married George Morganakis Grogos.
    Generosa Rand LaGaye Ammon was the daughter of Marie Theresa LaGaye of Laguna Beach, CA.
    Robert was bludgeoned to death by Generosa's boyfriend Daniel Pelosia, who she later married.
    The house was inherited by Robert and Generosa's adopted children Gregory and Alexa R. Ammon.
    In 2017 the six-bedroom, six-and-a-half-bath, 7,000-square-foot house and 2.2 acres were for sale. The asking price was $2.7 million.

Anderson, Edward Ewen (1895-1970)

Occupation(s):	financier - vice-president and director, Discount Corporation of New York; trustee, East River Savings Bank
Marriage(s):	1933-1965 – Helen Natalie Johnson (d. 1965) - capitalist - president, 51st Street Corp. (real estate firm) Civic Activism: president, Women's National Republican Club, 1954-1958*; trustee, Young Women's Christian Association, NYC; trustee, Children's Aid Society; president, Ladies Village Improvement Society, East Hampton; trustee, Guild Hall, East Hampton
Address:	Jericho Lane, East Hampton
Name of estate:	*Up-the-Hill*
Year of construction:	
Style of architecture:	
Architect(s):	
Landscape architect(s):	
House extant:	unconfirmed
Historical notes:	

The Book of the Hamptons, 1958 lists Edward Ewen and Helen N. Johnson Anderson as residing at *Up-the-Hill* on Jericho Lane, East Hampton.

He was the son of General Edward D. Anderson.

Helen Natalie Johnson Anderson was the daughter of J. Bent Johnson of Washington, DC. Her sister Lilyann married Willard Fiske Place of East Hampton and, later, Joseph B. Terbell.

*Mrs. Anderson was against having a woman serve as President of the United States.

Andrews, William Loring (1837-1920)

Occupation(s):	financier - trustee, Bank for Savings, NYC; director, Continental Insurance Co.
	industrialist - partner, Loring Andrews and Co. (later, Loring Andrews and Sons) (hide and leather firm); partner, Loring Andrews and Sons
	writer - *New Amsterdam, New Orange, New York*, 1898;
	Fragments of American History, 1898;
	Old Book Sellers of New York;
	A Trio of French Engravers, 1899;
	Portraiture of American Revolutionary War;
	James Lyne's Survey, 1900;
	Gossip About Book Collecting, 1900;
	Paul Revere and His Engravings;
	Iconography of Battery and Castle;
	Treatyse of Fysshynge Wyth An Angle, 1903;
	New York as Washington Knew It After the Revolution, 1906;
	Sportsmen and Binder of Angling Books, 1907;
	The Heavenly Jerusalem;
	Catalogue of Early Printed Books Given to Yale University, 1912
Civic Activism:	manager, House of Refuge, Randall's Island, NYC;
	trustee, School District #1, Town of Islip, Islip, NY;
	member, executive board, Metropolitan Museum of Art, NYC;
	a founder, Grolier Club, NYC;
	a founder and president, Society of Iconophiles of New York
Marriage(s):	1860-1920 – Jane Elizabeth Crane (1840-1930)
	- Civic Activism: trustee, Women's Hospital; trustee, National Society of Colonial Dames
Address:	153 De Forest Road, Montauk
Name of estate:	
Year of construction:	1883
Style of architecture:	Beach Cottage
Architect(s):	McKim, Mead & White designed the house
	Francis Fleetwood, 1992 alterations (for Donovan)
Landscape architect(s):	Frederick Law Olmstead designed the site plan
Builder:	Mead & Taft
House extant: yes	
Historical notes:	

The house, which is on the National Register of Historic Places, is one of the Montauk Association's "Seven Sisters." It was owned by Andrews.

He was the son of Loring and Caroline Catherine Delamater Andrews.

Jane Elizabeth Crane Andrews was the daughter of Theodore and Margaret B. Crane of New York.

[For information about the Andrews' West Islip estate *Pepperidges, see* Spinzia, *Long Island's Prominent South Shore Families –* Andrews entry.]

The house was later owned by the estate of Dr. Cornelius Rea Agnew which deeded it to the Eye and Ear Infirmary of New York. The hospital immediately sold it to Frederick and Myra Upright. The Uprights sold the house to Miss H. Corinne Wagner who sold it to George and Emma Vogel. In 1981 the Vogels sold the house to Cornelius Peter and Roberta Gosman Donovan, Jr.

In 2012 Mrs. Donovan sold the house for $12 million.

In 2016 the 3,800-square-foot, four-bedroom, two-and-a-half bath house and 2.3 acres were again for sale. The asking price was $18.5 million. The annual taxes were $15,522.

Appleton, Robert Wilmarth (1875-1948)

Occupation(s):	capitalist - partner, Appleton, McKibbin, & Co., NYC (real estate firm)
Civic Activism:	president, East Hampton Riding Club; member, executive committee, East Hampton Associates
Marriage(s):	M/1 – 1897-div. – Mary Horsman (1871-1864)
	M/2 – Katharine Semple Jordan (1877-1949)
Address:	31 Old Beach Lane, East Hampton
Name of estate:	*Nid de Papillion*
Year of construction:	1917
Style of architecture:	Cotswold
Architect(s):	Frank Eaton Newton designed the house (for Appleton)
Landscape architect(s):	
Builder:	Edward M. Gay
House extant: yes	
Historical notes:	

The house, originally named *Nid de Papillion*, was built by Robert Wilmarth Appleton.

The *Social Register Summer, 1921* lists Robert and Katharine Jordan as residing at *Nid de Papillion* in East Hampton.

Mary Horsman Appleton was the daughter of Edward Imeson and Florence Lewis Benton Horsman, Sr. of Brooklyn. Mary later married Spencer Swain of Brooklyn and, subsequently, Murray Herbert La Mont of Brooklyn and resided in Woodmere. [*See* Spinzia, *Long Island's Prominent Families in the Town of Hempstead* – La Mont entry.]

Robert Wilmarth and Mary Horsman Appleton's daughter Mary married William Harman Brown III. Their daughter Florence married James Clarke Milholland and resided in Hewlett Harbor and, later, John Mingus Dodd, Jr. of *The Kennels* in East Hampton. [*See* Spinzia, *Long Island's Prominent Families in the Town of Hempstead* – Milholland entry.]

Katharine Semple Jordan Appleton was the daughter of Nathan Edmund and Sarah Semple Jordan. She had previously been married to George Wright Peavey, the son of Frank Hutchison and Mary Dibble Wright Peavey of Minneapolis, MN.

Appleton died as result of falling from the sixth floor of a Palm Beach hotel. [*The New York Times* January 5, 1948, p. 21.]

The house, which is on the National Register of Historic Places, was later owned by James Loring Johnson who continued to call it *Nid de Papillion*.

Aspinwall, James Lawrence (1854-1936)

Occupation(s):	architect* - partner, Renwick, Aspinwall, and Russell, NYC;
	partner, Renwick, Aspinwall, and Tucker, NYC;
	partner, Renwick, Aspinwall, and Guard, NYC
Civic Activism:	trustee, New York Infirmary for Women and Children;
	treasurer, St. Luke's Association of Grace Episcopal Church, NYC
Marriage(s):	1891-1892 – Mary Morris Carnochan (d. 1892)
Address:	Briar Patch Road, East Hampton
Name of estate:	
Year of construction:	1904
Style of architecture:	Modified Salt-Box**
Architect(s):	James Lawrence Aspinwall designed his own house
Landscape architect(s):	
Builder:	Thomas E. Babcock
House extant: yes	
Historical notes:	

   The house, which was originally designed as a modified salt-box, was built by James Lawrence Aspinwall.
   He was the son of James Scott and Margaret Maxwell Aspinwall of NYC.
   Mary Morris Carnochan Aspinwall was the daughter of Dr. John Murray Carnochan of NYC.
   Aspinwall did not remarry after Mary's death.
   *Among the architectural projects with which he was involved were St. Patrick's Cathedral, NYC, and the stone spire of Grace Episcopal Church, NYC. He designed the buildings for the American Society for the Prevention of Cruelty to Children; the American Society for Prevention of Cruelty to Animals; New York Infirmary for Women and Children; and the American Express Building.
   **The house was later transformed, by later alterations, into an eclectic style.

Ashplant, Frederick Bryant, Sr. (1895-1973)

Occupation(s):	financier - chief foreign exchange trader, Bank of Montreal, NYC; a founder, with Gordon Saunders, Saunders, Ashplant and Co., NYC (investment banking firm); a founder and partner, F. B. Ashplant and Co., NYC (stock brokerage firm); investment advisor, Bank of N. T. Butterfield & Sons, Ltd, Hamilton, Bermuda; consultant to International Monetary Fund
Civic Activism:	president and historian, Canadian Society of New York; president, Baptist Union of Brooklyn and Long Island; president, Ridgewood Art Association
Marriage(s):	M/1 – 1929-1957 – Frances Balfour Begg (1897-1957) M/2 – 1959-1973 – Dorothy Crouch
Address:	Lily Pond Lane and Cottage Avenue, East Hampton
Name of estate:	*The Dolphins*
Year of construction:	1899
Style of architecture:	Shingle
Architect(s):	George A. Eldredge designed and built 1899 alterations to the house and 1902 stables (for Strong)
Landscape architect(s):	
Builder:	Thomas E. Babcock
House extant:	unconfirmed

Nassau County Museum Collection has photographs of the estate.
Historical notes:

In 1899 Theron George Strong purchased Dan Talmage's *Red Cottage*. He altered the house and renamed it *The Dolphins*. In 1941 Mrs. Strong sold it to Ashplant. [*The East Hampton Star* October 9, 1941, p. 1.]

The Blue Book of The Hamptons, 1958 lists Frederick B. Ashplant [Sr.] as residing at *The Dolphins*, Lily Pond Lane and Cottage Avenue, East Hampton.

He was the son of Henry Brimsmead and Alice Amelia Hargreaves Ashplant of London, Ontario, Canada.

Frances Balfour Begg Ashplant was the daughter of William and Elizabeth Margaret Serymgeour Begg.

Frederick Bryant and Frances Balfour Begg Ashplant, Sr.'s son William married Dr. Irene Labourdette, the daughter of Pierre Labourdette of Lincoln Park, NJ. Their son Frederick Bryant Ashplant, Jr. resided in Pine Lake, NJ.

Dorothy Crouch Ashplant was the daughter of Franklin B. Crouch. She had previously been married to Joseph Harris.

Ashplant, Frederick Bryant, Sr. (1895-1973)

Occupation(s):	*[See previous entry.]*
Civic Activism:	*[See previous entry.]*
Marriage(s):	M/1 – 1929-1957 – Frances Balfour Begg (1897-1957) M/2 – 1959-1973 – Dorothy Crouch
Address:	Drew Lane, East Hampton
Name of estate:	
Year of construction:	
Style of architecture:	
Architect(s):	
Landscape architect(s):	
Builder:	
House extant:	unconfirmed

Historical notes:

Ashplant purchased Mary Louise Woodin Miner's residence *Mi Dune*. [*The East Hampton Star* November 23, 1944, p. 8.]
[See previous entry for family information.]
In 1961 he sold the house to Edward Durell Stone, Sr. [*The East Hampton Star* May 4, 1961, p. 4.]

Aubert, Marion Eugenia Bragg (1886-1971)

Civic Activism:	founder and benefactor, a hospital for children at Autevil, France, during World War I;
	established a rest house for American officers in Paris, France, through the Red Cross during World War I
Marriage(s):	M/1 – div. 1920 – Harry Langdon Laws III (1880-1955)
	- capitalist - vice-president and director, Catherine Sugar Co., Inc., Lobdell, LA;
	chairman of board, Harry L. Laws and Co, Inc., Cinclare, LA (planters and processors of cane sugar);
	director, Texas and Pacific Railway
	M/2 – 1921-div. 1926 – Ludvig Caesar Martin Aubert II (b. 1878)
	- diplomat - Norwegian Consul General, Montreal, Canada, 1921;
	Norwegian Envoy Extraordinary and Minister Plenipotentiary to Japan, 1932
Address:	Star Island Road, Montauk
Name of estate:	*Star Acres*
Year of construction:	1929
Style of architecture:	Modified French Country
Architect(s):	Walker and Gillette designed the house (for Bragg)
Landscape architect(s):	Olmstead, 1929-1930 (for Bragg)
House extant: yes	
Historical notes:	

   The house was built by the noted automobile and speedboat racer Caleb Smith Bragg. The estate was later owned by Caleb's sister Marion who called it *Star Acres*.

   Marion and Caleb were the children of Caius and Eugenia Hofer Bragg of Cincinnati, OH.

   The *Social Register Summer, 1949* lists Marion B. Aubert as residing at *Star Acres* in Montauk.

   Harry Langdon Laws III was the son of Harry Langdon and Florence Bradford Laws, Jr. of Cincinnati, OH. He subsequently married Louise Kohlsaat.

   Harry Langdon and Marion Eugenia Bragg Law III's son Eugene married Mary Brickell, the daughter of William B. Brickell.

   Ludvig Caesar Martin Aubert II was the son of Julius Henrik Vihelm Adelsten and Sigrid Eriksdatter Aubert. Ludvig subsequently married Ruth Lilly Margaretha Swanstrom.

   By the mid-1950s Mrs. Aubert had relocated to Arizona.

   In 1987 the estate, which consists of the main residence and several service buildings, was listed on the National Register of Historic Places. They are currently used as villas at the Montauk Yacht Club Resort and Marina.

   [For information on Mrs. Aubert's Muttontown residence *Eight Acres*, see Spinzia, *Long Island's Prominent North Shore Families, vol. I* – Aubert entry.]

Austin, William Gage (1882-1952)

Occupation(s):	financier - member, Union Trust Co., NYC
	industrialist - officer, Acme Furnace Equipment Co., NYC
Marriage(s):	1912-1952 – Adelaide Louise Douglas (1883-1979)
Address:	Bluff Road, Amagansett
Name of estate:	
Year of construction:	
Style of architecture:	
Architect(s):	
Landscape architect(s):	
House extant:	unconfirmed
Historical notes:	

The Book of the Hamptons, 1958 lists Mrs. William Gage Austin as residing on Bluff Road, Amagansett.
She was the daughter Henry Douglas of NYC. Her brother John was a noted Manhattan surgeon.
William Gage Austin was the son of William Henry Harrison and Eleanor Florence Gage Austin of NYC.
William Gage and Adelaide Louise Douglas Austin's daughter Eleanor married Edwin Van Valkenburg Sutherland, the son of Hugh Brock Sutherland of Germantown, PA. Their daughter Janet married William Dickinson Hart, Jr. of Stamford, CT, and resided in Stamford.

Avedon, Richard (1923-2004)

Occupation(s):	professional photographer - fashion and portrait photographer, *Harper's Bazaar*, *Vogue*, *New Yorker*
	writer - *Observations*, 1959;
	Portraits, 1976;
	Avedon Photographs 1947-1977, 1978;
	In the American West, 1985;
	Richard Avedon, 1993 (autobiography);
	Evidence: 1944-1994, 1994;
	The Sixties, 1999
Marriage(s):	M/1 – 1944-div. 1949 – Dorcas Marie Nowell (1925-2011)
	(aka Doe Avedon; Betty Harper)
	- model
	entertainers and associate professions -
	Broadway and motion picture actress
	M/2 – 1951-2004 – Evelyn Franklin (d. 2004)
Address:	430 Old Montauk Highway, Montauk
Name of estate:	
Year of construction:	1980
Style of architecture:	Cape Cod
Architect(s):	Frederick Stelle, alterations, 2009
Landscape architect(s)	
House extant:	yes
Historical notes:	

The 3,500-square-foot, five-bedroom, four-and-a-half-bath house was built by Richard Avedon.
He was the son of Jacob Israel and Amne Polonsky Avedon.
Dorcas Marie Nowell Avedon was orphaned at the age of twelve and raised by a wealthy Old Westbury estate owner for whom her father was a butler. She later married actor Donald Matthews and, subsequently, director Donald Siegel.
Richard and Evelyn Franklin Avedon's son John married Elizabeth Paul and Maura Moynihan.
In 1998 Avedon listed the house for sale. The asking price was $10 million.

Avery, Edward Strong (1871-1937)

Occupation(s):	attorney
	financier - trust and law officer, Van Norden Trust Co., 1903; president, Van Dyck Estate Co. (investment firm)
Marriage(s):	1909-1937 – Rebecca Janet Gilfillan (b. 1880)
Address:	Lily Pond Lane, East Hampton
Name of estate:	
Year of construction:	1914
Style of architecture:	Ranch
Architect(s):	John Custis Lawrence designed the house (for Avery)*
Landscape architect(s):	
House extant: yes	
Historical notes:	

The house was built by Edward Strong Avery.

The *Social Register Summer, 1915* and *1921* list Edward S. and Rebecca J. Gilfillan Avery as residing in East Hampton.

He was the son of Dr. Henry Newell and Mrs. Catherine Seabring Fowler Avery.

Rebecca Janet Gilfillan Avery was the daughter of John Bachop and Rebecca Corse Oliphant Gilfillan.

Edward Strong and Rebecca Janet Gilfillan Avery's son Gilfillan, who resided in Cold Spring Harbor, married Anne Douglas Meding, the daughter of Dr. Charles Bramman Meding of Manhattan, and, subsequently, Joan Pulling, the daughter of Edward Pulling.

*In 1961 alterations were made to the house.

Ayer, Frederick, III (b. 1938)

Occupation(s):	professional photographer - freelance
Marriage(s):	1974 – Claire Sylvie Labourel
	- attorney - member, Clifford–Turner and Co.
Address:	81 Ocean Avenue, East Hampton
Name of estate:	
Year of construction:	
Style of architecture:	Colonial Revival
Architect(s):	
Landscape architect(s):	
House extant: yes	
Historical notes:	

The *Social Register Summer, 2001* lists Frederick and Claire Labourel Ayer III as residing at 81 Ocean Avenue, East Hampton.

He is the son of Frederick and Elizabeth Jenney Ayer II of Hewlett and Locust Valley. [*See* Spinzia, *Long Island's Prominent Families in the Town of Hempstead* – Ayer entry – and *Long Island's Prominent North Shore Families, vol. I* – Ayer entry.] Frederick's mother subsequently married Richard Draper Richards and resided at *Little Too Close* in East Hampton.

Claire Sylvie Labourel Ayer is the daughter of André Guy and Marie Jeanne Desclaux Labourel of Paris, France.

Frederick and Claire Sylvie Labourel Ayer III's son Andrew resides in Shanghai, China. Their son Alexander resides in Paris, France.

In 2009 the house was remodeled.

The four-bedroom, five-bath, 3,200-square-foot house and 0.99 acre were for sale in 2015. The asking price was $8 million.

Backus, Henry Clinton (1848-1908)

Occupation(s): attorney -   partner, Beebe, Wilcox, and Hobbs

Marriage(s): 1890-1908– Harriet Ivins Davis (1868-1941)
- Civic Activism: vice-president, Woman's Municipal League;
member, board of managers, New York Colored
Orphan Asylum;
actively opposed woman's suffrage*

Address: Lily Pond Lane, East Hampton
Name of estate: *Tranquility*
Year of construction:
Style of architecture:
Architect(s):
Landscape architect(s):
House extant: unconfirmed
Historical notes:

   The *Social Register Summer, 1915* lists Harriet Ivins Davis Backus as residing at *Tranquility* in East Hampton. She was the daughter of Wilmer and Jane Hastings Davis.
   Henry Clinton Backus was the son of Charles Chapman and Harriet Newell Baldwin Backus of Utica, NY.
   Henry Clinton and Harriet Ivins Davis Backus's son Clinton, a bachelor, died at the age of thirty-five. Their daughter Harriet was an infant at the time of her death.
   By 1929 Mrs. Backus had relocated to *Tranquility* in Vermont.
   [For information about Mrs. Backus' Garden City residence, *see* Spinzia, *Long Island's Prominent Families in the Town of Hempstead* – Backus entry.]
   *For other Long Islanders involved in the suffrage movement *see* Raymond E. Spinzia, "Winning the Franchise: Long Island Activists in the Fight for Woman's Suffrage and Their Opponents, Long Island's Anti-Suffragists." wwwspinzialongislandestates.com.

Bacon, Clarence Everett, Jr. (1890-1989)

Occupation(s):	financier - partner, Spencer, Trask, and Co. (investment banking firm)
	industrialist - director, Colorado Fluorspar Corp.;
	treasurer and director, Yaddo Corp.;
	director, Compania Metallugica Mexicana;
	director, Fresnillo Corp.
	capitalist - partner, president, treasurer, and director, Broadway Realty Co., NYC;
	vice-president and treasurer, 880 Fifth Avenue Corp., NYC;
	vice-president, Mexican Northern Railroad
Civic Activism:	trustee, Bennett College, Greensboro, NC;
	trustee, Spelman College, Atlanta, GA;
	trustee, Atlanta University, Atlanta, GA;
	trustee, Morehouse College, Atlanta, GA;
	trustee, Southern Education Foundation, Inc.;
	trustee, Federal Council of Churches of Christ in America;
	governor, Association of Stock Exchange Firms, 1925-1936;
	president, YMCA, Montclair, NJ;
	president and trustee, Montclair Community Chest;
	director, Hook Pond Associates
Marriage(s):	M/1 – 1915-div. 1947 – Eva Peabody (1890-1984)
	M/2 – 1947-1983 – Ramona Elsie Diller (1915-1983)
Address:	East Dune Lane, East Hampton
Name of estate:	*Dune Gate*
Year of construction:	
Style of architecture:	
Architect(s):	
Landscape architect(s):	
House extant: unconfirmed	
Historical notes:	

The Blue Book of The Hamptons, 1965 lists Mr. and Mrs. C. Everett Bacon [Jr.] as residing on East Dune Lane, East Hampton. *The Blue Book of The Hamptons, 1987* lists C. Everett Bacon [Jr.] as residing at *Dune Gate*, East Dune Lane, East Hampton.
  He was the son of Clarence Everett and Katharine Sedgewick Whiting Bacon, Sr.
  Eva Peabody Bacon was the daughter of Charles Jones and Helen Hoyt Peabody of New York.
  Charles Everett and Eva Peabody Bacon, Jr.'s daughter Anne married Stuart C. Lowe.
  In 1966 Bacon was inducted into the National Football Foundation Hall of Fame.

Bailey, Dr. Theodorus, II (1874-1947)

Occupation(s):	physician - gastro-enterologist
	capitalist - president, McKnight Realty Co.;
	president, Foos Realty Co.;
	president, Bailwick Inc. (realty firm);
	president, Major Dania Inc. (realty firm)
	educator - instructor, Polyclinic Medical School;
	professor, New York School of Clinical Medicine
Marriage(s):	1902-1947 – Alice Van Benschoten Foos (1881-1964)
	- Civic Activism: vice-chair and treasurer, Republican Committee of One Hundred
Address:	Dunemere Lane, East Hampton
Name of estate:	*Dunemere*
Year of construction:	c. 1891
Style of architecture:	Shingle
Architect(s):	Joseph Greenleaf Thorp designed the house (for J. N. Steele, Sr.)
Landscape architect(s):	
House extant: unconfirmed	
Historical notes:	

    The house, originally named *Dunemere,* was built by The Reverend James Nevett Steele, Sr. It was later owned by Clarence Hopkins Hensel, who continued to call it *Dunemere*. In 1928 Hensel sold the house to Bailey. [*The East Hampton Star* May 17, 1929, p. 7.]

    The *Social Directory of Southampton, Long Island, 1931* lists Dr. Theodorus and Mrs. Alice Van B. Foos Bailey [II] as residing on Dunemere Lane, East Hampton. The *Social Register Summer, 1932* lists *Dunemere* as the name of their residence.

    He was the son of Edmund S. Bailey and the grandson of Rear Admiral Theodorus Bailey who was second in command in the Civil War battle for New Orleans.

    Alice Van Benschoten Foos Bailey was the daughter of Lamar and Mary King Fellows Foos.

    Dr. Theodorus and Mrs. Alice Van Benschoten Foos Bailey II's daughter Rosalie married James Leo Gaffey, Jr. Their daughter Dorothea married Harold Alvin Chandor, Jr. and, subsequently, Henry James Jackman. Their daughter Gertrude married Lawrence Gahagan. Their daughter Elsa married Fridolin Joseph Blumer, the son of Adam Blumer.

    In 1944 the house was purchased by Delos Walker. [*The East Hampton Star* June 24, 1944, p. 1.]

Baker, John T., Sr. (1842-1947)

Occupation(s):	
Marriage(s):	
Address:	Lily Pond Lane, East Hampton
Name of estate:	
Year of construction:	1907
Style of architecture:	Shingle
Architect(s):	John Custis Lawrence designed the house (for Baker)
Landscape architect(s):	
Builder:	Thomas E. Babcock
House extant: yes	
Historical notes:	

    The house was built by John T. Baker Sr.

    He was born in Watertown, NY, and resided in Plainfield, NJ.

    The *Long Island Society Register, 1929* list Mr. and Mrs. John T. Baker [Jr.] as residing on Lily Pond Lane, East Hampton.

    The house was later owned by his son John T. Baker, Jr.

Baker, Lawrence Adams, Sr. (1890-1980)

Occupation(s):	attorney - specialist in Federal tax law; partner, Winthrop, Stimson, Putnam, and Roberts; partner, Baker, Selby, and Rutter
Civic Activism:	president, United States Lawn Tennis Association; member, Davis Cup advisory committee; a founder, Tennis Education Foundation, Newport, RI (now, Tennis Foundation and Hall of Fame); secretary, treasurer, and vice-president, United States Lawn Tennis Association; governor, Devon Yacht Club, Amagansett; director, Maidstone Club, East Hampton
Marriage(s):	1916-1964 – Marjorie Russ (1893-1964)
Address:	95 Main Street, East Hampton
Name of estate:	*Baker's Acres*
Year of construction:	1740
Style of architecture:	Dutch Colonial
Architect(s):	
Landscape architect(s):	
House extant: yes	
Historical notes:	

The house was previously owned by Winthrop Gardiner, Sr. who called it *Deurcant House*. In 1924 Gardiner moved the house further back on property and enlarged the house at the same time. The house was later owned by Baker who called it *Baker's Acres*.

The *Social Register Summer, 1958* lists Lawrence A. and Marjorie Russ Baker [Sr.] as residing at 95 Main Street, East Hampton. *The Blue Book of The Hamptons, 1973* lists *Baker's Acres* as the name of their residence.

He was the son of James Marion and Mary Adams Baker.

Marjorie Russ Baker was the daughter of Charles P. Russ.

Their son Lawrence Adams Baker, Jr. married Cynthia Cheatham, the daughter of Owen Cheatham and resided in Palm Beach, FL.

The house currently houses the Ladies Village Improvement Society's Thrift and Book Shops.

Baldwin, Alexander Rae, III (b. 1958)
aka Alec Baldwin

Occupation(s):	entertainers and associated professions -
	stage, television, and motion picture actor;
	announcer, New York Philharmonic
	capitalist - producer
	journalist - columnist, *The Huffington Post*
	writer - co-author, with Mark Tabb, *A Promise to Ourselves: A Journey Through Fatherhood and Divorce*, 2008
Civic Activism:	trustee, People for the American Way;
	trustee, New York Philharmonic, NYC;
	co-chairman and trustee, Hamptons International Film Festival;
	donated $1 million to East Hampton Free Library
Marriage(s):	M/1 – 1993-div. 2002 – Kimila Ann Basinger (b. 1953)
	(aka Kim Basinger)
	- entertainers and associated professions -
	television and motion picture actress
	capitalist - producer
	M/2 – 2012 – Hilaria Lynn Thomas (b. 1984)
	- capitalist - co-owner, Yoga Vida Studio, NYC
	yoga instructor
	journalist - lifestyle correspondent, *Extra*
Address:	341 Town Lane, Amagansett
Name of estate:	
Year of construction:	2015
Style of architecture:	Contemporary
Architect(s):	Edward M. Gay, 1914
	alterations (for Hamlin)
Landscape architect(s):	
Builder:	Edward M. Gay (for Hamlin)
	Jeffrey Colle (for Baldwin)
House extant:	no*

Historical notes:

   Nathaniel Baker's 1680s house was purchased by Samuel Schellinger who enlarged it in 1797. The house was purchased in 1913 by Harry Leon Hamlin who moved it from Main Street to what was to become his 325-acre Town Lane dairy farm *Stony Hill Farm*. [*The East Hampton Star* October 3, 1913, p. 3, and Carleton Kelsey and Lucinda Mayo, *Images of America: Amagansett* (Dover, NH: Arcadia Publishing, 1997), p. 12.] In 1949 it was purchased from Mrs. Hamlin by Jeffrey Brackett Potter who continued to call it *Stony Hill Farm*. [*The East Hampton Star* November 17, 1949, p. 4.]

   The main residence was purchased by Michael Minkoff who flipped it to Baldwin in 1996. In 2015 Baldwin substantially enlarged and remodeled the house into a contemporary style.

   He is the son of Alexander Rae and Carol Newcomb Martineau Baldwin, Jr. of Massapequa.

   Kimila Ann Basinger Baldwin is the daughter of Donald Wade and Ann Lee Cordell Basinger. Kimila was previously married to Ron Snyder–Britton.

   Alexander Rae and Kimila Ann Basinger Baldwin II's daughter Ireland is not married.

   Both Alexander and Kimila have won numerous awards for their acting.

   Alexander Rae and Hilaria Lynn Thomas Baldwin III's daughter Carmen was born in 2013.

   *A portion of the original interior remains.

Barbour, William Stanton (1905-1988)

Occupation(s):	capitalist - importer of Bolivian goods
Marriage(s):	1930-1988 – Martha Buckham Benedict (1907-1989) - Civic Activism: translated books into Braille for the Library of Congress
Address:	Lily Pond Lane, East Hampton
Name of estate:	
Year of construction:	
Style of architecture:	
Architect(s):	
Landscape architect(s):	
Builder:	Dayton and Dayton
House extant: unconfirmed	
Historical notes:	

   The house was built by Dr. James Craig Joyner. [*The East Hampton Star* January 24, 1957, p. 1.] In 1941 Barbour purchased the house. [*The East Hampton Star* October 23, 1941, p. 1.]
   The Blue Book of The Hamptons, 1973 lists Mr. and Mrs. W. Stanton Barbour as residing on Lily Pond Lane, East Hampton.
   He was the son of John Edwards and Katherine Stanton Niven Barbour of Paterson, NJ.
   Martha Buckham Benedict Barbour was the daughter of James Dewey and Ada Platt Benedict of Montclair, NJ.
   William Stanton and Martha Buckham Benedict Barbour's daughter Joan married Robert David Rogers, the son of Ralph Burton Rogers of Dallas, TX. Their daughter Susanne married Charles Seymour Bullock, Jr. of Cold Spring-on-Hudson, NY. Their daughter Katherine married Ogden Hillyer Sutro, of the son of Ogden Winne Sutro of Hamden, CT, and Hartwood, NY.

Baron, Ronald Stephen (b. 1943)

Occupation(s):	financier - a founder and partner, Herzfeld and Baron (stock brokerage firm); founder and president, Baron Capital Management attorney
Civic Activism:	founder, Baron Capital Foundation
Marriage(s):	1978 – Judy Bernard - computer system specialist, Chase Manhattan Bank
Address:	Further Lane, East Hampton
Name of estate:	
Year of construction:	2009
Style of architecture:	Elizabethan Revival
Architect(s):	Hart Howerton designed the house (for Baron)
Landscape architect(s):	
House extant: yes	
Historical notes:	

   The 28,000-square-foot house was built by Ronald Stephen Baron on forty acres of vacant land that he purchased from Mrs. Louise Adelaide de Menil Carpenter for $103 million.
   He is the son of Morton and Marian Baron of West Allenhurst, NJ.
   Judy Bernard Baron is the daughter Leon and Sylvia Bernard.

Bartlett, Edward Everett, Jr. (1885-1961)

Occupation(s):	financier - partner, Gwathmey and Co., NYC, 1909-1926 (cotton brokerage firm) (merged with A. A. Housman & Co. becoming E. A. Pierce and Co., a stock brokerage firm);
	partner, E. A. Pierce and Co., 1926-1929 (stock brokerage firm);
	partner, Merrill, Lynch, Pierce, Fenner, and Beane (with became Merrill Lynch and Co.; and now, after acquisition by Bank of America in 2009, Bank of America Merrill Lynch, banking and wealth management division);
	vice-president, New York Cotton Exchange, 1921-1923;
	president, New York Cotton Exchange, 1923-1925;
	chairman of board, New York Stock Exchange, 1938-1941;
	chairman, New York Stock Exchange Quotation Co.;
	director, New York Stock Exchange Clearing House
Civic Activism:	president, American Red Cross, West Palm Beach, FL, chapter;
	chairman of board, Guild Hall, East Hampton
Marriage(s):	M/1 – 1911-1919 – Anna Katherine Schnakenberg (1883-1919)
	M/2 – 1932-1944 – Christine Hill (1891-1944)
	M/3 – 1945-1961 – Virginia McClellan (1905-1995)
Address:	Further Lane, Amagansett
Name of estate:	*Furtherlane*
Year of construction:	c. 1915
Style of architecture:	Modified French Chateau
Architect(s):	Hewitt and Bottomley designed the house (for E. E. Bartlett, Jr.)
Landscape architect(s):	
House extant: yes	
Historical notes:	

The 6,000-square-foot, six-bedroom, six-bath house, originally named *Furtherlane*, was built by Edward Everett Bartlett, Jr.

The *Long Island Society Register, 1929* lists Edward E. Bartlett [Jr.] as residing at *Furtherlane* in Amagansett.

He was the son of Edward Everett and Jessie Irving Mitchell Bartlett, Sr. of Manhattan.

Anna Katherine Schnakenberg Bartlett was the daughter of Daniel and Elizabeth Gillespie Schnakenberg, Sr. of Staten Island, NY.

Edward Everett and Anna Katherine Schnakenberg Bartlett, Jr.'s daughter Elizabeth married William Madden.

Virginia McClellan Bartlett was the daughter of George Robert and Marie M. McClellan of Manhattan. She had previously been married to Guertin Tuttle.

The house and 4+ acres were for sale in 2012. The asking price was $21.5 million.

Barton, Flora Benjamin McAlpin (1894-1964)

Marriage(s):	M/1 – 1918-div. 1928 – Charles Pierce Barton, Jr. (1890-1955)
	  - engineer
	    politician - member, Federal Housing administration, 1941
	    writer - *The Boys of Bob's Hill;*
	        The Trail Makers, 1919
	M/2 – 1936 – Roy Clinton Seeley (1891-1976)
	  - capitalist - president, R. C. Seeley, Los Angeles, CA
	        (real estate agency)

Address:	Lee Avenue, East Hampton
Name of estate:	
Year of construction:	1915
Style of architecture:	Shingle

Architect(s):	John Custis Lawrence designed
	  the house (for Quackenbush);
	  alterations, 1929 (for Barton)

Landscape architect(s):	
Builder:	
House extant:	yes
Historical notes:	

The house was built by Schuyler Quackenbush. It was later owned by Flora Benjamin McAlpin Barton.

The *Social Directory of Southampton, Long Island, 1931* lists Flora B. McAlpin as residing on Lee Avenue, East Hampton.

She was the daughter of George Lodowich and Sallie Blanche Benjamin McAlpin, Sr. of *Dune Alpin* in East Hampton. Flora's sister Dorothy married Alfred Dennis Bell of East Hampton. Her sister Jeannette married A. Musgrave Hyde.

Charles Pierce and Flora Benjamin McAlpin Barton, Jr.'s daughter Jeannette married Max L. Green, Jr. of Los Angeles, CA.

Roy Clinton Seeley was the son of Aron and Kate Sutherland Seeley of Los Angeles.

Bates, Jerome Elliott (1841-1926)

Occupation(s):	industrialist - president, J. E. Bates & Co., Worcester, MA (shoe manufacturing firm)
Marriage(s):	1873-1926 – Eliza Whitmore Barnes (1853-1931)
Address:	41 Ocean Avenue, East Hampton
Name of estate:	*Dune Pasture*
Year of construction:	18th Century
Style of architecture:	Victorian (after being remodeled)
Architect(s):	
Landscape architect(s):	
House extant:	yes
Historical notes:	

In 1884 the house was moved from Main Street and remodeled in 1898.

The *Long Island Society Register, 1929* lists Eliza Whitmore Barnes Bates as residing at *Dune Pasture* in East Hampton.

Jerome Elliott Bates was the son of Walter and Mary Jacobs Elliott Bates.

Jerome Elliott and Eliza Whitmore Barnes Bates' son Leonard married Zillah Genung, the daughter of Edward P. Genung of Brooklyn, and resided in Brooklyn. Their daughter Clara married Howard Clarke of Brooklyn and resided in White Plains, NY. Their daughter Ethel did not marry.

Baxter, Ann Wright (1922-2007)

Civic Activism:	trustee, University Hospital, Cleveland, OH;
	trustee, Rainbow Hospital, Cleveland, OH;
	trustee, Visiting Nurse Service, NYC;
	trustee, Turtle Bay Music School;
	president and member, board of managers, East Hampton Free Library;
	trustee, D'Amico Art Barge

Marriage(s):   M/1 – 1941-div. 1953 – Matthew Andrews Baxter, Sr. (1920-1979)
- industrialist -   chairman of board, Ohio Bronze Powder Co., Cleveland, OH

M/2 – 1966 – Elmore Coe Kerr, Jr. (1914-1973)
- merchant -   founder and president, E. Coe Kerr Gallery, Inc., NYC (art gallery);
president and director, M. Knoedler & Co., Inc. (art gallery)
financier -   director, Chemical Bank
Civic Activism: director, Federation des Alliances Francaise

M/3 – 1990-2000 – David R. Williams, Jr. (1922-2000)
- capitalist -   a founder, Williams Brothers, Tulsa, TX (later, Williams Companies) (largest oil and gas pipeline company in the country in 1960s);
chairman of board, Williams Companies;
president, Williams Brothers Engineering Co.

Address:	Woods Lane, East Hampton
Name of estate:	
Year of construction:	
Style of architecture:	Shingle
Architect(s):	
Landscape architect(s):	
Builder:	
House extant: yes	
Historical notes:	

The Blue Book of The Hamptons, 1958 lists Ann Wright Baxter as residing on Woods Lane, East Hampton.
   She was the daughter of John Howie and Anne M. Ryan Wright, Jr. of East Hampton.
   Matthew Andrews Baxter, Sr. was the son of Charles McGhee and Marcella Virginia Andrews Baxter of Cleveland, OH. Matthew's paternal grandparents George White and Margaret White McGhee Baxter resided at *Cherokee Cottage* in East Hampton.
   Matthew Andrews and Ann Wright Baxter, Sr.'s son Matthew Andrews Baxter, Jr. married Kate Davis Putnam, the daughter of Henry W. Putnam.
   The Blue Book of The Hamptons, 1973 lists Ann Wright Kerr as residing at 68 Woods Lane, East Hampton.
   Elmore Coe Kerr, Jr. was the son of Elmore Coe and Marian Lyman Smyth Kerr, Sr. of Mill Neck. [*See* Spinzia, *Long Island's Prominent North Shore Families, vol. I* – Kerr entry.] Elmore had previously been married to Mallory Mixsell, the daughter of Dr. Harold Ruckman and Mrs. Charlotte Mallory Mixsell of *Forest Edge* in Matinecock. [*See* Spinzia, *Long Island's Prominent North Shore Families, vol. I* – Mixsell entry.] After his divorce from Mallory, Kerr married Sara Nichols.

Baxter, George White (1855-1929)

Occupation(s):	politician - governor, Territory of Wyoming, 1886
	capitalist - established large cattle ranches near Fort Washakie, Colorado; general manager, Western Union Beef Co.; president and general manager, North American Cattle Co.; president and general manager, Frontier Land and Cattle Co.
Civic Activism:	a founder, Society of Indian Wars; suffrage*
Marriage(s):	1880-1929 – Margaret White McGhee (1858-1942)
Address:	Lee Avenue, East Hampton
Name of estate:	*Cherokee Cottage*
Year of construction:	1890
Style of architecture:	Shingle
Architect(s):	
Landscape architect(s):	
Builder:	John Aldrich
House extant:	yes
Historical notes:	

The house, originally located at the corner of Ocean Avenue and Pudding Hill Lane, was built by Mrs. William Draper. It was later owned by Baxter, who moved it to its present location in 1919.

The *Long Island Society Register, 1929* lists George White and Margaret W. McGhee Baxter as residing at *Cherokee Cottage* in East Hampton.

He was the son of John and Orra Alexander Baxter of Henderson, NC.

Margaret White McGhee Baxter was the daughter of Charles McClung and Cornelia Humes White McGhee of Knoxville, TN.

George White and Margaret White McGhee Baxter's daughter Cornelia married Hugh Tevis, Sr. of San Francisco and, later, Evelyn Toulmin of London, England. Their daughter Margaret married Albert Volney Foster and resided in Lake Forest, IL. Their daughter Katherine married Russell Burrage of Boston, MA. Their daughter Eleanor married Chauncey Perry Beadleston with whom she resided in Hewlett Bay Park. Eleanor later married James Clarke Milholland of Hewlett Harbor. [*See* Spinzia, *Long Island's Prominent Families in the Town of Hempstead* – Beadleston and Milholland entries.] Their son Charles married Marcella Virginia Andrews, the daughter of Matthew Andrews of Cleveland, OH.

*Baxter assisted in framing the constitution under which Wyoming was admitted into statehood. He authored the clause that extended suffrage to women. [For other Long Islanders involved in the suffrage movement *see* Raymond E. Spinzia, "Winning the Franchise: Long Island Activists in the Fight for Woman's Suffrage and Their Opponents, Long Island's Anti-Suffragists." wwwspinzialongislandestates.com.]

[For information about the Baxters' Greenvale residence, *see* Spinzia, *Long Island's Prominent North Shore Families, vol. I* – Baxter entry.]

In 1940 Miss Martha Arrington Burke, the sister of Mrs. Clarence F. Alcott of East Hampton, purchased *Cherokee Cottage* from Mrs. Baxter. [*The New York Times* May 6, 1940, p. 19.]

Beale, Phelan, Sr. (1881-1956)

Occupation(s):	attorney - partner, Bouvier, Caffey, and Beale (later, Bouvier and Beale)
Civic Activism:	president, New York Southern Society; treasurer, University of the South, Sewanee, TN; member, executive committee, East Hampton Associates
Marriage(s):	M/1 – 1917-div. 1946 – Edith Ewing Bouvier (1895-1977)
	M/2 – 1947-1956 – Dorothy D. Durham (1906-1975)
Address:	3 West End Avenue, East Hampton
Name of estate:	*Grey Gardens*
Year of construction:	1897
Style of architecture:	Shingle
Architect(s):	Joseph Greenleaf Thorp designed the house (for F. S, Phillips)
	Eugene Lawrence Futterman, 1980 alterations (for Bradlee)
Landscape architect(s):	Anna Park Gilman Hill designed her own gardens, with Ruth Dean, 1914
	Victoria Fensterer, 1985- (for Bradlee)
Builder:	George A. Eldredge

House extant: yes*
Nassau County Museum Collection has photographs of the estate.
Historical notes:

The house was built by Fleming Stanhope Phillips. In 1913 it was sold to Robert Carmer Hill, who named it *Grey Gardens*. In 1924 Hill sold the house to Beale, who continued to call it *Grey Gardens*. As part of his divorce settlement, Beale deeded the house to his wife Edith.

The *Social Register Summer 1921* lists Phelan and Edith E. Bouvier Beale as residing in East Hampton.

He was the son of Jesse Drew and Caroline Blount Phelan Beale, Jr. of Chattanooga, TN.

Edith Ewing Bouvier Beale was the daughter of John Vernou and Maude Francis Sergeant Bouvier, Jr. of *Little House* and *Lasata* in East Hampton. Edith's brother William married Emma Louise Stone, who resided in Southampton. [*See* Spinzia, *Long Island's Prominent Families in the Town of Southampton* – Bouvier entry.] Her sister Maude married John Ethelbert Davis and resided in Ridgefield, CT. Her sister Michelle married Henry Clarkson Scott, Sr. with whom she resided in Woodmere and, later, Harrington Putnam with whom she resided in East Hampton. [*See* Spinzia, *Long Island's Prominent Families in the Town of Hempstead* – Scott entry.] Her brother John Vernou Bouvier III, who resided at *Rowdy Hall* and, later, at *Little House* in East Hampton, married Janet Norton Lee.

Phelan and Edith Ewing Bouvier Beale, Sr.'s daughter Edith, who resided at *Grey Gardens* with her mother, did not marry. Their son Bouvier Beale, Sr. married Katharine Ridgely Jones, the daughter of Nicholas Ridgely and Katharine Black Jones of *Edgewood* in Glen Cove, and resided in Glen Cove. [*See* Spinzia, *Long Island's Prominent North Shore Families, vol. I* – Beale and Jones entries.] Their son Phelan Beale, Jr. married Roselia Ramsey and resided in Oklahoma City, OK.

The Beales' daughter Edith sold the house in 1979 to Benjamin Crowninshield Bradlee, Sr., who continued to call it *Grey Gardens*.

Dorothy D. Durham Beale was the daughter of Dillard D. and Estelle Durham.

*Alterations were made to the house c. 1972 and in 1980.

The house is on the National Register of Historic Places.

In 2017 the seven-bedroom, six-bath, 6,000-square-foot house and 1.7 acres were for sale. The asking price was $19.995 million.

Beard, Jeremiah Robinson, Jr.

Occupation(s):	capitalist - director, Beard's Erie Basin, Inc., Brooklyn (maritime terminal)
Marriage(s):	M/1 – 1933-div. 1938 – Elizabeth F. Bumiller
	M/2 – 1942 – Lillian H. Osborn (d. 1988)
	- Civic Activism: recording secretary, Garden Club of East Hampton
Address:	122 Egypt Lane, East Hampton
Name of estate:	
Year of construction:	
Style of architecture:	
Architect(s):	
Landscape architect(s):	
House extant: yes	
Historical notes:	

Jeremiah Robinson Beard, Jr. was the son of Jeremiah Robinson and Grace Benedict Beard, Sr.

Elizabeth F. Bumiller Beard was the daughter of Eckley B. Bumiller of NYC. She had previously been married to E. Thurston Clarke of NYC. After her divorce from Beard she married Vanderburgh Johnstone.

Jeremiah Robinson and Elizabeth F. Bumiller Beard, Jr.'s daughter Susan married David King Bryant, the son of Arthur King Bryant of Seattle, WA.

The *Social Register, 1977* lists Jeremiah R. and Lillian H. Osborn Beard [Jr.] as residing at 122 Egypt Lane in East Hampton.

She was the daughter of Percy George Osborn of Glasgow, Scotland.

Jeremiah Robinson and Lillian H. Osborn Beard, Jr.'s daughter Linda married James Howell Brandi, the son of Frederic H. Brandi of New York.

In 2014 the three-bedroom, three-bath, ranch-style guest house and 1.06 acres were for sale. The asking price was $8.95 million.

Beard, Peter Hill (1938-2020)

Occupation(s):	professional photographer – The Peter Beard Studio
	writer - *The End of the Game*, 1965; *Eyelids of Morning*, 1973; *Longing for Darkness*, 1975; *Zara's Tales*, 2004; *Germany*, 2006
Marriage(s):	M/1 – 1967-div. 1970 – Mary Olivia Cochran Cushing (1938-2010)
	M/2 – 1982-div. 1986 – Cheryl Rae Tiegs (b. 1947)
	- model
	fashion designer - Cheryl Tiegs Sportswear; line of wigs and hair accessories for Revlon
	Civic Activism: C.O.A.C.H. Kids and the Earth Conservation Corp.; spokeswoman, City of Hope; ambassador, International Planned Parenthood Foundation
	M/3 – 1986-2020 – Nejama Khanum
Address:	Old Montauk Highway, Montauk
Name of estate:	
Year of construction:	
Style of architecture:	
Architect(s):	
Landscape architect(s):	
House extant: yes	
Historical notes:	

In 1977 Beard's previous house in Montauk was destroyed by fire.

He was the son of Anson McCook and Roseanne Hoar Beard, Jr. of Islip. [*See* Spinzia, *Long Island's Prominent South Shore Families* – Beard entry.] Peter's grandparents Anson McCook and Ruth Hill Beard, Sr. and Friend and Virginia Goffe Hoar resided in Southampton. [*See* Spinzia, *Long Island's Prominent Families in the Town of Southampton* – Beard and Hoar entries.]

Mary Olivia Cochran Cushing Beard was the daughter of Howard Gardiner and Mary Callender Ames Cushing, Sr. of Newport, RI. She subsequently married James Julian Coleman, Jr.

Cheryl Rae Tiegs Beard is the daughter of Theodore and Phyllis Tiegs. Cheryl had previous been married to Stanley John Dragoti. She later married Anthony Peck, the son of actor Gregory Peck, and, subsequently, Rod Stryker.

Peter Hill and Nejama Khanum Beard's daughter Zara was born in 1988.

Beardsley, Samuel Arthur, Sr. (1856-1932)

Occupation(s):	attorney -	partner, Beardsley, Burdick and Beardsley, Utica, NY;
		partner, Beardsley and Beardsley, Utica, NY;
		partner, Beardsley and Hemmens, NYC;
		partner, Beardsley and Taylor, NYC;
		special city judge, Utica, NY, 1886-1888;
		city judge, Utica, NY, 1888-1892
	capitalist -	director, Edison Co. (electric utility firm);
		director, United Electric Light & Power Co.;
		president, Consolidated Telegraph & Electrical Subway Co., NYC;
		secretary and treasurer, Harway Improvement Co.;
		a founder and director, Utica Gas & Electric Co.;
		director, Glens Falls Gas and Electric Light Co.;
		director, General Electric Light & Fuel Co.;
		director, Consolidated Light and Power Co.
	financier -	director, Utica City National Bank
Civic Activism:		chairman, New York State Board of Railroad Commissioners, 1892-1896
Marriage(s):		M/1 – 1881-1916 – Elizabeth Ann Hopper (1857-1916)
		M/2 – 1927-1932 – Lillian Valerie Ella Walpole–Moore

Address: Lee Avenue, East Hampton
Name of estate:
Year of construction: 1900
Style of architecture: Shingle
Architect(s): William Strom designed the house
 (for S. A. Beardsley)
Landscape architect(s):
Builder: Frank Grimshaw, house and 1901 stables
House extant: no
Nassau County Museum Collection has photographs of the estate.
Historical notes:

 The house was built by Samuel Arthur Beardsley, Sr.
 He was the son of Arthur Moore and Louise Howland Adams Beardsley of Utica, NY, and a descendant of Presidents John Adams and John Quincy Adams.
 Elizabeth Ann Hopper Beardsley was the daughter of Thomas Hopper of Utica, NY.
 Samuel Arthur and Elizabeth Ann Hopper Beardsley, Sr.'s daughter Louise married Robert Peebles Kernan, the son of John D. Kernan of Utica, NY. Their son Thomas, who resided in East Hampton, married Louise Tousey and, later, Edith Armstrong. Their son Samuel Arthur Beardsley, Jr. married Emily Gale Loery and resided in Utica, NY.
 Lillian Valerie Ella Walpole–Moore Beardsley was the daughter of Arthur William Moore of Victoria, Australia, and a descendant of the English statesman Horace Walpole. Her grandfather John Moore was Secretary of State for Australia.
 [See following entry for additional family information.]

Beardsley, Thomas Hopper (1882-1962)

Occupation(s):	attorney - partner, Beardsley and Hemmens, NYC; partner, Beardsley and Taylor
	capitalist - director, Consolidated Telegraph; director, Electric Subway Co.
	financier - trustee, South Brooklyn Savings Bank
Civic Activism:	member, Legal Advisory Board, Brooklyn, during World War I
Marriage(s):	M/1 – 1907-div. 1931 – Louise Tousey (b. 1880)
	M/2 – 1931-1962 – Edith Armstrong
Address:	Middle Lane, East Hampton
Name of estate:	
Year of construction:	1933
Style of architecture:	
Architect(s):	
Landscape architect(s):	
Builder:	Charles Rush
House extant: unconfirmed	
Historical notes:	

    The house was built by Mark Ainslie Nobel. [*The East Hampton Star* August 4, 1933, p. 6.] It was later owned by Beardsley. [*The East Hampton Star* January 24, 1946, p. 5.]
    Thomas Hopper Beardsley was the son of Samuel Arthur and Elizabeth Ann Hopper Beardsley, Sr. of East Hampton.
    Louise Tousey Beardsley was the daughter of John Euart and Nellie Elderkin Tousey of Brooklyn. Louise subsequently married Paul E. Vernon of Garden City.
    Thomas Hopper and Louise Tousey Beardsley's daughter Elizabeth married Philip Cooke Sayres, the son of John Hunting Sayres of Brooklyn and, later, Allan Truesdall Leverich, the son of Lewis G. Leverich of Garden City.
    The *Social Register Summer, 1951* lists Thomas H. and Edith Armstrong Beardsley as residing on Middle Lane, East Hampton.
    She was the daughter of John Armstrong of NYC.
[See previous entry for additional family information.]

Beaumont, Perry H. (b. 1961)

Occupation(s):	financier - president, Alpha Global Advisors, East Hampton; founder, Bedotcome (career counseling firm); managing director, Financial Economics, 2008; co-head of global fixed income, AXA Management, 1999-2001; managing director, Morgan Stanley Wealth Management, 1996-1999; senior vice-president, Lehman Brothers, 1993-1996; head of market risk management for the Americas, UBS, 1990-1993; financial strategist, Swiss Bank Corp NY; bond fund analyst, Kidder, Peabody and Co. inventor - created computer method and apparatus for aggregating and segmenting probalistic distributions, 2008 educator - adjunct faculty, Fordham University, The Bronx, NY writer - *Financial Engineering Principles*, 2003; *Fixed-Income Synthetic Assets*
Civic Activism:	volunteer, Invest Write Program at SIFMA
Marriage(s):	Alexandra *[unable to determine maiden name]*
Address:	82 Woods Lane, East Hampton
Name of estate:	
Year of construction:	1912
Style of architecture:	Dutch Colonial Revival
Architect(s):	Joseph Greenleaf Thorp designed the house (for Flannery)
Landscape architect(s)	
House extant:	yes
Historical notes:	

The 5,500-square-foot, seven-bedroom house was built by John Flannery. It was later owned by Beaumont.
In 2005 Michael P. and Erin M. Callan Thompson purchased the house from Beaumont for $3.93 million.
In 2008 Michael sold the house to Erin for $495,000. The transaction may have been part of their divorce settlement.
In 2013 Erin and her new husband Anthony Montella sold the house to Christopher J. and Tannaz Fiore for $3.75 million.

Becker, Harold (b. 1928)

Occupation(s):	entertainers and associated professions - television commercials director; motion picture producer and director professional photographer
Marriage(s):	Susan E. *[unable to determine maiden name]* - entertainers and associate professions - motion picture costume designer educator - fashion design, University of Illinois, Champaign–Urbana, IL
Address:	Town Line Road, East Hampton
Name of estate:	
Year of construction:	1969
Style of architecture:	Modern
Architect(s):	Norman Jaffe designed the house (for Becker)
Landscape architect(s)	
Builder:	Robert Gruber and David Stoeckert
House extant:	yes
Historical notes:	

The house was built by Harold Becker.

Beckers, William Kurt (1900-1989)

Occupation(s):	financier - partner, Spencer, Trask, and Co.; partner, Hornblower and Weeks; vice-president, Shearson Lehman Brothers (investment banking firm) industrialist - director, Mohawk Paper Mills, Inc.
Civic Activism:	chairman of board of governors, New York Stock Exchange; president, Maidstone Club, East Hampton
Marriage(s):	1929-1985 – Annadel Kelly (1907-1985) - Civic Activism: treasurer, Garden Club of East Hampton
Address:	Highway Behind the Pond, East Hampton
Name of estate:	
Year of construction:	
Style of architecture:	
Architect(s):	
Landscape architect(s):	
House extant: unconfirmed	
Historical notes:	

The Blue Book of The Hamptons, 1958 lists Mr. and Mrs. William K. Beckers as residing on Highway Behind the Pond, East Hampton.
   He was the son of William Gerhardt and Antoinette Pothen Beckers of NYC.
   Annadel Kelly Beckers was the daughter of Bernard P. Kelly of NYC.
   William Kurt and Annadel Kelly Beckers' daughter Antoinette married Robert William MacNamara, Sr., the son of William Kelly MacNamara of West Medford, MA, and resided in Wellesley, MA. Their daughter Annadel married James Timpson, the son of Carl William and Marcelle E. Vallon Timpson, Sr. of *Windy Top* in Hewlett Harbor, and resided in Bernardsville, NJ. [*See* Spinzia, *Long Island's Prominent Families in the Town of Hempstead* – Timpson entry.]
   By 1973 Beckers had relocated to East Dune Lane, East Hampton.

Beebe, William Nottingham, Sr. (1903-1985)

Occupation(s):	financier - manager, bond department, Stillman, Maynard, and Co.
Marriage(s):	1924-1981 – Margaret Louise Weeks (1903-1981)
Address:	Highway Behind the Pond, East Hampton
Name of estate:	
Year of construction:	
Style of architecture:	
Architect(s):	
Landscape architect(s):	
House extant: unconfirmed	
Historical notes:	

The Blue Book of The Hamptons, 1973 lists Mr. and Mrs. William N. Beebe as residing on Highway-Behind-the-Pond, East Hampton.
   He was the son of Clifford Dwight and Helen Maud Chapin Beebe.
   Margaret Louise Weeks Beebe was the daughter of John Lafayette and Margaret Clarbaugh Weeks of East Hampton.
   William Nottingham and Margaret Louise Weeks Beebe, Sr.'s son Daniel married Patricia Ann Sullivan, the daughter of Edward C. Sullivan of Pittsburgh, PA. Their son William Nottingham Beebe, Jr. resided in Englewood, NJ, and Camden, SC.

Bell, Alfred Dennis, Sr. (1886-1961)

Occupation(s):	politician - member, New York State legislature
Civic Activism:	president, East Hampton Associates
Marriage(s):	M/1 – 1908-div. 1916 – Dorothy Perry (d. 1971)
	M/2 – div. c. 1937 – Dorothy McAlpin (1887-1971)
	M/3 – 1937-1961 – Helen Burt Holmes (1887-1961)
Address:	Georgica Road, East Hampton
Name of estate:	
Year of construction:	c. 1915
Style of architecture:	Modified Colonial Revival
Architect(s):	John Custis Lawrence, 1928 alterations (for A. D. Bell, Sr.)
Landscape architect(s):	
House extant: yes	
Historical notes:	

The house was built by Dr. Frederick Lester Stanton. It was purchased by Bell in 1928.

He was the son of James Christy and Mary Eliza Dennis Bell, Sr. His brother James Christy Bell, Jr. married Louise Tiffany Frank, the daughter of Charles Augustus and Louise Clark Read Frank of *Charlon House* in Glen Cove, and resided at *Stramore* in Upper Brookville. [*See* Spinzia, *Long Island's Prominent North Shore Families, vol. 1* – Bell and Frank entries.]

Dorothy Perry Bell was the daughter of Dr. Safford Goodwin and Mrs. Frances Shedd Thomas Perry. Dorothy subsequently married Leonard C. Hammond and resided in Washington, CT.

Alfred Dennis and Dorothy Perry Bell, Sr.'s son Alfred Dennis Bell, Jr. married Marjorie Ramsay Blyth, the daughter of Charles Blyth of Burlingame, CA.

The *Social Register Summer, 1932* lists Alfred D. and Dorothy McAlpin Bell [Sr.] as residing in East Hampton.

She was the daughter of George Lodowich and Sallie Blanche McAlpin, Sr. of *Dune Alpine* in East Hampton.

Alfred Dennis and Dorothy McAlpin Bell, Sr.'s daughter Shirley married William Harold Murphy of Lake Placid, NY. Their daughter Nancy married Joseph C. Belden, Jr. of Lake Forest, IL. Their daughter Dorothy married Dr. Auley McRae Crough, Jr. of Wilmington, DE.

Helen Burt Holmes Bell was the daughter of Francis Hutchins and Mary Burt Holmes. Helen had previously been married to Samuel F. Streit.

Bell, Dr. Dennistoun Mildeberger (1879-1954)

Occupation(s):	physician
Marriage(s):	M/1 – 1905-1947 – Frances A. Dolan (1885-1947)
	M/2 – Agnes C. Loftus (1883-1968)
Address:	off Springs – Amagansett Road, Amagansett
Name of estate:	*Broadview*
Year of construction:	c. 1916
Style of architecture:	Neo-Georgian
Architect(s):	Trowbridge and Livingston designed the house (for D. M. Bell)
Landscape architect(s):	
Builder:	William Crawford
House extant: no; destroyed by fire, 1991	
Historical notes:	

The twenty-one-room house, originally named *Broadview*, was located on Gardiner's Bay. It was built by Dr. Dennistoun Mildeberger Bell. Bell's estate eventually encompassed over five hundred acres.

He was the son of Dr. Christopher M. and Mrs. Mary Norris Bell.

Frances Dolan Bell was the daughter of Richard Vincent and Mary Jane Scanlon–Scanlon Dolan of Pennsylvania.

Dr. Dennistoun Mildeberger and Mrs. Frances Dolan Bell's daughter Mary married Benjamin Rabe. Their son William married Alice Conklin Miller, the daughter of Joseph Francis Miller of Montauk.

Agnes C. Loftus Bell was the daughter of John and Winnifred Loftus.

In 1988 Reginald F. Lewis purchased the estate from Amagan, Inc. He was the owner of the house at the time it was destroyed by fire.

Bell, Emily Carrington Trowbridge (1884-1933)

Marriage(s):	M/1 – 1902-div. 1915 – Frederick Gallatin II (1880-1956)
	- financier - partner, Smith and Gallatin (stock brokerage firm)
	M/2 – 1915- div. – John S. Garvan, Sr. (1880-1954)
	- merchant - P. Garvan, Inc. (paper and paper stock dealers)
	financier - director, Riverside Trust Co.
	Civic Activism: trustee, John S. Garvan Foundation
	M/3 – 1922 – George Newell Bell (1880-1945)
	- attorney
Address:	Apaquogue Road, East Hampton
Name of estate:	
Year of construction:	c. 1920
Style of architecture:	Colonial Revival
Architect(s):	Aymar Embury II
Landscape architect(s):	
House extant: yes	
Historical notes:	

   The *Social Directory of Southampton, Long Island, 1931* lists Emily C. Trowbridge Bell as residing on Apaquogue Road, East Hampton.
   She was the daughter of Edwin Dwight and Harriet Carrington Trowbridge of NYC.
   Frederic Gallatin was the son of James and Elizabeth Hill Dawson Gallatin of New York.
   Frederic and Emily Carrington Trowbridge Gallatin's daughter Frederica married Albert Francis Donahue, the son of Peter J. Donahue of Dorchester, MA. Their daughter Nancy married Edward Wanner Burns.
   John S. Garvan, Sr. was the son of Patrick and Mary Carroll Garvan of East Hartford, CT. John's brother Francis married Mabel Brady and resided at *Roslyn House* in Old Westbury. His sister Genevieve, who resided at *Inisfada* in North Halls, married Nicholas Frederic Brady and, later, William J. Macaulay. [*See* Spinzia, *Long Island's Prominent North Shore Families, vol. 1* – Brady and Garvan entries.]
   George Newell Bell was the son of George and Edna Shaw Newell Bell of *Belfort* in New Brighton, Staten Island, NY.

Bell, Dr. James Finley (1860-1936)

Occupation(s):	physician - known for bacteriological studies of milk and its role in infant health;
	staff, State Hospital, Wards Island, NY;
	staff, Brentwood Sanitarium, Brentwood, NY;
	founder, Englewood Baby Dispensary, Englewood, NJ
Marriage(s):	1883-1936 – Cordella Mayes
Address:	10 Pantigo Road, East Hampton
Name of estate:	
Year of construction:	1895
Style of architecture:	Dutch Colonial Revival
Architect(s):	
Landscape architect(s):	
Builder:	George A. Eldredge
House extant: unconfirmed	
Historical notes:	

   The house was built by Dr. James Finley Bell.
   Dr. James Finley and Mrs. Cordella Mayes Bell's son William Washington Bell married Harriet Darling Holran, the daughter of Francis P. Holran of Englewood, NJ, and resided in Tenafly, NJ. Their son Dr. Alfred Loomis Bell married Grace Pauline Seidel, the daughter of William R. Seidel, and resided in Tenafly, NJ. Their daughter Lillian married George V. Harvey and resided in Englewood, NJ. Their daughter Evaline married Norman Theodore Anthony and resided in Tenafly, NJ. Their son Samuel resided in River Ridge, NJ.

Bellas, Alfred Constantine (b. 1942)

Occupation(s):	financier - Dillon, Read and Co., Inc., NYC;
	vice-president, Goldman Sachs and Co., NYC;
	general partner, Loeb, Rhoades and Co., NYC;
	vice-president, Loeb, Rhoades, Hornblower, Inc., NYC;
	chairman of board, Neuberger, Berman Trust Co., NYC;
	managing director, Offibank;
	vice-president, Shearson, Lehman Brothers, NYC
	attorney
Civic Activism:	director, Lincoln Center for the Performing Arts, Inc., NYC;
	treasurer, director, and chairman, finance committee, Lincoln Center Constituent Development Project, Inc., NYC;
	chairman of board, American Ballet, NYC;
	director and treasurer, Guild Hall, East Hampton;
	member, board of regents and chairman of finance committee, The Mercerburg Academy;
	chairman of investment committee, Century Association;
	trustee, St Mary's Foundation for Children

Marriage(s):
    M/1 – 1970-div. – Selina Schroeder Croll
        (aka Tina Croll)
      - entertainers and associated professions -
        dancer;
        choreographer
    M/2 – 1978 – Kathryn Mazzo (b. 1946)
        (aka Kay Mazzo)
      - entertainers and associated professions -
        ballet dancer, New York City Ballet
        Civic Activism: co-chair, faculty committee, School of American Ballet, NYC

Address:	43 Dunemere Lane, East Hampton
Name of estate:	
Year of construction:	1886
Style of architecture:	Shingle with Dutch elements
Architect(s):	Joseph Greenleaf Thorp designed the house (for S. F. Johnson)
Landscape architect(s):	
Builder:	George A. Eldredge
House extant: yes	
Historical notes:	

    The six-bedroom, five-and-a-half-bath, 5,500-square-foot house was built by Servetus Fisher Johnson. It was later owned by Bellas.
    He is the son of Constantine Michael and Kiki Michalopoulos Bellas of Ohio.
    Selina Schroeder Croll Bellas is the daughter of Joseph D. Croll of NYC and a descendant of the last Dutch governor of New Amsterdam and Governor John Winthrop of the Massachusetts Bay Colony.
    Kathryn Mazzo Bellas is the daughter of F. Alfred Mazzo of Evanston, IL.

Benjamin, Park, III (1849-1922)
aka Park Benjamin, Jr.

Occupation(s): attorney - specialized in patent law
journalist - associate editor, *Scientific American*, 1872-1878
publisher - editor-in-chief, *Appleton's Cyclopedia of Applied Mechanics*, 1878-1891
writer - *Shakings or Etchings from United States Naval Academy*, 1867;
Wrinkles and Recipes, 1875;
The End of New York, 1881;
The Age of Electricity, 1886;
The Voltaic Cell, 1892;
The History of Electricity, 1895;
The Early History of the United States Naval Academy;
numerous articles in journals & newspapers

Marriage(s): 1891-1922 – Ida E. Crane (1866-1922)

Address: Buel Lane, East Hampton
Name of estate:
Year of construction:
Style of architecture:
Architect(s):
Landscape architect(s):
House extant: unconfirmed
Historical notes:

The *Social Register, Summer 1915* lists Park and Ida E. Crane Benjamin [III] as residing in East Hampton. The Benjamins were renting the William Everest house.

He was the son of Park and Mary Brower Western Benjamin, Jr. of Manhattan.

Ida E. Crane Benjamin was institutionalized in 1910. [*The New York Times* September 13, 1922, p. 18.] When Benjamin refused to pay his wife's hospital bills, they were paid by his son-in-law Enrico Caruso.

Park and Ida E. Crane Benjamin III's daughter Dorothy, who married the famed tenor Enrico Caruso, Ernest A. Ingram, and, subsequently, Dr. Charles Adams Holder, resided in Southampton. [*See* Spinzia, *Long Island's Prominent Families in the Town of Southampton* – Caruso entry.] Their daughter Marjorie married John Wolf Clark and, later, William T. Glenney. Their daughter Gladys married Frederick Worth Goddard of New York and resided in Plainfield, NJ. Their son Romeyn was a bachelor. Their son Park Benjamin IV married Katherine Ward Doremus, the daughter of Dr. Charles Avery Doremus, and, later, Gladys Lanphere, the daughter of Lamkin Lanphere. Katherine had Park imprisoned for failure to provide child support. [*The New York Times* May 20, 1924, p. 44.]

Benjamin disinherited his children and adopted their governess Anna Marie Bochi who inherited his fortune. She married her attorney Arthur Louis Fullman.

Benjamin relocated to Westhampton Beach. [*See* Spinzia, *Long Island's Prominent Families in the Town of Southampton* – Benjamin entry.]

Benjamin, William Wallace, Jr. (1872-1902)

Occupation(s):	
Marriage(s):	Florence Almira Briggs (1868-1934)
	- Civic Activism: president, Garden Club of East Hampton
Address:	Crossways, East Hampton
Name of estate:	*Crossways*
Year of construction:	1902
Style of architecture:	Shingle
Architect(s):	George A. Eldredge and John Custis Lawrence designed the house (for W. W. Benjamin, Jr.)
Landscape architect(s):	Marian Cruger Coffin designed the perennial garden with privet arch, the small pool, and long grass allee, c. 1928 (for Mrs. W. W. Benjamin, Jr.)
Builder:	George A. Eldredge

House extant: yes
Nassau County Museum Collection has photographs of the estate.
Historical notes:

   The house, originally named *Crossways*, was built by William Wallace Benjamin, Jr.
   He was the son of William Wallace and Delia Ann Flint Benjamin, Sr. of Sing Sing [Ossining], NY.
   Florence Almira Briggs Benjamin was the daughter of Pierson Douglas and Lucy Rockefeller Briggs of Cleveland, OH. Florence's sister Sallie married George Lodowich McAlpin, Sr. and resided at *Dune Alpin* in East Hampton.
   William Wallace and Florence Almira Briggs Benjamin, Jr.'s daughter Lucy married Morgan Witter Rogers and resided in South Kingstown, RI. Their son William Wallace Benjamin III later owned the house.
[See following entry for additional family information.]
   It was subsequently owned by Alexander Neil Lilley, Sr. who continued to call it *Crossways*.

Benjamin, William Wallace, III (b. 1898)

Occupation(s):	capitalist - real estate
Marriage(s):	M/1 – 1924-1952 – Candace Catlin Woodruff (1902-1952)
	- Civic Activism: director, East Hampton Visiting Nurse Association, Inc.
	M/2 – 1958 – Dorothy Patience Du Croz
Address:	Crossways, East Hampton
Name of estate:	*Crossways*
Year of construction:	1902
Style of architecture:	Shingle
Architect(s):	George A. Eldredge and John Custis Lawrence designed the house (for W. W. Benjamin, Jr.)
Landscape architect(s):	Marian Cruger Coffin designed perennial garden with privet arch, the small pool, and long grass allee, c. 1928 (for Mrs. W. W. Benjamin, Jr.)

House extant: yes
Historical notes:

   The house, originally named *Crossways*, was built by William Wallace Benjamin, Jr. It was later owned by his son William Wallace Benjamin III.
   Candace Catlin Woodruff Benjamin was the daughter of Judge James Parsons Woodruff of Litchfield, CT.
   William Wallace and Candace Catlin Woodruff Benjamin III's daughter Barbara married Boughton Cobb, Jr., the son of Boughton and Edith McKeever Cobb, Sr. of *The Chimney* in Hewlett Bay Park. [*See* Spinzia, *Long Island's Prominent Families in the Town of Hempstead* – Cobb entry.] Their daughter Candace married Honore Martyn Owen, Jr. of Decatur, IL.
   Dorothy Patience Du Croz Benjamin was the daughter of Francis Du Croz of Surry, England. She had previously been married to the Honorable Patrick William May, the son of Sir George Ernest May, the first Baron May, and Lily Julia Straus May. Dorothy's second husband was the actor Roland Young, who starred in the 1937 motion picture "Topper" with Cary Grant and Constance Bennett.
[See previous entry for additional family information.]
   It was subsequently owned by Alexander Neil Lilley, Sr. who continued to call it *Crossways*.

Bennett, Russell Conwell, Sr. (1892-1976)

Occupation(s):	industrialist - chairman of board, R. C. Bennett Box and Pallet Co., Englewood, NJ; partner, Corrugated Container Co., Columbus, OH
Marriage(s):	M/1 ____ M/2 – 1952-1976 – Katharine Irene Edwards (1910-2003) - nurse
Address:	West End Avenue, East Hampton
Name of estate:	
Year of construction:	1928
Style of architecture:	Modified Neo-Tudor
Architect(s):	Robert Tappan designed the house (for N. A. Campbell, Sr.)
Landscape architect(s):	
House extant: no; demolished in 1995	
Historical notes:	

The house, originally named *Camelot*, was built by Nathaniel Adams Campbell, Sr. In 1945 Mrs. Campbell sold it to Bennett. [*The Country Review* October 18, 1945, p. 7.]

The house, which is on the National Register of Historic Places, was later owned by Lydia Stokes.
[See following entry for additional family information.]

Bennett, Russell Conwell, Sr. (1892-1976)

Occupation(s):	industrialist - chairman of board, R. C. Bennett Box and Pallet Co., Englewood, NJ; partner, Corrugated Container Co., Columbus, OH
Marriage(s):	M/1 ____ M/2 – 1952-1976 – Katharine Irene Edwards (1910-2003) - nurse
Address:	21 North Main Street, East Hampton
Name of estate:	
Year of construction:	
Style of architecture:	Neo-Federal
Architect(s):	
Landscape architect(s):	
House extant: yes	
Historical notes:	

The Blue Book of The Hamptons, 1973 lists Russell C. and Katharine Edwards Bennett as residing at 21 North Main Street, East Hampton.

Katharine Edwards Bennett was the daughter of Dr. David and Mrs. Carrie Mulford Edwards of East Hampton.

Russell C. and Katharine Edwards Bennett, Sr.'s son Gunnar married Beatrice Branch Briggs, the daughter of James Branch and Virginia C. Moore Briggs of *Beehive* in East Hampton.

In 2013 the 6,000+-square-foot, six-bedroom, four-and-a-half-bath house and 3.5 acres were for sale. The asking price was $3.95 million.

Benson, Arthur W. (1812-1889)

Occupation(s):	capitalist - developer of Bensonhurst section of Brooklyn; one of nine investors in the Brooklyn Bridge; owner, sheep farm, Montauk; president, Brooklyn Gas Co.
	financier - director, Brooklyn Savings Bank
Civic Activism:	trustee, Brooklyn Hospital; trustee, Packer Collegiate Institute, Brooklyn Heights; trustee, Brooklyn Academy of Music; trustee, Brooklyn Dispensary; trustee, Greenwood Cemetery, Brooklyn; trustee, Brooklyn Polytechnic Institute
Marriage(s):	Jane Ann Marks (1829-1913)
Address:	115 De Forest Road, Montauk
Name of estate:	*Weeweecho*
Year of construction:	1883
Style of architecture:	Beach Cottage
Architect(s):	McKim, Mead & White designed the house (for Benson)
Landscape architect(s):	Frederick Law Olmsted designed the site plan (for Benson)
Builder:	George A. Eldredge & Son, 1914 alterations (for Mary Benson)
	Mead & Taft

House extant: yes
Historical notes:

The 4,000-square-foot house, originally named *Weeweecho*, was built by Arthur W. Benson. Benson also owned all of Plum Island. [*The Brooklyn Daily Eagle* September 9, 1883, p. 1.]

He was the son of John Benson, Sr.

Jane Ann Marks Benson was the daughter of Dennis and Almira Bacon Marks.

Arthur W. and Jane Ann Marks Benson's granddaughter Thyrza married Montague Flagg II, with whom she resided at *Applewood* in Upper Brookville, and, later, Harold Fowler with whom she resided at *Middlebrook* in Far Hills, NJ, and *Hither House* in Southampton. [*See* Spinzia, *Long Island's Prominent North Shore Families, vol. 1* – Flagg entry – and *Long Island's Prominent in the Town of Southampton* – Fowler entry.] Their son Frank married Elizabeth Woodbridge Are, the daughter of Robert and Olivia Phelps Are.

The house was inherited by the Bensons' daughter Mary, who did not marry. The *Brooklyn Blue Book and Long Island Society Register, 1918* lists Mary Benson as residing at *Weeweecho* in Montauk.

The house was later owned by Marion Bolton Marsh, who called it *Windway*, and, then, by her daughter Penelope and son-in-law Holger Lundbergh, who renamed it *Bayberry*. In 1981 is was purchased by Charles Matthew Levi.

In 1995 the house sold for $700,000.

Betner, Benjamin Carlton, Jr. (1908-1970)

Occupation(s):	industrialist - president, Benjamin C. Betner Co., Devon, PA (manufacturer of bags from paper, foil, cellophane, laminate, glassine, plastic, and wax paper) (merged into Continental Can); vice-president, Continental Can Co.
Marriage(s):	M/1 – 1932-div. 1948 – Josephine Lee Auchincloss (1912-2005) M/2 – div. – Rosamund Saltonstall Auchincloss (1907-1971) M/3 – Frances Louise Weeks
Address:	Lily Pond Lane, East Hampton
Name of estate:	
Year of construction:	
Style of architecture:	
Architect(s):	
Landscape architect(s):	
House extant: unconfirmed	
Historical notes:	

Benjamin Carlton Betner, Jr. was the son of Benjamin Carlton and Olyve Mayfields Ballard Betner, Sr.

Josephine Lee and Rosamund Saltonstall Auchincloss Betner were the daughters of Charles Cooke and Rosamond Saltonstall Auchincloss of *Builtover* in Roslyn Heights. After her divorce from Betner, Josephine married Harry Ingersoll Nicholas III, the son of Harry Ingersoll and Dorothy Snow Nicholas II of *Rolling Hill Farm* in Muttontown. [*See* Spinzia, *Long Island's Prominent North Shore Families*, vol. I – Auchincloss entry – and *vol. II* – Nicholas entry.] Rosamund Saltonstall Auchincloss Betner had previously been married to James Lee Burton, Jr. of Cold Spring Harbor. After her divorce from Betner, she married Thomas Campbell Plowden–Wardlaw.

Benjamin Carlton and Josephine Lee Auchincloss Betner, Jr.'s daughter Josephine married Alexander Dunn Mallace, the son of Malcolm G. Mallace of Providence, RI, and resided in San Marino, CA. Their daughter Cynthia married Simon David Manonian, the son of Jacques Manonian of Grenoble, France. Their daughter Nina married John Troxell, the son of Harry L. Troxell of Narberth, PA.

Frances Louise Weeks Betner was the daughter of John Lafayette and Margaret Louise Clarbough Weeks of East Hampton. Frances had previously been married to David Balderston Stone, the son of Robert E. Stone of Brookline, MA, and, later, to Bruce Edgar Ryan of East Hampton.

Betts, Hobart Dominick, Sr. (1872-1934)

Occupation(s):	industrialist - vice-president and treasurer, Thomas and Betts Co. (manufacturer of electrical specialties)
Marriage(s):	1903-c. 1926 – Josephine Gould (1879-1926)
Address:	Main Street, East Hampton
Name of estate:	
Year of construction:	
Style of architecture:	
Architect(s):	
Landscape architect(s):	
House extant: unconfirmed	
Historical notes:	

The *Long Island Society Register, 1929* lists Hobart D. Betts [Sr.] as residing on Main Street, East Hampton.

He was the son of George Whitefield and Margaret E. Dominick Betts, Sr. of Englewood, NJ.

Josephine Gould Betts was from Wellesley, MA.

Hobart Dominick and Josephine Gould Betts, Sr.'s son Hobart Dominick Betts, Jr. married Elizabeth Vosseller Higgins, the daughter of Judiah Higgins of Flemington, NJ. After Hobart's untimely death, Elizabeth married John C. Swartley, Jr.

Despondent over his wife's death and his son's suicide, Hobart Dominick Betts, Sr. took his own life by plunging from the tenth floor of his Park Avenue apartment. [*The New York Times* October 30, 1934, p. 42.]

Bianchi, Albert William (1900-1956)

Occupation(s): financier - a founder, Zwetsch Heinzelman and Co., Inc. (utility
         brokerage firm);
   partner, Carl M. Loeb and Co. (stock brokerage firm);
   partner, Pyne, Kendall, and Hollister (stock brokerage firm)

Marriage(s): 1925-1956 – Gladys Wilckes (1903-1975)
   - Civic Activism: co-chair, Guild Hall Rehabilitation Fund, East Hampton

Address: Further Lane, East Hampton
Name of estate:
Year of construction:
Style of architecture:
Architect(s):
Landscape architect(s):
House extant: unconfirmed
Historical notes:

In 1950 Bianchi purchased a poultry house and converted it into his residence. [*The East Hampton Star* October 5, 1950, p. 1.]

The Blue Book of The Hamptons, 1958 lists Mrs. Albert W. Bianchi as residing on Further Lane, East Hampton.

She was the daughter of Felix Wilckes of Manhattan. She subsequently married Arthur B. Marvin, the son of William Bradbury Marvin of Montclair, NJ, and resided in Manhattan.

Albert William Bianchi was the son of William Bianchi of Central Park West, NYC, and Patchogue.

Albert William and Gladys Wilckes Bianchi's son William married Louise Kennedy, the daughter of William Walker and Louise Leeds Kennedy of *Plandome Mills* in Plandome Manor. [*See* Spinzia, *Long Island's Prominent North Shore Families, vol. I* – Kennedy entry.]

Binn, Moreton (b. 1936)
aka Moreton Binstock

Occupation(s): capitalist - chairman of board and CEO, Atwood Richards Inc., NYC
         (international bartering firm);
   co-founder, with his wife Marisol, Xpres Spa;
   owner, Pen-Mar Farm, Muttontown (80-acre horse-breeding farm)

Civic Activism: co-founder, with his wife Marisol, Charitable Foundation for Animals,
   Ridgefield, CT;
   founder, Moreton Binstock Scholarship

Marriage(s): M/1 – 1960-1997 – Penny Schwartz (1938-1997)
   - clinical psychologist
       educator - faculty member, Queens College, Flushing, NY;
          faculty member, Kingsborough Community College,
          Brooklyn, NY;
          professor of psychology, Adelphi University, Garden City
   M/2 – Marisol Fernandes (b. 1967)
   - capitalist - co-founder, with her husband Moreton, Xpres Spa
       Civic Activism: co-founder, with her husband Moreton, Charitable
          Foundation for Animals, Ridgefield, CT

Address: Further Lane, Amagansett
Name of estate:
Year of construction: 2001
Style of architecture: Eclectic Colonial Revival
Architect(s):
Landscape architect(s)
House extant: yes
Historical notes:

Penny Schwartz Binn was the daughter of William and Hattie Schwartz.

Moreton and Penny Schwartz Binn's son Jason married Haley Phyliss Lieberman, the daughter of Alan R. and Diane Lieberman of Aventura, FL. Their son Jonathan resides in Washington, DC.

In 2007 Binn sold the 9,000-square-foot, five-bedroom, eight-bath house to Vinayak Singh for $9.5 million.

In 2012 Singh listed the house for sale. The asking price, which represented a $1 million loss for Singh, was $8.5 million.

Bisco, Leonard Gerard (1903-2002)

Occupation(s):	attorney - partner, Newman and Bisco, NYC
Marriage(s):	M/1 – 1926-div. 1937 – Dorothy Rabinowitz
	M/2 – 1938-1955 – Loretta *[unable to determine maiden name]* (d. 1955)
Address:	86 Lily Pond Lane, East Hampton
Name of estate:	
Year of construction:	1901
Style of architecture:	Neo-Tudor
Architect(s):	Joseph Greenleaf Thorp designed the house (for J. R. Paxton, Sr.)
Landscape architect(s):	
Builder:	George A. Eldredge
House extant: yes	
Historical notes:	

The house, originally named *Windward*, was built by The Reverend John Randolph Paxton, Sr. It was later owned by his daughter Mary Elkins Paxton Hamlin who continued to call it *Windward*. In 1946 Mrs. Hamlin sold the house to Bisco. [*The East Hampton Star* February 14, 1946, p. 5.]

He was the son of Herman S. and Lizzie Bisco of Brooklyn, NY.

Leonard Gerard and Dorothy Rabinowitz Bisco's daughter Susan married Michael D. Aaron, the son of Jack Aaron of Westhampton Beach.

In 1963 the house was purchased by Alvin Gibbs Fox. [*The East Hampton Star* April 23, 1964, p. 3.] It was later owned by Carol Ann Morgan who, in 2010, sold the house for $25.5 million.

Alterations to the house were made in 1906 and 1926.

Bishop, Bennett (1862-1935)

Occupation(s):	electrical engineer
	capitalist - breeding and selling polo ponies
Marriage(s):	M/1 – 1892-div. 1904 – Grace Kellogg Scoville (b. c. 1865)
	M/2 – 1931-1935 – Marion Eloise Antman (b. 1870)
Address:	4 Ocean Avenue, East Hampton
Name of estate:	*Pudding Hill*
Year of construction:	c. 1887
Style of architecture:	Shingle
Architect(s):	Isaac Henry Green II designed the house and the 1906 extension (for E. Herrick)*
Landscape architect(s):	
House extant: yes	
Historical notes:	

The house, originally named *Pudding Hill*, was built by Dr. Everett Herrick. It was later owned by his brother-in-law James Bishop Ford; by Ford's cousin Bennett Bishop; and, subsequently, by John Richard Peddy. Ford, Bishop, and Peddy continued to call the house *Pudding Hill*.

Bennett Bishop was the son of James and Mary Faugeres Ellis Bishop. His brother Dr. Louis Faugeres Bishop, Sr. married Charlotte Dater Gruner and resided at *Bishopgate* in East Hampton.

Marion Eloise Antman Bishop was the daughter of John Antman of Suffolk, MA.

On the eve of Bishop's marriage to Marion his nephew Dr. Louis Faugeres Bishop, Jr. filed papers in the courts declaring Bennett incompetent and accused him of squandering the $1,205,000 inheritance he had received from his cousin James Bishop Ford. Bennett was declared competent and his nephew had to pay all legal costs. [*The New York Times* June 30, 1931, p. 7, and July 21, 1931, p. 24.]

[See Bishop and Ford entries for additional family information.]

*For Green's other commissions, see Spinzia, *Long Island's Prominent South Shore Families: Their Estates and Their Country Homes in the Towns of Babylon and Islip.*

Bishop, Dr. Louis Faugeres, Jr. (1901-1986)

Occupation(s):	physician - clinical cardiologist
	writer - *Myself When Young: Growing Up in New York, 1901-1925*;
	The Birth of a Specialty: A Diary of an American Cardiologist, 1926-1972
Civic Activism:	president, American College of Cardiology, 1960-1961;
	a founder and president, American College of Sports Medicine, 1958-1959
Marriage(s):	1925-1986 – Kathleen Sinclair (1905-1992)
	- Civic Activism: director, East Hampton Visiting Nurse Association, Inc.;
	director, Ladies Village Improvement Society, East Hampton
Address:	18 Ocean Avenue, East Hampton
Name of estate:	*Holiday*
Year of construction:	1928
Style of architecture:	Georgian with French Country elements
Architect(s):	L. Bancel LaFarge designed the house (for L. F. Bishop, Jr.)
Landscape architect(s):	
House extant: yes*	
Historical notes:	

The house, originally named *Holiday*, was built by Dr. Louis Faugeres Bishop, Jr.

The *Social Directory of Southampton, Long Island, 1931* lists Dr. Louis Faugeres and Mrs. Kathleen Sinclair Bishop, Jr. as residing on Ocean Avenue, East Hampton. The *Social Register Summer, 1945* lists *Holiday* as the name of their residence.

He was the son of Dr. Louis Faugeres and Mrs. Charlotte Dater Gruner Bishop, Sr. of East Hampton.

Kathleen Sinclair Bishop was the daughter of Earle Westwood and Blanche Stich Sinclair of *Fairlawn* in East Hampton.

Dr. Louis Faugeres and Mrs. Kathleen Sinclair Bishop, Jr.'s daughter Anne married Alexander Cannon and resided in New York City. Their daughter Barbara married Stuart Hall Bartle and resided in Manhattan. Their daughter Mary married Robert Plant Millspaugh, the son of Francis C. Millspaugh of Swampscott, MA, and resided in Huntington. Their son Louis Faugeres Bishop III married Alexandra Griggs.

[See other Bishop entries for additional family information.]

In 1962 Bishop sold the house to Socrates George Gainis, Sr. for $52,500. [*The East Hampton Star* March 15, 1962, p. 4, and June 14, 1962, p. 4.]

*The house sustained damage from a fire in 1985 and was remodeled in 1986 and 2013. [*The East Hampton Star* January 2, 1986, p. 16.]

In 2014 the 6,000-square-foot, seven-bedroom, five-and-a-half-bath house and 1.48 acres were for sale. The asking price was $13.9 million. In 2015 the price was reduced to $11.5 million. In 2019 it was reduced to $7.995 million.

Bishop, Dr. Louis Faugeres, Sr. (1864-1941)

Occupation(s):	physician - St. Luke's Hospital, 1889-1892; visiting physician, Lincoln Hospital; physician, Mercy Hospital, Hempstead, NY
	writer - *Heart Disease and Blood Pressure as Affecting the Heart, Brain, Kidneys, and General Circulation*; *Arteriosclerosis*; *Heart Troubles: Their Prevention and Relief*; *Heart Disease, Blood Pressure, and Nauheim Treatment*; *A Key to the Electro-cardiograms*; co-author, *History of Cardiology*; co-translator, *Mechanism of the Heart*; numerous articles in medical journals
Civic Activism:	trustee, New York Academy of Medicine; trustee, Good Samaritan Dispensary; director, School for the Deaf; director, Museum of the American Indian; director, Society for Relief of Widows and Orphans; treasurer, Rutgers University, New Brunswick, NJ
Marriage(s):	1899-1941 – Charlotte Dater Gruner (1876-1966)
Address:	Woods Lane, East Hampton
Name of estate:	*Bishopgate*
Year of construction:	
Style of architecture:	
Architect(s):	
Landscape architect(s):	
House extant: yes	
Historical notes:	

The *Social Directory of Southampton, Long Island, 1931* lists Dr. Louis Faugeres and Mrs. Charlotte D. Gruner Bishop [Sr.] as residing on Woods Lane, East Hampton.

He was the son of James and Mary Faugeres Ellis Bishop.

Charlotte Dater Fruner Bishop was the daughter of Siegfried and Annie Josephine Dater Gruner.

Dr. Louis Faugeres and Mrs. Charlotte Dater Gruner Bishop, Sr.'s son Dr. Louis Faugeres Bishop, Jr. married Kathleen Sinclair and resided in East Hampton.

[See previous Bishop entries for additional family information.]

Bishopric, Allison, Jr. (1900-1998)

Occupation(s):	industrialist - vice-president, Bishopric Manufacturing Co.
Marriage(s):	M/1 – 1926-div. 1930 – Sarah Elizabeth Robbins (b. 1903)
	M/2 – 1933-1991 – Marjorie Lee Collins (1911-1991)
	- Civic Activism: a founder, Merry G. Round Mews; board member, The Nathaniel Witherell Auxiliary
Address:	10 Cross Highway, Amagansett
Name of estate:	*Windy Dune*
Year of construction:	c. 1910
Style of architecture:	Mediterranean Villa
Architect(s):	Tietig and Lee designed the house (for J. Rawson, Jr.)
	Christopher Bickford, 1992-1994 alterations (for Cookson)
	Rich Hirt, 2003-2006 alterations (for Cookson)
Landscape architect(s):	
House extant: yes	
Historical notes:	

The 7,000-square-foot house, originally named *Red Roof*, was built by Joseph Rawson, Jr. Its name was changed to *Windy Dune* after its terra cotta roof was lost in the 1938 hurricane. The house was later owned by Allison Bishopric who called it *Windy Dune*.

He was the son of Allison and Adelia Fern Gazlay Bishopric, Sr. of Cincinnati, OH.

Sarah Elizabeth Robbins Bishopric was the daughter of Sabin and Ruth Reed Robbins of Cincinnati, OH. Sarah subsequently married William Ernst Minor, Jr.

Marjorie Lee Collins Bishopric was the daughter of William R. and Lucy Rawson Collins of Cincinnati, OH.

Allison and Marjorie Lee Collins Bishopric, Jr.'s daughter Lucy, who subsequently owned the house, married Carl Edward Bolch, Jr., Jean-Charles Sprunger, and Steven D. Cookson.

Blackburn, Wilmuth Earle (1909-1978)

Occupation(s):	financier - member, Halsey, Stuart, and Co., Hartford, CT (investment (banking firm)
Civic Activism:	vice-commodore, Devon Yacht Club, Amagansett
Marriage(s):	1942-1978 – Elizabeth Detwiller Campbell (1912-1988)
Address:	West End Avenue, East Hampton
Name of estate:	*West Side Story*
Year of construction:	
Style of architecture:	
Architect(s):	
Landscape architect(s):	
House extant: unconfirmed	
Historical notes:	

The Blue Book of the Hamptons, 1973 lists W. Earle and Betty [Elizabeth] Campbell Blackburn as residing at *West Side Story*, West End Road [Avenue], East Hampton.

He was the son of Wilmuth Evert and Rita Mable Chapman Blackburn of Summit, NJ.

Elizabeth Campbell Blackburn was the daughter of Nathaniel Adams and Elizabeth Warne Detwiller Campbell, Sr. of *Camelot* in East Hampton.

Wilmuth Earle and Elizabeth Detwiller Campbell Blackburn's daughter Selena married Lincoln Kinnicutt of West Hartford, CT, and resided in Weston, MA.

Blair, Montgomery, II (1865-1944)

Occupation(s):	attorney
Marriage(s):	1895-1939 – Edith Draper (1874-1939) |//
- Civic Activism: a founder, Potomac School, 1904, McLean, VA; oversaw creation of Falkland Garden Apartments, Silver Springs, MD (boarding house for women)

Address: Ocean and Lee Avenues, East Hampton
Name of estate:
Year of construction:
Style of architecture:
Architect(s):
Landscape architect(s):
House extant: unconfirmed
Historical notes:

    The *Long Island Society Register, 1929* lists Montgomery and Edith Draper Blair [II] as residing at the corner of Ocean and Lee Avenues, East Hampton.
    He was the son of United States Postmaster General Montgomery and Mrs. Mary Elizabeth Woodbury Blair, Sr. of Washington, DC,
    Edith Draper Blair was the daughter of General William Franklin and Mrs. Lydia Warren Draper of Massachusetts.
    Montgomery and Edith Draper Blair II's daughter Edith married Rear Admiral Adolphus Staton and resided in Washington, DC. Their daughter Minna married Stephen Olin Richey. Their daughter Virginia married Robert Clymer Brooks and resided in Philadelphia, PA. Their daughter Ellen married Benjamin Lowndes and resided in Chevy Chase, MD. Their son Charles married Rosalind Mellor and resided in Charleston, WV. Their son William married Mary Eula Mason. Their son Montgomery Blair III married Virginia Augusta Mason, the daughter of Charles Mason.
    Blair House, the family's ancestral homes in Washington, DC, for over one hundred years, was purchased by the federal government in 1942. The Blairs' daughter Edith is reputed to have been the last Blair to be born in *Blair House*.

Blakeman, Emma Augusta Terbell (1845-1921)

Marriage(s): ____ Blakeman

Address: Terbell Lane, East Hampton
Name of estate:
Year of construction: 1901
Style of architecture: Shingle
Architect(s):
Landscape architect(s):
Builder: Frank Grimshaw
    S. C. Grimshaw (plumbing firm)

House extant: yes
Historical notes:

    The house was built by Emma Augusta Terbell Blakeman. [*The East Hampton Star* January 18, 1901, p. 5.]
    She was the daughter of Henry S. and Hannah Dyer Terbell of East Hampton. Emma's brother Edward married Elijean Stites, the daughter of Elijah Stites of New York and resided at *Maidstone Hall* in East Hampton.
    In 1912 the house was sold to William Walker Green. [*The East Hampton Star* October 18, 1912, p. 5.]

Bogert, Edward Osgood (1894-1956)

Occupation(s):
Civic Activism: president, Guild Hall Players, East Hampton

Marriage(s): M/1 – 1922-div. – Esther Jean Bochman (1897-1952)
M/2 – 1933-1956 – Elizabeth Wood (1897-1985)

Address: Apaquogue and Jones Roads, East Hampton
Name of estate:
Year of construction: Colonial
Style of architecture:
Architect(s):
Landscape architect(s):
House extant: unconfirmed
Historical notes:

He was the son of Henry Lawrence and Caroline Lawrence Osgood Bogert, Sr. of Flushing, NY. Edward's brother Henry Lawrence Bogert, Jr. married Elizabeth Blodget Sanford, the daughter of George Baylies and Caroline Blodget Sanford of *The Byways* in Lawrence, and resided in Lawrence. [*See* Spinzia, *Long Island's Prominent Families in the Town of Hempstead* – Bogert and Sanford entries.]

Esther Jean Bachman Bogert was the daughter of Charles Francis Bachman of Philadelphia, PA.

Edward Osgood and Esther Jean Bachman Bogert's daughter Cynthia married Charles S. Fischer. Their daughter Jean did not marry.

The Blue Book of The Hamptons, 1958 lists Edward O. and Elizabeth Wood Bogert as residing on Apaquogue Road, East Hampton.

She was the daughter of Robert Williams and Gertrude Ames Wood, Jr. of East Hampton, who had purchased the Miller homestead in 1908. [*The East Hampton Star* August 18, 1955, p. 2.] Elizabeth's sister Margaret Wood (aka Margo White), who resided in Lawrence, married Victor Gerald White, Sr. and, later, Arthur Ulysses Newton. [*See* Spinzia, *Long Island's Prominent Families in the Town of Hempstead* – Newton and White entries.]

Edward Osgood and Elizabeth Wood Bogert's daughter Elizabeth married Lawrence Richmond Hotckiss, the son of Ralph R. Hotckiss of Westport, CT, and resided in Amagansett. Elizabeth and her brother Robert continued to reside at the house after the death of their parents.

Bogert, George Henry (1864-1944)

Occupation(s): artist - landscape paintings*

Marriage(s): 1898 – Margaret Austin Merryman (1867-1958)

Address: Pantigo Road, East Hampton
Name of estate:
Year of construction:
Style of architecture:
Architect(s):
Landscape architect(s):
House extant: unconfirmed
Historical notes:

The *Social Register Summer, 1915* lists George H. and Margaret Merryman Bogert as residing in East Hampton.

He was the son of Henry and Helen Anderson Evans Bogert of NYC.

Margaret Austin Merryman Bogert was the daughter of Joseph Purnell and Eleanor J. Lucas Merryman of Baltimore, MD.

George Henry and Margaret Austin Merryman Bogert's son Austin was a youth at the time of his death. Their daughter Eleanor married Charles Bradford Welles, the son of Charles T. Welles of Hartford, CT, and resided in North Haven, CT.

*Bogert's paintings can be found in several of the nation's major art museums.

Bon Jovi, Jon (b. 1962)
aka John Francis Bongiovi, Jr.

Occupation(s):	entertainers and associated professions -
	singer - founder, Bon Jovi rock band;
	motion picture and television actor
	composer - songwriter*
	restaurateur - partner, The Blue Parrot Restaurant, East Hampton
Civic Activism:	founder, The Bon Jovi Soul Foundation;
	member, White House Council for Community Solutions (Obama
	administration);
	ambassador, Habitat for Humanity
Marriage(s):	1989 – Dorothea Hurley (b. 1962)
	- restaurateur - partner, The Blue Parrot Restaurant, East Hampton
	educator - karate instructor
Address:	6 Lily Pond Lane, East Hampton
Name of estate:	
Year of construction:	1899
Style of architecture:	Shingle
Architect(s):	Joseph Greenleaf Thorp designed
	the house (for E. C. Potter)
Landscape architect(s):	
Builder:	George A. Eldredge
House extant: yes	
Historical notes:	

    The eleven-bedroom house, originally named *A–Y–Mor*, was built by Eugene Clifford Potter. The house was owned by J. J. O'Connell. In 2004 Bon Jovi purchased the house for $7.6 million.
    He is the son of John Francis and Carol Sharkey Bongiovi, Sr. of New Jersey.
    Dorothea Hurley Bon Jovi is the daughter of Donald and Dorothy Pawlyk Hurley.
    *In 2009 Bon Jovi was inducted into the Songwriter's Hall of Fame.

Bonner, Marie Louise Clifford

Marriage(s):	1894-1911 – Frederic Bonner (1856-1911)
	- publisher - an owner and senior editor of the *Ledger*, NY
	Civic Activism: member, art committee, Union Club, NYC
Address:	Lily Pond Lane, East Hampton
Name of estate:	*Pond House*
Year of construction:	
Style of architecture:	
Architect(s):	
Landscape architect(s):	
House extant: unconfirmed	
Historical notes:	

    The *Long Island Society Register, 1929* lists Marie L. Clifford Bonner as residing at *Pond House* on Lily Pond Lane, East Hampton.
    She was the daughter of Robert H. Clifford.
    Frederic Bonner was the son of Robert and Jane Bonner.

Boots, Dr. Ralph Henderson, Sr. (1891-1968)

Occupation(s): physician - Rockefeller Hospital, NYC, 1919-1923;
surgeon, Presbyterian Hospital, NYC (which became
Columbia–Presbyterian Hospital)

Marriage(s): 1928-1968 – Lois Kingsley (1905-1991)

Address: Dunemere Lane, East Hampton
Name of estate: *The White Elephant*
Year of construction:
Style of architecture:
Architect(s):
Landscape architect(s):
House extant: unconfirmed
Historical notes:

   The *Social Register Summer, 1945* lists Dr. Ralph H. and Mrs. Lois Kingsley Boots [Sr.] as residing at *The White Elephant* on Dunemere Lane, East Hampton.
   He was the son of John Sheridan and Elizabeth McPherson Boots of New Brighton, PA.
   Lois Kingsley Boots was the daughter of Darwin Pearl and Josephine Ignatius McCall Kingsley, Sr. of East Hampton. Lois' brother John married Elizabeth Heron Curry, the daughter of Henry Milo Curry of Pittsburgh, PA, and resided in Kennebunkport, ME. Her brother Darwin Pearl Kingsley, who married Heywood Mason Butler and, later, Elizabeth Eckhart resided in Hewlett. [*See* Spinzia, *Long Island's Prominent Families in the Town of Hempstead* – Kingsley entry.]
   Dr. Ralph Henderson and Mrs. Lois Kingsley Boots, Sr.'s twenty-five-year-old son Ralph Henderson Boots, Jr. died in an automobile accident while a student at the Army Language School in Monterey, CA. Their daughter Lois married Richard Lindabury Berry, the son of Robert L. Berry, and resided in Darien, CT.

Borden, Lewis Mercer, Sr. (1879-1935)

Occupation(s): merchant - a founder and vice-president, A. Jaeckel & Co., NYC
(furriers);
director, Abercrombie & Fitch Co. (sporting goods firm)
industrialist - director, Borden Co., 1911-1935
capitalist - director, Borden Realty Co.

Marriage(s): 1906-1935 – Marie Jaeckel (d. 1945)
- Civic Activism: governor, Riding Club of East Hampton

Address: 44 Woods Lane, East Hampton
Name of estate: *Seaholme*
Year of construction: 1899
Style of architecture: Shingle
Architect(s): Joseph Greenleaf Thorp designed
the house (for Cammann)
Landscape architect(s):
House extant: yes
Builder: George A. Eldredge
Historical notes:

   The house, originally named *Seaholme*, was built by George Philip Cammann, Jr. In 1914 Cammann sold the house to Borden who continued to call it *Seaholme* and who, in 1915, made alterations to it.
   The *Social Register Summer, 1932* lists Lewis M. and Marie Jaeckel Borden as residing at *Seaholme* in East Hampton.
   He was the son of John Gail and Ellen Lovisa Graves Borden.
   Marie Jaeckel Borden was the daughter of Adelbert Jaeckel.
   Lewis Mercer and Marie Jaeckel Borden, Sr.'s daughter Penelope married Summitt Edward Boone. Their son Adelbert married Lesley Stoddart Smith, the daughter of Morris A. Smith of Hastings-on-Hudson, NY. Their son Lewis Mercer Borden, Jr. died in 1922. Their son Gail Borden II married Margaret Henry, the daughter of DeWitt Henry of Philadelphia, and later, Elsa Tvedt, the daughter of Nelson Tvedt of Bergen, Norway.
   In 1959 the house became the Jewish Center of the Hamptons.

Boughton, Edward Smith (1863-1916)

Occupation(s):	publisher - in 1890 he purchased *The East Hampton Star*
	journalist - *Danbury Republican*, Danbury, CT;
	Thomaston Express, Thomaston, CT
Marriage(s):	1886-1916 – Bertha Emeline Welby (1865-1946)
	- publisher - *The East Hampton Star*
Address:	Newtown Lane, East Hampton

Name of estate:
Year of construction:
Style of architecture:
Architect(s):
Landscape architect(s):
House extant: unconfirmed
Historical notes:

Edward Smith Boughton was the son of Minot Smith and Mary Benjamin Boughton.

Bertha Emeline Welby Boughton was the daughter of Henry and Matilda Hawthorne Arnold Welby.

Edward Smith and Bertha Emeline Welby Boughton's daughter Clara married Frederick Wohlfert. Their son Lewis was a teenager when he died in 1918. Their daughter Helen married Paul V. Reutershan. Their daughter Marion married Dermott J. Dillon. Their daughter Barbara married Charles Grainger. Their son Clifford married Doris Chandler. Their son Welby married Florence Thomas. Their daughter Mildred married Vinton Mitchell.

Bouvier, John Vernou, Jr. (1865-1948)

Occupation(s):	attorney
	financier - partner, M. C. Bouvier and Co. (stock brokerage firm)
Civic Activism:	president, board of education, Nutley, NJ;
	president, Sons of the Revolution;
	trustee, New York Foundling Hospital, NYC;
	trustee, New York Historical Society, NYC;
	director, Maidstone Club, East Hampton
Marriage(s):	1890-1940 – Maude Frances Sergeant (1869-1940)
Address:	Apaquogue Road, East Hampton
Name of estate:	*Little House**
Year of construction:	
Style of architecture:	Modified Colonial Revival
Architect(s):	
Landscape architect(s):	Victoria Fensterer designed pergola plantings

House extant: yes
Historical notes:

John Vernou Bouvier, Jr. purchased the house in 1914 and resided at *Little House* until 1926 when he purchased *Lasata*, which was also in East Hampton.

He was the son of John Vernou and Caroline Maslin Ewing Bouvier, Sr.

Maude Frances Sergeant Bouvier was the daughter of William Roberts and Edith Matilda Leaman Sergeant.

John Vernou and Maude Frances Sergeant Bouvier, Jr.'s son William married Emma Louise Stone who resided in Southampton. [*See* Spinzia, *Long Island's Prominent Families in the Town of Southampton* – Bouvier entry.] Their daughter Edith married Phelan Beale, Sr. and resided at *Grey Gardens* in East Hampton. Their daughter Maude married John Ethelbert Davis and resided in Ridgefield, CT. Their daughter Michelle married Henry Clarkson Scott, Sr. with whom she resided in Woodmere. [*See* Spinzia, *Long Island's Prominent Families in the Town of Hempstead* – Scott entry.] Their daughter Caroline died at the age of two. Their son John Vernou Bouvier III, who resided at *Rowdy Hall* and, later, at *Little House* in East Hampton, married Janet Norton Lee.

*Little House, which was also known as *Wildmoor*, was later owned by John Vernou Bouvier III.

In 1960 the house was purchased by Adolph Gottlieb who converted the garage into his art studio.

Bouvier, John Vernou, Jr. (1865-1948)

Occupation(s):	*[See previous entry.]*
Civic Activism:	*[See previous entry.]*
Marriage(s):	1890-1940 – Maude Frances Sergeant (1869-1940)
Address:	121 Further Lane, East Hampton
Name of estate:	*Lasata**
Year of construction:	1917
Style of architecture:	Mediterranean
Architect(s):	Arthur C. Jackson designed the house (for G. W. Schurman)
	Ferguson and Shamamian, alterations (for Krakoff)
Landscape architect(s):	Charles Nassau Lowrie, Sr. (for G. W. Schurman)
	Perry Guillot (for Krakoff)
Builder:	Edward M. Gay
House extant:	yes**
Historical notes:	

    The ten-bedroom, eleven-and-a-half-bath, 8,500-square-foot house, originally named *Beachclose*, was built by George Wellington Schurman. In 1923 Schurman sold the house to Laura Elizabeth Young Martin, who died in 1924. Lion Gardiner purchased it in 1925 and sold it to Mrs. Maude Frances Sergeant Bouvier. Mrs. Bouvier deeded it to her husband in 1935. The Bouviers called the house *Lasata*.

   [See previous entry for family information.]

    In 1950 the house was sold to Frances May Archbold Hufty. In the early 1960s the house was purchased by Joseph Ansbro Meehan. It was purchased in 2006 by Reed and Delphine Krakoff, who, in 2016, listed the house and 7.15 acres for sale. The asking price was $38.995 million.

   *Lasata is Native American for Place of Peace.

   **The stables were demolished.

Bouvier, John Vernou, III (1891-1957)

Occupation(s):	financier independent stockbroker
Marriage(s):	1928-1940 – Janet Norton Lee (1907-1989)
	- Civic Activism: director, Robert E. Lee Association
Address:	111 Egypt Lane, East Hampton
Name of estate:	*Rowdy Hall**
Year of construction:	Early- to mid-eighteenth century
Style of architecture:	Colonial
Architect(s):	Joseph Greenleaf Thorp, 1926
	alterations (for Mrs. Hamlin)
Landscape architect(s):	
House extant: yes	
Historical notes:	

    The house was originally the Osborn family's residence. It was later owned by David Huntting and then by his adopted daughter Annie who utilized it as a boarding house. In 1895 the house was moved from Main Street to Gay Lane. In 1925 it was purchased by Mrs. Mary Elkins Paxton Hamlin who moved it to Egypt Lane. [*The East Hampton Star* November 15, 1934, p. 5.]
    *Bouvier had a long-term lease on the house.
    John Vernou Bouvier III was the son of John Vernou and Maude Francis Sergeant Bouvier of *Little House* and *Lasata* in East Hampton.
    Janet Norton Lee Bouvier was the daughter of James Thomas and Margaret A. Merritt Lee of East Hampton. Janet later married Hugh Dudley Auchincloss, Jr. and, subsequently, Bingham Willing Morris with whom she resided at *Pra–Qua–Les* in Southampton. [*See* Spinzia, *Long Island's Prominent Families in the Town of Southampton* – Morris entry.]
    John Vernou and Janet Norton Lee Bouvier III's daughter Jacqueline married President John Fitzgerald Kennedy and, subsequently, Aristotle Onassis. Their daughter Caroline (aka Lee) married Michael Temple Canfield, Prince Stanislaw Albrecht Radziwill, and, subsequently, Herbert David Ross.
    John Vernou Bouvier III also had two illegitimate children, a son who died in an automobile accident in England and a daughter who was murdered while living in the Middle East. [David Heyman. *A Woman Named Jackie.* (New York: Carol Communications, 1989), p. 56.]
    By the 1930s Bouvier was residing at his parents' former East Hampton residence *Little House*.
    In 1953 the house was purchased from Mrs. Hamlin by Robert Barnes who made alterations and repairs to it and, in 1954, sold the house to Henry Sanford Thorne. [*The East Hampton Star* November 26, 1953, p. 4, and June 17, 1954, p. 7.] In 2003 the house was listed for sale. The asking price was $2.25 million.

Bowne, Robert Southgate (1842-1896)

Occupation(s):	financer - director, Queens County Bank
Civic Activism:	a founder, Maidstone Club, East Hampton; trustee, Village of Flushing
Marriage(s):	1864-1896 – Jessie Draper (1846-1925)
Address:	32 Ocean Avenue, East Hampton
Name of estate:	*Clifford-by-the-Sea*
Year of construction:	1889
Style of architecture:	Shingle
Architect(s):	
Landscape architect(s):	
Builder:	James L'Hommedieu
House extant: yes	
Historical notes:	

   The twelve-bedroom, eight-and-a-half-bath, 8,000-square-foot house, originally named *Clifford-by-the-Sea*, was built by Robert Southgate Bowne.
   He was a descendant of Flushing's patentee John Bowne, who erected the historic *Bowne House* which still stands in Flushing.
   Jessie Draper Bowne was the daughter of William Bemis and Elizabeth Haggerty Draper.
   Robert Southgate and Jessie Draper Bowne's daughter Elizabeth married Harris Duncomb Colt of New York. Their son Frederick married Alice Holbrook and resided in Flushing. Their son Francis married Gertrude Travers, the daughter of Edward Montague Travis. Their son Walter married Katherine Guild.
   The house was later owned by Bernard Zamichow. [*The East Hampton Star* March 22, 1979, p. 22.]

Bracken, James W. (1894-1975)

Occupation(s):	financier - investment counselor, Scudder, Stevents, and Clark; manager, investment department, INA Corp. (Insurance Company of North America)
Civic Activism:	trustee, Dunwoody Home, Newtown Square, PA; president, Rosemont–Villanova Civic Association; trustee, Southern Home for Children; trustee, Morris Animal Refuge
Marriage(s):	Katharine Davis (d. 1984)
Address:	Further Lane, Amagansett
Name of estate:	
Year of construction:	
Style of architecture:	
Architect(s):	
Landscape architect(s):	
House extant: unconfirmed	
Historical notes:	

   The Blue Book of The Hamptons, 1958, 1965, and *1973* list James W. and Katharine Davis Bracken as residing on Further Lane, Amagansett.

Brackenridge, Gavin, Jr. (b. 1944)

Occupation(s):	financier -	director, Greig Middleton (later, Gerrard Investment Management); member, Charles Stanley and Co; vice-president, Deutsch Bank
	capitalist -	vice-president, Editions Fenwick (creates and markets business games); owner and president, Gavin Brackenridge & Co., Inc., NYC (executive relocation firm); vice-president, Executive Home Settlers; member, Barbara Cleary's Realty Guild
	publisher -	founder, The Agency Book (annual catalogue of advertising agency brand assignments)

Marriage(s): M/1 – 1971 – Caroline Dodd Lynch
M/2 – 1980 – Mary Kathryn McDonnell

Address: Woods Lane, East Hampton
Name of estate:
Year of construction:
Style of architecture:
Architect(s):
Landscape architect(s):
House extant: unconfirmed
Historical notes:

The Blue Book of The Hamptons, 1973 lists Gavin and Caroline Lynch Brackenridge, Jr. as residing at 26 Woods Lane, East Hampton.

He was the son of Gavin and Anne Ingersoll Brackenridge, Sr., who had previously owned the house.

Caroline Dodd Lynch Brackenridge is the daughter of Edmund Ambrose and Florence Dodd Sullivan Lynch, Jr. of *Holly House* in Lawrence. [*See* Spinzia, *Long Island's Prominent Families in the Town of Hempstead* – Lynch entry.]

Gavin and Caroline Dodd Brackenridge, Jr.'s daughter Ann married Peter W. McCallum.

[See following entry for additional family information.]

By 2008 the Brackenridges' address was listed as 30A Woods Lane, East Hampton.

Brackenridge, Gavin, Sr. (1894-1965)

Occupation(s): financier - vice-president and director, General Motors Acceptance Corp.

Marriage(s): 1930-1965 – Anne Ingersoll (1904-1968)
- Civic Activism: member, entertainment committee, The Maidstone Club, East Hampton

Address: Woods Lane, East Hampton
Name of estate:
Year of construction:
Style of architecture:
Architect(s):
Landscape architect(s):
House extant: no
Historical notes:

In 1893 Adrian Hoffman Larkin remodeled the South End School as his residence which he called *Green Frog*. [*The East Hampton Star* September 30, 1965, p. 2.] By 1900 it was owned by Clara Cooper Stratton. [*The East Hampton Star* February 9, 1900, p. 5.] The house was later owned by Miss Hedwig Monberg who, in 1954, sold the house to Brackenridge. [*The East Hampton Star* March 4, 1954, p. 2, and June 24, 1954, p. 2.]

The Blue Book of The Hamptons, 1958 lists Mr. and Mrs. Gavin Brackenridge [Sr.] as residing on Woods Lane, East Hampton.

He was the son of John C. Brackenridge of Kew Gardens, NY.

Ann Ingersoll Brackenridge was the daughter of Charles H. and Eleanor Bond Ingersoll of Llewellyn Park, West Orange, NJ. Anne's sister Jane married Joseph Durand Scheerer and resided in East Hampton.

Gavin and Anne Ingersoll Brackenridge, Sr.'s daughter Belinda married R. Bradley Ward, the son of Ralph B. Ward of Suffern, NY. Their son Gavin Brackenridge, Jr. was married to Caroline Dodd Lynch and, subsequently, to Kathryn McDonnell.

[See previous entry for additional family information.]

Bradlee, Benjamin Crowninshield, Sr. (1921-2014)

Occupation(s):	publisher - a founder, *New Hampshire Post*;
	vice-president and director, *The Washington Post**
	journalist - *New Hampshire Post*, *The Washington Post*, and *Educational Exchange*;
	Washington bureau chief, *Newsweek*;
	managing editor, *The Washington Post**
	intelligence agent - United States Navy during World War II
	capitalist - director, Independent News and Media Group (foreign radio stations and cable telecoms and over 200 foreign newspapers and magazines)
	writer - *A Special Grace*, 1964;
	Conversations With Kennedy, 1975;
	A Good Life: Newspapering and Other Adventures, 1995
Civic Activism:	endowed chair at John F. Kennedy School of Government, Harvard University, Cambridge, MA;
	chairman of board, Historic St. Mary's City Commission, St. Mary's City, MD (Maryland's first capital);
	trustee, St. Mary's College, St. Mary's City, MD;
	chairman of board, fund drive, Children's Hospital, Washington, DC
Marriage(s):	M/1 – 1942-div. 1955 – Jean Saltonstall (1921-2011)
	M/2 – 1956-div. 1975 – Antoinette Eno Pinchot (1924-2011)
	- journalist - *Vogue* magazine
	M/3 – 1978-2014 – Sally Quinn (b. 1941)
	- journalist - *The Washington Post,* Washington, DC;
	The New York Times, NYC
	entertainers and associate professions -
	co-anchor, "CBS Morning News"
	writer - *The Party: A Guide to Adventurous Entertainment*, 1997;
	We're Going to Make You a Star, 1975 (autobiography);
	Regrets Only, 1986;
	Finding Magic, 2017
	Civic Activism: board vice-chair, fund drive, Children's Hospital, Washington, DC
Address:	3 West End Avenue, East Hampton
Name of estate:	*Grey Gardens*
Year of construction:	1897
Style of architecture:	Shingle
Architect(s):	Joseph Greenleaf Thorp designed the house (for F. S. Phillips)
	Eugene Lawrence Futterman, 1980 alterations (for Bradlee)
Landscape architect(s):	Anna Park Gilman Hill designed her own gardens, with Ruth Dean, 1914
	Victoria Fensteer, 1985- (for Bradlee)
Builder:	George A. Eldredge

House extant: yes**
Nassau County Museum Collection has photographs of the estate.
Historical notes:

   The house was built by Fleming Stanhope Phillips. In 1913 it was sold to Robert Carmer Hill, who named it *Grey Gardens*. In 1924 Hill sold the house to Phelan Beale, Sr. who continued to call it *Grey Gardens*. As part of his divorce settlement, Beale deeded the house to his wife Edith. The Beales' daughter Edith sold the house in 1979 to Bradlee, who continued to call it *Grey Gardens*.
   He was the son of Frederick Josiah and Josephine deGersdroff Bradlee, Jr. of Boston, MA.

Bradlee, Benjamin Crowninshield, Sr. (cont'd)

Jean Saltonstall Bradlee was the daughter of John L. and Gladys Durrant Rice Saltonstall of *Topsfield*, MA, and the granddaughter of Dr. Clarence Charles and Mrs. Jeannie Terry Durrant Rice of East Hampton. Jean's sister Elizabeth married August Belmont IV, the son of August and Alice Wall deGoicouria Belmont III of Bay Shore. [*See* Spinzia, *Long Island's Prominent South Shore Families* – Belmont entries.] Jean subsequently married Oscar William Hausserman, Jr. and resided in Cambridge, MA.

Benjamin Crowninshield and Jean Saltonstall Bradlee, Sr.'s son Benjamin Crowninshield Bradlee, Jr., who married ABC News' chief foreign correspondent Martha Raddatz and, later, Jan Saragoni, followed the family's journalistic tradition by becoming the editor of *The Boston Globe*.

Antoinette Eno Pinchot Bradlee was the daughter of Amos Richards Eno and Ruth Pickering Pinchot of Milford, PA. She had previously been married to Steuart Lansing Pittman II, the son of Ernest Wetmore and Estelle Young Romeyn Pittman of Lawrence and East Hampton. [*See* Spinzia, *Long Island's Prominent in the Town of Hempstead* – Pittman entry.] Antoinette's sister Mary married Cord Meyer IV, the son of Cord and Katharine Blair Thaw Meyer III of *Little River Farm* in North Hampton, NH, and the grandson of Cord and Cornelia M. Covert Meyer II of *The Cove* in Kings Point. [*See* Spinzia, *Long Island's Prominent North Shore Families, vol. I* – Meyer entry.] Cord Meyer IV was the Chief of Covert Action Staff of the Directorate of Plans for the CIA's worldwide clandestine activities. His wife Mary was murdered in 1964 while walking along the former tow path of the Chesapeake and Ohio Canal in Georgetown, VA.
[*See* Raymond E. Spinzia, "Adultery, Drugs, Murder, Untimely Deaths, and Long Island's Prominent Families: A Tangled Web." www.spinzialongislandestates.com and Judith Ader Spinzia, "Women of Long Island: Cornelia Bryce Pinchot, Feminist, Social-Activist – The Long Islander Who Became First Lady of Pennsylvania." www.spinzialongislandestates.com.]

Benjamin Crowninshield and Antoinette Eno Pinchot Bradlee, Sr.'s son Dominic, who resides in Milford, PA, married Lesley Marshall.

Sally Quinn Bradlee is the daughter of General William Wilson and Mrs. Bette Williams Quinn.

Benjamin Crowninshield and Sally Quinn Bradlee, Sr.'s son Josiah (Quinn) married Pary Williamson.

*It was during Bradlee's tenure at *The Washington Post* that Bernstein and Woodward uncovered the Watergate scandal. [*See* Northrup entry in this volume for additional Watergate information.]

**Alterations were made to the house c. 1972 and in 1980.

The house is on the National Register of Historic Places.

In 2017 the seven-bedroom, six-bath, 6,000-square-foot house and 1.7 acres were for sale. The asking price was $19.995 million.

Bradley, Andrew Coyle (1844-1902)

Occupation(s):	attorney - judge - associate Supreme Court justice, District of Columbia*
	educator - professor of law, Columbia University, Washington, DC
Marriage(s):	1872-1902 – Sue H. Young (1847-1930)
Address:	56 Woods Lane, East Hampton
Name of estate:	
Year of construction:	1900
Style of architecture:	Modified Dutch Colonial Revival
Architect(s):	Joseph Greenleaf Thorp designed the house (for Bradley)
Landscape architect(s):	
House extant: yes	
Historical notes:	

The 9,000-square-foot, six-bedroom, three-and-a-half-bath house was built by Andrew Coyle Bradley.

He was the son of Charles and Ann Catharine Coyle Bradley of Washington, DC.

Sue H. Young Bradley was the daughter of William Proby and Susan Bradford Grice Young.

Andrew Coyle and Sue H. Young Bradley's children Sue, Grace, and Kathleen were youths at the time of their deaths. Their son Andrew Young Bradley married Julia Augusta Kellogg, the daughter of Sanford Cobb and Frances Breckinridge Kellogg. Their son Charles married Ann Phelps Brown, the daughter of Sevellon Alden and Sally Maynadier Phelps Brown.

*Bradley presided over the trial of Henry Osborne Havemeyer, the founder and president of American Sugar Refining Company which controlled more than fifty-percent of the nation's sugar refining. Bradley instructed the jury to bring in a verdict of not guilty. [*The New York Times* May 16, 1902, p. 5.] [*See* Spinzia, *Long Island's Prominent South Shore Families* – Havemeyer entry.]

The house was later owned by Judith Lachman.

The house and two acres were for sale in 2014. The asking price was $3.95 million.

Bragg, Caleb Smith (1885-1943)

Occupation(s):	engineer
	inventor - co-inventor, with Victor W. Kliesrath, Bragg–Kliesrath automobile brake
	diplomat - attaché, United States Embassy, Paris, France, 1914
	industrialist - vice-president, Glen L. Martin Co. (airplane manufacturer);
	co-founder, Wright–Martin Co. (airplane manufacturer);
	director, Wright Aeronautical Corp.;
	president, Bragg–Kliesrath Corp., Long Island City (automobile brake manufacturer) (later, Bendix Aviation Corp.);
	director, Bendix Aviation Corp.;
	vice-president, Bendix Marine Products Co.;
	president, Langley Aviation Corp. (built molded plastic and plywood planes for private use);
	vice-president and consulting engineer, C. M. Keys Aircraft Service, Inc.
	capitalist - director, Montauk Beach Development Co.
Civic Activism:	governor, Aero Club of America;
	governor, Montauk Yacht Club Resort and Marina
Marriage(s):	bachelor
Address:	Star Island Road, Montauk
Name of estate:	
Year of construction:	1929
Style of architecture:	Modified French Country
Architect(s):	Walker and Gillette designed the house (for Bragg)
Landscape architect(s):	Olmstead, 1929-1930 (for Bragg)
House extant: yes	
Historical notes:	

The house was built by the noted automobile and speedboat racer Caleb Smith Bragg.

He was the son of Caius and Eugenia Hofer Bragg of Cincinnati, OH. Caleb's sister Marion, who resided in at *Eight Acres* in Muttontown, married Harry Langdon Laws III and, later, Ludvig Caesar Martin Aubert II. [*See* Spinzia, *Long Island's Prominent North Shore Families, vol. I* – Aubert entry.] Marion later owned Caleb's Montauk estate which she called *Star Acres*. By the mid-1950s she had relocated to Arizona.

In 1987 the estate, which consists of the main residence and several service buildings, was listed on the National Register of Historic Places. They are currently used as villas by the Montauk Yacht Club Resort and Marina.

Breen, Daniel Anthony, Jr. (1928-2016)

Occupation(s):	advertising executive - marketing representative, director of sales promotion, and co-director of industry marketing, IBM
	financier - vice-president, National Securities and Research (mutual fund firm);
	director, partner, and president, Fayez, Sarofim, & Co. (assets management firm);
	founder, Daniel Breen & Co. (asset management firm);
	founder, Breen Trust Co. (asset management firm)
Marriage(s):	1961-2016 – Margaret Patricia McCloskey (d. 2018)
	- Civic Activism: trustee, Houston Grand Opera;
	trustee, Houston Ballet Foundation;
	trustee, Health Science Center, University of Texas, Austin, TX;
	trustee, Texas Partners School of Nursing, Austin, TX;
	trustee, Gathering Place;
	trustee, The Hobby Center for Performing Arts
Address:	32 Middle Lane, East Hampton
Name of estate:	*Furtherfield*
Year of construction:	1930-1931
Style of architecture:	Neo-Federal
Architect(s):	Aymar Embury II designed the house (for G. H. Roberts, Jr.)
Landscape architect(s):	Ruth Bramley Dean, 1930 (for G. H. Roberts, Jr.)
	Mary Lois Deputy Lamson, c. 1941 (for G. H. Roberts, Jr.)

House extant: yes
Nassau County Museum Collection has photographs of the estate.
Historical notes:

The 8,268-square-foot, six-bedroom, five-bath house, originally named *Furtherfield*, was built by George Hewitt Roberts, Jr. It was later owned by Breen who continued to call it *Furtherfield*.

The Blue Book of the Hamptons, 2008 lists Daniel Anthony and Margaret Patricia McCloskey Breen [Jr.] as residing at *Furtherfield*, 32 Middle Lane, East Hampton.

He was the son of Daniel Anthony and Helen Frances Brady Breen, Sr. of Kansas City, MO.

Margaret Patricia McCloskey Breen is the daughter of John Bernard McCloskey of New York.

Daniel Anthony and Margaret Patricia McCloskey Breen, Jr.'s son Patrick married Erin Alison McClure, the daughter of Leon Edward McClure of Austin, TX. Their son Daniel Anthony Breen III married Dionne Delery. Their son John married Zoe Pennebaker. Their son Thomas married McCheney Hortenstine. Their son Michael married Erin Suzanne McClung, the daughter of Dr. Douglas Lauren McClung of Houston, TX.

In 2017 the house and 5.2 acres were for sale. The asking price was $29.95 million. The annual taxes were $60,378. The estate sold in 2017 for $25 million.

Breinin, Dr. Goodwin Milton (1918-2011)

Occupation(s):	educator - professor of ophthalmology, Bellevue Hospital, NYC; visiting professor and consultant, Hailie Selassie University Foundation, Ethiopia, 1972
	physician - chairman, ophthalmology department, New York University Bellevue Medical Center, NYC, 1959-2000; director of eye service, Bellevue and University Hospitals, NYC, 1959-2000; chairman of board, New York University Bellevue Medical Center, NYC, 1975-1977; chief consultant, Veterans Administration Hospital, Manhattan Eye, Ear, and Throat, St. Vincent's, Beth Israel, and Lenox Hill Hospitals
	writer - *The Electrophysiology of Extraocular Muscle: With Special Reference to Electromyography,* 1962
Civic Activism:	member, vision commission, National Research Council, 1960-1965; chairman, vision research training committee, National Institutes for Neurological Diseases and Blindness, 1963-1964; chairman, National Reserve Review Committee, 1976-1977; member, advisory board, National Council to Combat Blindness; president, Council for United States and Soviet Socialist Republic Health Exchange, 1977; member, American committee, International Agency for Prevention of Blindness; president, Second International Symposium in Visual Optics, 1982, Tucson, AZ
Marriage(s):	1947-2005 – Rose-Helen Kopelman (1827-2005) - artist art historian, Institute of Fine Arts, NYC
Address:	Lily Pond Lane, East Hampton
Name of estate:	
Year of construction:	c. 1951
Style of architecture:	
Architect(s):	
Landscape architect(s):	
Builder:	
House extant: unconfirmed	
Historical notes:	

The house was built by Gerald Maxwell Geddes. [*The East Hampton Star* May 31, 1951, p. 4.] In 1974 it was purchased by Breinin. [*Sag Harbor Express* March 14, 1974, p. 7.]

He was the son of Dr. Louis and Mrs. Mary Mirsky Breinin of Miami, FL.

Rose-Helen Kopelman Breinin was the daughter of Barnett Eugene and Sarah L. Kopelman of NYC.

Dr. Goodwin Milton and Mrs. Rose-Helen Kopelman Breinin's daughter Constance married Nigel Malcolm Paton, the son of Malcolm Bolding Paton of Weybourne, Norfolk, England. Their son Bartley married Rachel Gelin, the daughter of Jacques B. Gelin of Rockville, MD.

Brett, Philip Milledoler, Jr. (1908-1988)

Occupation(s):	financier - member, Stillman, Maynard, and Co. (stock brokerage firm); member, H. G. Wellington and Co. (stock brokerage firm)
Civic Activism:	trustee, Judson Health Center, NYC; trustee, Fund for the Blind
Marriage(s):	M/1 – 1935-div. 1962 – Elizabeth Minot Weld (1913-1982)
	M/2 – 1971-1988 – Mary Baldwin Schwab (1925-1997)
	- Civic Activism: member, board of managers, East Hampton Free Library
Address:	Ocean Avenue, East Hampton
Name of estate:	
Year of construction:	
Style of architecture:	
Architect(s):	
Landscape architect(s):	
House extant: unconfirmed	
Historical notes:	

    Philip Milledoler Brett, Jr. was the son of Philip Milledoler and Margaret Strong Brett, Sr. of *White Staunton* in Greenwich, CT.
    Elizabeth Minot Weld Brett was the daughter of Christopher Minot Weld. She subsequently married Joseph Farrell Haskel.
    Philip Milledoler and Elizabeth Minot Weld Brett, Jr.'s daughter Elizabeth married Robert David Webster. Their daughter Katryna married George Gardner Herrick and, later, Neil Carothers, III. Their son Philip Milledoler Brett III married Anne Lenox Alexandre, the daughter DeWitt Loomis Alexandre of Far Hills, NJ.
    The Blue Book of The Hamptons, 1973 lists Philip M. and Mary Schwab Brett, Jr. as residing on Ocean Avenue, East Hampton.
    She was the daughter of Hermann Casper and Ruth Baldwin Bliss Schwab of *Chicken Valley Farm* in Old Brookville. [*See* Spinzia, *Long Island's Prominent North Shore Families, vol. II* – Schwab entry.] Mary had previously been married to Henry Lawrence Pool with whom she resided at Ocean Avenue, East Hampton.

Breyer, Henry William, III (1930-2019)

Occupation(s):	industrialist - president, Tycoon Fin-Nor (manufacturer of fishing tackle)
Marriage(s):	1959-2019 – Joanne Braatz (b. 1937)
	- Civic Activism: chair, hostesses committee, New York Arthritis and Rheumatism Foundation benefit, 1964
Address:	40 Lee Avenue, East Hampton
Name of estate:	
Year of construction:	c. 1960s
Style of architecture:	French Country
Architect(s):	
Landscape architect(s):	
Builder:	
House extant: yes	
Historical notes:	

    The *Social Register, 2002* lists Henry W. and Joanne Braatz Breyer III as residing at 40 Lee Avenue, East Hampton.
    He was the son of Henry William and Margaret McKee Breyer, Jr. of Haverford, PA, and heir to the Breyers ice cream fortune.
    Joanne Braatz Breyer is the daughter of Clayton O. Braatz of South Orange, NJ, and Cutchogue, LI.
    In 2010 Breyer listed the 7,500-square-foot house and two guest houses for sale. The asking price was $27 million.

Briggs, James Branch (1923-1999)

Occupation(s):	advertising executive - vice-president, Wasey, Ruthrauff, and Ryan (advertising firm); president, J. Branch Briggs (advertising and public relations firm)
Marriage(s):	1943-1997 – Virginia Catherine Moore (1923-1997)
Address:	19 Lee Avenue, East Hampton
Name of estate:	*Beehive*
Year of construction:	1899
Style of architecture:	Shingle
Architect(s):	Joseph Greenleaf Thorp designed the house (for F. G. Potter)
Landscape architect(s):	
Builder:	Loper Brothers
House extant: yes	
Historical notes:	

The 10,000-square-foot, ten-bedroom house was built by Frederick Gaul Potter. It was later owned by John Richard Keim who sold it to Lamon Vanderburg Harkness in 1914. [*The East Hampton Star* January 22, 1915, p. 5.] Briggs, who subsequently purchased the house, called it *Beehive*.

The Blue Book of The Hamptons, 1965 lists James B. and Virginia C. Moore Briggs as residing at *Beehive* at 123 Lee Avenue, East Hampton.

He was the son of Stephen Foster and Beatrice Branch Briggs.

James Branch and Virginia Catherine Moore Briggs' daughter Beatrice married Gunnar Broval Bennett, the son of Russell C. and Katharine Edwards Bennett of East Hampton; Nick Farina; and Dick Simpson. Their daughter Stephanie married Peter Gibbon–Neff. Their daughter Melanie married Jeffrey Paul Donaldson, the son of James R. Donaldson of East Hampton. Their son Timothy was twenty-four years old when he was killed in an automobile accident.

The house was later owned by Chevy Chase and, then, by Peter Gabriel Terian. In 2010 Mrs. Terian placed it on the market; the asking price was $21 million.

Brisbane, Arthur (1863-1936)

Occupation(s):	journalist - reporter, *New York Sun*, NYC, 1883-1887;
	managing editor, *Evening Sun*, 1887-1890;
	managing editor, *New York World*, NYC, 1890-1897;
	managing editor, *Evening Journal*, 1897-1921;
	editor, *Chicago Herald and Examiner*, Chicago, IL
	publisher - owner, *Washington Times*, Washington, DC, 1917-1919;
	owner, *Evening Wisconsin*, 1918-1919
	capitalist - extensive Manhattan real estate holdings;
	built and owned Ritz Tower Apartment Building, NYC
	writer - *Mary Baker Glover Eddy*, 1908
Civic Activism:	a founder, Museum of the City of New York;
	deeded 1,200 acres to State of New Jersey for the establishment of Allaire State Park and Historic Village*;
	suffragist lecturer**
Marriage(s):	1912-1936 – Phoebe Cary (1890-1967)
Address:	De Forest Road, Montauk
Name of estate:	
Year of construction:	1883
Style of architecture:	Beach Cottage
Architect(s):	McKim, Mead & White designed the house (for Agnew)
Landscape architect(s):	Frederick Law Olmsted designed the site plan (for Agnew)
Builder:	Mead and Taft
House extant: yes	
Historical notes:	

 The house is one of the Montauk Association's "Seven Sisters." It was owned by Dr. Cornelius Rea Agnew, Sr. It was later owned by Brisbane.

 He was the son of Albert and Sarah White Brisbane of Buffalo, NY.

 Phoebe Cary Brisbane was the daughter of Seward and Emily Scatcherd Cary of Hempstead and Buffalo, NY.

 Arthur and Phoebe Cary Brisbane's daughter Sarah married John Reagan "Tex" McCrary, Jr. and resided in Manhasset. [*See* Spinzia, *Long Island's Prominent North Shore Families, vol. I* – McCrary entry.] Sarah subsequently married Chase Mellen, Jr., the son of Chase and Lucy Cony Manley Mellen, Sr. of Garden City. Their daughter Eleanor married Solon Chester Kelly III and, subsequently, Ewing Reginald Philbin, Jr., the son of Ewing Reginald and Harriet M. Woodward Philbin, Sr. of *Pine Tree House* in Hewlett Bay Park. Their daughter Alice married E. Haring Chandor, the son of Reginald M. Chandor, and, subsequently, David Dows, Jr. Their daughter Emily did not marry. Their son Seward married Doris Fauser and resided in Upper Brookville.

 [For information about Brisbane's East Meadow residence, *see* Spinzia, *Long Island's Prominent Families in the Town of Hempstead* – Brisbane entry.]

*The Historic Village at Allaire in Allaire State Park is an interpretive restoration of an early 19th-century New Jersey iron producing community.

 **For other Long Islanders involved in the suffrage movement *see* Raymond E. Spinzia, "Winning the Franchise: Long Island Activists in the Fight for Woman's Suffrage and Their Opponents, Long Island's Anti-Suffragists." wwwspinzialongislandestates.com.

 The house was later owned by L. W. Miller; Grant Adams; Erik Eastman; and, subsequently, by Hazanne Smith, who restored the house after it was damaged by fire in 1992.

Brockman, Daniel David (1904-1990)

Occupation(s):	attorney - specialized in tax law
	accountant - president, C. D. Giles & Co.
Civic Activism:	a founder, Free Classical Music Concerts in Central Park;
	a founder and director, American Symphony Orchestra;
	prominent supporter in effort to save Carnegie Hall from demolition;
	established Playhouse Project master class
Marriage(s):	Elizabeth [unable to determine maiden name]
	- Civic Activism: established Playhouse Project master class; trustee, East Hampton Historical Society
Address:	80 Huntting Lane, East Hampton
Name of estate:	*The Playhouse*
Year of construction:	1917
Style of architecture:	Neo-Tudor
Architect(s):	Francis Burrall Hoffman, Jr. designed *The Playhouse* 1917 (for L. E. Woodhouse)
	Richard Webb converted *The Playhouse* into a residence

Landscape architect(s):
House extant: yes
Historical notes:

Built originally as a playhouse by Lorenzo Easton Woodhouse, it was converted into a residence. Brockman purchased *The Playhouse* in 1958 and continued to call it *The Playhouse*.

Daniel David and Elizabeth Brockman's daughter Jolie married Gordon Hammer and, subsequently, Charles M. Kinsolving, Jr. Their son Richard married Marjorie LaRowe, the daughter of Franklin Hewitt LaRowe of Massapequa, and, later, Mirra Ellen Bank, the daughter of Michael L. and Julia Bank. Their daughter Susan was not married at the time of her death in 2001.

The Playhouse is on the National Register of Historic Places.

Broderick, Matthew (b. 1962)

Occupation(s):	entertainers and associated professions - stage, motion picture, and television actor
Marriage(s):	1997 – Sarah Jessica Parker (b. 1965)
	- entertainers and associated professions - stage, motion picture, and television actress; television program producer
	industrialist - founder, Lovely, 2005 (perfume line); founder, Covet, 2007 (perfume line); founder, Bitten, 2007 (fashion line of clothes)
Address:	401 Marine Boulevard, Amagansett
Name of estate:	
Year of construction:	
Style of architecture:	Beach House
Architect(s):	
Landscape architect(s):	

House extant: yes
Historical notes:

Matthew Broderick is the son of James Joseph and Patricia Biow Broderick.

Sara Jessica Parker Broderick is the daughter of Stephen and Barbara Keck Parker.

The Brodericks' son James was born in 2002. Their twin daughters Marion and Tabitha were born in 2009 via a surrogate.

Bronaugh, Frederick Lewis (1871-1946)

Occupation(s):	industrialist - vice-president and sales manager, A & M Karagheusian, Inc. (manufacturer and importer of rugs and carpets)
Civic Activism:	a founder, Institute of Carpet Manufacturers of America; director, Maidstone Club, East Hampton
Marriage(s):	1902-1946 – Sue Robertson (1878-1975)
Address:	67 Woods Lane, East Hampton
Name of estate:	*Elsufral*
Year of construction:	1900
Style of architecture:	Colonial Revival
Architect(s):	
Landscape architect(s)	
House extant: yes	
Historical notes:	

    The compound consists of a 6,000-square-foot, three-story, six-bedroom main residence and a turn-of-the-century guest cottage.

    The *Social Register Summer, 1945* lists Frederick L. and Sue Robertson Bronaugh as residing at *Elsufral* in East Hampton. *The Blue Book of The Hamptons, 1958* lists the address as 67 Woods Lane, East Hampton.

    He was the son of Frederick Peyton and Helen H. Myers Bronaugh.

    Frederick Lewis and Sue Robertson Bronaugh's daughter Elinor, who subsequently owned the house, married Alex John Pagel, Jr. of Stockholm, Sweden.

    In 2015 the 2.75-acre estate was for sale. The asking price was $4.995 million; the annual taxes were $19,169.

Bronfman, Edgar Miles, Jr. (b. 1955)

Occupation(s): capitalist - chairman of board, Global Thermostat (develops technology
    for direct air capture of carbon dioxide);
    CEO and chairman of board, Warner Music Group, Inc.,
      2004-2011;
    motion picture and Broadway producer
industrialist - president, House of Seagram (beverage firm);
    CEO, Seagram and Sons, Inc. (beverage firm)
composer - songwriter

Civic Activism: established the Clarissa and Edgar Bronfman, Jr. Foundation

Marriage(s): M/1 – 1979-div. 1991 – Sherry Brewer
    - entertainers and associated professions -   actress
M/2 – 1993 – Clarissa Alcock
    - Civic Activism: trustee, the Museum of Modern Art, NYC;
      board vice-chair, Carnegie Hall, NYC;
      trustee, The Nightingale–Bamford School, NYC

Address: 428 Further Lane, Amagansett
Name of estate:
Year of construction: 1982
Style of architecture: International
Architect(s): Charles Gwathmey designed
  the house (for de Menil)
Charles Gwathmey designed 1990
  alterations (for Bronfman)
Landscape architect(s)
House extant: yes*
Historical notes:

    The 11,000-square-foot house, originally named *Toad Hall*, was built by Francois de Menil. In 1988 de Menil sold the house to Lawrence Gilbert Gagosian. In 1990 it was purchased by Bronfman.
    He is the son of Edgar Miles and Ann Loeb Bronfman, Sr.
    Edgar Miles and Sherry Brewer Bronfman, Jr.'s son Benjamin married Mathangi Arulpragasam. Their daughter Hannah married Brendan Fallis.
    Clarissa Alcock Bronfman is the daughter of Frank Alcock, a Venezuelan oil executive of British descent.
    Edgar Miles and Clarissa Alcock Bronfman, Jr. have four children—Aaron, Erick, Bettina, and Clarissa.
    *In 2011 there was a serious fire in the main residence. In 2014 there was a fire in the guest house.

Brown, Anthony Coates

Occupation(s): financier - member, Eastman Dillon Union Securities and Co.

Marriage(s): 1962 – Winifred Lee d'Olier
    - Civic Activism: director, Mayor's Voluntary Action Center, NYC

Address: 3 Clover Leaf Lane, East Hampton
Name of estate: *Clover Cottage*
Year of construction:
Style of architecture:
Architect(s):
Landscape architect(s)
House extant: yes
Historical notes:

    The *Social Register Summer, 2001* lists Anthony C. and Winifred Lee d'Olier Brown as residing at 3 Clover Leaf Lane, East Hampton. *The Blue Book of The Hamptons, 2008* list the name of their residence as *Clover Cottage.*
    He is the son of Phillip Wilson Tate and Aralene P. Miller Brown, Sr. of East Hampton.
    Winifred Lee d'Olier Brown is the daughter of Franklin Woolman and Margaret Winifred Lee d'Olier, Jr. of East Hampton.
    Anthony Coates and Winifred Lee d'Olier Brown's daughter Leelee married Robert Douglas Jaffe.

Brown, Lathrop (1883-1959)

Occupation(s):	real estate agent - partner, Charles S. Brown Co. (later, Brown, Wheelock, Harris, & Co.; now, Brown, Harris, Stevens (real estate brokerage firm)*; director, Brown, Wheelock, Harris, & Co.; director, Brown, Harris, Stevens
	publisher - director, G. Schirner & Co. (music publisher)
	financier - director, Commonwealth Insurance Co.
	politician - member, United States Congress, NYS First Congressional District; examiner, Railway Wage Commission
	statesman - special assistant to Secretary of the Interior Franklin Knight Lane, 1917-1918; secretary, President Woodrow Wilson's Industrial Conference, 1919
Marriage(s):	1911-1959 – Helen Chamblet Hooper (1891-1978) - Civic Activism: donated 1,600 acres of coastal land to California for a state park
Address:	off Old Montauk Highway, Montauk
Name of estate:	*The Windmill*
Year of construction:	1922-1923
Style of architecture:	Eclectic
Architect(s):	Peabody, Wilson, and Brown designed the house (for L. Brown)
Landscape architect(s)	
House extant: no**	
Historical notes:	

 The house, originally named *The Windmill*, was built by Lathrop Brown.
 The *Social Register Summer, 1932* lists Lathrop and Helen Hooper Brown as residing at *The Windmill* in Montauk.
 He was the son of Charles Stelle and Lucy Barnes Brown, Sr. of *Ardshiel* in Mount Kisco, NY.
 *President Theodore Roosevelt's brother-in-law was a partner in the real estate brokerage firm of Charles S. Brown Co.
 His brother Archibald was a noted architect and partner in the firm of Peabody, Wilson, and Brown. He was married to Helen Parrish and, later, Eleanor Stockstrom and resided at *Four Fountains* in Southampton. [*See* Spinzia, *Long Island's Prominent Families in the Town of Southampton* – Brown entry.] His sister Lucy married William J. Engle and resided in Manhattan. His brother Charles Stelle Brown, Jr. married Mary Jay Schieffelin and also resided in Manhattan.
 Helen Chamblet Hooper Brown was the daughter of Robert and Helen Angler Ames Hooper of Boston, MA. Lathrop's wife had inherited $10 million when she was orphaned at the age of fifteen.
 Lathrop and Helen Chamblet Hooper Brown's daughter Halla married Arthur B. Rosenbaum. Their daughter Camilla married Robert Warren Canfield, the son of George F. Canfield of NYC and *Farmlands* in Peekskill, NY, and, later, Mathew Comstock Jenkins.
 Lathrop and President Franklin Delano Roosevelt were classmates at Groton, roommates at Harvard, and served as best man at each other's weddings.
 **In 1942 Brown sold the estate to the federal government which demolished the house and incorporated the estate's land into Camp Hero. After World War II the land was incorporated into Camp Hero State Park. The John Dudley Edwards Wainscott Windmill, which Brown had purchased in 1922 and moved to his Montauk residence, was deeded by Brown for one dollar to the Georgica Association in Wainscott, which moved the windmill back to Wainscott. The windmill has been on the National Register of Historic Places since 1978. [*See* Spinzia, *Long Island: A Guide to New York's Suffolk and Nassau Counties,* Hippocrene Books, New York, third edition, 2009, p. 81.]

Brown, Philip Wilson Tate, Sr. (1900-1975)

Occupation(s):	financier - partner, Charles D. Barney and Co. (stock brokerage firm) (later, Smith Barney and Co.)
	partner, Smith Barney and Co. (stock brokerage firm) (now, Morgan Stanley Smith Barney) (investment banking firm)
Civic Activism:	governor, American Stock Exchange;
	director, Maidstone Club, East Hampton
Marriage(s):	1929-1975 – Aralene Paul Miller
Address:	Pudding Hill Lane, East Hampton
Name of estate:	
Year of construction:	
Style of architecture:	
Architect(s):	
Landscape architect(s)	
House extant: unconfirmed	
Historical notes:	

The Blue Book of The Hamptons, 1973 lists Phillip W. and Aralene P. Miller Brown as residing on Pudding Hill Lane, East Hampton.

He was the son of Robert E. Brown.

Aralene Paul Miller Brown was the daughter of Walter Pawson Miller of Germantown, PA.

Phillip Wilson Tate and Aralene Paul Miller Brown, Sr.'s son Anthony married Winifred Lee d'Olier, the daughter of Franklin and Margaret Winifred Lee d'Olier, Jr. of East Hampton. Their son Phillip Wilson Tate Brown, Jr. married Diane Smith, the daughter of Homer Smith; Helen Madelyn Kinnucan, the daughter of Henry L. Kinnucan of Grosse Pointe Farms, MI; and, subsequently, Nancy E. Burke with whom he resided in Salisbury, CT.

Browne, Christopher H. (1946-2009)

Occupation(s):	financier - managing director, Tweedy, Browne, and Co. (private investment firm);
	president, Tweedy, Browne Funds (mutual fund group)
	educator - faculty, John F. Kennedy School of Government, Harvard University, Cambridge, MA
	writer - *The Little Book of Value Investing*, 2006
Civic Activism:	donated $10 million to the University of Pennsylvania, Philadelphia, PA;
	established Christopher H. Browne Center for Immunology and Immune Diseases, Rockefeller University, NYC;
	chairman of board of overseers, School of Arts and Sciences, University of Pennsylvania, Philadelphia, PA;
	trustee, The Paley Center for Media, NYC;
	director, Institute for Classical Architecture and Art, NYC;
	trustee, Long Island Chapter of The Nature Conservancy;
	trustee, Guild Hall, East Hampton
Marriage(s):	bachelor
Address:	Middle Lane, East Hampton
Name of estate:	*Chateau Amorois*
Year of construction:	1998
Style of architecture:	Contemporary French Country
Architect(s):	Boris Baranovich designed the house (for Browne)
Landscape architect(s)	Christopher H. Browne designed his own landscaping*
Builder:	Trunzo Contracting, Inc.
House extant: yes	
Historical notes:	

The five-bedroom house, originally named *Chateau Amorois*, was built by Christopher H. Browne.

He was the son of Howard Browne.

*Browne spent several years landscaping the property prior to building the house.

Browne, Christopher H. (1946-2009)

Occupation(s):	*[See previous entry.]*
Marriage(s):	bachelor
Address:	60 Further Lane, East Hampton
Name of estate:	
Year of construction:	2007
Style of architecture:	Modern
Architect(s):	Andrew S. Gordon designed the house (for Browne)
Landscape architect(s)	Christopher H. Browne and Andrew S. Gordon

House extant: unconfirmed
Historical notes:

The 9,000-square-foot, four-bedroom, one-story house with two guest suites was built by Christopher H. Browne on property he purchased from Elizabeth Fondaras. Prior to Fondaras' ownership, the property was owned by Robert Dudley Roberts, Jr., who purchased East Hampton's historic Dominy clock shop and cabinet shop in 1946. He relocated them to his Further Lane property where he had them joined together as a single building.
[See previous entry for family information.]
After a bitter legal battle, Browne's partner of ten years, artist, architect, and landscape architect Andrew S. Gordon inherited the house and Browne's fortune. Upon Gordon's death in 2014 the inheritance reverted to Browne's family.
In 2014 the estate and 18 acres were purchased for $147 million by Barry Rosenstein who intends to demolish the main residence and build a new one on the site. Plans are in progress to relocate the Dominy buildings to a site in the village where they will be open to the public as a museum.

Buddenhagen, Frederick Leonard

Occupation(s):	financier - chairman of board, Arab International Center for Commerce and Industry; president, Arab American Capital Corp.; vice-president, Trident Investment Management, Inc.
	writer - *Internal Entrepreneurship as a Corporate Strategy for New Product Development*, 1967
Marriage(s):	M/1 ____
	M/2 – 1978 – Kathleen Ingrid Burns
	- Civic Activism: director, L. W. Frohlich Family Fund
Address:	15 Hither Lane, East Hampton
Name of estate:	
Year of construction:	
Style of architecture:	
Architect(s):	
Landscape architect(s):	

House extant: yes
Historical notes:

The *Social Register Summer, 2000* lists Frederick L. and Kathleen I. Burns Buddenhagen as residing at 15 Hither Lane, East Hampton.
He is the son of Frederick E. Buddenhagen of Akron, OH.
Kathleen Ingrid Burns Buddenhagen is the daughter of Thomas Robert and Ingrid Lily Frohlich Burns of East Hampton. Kathleen had previously been married to Thomas Preston Bartle, Jr.
In 2004 Mrs. Buddenhagen sold the house for $3.2 million.

Buek, Gustav H. (1850-1927)
aka Gustavus H. Buek

Occupation(s):	industrialist - partner, Buek and Lindner (later, G. H. Buek; subsequently, American Lithographic Co.); vice-president, director, and art manager, American Lithographic Co.; president, and director, Alco–Gravure Inc. (printing division of Crowell–Collier Publishing Co.)
	publisher - director, Crowell–Collier Publishing Co.
Marriage(s):	1873-1927 – Hannah Louise Valentine (1852-1941)
Address:	14 James Lane, East Hampton
Name of estate:	*Home Sweet Home*
Year of construction:	c. 1680
Style of architecture:	Saltbox
Architect(s):	
Landscape architect(s):	
House extant: yes	
Historical notes:	

In 1907 Buek purchased the ancestral home of John Howard Payne.
He was the son of Herman and Augusta Stiemers Buek of Brooklyn.
In 1928 the Village of East Hampton purchased the house. [*The East Hampton Star* June 22, 1928, p. 1.]
The house is on the National Register of Historic Places and is currently open to the public as a museum.

Bunshaft, Gordon (1909-1990)

Occupation(s):	architect - partner, Skidmore, Owings, & Merrill (later, SOM); partner, SOM
Civic Activism:	member, United States Commission of Fine Arts; trustee, Museum of Modern Art, NYC, 1963-1972; trustee, Carnegie–Mellon University, Pittsburgh, PA
Marriage(s):	1943-1990 – Nina Elizabeth Wayler (d. 1994) - entertainers and associated professions - motion picture actress Civic Activism: donated *Travertine House* and her art collection to the Museum of Modern Art, NYC; founder - The Nina and Gordon Bunshaft Fund
Address:	84 Georgica Close Road, East Hampton
Name of estate:	*Travertine House*
Year of construction:	1963
Style of architecture:	Modern
Architect(s):	Gordon Bunshaft designed his own residence
Landscape architect(s)	
House extant: no; demolished 2004	
Historical notes:	

The 2,300-square-foot, two-bedroom house, originally named *Travertine House*, was built by Gordon Bunshaft.
He was the son of David and Yelta Bunshaft of Buffalo, NY.
Gordon and Nina Elizabeth Wayler Bunshaft did not have children.
In 1995 Martha Stewart purchased the house from the Museum of Modern Art for $3.2 million. Martha had architect John Pawson gut the house's interior and was preparing to renovate it when she became involved in litigation over shrubbery and a service building which she planned to erect. Martha transferred the house's gutted shell to her daughter Alexis, who sold it to Donald H. Maharan in 2004 for $9.5 million. Maharan demolished the house and built a new residence on the property.

Burchell, Henry J., Jr. (1870-1959)

Occupation(s):	capitalist - realtor
	educator - instructor, Latin and Greek, Columbia University, NYC, and Barnard College, NYC
Civic Activism:	director, Casa Italiana (Columbia University Italian Cultural Center);
	secretary, Italy–America Society;
	director, Mulberry Community Center
Marriage(s):	1900-1951 – Candida Paleari (1869-1951)
	- Civic Activism: a founder, American Committee to Aid Soldiers Crippled in the War during World War I*
Address:	Huntting Lane, East Hampton
Name of estate:	*Gay Cottage*
Year of construction:	
Style of architecture:	
Architect(s):	
Landscape architect(s)	
House extant: unconfirmed	

Historical notes:

The *Social Register Summer, 1915* lists Henry J. and Candida Paleari Burchell as residing at *Gay Cottage* on Huntting Lane, East Hampton.

She was the daughter of Mario and Antoinetta de Monti Paleari of Milan, Italy.

Henry J. and Candida Paleari Burchell, Jr.'s daughter Mary married ____ Matthews.

*Candida was awarded the Gold Medal of the Italian Red Cross for her services during World War I.

Burke, Oscar Moech (1883-1959)

Occupation(s):	industrialist - president, Manhattan Soap Co. (merged into Purex Corp. in 1956)
Civic Activism:	a founder and director, Gardiner's Bay Boat Club
Marriage(s):	M/1 – 1913-div. 1920 – Helen Edna Marston (1893-1969)
	M/2 – January 1926-div. July 1926 – Helen Margaret Kelly (1884-1952)
	M/3 – 1934 – Cicely Mary Hilger
	M/4 – 1942-1959 – Marguerite Stone (d. 1969)
Address:	Georgica Road, East Hampton
Name of estate:	
Year of construction:	
Style of architecture:	
Architect(s):	
Landscape architect(s):	
House extant: unconfirmed	

Historical notes:

The *Social Register Summer, 1915* lists Oscar M. and [Helen] Edna Marston Burke as residing in East Hampton.

In 1919 Oscar purchased Mrs. Harriet Taylor's residence. It had previously been owned by Bishop Greer. [The *East Hampton Star* October 3, 1919, p. 5.]

Burke was the son of Frank Gaius and Joanna Arrington Burke, Sr. of New York. Oscar's sister Lucie married Clarence Frank Alcott and resided in East Hampton.

Helen Edna Marston Burke was the daughter of Edwin Sprague and Emma Doty Marston of New York. She subsequently married Robert Livingston Beekman, the Governor of Rhode Island.

Oscar Moech and Helen Edna Marston Burke's son Edwin married Virginia Consuelo Smith, the daughter of Edward Tailer and Consuelo Vanderbilt Smith of *Iradell* in Sands Point, and resided in Far Hills, NJ. [*See* Spinzia, *Long Island's Prominent North Shore Families, vol. II* – Smith entry – and Raymond E. Spinzia "Adultery, Drugs, Murder, Untimely Deaths, and Long Island's Prominent Families: A Tangled Web" www.spinzialongislandestates.com.]

Helen Margaret Kelly Burke was the daughter of Edward Kelly of New York. She had previously been married to Frank Jay Gould; Ralph Hill Thomas; and Prince Noureddin Vlora of Albania.

Cicely Mary Hilger Burke was the daughter of John Hilger of St. Louis, MO. She had previously been married to Walter Scott Cameron of Hempstead and *Wee Home* in Southampton. [*See* Spinzia, *Long Island's Prominent Families in the Town of Hempstead* and *Long Island's Prominent Families in the Town of Southampton* – Cameron entries.] Cicely retained ownership of Cameron's other Southampton house *Lochiel* where she resided with Burke.

Marguerite Stone Burke was the daughter of Francis William Stone of New York and Philadelphia, PA. She had previously been married to William Cameron and John Hamilton Inman, Jr.

Burnett, Eugene Rodney (1880-1956)

Occupation(s):	financier - member, New York Cotton Exchange
Marriage(s):	Emma Darrow (1875-1953)
Address:	Georgica Road, East Hampton

Name of estate:
Year of construction:
Style of architecture:
Architect(s):
Landscape architect(s):
House extant: unconfirmed
Nassau County Museum Collection has photographs of the estate.
Historical notes:

    The *Long Island Society Register, 1929* lists E. R. and Emma Darrow Burnett as residing on Georgica Road, East Hampton.

    Emma Darrow Burnett was the daughter of Rufus Darrow. She had previously been married to Charles Goodhue Dodd, the son of John Mingus Dodd, Jr. of East Hampton. Emma's brother Daniel married Florence Lander and resided in East Hampton.

Burns, Thomas Robert (d. 1995)

Occupation(s):	publisher - vice-president, sales and marketing, Doubleday and Co., Garden City, NY
Civic Activism:	trustee, L. W. Froblich Charitable Trust

Marriage(s):	1953-1995 – Ingrid Lily Froblich (1913-2009)
	- fashion model
	    Civic Activism: trustee, International House;
	                                 trustee, L. W. Froblich Trust

Address:	32 Davids Lane, East Hampton

Name of estate:
Year of construction:
Style of architecture: Colonial Revival
Architect(s):
Landscape architect(s)
House extant: yes
Historical notes:

    The Blue Book of The Hamptons, 1973 lists Thomas R. and Ingrid L. Froblich Burns as residing at 32 Davids Lane, East Hampton.

    Ingrid Lily Froblich Burns was the daughter of Leopold Froblich of Austria, who died in a Nazi concentration camp.

    Thomas Robert and Ingrid Lily Froblich Burns' daughter Madeleine married Laurence Laird Davis, Jr. and, later, Robert Lyman Miller, the son of Paul Albert Miller. Their daughter Kathleen married Thomas Preston Bartle, Jr. and, subsequently, Frederick Leonard Buddenhagen with whom she resides in East Hampton.

    By 1987 the Burnses had relocated to *Georgica Cove* at 6 La Forest Lane, East Hampton.

Burton, Jane Erdmann (1910-1985)

Civic Activism:	member, National Watershed Congress, 1963-1965;
	member, women's board, Navy League, NYC;
	member, women's auxiliary commission during World War II;
	trustee, Home for New York Aged and Indigent Families;
	committee member, St. Barnabas House, 1962-1965;
	member, woman's auxiliary board, William Waldo Burton Memorial Home, New Orleans, LA;
	director, Christian Women's Exchange, Herman–Grima House;
	director, Friends of the Cabildo, New Orleans, LA;
	director, Gallier House, New Orleans, LA;
	trustee, Caroline Dorman Nature Preserve, Natchiloches, LA;
	trustee, Live Oak Gardens, Jefferson Island, LA;
	vice-chair, conservation committee, Garden Club of America, 1962-1965;
	director, Southeastern Architectural Archives
Marriage(s):	1934-div. 1954-remarried 1956-div. – William Lafayette Burton II (1910-1957) - financier - a founder, William L. Burton and Co. (stock brokerage firm)
Address:	89 Lily Pond Lane, East Hampton
Name of estate:	*Coxwould*
Year of construction:	1912
Style of architecture:	Coxwold
Architect(s):	Albro and Lindeberg designed the house (for Erdmann)
Landscape architect(s):	Edwina Von Gal designed gardens (for Schulman)*
Builder:	Smith and Davis
House extant: yes	
Historical notes:	

   The eight-bedroom, eight-bath, 9,000-square-foot house, originally named *Coxwould*, was built by Dr. John Frederick Erdmann. It was later owned by his daughter Jane Erdmann Burton.
   William Lafayette Burton II was the son of William Waldo Burton.
   Jane subsequently married Francisco Aurelio Gonzalez of Southampton and, then, Morgan Whitney.
   In 1954 Mrs. Burton sold the house to Dayton Hedges and in 1955 built a house on Gracie Lane. [*The East Hampton Star* August 5, 1954, p. 1, and June 16, 1955, p. 12.] In 1956 she was residing at *Dune House* on a private road off Lily Pond. [*The East Hampton Star* January 5, 1956, p. 1.]
   In 1958 Hedges' son Burke Osborn Hedges purchased the house. [*The East Hampton Star* July 3, 1958, p. 4.] It was then owned by Joseph Weinstein and, subsequently, by Lowell M. Schulman who renamed it *Beechwood*. In 2012 the house was for sale by Schulman. The asking price was $24.95 million; the annual taxes were $60,000.
   *Edwina Von Gal created fifteen garden rooms that were inspired by English gardens.

Butler, Howard Russell, Sr. (1856-1934)

Occupation(s):	attorney
	educator - assistant professor of physics, Princeton University, Princeton, NJ
	capitalist - secretary, Gold and Stock Telegraph Co., 1879; secretary, American Speaking Telephone Co., 1880; president, Carnegie Music Hall, NYC, 1896-1905
	writer - *Painter and Space*; *Synopsis of the Covenant With Comment*, 1919 (pamphlet); *The Covenant Gutted*, 1919 (pamphlet)
	artist - awarded several medals for his artwork*
Civic Activism:	a founder and first president, American Fine Arts Society, 1889-1906; president, National Academy Association; vice-president, National Academy of Design; supervisor, American Museum of Natural History, 1925
Marriage(s):	1890-1934 – Virginia Hays (1866-1945)
Address:	West End Avenue, East Hampton
Name of estate:	*Bay Bush*
Year of construction:	1893
Style of architecture:	Beach Cottage
Architect(s):	
Landscape architect(s):	
Builder:	Babcock and Grimshaw
	Asa Otis Jones, 1906 additions (for H. R. Butler, Sr.)**

House extant: unconfirmed
Historical notes:

 The house, originally named *Bay Bush*, was built by Howard Russell Butler, Sr.
 The *Social Register Summer, 1915* lists Howard Russell and Virginia Hays Butler [Sr.] as residing at *Bay Bush* in East Hampton.
 He was the son of William Allen and Mary Russell Marshall Butler, Sr. of Manhattan.
 Virginia Hays Butler was the daughter of William J. and Helen Dummer Hays of Manhattan.
 Howard Russell and Virginia Hays Butler Sr.'s daughter Helen died in infancy. Their son Howard Russell Butler, Jr. married Caroline Mott Frost, the daughter of Dr. Conway Frost of Clinton, NY.
 *Butler's artwork won medals at expositions at Paris, 1889; Atlanta, 1895; Philadelphia Temple, 1888; Paris, 1900; Buffalo, 1901; and honorable mention at the Paris Salon, 1886.
 **He made a forty-square-foot extension to the house in 1900 and added a twenty-five- by nineteen-foot art gallery in 1906.
 In 1916 the house was sold to Miss Emma Louise Stone who made extensive alterations. [*The East Hampton Star* November 3, 1916, p. 5.]

Butler, William Allen, III (1886-1971)

Occupation(s):

Marriage(s): 1921-1950 – Vivienne Randolph Moncure (1885-1950)

Address: Middle Lane, East Hampton
Name of estate: *Crestmere*
Year of construction:
Style of architecture:
Architect(s):
Landscape architect(s):
House extant: unconfirmed
Historical notes:

    The *Long Island Society Register, 1929* lists William Allen and Vivienne R. Moncure Butler, Jr. [III] as residing on Middle Lane, East Hampton.
    He was the son of William Allen and Louise Terry Collins Butler, Jr. of *To Windward* in Southampton. [*See* Spinzia, *Long Island's Prominent Families in the Town of Southampton* – Butler entry.] His sister Lydia married Maitland Dwight and resided at *Chipperkyle* in Bedford, NY. His sister Louise married William Edgar Shepherd, Jr. His brother Lyman died in 1917 after returning from the Mexican border campaign. His brother Charles married Dorothy P. Black and resided in Olai, CA.
    Vivienne Randolph Moncure Butler was the daughter of William S. and Belle Chapman Moncure of Richmond, VA.
    William Allen and Vivienne R. Moncure Butler III's daughter Mary did not marry.

Calicchio, John

Occupation(s): shipping - chairman of board, Apex Bulk Carriers, LLC (dry bulk shipping firm)
capitalist - chairman of board, Argo International Corp. (distributor of mechanical and electric equipment);
sole owner, Delcal Enterprises, Inc. (holding company);
chairman of board, Argo Turboserve Corp. (distributor of inventory control systems);
president and CEO, Argo Marine Supply Co.

Civic Activism: trustee and director, Solomon R. Guggenheim Foundation;
major benefactor, Children's Cancer and Blood Foundation

Marriage(s): Millicent E. *[unable to determine maiden name]* (aka Lee Calicchio)
 - merchant - Lee Calicchio Ltd., NYC (antique firm)

Address: 306 Georgica Road, East Hampton
Name of estate:
Year of construction:
Style of architecture: French Chateau
Architect(s):
Landscape architect(s):
House extant: yes
Historical notes:

    John Calicchio is the son of Thomas Calicchio.
    John and Millicent E. Calicchio's daughter Lisa married Donald J. Jackson, the son of Alfred George and Helen Jackson. Their son Thomas married Carol Ann DiScala, the daughter of Francis J. DiScala of Norwalk, CT.
    In 2017 the five-bedroom, six-bath, 5,888-square-foot house and 2.7 acres were for sale. The asking price was $6.95 million.

Callan, Erin M. (b. 1965)

Occupation(s):	attorney - member, Simpson, Thacher, and Bartlett (specialized in taxes)
	financier - CFO, Lehman Brothers, 2007-2008; member, Credit Suisse, 2009-2009; managing director, Global Finance Solutions
Marriage(s):	M/1 – div. 2008 – Michael P. Thompson
	M/2 – Anthony Montella
	- New York City fireman, retired
Address:	82 Woods Lane, East Hampton
Name of estate:	
Year of construction:	1912
Style of architecture:	Dutch Colonial Revival
Architect(s):	Joseph Greenleaf Thorp designed the house (for Flannery)
Landscape architect(s):	
House extant: yes	
Historical notes:	

The 5,5000-square-foot, seven-bedroom house was built by John Flannery.

Michael P. and Erin M. Callan Thompson purchased the house in 2005 from Perry H. and Alexandra Beaumont for $3.93 million. In 2008 Michael sold the house to Erin for $495,000. The transaction may have been part of their divorce settlement.

In 2013 Anthony and Erin sold the house to Christopher J. and Tannaz Fiore for $3.75 million.

Cammann, George Philip, Jr. (1861-1920)

Occupation(s):	capitalist - secretary and director, Almy Realty Corp.
Marriage(s):	1894-1920 – Jean Buchanan Gallatin (1873-1955)
Address:	44 Woods Lane, East Hampton
Name of estate:	*Seaholme*
Year of construction:	1899
Style of architecture:	Shingle
Architect(s):	Joseph Greenleaf Thorp designed the house (for Cammann)
Landscape architect(s):	
Builder:	George A. Eldredge
House extant: yes	
Historical notes:	

The house, originally named *Seaholme*, was built by George Philip Cammann, Jr. [*The East Hampton Star* November 25, 1898, p. 5.]

The *Social Register Summer, 1910* lists George P. and Jean B. Gallatin Cammann as residing at *Seaholme* in East Hampton.

He was the son of Dr. George Philip and Mrs. Catherine Lorillard Cammann, Sr. Dr. Cammann invented the biauricular stetho-scope.

Jean Buchanan Gallatin Cammann was the daughter of Frederic and Amy Goelet Gerry Gallatin, Sr. of *Breezy Lawn* in East Hampton. Jean's sister Almy married Howland Pell and resided in Tuxedo Park, NY. Her sister Mary married William Warner Hoppin, Jr. and resided at *Friendship Hill* in Old Brookville [*See* Spinzia, *Long Island's Prominent North Shore Families, vol. 1* – Hoppin entry.] Her brother Rolaz married Emily Lorillard Morris and resided at *Chepstow* in Newport, RI. Her brother Goelet married Edith Church Post, the daughter of Charles Alfred and Caroline de Trobriand Post of *Strandhome* in Bayport, and resided in Bellport. [*See* Spinzia, *Long Island's Prominent South Shore Families* – Post entry.] Her brother Albert Gallatin III married Margaret Hoffman Hackstaff, the daughter of Charles Ludovic Hackstaff of East Hampton, and resided in Southampton.

George Philip and Jean Buchanan Gallatin Cammann, Jr.'s son Philip married Elizabeth Wolcott Merchant. Their son Frederic married Katharine J. Blackwell, the daughter of George E. Blackwell of New York City, and, later, Margaret Ripley with whom he resided in Morrisville, PA.

In 1914 Cammann sold the house to Lewis Mercer Borden, Sr., who continued to call it *Seaholme*.

In 1959 the house became the Jewish Center of the Hamptons.

Cammann, Roy Lennox (1896-1974)

Occupation(s):	industrialist - vice-president, Allied Chemical Co.
Marriage(s):	Naomi Clele Conde (1904-1986)
Address:	Lily Pond and Hedges Lanes, East Hampton
Name of estate:	
Year of construction:	1917
Style of architecture:	
Architect(s):	
Landscape architect(s):	
Builder:	
House extant:	unconfirmed
Historical notes:	

    The house was built by John LaRue Helm, Jr. In 1923 Mrs. Helm sold it to James Andrew Moffett, Jr. who called it *Inadune*. [*The East Hampton Star* March 16, 1923, p. 5.] In 1937 Moffett sold the house to John Lafayette Weeks. [*The East Hampton Star* January 28, 1937, p. 1.] In 1951 it was purchased by Cammann. [*The East Hampton Star* May 3, 1951, p. 1.]

    The Blue Book of the Hamptons, 1958 lists Mr. and Mrs. Roy Lennox Cammann as residing on Lily Pond and Hedges Lanes.

Campbell, David (b. 1944)

Occupation(s):	financier - a founder and CEO, Global Minerals and Metals Corp. (commodity trading firm)
Marriage(s):	
Address:	38 Mathews Road, East Hampton
Name of estate:	*Burnt Point*
Year of construction:	1997
Style of architecture:	Dutch Colonial Revival
Architect(s):	Francis Fleetwood designed the house (for Campbell)
Landscape architect(s)	
House extant:	yes
Historical notes:	

    The house, originally named *Burnt Point*, was built by David Campbell.

    In 2005 the 18,000-square-foot house was purchased by Stewart J. Rahr for $45 million. In 2015 he listed the house for sale. The asking price was $95 million.

Campbell, Nathaniel Adams, Jr. (b. 1909)

Occupation(s):	writer - songwriter
Marriage(s):	
Address:	19 Woods Lane, East Hampton
Name of estate:	
Year of construction:	
Style of architecture:	
Architect(s):	
Landscape architect(s):	
House extant: unconfirmed	
Historical notes:	

The Blue Book of The Hamptons, 1973 lists Nathaniel A. Campbell [Jr.] as residing at 19 Woods Lane, East Hampton. He was the son of Nathaniel Adams and Elizabeth Warne Detwiller Campbell, Sr. of *Camelot* in East Hampton.
[See following entry for additional family information.]

Campbell, Nathaniel Adams, Sr. (1869-1944)

Occupation(s):	capitalist - partner, Campbell & Huffer (exporting firm); president and director, Atlantic & Western Railroad; vice president, St. Louis and Southwestern Railroad
	financier - trustee, American Savings Bank
	industrialist - director, Concrete Steel Co.; director, Old Dominion Iron & Steel Works
Civic Activism:	secretary, Devon Yacht Club, Amagansett; director, Maidstone Club, East Hampton; a founder, Sleepy Hollow Club; a founder, Ardsley Club
Marriage(s):	1905-1944 – Elizabeth Warne Detwiller (1873-1960) - Civic Activism: member, executive committee, East Hampton Women's Republican Club
Address:	West End Avenue, East Hampton
Name of estate:	*Camelot*
Year of construction:	1928
Style of architecture:	Modified Neo-Tudor
Architect(s):	Robert Tappan designed the house (for N. A. Campbell, Sr.)
Landscape architect(s):	
House extant: no; demolished in 1995	
Historical notes:	

The house, originally named *Camelot*, was built by Nathaniel Adams Campbell, Sr.
He was the son of John and Frances K. Maycock Campbell.
Elizabeth Warne Detwiller Campbell was the daughter of John Jacob and Arabelle Knecht Detwiller.
Nathaniel Adams and Elizabeth Warne Detwiller Campbell, Sr.'s daughter Elizabeth married Wilmuth Earle Blackburn, the son of Wilmuth Everet and Rita Mabel Chapman Blackburn of Summit, NJ, and resided at *West Side Story* in East Hampton. Their son Nathaniel Adams Campbell, Jr. resided in East Hampton.
[See previous entry for additional family information.]
In 1945 Mrs. Campbell sold the house to Russell Conwell Bennett, Sr. [*The County Review* October 18, 1945, p. 7.]
The house, which is on the National Register of Historic Places, was later owned by Lydia Stokes.

Carlson, Dr. Earl R. (1897-1974)

Occupation(s):	physician - neurologist, cerebral palsy authority
	writer - *Born That Way*, 1941 (autobiography)
Civic Activism:	established Carlson Foundation;
	co-founder, American Academy of Cerebral Palsy;
	founder, first cerebral palsy clinic, Neurological Institute, Presbyterian Medical Center, NYC, 1932;
	established schools for those affected by cerebral palsy in East Hampton, and in Miami and Pompano Beach, FL
Marriage(s):	Ilse Schneider (b. 1893)
	- nurse
Address:	Terbell Lane, East Hampton
Name of estate:	
Year of construction:	c. 1900
Style of architecture:	Adamesque
Architect(s):	
Landscape architect(s):	
House extant: no*	
Historical notes:	

The house, originally named *Lockdune*, was built by Williston Benedict Lockwood. It was later owned by Laurette Helen Cooney Manners and, then, by Paul Joseph Moranti. In 1936 it was purchased by Carlson who used it as a school for children afflicted with cerebral palsy with which he also was afflicted and for which his alcoholic father often threatened to beat him. [*The East Hampton Star* August 27, 1936, p. 4, and July 11, 1974, p. 2.]

The Carlsons did not have children.

The house was later owned by Charles A. Julianelli.

*The carriage house is extant.

**Carpenter, Louise Adelaide de Menil (b. 1935)
aka Adelaide de Menil***

Occupation(s):	professional photographer under the name Adelaide de Menil
Civic Activism:	founding benefactor and council member, Menil Foundation; donated eight historic buildings and $2 million for their upkeep to the Town of East Hampton
Marriage(s):	Edmund Snow Carpenter (1922-2011)

    - educator -
        taught anthropology,
            University of Toronto;
            New School for Social Research, NYC;
            Center for Visual Anthropology, Harvard University, Cambridge, MA;
            Adelphi University, Garden City, NY;
            New York University, NYC;
            held Carnegie chair, University of California, Santa Cruz;
            chairman, anthropology department, University of California, San Fernando Valley State College;
            held research professorship, University of Papua, New Guinea
    entertainers and associated professions -
        produced and hosted "Explorations" on CBS television
    writer - co-author, "Georgia Sea Island Singers", 1964 (documentary);
        collaborator, "Buck Dancer", 1965 (short film);
        Patterns That Connect, 1996;
        They Became What They Beheld, 1971
    scientist - numerous anthropological sites
    Civic Activism: a founding benefactor, Menil Foundation

Address:	Further Lane, East Hampton
Name of estate:	
Year of construction:	1923
Style of architecture:	
Architect(s):	
Landscape architect(s):	
House extant: no; 2007**	
Historical notes:	

    The house was built by Adelaide de Menil Carpenter by merging the 1700s *Purple House* with a historic barn to create a three-bedroom house.
    She is the daughter of Baron Jean Marie Joseph Menu and Dominique Isaline Zelia Henrietta Clarisse Schlumberger de Menil of Houston, TX. Adelaide's brother Francois married Susan Kadin Silver and resided at *Toad Hall* in Amagansett.
    Edmund Snow Carpenter was the son of Fletcher Hawthorne and Agnes Barbara Wright Carpenter of Rochester, NY. Edmund had previously been married to Florence Ofelia Camara, the daughter of Allonso and Marion Camara, and Virginia York Wilson, the daughter of Ronald York Wilson of Canada.
    *Other member of the de Menil family referred to themselves as Menil.
    **In 2006 the forty-acre estate was listed for sale. *Purple House* and the historic barn along with six other historic buildings were donated by Mrs. Carpenter to the Town of East Hampton. *Purple House* became part of the town's Town Hall on Pantigo Road. The estate was purchased by Ronald Stephen Baron who built a new house on the site.

Carr, Eleanor Maitland DeGraff

Civic Activism:	donated a Tiffany clock to the East Hampton Free Library in memory of her father
Marriage(s):	1919-1956 – Dr. Frank Clyde Carr, Sr. (1886-1956) - physician - ear, nose, and throat specialist, New York Eye and Ear Infirmary, NYC
Address:	20 Apaquogue Road, East Hampton
Name of estate:	*Cherridune*
Year of construction:	1901
Style of architecture:	Modified Shingle
Architect(s):	
Landscape architect(s)	
Builder:	Francis E. Grimshaw, Jr.
House extant: yes	
Historical notes:	

The house was built by Angeline Ensign Newman. It was later owned by James Wilde DeGraff who called it *Cherridune* and, then, by his daughter Eleanor, who continued to call it *Cherridune*.

Eleanor's brother Robert married Dorcas Marie Bomann and resided at *Wood Hollow* in Mill Neck. [*See* Spinzia, *Long Island's Prominent North Shore Families, vol. I* – DeGraff entry.]

Dr. Frank Clyde Carr, Sr. was the son of Dr. John Wesley Carr, Sr. of Murray, KY.

Dr. Frank Clyde and Mrs. Eleanor Maitland DeGraff Carr, Sr.'s son John Wesley Carr II married Julie Yvonne Webb, the daughter of Brodis H. Webb of Montgomery, AL, and, later, Marion Alofs, the daughter of Edward J. Alofs of Pasadena, CA. Their son James married Marie McCabe and resided in Manhasset and in New Hyde Park. Their son Robert resided in New Hampshire. Their son Frank Clyde Carr, Jr. married but in 1983 became a Roman Catholic priest in Yuma, AZ.

By 1965 the Carrs had relocated to *Dunfour*.

The Blue Book of The Hamptons, 1965 lists Mrs. Frank C. Carr as residing at *Dunfour* at the intersection of Apaquogue Road and Hedges Lane, East Hampton.

Cherridune was for sale in 2014. It included the 7,400-square-foot house with nine bedrooms, six full bathrooms, two half bathrooms, a guest house which was originally the chauffeur's cottage, and one acre. The asking price was $6.95 million.

Carse, Donald Rede, Sr. (1899-1971)

Occupation(s):	industrialist - vice-president, Standard Car Manufacturing Co.
Civic Activism:	governor, Devon Yacht Club, Amagansett
Marriage(s):	M/1 – 1927-div. 1932 – Catherine Fowler Clarke (1900-1935) M/2 – 1939-1971 – Caroline Louise Doerr (1911-1988) - Civic Activism: chair, Ladies Village Improvement Society Fair, 1951
Address:	Pudding Hill Lane, East Hampton
Name of estate:	
Year of construction:	
Style of architecture:	
Architect(s):	
Landscape architect(s):	
House extant: unconfirmed	
Historical notes:	

Donald Rede Carse, Sr. was the son of John Bradley and Anne Reed Williams Carse, Sr. of *End Cottage* in East Hampton.

Catherine Clarke Carse was the daughter of Audley and Lulu Edith Carscallen Clarke of Jamestown, RI, and Brooklyn, NY. She had previously been married to Karl Russell Whitmarsh. After divorcing Carse she married A. A. Bint.

The Blue Book of The Hamptons, 1958 lists Donald Rede and Caroline Doerr Carse [Sr.] as residing on Pudding Hill Lane, East Hampton.

She was the daughter of George Valentine Doerr of Minneapolis, MN.

Donald Rede and Caroline Louise Doerr Carse, Sr.'s daughter Anne married Anthony Marcus Paul, the son of Arthur Aubrey Paul of Brisbane, Australia. Their son Donald Rede Carse, Jr. married Isabelle Dolores Wedemeyer, the daughter of Frederick J. Wedemeyer. Their daughter Shirley married ____ Oliver.

[See following entry for additional family information.]

Carse, John Bradley, Sr. (1864-1945)

Occupation(s):	industrialist - chairman, advisory committee, U.S. Steel Corp. (now, USX);
	vice-president, treasurer, and director, Carse Brothers Co., 1892-1903;
	secretary, treasurer, and director, Thomas Kane & Co., 1897-1903;
	vice-president and director, Manufacturers Stove Repair Co., 1898-1903
Civic Activism:	director, Maidstone Club, East Hampton;
	governor, Devon Yacht Club, Amagansett;
	director, YMCA, NYC
Marriage(s):	1896-1939 – Anna Reed Williams (d. 1939)
Address:	70 Dunemere Lane, East Hampton
Name of estate:	*End Cottage*
Year of construction:	1905
Style of architecture:	Shingle
Architect(s):	Joseph Greenleaf Thorp designed the house (for C. A. B. Randell)
Landscape architect(s):	
Builder:	Thomas E. Babcock
House extant: yes	
Historical notes:	

The house was built by Caroline Amelia Boardman Randell. In 1919 it was purchased by Carse, who called it *End Cottage*. [*The East Hampton Star* Mary 20, 1971, p. 2.]

The *Long Island Society Register, 1929* lists John Bradley and Anne R. Williams Carse [Sr.] as residing at *End Cottage* in East Hampton. The *Social Directory of Southampton, Long Island, 1931* lists their address as Dunemere Lane.

He was the son of Thomas and Matilda Bradley Carse.

Anne Reed Williams Carse was a Mayflower descendant.

John Bradley and Anne Reed Williams Carse, Sr.'s son Donald, who resided in East Hampton, married Catherine Clarke and, later, Caroline Louise Doerr. Their son John Bradley Carse, Jr. died at the age of six.

[See previous entry for additional family information.]

The house was later owned by Norman Smith Cleaves. [*The East Hampton Star* January 5, 1934, p. 5.]

Carson, William Moore, Sr. (1858-1920)

Occupation(s):	capitalist - president, Guantanamo Co. (sugar importer)
Civic Activism:	secretary, Maidstone Club, East Hampton
Marriage(s):	1890-1920 – Jean Maclay Williams (1855-1935)
	- Civic Activism:
	donated J. W. Audubon's painting "The Last Resort" to the
	American Museum of Natural History, NYC
Address:	Lee Avenue, East Hampton
Name of estate:	
Year of construction:	1899
Style of architecture:	Colonial Revival with Federal elements
Architect(s):	Leinau and Nash designed
	the house (for Carson)
Landscape architect(s):	
Builder:	Asa Otis Jones, 1899
	Asa Otis Jones, 1901 alterations
	(for Carson)
House extant: yes*	
Historical notes:	

   The house was built by William Moore Carson, Sr.
   The *Social Register Summer, 1910* lists William Moore and Jean Maclay Williams Carson [Sr.] as residing in East Hampton.
   He was the son of Joseph and Matilda Graydon Moore Carson of Mount Kisco, NY, and Baltimore, MD.
   Jean Maclay Williams Carson was the daughter of John S. and Mary Pentz Williams.
   William Moore and Jean Maclay Williams Carson, Sr.'s daughter Elizabeth married Charles McGhee Tyson and, later, Logan Fox. Their daughter Rosetta married Laurence Van Post Schwab, the son of The Reverend Laurence Henry and Margaret Paris Schwab, and, later, Charles A. Blein, Their son William Moore Carson, Jr. married Elise Pollard Sortwell.
   *In 1901 a west wing was added to the house.
   In 1920 the house was purchased by Earle Westwood Sinclair. [*The East Hampton Star* July 30, 1920, p. 6.]
   In 1945 it was purchased by Robert Elliot McCormick. [*The East Hampton Star* November 8, 1945, p. 1.]
   In 1946 McCormick sold the house to Walter Bartow Duryea. [*The East Hampton Star* February 20, 1947, p. 6.]
   It was later owned by David Hall McConnell III. [*The East Hampton Star* May 20, 1965, p. 2.]

Caruso, Enrico (1873-1921)

Occupation(s):	entertainers and associated professions - international opera star

Marriage(s):	1918-1921 – Dorothy Park Benjamin* (1893-1955)
	  - industrialist - a founder, Dorothy Caruso Reproducing Studio, NYC (a personal phonographic record manufacturing firm)
	    writer - *Enrico Caruso: His Life*, 1945;
	    Dorothy Caruso: A Personal History, 1952;
	    Wings of Song (co-authored with Torrance Goddard)

Address:	Montauk Highway, East Hampton
Name of estate:	*Près Choisis / The Creeks*
Year of construction:	1898-1899
Style of architecture:	Italian Villa
Architect(s):	Grosvenor Atterbury designed the house (for A. Herter)
Landscape architect(s):	Albert and Adele McGinnis Herter designed their own gardens Alfonso Ossorio designed his own gardens
Builder:	Frank Grimshaw

House extant: yes**
Nassau County Museum Collection has photographs of the estate.
Historical notes:

    The house, originally named *Près Choisis*, was built by Albert Herter who later renamed it *The Creeks*.
    In 1920 Enrico and Dorothy Benjamin Caruso rented *The Creeks*. [John H. Davis. *The Bouviers: Portrait of an American Family*. (New York: Farrar, Straus & Giroux, 1969), p. 258.]
    He was the son of Marcellino and Anna Baldine Caruso of Naples, Italy.
    Dorothy Benjamin Caruso was the daughter of Park and Ida E. Crane Benjamin III of East Hampton. Her father was opposed to her marriage to Caruso because of Caruso's nationality and age. The fact that Mr. Benjamin was eighteen years older than his wife seemed to be irrelevant. He would later disinherit his daughter. After Caruso's death Dorothy married Ernest A. Ingram and, subsequently, Dr. Charles Adams Holder.
    *After her divorce from Holder she resumed the use of the surname Caruso and resided in Southampton. [*See* Spinzia, *Long Island's Prominent Families in the Town of Southampton* – Caruso entry.]
    In 1951 Albert Herter's son Christian sold the estate to Alfonso Angel Ossorio, who bequeathed it to his longtime companion Edward F. Dragon. Both Ossorio and Dragon continued to call the estate *The Creeks*. In the 1990s Dragon sold the estate to Ronald Owen Perelman, who made extensive alterations.
    The estate's stables were added in 1899 and a studio was added in 1912.
    **In 2018 a portion of the house was damaged by fire.

Cater, Louise Bowers (1864-1953)

Occupation(s):	capitalist - proprietor, The Apaquogue; proprietor, with Mrs. R. W. Hawkesworth, West End Shore Club, Long Branch, NJ; co-proprietor, Iceland, NYC (ice-skating rink); co-proprietor, with Mrs. R. W. Hawkesworth, dance studio, NYC
Marriage(s):	1894-1911 – Arthur Aymar Carter (1867-1911) - merchant - a founder, Molancuit Cattle & Feed Co., Jersey City, NJ, 1903 Civic Activism: director, Staten Island Cricket and Baseball Club
Address:	72 Apaquogue Road, East Hampton
Name of estate:	*The Apaquogue House*
Year of construction:	c. 1884
Style of architecture:	Federal
Architect(s):	
Landscape architect(s)	
Builder:	Edward M. Gay, 1912 addition (for Mrs. A. A. Cater)*

House extant: yes
Historical notes:

Edward A. LaForest, who had been blind since 1865, died in his East Orange, NJ, home of injuries sustained in a fall down the stairs in his East Hampton residence. As a result of his disability, his wife Helen had attended to their financial affairs. She purchased Abraham D. Candy's East Hampton boarding house and 107-acre farm. When the boarding house was destroyed by fire, she built a new boarding house. The LaForests' son Henry, who purchased the boarding house and the farm from his mother in 1895, named it The Apaquogue. [*The East Hampton Star* March 22, 1895, p. 5; May 17, 1895, p. 5; and June 7, 1895, p.1.] By 1889 ownership had reverted back to his mother. In 1901 Helen LaForest sold it to B. H. Van Scoy and E. H. Dayton. [*Suffolk County News* April 27, 1889, p. 1, and *The East Hampton Star* October 25, 1901, p. 5.] In 1912 the house was sold to Mrs. Cater of Long Branch, NJ, Staten Island, and Manhattan.

The *Social Register Summer, 1910* lists Arthur Aymar and Louise Bowers Cater as residing in New Dorp, Staten Island, NY.

He was the son of Aymar Cater of Barnet, Herts, England.

Louise Bowers Cater was the daughter of Henry and Louise W. Bowers. Her sister Marion married Bradish Johnson Carroll, Sr., the son of Dr. Alfred Ludlow and Mrs. Lucy Johnson Carroll of Bay Shore. [*See* Spinzia, *Long Island's Prominent South Shore Families* – Carroll and Johnson entries.]

Arthur Aymar and Louise Bowers Cater's daughter Louise was an infant at the time of her death in 1898. Their son Aymar A. Cater married Sarah Louise Payne, the daughter of Charles Leicester Payne of Montclair, NJ, and resided in McLean, VA.

In 1919 Mrs. Cater sold it the house to Julian Southall Myrick who used it as his summer residence which he called *Apaquogue*.

In 2019, after one hundred years of ownership by Myrick's extended family, the 10,000-square-foot, sixteen-bedroom, seven-bath house and four acres were for sale. The asking price was $16.9 million.

In 1893 the front porch was added. [*The East Hampton Star* November 24, 1893, p. 5.]

In 1894 houses were built for the employees. [*The East Hampton Star* June 8, 1894, p. 5.]

*Gay's 1912 addition consisted of the installation of seven bathrooms and a rear extension for servant's quarters. [*The East Hampton Star* March 22, 1912, p. 5.]

Cavett, Richard Alva (b. 1936)
aka Dick Cavett

Occupation(s): entertainers and associated professions* -
- stand-up comic;
- actor - "Phil Silvers Show", "Body and Soul", "Playhouse 90", and several other television programs;
- talent coordinator. Jack Parr's "The Tonight Show";
- television host - ABC's "This Morning"; "The Dick Cavett Show"
- writer - Jack Parr's "The Tonight Show"; Johnny Carson's "The Tonight Show"; "The Merv Griffin Show"; co-authored, with Christopher Porterfield, *Cavett*, 1974 (autobiography); *Eye on Cavett*, 1983

Marriage(s): M/1 - 1964-2006 – Caroline Nye McGeoy (1936-2006) (aka Carrie Nye)
- entertainers and associated professions -
  - Broadway, motion picture, and television actress

M/2 – 2010 – Martha Rogers
- writer - customer strategy books and articles in professional journals
- educator - adjunct professor, Fuqua School of Business, Duke University, Durham, NC
- advertising executive - co-founder and partner, Peppers & Rogers Group

Address: 165 De Forest Road, Montauk
Name of estate:
Year of construction: 1883
Style of architecture: Beach Cottage
Architect(s): McKim, Mead & White designed the house
Landscape architect(s): Frederick Law Olmstead designed the site plan
Builder: Mead & Taft
House extant: no; destroyed by fire, 1997***
Historical notes:

   The house is one of the Montauk Association's "Seven Sisters." It was owned by Alexander Ector Orr. It was owned later by James L. Darby prior to being purchased in 1924 by Harrison Tweed who called it *Tick Hall*. It was purchased by Cavett who also bought the house on the adjacent property which was built by Henry Grant de Forest.
   Richard Alva Cavett, the son of Alva B. and Erabel Richards Cavett, was born in Gibbon, NE.
   *Cavett was nominated for over ten Emmy Awards of which he won three.
   Carolyn Nye McGeoy Cavett was born in Greenwood, MS.
   **She was nominated for a Tony Award for her portrayal of Helen Walsingham in "Half a Sixpence."
   ***The house was owned by Cavett when it was destroyed by fire in 1997. He built a contemporary version similar to the original house on the site. The new house was designed by James Hadley.
   In 2017 the 7,000-square-foot house was for sale by Cavett. The asking price was $62 million. The annual taxes were $50,000. In 2018 the price was lowered to $48.5 million.

Chace, Franklin M. (1880-1974)

Occupation(s):	capitalist - partner, with his brother Carl Smith Chace, Chace and Chace, Inc. (real estate and insurance firm)
Marriage(s):	1940-1974 – Jeanetta Chalmers Jameson (1895-1977) - Civic Activism: trustee, American Platform Guild
Address:	117 Main Street, East Hampton
Name of estate:	*Gone With the Wind*
Year of construction:	c. 1799
Style of architecture:	Georgian*
Architect(s):	Isaac Henry Green II designed 1889 alterations** Joseph Greenleaf Thorp designed 1905 interior and exterior alterations
Landscape architect(s):	Mary Lois Deputy Lamson (for Douglas)

House extant: yes
Historical notes:

*The Georgian-style house was built by Jeremiah Miller IV. It was later owned by Edward de Rose who remodeled it, changing the architecture from Georgian to Colonial Revival, and named it *Millfield*. In c. 1885 de Rose also built a guest cottage on the property in an eclectic windmill style.

In 1910 it was owned by Thomas Lincoln Manson III and, then, by his daughter Dorothea and son-in-law Kiliaen Van Rensselaer. Both Manson and Van Rensselaer continued to call it *Millfield*.

The Colonial Revival-styled house was owned by Graham Douglas and by Chace. The Chaces called the house *Gone With the Wind*. [*The East Hampton Star* October 30,1947, p. 5.]

The *Social Register Summer, 1950* lists Franklin M. and Jeanetta C. Jameson Chace as residing on Main Street, East Hampton.

He was the son of Amos Mason and Pastora Forest Smith Chace of Boston, MA.

Jeanetta Chalmers Jameson Chace was the daughter of Dr. Patrick Chalmers and Mrs. Sarah Jane Stanmer Jameson of Brooklyn.

By 1973 the house was owned by Richard Vincent Hare.

**For Green's other commissions, *see* Spinzia, *Long Island's Prominent South Shore Families: Their Estates and Their Country Homes in the Towns of Babylon and Islip*.

Chalif, Seymour Hunt (b. 1927)

Occupation(s):	attorney - member, Hale, Kaye, and Brennan, NYC; partner, Kaye, Scholer, Fierman, Hays, and Handler, NYC; partner, London, Buttenwieser and Chalif, NYC
	capitalist - director, U. S. Home Corp., Clearwater, FL (single family home builder)
	industrialist - secretary, Colorite Plastics, Inc., Paterson, NJ
Marriage(s):	1954-2019 – Rona Miriam Stern (1933-2019) (aka Ronnie Chalif) - artist Civic Activism: co-founder and president, Neuropathy Association
Address:	Terbell Lane, East Hampton
Name of estate:	
Year of construction:	1964
Style of architecture:	Modern
Architect(s):	Julian and Barbara Neski designed the house (for Chalif)
Landscape architect(s):	
Builder:	H. H. Wilde

House extant: yes*
Historical notes:

The house was built by Seymour Hunt Chalif.

He is the son of Hyman and Sarah Chalif of New York.

Rona Miriam Stern Chalif was the daughter of Norman and Ruth London Stern of Great Neck.

Seymour Hunt and Rona Miriam Stern Chalif's son John married Janet Carol Abrams, the daughter of William P. Abrams of Huntington, WV, and resided in Palm Beach, FL. Their son Peter resides in Llewellyn Park, NJ.

The house was later owned by Frederic Milton Seegal.

*Extensive additions have been made to the house.

Chanos, James Steven (b. 1957)

Occupation(s):	financier - analyst, Blyth Eastman Dillon, Chicago, IL; analyst, Gifford Securities; analyst, Paine, Webber vice-president and analyst, Deutsch Bank Capital Corp.; founder, managing partner and president, Kynikos Associates (hedge fund with focuses on short selling); chairman of board, Coalition of Private Investment Companies
	educator - lecturer, School of Management, Yale University, New Haven, CT
Civic Activism:	trustee, Citizens Budget Commission, Yale University, New Haven, CT; president, board of trustees, The Browning School, NYC; trustee, The Nightingale–Bamford School, NYC; trustee, The New York Historical Society, NYC
Marriage(s):	div. 2006 – Amy *[unable to determine maiden name]* - Civic Activism: a founder, Miracle House, NYC
Address:	Further Lane, East Hampton
Name of estate:	
Year of construction:	
Style of architecture:	Shingle with Dutch Colonial elements
Architect(s):	
Landscape architect(s):	
House extant: yes	
Historical notes:	

Chanos was born in Milwaukee, WI, into a Greek-American family.
In 2007 the house was purchased for $18 million by Steven A. Cohen.

Chapman, Benjamin Gaines, Jr. (1883-1962)

Occupation(s):	financier - president, American Central Life Insurance Co., St. Louis, MO
Civic Activism:	director, Maidstone Club, East Hampton; co-chairman, membership committee, Guild Hall, East Hampton
Marriage(s):	Lucile Campbell (d. 1978) - Civic Activism: chair, greens committee, Ladies Village Improvement Society, East Hampton
Address:	Pudding Hill Lane, East Hampton
Name of estate:	
Year of construction:	
Style of architecture:	
Architect(s):	
Landscape architect(s):	
Builder:	Robert Seervelt, 1940 alterations (for Chapman)
House extant: unconfirmed	
Historical notes:	

In 1940 Chapman purchased the Carlisle Joyslin Gleason house *Greyshingles*. [*The East Hampton Star* September 26, 1940, p. 5.] *The Blue Book of The Hamptons, 1958* lists B. G. and Lucile Campbell Chapman, Jr. as residing on Pudding Hill Lane, East Hampton.

He was the son of Benjamin Gaines and Louise Hopkins Chapman, Sr. of Michigan.

Lucile Campbell Chapman was the daughter of Edward Taylor Campbell of St. Louis, MO.

Benjamin Gaines and Lucile Campbell Chapman, Jr.'s daughter Alice married Arthur Furber Greer, the son of James A. Greer of Berkeley, CA. Their daughter Jacquelin married Robert Arnold Sherman, Jr. of Westerly, RI. Their son Benjamin Gaines Chapman III married Lauren Grinnell Edgar, the daughter of Robert Bone Edgar of Scranton, PA.

By 1973 Mrs. Chapman had relocated to Barnes Lane, East Hampton.

Chase, Chevy (b. 1943)
aka Cornelius Crane Chase

Occupation(s):	entertainers and associated professions - actor/comedian writer - motion picture and television scripts

Marriage(s):	M/1 – 1973-div. 1976 – Suzanne Hewitt
	M/2 – 1976-1980 – Jacqueline Jean Carlin (b. 1942)
	    - entertainers and associated professions - actress
	M/3 – 1982 – Jayni Ann Luke (b. 1957)
	    - writer - co-author, *Blueprint for a Green School*, 1995;
	        scripts for television shows and documentaries
	    Civic Activism: a founder, Center for Environmental Education;
	        member of board, Friends of the Earth

Address:	19 Lee Avenue East Hampton
Name of estate:	
Year of construction:	1899
Style of architecture:	Shingle
Architect(s):	Joseph Greenleaf Thorp designed the house (for F. G. Potter)
Landscape architect(s):	
Builder:	Loper Brothers
House extant: yes	
Historical notes:	

The 10,000-square-foot, ten-bedroom house was built by Frederick Gaul Potter. It was later owned by John Richard Keim who sold it to Lamon Vanderburg Harkness in 1914. [*The East Hampton Star* January 22, 1915, p. 5.] James Branch Briggs, who subsequently purchased the house, called it *Beehive*. It was then owned by Chase.

Born Cornelius Crane Chase, he is the son of Edward Tingsley and Cathalene Parker Browning Chase of *Cranberry Bog* in East Hampton and a Mayflower descendant.

Jacqueline Jean Carlin Chase was born in Essex Fells, NJ. She was the first female actor to appear on "Saturday Night Live." Jacqueline subsequently married Peter Bryan Cannon and Terence Paul Jorden, aka Terry Melcher.

Jayni Ann Luke Chase was born in Los Angeles, CA.

Cornelius Crane and Jayni Ann Luke Chase's daughter Cydney married Ryan Bartell. Their daughter Caley is a writer, actress, and producer. Their daughter Emily works for Aspen Center for Environmental Studies.

[See following entry for additional family information.]

In 2001 the house was purchased from Chase by Peter Gabriel Terian for $10.1 million. In 2010 Mrs. Terian placed the house on the market; the asking price was $21 million.

Chase, Edward Tinsley (1919-2005)

Occupation(s):	publisher - editor-in-chief, New American Library;
	vice-president, G. P. Putnam's;
	vice-president, Berkley Books;
	vice-president, *The New York Times,* NYC;
	editor-in-chief, Time Books;
	senior editor, Scribner / Macmillan
	educator - taught English, Stanford University, Stanford, CA
Marriage(s):	M/1 – 1941-div. 1949 – Cathalene Parker Browning (1923-2005)
	(aka Cathalene Crane)
	- entertainers and associated professions - concert pianist; librettist
	M/2 – 1949-2005 – Ethelyn Atha (b. 1923)
	- entertainers and associated professions - songwriter*
	Civic Activism: chair, Academy of American Poets
Address:	15 Jones Road, East Hampton
Name of estate:	*Cranberry Bog*
Year of construction:	
Style of architecture:	
Architect(s):	
Landscape architect(s):	
Builder:	Dayton and Dayton, 1957 alterations (for Buckwalter)
House extant: yes	
Historical notes:	

　　Edward Tinsley Chase was the son of Edward Leigh and Mabel Penrose Tinsley Chase of Woodstock, NY.
　　Cathalene Parker Browning Chase was the daughter of Admiral Miles Rutherford and Mrs. Cathalene Isabella Parker Browning. As commander of the carriers USS *Hornet* and USS *Enterprise*, Browning participated in the naval battles of Midway, Guadalcanal, Eastern Solomon's, Santa Cruz Islands, Gilbert Islands, Marshall Islands, and New Guinea. Cathalene later assumed the surname of her step-father Cornelius Vanderbilt Crane. She had previously been married to Lawrence Widdoes. After her divorce from Chase, she married John Cederquist.
　　Edward Tinsley and Cathalene Parker Browning Chase's son Cornelius Crane Chase (aka Chevy Chase), who also resided in East Hampton, married Suzanne Hewitt; Jacqueline Jean Carlin; and, later, Jayni Luke.
　　The Blue Book of The Hamptons, 1973 list Edward Tinsley and Ethelyn Atha Chase as residing at *Cranberry Bog* on Jones Road, East Hampton.
　　She was the daughter of Joseph Samuel and Ethel Atha of Kansas City, MO.
　　Edward Tinsley and Ethelyn Atha Chase's daughter Cynthia married Jonathan Dwight Culler and resided in Ithaca, NY. Their son Edward Thornton Chase married Joan Harriet Gregory and resides in Mount Vernon, NY. Their daughter Daphine married Sidney Val Smith, Jr. of Houston, TX, and, later, Frank A. Rowe with whom she resides in Bryn Mawr, PA.
　　*In 1995 Ethelyn received the Distinguished Service to the Arts Award.
　　[See previous entry for additional family information.]
　　In 1956 the house was purchased from Mrs. Chase by Mrs. Florence F. Buckwalter who had an addition added to the house. [*The East Hampton Star* February 28, 1957, p. 1.]

Chatfield, Henry Houston (1917-1991)

Occupation(s):	attorney - partner, Walker and Chatfield, Cincinnati, OH
Marriage(s):	1945-1991 – Margaret Anna Tince Rowe (1913-1998)
Address:	Cross Highway, Amagansett
Name of estate:	*Devon*
Year of construction:	c. 1910
Style of architecture:	Mediterranean Villa
Architect(s):	Tietig & Lee designed the house (for R. Levering, Sr.)
Landscape architect(s):	
House extant: yes	
Historical notes:	

The house, originally named *Devon*, was built by Richmond Levering, Sr. In 1920 it was purchased by M. Materson. [*The East Hampton Star* October 22, 1920, p. 6.] In 1930 it was purchased by John Louis Kuser, Jr. from Ardis J. Reynolds. [*The East Hampton Star* October 3, 1930, p. 1.] In c. 1946 the house was purchased by George Epworth Devendorf who called it *El Pasaiso*. [*The East Hampton Star* July 18, 1946, p. 2.] It was later owned by Chatfield who called it *Devon*.

The Blue Book of The Hamptons *1979* and *1987* list Henry H. and Margaret A. Rowe as residing at *Devon*, Cross Highway, Amagansett.

He was the son of William Hayden and Elizabeth Wolcott Henry Chatfield of Cincinnati, OH.

Margaret Anna Tince Rowe Chatfield was the daughter of John Jay and Grace Sherlock Probasco Rowe, Sr. of Cincinnati, OH, and *Devon* in Amagansett.

Henry Houston and Margaret Anna Tince Rowe Chatfield's son Charlton married Sandra Margaret McCullough, the daughter of Robert W. McCullough of Riverside, CT. Their son George married Michelle Lillian Walton.

Chauncey, Alexander Wallace (1891-1973)

Occupation(s):	attorney - member, William A. Read and Co., 1915-1916 (later, Dillon, Read, and Co.)
	financier - partner, Chauncey, Hayes and Lord, 1919-1922 (investment banking firm)
	industrialist - vice-president, A. W. Chauncey Technitrol Engineering Co. (manufacturer of electronic components);
	vice-chairman and director, Interchemical Corp., NYC, 1937-1959;
	director, Millprint Inc.;
	director, International Printing Ink Ltd.;
	director, Ault & Wiborg Corp.;
	vice president and secretary, Ruxton, Inc. (printing ink firm);
	director, International Printing Ink Corp., 1928-1937
	capitalist - proprietor, Cove Hollow Farm, East Hampton, NY;
	director, Chauncey Real Estate Corp.
Civic Activism:	president, Maidstone Club, East Hampton;
	president and director, Greenwood Cemetery, Brooklyn, NY;
	trustee, Village of East Hampton;
	a founder and director, East Hampton League, 1945;
	governor, Devon Yacht Club, Amagansett
Marriage(s):	1919-1971 – Louise Ginnel Ruxton (1894-1971)
	- Civic Activism: donated artworks to Metropolitan Museum of Art, NYC;
	director, Ladies Village Improvement Society, East Hampton
Address:	Apaguogue Road, East Hampton
Name of estate:	*Our Place*
Year of construction:	1936
Style of architecture:	Modified Neo-Georgian
Architect(s):	Aymar Embury II designed the house (for Chauncey)
Landscape architect(s):	
House extant: yes	
Historical notes:	

The house, originally named *Our Place*, was built by Alexander Wallace Chauncey.

The Blue Book of The Hamptons, 1958 lists A. Wallace and Louise G. Ruxton Chauncey as residing at *Our Place* on Apaquogue Road, East Hampton.

He was the son of George W. and Adelaide Sheldon Chauncey of Brooklyn.

Louise Ginnel Ruxton Chauncey was the daughter of Philip and Louise Virginia DeWitt Ruxton of *Cairnhill* in East Hampton. Louise's sister Frances married William Christian Heppenheimer, Jr. and resided in East Hampton.

The Chaunceys did not have children.

The house was subsequently owned by their nephew William Christian Heppenheimer III.

Cheek, Frank Louis, Sr. (1894-1968)

Occupation(s):	financier - member, advisory board, Chemical National Bank, Brooklyn, NY
	industrialist - vice-president and general manager, Cheek–Neal Coffee Co., Nashville, TN [became Maxwell House Coffee]
Civic Activism:	vice-president and executive secretary, Merchants and Manufacturers Association of Bush Terminal, Brooklyn, NY;
	vice-president, Brooklyn Chamber of Commerce, Brooklyn, NY
Marriage(s):	M/1 – ____ Hale
	M/2 – 1921 – Marie Ethel Walters (b. 1902)
Address:	Apaquogue Road, East Hampton
Name of estate:	
Year of construction:	
Style of architecture:	
Architect(s):	
Landscape architect(s):	
House extant: unconfirmed	
Historical notes:	

The *Social Directory of Southampton, Long Island, 1931* lists Frank L. and Marie W. Walters Cheek [Sr.] as residing on Apaquogue Road, East Hampton.

He was the son of Joel Owsley and Minnie H. Ritchey Cheek of Nashville, TN.

Marie Ethel Walters Cheek was the daughter of Martin F. Walters of Appleton, WI.

Chisholm, Edward de Clifford (1871-1941)

Occupation(s):	financier - a founder and partner, Chisholm and Chapman (stock brokerage firm)
Marriage(s):	1898 -1941 – Edith Seymour Johnson (1875-1951)
Address:	Georgica Road and Crossings, East Hampton
Name of estate:	*Onadune*
Year of construction:	1903
Style of architecture:	Shingle
Architect(s):	John Custis Lawrence designed the house (for S. F. Johnson)*
	Peter Cook, 1992 alterations (for Shafran)
Landscape architect(s):	
Builder:	George A. Eldredge
House extant: yes	
Historical notes:	

The thirty-three-room, thirteen-bedroom, nine-bath house, originally named *Onadune*, was built by Servetus Fisher Johnson. It was later owned by his daughter Edith and son-in-law Edward de Clifford Chisholm who continued to call it *Onadune*.

The *Social Directory of Southampton, Long Island, 1931* lists Edward de Clifford and Edith Seymour Johnson Chisholm as residing at *Onadune*.

He was the son of Judge Walter Scott and Mrs. Eliza Clifford Anderson Chisholm of Savannah, GA.

Edward de Clifford and Edith Seymour Johnson Chisholm's daughter Edith married Dashiell Livingston Madeira and resided in Charlottesville, VA. Their daughter Sarah married Selwyn Kip Farrington, Jr., the son of Selwyn Kip and Elizabeth Taylor Farrington, Sr., and resided in East Hampton.

In 1940 the house was owned by Dr. Frank Earl Adair, who called it *Sherwood*. In 1992 it was purchased by Irving Shafran.

*Alterations to the house were made in 1907 and in 1992.

Church, Richard Newton Loomis (1892-1943)

Occupation(s):	industrialist - member, Church and Dwight Co., Inc.
Civic Activism:	a founding member, Committee of One Hundred (promoted civic interest in Montauk)
Marriage(s):	1914-1943 – Dorothy Elizabeth Bennett (1889-1970)
Address:	*[unable to confirm street address],* Montauk
Name of estate:	
Year of construction:	1932
Style of architecture:	
Architect(s):	
Landscape architect(s):	
Builder:	Matthew Construction Co., Princeton, NJ
House extant: unconfirmed	
Historical notes:	

   The house was built by Richard Newton Loomis Church on property he purchased from David E. Osborn. [*The East Hampton Star* February 26, 1932.]

   He was the son of James Austin and Nellie Eliza Loomis Church, Sr. and an heir to the Church & Dwight Co. fortune, makers of Arm & Hammer Baking Soda. [*The New York Times* February 20, 1943, p. 13.]

   Dorothy Elizabeth Bennett Church subsequently married Maximillian F. Kaminski and resided in Palm Springs, FL.

   Richard Newton Loomis and Dorothy Elizabeth Bennett Church's daughter Cynthia married Robert Charles Boomhower, Sr. and resided in Palm Springs, FL. Their son Richard Bennett Church married Janice Roselind Caudill, the daughter of Howard F. Caudill of Arlington Heights, IL, and resided in Wainscott.

   [For R. N. L. Church's Kings Point residence *The Point*, see Spinzia, *Long Island's Prominent North Shore Families, vol. 1* – Church entry.]

Citron, Casper Henry (1919-2002)

Occupation(s):	entertainers and associated professions - "Casper Citron Interviews" (syndicated radio talk show which originated from New York City's Algonquin Hotel)*
	journalist - *The Village Voice* (political columnist)
	writer - *John V. Lindsey and the Silk Stocking Story*
Marriage(s):	M/1 – 1948 – Anne Louise Zabriskie
	M/2 – 1970 – Dr. Fiona Margaret Graham (b. 1929) - physician - surgeon
Address:	La Forest Road, East Hampton
Name of estate:	
Year of construction:	
Style of architecture:	
Architect(s):	
Landscape architect(s):	
House extant: unconfirmed	
Historical notes:	

   The Blue Book of The Hamptons, 1958 lists Mr. and Mrs. Casper H. Citron as residing on La Forest Road, East Hampton [Apaquogue].

   He was the son of Henry Casper and Minna Wright Citron of New York.

   Anne Louise Zabriskie Citron was the daughter of Charles Lemaire and Frances Mary Hyde Zabriskie of Cooperstown, NY. She subsequently married John Harmon Noble with whom she resided in Essex, NJ, and Pasadena, CA.

   Casper Henry and Anne Louise Zabriskie Citron's son Steven married Mary Louise Jachym, the daughter of Edward F. Jachym of Windsor, CT, and resides in Purdy's, NY. Their daughter Christiane married David Anson Clive Moore, the son of William C. Moore of Washington, DC, and resides in Denver, CO. Their daughter Allsande married William Alan Slivka, the son of Andrew Slivka of Cleveland, OH, and resides in Morristown, NJ.

   Fiona Margaret Graham Citron was the daughter of Henry Archibald Robert and Margaret Beatrice Lopes Graham. Fiona had previously been married to Jarvard S. Idriss.

   *Citron was noted for his long interviews. His radio guests included Martin Luther King Jr.; Robert F. Kennedy; Henry Kissinger; and Presidents Dwight D. Eisenhower and Jimmy Carter.

Claiborne, Craig (1920-2000)

Occupation(s):	journalist - editor, *Gourmet Magazine*;
	food editor and restaurant critic, *The New York Times*
	writer - *The New York Times Cookbook*, 1961;
	The New York Times Menu Cook Book, 1966;
	The New York Times International Cookbook, 1971;
	Craig Claiborne's Favorites from The New York Times, vol. 1, 1975;
	Craig Claiborne's Favorites from The New York Times, vol. 2, 1976;
	Craig Claiborne's Favorites from The New York Times, vol. 3, 1977;
	Craig Claiborne's Favorites from The New York Times, vol. 4, 1978;
	Cooking with Herbs and Spices, 1977;
	Veal Cookery, 1980
	(co-authored with Pierre Franey);
	Classic French Cooking, 1978 (Time-Life Foods of the World)
	(co-authored with Pierre Franey);
	Craig Claiborne's New York Times Cookbook, 1980
	(co-authored with Pierre Franey);
	A Feast Made for Laughter, 1982 (autobiography);
	The Master Cooking Course, 1982
	(co-authored with Pierre Franey);
	Cooking with Craig Claiborne and Pierre Franey, 1985;
	Craig Claiborne's Memorable Meals, Menus, Memories and Recipes from over Twenty Years of Entertaining, 1985;
	Craig Claiborne's The New York Times Food Encyclopedia, 1985;
	Craig Claiborne's Gourmet Diet, 1985
	(with Pierre Franey);
	Craig Claiborne's Southern Cooking, 1987;
	Elements of Etiquette: A Guide to Table Manners in an Imperfect World, 1992;
	The Chinese Cookbook, 1992
	(co-authored with Virginia Lee);
	Craig Claiborne's Kitchen Primer, 1993;
	The Best of Craig Claiborne: 1,000 Recipes from His New York Times Food Columns and Four of His Classic Cookbooks, 1999
Marriage(s):	bachelor
Address:	15 Clamshell Avenue, East Hampton
Name of estate:	
Year of construction:	1979
Style of architecture:	
Architect(s):	Craig Claiborne designed his own residence
Landscape architect(s):	
House extant: yes	
Historical notes:	

The house was built by Craig Claiborne.
He was the son of Lewis Edmond and Kathleen Craig Claiborne of Mississippi.
In 2013 the house and 2.3 acres sold for $1.7 million.

Clark, Evans (1888-1970)

Occupation(s):	attorney
	educator - instructor of government, Princeton University, Princeton, NJ., 1913-1917
	journalist - associate editor, *The Utilities Magazine*, 1917-1919; a founder and managing editor, *The Labor Bureau Inc.*, 1920-1924 (business journal); associate editor, *Advertisers Weekly*, 1924-1925; editor, *The New York Times*, 1954-1962
	writer - *Financing the Consumer*, 1930; *Boycotts and Peace*, 1932; *How to Budget Health*, 1933; *International Debts of the United States*, 1933; *Stock Market Control*, 1934
	capitalist - a founder, Health Insurance Plan (health care provider)
Civic Activism*:	director, Twentieth Century Fund, 1928-1953 (specializes in economic research and public education on economic problems);
	a founder, Public Affairs Committee;
	secretary, Council for Democracy, 1940-1949;
	trustee, Spring Hill School, 1933-1938;
	trustee, Film Council of America, 1948-1952;
	director, New York State Citizens Council, 1944-1950;
	trustee, Joint Council on Economic Education, 1952-1953;
	economic advisor, Housing Authority, NYC, 1935-1937;
	chairman of board, New York State Adjustment Board of the National Recovery Administration, 1935
Marriage(s):	1915-1970 – Mary Frederika Kirchwey (1893-1976) (aka Freda Kirchwey)
	- journalist** - general reporter, *New York Morning Telegraph*; editor, *New York Magazine*; editor, *Every Week*, 1917-1918; reporter, *New York Sunday Tribune*, 1918
	publisher - managing editor, vice-president, and publisher, *Nation*
Address:	Springs – Fireplace Road, Springs
Name of estate:	
Year of construction:	
Style of architecture:	
Architect(s):	
Landscape architect(s):	
House extant: unconfirmed	
Historical notes:	

The Blue Book of The Hamptons, 1965 lists Evans and Freda Kirchwey Clark as residing on Fireplace Road [Springs – Fireplace Road], East Hampton [Springs].

He was the son of Dr. William Brewster and Mrs. Fanny H. Cox Clark of NYC.

Mary Frederika Kirchwey Clark was the daughter of George Washington and Dora Child Wendell Kirchwey.

Evans and Mary Frederika Kirchwey Clark's sons Brewster and Jeffery died in childhood. Their son Michael married Edmee Jahier, the daughter of Paul Jahier of Algiers, Algeria, and, later, Makiko Kanada.

*Evans was strongly committed to Socialist, Communist, and liberal socio-economic views.

**Mary was committed to liberal positions. She was anti-Fascist, pro-Soviet, and anti-Communist.

Clark, Ivor Bache, Sr. (1891-1960)

Occupation(s):	financier - founder and chairman of board, Ivor B. Clark Co., Inc., NYC (mortgage specialists)*;
	trustee, Union Dime Savings Bank
	capitalist - at the age of sixteen Clark built houses in Brooklyn
Civic Activism:	a founder, Albert Einstein College of Medicine, Yeshiva University, NYC;
	a founder, Beth David Hospital, NYC;
	governor, Real Estate Board of New York;
	member, Metropolitan Fair Rent Committee, NYC;
	trustee, Boy Scouts of America;
	governor, Devon Yacht Club, Amagansett
Marriage(s):	M/1 – 1914-div. – Florence Lee Loveland (1892-1948)
	M/2 – Jessie E. Gillies (d. 1965)**
Address:	Further Lane, Amagansett
Name of estate:	*Driftwood*

Year of construction:
Style of architecture:
Architect(s):
Landscape architect(s)
House extant: unconfirmed
Historical notes:

    Florence Lee Loveland Clark was the daughter of John Winthrop and Florence Lee Partridge Loveland, Sr. of Englewood, NJ. She later married Lawrence Edward Barron, the son of Mark William and Julia O'Brien Barron, and, subsequently, Harry Herbert Griswold.
    The *Social Register Summer, 1950* lists Ivor B. and Jessie E. Gillies Clark as residing at *Driftwood* on Further Lane, Amagansett.
    Ivor Bache and Jessie E. Gillies Clark, Sr.'s daughter Elizabeth married Theodore Frelinghuysen Talmadge, the son of John Frelinghuysen and Louise Thorne Ditmas Talmadge of *Tollemache House* in East Hampton, and resided in New Canaan, CT. Their daughter Pamela married Christopher Charles Coyne, Jr. of Moline, IL, and, later, William S. Wellington. Their son Ivor Bache Clark, Jr. married Mary Ellen Riddle, the daughter of Andrew M. Riddle of Denver, CO, and, Pamela Ruth Slay, the daughter of Arthur Herbert Slay. Their daughter Jean married Theodore Talmage.
    *As a youth, Ivor wrote to J. P. Morgan advising Morgan he was paying too much interest on his mortgages. When they met, Morgan's greetings to Clark were "What fool asked you to come here?" Clark replied, "You're the fool who sent for me." From then on Clark managed Morgan's mortgage financing. [*The New York Times* January 23, 1960, p. 21.]
    **Mrs. Clark was residing at *Driftwood* at the time of her death.

Clarke, Thomas Benedict, Sr. (1848-1931)

Occupation(s):	industrialist - linen and lace collar and cuff manufacturer
	educator - president, New York School of Applied Design for Women, NYC
	merchant - president, Art House, NYC (specialized in sale of Chinese and Japanese ceramics and Eastern and Middle Eastern art)
	writer - *Catalogue of Thomas B. Clarke Collection of American Pictures,* 1899
Civic Activism:	established Clarke Composition Prize at National Academy of Design;
	vice-president, Southampton Club;
	chairman of art committee, Union League Club of New York;
	a founder, Suffolk Hunt Club, 1910
Marriage(s):	1871-1920 – Fanny Eugenia Morris (1852-1920)
Address:	Ocean Avenue, East Hampton
Name of estate:	*The Lanterns*
Year of construction:	1892
Style of architecture:	
Architect(s):	
Landscape architect(s):	
House extant: unconfirmed	
Historical notes:	

    The *Social Register Summer, 1910* and *1915* list Thomas B. and Fanny E. Morris Clarke [Sr.] as residing at *The Lanterns* in East Hampton.

    He was the son of George Washington and Mary J. Clarke of NYC.

    Fanny Eugenia Morris Clarke was the daughter of John J. Morris, President of the New York City Board of Aldermen in Mayor Havemeyer's administration.

    Thomas Benedict and Fanny Eugenia Morris Clarke, Sr.'s daughter Grace married Richard Heber Newton, Jr. of *Box Farm* in Water Mill. He was the son of The Reverend Richard Heber and Mrs. Mary Elizabeth Lewis Newton, Sr. of East Hampton. [*See* Spinzia, *Long Island's Prominent Families in the Town of Southampton* – Newton entry.] Their son Thomas Benedict Clarke, Jr., who lived in Darien CT, married the actress Elsie Louise Ferguson and, subsequently, Camilla Granchez Sanborn. Thomas, who had attempted suicide in 1942 by shooting himself in the temple, died in 1958.

    Thomas Benedict Clarke, Sr. purchased the Suffolk Hunt Club in Southampton and remodeled it into his residence.

    [For information about the Clarkes' Southampton residence *Lindenland, see* Spinzia, *Long Island's Prominent Families in the Town of Southampton* – Clarke entry.]

    In 1915 Clarke sold *The Lanterns* to James Lawrence Ogden, Jr. [*The East Hampton Star* November 19, 1915, p. 5.]

    Clarke's New York City residence is now the Collectors Club of New York.

Cleaves, Norman Smith (1892-1951)

Occupation(s):	capitalist - building contractor (built several homes in East Hampton area); owned a movie theater
	merchant - owned a hardware store on Main Street, East Hampton
Marriage(s):	M/1 – 1915-1946 – Edith Hallock Lester (1893-1946)
	M/2 – 1946-1951 – Ruth R. Lane (1902-1989)
Address:	70 Dunemere Lane, East Hampton
Name of estate:	
Year of construction:	1905
Style of architecture:	Shingle
Architect(s):	Joseph Greenleaf Thorp designed the house (for Mrs. Randell)
Landscape architect(s):	
Builder:	Thomas E. Babcock
House extant: yes	
Historical notes:	

The house was built by Caroline Amelia Boardman Randell. In 1919 it was purchased by John Bradley Carse, Sr. who called it *End Cottage*. [*The East Hampton Star* May 20, 1971, p. 2.] It was later owned by Cleaves. [*The East Hampton Star* January 5, 1934, p. 5.]

He was the son of George and Elizabeth Cass Cleaves.

Edith Hallock Lester Cleaves was the daughter of William B. and Ada M. Hallock Lester.

Norman Smith and Edith Hallock Lester Cleaves' daughter Evelyn married Lyndon Wood English, who was killed in World War II. He was the son of Dr. William H. English of Rochester, NY. She later married James N. Edwards, the son of David Edwards and Dr. Francis L. Cooper of East Hampton.

Ruth R. Lane Cleaves had previously been married to ____ Robinson.

Clements, Hurin Martin (1870-1936)

Occupation(s):	capitalist - president, Clements & Sons, NYC (importing firm);
	president, Java Coconut Oil Co. (import / manufacturing firm);
	president, Brazilian Babassu (oil exporting firm)
Civic Activism:	a founder, Pine Valley Golf Club, Clementon, NJ
Marriage(s):	Lily Clapp Morrison (1875-1965)
Address:	Lily Pond Lane, East Hampton
Name of estate:	
Year of construction:	
Style of architecture:	
Architect(s):	
Landscape architect(s):	
House extant: unconfirmed	
Historical notes:	

The *Long Island Society Register, 1929* lists Hurin M. and Lily Morrison Clements as residing on Lily Pond Lane, East Hampton.

He was the son of Alfred Ludlow and Lou Buckley Clements.

Lily Clapp Morrison Clements was the daughter of George Augustus and Frances Norton Morrison.

Hurin Martin and Lily Clapp Morrison Clements' daughter Elizabeth married Newcomb Debovoise Cole, the son of Newcomb B. Cole, and resided in Manhattan. Their son Hurin Morrison Clements married Elizabeth McKinney, the daughter of James Harry McKinney, Sr. of Pittsburgh, PA. Their son Ludlow died in 1929 at the age of nineteen.

Cloud, Chester Marts (1884-1948))

Occupation(s):	financier - manager, New York branch office, Fidelity and Deposit; general manager, E. B. Quackenbush (insurance firm)
	industrialist - director, Universal Bitters Co., NY
Civic Activism:	trustee, Village of Southampton;
	trustee, Village of East Hampton;
	trustee, Guild Hall, East Hampton;
	governor, Devon Yacht Club, Amagansett
Marriage(s):	1909-1948 – May Christine Walther (1883-1948)
Address:	34 Hither Lane, East Hampton
Name of estate:	*Prim Close*
Year of construction:	
Style of architecture:	Colonial Revival
Architect(s):	
Landscape architect(s):	

House extant: yes

Historical notes:

In 1925 Mary Lange DeVries (aka Mary MacKinnon) purchased the house and ten acres from Thomas Robinson. [*The East Hampton Star* December 11, 1925, p. 7.] In 1930 Cloud purchased the house from Mrs. DeVries. [*The East Hampton Star* March 7, 1930, p. 5.]

The *Social Directory of Southampton, Long Island, 1931* lists Chester M. and May C. Walther Cloud as residing at *Prim Close* on Hither Lane, East Hampton.

He was the son of Josiah Glover and Louella W. Marts Cloud.

May Christine Walther was the daughter of George W. Walther of Baltimore, MD.

In 1946 Irwin Hewlett Cornell purchased the house from Cloud. [*The East Hampton Star* October 3, 1946, p. 5.]

In 1963 it was purchased by Charles Francis Preusse. [*The East Hampton Star* May 16, 1963, p. 4.]

Cobb, Henry Ives, Sr. (1859-1931)

Occupation(s):	architect*
	capitalist - president, Forty-Two Broadway Co.;
	president, John Jay Realty Co.
Civic Activism:	vice-president, Merchants' Association
Marriage(s):	1882-1931 – Emma Martin Smith (1859-1944)
Address:	Dunemere Lane, East Hampton
Name of estate:	
Year of construction:	
Style of architecture:	
Architect(s):	
Landscape architect(s):	

House extant: unconfirmed

Historical notes:

The *Long Island Society Register, 1929* lists Henry Ives and Emma M. Smith Cobb [Sr.] as residing on Dunemere Lane, East Hampton.

He was the son of Albert Adams and Mary Russell Chandler Cobb of Brookline, MA.

Emma Martin Smith Cobb was the daughter of Augustus Fitzalan and Lucy Ann Elliot Smith of New York.

Henry Ives and Emma Martin Smith Cobb, Sr.'s son Boughton married Edith McKeever and resided at *The Chimney Corner* in Hewlett Bay Park. Their son Henry Ives Cobb, Jr., who resided in Hewlett, married Carolyn S. Postlethwaite and, later, Gwendolyn Wickersham, the daughter of George Woodward and Mildred Wendell Wickersham of *Marshfield* in Lawrence. [*See* Spinzia, *Long Island's Prominent Families in the Town of Hempstead* – Cobb and Wickersham entries.] Their daughter Leonore married Robert Amory, Jr. of Boston, MA. Their son Cleveland married Priscilla Baldwin, the daughter of Joseph Clark Baldwin, Jr. of *Shallow Brook Farm* in Mount Kisco, NY. Priscilla had previously been married to Lewis Thompson Preston, Sr., the son of Ralph Julius and Elizabeth Thompson Preston of *Ivy Hall* in Jericho. She had also been previously married to Thomas Archer Morgan, the son of Edwin Morgan III of *Wheatley* in Old Westbury. [*See* Spinzia, *Long Island's Prominent North Shore Families, vol. I* – Morgan entry – and *vol. II* – Preston entry.] She subsequently married Robert A. Jordan. Their son Chandler married Beatrice Carpenter, the daughter of Charles Whitney Carpenter of Manhattan, and resided in New York City.

*Cobb was the first architect to utilize steel skeleton framing in the construction of tall buildings.

Cobb, Irvin Shewsbury (1876-1944)

Occupation(s):	writer - wrote over 64 humorous short stories and books
	journalist - editor, *Paducah Daily News*, Paducah, KY;
	staff correspondent, *Evening Post*, Louisville, KY, 1898-1901;
	managing editor, *Paducah News Democrat*, Paducah, KY;
	staff writer, *Evening World*, NYC;
	war correspondent, *Saturday Evening Post*
Civic Activism:	suffrage* - suffragist lecturer;
	honorary editor, suffrage article in *Puck*, 1915;
	member Men's League for Woman's Suffrage of the State of New York
	a founder and governor, Montauk Swordfish Club
Marriage(s):	1900-1944 – Laura Spencer Baker (1877-1967)
Address:	Hither Lane, East Hampton
Name of estate:	*Back Home*
Year of construction:	1916
Style of architecture:	Colonial Revival
Architect(s):	
Landscape architect(s):	
House extant: unconfirmed	
Historical notes:	

    The house was built by Theodore Wilson Morris, Jr. [*The East Hampton Star* March 10, 1916, p. 5.]
    Cobb purchased the house in 1927 from Morris. [*The East Hampton Star* October 7, 1927, p. 1, and May 2, 1935, p. 5.]
    The *Social Directory of Southampton, Long Island, 1931* lists Irvin S. and Laura Baker Cobb as residing at *Back Home* on Hither Lane, East Hampton.
    He was the son of Joshua Clark and Manie Marshall Saunders Cobb.
    Laura Spencer Baker Cobb was the daughter of Marcus Stevens Baker of Savannah, GA.
    Irvin Shewsbury and Laura Spencer Baker Cobb's daughter Elisabeth married Alton A. Brody and, later, ____ Rogers.
    Justin O'Brien Haynes purchased the house from Cobb in 1940 for $27,500. [*The New York Times* February 11, 1940, p. 127.]
  *For other Long Islanders involved in the suffrage movement *see* Raymond E. Spinzia, "Winning the Franchise: Long Island Activists in the Fight for Woman's Suffrage and Their Opponents, Long Island's Anti-Suffragists." wwwspinzialongislandestates.com.

Cockcroft, Edward Truesdell, Sr. (b. 1880)

Occupation(s):	interior designer
	merchant - antiques dealer
Marriage(s):	1904 – Viola A. Baker
Address:	88 Lily Pond Lane, East Hampton
Name of estate:	*Little Burlees*
Year of construction:	1905
Style of architecture:	Neo-Italian Renaissance
Architect(s):	Albro and Lindeberg designed the house (for Cockcroft)

Landscape architect(s):
House extant: no; destroyed by fire in 2008
Historical notes:

   The house, originally named *Little Burlees*, was built by Edward Truesdell Cockcroft, Sr.
   The *Social Register Summer, 1915* lists Edward T. and Viola Baker Cockcroft [Sr.] as residing at *Little Burlees* in East Hampton.
   He was the son of John Voohees and Sarah Hubbard Truesdell Cockcroft of Ossining, NY.
   Viola A. Baker Cockcroft was the daughter of John S. Baker. She had previously been married to Dr. John Newell Tilden, Sr., the son of Elihu and Mary Lounsbury Tilden of Onondaga, NY.
   Edward Truesdell and Viola Baker Cockcroft, Sr.'s son John married Cecilia Lee, the daughter of James Wideman Lee, Jr. of Rye, NY, and, later, Cynthia Mary Spencer, the daughter of Kingsland Spencer of Tarrytown, NY. Their son Edward Truesdell Cockcroft, Jr. died in 1918 at the age of eleven.
   In 1912 the house was purchased by Tyler Morse. [*The East Hampton Star* August 16, 1912, p. 5.] The house was owned from 1936 to 1994 by Franklin Woolman d'Olier, Jr. In 1994 it was purchased by Jonathan Everett Sandelman for $2.15 million. He was the owner of the house when it was destroyed by fire.

Cody, Frederick (1874-1936)

Occupation(s):	advertising executive - vice-president, McCann Erikson Inc.
	financier - manager, New York Life Insurance Co., Detroit, MI; supervisor, Fidelity Mutual Life Insurance, Michigan and Ohio
	educator - principal, Webster School, Detroit, MI
Marriage(s):	1899-1936 – Lucille Stedman
Address:	18 Further Lane, East Hampton
Name of estate:	*Fairways*
Year of construction:	1928
Style of architecture:	Mediterranean
Architect(s):	John Custis Lawrence designed the house (for Cody)

Landscape architect(s):
House extant: yes
Builder: Edward M. Gay
Historical notes:

   The twenty-room house, originally named *Fairways*, was built by Frederick Cody.
   He was the son of Thomas and Clarissa Kipp Cody of Belleville, MI.
   Lucille Stedman Cody was the daughter of The Reverend William H. and Mrs. Belle Kimberlin Stedman.
   Edward Renick Alexander, Sr. of Washington, DC, purchased the house in 1940 from Mrs. Cody for $35,000 and renamed it *Sterling-Haven*. [*The New York Times* February 11, 1940, p. 147.]

Cogan, Marshall Stuart (b. 1937)

Occupation(s):	financier - research analyst, Carter, Berlind, and Weill (investment banking firm);
	partner, Cogan, Berlind, and Weill (investment banking firm)
	merchant - founder, United Automobile Group (later, Penske Automotive Group) (automobile and truck dealership franchises)
	publisher - owner, *Arts & Auction* magazine
	restaurateur - owner, 21 Club, NYC
	industrialist - chairman of board and CEO, Trace International Holdings, Inc. (manufacturer of carpets and polyurethane foam);
	director, Ener 1 (manufacturer of lithium-ion batteries);
	CEO, Knoll International (office furniture manufacturing firm);
	chairman of board, Foamex International (holding company);
	chairman of board and director, Sheller–Globe Corp. (automobile parts manufacturing firm)
Civic Activism:	trustee, Boston Latin School;
	trustee, New York University Medical Center, NYC;
	established Marshall Cogan Fine Arts Book Fund, Harvard University, Cambridge, MA;
	director, American Friends of Israel Museum;
	director, Museum of Modern Art, NYC
Marriage(s):	1961 – Maureen Nancy Abramson (b. 1946)
	- publisher - board chair, *Arts & Auction* magazine, 1984-1998
	Civic Activism: trustee, Columbia University, NYC;
	director, American Friends of Israel Museum;
	trustee, Children's Defense Fund;
	trustee, Turnaround for Children;
	board chair, Israel Museum International Council
Address:	34 Terbell Lane, East Hampton
Name of estate:	
Year of construction:	1971
Style of architecture:	International
Architect(s):	Charles Gwathmey designed the house (for Cogan)
Landscape architect(s)	
House extant: no	
Historical notes:	

The house was built by Marshall Stuart Cogan.
He is the son of Meyer Cogan.
Maureen Nancy Abramson Cogan is the daughter of Dr. Daniel Abramson of Brookline, MA.
Marshall Stuart and Maureen Nancy Abramson Cogan's son Andrew married Lori Finkel and resides in Shelter Island, NY. Their daughter Stephanie married Dr. John George Golfinos, the son of Dr. Argyrios Golfinos of Atlantic Beach, NY.
The house was later owned by Joseph Fredrick Cullman III and, subsequently, by Gary L Fuhrman who razed the house and built a new residence.

Cohen, Peter Anthony (b. 1946)

Occupation(s):	financier - chairman of board and CEO, Cowen, Inc. (investment banking firm);
	chairman of board and CEO, Shearson Lehman Brothers (later, Lehman Hutton);
	chairman of board and CEO, Shearson Lehman Hutton;
	chairman of board, Cowen Group;
	vice-chairman of board and director, Republic New York Corp.;
	chairman of board, Ramius Capital
	industrialist - director, Olivetti (typewriter manufacturer; now, computer manufacturing firm)
Marriage(s):	M/1 – Karen Mae Deutsch
	M/2 – Brooke Goodman
	- flight attendant, American Airlines
	Civic Activism:
	member, board of visitors, School of Human Ecology, University of Wisconsin, Madison, WI;
	director, The Ovarian Cancer Research Fund, Inc., NYC;
	a founder, Randall's Island Park Alliance
Address:	77 Cross Highway, East Hampton
Name of estate:	
Year of construction:	1982
Style of architecture:	Modern
Architect(s):	Norman Jaffe designed the house (for P. A. Cohen)
Landscape architect(s):	
House extant: yes	

Historical notes:

   The five-bedroom, five-bath, 7,000-square-foot house was built by Peter Anthony Cohen.

   He is the son of Sidney B. and Florence Cohen of Rockville Centre, NY.

   Karen Mae Deutsch Cohen is the daughter of Frank Deutsch of Cincinnati, OH.

   Peter Anthony and Karen Mae Deutsch Cohen's daughter Lauren married David Lawrence Ronick, the son of Ted M. and Beverly A. Ronick of New York, and, later, Dr. Christopher Edward Starr, the son of Edward J. Starr of Dover, DE. Their son Andrew married Elizabeth Cook Stewart, the daughter of John K. and Sara Stewart of Riverside, CT.

   In 1988 the house was for sale by Cohen. The asking price was $6.75 million. It was purchased in 2002 by Arthur Goodhart Altschul, Jr., who restored the house to its original appearance.

   In 2019 the house was again listed for sale. The asking price was $6.495 million.

Cohen, Steven A. (b. 1956)

Occupation(s):	financier - trader, Gruntal & Co.;
	founder, SAC Capital Partners (hedge fund)
	capitalist - minority owner, New York Mets (baseball team)
Civic Activism:	founder, Steven and Alexandra Cohen Foundation;
	trustee, Brown University, Providence, RI;
	trustee, Robin Hood Foundation (established to alleviate poverty in NYC)
Marriage(s):	M/1 – 1979-div. 1990 – Patricia Finke (b. 1952)
	M/2 – 1992 – Alexandra Garcia (b. 1944)
Address:	Further Lane, East Hampton
Name of estate:	
Year of construction:	
Style of architecture:	Contemporary
Architect(s):	
Landscape architect(s)	
House extant: yes	

Historical notes:

   In 2013 Steven A. Cohen paid $60 million for the 10,000-square-foot, seven-bedroom house which be purchased from Robert Brian McKeon's estate. At the time, Cohen owned a house on Further Lane which he had purchased in 2007 for $18 million from James Steven Chanos.

   Steven A. and Alexandra Garcia Cohen have four daughters.

Cohn, Maurice J. (1931-2015)

Occupation(s):	financier - CEO and co-founder, with Bernard Lawrence Madoff, Cohmad Securities*
Civic Activism:	trustee, North Shore – Long Island Health System; donated, with his wife, Marilyn and Maurice Cohn Trauma Center, North Shore University Hospital, Manhasset, NY; trustee, Northwell Health
Marriage(s):	Marilyn B. *[unable to determine maiden name]* - Civic Activism: donated, with her husband, Marilyn and Maurice Cohn Trauma Center, North Shore University Hospital, Manhasset, NY
Address:	54 Sandpiper Lane, Amagansett
Name of estate:	
Year of construction:	1972
Style of architecture:	International
Architect(s):	Charles Gwathmey designed the house (for M. J. Cohen)
Landscape architect(s)	
House extant: yes	
Historical notes:	

The four-bedroom house was built by Maurice J. Cohn.
In 2013 Cohn sold the house for $11 million.
*Cohmad is a merging of the name Cohn and Madoff.

Cole, John Nelson, Jr. (1889-1961)

Occupation(s):	financier - governor, New York Stock Exchange industrialist - president, Planographic Equipment Co.
Civic Activism:	a founder and vice-president, East Hampton League, 1945
Marriage(s):	1922-1961 – Helen Marr Dodd (1902-1967) - interior designer - president, Helen Cole Inc., NYC*
Address:	West End Avenue, East Hampton**
Name of estate:	*Bayberry*
Year of construction:	1927
Style of architecture:	Shingle
Architect(s):	
Landscape architect(s):	
House extant: unconfirmed	

Nassau County Museum Collection has photographs of the estate.
Historical notes:

The house, originally named *Bayberry*, was built by John Nelson Cole, Jr.
The *Long Island Society Register, 1929* lists John N. and Helen Marr Dodd Cole as residing on Apaquogue Road [West End Avenue], East Hampton.
He was the son of The Reverend John Nelson Cole, Sr.
Helen Marr Dodd Cole was the daughter of Charles Goodhue and Emma Darrow Dodd. Helen's mother subsequently married Eugene Rodney Burnett of East Hampton.
John Nelson and Helen Marr Dodd Cole, Jr.'s son Charles married Cynthia Whitehead, the daughter of Lyman Whitehead, Jr. of Syosset. Their daughter Jane married John Alexander Graves, the son of John A. Graves of Fort Worth, TX, and resided in Fort Worth. Their son John Nelson Cole III married Cynthia Waterbury, the daughter of C. Livingston Waterbury of Manhattan, and resided in Kennebunkport, ME.
*Helen also designed windows for major New York City department stores and decorated the interior of the New York City pavilion at the 1939 World's Fair. [*The New York Times* December 21, 1967, p. 37.]
**The Coles resided at this address for thirty-five years.
The house was later owned in c. 1952 by George Adam Rentschler, Jr., who called it *Summertime*, and, subsequently, by Charles Schuveldt Dewey, Jr. [*The East Hampton Star* January 3, 1952, p. 1, and April 28, 1960, p.11.]

Coleman, Helen Douglas Rulison (1867-1955)

Civic Activism:	member, board of managers, St. Luke's Hospital, NYC
Marriage(s):	1891-1929 – Charles Philip Coleman (1866-1929)

    - industrialist - purchasing agent and assistant to president, Bethlehem Steel Co., 1897-1898;
        president, Saurer Motor Co.;
        president, Mount Hope Bridge Co.;
        president, International Motor Co., 1911-1913;
        vice-president, International Steam Pump Co., 1913;
        director, Worthington–Simpson Ltd.;
        president, Worthington Pump and Machinery Co., 1916-1918;
        secretary and treasurer, Singer Sewing Machine Co., 1903-1910;
    capitalist - assistant general superintendent, Lehigh Valley Railroad, 1898-1903
    Civic Activism: director, American–Russian Chamber of Commerce

Address: Terbell Lane, East Hampton
Name of estate:
Year of construction:
Style of architecture:
Architect(s):
Landscape architect(s)
House extant: unconfirmed
Historical notes:

    In 1929 Mrs. Coleman purchased the Gilmartin residence. [*The East Hampton Star* November 8, 1929, p. 4.]

    The *Social Directory of Southampton, Long Island, 1931* lists Helen D. Rulison Coleman as residing on Terbell Lane, East Hampton.

    She was the daughter of The Right Reverend Nelson Summerville Rulison, the Second Protestant Episcopal Bishop of Central Pennsylvania, and Mrs. George Blanche Rice Rulison.

    Charles Philip Coleman was the son of William Wheeler and Ellen Gibbons Hiss Coleman of Baltimore, MD.

    Charles Philip and Helen Douglas Rulison Coleman's son Douglas married Elinor Payson and resided in Harbourton, NJ. Their son Leighton married Jane Gardner Fraser, the daughter of George Corning Fraser of Morristown, NJ, and resided in Stonybrook.

    In 1946 the house was purchased by Ernest Wetmore Pittman. [*The East Hampton Star* August 21, 1947, p. 2.]

    In 1965 the roof of the house sustained fire damage ignited by sparks from the chimney. [*The East Hampton Star* June 17, 1965, p. 3.]

Coler, Dr. Eugene Seeley (1896-1953)

Occupation(s): physician - obstetrics and gynecology, Sloan Hospital for Women, NYC

Marriage(s): 1919-1953 – Helen Danforth Geer (b. 1895)

Address: Apaquogue Road, East Hampton
Name of estate: *Windrow*
Year of construction:
Style of architecture:
Architect(s):
Landscape architect(s)
House extant: unconfirmed
Historical notes:

    The *Social Register Summer, 1950* lists Dr. Eugene S. and Mrs. Helen D. Geer Coler as residing at *Windrow* in East Hampton.
    He was the son of William Nichols and Lillie Seeley Coler, Jr. and a World War I air ace credited with sixteen victories while serving in the British Flying Corps and the Royal Air Force.
    Helen Danforth Geer Coler was the daughter of Walter Danforth and Mary Wiley Potter Geer, Sr. of Long Beach, NY. Helen subsequently married Harold Goodwin of Dedham, England.
    Dr. Eugene Seeley and Mrs. Helen Danforth Geer Coler's son William married Rosemary Dalzell, the daughter of Ernest Dalzell of New Bedford, MA. Their daughter Helene married Richard Seymour Jackson, the son of John Day and Rose Marie Herrick Jackson of Amagansett; David F. Seiferheld, the son of Sigmund Seiferheld; and, subsequently, Walter Muensterberger, the son of Alfred Muensterberger.
    In 1954 the house was purchased by Alexander Mellon Laughlin, Sr. [*The East Hampton Star* June 3, 1954, p. 7.]

Collins, William Bradley Isham, Sr. (1912-1996)
aka Bradley Isham Collins

Occupation(s):

Marriage(s): 1952 – Mary Carol Ohmer

Address: 24 Huntting Lane, East Hampton
Name of estate: *Briar Patch*
Year of construction:
Style of architecture:
Architect(s):
Landscape architect(s)
House extant: unconfirmed
Historical notes:

    The *Social Register Summer, 1958* lists Bradley I. and M. Carol Ohmer Collins as residing on Huntting Lane, East Hampton. *The Blue Book of The Hamptons, 1958* lists their address as 24 Huntting Lane, East Hampton.
    He was the son of Minturn Post and Flora Isham Collins, Sr. of East Hampton.
    Mary Carol Ohmer Collins was the daughter of Raymond Michael and Agnes Louise Cantwell Ohmer, Sr. of Dayton, OH.
    William Bradley Isham and Mary Carol Ohmer Collins, Sr.'s son James married Virginia Dance Donelson. Their daughter Carol married Livingston Ludlow Biddle IV of Bryn Mawr, PA. Their son William Bradley Isham Collins, Jr. (aka Bradley Isham, Jr.) married art historian and author Amy Fine and resides in NYC.

Combs, Sean John (b. 1969)
aka Puff Daddy, Daddy, and P. Diddy

Occupation(s):	entertainers and associated professions -
	rapper; record producer; actor*;
	talent director, Uptown Records;
	a founder, Bad Boy Records;
	producer, "Making the Band", MTV special
	industrialist - a founder, Sean John (line of clothing);
	a founder, I am King (a line of men's cologne);
	principle, Ciroc vodka;
	owner, Enyce (line of clothing)
	restaurateur - Justin's, NYC;
	Justin's, Atlanta, GA
Civic Activism:	founder, Daddy's House Social Programs (helps inner city youth);
	trustee, New York Mission Society, NYC
Marriage(s):	bachelor**
Address:	40 Hedges Banks Drive, East Hampton
Name of estate:	
Year of construction:	1989
Style of architecture:	Modern
Architect(s):	Bruce Dean Nagel designed the house (for Shyer)

Landscape architect(s)
House extant: yes
Historical notes:
  The house was built by Henry Shyer. It was later owned by Combs.
  He is the son of Melvin and Janice Combs of Mount Vernon, NY.
  *Combs has a star on Hollywood's Walk of Fame.
  **While still a bachelor, he has five children.

Conway, Edmund Virgil, II (1884-1949)

Occupation(s):	financier - controller, treasurer, and chief accounting officer, Montauk Beach Company;
	auditor, Osborne Trust Company, East Hampton
Civic Activism:	a founder, trustee and treasurer, Montauk Community Church;
	secretary and treasurer, Montauk Fire Department;
	treasurer, Montauk Board of Education;
	a founder and treasurer, Montauk Community Church
Marriage(s):	1928-1949 – Dorothea Brandes (1897-1967)
	- nurse
	Civic Activism: a founder, Montauk Chapter, American Women's Volunteer Service during World War I and II;
	first treasurer, Montauk Village Association;
	president, Women's Guild of Montauk Community Church;
	trustee and treasurer, Montauk Community Church
Address:	*[unable to confirm street address]*, Montauk

Name of estate:
Year of construction:
Style of architecture:
Architect(s):
Landscape architect(s):
House extant: unconfirmed
Historical notes:
  Edmund Virgil and Dorothea Brandes Conway II's son William married Florence Clark Scott, the daughter of William Maxwell Scott, Jr. of Bryn Mawr, PA, and resided in New Orleans, LA. Their son Edmund Virgil Conway III, who resided in Bronxville and Montauk, married Audrey Joan Oehler and, later, Elaine Wingate.
  [See following entry for additional family information.]

Conway, Edmund Virgil, III (1929-2015)

Occupation(s):	attorney -	member, Debevoise, Plimpton, and McLean, NYC; member, Debevoise, Plimpton, Lyons, and Gates, NYC
	capitalist -	director, Urstadt, Biddle Properties; director, Union Pacific Corp.; director, Consolidated Edison
	financier -	director, Atlantic Mutual Insurance Co.; chairman of board and president, Seaman's Bank for Savings; chairman of board, Rittenhouse Advisors (financial advisors)
	politician -	Deputy Superintendent of New York State Banks (Rockefeller administration); chairman of board, New York City Audit Department; chairman of board, Metropolitan Transit Authority (Pataki administration); chairman of board Temporary Commission on Water Supply Needs of Southern New York State; member, Governor Pataki's "kitchen cabinet"

Civic Activism: **
president, New York Young Republican Club;
trustee, Colgate University;
trustee, Pace University;
chairman of board, Financial Accounting Standard Advisory Council;
vice-chairman of board, New York City Partnership and Chamber of
 Commerce and Industry;
member, board of governors, Brooklyn Heights Association;
trustee, Kindergarten Society;
member, executive committee, Plymouth Church of the Pilgrims

Marriage(s):
M/1 – 1951 – Audrey Joan Oehler
 - assistant to president, Frew Hall Travel, Inc.
M/2 – Elaine Wingate
 - Civic Activism: **

Address: 5 Oceanview Terrace, Montauk
Name of estate:
Year of construction: 1967
Style of architecture: Beach Cottage
Architect(s):
Landscape architect(s):
House extant: unconfirmed
Historical notes:

  Edmund Virgil Conway III was the son of Edmund Virgil and Dorothea Brandes Conway II of Montauk.
  Audrey Joan Oehler Conway is the daughter of Harry Williams Oehler of St. Paul, MN.
  Edmund Virgil and Audrey John Oehler Conway III's daughter Allison married Richard Brian Carey. Their daughter Sarah resides in Montauk.
  **Edmund and Elaine funded the visitor's center at the Montauk Lighthouse.
  In 2016 the 2,250-square-foot, four-bedroom, five-and-a-half-bath house was for sale. The asking price was $6.75 million.

Cook, Francis Howell (1899-1969)

Occupation(s):	industrialist - McCord Manufacturing Co., Detroit, MI
Marriage(s):	1925-1969 – Janet McCord (d. 1971)
Address:	78 Egypt Lane, East Hampton
Name of estate:	
Year of construction:	
Style of architecture:	
Architect(s):	
Landscape architect(s):	
House extant: unconfirmed	
Historical notes:	

The Blue Book of The Hamptons, 1958 lists Mr. and Mrs. H. Cook as residing at 78 Egypt Lane, East Hampton.

He was the son of Henry Francis and Lena Marianna Fahys Cook of *Clench–Warton* in North Haven. [*See* Spinzia, *Long Island's Prominent Families in the Town of Southampton* – Cook entry.] His sister Edith married James Alexander Edwards, Jr. His brother Joseph married Theresa S. Lesher and resided at *Cedarcroft* in Rye, NY. His sister Maria married Howard Brush Dean, Sr., the son of Herbert Hollingshead and Marion Atwater Brush Dean of *Deanlea* in Lattingtown, and resided in Garden City. [*See* Spinzia, *Long Island's Prominent North Shore Families, vol. I*, and *Long Island's Prominent Families in the Town of Hempstead* – Dean entries.] Marie subsequently married Dudley DeVore Roberts, Jr. with whom she resided in East Hampton. His sister Madeleine married Theodore P. Dixon, the son of Courtland P. Dixon.

Janet McCord Cook was the daughter of David Walter and Fannie Eliza Davis McCord of *Hither House* in East Hampton. Janet's sister Dorothy married William Jackson Lippincott, the son of Jason Evans and Minnie Stewart Horner Lippincott of Cincinnati, OH, and resided in Oyster Bay. [*See* Spinzia, *Long Island's Prominent North Shore Families, vol. I* – Lippincott entry.]

Francis Howell and Janet McCord Cook's daughter Jean married Dr. Henry Charles Barkhorn, Jr. of Newark, NJ, and resided in East Hampton.

[See following entry for additional family information.]

Cook, Harry (1893-1956)

Occupation(s):	financier - partner, Hornblower and Weeks (stock brokerage firm)
	industrialist - vice-president, Fahys Watch Case Co., Sag Harbor, NY
Civic Activism:	director, Southampton Hospital
Marriage(s):	1925-1956 – Lela Harkness Edwards (1903-1980)
	- Civic Activism: treasurer, Republican Volunteers for Nixon - Lodge
Address:	Hither Lane, East Hampton
Name of estate:	*Holly Hall*
Year of construction:	1932
Style of architecture:	Colonial Revival
Architect(s):	Ritzema and Perry designed the house (for H. Cook)
Landscape architect(s):	
House extant: yes	
Historical notes:	

The house, originally named *Holly Hall*, was built by Harry Cook.

The *Social Register Summer, 1945* lists Harry and Lela Harkness Edwards Cook as residing at *Holly Hall* on Hither Lane, East Hampton.

He was the son of Henry Francis and Lena Marianna Fahys Cook of *Clench–Warton* in North Haven. [*See* Spinzia, *Long Island's Prominent Families in the Town of Southampton* – Cook entry.]

Lela Harkness Edwards Cook was the daughter of Dr. Ogden Matthias and Mrs. Lela Harkness Edwards, Jr. of *Walnut Hall Farm* in Donerall, KY, Pittsburgh, PA, and East Hampton and the granddaughter of Steven V. Harkness, a founder of Standard Oil. She subsequently married A. Burton Closson of Cincinnati, OH.

The *Long Island Society Register, 1929* lists Harry and Lela H. Edwards Cook as residing at *The Little House* in Sag Harbor. *The Blue Book of The Hamptons, 1958* lists Mrs. Harry Cook as residing at *Holly Hall* on Hither Lane, East Hampton.

Harry and Lela Harkness Edwards Cook's daughter Lela married George Esterbrook Brown, Jr. and resided in Manhattan.

[See previous entry for additional family information.]

Cookson, Lucy Allison Bishopric (b. 1943)

Occupation(s):	artist
	merchant - founder and president, Thumbelina Needlework Design and Collection, East Hampton
	educator - kindergarten through high school
Marriage(s):	M/1 – 1964 – Carl Edward Bolch, Jr. (b. 1943)
	M/2 – 1986 – Jean-Charles Sprunger (1944-2009)
	- artist - lamp designer
	M/3 – Steven D. Cookson
Address:	18 Cranberry Lane, Amagansett
Name of estate:	
Year of construction:	1910
Style of architecture:	Shingle
Architect(s):	Tietig and Lee designed the house (for J. H. Levering)
Landscape architect(s):	
Builder:	Thomas E. Babcock
House extant: unconfirmed	
Historical notes:	

The 4,896-square-foot, six-bedroom house was built by Richmond Levering, Sr. for his mother Julia Henderson Levering after the death of her husband. In 1930 it was purchased by Jorje Ezequiel Zalles. [*The New York Times* April 6, 1930, p. 52.] The house was later owned by Richard Seymour Jackson. In 1986 it was purchased by Lucy Allison Bishopric Cookson.

[See following entry for family information.]

In 2014 the main residence, a two-bedroom, one-bath guest house, and 5.2 acres were for sale. The asking price was $13 million. In 2015 the price was reduced to $11.8 million.

Cookson, Lucy Allison Bishopric (b. 1943)

Occupation(s):	*[See previous entry.]*
Marriage(s):	M/1 – 1964 – Carl Edward Bolch, Jr. (b. 1943)
	M/2 – 1986 – Jean-Charles Sprunger (1944-2009)
	- *[See previous entry.]*
	M/3 – Steven D. Cookson
Address:	10 Cross Highway, Amagansett
Name of estate:	*Windy Dune*
Year of construction:	c. 1910
Style of architecture:	Mediterranean Villa
Architect(s):	Tietig and Lee designed the house (for J. Rawson, Jr.)
	Christopher Bickford, 1992-1994 alterations (for Cookson)
	Rich Hirt, 2003-2006 alterations (for Cookson)
Landscape architect(s):	
House extant: yes	
Historical notes:	

The 7,000-square-foot house, originally named *Red Roof*, was built by Joseph Rawson, Jr. The house was later owned by Allison Bishopric, Jr. who called it *Windy Dune*. Its name was changed to *Windy Dune* after its terra cotta roof was lost in the 1938 hurricane. Allison and Marjorie Lee Collins Bishopric, Jr.'s daughter Lucy, who subsequently owned the house, continue to call it *Windy Dune*.

Carl Edward and Lucy Allison Bishopric Bolch, Jr.'s daughter Allison married Crawford Cotten Moran.

Jean-Charles Sprunger was the son of Virgil and Clair Lenoir Sprunger of Switzerland.

Coppell, Herbert (1874-1931)

Occupation(s):	attorney
	financier - partner, Maitland, Coppell, and Co. (stock brokerage firm);
	president, Superior Investment Co.
	industrialist - large iron interests in Great Lakes region
Marriage(s):	1897-1931 – Georgie Estelle Myers (1873-1933)
Address:	Lily Pond Lane, East Hampton
Name of estate:	*White-Cottage-By-the-Sea*
Year of construction:	1920
Style of architecture:	Modified Shingle
Architect(s):	John Custis Lawrence designed the house (for Coppell)
	Robert Tappin designed 1928 alterations (for Coppell)
Landscape architect(s):	
Builder:	Edward M. Gay
House extant: yes	
Historical notes:	

The house, originally named *White-Cottage-By-the-Sea*, was built by Herbert Coppell.

The *Long Island Society Register, 1929* lists Herbert and Georgie Myers Church Coppell as residing at *White-Cottage-By-the-Sea* on Lily Pond Lane, East Hampton.

He was the son of George and Helen Hoffman Gillingham Coppell of Manhattan. Herbert's brother Arthur married Mary Stewart Bowers, the daughter of John M. Bowers of New York. His sister Mary married Edgar H. Booth.

Georgie Estelle Meyers Coppell was the daughter of George Smith and Mary Buchanan Myers. Georgie's father George was a founder of Liggett and Myers Tobacco Company. She had previously been married to Samuel Christy Church.

In 1933 the house was purchased by Frederick Behrens Ryan, Sr. who renamed it *East of 69*. [*The East Hampton Star* October 24, 1935, p. 21.]

The house, which is listed on The National Register of Historic Places, was later owned by Elie Hirschfeld who, in 2002, completely renovated it.

In 2011 it was rented by President Clinton.

In 2015 Hirschfeld listed the 10,000-square-foot house, with eight bedrooms, nine full bathrooms, and two half bathrooms, for sale. The asking price was $32.5 million.

Cordier, Auguste Julien, Jr. (1891-1949)

Occupation(s):	industrialist - president and director, Lalance & Grosjean Manufacturing Co. (manufacturer of stainless-steel cookware and sheet metal ware)
Civic Activism:	director, Maidstone Club, East Hampton
Marriage(s):	M/1 – 1921-div. 1937 – Helen Ogden Wood
	M/2 – 1937-1949 – Betsy Page
Address:	Lily Pond Lane, East Hampton
Name of estate:	*Kyalami*
Year of construction:	1901
Style of architecture:	Shingle
Architect(s):	James Brown Lord designed the house (for Drew)
Landscape architect(s):	
Builder:	George A. Eldredge
House extant: no	
Historical notes:	

The house, originally named *Kyalami*, was built by John Drew, Jr. It was later owned by Drew's daughter Louise Devereaux. In 1929 Louise sold the house to Cordier who continued to call it *Kyalami*. [*The East Hampton Star* October 11, 1929, p. 1.]

The *Social Directory of Southampton, Long Island, 1931* lists Auguste J. and Helen Ogden Wood Cordier [Jr.] as residing on Lily Pond Lane, East Hampton. The *Social Register Summer, 1937* lists *Kyalami* as the name of their residence.

He was the son of Auguste Julien and Alice Marie Grosjean Cordier, Sr. of Woodhaven, NY.

Helen Ogden Wood Cordier was the daughter of Howard Ogden and Julia Curtis Twichell Wood, Sr. of East Hampton.

Auguste Julien and Helen Ogden Wood Cordier, Jr.'s daughter Helen married Dr. Thomas Nelson Page Johns, the son of Dr. Frank Stoddert Johns of Richmond, VA, and resided in East Hampton.

Betsy Page Cordier was the daughter of The Reverend Frank Page of Fairfax, VA. She had previously been married to Norman Jay Gaynor, Sr., the son of New York City Mayor William Jay Gaynor, who resided at *Deepwells* in St. James. [*See* Spinzia, *Long Island: A Guide to New York's Suffolk and Nassau Counties* – *Deepwells Farm* – Estate of William Jay Gaynor – *Deepwells*, St. James.] Norman's sister Marion married Ralph Heyward Isham of Glen Head; Congrove Jackson of Oyster Bay; and Frank C. Kurt. [*See* Spinzia, *Long Island's Prominent North Shore Families, vol. I* – Isham entry.] His sister Ruth married John Townsend Rennard and resided in Uniondale. She later married Dudley Gautier Bird, the son of Oliver William and Clara Gautier Bird, Jr. of *Green Hedge* in Uniondale. [*See* Spinzia, *Long Island's Prominent North Families in the Town of Hempstead* – Bird and Rennard entries.] His sister Gertrude married William Seward Webb, Jr. and resided in Old Westbury. [*See* Spinzia, *Long Island's Prominent North Shore Families, vol. II* – Webb entry.] His sister Helen married Edward T. Bedford II and, later, Whitney Kernochan, the son of J. Frederick Kernochan of Manhattan.

In c. 1944 the house was purchased by Louis Rice Wasey. [*The East Hampton Star* November 23, 1944, p. 1.]

Cornell, Irwin Hewlett (1881-1963)

Occupation(s):	industrialist - vice-president, J. B. & J. M. Cornell Co., (iron foundry); assistant secretary, secretary, statistician, manager of sales, and vice president, St Joseph Lead Co.; director, Cornell Iron Works, Long Island City, NY
Civic Activism:	chairman, board of trustees, Guild Hall, East Hampton
Marriage(s):	M/1 – 1902-1934 – Ruth Arven Jones (1880-1934) M/2 – 1935-1960 – Adelaide Pendergast (d. 1960) - Civic Activism: director, Yorkville Community Association
Address:	34 Hither Lane, East Hampton
Name of estate:	
Year of construction:	
Style of architecture:	Colonial Revival
Architect(s):	
Landscape architect(s):	
House extant: yes	
Historical notes:	

In 1925 Mary Lange DeVries (aka Mary MacKinnon) purchased the house and ten acres from Thomas Robinson. [*The East Hampton Star* December 11, 1925, p. 7.] In 1930 the house was purchased from Mrs. DeVries by Chester Marts Cloud. [*The East Hampton Star* March 7, 1930, p. 5.] In 1946 Cornell purchased it from Cloud. [*The East Hampton Star* October 3, 1946, p. 5.]

He was the son of John Milton and Sarah Ann Keen Cornell.

Ruth Arven Jones Cornell was the daughter of Dwight Arven and Emily Lefferts Jones of Englewood, NJ.

Irwin Hewett and Ruth Arven Jones Cornell's daughter Emily married Harold McIntyre Grout, Jr. of Troy, NY. Their daughter Arven married Charles Sumner Stedman, Jr. Their daughter Ruth married Louis Fleitman Watjen, the son of Louis Watjen of Greenwich, CT.

Adelaide Pendergast Cornell was the daughter of J. Lynch and Josephine Archer Jacobsen Pendergast. Adelaide had previously been married to Lawrence T. Durant of NYC.

In 1963 the house was purchased by Charles Francis Preusse. [*The East Hampton Star* May 16, 1963, p. 4.]

Cornell, William Frank (1896-1976)

Occupation(s):	industrialist - president, International Printing division, Interchemical Corp.
Marriage(s):	1917-1976 – Clara Heins (d. 1984)
Address:	67 Davids Lane, East Hampton
Name of estate:	
Year of construction:	
Style of architecture:	
Architect(s):	
Landscape architect(s):	
House extant: unconfirmed	
Historical notes:	

The Blue Book of The Hamptons, 1973 lists W. Frank and Clara Heins Cornell as residing at 67 Davids Lane, East Hampton.

Clara Heins Cornell was the daughter of Henry Heins of Roanoke, VA.

William Frank and Clara Heins Cornell's daughter Patricia married Renton Kirkwood Brodie, Jr. and resided in Cincinnati, OH. Their daughter Ann married Frank Davis Campion, the son of Edward W. Campion of Columbus, OH; A. Hunter Bowman, the son of Luther Lee Bowman; and, subsequently, Dwight J. Thompson with whom she resided in Santa Barbara, CA.

In 1955 the house was purchased by John White Geary III. [*The East Hampton Star* June 9, 1955, p. 4.]

Cory, David Cleveland (1912-1986)

Occupation(s):	engineer - Lamont, Corliss & Co.
	capitalist - real estate developer – Sea Bluff, Amagansett (residential community)
	advertising executive - founder and president, David C. Cory Marketing Services, Englewood, NJ
	financier - director, United Jersey Bank, Hackensack, NJ (later, Hackensack United Jersey Bank);
	director, Hackensack United Jersey Bank
Civic Activism:	president, Sea Bluff Association;
	treasurer, secretary, and governor, Devon Yacht Club, Amagansett;
	a founder, vice-president, secretary, and treasurer, South Fork Country Club, Amagansett
Marriage(s):	1938-1986 – Constance Thayer (1912-1999)
	- educator - teacher, Morrow School, Englewood, NJ
Address:	Sandpiper Lane, Amagansett
Name of estate:	*Sea Bluff*
Year of construction:	1959
Style of architecture:	
Architect(s):	
Landscape architect(s):	
House extant: unconfirmed	
Historical notes:	

The house, originally named *Sea Bluff*, was built by David Cleveland Cory.

The Blue Book of The Hamptons, 1973 lists David Cleveland and Constance Thayer Cory as residing at *Sea Bluff* on Sandpiper Lane, Amagansett.

He was the son of Robert Haskell and Julia Bulkey Cady Cory, Jr. of Englewood, NJ, and the grandson of the noted architect Josiah Cleveland Cady.

Constance Thayer Cleveland Cory was the daughter of Charles Martin Thayer of Worcester, MA.

David Cleveland and Constance Thayer Cory's son Christopher married Laura Page Williams, the daughter of Gordon Page Williams of New York and Washington, DC; Susan B. Lyle; and Helen Hinda Seldon, the widow of Everett Tennant Rattray, and resides in East Hampton. Their daughter Constance married Laura's brother Roger Clark Williams. Their daughter Eleanor married Joel William Gressel III and resided in Manhattan. Their son Robert Haskel Cory III married Elean Ann Reingoldas of Worcester, MA, and resided in Lawrence, MA. Their son Hoyt resides in California.

[See following entry for further family information.]

Cory, Helen Hinda Seldon (b. 1934)

Occupation(s):	journalist – weekly column, *The East Hampton Star*
	publisher - president, *The East Hampton Star*;
	founder and president, *Sag Harbor Herald*
Marriage(s):	M/1 – 1960-1980 – Everett Tennant Rattray (1932-1980)

        - journalist - editor, *The East Hampton Star*
          writer - *The South Fork: Land and People of Long Island*, 1979;
              The Adventure of Jeremiah Dimon, 1985 (novel)
          Civic Activism: member, advisory commission, Fire Island National Seashore;
              director, East Hampton Historical Society;
              a founder, East Hampton Town Marine Museum, Amagansett

M/2 – 1995 – Christopher Thayer Cory (b. 1940)
    - public relations executive -
        director, public affairs, Carnegie Council on Children, 1975-1978;
        manager, editorial services, Philip Morris, Inc., 1983-1991;
        director, college relations, Connecticut College, New London, CT, 1991-1996;
        director, public relations, Long Island University, 1996-2001;
        director of communications, International Longevity Center, NYC, 2001-2002;
        executive director of public information, Pace University, NYC, 2002-
    journalist - correspondent, *Time* magazine, 1962-1965;
        Boston bureau chief, *Time* magazine, 1965-1967;
        associate editor, *Time* magazine, 1967-1972;
        managing editor, *Psychology Today*, 1978-1983
    writer - articles for *Learning* magazine

Address: Edwards Lane, East Hampton
Name of estate:
Year of construction:
Style of architecture:
Architect(s):
Landscape architect(s):
House extant: yes
Historical notes:

    The house was previously owned by Jeannette Frances Edwards Rattray. It was later owned by her son Everett and, then, by his wife Helen.
    She was the daughter of Abraham H. and Yetta Seldon of Bayonne, NJ.
    Everett Tennant Rattray was the son of Arnold Elsmere and Jeannette Frances Rattray.
    Everett Tennant and Helen Hinda Seldon Rattray's daughter Bess married Paul Gartside, the son of Robert and Norma Gartside of Canada. Their son David married Lisa Ann Heilbrunn, the daughter of Dr. Karl and Mrs. Elaine Heilbrunn of NYC.
    Christopher Thayer Cory was the son of David Cleveland and Constance Thayer Cory of *Sea Bluff* in Amagansett. Christopher had previously been married to Laura Page Williams, the daughter of Gordon Page Williams, and Susan B. Lytle.
    [See previous entry for additional family information.]

Couric, Katie (b. 1957)
aka Katherine Anne Couric

Occupation(s):	journalist - global anchor, Yahoo News
	entertainers and associated professions -
	television news programs, NBC, CBS, ABC;
	"Katie" (syndicated daytime talk show, Disney ABC Domestic
	Television)
	writer - *The Best Advice I Ever Got*, 2011
Civic Activism:	director, The Robin Hood Foundation (established to alleviate poverty in NYC)
Marriage(s):	M/1 – 1989-1998 – John Paul Monahan III (1956-1998)
	- attorney - Hunton and Williams, NYC;
	legal analyst, NBC News, 1996-1997
	M/2 – 2014 – John P. Moler (b. 1963)
	- financier - banking division, First Boston Corp.;
	head of mergers and acquisitions, Brown Brothers Harriman (investment banking firm)
Address:	15 Amy's Lane, East Hampton
Name of estate:	
Year of construction:	
Style of architecture:	Modified Shingle with Dutch Revival Elements
Architect(s):	
Landscape architect(s)	Clara Couric (for K. Couric)
House extant: yes	
Historical notes:	

  Katie Couric purchased the 7,000-square-foot, seven-bedroom, six-bath house in 2006 for $6.3 million.
  She is the daughter of John Martin and Elinor Hene Couric of Virginia.
  John Paul Monahan III was the son of John Paul and Carol Monahan, Jr. of Rehoboth, DE.
  John Paul and Katie Couric Monahan III's daughter Elinor was born in 1991. Their daughter Caroline was born in 1996.
  In 2004 Couric was inducted into the Television Hall of Fame.

Coy, James Joseph. Jr. (1881-1948)

Occupation(s):	entertainers and associated professions -
	extra in the Broadway play "The Pit", starring Douglas Fairbanks, Sr.;
	actor, Ringling Brothers, Barnum and Bailey Circus, 1910
	member, New York City Police's famous bomb squad, 1914-1918*
	member, New York City Police homicide squad, 1918-1920
	member, New York City Police pickpocket and gangster squad, 1920-1921
	member, New York City Police safe and loft squad, 1925-1926
	commander, New York City jewelry squad, 1930
	acting captain, New York City Police
	manager, private detective agency (after retiring from the police force)
	intelligence agent - military intelligence during World War I
Marriage(s):	Esther McGrann (1885-1977)
Address:	*[unable to confirm street address]*, East Hampton
Name of estate:	
Year of construction:	
Style of architecture:	
Architect(s):	
Landscape architect(s):	
House extant: yes	
Historical notes:	

    James Joseph Coy, Jr. was the son of James Joseph and Minnie Meyer Coy, Sr.
    James Joseph and Esther McGrann Coy, Jr.'s daughter Stephanie married Arnold Zavell and resided in East Hampton. She later married ____ Cartwright. Their daughter Mary married Nelson C. Osborne, Jr. and resided in Irvington-on-the-Hudson, NY, and East Hampton. Their son James Joseph Coy III married Evelyn Poppiti and resided in East Hampton.
    [See following entry for additional family information.]
    *As a member of Thomas Joseph Tunney's bomb squad, Coy was instrumental in the capture of the German saboteur and inventor of the rudder bomb Robert Fay. [*See* Raymond E. Spinzia "The Involvement of Long Islanders in the Events Surrounding German Sabotage in the New York Metropolitan Area 1914-1917." wwwspinzialongislandestates.com.]

Coy, James Joseph, III (1913-2003)

Occupation(s):	financier - vice-president, James Talcott and Co. (commercial
	finance firm);
	director, First Investors Corp.
	attorney - assistant general counsel, General Motors Corp.
	industrialist - secretary, General Motors Corp.
Marriage(s):	1939-2003 – Evelyn Poppiti
Address:	90 Buell Lane, East Hampton
Name of estate:	
Year of construction:	1904
Style of architecture:	
Architect(s):	
Landscape architect(s):	
House extant: yes	
Historical notes:	

    In 1960 Coy purchased the residence of Mrs. W. F. Mann. [*The East Hampton Star* May 26, 1960, p. 4.]
    The Blue Book of The Hamptons, 1965 lists James J. and Evelyn Poppiti Coy [III] as residing at 90 Buell Lane, East Hampton.
    He was the son of James Joseph and Esther McGrann Coy, Jr. of East Hampton.
    James Joseph and Evelyn Poppiti Coy III's daughter Jamie married Edward Bruce Wallace, Jr. of Garden City and East Hampton. Their son Gregory died in 1994. Their son Christopher married Joann Owen.
    [See previous entry for additional family information.]
    The 2,000-square-foot, five-bedroom, three-and-a-half-bath house and 0.33 acres was sold in 2011 for $1.45 million.

Craig, Dr. Stuart Lessley (1885-1972)

Occupation(s):	physician* - surgeon and director, New York Eye and Ear Infirmary, NYC;
	consulting surgeon, Rockefeller Institute
Civic Activism:	president, Ontological Association;
	trustee, New York Academy of Medicine, NYC
Marriage(s):	1923-1964 – Mary Peronneau de Saussure (1890-1964)
Address:	Ocean Avenue and Jefferys Lane, East Hampton
Name of estate:	
Year of construction:	c. 1872
Style of architecture:	Italianate
Architect(s):	Charles Peter Beauchamp Jefferys
	designed his own residence**
Landscape architect(s):	
House extant: yes	
Historical notes:	

The house, originally named *Sommariva*, was built by Charles Peter Beauchamp Jefferys, Sr. It was inherited by his daughter Marie and son-in-law Henry Lee Hobart, who moved the house about one hundred yards east to its present site. The house was later owned by Abraham Mills, who called it *The Chalet*, and, subsequently, by Craig.

Mary Peronneau de Saussure Craig was the daughter of James Peronneau and Annie Isabella Laurens de Saussure.

Dr. Stuart Lessley and Mrs. Mary Peronneau de Saussure Craig's daughter Jeanne married Lawrence L. Davis and resided in Brookville. Their son Judge Stuart Laurens Craig married Eleanor Bradford Spencer, the daughter of Harold Bennett Spencer.

*Dr. Craig was a witness at Gloria Vanderbilt's 1934 custody trial. [*The New York Times* May 24, 1972, p. 50.]

The house is on the National Register of Historic Places.

**The 1914 alterations to the house were made by the Hobarts.

Crane, Thomas (1865-1943)

Occupation(s):	industrialist - partner, Crane and Breed (furniture manufacturer)
Civic Activism:	trustee - Village of East Hampton, 1932-1940
Marriage(s):	
Address:	46 Dunemere Lane, East Hampton
Name of estate:	
Year of construction:	1926
Style of architecture:	Colonial Revival
Architect(s):	
Landscape architect(s):	
Builder:	Edward M. Gay
House extant: unconfirmed	
Historical notes:	

The house was built by Thomas Crane. [*The East Hampton Star* August 14, 1945, p. 1.]

In 1945 the house was purchased by Halfred Alfred Langben from the Oteco Corporation. [*The East Hampton Star* November 8, 1945, p. 1.]

Creel, Alexandra Diodati Gardiner (1910-1990)

Marriage(s): 1932-1990 – James Randall Creel, Jr. (1904-1990)
- attorney - assistant U. S. attorney, Southern District of New York, 1933-1939;
judge, Court of Special Sessions, NYC

Address: Gardiner's Island
Name of estate: *Manor House*
Year of construction: 1947
Style of architecture: Georgian Revival
Architect(s):
Landscape architect(s)
House extant: yes
Historical notes:

    The *Manor House* was built by Miss Sarah Diodati Gardiner. It was later owned by her nephew Robert David Lion Gardiner and his sister Alexandra.
    She was the daughter of Robert Alexander and Nora Loftus Gardiner of *Maidstone Hall* in East Hampton.
    James Randall Creel, Jr. was the son of James Randall Creel, Sr. of Kansas City, MO.
    James Randall and Alexandra Diodati Gardiner Creel, Jr.'s daughter Alexandra, who resides on Gardiner's Island, married Peter Francis Tufo II, the son of Dr. and Mrs. Gustave Francis Tufo of Chicago, IL, and, later, Robert Guestier Goelet, the son of Robert Walton and Anne Marie Guestier Goelet. Their son James Randall Creel, Jr. [III] married Giulia Pallavicini, the daughter of Alessandro Mario Lugi Pietro and Margaret Roosevelt Pallavicini of Rome Italy, and the granddaughter of George Emlen and Julia Morris Addison Roosevelt, Sr. of *Gracewood* in Cove Neck. [*See* Spinzia, *Long Island's Prominent North Shore Families, vol. II* – Roosevelt entry.] James later married Diana Millicent Forman, the daughter of Lawrence Carter Forman of Greenwich, CT; Maria del Carmen Camba; and, subsequently, Marion D. Von Mayrhauser.
    [For information about the Creels' Mill Neck residence, see Spinzia, *Long Island's Prominent North Shore Families, vol. I* – Creel entry.]

Cullman, Joseph Fredrick, III (1912-2004)

Occupation(s):	industrialist - CEO, Philip Morris Co., 1957-1978
	writer - *I'm a Lucky Guy*, 1998 (autobiography)
Civic Activism:	established Joseph and Joan Cullman Conservation Foundation;
	endowed Joseph F. Cullman Library of Natural History, Smithsonian Institution, Washington, DC;
	endowed Joseph F. Cullman Professorship, Yale University, New Haven, CT;
	chairman of board, Atlantic Salmon Federation;
	director, World Wildlife Fund;
	founder, Cullman Wildlife Project, Tanzania;
	chairman, executive committee, Tobacco Institute;
	chairman of board, U. S. Open, Forest Hills, NY, 1969 and 1970;
	president and chairman of board, International Tennis Hall of Fame, 1982-1988
Marriage(s):	M/1 – 1935-div. 1974 – Susan Lehman (1914-1994)
	M/2* – Joan Paley (1924-2004)
	- board vice-chair, Lincoln Center, NYC;
	trustee, The Jewish Center of the Hamptons
Address:	34 Terbell Lane, East Hampton
Name of estate:	
Year of construction:	1971
Style of architecture:	International
Architect(s):	Charles Gwathmey designed the house (for Cogan)
Landscape architect(s)	
House extant: no	
Historical notes:	

    The house was built by Marshall Stuart Cogan. It was later owned by Cullman.
    He was the son of Joseph Fredrick and Frances Wolff Cullman, Jr.
    Susan Lehman Cullman was the daughter of Harold Mayer and Cecile Sigmund Lehman of *Willowpond* in Tarrytown, NY.
    Joseph Fredrick and Susan Lehman Cullman III's daughter Dorothy married Norman J. Treisman and resides in Briarcliff Manor, NY.
    Joan Paley Cullman was the daughter of Peter J. Paley of Woodmere. She had previously been married to Barnard Sachs Straus.
    *Joseph and Joan married, divorced, and, later, remarried each other.
    The house was subsequently owned by Gary L. Fuhrman who razed it to build a new residence.

Culver, Austin H. (1863-1944)

Occupation(s):	capitalist - partner, Lee and Culver (built and owned Three Mile Harbor Pavilion); owned, Maidstone Bath House
	financier - director, Osborne Trust Co., East Hampton
Civic Activism:	chairman, East Hampton War Price and Rationing Board, 1943;
	member, Village of East Hampton Zoning Board;
	member, Village of East Hampton Board of Appeals;
	member of board, Village of East Hampton;
	director, East Hampton Neighborhood Association;
	president, East Hampton Boards of Trade;
	treasurer, Maidstone Fire Department District No. 1
Marriage(s):	1885-1944 – Isabelle Amelia Terry (1864-1945)
Address:	Dunemere Lane, East Hampton
Name of estate:	
Year of construction:	1911
Style of architecture:	Four Square
Architect(s):	
Landscape architect(s):	
Builder:	Edward M. Gay
House extant: yes	
Historical notes:	

The house was built by Austin H. Culver. [*The East Hampton Star* October 6, 1911, p. 4.]
He was the son of Josiah and Mary Hedges Conklin Culver of Wainscott.
Isabella Amelia Terry Culver was the daughter of Egbert H. and Mary Anna Tyler Terry of East Moriches.
Austin H. and Isabella Amelia Terry Culver's daughter Mary married Ernest F. Clifford and resided in Jamaica, NY.
In 1944 Mrs. Culver sold the house to Ida May Barbery. [*The East Hampton Star* November 23, 1944, p. 1.]

Cummins, Stephen Swete (1851-1945)

Occupation(s):	merchant - partner with Hingston Smith, The Hingston Smith Arms Co. (Canadian trading post)
	industrialist - director, The Bishop Engraving and Printing Co., Winnipeg, Canada
	financier - director, Bank of Montreal, Montreal, Canada; director, Northern Crown Bank; director, Lancashire Life Insurance Co.
Civic Activism:	a founder, St. George's Snowshoe Club
Marriage(s):	M/1 – 1906-1908 – Emma Douglas Arrowsmith (1846-1908)
	M/2 – 1919 – Virginia P. Kent (1870-1952)
	- writer - *On Wind of Chance*, 1931 (poetry); *Pierre: Or a Parisian and a Puritan*, 1949 (poetry)
	publisher - a founder and editor, *Lyric Magazine*
	Civic Activism: established The Lyric Foundation, 1949*; suffragist**
Address:	63 Huntting Lane, East Hampton
Name of estate:	*Greycroft*
Year of construction:	1894
Style of architecture:	Shingle
Architect(s):	Isaac Henry Green II designed the house (for L. G. Woodhouse)***
	George A. Eldredge designed 1897 alterations
	Robert Arthur Morton Stern designed 1980-1981 alterations to playhouse

Landscape architect(s):
House extant: yes
Nassau County Museum Collection has photographs of the estate.
Historical notes:

 The house, originally named *Greycroft*, was built by Lorenzo Guernsey Woodhouse.
 Stephen Swete Cummins was the son of John Z. and Louannie Huddleston Cummins of Gambi, Quebec, Canada. In 1938 Stephen returned to Winnipeg, Canada. [*The Winnipeg Tribune* August 20, 1945, p. 8.]
 Emma Douglas Arrowsmith Cummins was the daughter of Edgar Arrowsmith of New York. She had previously been married to Lorenzo Guernsey Woodhouse with whom she resided at *Greycroft* in East Hampton.
 The *Social Directory of Southampton, 1931* lists Stephen S. and Virginia P. Kent Cummins as residing at *Tidetop* [*Tide Top*], Lily Pond Lane, East Hampton.
 She had previously been married to Louis Magee of Boston, MA, with whom she resided in Manhattan. By 1950 Virginia had relocated to *Tides Turn* in East Hampton.
 *The Lyric Foundation was established to promote simplicity, clarity, and discipline in the writing of poetry.
 **For other Long Islanders involved in the suffrage movement *see* Raymond E. Spinzia, "Winning the Franchise: Long Island Activists in the Fight for Woman's Suffrage and Their Opponents, Long Island's Anti-Suffragists." wwwspinzialongislandestates.com.
 ***For Green's other commissions, *see* Spinzia, *Long Island's Prominent South Shore Families: Their Estates and Their Country Homes in the Towns of Babylon and Islip.*

Cushman, Blinn Sill, Jr. (1907-1980)

Occupation(s):	capitalist - staff supervisor, Bell Telephone Exhibit at New York's World Fair; general personnel supervisor, New York Telephone Co.
Marriage(s):	M/1 – 1931-div. – Edith Marie Macon (1909-1985) - educator - first director of school lunch programs, Connecticut Department of Education, 1943 writer - articles on nutrition Civic Activism: a founder, Connecticut Nutritional Council; president, American Food Service Association; president, Connecticut Dietetic Association M/2 – 1949-1980 – Dorothy Quincy Lawrence (d. 1981)
Address:	98 Jericho Lane, East Hampton
Name of estate:	
Year of construction:	
Style of architecture:	
Architect(s):	
Landscape architect(s):	
House extant:	unconfirmed
Historical notes:	

The Blue Book of The Hamptons, 1973 lists Blinn Sill and Dorothy Q. Lawrence Cushman [Jr.] as residing at 98 Jericho Lane, East Hampton. They had previously resided on Main Street in Wainscott.

He was the son of Blinn Sill and Jessie R. Manley Cushman, Sr. of Ithaca, NY.

Edith Marie Macon Cushman was the daughter of William Watts and Maud Evelyn Andruss Macon of Brooklyn, Rochester, NY, and Ithaca, NY. Edith subsequently married ____ Blakeley.

Blinn Sill and Edith Marie Macon Cushman, Jr.'s son Richard died in 1946 at the age of nine.

Dorothy Quincy Lawrence Cushman was the daughter of Effingham and Dorothy Quincy Gookin Lawrence II of Cold Spring Harbor. [*See* Spinzia, *Long Island's Prominent North Shore Families, vol. I* – Lawrence entry.] She had previously been married to George Hopper Fitch.

Blinn Sill and Dorothy Quincy Lawrence Cushman, Jr.'s son Andrew married Alison Gregg McCall, the daughter of Julien Lachicotte McCall of Hunting Valley, OH.

Dana, Robert Bingham (1884-1961)

Occupation(s):	capitalist - president, R. B. Dana Co. (sales agency for New York Insulated Wire division, General Electric Co.)
Marriage(s):	1912-1961 – Laura Grace Maclay (1882-1968)
Address:	Indian Wells Highway, Amagansett
Name of estate:	
Year of construction:	
Style of architecture:	
Architect(s):	
Landscape architect(s):	
House extant:	unconfirmed
Historical notes:	

The Blue Book of The Hamptons, 1965 lists R. Bingham and L. Grace Maclay Dana as residing on Indian Wells Highway, Amagansett.

He was the son of Robert Knight and Lucretia Saltonstall Bonnett Dana.

Laura Grace Maclay Dana was the granddaughter of New York City Mayor William Frederick and Mrs. Sarah Craig Havemeyer and the daughter of Major Isaac Walker and Mrs. Laura A. Havemeyer Maclay. Major Maclay helped to carry President Lincoln to Peterson's house after the President had been shot at Ford's Theater.

Robert Bingham and Laura Grace Maclay Dana's daughter Lucia married Baird Jensenius Simpson, the son of James Baird Simpson, and, later, Allen K. Eastman. Their daughter Laura married William V. N. Carroll.

Darrow, Daniel (1867-1931)

Occupation(s):	merchant - vice-president, General Builders Supply Corp.
	capitalist - president, Equity Securities & Realty Corp., NYC; president, Darrow Holding Co.; treasurer, Scarsdale Corp.
Marriage(s):	Florence Lander (d. 1950)
Address:	Lily Pond Lane, East Hampton
Name of estate:	*Mayfair House*
Year of construction:	
Style of architecture:	
Architect(s):	
Landscape architect(s):	
House extant:	unconfirmed
Historical notes:	

The *Long Island Society Register, 1929* lists Daniel Darrow as residing on Lily Pond Lane, East Hampton.

He was the son of Rufus Darrow. Daniel's sister Emma married Charles Goodhue Dodd, the son of John Mingus Dodd, Jr. of East Hampton, and, later, Eugene Rodney Burnett with whom she resided in East Hampton.

Daniel and Florence Lander Darrow's daughter Jean married Russell Davidson Robinson, the son of William Russell Robinson and resided in Great Neck. Their son Rufus Darrow II married Betty Cummings and resided in Hamden, CT.

In 1944 Mrs. Darrow sold the house to Harold Willis Nichols, Sr. who called it *Crow Nest*. [*The East Hampton Star* November 23, p. 1.]

Davies, Francis Herbert (1849-1906)

Occupation(s):	financier - member, Henry Clews and Co. (investment banking firm)
Marriage(s):	1876-1906 – Cornelia Scott Rokenbaugh (1847-1906)
Address:	50 Ocean Avenue, East Hampton
Name of estate:	*Tidelands*
Year of construction:	1899
Style of architecture:	Shingle
Architect(s):	Joseph Greenleaf Thorp designed the house (for F. H. Davies)
	John Custis Lawrence designed the 1910 alterations
Landscape architect(s):	
Builder:	Howard Emslie & Son, house
	George A. Eldredge, alterations
House extant:	yes
Historical notes:	

The house, originally named *Tidelands*, was built by Francis Herbert Davies. [*The East Hampton Star* April 19, 1907, p. 5.]

He was the son of New York State Chief Justice of the Court of Appeals Henry Ebenezer and Mrs. Rebecca Waldo Tappan Davies of New York. Francis' brother Julien married Alice Martin and resided at *Timber Point* in Great River. [*See* Spinzia, *Long Island's Prominent South Shore Families* – Davies entry.]

Cornelia Scott Rokenbaugh Davies was the daughter of Henry Scott and Jeanette E. Eager Rokenbaugh of *Villa Avalon* in Bay Shore. [*See* Spinzia, *Long Island's Prominent South Shore Families* – Rokenbaugh entry.]

Francis Herbert and Cornelia Scott Rokenbaugh Davies' daughter Helen married Charles E. Tainter of Flushing, NY. Their daughter Lucy married Dr. Samuel Swift, the Mayor of Yonkers, NY.

The house was later owned by H. C. Thorpe and, subsequently, by Stephen J. Heyman.

Davis, Charlotte Frances Rowe (1894-1922)

Marriage(s):	M/1 – 1914-1922 – Edward Mailler Radway (1888-1922)
	- capitalist - president, Richvein Coal Co., Cincinnati, OH;
	president, Russell Producing Co., Cincinnati, OH
	M/2 – 1926-1942 – Chase Henchman Davis (1891-1942)
	- industrialist - Tri-State Ignition Co., Cincinnati, OH
Address:	21 Jefferys Lane, East Hampton
Name of estate:	
Year of construction:	
Style of architecture:	
Landscape architect(s)	
House extant: yes	
Historical notes:	

    Charlotte Frances Rowe Davis was the daughter of William Stanhope and Margaret Anna Richardson Rowe, Sr. of Amagansett.
    Edward Mailler Radway was the son of Dr. John Symonds and Mrs. Mary Anna Mailler Radway of Quogue. [*See* Spinzia, *Long Island's Prominent Families in the Town of Southampton* – Radway entry.]
    Edward Mailler and Charlotte Frances Rowe Radway's son John married Mary Mitchell, the daughter of John Ledyard Mitchell of Cincinnati, OH; Judith Ann Dawson; and Placidia Knowlton.
    Chase Henchman Davis was the son of Nathaniel Henchman and Jeannette Alice Skinner Davis of Cincinnati, OH.
    In 1964 Danna Merrian Raymond purchased the house. [*The East Hampton* Star May 28, 1964, p. 4.]

Davis, George Samler (1858-1931)

Occupation(s):	educator - teacher, New York City School System, 1880-1887;
	assistant principal, Grammar School 83, NYC;
	assistant superintendent, New York City School System,
	1887-1896;
	associate superintendent, New York City School System,
	1896-1908;
	president, Normal College (later, Hunter College of City
	of New York), 1908;
	president, Hunter College of City of New York, 1908-1929
Marriage(s):	1888-1913 – Emilia Wickham Suydam (1863-1913)
Address:	Indian Wells Highway, Amagansett
Name of estate:	
Year of construction:	1884
Style of architecture:	Shingle
Architect(s):	
Landscape architect(s):	
House extant: unconfirmed	
Historical notes:	

    The house was built by George Samler Davis.
    He was the son of Robert Vernon and Mary Schiefflin Samler Davis, Sr.
    Emilia Wickham Suydam Davis was the daughter of John Henry and Emilia Wickham Suydam of New York.
    George Samler and Emilia Wickham Suydam Davis' daughter Margaret married Harry MacNaughton Farlow. Their daughter Emilia married Fletcher Donoghue Dodge.
    The house was inherited by his sister Miss Genevieve Mansfield Davis. [*The East Hampton Star* June 5, 1931, p. 5.]

Davis, Vernon Mansfield (1855-1931)

Occupation(s):	attorney - partner, Davis, Cohen, and McWilliam:
	assistant district attorney, New York County, 1885-1897;
	district attorney, New York County, 1897-1901;
	judge, Supreme Court of New York for First District, 1916
	educator - instructor of Greek and mathematics, College of the City of New York
	politician - commissioner of education, New York City, 1902
Civic Activism:	president, Society for the Prevention of Cruelty to Children;
	trustee, Cathedral of St. John the Divine, NYC;
	delegate, triennial general convention of the Protestant Episcopal Church;
	member, standing committee, New York Protestant Episcopal Church;
	vestryman and clerk of the vestry, St. Andrew's Church, NYC (later, Trinity Church);
	vestryman, St. Luke's Church, East Hampton
Marriage(s):	1885-1920 – Harriet Lobdell (1863-1920)
Address:	Indian Wells Highway, Amagansett
Name of estate:	*Half-a-Gale*
Year of construction:	1892
Style of architecture:	Beach Cottage
Architect(s):	
Landscape architect(s):	
Builder:	Grimshaw and Babcock
House extant: unconfirmed	
Historical notes:	

The house, originally named *Half-a-Gale*, was built by Vernon Mansfield Davis.
The *Social Register Summer, 1923* lists Vernon Mansfield Davis as residing at *Half-a-Gale* in Amagansett.
He was the son of Robert Vernon and Mary Schiefflin Samler Davis.
Harriet Lobdell Davis was the daughter of The Reverend Francis and Mrs. Julia Almira Danforth Lobdell.

Day, Thomas Mills, Jr. (1892-1953)

Occupation(s):	capitalist - treasurer, International Telephone and Telegraph Co.
Marriage(s):	1941-1953 – Agnes Roudebush (1895-1975)
	- Civic Activism: president of board, Graham School;
	member, board of managers, East Hampton Free Library
Address:	Ocean Avenue and Hook Pond Lane, East Hampton
Name of estate:	
Year of construction:	
Style of architecture:	
Architect(s):	
Landscape architect(s):	
House extant: unconfirmed	
Historical notes:	

The Blue Book of The Hamptons, 1973 lists Agnes Roudebush Day as residing at Ocean Avenue and Hook Pond Lane, East Hampton.
   She was the daughter of John Heywood and Vallory Odell Roudebush of *Stonybroke* in East Hampton. Agnes has previously been married to Reginald Satterlee Willis with whom she resided in Kings Point. [*See* Spinzia, *Long Island's Prominent North Shore Families, vol. II* – Willis entry.] Her sister Roseanne married Lawrence Larkin, the son of Adrian Hoffman and Katherine Bache Satterthwaite Larken of *Les Alouettes* in Southampton, and resided in East Hampton. [*See* Spinzia, *Long Island's Prominent Families in the Town of Southampton* – Larkin entry.]
   Thomas Mills Day, Jr. was the son of Thomas Mills and Anna Perkins Smith Day, Sr. of Plainfield, NJ.

Dean, Howard Brush, Jr. (1921-2001)

Occupation(s):	financier - partner, Harris Upham and Co. (later, Smith, Barney, Harris, Upham, and Co.; now, Salomon Smith Barney) (investment banking firm); vice-president, Dean Witter Reynolds (now, Morgan Stanley Smith Barney) (investment banking firm)
Civic Activism:	member, board of governors, Investment Banking Association; member, board of governors, American Stock Exchange; member, board of governors, Stock Exchange Firms; trustee, Browning School, NYC; trustee, Pomfert School, Pomfert, CT; chairman of board, St. George's School, Newport, RI; director, Hospital for Special Surgery, NYC; director, Freedom Institute, NYC; vice-president, Maidstone Club, East Hampton
Marriage(s):	1947-2001 – Andree Belden Maitland (b. 1929) - appraiser - president, Art Associates, NY (art consulting firm)
Address:	Hook Pond Lane, East Hampton
Name of estate:	
Year of construction:	
Style of architecture:	
Architect(s):	
Landscape architect(s):	
House extant: yes	
Historical notes:	

The house was built by Howard Brush Dean, Jr.

The Blue Book of The Hamptons, 1973 lists Howard B. and Andree B. Maitland Dean [Jr.] as residing on Hook Pond Lane, East Hampton. The Deans had previously owned James Sheafe Satterthwaite, Sr.'s house.

He was the son of Howard Brush and Maria Fahys Cook Dean, Sr. of Garden City.

Andree Belden Maitland Dean was the daughter of James William and Sylvia Wigglesworth Maitland of Hewlett Bay Park. [*See* Spinzia, *Long Island's Prominent Families in the Town of Hempstead* – Dean and Maitland entries.]

Howard Brush and Andree Belden Maitland Dean, Jr.'s son James married Virginia Dorothy Lynch, the daughter of Edmund Calvert and Caroline Hudson Lynch, Jr. of *Floralyn* in Lattingtown. [*See* Spinzia, *Long Island's Prominent North Shore Families, vol. 1* – Lynch entry.] Their son William married Beth Ann Morley, the daughter of Dr. John J. Morley of Dedham and Truro, MA. Their son Dr. Howard Brush Dean III married Dr. Judith Ellen Steinberg, the daughter of Dr. Herman and Dr. Ethel Bookhalter Steinberg of Roslyn, and resides in Vermont. Dean served as Governor of Vermont from 1991-2003 and was unsuccessful in becoming the Democratic candidate for the presidency in the 2004 election. He then headed the Democratic National Committee through the 2008 election.

DeFelice, Gian Palo

Occupation(s):	Alitalia pilot
	restaurateur - partner, Estia's Little Kitchen, Sag Harbor; partner, *Tutto il Giorno;* Southampton, NYC, Sag Harbor
Marriage(s):	Gabby Karan
	- restaurateur - partner, Estia's Little Kitchen, Sag Harbor; partner, *Tutto il Giorno;* Southampton, NYC, Sag Harbor
Address:	88 Bull Path, East Hampton
Name of estate:	*Abbey Cottage*
Year of construction:	
Style of architecture:	Tuscan
Architect(s):	
Landscape architect(s)	
House extant: yes	
Historical notes:	

The 3,500-square-foot, five-bedroom, five-and-a-half-bath house was built by Gian Palo DeFelice. Gabby Karan DeFelice is the daughter of Mark and Donna Ivy Faske Karan of East Hampton.

In 2015 the DeFelices listed the house for sale. The asking price was $2.7 million.

de Forest, Henry Grant (1820-1889)

Occupation(s):	attorney - partner, Weeks, Forster, and de Forest (later, Weeks and de Forest)
	capitalist - partner, W. W. de Forest (importer of South American products)
Civic Activism:	chairman, Ways and Means Committee, New York Bible Society; member, board of managers, Presbyterian Hospital, NYC
Marriage(s):	1847-1889 – Julia Mary Weekes (1827-1896)
	- Civic Activism: member, district committee, Charity Organization Society of the City of New York
Address:	De Forest Road, Montauk
Name of estate:	
Year of construction:	1883
Style of architecture:	Beach Cottage with Queen Anne elements
Architect(s):	McKim, Mead, & White designed the house
Landscape architect(s):	Frederick Law Olmstead designed the site plan
Builder:	Mead & Taft
House extant: yes	
Historical notes:	

The house is one of the Montauk Association's "Seven Sisters." It was owned by Henry Grant de Forest of *Nethermuir* in Laurel Hollow.

He was the son of Lockwood and Mehetable Wheeler de Forest.

Julia Mary Weekes de Forest was the daughter of John Abeel and Alice H. Delano Weekes, Sr. Her brother John, who resided at *Tranquility* in Oyster Bay Cove, married Estelle Durant and, later, Elsa Adele Schreiter. [*See* Spinzia, *Long Island's Prominent North Shore Families, vol. II* – Weekes entry.]

Henry Grant and Julia Mary Weekes de Forest's son Robert married Emily Johnston, the daughter of John Taylor and Frances Collen Johnston, and resided at *Wawapek* in Cold Spring Harbor. Their son Lockwood de Forest II married Meta Kemble and resided in Manhattan. Their daughter Julia, who did not marry, resided at *Airslie* in Laurel Hollow. Their son Henry Wheeler de Forest, who inherited *Nethermuir* and *Airslie*, married Julia Gilman Noyes; the daughter of Charles Phelps and Emily Hoffman Gilman Noyes of St. Paul, MN.

[For information about the de Forest family's estates on Long Island's North Shore, *see* Spinzia, *Long Island's Prominent North Shore Families, vol. I* – de Forest entries.]

The house was later purchased by Richard Alva Cavett who used it as a rental.

DeGraff, James Wilde (1862-1956)

Occupation(s):	merchant - a founder and president, DeGraff and Palmer (wholesale notion firm)
Civic Activism:	trustee, Muhlenberg Hospital, Plainfield, NJ, 1918; president, East Hampton Associates
Marriage(s):	1890-1951 – Carrie Thompson Milliken (1867-1951)
Address:	20 Apaquogue Road, East Hampton
Name of estate:	*Cherridune*
Year of construction:	1901
Style of architecture:	Modified Shingle
Architect(s):	
Landscape architect(s):	
Builder:	Francis E. Grimshaw, Jr.
House extant: yes	
Historical notes:	

The house was built by Angeline Ensign Newman. It was later owned by DeGraff who called it *Cherridune*.

The *Social Directory of Southampton, Long Island, 1931* lists James W. DeGraff as residing on Apaquogue Road, East Hampton.

He was the son of Liverius and Alice Fair DeGraff. James' sister Neltje married Frank Nelson Doubleday and resided at *Effendi Hill* in Mill Neck and at a second unnamed residence in Mill Neck. [*See* Spinzia, *Long Island's Prominent North Shore Families, vol. 1* – Doubleday entry.]

Carrie Thompson Millikin DeGraff was the daughter of Samuel Milliken of Plainfield, NJ.

James Wilde and Carrie Thompson Milliken DeGraff's son Robert married Dorcas Marie Bomann, the daughter of George A. Bomann of Plainfield, NY, and resided at *Wood Hollow* in Upper Brookville. [*See* Spinzia, *Long Island's Prominent North Shore Families, vol. 1* – DeGraff entry.] Their daughter Eleanor, who later owned *Cherridune*, married Dr. Frank Clyde Carr, Sr. The Carrs subsequently relocated to *Dunfour* in East Hampton.

In 1943 DeGraff purchased W. Howard O'Brien's Egypt Lane residence. [*The East Hampton Star* August 10, 1944, p. 1.]

In 2014 *Cherridune* was for sale. It included the 7,400-square-foot house with nine bedrooms, six full bathrooms, two half bathrooms, a guest house which was originally the chauffeur's cottage, and one acre. The asking price was $6.95 million.

de Kay, Charles (1848-1935)

Occupation(s):	journalist - art and literary critic, *The New York Times*, 1876-1894; art editor, *The New York Evening Post*, 1907; associate editor, *Art World*
	writer - numerous poems and short sketches in periodicals; *The Bohemian: A Tragedy of Modern Life*, 1878; *Hesperus and Other Poems*, 1880; *The Vision of Nimrod: An Oriental Romance*, 1881; *The Vision of Ester*, 1882; *The Love of Poems of Louis Barnaval*, 1883; *Barye: His Life and Work*, 1889; *Familiar Letters of Heinrich Heine*, 1890; translations of books by and about Alphonse Daudet, 1898; *The Art Work of Louis Comfort Tiffany*, 1914 (from material dictated to de Kay by Louis Comfort Tiffany)
	diplomat - consul-general, Berlin, Germany, 1894-1897 (Arthur and Cleveland administrations)
Civic Activism:	a founder, Authors Club, 1881; a founder, Fencer's Club, 1882; a founder, City Club, 1892; a founder and vice president, National Sculpture Society, 1892; a founder, National Arts Club, 1898; director, Artist–Artisan Institute of New York
Marriage(s):	1888-1935 – Lucy Edwalyn Coffey (1867-1949)
	- entertainers and associated professions - actress
	writer - *Adventures of a Young Wife in the Nineties*; *Coals of Fire* (a play)
Address:	Georgica Road, East Hampton
Name of estate:	*Abrigada*
Year of construction:	1907-1908
Style of architecture:	
Architect(s):	
Landscape architect(s):	
House extant:	no
Historical notes:	

The house, originally named *Abrigada*, was built by Charles de Kay.

The *Social Register Summer, 1915* lists Charles and L. Edwalyn Coffey de Kay as residing at *Abrigada* in East Hampton.

He was the son of George Coleman and Janet Halleck Drake de Kay.

Lucy Edwalyn Coffee de Kay was the daughter of Edward Lees and Lucy Edwalyn Haxall Coffee of Virginia.

Charles and Lucy Edwalyn Coffee de Kay's daughter Phyllis married Edward Basil Bury, the son of John B. Bury of Cambridge, England. She subsequently married John Hall Wheelock, the son of Dr. William Efner and Mrs. Emily Charlotte Hall Wheelock of *Wuthering* in East Hampton, and resided at *Wuthering*. Their daughter Katharine married Robert Woodhouse Barbour and resided in Manhattan. Their daughter Marion married Dr. Peyton Rous, the son of Charles Rous of Manhattan, and resided in New York City. Their son Rodman married Ann W. Craven and resided in Port Washington. Their son Ormonde married Margaret McClure and resided in East Hampton.

[See following entry for additional family information.]

de Kay, Ormonde, Sr. (1900-1980)

Occupation(s):	financier - stockbroker
Civic Activism:	director and secretary, Preservation Society of the East End
Marriage(s):	Margaret McClure (1900-1974) - Civic Activism: vice-chair, Hobby Show for Older Persons; co-chair, Children's Health Service
Address:	Jones Road, East Hampton
Name of estate:	
Year of construction:	1958
Style of architecture:	
Architect(s):	
Landscape architect(s):	
House extant: unconfirmed	
Historical notes:	

The house was built by Ormonde de Kay, Sr. [*The East Hampton Star* June 19, 1958, p. 1.]

The Blue Book of The Hamptons, 1973 lists Ormonde and Margaret McClure de Kay as residing on Jones Road, East Hampton.

He was the son of Charles and Lucy Edwalyn Coffey de Kay of *Abrigada* in East Hampton.

Margaret McClure de Kay was the daughter of John Franklin and Helen Hayes McClure.

Ormonde and Margaret McClure de Kay, Sr.'s son George married Mary Lawrence Elliman, the daughter of Douglas Ludlow Elliman of NYC, and, later, Miranda Knickerbocker, the daughter of Pulitzer prize winner Herbert R. Knickerbocker, with whom he resided at *The Hill* in Stonington, CT. Their son James married Helen Lopachyk. Their son Ormonde de Kay, Jr. married Barbara Ellen Scott, the daughter of John Lennox Scott of Seattle, WA. Barbara had previously been married to Philip James Roosevelt, Jr., the son of Philip James and Jean Schermerhorn Roosevelt Roosevelt, Sr. of *Dolonar* in Cove Neck. [*See* Spinzia, *Long Island's Prominent North Shore Families, vol. II* – Roosevelt entries.]

[See previous entry for additional family information.]

de Kooning, Willem (1904-1997)

Occupation(s):	artist - abstract expressionist educator - Black Mountain College, Ashville, NC, 1948; Yale School of Art, New Haven, CT, 1950-1951
Marriage(s):	1943-1989 – Elaine Marie Catherine Fried (1918-1989) - artist - abstract expressionist journalist - editorial associate, *Art News*
Address:	Accabonac Road, East Hampton
Name of estate:	
Year of construction:	1959
Style of architecture:	Eclectic
Architect(s):	
Landscape architect(s):	
House extant: yes	
Historical notes:	

In 1959 de Kooning purchased five acres from sculptor Wilfrid Zogbaum and built his combination house and studio.

Born in Rotterdam, The Netherlands, Willem was the son of Leendert and Cornelia Nobel de Kooning.

Elaine Marie Catherine Fried de Kooning was the daughter of Charles Frank and Mary Ellen O'Brien Fried of the Sheepshead Bay section of Brooklyn, NY.

Willem's illegitimate daughter Johanna (aka Lisa) married Christian Villeneuve and resided on Woodbine Drive in the Springs section of East Hampton.

Willem and Elaine de Kooning did not have children.

De Koven, Louis Besant Wadsworth (1881-1938)

Occupation(s): financier - member, Knickerbocker Trust Co.;
member, J. W. Davis (stock brokerage firm)

Marriage(s): 1917-1938 – Amy Hawxhurst Mills (1872-1947)

Address: Woods Lane, East Hampton
Name of estate: *Bruton Braes*
Year of construction:
Style of architecture:
Architect(s):
Landscape architect(s):
House extant: no*
Historical notes:

The *Social Directory of Southampton, Long Island, 1931* lists Louis B. and Amy H. Hill De Koven as residing at *Bruton Braes* on Woods Lane, East Hampton.
He was the son of Le Roy and Alice Bennett De Koven.
Bruton Braes was demolished in 1943. [*The East Hampton Star* November 25, 1943, p. 5.]

de Liagre, Alfred, Jr. (1904-1987)
aka Alfred Gustav Etienne de Liagre, Jr.

Occupation(s): entertainers and associated professions -
Broadway actor, director, and producer

Marriage(s): Mary Rogers (1913-2009)
(aka Mary Howard)
- entertainers and associated professions -
Ziegfeld Follies and motion picture actress
Civic Activism: a founder, Recording for the Blind;
trustee, American Academy of Dramatic Art;
trustee, Princess Grace Foundation

Address: 42 Highway Behind the Pond, East Hampton
Name of estate: *Swan Cove*
Year of construction: c. 1903
Style of architecture: Modified Colonial Revival
Architect(s):
Landscape architect(s):
House extant: no; demolished*
Historical notes:

Gerald Clery Murphy and, his wife, Sara Sherman Wiborg Murphy remodeled the dairy barn of Sara's parents' estate *The Dunes* into their residence which they called *Swan Cove*. In 1959 the noted actor Robert Montgomery purchased the house. In 1973 it was purchased from Montgomery by de Liagre. [*The East Hampton Star* March 1, 1973, p. 4.] Both Montgomery and de Liagre continued to call it *Swan Cove*. Because the house had a pink stucco exterior, it is sometimes referred to as *Pink House*.
The Blue Book of The Hamptons, 1973 lists Alfred and Mary Howard de Liagre, Jr. as residing on Highway Behind the Pond, East Hampton. *The Blue Book of The Hamptons* lists the address as 42 Highway Behind the Pond, East Hampton.
In 1955 the guest house was built. [*The East Hampton Star* June 16, 1955, p. 12.]
Mrs. de Liagre was residing at their residence at the time of her death.
In 2009 the 3,500-square-foot, five-bedroom house was purchased by Peter Jay Solomon for $19 million. [*The East Hampton Star* April 15, 2019, p. 5.]
*In 2010 Solomon demolished the house and built a new residence on the site. [*The East Hampton Star* December 2, 2010, p. 3.]

Della Femina, Jerry (b. 1936)
aka Gennaro Tomas Della Femina

Occupation(s):	advertising executive -
	    co-founder, with Ron Travisano; and chairman of board, Della Femina, Travisano; & Partners, NYC and Los Angeles;
	    copy editor, Daniel & Charles;
	    member, Delehanty, Kurnit, and Geller;
	    creative supervisor, Ted Bates Advertising;
	    founder, Jerry, Inc., 1992 (later, Jerry & Ketchum; then, Femina, Jerry, and Partners);
	    chairman of board, Della Femina, McNamee WCRS, Inc.
	restaurateur - owner, Della Femina, East Hampton
	publisher - co-publisher, *The Independent*, East Hampton
	writer - *From Those Wonderful Folks Who Gave You Pearl Harbor*, 1970;
	    Jerry Della Femina: An Italian Grows in Brooklyn, 1978

Marriage(s):	M/1 – Barbara *[unable to determine maiden name]*
	    - financier - assistant treasurer, Chemical Bank
	      public relations executive - public relations consultant
	M/2 – 1983 – Judith Carol Licht (b. 1946)
	    - entertainers and associated professions -
	      television anchor and reporter, WNEW, WCBS, WYNW, WABC, WNYE
	    journalist - fashion columnist:
	      The Huffington Post;
	      Details, NY;
	      The Daily News

Address:	20 Drew Lane, East Hampton
Name of estate:	
Year of construction:	
Style of architecture:	Contemporary with French Country Elements
Architect(s):	
Landscape architect(s)	
House extant: yes	
Historical notes:	

   In 1987 Jerry Della Femina purchased the house, which had been uninhabited for many years and in need of refurbishing, from Leonard Stern for $3.4 million. Della Femina spent an additional $6 million on remodeling the house.
   He is the son of Michael Della Femina of Brooklyn, NY.
   Jerry and Barbara Della Femina's daughter Donna married Adam Jay Hart, the son of Allen M. Hart of Valley Stream. Their son Michael married Jeanne Fulleton, the daughter of John and Jean Fulleton. Their daughter Jodi married John Kim.
   Judith Carol Licht Della Femina is the daughter of Bernard and Eleanor Licht of Brooklyn. She had previously been married to Eugene V. Wolsk, the son of Isidore Wolsk of Baldwin Harbor, NY.
   In 2012 Della Femina sold the house to David Zaslav for $24.5 million.

de Menil, Francois (b. 1945)
aka Francois Conrad Thomas de Menil

Occupation(s):	architect		
	entertainers and associated professions -		
	motion picture director:	"Evening of Light", 1969;	
		"Crush Proof", 1972;	
		"North Star: Mark di Suvero", 1978;	
		"Max Ernst Hanging", 2009;	
	actor -	"Homeo", 1967;	
		"Crush Proof", 1972	
	capitalist -	motion picture producer:-	"Evening of Light", 1969;
			"Gixmo!", 1977;
			"Stir Crazy", 1980
		play producer:	"Beyond Therapy";
			"The Wake of Jamey Foster"

Civic Activism: trustee, Cooper Union, NYC;
trustee and founding benefactor, Menil Foundation

Marriage(s): 1985 – Susan Kadin Silver (b. 1958)
- entertainers and association professions - designer
  writer - co-editor, *Angels and Franciscans*;
  co-editor, *Innovative Architecture from Los Angeles and San Francisco and Sanctuary*;
  The Spirit In/Of Architecture
  Civic Activism: director and president, Byzantine Fresco Foundation;
  trustee, Allen–Stevenson School, NY;
  member, President's Counsel of Cooper Union, NYC;
  trustee, Smithsonian National Design Museum, Cooper Hewitt, NYC;
  member, Committee on Architecture and Design, Museum of Modern Art, NYC;
  a founder, National Council, American Film Institute;
  founding benefactor, Menil Foundation

Address: 428 Further Lane, Amagansett
Name of estate: *Toad Hall*
Year of construction: 1982
Style of architecture: International
Architect(s): Charles Gwathmey designed
  the house (for de Menil)
  Charles Gwathmey, 1990
  alterations (for Bronfman)
Landscape architect(s)
House extant: yes*
Historical notes:

  The 11,000-square-foot house, originally named *Toad Hall*, was built by Francois de Menil.
  He is the son of Baron Jean Marie Joseph Menu and Dominique Isaline Zelia Henrietta Clarisse Schlumberger de Menil of Houston, TX. Francois' sister Adelaide married the noted anthropologist Edmund Snow Carpenter and resided in East Hampton.
  Susan Kadin Silver de Menil is the daughter of Robert J. and Sandra Kadin Silver of NYC.
  In 1988 de Menil sold the house to Lawrence Gilbert Gagosian.
  In 1990 it was purchased by Edgar Miles Bronfman, Jr.
  *In 2011 there was a serious fire in the main residence. In 2014 there was a fire in the guest house.

De Niro, Robert, Jr. (b. 1943)

Occupation(s):	entertainers and associated professions -
	director;
	motion picture and television actor*
	capitalist - co-founder, TriBeCa Productions (film studio);
	owner, Greenwich Hotel, NYC
	restaurateur - co-owner with Stewart Lane, TriBeCa Grill, NYC;
	owner, *Locanda Verde* restaurant in Greenwich Hotel, NYC
Civic Activism:	donated his film archives to Harry Ransom Center, University of Texas, Austin, TX, 1987;
	co-founder, Tribecca Film Festival, NYC;
	president of jury, Fifteenth Moscow Film Festival, 1987;
	president of jury, Sixth Cannes Film Festival, 2011
Marriage(s):	M/1 – 1976-div.-1988 – Diahnne Eugenia Abbott (b. 1945)
	(aka Diahnne Dea)
	- entertainers and associated professions -
	singer;
	motion picture actress
	M/2 – 1997 – Grace Hightower (b. 1955)
	- entertainers and associated professions -
	singer;
	motion picture actress
	Civic Activism: trustee, New York Women's Foundation;
	trustee, New York Fund for Public Schools;
	founder, Grace Hightower and Coffees of Rwanda, 2013 (project to improve Rwandan livelihoods by marketing their products)
Address:	242 Old Montauk Highway, Montauk
Name of estate:	
Year of construction:	
Style of architecture:	
Architect(s):	
Landscape architect(s)	
House extant: yes*	
Historical notes:	

    Robert De Niro is the son of Robert and Virginia Admiral De Niro, Sr. of NYC.
    Robert and Diahnne Eugenia Abbott De Niro, Jr.'s son Raphael married Claudine De Matos of East Hampton.
    Robert and Grace Hightower De Niro, Jr.'s son Elliot was born in 1998. Their daughter Helen was born in 2011 via a surrogate.
    *De Niro received the Best Supporting Actor Award for his performance in "The Godfather." He was nominated for Best Actor for "Taxi" and nominated for Best Supporting Actor for his performance in "Silver Linings Playbook."

De Palma, Brian Russell (b. 1940)

Occupation(s):	entertainers and associated professions - motion picture director
	writer - screenwriter
Marriage(s):	M/1 – 1979-div. 1983 – Nancy Allen (b. 1950)
	- entertainers and associated professions - television and motion picture actress
	Civic Activism: executive director, weSPARK Cancer Support Center
	M/2 – 1991-div.1993 – Gale Anne Hurd (b. 1955)
	- entertainers and associated professions - founder, Pacific Western Productions (produces motion pictures)
	writer - screenwriter
	Civic Activism: recording secretary, Producers Guild of America; governor, Academy of Motion Picture Arts and Sciences
	M/3 – 1995-div. 1997 – Darnell Gregorio (aka Darnell Gregorio–De Palma)
	- entertainers and associated professions - actress
	restaurateur - partner, with her husband Edoardo Baldi, Tuscan Restaurant, Beverly Hills, CA
Address:	82 Pantigo Road, East Hampton
Name of estate:	
Year of construction:	1999
Style of architecture:	Contemporary
Architect(s):	
Landscape architect(s)	
House extant: yes	
Historical notes:	

   In 2013 DePalma purchased the 3,5000-square-foot house for $2.95 million.
   He is the son of Dr. Anthony Frederico and Mrs. Vivienne Muti De Palma.
   Nancy Allen De Palma is the daughter of Eugene and Florence Allen of Yonkers, NY. Nancy later married Craig Shoemaker and, subsequently, Randy Bailey.
   Gale Ann Hurd is the daughter of Frank E. and Lolita Espiau Hurd of Palm Springs, CA. Gale had previously been married to James Cameron. After her divorce from De Palma, she married Jonathan Hensleigh.
   Brian Russell and Gale Anne Hurd De Palma's daughter Lolita was born in 1991.
   Darnell Gregorio De Palma had previously been married to Keith Holland. After her divorce from De Palma, she married Edoardo Baldi.
   Brian Russell and Darnell Gregorio De Palma's daughter Piper was born in 1996.
   In 2006 the house sold for $3.2 million.

de Rose, Edward (1836-1916)

Occupation(s):	capitalist - director, Continental Construction Co.
Civic Activism:	a founder and director, Maidstone Club, East Hampton
Marriage(s):	M/1 – 1870-1886 – Julia Mathilda Varnum (1840-1886)
	M/2 – 1901-1916 – Susan Graham Varnum (1864-1943)
Address:	117 Main Street, East Hampton
Name of estate:	*Millfield*
Year of construction:	c. 1799
Style of architecture:	Georgian*
Architect(s):	Isaac Henry Green II designed 1889 alterations**
	Joseph Greenleaf Thorp designed 1905 interior and exterior alterations
Landscape architect(s):	Mary Lois Deputy Lamson (for Douglas)

House extant: yes
Historical notes:

*The house was built by Jeremiah Miller IV. It was later owned by Edward de Rose who remodeled it, changing the architecture from Georgian to Colonial Revival, and named it *Millfield*. In c. 1885 de Rose also built a guest cottage on the property in an eclectic windmill style.

By 1910 the de Roses had relocated to Southampton. The *Social Register Summer, 1910* lists Edward and Susan G. Varnum de Rose as residing at *Westover* in Southampton. [*See* Spinzia, *Long Island's Prominent Families in the Town of Southampton* – de Rose entry.]

She was the daughter of James Mitchell and Helen Taylor Varnum. James was included in Ward McAllister's list of society's elite "400."

In 1930 Edward and Susan Graham Varnum de Rose's daughter Rose attempted suicide by stabbing herself six times while visiting Havana, Cuba. [*The New York Times* March 11, 1930, p. 18.]

In 1910 the Colonial Revival-style house was owned by Thomas Lincoln Manson III and, then, by his daughter Dorothea and son-in-law Kiliaen Van Rensselaer. Both Manson and Van Rensselaer continued to call the estate *Millfield*.

In 1945 the Colonial Revival-styled house which is on the National Register of Historic Places, was owned by Graham Douglas. By 1950 it was owned by Franklin M. Chace who called it *Gone With the Wind*. By 1973 the house was owned by Richard Vincent Hare.

**For Green's other commissions, *see* Spinzia, *Long Island's Prominent South Shore Families: Their Estates and Their Country Homes in the Towns of Babylon and Islip.*

Deutsch, Donny (b. 1957)
aka Donald Jay Deutsch

Occupation(s):	advertising executive - partner and, later, president, David Deutsch Associates (later, Deutsch Inc.); chairman of board and president, Deutsch Inc.
	entertainers and associated professions - television guest and host of Saturday Night Politics on MSNBC; managing partner, Deutsch Open City (independent motion picture production firm)
	writer - co-author, with Peter Knobler, *After Wrong, Never in Doubt*, 2005
Civic Activism:	member, executive committee, University of Pennsylvania School of Social Policy and Practice, Philadelphia, PA; director, Michael J. Fox Parkinson's Foundation
Marriage(s):	2000-div. 2005 – Stacy Josloff
Address:	12 and 14 Tyson Lane, East Hampton
Name of estate:	
Year of construction:	
Style of architecture:	
Architect(s):	
Landscape architect(s)	

House extant: yes
Historical notes:

Donny Deutsch purchased the house in 2007 from ____ Tyson for $29 million.

Born in Hollis Hills, NY, he is the son of David Deutsch.

In 2010 Donny sold the house to Howard Stanley Marks for $30 million.

De Vecchi, Robert Paolo (1930-2015)

Occupation(s):
Civic Activism: European director, The Conference Board;
director, Inner Cities Program;
New York representative, Save the Children Foundation;
president and CEO, International Rescue Committee;
executive director, National Industrial Conference Board, NY (private refugee assistance organization)

Marriage(s): M/1 – 1957-div. – Florence Lincoln Sloan
M/2 – 1983-2009 – Elizabeth Stettinius Trippe (1932-2009)
- Civic Activism: president, Project Orbis (converted a jetliner and equipping it for eye surgery and ophthalmology);
trustee, New York Association for the Blind;
trustee, Institute of Visual Science;
trustee, National Home Care Council;
trustee, Eugene O'Neill Theater Center;
trustee, Outward Bound;
trustee, Ackerman Institute

Address: 39 Dunemere Lane, East Hampton
Name of estate:
Year of construction:
Style of architecture:
Architect(s):
Landscape architect(s):
House extant: yes
Historical notes:

The house is the former carriage house of Elizabeth's grandparents Charles White Trippe, Sr.

Robert Paolo De Vecchi is the son of Robert and Margaret Shaw De Vecchi of *Tebola Farm* in Washington Crossing, PA.

Florence Lincoln Sloan De Vecchi is the daughter of George Arthur and Florence Lincoln Sloan who resided at *Woodwinds* on Vineyard Lane, Greenwich, CT.

Robert Paolo and Florence Lincoln Sloan De Vecchi's daughter Margaret married Peter Johnstone Smith, the son of Albert Oliver Smith of Milton, MA. Their daughter Angela married Paul Smyke.

The *Social Register Summer, 2001* lists Robert P. and Betsy S. Trippe De Vecchi as residing at 39 Dunemere Lane, East Hampton. She was the daughter of Juan Terry and Elizabeth Stettinius Trippe of East Hampton and had previously been married to William H. Duke; William Angus Douglass; and Stuyvesant Wainwright II of *Green Oaks* in Wainscott.

In 2017 the 4,000-square-foot, six-bedroom, five-and-a-half-bath house sold for $3.95 million.

Devendorf, Alfred Ervin (b. 1935)

Occupation(s):	attorney - partner, Pacifico, DiGregorio, and Pacifico, Mineola; assistant district attorney, Nassau County, 1973-1976; counsel, Nassau County Commissioner of Health, 1976-1980
	politician - executive assistant, Nassau County Commissioner of Health
	capitalist - coordinator, sales promotions, Long Island Lighting Co., 1966-1968
Civic Activism:	president, board of trustees, Children's House, Inc., Mineola; director, Long Island Council on Alcoholism and Drug Dependence; president, North Shore Interfaith Nutrition Network, Glen Cove, 1995-1996; president, Locust Valley Republican Club, 1980
Marriage(s):	1965 – Barbara Jean Lancaster (aka Bonnie Devendorf) - real estate agent - sales manager and vice president, Daniel Gale Sotheby's International Realty, Locust Valley
Address:	15 Conklin Terrace, East Hampton
Name of estate:	*El Paraiso*
Year of construction:	2003
Style of architecture:	Contemporary Long Island Farm House
Architect(s):	
Landscape architect(s):	
House extant: yes	
Historical notes:	

In 2004 the house was purchased by Devendorf.

The Blue Book of The Hamptons, 2008 lists Alfred E. and Bonnie Lancaster Devendorf as residing at *El Paraiso*, 15 Conklin Terrace, East Hampton.

He is the son of George Epworth and Adelina Spinetti Devendorf of Lake Success and Amagansett. [*See* Spinzia, *Long Island's North Shore Prominent, vol. I* – G. E. Devendorf entry.]

Barbara Jean Lancaster Devendorf is the daughter of John Howard and Phyllis Elaine Metcalf Lancaster of Bellport.

The Devendorfs' daughter Diana married John Clayton Rice, the son of Anton and Carol Rice of Stamford, CT. Their son George Epworth Devendorf II married Susan Romanski.

[For information on the Devendorfs' Matinecock residence, *see* Spinzia, *Long Island's North Shore Prominent, vol. I* – A. E. Devendorf entry.]

[See following entry for additional family information.]

Devendorf, George Epworth (1891-1984)

Occupation(s):	financier - vice-president and manager of investment division, Stone and Webster Corp., 1935-1945 (investment banking firm); vice-president and manager of investment division, American Founders Corp. (investment banking firm); president, American Investment Corp. (investment banking firm)
	capitalist - chairman, Patchogue Electric Light Co. (which was absorbed into Long Island Lighting Co. in 1963), 1945-1963; chairman of board, Consolidated Electric & Gas Co.
Marriage(s):	Adelina Spinetti (d. 1987)
Address:	Cross Highway, Amagansett
Name of estate:	*El Paraiso*
Year of construction:	1910
Style of architecture:	Mediterranean Villa
Architect(s):	Tietig and Lee designed the house (for R. Levering, Sr.)
Landscape architect(s):	
House extant:	
Historical notes:	

The house, originally named *Devon*, was built by Richmond Levering, Sr. In 1920 it was purchased by M. Materson. [*The East Hampton Star* October 22, 1920, p. 6.] In 1930 it was purchased by John Louis Kuser, Jr. from Ardis J. Reynolds. [*The East Hampton Star* October 3, 1930, p. 1.] In c. 1946 the house was purchased by Devendorf who called it *El Paraiso*. [*The East Hampton Star* July 18, 1946, p. 2.]

The Blue Book of The Hamptons, 1958 lists George E. and Adelina Spinetti as residing at *El Paraiso* in the Devon Colony section of Amagansett.

He was the son of Luther A. and Anna Jane McCall Devendorf.

The Devendorfs' son Donald married Jacqueline Gertz Byrne, the daughter of John P. Bryne of Upper Montclair, NJ. Their daughter Corina married Charles John Vernilye of Brooklyn. Their son Andres, who was the proprietor of the Maidstone Arms in East Hampton, was a bachelor. Their son John married Carol Fennelly, the daughter of Leo C. Fennelly of East Hampton. Their son Alfred married Barbara Jean Lancaster, the daughter of John H. Lancaster of Bellport, and resided in East Hampton and Matinecock.

By 1966 the Devendorfs had relocated to East Hampton.

[For information on the Devendorfs' Lake Success residence, *see* Spinzia, *Long Island's North Shore Prominent, vol. I* – Devendorf entry.]

[See previous entry for additional family information.]

It was later owned by Henry Houston Chatfield who called it *Devon*.

Devereaux, Jack (1881-1958)

Occupation(s):	entertainers and associated professions - director and actor - appeared in: *The Sentimental Lady*, 1915; *Grafters*, 1917; *The Jinx Jumper*, 1917; *American – That's All*, 1917; *The Man Whom Made Good*, 1917; *Her Father's Keeper,* 1917; *A Successful Failure*, 1917; *Romeo's Dad*, 1919; *Superstition*, 1922
	capitalist - a founder, Devsilck, Inc. (produced plays)
Marriage(s):	1917-1954 – Louise Drew (1882-1954)
	- entertainers and associated professions - actress
	Civic Activism: president, Twelfth Night Club
Address:	Drew Lane, East Hampton
Name of estate:	
Year of construction:	
Style of architecture:	
Architect(s):	
Landscape architect(s):	
House extant: unconfirmed	
Historical notes:	

The house was built by Jack Devereaux. [*The East Hampton Star* June 25, 1959, p. 9.]

The *Social Directory of Southampton, Long Island, 1931* lists Jack and Louise Drew Devereaux as residing on Drew Lane, East Hampton.

Louise Drew Devereaux was the daughter of John and Josephine Baker Drew, Jr. of East Hampton.

Jack and Louise Drew Devereaux's son John Drew Devereaux subsequently owned the house.

[See the following entry for additional family information.]

Devereaux, John Drew (1918-1995)

Occupation(s):	entertainers and associated professions - Broadway actor, director, and stage manager
Marriage(s):	M/1 – 1941-div. – Susan Fox
	M/2 – 1949-div. – Pauline Estelle Lord (b. 1920)
	- journalist - reporter, *The Republican*, Springfield, MA
	publisher - editor, Magna Publications; editor, General Service Publishing Co., NYC
	M/3 – Jane Henderson
	- entertainers and associated professions - Broadway actress
Address:	Drew Lane, East Hampton
Name of estate:	
Year of construction:	
Style of architecture:	
Architect(s):	
Landscape architect(s):	
House extant: unconfirmed	
Historical notes:	

The house was built by Jack Devereaux. [*The East Hampton Star* June 25, 1959, p. 9.] It was later owned by his son John. [*The East Hampton Star* March 9, 1972, p. 11.]

Susan Fox Deveraux was the daughter of J. Bertram Fox.

Pauline Estelle Lord Deveraux was the daughter of Dr. Maurice Edwin Lord, Sr. of Skowhegan, MA.

Jane Henderson Deveraux was the daughter of Sir Guy Wilmot McLintock Henderson.

[See the previous entry for additional family information.]

Devine, James Joseph (1889-1958)

Occupation(s):	educator - public school teacher, West Virginia
	advertising executive -
	president, Devine–Tenney Corp. (sold advertising in newspapers);
	president, J. J. Devine and Associates (sold advertising in newspapers)
	publisher - co-owner, *The Clarksburg Telegram*, Clarksburg, WV;
	owned ten daily newspapers in the East and in the West
	financier - trust officer, Empire Bank, Clarksburg, WV
Marriage(s):	1912-1958 – Mary Frances Ryan
Address:	Egypt Lane, East Hampton

Name of estate:
Year of construction:
Style of architecture:
Architect(s):
Landscape architect(s):
House extant: unconfirmed
Historical notes:

    James Joseph and Mary Frances Ryan Devine's son Charles, who resided at *The Belfry* in Marlborough, MA, married Elizabeth Atwood Wyckoff, the daughter of Herbert Ashton Wyckoff of Green Farms, CT; Louise Culver Williams, the daughter of Rodney W. Williams; and, later, Cynthia Smathers Healey, the daughter of Justin O'Brien and Virginia Smathers Healey of East Hampton. Their daughter Katherine married Neil Anderson McConnell of East Hampton, the son of David Hall and Marjorie Anderson McConnell. Katherine subsequently married the noted actor Sterling Hayden. Their son Joseph married Margaret Dowdney and, later, Nina Cave, the daughter of Dr. Henry W. Cave. Their daughter Betty married George Byron Smith II of New York. Their son James married Eleanor Virginia Edwards, the daughter of Ernway Edwards of Evanston, IL.

    Mary's sister Anne married John Howie Wright, Sr. and resided in East Hampton.

    In 1947 the house was purchased by Dr. Mario Scandiffio. [*The East Hampton Star* August 28, 1947, p.1.]

DeVoe, Raymond Forsyth, Sr. (1894-1977)

Occupation(s):	financier - a founder and partner, DeVoe, Dyke, and Sperry (stock brokerage firm);
	vice-president and director, Harriman, Ripley, and Co. (investment banking firm)
	industrialist - partner, Robert Gair Co. (paper manufacturing firm) (merged into Continental Can Co.);
	vice-president and director, Continental Can Co.
	capitalist - a founder, Central Telephone Company of Florida
Marriage(s):	M/1 – 1928-1968 – Madeline Fagan (1895-1968)
	M/2 – Dorothy I. Williams
Address:	97 Egypt Lane, East Hampton

Name of estate:
Year of construction:
Style of architecture:
Architect(s):
Landscape architect(s):
House extant: unconfirmed
Historical notes:

    The Blue Book of The Hamptons, 1958 lists Mr. and Mrs. Raymond DeVoe [Sr.] as residing at 97 Egypt Lane, East Hampton.

    He was the son of Harkness DeVoe of NYC. Raymond represented the twelfth generation of the DeVoe family that had settled in Manhattan in 1645. DeVoe Park and DeVoe Terrace in The Bronx are named for his family.

    Madeline Fagan DeVoe was the daughter of Lawrence Fagan of NYC.

    Raymond Forsyth and Madeline Fagan DeVoe, Sr.'s daughter Jacqueline married Prince Henri de Bourbon of Paris France, and, later, Roy Sarles Durstine, Jr. of East Hampton. Their daughter Madelon married Truman MacDonald Talley and resided in Manhattan. Their son Lawrence married Natalie Smissart, the daughter of Leonard A. Smissart of New Canaan, CT. Their son Richard married Ruth McDowell, the daughter of James H. McDowell of Katonah, NY, and, later, ____ Morris. Their son Raymond Forsyth DeVoe, Jr., who coined the stock market phrase "dead cat bounce," married Anne Elizabeth Fosbroke, the daughter of Hughell E. W. Fosbroke.

    Dorothy I. Williams DeVoe had previously been married to ____ Dwyer.

DeVries, Mary Lange (1890-1962)
aka Mary MacKinnon

Occupation(s):	artist - creator of the Lux girl image; illustrator for *Vogue*, *Harper's Bazaar*, and Sears & Roebuck catalog
	educator - founder of The East Hampton Summer School of Applied Art
Civic Activism:	a founder, Society of Four Arts Museum and Library, Palm Beach, FL
Marriage(s):	M/1 – Archibald Angus MacKinnon (1891-1918)
	- artist - illustrator and etcher
	M/2 – div. 1928 – John T. DeVries
	- artist
	M/3 – 1930-1958 – Frederick Johnson, Sr. (1873-1958)
	- capitalist - real estate
	Civic Activism: a founder and president, Bath and Tennis Club, Palm Beach, FL;
	a founder and vice-president, Everglades Club;
	a founder, Seminole Club
Address:	34 Hither Lane, East Hampton
Name of estate:	
Year of construction:	
Style of architecture:	Colonial Revival
Landscape architect(s)	
House extant: yes	
Historical notes:	

  In 1925 Mary Lange DeVries purchased the house and ten acres from Thomas Robinson. [*The East Hampton Star* December 11, 1925, p. 7.]
  She was the daughter of Louis and Agnes Lange of Manhattan.
  Archibald Angus MacKinnon was the son of Malcolm MacKinnon of East Orange, NJ.
  At the time of her divorce from DeVries, Mary owned six houses, two of which were on Long Island. In addition to her East Hampton house, she owned a house in Old Westbury. Her substantial income was derived from her work as an illustrator and society portrait painter.
  In 1930 the house was purchased by Chester Marts Cloud. [*The East Hampton Star* March 7, 1930, p. 5.]
  In 1946 it was purchased from Cloud by Irwin Hewlett Cornell. [*The East Hampton Star* October 3, 1946, p. 5.]
  In 1963 the house was purchased by Charles Francis Preusse. [*The East Hampton Star* May 16, 1963, p. 4.]

Dewey, Charles Schuveldt, Jr. (1908-1974)

Occupation(s):	financier - financial advisor
	statesmen - secretary to his father who was Assistant Secretary of Treasury, 1924-1927
	intelligence agent - member of OSS during World War II
Civic Activism:	president of board, Guild Hall Center for the Visual and Performing Arts, East Hampton
Marriage(s):	M/1 – div. 1955 – Marjorie Sawyer Goodman (1914-2009)
	- interior decorator - Dan Cooper, NYC
	capitalist - operated Mt. Gabriel in the Laurentians (ski lodge); owner, High Time Farm, Bedminster, NJ (grain and pedigree cattle farm)
	Civic Activism: a founder, Les Jeunes de'L'Alliane Francaise; trustee, Junior Council; trustee, International Council; member, Committee for the Research Library, New York Public Library, NYC; member of committee, Women's Council, New York Public Library, NYC; founder, Committee for Dance Collection, New York Public Library, NYC; chairman of board, Guild Hall, East Hampton, 1966
	M/2 – 1955-1974 – Catherine Harriet Kresge (1908-1990)
	- Civic Activism: chair, drama committee, Guild Hall, East Hampton, 1964; chair, art committee, Guild Hall, East Hampton, 1965

Address:	West End Avenue, East Hampton
Name of estate:	
Year of construction:	1927
Style of architecture:	Shingle
Architect(s):	
Landscape architect(s):	

House extant: unconfirmed
Nassau County Museum Collection has photographs of the estate.
Historical notes:

  The house, originally named *Bayberry*, was built by John Nelson Cole, Jr. In c. 1952 it was purchased by George Adam Rentschler, Jr., who called it *Summertime*. [*The East Hampton Star* January 3, 1952, p. 1.] In 1960 Dewey purchased the house. [*The East Hampton Star* April 28 1960, p. 11.]
  He was the son of Charles Schuveldt and Suzette de Marigny Hall Dewey, Sr. of Illinois.
  Marjorie Sawyer Goodman Dewey was the daughter of Kenneth Sawyer and Marjorie Robbins Goodman. She subsequently married Robert D. Graff.
  Charles Schuveldt and Marjorie Sawyer Goodman Dewey, Jr.'s daughter Ariane married José Espiritu Aruego, the son of José M. Aruego of Manila, The Philippines. Their son Kenneth, who was a bachelor, died in 1972 at the age of thirty-eight when the plane he was piloting crashed in a wooded area near Orange, NJ.
  The Blue Book of The Hamptons, 1973 lists Charles S. and Catherine Kresge Dewey [Jr.] as residing on West End Road [Avenue], East Hampton.
  She was the daughter of Sebastian Spering Kresge, the founder of the Kresge Department Store chain, and his wife Anna Emma Harvey Kresge. Catherine had previously been married to Baron Carl Carlson Wijki of Sweden and Charles B. G. Murphy, the son of Fred Towlsey Murphy of Detroit, MI.

Dickerman, William Carter, Sr. (1874-1946)

Occupation(s):	industrialist - partner with his father, Milton Car Works, Milton, PA (railroad car manufacturing firm);
	vice-president, American Car & Foundry Co.;
	president and chairman of board, American Locomotive Co., 1929-1940;
	director, Milton Manufacturing Co.;
	chairman of board, Alco Products, Inc.;
	director, Montréal Locomotive Works, Ltd.;
	director, General Steel Casting Corp.;
	director, Carter Carburetor Co.;
	director, Super Heater Co.;
	director, American Car & Foundry Motors Co.;
	director, Flannery Bolt Co.;
	director, Shippers Car Line Corp.
	capitalist - director, United Gas Improvement Co.;
	director, American Car & Foundry Export Co.;
	director, American–Canadian Properties Corp.
	writer - railroad related articles in journals
	financier - director, American Car & Foundry Securities Co.;
	director, First Milton National Bank, Milton, PA
Civic Activism:	director, American Arbitration Association;
	director, United States Chamber of Commerce;
	member, advisory council, United States Department of Commerce (FDR administration);
	trustee, Lehigh University, Bethlehem, PA;
	president, Brackett Lectures, Princeton University, Princeton, NJ;
	trustee, Southampton Hospital;
	governor, Riding Club of East Hampton;
	member, advisory board, East Hampton Free Library
Marriage(s):	1905-1947 – Alice Carter (1868-1959)
	- Civic Activism: founder, Training School for Kindergarten Teachers, 1904 (later, Illman–Garter Unit for Kindergarten–Primary Teachers), University of Pennsylvania, Philadelphia, PA;
	president, New York Kindergarten Association;
	founder, music department, Bryn Mawr College, Bryn Mawr, PA;
	donated the area known as the Old Sheep Pound to the Village of East Hampton for use as a park;
	established the Charles H. Dickerman Memorial Trophy, Maidstone Club, East Hampton
Address:	Lee Avenue, East Hampton
Name of estate:	*Dune Dee*
Year of construction:	1901
Style of architecture:	Colonial Revival
Architect(s):	George Keister designed the house (for G. L. McAlpin, Sr.)
	John Custis Lawrence, alterations
Landscape architect(s):	
Builder:	Asa Otis Jones, house
	Frank Grimshaw, 82-foot-long stable, 1901

House extant: no; demolished in 1950
Historical notes:

The 60- x 104-foot, four-floor, fifty-foot-high house, originally named *Dune Alpin*, was built by George Lodowich McAlpin, Sr. [*The East Hampton Star* November 2, 1900, p. 5; November 23, 1900, p. 5; November 30, 1900, p. 5; January 4, 1901, p. 5; and April 19, 1901, p. 5.] In 1929 it was purchased by Dickerman who renamed it *Dune Dee*. [*The East Hampton Star* March 29, 1929, p. 1.]

Dickerman, William Carter, Sr. (cont'd)

The *Social Directory of Southampton, Long Island, 1931* lists William Carter and Alice Carter Dickerman [Sr.] as residing at *Dune Dee* in East Hampton.
He was the son of Charles Heber and Joy Ivy Carter Dickerman of Milton, PA.
Alice Carter Dickerman was the daughter of William Thornton Carter of Philadelphia, PA.
William Carter and Alice Carter Dickerman, Sr.'s daughter Joy married Orson Luer St. John and, later, Jessie F. Sammis, Jr. Their daughter Honour married James Oliver Brown and resided in New York. Their daughter Cornelia married Ernest Lee Jahnchke, Jr. and resided in Greenwich, CT. Their twenty-seven-year-old bachelor son Charles, who had suffered from a valvular heart ailment since childhood, died of a heart attack. [*The New York* Times January 12, 1937, p. 24.] Their son William Carter Dickerman, Jr. married Marion LaBau Browne and resided in Charleston, WV.
In 1949 the estate, which consisted of a twenty-one-room, twelve-bedroom, nine-bath main residence with a music room with murals of the dunes painted by Hamilton King of *Spindrift* in East Hampton, a garage with two apartments, and a children's playhouse, and 7.37 acres were listed for sale by Mrs. Dickerman. The asking price was $100,000. It was purchased by Thomas S. Nichols who sold it to Jay Holmes in 1950. Holmes demolished the house to build his new residence. [*The East Hampton Star* October 5, 1950, p. 5.]

Dodd, John Mingus, III (1896-1970)

Occupation(s): financier - member, Finch, Wilson, and Co.

Marriage(s): M/1 – Helen Price Barclay Riordan
M/2 – 1937-1970 – Florence Appleton (1898-1987)

Address: Dunemere Lane, East Hampton
Name of estate: *The Kennels*
Year of construction:
Style of architecture:
Architect(s):
Landscape architect(s):
House extant: unconfirmed
Nassau County Museum Collection has photographs of the estate.
Historical notes:

In 1929 Dodd purchased the house from Juan Terry Trippe. [*The East Hampton Star* October 11, 1929, p. 1.]
The *Social Directory of Southampton, Long Island, 1931* lists John M. and Helen P. Riordan Dodd [III] as residing on Dunemere Lane, East Hampton.
She was the daughter of James and Edith L. Price Riordan of NYC. Helen had previously been married to Wilfred Wood, the son of Frederic and Caroline Cheesman Wood, with whom she resided in East Hampton.
The *Social Register Summer, 1950* lists John M. and Florence Appleton Dodd [III] as residing at *The Kennels* in East Hampton.
She was the daughter of Robert Wilmarth Appleton of *Nid de Papillion* in East Hampton. Florence had previously been married to James Clarke Milholland with whom she resided in Hewlett Harbor. [*See* Spinzia, *Long Island's Prominent Families in the Town of Hempstead* – Milholland entry.] Her son Peter Milholland resided in East Hampton.
John Mingus and Florence Appleton Dodd, III's daughter Patricia married Ronald Goodall Frazer, the son of Alexander and Mary Goodall Nicoll Frazer of *Wilsheron* in East Hampton, and resided in East Hampton.

Dodge, Washington, Jr. (1907-1974)

Occupation(s):	journalist - financial editor, *Time* magazine, 1929-1983;
	editor, *Architectural Forum*;
	editor, *Fortune* magazine
	publisher - "Washington Dodge Letter," 1937-1957;
	director, Holt, Rinehart & Winston, Inc.
	financier - partner, Weisenberger and Co., 1941-1944 (stock brokerage
	firm);
	partner, Robert Rutter and Co., 1944-1969;
	vice-president, Clark Dodge and Co., 1969-1972;
	partner, Cady Roberts, and Co. (stock brokerage firm);
	director, A. C. Spaulding (stock brokerage firm);
	vice-president, Kidder Peabody and Co (stock brokerage firm)
	public relations executive - member, Barrett and Co., 1933-1937
Civic Activism:	editor, *Yale Literary Magazine*;
	editor, *Yale Daily News*
Marriage(s):	M/1 – 1932-div. 1939 – Helen Kent Hubbard (1904-1983)
	M/2 – 1941-1974 – Helen Manning Brown (1904-1983)
Address:	Bluff Road, Amagansett
Name of estate:	*Ironsides*
Year of construction:	
Style of architecture:	
Architect(s):	
Landscape architect(s):	
House extant: unconfirmed	
Historical notes:	

    Washington Dodge, Jr. was the son of Dr. Washington and Mrs. Ruth Vidaver Dodge, Sr. of San Francisco, CA. As a youth of five, he and his parents were aboard the *Titanic* when it struck an iceberg and sank. Fortunately, all three managed to survive the disaster.

    Helen Kent Hubbard Dodge was the daughter of E. Kent and Helen Keep Otis Hubbard of *Arawana* in Middletown, CT. She subsequently married Peter Joseph Ferrara.

    Washington and Helen Kent Hubbard Dodge, Jr.'s son Jonathan married Cynthia Warner Vodrey, the daughter of Joseph Kelley Vodrey of Canton, OH, and resided in Los Angeles, CA. Their son Kent Hubbard Dodge, Sr. married Ardys L. Hough, the daughter of David B. Hough of Akron, OH, and resided in Summit, NJ, and Camden, MA.

    The Blue Book of The Hamptons, 1973 lists Washington and Helen Manning Brown Dodge [Jr.] as residing at *Ironsides* on Bluff Road, Amagansett.

    She was the daughter of noted architect Archibald Manning and his wife Caroline Helen Parish Brown, Sr. of *The Studio* and *Four Fountains* in Southampton and a descendant of Commodore Cornelius Vanderbilt. Helen had previously been married to Herbert Dudley Hale, Sr. [*See* Spinzia, *Long Island's Prominent Families in the Town of Southampton* – Brown and Parish entries.]

    Washington and Helen Manning Brown Dodge, Jr.'s son Arthur married Mary Therese Grossman and, later, Marysea Nina Dolenka.

d'Olier, Franklin Woolman, Jr. (1911-2000)

Occupation(s):	industrialist - General Refractory Co., Philadelphia, PA
Civic Activism:	member of Devon Yacht Club Junior Committee, Amagansett
Marriage(s):	1936-1991 – Margaret Winifred Lee (1912-1991)
Address:	88 Lily Pond Lane, East Hampton
Name of estate:	
Year of construction:	1905
Style of architecture:	Neo-Italian Renaissance
Architect(s):	Albro and Lindeberg designed the house (for Cockcroft)
Landscape architect(s):	

House extant: no; destroyed by fire in 2008
Historical notes:

The house, originally named *Little Burlees*, was built by Edward Truesdell Cockcroft, Sr. In 1912 it was purchased by Tyler Morse. [*The East Hampton Star* August 16, 1912, p. 5.] The house was purchased d'Olier in 1936.

He was the son of Franklin Woolman and Helen K. d'Olier, Sr. of Morristown, NJ.

Margaret Winifred Lee d'Olier was the daughter of James Thomas and Margaret Merritt Lee of East Hampton. Margaret's sister Janet married John Vernou Bouvier II and, later, Hugh Dudley Auchincloss, Jr. She subsequently married Bingham Willing Morris with whom she resided at *Pra–Qua–Les* in Southampton. [*See* Spinzia, *Long Island's Prominent Families in the Town of Southampton* – de Rose entry.]

Franklin Woolman and Margaret Winifred Lee d'Olier, Jr.'s daughter Anne married John W. Mullen III of Dallas, TX. Their daughter Winifred married Anthony Coates Brown, the son of Phillip Wilson Tate and Aralene P. Miller Brown, Sr. of East Hampton.

In 1994 the house was purchased from d'Olier by Jonathan Everett Sandelman for $2.15 million. He was the owner of the house when it was destroyed by fire.

Donoho, Gaines Ruger (1857-1916)
aka Ruger Donoho

Occupation(s):	artist - impressionist*
Marriage(s):	1894-1916 – Emily Matilda Ackley (1862-1939)
Address:	Egypt Lane, East Hampton
Name of estate:	*Willow Bend/Under the Willows*
Year of construction:	c. 1725-1750
Style of architecture:	Colonial**
Architect(s):	
Landscape architect(s):	Gaines Ruger Donoho designed his own gardens

House extant: unconfirmed
Historical notes:

Donoho purchased the house in 1891. [John Esten. *Hampton Gardens: 350 Years* (New York: Rizzoli, 2008), p. 22.]

The *Social Register Summer, 1915* lists [Gaines] Ruger and Matilda Ackley Donoho as residing at *Willow Bend* in East Hampton. The *Social Register Summer 1921* and *1923* list the name of their residence as *Under the Willows*.

He was the son of Robert and Julia Sophia Ruger.

Matilda Ackley Donoho was the daughter of Thomas W. and Caroline Owen Ackley of Manhattan.

*Donoho was awarded several medals for his artwork.

The house was purchased in 1919 by Frederick Childe Hassam who continued to call it *Willow Bend*. In 1940 the house was purchased by Wilfred Wood of Morristown, NJ. [*The New York Times* December 8, 1940, p. 221.]

**The house was modified into Shingle style of architecture.

Donovan, Roberta Gosman (1932-2018)

Occupation(s):	restaurateur - manager, Gosman's Restaurant and Dock, Montauk (500-seat waterfront restaurant)
Civic Activism:	a founder, Music for Montauk; chair, Montauk Citizens Advisory Committee; trustee, Montauk Chamber Society; member, Town of East Hampton Planning Board
Marriage(s):	1978 – Cornelius Peter Donovan, Jr. (1927-1986) (aka Con Donovan) - publisher - chairman of board, Donovan Communications (publisher of *Girl Talk* magazine)
Address:	153 De Forest Road, Montauk
Name of estate:	
Year of construction:	1883
Style of architecture:	Beach Cottage
Architect(s):	McKim, Mead & White designed the house Francis Fleetwood, 1992 alterations (for Donovan)
Landscape architect(s):	Frederick Law Olmstead designed the site plan
Builder:	Mead & Taft
House extant: yes	
Historical notes:	

The house, which is on the National Register of Historic Places, is one of the Montauk Association's "Seven Sisters." It was owned by William Loring Andrews. The house was later owned by the estate of Dr. Cornelius Rea Agnew which deeded it to the Eye and Ear Infirmary of New York. The hospital immediately sold it to Frederick and Myra Upright. The Uprights sold the house to Miss H. Corinne Wagner who sold it to George and Emma Vogel. In 1981 the Vogels sold the house to Gosman.

She was the daughter of Robert H. and Mary Ellen Harrington Gosman of Amagansett.

Cornelius Peter Donovan, Jr. was the son of Cornelius Peter and Martha M. Donovan, Sr. of Bronxville, NY.

In 2012 Donovan sold the house for $7 million.

In 2016 the 3,800-square-foot, four-bedroom, two-and-a-half-bath house and 2.3 acres were again for sale. The asking price was $18.5 million. The annual taxes were $15,522.

Dougherty, Bertha Shults (1892-1973)

Civic Activism:	donated Native American artifacts to the Metropolitan Museum of Art, NYC
Marriage(s):	1917-div. – Russell Keresey Dougherty (1888-1944) - industrialist - Argonaut Oil
Address:	Jones Road, East Hampton
Name of estate:	*Westmeath*
Year of construction:	
Style of architecture:	
Architect(s):	
Landscape architect(s):	
House extant: unconfirmed	
Historical notes:	

The house, originally named *Westover*, was built by Mary Breck Vaill Talmage. It was later owned by her son Rockwell Dwight Talmage who sold the house to Hamilton Jackson Starke in 1936. [*Union Times* December 20, 1936, p. 21.] In 1946 Bertha purchased the house from Starke and renamed it *Westmeath*. [*The East Hampton Star* March 28, 1946, p. 6.]

The *Social Register Summer, 1951* lists Bertha Shults Dougherty as residing at *Westmeath* on Jones Road, East Hampton.

She was the daughter of John H. and Daisy Beard Shults, Jr.

Russell Keresey Dougherty was the son of Andrew and Nannette Keresey Dougherty of Brooklyn Heights, NY.

Dougherty, Frazer Lowber Welsh (b. 1922)

Occupation(s): capitalist - a founder and president, LTV (East Hampton television station);
president, East Hampton Studios;
president, Plum TV Cable Station;
president, North Fork Retrofit, Greenport (energy analyzing firm);
partner, Robert B. Gersin Associates (industrial design firm)
artist

Marriage(s): M/1 – 1943-div – Page Caroline Huidekoper (b. 1918)
- press attaché, U. S. Embassy, London, 1938-1940 (for Ambassador Joseph P. Kennedy)
journalist - *The Washington Times–Herald*, Washington, DC (political journalist)
writer - *Through the Looking Glass Darkly: A Political Fantasy*, 1963;
How to Cook Reagan's Goose, 1984
M/2 – 1963-2001 – Frances Ann Cannon (1918-2001)
- entertainers and associated professions -
co-founder, National Repertory Theater;
co-founder, Musical Theater Works, Greenwich Village, NYC
Civic Activism: chair of board, John Drew Theater, East Hampton
M/3 – 2006-2011 – Eleanor Sage (1939-2011)
- interior designer - owned interior design and architectural firm, Miami and New York
Civic Activism: a founder and president, Music Festival of the Hamptons

Address: 27 Drew Lane, East Hampton
Name of estate:
Year of construction: 1920
Style of architecture: Shingle
Architect(s): John Custis Lawrence designed the house (for F. K. Hollister)
Richard A. Cook of CookFox Associates designed 2007 alterations (for Rosenstein)
Landscape architect(s): Paula Hayes (for Rosenstein)
Builder: Edward M. Gay (for F. K. Hollister)
Bulgin & Associates, 2007 alterations (for Rosenstein)

House extant: yes
Historical notes:

The house was built by Dr. Frederick Kellogg Hollister. In 1939 Mrs. Hollister sold it to Jesse William Sweetser, Sr. [*The East Hampton Star* June 22, 1939, pp. 1 and 5.] In 1941 Alexander Fraser purchased the house from Sweetser who called it *Wilsheron*. [*The East Hampton Star* October 23, 1941, p. 5.] In 1960 Frances Ann Cannon (Hersey) Dougherty purchased it from Fraser. [*The East Hampton Star* April 28, 1960, p. 11.]

Frazer Lowber Welsh Dougherty was the son of Graham and Maria Frazer Dougherty, Sr. of *Woodley* in Berryville, VA.

Page Caroline Huidekoper Dougherty is the daughter of Prescott Foster and Ann Adelaide Nelson Huidekoper, Sr. Page subsequently married Adlai Stevenson's speech writer Thomas W. Wilson, Jr.

Frazer Lowber Welsh and Caroline Huidekoper Dougherty's son Rush resided in Sagaponack. Their daughter Ariel is a feminist film maker. Their son Frazer Page Dougherty resides in East Marion.

Frances Ann Cannon Dougherty was the daughter of Martin L. Cannon of Charlotte, NC, and an heir to the Cannon towel fortune. She had previously been married to Pulitzer Prize author John Hersey.

Eleanor Sage Dougherty was the daughter of Dr. John E. and Mrs. Riva Moiseivitch Sage. Eleanor had previously been married to ____ Howard.

In 2005 Mrs. Dougherty's husband sold the house to Barry Rosenstein for $19.2 million. [*The East Hampton Star* June 23, 2005, p. 35.]

In 2017 Rosenstein listed the house for sale. The asking price was $70 million.

In 2019 the 10,425-square-foot, nine-bedroom, thirteen-bath house, a separate two-bedroom caretakers/guest cottage, and 1.567 acres was again for sale. The asking price was $52.5 million.

Douglas, Graham

Occupation(s):

Marriage(s):

Address: 117 Main Street, East Hampton
Name of estate:
Year of construction: c. 1799
Style of architecture: Georgian
Architect(s): Isaac Henry Green II designed
    1889 alterations*
Joseph Greenleaf Thorp designed 1905
    interior and exterior alterations
Landscape architect(s): Mary Lois Deputy Lamson (for Douglas)
House extant: yes
Historical notes:

    The house, which is on the National Register of Historic Places, was built by Jeremiah Miller IV. It was later owned by Edward de Rose who remodeled it, changing the architecture from Georgian to Colonial Revival, and named it *Millfield*. In c. 1885 de Rose also built a guest cottage on the property in an eclectic windmill style.

    In 1910 the Colonial Revival-style house was owned by Thomas Lincoln Manson III and then by his daughter Dorothea and son-in-law Kilian Van Rensselaer. Both Manson and Van Rensselaer continued to call the estate *Millfield*.

    In 1945 the house was owned by Graham Douglas.

    By 1950 it was owned by Franklin M. Chace who called it *Gone With the Wind*. By 1973 the house was owned by Richard Vincent Hare.

    *For Green's other commissions, *see* Spinzia, *Long Island's Prominent South Shore Families: Their Estates and Their Country Homes in the Towns of Babylon and Islip.*

Douglas, Robert Graham Dunn (d. 1967)
aka Robert Graham Dunn Douglass

Occupation(s):

Marriage(s):

Address: 181 Main Street, East Hampton
Name of estate:
Year of construction:
Style of architecture: Elizabethan
Architect(s): Joseph Greenleaf Thorp, 1910
    alterations (for Poor)
Eric Woodward, 1996 alterations
    (for Reiswig)
Landscape architect(s):
House extant: yes
Historical notes:

    In 1899 Poor purchased the former Daniel Howe/Thomas Baker residence. [*The East Hampton Star* June 2, 2005, p. 44.] In 1943 the house was purchased by Douglas. [*The East Hampton Star* July 1, 1943, p. 1.]

    He was the son of Robert Dunn Douglass of Llewellyn Park, NJ, and *Camp Blythmere* in Saranac Lake, NY.

    His daughter Diana married Frank Quarles Barstow, the son of William A. Barstow of Manhattan.

    In 1959 Harry Wilfred Watts purchased the house from Douglas. [*The East Hampton Star* April 16, 1959, p. 1.] In 1973 Mrs. Watts donated it to the Southampton Hospital. [*The East Hampton Star* May 25, 1973, p. 20.]

    In 1996 the house was purchased by Gary D. and Rita Reiswig who remodeled it into The Baker House 1650, a bed and breakfast inn. In 2004 the Reiswigs listed it for sale. The asking price was $3.95 million.

    It was purchased by Robert and Antonella Rosen.

Dowdney, Louis Purcell (1884-1946)

Occupation(s):	capitalist - president and director, General Realty and Utilities Co.; partner, Dowdney & Richard (real estate firm)
Civic Activism:	member, Real Estate Board of New York
Marriage(s):	1916-1946 – Margaret Genevieve Emerson (1895-1984)
Address:	14 Huntting Lane, East Hampton
Name of estate:	
Year of construction:	1899
Style of architecture:	Shingle
Architect(s):	
Landscape architect(s):	
House extant: yes	
Historical notes:	

The Blue Book of The Hamptons, 1958 lists Mrs. Louis Dowdney as residing at 14 Huntting Street [Lane], East Hampton.

She was the daughter of Samuel D. Ingham and Juliet Strohm Emerson, Sr. of Pittsburgh, PA.

Louis Purcell Dowdney was the son of Abram and Lilian Purcell Dowdney of Manhattan and the grandson of Samuel D. Ingham, who served as Secretary of the Treasury during the Andrew Jackson administration. Suffering from severe arthritis and under the care of a private nurse, Louis died as a result of a fall from his fifth floor Park Avenue apartment. [*The New York Times* November 11, 1946, p. 43.]

Louis Purcell and Genevieve Emerson Dowdney's daughter Louise married William Rogers Deering, who resided at *Roseneath* in Laurel Hollow, and, later, William Leeson Pollok, the son of Thomas Condell Pollok of Leonia, NY. [*See* Spinzia, *Long Island's Prominent North Shore Families, vol. 1* – Deering entry.] Their son Samuel married Ella Heyward Palmer, the daughter of Paul Trapier and Eloise Lynah Palmer of *Rockland Plantation* in Charleston, SC. Their daughter Margaret married Joseph Edward Devine, the son of James J. Devine of Pelham, NY, and, later, Leonard Albert Watson, Jr. Their son John married Margaret Moffat, the daughter of John Gilchrist Moffat of Scranton, PA, and, subsequently, Nancy Anne Lutkins, the daughter of Theodore LaRue Lutkins of *Proud Pines*, Towners, NY.

The Blue Book of The Hamptons, 1965 lists Dickson Bayard and Sue C. Bucknell Potter as residing at this house which they called *Falaise Farm*.

In 2017 the five-bedroom, three-bath, 3,045-square-foot house was for sale. The asking price was $3.9 million.

Dowling, Robert Whittle (1895-1973)

Occupation(s):	capitalist -	director, Waldorf–Astoria Corp., NYC;
		chairman of board, Pierre Service Corp., NYC (manages Pierre Hotel, NYC);
		president, Carnegie Hall Corp., NYC;
		vice-president, Starrett Brothers & Eken (construction company);
		chairman of board, City Investment Co. (New York real estate development and holding firm);
		director, National City Realty Corp.;
		director, United Artists Corp.;
		Broadway play and motion picture producer;
		proprietor, Carlyle Hotel, NYC;
		director, General Development Corp.
	financier -	director, Home Title Guaranty Co.;
		director, New York Life Insurance Co.;
		director, City Bank Farmers Trust Co.;
		director, East River Savings Bank;
		director, Emigrant Savings Bank
	merchant -	director, R. H. Macy & Co. (department store chain)

Civic Activism: Cultural Executive of the City of New York;
trustee, John F. Kennedy Center for the Performing Arts, Washington, DC;
president, arts advisory committee, National Cultural Center, Washington, DC;
chairman of board, citizen's committee, New York Shakespeare Festival, NYC;
donated $3 million for the establishment of Dowling College, Oakdale, NY;
trustee, Lenox Hill Hospital, NYC;
director, Commerce and Industry Association of New York;
chairman, fund raising committee, American National Theatre and Academy;
president, National Urban League, 1950-1956;
director, Boy Scouts of America

Marriage(s):
M/1 – 1919-div. 1931 – Ethel Finch Robertson
M/2 – 1934-div. 1968 – Alice Bevier Hall (1899-1970)
  - Civic Activism: president, Spence–Chapin Adoption Service, NYC;
              a founder, Harlem–Dowling Children's Service, NYC
M/3 – 1968-1973 – Audrey A. Reber

Address: Windmill Lane, East Hampton
Name of estate: *South Wind*
Year of construction: 1778
Style of architecture: Colonial Cape Cod Style
Architect(s):
Landscape architect(s):
House extant: yes
Historical notes:

The *Social Register Summer 1950* lists Robert W. and Alice B. Hall Dowling as residing on Lily Pond Lane, East Hampton.

In 1951 Dowling purchased nine acres on Windmill Lane and moved the c. 1780 Conklin house from Amagansett, a 1751 saltbox-style house from Springs, a c.1780 house from Egypt Lane in East Hampton, and an 1802 gristmill from Bridgehampton to the site.

He was the son of Robert Emmet and Minetta Linck Dowling of Manhattan.

Ethel Finch Robertson Dowling was the daughter of Norman Alfred and Jennie Finch Robertson of NYC.

Alice Bevier Hall Dowling was the daughter of Henry J. S. Hall of *Yew Tree Farm* in Smithtown and *Moorlawn* in East Hampton. Alice had previously been married to William A. Bartle, Jr. of Washington, DC.

Robert Whittle and Alice Bevier Hall Dowling's daughter Ruth married Lawrence W. A. Newman, the son of Leon B. Newman of Boston, MA.

Audrey A. Reber Dowling was the daughter of Robert Lane Reber of Denver, CO. She had previously been married to ___ Williams of Boston, MA.

The compound was later owned by William Edward Simon, Sr.

Downey, Robert, Jr. (b. 1965)

Occupation(s):	entertainers and associated professions -
	actor;
	a founder, with his wife Susan, Team Downey (a production firm)
Civic Activism:	trustee, Anti-Recidivison Coalition
Marriage(s):	M/1 – 1992-div. 2004 – Deborah Falconer (b. 1965)
	- entertainers and associated professions -
	actress and musician
	M/2 – 2005 – Susan Nicole Levin (b. 1973)
	- entertainers and associated professions -
	co-president, Dark Castle Entertainment;
	executive vice president of production, Silver Pictures;
	a founder, with her husband Robert, and president,
	Team Downey, (a production firm)
Address:	123 Main Street, East Hampton
Name of estate:	
Year of construction:	c. 1895
Style of architecture:	Eclectic
Architect(s):	
Landscape architect(s):	
House extant: yes	
Historical notes:	

   The house was built by Edward de Rose as a guest house on his estate, *Millfield*. It was later owned by Harold Jack Rosinsky who sold the house to Kenneth Sidney Kuchin in 1998 for $2.16 million.
   In 2015 the house, which had been enlarged over the years, was for sale. The asking price was $11.9 million. In 2017 it was purchased by Downey.
   He is the son of Robert and Elsie Ann Ford Downey, Sr.

Draper, Frances S. Haggerty (1810-1905)

Marriage(s):	1834-1866 – Simeon Draper, Jr. (1804-1866)

- financier - a founder and director, The Building Associations Fire
    Insurance Co.;
    president, The Citizen's Mutual Loan and Accumulation
        Fund Association;
    a founder, National Union Life and Limb Insurance Co.
        (later Metropolitan Life Insurance Co.)
- auctioneer - founder, Simeon Draper Co. (later, John H. Draper Co.)
    (had monopoly on tea and coffee sales)
- politician - member, New York State Whig Central Committee;
    chairman of board, Board of Tea Governors (in charge of
        New York City charities);
    Commissioner of Public Charities and Collections;
    New York City Provost Marshal, 1862;
    Collector of Customs, Port of New York, 1864-1865;
    government cotton agent, Port of New York (had complete
        charge of all cotton received in the port);
    president of board, Metropolitan Police Commissioners, NYC

Address:	67 Ocean Avenue, East Hampton
Name of estate:	*Duneside*
Year of construction:	c. 1871
Style of architecture:	Colonial Revival (after 1901 remodeling)
Architect(s):	
Landscape architect(s)	
Builder:	Stafford Tillinghast, 1899 alterations
	Asa Otis Jones, 1890 alterations (for Draper)

House extant: yes
Historical notes:

    The house, originally named *Sea Side Cottage*, was built by The Reverend Stephen Lyon Mershon, Sr. It was later owned by Richmond Mayo–Smith. The house was purchased from Mayo–Smith by Mrs. Draper.

    The *Social Register Summer, 1904* lists Frances S. Haggerty Draper as residing at *Duneside* in East Hampton.

    She was the daughter of John and Maria Allair Haggerty.

    Simeon Draper, Jr. was the son of Simeon and Mary Bemis Draper, Sr. of Massachusetts.

    Simeon and Frances S. Haggerty Draper, Jr.'s daughters Marie and Fanny did not marry. Their son Henry married Gertrude Aletta Van Dervoort, the daughter of Joseph Burroughs and Letitia Van Wyck Van Dervoort. Their son Julian was an infant at the time of his death.

Drew, John, Jr. (1853-1927)

Occupation(s):	entertainers and associated professions - actor
Civic Activism:	founder and member, first board of governors, Devon Yacht Club, Amagansett
Marriage(s):	1880-1918 – Josephine Baker (1854-1918)
Address:	Lily Pond Lane, East Hampton
Name of estate:	*Kyalami*
Year of construction:	1901
Style of architecture:	Shingle
Architect(s):	James Brown Lord designed the house (for Drew)
Landscape architect(s):	
Builder:	George A. Eldredge

House extant: no
Historical notes:

    The house, originally named *Kyalami*, was built by John Drew, Jr.

    He was the son of John and Louisa Lane Drew, Sr. of Philadelphia, PA.

    Josephine Baker Drew was the daughter of Alexina Fisher Baker of Philadelphia, PA.

    John and Josephine Baker Drew, Jr.'s daughter Louise, who later owned the house, married Jack Devereaux and resided in East Hampton.

    In 1929 Louise sold the house to Auguste Julien Cordier, Jr. who continued to call it *Kyalami*. [*The East Hampton Star* October 11, 1929, p. 1.]

    In 1944 it was purchased by Louis Rice Wasey. [*The East Hampton Star* November 23, 1944, p. 1.]

Drexler, Millard S. (b. 1944)
aka Mickey Drexler

Occupation(s):	merchant - director, president CEO, The Gap, Inc.;
	CEO and chairman of board, J. Crew Group, Inc.;
	CEO and chairman of board, Madewell, Inc.;
	president, Old Navy, Inc.;
	president and CEO, Ann Taylor Stores;
	vice-president, Abraham and Straus
	industrialist - director, Apple, Inc.;
	director, Jand, Inc.
Civic Activism:	director, Teach for America, Inc.;
	member, board of advisors, Common Sense Media, Inc.;
	co-founder, with his wife Peggy, The Peggy and Millard Drexler Foundation
Marriage(s):	1969 – Peggy F. *[unable to determine maiden name]*
	- educator - gender scholar, Stanford University;
	assistant professor of psychiatry, Weill Medical College of Cornell University;
	director, New York University Child Study Center
	writer - co-author, with Linden Gross, *Boys Without Men*, 2005;
	Our Fathers Ourselves, 2011;
	numerous articles in journals
	Civic Activism: co-founder, with her husband Millard, The Peggy and Millard Drexler Foundation
Address -	16 Cliff Drive, Montauk
Name of estate:	
Year of construction:	1931
Style of architecture:	Colonial Revival
Architect(s):	Rolf W. Bauhan designed the compound (for Church)
	Thierry W. Despont designed the 2007 alterations (for Drexler)
Landscape architect(s):	Miranda Brooks (for Lindemann)
House extant: yes	
Historical notes:	

The compound, which consists of a seven-bedroom main residence, four guest houses, a three-car garage, and a stable, was built by Richard E. Church. It remained in the Church family until 1971 when it was purchased for $225,000 by Andy Warhol and Paul Morrissey, who called it *Eothen*. In 2007 Morrissey sold the estate to Drexler for $27 million.

In 2015 Drexler sold the main residence, guest houses, garage, and 5.6 acres to Adam Marc Lindemann for $50 million. The equestrian portion of the property remained on the market.

Dubow, Arthur Myron (1933-1999)

Occupation(s):	attorney -	associate, Webster, Sheffield, Fleischmann, and Chrystie, NYC, 1960-1964
	financier -	director and vice-president Back Bay Enterprises, Inc., Boston, MA;
		director and president, Backorient Holding Corp, Boston, MA;
		president, Korean Capital Corporation, NYC;
		president, Fortune Capital Ltd., Boston, MA, and NY;
		chairman of board, Institutional Shareholder Services;
		director, Castle Convertible Fund, Inc.;
		director, Spectra Funds, Inc.;
		director, Alger Funds;
		director, Coolidge Investment Corp.
	capitalist -	director and president, Boston Company Energy Advisers;
		president, Fourth Estate, Inc.;
		chairman of board, Sulpetro Canada, Ltd.
Civic Activism:		member, National Advance Committee on Accreditation and Institutional Eligibility, U. S. Department of Education;
		member, visiting committee, Center for Science and Institutional Affairs, Harvard University, Cambridge, MA;
		director, Institute for Educational Leadership;
		director, Thomas Jefferson Forum;
		established Arthur Dubow Foundation
Marriage(s):		M/1 – 1962-div. 1983 – Isabella Goodrich Breckinridge
		M/2 – 1986 – Barbara J. Shattuck
Address:		Briar Patch Road, East Hampton
Name of estate:		
Year of construction:		1900
Style of architecture:		Modified Salt Box
Architect(s):		
Landscape architect(s):		
Builder:		George A. Eldredge
House extant: yes		
Historical notes:		

    The combination of house and art studio was built by Edward Emerson Simmons. It was later owned by Dubow.
He was the son of David and Matilda Polster Dubow.
    Isabella Goodrich Breckinridge Dubow is the daughter of Charles David Goodrich Breckinridge and the great-granddaughter of Benjamin Franklin Goodrich, the founder of B. F. Goodrich Tire Company. She was also a descendant of United States Vice-President John Cabell Breckinridge who later became Secretary of War for the Confederate States of America.
    Arthur Myron and Isabella Goodrich Breckinridge Dubow's son Charles married Tatyana Alexandra Eugenie Yassukovich, the daughter of Stanistas M. Yassukovich of London and Gloucestershire, England, and, later, Melinda Ely, the daughter of C. Geist Ely of New York.
    Barbara J. Shattuck Dubow had previously been married to Arthur Eugene Kohn.

Duffield, The Reverend Dr. Howard (1854-1941)

Occupation(s):	clergy- minister, Presbyterian Church, Lecock, PA; minister, Beverly, NJ; minister, Detroit, MI; minister, Old First Presbyterian Church, NYC, 1891-1918
Civic Activism:	director, Princeton Theological Seminary; director, Leake and Watts Orphan House; director, Sailors Snug Harbor, NYC; member, board of managers, Presbyterian Hospital, NYC
Marriage(s):	1877-1936 – Katharine Nash Greenleaf (1852-1936)
Address:	318 Bluff Road, Amagansett
Name of estate:	*Dune Crest*
Year of construction:	1903
Style of architecture:	Mediterranean
Architect(s):	
Landscape architect(s):	
House extant: yes	
Historical notes:	

The house, originally named *Dune Crest*, was built by The Reverend Dr. Howard Duffield.

The *Social Register Summer, 1915* lists The Reverend and Mrs. Katharine N. Greenleaf Duffield as residing at *Dune Crest* in Amagansett.

He was the son of John T. and Sarah Elizabeth Duffield.

Katharine Nash Greenleaf Duffield was the daughter of Thomas and Eleanor Leal Greenleaf.

Howard and Katharine Nash Greenleaf Duffield's daughters Winifred and Katharine did not marry. Their son Stuart resided in Los Angeles, CA.

The 5,000-square-foot, six-bedroom house, with five and a half bathrooms, was later owned by Kathleen Turner. In 2010 Turner sold it for $3.9 million.

Duke, Anthony Drexel, Sr. (1918-2014)

Occupation(s):	capitalist - vice president, Duke International Import and Export Co.; president, A. D. Duke Realty, Inc., NY
	financier - director, American National Bank; member, executive committee, Florida Growth Fund
	writer - *The Voyage of My Life* (with Richard Firstman)
Civic Activism*:	founder and president, Boys Harbor, East Hampton (later, The Harbor for Boys and Girls), 1937;
	president and chairman of board, Boys and Girls Harbor, East Hampton;
	commissioner, New York City Youth Board (Robert F. Wagner administration);
	delegate, International Conference on Private Sector Initiatives, 1986;
	member, advisory council, United States Naval Academy, Annapolis, MD;
	vice-chairman of trustees, Duke University, Durham, NC;
	trustee, Rumsey Hall School, Washington Depot, CT;
	member, International Rescue Committee;
	trustee, The Achelis Foundation;
	trustee, Bodman Foundation;
	National Committee of American Foreign Policy;
	trustee, New York University Medical Center Child Study Center, NYC;
	member, Duke University Provost Advisory Committee, Durham, NC;
	a founder and director, East Hampton Health Care Foundation;
	director, Maidstone Club, East Hampton
Marriage(s):	M/1 – 1939-div. 1947 – Alice Noel Rutgers
	M/2 – 1947-div. – Elizabeth Ordway (1925-1984)
	- Civic Activism: established Elizabeth Ordway Dunn Foundation with a bequest of $10 million (historic and environmental projects)
	M/3 – 1957-div. – Diane M. Douglas (1933-2015)
	- restaurateur - manager, Donald Bruce White Catering, NYC
	Civic Activism: member, Village of Southampton Planning Board
	M/4 – 1975-2014 – Maria De Lourdes Alcebo (b. 1947)
	- Civic Activism: president, Fundacion Armistad Foundation (to bridge relations between Cuba and the United States);
	director, Protective One;
	vice-president, The Harbor for Boys and Girls, East Hampton;
	member, Women's Commission of International Rescue Committee;
	member, Provost Advisory Committee on International Affairs, Duke University, Durham, NC
Address:	180 Springy Banks Road, East Hampton
Name of estate:	*Harbor House*
Year of construction:	
Style of architecture:	Shingle
Architect(s):	
Landscape architect(s):	
House extant: yes	
Historical notes:	

The Blue Book of The Hamptons, 1958 lists Mr. and Mrs. Anthony Drexel Duke [Sr.] as residing on Springy Banks Road, East Hampton.

Duke, Anthony Drexel, Sr. (cont'd)

Anthony Drexel Duke, Sr. was the son of Angier Buchanan and Cordelia Drexel Biddle Duke. After her husband's death, Cordelia married Thomas Marko Robertson and resided at *Wyndecote* in Southampton and *Guinea Hollow Farm* in Old Westbury. [*See* Spinzia, *Long Island's Prominent Families in the Town of Southampton* and *Long Island's Prominent North Shore Families, vol. II* – Robertson entries.]

Alice Noel Rutgers Duke was the daughter of Nicholas Gouverneur Rutgers, Jr. of Rumson, NJ. She subsequently married Marshall Jewell Dodge, Jr., the son of Marshall Jewell and Priscilla Dixon Barnes Dodge, Sr. of *Brightside* in Southampton. [*See* Spinzia, *Long Island's Prominent Families in the Town of Southampton* – Dodge entry.]

Anthony Drexel and Alice Noel Rutgers Duke, Sr.'s son Anthony Drexel Duke, Jr. married Barbara Briggs Foshay, the daughter of William Ward Foshay, and, subsequently, Olga Cabrer King, the daughter of Augustin Cabrer of Humacao, Puerto Rico.

Elizabeth Ordway Duke was the daughter of Lucius Pond and Josephine Green Ordway, Jr. Elizabeth subsequently married John Richard Dunn.

Anthony Drexel and Elizabeth Ordway Duke, Sr.'s daughter ____ married David Burrell McSherry. Their son John married Beatriz Alcebo, the daughter of José Alcebo of Miami, FL. Their daughter Josephine married John Marshall Geste Brown, Jr.

Diane M. Douglas Duke was the daughter of Barclay Koutze and Jane Elizabeth Foster Douglas. Elizabeth later married Hunter Goodrich, Jr. with whom she resided at *Cairn Cote* in Southampton and, subsequently George D. F. Lamborn.

Anthony Drexel and Diane M. Douglas Duke, Sr.'s son Douglas married Laura Lee Liptrot, the daughter of Peter Atherton Liptrot of East Hampton.

Marie De Lourdes Alcebo Duke is the daughter of José Antonio Alcebo, Sr. of Cuba. She had previously been married to ____ Longaray.

Anthony Drexel and Maria De Lourdes Alcebo Duke, Sr.'s son Washington Alcebo Duke married Sarah Rothwell.

*Because of his charitable work, Duke was named a "living landmark" by the New York Landmark Conservancy.

In 2016 the six-bedroom, five-and-a-half-bath house was for sale.

Dunbar, Arthur T.

Occupation(s):

Marriage(s):

Address: Lee Avenue, East Hampton
Name of estate:
Year of construction: 1903
Style of architecture: Shingle
Architect(s): George A Eldredge designed
    the house (for A. T. Dunbar)

Landscape architect(s):
Builder: George A. Eldredge
    T. E. Babcock, 1903 additions

House extant: yes
Historical notes:

The house was built by Arthur T. Dunbar.

The *Brooklyn Blue Book and Long Island Society Register, 1921* lists A. T. Dunbar as residing on Lee Avenue, East Hampton.

In 1927 the furnished house and stables on 2 1/2 acres were put up for auction. [*The New York Times* August 20, 1927, p. 26.]

Dunn, Dr. James Manning (1887-1956)

Occupation(s):	physician -	ophthalmology surgeon; chief, medical rehabilitation, Veterans' Hospital, Seattle, WA; assistant chief, physical medicine and rehabilitation, Veterans' Hospital, Washington, DC
	educator -	assistant commandant, Enlisted Technicians School, Lawson General Hospital, Atlanta, GA; chief, Women's Army Corps Enlisted Technicians School, Fort Oglethorpe, GA

Marriage(s): M/1 – 1917-1918 – Alice Aurora (d. 1918)
M/2 – 1925-1956 – Marguerite Ritzer
- educator - English teacher, East Hampton High School

Address: 27 Edwards Lane, East Hampton
Name of estate:
Year of construction: c. 1840
Style of architecture: Modified Federal
Architect(s):
Landscape architect(s):
Builder: George A. Eldredge, architectural details
House extant: yes*
Historical notes:

In 1940 Dunn moved the Charles Osborne house from Main Street to Edwards Lane. [*The East Hampton Star* June 20, 1940, p. 5.]

He was the son of Hugh Francis and Catharine Daily Dunn of Troy, NY.

Alice Aurora Dunn was the daughter of Charles Ganser Aurora.

James Manning and Alice Aurora Dunn's daughter Alice married Albert Southard Knight, Jr. of Niagara Falls, NY.

In 1958 the house was purchased by Irvin Bruce Tiedeman, Sr. [*The East Hampton Star* May 1, 1958, p. 5.]

*Alterations to the house were made by Dunn and Tiedeman.

Duryea, Walter Bartow (1876-1954)

Occupation(s): merchant - wholesale dry goods

Marriage(s): 1904-1954 – Ella Louise Mairs (1878-1964)
    (aka Ellen Louise Mairs)

Address: Lee Avenue, East Hampton
Name of estate:
Year of construction: 1899
Style of architecture: Colonial Revival with Federal elements
Architect(s): Leinau and Nash designed
    the house (for Carson)
Landscape architect(s):
Builder: Asa Otis Jones, 1899;
    1901 alterations (for Carson)
House extant: yes*
Historical notes:

    The house was built by William Moore Carson, Sr. In 1920 it was purchased by Earle Westwood Sinclair. [*The East Hampton Star* July 30, 1920, p. 6.] In 1945 Robert Elliott McCormick purchased Earle Westwood Sinclair's residence *Fairlawn*. In 1946 he sold it to Duryea. [*The East Hampton Star* November 8, 1945, p. 1, and February 20, 1947, p. 6.]

    The Blue Book of The Hamptons, 1958 lists Walter Bartow and Ella Louise Mairs Duryea as residing on Lee Avenue, East Hampton.

    He was the son of Albert Edwin and Eliza Ferdon Bartow Duryea of Nyack, NY.

    Ella Louise Mairs Duryea was the daughter of William Henry and Ellen A. Olney Mairs of Brooklyn. Her brother Olney Blanchard Mairs, Sr. married Eva Eugenie Ward, the daughter of Joseph Alexander Ward, and resided in East Hampton.

    Walter Bartow and Ella Louise Mairs Duryea's son William Mairs Duryea, Sr., who resided in Old Westbury, married Marjorie Elwell Simonds, the daughter of William Robinson and Henrietta Louise Jones Simonds of *Williston House* in Southampton and *Wyndemoor* in Sayville, and, later, Mary Atwell, the daughter of George Joseph and Mary Atwell of Woodmere and Old Westbury. [*See* Spinzia, *Long Island's Prominent Families in the Town of Southampton* – Simonds entry; *Long Island's Prominent South Shore Families* – Simonds entry; *Long Island's Prominent Families in the Town of Hempstead* – Atwell entry; and *Long Island's Prominent North Shore Families, vol. I* – Atwell entry.]

    *In 1901 a west wing was added to the house.

    The house was later owned by David Hall McConnell III. [*The East Hampton Star* May 20, 1965, p. 2.]

DuVal, Guy (1859-1949)

Occupation(s):	capitalist - partner, W. A. & A. M. White (importer and manufacturer of fur), Danbury, CT; secretary, Brooklyn Warehouse and Storage Co.; trustee, Washington Water Power Co. financier - director, Farmers Loan & Trust Co.
Civic Activism:	treasurer, Brooklyn Bureau of Charities; vice-president, Brooklyn Heights Association; president, Long Island Historical Society, Brooklyn; a founder and director, Brooklyn Chamber of Commerce; vice-chairman, Brooklyn Chapter, American Red Cross; president, Brooklyn Children's Aid Society
Marriage(s):	1894-1948 – Florence Fairbanks (d. 1948) - Civic Activism: treasurer, Graham Home for Old Ladies, Brooklyn
Address:	De Forest Road, Montauk
Name of estate:	*Awepesha*
Year of construction:	1883
Style of architecture:	Beach Cottage with Queen Anne elements
Architect(s):	McKim, Mead & White designed the house (for A. M. Hoyt)
Landscape architect(s):	Frederick Law Olmsted designed the site plan (for A. M. Hoyt)
Builder:	Mead & Taft

House extant: yes
Historical notes:

The 7,000-square-foot house is one of the Montauk Association's "Seven Sisters." It was owned by Alfred Miller Hoyt and, later, by DuVal who called it *Awepesha*.

The *Long Island Society Register, 1929* lists Guy and Florence Fairbanks DuVal as residing at *Awepesha* in Montauk.

He was the son of William DuVal of Brooklyn.

Florence Fairbanks DuVal was the daughter of David B. and Mary Sophia Cotton Fairbanks of Brooklyn.

The house was later owned by Florence Biggs and, then, by Sidney and Winnifred Goddard, who remodeled it into The Grand View Manor restaurant. It subsequently became the residence of Dr. Dewey and Mrs. Hilda Smith.

Eastman, Joseph (1853-1920)

Occupation(s):	financier - director, West Side Bank, NYC capitalist - exporter
Marriage(s):	1881-1903 – Harriet Collyer (d. 1903)
Address:	Ocean and Lee Avenues, East Hampton
Name of estate:	
Year of construction:	1899
Style of architecture:	Shingle
Architect(s):	Joseph Greenleaf Thorp designed the house (for W. G. Smith) John Custis Lawrence, 1916 alterations (for Eastman)
Landscape architect(s):	

House extant: yes
Historical notes:

The house was built by Warren G. Smith. In 1916 it was purchased by Eastman from Mrs. Smith. [*The East Hampton Star* September 15, 1916, p. 7.]

The *Social Register Summer, 1915* lists Joseph Eastman as residing in East Hampton.

He was the son of Timothy P. and Lucy Putnam Eastman of New York.

Harriet Collyer Eastman was the daughter of The Reverend Robert and Mrs. Ann Armitage Collyer of New York.

Joseph and Harriet Collyer Eastman's daughter Anne married Reginald F. Wigham, Sr. and resided at *Sunnycroft* in Southampton. [*See* Spinzia, *Long Island's Prominent Families in the Town of Southampton* – Wigham entry.] Their son Norman married Frances Ernst and resided in Scarsdale, NY.

The twelve-room house was sold at auction in 1937 to James Thomas Lee. [*The New York Times* September 29, 1937, p. 41.]

Edwards, Harkness, Sr. (1905-1946)

Occupation(s):	capitalist - manager, Walnut Hill Farm, Donerail, KY (horse breeding farm)
Civic Activism:	vice-president, Grand Circuit Racing; president and director, Trotting Horse Breeders Association
Marriage(s):	1927-1946 – Mary Bedell Suydam (1907-1993)
Address:	18 Lee Avenue, East Hampton
Name of estate:	
Year of construction:	1899
Style of architecture:	Shingle
Architect(s):	Joseph Greenleaf Thorpe designed the house (for Hackstaff)
Landscape architect(s):	
Builder:	Loper Brothers George A. Eldredge, 1902 alterations*

House extant: yes
Historical notes:

The 7,500-square-foot, eight-bedroom, seven-and-a-half bath house, originally named *Tarriawyle*, was built by Charles Ludovic Hackstaff. It was later owned by Edwards.

He was the son of Dr. Ogden Matthias and Mrs. Lela Harkness Edwards, Jr. of *Dunehurst* in East Hampton.

Mary Adele Suydam Edwards was the daughter of Moses Bedell Suydam of Pittsburgh. She subsequently married Sherman Jenney, the son of William Sherman and Nina Bevan Jenney of *Little Close* in East Hampton.

Harkness and Mary Bedell Suydam Edwards, Sr.'s son Harkness Edwards, Jr. married Gladys Barker.

*The 1902 addition of the south facade was built by Eldredge. In 1969 the front porch was enclosed.

The house was later owned by Stephen Kniznick Robert.

In 2012 it was for sale by Robert; the asking price was $18.5 million. It was sold for $14.9 million in 2014.

Edwards, James Cook, Sr. (1922-1996)

Occupation(s):	attorney financier - vice-president, Douglas T. Johnson and Co. (financial advising firm); founder and president, James C. Edwards and Co. (financial advising firm)
Civic Activism:	president, Maidstone Club, East Hampton
Marriage(s):	1951-1996 – Sally Ann Matson (b. 1926) - Civic Activism: a founder and benefactor, East Hampton Healthcare Foundation
Address:	19 Hook Pond Lane, East Hampton
Name of estate:	
Year of construction:	
Style of architecture:	
Architect(s):	
Landscape architect(s):	

House extant: unconfirmed
Historical notes:

The Blue Book of The Hamptons, 1973 lists James C. and Sally A. Matson Edwards as residing on Hook Pond Road [sic], East Hampton.

He was the son of James A. and Edith Cook Edwards of North Haven.

Sally Ann Matson Edwards was the daughter of David Hayse Matson of Reforma, Mexico.

James Cook and Sally Ann Matson Edwards, Sr.'s daughter Anne married Thomas Bayard McCabe III of Haverford, PA, and resided in Haverford, PA. Their son James Cook Edwards, Jr., who resided in East Hampton, married Barbara Hartley Lord, the daughter of James Couper and Barbara Stuart Harley Lord, Jr. of Southampton. [*See* Spinzia, *Long Island's Prominent Families in the Town of Southampton* – Hartley and Lord entries.]

In 1955 the house was remodeled. [*The East Hampton Star* June 16, 1955, p. 12.]

Edwards, James McPherson (1849-1920)

Occupation(s):	capitalist - vice-president and general manager, Louisville, New Orleans, and Texas Railroad; president, Yonkers Street Railroad, Yonkers, NY; president, Detroit United Railroad, Detroit, MI
	industrialist - president, Alkali Works, Saltville, VA; president, Castner Electrolytic Alkali Co., Niagara Falls, NY
Marriage(s):	Elizabeth Erwin Scudder (1847-1920)
Address:	Georgica Road, East Hampton
Name of estate:	
Year of construction:	1914
Style of architecture:	Colonial Revival
Architect(s):	John Custis Lawrence designed the house (for J. Mc. Edwards)
Landscape architect(s):	
Builder:	Edward M. Gay
House extant: yes	
Historical notes:	

The house was built by James McPherson Edwards.
The *Social Register Summer, 1915* lists James M. and Elizabeth E. Scudder Edwards as residing in East Hampton.
He was the son of Mordacai E. and Martha Jane Fullton Edwards.
Elizabeth Erwin Scudder Edwards was the daughter of Alexander McLean and Susan Clarke Scudder.
James McPherson and Elizabeth Erwin Scudder Edwards' daughter married William Andrew Lockwood and resided at *Ivy Cottage* in East Hampton. Their daughter Marian married George De Witt Williamson, the son of David B. and Mary Butler Williamson. Their son James Alexander Edwards married Edith E. Cook, the daughter of Henry Francis and Lena Marianna Fahys Cook of *Clench-Warton* in North Haven. [*See* Spinzia, *Long Island's Prominent Families in the Town of Southampton* – Cook and Fahys entries.] Their son Allen married Christine Muir Russell and resided in Detroit, MI.
By 1919 Edwards had relocated to Apaquogue Road.

Edwards, Dr. Ogden Matthias, Jr. (1869-1940)

Occupation(s):	physician - pediatrician
	educator - professor of pediatrics, University of Pittsburgh, Pittsburgh, PA;
	dean, School of Medicine, University of Pittsburgh, Pittsburgh, PA, 1917-1919
	financier - director, Commonwealth Trust Co., Pittsburgh, PA
Civic Activism:	a founder and chairman of board, Allegheny County Medical Society Milk Commission;
	president, American Association of Medical Milk Commission;
	trustee, University of Pittsburgh, Pittsburgh, PA;
	trustee, Shady Side Academy;
	trustee, Presbyterian Hospital, NYC;
	commodore, Devon Yacht Club, Amagansett
Marriage(s):	1898-1940 – Lela Harkness (1873-1946)
Address:	10 Lee Avenue, East Hampton
Name of estate:	*Dunehurst*
Year of construction:	1898-1899
Style of architecture:	Shingle
Architect(s):	Cyrus Lazelle Warner Eidlitz designed the house (for Quackenbush)
Landscape architect(s):	
Builder:	George A. Eldredge
House extant: yes	
Historical notes:	

The house was built by Schuyler Quackenbush. It was later owned by Edwards.

The *Long Island Society Register, 1929* lists Dr. Ogden M. and Mrs. Lela Harkness Edwards, Jr. as residing at *Dunehurst* in East Hampton.

He was the son of Ogden Matthias and Sara Anderson Herron Edwards, Sr. of Pittsburgh, PA.

Lela Harkness Edwards was the daughter of Lamon Vanderburg and Martha Frances Johnson Harkness of Lexington, KY, and East Hampton.

Dr. Ogden Matthias and Mrs. Lela Harkness Edwards, Jr.'s daughter Martha married John McKelvy Lazear and resided in Manhattan. Their daughter Lela married Harry Cook, the son of Henry Francis and Lena Marianna Fahys Cook of *Clench–Warton* in North Haven, and resided at *Holly Hall* in East Hampton. [*See* Spinzia, *Long Island's Prominent Families in the Town of Southampton* – Cook entry.] Their son Harkness married Mary Adele Suydam and resided in East Hampton and at *Walnut Hall Farm* in Donerail, KY. Their daughter Katherine, who married Harold Willis Nichols Jr., inherited the estate and continued to call it *Dunehurst*.

In 2016, the approximately 10,000-square-foot house, with ten bedrooms and six and a half bathrooms, and 3.3 acres were for sale. The asking price was $18.95 million.

Edwards, Walter, Jr. (1834-1895)

Occupation(s):	attorney
Civic Activism:	a founder, Georgica Association
Marriage(s):	Camilla Davis Leonard (1838-1936)
Address:	40 Georgica Association Road, East Hampton
Name of estate:	*Kilkare*
Year of construction:	c. 1877
Style of architecture:	Shingle
Architect(s):	
Landscape architect(s):	Andrew Graham, stone wall surrounding pool (for Kennedy)
Builder:	Asa Otis Jones, enlarged the house, 1901 (for Mrs. W. Edwards)

House extant: yes
Historical notes:

The house, originally named *Kilkare*, was built by Walter Edwards, Jr.

The *Social Register, August 1897* lists Camilla Leonard Edwards as residing at *Kilkare* in Wainscott [East Hampton].

Walter and Camilla Davis Leonard Edwards, Jr.'s son William later inherited *Kilkare*. He married Susan Sherman White, the daughter of Charles Atwood and Frances Spencer Eaton White of New Haven, CT, who were descendants of Roger Sherman, a signer of the Declaration of Independence. Susan's sister Mabel married Secretary of State and Secretary of War Henry Lewis Stimson with whom she resided at *Highold* in West Hills, Long Island. [*See* Spinzia, *Long Island's Prominent North Shore Families, vol. II* – Stimson entry.]

The house remained in the Edwards family until 1975 when it was sold to Michael John Kennedy. The Kennedys continued to call it *Kilkare*. In 2017 Mrs. Kennedy listed the 5,000-square-foot, seven-bedroom, seven-and-a-half-bath house for sale. The asking price was $55 million.

Edwards, William Henry Leonard (1870-1937)

Occupation(s):	attorney - assistant district attorney, NYC; partner, Edwards, Murphy, and Minton
Marriage(s):	1898-1937 – Susan Sherman White (1870-1949)
Address:	40 Georgica Association Road, East Hampton
Name of estate:	*Kilkare*
Year of construction:	c. 1877
Style of architecture:	Shingle
Architect(s):	
Landscape architect(s):	Andrew Graham, stone wall surrounding pool (for Kennedy)
Builder:	Asa Otis Jones, enlarged the house, 1901 (for Mrs. W. Edwards)

House extant: yes
Historical notes:

The house originally named *Kilkare*, was built by Walter Edwards, Jr. It was inherited by his son William who continued to call it *Kilkare*.

Susan Sherman White Edwards was the daughter of Charles Atwood and Frances Spencer Eaton White of New Haven, CT, who were descendants of Roger Sherman, a signer of the Declaration of Independence. Susan's sister Mabel married Secretary of State and Secretary of War Henry Lewis Stimson with whom she resided at *Highold* in West Hills, Long Island. [*See* Spinzia, *Long Island's Prominent North Shore Families, vol. II* – Stimson entry.]

William Henry Leonard and Susan Sherman White Edwards' son Henry died in 1908 at the age of two. Their daughter Camilla married Francis Osborn Noble, the son of Dr. Eugene Allen and Mrs. Lillian Osborn Noble of New York, and resided at *Solidago* in East Hampton. Their son Jonathan resided in Mount Kisco, NY.

The house remained in the Edwards family until 1975 when it was sold to Michael John Kennedy. The Kennedys continued to call it *Kilkare*. In 2017 Mrs. Kennedy listed the 5,000-square-foot, seven-bedroom, seven-and-a-half-bath house for sale. The asking price was $55 million.

Eidlitz, Cyrus Lazelle Warner (1853-1921)

Occupation(s):	architect - partner, Eidlitz & McKenzie*
	[See architect appendix in this volume for Eidlitz's commissions in East Hampton.]
	capitalist - director, East Hampton Electric Light Co.
Civic Activism:	a founder, Maidstone Club, East Hampton
Marriage(s):	1877-1921 – Jennie Turner Dudley (1854-1935)
Address:	58 Ocean Avenue, East Hampton
Name of estate:	*Overlea*
Year of construction:	1897
Style of architecture:	Shingle with Queen Anne elements
Architect(s):	Cyrus Lazelle Warner Eidlitz designed his own house and the 1898 and 1901 alterations
Landscape architect(s):	
House extant: yes	
Historical notes:	

The house, originally named *Overlea*, was built by Cyrus Lazelle Warner Eidlitz.

The *Social Register Summer, 1921* lists Cyrus L. W. and Jennie T. Dudley Eidlitz as residing at *Overlea* in East Hampton.

He was the son of Leopold and Harriet Armanda Lazelle Warner Eidlitz of New York. Cyrus' sister Harriet married Schuyler Quackenbush and resided in East Hampton.

The *Long Island Society Register, 1929* lists Jennie T. Dudley Eidlitz as residing at *Overlea* in East Hampton.

She was the daughter of Joseph Dana and Caroline Felthousen Dudley of Buffalo, NY.

Cyrus Lazelle Warner and Jennie Turner Dudley Eidlitz's daughter Caroline married Alexander Ladd Ward and resided in Manhattan. Their daughter Marion married John Butler Jameson and resided in Concord, NH.

*Eidlitz and Andrew C. Mackenzie designed The New York Times building in Manhattan.

The house was later owned by Carl William Gram, Jr. who called it *Maya* and, subsequently, by Mrs. Anne Woodin Harvey Gerli who continued to call it *Maya*.

Eldredge, George A. (1854-1924)

Occupation(s):	capitalist - a founder and director, Home Water Company of East Hampton;
	builder, East Hampton area;
	managing director, East Hampton Electric Light Co.
	financier - director, East Hampton National Bank
Civic Activism:	trustee, Town of East Hampton
Marriage(s):	Mary *[unable to determine maiden name]*
	- Civic Activism: president, Ladies Village Improvement Society, East Hampton, 1928
Address:	Cottage Avenue, East Hampton
Name of estate:	
Year of construction:	1873-1874
Style of architecture:	High Victorian Gothic
Architect(s):	Joseph Greenleaf Thorp, 1899 alterations (for Mrs. MacKay)*
Landscape architect(s):	
House extant: unconfirmed	
Historical notes:	

By 1887 The Reverend William R. MacKay had purchased the house from the firm of Dan Talmage's Sons. In 1919 Eldredge purchase the house for use as a rental.

He is the son of George Eldredge of East Hampton.

*Additional alterations to the house were made by Eldredge.

Eldredge, George A. (1854-1924)

Occupation(s):	*[See previous entry.]*
Marriage(s):	Mary *[unable to determine maiden name]* - *[See previous entry.]*
Address:	41 Huntting Lane, East Hampton
Name of estate:	
Year of construction:	1901
Style of architecture:	Shingle
Architect(s):	George A. Eldredge
Landscape architect(s):	
Builder:	George A. Eldredge
House extant: yes	
Historical notes:	

The house was built by George A. Eldredge.
[See previous entry for family information.]

Elliott, William, Jr. (1895-1945)

Occupation(s):	financier - stockbroker
Marriage(s):	1924-1942 – Glory Thomas (1898-1942) - writer - authored magazine articles Civic Activism: member, board of managers, Junior League
Address:	Georgica Road, East Hampton
Name of estate:	
Year of construction:	
Style of architecture:	
Architect(s):	
Landscape architect(s):	
House extant: unconfirmed	
Historical notes:	

   William Elliott, Jr. was the son of William and Minnie Fowler Elliot, Sr. of Manhattan.
   Glory Thomas Elliott was the daughter of Augustus and Lisle U. Colby Thomas of East Hampton. Glory's brother Luke, who married Dorothy Stuart Mahoney, the daughter of James Augustin Mahoney of Manhattan, and, later, Elizabeth Clarkson, resided also in East Hampton.
   William and Glory Thomas Elliott, Jr.'s son William Graeme Elliott married Lydia Taylor, the daughter of James Blackstone and Aileen B. Sedgwick Taylor, Jr. of *Sunset House* in Cove Neck. [*See* Spinzia, *Long Island's Prominent North Shore Families, vol. II* – Taylor entry.] Their son William Elliott III married Susanne Smith.
   Mrs. Elliott committed suicide in the bedroom of her East Hampton residence. [*The New York Times* August 20, 1942, p. 14.]

Ely, John Ingraham (1913-1997)

Occupation(s):	attorney - partner, Wiggin and Day
Civic Activism:	governor, Devon Yacht Club, Amagansett
Marriage(s):	1939-1995 – Harriet Jackson (1917-1995)
	- Civic Activism: established Alice Stuart Ely Book Fund, Bryn Mawr College Library, Bryn Mawr, PA, 1967

Address: Further Lane, Amagansett
Name of estate: *Hell-Gate*
Year of construction:
Style of architecture:
Architect(s):
Landscape architect(s)
House extant: unconfirmed
Historical notes:

In 1944 Ely purchased the house from Mrs. Barbara Comstock. [*The East Hampton Star* November 23, 1944, p. 6.]

The Blue Book of The Hamptons, 1973 lists John Ingraham and Harriet Jackson Ely as residing at *Hell-Gate* on Further Lane, Amagansett.

He was the son of Heman and Anna Burt Ely.

Harriet Jackson Ely was the daughter of John Day and Rose Marie Herrick Jackson of Amagansett.

John Ingraham and Harriet Jackson Ely's son Robert Ely (aka Robert Moulton-Ely) married Alice Fairchild Moulton, the daughter of David Richard Moulton of Lake Forest, IL. Their daughter Harriet married David H. Griesinger. Their daughter Nancy married William Robert Kales II, the son of Robert Gray Kales of Grosse Pointe Farms, MI. Their daughter Alice married Leroy Ralph Chapman, the son of Martin J. Chapman. Their daughter Mary married Charles M. Brennan. Their son Richard married Marion Wade Campbell, the daughter of Charles E. Campbell of Darien, CT, and resided in Ossipee, NH. Their daughter Jane married John Inman Pearce, Jr., the son of John Inman and Joan Ball Pearce, Sr.

Ely, Laurence Driggs, Sr. (1890-1958)

Occupation(s):	capitalist – vice-president, Lamont, Corliss & Co. (importing firm)
	industrialist - chairman of board, Talco Engineering Co., New Haven, CT;
	a founder, Sirin Mills Co.,
	president, Ross Soda Fountain Co., NYC;
	a founder and president, Reeves–Ely Laboratories, Inc., NYC
Marriage(s):	1916-1958 – Gladys Ione Noggle (1893-1981)

Address: Crossroads, East Hampton
Name of estate: *Olde Trees*
Year of construction:
Style of architecture:
Architect(s):
Landscape architect(s):
House extant: unconfirmed
Historical notes:

The Blue Book of The Hamptons, 1958 list Laurence Driggs and Gladys Nagel [sic] as residing at *Olde Trees* in East Hampton.

He was the son of Newell William and Florence Nightingale Ely of Evart, MI.

Laurence Driggs and Gladys Noggle Ely, Sr.'s son John married Marion Salvesen, the daughter of Conrad Thor and Olanda Salvesen, and resided in Sag Harbor. Their daughter Karen married Roger Harvey Thiele of *Taramar* in East Hampton. Their son Laurence Driggs Ely, Jr. married Elizabeth Duhrssen.

In 1958 the house was purchased by R. Lynn Baker. [*The East Hampton Star* June 19, 1958, p. 1.]

Embury, Aymar, II (1880-1966)

Occupation(s):	architect*
	writer - *One Hundred Country Houses;*
	The Dutch Colonial House;
	Country Houses;
	Early American Churches;
	The Livable House;
	The Aesthetics of Engineering Construction
Civic Activism:	member, New York States Memorial Commission (Lehman administration);
	member, President's Advisory Committee on Architecture, 1934-1943
Marriage(s):	M/1 – 1904-div. – Dorothy Coe
	M/2 – 1923-1932 – Ruth Bramley Dean (1889-1932)
	- landscape architect**
	writer - *The Livable House; Its Garden,* 1917;
	One Hundred Country Houses, 1909
	M/3 – 1934-div. – Josephine Bound
	M/4 – Jane E. Schabbehar (1910-1995)
Address:	223 Main Street, East Hampton
Name of estate:	*Third House*
Year of construction:	early 18th century
Style of architecture:	Colonial
Architect(s):	Aymar Embury II designed his own alterations, 1929*
Landscape architect(s):	Ruth Bramley Dean designed her own landscaping, c. 1930**

House extant: yes
Historical notes:

   The house was built by Isaac W. Miller. In 1927 Embury purchased it and named it *Third House*, because it was his third residence.
   He was the son of Aymar and Fannie Miller Bates Embury, Sr. of Manhattan.
   Dorothy Coe Embury was the daughter of Edward P. Coe.
   Aymar and Dorothy Coe Embury II's son Edward married Marguerite Jane Haynes, the daughter of George Allison Haynes of Manhattan. Their son Peter married Janet Upjohn, the daughter of William Harold Upjohn. Their son Aymar Embury III died during infancy.
   Ruth Bramley Dean Embury was the daughter of Alexander S. and Emma Dean of Wilkes–Barre, PA.
   Aymar and Ruth Bramley Dean Embury II's daughter Judith married Hugh Hack.
   Josephine Bound Embury was the daughter of Charles Fiske and Mary Josephine Richards Bound, Sr. Josephine subsequently married Richard Caldwell Millett, the son of Stephen C. Millet.
   Jane E. Schabbehar Aymar was the daughter of George Edward and Helena Cecilia Trube Schabbehar, Sr. Jane subsequently married Robert Steiner Benepe.
   In 2012 the house sold for $825.000.
   In 2016 restoration of the house was begun.
   *For Aymar Embury II's Long Island residential commissions, *see* architect appendices in Spinzia, *Long Island's Prominent North Shore Families, vol. II*; *Long Island's Prominent Families in the Town of Hempstead;* and *Long Island's Prominent Families in the Town of Southampton.*
   **For Ruth Bramley Dean [Embury]'s residential commissions on Long Island, *see* landscape architect appendices in Spinzia, *Long Island's Prominent North Shore Families, vol. II*, and *Long Island's Prominent Families in the Town of Hempstead.*

Eno, Alfred Joseph (d. 1953)

Occupation(s):	financier - a founder, Alfred J. Eno and Co. (stock brokerage firm)
	real estate agent - Queens County, NY, and East Hampton
Civic Activism:	secretary, Queens Borough chapter, National Progressive Party;
	president, Long Island Automotive League, 1908
Marriage(s):	1897-1953 – Eva Walling (1878-1961)
	- attorney
	capitalist - school for children;
	owned employment agency
	Civic Activism: suffrage*:
	- suffragist;
	chair, Borough of Queens chapter, Woman's
	Suffrage Party, 1912-1914;
	chair, Queens Village chapter, Woman's
	Suffrage Party;
	publisher, The Queensboro Equality
	(a broadsheet that advocated for Woman's
	Suffrage);
	delegate to state Federation of Women's Clubs;
	chair, women workers committee, Queens Borough
	chapter, National Progressive Party;
	corresponding secretary, Women's Press Club, NYC
Address:	Osborn Lane, East Hampton
Name of estate:	
Year of construction:	
Style of architecture:	
Architect(s):	
Landscape architect(s):	
House extant: unconfirmed	
Historical notes:	

   Alfred Joseph Eno was the son of Joseph Alfred Eno of Newark, NJ.
   Eva Walling Eno was the daughter of Jonathan Sproul and Katherine Applegate Walling of Monmouth County, NJ.
   Alfred Joseph and Eva Walling Eno's son Ralph died in 1908 at the age of eight.
   By 1951 the Enos were residing on Springs Road. [*The East Hampton Star* June 14, 1951, p. 7.] By 1953 they had relocated to Springs – Fireplace Road. [*The East Hampton Star* January 29, 1953, p. 6.]
   *For other Long Islanders involved in the suffrage movement *see* Raymond E. Spinzia, "Winning the Franchise: Long Island Activists in the Fight for Woman's Suffrage and Their Opponents, Long Island's Anti-Suffragists." wwwspinzialongislandestates.com.

Entenmann, Charles, Sr. (b. 1929)

Occupation(s):	industrialist - secretary, Entenmann's Inc., Bay Shore*
Civic Activism:	chairman, Town of Islip Republican campaign, 1969; vice-president, Bay Shore School Board; secretary, Long Island Association of Commerce and Industry; president, Bay Shore Tuna Club
Marriage(s):	1951-2014 – Nancy Lee Drake (1930-2014) - Civic Activism: neighborhood chair, Bay Shore–Brightwaters Council of Girl Scouts; director, Girl Scout Council of Suffolk County, NY
Address - Name of estate:	93 Prospect Hill Lane, Montauk
Year of construction:	2005
Style of architecture:	Eclectic
Architect(s):	
Landscape architect(s):	
House extant: yes	
Historical notes:	

Charles Entenmann, Sr. is the son of William Charles and Martha Clara Schneider Entenmann, Jr. of Bay Shore. His brother Robert, who resides in Bay Shore, Riverhead, and Montauk, married Mary L. Bayer. His brother William Charles Entenmann III married Christine Sutton and resided in Bay Shore and at *Timber Bay Farm* in Old Westbury. [*See* Spinzia, *Long Island's Prominent South Shore Families* – Entenmann entries – and *Long Island's Prominent North Shore Families, vol. I* – Entenmann entry.]

Nancy Lee Drake Entenmann was the daughter of Arthur and Hazel Drake of Bay Shore.

Charles and Nancy Lee Drake Entenmann, Sr.'s daughter Susan married James Cook, the son of George Cook of Fort Wayne, IN. Their daughter Barbara married ____ Thompson.

*Entenmann's Inc. was purchased in 1978 by Warner–Lambert Co. In 1982 it was purchased by General Foods Corp. In 1985 General Foods was acquired by Philip Morris and became part of Kraft Foods. In 1995 Entenmann's was acquired by CPC International (Bestfoods). In 2000 Bestfoods was purchased by Unilever which sold it to Weston in 2001. In 2008 Entenmann's was acquired by the Mexican conglomerate Grupa Bimbo. In July of 2014 the company ended its baking operation in Bay Shore but continued its store, sales, and distribution at the Bay Shore facility.

The 4,500-square-foot, five-bedroom, six-and-a-half-bath house incorporates a pre-existing lighthouse into the structure.

The house was for sale in 2007. The asking price was $3.295 million. It sold in 2009 for $2.2 million.

[For information about the Entenmanns' Bay Shore residences, see *Long Island's Prominent South Shore Families* – Entenmann entries.]

Entenmann, Robert William, Sr. (1928-2016)

Occupation(s):	industrialist - vice-president, president, and chairman of board, Entenmann's, Inc., Bay Shore
	capitalist - a founder and co-owner, with his daughter Jacqueline, Martha Clara Vineyards, Riverhead*
	financier - director and partner, First Long Investors, Inc., Jericho, NY (wealth management firm)
Civic Activism:	chairman, fund raising committee, American Cancer Society of Suffolk County, NY, 1970-1971;
	trustee, American Cancer Society of Suffolk County, NY;
	trustee, Y. M. C. A.;
	member, Board of Fire Commissioners, Bay Shore;
	captain, Bay Shore Hose Company
Marriage(s):	div. – Mary L. Bayer
Address:	642 Old Montauk Highway, Montauk
Name of estate:	
Year of construction:	
Style of architecture:	Modern
Architect(s):	
Landscape architect(s):	
House extant: yes	
Historical notes:	

    Robert William Entenmann, Sr. was the son of William Charles and Martha Clara Schneider Entenmann, Jr. of Bay Shore. His brother Charles married Nancy Lee Drake and resided in Bay Shore and Montauk. His brother William Charles Entenmann III married Christine Sutton and resided in Bay Shore and at *Timber Bay Farm* in Old Westbury [*See* Spinzia, *Long Island's Prominent South Shore Families* – Entenmann entries – and *Long Island's Prominent North Shore Families, vol. I* – Entenmann entry.]
    Mary L. Bayer Entenmann is the daughter of Charles J. and Louise ____ Bayer, Sr. of Central Islip.
    Robert William and Mary L. Bayer Entenmann, Sr.'s daughter Jacqueline married John Connolly and, later, Jason Damianos, the son of the founder of Pindar Vineyards, Dr. Herodotis Damianos.
    *The 200-acre Martha Clara Vineyards, which was named after Robert's mother, was for sale in 2014. The asking price was said to be $29 million.
    Entenmann's 3,000-square-foot house was for sale in 2012. The asking price was just under $10 million.
    [For information about the Entenmanns' East Islip and Bay Shore residences, see *Long Island's Prominent South Shore Families* – Entenmann entries.]

Ephron, Nora (1941-2012)

Occupation(s): journalist - reporter, *New York Evening Post*;
women's issues column, *Esquire Magazine*;
articles, *Women's Wear Daily*;
article, *Cosmopolitan*
writer - *Silkwood*, 1983 (novel);
Heartburn, 1986 (novel);
Imaginary Friends, 2002 (play)
entertainers and associated professions -
wrote screenplay and produced:
When Harry Met Sally, 1989;
Cookie, 1989;
My Blue Heaven, 1990;
wrote and directed:
This is My Life, 1992;
co-authored with her sister Delia Ephron, *Sleepless in Seattle*, 1993;
Mixed Nuts, 1994;
wrote, directed, and produced:
Michael, 1996;
You've Got Mail, 1998;
Bewitched, 2005;
Julie and Julia, 2009

Marriage(s): M/1 – 1967-div. 1976 – Dan Greenberg
- writer
M/2 – 1976-div. 1980 – Carl Bernstein (b. 1944)
- journalist - reporter, *Washington Post* (broke Watergate scandal);
numerous free-lance articles;
Washington Bureau Chief and senior correspondent, ABC News, 1980-1984;
writer - co-authored with Bob Woodward, *All the President's Men*, 1974;
The Final Days, 1976;
co-authored with Marco Politi, *His Holiness: John Paul II and the History of Our Times*, 1996;
The Secret Man, 2005;
Loyalties: *A Son's Memoir*, 1989;
A Woman in Charge: The Life of Hillary Rodham Clinton, 2007
Civic Activism: president, B'nai Brith
M/3 – 1987-2012 – Nicholas Pileggi, Jr. (b. 1933)
- writer - *Private Eye*, 1987 (novel);
Loyalty and Betrayal, 1994;
Vegas (television series);
wrote novel and screenplay:
Wiseguy: Life in a Mafia Family, 1986 (adapted into movie "Goodfellas", 1990);
Casino: Love and Honor in Las Vegas (adapted into movie "Casino", 1995);
wrote screenplay:
City Hall, 1996
entertainers and associated professions -
wrote and produced:
King of South Beach, 2007;
American Gangster, 2007

Ephron, Nora (cont'd)

Address: 115 Apaquogue Road, East Hampton
Name of estate:
Year of construction:
Style of architecture: Shingle
Architect(s):
Landscape architect(s):
House extant: yes
Historical notes:

The five-bedroom, four-bath, 4,000-square-foot house was previously owned by Alfred Valentine Leaman, Jr. who called in *Sunset Cottage*, and, then, by his son Alfred Valentine Leaman III. It was subsequently owned by Ephron.

She was the daughter of Henry R. and Phoebe Wolkind Ephron.

Carl Bernstein is the son of Alfred and Sylvia Walker Bernstein. Carl had previously been married to Carol Honsa. After his divorce from Nora, he married Christine Kuehbeck.

Nicholas Pileggi is the son of Nicholas and Susan Defaslo Pileggi, Sr.

Erdmann, Dr. John Frederic (1864-1954)

Occupation(s): physician - surgeon*
educator - professor of practical anatomy, New York University, NYC;
professor of surgery, Bellevue Hospital Medical College, NYC

Civic Activism: governor, Devon Yacht Club, Amagansett;
a founder and governor, Montauk Swordfish Club

Marriage(s): 1894-1952 – Georgiana Therese Wright (1868-1952)

Address: 89 Lily Pond Lane, East Hampton
Name of estate: *Coxwould*
Year of construction: 1912
Style of architecture: Coxwold
Architect(s): Albro and Lindeberg designed the house (for Erdmann)
Landscape architect(s): Edwina Von Gal designed the gardens (for Schulman)**
Builder: Smith and Davis
House extant: yes
Historical notes:

The eight-bedroom, eight-bath, 9,000-square-foot house, originally named *Coxwould*, was built by Dr. John Frederic Erdmann.

The *Social Register Summer, 1921* lists Dr. John F. and Mrs. Georgianna T. Wright Erdmann as residing on Lily Pond Lane in East Hampton.

He was the son of Zacharia and Maria Elizabeth Lippert Erdmann.

Georgianna Therese Wright Erdmann was the daughter of George Waterman and Georgiana Sturtevant Taft Wright of Providence, RI.

Dr. John Frederic and Mrs. Georgianna Therese Wright Erdmann's son Sturtevant married Wilma Kohler and resided in New Canaan, CT. Their daughter Olivia married John Louis Kuser, Jr. and resided in Amagansett and at *Strawberry Hill* in Titusville, NJ. Their daughter Jane, who subsequently owned *Coxwould* married William Lafayette Burton II, with whom she resided in East Hampton; Frank Aurelio Gonzalez, with whom she resided in Southampton; and, later, Morgan Whitney.

*At the age of twenty-nine, Erdmann assisted the surgeon who removed a cancerous portion of President Grover Cleveland's upper jaw. Fearful of a financial panic, the operation was done clandestinely aboard a yacht on Long Island Sound while the President was seated in a chair. [*The New York Times* March 28, 1954, p. 89.] During his medical career Erdmann performed over 20,000 operation including chest surgery on tenor Enrico Caruso.

In 1954 Mrs. Burton sold the house to Dayton Hedges. [*The East Hampton Star* August 5, 1954, p. 1.] In 1958 Hedges' son Burke Osborn Hedges purchased the house. [*The East Hampton Star* July 3, 1958, p. 4.] It was then owned by Joseph Weinstein and, subsequently, by Lowell M. Schulman who renamed it *Beechwood*. In 2012 the house was for sale by Schulman. The asking price was $24.95 million; the annual taxes were $60,000.

**Edwina Von Gal created fifteen garden rooms which were inspired by English gardens.

Erwin, Daniel Peart, Jr. (b. 1903)

Occupation(s):	
Marriage(s):	M/1 – 1925-div. 1931 – Mary Moore (1903-1977)
	M/2 – 1933-div. 1940 – Roma Virginia Volck (1917-1985)
	(aka Doris Dudley)
	- entertainers and associated professions - actress
	M/3 –1943 – Camilla Woodward Livingston (1902-1978)
Address:	13 Fithian Lane, East Hampton
Name of estate:	
Year of construction:	
Style of architecture:	
Architect(s):	
Landscape architect(s)	
House extant: unconfirmed	

Historical notes:

Daniel Peart Erwin was the son of Daniel Peart Erwin, Sr. of Indianapolis, IN.

Mary Moore Erwin was the daughter of David Thomas and Mary P. Earle Moore of Westbury.

Roma Volck Erwin was the daughter of Adelbert Volck of NYC. She later married Gordon P. Franklin and, subsequently, Jack Jenkins.

The Blue Book of The Hamptons, 1958 lists Daniel Peart and Camilla Woodward Livingston Erwin as residing at 13 Fithian Lane, East Hampton.

She was the daughter of Johnston and Nathalie Fellows Moss Livingston II and the granddaughter of Robert Cambridge and Maria Whitney Livingston III of *Lakeside* in Islip. [*See* Spinzia, *Long Island's Prominent South Shore Families* – Livingston entry.] Camilla had previously been married to Donald McVickar, the son of Henry Goelet and Janet Lansing McVickar of *Pondacre* in East Norwich. [*See* Spinzia, *Long Island's Prominent North Shore Families, vol. I* – McVickar entry.] Her half-brother Johnston Livingston III resided in East Hampton.

Ethridge, George (1866-1941)

Occupation(s):	advertising executive - founder and treasurer, George Ethridge Co.*
	journalist - a founder and editor, "Department of Commercial Art",
	NYC, in *Printer's Ink*
	financier - director, Central Mercantile Bank, NY
Civic Activism:	trustee, American Defense Society;
	trustee, St. Agnes Day Nursery, NYC;
	member, nominating committee, Maidstone Club, East Hampton
Marriage(s):	1894-1941 – Julia Dinsmore Flandrau (1872-1941)
	- Civic Activism: secretary, St. Agnes Day Nursery, NYC;
	president, Ladies Village Improvement Society
Address:	68 Woods Lane, East Hampton
Name of estate:	
Year of construction:	1902
Style of architecture:	Shingle
Architect(s):	Isaac Henry Green II designed
	the house (for E. M. Schmidt)**
Landscape architect(s):	
Builder:	Breckenridge and Ashby
House extant: yes	

Historical notes:

The house was built by Max Eberhardt Schmidt. It was later owned by Ethridge.

The *Social Directory of Southampton, Long Island, 1931* lists George and Julia D. Flandrau Ethridge as residing on Woods Lane, East Hampton.

He was the son of Alfred and Abby Murdock Ethridge of Rome, NY.

Julia Dinsmore Flandrau Ethridge was the daughter of Thomas Macomb and Clarissa Foote Flandrau.

*Ethridge introduced advertising psychology into advertising illustrations.

In 1943 the house was purchased by Mrs. John Howie Wright, Jr. [*The East Hampton Star* July 1, 1943, p. 5.]

In 2009 the five-bedroom house was for sale. The asking price was $3.95 million.

**For Green's other commissions, *see* Spinzia, *Long Island's Prominent South Shore Families: Their Estates and Their Country Homes in the Towns of Babylon and Islip*.

Evans, Benjamin Franklin (1843-1913)

Occupation(s):	financier - founder and president, Evans, Conger, & Breyer, Inc. (insurance brokerage firm); banker
Marriage(s):	1869-1913 – Harriet Cassard Bonbright (1847-1933)
Address:	Lily Pond Lane, East Hampton
Name of estate:	*Dunemead*
Year of construction:	1913
Style of architecture:	Shingle
Architect(s):	John Custis Lawrence designed the house (for Evans)
Landscape architect(s):	
Builder:	Smith and Davis built the house R. S. Parsons, electrical S. C. Grimshaw, plumbing S. J. Lynch, masonry

House extant: yes
Historical notes:

    The twelve-bedroom, four-bath house, originally named *Dunemead*, was built by the Benjamin Franklin Evans.
    The *Social Register Summer, 1919* lists Harriet C. Bonbright Evans as residing at *Dunemead* in East Hampton. The *Social Directory of the Hamptons, 1931* lists Harriet C. Bonbright Evans as residing on Lily Pond Lane, East Hampton.
    She was the daughter of William and Elizabeth Cross Bonbright.
    Benjamin Franklin Evans was the son of Jason Evans.
    Benjamin Franklin and Harriet Cassard Bonbright Evans' daughter Madeline married David Hunter McAlpin II and resided in East Hampton. Their daughter Elizabeth married Oliver Chandler Billings, Sr. and resided in Morristown, NJ. Their daughter Harriet did not marry. Their daughter Mary married Walter S. Cramp.
    The house was later owned by Malcolm Evans McAlpin who continued to call it *Dunemead*.
    In 2002 it was for sale. The asking price was $27 million. [*The New York Times* September 15, 2002, p. E118.]

Evans, James Hurlburt (1920-2015)

Occupation(s):	attorney
	capitalist - chairman of board, Union Pacific Railroad; chairman of board, Union Pacific Corp.; director, American Telegraph and Telephone Co.; director, The Anaconda Co.
	financier - chairman of board, The Seamen's Bank; president, Dun & Broadstreet; attorney and loan officer, Harris Trust and Saving Bank; director, Citicorp/Citibank; director, Metropolitan Life Insurance Co.
	industrialist - director, Bristol Myers Co.; director, General Motors Corp.
Civic Activism:	trustee, Recreatub Foundation; chairman of board, Central Park Conservancy; trustee, New York Presbyterian Hospital, NYC; trustee, University of Chicago; chairman, board of trustees, Centre College, Danville, KY; co-chairman, John F. Kennedy Center for the Performing Arts, Washington, DC; governor, American National Red Cross; trustee, Rockefeller Brothers Fund; endowed the Eric B. Evans Scholarship, Centre College, Danville, KY; trustee, National Recreation and Park Association; member, Citizens Advisory Committee on Environmental Quality
Marriage(s):	M/1 – 1944-div. – LoRaine Bertram (1921-2009)
	M/2 – 1984-2015 – Mary Catherine Johnston (1930-2014)
Address:	32 Windmill Lane, East Hampton
Name of estate:	
Year of construction:	1986
Style of architecture:	Contemporary
Architect(s):	
Landscape architect(s):	
Builder:	Patrick Trunzo
House extant: yes	
Historical notes:	

The house was built by James Hurlburt Evans.
He was the son of James L. and Marie Hurlburt Evans.
LoRaine Bertram Evans was the daughter of Frederick A. and Ruth E. Martin Bertram.
James Hurlburt and LoRaine Bertram Evans' son Eric died in 1996 of complications from liver transplant surgery. Their daughter Carol married Thomas Craig Jepperson. Their daughter Joanie married Richard Madsen.
The Blue Book of The Hamptons, 1992 lists James H. and Mary Catherine Johnston Evans as residing on Windmill Lane, East Hampton.
She was the daughter of Paul X. and Helen Elizabeth Alford Johnston. Mary had previously been married to Benjamin Thomas Head.
In 2019 the estate of Evans listed the 5,500-square-foot, five-bedroom, six-bath main residence with a three-bedroom 1950's guest house and 6.5 acres for sale. The asking price was $60 million.

Farrington, Selwyn Kip, Jr. (1904-1983)

Occupation(s):	financier - partner, George and Farrington (stock brokerage firm)
	writer - 21 sports, railroad, maritime, and pet books
	journalist - saltwater editor, *Field and Stream*, 1937-1972
	public relations executive - member, Kelly Nelson
Civic Activism:	founder, international tuna cup competition;
	director, Maidstone Club, East Hampton
Marriage(s):	1934-1983 – Sarah H. Chisholm (aka Chise Farrington) (1907-1992)
	- writer - *Women Can Fish*, 1951
	journalist - articles for *Harper's Bazaar*, *Vogue*, and *Mademoiselle*
Address:	Dune Meadows, East Hampton
Name of estate:	*Finning Out*
Year of construction:	
Style of architecture:	
Architect(s):	
Landscape architect(s)	
House extant: unconfirmed	
Historical notes:	

The Blue Book of The Hamptons, 1973 and the *Social Register Summer, 1969* list S. Kip and Sarah H. Chisholm Farrington, Jr. as residing at *Finning Out* on Dune Meadows, East Hampton.

He was the son of Selwyn Kip and Elizabeth Josephine Taylor Farrington, Sr. His mother Elizabeth subsequently married Ira Andruss Kip, Jr. with whom she resided in Hewlett Bay Park and, later, East Hampton. [*See* Spinzia, *Long Island's Prominent Families in the Town of Hempstead* – Kip entry.]

Sarah H. Chisholm Farrington was the daughter of Edward and Edith Seymour Johnson de Clifford Chisholm of *Overdune* in East Hampton.

Sarah held seven world fishing records.

Fennelly, Leo C. (1897-1979)

Occupation(s):	attorney - partner, Fennelly, Eagan, Nager, and Lage;
	partner, Fennelly, Douglas, Eagan, Nager, and Voorhees;
	assistant United States attorney, 1934-1939;
	special assistant to United States Attorney General,
	1939-1940
Marriage(s)	1928-1979 – Edith Louise Buhler (1901-1986)
Address:	Lily Pond Lane, East Hampton
Name of estate:	
Year of construction:	
Style of architecture:	
Architect(s):	
Landscape architect(s):	
House extant: yes	
Historical notes:	

The Blue Book of The Hamptons, 1973 lists Leo C. and Edith L. Buhler Fennelly as residing on Lily Pond Lane in East Hampton.

He was the son of Michael and Mary Fennelly.

Edith Louise Buhler Fennelly was the daughter of Carl Conrad and Martha Caroline Warburg Buhler of NYC.

Leo C. and Edith Louise Buhler Fennelly's daughter Carol married John J. Devendorf, the son of George Epworth and Adelina Spinetti Devendorf of Lake Success and *El Paraiso* in Amagansett. [*See* Spinzia, *Long Island's Prominent North Shore Families* – Devendorf entry.] Carol later married Waldo Hutchins III with whom she resided in Glen Head. Their daughter Marcia married George W. Gowen II, the son of Franklin Crosbie and May Elizabeth Klein Gowen, and resided in East Hampton.

Finkbeiner, Dr. John A. (1917-1996)

Occupation(s):	physician - Chief of Oncology, Lenox Hill Hospital, NYC
Civic Activism:	president, New York State Medical Society
Marriage(s):	M/1 – 1946-div. 1952 – Jean Adelaide Kerr (1915-2010)
	M/2 – 1955-div. – Sarah Frances Getman (1913-1976)
	M/3 – Mary Stuart (1910-1976)
Address:	Jericho Road, East Hampton
Name of estate:	*Second Dune*
Year of construction:	
Style of architecture:	
Architect(s):	
Landscape architect(s)	
House extant: unconfirmed	
Historical notes:	

The Blue Book of The Hamptons, 1973 lists Dr. and Mrs. John A. Finkbeiner as residing on Jericho Lane, East Hampton.

The East Hampton Star July 10, 1969, p. 4, lists the estate name as *Second Dune*.

He was the son of Daniel T. Finkbeiner of Harrisburg, PA.

Jean Adelaide Kerr Finkbeiner was the daughter of William Walter Kerr of *Ravenscraig*, Seafield, Roslin, Scotland. She subsequently married John E. Watson of York, PA.

Sarah Francis Getman Finkbeiner was the daughter of William and Adelyn F. Brown Getman. She had previously been married to Ralph Hudson Plumb, the son of Ralph and Julia Cary Plumb of Buffalo, NY.

Mary Stuart Finkbeiner was the daughter of William and Xena Leper Stuart of Missouri.

Fish, Sidney Webster (1885-1950)

Occupation(s):	attorney
Marriage(s):	M/1 – 1915-1937 – Olga Wiborg (1889-1937)
	M/2 – 1939-1950 – Esther Foss (1984-1954)
Address:	New Highway, East Hampton
Name of estate:	
Year of construction:	
Style of architecture:	
Architect(s):	
Landscape architect(s)	
House extant: unconfirmed	
Historical notes:	

The *Social Directory of Southampton, Long Island, 1931* lists Sidney W. and Olga Wiborg Fish as residing on New Highway, East Hampton.

His father was Stuyvesant Fish, Sr., president of the Illinois Railroad. His mother was the famous Newport socialite Marion Graves Anton Fish, known for her bizarre formal dinner parties at which domestic pets were the guests of honor. Sidney's sister Marion married Albert Zebriskie Gray of *Orchard Farm* in Old Westbury. [*See* Spinzia, *Long Island's Prominent North Shore Families, vol. I* – Gray entry.]

Olga Wiborg Fish was the daughter of Frank Bestow and Adeline Moulton Sherman Wiborg of *The Dunes* in East Hampton. Olga's sister Mary did not marry. Her sister Sara married Gerald Clery Murphy, the son of Patrick Francis and Ann Ryan Murphy of *Agawam* in Southampton, and resided at *Swan Cove* in East Hampton. [*See* Spinzia, *Long Island's Prominent Families in the Town of Southampton* – Murphy entry.]

Esther Foss Fish was the daughter of Governor Eugene Noble Foss of Massachusetts. She had previously been married to George Gordon Moore and Aidan Roark.

[For information about Fish's Old Brookville residence, see Spinzia, *Long Island's Prominent North Shore Families, vol. I* – Fish entry.]

In 1940 the house was purchased by Ledyard Mitchell. [*The East Hampton Star* September 12, 1940, p. 5.]

Fisher, Carl Graham, Sr. (1874-1939)

Occupation(s): industrialist - manufacturer of Prest-o-Lite (standard headlight in
  early automobiles)
  merchant - partner, with Barney Oldfield, Fisher Automobile Co.,
   Indianapolis, IN (Packard, Stutz car, and Reo truck
   dealership)
  capitalist - developer of the City of Miami, FL*;
   a founder, Indianapolis Motor Speedway, Indianapolis, IN;
   organized and helped build the Lincoln Highway (east-west
    highway across the country;
   organized and helped build the Dixie Highway (north-south
    highway);
   began the development of Montauk, LI**

Marriage(s): M/1 – 1909-div.1926 – Jane Watts (1887-1968)
  M/2 – 1927-1939 – Margaret Eleanor Collier

Address: De Forest Road, Montauk
Name of estate:
Year of construction: 1883
Style of architecture: Beach Cottage
Architect(s): McKim, Mead & White designed
  the house
  Francis Fleetwood, c. 1994
   alterations (for Dennis)
Landscape architect(s): Frederic Law Olmstead designed
  the site plan
House extant: yes
Historical notes:
  The house is one of Montauk Association's "Seven Sisters." It was owned by Henry Sanger and, later, by Fisher.
  He was the son of Albert Harvey and Ida Graham Fisher, Sr.
  Jane Watts Fisher was the step-daughter of James Buchanan Watts. She subsequently married Robert Johnson of New York.
  Carl Graham and Jane Watts Fisher, Sr.'s son Carl Graham Fisher, Jr. died in infancy.
  Margaret Eleanor Collier Fisher subsequently married Howard W. Lyon of New York.
  *Because of his development of Miami, Fisher was adjudged by a panel of fifty-six historians and writers as one of the fifty most influential people in the history of Florida.
  **Fisher's development of some 10,000 acres in Montauk, the "Miami Beach of the North," was never completed. After suffering severe losses in the 1929 stock market crash, Fisher declared bankruptcy in 1932.
  The house was later owned by Frank and Helen Hourtel and, then, by Thomas Dennis.
  [For information about Fisher's North Shore residence, *see* Spinzia, *Long Island's Prominent North Shore Families, vol. I* – Fisher entry.]

Fisher, Carl Graham, Sr. (1874-1939)

Occupation(s): *[See previous entry.]*

Marriage(s): M/1 – 1909-div.1926 – Jane Watts (1887-1968)
  M/2 – 1927-1939 – Margaret Eleanor Collier

Address: 44 Foxboro Road, Montauk
Name of estate:
Year of construction: 1927
Style of architecture: Colonial Revival
Architect(s): Arthur B. Wood designed
  the house (for Fisher)
Landscape architect(s):
House extant: yes
Historical notes:
  The six-bedroom, six-and-a-half-bath, 8,000-square-foot house was built by Carl Graham Fisher, Sr.
  [See previous entry for additional information.]
  It was later owned by Robert Macomber Akin, Jr., who called it *Hilltop House*.
  In 2016 the main residence, a guest house, and 7.6 acres were for sale. The asking price was $10.5 million.

Fleetwood, Francis (1946-2015)

Occupation(s):	architect - member, Pielstick & Roselack, Aspen, CO; a founder, Fleetwood & McMullan, 1980* *[See Architects appendix in this volume for Fleetwood's commissions in East Hampton.]*
Marriage(s):	Stephanie Turner
Address:	85 Ocean View Lane, Amagansett
Name of estate:	
Year of construction:	1988
Style of architecture:	Contemporary
Architect(s):	Francis Fleetwood designed his own residence
Landscape architect(s):	
House extant: yes	
Historical notes:	

The four-bedroom, four-and-a-half-bath, 3,600-square-foot house was built by Francis Fleetwood.
He was the son of Harvey and Dr. Maria Freile Fleetwood.
Stephanie Turner Fleetwood had previously been married to ____ Orhan.
*Fleetwood designed over two hundred house in The Hamptons.
In 2016 the house and 33.67 acres sold for $14.25 million.

Fleming, Henry Stuart (1863-1938)

Occupation(s):	capitalist - president, Louisiana Southern Railway Co. industrialist - director, Middle States Petroleum Co.
Marriage(s):	M/1 – 1905-1927 – Caroline M. Pelgram (1872-1927) - Civic Activism: suffragist* M/2 – 1933-1938 – Thelma Jacobsen Odegaarden
Address:	Woods Lane, East Hampton
Name of estate:	*The Green Flag*
Year of construction:	
Style of architecture:	
Architect(s):	
Landscape architect(s)	
House extant: unconfirmed	
Historical notes:	

The *Social Register Summer, 1915* lists Henry Stuart and Caroline M. Pelgram Fleming as residing at *The Green Flag* in East Hampton.
He was the son of Joseph and Emma L. Scherzer Fleming of Philadelphia, PA.
Caroline M. Pelgram Fleming was the daughter of Charles R. and Eliza Bollery Pelgram of Paterson, NJ.
Henry Stuart and Caroline M. Pelgram Fleming's daughter Elizabeth married Ralph Emerson Stone, the son of Frederick Condit Stone of Peekskill, NY, and resided in Lake Waccabuc, NY.
By 1929 the Flemings had relocated to Southampton. [*See* Spinzia, *Long Island's Prominent Families in the Town of Southampton* – Fleming entry.]
*For other Long Islanders involved in the suffrage movement *see* Raymond E. Spinzia, "Winning the Franchise: Long Island Activists in the Fight for Woman's Suffrage and Their Opponents, Long Island's Anti-Suffragists." wwwspinzialongislandestates.com.

Fleming, Matthew Corry, Sr. (1864-1946)

Occupation(s):	attorney* - partner, Dexter, Osborn, Fleming, and Whittlesey, NYC; counsel, Armstrong Investigating Commission, NYC, 1905-1906
	industrialist - director, Phelps Dodge Corp.; director, Phelps Dodge Mercantile Co.
	capitalist - director, Pardee Co.
Civic Activism:	trustee and secretary, Presbyterian Hospital, NYC;
	director, Bowery branch, Young Men's Christian Association (Y.M.C.A.);
	trustee and treasurer, Princeton University, Princeton, NJ;
	member, first board of governors, Devon Yacht Club, Amagansett
Marriage(s):	1893-1946 – Angeline Wilson (1871-1960)
Address:	Lily Pond Lane, East Hampton
Name of estate:	
Year of construction:	
Style of architecture:	
Architect(s):	
Landscape architect(s):	
House extant: unconfirmed	
Historical notes:	

The *Long Island Society Register, 1929* lists Matthew C. and Angeline Wilson Fleming [Sr.] as residing on Lily Pond Lane, East Hampton.

He was the son of Ebenezer Caldwell and Rachel Corry Fleming.

Angeline Wilson Fleming was the daughter of Moses F. Wilson of Cincinnati, OH.

Matthew Corry and Angeline Wilson Fleming, Sr.'s son Matthew Corry Fleming, Jr. married Dorothy Stevens, the daughter of Richard Stevens of *Manor House*, Castle Point, Hoboken, NJ, and resided in Princeton, NJ.

*In 1905 Fleming was chosen to be a special assistant to Governor Charles Evan Hughes' investigation of the insurance companies. [*The East Hampton Star* February 28, 1946, p. 1.]

Flinn, George Hamilton, Sr. (1875-1929)

Occupation(s):	capitalist - founder, George H. Flinn Corp. (later, Booth & Flinn) (construction firm)*; chairman of board, Booth & Flinn
Marriage(s):	1900-1929 – Clara Louise Negley (1877-1966)
Address:	27 Drew Lane, East Hampton
Name of estate:	
Year of construction:	1920
Style of architecture:	Shingle
Architect(s):	John Custis Lawrence designed the house (for F. K. Hollister) Richard A. Cook of CookFox Associates designed 2007 alterations (for Rosenstein)
Landscape architect(s):	Paula Hayes (for Rosenstein)
Builder:	Edward M. Gay (for F. K. Hollister) Bulgin & Associates, 2007 alterations (for Rosenstein)

House extant: yes
Historical notes:

The house was built by Dr. Frederick Kellogg Hollister and rented by Flinn.

The *Long Island Society Register, 1929* lists George Hamilton and Sara Louise Negley Flinn [Sr.] as residing on Drew Lane, East Hampton.

He was the son of Senator William and Mrs. Mary Galbraith Flinn of Pittsburgh, PA.

Clara Louise Negley Flinn was the daughter of Daniel Charles and Lillie Berry Negley of Pittsburgh, PA.

George Hamilton and Clara Louise Negley Flinn, Sr.'s daughter Louise married Stuyvesant Wainwright, Jr., the son of Dr. Stuyvesant and Mrs. Caroline Smith Snowden Wainwright, Sr. of Rye, NY, and resided at *Duckwood* in Hampton Bays. [*See* Spinzia, *Long Island's Prominent Families in the Town of Southampton* – Wainwright entry.] Their son Lawrence married Marion de Vlaming. Their son George Hamilton Flinn II married Evelyn Lilley.

[See other entries for additional family information.]

*Flinn's construction company built the Holland Tunnel under the Hudson River and a number of New York City's subway tunnels.

In 1939 Mrs. Hollister sold the house to Jesse William Sweetser, Sr. [*The East Hampton Star* June 22, 1939, pp. 1 and 5.]

In 1941 Alexander Fraser purchased it from Sweetser and called it *Wilsheron*. [*The East Hampton Star* October 23, 1941, p. 5.]

In 1960 Frances Ann Cannon (Hersey) Dougherty purchased the house from Fraser. [*The East Hampton Star* April 28, 1960, p. 11.]

In 2005 her husband Frazer Lowber Welsh Dougherty sold it to Barry Rosenstein for $19.2 million. [*The East Hampton Star* June 23, 2005, p. 35.]

In 2017 Rosenstein listed the house for sale. The asking price was $70 million.

In 2019 the 10,425-square-foot, nine-bedroom, thirteen-bath house, a separate two-bedroom caretakers/guest cottage and 1.567 acres were again for sale. The asking price was $52.5 million.

Flinn, Lawrence, Jr. (b. 1936)

Occupation(s):	financier - member, Morgan Stanley & Co. (investment banking firm); member Bogdan Co. (venture capital firm)
	capitalist - a founder, Washington Cable Co. (television cable firm); president, Vestal Video, Binghamton, NY (television cable firm) (later, Video Cablevision, Inc.); president, Tri-Town Video, Inc. (television cable firm); president, United Video of St. Louis, Inc., St. Louis, MO (television cable firm); president, United Video Cablevision of Hawaii, Inc., Hawaii; president, United Video Cablevision, Jackson, OH; director, Lodgenet Entertainment Group; CEO and chairman of board, United Video Satellite Group, Inc.
Civic Activism:	trustee, The Hotchkiss School, Lakeville, CT; member, board of overseers, Columbia Business School, NYC; trustee, Jupiter Medical Center Foundation; a founder, with his wife Stephanie, Stephanie and Lawrence Flinn, Jr. Charitable Trust
Marriage(s):	M/1 – 1955 – Linda Gilbert Scott (aka Linda Scott) - artist*
	M/2 – 1965 – Stephanie Hanes Strubling - artist - portrait painter
	Civic Activism: director and secretary, Girls Club of America, Inc.; a founder, with her husband Lawrence, Stephanie and Lawrence Flinn, Jr. Charitable Trust
Address:	97 Egypt Lane, East Hampton
Name of estate:	
Year of construction:	
Style of architecture:	
Architect(s):	
Landscape architect(s)	
House extant:	unconfirmed
Historical notes:	

    Lawrence Flinn, Jr. is the son of Lawrence and Marion de Vlaming Flinn, Sr.
    In 1973 he purchased the house from Phyllis Stockton B. Wilkinson for $105,000. [*The East Hampton Star* August 9, 1973, p. 17.]
    Linda Gilbert Scott Flinn is the daughter of Martin L. and Helen Boors Scott of New York. Linda later married Richard Pitts.
    *Linda's fifty-foot-tall "Stargazer" sculpture is located on Route 111 in Manorville.
    The *Social Register Summer, 1982* lists Lawrence and Stephanie H. Strubling Flinn, Jr. as residing at 97 Egypt Lane, East Hampton.
    She is the daughter of Philip Henry and Elizabeth Leigh Hanes Strubling, Jr. of Chestnut Hill, PA.
    Lawrence and Stephanie Hanes Strubling Flinn, Jr.'s daughter Marion married John Henry Moulton, the son of Everts Moulton of Las Cruces, NM. Their daughter Adriane did not marry.
[See other Flinn entries for additional family information.]
    By 1992 the Flinns had relocated to Spaeth Lane, East Hampton.
    In 2008 they were residing at *Over Hook*, 6 Maidstone Lane, East Hampton.

Flinn, Lawrence, Sr. (1910-1945)

Occupation(s):	financier - vice-president and treasurer, Institute of Applied Ecometrics, Inc., NYC
	educator - lecturer, University of North Carolina, Chapel Hill, NC
Marriage(s):	1930-1945 – Marion de Vlaming (1906-1969)
	- Civic Activism: assistant treasurer, Guild Hall Rehabilitation Fund, East Hampton
Address:	Lily Pond Lane, East Hampton
Name of estate:	*Sea Song*
Year of construction:	1916
Style of architecture:	Cotswold
Architect(s):	Grosvenor Atterbury designed the house and the 1925 gardener's cottage (for Woodin, Sr.) *[attributed]*
Landscape architect(s)	Marian Cruger Coffin, 1927 (for Woodin, Sr.)

House extant: yes
Historical notes:

In 1941 Lawrence Flinn, Sr. purchased the William Harman Woodin estate *Dune House* and renamed it *Sea Song*. [*The East Hampton Star* October 23, 1941, p. 1, and May 31, 1945, p. 1.]

Lawrence Flinn, Sr. was killed in World War II at the Battle for the Rhine. He was the son of George Hamilton and Sara Louise Negley Flinn, Sr. of East Hampton and Pittsburgh, PA.

The Blue Book of The Hamptons, 1965 lists Marion de Vlaming Flinn as residing at *Sea Song* on Lily Pond Lane, East Hampton.

She was the daughter of Adrian Stanfield de Vlaming of Roxboro, NC. Marion subsequently married Thomas F. Tuohy, Jr.

Lawrence and Marion de Vlaming Flinn, Sr.'s son George Hamilton Flinn II married Kendall Dayton Murphey, the daughter of Chauncey Hulburt Murphey, Jr. of South Salem, NY, and, later, Genie Lord. Their son Michael married Elizabeth Jamison Foulke, the daughter of Joseph William Foulke of St. Louis, MO, and, later, Ann D. Gulliver with whom he resided on Shelter Island. Their son Lawrence Flinn, Jr., who resides in East Hampton, married Linda Gilbert Scott and, later, Stephanie Hanes Strubling.

[See other Flinn entries for additional family information.]

The house was later owned by Donald J. Bruckman.

Ford, James Bishop (1845-1928)

Occupation(s):	industrialist - treasurer, Meyer Rubber Co.;
	vice-president, United States Rubber Co.
Civic Activism:	donated $400,000 to Peekskill Military Academy;
	donated Herrick Park in East Hampton in memory of his sister Harriet Ford Herrick;
	trustee, Museum of the American Indian, Heye Foundation
Marriage(s):	bachelor
Address:	4 Ocean Avenue, East Hampton
Name of estate:	*Pudding Hill*
Year of construction:	c. 1887
Style of architecture:	Shingle
Architect(s):	Isaac Henry Green II designed the house and the 1906 extension (for E. Herrick)*

Landscape architect(s):
House extant: yes
Historical notes:

The house, originally named *Pudding Hill*, was built by Dr. Everett Herrick. It was later owned by Ford, who was Herrick's brother-in-law.

James Bishop Ford was the son of John Ross and Ann Elizabeth Bishop.

The house was later owned by Ford's cousin Bennett Bishop and, subsequently, by John Richard Peddy. Both Bennet Bishop and John Richard Peddy continued to call the house *Pudding Hill*.

*For Green's other commissions, *see* Spinzia, *Long Island's Prominent South Shore Families: Their Estates and Their Country Homes in the Towns of Babylon and Islip.*

Ford, William Clay, Sr. (1925-2014)

Occupation(s):	industrialist - head of Continental Division, Ford Motor Co., Detroit, MI; director, Ford Motor Co., Detroit MI
	capitalist - held controlling interest in Detroit Lions (National Football League team); chairman of board, Detroit Cougars (professional soccer team)
Marriage(s):	1947-2014 – Martha Parke Firestone (b. 1925)
	- capitalist - majority owner and chairman of board, Detroit Lions (National Football League team)
	Civic Activism: trustee, Henry Ford Health System, Detroit, MI
Address:	15 Nichols Lane, East Hampton
Name of estate:	*Dunemere*
Year of construction:	1963
Style of architecture:	
Architect(s):	Mott B. Schmidt designed the house (for W. C. Ford, Sr.)
Landscape architect(s):	
House extant: yes	
Historical notes:	

The Blue Book of The Hamptons, 1973 lists William Clay and Martha Firestone Ford [Sr.] as residing on Nichols Lane, East Hampton.

Their first house on Nichols Lane was destroyed by fire. They immediately built a new house on the site. [*The East Hampton Star* February 14, 1963, p. 1, and May 30, 1963, p. 4.]

He was the son of Edsel Bryant and Eleanor Lowthian Clay Ford. William's brother Henry Ford II, who resided in Southampton, married Anne McDonnell, the daughter of James Francis and Anna Loretta Murray McDonnell Sr. of *East Wickapogue Cottage* in Southampton; Maria Christina Vettore; and, subsequently, Kathleen DuRoss. [*See* Spinzia, *Long Island's Prominent Families in the Town of Southampton* – Ford and McDonnell entries.]

Martha Parke Firestone Ford is the daughter of Harvey Samuel and Elizabeth Parke Firestone, Jr.

William Clay and Martha Parke Firestone Ford, Sr.'s daughter Martha married Peter Christopher Morse. Their daughter Shelia married William Justus Brock, the son of James Earl Brock of Grosse Point, MI, and, later, Steven Hamp. Their daughter Elizabeth married Charles Kontulis II, the son of Charles Phedon and Marilyn Kontulis of Locust Valley.

Foss, Martin Moore, Sr. (1878-1953)

Occupation(s):	publisher - in charge of book publishing, Baker & Taylor, Co., 1901-1907 (book wholesaler and publisher); manager, book department, Hill Public Co., 1907-1909; a founder and president, McGraw–Hill Book Co.
Marriage(s):	M/1 – div. 1921 – Alice Leary M/2 – 1921-1926 – Elizabeth M. Laing (b. 1894) M/3 – 1929-div. 1946 – Sarah J. Bush (aka Sally Bush) (1895-1973)
Address:	11 Egypt Lane, East Hampton
Name of estate:	
Year of construction:	
Style of architecture:	
Architect(s):	
Landscape architect(s):	
House extant: unconfirmed	
Historical notes:	

Martin Moore Foss was the son of Savillian Fuller and Nellie Juliet Moore Foss.

Alice Leary Foss subsequently married Ralph Woodford St. John, the son of The Reverend Henry Woodford and Mrs. Mary Ann Tanner St. John.

Elizabeth M. Laing Foss was the daughter of George and Fannie Henshaw Laing. Elizabeth later married Frederick Proctor, Louis De Jonge Tim, and, subsequently, John J. MacWilliams, Sr.

In 1944 Sarah J. Bush Foss purchased Josiah Peter Marvel's Egypt Lane residence which was known as Lorenzo Easton Woodhouse's Thorpe cottage.

The *Social Register Summer, 1946* lists Martin M. and Sarah Bush Foss [Sr.] as residing on Egypt Lane, East Hampton.

She had previously been married to ____ Bullard. After her divorce from Foss, Sarah married Henry Sanford Thorne with whom she resided at *Rowdy Hall* in East Hampton.

Martin Moore and Sarah Bush Foss, Sr.'s daughter Patricia married Robert Montgomery Donaldson II of Montclair, NJ, and, later, Millard J. Bloomer, Jr.

In 1947 the house was purchased by Fielding S. Robinson. [*The East Hampton Star* May 1, 1947, p. 5.]

Fox, Alvin Gibbs (1927-1964)

Occupation(s):	scientist - physicist in neurological research, College of Physicians and Surgeons, NYC; physicist in neurological research, New York University School of Medicine, NYC
Marriage(s):	1951-1964 – Nancy Louise O'Connell
Address:	86 Lily Pond Lane, East Hampton
Name of estate:	
Year of construction:	1901
Style of architecture:	Neo-Tudor
Architect(s):	Joseph Greenleaf Thorp designed the house (for J. R. Paxton, Sr.)
Landscape architect(s):	
Builder:	George A. Eldredge
House extant: yes	
Historical notes:	

The house, originally named *Windward*, was built by The Reverend John Randolph Paxton, Sr. It was later owned by his daughter Mary Elkins Paxton Hamlin who continue to call it *Windward*. In 1946 Mrs. Hamlin sold the house to Leonard Gerard Bisco. [*The East Hampton Star* February 14, 1946, p. 5.] In 1963 it was purchased by Fox. [*The East Hampton Star* April 23, 1964, p. 3.]

He was the son of Alanson Gibbs and Mary Cumming Humstone Fox of Brooklyn, NY.

Nancy Louise O'Connell Fox was the daughter of John Joseph O'Connell of Springfield, MA. She later married Francis Bryan Williams, Jr. of Richmond, VA, Alan Gordon, and Warren Smith.

Alvin Gibbs and Nancy Louise O'Connell Fox's daughter Brenda married Peter Johannes Gall, the son of Hannes Gall of Vienna, Austria. Their daughter Susan married Michael Philip Jarvis, the son of Kaye Jarvis of Washington.

The house was later owned by Carol Ann Morgan who sold it for $25.5 million in 2010.

Alterations to the house were made in 1906 and 1926.

Francisco, Donald W., Sr. (1891-1973)
aka Don Francisco

Occupation(s):	industrialist - fruit inspector, Chicago office, California Fruit Growers Exchange (later, Sunkist Growers)
	advertising executive - assistant advertising executive, Fruit Growers Exchange, 1915-1916;
	president, Lord and Thomas, 1921-1940 (advertising agency);
	vice-president and director, J. Walter Thompson Co., 1945-1956 (advertising agency)
	educator - lecturer, Michigan State University, Lansing, MI, 1956-1957
Civic Activism:	a founder and assistant coordinator, Voice of America in the Eastern Hemisphere;
	director, Association of Advertisers, 1920-1921;
	president, Pacific Advertising Club of the World, 1921-1923;
	director, National Outdoor Advertising Bureau, 1925;
	director, Advertising Federation of America, 1928-1932;
	governor, American Association of Advertising Agencies, 1937-1939;
	member, United States Mass Media Committee, UNESCO, 1945-1946;
	vice-president and director, Brand Names Foundation, 1952-1955;
	trustee, Michigan State Development Fund, 1956-1958;
	trustee, International House, NYC, 1959-1973;
	director, National Commission on Alcoholism;
	president, Advertising Club, Los Angeles, CA
Marriage(s):	1915-1973 – Constance M. Little (1896-1991)
Address:	Further Lane, Amagansett
Name of estate:	*Windward*
Year of construction:	
Style of architecture:	
Architect(s):	
Landscape architect(s):	
House extant: unconfirmed	
Historical notes:	

In 1952 Francisco purchased the house from James Perkins. [*The East Hampton Star* October 16, 1952, p. 3.]

The Blue Book of The Hamptons, 1973 lists Mr. and Mrs. Don Francisco [Sr.] as residing at *Windward* on Further Lane, East Hampton.

He was the son of Will and Lillian Burgdorf Francisco of Lansing, MI.

Constance M. Little Francisco was the daughter of Charles Little of Passaic, NJ.

Donald W. and Constance M. Little Francisco, Sr.'s son Donald W. Francisco, Jr. married Doris O'Meara and resided in South Norwalk, CT.

Perkins had twice made alterations to the house. [*The East Hampton Star* January 14, 1954, p. 1.]

Franey, Pierre (1921-1996)

Occupation(s):
 chef - French Pavilion, New York World's Fair, 1939;
  executive chef, Le Pavilion, NYC, 1952-1960;
  executive chef, La Cote Basque;
  executive chef, Hedges Inn, East Hampton
 restaurateur - vice-president, Howard Johnson, 1960-1975 (created menus and recipes)
 journalist - "The 60 Minute Gourmet", (a syndicated column which appeared in over 360 newspapers);
  "Kitchen Equipment" column, *The New York Times*;
  co-authored, with Craig Claiborne, weekly food articles and restaurant reviews, *The New York Times*
 publisher - co-published, with Craig Claiborne, food and restaurant newsletter
 entertainers and associated professions -
  PBS series: *"Cuisine Rabide"*;
   "Cooking in America";
   "Cooking in France";
   "Cooking in Europe"
 writer - *Pierre Franey's Kitchen*, 1982;
  The New York Times 60 Minute Gourmet, 1984;
  Pierre Franey's Low-Calorie Gourmet, 1984;
  The New York Times More 60 Minute Gourmet, 1986;
  Pierre Franey's Cooking in France, 1994;
  Pierre Franey's Cooking in America, 1997;
  Cooking with The 60 Minute Gourmet, 1999;

  co-authored, with Richard Flaste & Bryan Miller, *A Chef's Tale*, 1994;

  co-authored, with Craig Claiborne:
   Classic French Cooking, 1970;
   Veal Cookery, 1978;
   The New York Times Cookbook, 1980;
   The Master Cooking Course, 1982;
   Cooking with Craig Claiborne and Pierre Franey, 1985;
   Craig Claiborne's Gourmet Diet, 1985;

  co-authored, with Bryan Miller:
   The Seafood Cookbook, 1986;
   Cuisine Rabide, 1989;

  co-authored, with Claudia Franey Jensen, *Pierre Cooks with His Friends*, 1997

Marriage(s):
 1948-1996 – Elizabeth Chardenet (1922-2008)
  - capitalist - purchasing agent, Scandinavian Airlines
  Civic Activism: chair, annual Fisherman's Fair, Springs;
   a founder, Cape Gardiner Civic Association, 1964
    (later, Accabonac Protection Committee);
   trustee, Town of East Hampton, 1984 and 1985;
   trustee, Nature Conservancy, East End Chapter

Franey, Pierre (cont'd)

Address: 210 Old Stone Highway, East Hampton
Name of estate:
Year of construction: 1965
Style of architecture: Colonial Revival
Architect(s):
Landscape architect(s):
House extant: yes
Historical notes:

The Franeys relocated to this address in 1977 from Gerard Drive, East Hampton.
He was the son of Aristide and Charlotte ____ Franey of Saint Vinnemer, Yonne, France.
Elizabeth Chardenet Franey was the daughter of Auguste and Lucille ____ Chardenet of Lynbrook, NY.
Pierre and Elizabeth Chardenet Franey's daughter Diane, who resides in East Hampton, married Dr. Vadim M. Schaldenko. Their daughter Claudia married Richard Jensen, the son of Edward Jensen of Wantagh, NY, and resides in Larchmont, NY. Their son Jacques resides in Amagansett.
The 2,200-square-foot, three-bedroom, two-bath house and 2.77 acres were for sale in 2014. The asking price was $855,000.

Frankel, Evan M. (1900-1991)

Occupation(s): capitalist - partner, Ross–Frankel, Inc. (Depression era commercial construction);
built and owned apartment buildings on Manhattan's Lower East Side;
land developer, East Hampton, NY;
backed Broadway plays – "Gramercy Ghost";
"The Medium";
"Gentlemen Prefer Blonds";
"Billy Budd"

Civic Activism: established Evan M. Frankel Foundation, 1978;
co-founder, with Jacob M. Kaplan, and chairman, Jewish Center of the Hamptons

Marriage(s): bachelor

Address: Hither Lane, East Hampton
Name of estate: *Brigadoon*
Year of construction: 1946
Style of architecture: Modified Cotswold
Architect(s):
Landscape architect(s):
House extant: yes
Historical notes:

In 1946 Frankel purchased the remains of the former Dr. Clarence Charles Rice estate and converted its carriage house into his residence, which he called *Brigadoon*. At the same time he sunk a swimming pool into the foundation of the former Rice residence.
In 1995 the house was sold for $4.76 million. The proceeds went to the Evan M. Frankle Foundation.

Fraser, Alexander (1890-1975)

Occupation(s):	industrialist - president, Shell Petroleum Corp. (later, Shell Oil Co); president and chairman of board, Shell Oil Co.
	financier - director, Mercantile Trust
Civic Activism:	secretary, Inter-Allied Petroleum Council during World War I;
	chairman of board, Ford Fund for Adult Education;
	trustee, American University, Beirut, Lebanon;
	trustee, St. Louis Symphony Society;
	trustee, Guild Hall, East Hampton;
	vice-president, Williamsburg restoration committee;
	treasurer, Maidstone Club, East Hampton
Marriage(s):	Mary Goodall Nicoll (1898-1969)
Address:	27 Drew Lane, East Hampton
Name of estate:	*Wilsheron*
Year of construction:	1920
Style of architecture:	Shingle
Architect(s):	John Custis Lawrence designed the house (for F. K. Hollister)
	Richard A. Cook of CookFox Associates designed 2007 alterations (for Rosenstein)
Landscape architect(s):	Paula Hayes (for Rosenstein)
Builder:	Edward M. Gay (for F. K. Hollister)
	Bulgin & Associates, 2007 alterations (for Rosenstein)

House extant: yes
Historical notes:

    The house was built by Dr. Frederick Kellogg Hollister. In 1939 Mrs. Hollister sold it to Jesse William Sweetser, Sr. [*The East Hampton Star* June 22, 1939, pp. 1 and 5.] In 1941 Fraser purchased the house from Sweetser.
    The Blue Book of The Hamptons, 1958 lists Alexander and Mary Goodall Nicoll Fraser as residing at *Wilsheron*, Drew Lane, East Hampton.
    He was born in Glasgow, Scotland.
    Mary Goodall Nicoll Fraser was born in Glasgow, Scotland.
    Alexander and Mary Goodall Nicoll Fraser's son Ronald married Sophia Seymour Porter, the daughter of Rutger Bleecker Porter of Tucson, AZ, and, later, Patricia Dodd with whom he resided in East Hampton. Their son William married Minette Adams, the daughter of Stephen Seymour and Elizabeth Lewis Powell Adams of St. Louis, MO, and resided in Memphis, TN. Their daughter Sheila married Thomas Parker Bowman, the son of United States Consul General to South Africa Thomas DeWitt Bowman.
    The house was later owned by Mrs. Francis Ann Cannon (Hersey) Dougherty and, then, by Barry Rosenstein who listed it for sale for $70 million in 2017. In 2019 it was again for sale, listed for $52.5 million.

Fraser, Ronald Goodall (1932-2017)

Occupation(s):	advertising executive - Weightman Group, Philadelphia, PA; Procter & Gamble, Co.
Civic Activism:	New York director, Christian Ministries, NY (Christian outreach)
Marriage(s):	M/1 – 1957-1965 – Sophia Seymour Porter (d. 1965)
	M/2 – 1966-2016 – Patricia Dodd (1939-2016)
	- Civic Activism: executive, Christian Ministries, NY (Christian outreach)
Address:	Apaquogue Road, East Hampton
Name of estate:	
Year of construction:	
Style of architecture:	
Architect(s):	
Landscape architect(s):	
House extant: yes	
Historical notes:	

He was the son of Alexander and Mary Goodall Nicoll Fraser of *Wilsheron* in East Hampton.

Sophia Seymour Porter Fraser was the daughter of Rutger Bleecker Porter of Tucson, AZ.

Ronald Goodall and Sophia Seymour Porter Fraser's daughter Nina married Peter Muscato. Their daughter Allison did not marry.

The Blue Book of The Hamptons, 1992 lists Ronald G. and Patricia Dodd Fraser as residing on Apaquogue Road in East Hampton.

She was the daughter of John Mingus and Florence Appleton Dodd III of *The Kennels* in East Hampton.

Ronald Goodall and Patricia Dodd Fraser's daughter Jennifer married Bruce Webster Gregory, the son of Alan Gill Trexler and Robin Doumar Mossman Gregory of Dallas, TX. Their son Ian married Suzanne C. Middleton.

Friedman, Marvin Ross

Occupation(s):	attorney - Friedman and Friedman, Coral Gables, FL
	merchant - dealer in 20th century art
Marriage(s):	Sheila Natasha Simrod (1943-1993)
	- fashion designer
	writer - *The Art Museum*, 1995
Address:	30 Woods Lane, East Hampton
Name of estate:	
Year of construction:	1895
Style of architecture:	Dutch Colonial
Architect(s):	Isaac Henry Green II designed the house (for Annie Huntting)*
Landscape architect(s):	
Builder:	Philip Ritch
	George A. Eldredge, addition of new kitchen and servants' quarters, 1898**
House extant: yes	
Historical notes:	

The house was built by Annie Huntting. In 1909 she sold it to E. T. Dayton. [*The East Hampton Star* May 7, 1909, p. 5.] In the 1970s it was purchased by Friedman.

Marvin Ross and Sheila Natasha Simrod Friedman's daughter Natasha married Daniel Efren Tauber, the son of Ronald and Adele Tauber of New York.

*For Green's other commissions, *see* Spinzia, *Long Island's Prominent South Shore Families: Their Estates and Their Country Homes in the Towns of Babylon and Islip.*

**In 1897 the house was also enlarged. In 1909 a new addition was added to the rear of the house and a separate cottage was built.

Fuhrman, Gary L.

Occupation(s):	financier - member, Arnhold and S. Bleichroeder, Inc. (investment banking firm);
	a founder, CEO, chairman of board, and treasurer, GF Capital Management and Advisors, LLC (private equity firm);
	director and vice-president, Natixia Securities Associates, LLC (investment banking firm)
	industrialist - director, Melodeo, Inc. (wireless software firm);
	director, Precise Software Solutions, Ltd.
	merchant - director, Medical Resources, Inc. (medical equipment and furnishings supplier)
Civic Activism:	trustee, Garden of Dreams Foundation;
	trustee, Dwight School Foundation, NYC;
	governor, Dwight School
Marriage(s):	Dorian Flynn
	- advertising executive – director of fashion advertising, *Elle* magazine Civic Activism: trustee, East Hampton Historical Society;
	a founder, Parents Against Vaping e-Cigarettes
Address:	34 Terbell Lane, East Hampton
Name of estate:	
Year of construction:	
Style of architecture:	Shingle
Architect(s):	
Landscape architect(s)	
House extant: yes	
Historical notes:	

Dorian Flynn is the daughter of Edward Patrick Flynn.
In 2005 the house sold for $7.7 million.
The Fuhrmans razed the Gwathmey-designed house to build a new residence.

Fuller, Edward Reinow (1896-1964)

Occupation(s):	advertising executive -
	member, advertising department, Butterick Publishing Co., Chicago, IL (purchased by American Can Company in 1967 and renamed the Butterick Fashion Marketing Co.; now part of The McCall Pattern Co.)*;
	account executive, J. Walter Thompson Co., NYC (advertising firm)
	industrialist - president, Luxor Ltd., Chicago, IL (cosmetics firm); founder, Sylvan Seal Milk, Inc., Philadelphia, PA (later, Borden Milk)**
Civic Activism:	chairman, March of Dimes drive of National Foundation for Infantile Paralysis
Marriage(s):	1923-1964 – Edna Schlesier (b.1899)
Address:	Lee Avenue, East Hampton
Name of estate:	*Tall Trees*
Year of construction:	1955
Style of architecture:	
Architect(s):	
Landscape architect(s):	
House extant: unconfirmed	
Historical notes:	

    The house was built by Edward Reinow Fuller. [*The East Hampton Star* June 16, 1955, p. 12.]
    The Blue Book of The Hamptons, 1958 lists Edward R. and Edna Schlesier Fuller as residing at *Tall Trees* on Lee Avenue, East Hampton.
    He was the son of Charles Spencer and Clara Espenett Fuller of Madison, WI.
    Edna Schlesier Fuller was the daughter of Edwin E. and Susan M. Schlesier of Forest Hills, NY. Edna subsequently married Stuart A. Prosser of Southampton.
    *Butterick Publishing Company was the first publisher to distribute graded sewing patterns.
    **Sylvan Seal Milk is considered to be the first company to package milk solely in paper cartons.
    In 1964 the house was purchased by Edward Whitney. [*The East Hampton Star* May 7, 1964, p. 4.]

Furman, Roy Lance (b. 1940)

Occupation(s):	attorney
	financier - chairman of board, Jefferies Capital Partners (private equity funds);
	a founder and CEO, Furman Selz, LLC (investment banking firm);
	vice-chairman of board, ING Barings, LLC
	entertainers and associated professions - producer, Broadway plays
Civic Activism:	chairman of board, Lincoln Center for the Performing Arts, NYC;
	chairman of board, Film Society of Lincoln Center, NYC;
	a founder, with his wife Frieda, Frieda and Roy Furman Foundation Center, NYC;
	chairman of board, Brooklyn College Foundation;
	chairman of board, Harvard Law School Fund;
	finance chairman, Democratic National Committee, 1992-1993
Marriage(s):	1965-2013 – Frieda Anne Bueler (d. 2013)
	- educator - teacher, Chapaqua, NY, school district
	Civic Activism: a founder, with her husband Roy, Frieda and Roy Furman Foundation Center, NYC
Address:	50 Broadview Road, Amagansett
Name of estate:	
Year of construction:	1955
Style of architecture:	Modified Shingle
Architect(s):	
Landscape architect(s):	
House extant: yes	
Historical notes:	

The seven-bedroom, eight-and-a-half-bath, 9,000-square-foot house was built by Barry Sonnenfeld. It was later owned by Furman.

He is the son of Joseph M. and Frances Furman of Brooklyn.

Frieda Anne Bueler Furman was the daughter of Jerome Bueler of Asbury Park, NJ.

Roy Lance and Frieda Anne Bueler Furman's daughter Jill married Richard Willis and, later, Andrew Blauner. Their daughter Stephanie married Nicholas Darrow.

In 2014 Furman sold the house to Harvey Weinstein for $11.65 million.

In 2018 Weinsten sold it for $10 million.

Gagosian, Lawrence Gilbert (b. 1945)

Occupation(s):	merchant - founder, Gagosian Gallery (chain of 12 art galleries)
Civic Activism:	trustee, Jazz at Lincoln Center, NYC;
	trustee, Institute of Fine Arts, New York University, NYC
Marriage(s):	bachelor
Address:	428 Further Lane, Amagansett
Name of estate:	
Year of construction:	1982
Style of architecture:	International
Architect(s):	Charles Gwathmey designed the house (for de Menil);
	1990 alterations (for Bronfman)
Landscape architect(s)	
House extant: yes*	
Historical notes:	

The 11,000-square-foot house, originally named *Toad Hall*, was built by Francois de Menil. In 1988 it was purchased from de Menil by Gagosian.

He is the son of Ara and Ann Louise Toakin Gagosian of Los Angeles.

Gagosian does not have children although it is rumored that he was married for sixteen days.

In 1990 the house was purchased by Edgar Miles Bronfman, Jr.

*In 2011 there was serious fire in the main residence. In 2014 there was a fire in the guest house.

Gallagher, Thomas (b. 1944)

Occupation(s):	capitalist - senior managing director and head, isi Policy RE at Icm Holdings (supplier to oil industry)
Marriage(s):	Alice Jarcho (b. 1946) - financier - stock trader, Loews Corp; vice-president, Oppenheimer and Co., 1976
Address:	52 Ruxton Road, East Hampton
Name of estate:	*Cove Hollow Farm*
Year of construction:	1987
Style of architecture:	Shingle
Architect(s):	
Landscape architect(s):	
House extant: yes	
Historical notes:	

In 2010 Thomas Gallagher purchased the 3,200-square-foot, four-bedroom, three-bath house from Stephen Allen Schwarzman for $6.25 million.

Alice Jarcho Gallagher is the daughter of Ralph and Lillian Baron Jarcho of Manhattan.

Gallatin, Frederic (1841-1927)

Occupation(s):	attorney
Marriage(s):	1866-1917 – Amy Goelet Gerry (1840-1917)
Address:	Ocean Avenue, East Hampton
Name of estate:	*Breezy Lawn*
Year of construction:	1878-1880
Style of architecture:	Stick-style
Architect(s):	James Renwick, Jr. designed the house (for F. Gallatin)
Landscape architect(s):	Charles Nassau Lowrie, Sr. (for Leonard)
House extant: no; demolished in 1930s	
Historical notes:	

The house, originally named *Breezy Lawn*, was built by Frederic Gallatin.

The *Social Register Summer, 1910* lists Frederic and Amy G. Gerry Gallatin as residing in East Hampton.

He was the son of James Albert Rolaz and Mary Lucille Stevens Gallatin, Sr.

Amy Goelet Gerry Gallatin was the daughter of Thomas Russell and Hannah Green Goelet Gerry.

Frederic and Amy Goelet Gerry Gallatin's daughter Jean married George Philip Camman, Jr. and resided in East Hampton. Their daughter Amy married Howland Pell and resided in Tuxedo Park, NY. Their daughter Mary married William Warner Hoppin, Jr., the son of William Warner and Katharine Beekman Hoppin, Sr. of Manhattan, and resided at *Friendship Hill* in Old Brookville. [*See* Spinzia, *Long Island's Prominent North Shore Families, vol. 1* – Hoppin entry.] Their son Rolag married Emily Lorillard Morris and resided at *Chepstow* in Newport, RI. Their son Goelet married Edith Church Post, the daughter of Charles Alfred and Caroline de Trobriand Post of *Standhome* in Bayport, and resided in Blue Point. [*See* Spinzia, *Long Island's Prominent South Shore Families* – Post entry.] Their son Albert Gallatin II married Margaret Hoffman Hackstaff, the daughter of Charles Ludovic Hackstaff of East Hampton, and resided in Southampton. [*See* Spinzia, *Long Island's Prominent Families in the Town of Southampton* – Gallatin entry.]

In 1919 the house was purchased by Stephen Joseph Leonard, Sr., who renamed it *Waterwood*. [*The East Hampton Star* March 15, 1979, p. 22.]

In 1943 the Hook Pond Corporation purchased the estate's grounds for development. [*The East Hampton Star* October 10, 1968, p. 16.]

Gallatin, James (1846-1890)

Occupation(s):	
Civic Activism:	founder and first president, Society for Improving the Condition of the Poor;
	treasurer, Village of East Hampton
Marriage(s):	Elisabeth Hill Dawson (1843-1928)
Address:	4 Pudding Hill Lane, East Hampton
Name of estate:	*The Rainbow*
Year of construction:	1889
Style of architecture:	Shingle
Architect(s):	
Landscape architect(s):	
Builder:	James L'Hommedieu
House extant: yes	
Historical notes:	

The house, originally named *The Rainbow*, was built by James Gallatin.

The *Social Register Summer, 1910* lists James and Elisabeth Dawson Gallatin as residing at *The Rainbow* in East Hampton.

He was the son of Albert Rolaz and Mary Lucille Stevens Gallatin, Sr.

Elisabeth Hill Dawson Gallatin was the daughter of Benjamin Frederick and Elisabeth Osborne Dawson.

James and Elisabeth Hill Dawson Gallatin's daughter Helen married George Kidder Davis, the son of Andrew Jackson and Louisa Dana Davis of Wilkes Barre, PA; Charles Newbold Welsh, the son of John Lowber and Maria Newbold Welsh; and, later, Baron Emile Christian De Stubner. Their son Francis married Harriet Lawrence Bogart, the daughter of Charles Ludlow and Julia T. Hamilton Bogart, and, later, Dorothy C. Brady. Their daughter Elizabeth married John de Courcy Ireland, the son of John B. Ireland of NYC. Their son Albert married Beatrice Armall. Their son James Nicholson Gallatin, who also later owned the house, married Pauline Munroe Cory and, later, Ida Robinson Adams.

[See other Gallatin entries for additional family information.]

The house was later owned by Martin Gordon. [*The East Hampton Star* March 22, 1979, p. 22.]

Gallatin, James Nicholson (1878-1916)

Occupation(s):	financier - stockbroker
	merchant - proprietor, florist shop, Fifth Avenue, NYC
Marriage(s):	M/1 – 1902-div. 1903 – Pauline Munroe Cory (1874-1960)
	M/2 – 1907-div. 1911 – Ida Robinson Adams (b. 1874)
Address:	4 Pudding Hill Lane, East Hampton
Name of estate:	
Year of construction:	1889
Style of architecture:	Modified Colonial Revival with Shingle elements
Architect(s):	
Landscape architect(s):	
Builder:	James L'Hommedieu
House extant: yes	
Historical notes:	

The house was built by James Gallatin. It was later owned by his son James Nicholson Gallatin.

He was the son of James Nicholson and Elizabeth Dawson Gallatin of East Hampton.

James' 1902 engagement to the actress Edna Wallace was terminated in June of the same year.

Pauline Munroe Cory Gallatin was the daughter of David Monroe and Ellen Cory of Manhattan. She later married Joseph Stevens Ulman and, subsequently, Sir Claude Edward Marjoribanks Dansey of London, England.

Ida Robinson Adams Gallatin was the daughter of gambler Albert J. ("Al") Adams, who was known as "the policy king" of Providence, RI, and Mrs. Isabella Adams. Ida was later married to Francis Baldwin Anderson; the marriage lasted one week.

[See other Gallatin entries for additional family information.]

Gardiner, David Lion, Sr. (1784-1844)

Occupation(s):	attorney
	politician - New York State Senator, First District, 1824-1828
	writer - *Chronicles of East Hampton*
Marriage(s):	1815-1844 – Juliana MacLachlan (1799-1864)
Address:	129 Main Street, East Hampton
Name of estate:	*White House*
Year of construction:	1835
Style of architecture:	
Architect(s):	
Landscape architect(s):	
House extant:	no; demolished in 1939
Historical notes:	

The almost one-hundred-year history of the Gardiner family's association with *White House* is a dizzying sequence of names, interfamily relationships that encompass litigation between First Lady Julia Tyler and her brother David Lion Gardiner, Jr. over ownership, adoption, and the transfer of ownership from one branch of the family to another branch and its accompanying animosity. The following is an abbreviated version of ownership:

The house was built by John Dimon. It was later owned by Gardiner who called it *White House*.
He was the son of Abraham and Phebe Dayton Gardiner.
Juliana MacLachlan Gardiner was the daughter of Michael MacLachlan.
*While sailing aboard the USS *Princeton* with President Tyler David Lion Gardiner, Sr. was killed when a canon exploded.
David Lion and Juliana MacLachlan Gardiner, Sr.'s daughter Juliana (aka Julia) married President John Tyler. Their son Alexander was a Clerk of the United States Circuit Court and an unofficial aide to President Tyler. Their son David Lion Gardiner, Jr., who later owned *White House*, married Sarah Gardiner Thompson. They divided their time between East Hampton and *Sagtikos Manor* in West Bay Shore which he also owned. [*See* Spinzia, *Long Island's Prominent South Shore Families in the Towns of Babylon and Islip* – Gardiner entry.] Their daughter Margaret married John Henry Beekman, the son of Henry and Catherine McPhgaedris Livingston Beekman. In 1850, just two years after they were married, John accidently shot himself and died while on a hunting trip. In 1857 the thirty-four-year-old Margaret died after consuming poison. John and Margaret's son Henry was killed in a riding accident.

In 1937 both *White House* and Gardiner's Island were purchased by David Lion Gardiner, Jr's daughter Sarah Diodati Gardiner who, in 1939, demolished *White House* and built a new house on the site which she called *White House*.

Gardiner, Robert Alexander (1863-1919)

Occupation(s):	
Marriage(s):	1909-1919 – Nora Loftus (1871-1955)
Address:	47 Ocean Avenue, East Hampton
Name of estate:	*Maidstone Hall*
Year of construction:	1869-1870
Style of architecture:	Colonial Revival
Architect(s):	Walter E. Brady, 1901 alterations which transformed house from Stick-style to Colonial Revival (for E. D. Terbell)*
	David Mann, 1990, alterations
Landscape architect(s):	Lear + Mahoney, 1990
Builder:	George Eldredge, 1895 alterations (for H. S. Terbell)
	Jeffery Colle, 1990 alterations

House extant: yes
Nassau County Museum Collection has photographs of the estate.
Historical notes:

    The house, originally named *Maidstone Hall*, was built by Henry S. Terbell, Sr. It was inherited by his son Edward Dyer Terbell. In 1901 he had the original 1869-1870 Stick-style house redesigned into a Colonial Revival style, which he then named *Maidstone Hall*. In 1908 Edward sold the house to Arthur Kennedy. [*The East Hampton Star* November 6, 1908, p. 5.] In 1915 Kennedy sold it to Robert Alexander Gardiner, who, in 1915, made extensive alterations and continue to call the house *Maidstone Hall*.

    The *Social Register Summer, 1921* lists Robert A. and Nora Loftus Gardiner as residing at *Maidstone Hall* in East Hampton.

    He was the son of David Lyon and Sarah Gardiner Thompson Gardiner of Gardiner's Island.

    Nora Loftus Gardiner was the daughter of Lindsay C. Loftus of Mount Loftus, Kilkenny County, Ireland, and the subject of a marble sculpture by Rodin.

    Robert Alexander and Nora Loftus Gardiner's son Robert David Lion Gardiner, who became Gardiner's Island's Sixteenth Lord of the Manor, married Eunice Bailey. *[See following entry.]* Their daughter Alexandra secretly married James Randall Creel, Jr., the son of James Randall Creel, Sr. of Kansas City, MO, at the Cathedral of the Incarnation in Garden City without even informing her mother that she had been engaged. Upon hearing of the marriage Mrs. Gardiner went to the office of the Dean of the Cathedral to see the marriage record. After waiting for two hours to view the records, Mrs. Gardiner called the Garden City police. During the heated discussion that ensued after the arrival of the police, the Dean of the Cathedral asked the police to eject Mrs. Gardiner, her secretary, and her son Robert David Lion Gardiner from the building. Mrs. Gardiner later filed charges against the dean to which he responded that the marriage records were "church – not public property." [*The New York Times* June 12, 1932, p. 14, and June 13, 1932, p. 2.] Judge James Randall and Mrs. Alexandra Diodati Gardiner Creel, Jr. were residing on Gardiner's Island and in Mill Neck at the time of their deaths. [*See* Spinzia, *Long Island's Prominent North Shore Families, vol. I* – Creel entry.]

    *Alterations were made to the house in 1895, 1901, 1908, 1915, and in 1990.

Gardiner, Robert David Lion (1911-2004)

Occupation(s):	financier - member, Empire Trust Co.
	capitalist - extensive commercial real estate holdings
	intelligence agent - naval intelligence officer during World War II
Civic Activism:	established the Robert David Lion Gardiner Foundation (supports study of New York and Suffolk County history)
Marriage(s):	1961-2004 – Eunice Bailey (1928-2011)
	- British fashion model
Address:	Gardiner's Island
Name of estate:	*Manor House*
Year of construction:	1947
Style of architecture:	Georgian Revival
Architect(s):	
Landscape architect(s):	
House extant: yes	
Historical notes:	

After the 1774 house was destroyed by fire in 1947, the third *Manor House* was built by Miss Sarah Diodati Gardiner the same year.

Because the Fourteenth Proprietor of Gardiner's Island, Winthrop Gardiner, Jr. did not have an heir, Sarah purchased the island from him in 1937 and bequeathed it equally to her nephew Robert David Lion Gardiner and her niece Alexandra Gardiner Creel (Mrs. James Randall Creel, Jr.) with the stipulation that the island be passed on to their heirs. Since Robert did not have an heir, Alexandra's inheritance was passed on to her daughter Alexandra Gardiner Creel Goelet (Mrs. Robert Guestier Goelet). A long-standing and very vocal dispute between Robert and the Creel/Goelet families over the maintenance and disposition of the island was finally resolved with the death of Robert, where upon the entire title to the island passed to Mrs. Goelet.

Gardiner, Robert David Lion (1911-2004)

Occupation(s):	*[See previous entry.]*
Civic Activism:	*[See previous entry.]*
Marriage(s):	1961-2004 – Eunice Bailey (1928-2011)
	- *[See previous entry.]*
Address:	127 Main Street, East Hampton
Name of estate:	*White House*
Year of construction:	c. 1939
Style of architecture:	Mediterranean
Architect(s):	Wyeth and King designed the house (for S. D. Gardiner)
Landscape architect(s):	
House extant: yes	
Historical notes:	

The ten-bedroom house, with eight and a half bathrooms, originally named *White* House, was built by Miss Sarah Diodati Gardiner. It was later owned by her nephew Robert David Lion Gardiner, who continued to call it *White House*.

He was the son of Robert Alexander and Nora Loftus Gardiner of *Maidstone Hall* in East Hampton.

Eunice Bailey Gardiner was the daughter of Alfred Bailey of London, England. She had previously been married to gold mine heir William Pitt Oakes II, whose father Sir Harry Oakes was murdered in the Bahamas in 1943 under questionable circumstances that involved the Duke and Duchess of Windsor. According to a friend of the authors Wesley F. L. Gardiner, Robert David's claim to being the oldest surviving Gardiner was not accurate. As Wes put it, "I distinctly remember Cousin Bob's birth."

Robert David Lion and Eunice Bailey Gardiner did not have children.

In 2011 the house on 5.5 acres was for sale. The asking price was $29 million.

Gardiner, Miss Sarah Diodati (1862-1953)

Occupations:	writer - *Early Memories of Gardiner's Island*, 1947; editor of her Aunt Margaret Gardiner's *Leaves From a Young Girl's Diary*, 1926
Marriage(s):	unmarried
Address:	127 Main Street, East Hampton
Name of estate:	*White House*
Year of construction:	c.1939
Style of architecture:	Mediterranean
Architect(s):	Wyeth and King designed the house (for S. D. Gardiner)
Landscape architect(s):	
House extant:	yes
Historical notes:	

Sarah Diodati Gardiner demolished David Lion Gardiner, Sr.'s *White House* and built a ten-bedroom house, with eight and a half bathrooms, which she named *White House*. She also built the current, third *Manor House* on Gardiner's Island. Both houses, the second *White House* and the *Manor House,* were later owned by her nephew Robert David Lion Gardiner.

The *Social Register Summer, 1945* lists Miss Sarah Diodati Gardiner as residing at *White House* in East Hampton.

She was the daughter of David Lion and Sarah Gardiner Thompson Gardiner, Jr.

In 2011 the house on 5.5 acres was for sale. The asking price was $29 million.

Gardiner, Winthrop, Jr. (1912-1980)

Occupation(s):	capitalist - aviation executive
Civic Activism:	racing vice-chairman, International Whaling Races; president, Sagaponack Club (beach club); director, Mid-Ocean Bath and Tennis Club, Bridgehampton
Marriage(s):	M/1 – 1936-div. 1937 – Mildred Helen Shay (1911-2005)

    - entertainers and associated professions -
      motion picture actress
  M/2 – 1938-div. 1941 – Bethany Ann Beckwick (d. 2002)
    - model
  M/3 – 1942-div. 1949 – Frances Weinman (1914-1989)
  M/4 – 1949-div. 1956 – Sonja Henje (1912-1969)
    - entertainers and associated professions - figure skater*;
                                              Ice Capades performer;
                                              motion picture actress
    Civic Activism: donated 250 paintings and an art museum
                          building to Norway
  M/5 – 1956-1975 – Elizabeth Neher (1926-1975)
  M/6 – 1975-1980 – Nancy Deere Wiman (1912-1981)
    - entertainers and associated professions - stage actress
    Civic Activism: donated $1 million to Duke University for
                          neuroscience research

Address:	36 James Lane, East Hampton
Name of estate:	*The Mill Cottage / Hill Cottage / Mill Cottage**
Year of construction:	1870
Style of architecture:	Colonial Revival
Architect(s):	
Landscape architect(s):	

House extant: yes
Historical notes:

    Winthrop Gardiner, Jr., who became the Fourteenth Lord of the Manor, was the son of Winthrop and Isabel Tasher Lemmon Gardiner, Sr. of Gardiner's Island and East Hampton.

    Mildred Helen Shay Gardiner was the daughter of Joseph A. and Lilian Shay. Mildred had previously been married to Thomas Francis Murphy. After her divorce from Gardiner, she married Geoffrey Steel.

    Bethany Ann Beckwick Gardiner was the daughter of Dr. J. Holden and Mrs. Ann Coleman Beckwick. She later married Dana Gibson Noble and, subsequently, Alfred Corning Clark II.

    Frances Weinman Gardiner was the daughter of William J. and Caroline Weinman of Atlanta and Carterville, GA. Frances had previously been married to William Carroll Latimer. After her divorce from Gardiner, she married Horatio A. Luro.

    Sonja Henje Gardiner was the daughter of Wilhelm and Selma Henie of Oslo, Norway. She was a three-time Olympic Champion (1928, 1932, and 1936), a ten-time World Champion (1927-1936), and six-time European Champion (1931-1936). Sonja won more Olympic and World figure skating titles than did any other ladies figure skater. She had previously been married to Daniel Reid Topping, Sr. of *Fairlea* in Southampton. After her divorce from Gardiner she married Niels Ornstad. [*See* Spinzia, *Long Island's Prominent Families in the Town of Southampton* – Topping entry.]

    Elizabeth Neher Gardiner was the daughter of Marion Neher of Columbus and Granville, OH. She had previously been married to Gordon Miles Copp.

    Nancy Deere Wiman Gardiner was the daughter of Dwight Deere and Dorothea Stewart Stephens Wiman of Greenwich, CT, and a descendant of John Deere, the founder of the farm equipment manufacturing firm of Deere and Co. Nancy had previously been married to Arthur William Carter, Jr. of Los Angeles. Their daughter Katherine Theresa Carter married John Nicholas Regan, Jr., the son of John Nicholas and Kathleen Maguire Regan, Sr. of East Hampton. Nancy's second husband, William Thomson Wakeman, became a paraplegic at the age of forty-five after Nancy shot him in the back in 1967. William died two years later. Nancy was convicted of aggravated assault and sentenced to five years' probation. In the divorce proceedings which were in progress at the time of Winthrop's death, Gardiner sued Nancy for alimony.

    **The Blue Book of The Hamptons, 1958* lists the name of Gardiner's residence as *The Mill Cottage*; *The Blue Book of The Hamptons, 1965* lists it as *Hill Cottage;* and *The Blue Book of The Hamptons, 1973* lists it as *Mill Cottage*.

    Gardiner did not have children.

    The house was inherited from Winthrop by his sister Isabel and her husband Olney Mairs Gardiner.

[See following entry for additional family information.]

    In 2014 the house was for sale for $12.95 million by Olney Mairs Gardiner.

    It was purchased by the Town of East Hampton for $9.625 million.

Gardiner, Winthrop, Sr. (1887-1970)

Occupation(s):	
Marriage(s):	1911-1957 – Isabel Tasher Lemmon (1878-1957)
Address:	95 Main Street, East Hampton
Name of estate:	*Deurcant House*
Year of construction:	1740
Style of architecture:	Dutch Colonial
Architect(s):	
Landscape architect(s):	

House extant: yes
Historical notes:

   Winthrop Gardiner, Sr. was the son of John Lyon and Elizabeth Coralie Livingston Jones Gardiner from whom he inherited Gardiner's Island becoming the Thirteenth Lord of the Manor.

   Isabel Tasher Lemmon Gardiner was the daughter of John Southgate and Frances Addison Carter Dulany Lemmon of Baltimore, MD.

   Winthrop and Isabel Tasher Lemmon Gardiner, Sr.'s daughter Isabel married Olney Blanchard Mairs, Jr., the son of Olney Blanchard and Eugenie Ward Mairs, Sr. of East Hampton, and resided in East Hampton. Their daughter Frances married Edward Gardiner and, later, Philip Collins and resided in East Hampton and in South Boston, VA. Their son Winthrop Gardiner, Jr., who inherited Gardiner's Island and also lived in East Hampton, married Mildred Helen Shay; Bethany Ann Beckwick; Frances Weinman; Sonja Henje; Elizabeth Neher; and Nancy Deere Wiman.

   In 1924 Winthrop Gardiner, Sr. moved the house further back on the property and enlarged the house at the same time.
[See previous entry for additional family information.]
   The house was later owned by Lawrence Adams Baker, Sr. who called it *Baker's Acres*.
   The house currently houses the Ladies Improvement Society Thrift and Book Shops.

Garni, Adolph (1886-1954)
aka Adolf Garni

Occupation(s):	shipping -	vice-president and treasurer, W. R. Grace & Co.; shipping director, Gulf and South American Steamship Co.
	capitalist -	director, Eastern Air Lines; director, Grace Line; director, Pan-American-Grace Airways
	industrialist -	vice-president, chairman of board, and treasurer, Nitrate Agencies Ltd.
Marriage(s):	Altana Birchett (1892-1946)	
Address:	Essex Street, Montauk	
Name of estate:		
Year of construction:		
Style of architecture:	Neo-Tudor	
Architect(s):		
Landscape architect(s):		
Builder:	Pearson Construction Co., new wing for additional 2 bedrooms and 2 bathrooms, 1931 (for Garni)	
	Edward Pospisil, additions to house, 1933 (for Garni); new garage, servants' quarters and playroom with old garage becoming living quarters, 1935 (for Garni)	

House extant: yes
Historical notes:

   Garni purchased the house in 1930. [*The New York Times* April 6, 1930, p. 52.]
   Altana Birchett Garni was the daughter of Alfred Birchett, Sr.
   The Garnis' daughter Adelaide married Francis Joseph Henry, the son of Frank Henry of London, Ontario, Canada. Their son Birchett married Jean Millicent McNeel, the daughter of Robert Mills McNeel, Jr. of Miami, FL.
   In 1955 the house was sold to M. V. Alfis of River Edge, NJ. [*The East Hampton Star* October 6, 1955, p. 8.]

Garten, Jeffery E. (b. 1946)

Occupation(s): statesman - Under Secretary of Commerce for International Trade (Clinton administration)
educator - professor for international trade, finance, and business, Yale School of Management, Yale University, New Haven, CT;
dean, Yale School of Management, Yale University, New Haven, CT
financier - managing director, Blackstone Group;
managing director, Lehman Brothers;
director, Aetna Corp.;
director, Suisse Asset Management;
member, board of managers, Standard and Poor's;
member, advisory board, Miller Buckfire (financial restructuring firm)
industrialist - director, Alcan Inc. (Canadian mining and aluminum manufacturing firm)
writer - *A Cold Peace*, 1992;
The Big Ten, 1997;
Riding the Tigers, 1998;
The Mind of the CEO, 2001;
The Politics of Fortune, 2002
journalist - numerous newspaper and magazine articles;
monthly columnist, *Business Week*, 1997-2005
capitalist - chairman of board, Garten, Rothkopf (global consulting firm);
director, Calpine Energy Corp. (electric utility);
director, The Conference Board (provides businesses with practical knowledge to improve their performance)
merchant - director, CarMax, Inc.

Civic Activism: trustee, The International Rescue Committee

Marriage(s): 1986 – Ina Rosenberg (b. 1948)
- entertainers and associated professions -
host, "Barefoot Contessa" (Food Network cooking program)*
journalist - magazine columns;
writer - *The Barefoot Contessa Cookbook*, 1999;
Barefoot Contessa Parties, 2001;
Barefoot Contessa Family Style, 2002;
Barefoot Contessa in Paris, 2004;
Barefoot Contessa at Home, 2006;
Barefoot Contessa: Back to Basics, 2008;
Barefoot Contessa: How Easy Is That?, 2010;
Barefoot Contessa: Foolproof, 2012
budget analyst, Office of Management and Budget (Ford and Carter administrations)
merchant - owner, Barefoot Contessa Store, Westhampton Beach (specialty food store), 1978;
founder, Barefoot Contessa Pantry (packaged convenience foods)
Civic Activism: member, design review board of East Hampton

Garten, Jeffery E. (cont'd)

Address: Buell Lane, East Hampton
Name of estate:
Year of construction:
Style of architecture: Shingle
Architect(s): Frank Greenwald designed a separate structure called *The Barn* housing a test kitchen (for Garten)
Landscape architect(s):
Builder:
House extant: yes
Historical notes:

Jeffery E. Garten is the son of Melvin and Ruth Garten.
Born in Brooklyn, Ina Rosenberg Garten is the daughter of Dr. Charles H. and Florence Rosenberg.
*In 2005 her program was nominated for Daytime Emmy Award and in 2009 her program won Daytime Emmy Award.

Geddes, Gerald Maxwell (1911-1982)

Occupation(s): financier - partner, Clark, Dodge, and Co. (stock brokerage firm)

Marriage(s): M/1 – 1945-1971 – Elizabeth C. Kip (1914-1971)
M/2 – 1972-1982 – Judith C. Harris (1927-2011)

Address: Lily Pond Lane, East Hampton
Name of estate:
Year of construction: c. 1951
Style of architecture:
Architect(s):
Landscape architect(s):
House extant: unconfirmed
Historical notes:

The house was built by Gerald Maxwell Geddes. [*The East Hampton Star* May 31, 1951, p. 4.]
The Blue Book of The Hamptons, 1965 lists Gerald Maxwell and Elizabeth C. Kip Geddes as residing on Lily Pond Lane, East Hampton.
He was the son of Donald Grant and Grace Lester Maxwell Geddes, Sr. of Glen Cove. [*See* Spinzia, *Long Island's Prominent North Shore Families, vol. I* – Geddes entry.]
Elizabeth C. Kip Geddes was the daughter of William Ruloff and Mildred F. Corwin Kip of *The Moorings* in Greenport and *Akony* in Rhinebeck, NY. She had previously been married to Hyatt Von Dehn.
Gerald Maxwell and Elizabeth C. Kip Geddes' son Gerald Kip Geddes married Annette Louise Lonyo (aka Longnon), the daughter of Louis and Jane Edwards Lonyo III of Grosse Pointe, MI, and resides in Southampton. [*See* Spinzia, *Long Island's Prominent Families in the Town of Southampton* – Geddes entry.] Their son Douglas married Jean Theresa Laurino; the daughter of Anthony Laurino of Daytona Beach, FL, and resides in Amagansett.
The Blue Book of The Hamptons, 1973, lists Gerald Maxwell and Judith C. Harris Geddes as residing on Lily Pond Lane, East Hampton.
Judith was the daughter of Robert Mallory and Abbeline Coffey Harris. She had previously been married to Judge Paul Douglas of Palm Beach, FL.
In 1974 the house was purchased by Dr. Goodwin Milton Breinin. [*Sag Harbor Express* March 14, 1974, p. 7.]

Geffen, David Lawrence (b. 1943)

Occupation(s):	entertainers and associate professions -
	member, William Morris Agency (talent agency);
	vice-chairman of board, Warner Brothers (motion picture studio);
	founder, Geffen Film Co.;
	a founder, with Steven Spielberg and Jeffery Katzenberg, Dream Works SKG (motion picture studio)
	capitalist - co-founder, with Elliot Roberts, Asylum Records;
	founder, Geffen Records
Civic Activism:	donated $5 million to UCLA's Westwood Playhouse, Los Angeles, CA;
	donated $300 million to UCLA School of Medicine, Los Angeles, CA;
	benefactor, New York University School of Medicine, NYC;
	donated $100 million to New York's Lincoln Center's Avery Fisher Hall (renamed Donald Geffen Hall), NYC;
	one of the largest patrons of God's Love We Deliver (a non-profit charity which delivers donated restaurant meals to home bound people with AIDS), NYC
Marriage(s):	bachelor
Address:	West End Road, East Hampton
Name of estate:	
Year of construction:	
Style of architecture:	Modified Shingle
Architect(s):	
Landscape architect(s):	
House extant: yes	
Historical notes:	

In 2014 Geffen purchased *Cody House*, the estate of Steven Jay Ross.

The estate consisted of a 7,500-square-foot, six-bedroom, six-bath main residence, a three-bedroom guest house, and 5.5 acres.

He is the son of Abraham and Batya Volovskaya Geffen of Brooklyn, NY.

Gerli, David Charles, Sr. (1911-2009)

Occupation(s):	industrialist - vice-president, Allentown Silk Co., Allentown, PA (textile firm); president, Gerli & Co., Inc. (textile firm)

Marriage(s):	M/1 – 1935-div. – Genevieve Wren (b. 1912)
	M/2 – 1942-div. 1952 – Jacqueline Kneip (1918-1990)
	  - entertainers and associated professions -
	    motion picture actress
	    model
	M/3 – 1953-div. 1954 – Bessie Sims (aka Billie Sims)
	M/4 – 1959 – Michelle Dale (d. 1972)
	M/5 – 1974-2009 – Anne Woodin Harvey (1923-2016)
	  - Civic Activism: president, Junior League of New York;
	    president, Garden Club of East Hampton;
	    board member, Ladies Village Improvement Society, East Hampton;
	    vice-president, United States Figure Skating Association;
	    president, Women's Prison Association;
	    president, Girls' Service League;
	    president, Foundation House

Address:	58 Ocean Avenue, East Hampton
Name of estate:	*Maya*
Year of construction:	1897
Style of architecture:	Shingle with Queen Anne elements
Architect(s):	Cyrus Lazelle Warner Eidlitz designed his own house and the 1898 and 1901 alterations

House extant: yes
Historical notes:

The house, originally named *Overlea*, was built by Cyrus Lazelle Warner Eidlitz. It was later owned by Gerli, who called it *Maya*, and, then, by his fifth wife, Mrs. Anne Woodin Harvey Gerli, who continued to call it *Maya*. Anne had previously been married to Carl William Gram, Jr. with whom she resided at *Maya*.

David Charles Gerli, Sr. was the son of Emanuel Gerli of Smithtown, NY. David's sister Diane married Daniel Nelson Adams, the son of Daniel Crouse and Katharine Hamlin Osterhoudt Adams of East Hampton.

Genevieve Wren Gerli was the daughter of Dr. Alphonse A. Wren of New York. She subsequently married Frederick Ham.

David Charles and Genevieve Wren Gerli, Sr.'s daughter Joan married Christopher Hempstead, the son of Robert Weir and Maria Luisa Hempstead. Their son David Charles Gerli, Jr. married Blanquita Rosa Champsaur.

Jacqueline Kneip Gerli was the daughter of Edgar Kneip of Oak Park, IL. She had previously been married to Robert Wieland, the son of Christian Wieland of Chicago, IL. After her divorce from Gerli she married David Graham Legget III.

David Charles and Jacqueline Kneip Gerli, Sr.'s daughter Carole married Giovanni Carlos Tommaso, the son of Dr. Guiseppe Tommaso of Florence, Italy, and, later, ____ Pfeuti. Their daughter Eden married David Graham Legget IV and, later, ____ Ljungberg with whom she resided in Stockholm, Sweden.

Bessie Sims Gerli was the daughter of Simpson Henry Sims of Dallas, TX. She had previously been married to ____ Miller. After her divorce from Gerli, she resumed the use of her maiden name.

The Blue Book of The Hamptons, 2008 lists David C. and Anne Woodin Harvey Gerli as residing at *Maya*, 58 Ocean Avenue, East Hampton.

She was the daughter of Olin Frisbee and Ann Jessip Woodin Harvey, Jr. and the granddaughter of Secretary of the Treasury William Hartman Woodin, Sr. and his wife Annie Jessip Woodin of *Dune House* in East Hampton.

Gianis, Socrates George, Sr. (1917-2011)

Occupation(s):	financier - founder, Gianis and Co. (investment banking firm)
	educator - co-founder, Boys Town, Tel Aviv (1,000-student trade school)
Marriage(s):	M/1 – 1943-div. – Natalie Simpkins
	M/2 – Tamara Victoria Clement
	- artist
Address:	18 Ocean Avenue, East Hampton
Name of estate:	
Year of construction:	1928
Style of architecture:	Georgian with French Country elements
Architect(s):	L. Bancel LaFarge designed the house (for L. F. Bishop, Jr.)
Landscape architect(s):	
House extant:	yes*
Historical notes:	

The house, originally named *Holiday*, was built by Dr. Louis Faugeres Bishop, Jr. In 1962 Gianis purchased it for $52,500. [*The East Hampton Star* March 15, 1962, p. 7, and June 14, 1962, p. 4.]

He was the son of George and Viola Vasiliki Gianis.

Natalie Simpkins Gianis was the daughter of Willard S. and Augusta Prescott Simpkins of Bedford Hills, NJ. Natalie subsequently married Robert Hamill Workum, the son of Fifield Workum, and resided in Calgary, Canada.

Socrates George and Natalie Simpkins Gianis, Sr.'s son Augustus married Beverly Ruth Rollins, the daughter of George W. Rollins of Billings, MT, and resides in Canada. Their sons Gregory and Christopher also reside in Canada.

Tamara Victoria Gianis is the daughter of Jean Horatio and Victoria Boshko Clement of New York.

Socrates George and Tamara Victoria Clement Gianis, Sr.'s son Alexander resides in East Hampton. In 1999 their daughter Victoria fell from her sixteenth floor room in New York City's Plaza Hotel. Their son Socrates George Gianis, Jr. resides in Sag Harbor.

*The house sustained damage from a fire in 1985 and was remodeled in 1986 and 2013. [*The East Hampton Star* January 2, 1986, p. 16.]

In 2014 the 6,000-square-foot, seven-bedroom, five-and-a-half-bath house and 1.48 acres were for sale. The asking price was $13.9 million. In 2015 the price was reduced to $11.5 million. In 2019 it was reduced to $7.995 million.

Gleason, Carlisle Joyslin (1874-1940)

Occupation(s):	attorney -	partner, James Schell and Elkins, NYC;
		partner, Gleason, McLanachan, Merritt, and Ingraham, NYC
	financier -	director, American Fidelity Co.
	industrialist -	director, Phelps Dodge Copper Products Corp.;
		director, Habershaw Cable & Wire Corp.;
		director, Charles Hardy Inc.;
		director, Hardy Metallurgical Co.;
		director, American Copper Products Corp.;
		director, British–American Tube Co.;
		director, Eiseman Magneto Seymour Manufacturing Co.;
		director, Seymour Corporation of Delaware;
		director, Mullite Refractories Corp.
	capitalist -	director, Bulwark Corp.;
		director, Eastern Building Corp.;
		director, Dunmovin Corp.;
		director, Brazilian Babassu Corp. (grower and importer of Brazilian nuts);
		vice-president and director, New York Postal Station, Inc.;
		vice-president and director, Union Estates Corp.;
		director, Varick Corp.;
		director, Margay Oil Corp.
Civic Activism:		secretary and director, Maidstone Club, East Hampton
Marriage(s):		1902-1940 – Ellen L. Fifield (1875-1949)
		- Civic Activism: president, Garden Club of East Hampton
Address:		Pudding Hill Lane, East Hampton
Name of estate:		*Greyshingles*
Year of construction:		
Style of architecture:		
Architect(s):		
Landscape architect(s):		
Builder:		Robert Seerveld, 1940
		alterations (for Chapman)
House extant: unconfirmed		
Historical notes:		

The *Long Island Society Register, 1929* lists Carlisle J. and Ellen Fifield Gleason as residing at *Greyshingles* on Pudding Hill Lane, East Hampton.

He was the son of Louis Pomeroy and Anne Louise Timothy Gleason of Montpelier, NH.

Ellen L. Fifield Gleason was the daughter of Benjamin Franklin and Lucy Hubbard Fifield of Vermont.

Carlisle Joyslin and Ellen L. Fifield Gleason's daughter Louise married Frederic Stanton Withington, Jr. of Rutherford, NJ, and resided in Washington, DC. Their daughter Elizabeth married James A. Moffett II, the son of George Monroe and Madeline Buckner Moffett, Sr. of *Les Bois* in Old Brookville. [*See* Spinzia, *Long Island's Prominent North Shore Families, vol. I* – Moffett entry.]

In 1940 the house was purchased by Benjamin Gaines Chapman, Jr. [*The East Hampton Star* September 26, 1940, p. 5.]

Godwin, Courtlandt (b. 1871)

Occupation(s):	merchant - Powell & Campbell, NYC (shoe store)
Marriage(s):	1901-1953 – Sara Woodbury Sylvester Hedge (1881-1953)
Address:	Apaquogue Road, East Hampton
Name of estate:	*Crowland*
Year of construction:	
Style of architecture:	
Architect(s):	
Landscape architect(s):	
House extant: unconfirmed	
Historical notes:	

In 1929 Godwin purchased the house from Stephen G. Williams. [*The East Hampton Star* October 11, 1929, p. 1.]

The *Social Directory of Southampton, Long Island, 1931* lists Mr. and Mrs. Courtlandt Godwin as residing on Apaquogue Road, East Hampton. The *New York Social Register, 1933* lists the name of the Godwin's residence as *Crowland*.

He was the son of Joseph H. Godwin, Jr. and the grand-nephew of President Zachary Taylor.

Sara Woodbury Sylvester Hedge Godwin was the daughter of Charles Gorham and Emma W. Bremer Hedge.

Courtlandt and Sara Woodbury Sylvester Hedge Godwin's daughter Jacqueline married Terrence Harp and resided in Baltimore, MD. Their daughter Doris married Ira Lawrence Hill, the son of Thomas Hill and, later, George W. Pierpont with whom she resided in East Hampton and in Boulder, CO. Their daughter Priscilla married H. Pierson Mapes, the son of Herbert Mapes, and resided at *Smith House Farm* in Sloatsburg, NY. Their son Gorham married Bernadine Thole, the daughter of George J. Thole of Brooklyn.

Goelet, Alexandra Gardiner Creel (1939-1990)

Marriage(s):	M/1 – 1964-div. – Peter Francis Tufo (b. 1938)

- attorney - member, Davis, Polk, Wardwell, Sunderland, and Kiendl;
  chief counsel, New York City Department of Investigation
    (Lindsay administration);
  a founder and partner, Tufo, Johnston, and Zuccotti, NYC;
  partner, Milbank, Tweed, Hadley, and McCloy, NYC
- politician - Assistant to New York City Mayor (Lindsay administration)
- financier - managing director of investment banking, Merrill, Lynch
    & Co.;
  senior advisor, Lazard, Freres & Co.
- entertainers and associated professions -
  host, "The Cost of Crime" (Metromedia television series);
  host, "Save Our Schools" (Metromedia television series)
- diplomat - United States Ambassador Extraordinary and Plenipotentiary
    to Hungary, 1997-2001 (Clinton administration)
- Civic Activism: chairman of board, New York City Board of Correction
    (Lindsay and Koch administrations);
  chairman of board and CEO, New York State Thruway
    Authority, 1989-1996;
  member, New York City Commission on Education,
    NYC;
  president, Yale School Association.

M/2 – 1976-1990 – Robert Guestier Goelet (1924-2019)
- capitalist - president and director, Goelet Realty Co.;
  vice-president and director, Goelet Estate Co.;
  chairman of board, Rhode Island Corp. (family holding
    company)
- financier - director, Chemical Bank
- Civic Activism: president of board, American Museum of Natural
    History, NYC;
  president of board, New York Historical Society, NYC;
  president of board, French Institute;
  president of board, New York Zoological Society;
  treasurer and director, National Audubon Society

Address:	Gardiner's Island
Name of estate:	*Manor House*
Year of construction:	1947
Style of architecture:	Georgian Revival
Architect(s):	
Landscape architect(s)	
House extant:	yes
Historical notes:	

The *Manor House* was built by Miss Sarah Diodati Gardiner after the 1774 house was destroyed by fire in 1947. It was later owned by her nephew Robert David Lion Gardiner and his sister Alexandra Diodati Gardiner Creel who married James Randall Creel, Jr. The island was subsequently owned by the Creels' daughter Alexandra.

[For information about the Creels' Mill Neck residence, *see* Spinzia, *Long Island's Prominent North Shore Families, vol. I* – Creel entry.]

Peter Francis Tufo is the son of Dr. and Mrs. Gustave Francis Tufo of Chicago, IL. Peter remarried and resided in Southampton. [*See* Spinzia, *Long Island's Prominent Families in the Town of Southampton* – Tufo entry.]

Robert Guestier Goelet was the son of Robert Walton and Anne Marie Guestier Goelet.

Gordon, George Breed (1860-1927)

Occupation(s):	attorney - partner, Gordon, Smith, Buchanan, and Scott industrialist - director, Boorum & Pease Co., Brooklyn (manufacturer of blank notebooks)
Civic Activism:	president, Pennsylvania Bar Association; trustee, University of Pittsburgh
Marriage(s):	1889-1927 – Mary Edwards Boorum (1862-1934) - established Katherine Edward Gordon scholarship for architecture, American Academy, Rome, Italy; a founder, Industrial Home for Crippled Children
Address:	Lily Pond Lane, East Hampton
Name of estate:	
Year of construction:	c. 1890
Style of architecture:	Modified Colonial Revival
Architect(s):	
Landscape architect(s):	John Custis Lawrence, 1910 garage (for Gordon)
Builder:	Edward M. Gay, 1910 garage (for Gordon)

House extant: unconfirmed
Historical notes:

The house was built by Anna Mary Brown Ireland. [*The East Hampton Star* May 16, 1940, p. 2.] In 1909 it was purchased by Gordon. [*The East Hampton Star* October 8, 1909, p. 5.]

The *Social Register Summer, 1910* (Pittsburgh section) lists George B. and Mary E. Boorum Gordon as residing in East Hampton.

He was the son of Alexander Gordon, Sr.

Mary Edwards Boorum Gordon was the daughter of William Burger and Amelia Ogden Whiting Boorum, Sr. of Brooklyn.

George Breed and Mary Edwards Boorum Gordon's daughter died in 1917 at the age of twenty. Their son William died in 1902 at the age of twelve.

In 1920 the house was purchased by Edward Elliott Jenkins from Mrs. Gordon. [*The East Hampton Star* October 1, 1920, p. 5.]

In 1926 it was purchased by Jessie Spaulding II who named the house *Pineleigh*. [*The East Hampton Star* November 17, 1933, p. 4.]

Gosman, Mary Ellen Harrington (1909-1997)

Occupation(s):	restaurateur - a founder, with her husband Robert, Gosman's Restaurant and Dock, Montauk (500-seat waterfront restaurant)
Marriage(s):	1932-1982 – Robert H. Gosman (d. 1982) - restaurateur - co-founder, Gosman's Restaurant and Dock, Montauk merchant - founder, Bob Gosman and Co., Inc., Montauk (wholesale seafood firm)
Address:	162 Fairview Avenue, Montauk
Name of estate:	
Year of construction:	1928
Style of architecture:	Eclectic Dutch Farmhouse
Architect(s):	Arthur B. Wood designed his own residence

Landscape architect(s):
House extant: yes
Historical notes:

The house, which has been extensively altered over the years, was built by Arthur B. Wood. It was later owned by Lindsey Hopkins, Jr. In 1966 the house was purchased by Gosman.

She was the daughter of Hubert James and Margaret Shannon Harrington Gosman of Cloonkerin, Ireland.

Mary sold the house to Marion Daily who listed it for sale in 2018. The asking price was $1.9 million.

Gossler, Philip Green, Jr. (1901-1978)

Occupation(s):	
Marriage(s):	M/1 – 1930-div. 1939 – Germaine Adelaide de Baume (1891-1986) M/2 – 1943-1974 – Dorothy Donaldson (d. 1974) - Civic Activism: vice-president, Ladies Village Improvement Society, East Hampton
Address:	128 Main Street, East Hampton
Name of estate:	
Year of construction:	c. 1780
Style of architecture:	Colonial
Architect(s):	Lear + Mahoney
Landscape architect(s):	
House extant: yes	
Historical note:	

 The 3,500-square-foot historic house has five bedrooms and three and a half bathrooms. It was the former Sherrill homestead. The house was purchased and enlarged by Gossler in 1956. [*The East Hampton Star* June 6, 1957, p. 7.]

 Philip Green Gossler, Jr. was the son of Philip Green and Mary Claflin Gossler, Sr. of *Highfield* in Brookville. [*See* Spinzia, *Long Island's Prominent North Shore Families, vol. I* – Gossler entry.]

 Germaine Adelaide de Baume Gossler had previously been married to Arthur Read Christie. After her divorce from Gossler, she married Henry Rogers Benjamin, Sr. of *Lake House* in Southampton and, later, James H. R. Cromwell. [*See* Spinzia, *Long Island's Prominent Families in the Town of Southampton* – Benjamin entry.]

 The Blue Book of The Hamptons, 1958 and *1973* list Philip and Dorothy Donaldson Gossler as residing at 128 Main Street, East Hampton.

 She was the daughter of Keith Donaldson and had previously been married to Lawrence Wordsworth Snell, Jr. of Manhattan.

Gottlieb, Adolph (1903-1974)

Occupation(s):	artist - sculptor and abstract expressionist painter
Civic Activism:	a founder, with his wife Esther, Adolph and Esther Gottlieb Foundation; a founder, "The Ten", 1935 (devoted to expressionist and abstract painting); a founder, New York Artist Painters, 1943
Marriage(s):	1932-1974 – Esther Dick (1907-1988) - educator, dean of girls, Fashion Industries High School, NYC; Civic Activism: a founder, with her husband Adolph, and president, Adolph and Esther Gottlieb foundation
Address:	Apaquogue Road, East Hampton
Name of estate:	
Year of construction:	
Style of architecture:	Modified Colonial Revival
Architect(s):	
Landscape architect(s):	Victoria Fensterer designed the pergola plantings
House extant: yes	
Historical notes:	

 The house was previously owned by John Vernou Bouvier, Jr., who called it *Little House*. It was later owned by his son John Vernou Bouvier III, who called it *Wildmoor*. In 1960 the house was purchased by Gottlieb, who converted the garage into his art studio.

 He was the son of Emil and Elsie Berger Gottlieb of Manhattan.

 The Gottliebs did not have children.

Gowen, George W., II (b. 1929)

Occupation(s):	attorney -	partner, Dunnington, Bartholow, and Miller, NYC, 1966-1985;
		partner, Fryer, Ross, and Gowen, NYC, 1986-1994;
		general counsel, United States Tennis Association*;
		counsel, United States Olympic Committee;
		chief of legal committee, Explorers Club
	financier -	director, Paine Weber Cashfund, Inc.;
		director, Royal Military Academy Funds, Inc.
	educator -	adjunct professor, New York University Graduate School of Business Administration
	writer -	*Talk of Many Things: Law, Sports, Politics, Nature*, 2014

Civic Activism: president and chairman of board, American Society for the Prevention of Cruelty to Animals;
director and chairman, executive committee, National Park Foundation;
chairman of board, Scenic Hudson, Inc., 1984-1987;
president, United States Olympic Federation, since 1996;
trustee, Lenox Hill Hospital, NYC;
chairman of board, Voltaire Society of America;
trustee, Christodora (wilderness camp for inner-city youths);
member, United Nations Human Rights Commission;
secretary, Maidstone Club, East Hampton

Marriage(s): 1959-2019 – Marcia Ann Fennelly (1936-2019)
- public relations executive -
managing director, Center for Special Care, NYC
Civic Activism: president, Garden Club of East Hampton;
trustee, YWCA Camping Service

Address: 53 Lily Pond Lane, East Hampton
Name of estate:
Year of construction: 1913
Style of architecture: Shingle
Architect(s): John Custis Lawrence designed the house (for Hollister)
Landscape architect(s):
House extant: yes
Historical notes:

The house was built by Dr. Frederick Kellogg Hollister. It was later owned by Gowen.
The Blue Book of The Hamptons, 2008 lists George W. and Marcia A. Fennelly Gowen II as residing at 53 Lily Pond Lane in East Hampton.
He is the son of Franklin Crosbie and May Elizabeth Klein Gowen.
Marcia Ann Fennelly Gowen was the daughter of Leo C. and Edith Louise Buhler Fennelly of East Hampton.
George W. and Marcia Ann Fennelly Gowen II's daughter Cynthia married William Michael Crawford, the son of Carroll E. Crawford of Wayzata, MN. Their daughter Lee married Jeffrey Andrew Marine, the son of Gary and Marion Marine of Chadds Ford, PA.
*In 2006 Gowen was inducted into the Eastern Tennis Hall of Fame.

Grace, Morgan Hatton, Jr. (1906-1995)

Occupation(s): financier - partner, Sterling, Grace, and Co. (stock brokerage firm)

Marriage(s): 1938-1995 – Natalie O. Watts (1909-2008)
- entertainers and associated professions -
member, Blue Hill Troupe (specialized in Gilbert and Sullivan operettas)

Address: 85 Lee Avenue, East Hampton
Name of estate:
Year of construction:
Style of architecture:
Architect(s):
Landscape architect(s):
House extant: yes
Historical notes:

In c. 1952 Grace purchased the house of John Kirkland Weeks, Sr. [*The East Hampton Star* January 3, 1952, p. 1.]

The Blue Book of The Hamptons, 1958 lists Morgan H. and Natalie O. Watts Grace, Jr. as residing on Lee Avenue, East Hampton. *The Blue Book of The Hamptons, 2003* lists the address as 85 Lee Avenue, East Hampton.

He was the son of Morgan Hatton and Ruth Agnes Eden Grace, Sr. of *Lismore* in Kings Point. His brother Oliver married Ann Chilton McDonnell; Jeanne DeVol; and Lorraine Graves, with whom he resided at *Yellowbanks* in Cove Neck. [*See* Spinzia, *Long Island's Prominent North Shore Families, vol. I* – Grace entries.] Their brother David married Nancy Major Erskine, the daughter of Howard M. Erskine of Bronxville, NY.

Natalie O. Watts Grace was the daughter of Edward Everett Watts, Sr.

Morgan Hatton and Natalie O. Watts Grace, Jr.'s daughter Natalie married William H. Brinckerhoff of Lyon, France, and resided in Locust Valley and in East Hampton. Their son Morgan Hatton Grace III married Robin Weaver Rutherford, the daughter of Jay Rutherford, and resides in Washington, DC, and in Southampton.

Graham, Lucie Wilshire (1882-1963)

Marriage(s): James Leonard Graham, Sr. (1875-1936)
- industrialist - Carnegie Steel Co., Pittsburgh, PA

Address: New Highway, East Hampton
Name of estate:
Year of construction: 1941
Style of architecture:
Architect(s):
Landscape architect(s):
House extant: unconfirmed
Historical notes:

The house was built by Mrs. Marjorie Holland McKittrick. [*The Brooklyn Daily Eagle* April 21, 1940, p. 20.] It was purchased in 1941 by Mrs. Graham. [*The East Hampton Star* October 23, 1941, p. 5.]

Lucie Wilshire Graham was a descendant of Chief Justice John Marshall.

James Leonard and Lucie Wilshire Graham, Sr.'s daughter Marjorie married Frank Whittesley Berrien, the son of F. D. Berrien of Brookline, MA, and, later, Newton Cooke Boykin, the son of Elias Miller and Lucy Carter Cooke Boykin. Their son James Leonard Graham, Jr. married Gretchen Swindle of Hardin, MT, and resided in Sheridan, WY.

Gram, Carl William, Jr. (1915-1973)

Occupation(s):	industrialist - chairman of board, Actronics, Inc. (electronic controls manufacturing firm)
Civic Activism:	director, United States Olympic Committee; vice-president, United States Figure Skating Association; director, Maidstone Club, East Hampton
Marriage(s):	1946-1973 – Anne Woodin Harvey (1923-2016)

- Civic Activism:
    - president, Junior League of New York;
    - president, Garden Club of East Hampton;
    - board member, Village Preservation Society, East Hampton;
    - vice-president, United States Figure Skating Association;
    - president, Women's Prison Association;
    - president, Girls Service League;
    - president, Foundation House;
    - chair, ladies tennis committee, Maidstone Club, East Hampton;
    - chair, alumni association, Nightingale-Barnford School

Address:	58 Ocean Avenue, East Hampton
Name of estate:	*Maya*
Year of construction:	1897
Style of architecture:	Shingle with Queen Anne elements
Architect(s):	Cyrus Lazelle Warner Eidlitz designed his own house and the 1898 and 1901 alterations

House extant: yes
Historical notes:

The house, originally named *Overlea*, was built by Cyrus Lazelle Warner Eidlitz. It was later owned by Gram who called it *Maya* and, then, by Mrs. Gram.

The Blue Book of The Hamptons, 1965 lists Carl W. and Anne Woodin Harvey Gram, Jr. as residing at *Maya* on Ocean Avenue, East Hampton.

He was the son of Carl William Gram, Sr. of Boston, MA, and Strasburg, PA.

Anne Woodin Harvey Gram was the daughter of Olin Frisbee and Annie Jessip Woodin Harvey, Jr. and the granddaughter of Secretary of the Treasury William Hartman Woodin, Sr. and his wife Annie Jessup Woodin of *Dune House* in East Hampton. Anne later married David Charles Gerli, Sr. with whom she continued to reside at *Maya*.

Carl William and Anne Woodin Harvey Gram, Jr.'s daughter Ann married Edward Townsend Shean, Jr. of East Hampton. Their daughter Mary married Francis Hopkinson Van Deventer, Jr. of Greenwich, CT. Their daughter Carol married George Selak, Jr. of New York.

Greary, John White, III (1897-1956)
aka John White Greary, Jr.

Occupation(s):	capitalist - partner, George H. McFadden & Brothers (cotton exporting firm)
	industrialist - manager, American Viscore Corp. (synthetic fiber manufacturing firm)
Civic Activism:	vice-president, Export Managers Club;
	vice-president, Textile Association of the United States
Marriage(s):	1917-1956 – Elizabeth English Wister (1896-1983)
Address:	67 Davids Lane, East Hampton
Name of estate:	
Year of construction:	
Style of architecture:	
Architect(s):	
Landscape architect(s):	
House extant: unconfirmed	
Historical notes:	

   In 1955 Greary purchased the William Frank Cornell residence. [*The East Hampton Star* June 9, 1955, p. 4.]
   Greary was the son of John White and Mary de Forest Harrison Greary, Jr. His grandfather, John White Greary, Sr., was a general in the Civil War, governor of Pennsylvania, and governor of the Kansas Territory.
   Elizabeth English Wister Greary was the daughter of Charles Jones and Elizabeth English Morgan Wister.
   John White and Elizabeth English Wister Greary III's daughter Louise married Edward Cameron Kirk Read, the son of Conyers and Edith Coulson Kirk Read. Their daughter Mary married Guilliamem Aertsen and resided at *Luzon Cottage* in Torresdale, PA.

Green, Adolph (1914-2002)

Occupation(s):	entertainers and associated professions - lyricist and playwright*
Marriage(s):	M/1 – 1941-div. – Elizabeth Reitell (1920-2001)
	- entertainers and associated professions - designed dance costumes; play producer; assistant to Arthur Miller
	writer - editor and writer, Columbia River Inter-Tribal Fish Commission, Portland, OR
	Civic Activism: environmental lecturer; director, Montana Wilderness Association
	M/2 – 1945-1953 – Allyn Ann McLerie (1926-2018)
	- entertainers and associated professions - actress; dancer; singer
	M/3 – 1960-2002 – Phyllis Newman (1933-2019)
	- entertainers and associate professions - actress; singer
	Civic Activism: founder, Phyllis Newman Women's Health Initiative
Address:	Georgica Road, East Hampton
Name of estate:	
Year of construction:	1895
Style of architecture:	Neo-Tudor
Architect(s):	Joseph Greenleaf Thorp designed the house (for Spring)
	Howard Greenley, 1915 alterations (for Roberts)
	Spencer Fullerton Weaver, Sr., 1925 alterations (for himself)
Landscape architect(s):	John Raum, 1917 (for Roberts)
	Jacob John Spoon designed the swimming pool (for Weaver)
Builder:	Philip Ritch

House extant: no**
Nassau County Museum Collection has photographs of the estate.
Historical notes:

The house, originally named *Winklehawk*, was built by Preston Brady Spring, Sr. In 1915 it was purchased by Walter Scott Roberts. [*The East Hampton Star* August 6, 1915, p. 5; December 13, 1918, p. 5; and June 8, 1944, p. 3.] In 1925 the house was purchased by Spencer Fullerton Weaver, Sr. who renamed it *Spencecliff*. In 1949 it was purchased by William Seligson who subdivided the estate's property into six building lots. [*The East Hampton Star* January, 13, 1955, p. 5, and June 16, 1955, p. 12.] The house was subsequently owned by Green.

He was the son of Daniel and Helen Weiss Green of The Bronx, NY.

Elizabeth Reitell Green was the daughter of Charles and Jane Myer Reitell of Elmira, NY. Elizabeth had previously been married to John Hammond. After her divorce from Adolph, she married Eldon Smith.

Allyn Ann McLerie Green was the daughter of Allyn Gordon and Vera Alma Stewart McLerie. Allyn subsequently married George Gaynes (aka George Jongejans), the son of Gerrit and Iya Grigorieva de Gay Jongejans of Finland.

Phyllis Newman Green was the daughter of Sigmund and Rachel Newman.

Adolph and Phyllis Newman Green's son Adam is a songwriter. Their daughter Amanda married Dr. Jeffrey Kaplan of NYC.

*In 1980 Adolph was inducted into the Songwriters Hall of Fame. In 1981 he was inducted into the American Theatre Hall of Fame.

**In 1969 the house was destroyed by fire during a wedding at Green's estate when a caterer's gas line leaked and ignited.

Green, William Walker (1855-1924)

Occupation(s):	attorney - partner, Alexander and Green
Marriage(s):	Jessica R. Thayer (d. 1947)
Address:	Terbell Lane, East Hampton
Name of estate:	*End of the Lane*
Year of construction:	1901
Style of architecture:	Shingle
Architect(s):	
Landscape architect(s):	
Builder:	Frank Grimshaw
	S. C. Grimshaw (plumbing firm)

House extant: yes
Historical notes:

The house was built by Mrs. Emma Augusta Terbell Blakeman. In 1912 it was purchased by Green. [*The East Hampton Star* January 18, 1901, p. 5, and October 18, 1912, p. 5.]

The *Social Register Summer, 1915* lists William Walker and Jessica R. Thayer Green as residing at *End of the Lane* in East Hampton.

He was the son of Ashbell and Louise Buloid Walker, Sr.

William Walker and Jessica R. Thayer Green's daughter Helen married Oswald Kirby and, later, ____ Sare. Their daughter Jessica married James McMann.

In 1939 Leighton Stevens purchased the house from Mrs. Green. [*The New York Times* May 28, 1939, p. D3.]

Greene. Anne Johnston Sawyer (1920-2003)

Occupation(s):	financier - director, First National Bank (now, National City Bank)
Civic Activism:	director, Dayton United Way, Dayton, OH;
	director, Dayton Area Chamber of Commerce, Dayton, OH;
	director, Dayton Foundation, Dayton, OH;
	president, Community Welfare Council;
	vice-president, Dayton Art Institute, Dayton, OH;
	member of board, Dayton Black Cultural Festival, Dayton, OH;
	board chair, Dayton Human Relations Commission, Dayton, OH
Marriage(s):	M/1 – 1940-div. – John Pattison Williams, Sr. (1915-1973)
	- capitalist - president and chairman of board, Easty Industries, Dayton, OH (owns and operates WEZE radio station, Boston, MA);
	vice-president, Great Trails Broadcasting Corp.
	Civic Activism: vice-president, Ohio Association of Broadcasters
	M/2 – 1957-1997 – John Bradley Greene II (1911-1997)
	- financier - partner, Greene & Brock (stock brokerage firm); partner, Greene and Ladd (later, Cowan & Co.) (stock brokerage firm)
Address:	Oceanview Lane, Amagansett
Name of estate:	*Devon House*
Year of construction:	1909
Style of architecture:	Mediterranean Villa
Architect(s):	Tietig and Lee designed the house (for W. C. Procter)
Landscape architect(s):	
House extant: yes	
Historical notes:	

The seven-bedroom, five-bath house was built by William Cooper Procter.

It was later owned by Procter's niece Mary Elizabeth Johnston, who called it *Devon House*. In 1967 she bequeathed *Devon House* and its furnishings to her niece Anne Johnston Sawyer Greene.

Anne was the daughter of United States Secretary of Commerce Charles W. Sawyer and Mrs. Margaret Sterrer Johnston Sawyer.

John Pattison Williams, Sr. was the son of George Lathrop and Elise Grace Burkham Williams.

John Pattison and Anne Johnston Sawyer Williams, Sr.'s son John Pattison Williams, Jr. married Janie Coates–Cartwright Pepper, the daughter of John Arthur Reid Pepper. Their daughter Mary married Geoffrey Welles Smith, the son of Frederick Coe Smith.

The Blue Book of The Hamptons, 1987 lists John Bradley and Anne Johnston Sawyer Greene as residing at *Devon House* on Oceanview Lane in Amagansett.

He was the son of George Shaw and Daisy Talbott Brown Greene. John had previously been married to Gertrude Stern.

In 1987 Jack Dobbs McSpadden, Jr. purchased the house from Mrs. Greene and continued to call it *Devon House*.

Greer, The Reverend David Hummell (1844-1919)

Occupation(s):	clergy - bishop, Protestant Episcopal Church
	writer - *Moral Power of History*, 1890;
	From Things to God, 1893;
	The Preacher and His Place, 1895;
	Visions, 1898
Marriage(s):	1869 – Caroline Augusta Keith
Address:	Georgica Road, East Hampton
Name of estate:	*Yondermere*
Year of construction:	
Style of architecture:	
Architect(s):	
Landscape architect(s):	
House extant:	unconfirmed
Historical notes:	

The *Social Register Summer, 1903* lists The Reverend David H. and Mrs. Caroline A. Keith Greer as residing at *Yondermere* in East Hampton.

He was the son of Jacob Rickard and Elizabeth Yellott Armstrong Greer of Wheeling, WV.

Caroline Augusta Keith Greer was the daughter of Quincy Adams and Priscilla Dean Hathaway Keith.

The Reverend David Hummell and Caroline Augusta Keith Greer's son William married Louise Noel, the daughter of Auguste and Emilie Raberg Noel, Sr. of Manhattan, and resided at *Flower de Hundred* in Matinecock. [*See* Spinzia, *Long Island's Prominent North Shore Families, vol. 1* – Greer entry.] Their daughter Jean married Franklin W. Robinson. Their daughter Mary married Thomas S. McLane, the son of Dr. James W. McLane. Their son Lawrence married Georgiana Oakes and resided in East Hampton

[See following entry for additional family information.]

Greer, Lawrence (1872-1925)

Occupation(s):	attorney - partner, Pierce and Greer;
	general counsel, Western Maryland Railway Co.;
	assistant general counsel, Wabash Railway Co.;
	general counsel, New Jersey, Indiana & Illinois Railway Co.;
	counsel to board, The Denver & Rio Grande Western Railway Co.;
	general counsel, St. Louis Southwestern Railway Co.
	capitalist - chairman of board, Western Maryland Railway Co.;
	director, New Jersey, Indiana & Illinois Railway Co.;
	director, St Louis Southwestern Railway Co.
Civic Activism:	trustee, Rockaway Hunt Club, Lawrence, NY;
	trustee, Turf and Field Club, Belmont Park, Elmont, NY
Marriage(s):	1896-1925 – Georgiana Oakes (1873-1959)
Address:	Apaquague Road, East Hampton
Name of estate:	
Year of construction:	
Style of architecture:	
Architect(s):	
Landscape architect(s):	Nellie Beatrice Osborn Allen, c. 1927
	(for C. H. McCall)
House extant:	unconfirmed

Nassau County Museum Collection has photographs of the estate.

Historical notes:

Lawrence Greer was the son of the Right Reverend David Hummell and Mrs. Caroline Augusta Keith Greer of *Yondermere* in East Hampton.

Georgiana Oakes Greer was the daughter of Thomas Fletcher and Abby Rogers Haskell Oakes.

Lawrence and Georgiana Oakes Greer's daughter Dorothy married Robert C. Myles, Jr. of Manhattan.

[See previous entry for additional family information.]

The house was later owned by Clifford Hyde McCall, Sr. who called it *Kipsveen*. [*The East Hampton Star* December 25, 1935, p. 2.] In 1955 it was purchased by Count Leonardo Mercati. [*The East Hampton Star* November 8, 1951, p. 5.]

Gribetz, Lester (b. 1930)

Occupation(s):	industrialist - senior vice-president, Waterford / Wedgwood Corp., 2008-2009;
	senior vice-president, Hartman Luggage, 2009-2012;
	director and president, Lenox Corp.
	merchant - vice-chairman of board, Bloomingdales, 1975-1991;
	vice president for fashion, Macy's Home Store;
	chairman of board and CEO, Macy's Inc.
Civic Activism:	trustee, God's Love We Deliver (a non-profit charity organization which delivers donated restaurant meals to home bound people with AIDS), NYC

Marriage(s):

Address:	467 Further Lane, Amagansett
Name of estate:	
Year of construction:	1955
Style of architecture:	Colonial Revival
Architect(s):	
Landscape architect(s):	
House extant: yes	
Historical notes:	

In 2013 Lester Gribetz purchased the 3,000-square-foot, four-bedroom, three-bath house for $3.7 million. He was the son of Herman and Celia Gribetz of NYC.

Gruen, Robert L. (b. 1913)

Occupation(s):	architect - president, Gruen Associates (industrial design firm)
Civic Activism:	president, Industrial Designer's Institute
Marriage(s):	Miriam Livingston (1912-1978)
Address:	199 Main Street, East Hampton
Name of estate:	
Year of construction:	1836
Style of architecture:	
Architect(s):	
Landscape architect(s):	
House extant: yes	
Historical notes:	

The house was originally the residence of James M. Hedges. It was later owned by Gruen.
The Blue Book of The Hamptons, 1973 lists Robert L. and Miriam Livingston Gruen as residing at 199 Main Street, East Hampton.
Robert L. and Miriam Livingston Gruen's daughter Andrea married Mac–Antoine Lombardi, the son of Baron Antonio Lombardi of Bologna, Italy, and Caracas, Venezuela. Their daughter Pamela married Hugh Ruse.

Gruss, Martin David (b. 1943)

Occupation(s):	financier - partner, Gruss and Co., NYC (arbitrage investment firm)
Civic Activism:	a founder, with his wife Audrey, Audrey and Martin Gruss Foundation; donated $42 million to Israel Museum, Jerusalem; chairman, The Caroline and Joseph S. Gruss Monument Funds
Marriage(s):	M/1 – 1973-div. 1988 – Agneta *[unable to determine maiden name]* (b. 1945)

- merchant - co-founder, Swedish Cottage, NYC (Swedish Country furnishings)

M/2 – 1988 – Audrey M. Butvay (b. 1942)
- model
- advertising executive - assistant to vice-president, Revlon; director of advertising and fashion, J. P. Stevens hosiery division; manager of sales promotion, Elizabeth Arden; founder, International Creative Marketing
- industrialist - co-founder and president, Terme di Saturnia (skin care firm)

Civic Activism:
- president and a founder, with her husband Martin, Audrey and Martin Gruss Foundation;
- trustee, Lincoln Center for the Performing Arts, NYC;
- trustee, Lenox Hill Neighborhood House, NYC;
- board member, The Public Theater / New York Shakespeare Festival, NYC;
- member, Chairman's Council, Metropolitan Museum of Art, NYC;
- member, International Advisory Council, Guggenheim Museum, NYC;
- member, advisory council, Literacy Partners;
- trustee, The Hospice Guild;
- trustee, The Preservation Council;
- a founder, Kravis Center for the Performing Arts, Palm Beach, FL;
- trustee, American Friends of Victoria & Albert Museum, London, England;
- member, advisory board, FAI (Italian architectural preservation organization);
- a founder, Hope for Depression Research Foundation;
- board member, Byrd Hoffman Water Mill Foundation;
- board member, Southampton Hospital;
- a founder, US-Baltic Foundation;
- a founding board member, American Lithuanian Economic Development Advisory Council

Address:	Heller Lane, East Hampton
Name of estate:	
Year of construction:	1978
Style of architecture:	Modern
Architect(s):	Norman Jaffe designed the house (for Gruss)
Landscape architect(s):	
House extant: yes	
Historical notes:	

The house was built by Martin David Gruss.
He is the son of Joseph Saul and Caroline Zelaznik Gruss.
Agneta Gruss was born in Sweden. She later married James Joseph Gillin.
Martin David and Agneta Gruss' son Joshua married Shoshanna Lonstein, the daughter of Zach and Betty Lonstein of New York, and, later, Jessica Elizabeth Siebel, the daughter of Kenneth F. and Judith A. Siebel of Ross, CA.
Audrey M. Butvay Gruss was born in Kaunas, Lithuania. She had previously been married to Dr. Ralph J. Nach.

Gruzen, Barnet Sumner (1903-1974)

Occupation(s):	architect - partner, Kelly and Kruzen; partner, Gruzen and Partners
Civic Activism:	president, American Technion Society; chairman, architectural division, United Jewish Appeal of New York City, 1951; chairman of board, Federated Jewish Philanthropies of New York City, 1952-1953
Marriage(s):	1930-1974 – Ethel Bernstein Brof (1905-1980) - entertainers and associated professions - singer, Metropolitan Opera, NYC
Address:	Further Lane and Skimhampton Road, Amagansett

Name of estate:
Year of construction:
Style of architecture:
Architect(s):
Landscape architect(s):
House extant: unconfirmed
Historical notes:

   Born in Riga, Latvia, Barnet Sumner Gruzen was the son of Max and Ida Friedman Gruzen.
   Ethel Bernstein Brof Gruzen was the daughter of Julius and Rebecca Bernstein Brof.
   Barnet Sumner and Ethel Bernstein Gruzen's son Maxson married Lynn Jay Winter, the daughter of Elmer L. Winter of Milwaukee, WI. Their son Jordan resided in Amagansett.
[See following entry for additional family information.

Gruzen, Jordan Lee (1934-2015)

Occupation(s):	architect - partner, Kell & Gruzen (later, Gruzen Partners; then, Gruzen Partnership; and subsequently, iBi Group Gruzen & Stanton)
Civic Activism:	co-founder, Action Group for Better Architecture; a founder, Knickerbocker Chamber Orchestra; a founder, Interfaith Community
Marriage(s):	M/1 – 1960-div. – Joan Ellen Greenberg M/2 – 1976-2015 – Lee Ferguson (b. 1946) - entertainers and associated professions - production associate, NBC News program "Today" writer - *Raising Your Jewish–Christian Child*, 1988
Address:	off Further Lane, Amagansett

Name of estate:
Year of construction: 1984
Style of architecture: Modern
Architect(s): Jordan Lee Gruzen designed his own residence
Landscape architect(s)
House extant: yes
Historical notes:

   The house was built by Jordan Lee Gruzen.
   He was the son of Barnet Sumner and Ethel Bernstein Brof Gruzen of Amagansett.
   Joan Ellen Greenberg Gruzen was the daughter of Oscar Greenberg of Jersey City, NJ. She subsequently married Monroe Levinson (aka Mon Levinson).
   Jordan Lee and Joan Ellen Greenberg Gruzen's son Alexander married Karen Malcolm Voss, the daughter of Edward C. Voss, Jr. of Wheeling, WV.
   Lee Ferguson Gruzen is the daughter of Clinton P. Ferguson of Marston Mills, MA.
   Jordan Lee and Lee Ferguson Gruzen's daughter Georgia, who is a freelance film maker, resides in Altadena, CA. Their daughter Rachael resides in Amagansett.
[See previous entry for additional family information.]

Gunster, Joseph Frederick (1894-1979)

Occupation(s):	attorney - partner, Gunster, Yoakley, Criser, and Stewart; Assistant City Solicitor, Scranton, PA
Civic Activism:	chairman of board, Scranton Airport Commission; president, Lackawanna Historical Society; president, Scranton Chamber of Commerce; president, Scranton Council of Social Agencies; president, Bath and Tennis Club, Palm Beach, FL; president, Society of the Four Arts, Palm Beach, FL; president, Palm Beach Civic Association; governor, Devon Yacht Club, Amagansett; president and trustee, Guild Hall, East Hampton, 1946-1948
Marriage(s):	1938-1964 – Harriet Ruth Harris (d. 1964) - Civic Activism: president, Garden Club of East Hampton
Address:	Hither Lane, East Hampton
Name of estate:	*Ten Elms*
Year of construction:	
Style of architecture:	
Architect(s):	
Landscape architect(s):	
House extant: unconfirmed	
Historical notes:	

The Blue Book of The Hamptons, 1965 lists Joseph Frederick Gunster as residing at *Ten Elms* on Hither Lane, East Hampton.

He was the son of Judge Frederick William and Mrs. Margaret Brehl Gunster of Scranton, PA.

Harriet Ruth Harris Gunster was the daughter of Walter Frederick Harris. She had previously been married to Standard Oil founder Horace Hutchins Work, Sr. of *Beechwood* in Madison, NJ.

The Gunsters did not have children.

In 1965 the house was purchased by Arthur Stanton. [*The East Hampton Star* May 5, 1966, p. 4.]

Gwathmey, Charles (1938-2009)

Occupation(s):	architect -	partner, Gwathmey, Siegel, and Associates
		[See Architects appendix in this volume for Gwathmey's commissions in East Hampton.]
	educator -	member of faculty, Cooper Union for Advancement of Science and Art, NYC;
		member of faculty, Princeton, NJ;
		member of faculty, Columbia University, NYC;
		member of faculty, University of Pennsylvania, Philadelphia, PA;
		member of faculty, University of Texas, Austin, TX;
		member of faculty, University of California, Los Angeles, CA;
		member of faculty, Yale University, New Haven, CT;
		member of faculty, Harvard University, Cambridge, MA;
		member of faculty, William A. Bernoudy Resident Architect, American University, Rome, Italy
Civic Activism:		president, board of trustees, The Institute for Architecture and Urban Studies

Marriage(s): M/1 – 1962-div. – Emily Margolin
- writer - *Trick or Treat*, 2001;
  On Earth as it is in Heaven;
  Lots of Luck, 1994;
  A Box of Kisses;
  Signs of Our Times;
  An Enchantment of Elephants, 1993;
  Sister Sets, 1997;
  Wholly Cow, 1988

M/2 – 1974 – Bette-Ann Damson (b. 1939)
- industrialist - president, Polo Ralph Lauren (manufacturer of women's and men's clothing and accessories)

Address: 122 Bluff Road, Amagansett
Name of estate:
Year of construction: 1965
Style of architecture: Modern
Architect(s): Charles Gwathmey designed the house and art studio (for R. Gwathmey, Jr.)
Charles Gwathmey, 2001 alterations (for himself)
Landscape architect(s)
Builder: John Caramagna
House extant: yes
Historical notes:

The 1,200-square-foot-house and art studio were built by Robert Gwathmey, Jr. In 2001 they were inherited by the Gwathmeys' son Charles.

Emily Margolin Gwathmey is the daughter of Benjamin and Annette Lief Margolin of NYC.

Charles and Emily Margolin Gwathmey's daughter Ann lives in Los Angeles, CA.

Bette-Ann Damson Gwathmey is the daughter of Harry C. and Ethel Brody Damson. Bette-Ann had previously been married to Robert Steel, Sr.

Gwathmey, Robert, Jr. (1903-1988)

Occupation(s):	artist - socialist realist painter
	educator - drawing, Temple University, Philadelphia, PA, 1930-1932;
	painting and drawing, Beaver College, Glenside, PA, 1930-1937;
	instructor, Carnegie Institute of Technology, Pittsburgh, PA, 1939-1942;
	life drawing, Cooper Union School of Art, NYC, 1942-1968;
	painting, New School for Social Research, NYC, 1946-1949;
	Boston University, Boston, MA, 1968-1969
Civic Activism:	vice-president, Artist Union
Marriage(s):	1935-1988 – Rosalie Dean Hook (1908-2001)
	- artist - textile designer
	professional photographer
	journalist - writer, editor, reviewer, *Photo Notes*
Address:	122 Bluff Road, Amagansett
Name of estate:	
Year of construction:	1965
Style of architecture:	Modern
Architect(s):	Charles Gwathmey designed the house and art studio (for R. Gwathmey, Jr.)
	Charles Gwathmey, 2001 alterations (for himself)
Landscape architect(s)	
Builder:	John Caramagna
House extant: yes	
Historical notes:	

The 1,200-square-foot-house and art studio were built by Robert Gwathmey, Jr.
He was the son of Robert and Eva Mortimer Harrison Gwathmey, Sr. of Virginia.
Rosalie Dean Hook Gwathmey was the daughter of Charles Christian and Ida MacDonald Hook of Charlotte, NC.
The house complex was subsequently owned by the Gwathmeys' son Charles.

Haag, Joseph, Jr. (1895-1958)

Occupation(s):	capitalist - president, Todd Drydock & Repair Corp., Brooklyn, NY
	industrialist - president, Todd Shipyard Corp.;
	president, Todd Combustion Equipment Corp.
Marriage(s):	Camilla Ashurst (1896-1966)
Address:	Jones Road, East Hampton
Name of estate:	
Year of construction:	
Style of architecture:	Cottage
Architect(s):	
Landscape architect(s):	
House extant: unconfirmed	
Historical notes:	

In 1943 Haag purchased William Raywood Maloney, Jr.'s residence *Glendella*. [*The East Hampton Star* November 25, 1943, p. 1.]
He was the son of Joseph and Nellie Grandon Haag, Sr.

Hackstaff, Charles Ludovic (1854-1926)

Occupation(s):	
Civic Activism:	a founder, St. Luke's Episcopal Church, East Hampton
Marriage(s):	1882-1908 – Margaret Euphemia Hoffman (1861-1908)
	- Civic Activism: member, Committee on History and Tradition of the Colonial Dames of the State of New York
Address:	18 Lee Avenue, East Hampton
Name of estate:	*Tarriawyle*
Year of construction:	1899
Style of architecture:	Shingle
Architect(s):	Joseph Greenleaf Thorp designed the house (for Hackstaff)
Landscape architect(s):	
Builder:	Loper Brothers
	George A. Eldredge, 1902 additions*

House extant: yes
Historical notes:

The 7,500-square-foot, eight-bedroom, seven-and-a-half-bath house, originally called *Tarriawyle*, was built by Charles Ludovic Hackstaff.

The *Social Register Summer, 1910* lists Charles L. Hackstaff as residing at *Tarriawyle* in East Hampton.

He was the son of William G. and Anna Garr Hackstaff.

Margaret Euphemia Hoffman Hackstaff was the daughter of The Reverend Eugene Augustus and Mrs. Mary Cooke Elmendorf Hoffman.

Charles Ludovic and Margaret Euphemia Hoffman Hackstaff's daughter Margaret married Albert Gallatin III, the son of Frederic and Almy Goelet Gerry Gallatin of *Breezy Lawn* in East Hampton, and resided in Southampton. [*See* Spinzia, *Long Island's Prominent Families in the Town of Southampton* – Gallatin entry.] Their daughter Mai married Dr. John Baldwin Walker, Sr., the son of The Reverend Avery Skinner and Mrs. Rosanna Baldwin Walker, and resided at *Tarriawyle* in East Hampton. Their daughter Caryl married Howard Ogden Wood, Jr. and resided in Lawrence and at *Tarriawyle* in East Hampton. [*See* Spinzia, *Long Island's Prominent Families in the Town of Hempstead* – Wood entry.]

*The 1902 addition on the south facade was built by Eldredge. In 1969 the front porch was enclosed.

The house was later owned by Harkness Edwards, Sr. and, subsequently, by Stephen Kniznick Robert.

In 2012 the house and 1.9 acres were for sale by Robert. The asking price was $18.5 million. It was sold for $14.9 million in 2014.

Hall, William Claiborne (1881-1937)

Occupation(s):	industrialist - vice-president, Atlanta Terra Cotta Co., Atlanta, GA
Marriage(s):	1909-1937 – Christine Collings (1883-1974)
	- Civic Activism: president, Ladies Village Improvement Society; treasurer, Guild Hall, East Hampton
Address:	Apaquogue Road, East Hampton
Name of estate:	
Year of construction:	
Style of architecture:	
Architect(s):	
Landscape architect(s):	

House extant: unconfirmed
Historical notes:

The *Social Directory of Southampton, Long Island, 1931* lists William Claiborne Hall as residing on Apaquogue Road, East Hampton.

He was the son of William Cornelius and Mary Suzette Thomas Hall.

Christine Collings Hall was the daughter of Crittendon Collings, a founder of Standard Oil.

William Claiborne and Christine Collings Hall's daughter Noel married Joseph Still Clark, Jr., the son of Joseph Still and Kate R. Avery Clark, Sr., of *Kate's Hall* in Southampton and, later, Cuthbert Russell Train, the son of Admiral Charles Russell Train. [*See* Spinzia, *Long Island's Prominent Families in the Town of Southampton* – Clark entry.] Their daughter Edith married Frederick T. Merrill, Sr. with whom she resided in East Hampton, and, later, Harding F. Bancroft with whom she resided in Washington.

Halsted, Dr. Harbeck (1890-1967)

Occupation(s):	physician - obstetrician and gynecologist, Sloan Hospital for Women, NYC;
	consulting physician, Southampton Hospital, Southampton, NY;
	consulting physician, Margaret Hague Maternity Hospital, Jersey City, NJ
	educator - professor, College of Physicians and Surgeons, Columbia University, NYC
Marriage(s):	Hedi Klaschke (d. 1966)
	- Civic Activism: chair, ladies golf committee, Maidstone Club, East Hampton
Address:	14 Mill Hill Lane, East Hampton
Name of estate:	
Year of construction:	
Style of architecture:	Shingled Cottage
Architect(s):	
Landscape architect(s):	
House extant: yes	
Historical notes:	

In 1964 Halsted sold his Cottage Avenue house to Richard Pelzman and rented the Mill Hill Lane house from Mrs. Helen Kennedy. [*The East Hampton Star* October 8, 1964, p. 4.]

The Blue Book of The Hamptons, 1965 lists Dr. Harbeck and Mrs. Halsted as residing at 14 Mill Hill Lane, East Hampton.

The Halsteds did not have children.

In 2016 the four-bedroom, three-bath, 2,700-square-foot Mill Lane house was for sale. The asking price was $2.4 million.

Hamilton, Chico (1921-2013)
aka Foreststorn Hamilton

Occupation(s):	entertainers and associated professions -
	jazz drummer*;
	motion picture actor;
	composer;
	band leader, Chico Hamilton Trio, Sextet, and Quintet
	educator - faculty member, Parsons New School of Jazz and Contemporary Music, NYC;
	faculty member, Mannes College of Music, New School University, NYC
Marriage(s):	1941-2008 – Helen *[unable to determine maiden name]* (1924-2008)
	- financier - member, AEA (investment firm)
Address:	Water Hole Road, East Hampton
Name of estate:	
Year of construction:	1973
Style of architecture:	Modern
Architect(s):	Norman Jaffe designed the house (for C. Hamilton)
Landscape architect(s)	
House extant: unconfirmed	
Historical notes:	

The house was built by Chico Hamilton.

He was the son of Jesse and Pearl Lee Gonzales Hamilton of Texas.

*Chico performed with Count Basie's Orchestra and provided backup for Lena Horne from 1948 to 1955 before forming his own band in 1955.

Hamilton, Gordon C. (1916-2008)

Occupation(s):	advertising executive - director of public relations, Texaco
	journalist - editor, *Newsweek* magazine;
	member, *The Literary Digest*;
	reporter, *Daily Mirror*
Marriage(s):	1948 – Constance Rose
Address:	Middle Lane, East Hampton
Name of estate:	
Year of construction:	1955
Style of architecture:	
Architect(s):	
Landscape architect(s)	
House extant: unconfirmed	
Historical notes:	

The house was built by Gordon C. Hamilton. [*The East Hampton Star* June 16, 1955, p. 12.]
The Blue Book of The Hamptons, 1973 lists Gordon C. and Constance Rose Hamilton as residing on Middle Lane, East Hampton.
He was the son of Clayton Hamilton of New York.
Constance Rose Hamilton was the daughter of William A. and Grace Johnson Rose, Sr. of Milford, CT.
Gordon C. and Constance Rose Hamilton's daughter Kim married John Frederick Gottshall, the son of Thomas H. Gottshall of Boyertown, PA.

Hamlin, Harry Leon (1861-1934)

Occupation(s):	capitalist - proprietor, Grand Opera House, Chicago, IL
Civic Activism:	a founder, East Hampton Riding Club; governor, Maidstone Club, East Hampton
Marriage(s):	M/1 – 1888-1892 – Katharine Dimon (d. 1892)
	M/2 – 1902-1934 – Mary Elkins Paxton (1875-1958)
	- restaurateur - East Hampton
	Civic Activism: president, Ogonitz Association; member, executive committee, East Hampton Women's Republican Club; trustee, Guild Hall, East Hampton; a founder, East Hampton Riding Club; member, East Hampton War Memorial committee, 1924
Address:	341 Town Lane, Amagansett
Name of estate:	*Stony Hill Farm*
Year of construction:	1914
Style of architecture:	Colonial Revival
Architect(s):	Edward M. Gay, 1914 alterations (for Hamlin)
Landscape architect(s):	
Builder:	Edward M. Gay (for Hamlin)
	Jeffrey Colle (for Baldwin)
House extant: no*	
Historical notes:	

    Nathaniel Baker's 1680s house was purchased by Samuel Schellinger who enlarged it in 1797. It was purchased in 1913 by Harry Leon Hamlin who moved it from Main Street to what was to become his 325-acre Town Lane dairy farm *Stony Hill Farm*. [*The East Hampton Star* October 3, 1913, p. 3, and Carleton Kelsey and Lucinda Mayo, *Images of America: Amagansett* (Dover, NH: Arcadia Publishing, 1997), p. 12.]

    The *Social Register Summer, 1923* lists Harry L. and Mary Elkins Paxton Hamlin as residing at *Stony Hill Farm* in Amagansett.

    He was the son of John Austin and Mary Ellen Donovan Hamlin.

    Katharine Dimon Hamlin was the daughter of John Dimon.

    Mary Elkins Paxton Hamlin was the daughter of The Reverend John Randolph and Mrs. Mary Lindsey Paxton, Sr. of *Windward* in East Hampton.

    Harry Leon and Mary Elkins Paxton Hamlin's daughter Judith married a descendant of William the Conqueror, Charles Percy Frederick North, the son of Frederick Keppel and Grace Feilding North, and resided in England.

    In 1949 the house was purchased from Mrs. Hamlin by Jeffery Brackett Potter who continued to call it *Stony Hill Farm*. [*The East Hampton Star* November 17, 1949, p. 4.] The main residence was purchased by Michael Minkoff who flipped it to Alexander Rae Baldwin III (aka Alec Baldwin) in 1996. In 2015 Baldwin substantially enlarged and remodeled the house into a contemporary style.

    *Some portions of the interior remain.

Hamlin, Harry Leon (1861-1934)

Occupation(s):	*[See previous entry.]*
Civic Activism:	*[See previous entry.]*
Marriage(s):	M/1 – 1888-1892 – Katharine Dimon (d. 1892)
	M/2 – 1902-1934 – Mary Elkins Paxton (1875-1958)
	- *[See previous entry.]*
Address:	74 James Lane, East Hampton
Name of estate:	
Year of construction:	1873
Style of architecture:	Colonial Revival
Architect(s):	
Landscape architect(s):	
Builder:	E. Marvin Conklin, 1935 alterations
	(for Mrs. Hamlin)
House extant: yes	
Historical notes:	

   The house was built by John Daniel Hedges. In 1935 it was purchased by Mrs. Mary Elkins Paxton Hamlin who enlarged the house for use as an inn.
   [See previous entry for family information.]
   In 1954 Mrs. Hamlin sold the house to Henri Remy Soule who called it The Hedges Inn.
   The house, which is on the National Register of Historic Places, is currently The Hedges Inn.

Hamlin, Mary Elkins Paxton (1875-1958)

Occupation(s):	*[See previous entry.]*
Civic Activism:	*[See previous entry.]*
Marriage(s):	1902-1934 – Harry Leon Hamlin (1861-1934)
	- *[See previous entry.]*
Address:	111 Egypt Lane, East Hampton
Name of estate:	*Rowdy Hall*
Year of construction:	early-to-mid-eighteenth century
Style of architecture:	Colonial
Architect(s):	Joseph Greenleaf Thorp, 1926 alterations
	(for Mrs. Harry L. Hamlin)
Landscape architect(s):	
House extant: yes	
Historical notes:	

   The house was originally the Osborn family residence. It was later owned by David H. Huntting and, then, by his adopted daughter Annie who utilized it as a boarding house. In 1895, the house was moved from Main Street to Gay Lane. In 1925 it was purchased by Mrs. Hamlin who moved it to Egypt Lane. [*The East Hampton Star* November 15, 1934, p. 5.]
   In 1953 the house was purchased from Mrs. Hamlin by Robert Barnes who made alterations and repairs to it and, in 1954, sold the house to Henry Sanford Thorne. [*The East Hampton Star* November 26, 1953, p. 4, and June 17, 1954, p. 7.]
   In 2003 the house was listed for sale. The asking price was $2.25 million.

Hamlin, Mary Elkins Paxton (1875-1958)

Occupation(s):	*[See previous entry.]*
Civic Activism:	*[See previous entry.]*
Marriage(s):	1902-1934 – Harry Leon Hamlin (1861-1934)
	- *[See previous entry.]*
Address:	86 Lily Pond Lane, East Hampton
Name of estate:	*Windward*
Year of construction:	1901
Style of architecture:	Neo-Tudor
Architect(s):	Joseph Greenleaf Thorp designed the house (for J. R. Paxton, Sr.)
Landscape architect(s):	
Builder:	George A. Eldredge
House extant: yes	
Historical notes:	

    The house, originally named *Windward*, was built by The Reverend John Randolph Paxton, Sr. It was later owned by his daughter Mary Elkins Paxton Hamlin who continued to call it *Windward*.
    The *Social Register Summer, 1932* lists Harry L. and Mary Elkins Paxton Hamlin as residing at *Windward* in East Hampton.
    He was the son of John Austin and Mary Ellen Donovan Hamlin of Chicago, IL.
    Harry Leon and Mary Elkins Paxton Hamlin's daughter Judith married Charles Percy Frederick North, the son of Frederick North of *Rougham Hall* in Norfolk, England.
    In 1946 Mrs. Hamlin sold the house to Leonard Biscoe. [*The East Hampton Star* February 14, 1946, p. 5.]
    In 1963 the house was purchased by Alvin Gibbs Fox. [*The East Hampton Star* April 23, 1964, p. 3] It was later owned by Carol Ann Morgan, who, in 2010, sold the house for $25.5 million.
    Alterations were made to the house in 1906 and 1929.

Hammond, John Carnahan (1898-1948)

Occupation(s):	publisher - *The Clinton Courier*, Clinton, NY
	financier - assistant head, trust department, Guaranty Trust Co.
	writer - co-editor, *The Atom in the Audience*, 1941 (30 years of his father's reviews)
Marriage(s):	M/1 – Charlotte Marshall
	M/2 – 1940-1948 – Charlotte Maurice (1909-1986)
Address:	Hither Lane, East Hampton
Name of estate:	*Aunt Phoebe's*
Year of construction:	
Style of architecture:	
Architect(s):	Joseph Greenleaf Thorp, 1926 alterations (for P. Hammond)
Landscape architect(s):	
House extant: unconfirmed	
Historical notes:	

    Hammond inherited the house from his father Percy.
    Charlotte Marshall Hammond was the daughter of George Holbrooke and Ethel Maurice. Charlotte had previously been married to Charles Morris.
    [See following entry for additional family information.]

Hammond, Percy (1873-1936)

Occupation(s):	journalist - editor, *News Advertiser*, Chillicothe, OH;
	police reporter, City Press Association, Chicago, IL;
	drama critic, *Evening Post*, Chicago, IL;
	drama critic, *Tribune*, Chicago, IL;
	drama critic, *New York Tribune* (later, *Herald Tribune*);
	drama critic, *Herald Tribune*, NYC
	writer - *But Is It Art?* 1927
Marriage(s):	1896-1935 – Florence Carnahan (d. 1935)
Address:	Hither Lane, East Hampton
Name of estate:	*Aunt Phoebe's*
Year of construction:	
Style of architecture:	Colonial Revival
Architect(s):	Joseph Greenleaf Thorp, 1926
	alterations (for P. Hammond)
Landscape architect(s)	
House extant: unconfirmed	
Historical notes:	

    In 1926 Hammond bought the former Edward's house, moved it from Main Street to Hither Lane, remodeled it, and named the house *Aunt Phoebe's* in honor of Mrs. John Huntting. [*The East Hampton Star* April 30, 1936, pp. 2 and 8; April 20, 1939, p. 2; and February 25, 1965, p. 7.]

    The *Long Island Society Register, 1929* lists Mr. and Mrs. Percy Hammond as residing on Hither Lane, East Hampton. He was the son of Alexander and Charlotte Hunter Hammond of Cadiz, OH.

    Florence Carnahan Hammond was the daughter of Andrew Henderson Carnahan of Cadiz, OH.

    Percy and Florence Carnahan Hammond's son John married Charlotte Marshall.

[See previous entry for additional family information.]

Hand, John White (1865-1949)

Occupation(s):	merchant - owner, Quaker Oak Farm (peach orchard);
	salesman for hot air furnace firm
Civic Activism:	chairman, Committee to Improve Three Mile Harbor Waterway
Marriage(s):	1909-1949 – Mary Coolidge (1874-1957)
	- educator - high school music teacher
	Civic Activism: chair, East Hampton Chapter, American Red Cross, 1940;
	secretary and manager, East Hampton Free Library;
	chair, nominating committee, Ladies Village Improvement Society, East Hampton;
	president, Ladies Village Improvement Society, East Hampton;
	co-founder, Mother's Club, East Hampton;
	chair, East Hampton Chapter, Home Service;
	director, Southampton Hospital
Address:	Huntting Lane, East Hampton
Name of estate:	
Year of construction:	1898
Style of architecture:	
Architect(s):	Joseph Greenleaf Thorp designed
	the house (for Hand)
Landscape architect(s):	
House extant: yes	
Historical notes:	

    The house was built by John White Hand.

    He was the son of George and Eliza Abigail White Hand.

    Mary Coolidge Hand was the daughter of Charles and Cornelia Coolidge.

    John White and Mary Coolidge Hand's son John Coolidge White married Emily Porter Shaw, the daughter of Leland H. Shaw of Poughkeepsie, NY.

    By 1949 the Whites had relocated to Newtown Lane.

Hanke, George Frederick Robert, Sr.

Occupation(s):	attorney
	financier - financial analyst, Scudder, Stevens, and Clark (investment banking firm)
	capitalist - president and CEO, Polaris Arts Ltd., New York and London, England (motion picture and stage production firm); president, New York Repertory Theater Co.
Civic Activism:	vice president and general counsel, The Asia Society, NYC;
	trustee, Flagler College, St. Augustine, FL;
	vice-president, Henry Morrison Flagler Museum, Palm Beach, FL
Marriage(s):	M/1 – 1960 – Mary Vincent Martin
	M/2 – Lynn S. Washburn
	- capitalist - motion picture producer
Address:	15 Lily Pond Lane, East Hampton
Name of estate:	
Year of construction:	
Style of architecture:	
Architect(s):	
Landscape architect(s)	
House extant: unconfirmed	
Historical notes:	

George Frederick Robert Hanke, Sr. is the son of Ralph Frederick Herman and Jean Flagler Hanke and the great-grandson of Henry Morrison Flagler.

Mary Vincent Martin Hanke is the daughter of Williams Swift Martin II of Georgetown, VA.

George Frederick Robert and Mary Vincent Martin Hanke, Sr.'s son John Vincent Hanke married Holly Hayes.

The *Social Register Summer, 1982* lists G. F. Robert and Lynn S. Washburn Hanke [Sr.] as residing on Lily Pond Lane, East Hampton.

She is the daughter of George and Anne Gibson Clark Washburn of *Tree House* in East Hampton.

Hansen, Curt Eric (1891-1974)

Occupation(s):	industrialist - manager, Chisholm–Moore Manufacturing Co. (manufacturer of chain hoists, trollies, and cranes); partner, Colston, Heald, & Trail
Marriage(s):	1917-div. 1925 – Evine Richard (1895-1974)
	- Civic Activism: president, Ladies Village Improvement Society, East Hampton
Address:	Woods Lane, East Hampton
Name of estate:	
Year of construction:	
Style of architecture:	
Architect(s):	
Landscape architect(s):	
House extant: unconfirmed	
Historical notes:	

The *Social Register Summer, 1921* lists Curt Eric and Evine Richard Hansen as residing on Woods Lane, East Hampton.

He was the son of Carl E. and Gertrude Dollen Hansen.

Evine Richard Hansen was the daughter of Edwin Auguste and Alice Bartow Moore Richard, Sr. Evine subsequently married Clifford Hyde McCall, Sr. and resided with him at *Kipsveen* in East Hampton. Evine's brother Auguste married Rita Conway and resided in East Hampton.

Curt Eric and Evine Richard Hansen's son Eric married Susan Mayne Kelsey, the daughter of Stephen Tomlinson and Anne Louise Silver Kelsey of *Leecott* in East Hampton and resided in Darien, CT. Their son Edwin married Sarah Eveleth Campbell, the daughter of David Campbell of Milton, MA.

Hardy, Charles J., Jr. (1895-1973)

Occupation(s):	attorney - partner, Hardy, Stancliffe, and Hardy; partner, Hardy, Peal, Rawlings, Werner, and Maxwell industrialist - chairman of board, ACF Industries, Inc. (formally American Car and Foundry Co.); director, Fasteners, Inc.; director, Philips Screw Co.; director, Pollard–Alling Co. publisher - owner, Journal News, Nyack, NY; president, Landrock Publishing Corp., Nyack, NY
Marriage(s):	M/1 – 1921-div. 1948 – Helen E. Mueller M/2 – 1948-1973 – Mattie–King Shropshire
Address:	Lily Pond Lane, East Hampton
Name of estate:	
Year of construction:	
Style of architecture:	
Architect(s):	
Landscape architect(s)	
House extant: unconfirmed	
Historical notes:	

Charles J. Hardy, Jr. was the son of Charles J. and Virginia Taylor Hardy, Sr. of Hampton Bays. [*See* Spinzia, *Long Island's Prominent Families in the Town of Southampton* – Hardy entry.]

Helen E. Mueller Hardy was the daughter of E. T. Mueller of Mount Vernon, NY.

Charles J. and Helen E. Mueller Hardy, Jr.'s daughter Ruth married Charles G. Miller, Jr. of Rye, NY, and resided in Bridgehampton.

The Blue Book of The Hamptons, 1958 lists Charles J. and Mattie–King Shropshire Hardy, Jr. as residing on Lily Pond Lane, East Hampton.

She was the daughter of John Henry and Juanita Eugenia Shropshire of Texas. Mattie had previously been married to Richard G. Massock.

In 1965 the twenty-room house was damaged by fire while the Hardys were not at home; arson was suspected. *[The East Hampton Star* November 18, 1965, p. 1.]

Hare, Richard Vincent (1922-2002)

Occupation(s):	interior designer - showrooms in Manhattan and Main Street, East Hampton
Civic Activism:	member, advisory committee, New York Exchange for Women's Work
Marriage(s):	1950 – Anne Elizabeth Haddock - model
Address:	117 Main Street, East Hampton
Name of estate:	
Year of construction:	c. 1799
Style of architecture:	Georgian*
Architect(s):	Isaac Henry Green II designed 1889 alterations** Joseph Greenleaf Thorp designed 1905 interior and exterior alterations
Landscape architect(s):	Mary Lois Deputy Lamson (for Douglas)

House extant: yes
Historical notes:

*The Georgian-style house was built by Jeremiah Miller IV. In 1885 Edward de Rose purchased the house, remodeled it from Georgian to Colonial Revival, and renamed it *Millfield*. In c. 1885 de Rose also built a guest cottage on the property in an eclectic windmill style. In 1910 the Colonial-Revival-style house was owned by Thomas Lincoln Manson III and, then, by his daughter Dorothea and son-in-law Kilian Van Rensselaer. Both Manson and Van Rensselaer continued to call the estate *Millfield*. In 1945 the house, which is on the National Register of Historic Places, was owned by Graham Douglas. By 1950 it was owned by Franklin M. Chace. It was later owned by Hare.

The Blue Book of The Hamptons, 1973 lists Richard V. Hare as residing at 117 Main Street in East Hampton.

He was the son of Harry Gradzinsky and Anita Cecilia Aronson Hare of Cornwall-on-Hudson, NY.

Anne Elizabeth Haddock Hare was the daughter of William Charlton and Helen Gormley Haddock, Jr. of Rydal, PA.

Richard Vincent and Ann Elizabeth Haddock Hare's son Stephen was a bachelor at the time of his death at age thirty-six. Their son Nicholas resides in Darien, CT.

The 2,380-square-foot house had four bedrooms and three bathrooms.

By 1992 the Hares had relocated to *Es Moli* on Cranberry Lane, Amagansett.

**For Green's other commissions, *see* Spinzia, *Long Island's Prominent South Shore Families: Their Estates and Their Country Homes in the Towns of Babylon and Islip*.

Harkness, Lamon Vanderburg (1850-1916)

Occupation(s):	industrialist - major stockholder and director, Standard Oil Corp.
	capitalist - California real estate, mine, and cattle holdings
Marriage(s):	1872 – Martha Frances Johnson
Address:	19 Lee Avenue, East Hampton
Name of estate:	
Year of construction:	1899
Style of architecture:	Shingle
Architect(s):	Joseph Greenleaf Thorp designed the house (for F. G. Potter)
Landscape architect(s):	
Builder:	Loper Brothers
House extant: yes	
Historical notes:	

The 10,000-square-foot, ten-bedroom house was built by Frederick Gaul Potter. It was later owned by John Richard Keim who sold it to Harkness in 1914. [*The East Hampton Star* January 22, 1915, p. 5.]

He was the son of Stephen Vanderburg and Laura Osborn Harkness.

Martha Frances Johnson Harkness was the daughter of Elias Johnson of Wauseon, OH.

Lamon Vanderburg and Martha Frances Johnson Harkness' daughter Lela married Dr. Ogden Matthias Edwards and resided at *Dunehurst* in East Hampton. Their daughter Laura married Abraham Kingsley Macomber. Their son Harry married Marie Moss Marbeck and, later, Florence Steuber.

The house was later owned by James Branch Briggs, who called it *Beehive*; Chevy Chase; and, then, Peter Gabriel Terian. In 2010 Mrs. Terian placed the house on the market; the asking price was $21 million.

Harper, Marion Clay, Jr. (1916-1989)

Occupation(s):	advertising executive - president and chairman of board, Interpublic, Inc. (advertising firm);
	president, McCann–Erikson (advertising firm)
Marriage(s):	M/1 – 1942-div. 1960 – Virginia Millan Epes
	M/2 – 1963 – Valerie Feit
	- fashion consultant
Address:	211 East Lake Drive, Montauk
Name of estate:	
Year of construction:	1929
Style of architecture:	Modified French Chateau
Architect(s):	K. B. C. Smith designed the house (for Wasey)
Landscape architect(s)	
House extant: unconfirmed	
Historical notes:	

The fourteen-room house was built by Carl Graham Fisher, Sr. It was later owned by Louis Rice Wasey. In 1955 Harper purchased the house from Wasey and converted it into a private club called Captain's Marina. [*The New York Times* December 8, 1955, p. 65.] Beginning in the 1960s, President Nixon was a frequent guest at the club.

Marion Clay Harper, Jr. was the son of Marion Clay and Lotos Alexander Harper, Sr. of *Pendella Farm* in Bucks County, PA.

Virginia Millan Epes Harper was the daughter of Horace Hardaway and Glenda Reid Millan Epes, Sr. Virginia subsequently married Lewis B. Jennings with whom she resided in Arnold, MD.

Marion Clay and Virginia Millan Epes Harper, Jr.'s son Stephen married Josephine Garrett Angevin, the daughter of The Reverend Jay Angevin. Their son Clinton married Macarena Panigua Fuentes.

Valerie Feit Harper was the daughter of Dr. Herman and Mrs. Clair Feit.

Marion Clay and Valerie Feit Harper, Jr.'s daughter Victoria married Richard Mestres Moeser, the son of Charles R. Moeser, Jr. of Cincinnati, OH.

In 2003 the club was purchased by Double K. Management Company which refurbished the premises and operates it as the Montauk Lake Club & Marina.

Harris, William Victor (1869-1943)
aka Victor Harris

Occupation(s):	entertainers and associated professions -
	assistant conductor, Metropolitan Opera, NYC;
	conductor, St. Cecilia Club, 1902-1936;
	singing coach
	composer
Civic Activism:	a founder, St. Cecilia Club (music ensemble)
Marriage(s):	1916-1943 – Catherine Lawrence Richardson (1890-1970)
	- Civic Activism: president, St. Cecilia Club;
	president, New York Club;
	president, auxiliary, Polyclinic Hospital;
	president, Ladies Village Improvement Society, East Hampton;
	member, executive committee, East Hampton Women's Republican Club;
	trustee, Guild Hall, East Hampton;
	secretary, Guild Hall Rehabilitation Fund, East Hampton
Address:	Drew Lane, East Hampton
Name of estate:	*Dune Home*
Year of construction:	
Style of architecture:	
Architect(s):	
Landscape architect(s):	
House extant:	unconfirmed
Historical notes:	

   The *Long Island Society Register, 1929* lists [William] Victor and Catherine Lawrence Richardson Harris as residing on Drew Lane, East Hampton.
   The *Social Register Summer, 1950* lists *Dune Home* as the name of their residence.
   He was the son of Jacob and Hannah Harris of Manhattan.
   Catherine Lawrence Richardson Harris was the daughter of S. H. Richardson of Manhattan.
   William Victor and Catherine Lawrence Richardson Harris' son Victor Stevens Harris married Geraldine Schuyler, the daughter of Charles Stanley Schuyler of Edgewater Park, NJ. Their daughter Mary married Alan Gilchrist, the son of Edmund B. Gilchrist, Sr. of Chestnut Hill, Philadelphia, PA, and, later, Timothy Wetherill Knipe. Their daughter Cecilia married John Sanger Williams, the son of William F. Williams of Towson, MA. Their son David married Susie Skidmore, the daughter of James Bond Skidmore of *Honeysuckle Hedge* in East Hampton, and resided in Greenwich, CT.

Hartley, Theodore Ringwalt (b. 1935)

Occupation(s):	entertainers and associated professions - actor; producer
	capitalist - partner, Pavilion Communications (later, RKO pictures); chairman of board, RKO Pictures
	financier - investment banker; vice-president, First Western Corp.
Civic Activism:	co-founder, with wife Dina, The Story Project (for literacy);
	co-founder, with wife Dina, Hartley–Merrill International Screenwriting Award
Marriage(s):	1989-2017 – Nedenia Marjorie Hutton (1923-2017) (aka Dina Merrill)
	- financier - director, E. F. Hutton and Co. (investment banking firm); chairman, compensation and benefits committee, and director, Lehman Brothers (investment banking firm)
	capitalist - partner, Pavilion Communications (later, RKO Pictures); vice-chairman of board, RKO Pictures
	entertainers and associated professions - actress
	industrialist - president, Amaranthe (cosmetic manufacturer)
	Civic Activism: a founder and trustee, Eugene O'Neill Theater Center, NYC;
	trustee, John F. Kennedy Center for the Performing Arts, Washington, DC;
	vice-president, New York City Mission Society, NYC;
	a founder, Juvenile Diabetes Foundation;
	vice-chair, Republican Pro-Choice Coalition;
	trustee, Population Resource Council;
	trustee, Paley Center for Media, NYC;
	director, Project Orbis (teaches eye care & surgical techniques worldwide);
	co-founder, with husband Ted, The Story Project;
	co-founder, with husband Ted, Hartley–Merrill International Screenwriting Award
Address:	9 West Dune Lane, East Hampton
Name of estate:	
Year of construction:	
Style of architecture:	
Architect(s):	
Landscape architect(s):	
House extant: yes	
Historical notes:	

The Blue Book of The Hamptons, 1997 lists Theodore R. and Nedenia Hutton Hartley as residing at 9 West Dune Road, East Hampton. Their previous East Hampton residence was on Highway Behind the Pond.

He was born in Omaha, NE, and raised on a farm in Iowa after which he attended Annapolis and served as a carrier-based pilot, as a congressional liaison for the Pentagon, and as a presidential aide. Following severe back injuries after his F9F8 fighter jet crashed during a carrier landing, Hartley turned to investment banking, attending Harvard Business School, and eventually pursued an acting career.

Nedenia Marjorie Hutton Hartley was the daughter of Edward Francis and Marjorie Merriweather Post Hutton, who resided at *Hillwood* in Brookville. She had previously been married to Stanley Maddox Rumbough, Jr. of East Hampton and Old Brookville. He was the son of Stanley and Elizabeth Morse Colgate Rumbough, Sr. of *Elston Oaks* in Lloyd Harbor. [*See* Spinzia, *Long Island's Prominent North Shore Families, vol. I* – Hutton entry – and vol. II – Post and Rumbough entries.] After her divorce from Rumbough, Nedenia married the actor, director, and writer Cliff Robertson, who resided in East Hampton and Water Mill, and, later, Hartley. [*See* Spinzia, *Long Island's Prominent Families in the Town of Southampton* – Robertson entry.]

Hassam, Frederick Childe (1859-1935)
aka Childe Hassam

Occupation(s):	artist - painter, etcher
Civic Activism:	first president, New York Water-Color Club, 1890-1896; president, Ten American Painters, NYC
Marriage(s):	1884-1935 – Kathleen Maude Doane (1862-1946)
Address:	Egypt Lane, East Hampton
Name of estate:	*Willow Bend*
Year of construction:	c. 1725-1750
Style of architecture:	Colonial*
Architect(s):	
Landscape architect(s):	Gaines Ruger Donoho designed his own gardens

House extant: unconfirmed
Historical notes:

    Gaines Ruger Donoho purchased the house in 1891. [John Esten. *Hampton Gardens: 350 Years* (New York: Rizzoli, 2008), p. 22.] In 1919 Hassam purchased the house.
    The *Long Island Society Register, 1929* lists Childe and Maude Doane Hassam as residing at *Willow Bend* in East Hampton.
    He was the son of Frederick Fitch and Rosa Delia Hawthorne Hassam of Boston, MA.
    Kathleen Maude Doane Hassam was the daughter of Thomas Coffin and Maria Perry Doane.
    The Hassams did not have children.
    In 1940 Wilfred Wood purchased the house. [*The New York Times* December 8, 1940, p. 221, and *The East Hampton Star* August 22, 1940, p. 1.]
    *The house was modified into Shingle style of architecture.

Hattersley, Lelia Marie Chopin (1879-1962)

Marriage(s):	1905-1909 – Frederick Robert Hattersley (1879-1909) - financier - secretary, F. Hattersley Brokerage and Commission Co., St. Louis, MO
Address:	Egypt Lane, East Hampton
Name of estate:	*Captain's House*
Year of construction:	
Style of architecture:	
Architect(s):	
Landscape architect(s)	

House extant: unconfirmed
Historical notes:

    In 1930 Mrs. Hattersley purchased the Dickinson house and remodeled it as her residence. [*The East Hampton Star* September 12, 1930, p. 7.]
    The *Social Directory of Southampton, Long Island, 1931* lists Mrs. Lelia Hattersley as residing on Egypt Lane, East Hampton. The *Social Register Summer, 1937* lists the name of her residence as *Captain's House*.
    She was the daughter of Aurelian Roselius Oscar and Kate O'Flaherty Chopin.
    Frederick Robert Hattersley was the son of Frederick Hattersley.
    Frederick Robert and Lelia Marie Chopin Hattersley's son Robert married Virginia Luke, the daughter of John Guthrie Luke of New York, and resided at *Cherry Leaze* in Glen Head. [*See* Spinzia, *Long Island's Prominent North Shore Families, vol. I* – Hattersley entry.]

Haupt, Melville I. (1918-2014)

Occupation(s):	industrialist - president, Melville Knitwear Co., Inc., Lawrence, NY
Civic Activism:	chairman of board, Masonic division, Federation of Jewish Philanthropies; chairman of board, Excelsior apartment building, NYC
Marriage(s):	1941-div. – Rita Gradinger (b. 1919) - real estate agent
Address:	43 Gilbert Path, Amagansett
Name of estate:	
Year of construction:	1976
Style of architecture:	International
Architect(s):	Charles Gwathmey designed the house (for Haupt)
Landscape architect(s)	
House extant:	yes

Historical notes:

The house was built by Melville I. Haupt.

He is the son of Samuel and Janet Manheimer Haupt.

Rita Gradinger Haupt is the daughter of Benjamin and Dora Sternberg Gradinger of Far Rockaway, NY. Rita subsequently married ____ Mayer.

Melville I. and Rita Gradinger Haupt's daughter Leslie married Jay Phillip Mayesh, the son of Samuel Mayesh of Rock Island, IL. Their son Samuel married Rosalina Leung. Their daughter Debra married Steven Saltzman.

Havens, Valentine Britton (1889-1948)

Occupation(s):	attorney - partner, Holmes, Lynn, Paul, and Havens, 1922-1925; partner, Holmes, Paul, and Havens, 1926-1930; partner, Olcott, Holmes, Glas, Paul, and Havens, 1930-1932; partner, Olcott, Havens, Wandless, and Stitt educator - lecturer, Brooklyn Law School, 1922-1941 industrialist - director, Radio Frequency Laboratories, Inc., Boonton, NJ*; director, Aircraft Radio Corp, Boonton, NJ; director, Tech-Art Plastics Co. (molds for plastic articles); director, Greenville Finishing Co., Greenville, SC (textile firm)
Marriage(s):	M/1 – 1919-div. 1935 – Nellie F. Laycock (1891-1973) - Civic Activism: volunteer nurse, London England, hospital during World War I; treasurer, Bridgehampton Child Care Center; director, Brooklyn Free Kindergarten Society, 1935-1936 M/2 – 1935-div. 1943 – Louise Richmond Kitchen M/3 – 1943-div. 1945 – Katherine Seymour Mapp
Address:	80 Dunemere Lane, East Hampton
Name of estate:	
Year of construction:	1913
Style of architecture:	Modified Norman
Architect(s):	John Custis Lawrence designed the house (for Voorhees)
Landscape architect(s):	
Builder:	Edward M. Gay
House extant:	yes

Historical notes:

In 1936 Havens purchased the Dr. James Ditmars Voorhees residence. [*The East Hampton Star* December 17, 1936, p. 5.]

He was the son of Edwin Taylor and Edith Murphy Havens of Brooklyn.

Valentine Britton and Nellie F. Laycock Havens' son Leston married Nancy Leigh Tucker, the daughter of The Reverend William LeGrand Tucker.

Louise Richmond Kitchen Havens had previously been married to Henry Daniels Mygatt, the son of Frederic E. Mygatt of Plainfield, NJ.

Katherine Seymour Mapp Havens was the daughter of Dr. Cortez Jefferson Mapp, DDS, of Manhattan.

*In 1922, as a young Army lieutenant general, James H. (Jimmy) Doolittle made the first "blind flight" take-off and landing at Mitchell Field in Garden City using Radio Frequency Laboratories equipment.

The house was later owned by Irving Howland Taylor.

Haverland, Michael Robert (b. 1967)

Occupation(s):	architect - founder, Michael Haverland Design
	educator - assistant professor, Yale School of Architecture, New Haven, CT;
	director, Yale Urban Design Workshop, Yale School of Architecture, New Haven, CT (community-based design center)
Marriage(s):	bachelor
Address:	73 Cove Hollow Road, East Hampton
Name of estate:	
Year of construction:	2004
Style of architecture:	Modern
Architect(s):	Michael Robert Haverland designed his own residence
Landscape architect(s)	
House extant: yes	
Historical notes:	

The 3,000-square-foot house was built by Michael Robert Haverland.

Hayden, William Martin, Sr. (1906-1980)

Occupation(s):	
Civic Activism:	governor, Devon Yacht Club, Amagansett
Marriage(s):	1932-1979 – Rose Miller Betts (1906-1979)
	- educator - teacher
Address:	Indian Wells Highway, Amagansett
Name of estate:	*Half-a-Gale*
Year of construction:	c. 1951
Style of architecture:	
Architect(s):	
Landscape architect(s)	
House extant: unconfirmed	
Historical notes:	

    The house, originally named *Half-a-Gale*, was built by William Martin Hayden, Sr. [*The East Hampton Star* June 14, 1951, p. 9.]
    The Blue Book of The Hamptons, 1973 lists William M. and Rose Miller Betts Hayden [Sr.] as residing at *Half-a-Gale* on Indian Wells Highway in Amagansett.
    He was the son of William Finley and Anna Marguerite Martin Hayden.
    Rose Miller Betts Hayden was the daughter of The Reverend Robert Calvin and Mrs. Mary Wallace Betts.
    William Martin and Rose Miller Betts Hayden, Sr.'s daughter Elizabeth married William Blas Ryall Reiss, the son of Malcolm Reiss of Wilton, CT. Their son William Martin Hayden, Jr. resided in New Mexico.

Haynes, Justin O'Brien, Sr. (1902-1972)

Occupation(s):	financier - vice-president, Abacus Fund, Inc. (investment banking firm)
	industrialist - president, Crookes–Barnes Laboratories, Wayne, NJ. (pharmaceutical firm);
	director of investments, Bristol–Myers Co., 1940-1970 (which became Bristol–Meyer Squibb in 1989 with the merger of Bristol–Meyers Co., founded in 1887 by William McLaren Bristol and John Ripley Myers in Clinton, NY, and the Squibb Corp., founded in 1858 by Edward Robinson Squibb in Brooklyn) (prescription pharmaceutical manufacturer)
Marriage(s):	M/1 – 1928-div. 1943 – Virginia Smith Smathers (1903-1943)
	M/2 – 1945-1972 – Evelyn Green (1908-2001)
	- journalist - beauty editor, *Vogue* magazine
	Civic Activism: established Evelyn G. Haynes Fund at Spencer School (for study of classical architecture); member, New York City Landmarks Committee
Address:	Hither Lane, East Hampton
Name of estate:	
Year of construction:	
Style of architecture:	Colonial Revival
Architect(s):	
Landscape architect(s):	
House extant: unconfirmed	
Historical notes:	

The house was built by Theodore Wilson Morris, Jr. In 1927 it was purchased from Morris by Irvin Shewsbury Cobb, who called it *Back Home*. In 1940 Haynes purchased the house for $27,500 from Cobb. [*The New York Times* February 11, 1940, p. 147.]

He was the son of Clarence L. and Mary V. Haynes of Fort Wayne, IN.

Virginia Smith Smathers Haynes was the foster daughter of Elmer E. Smathers. She had previously married to Giles Greville Healey. In 1929, when Virginia's divorce from Healey was voided by the court, she technically became a bigamist. [*The Courier-News* February 27, 1929, p. 1.] Virginia committed suicide by ingesting twenty sleeping pills. Five years before her death she had had to have her leg amputated. [*The Brooklyn Daily Eagle* June 23, 1945, p. 1.]

Justin and Virginia Smith Smathers Haynes, Sr.'s daughter Cynthia married Merrill Chapin Krech, the son of Dr. Shepard and Mrs. Mary Stevens Chapin Krech of *Briar Patch* in East Hampton; C. Robert Devine, the son of James J. Devine of New York; and, subsequently, ____ de Fabiny. Their son Justin O'Brien Haynes, Jr. lives in Sussex, England.

Evelyn Green Haynes was the daughter of William Harris Green of Manhattan. She had previously been married to Fred John Hamm.

Justin O'Brien and Evelyn Green Haynes, Sr.'s daughter Sheila married the noted historian Sir John Hale of London, England. Their daughter Amanda married ____ Dale and resided in Manhattan.

Hedges, Burke Osborn (1912-1976)

Occupation(s):	statesman - Cuban Ambassador to Brazil, 1958-1959
	capitalist - director, American Airlines, Inc.
	industrialist - president, Compania Textilera Ariguanabo, Cuba
	(largest textile firm in Cuba)
Civic Activism:	president, Anglo-American Welfare Federation, Cuba;
	member, Consultive Council, Cuba;
	president, Industrial National Association of Cuba;
	president, American Club, Havana, Cuba
Marriage(s):	M/1 – 1959-div. – Maritza de Beche
	M/2 – Georgia Brown
Address:	89 Lily Pond Lane, East Hampton
Name of estate:	
Year of construction:	1912
Style of architecture:	Coxwold
Architect(s):	Albro and Lindeberg designed
	the house (for Erdmann)
Landscape architect(s):	Edwina Von Gal designed gardens
	(for Schulman)*
Builder:	Smith and Davis
House extant: yes	
Historical notes:	

    The eight-bedroom, eight-bath, 9,000-square-foot house, originally named *Coxwould*, was built by Dr. John Frederick Erdmann. It was later owned by his daughter Jane Erdmann Burton. In 1954 Mrs. Burton sold the house to Dayton Hedges. [*The East Hampton Star* August 5, 1954, p. 1.] It was later owned by his son Burke. [*The East Hampton Star* July 3, 1958, p. 4.]
    Maritza de Beche Hedges was the daughter of Francisco and Delie de Beche of Havana, Cuba.
    Burke Osborn and Georgia Brown Hedges' daughter Helen married Dr. Robert Allen Miller.
[See following entry for additional family information.]
    The house was later owned by Joseph Weinstein and, subsequently, by Lowell M. Schulman who renamed it *Beechwood*. In 2012 the house was for sale by Schulman. The asking price was $24.95 million; the annual taxes were $60,000.
    *Edwina Von Gal created fifteen garden rooms which were inspired by English gardens.

Hedges, Dayton (1884-1957)
aka William Dayton Hedges

Occupation(s):	capitalist - owner, Hedges Hotel, Shirley, NY
	industrialist - founder, Industria Textilera de Cuba (21 separate textile firms)
	politician - supervisor, Town of Brookhaven
Civic Activism:	president, American Club, Havana, Cuba;
	sponsored Jeannette Edwards Rattray's book *East Hampton: History Including Genealogies of Early Families* (proceeds from its sales went to establish Hedges Room in the East Hampton Free Library)
Marriage(s):	1907-1957 – Mary Elizabeth McCormick (1888-1957)
Address:	89 Lily Pond Lane, East Hampton
Name of estate:	
Year of construction:	1912
Style of architecture:	Coxwold
Architect(s):	Albro and Lindeberg designed the house (for Erdmann)
Landscape architect(s):	Edwina Von Gal designed gardens (for Schulman)*
Builder:	Smith and Davis

House extant: yes
Historical notes:

The eight-bedroom, eight-bath, 9,000-square-foot house, originally named *Coxwould*, was built by Dr. John Frederick Erdmann. It was later owned by his daughter Jane Erdmann Burton. In 1954 Mrs. Burton sold the house to Hedges. [*The East Hampton Star* August 5, 1954, p. 1.]

He was the son of Nathan Osborn and Theresa Miller Burke Hedges of Patchogue, NY.

Mary Elizabeth McCormick Hedges was the daughter of James H. and Mary Jane McCormick of Brooklyn.

Dayton and Mary Elizabeth McCormick Hedges' son James married Muriel Jean Mendals and, later, Elena Montalvo. In 1958 Dayton's son Burke Osborn Hedges purchased the house. [*The East Hampton Star* July 3, 1958, p. 4.]
[See previous entry for additional family information.]

The house was then owned by Joseph Weinstein and, subsequently, by Lowell M. Schulman who renamed it *Beechwood*. In 2012 the house was for sale by Schulman. The asking price was $24.95 million; the annual taxes were $60,000.

*Edwina Von Gal created fifteen garden rooms which were inspired by English gardens.

Hedges, Henry Denison (1854-1920)

Occupation(s):	merchant - house furnishings, Main Street, East Hampton
Civic Activism:	president, board of education, Union School District #1;
	trustee, First Presbyterian Church, East Hampton;
	assessor, East Hampton Village
Marriage(s):	1875-1911 – Ellen Osborn Howes (1855-1911)
Address:	29 Huntting Lane, East Hampton
Name of estate:	
Year of construction:	1903
Style of architecture:	Queen Anne
Architect(s):	
Landscape architect(s):	
Builder:	Asa Otis Jones

House extant: yes
Historical notes:

The seven-bedroom, eight-and-a-half bath, 7,000-square-foot house was built by Henry Denison Hedges.

He was the son of Stephen Lewis and Minerva Cartwright Hedges.

Ellen Osborn Howes Hedges was the daughter of Ezekiel and Hannah Osborn Howes.

Henry Denison and Ellen Osborn Howes Hedges' infant son died in 1888. Their daughter Fanny married Frank Benjamin Smith.

The house was purchased in 2007 by John Tarbet who completed its restoration in 2008. In 2010 he listed the house for sale. The asking price was $11.5 million. In 2010 the price was reduced to $10.9 million.

In 2019 it was again listed for sale. The asking price was $7.995 million.

Hedges, John Daniel (1839-1918)

Occupation(s):	financier - director, East Hampton National Bank
Marriage(s):	1864-1918 – Caroline Isabella Homan (1846-1923)
	- proprietor - The Hedges Inn, East Hampton
	Civic Activism: vice-president, board of managers, East Hampton Free Library;
	a founder and vice-president, Ladies Village Improvement Society, East Hampton;
	secretary, East Hampton Branch, Needlework Guild of America;
	secretary, Woman's Guild of East Hampton
Address:	Main Street, East Hampton
Name of estate:	
Year of construction:	1891
Style of architecture:	
Architect(s):	
Landscape architect(s):	
Builder:	Grimshaw & Babcock, 1892
	two-story carriage house
	Frank Grimshaw, 1897 barn

House extant: yes
Historical notes:

The house was built by John Daniel Hedges. [*The East Hampton Star* September 27, 1890, p. 5.]
He was the son of John N. and Eliza B. Fithian Hedges.
Caroline Isabella Homan Hedges was the daughter of Egbert V. and Caroline Conkling Homan.
John Daniel and Caroline Isabella Homan Hedges' son Daniel died at the age of twenty-three of typhoid fever.
In 1919 alterations were made to the house by Mrs. Hedges. [*The East Hampton Star* February 14, 1919, p. 5.]

Helier, David (1869-1931)

Occupation(s):	industrialist - partner, Helier & Long, NYC (handkerchief manufacturing firm)
Marriage(s):	1897-1931 – Blanche Uhlmann (1877-1975)
Address:	Ocean Avenue and Pudding Hill Lane, East Hampton
Name of estate:	
Year of construction:	
Style of architecture:	Queen Anne
Architect(s):	John Custis Lawrence designed
	1911 alterations (for Kelley)
Landscape architect(s):	
Builder:	Edward M. Gay, 1911 alterations

House extant: unconfirmed
Historical notes:

Helier purchased the William Vallandigham Kelley, Sr. residence.
Blanche Uhlmann Helier was the daughter of Simon and Caroline Mayer Uhlmann.
David and Blanche Uhlmann Helier's son Ambrose married Norma Porterfield, the daughter of James and Margaret Varner Porterfield, and resided in East Hampton.
Helier committed suicide in 1931 in the roof garden of his Manhattan residence.
The house was sold at auction in 1934 to settle his estate. [The East Hampton Star June 14, 1934, p. 5.]
Blanche subsequently married Richard Heber Newton, Jr. of *Box Farm* in Water Mill. [*See* Spinzia, *Long Island's Prominent Families in the Town of Southampton* – Newton entry.] He was the son of The Reverend Richard Heber and Mrs. Mary Elizabeth Lewis Newton, Sr. of *Dunecott* in East Hampton.

Helm, George Washington, Sr. (1897-1955)

Occupation(s):	attorney
Marriage(s):	M/1 – 1918-div. 1929 – Harriet Ayer Seymour (1899-1969)
	M/2 – 1937 – Hildegard Ault (1907-1969)
Address:	Jefferys Lane, East Hampton
Name of estate:	
Year of construction:	1935
Style of architecture:	
Architect(s):	
Landscape architect(s):	
Builder:	
House extant:	unconfirmed
Historical notes:	

The house was built by Clifford Rathbone Hendrix, Sr. [*The East Hampton Star* November 21, 1935, p. 5.] In 1940 Hendrix sold it to the Lane Realty Corporation. which, in 1942, sold it to Helm. [*The East Hampton Star* February 8, 1940, p. 1.]

He was the son of John LaRue and Lucy Amelia Washington Helm, Jr. of Louisville, KY, and East Hampton.

Harriet Ayer Seymour Helm was the daughter of Louis Allen and Harriet Ayer Seymour of New York. She subsequently married Valentine Everit Macy, Jr. of *Longlast* in East Hampton.

George Washington and Harriet Ayer Seymour Helm, Sr.'s son George Washington Helm, Jr. married Barbara Ginn, the daughter of Edwin Ginn.

Hildegard Ault Helm was the daughter of Lee B. and Hildegard von Steinweber Ault. She had previously been married to Ashby Wallingford Buchner III, the son of Ashby Wallingford and Anna Rives Longworth Buchner, Jr. Hildegard subsequently married Rolf Tjeder.

Helm, John E.

Occupation(s):	
Marriage(s):	
Address:	Nichols Lane, East Hampton
Name of estate:	
Year of construction:	1917
Style of architecture:	Modified Colonial Revival
Architect(s):	John Custis Lawrence designed the house (for J. E. Helm)
Landscape architect(s):	
Builder:	Edward M. Gay, house and 1917 garage
	C. Redford, plumbing and heating (for J. E. Helm)
House extant:	yes
Historical notes:	

The house was built by John E. Helm. [*The East Hampton Star* November 10, 1916, p. 5.]
He was from Louisville, KY.
In 1946 alterations were made to the house.

Helm, John LaRue, Jr. (c. 1845-1917)

Occupation(s):	merchant - partner, Meguiar, Helm, and Co., Louisville, KY (tobacco merchants);
	partner, Roland Webe and Co., Louisville, KY (tobacco merchants)
	financier - director, Fidelity and Trust Co.
Civic Activism:	director, Board of Trade, Louisville, KY;
	director, Tobacco Exposition, 1885;
	a founder and director, Hardin County Training and Trotting Association, 1892
Marriage(s):	1881-1917 – Lucy Amelia Washington (1861-1955)
Address:	Lily Pond and Hedges Lanes, East Hampton
Name of estate:	
Year of construction:	1917
Style of architecture:	
Architect(s):	
Landscape architect(s):	
Builder:	
House extant:	unconfirmed
Historical notes:	

The house was built by John LaRue Helm, Jr.

He was the son of Mrs. Lucinda Barbour Hardin Helm and Kentucky's Governor John LaRue Helm, Sr. of *Helm Place* in Harden County, KY. John was killed while crossing a street in Louisville, KY.

Lucy Amelia Washington Helm was the daughter of George Augustine and Jane Smith Washington of *Wessyngton Plantation* near Cedar Hill, TN. They were related to George Washington.

John LaRue and Lucy Amelia Washington Helm, Jr.'s daughter Jane married Ex Norton, Jr., the son of Ex and Lucy Moore Norton, Sr. of Staten Island, NY, and resided in Louisville, KY. Their daughter Emily married Malcolm Roderick MacClean, the son of Malcolm and Mary Mills MacLean, and resided in Savannah, GA. Their son George Washington Helm, Sr., who resided in East Hampton, married Harriet Ayer Seymour and, later, Hildegard Ault.

In 1923 Mrs. Helm sold the house to James Andrew Moffett, Jr. who called it *Inadune*. [*The East Hampton Star* March 16, 1923, p. 5.]

In 1937 Moffett sold it to John Lafayette Weeks. [*The East Hampton Star* January 28, 1937, p. 1.]

In 1951 the house was purchased by Roy Lennox Cammann. [*The East Hampton Star* May 3, 1951, p. 1.]

Helmuth, Dr. William Tod, Jr. (1862-1932)

Occupation(s):	physician - surgeon:
	    Helmuth House, NYC;
	    Laura Franklin Hospital, NYC;
	    Flower Hospital, NYC
	capitalist - proprietor, Helmuth House, NYC
	educator - professor of surgery, New York Homeopathic Medical College, NYC

Marriage(s):	1895-1932 – Isabel Spaulding Lockman (1871-1947)
	  - Civic Activism: president, Sarosis;
	    president, New York State Federation of Women's Clubs;
	    president, East Hampton Visiting Nurse Association, Inc.

Address:	Cottage Lane, East Hampton
Name of estate:	*Kumonin*
Year of construction:	
Style of architecture:	
Architect(s):	
Landscape architect(s):	
House extant:	unconfirmed
Historical notes:	

The *Social Register Summer, 1910* lists Dr. William Todd and Mrs. Isabel S. Lockman Helmuth [Jr.] as residing at *Kumonin* in East Hampton. The *Social Directory of Southampton, Long Island, 1931* lists Dr. William Tod and Mrs. Isabel S. Lockman Helmuth [Jr.] as residing on Cottage Lane, East Hampton.

He was the son of William Tod and Fannie Ida Pritchard Helmuth, Sr. of St. Louis, MO.

Isabel Spaulding Lockman Helmuth was the daughter of General John Thomas and Mrs. Harriet Hall Lockman.

Dr. William Tod and Mrs. Isabel Spaulding Lockman Helmuth, Jr.'s daughter Fannie married John Howard Beebe, the son of Howard Wade and Gertrude Baker Beebe of East Hampton. Their son William Tod Helmuth III married Margaret W. Kech and resided in East Hampton.

Hendrix, Clifford Rathbone, Sr. (1882-1953)

Occupation(s):	financier - member, Jacquelin and deCoppet (odd-lot brokerage firm)*

Marriage(s):	1920-1953 – Eugenia M. Terry (b. 1890)
	    (aka Gena Terry)
	  - Civic Activism: Red Cross volunteer during World War I

Address:	Jefferys Lane, East Hampton
Name of estate:	
Year of construction:	1935
Style of architecture:	
Architect(s):	
Landscape architect(s):	
Builder:	
House extant:	unconfirmed
Historical notes:	

The house was built by Clifford Rathbone Hendrix, Sr. [*The East Hampton Star* November 21, 1935, p. 5.]

He was the son of Joseph Clifford and Mary Alice Rathbone Hendrix of Brooklyn.

Eugenia M. Terry Hendrix was the daughter of John D. Terry of NYC.

Clifford Rathbone and Eugenia M. Terry Hendrix, Sr.'s daughter Eugenia married William Price Oliver Clarke, Jr. and resided in Wayne, PA. Their daughter Nancy married William MacKenzie MacLeod, the son of William MacLeod of Newport, RI. Their son Clifford Rathbone Hendrix, Jr., who resided in San Francisco, CA, married Helen Louise Robins, the daughter of James Hamilton Robins.

In 1940 Hendrix sold the house to the Lane Realty Corporation. which, in 1942, sold it to George Washington Helm, Sr. [*The East Hampton Star* February 8, 1940, p. 1, and October 8, 1942, p. 1.]

    *For Andre H. deCoppet's Islip estate *The Willows*, see Spinzia, *Long Island's Prominent South Shore Families* – deCoppet entry.]

Hensel, Clarence Hopkins (1888-1960)

Occupation(s):	financier - sales representative for the Wall Street firm of A. W. Benkert Co., Inc.
	capitalist - director, New York, Susquehanna and Western Railroad
Marriage(s):	
Address:	Dunemere Lane, East Hampton
Name of estate:	*Dunemere*
Year of construction:	c. 1891
Style of architecture:	Shingle
Architect(s):	Joseph Greenleaf Thorp designed the house (for J. N. Steele, Sr.)
Landscape architect(s):	
House extant: unconfirmed	
Historical notes:	

 The house, originally named *Dunemere*, was built by the Reverend James Nevett Steele, Sr. It was later owned by Hensel who continued to call it *Dunemere*.
 In 1928 Hensel sold the house to Dr. Theodorus Bailey II who also continued to call it *Dunemere*.
 In 1944 it was purchased by Delos Walker. [*The East Hampton Star* May 17, 1929, p. 7, and June 24, 1944, p.1.]

Heppenheimer, William Christian, III (1923-2009)

Occupation(s):	capitalist - proprietor, Cove Hollow Farm, East Hampton
	financier - member, Morgan Stanley Trust Co.
	industrialist - vice-president, Inmont (which merged into BASF) (printing ink, chemical, and adhesives firm)
Civic Activism:	trustee, Village of East Hampton;
	president of board, Southampton Hospital, 1982-1987;
	treasurer and president, Maidstone Club, East Hampton, 1973-1979;
	a founder, East Hampton Health Care Center;
	a founder, Urgent Care Center, East Hampton
Marriage(s):	1953-2009 – Emmeline Dore Sands (1929-2012)
Address:	Briar Patch Road, East Hampton
Name of estate:	
Year of construction:	1955
Style of architecture:	
Architect(s):	
Landscape architect(s):	
House extant: yes	
Historical notes:	

 The house was built for Heppenheimer as a wedding present by his uncle and aunt, Alexander Wallace and Louise Ginnel Ruxton Chauncey, who resided at *Our Place* in East Hampton.
 William Christian Heppenheimer III was the son of William Christian and Frances Ruxton Heppenheimer, Jr. of Manhattan and Newport, RI.
 Emmeline Dore Sands Heppenheimer was the daughter of Harold Aymar and Murial Winthrop Sands of Newport, RI.
 William Christian and Emmeline Dore Sands Heppenheimer III's daughter Anita married Hilary Halsted Holmes and resides in Wainscott. Their son William S. Heppenheimer married Martha J. Ball and resides in Sag Harbor.
 The Heppenheimers relocated to *Cove Hollow Farm*. In 1977 it was destroyed by fire. [*The East Hampton Star* November 24, 1977, p.5.]

Herrick, Anson Boulton, Sr. (1912-1989)

Occupation(s):	financier - vice-president, Herrick and Herrick (insurance brokerage firm)
Civic Activism:	head, Junior Yacht committee, Devon Yacht Club, Amagansett; donated five acres of land to Atlantic Double Dunes Preserve; president, Amagansett Beach Club
Marriage(s):	1938-1989 – Ruth Mary Burdett - Civic Activism: co-chair, volunteer services committee, Overlook Hospital, Summit, NJ
Address:	Bluff Road, Amagansett
Name of estate:	
Year of construction:	
Style of architecture:	
Architect(s):	
Landscape architect(s)	
House extant:	unconfirmed
Historical notes:	

The Blue Book of The Hamptons, 1973 lists Anson B. and Ruth M. Burdett Herrick [Sr.] as residing on Bluff Road in Amagansett.

He was the son of Newbold Lawrence and Pauline E. Boulton Herrick, Sr. of Woodsburgh, Long Island. [*See* Spinzia, *Long Island's Prominent Families in the Town of Hempstead* – Herrick entry.]

Ruth Mary Burdett Herrick was the daughter of Gilbert Underhill and Helen Emily Cornwall Burdett of Amagansett and a descendant of a signer of the Declaration of Independence.

Anson Boulton and Ruth Mary Burdett Herrick, Sr.'s son Anson Boulton Herrick, Jr. married Rossana Laura Garrow, the daughter of Douglas Garrow of Bellmore, and, later, Mary Lou Crandall with whom he resided in Southold. Their son William married Carol Kane Neilson, the daughter of Louis Neilson of Dorset, VT. Their son John married Elizabeth Scott Greene, the daughter of Frederick H. Greene, Jr. of Lincoln, MA. Their son Gilbert married Suzanne Pedlow Evans, the daughter of Richard Davies Evans of Springfield, PA.

Herrick, Dr. Everett (1830-1914)

Occupation(s):	physician capitalist - director, East Hampton Electric Light Co.
Civic Activism:	a founder, East Hampton Lawn Tennis Club; a founder and first president, Maidstone Club, East Hampton; chairman of board, New York Academy of Medicine; bequeathed $25,000 to East Hampton Free Library
Marriage(s):	1880-1912 – Harriet Ford (1847-1912) - Civic Activism: a founder, East Hampton Free Library; president of board, Lincoln Hospital and Home of the City of New York
Address:	4 Ocean Avenue, East Hampton
Name of estate:	*Pudding Hill*
Year of construction:	c. 1887
Style of architecture:	Shingle
Architect(s):	Isaac Henry Green II designed the house and the 1906 extension (for E. Herrick)*
Landscape architect(s):	
House extant:	yes
Historical notes:	

The house, originally named *Pudding Hill*, was built by Dr. Everett Herrick.

He was the son of Jonathan and Rhoda Everett Herrick.

Harriet Ford Herrick was the daughter of John Ross and Ann Elizabeth Bishop Ford.

The house was later owned by Herrick's brother-in-law James Bishop Ford; by Ford's cousin Bennett Bishop; and, subsequently, by John Richard Peddy, all of whom continued to call the house *Pudding Hill*.

*For Green's other commissions, *see* Spinzia, *Long Island's Prominent South Shore Families: Their Estates and Their Country Homes in the Towns of Babylon and Islip*.

Herter, Albert (1871-1950)

Occupation(s):	artist - portrait and mural painter*
	industrialist - president, Herter Looms, NYC (curtain, tapestry, rug, and furniture covering weaving firm)
	interior designer
	landscape architect
	educator, professor of art, Art Institute of Chicago, Chicago, IL
Marriage(s):	1893-1946 – Adele McGinnis (1869-1946)
	- artist - portrait painter
	Civic Activism: member, East Hampton War Memorial committee, 1924
Address:	Montauk Highway, East Hampton
Name of estate:	*Près Choisis / The Creeks*
Year of construction:	1898-1899
Style of architecture:	Italian Villa
Architect(s):	Grosvenor Atterbury designed the house (for A. Herter)
Landscape architect(s):	Albert and Adele McGinnis Herter designed their own gardens
	Rupert Barneby designed evergreen plantings (for Ossorio)
Builder:	Frank Grimshaw

House extant: yes**
Nassau County Museum Collection has photographs of the estate.
Historical notes:

    The house, originally named *Près Choisis*, was built by Albert Herter, who later renamed it *The Creeks*.
    He was the son of Christian and Mary Miles Herter of Manhattan.
    Adele McGinnis Herter was the daughter of John McGinnis.
    The *Long Island Society Register, 1929* lists Albert and Adele McGinnis Herter as residing at *Près Choisis* in East Hampton.
    The Herters' daughter Lydia did not marry. Their son Christian, who served as Governor of Massachusetts and, later, as United States Secretary of State, married Mary Caroline Pratt, the daughter of Frederick Bayley and Caroline Ames Pratt of *Poplar Hill* in Glen Cove. [*See* Spinzia, *Long Island's Prominent North Shore Families, vol. II*– Pratt entry.]
    *Herter's artwork included designs for magazine covers, illustrations, water-colors, stage settings, tapestries, cartoons, and textile designs.
    The estate's stables were added in 1899 and a studio was added in 1912.
    In 1951 Christian sold the estate to Alfonso Angel Ossorio, who bequeathed it to his long-time companion Edward F. Dragon. Both Ossorio and Dragon continued to call the estate *The Creeks*. In the 1990s Dragon sold the estate to Ronald Owen Perelman who made extensive alterations.
    The house is on the National Register of Historic Places.
    **In 2018 a portion of the house was damaged by fire.

Hess, Harry Bellas (1872-1960)

Occupation(s):	merchant - founder and president, National Bellas Hess & Co. (which merged with National Coat and Suit Co.) (mail order clothing firm)
Marriage(s):	1903-1960 – Mabel Bingham (d. 1981)
Address:	Buel Lane, East Hampton
Name of estate:	
Year of construction:	
Style of architecture:	
Architect(s):	
Landscape architect(s):	
House extant: unconfirmed	
Historical notes:	

The *Social Directory of Southampton, Long Island, 1931* lists Harry Bellas and Mabel Bingham Hess as residing on Buel Lane, East Hampton. The *Long Island Society Register, 1929* lists the Hesses as residing at *The Cedars* in Huntington [Huntington Station]. [*See* Spinzia, *Long Island's Prominent North Shore Families, vol. I* – Hess entry.]

He was the son of Samuel S. and Margarette Bellas Hess.

Mable Bingham Hess was the daughter of Charles Lyman and Jane Elizabeth Leonard Bingham of Chicago, IL.

Hess served during World Wars I and II as a member of the Secret Service during the former and as a special agent for the FBI during the latter.

*His firm was the third largest mail order clothing company in the United States.

Harry Bellas and Mabel Bingham Hess' daughter June married Thomas Aquin Kelly and resided in Croton, NY.

Heyman, Stephen J.

Occupation(s):	industrialist - managing partner, Nadel and Gussman, Midland, TX (oil and gas drilling firm); chairman of board, American Central Gas Co., Tulsa, OK
Civic Activism:	president and treasurer, Evergreen Foundation; co-established, with his wife Barbara, college scholarships
Marriage(s):	Barbara G. *[unable to determine maiden name]* - Civic Activism: co-established, with her husband Stephen, college scholarships
Address:	50 Ocean Avenue, East Hampton
Name of estate:	
Year of construction:	1899
Style of architecture:	Shingle
Architect(s):	James Greenleaf Thorp designed the house (for F. H. Davies) John Custis Lawrence designed 1910 alterations
Landscape architect(s):	
Builder:	Howard Emslie & Son, house George A. Eldredge, alterations
House extant: yes	
Historical notes:	

The house, originally named *Tidelands*, was built by Francis Herbert Davies. It was later owned by H. C. Thorpe and, subsequently, by Heyman.

Highet, Gilbert Albert (1906-1978)

Occupation(s): educator - fellow of classics, St. John's College, Oxford University, Oxford, England;
visiting associate professor of classics, Columbia University, NYC, 1937-1938;
professor, Greek and Latin, Columbia University, NYC, 1938-1972

entertainers and associated professions -
"People, Places and Books". weekly syndicated radio program carried by 300 stations in the United States, Canada, British Broadcasting Corporation, and Voice of America

journalist - chief literary critic, *Harper's* magazine, 1952-1954;
member, editorial advisory board, *Horizon* magazine

intelligence agent - member, MI6 (British espionage service)

writer -

An Outline of Homer, 1935;
Paideia: The Ideals of Greek Culture, 1939-1944
 (translation of *Paideia: Die Formung des Griechischen Menschen*);
The Classical Tradition: Greek and Roman Influences on Western Literature, 1949;
The Art of Teaching, 1950;
Another Solution, 1951
 (published in *Harper's* magazine);
People, Places and Books, 1953;
A Clerk of Oxenford, 1954;

Man's Unconquerable Mind, 1954;
The Migration of Ideas, 1954;
Juvenal the Satirist: A Study, 1954;
Poets in a Landscape, 1957;
Talents and Geniuses, 1957;
The Powers of Poetry, 1960;
The Anatomy of Satire, 1962;
Explorations, 1971;
The Immortal Profession: The Joys of Teaching and Learning, 1976;
The Speeches in Vergil's Aeneid, 1972

Marriage(s): 1932-1978 – Helen Clark MacInnes (1907-1985)
(aka Helen MacInnes)
- writer -

Above Suspicion, 1941;
Assignment in Brittany, aka *Cross Channel*, 1942;
The Unconquerable, aka *While Still We Live*, 1944;
Horizon, 1945;
Friends and Lovers, 1947;
Rest and Be Thankful, 1949;
Neither Five Nor Three, 1951;
I and My True Love, 1953;
Pray for a Brave Heart, 1955;
North from Rome, 1958;
Decision at Delphi, 1960;

The Venetian Affair, 1963;
Home Is the Hunter: A Comedy in Two Acts, 1964;
The Double Image, 1966;
The Salsburg Connection, 1968;
Message from Málaga, 1971;
The Snare of the Hunter, 1974;
Agent in Place, 1976;
Prelude to Terror, 1978;
The Hidden Target, 1980;
Cloak of Darkness, 1982;
Ride a Pale Horse, 1984

Address: 15 Jefferys Lane, East Hampton
Name of estate:
Year of construction: 1920
Style of architecture: Tuscan
Architect(s):
Landscape architect(s)
House extant: yes
Historical notes:

In 1957 Highet purchased Harry Wilfred Watts' residence. [*The East Hampton Star* March 28, 1957, p. 5.]
The Blue Book of The Hamptons, 1973 lists Dr. Gilbert and Mrs. Helen MacInnes Highet as residing at 15 Jefferys Lane, East Hampton.
 He was the son of Gilbert and Elizabeth Gertrude Boyle Highet of Glasgow, Scotland.
 Helen MacInnes Highet was the daughter of Donald and Jessica McDiarmid MacInnes of Glasgow, Scotland.
 Gilbert Albert and Helen Clark MacInnes Highet's son Gilbert Keith Highet married Eliot Brady, the daughter of James Cox Brady of Far Hills, NJ.
 The 5,000-square-foot, five-bedroom, five-and-a-half-bath house and 0.9 acres sold in 2015 for $6.5 million.

Hill, Robert Carmer (1869-1947)

Occupation(s):	industrialist - chairman of board, Pittsburgh Consolidation Coal Co.; a founder and vice-president, Madeira Hill & Co.; president, Avonmore Coal Co.; director, Northwestern Hanna Fuel Co.; director, Hanna Coal Co. Ltd., Toronto, Canada; president, Raven Run Coal Co.
	financier - trustee, Bank of New York; member, executive and real estate committee, Equitable Life Assurance Society of the United States; director, Eagle Fire Co.; director, Church Properties Fire Insurance Co.; director, Norwich Union Indemnity Co.; director, Parish Safe Deposit Co.
Civic Activism:	trustee, University of Pennsylvania, Philadelphia, PA; director, New York Post Graduate Hospital
Marriage(s):	1894-1947 – Anna Park Gilman (1875-1955) - writer - *Forty Years of Gardening*, 1938
Address:	3 West End Avenue, East Hampton
Name of estate:	*Grey Gardens*
Year of construction:	1897
Style of architecture:	Shingle
Architect(s):	Joseph Greenleaf Thorp designed the house (for F. S. Phillips) Eugene Lawrence Futterman, 1980 alterations (for Bradlee)
Landscape architect(s):	Ann Park Gilman Hill designed her own gardens, with Ruth Dean, 1914 Victoria Fensteer, 1985- (for Bradlee)
Builder:	George A. Eldredge

House extant: yes
Nassau County Museum Collection has photographs of the estate.
Historical notes:

    The house was built by Fleming Stanhope Phillips. In 1913 it was sold to Hill, who named it *Grey Gardens*.
    The *Social Register Summer, 1921* lists Robert Carmer and Anna P. Gilman Hill as resided at *Grey Gardens* in East Hampton.
    He was the son of William and Harriet Chapin Hill of Philadelphia, PA.
    Anna Park Gilman Hill was the daughter of Winthrop Sargent and Anna Park Gilman, Jr. of *Neiderhurst* in Palisades, NY.
    In 1924 Hill sold the house to Phelan Beale, Sr., who continued to call it *Grey Gardens*. As part of his divorce settlement, Beale deeded the house to his wife Edith.
    In 1979 the Beale's daughter Edith sold it to Benjamin Crowninshield Bradlee, Sr., who continued to call the house *Grey Gardens*.
    Alterations were made to the house in c. 1972 and in 1980.
    The house is on the National Register of Historic Places.
    In 2017 the 6,000-square foot, seven-bedroom, six-bath house and 1.7 acres were for sale. The asking price was $19,995 million.

Hillman, Murray (1922-2011)

Occupation(s): educator - statistics instructor, College of the City of New York, 1942-1943
public relations executive -
   director and president, Strategy Workshop of New York;
   vice-president and chairman of marketing plans, McCann–Erickson (later, Interpublic Group of Companies);
   vice-president, Interpublic Group of Companies
industrialist - president, Adam Hat Co.

Marriage(s): M/1 – 1946 – Harriet Chefetz (b. 1925)
M/2 – Marilyn [unable to determine maiden name]

Address: 992 Springs – Fireplace Road, East Hampton
Name of estate:
Year of construction: 1977
Style of architecture: Modern
Architect(s): Norman Jaffe designed the house (for Hillman)
Landscape architect(s)
House extant: yes
Historical notes:

   The three-bedroom, two-bath, 3,5000-square-foot house was built by Murray Hillman.
   He was the son of Abraham and Fannie Worton Hillman of The Bronx, NY.
   Harriet Chefetz Hillman was the daughter of Albert and Bessie Chefetz of Brooklyn. Harriet subsequently married Henri Arnold.
   Murray and Harriet Chefetz Hillman's daughter Linda married Michael Chayes; the son of Leo and Mathy Chayes.
   In 2019 the house was listed for sale. The asking price was $4.75 million.

Hinton, Alfred Post (1871-1940)

Occupation(s): capitalist - owned Manhattan apartment buildings
Civic Activism: treasurer, New York Bible Society

Marriage(s): Mabel Dominick (1863-1934)

Address: Georgica Road and Burnell Lane (now, Pudding Hill Lane), East Hampton
Name of estate: *Roads Meet*
Year of construction: 1905
Style of architecture:
Architect(s): John Custis Lawrence designed the house (for Hinton)
Landscape architect(s):
Builder: Thomas E. Babcock
House extant: unconfirmed
Historical notes:

   The eleven-bedroom, four-bath house, originally named *Roads Meet*, was built by Alfred Post Hinton at a cost of $12,000. [*The East Hampton Star* November 18, 1904, p. 5.]
   The *Long Island Society Register, 1928* lists Alfred Post and Mabel Dominick Hinton as residing at *Roads Meet* in East Hampton.
   He was the son of Dr. John Henry and Mrs. Sarah Elsworth Hinton.
   Mabel Dominick Hinton was the daughter of James William and Mary Day Wells Dominick. Mabel's sister Janet married Williston Benedict Lockwood and resided at *Lockdune* in East Hampton.
   Alfred Post and Mabel Dominick Hinton's daughter Eleanor married Delevan Munson Baldwin, the son of William Delevan Baldwin of New York. Their daughter Mabel married George Clarence Arvedson and resided in Grosse Pointe, MI. Their son John married Eleanor Vezin, the daughter of Oscar Vezin of Montclair, NJ.
   In 1929 Dederick Herman Schmidt purchased the house. [*The East Hampton Star* November 8, 1929, p. 12.]

Hinton, Dr. James William (1894-1973)

Occupation(s):	physician - heart specialist;
	surgeon, New York Post Graduate Hospital, NYC;
	surgical consultant, Norwalk General Hospital Norwalk, CT;
	surgical consultant, General Hospital, Jersey, City, NJ;
	surgical consultant, New York Women's Infirmary, NYC;
	surgical consultant, Southampton Hospital, Southampton, NY
	educator - professor of clinical surgery, New York University, NYC;
	professor of surgery, Columbia University, NYC;
	chairman, surgery department, New York Post Graduate Medical School and Hospital, NYC
	writer - over one hundred articles in medical journals
	Civic Activism: president, Eastern Surgical Society;
	president, New York Surgical Society, NYC;
	vice-president, New York Academy of Medicine, NYC;
	donated twenty-eight color lithographs of Civil War battle scenes to The William L. Clement Library, University of Michigan, Ann Arbor, MI
Marriage(s):	Jannett Williams Lord (1902-1963)
	- Civic Activism: co-chair, Guild Hall Rehabilitation Fund, East Hampton
Address:	7 Maidstone Lane, East Hampton
Name of estate:	*Foxall*
Year of construction:	c. 1940
Style of architecture:	
Architect(s):	
Landscape architect(s):	
House extant: no	
Historical notes:	

    The house, originally named *Foxall*, was built by Dr. James William Hinton. [*The Brooklyn Daily Eagle* April 21, 1940, p. 20.]

    The Blue Book of The Hamptons, 1958 lists Dr. J. William and Mrs. Jannett Lord Hinton as residing at *Foxall* in East Hampton. The *Social Register Summer, 1961* lists their address as 7 Maidstone Lane, East Hampton.

    He was the son of John Braxton and Anne Augusta Croswell Hinton.

    Jannett Williams Lord Hinton was the daughter of Dr. Jere Williams and Evelyn Pope Lord, Sr. of Baltimore, MD. Jannett had previously been married to William Ashton Tucker, the son of Henry and Sophie M. Ashton Tucker.

    The Hintons did not have children.

Hirschfeld, Elie (b. 1949)

Occupation(s):	attorney - member, Milbank, Tweed, Hadley, and McCloy (specialized in real estate law)
	capitalist - president, Hirschfeld Properties (real estate developer of Grant Sutton, Hotel Pennsylvania, Crown Plaza Hotel, Park Avenue Court, and Manhattan Mall)
	owner of over 1,000 apartments and 1 million square feet of commercial space in NYC metropolitan area
	producer - Broadway plays
Civic Activism:	established Hirschfeld Foundation;
	trustee, Brown University, Providence, RI;
	trustee, Long Island University, Brooklyn, NY;
	director, U.S. Board, Weizmann Institute of Science;
	a founding donor, Drama League Theater Center, NYC;
	trustee, St. Lukes–Roosevelt Hospital, NYC;
	governor, Young Real Estate Associates, NYC;
	trustee, New York Eye and Ear Hospital, NYC;
	regent, Long Island College Hospital;
	director, Jewish National Fund

Hirschfeld, Elie (cont'd)

Marriage(s):	M/1 – 1980-div. 1995 – Marcia Riklis (b. 1951)

- capitalist - board chair, Rapid–American Corp (a holding company);
  founder, MNRKLIS Family Management Co., LLC,
  Southampton, NY
- Civic Activism: director, United Jewish Appeal Federation of NY;
  director, New York Legal Assistance Group;
  director, Israel Policy Forum;
  trustee, The Institute for National Security Studies;
  founder, Marcia Riklis Family Foundation,
  Southampton, NY

M/2 – 1996-div. 2010 – Dr. Susan T. Aronson (b. 1961)
- physician - Medical College of Pennsylvania, Philadelphia, PA
- educator - professor of pediatrics, Hahneman University Hospital,
  Philadelphia, PA;
  professor of pediatrics, School of Medicine, University of
  Pennsylvania, Philadelphia, PA
- Civic Activism: president, Pennsylvania chapter, American Academy of
  Pediatrics;
  director, Early Childhood Linkage System, Pennsylvania
  Chapter of Pediatrics

M/3 – 2011 – Dr. Sarah J. Schlesinger
- industrialist - director, Arid (pharmaceutical firm)
- physician - attending physician, The Rockefeller University, NYC;
  staff pathologist, Armed Force Institute of Pathology,
  Washington, DC
- scientist - clinical investigator and immunologist, The Rockefeller
  University, NYC;
  research physician and pathologist, Walter Reed Army
  Institute of Research
- writer - articles in profession journals
- Civic Activism: a founding donor, Drama League Theater Center, NYC;
  co-director, Clinical Scholar Program, The Rockefeller
  University, NYC

Address:	Lily Pond Lane, East Hampton
Name of estate:	
Year of construction:	1920
Style of architecture:	Modified Shingle
Architect(s):	John Custis Lawrence designed the house (for Coppell)
	Robert Tappin designed 1928 alterations (for Coppell)
Landscape architect(s)	
Builder:	Edward M. Gay
House extant: yes	
Historical notes:	

   The house, originally named *White-Cottage-By-the-Sea*, was built by Herbert Coppell. In 1933 it was purchased by Frederick Behrens Ryan, Sr. who renamed it *East of 69*. [*The East Hampton Star* October 24, 1935, p. 21.] The house was later owned by Hirschfeld.

   He is the son of Abraham Jacob Ha Levie and Zipora Teicher Hirshfeld.

   Marcia Riklis Hirschfeld is the daughter of Meshulam and Judith Stern Riklis. Marcia was previously married to Benjamin Kletter, the son of David Kletter of Jerusalem, Israel. After her divorce from Elie, Marcia resumed the use of her maiden name.

   [For information about Marcia's Southampton residence, *see* Spinzia, *Long Island's Prominent Families in the Town of Southampton* – Riklis entry.]

   In 2002 Elie completely renovated the house.

   In the summer of 2011 the house was rented by President Clinton.

   In 2015 Hirschfeld listed the 10,000-square-foot, eight-bedroom house, with nine full bathrooms and two half bathrooms, for sale. The asking price was $32.5 million.

   The house is listed on The National Register of Historic Places,

Hirtenstein, Michael

Occupation(s):	capitalist - partner, EMM Group (hospitality management firm); a founder and vice-chairman of board, West Com Corp (communications solutions to financial firms); director, Tour GCX Partners (fractional ownership share in golf clubs)
Civic Activism:	founder, Hirtenstein Family Fund; trustee, Happy Hearts Fund (improves lives of children)
Marriage(s):	2012 – Christina Hale
Address:	230 and 234 Old Montauk Highway, Montauk
Name of estate:	
Year of construction:	2006
Style of architecture:	Modern
Architect(s):	James Biber of Pentagram designed the compound (for Levy–Church)
Landscape architect(s)	
House extant: yes	
Historical notes:	

The house was built by Kenneth Levy–Church.

In 2013 Hirtenstein purchased the 5,000-square-foot main residence and 2,400-square-foot guest house from Levy–Church for $13 million.

The main residence won the American Institute of Architects Award.

In 2018 it was sold by Hirtenstein. The asking price was $21 million.

Hiss, Alger (1904-1996)

Occupation(s):	attorney
	diplomat - advisor, Yalta Conference, 1945
	statesman - assistant to Secretary of State, Edward Reilly Stettinius, Jr.; Assistant to the Director , Office of Far Eastern Affairs; Special Assistant to the Director, Office of Special Political Affairs; Director of Office of Special Political Affairs; Executive Secretary, Dumbarton Oaks Conference; Secretary-General, United Nations Conference on International Organizations
	* *[See below.]*
	merchant - salesman, stationery and printing services to businesses
	writer - *In the Court of Public Opinion*, 1957; *Recollections of a Life*, 1988
Civic Activism:	president, Carnegie Endowment for International Peace, 1946-1949

Hiss, Alger (cont'd)

Marriage(s): M/1 – 1929-1984** – Priscilla Harriet Fansler (1903-1984)
- educator - English teacher, Potomac School, Washington, DC;
English teacher, Dalton School, NYC, 1947-1948
journalist - office manager, *Time* magazine;
copy editor, Harcourt, Brace & World, 1966;
senior editor, Golden Press, 1972;
editor, children's books, Western Publishing Co.
Civic Activism: member, executive board, Community Board #2
of the Democratic Party, NYC;
member, executive board, Village Independent
Democrats, Greenwich Village, NYC;
member, executive board, Democratic County
Committee of New York County
M/2 – 1984-1996 – Isabelle Dowden (1907-2000)
- writer - free-lance;
fashion model

Address: Old Stone Highway, Amagansett
Name of estate:
Year of construction:
Style of architecture:
Architect(s):
Landscape architect(s):
House extant: unconfirmed
Historical notes:

Alger Hiss was the son of Charles Alger and Lavinia Hughes Hiss of Baltimore, MD.

Priscilla Harriett Fansler Hiss was the daughter of Thomas L. Fansler of *Roadside Acres* in Frazier, PA. She had previously been married to Francis Thayer Hobson, the president of the book publishing firm of William Morrow.

*At Harvard Law School Hiss was a protégé of Felix Frankfurter who later became a United States Supreme Court Justice. He went on to clerk for United States Supreme Court Justice Oliver Wendell Holmes, Jr. In 1933 Hiss embarked on his career in the federal government as an attorney in the Agricultural Adjustment Administration. He then worked for the Nye Commission prior to transferring to the Justice Department as an assistant to Woodrow Wilson's son-in-law Francis B. Sayre. Subsequently, Hiss served as special assistant to the Director of the Office of Far Eastern Affairs and as special assistant and, later, as executive secretary at the Dumbarton Oaks Conference. In 1945 Hiss participated in the Yalta Conference, served as Secretary-General to the United Charter Conference, and became Director of the Office of Special Political Affairs prior to leaving government service in 1946.

In 1948 Whittaker Chambers, an acknowledged Communist, testified to the House Committee on Un-American Activities that Hiss had been a member of the Communist Party. Freshman Congressman Richard M. Nixon spearheaded the committee's investigation of Hiss which resulted in a mistrial to charges of perjury. In 1950 a second trial of Hiss resulted in what is, to this day, a highly controversial verdict of guilty, also to the charge of perjury. Hiss served three years, eight months, and five days in Pennsylvania's maximum security Lewisburg Penitentiary working in the commissary. (The prison is now a super-maximum security prison housing terrorists.) After his release from prison in 1954, Hiss continually filed appeals in an attempt to prove his innocence.

After a two-day search of Soviet intelligence archives in 1991 by Russian archivists, General Volkogonov, the head of the archives, stated that no evidence had been found to confirm that Hiss had ever been a Soviet spy or a member of the Communist Party.

Nixon is reputed to have said that without the Hiss case he would never have become Vice-President or President.

In 1948 Chambers attempted to commit suicide in his mother's home in Lynbrook. [*Newsday* April 7, 1952.]

Alger and Priscilla Harriet Fansler Hiss' son Anthony married Lois Metzger and lives in NYC.

**Alger and Priscilla Fansler Hiss separated in 1959 but did not divorce.

Isabelle Dowden Hiss was the daughter of Dawson and Elsie Ruckelshaus Dowden. Isabelle had previously been married to Malcolm Perry Johnson.

Hiss later relocated to a house on Osborne Lane in East Hampton.

Hobart, Garret Augustus, Jr. (1884-1941)

Occupation(s):	financier - vice-president, Paterson Savings Institution, Paterson, NJ
Civic Activism:	president, preliminary survey commission, Passaic County Park System, Passaic, NJ
Marriage(s):	1906-1941 – Caroline Frye Briggs (d. 1960)
Address:	Lee Avenue, East Hampton
Name of estate:	*T'Other House*
Year of construction:	c. 1900
Style of architecture:	Shingle
Architect(s):	
Landscape architect(s):	

House extant: yes
Nassau County Museum Collection has photographs of the estate.
Historical notes:

The house, originally named *T'Other House*, was built by Garret Augustus Hobart, Jr.
The *Long Island Society Register, 1929* lists Garret A. and Caroline Frye Briggs Hobart [Jr.] as residing at *T'Other House* in East Hampton.
He was the son of United States Vice-President Garret Augustus and Mrs. Esther Jane Tuttle Hobart, Sr.
Caroline Frye Briggs Hobart was the daughter of Frank Herbert and Alice Clifford Frye Briggs of Auburn, ME.
Garret Augustus and Caroline Frye Briggs Hobart, Jr.'s daughter Katharine married David E. Hand and resided at *Glen Ailsa* in Paterson, NJ. Their daughter Elizabeth married Henry Augustus Kingsbury, the son of Frederick Hutchinson Kingsbury of Montclair, NJ, and resided in Englewood, NJ. Their son Garret Augustus Hobart III married Manette Seeldrayers, the daughter of Rodolphe William Seeldrayers, and resided in Tuxedo Park, NY. Manette subsequently married Alfred Lee Loomis, Sr. with whom she resided in Tuxedo Park and in East Hampton.
In 1940 Charles Arthur Klotz of Chicago, IL, purchased the house for $17,000. [*The New York Times* February 11, 1940, p. 147.]

Hobart, Henry Lee (1845-1930)

Occupation(s):	merchant - president, Porto Rico Commercial Co.
	capitalist - president, L. Hobart & Co., Hoboken, NJ. (sugar importer and refining firm);
	director, Hoboken Tank & Storage Co.
	industrialist - director, Empire Cream Separator Co., Bloomfield, NJ
	Civic Activism: member of building committee, treasurer, and vice-president, Seamen's Church Institute of America;
	trustee, Community House Settlement
Marriage(s):	1888-1928 – Marie Elizabeth Jefferys (1860-1928)
	- writer - *Lady Catechism and the Child*, 1904;
	The Little Pilgrims of the Book Beloved, 1905;
	Vision of St. Agnes Eve, 1906;
	Athanasius, 1909;
	The Sunset Hour, 1911;
	The Great Trial, 1913
	Civic Activism: a founder, Society of Old East Hampton (East Hampton residents that resided in the village for 25 or more years)
Address:	Ocean Avenue and Jefferys Lane, East Hampton*
Name of estate:	*Sommariva*
Year of construction:	c. 1872
Style of architecture:	Italianate
Architect(s):	Charles Peter Beauchamp Jefferys designed his own house
Landscape architect(s):	
House extant: yes	
Historical notes:	

The house, originally named *Sommariva*, was built by Charles Peter Beauchamp Jefferys, Sr. It was inherited by his daughter Marie and son-in-law Henry Lee Hobart who continued to call it *Sommariva*.

The *Social Register Summer, 1921* lists Henry Lee and Marie E. Jefferys Hobart as residing at *Sommariva* in East Hampton.

He was the son of James Thomas and Anne Newell Hobart of Cincinnati, OH.

Henry Lee and Marie Elizabeth Jefferys Hobart's sixteen-year-old daughter Rosamond died in 1908. Their daughter Margaret, who inherited *Sommariva* from her father, married The Reverend George B. Myers, the Dean of the Holy Trinity Cathedral in Havana, Cuba. [*The East Hampton Star* April 18, 1930, p. 1.] Their son Charles died in 1910 at the age of sixteen.

*The Hobarts moved the house about 100 yards east to its present location.

The house, which is on the National Register of Historic Places, was later owned by Abraham Mills, who called it *The Chalet*, and, subsequently, by Dr. Stuart Lessley Craig.

Hoffman, David Lehman, Sr.

Occupation(s):	real estate agent - president, Sealy, Hoffman, and Sheehan, Glen Head, NY (commercial real estate brokerage and management firm); vice-president and director, Cross & Brown Real Estate Co.
Marriage(s):	M/1 – Anita Vogel - publisher - vice-president, Browne & Co. (financial printer) M/2 – 1977 – Ellen Rose Wheeler - entertainers and associated professions - member, Lester Lewis Associates (theatrical agent)
Address:	185 Georgica Road, East Hampton
Name of estate:	
Year of construction:	1967
Style of architecture:	Modern
Architect(s):	Richard Meier designed the house (for D. Hoffman) Stamberg Aferiat + Associates designed 1997 alterations (for A. V. Hoffman)*

Landscape architect(s):
House extant: yes
Historical notes:

The house was built by David Lehman Hoffman, Sr.

He is the son of Philip E. and Florence Lehman Hoffman.

Anita Vogel Hoffman is the daughter of Alfons and Bella Schneersohn Vogel.

David Lehman and Anita Vogel Hoffman, Sr.'s daughter Susan married Jonathan Arthur Hyman, the son of Dr. Allen I. and Mrs. Valerie Hyman of New York. Their son David Lehman Hoffman, Jr. married Linda Ruth Beinfield and resides in Riverside, CT. Their daughter Catherine married Richard Marc Glosser, the son of Paul L. and Rita Glosser of Johnstown, PA.

Ellen Rose Wheeler Hoffman is the daughter of Frank R. Wheeler, Jr. of Scarsdale, NY.

*After her divorce from David, Anita continued to reside in the house and commissioned Stamberg Aferiat + Associates to enlarge the house to 3,000 square feet.

Holleran, Francis Joseph (1898-1987)

Occupation(s):	financier - vice-president, First National City Bank, NYC (later, Citibank)
Marriage(s):	1934-1978 – Helen Ruppert Silleck (1907-1978)
Address:	Maidstone Lane, East Hampton

Name of estate:
Year of construction:
Style of architecture:
Architect(s):
Landscape architect(s):
House extant: unconfirmed
Historical notes:

In 1947 Holleran purchased the house from Clinton Stephen Lutkins. [*The East Hampton Star* September 18, 1947, p. 1.]

The Blue Book of The Hamptons, 1965 lists F. Joseph and Helen R. Silleck Holleran as residing on Maidstone Lane, East Hampton.

He was the son of F. L. Holleran of Clinton, Iowa.

Helen Ruppert Silleck Holleran was the daughter of Henry Garrison and Amanda Elizabeth Ruppert Silleck, Jr. of Greenwich, CT. She was the niece of the multimillionaire brewer Jacob Ruppert from whom, at the age of thirty-two, she inherited one-third of his $40 million estate. [*The New York Times* January 30, 1939.]

Francis Joseph and Helen Ruppert Silleck Holleran's daughter Glenna married Philip Ottley, the son of Gilbert and Gladys Howland Graham Ottley of *Wuff Woods* in Upper Brookville, and resided in Sun Valley, ID. Their son Romer married Deming Pratt, the daughter of Sherman and Ethel B. Schniewind Pratt of Lattingtown, and resided in Greenwich, CT. Their son Richard married Katherine Gayle Jones. [*See* Spinzia, *Long Island's Prominent North Shore Families, vol. II* – Ottley, Pratt, and Schniewind entries.]

Hollister, Dr. Frederick Kellogg (1869-1934)

Occupation(s):	*[See following entry.]*
Marriage(s):	1899-1934 – Harriet May Shelton (1876-1965)
	- *[See following entry.]*
Address:	Lily Pond Lane, East Hampton
Name of estate:	
Year of construction:	1910
Style of architecture:	Mediterranean
Architect(s):	Albro and Lindeberg designed the house (for F. K. Hollister)
Landscape architect(s):	
Builder:	E. W. Davis
House extant: yes	
Historical notes:	

The house was built by Dr. Frederick Kellogg Hollister.
He was the son of Samuel Whiting and Henriette Kellogg Trowbridge Hollister of Manhattan.
Harriet May Shelton Hollister was the daughter of Dr. George Gregory Shelton of New York City.
Dr. Frederick Kellogg and Mrs. Harriet May Shelton Hollister's daughter Margaret married Jessie Isidor Straus, Jr. (aka Jack Isidor Straus) who resided at *Green Pastures* in Jericho and *Crow's Nest* in Cove Neck. [*See* Spinzia, *Long Island's Prominent North Shore Families, vol. II* – Straus entry.] Their son George married Kathryn Foster, the daughter of William Lawrence Foster of Rochester, PA.

Hollister, Dr. Frederick Kellogg (1869-1934)

Occupation(s):	physician - Flower Hospital, NYC; Hahnemann Hospital, NYC (later, Fifth Avenue Hospital)
	educator - lecturer in pharmacology, New York Homeopathic Medical College, NYC
	writer - articles in medical journals
Civic Activism:	director, Maidstone Club, East Hampton; vice-president, East Hampton Associates
Marriage(s):	1899-1934 – Harriet May Shelton (1876-1965)
	- Civic Activism: a founder and president, Garden Club of East Hampton; founder, East Hampton Emergency Sewing and Knitting Guild, 1932; chair, East Hampton Settlement House Association
Address:	53 Lily Pond Lane, East Hampton
Name of estate:	
Year of construction:	1913
Style of architecture:	Shingle
Architect(s):	John Custis Lawrence designed the house (for Hollister)
Landscape architect(s):	
House extant: yes	
Historical notes:	

The house was built by Dr. Frederick Kellogg Hollister.
[See previous Hollister entry for family information.]
The house was later owned by George W. Gowen II.

Hollister, Dr. Frederick Kellogg (1869-1934)

Occupation(s):	*[See previous entry.]*
Marriage(s):	1899-1934 – Harriet May Shelton (1876-1965)
	- *[See previous entry.]*
Address:	27 Drew Lane, East Hampton
Name of estate:	
Year of construction:	1920
Style of architecture:	Shingle
Architect(s):	John Custis Lawrence designed the house (for F. K. Hollister)
	Richard A. Cook of CookFox Associates designed 2007 alterations (for Rosenstein)
Landscape architect(s):	Paula Hayes (for Rosenstein)
Builder:	Edward M. Gay (for F. K. Hollister)
	Bulgin & Associates, 2007 alterations (for Rosenstein)

House extant: yes
Historical notes:

The house was built by Dr. Frederick Kellogg Hollister.

In 1939 Mrs. Hollister sold it to Jesse William Sweetser, Sr. [*The East Hampton Star* June 22, 1939, pp. 1 and 5.]

In 1941 Alexander Fraser purchased the house from Sweetser and called it *Wilsheron*. [*The East Hampton Star* October 23, 1941, p. 5.]

In 1960 Frances Ann Cannon (Hersey) Dougherty purchased it from Fraser. [*The East Hampton Star* April 28, 1960, p. 11.]

In 2005 her husband Frazer Lowber Welsh Dougherty sold the house to Barry Rosenstein for $19.2 million. [*The East Hampton Star* June 23, 2005, p. 35.]

In 2017 Rosenstein listed the house for sale. The asking price was $70 million.

In 2019 the 10,425-square-foot, nine-bedroom, thirteen-bath house, a separate two-bedroom caretakers/guest cottage and 1.567 acres were again for sale. The asking price was $52.5 million.

[See first Hollister entry for family information.]

Holmes, Jay (1902-1981)

Occupation(s):	industrialist - director, Standard Brands
Civic Activism:	president, Holmes Foundation*;
	trustee, San Francisco Opera, San Francisco, CA;
	trustee, Natural History Museum, NYC;
	chairman, Village of East Hampton Planning Board;
	member, zoning commission, Town of East Hampton
Marriage(s):	M/1 – 1925-div. 1934 – Frances Sarah Peters (1905-1975)
	M/2 – 1936-div. – Jane Alcott (d. 1989)
	M/3 – Jacqueline Cary
Address:	Lee Avenue, East Hampton
Name of estate:	
Year of construction:	1950
Style of architecture:	
Architect(s):	
Landscape architect(s):	
Builder:	Dayton and Dayton
House extant: unconfirmed	
Historical notes:	

In 1950 Holmes purchased the former estate of George Lodowich McAlpin, Sr. and William Carter Dickerman, Sr. from Thomas S. Nicols. Holmes demolished the twenty-one-room house and built his new residence. [*The East Hampton Star* October 5, 1950, p. 5.]

Jay Holmes was the son of Dr. Christian R. and Mrs. Bettie Fleischmann Holmes of *The Chimneys* in Sands Point. [*See* Spinzia, *Long Island's Prominent North Shore Families, vol. I* – Holmes entry.]

Frances Sarah Peters Holmes was the daughter of Norman and Anne Darby Peters. Frances subsequently married Harry Cook Cushing III of *Oxon Hill* in East Norwich and *Muttontown Farm* in Brookville. [*See* Spinzia, *Long Island's Prominent North Shore Families, vol. I* – Cushing entries.]

Jay and Frances Sarah Peters Holmes' daughter Babette married William Prosser Hilmer, the son of Arthur C. Hilmer and, later, Frederick R. Wille of NYC. Their son John married Sarah Louise Andrews, the daughter of Martin L. Andrews of Chicago IL, and resided in Wilton, CT.

The Blue Book of The Hamptons, 1958 lists Mr. and Mrs. Jay Holmes as residing on Lee Avenue, East Hampton.

Jane Alcott Holmes was the daughter of Clarence Frank and Lucie Arrington Burke Alcott of East Hampton. Jane subsequently married Dudley DeVore Roberts, Jr. with whom she resided in East Hampton.

*The foundation was established in 1953. In 1957 Holmes began making small contributions to the Congress for Cultural Freedom, a front organization of the Central Intelligence Agency. In 1962 the foundation became a mechanism by which the agency was able to funnel its money into the Congress. [Frances Stoner Saunders, *The Cultural Cold War; the CIA and the World of Arts and Letters* (New York: The New Press, 1999), p. 136, and Raymond E. Spinzia, "To Look in the Mirror and See Nothing: Long Islanders and the Office of Strategic Services and Its Successor, the Central Intelligence Agency." wwwspinzialongislandestates.com]

Homans, Eugene Vanderpool (1908-1965)

Occupation(s):	financier - member, Prosser and Homans (insurance brokerage firm) (later, Eugene V. Homans Agency); president, Eugene V. Homans Agency
Marriage(s):	1932-1965 – Marian Bennett (1908-2013)
Address:	Egypt Lane, East Hampton
Name of estate:	*Sea Spray*
Year of construction:	1955
Style of architecture:	
Architect(s):	Aymar Embury II designed the house (for Mrs. Homans)
Landscape architect(s):	
Builder:	Terry and Dufrane
House extant: unconfirmed	
Historical notes:	

The house, originally named *The Sea Spray*, was previously owned by Walter B. Cowperthwaite.

The *Social Register Summer, 1945* lists Eugene V. and Marian Bennett Homas as residing at *Sea Spray* in East Hampton.

In 1955 Homans built a new house on Egypt Lane. [*The East Hampton Star* December 2, 1954, p. 5.] *The Blue Book of The Hamptons, 1958* lists the address as Egypt Lane.

He was the son of Sheppard and Loraine Eleanor Vanderpool Homans, Jr. of Westhampton Beach. [*See* Spinzia, *Long Island's Prominent Families in the Town of Southampton* – Homan entry.]

Marian Bennett Homans was the daughter of Clarence F. Bennett of New Britain, CT.

Eugene Vanderpool and Marian Bennett Homans' daughter Helen married Walter Gordon Thompson, the son of Lewis S. Thompson.

Both Eugene and Marian were prominent amateur golfers.

Hone, Harold (1882-1939)

Occupation(s):	engineer - Consolidated Edison (electric utility firm)
Marriage(s):	1900-1939 – Adele Tobler (1880-1960)
Address:	De Forest Road, Montauk
Name of estate:	
Year of construction:	
Style of architecture:	
Architect(s):	
Landscape architect(s)	
House extant: unconfirmed	
Historical notes:	

The *Social Register Summer, 1932* lists Harold and Adele Tobler Hone as residing at *Spindrift* in Montauk. *The Blue Book of The Hamptons, 1965* lists the address of their residence as De Forest Road, Montauk.

He was the son of Charles Russell Home and the great-grandson of New York City Mayor Philip Hone.

Adele Tobler Hone was the daughter of Eugene Walter and Charlotte Silverman Tobler. She had previously been married to Frank Henry Judd, Jr.

Harold and Adele Tobler Hone's daughter Olga married William Anderson Rogers of Little Neck, NY. Their daughter Charlotte married David George Reuter, the son of The Reverend William C. Reuter of Pekin, IL, and resided in Flushing, NY.

Hopkins, John Appleton Haven, Sr. (1872-1960)

Occupation(s):	financier - director and vice-president, Johnson and Higgins (insurance brokerage firm)
Civic Activism:	suffrage - ardent suffrage supporter*; chairman of board, Progressive Party of New Jersey; treasurer and vice chairman of board, National Progressive Party; chairman of board, Morristown Civic Association, Morristown, NJ; president of board, Buckley School Corp., NY; a founder and chairman of board, Citizens Union of New Jersey
Marriage(s):	M/1 – 1895-1899 – Hilda Elizabeth Stone (1872-1899)
	M/2 – 1901-div.1927 – Alison Low Turnbull (1880-1951)
	- merchant - proprietor, Marjane Ltd., NYC (women's apparel store)
	Civic Activism:
	suffrage -
	stood with the "Silent Sentinel" that picketed the White House;
	member, executive board, Congressional Union of Woman Suffrage;
	board chair, New Jersey National Woman's Party;
	president, Summer Shelter, Morristown, NJ;
	member, executive committee, Morris County Branch, State Charities Aid Society of New Jersey;
	member, board of managers, Speedwell Society;
	board chair, Ladies House Committee of Morristown Field Club, Morristown, NJ;
	member, executive committee, Women's Town Improvement, Morristown, NJ;
	member, executive committee, Morris County Corn Growing and Industrial Contests, Morris County, NJ
Address:	Georgica Road, East Hampton
Name of estate:	
Year of construction:	
Style of architecture:	
Architect(s):	
Landscape architect(s):	
House extant: unconfirmed	
Historical notes:	

   John Appleton Haven Hopkins, Sr. was the son of John Milton and Augusta Deblois Haven Hopkins.
   Hilda Elizabeth Stone Hopkins was the daughter of Charles Frances and Sallie English Stone.
   John Appleton Haven and Hilda Elizabeth Stone Hopkins, Sr.'s son John Appleton Haven Hopkins, Jr. married ____ Sommers and resided in Denver CO.
   The *Social Register Summer, 1921* lists J. Appleton H. and Alison L. Turnbull Hopkins [Sr.] as residing on Georgica Road in East Hampton.
   She was the daughter of Frank and Marion Louise Bates Turnbull of Morristown, NJ.
   John Appleton Haven and Alison Low Turnbull Hopkins, Sr.'s daughter Marion married Henry Coddington Meyer III. Their son Douglas married Margot Millham, the daughter of Frederick Tracy Millham of NYC, and resided in NYC.
   *For other Long Islanders involved in the suffrage movement *see* Raymond E. Spinzia, "Winning the Franchise: Long Island Activists in the Fight for Woman's Suffrage and Their Opponents, Long Island's Anti-Suffragists." wwwspinzialongislandestates.com.

Hopkins, Lindsey, Jr. (1908-1986)

Occupation(s):	capitalist -	owned chain of hotels which included the Montauk Manor;
		a founder and president, Montauk Beach Co.;
		chairman of executive committee, Carl G. Fisher Corp.;
		a founder, New Orleans Saints (National Football League franchise)
	industrialist -	director, Coco Cola Bottling Co.;
		director, Sperry Corp.;
		director, American Malting;
		director, American Hide & Leather;
	financier -	chairman of board, Security Trust;
		director, Northtrust Corp.
Civic Activism:	a founder and president, Montauk Historical Society	
Marriage(s):	1932-1986 – Dorothy Smith (1911-1989)	
Address:	162 Fairview Avenue, Montauk	
Year of construction:	1928	
Style of architecture:	Eclectic Dutch Farmhouse	
Architect(s):	Arthur B. Wood designed his own residence	

Landscape architect(s):
House extant: yes
Historical notes:

    The house, which has been extensively altered over the years, was built by Arthur B. Wood. It was later owned by Hopkins.
    He was the son of Lindsey and Leonora Balsley Hopkins, Sr.
    Dorothy Smith Hopkins was the daughter of James Allen and Nannette Carter Smith.
    Lindsey and Dorothy Smith Hopkins, Jr.'s son Lindsay Hopkins III married Wanda Saltmarsh. Their son Carter married Susan Richardson.
    In 1966 the house was purchased by Mary Ellen Gosman and later sold to Marion Daily.
    In 2018 Daily listed the house for sale. The asking price was $1.9 million.

Hopkinson, Russell (1899-1979)

Occupation(s):	industrialist - member, development department, United States Rubber; president, Hopkinson Laboratories (plastic, films, and safety glass researcher; manufacturer of chemicals for medicine); vice-president, Olin Mathieson Chemical Co.
Civic Activism:	treasurer, secretary, and president, Maidstone Club, East Hampton director, Southampton Hospital Association; trustee, Southampton Hospital
Marriage(s):	1922-1979 – Mary Barbey Lewis (1901-1986) - Civic Activism: vice-president, Garden Club of East Hampton; member, board of managers, and president, East Hampton Free Library; chair, United Fund Patient's Hospital Library committee; president, Ladies Village Improvement Society, East Hampton; chair, ladies tennis committee, Maidstone Club, East Hampton; vice-chair, Y.W.C.A.'s Robert's House, NYC; chair, Homemaker Service division, Children's Aid Society
Address:	Windmill Lane, East Hampton
Name of estate:	
Year of construction:	1952
Style of architecture:	
Architect(s):	Ritzema and Perry designed the house (for Hopkinson)
Landscape architect(s):	
Builder:	Dayton and Dayton
House extant:	unconfirmed
Historical notes:	

The house was built by Russell Hopkinson.
The Blue Book of The Hamptons, *1958* lists Mr. and Mrs. Russell Hopkinson as residing on Windmill Lane, East Hampton.
He was the son of Ernest and Bessie Barnes Hopkinson of NYC.
Mary Barbey Lewis Hopkinson was the daughter of Joshua Roger and Ida May Barbey Lewis of East Hampton.
Russell and Mary Barbey Lewis Hopkinson's daughter Barbara married Paul Renner Scheerer, Jr., the son of Paul Renner and Gladys Knight Scheerer, Sr. of Llewellyn Park, NJ, and resided in East Hampton. Their daughter Mary married Peter Dunham, the son of Carroll Dunham III and resided in New Canaan, CT. Their daughter Joan married John Worthington Harder, the son of Lewis F. Harder, and resided in Seattle, WA. Their son Peter married resided in Boston, MA.

Hoppin, Henry Preston (1917-1990)

Occupation(s):

Marriage(s): 1953 – Patricia Massinger (1929-1996)
(aka Jane Kennedy)

Address: Apaquogue Road, East Hampton
Name of estate:
Year of construction:
Style of architecture: Eclectic Cotswold
Architect(s):
Landscape architect(s):
House extant: no*
Nassau County Museum Collection has photographs of the house.
Historical notes:

In 1915 Edward Hull Jewett, Sr. purchased Mrs. William Strom's residence and called it *The Ink Pot*. [*The East Hampton Star* September 24, 1915, p. 5.] In 1958 Hoppin purchased the house. [*The East Hampton Star* October 2, 1958, p. 4, and March 25, 1965, p. 1.]

He was the son of John Jewell and Edith Jennie Preston Hoppin of South Orange, NJ.

Jane Kennedy Hoppin was the daughter of Charles Jerome and Carolyn Kennedy Massinger, Jr. Patricia was adopted by her grandparents David E. and Clair O'Donnell Kennedy of *Second House* in Montauk. Jane had previously been married to William C. Kuhns, Sr.

Henry Preston and Jane Kennedy Hoppin's daughter Jennie married Kevin James McCarthy of San Francisco, CA.

*The house was purchased in 1972 by Abraham Robert Towbin who sold it in 2009 for $26.5 million. The new owner allowed the East Hampton Fire Department to set fire to house as a training experience.

Howell, John White, Sr. (1857-1937)

Occupation(s):	engineer - chief engineer, General Electric Co.
	inventor - Howell Vometer (first reliable current pressure indicator); automatic machine for treating carbon filament; four-headed, vertical sealing machine, 1896; co-inventor with William Russell Burrows, stem-making machine, 1901
	writer - *History of the Incandescent Lamp*, 1927 (co-authored with Henry Schroeder)
	financier - trustee, Howard Savings Institution, Newark, NJ
Civic Activism:	trustee, Newark Museum Association, Newark, NJ; trustee, Marcus L. Ward Home, Maplewood, NJ
Marriage(s):	M/1 – 1889-1890 – Mary Cortland Drake (d. 1890)
	M/2 – 1895-1937 – Frederica Burckle Gilchrist (1871-1953)
	- Civic Activism: trustee, Newark Museum, Newark, NJ; trustee, Newark Public Library, Newark, NJ
Address:	Indian Wells Highway, Amagansett
Name of estate:	*Sandylands*
Year of construction:	
Style of architecture:	
Architect(s):	
Landscape architect(s):	
House extant: unconfirmed	
Historical notes:	

   John White Howell, Sr. was the son of Martin Armstrong and Abigail Lucetta Stout Howell of New Brunswick, NJ. The Howells' ancestor Edward Howell was a founder of Southampton, NY.
   Mary Cortland Drake Howell was the daughter of Edward Cortland Drake of Newark, NJ.
   The *Long Island Society Register, 1929* lists John White and Frederica B. Gilchrist Howell [Sr.] as residing at *Sandylands* on Indian Wells Highway, Amagansett. The *Social Directory of Southampton, Long Island, 1931* lists their address as Bluff Road, Amagansett.
   She was the daughter of New Jersey Attorney General Robert Gilchrist and Mrs. Frederica Beardsley Gilchrist of Bluff Road, Amagansett.
   John White and Frederica Burckle Gilchrist Howell, Sr.'s daughter Frederica married Albert Blake Williams. Their daughter Jane married Elijah Parish Lovejoy and resided in Amagansett. Their daughter Cornelia married Nathan Comfort Starr and resided in Chesham, NH. In 1928 their twenty-four-year-old son Robert died in an airplane accident while performing stunts. Their son John White Howell, Jr. married Clara W. Stone and resided in Nutley, NJ, and in Amagansett.

Hoyt, Alfred Miller (1828-1903)

Occupation(s):	financier -	partner, Jesse Hoyt and Co.;
		trustee, Bank for Savings, NYC;
		trustee, Continental Trust Co.;
		director, Fidelity and Casualty Co.;
		director, Merchants' Exchange National Bank;
		director, New York Produce Exchange Safe Deposit and Storage Co.;
		director, Bowling Green Safe Deposit Co.
	capitalist -	a founder, Flint & Pere Marquette Railroad;
		a founder, St. Peter Railroad (later, Chicago and Northwestern Railroad);
		president, Milwaukee Northern Railroad
Marriage(s):	1858-1903 – Rosina Elizabeth Reese (1835-1922)	
Address:	De Forest Road, Montauk	
Name of estate:		
Year of construction:	1883	
Style of architecture:	Beach Cottage with Queen Anne elements	
Architect(s):	McKim, Mead & White designed the house (for A. M. Hoyt)	
Landscape architect(s):	Frederick Law Olmstead designed the site plan (for A. M. Hoyt)	
Builder:	Mead & Taft	
House extant: yes		
Historical notes:		

    The 7,000-square-foot house is one of the Montauk Association's "Seven Sisters." It was owned by Alfred Miller Hoyt. He was the son of James Moody and Mary Nesbitt Hoyt.
    Rosina Elizabeth Reese Hoyt was the daughter of William James and Mary Elizabeth Sherman Reese.
    Alfred Miller and Rosina Elizabeth Reese Hoyt's daughter Florence married Dr. William Kelly Otis, the son of Dr. Fessenden Nott and Mrs. Francis Cooke Otis of Montauk. Their son Henry married Emy Lydig Otto, the daughter of Carl August and Margaret Mesier Lydig Otto. Their son John married Ethel Phelps Stokes, the daughter of Anson Phelps and Helen L. Stokes. Their daughter Mary did not marry. Their daughter Rosina married Gerald Beekman Hoppin, the son of William Warner and Katherine Beekman Hoppin, Sr. of NYC, and resided at *Four Winds* in Oyster Bay Cove. [*See* Spinzia, *Long Island's Prominent North Shore Families, vol. I* – Hoppin entry.] Their son Alfred, a bachelor, resided at *Red Maples* in Southampton. [*See* Spinzia, *Long Island's Prominent Families in the Town of Southampton* – Hoyt entry.]
    The house was later owned by Gary DuVal, who called it *Awepesha;* Florence Biggs; and Sidney and Winnifred Goodard, who remodeled it into a restaurant named The Grand View Manor. It subsequently became the residence of Dr. Dewey and Mrs. Hilda Smith.

Hufty, Frances May Archbold (1912-2010)

Civic Activism:	president and board chair, Archbold Station, Lake Placid, FL; vice-chair, Garden Club of America; president, Palm Beach Rehabilitation Center, Palm Beach, FL; trustee, Palm Beach United Way, Palm Beach, FL
Marriage(s):	1932-2001 – Mann Randolph Page Hufty (1907-2001) (aka Page Hufty) - financier - founder, Page Hufty, Inc. (later, Corroon & Black) (insurance brokerage firm – credited with investing variable annuities); director, Equity Corp., NYC; director, American Trust Co., Washington, DC; director, First National Bank of Palm Beach, Palm Beach, FL; director, Northern Insurance Co., Hartford, CT; director, Industrial Bank of Commerce; director, Equity Corp.; director, New York City Bank, NYC; a founder, Variable Annuity Life Insurance Company of America; director, Union Trust Co. capitalist - director, Bayway Terminal Corp. industrialist - director, North Central Texas Oil Company, Inc.; director, Bell Aircraft Corp., Buffalo, NY Civic Activism: chairman of board, America First Committee; trustee, Hufty Foundation; chairman of board, Columbia Lighthouse for the Blind; member of board, Columbia Hospital for Women
Address:	121 Further Lane, East Hampton
Name of estate:	
Year of construction:	1917
Style of architecture:	Mediterranean
Architect(s):	Arthur C. Jackson designed the house (for G. W. Schurman) Charles Nassau Lowrie, Sr. (for G. W. Schurman) Ferguson & Shamanian (for Krakoff)
Landscape architect(s):	Perry Guillot (for Krakoff)
Builder:	Edward M. Gay
House extant: yes*	
Historical notes:	

The ten-bedroom, eleven-and-a-half bath, 8,500-square-foot house, originally named *Beachclose*, was built by George Wellington Schurman. In 1923 Schurman sold the house to Laura Elizabeth Young Martin, who died in 1924. The estate was sold twice more before the Huftys took up residence. Lion Gardiner purchased it in 1925 and sold it to Mrs. Maude Frances Sergeant Bouvier, who called the house *Lasata*. Mrs. Bouvier deeded it to her husband in 1935. In 1950 the house was sold to Mrs. Hufty.

She was the daughter of John Foster and May Barron Archbold of *Chinquapin Plantation*, Thomasville, GA, and an heiress to the Standard Oil of New Jersey fortune.

Mann Randolph Page Hufty was the son of Malcolm A. and Mary Page Hufty of Washington, DC.

Mann Randolph Page and Frances May Archbold Hufty's daughter Alexandra married Michael Alfred Reynal, the son of Juan José Reynal; Miquel de Atucha; John A. Hayes III; and William G. Anlyan. Their daughter Page married Benjamin Griswold and, later, Ted Bell with whom she resided in Palm Beach, FL. Their daughter Frances married Carter Randolph Leidy, Jr. and resided at *Springhouse* in West Chester, PA. Their son John married Carolyn Jean Layton, the daughter of John Emerson Layton. Their daughter Mary, who resides in Palo Alto, CA, is a physician.

In the early 1960s the house was purchased by Joseph Ansbro Meehan. It was purchased in 2006 by Reed and Delphine Krakoff, who, in 2016, listed the house and 7.15 acres for sale. The asking price was $38.995 million.

*The stables were demolished.

Huntting, Miss Annie

Occupation(s): capitalist - owner, Rowdy Hall (boarding house)

Address: Main Street, East Hampton
Name of estate: *Rowdy Hall*
Year of construction: early-to-mid-eighteenth century
Style of architecture: Colonial
Architect(s): Joseph Greenleaf Thorp, 1926 alterations
  (for Mrs. Harry L. Hamlin)

Landscape architect(s):
House extant: yes
Historical notes:

The house was originally the Osborn family residence. It was later owned by David H. Huntting and then by his adopted daughter Annie who utilized it as a boarding house.

In 1895, the house was moved from Main Street to Gay Lane. In 1925 it was purchased by Mrs. Mary Elkins Paxton Hamlin who moved it to Egypt Lane. [*The East Hampton Star* November 15, 1934, p. 5.]

In 1953 the house was purchased from Mrs. Hamlin by Robert Barnes who made alterations and repairs to it and, in 1954, sold the house to Henry Sanford Thorne. [*The East Hampton Star* November 26, 1953, p. 4, and June 17, 1954, p. 7.]

In 2003 the house was listed for sale. The asking price was $2.25 million.

Huntting, Miss Annie

Occupation(s): capitalist - owned *Rowdy Hall* (boarding house)

Address: 30 Woods Lane, East Hampton
Name of estate:
Year of construction: 1895
Style of architecture: Dutch Colonial
Architect(s): Isaac Henry Green II designed the
  house (for Annie Huntting)*

Landscape architect(s):
Builder: Philip Ritch
  George A. Eldredge, 1898 addition
    of new kitchen and servants'
    quarters**

House extant: yes
Historical notes:

The house was built by Annie Huntting.

She was the adopted daughter of David H. and Phebe Edwards Huntting. [*The East Hampton Star* April 12, 1962, p. 9.]

In 1909 she sold the house to E. T. Dayton. [*The East Hampton Star* May 5, 1909, p. 5.]

*For Green's other commissions, *see* Spinzia, *Long Island's Prominent South Shore Families: Their Estates and Their Country Homes in the Towns of Babylon and Islip*.

In the 1970s the house was owned by Marvin Ross Friedman.

**In 1897 the house was also enlarged. In 1909 a new addition was added to the rear of the house and a separate cottage was built.

Hutton, John Laurence, Sr. (1889-1951)

Occupation(s):	industrialist - president, T. Shriver & Co., Inc., Harrison, NJ (chemical machinery processing firm)
Civic Activism:	director, Maidstone Club, East Hampton; vice-commodore, Devon Yacht Club, Amagansett
Marriage(s):	M/1 – 1918-1948 – Katherine Lyon (1896-1948)
	M/2 – 1950-1951 – Alice Pine (1899-1989)
Address:	Apaquogue Road, East Hampton
Name of estate:	*Peep O'Day*
Year of construction:	1922
Style of architecture:	
Architect(s):	
Landscape architect(s):	
House extant: unconfirmed	
Historical notes:	

The house, originally named *The Chimneys*, was built by George Albert Lembcke. [*The East Hampton Star* August 18, 1922, p. 5.] In 1940 Hutton purchased Lembcke's residence and remodeled it. [*The Brooklyn Daily Eagle* April 21, 1940, p. 20, and *The East Hampton Star* February 12, 1948, p. 1.]

The *Social Register Summer, 1945* lists John L. and Katherine Lyon Hutton [Sr.] as residing at *Peep O'Day* on Apaquogue Road, East Hampton.

He was the son of John and Amy Shriver Hutton of Manhattan.

Katherine Lyon Hutton was the daughter of Marvin Thomas and Frances H. Rudd Lyon of Brooklyn and East Hampton.

John Laurence and Katherine Lyon Hutton, Sr.'s son William married Virginia Consuelo Smith, the daughter of Earl Edward and Consuelo Vanderbilt Smith, Sr. of *Iradell* in Sands Point, and resided at *Peep O'Day* on Further Lane, East Hampton. [*See* Spinzia, *Long Island's Prominent North Shore Families, vol. II* – Smith entry.] Their son John Laurence Hutton, Jr. married Emily Clarisse Rutherfurd, the daughter of John Rutherfurd of Cold Spring Harbor, and resided in Morristown, NJ.

Alice Pine Hutton was the daughter of John B. Pine of Manhattan. She had previously been married to Chauncey B. Garver.

In 1951 the house was purchased by Robert McClellen Simonds. [*The East Hampton Star* January 3, 1952, p. 1.]

Hutton, William Langdon

Occupation(s):	industrialist - president, T. Shriver & Co., Inc., Harrison, NJ (chemical machinery processing firm)
Civic Activism:	treasurer and governor, Devon Yacht Club, Amagansett
Marriage(s):	1950-div. – Virginia Consuelo Smith (b. 1930) - Civic Activism: member, administrative board, Society of the Memorial Sloan–Kettering Cancer Center, NYC
Address:	Further Lane, East Hampton
Name of estate:	*Peep O'Day*
Year of construction:	1958
Style of architecture:	
Architect(s):	
Landscape architect(s):	
House extant: unconfirmed	
Historical notes:	

The house, originally named *Peep O'Day*, was built by William Langdon Hutton. [*The East Hampton Star* June 19, 1958, p. 1.]

The Blue Book of The Hamptons, 1958 lists William L. and Virginia C. Smith Hutton as residing at *Peep O'Day* on Further Lane, East Hampton.

He was the son of John Laurence and Katherine Lyon Hutton, Sr. of *Peep O'Day* in East Hampton.

Virginia Consuelo Smith Hutton was the daughter of Earl Edward and Consuelo Vanderbilt Smith, Sr. of *Iradell* in Sands Point. [*See* Spinzia, *Long Island's Prominent North Shore Families, vol. II* – Smith entry.] Virginia subsequently married Edwin Marston Burke, Sr., the son of Oscar Moech and Edna Marston Burke of East Hampton, and resided in Far Hills, NJ.

William Langdon and Virginia Consuelo Smith Hutton's daughter Consuelo married Henry White Scherr–Thoss, the son of Hans Christopher Scherr–Thoss of Litchfield, CT. Their daughter Linda married Francois Lamy and resides in France. Their daughter Muriel married Michel Louis Francois de Chabert–Osland and resided in Hobe Sound, FL. Their daughter Cynthia married Robert John Murphy, the son of William C. Murphy of Mount Lebanon, PA, and, later, ____ Mack.

Hyde, Frank Dana (1861-1957)

Occupation(s):	capitalist - partner, Hyde & McFarlin (construction firm which built a portion of 1893 Chicago World's Fair and alterations to Grand Central Terminal, NYC)
Marriage(s):	1907-1942 – Ada Evelyn Thomas (1867-1942)
Address:	Jones Road, East Hampton
Name of estate:	*Adana*
Year of construction:	
Style of architecture:	
Architect(s):	
Landscape architect(s):	
House extant: unconfirmed	
Historical notes:	

The *Long Island Society Register, 1929* lists Mr. and Mrs. Frank Dana Hyde as residing on Jones Road, East Hampton. *The East Hampton Star* October 10, 1930, p. 7, lists the name of their residence as *Adana*.

He was the son of Parley and Catherine Hyde.

Ada Evelyn Thomas Hyde had previously been married to Reuben Newton Mayfield, the son of Alexander Campbell and Winney Tate Short Mayfield.

Frank Dana and Ada Evelyn Thomas Hyde's daughter Frances married Edmond Bowen Quillan, the son of J. D. Quillan of Eastern Shore, MD, and resided in Berlin, MD.

Icahn, Carl Celian (b. 1936)

Occupation(s):	financier - stockbroker, 1961 (focused on risk arbitrage and option trading);
	founder and chairman of board, Icahn Enterprises, LP (diversified holding firm);
	founder, Icahn Associates (venture capital and private equity firm);
	founder, Icahn Capital
	merchant - director, Blockbuster (video rental firm);
	director, XO Communication;
	director, WestPoint Home
	industrialist - chairman of board, ImClone Systems (biopharmaceutical firm);
	director Railcar Industries
	capitalist - founder, Foxfield Thoroughbreds (horse breeding farm);
	director, Cadius Corp. (real estate)
Civic Activism:	founder, Icahn Scholar Program, Choate Rosemary Hall, Wallingford, CT;
	benefactor, Princeton University, Princeton, NJ;
	benefactor and trustee, Mount Sinai Hospital, NYC;
	a founder, Children's Rescue Fund;
	founder, Icahn House, The Bronx, NY (65-unit complex for homeless families of single pregnant women);
	founder, Icahn House East (homeless shelter);
	founder, Icahn House West (homeless shelter);
	founder, Icahn Charitable Foundation;
	founder of Super Pac with $150 million donation (to encourage corporate tax reform)
Marriage(s):	M/1 – 1979-div. 1999 – Liba Trejbal
	- entertainers and associate professions - ballerina from Czech Republic
	M/2 – 1999 – Gail Golden (b. 1953)
	- financier - vice-president, Icahn Associates (venture capital and private equity firm); stockbroker
	capitalist - Gutsy Women Travel (luxury trips for women); board chair, Lowestfare.com
	Civic Activism: trustee, Icahn Charitable Foundation; trustee, Foundation for Greater Opportunity; trustee, Children's Rescue Fund
Address:	16 Nichols Lane, East Hampton
Name of estate:	
Year of construction:	
Style of architecture:	Modified Colonial Revival
Architect(s):	
Landscape architect(s):	
House extant: yes	
Historical notes:	

   In 1989 Icahn purchased the Thiele house for $6.8 million and completely renovated it. [*The New York Times* October 22, 1989, section 21, p. 1.]

   He is the son of Michael and Bella Schnall Icahn of Far Rockaway, NY.

   Carl Celian and Liba Trejbal Icahn's son Brett is a bachelor. Their daughter Michelle is a digital control producer at Icahn Capital.

Ireland, Anna Mary Brown (1816-1891)

Marriage(s):	George Ireland, Jr. (1813-1873)
Address:	Lily Pond Lane, East Hampton
Name of estate:	
Year of construction:	c. 1890
Style of architecture:	Modified Colonial Revival
Architect(s):	
Landscape architect(s):	John Custis Lawrence, 1910 garage (for Gordon)
Builder:	Edward M. Gay, 1910 garage (for Gordon)

House extant: unconfirmed
Historical notes:

The house was built by Anna Mary Brown Ireland. [*The East Hampton Star* May 16, 1940, p. 2.]
She was the daughter of Aaron Brown.
George Ireland, Jr. was the son of George and Catharine Ireland, Sr.
George and Anna Mary Brown Ireland, Jr.'s daughter Anna died in 1854 at the age of four. Their daughters Catharine, Emma, Grace, and Mary did not marry.
    In 1909 it was purchased by George Breed Gordon. [*The East Hampton Star* October 8, 1909, p. 5.]
    In 1920 the house was purchased by Edward Elliott Jenkins from Mrs. Gordon. [*The East Hampton Star* October 1, 1920, p. 5.]
    In 1926 it was purchased by Jessie Spaulding II who named the house *Pineleigh*. [*The East Hampton Star* November 17, 1933, p. 4.]

Jackson, Elbert McGran (1896-1963)

Occupation(s):	artist - portrait painter; illustrator: *Colliers* magazine; *Saturday Evening Post*; *Cosmopolitan* magazine industrialist - designed and manufactured silk-screened fabrics in the estate's greenhouse
Marriage(s):	1927-1963 – Constance Cabell Wright (1902-1989)
Address:	Flamingo Road, Montauk
Name of estate:	
Year of construction:	mid to late 1920s
Style of architecture:	Spanish Colonial Revival
Architect(s):	Andrew Jackson Thomas designed his own residence and boathouse
Landscape architect(s):	

House extant: unconfirmed
Historical notes:

    The house was built by Andrew Jackson Thomas who also maintained a private zoo on the estate's property [*The East Hampton Star* September 20, 1945, p. 2.]. In 1931 the house was purchased by Dr. William Henry Walker, Jr. [*The East Hampton Star* August 28, 1931, p. 1.] In 1936 it was purchased by Jackson who made extensive alterations. [*The East Hampton Star* October 8, 1936, p. 3, and November 26, 1936, p. 3.]
    He was the son of William Elbert and Crowella Ruth Doughty Jackson of Augusta, GA.
    Constance Cabell Wright Jackson was the daughter of Boykin and Margaret Constance Cabell Wright of Augusta, GA. Her brother Boykin Cabell Wright, Sr. married Miriam Harriman, the daughter of Joseph Wright and Augusta Barney Harriman of *Avondale Farms* in Brookville, and resided at *Rolling Field* in Jericho, NY. [*See* Spinzia, *Long Island's Prominent North Shore Families*, vol. I – Harriman entry – and vol. II – Wright entries.]
    Elbert McGran and Constance Cabell Wright Jackson's daughter Constance married Dr. Richard Wheeler Darrell, the son of Norris and Doris Clare Williams Darrell of New York, and resided in New York.

Jackson, John Day (1868-1961)

Occupation(s):	journalist - Washington correspondent - *New York Evening News*; *Newark Evening News*; *New York Journal of Commerce*
	capitol correspondent - *Washington Times*
	publisher - owner, *New Haven Register*, New Haven, CT; an owner, *New Haven Journal–Courier*, New Haven, CT; president, *Worcester Gazette*, Worcester, MA
	financier - director, New Haven Bank, New Haven, CT
Civic Activism:	member, New Haven Board of Education, 1900-1910, 1927; member, State Commission for New Haven Armory; a founder, New Haven Community Hospital, New Haven, CT
Marriage(s):	1901-1961 – Rose Marie Herrick (1888-1977)
	- Civic Activism: established John Herrick Jackson Library; established John Herrick Jackson Fund, Yale University, New Haven, CT
Address:	88 Indian Wells Highway, Amagansett
Name of estate:	
Year of construction:	1909
Style of architecture:	Mediterranean
Architect(s):	
Landscape architect(s):	
Builder:	Frank M. Griffing
House extant: yes	
Historical notes:	

The seven-bedroom, nine-and-a-half bath, 6,5000-square-foot house, originally named *Willward Lodge*, was built by William L. Ward. It was later owned by Jackson.

The Blue Book of The Hamptons, 1965 lists Mr. and Mrs. John Day Jackson as residing on Indian Wells Highway, Amagansett.

He was the son of General Joseph Cooke and Mrs. Katharine Perkins Day.

Rose Marie Herrick Jackson was the daughter of John Wheeler and Ann Taylor Herrick of Elgin, IL.

John Day and Rose Marie Herrick Jackson's son John married Mary Keen Richardson, the daughter of H. Smith Richardson. Their son Lionel, who resided in East Hampton, married Patricia Woolsey and, later, Patricia Hope Johnstone. Their son Richard, who resided in Amagansett, married Helene Danforth Coler and, later, Jean W. Washburn. Their daughter Katharine married William Blain Reese, Jr. of Atlanta, GA, and resided in Havre de Grace, MD. Their daughter Harriet married John Ingraham Ely, the son of Heman and Anna Burt Ely, and resided at *Hedge-Gate* in Amagansett. Their son William, who was killed in World War II, married Mary Esther Krech, the daughter of Dr. Shephard and Mrs. Mary Stevens Chapin Krech, Sr. of *Briar Patch* in East Hampton. Their son Henry married Eleanor Miles Wardlaw.

In 2013 the house and 2.54 acres sold for $7.5 million.

Jackson, Lionel Stewart, Sr. (1915-1999)

Occupation(s):	publisher - co-owner, with his brother Richard, and, subsequently, owner, *New Haven Register*, New Haven, CT; CEO, Jackson Newspapers, New Haven, CT
	financier - director, Connecticut Bank and Trust Co.
Civic Activism:	director, Greater New Haven Chamber of Commerce, New Haven, CT; director, New Haven Symphony Orchestra, New Haven, CT; member, Connecticut Public Expenditure Council; trustee, Yale–New Haven Hospital, New Haven, CT; governor, Devon Yacht Club, Amagansett
Marriage(s):	M/1 – 1938-div. – Patricia Woolsey (1917-2004)
	M/2 – 1987-1999 – Patricia Hope Johnstone
	- Civic Activism: vice-president, women's board, Santa Barbara Museum of Art, Santa Barbara, CA
Address:	Apaquogue Road, East Hampton
Name of estate:	
Year of construction:	
Style of architecture:	
Architect(s):	
Landscape architect(s):	
House extant: unconfirmed	
Historical notes:	

The Blue Book of The Hamptons, 1973 lists Lionel Stewart and Patricia Woolsey Jackson [Sr.] as residing on Apaquogue Road, East Hampton.

He was the son of John Day and Rose Marie Herrick Jackson of Amagansett.

Patricia Woolsey Jackson was the daughter of Theodore Salisbury and Ruby Hilsman Woolsey, Jr. of New Haven, CT.

Lionel Stewart and Patricia Woolsey Jackson, Sr.'s daughter Suzanne married David Austin Salisbury, the son of John W. Salisbury and, later, John Gallup Cartier with whom she resided in NYC, Their daughter Sheila married Michael Francis Dorsey, the son of Dr. John M. Dorsey of Winnetka, IL, and, later, ____ Leach. Their Son Lionel Stewart Jackson, Jr. married Mary Shirley Billings, the daughter of Dr. William C. Billings of Bradford, CT.

Patricia Hope Johnstone Jackson was the daughter of Alexander Miller and Margaret Blackwood Weir Johnstone of Codsall, England. She had previously been married to Edward Timothy McAuliffe, Sr. of London, England.

In 2007 the house was listed for sale. The asking price was $19.95 million. It was purchased by Steven Spielberg.

Jackson, Richard Seymour (1910-1974)

Occupation(s):	journalist -	reporter, *New Haven Register*, New Haven, CT, 1934-1937;
		assistant to publisher, *New Haven Register*, New Haven, CT, 1956-1960;
		associate editor, *New Haven Register*, New Haven, CT
	publisher -	co-owner, with his brother Lionel, and, subsequently, owner, *New Haven Register*, New Haven, CT;
		publisher, *New Haven Journal–Courier,* New Haven, CT, 1951-1952;
		director, Carrington Publishing Co., New Haven, CT;
		director and president, Register Publishing Co.
Civic Activism:		president, Associate of Connecticut Dailies, 1942-1945;
		member, Mayor's Human Rights Committee, New Haven, CT, 1963-1964;
		member, Connecticut governor's clean air task force, 1966;
		member, Connecticut governor's clean water task force, 1968;
		member Connecticut's Environmental Quality Committee, 1970;
		director, New Haven Preservation Trust, 1961-1973;
		trustee, St Raphael Hospital, New Haven, CT;
		director, Gaylord Hospital, Wallingford, CT;
		secretary and governor, Devon Yacht Club, Amagansett;
		director, Amagansett Village Improvement Society
Marriage(s):		M/1 – 1942-div. 1954 – Helene Danforth Coler (d. 2003)
		- merchant - director, Seiferheld Gallery, NYC (art gallery)
		M/2 – 1956-1974 – Jean Wuertz Washburn (b. 1927)
Address:		18 Cranberry Lane, Amagansett
Name of estate:		
Year of construction:		1910
Style of architecture:		Shingle
Architect(s):		Tietig and Lee designed the house for J. H. Levering)
Landscape architect(s):		
Builder:		Thomas E. Babcock
House extant: yes		
Historical notes:		

   The 4,896-square-foot, six-bedroom house was built by Richmond Levering, Sr. for his mother Julia Henderson Levering after the death of her husband. In 1930 the house was purchased by Jorje Ezequiel Zalles, Sr. [*The New York Times* April 6, 1930, p. 52.] It was later owned by Jackson.
   The Blue Book of The Hamptons, 1964 lists Mr. and Mrs. Richard S. Jackson as residing on Cranberry Lane, Amagansett.
   He was the son of John Day and Rose Marie Herrick Jackson of Amagansett.
   Helen Danforth Coler Jackson was the daughter of Dr. Eugene Seeley and Mrs. Helen Geer Coler of *Windrow* in East Hampton. Helene later married David F. Seiferheld, the son of Sigmund Seiferheld and, subsequently, Werner Muensterberger, the son of Alfred Muensterberger.
   Richard Seymour and Helene Danforth Coler Jackson's daughter Helene married Winfield Scott Magill, the son of Winfield A. Magill of New Hope, PA. Their daughter Rosemary married Joseph P. Wells, the son of Dr. Richard D. Wells of Pittsburgh, PA.
   The Blue Book of The Hamptons, 1973 lists Jackson residing here with Jean W. Washburn.
   Jean Wuertz Washburn Jackson was the daughter of Ira Hedges and Ida E. Wuertz Washburn, Sr. of East Hampton. Jean later married Lawrence Irving Clarke, the son of James Clarke, and resided in Amagansett.
   In 1986 it was purchased by Lucy Allison Bishopric Cookson.
   The main residence, a two-bedroom, one-bath guest house, and 5.2 acres were for sale in 2014. The asking price was $13 million. In 2015 the price was reduced to $11.8 million.

Jaffe, Stanley Richard (b. 1940)

Occupation(s):	entertainers and associated professions - producer, director, and television series creator; partner, Jaffe–Lansing (independent production firm); president, Paramount Studios
Civic Activism:	co-founder, Melinda and Stanley R. Jaffe Foundation
Marriage(s):	M/1 – 1963-div. – Joan Ellen Goodman
	M/2 – 1986 – Melinda Jill Marciano
	- Civic Activism: co-founder Melinda and Stanley R. Jaffe Foundation
Address:	Lily Pond Lane, East Hampton
Name of estate:	
Year of construction:	
Style of architecture:	
Architect(s):	
Landscape architect(s):	
House extant: unconfirmed	
Historical notes:	

    In 1950 Charles E. Main purchased Leo Dewey Welch's residence and named it *Main House*. [*The East Hampton Star* October 5, 1950, p. 1.] In 1974 Main sold the house to Jaffe. [*The East Hampton Star* March 14, 1974, p. 5.]
    He is the son of Leo and Dora Bertha Bressler Jaffe.
    Joan Ellen Goodman Jaffe was from Clinton Corners, NY.

James, Ellery Sedgwick, Sr. (1895-1932)
aka William Ellery Sedgwick James, Sr.

Occupation(s):	financier -	partner, Brown Brothers and Co. (investment banking firm);
		director, Union Bank;
		director, International European Investing;
		director, Holland American Trading;
		director, A. C. James Co.
	capitalist -	director, People's Light and Power;
		director, Western Pacific Railroad;
		director, General Realty and Utilities;
		director, Swiss–American Electric and Equities Co.
Civic Activism:		director, Maidstone Club, East Hampton
Marriage(s):		1917-1932 – Louise Russell Hoadley (1896-1977)
		- Civic Activism: president, Ladies Village Improvement Society, East Hampton;
		president, Garden Club of East Hampton
Address:		57 West End Avenue, East Hampton
Name of estate:		*Heather Dune*
Year of construction:		1926
Style of architecture:		Modified Cotswold
Architect(s):		Roger Bullard designed the house (for E. S. James, Sr.)
Landscape architect(s):		Ellen Biddle Shipman, 1926 *[attributed]* (for E. S. James, Sr.)
Builder:		Frank Johnson

House extant: no; destroyed by fire, 2015*
Historical notes:

The house, originally named *Heather Dune*, was built by Ellery Sedgwick James, Sr.
He was the son of Henry Amman and Laura Brevoort Sedgwick James of *Blomioff* in East Hampton.
Louise Russell Hoadley James was the daughter of Russell Hotchkiss and Mary Eliot Betts Hoadley, Jr. of *Bonnie Bourne* in Southampton. Louise later married Richardson Wright, the son of George S. S. Wright of Philadelphia, PA. [*See* Spinzia, *Long Island's Prominent Families in the Town of Southampton* – Hoadley entry.] Louise's sister Helen married Lydig Hoyt and resided in Woodbury. [*See* Spinzia, *Long Island's Prominent North Shore Families, vol. 1* – Hoyt entry.] Their brother Sheldon was killed in World War I.
Ellery Sedgwick and Louise Russell Hoadley James, Sr.'s daughter Mary married Dr. Joseph Martin Ford, the son of James Howard Ford of Huntington, WV. Their daughter Laura married John William Sinclair, the son of Earl Westwood and Blanche Stich Sinclair of *Fairlawn* in East Hampton, and, later, H. Lincoln Foster, the son of Harry W. Foster of Morristown, NJ. Their son Ellery Sedgwick James, Jr. married Sarah Lispenard Steward Symington, the daughter of James M. Symington of Short Hills, NJ, and, later, Mary Ladds, the daughter of Herbert Preston Ladds of Shaker Heights, OH.
By 1958 Mrs. James had relocated to *Berrywold* on Hook Pond Lane, East Hampton.
[See previous entry of additional family information.]
The house was later owned by Jack A. Rounick who sold it in 1993 to Dr. Gary Feldstein. In 1998 Peter Morton purchased the house from Feldstein. It was owned by Morton at the time of the fire.
*The fire started when construction workers were attempting to repair a chimney's flashing with a welding torch in forty-mile-per-hour winds.

James, Laura Brevoort Sedgwick (1859-1907)

Civic Activism:	president, Society l'Alliance Francaise
Marriage(s):	1891-1907 – Henry Amman James (1854-1929)
	- attorney
	Civic Activism: director, Maidstone Club, East Hampton
Address:	West End Avenue, East Hampton
Name of estate:	*Blomioff*
Year of construction:	1891
Style of architecture:	Shingle with Dutch elements
Architect(s):	Joseph Greenleaf Thorp designed the 1894, 1896, and 1899 alterations (for Mrs. James)
Landscape architect(s):	
Builder:	George A. Eldredge, 1894, 1896, and 1899 alterations
House extant:	no
Historical notes:	

The house, originally named *Blomioff*, was built by Laura Brevoort Sedgwick prior to her marriage to Henry Amman James. She was the daughter of William Ellery and Constance Irving Brevoort Sedgwick. According to her daughter-in-law Mrs. William Ellery Sedgwick James, Sr., Laura was stunned when a farmer, dressed in striped trousers and a top hat, rowed across Georgica Pond to ask for her hand in marriage. [*The New York Times* July 13, 1958, p. 66.]

Henry Amman James was the son of Henry and Amelia Baber Cates James of Baltimore, MD.

Henry Amman and Laura Brevoort Sedgwick James' son Ellery married Louise Russell Hoadley and resided at *Heather Dune* in East Hampton. Their daughter Dorothy married George Griswold Haven and resided at *Sunny Slope* in Salisbury, CT.

[See following entry for additional family information.]

The house, which was on the National Register of Historic Places, was later owned by Juan Terry Trippe. In 1991 the house was purchased by Calvin Klein who built a new house on the site.

Jefferys, Charles Peter Beauchamp, Sr. (1831-1910)

Occupation(s):	engineer - designed Sand Patch Tunnel for Baltimore and Ohio Railroad
Civic Activism:	a founder, St. Luke's Church, East Hampton
Marriage(s):	1858-1908 – Elizabeth Miller (1837-1908)
	- writer - co-authored, with her son William Hamilton Jefferys, *The Great Mystery: Two Studies on the Same Subject One in the Book of Revelation the Other in the Book of Nature*, 1901
Address:	Ocean Avenue and Jefferys Lane, East Hampton*
Name of estate:	*Sommariva*
Year of construction:	c. 1872
Style of architecture:	Italianate
Architect(s):	Charles Peter Beauchamp Jefferys, Sr. designed his own house
Landscape architect(s):	
House extant:	yes
Historical notes:	

The house, originally named *Sommariva*, was built by Charles Peter Beauchamp Jefferys, Sr.

He was the son of Peter Jefferys of Worcestershire, England.

Elizabeth Miller Jefferys was the daughter of Edward Miller.

Charles Peter Beauchamp and Elizabeth Miller Jefferys, Sr.'s son Harry married Marie Celeste Klemm and resided at *Duneden* in East Hampton. Their son William married Lucy Sturgis Hubbard and resided in Philadelphia, PA. Their son Edward married Amy Elizabeth Faulconer, the daughter of Charles and Elizabeth Williams Emmons Faulconer of Philadelphia, and resided at *Journey's End* in Northeast, ME. Their son Charles Peter Beauchamp Jefferys, Jr. was an Episcopalian priest. Their twenty-three-year-old son Maximillian died in 1898.

The house, which is on the National Register of Historic Places, was inherited by their daughter Marie and son-in-law Henry Lee Hobart, who moved the house about 100 yards east to its present site. It was later owned by Abraham Mills, who called it *The Chalet*, and, subsequently, by Dr. Stuart Lessley Craig.

Jefferys, Harry Leapold (1869-1948)

Occupation(s):	financier - insurance executive
Civic Activism:	bequeathed his stamp collection to the Franklin Institute, Philadelphia, PA (it was later transferred to The Smithsonian Institution, Washington, DC);
	a founder, with his sister Marie, Society of Old East Hampton (East Hampton residents that resided in the village for 25 or more years);
	member, board of managers, Howard Hospital, Philadelphia, PA;
	commodore, Devon Yacht Club, Amagansett;
	member, executive committee, East Hampton Associates
Marriage(s):	1910-div. – Marie Celeste Klemm (1879-1968)
Address:	Georgica Road, East Hampton
Name of estate:	*Duneden*
Year of construction:	1912
Style of architecture:	
Architect(s):	
Landscape architect(s):	
House extant: unconfirmed	
Historical notes:	

The house, originally called *Duneden*, was built by Harry Leapold Jefferys. [*The East Hampton Star* November 23, 1944, p. 3.]

The *Social Register Summer, 1937* lists Harry L. and M. Celeste Klemm Jefferys, Sr. as residing at *Duneden* on Georgica Road, East Hampton.

He was the son of Charles Peter Beauchamp and Elizabeth Miller Jefferys, Sr. of *Sommariva* in East Hampton.

Harry Leapold and Marie Celeste Klemm Jefferys' son William died in 1919 at the age of three.

By 1958 Mrs. Jefferys had relocated to Apaquogue Road, East Hampton.

The Jefferyses did not have children.

[See previous entry for additional family information.]

Jenkins, Edward Elliott (1873-1954)

Occupation(s):	financier - chairman of board, Peoples National Bank, Warrenton, VA
Marriage(s):	1903-1954 – Evelyn Grimm (b. 1876)
Address:	Lily Pond Lane, East Hampton
Name of estate:	
Year of construction:	c. 1890
Style of architecture:	Modified Colonial Revival
Architect(s):	
Landscape architect(s):	John Custis Lawrence, 1910 garage (for Gordon)
Builder:	Edward M. Gay, 1910 garage (for Gordon)
House extant: unconfirmed	
Historical notes:	

The house was built by Anna Mary Brown Ireland. [*The East Hampton Star* May 16, 1940, p. 2.] In 1909 it was purchased by George Breed Gordon. [*The East Hampton Star* October 8, 1909, p. 5.] In 1920 the house was purchased by Jenkins from Mrs. Gordon. [*The East Hampton Star* October 1, 1920, p. 5.]

The *Social Register Summer, 1923* (Pittsburgh section) lists Edward E. and Evelyn Grimm Jenkins as residing in East Hampton.

He was the son of Thomas C. Jenkins of Pittsburgh, PA.

Evelyn Grimm Jenkins was the daughter of Daniel and Caroline F. Weyman Grimm of Franklin, PA.

Edward Elliott and Evelyn Grimm Jenkins' son Edward Kenneth Jenkins married Hannah C. Willets, the daughter of Samuel Willets of NY. Their son Alan married Barbara Hoffstot, the daughter of Henry Phipps Hoffstot of Manhattan, and resided in Warrington, VA.

In 1926 the house was purchased by Jessie Spaulding II who named the house *Pineleigh*. [*The East Hampton Star* November 17, 1933, p. 4.]

Jenney, William Sherman (1867-1946)

Occupation(s):	attorney - partner, Jenney, Ruger, and Marshall
	capitalist - vice president, Delaware, Lackawanna, & Western Railroad;
	a founder, Glenn–Alden Coal Co., Scranton, PA
Marriage(s):	1895-1937 – Nina George Bevan (1873-1937)
	- Civic Activism: a founder, Women's Heterodoxy Club; member, board of managers, East Hampton Free Library
Address:	140 Egypt Lane, East Hampton
Name of estate:	*Little Close*
Year of construction:	1917
Style of architecture:	Modified Cotswold
Architect(s):	Polhemus and Coffin designed the house (for Jenney)
Landscape architect(s):	
Builder:	Frank B. Smith

House extant: yes*
Nassau County Museum Collection has photographs of the estate.
Historical notes:

The 4,875-square-foot, eight-bedroom, four-and-a-half-bath house, originally named *Little Close*, was built by William Sherman Jenney.

The *Social Directory of Southampton, Long Island, 1931* lists Mr. and Mrs. William Sherman Jenney as residing at *Little Close* on Egypt Lane, East Hampton.

He was the son of Edwin Sherman and Marie Regula Saul Jenney of Syracuse, NY.

Nina George Bevan Jenney was the daughter of Dr. Thomas Bevan of Chicago, IL.

William Sherman and Nina George Bevan Jenney's daughter Elizabeth married Frederick Ayer II, who resided in Hewlett, Locust Valley, and Bellport. He was the son of Dr. James Cook and Mrs. Mary Candee Hancock Ayer of *Shadowland* in Glen Cove. [*See* Spinzia, *Long Island's Prominent North Shore Families, vol. I* – Ayer entries – and *Long Island's Prominent Families in the Town of Hempstead* – Ayer entry.] Elizabeth later married Richard Draper Richards and resided in East Hampton. Their son Sherman married Jane Lindsay Ewing, the daughter of William Ewing of *Willow Creek* in Mount Kisco, NY, and, later, Mary Bedell Suydam (Mrs. Harkness Edwards) of East Hampton. Their daughter Nina married Hector Bellinetti and resided in New York.

The house is on the National Register of Historic Places.

*The carriage house was razed.

The house, pool house, and 1.58 acres were for sale in 2014. The asking price was $22.5 million. In 2017 the price was reduced to $12.9 million. The taxes were $19,700.

Jewett, Edward Hull, Jr. (1898-1981)

Occupation(s):	financier - partner, Jewett and Shean, NYC (stock brokerage firm)
Marriage(s):	M/1 – 1925-div – Georgina Frances Morrison
	M/2 – 1942-1981 – Camilla L. Roy (1911-2014)
	- dietician, City Home and Cancer Hospital, Welfare Island, NYC
Address:	211 South Main Street, East Hampton
Name of estate:	
Year of construction:	
Style of architecture:	Shingle
Architect(s):	
Landscape architect(s):	

House extant: yes
Historical notes:

    The *Social Directory of Southampton, Long Island, 1931* lists Edward Hull and Georgina Morrison Jewett, Jr. as residing on Dunemere Lane, East Hampton.

    He was the son of Edward Hull and Maude Sherwood Jewett, Sr. of *The Ink Pot* in East Hampton.

    Georgina Frances Morrison Jewett was the daughter of George F. Morrison of South Orange, NJ. She subsequently married William C. Krueger, the son of Judge Gottfried Krueger, and with whom she resided in Short Hills, NJ.

    Edward Hull and Georgina Frances Morrison Jewett, Jr.'s son George married Margaret Rowe Nichols, the daughter of Harold Willis and Katherine Harkness Edwards Nichols II of Cincinnati, OH, and East Hampton. Their son Edward Hull Jewett III married Suzanne Macdonald Barnes, the daughter of Shepard Barnes of Short Hills, NJ.

    The Blue Book of The Hamptons, 1997 lists Edward Hull and Camilla Roy Jewett as residing at 211 South Main Street, East Hampton. She was the daughter of John Alexander and Eveline White Roy of West Barnet, VT.

    Edward Hull and Camilla L. Roy Jewett, Jr.'s son John married Kathleen Daly and, later, Betty Boyd.

[See following entry for additional family information.]

Jewett, Edward Hull, Sr. (1860-1944)

Occupation(s):	financier - partner, Hayden, Stone, and Co. (stock brokerage firm);
	partner, Jewett Brothers (stock brokerage firm)
Civic Activism:	chairman, nominating committee, Maidstone Club, East Hampton
Marriage(s):	M/1 – 1894-1894 – Rose Howard (b. 1871-1894)
	M/2 – 1897-1944 – Maude Sherwood (1873-1953)
	(aka Maude Sherwood)
	- artist - sculptress*
	Civic Activism: member, board of managers, East Hampton
	Free Library
Address:	Apaquogue Road, East Hampton
Name of estate:	*The Ink Pot*
Year of construction:	
Style of architecture:	Eclectic Cotswold
Architect(s):	
Landscape architect(s):	

House extant: no**
Nassau County Museum Collection has photographs of the house.
Historical notes:

    In 1915 Jewett purchased Mrs. William Strom's house.

    He was the son of Charles Henry and Mary Hull Jewett, Sr. of Brooklyn.

    Rose Howard Jewett was the daughter of Joseph and Jane Anna Gregg Howard, Jr.

    The *Long Island Society Register, 1929* lists Edward H. and Maude Sherwood Jewett [Sr.] as residing on Apaquogue Road, East Hampton.

    She was the daughter of John Dunn and Emmaline Catherine Zimmerman Sherwood of *Stone Lode* in Englewood, NJ.

    Edward Hull and Maude Sherwood Jewett, Sr.'s son John, who resided in San Francisco, CA, married Louise Achelis, the daughter of Johnfritz Achelis of New York, and, later, Betty Martin. Their son Edward Hull Jewett, Jr., who resided in East Hampton, married Georgina Frances Morrison and, later, Camilla L. Roy.

[See following entry for additional family information.]

*Among Maude's many works were the fountain at the Cleveland Museum of Art and her 1924 granite Soldiers and Sailors Memorial on East Hampton's Hook Mill Green.

    In 1958 Henry Preston Hoppin purchased the house. [*The East Hampton Star* October 2, 1958, p. 4.]

**It was purchased in 1972 by Abraham Robert Towbin, who sold it in 2009 for $26.5 million. The new owner allowed the East Hampton Fire Department to set fire to the house as a training experience.

Joel, Billy (b. 1949)
aka William Martin Joel

Occupation(s):	entertainers and associated professions - pianist and singer*
	composer - songwriter
	industrialist - co-owner, with Peter Neeham, Long Island Boat Co.
	merchant - owner, custom-made, retro-styled motorcycle store, Oyster Bay, NY
Civic Activism:	member, site selection committee, Rock and Roll Hall of Fame, Cleveland, OH;
	sponsor, Billy Joel Visiting Composer Series, Syracuse University, Syracuse, NY
Marriage(s):	M/1 – 1973-div. 1982 – Elizabeth Weber
	- entertainers and associated professions - Billy's manager
	M/2 – 1985-div. 1994 – Christie Brinkley (b. 1954)
	- model
	entertainers and associated professions - picture, Broadway, and television actress
	artist - illustrator
	industrialist - founder, Believe (perfume);
	founder of her own line of jewelry (manufactured by Swank)
	writer - *Christie Brinkley's Outdoor Beauty and Fitness Book,* 1983
	M/3 – 2004 – Katie Lee (b. 1981)
	(aka Kathleen Rebekah Lee)
	- entertainers and associated professions - television personality
	journalist - contributing editor, *Gotham*;
	column, "Katie's Kitchen," *Hamptons*
	writer - *The Comfort Table,* 2008;
	The Comfort Table: Recipes for Everyday Occasions, 2009;
	Groundswell, 2001 (novel)
	Civic Activism: member of board, Chefs for Humanity
	M/4 – 2015 – Alexis Roderick (b. 1980)
	- financier - senior risk officer, Morgan Stanley, Garden City, NY; stockbroker
Address:	330 Further Lane, East Hampton
Name of estate:	
Year of construction:	1980s
Style of architecture:	
Architect(s):	
Landscape architect(s):	
House extant: no	
Historical notes:	

  The house was built by Billy Joel.
  He is the son of Howard and Rosalind Nyman Joel of Hicksville, NY.
  Elizabeth Weber Joel had previously been married to John Small.
  Christie Brinkley Joel is the daughter of Herbert and Marjorie Bowling Hudson. She was later adopted by her mother's subsequent husband Donald Brinkley. Christie had previously been married to Jean–Francois Allaux. After her divorce from Joel, she married Richard Taubman and, later, Peter Halsey Cook.
  Billy and Christie Brinkley Joel's daughter Alexa Ray is a singer, songwriter, and pianist.
  [For information on Christie's Bridgehampton and North Haven residences, *see* Spinzia, *Long Island's Prominent Families in the Town of Southampton* – Brinkley entries.]
  Katie Lee Joel is the daughter of actress Kim Becker.
  [For information about Joel's Sagaponack residence, *see* Spinzia, *Long Island's Prominent Families in the Town of Southampton* – Joel entry.]
  *Joel has been inducted into the Rock and Roll Hall of Fame and into the Long Island Music Hall of Fame. He has been nominated for twenty-three Grammy awards of which he won six. In 2005 he received a star on Hollywood's Walk of Fame and in 2014 he was awarded the Gershwin Prize for Popular Song by the Library of Congress.
  In 2000 Joel sold the twelve-acre estate to Jerry Seinfeld for $32 million. Seinfeld demolished the house and built a new residence.

John, Davis W. (d. 1947)

Occupation(s):	industrialist - president, Folwell Woolen Manufacturing Co., Atlanta, GA
Marriage(s):	Jencie Callaway) (1875-1950) (aka Jencie Callaway–John) - entertainers and associated professions - opera singer
Address:	Bluff Road and Miankoma Lane, Amagansett
Name of estate:	
Year of construction:	
Style of architecture:	Beach Cottage
Architect(s):	
Landscape architect(s):	
House extant: unconfirmed	
Historical notes:	

The house was previously owned by Mrs. Georgia Avery Kendrick. In 1911 it was purchased by John for $8,000. Jencie Callaway John was the daughter of William A. and Mary E. Patillo Callaway.

Johnson, Miss Edith (1872-1947)

Civic Activism:	secretary and treasurer, Old East Hampton (families that resided in East Hampton for 25 years or more); corresponding secretary, The Colonial Dames of America
Marriage(s):	
Address:	Mill Hill Lane, East Hampton
Name of estate:	
Year of construction:	
Style of architecture:	
Architect(s):	
Landscape architect(s):	
House extant: unconfirmed	
Historical notes:	

The house was built by Edith Johnson. [*The East Hampton Star* October 9, 1947, p. 1.]
She was the daughter of Samuel William and Mary Newlin Verplanck Johnson.
[For additional family information see M. N. V. Johnson entry.]

Johnson, James Loring (b. 1944)

Occupation(s):	artist
Civic Activism:	chairman of board, Drumthwacket Foundation (for preservation of the New Jersey governor's mansion in Princeton, NJ); founder, Cape Branch Foundation; endowed chair in water resources and watershed ecology, Rutgers University, New Brunswick, NJ.
Marriage(s):	1975 – Gretchen Ann Wittenborn - Civic Activism: board chair, Matheny School and Hospital, Peapack, NJ
Address:	31 Old Beach Lane, East Hampton
Name of estate:	*Nid de Papillion*
Year of construction:	1917
Style of architecture:	Cotswold
Architect(s):	Frank Eaton Newton designed the house (for Appleton)
Landscape architect(s):	
Builder:	Edward M. Gay
House extant: yes	
Historical notes:	

The house, originally named *Nid de Papillion*, was built by Robert Wilmarth Appleton. It was later owned by Johnson and is now on the National Register of Historic Places.

The Blue Book of The Hamptons, 1997 lists James L and Gretchen Ann Wittenborn Johnson as residing at *Nid de Papillion*, Old Beach Lane, East Hampton.

He is the son of John Seward and Esther Underwood Johnson and an heir to the Johnson and Johnson pharmaceutical fortune.

Gretchen Ann Wittenborn is the daughter of John Richard and Sarah Alwood Wittenborn of Highland Park, NJ. Gretchen had previously been married to Sabin Tucker Snow, the son of William Brewster Snow of Plainfield, NJ.

James Loring and Gretchen Ann Wittenborn Johnson's daughter Gretchen married Mark Winslow Biedron, the son of Stanley Biedron of Far Hills, NJ. In 2003 their son James Wittenborn Johnson produced a provocative documentary entitled "Born Rich."

Johnson, Mary Newlin Verplanck (1840-1909)

Marriage(s):	1866-1881 – Samuel William Johnson (1837-1881)
	- industrialist - executive director, Garner Print Works, Wappinger Falls, NY
Address:	35 Dunemere Lane, East Hampton
Name of estate:	*The Ingle*
Year of construction:	
Style of architecture:	Flemish*
Architect(s):	
Landscape architect(s):	
House extant: yes	
Historical notes:	

    The house, originally named *The Ingle*, was built by Mary Newlin Verplanck Johnson.
    The *Social Register Summer, 1902* lists Mary Verplanck Johnson as residing at *The Ingle* in East Hampton.
    She was the daughter of William Samuel and Anna Biddle Newlin Verplanck.
    Samuel William Johnson was the son of Pierpont Edwards and Ann Dowdall Johnson. Samuel had previously been married to Caroline Garner who died in childbirth. She was the daughter of Thomas and Frances Mathilda Thorn Garner, Sr. of Bay Shore. [*See* Spinzia, *Long Island's Prominent South Shore Families* – Garner entry.]
    Samuel William and Mary Newlin Verplanck Johnson's son Charles Everest Johnson, Sr. married Mary Elizabeth Gordon. Their son Edwards Johnson, Sr. married Helen Crocker Sloat, the daughter of Henry Ransom and Carrie Ward Sloat whose family founded Sloatsburg, NY. Their daughter Edith, who remained unmarried, later owned the house and sold it in 1936 to James Bond Skidmore who renamed it *Honeysuckle Hedge*. [*The East Hampton Star* March 25, 1937, p. 1.]
    While hunting along Long Island's Great South Bay, Samuel accidentally shot himself in the foot which resulted in its amputation and his death.
    Samuel's brother-in-law William Thorn Garner had an estate in Bay Shore. Both William and his wife Mary perished when the yacht *Mohawk* capsized in a squall off Staten Island, NY. [*See* Spinzia, *Long Island's Prominent South Shore Families* – Garner entry.]
    *The house was remodeled by Skidmore.

Johnson, Rossiter (1840-1931)

Occupation(s):	journalist - assistant editor, *Rochester Democrat and Chronicle*, Rochester, NY, 1864-1868;
	editor, *Statesman*, Concord, NH
	publisher - associate editor, *American Cyclopaedia*;
	editor, *Annual Cyclopaedia*, 1883-1902;
	managing editor, *Cyclopaedia of American Biography*, 1886-1888;
	associate editor, *Standard Dictionary*, 1892-1904;
	a founder and editor, *Liber Scriptorium* 1893
	writer -

Little Classics, 1874;
editor, *The British Poets*, 1976;
Famous Single and Fugitive Poems, 1877;
Pay-day Poems, 1878;
Fifty Perfect Poems (with Charles A. Dana), 1882;
Authorized History of the World's Columbian Exposition (4 volumes), 1897;
editor, *The World's Great Books*, 1898-1901;
editor, *The Universal Cyclopaedia*, 1902-1906;
editor, *Fortier's History of Louisiana*, 1904;
editor, *Great Events by Famous Historians*, 1905;
editor, *The Literature of Italy* (with Dora Knowlton Ranous), 1906;
editor, *The Author's Digest*, 1908;
Phaeton Rogers, 1881 (novel);

A History of the French War, 1882;
A History of the War of 1812-1815, 1882;
Idler and Poet, 1883 (poems);
A History of the War of Succession, 1888;
The Hero of Manila, 1899;
The Story of the Constitution, 1906;
Morning Lights and Evening Shadows, 1902 (poems);
The Alphabet of Rhetoric, 1903;
The Clash of Nations, 1914;
Captain John Smith, 1915;
The Fight for the Republic, 1916;
Biography of Helen Kendrick Johnson, 1917;
The Grandest Playground in the World, 1918;
War of Secession;
The End of a Rainbow: An American Story

Civic Activism:	a founder, The People's University Extension Society;
	a founder and president, Society of the Genesee
Marriage(s):	M/1 – 1869-1917 – Helen Louise Kendrick (1844-1917)
	- writer -

Roddy's Romance, 1874;
Reality, known as "The Roddy Books";
Ideal;
Our Familiar Songs and Those Who Made Them, 1881;
editor, *The Nutshell Series*, 1884 (6 volumes);

Raleigh Westgate or Epimenides in Maine, 1889;
Women and the Republic: A Survey of the Woman Suffrage Movement in the United States, and a Discussion of the Claims and Arguments of Its Foremost Advocates, 1897;
Women's Place in Nature, 1917

Civic Activism: a founder, Meridian Club;
a founder, Guidon Club (an anti-suffragist club)*

M/2 – 1924-1931 – Mary Agnes Keys
- nurse

Address:	Bluff Road, Amagansett**
Name of estate:	*Thalatta Cottage*
Year of construction:	1893
Style of architecture:	Shingle
Architect(s):	Helen Louise Kendrick Johnson designed her own house
Landscape architect(s):	
Builder:	Frank M. Griffin

House extant: unconfirmed
Historical notes:

The *Social Register Summer, 1910* lists Rossiter and Helen Kendrick as residing at *Thalatta Cottage* in Amagansett.

He was the son of Reuben and Almira Alexander Johnson of Rochester, NY.

Helen Louise Kendrick Johnson was the daughter of Asabel Clark and Anne Elizabeth Hopkins Kendrick of Hamilton, NY.

Rossiter and Helen Louise Kendrick Johnson's daughter Florence did not marry.

The *Long Island Society Register, 1929* lists Dr. Rossiter and Mrs. Mary Agnes Keys Johnson as residing at *Thalatta Cottage* in Amagansett.

*For other Long Islanders involved in the anti-suffrage movement *see* Raymond E. Spinzia, "Winning the Franchise: Long Island Activists in the Fight for Woman's Suffrage and Their Opponents, Long Island's Anti-Suffragists." wwwspinzialongislandestates.com.

**The Johnsons previously resided at *Bluff* on Bluff Road.

Johnson, Servetus Fisher (1831-1904)

Occupation(s):	*[See following entry.]*
Marriage(s):	Sara L. Seymour (1846-1922)
Address:	Georgica Road and Crossways, East Hampton
Name of estate:	*Onadune*
Year of construction:	1903
Style of architecture:	Elizabethan
Architect(s):	John Custis Lawrence designed the house (for S. F. Johnson)
	Peter Cook, 1992 alterations (for Shafran)
Landscape architect(s):	
Builder:	George A. Eldredge
House extant: yes	
Historical notes:	

The thirty-three-room, thirteen-bedroom, nine-bath house, originally named *Onadune*, was built by Servetus Fisher Johnson.

He was the son of Major and Elizabeth Lee Jones Johnson.

The *Social Register Summer, 1910* lists Sara L. Seymour Johnson as residing at *Onadune* in East Hampton.

She was the daughter of David Lowrey and Maria Lucy Curtiss Seymour.

Servetus Fisher and Sara Seymour Johnson's daughter Edith and son-in-law Edward de Clifford Chisholm inherited the house and continued to call it *Onadune*. Their son Seymour, who resided at *Driftwood* in Sands Point, married Helen Dorothea Kane, the daughter of Walter Langford Kane of Newport, RI, and, later, Lillian Campeau, the daughter of Robert MacDougall Campeau of Detroit, MI. [*See* Spinzia, *Long Island's Prominent North Shore Families, vol. I* –Johnson entry.]

The house was later owned by Dr. Frank Earl Adair who called it *Sherwood* and, subsequently, by Irving Shafran.

Alterations were made to the house in 1907 and in 1992.

Johnson, Servetus Fisher (1831-1904)

Occupation(s):	financier -	member, Johnson, Byrne, and Johnson;
		partner, Gwynne, Johnson, and Day (investment banking firm);
		partner, Johnson and Boardman (investment banking firm);
		partner, S. F. Johnson (investment banking firm)
	capitalist -	director, East Hampton Electric Light Co.
Marriage(s):	Sara L. Seymour (1846-1922)	
Address:	43 Dunemere Lane, East Hampton	
Name of estate:		
Year of construction:	1886	
Style of architecture:	Shingle with Dutch elements	
Architect(s):	Joseph Greenleaf Thorp designed the house (for S. F. Johnson)	
Landscape architect(s):		
Builder:	George A. Eldredge	
House extant: yes		
Historical notes:		

The six-bedroom, five-and-a-half-bath, 5,500-square-foot house was built by Servetus Fisher Johnson as a rental.

Alterations were made to the house in 1981.

The house was later owned by Alfred Constantine Bellas.

Johnson, Servetus Fisher (1831-1904)

Occupation(s):	*[See previous entry.]*
Marriage(s):	Sara L. Seymour (1846-1922)
Address:	43A Dunemere Lane, East Hampton
Name of estate:	
Year of construction:	1896
Style of architecture:	Shingle with Dutch elements
Architect(s):	Joseph Greenleaf Thorp designed the house (for S. F. Johnson)
Landscape architect(s):	
House extant: yes	
Historical notes:	

The house was built by Servetus Fisher Johnson as a rental.

Johnston, Miss Mary Elizabeth (1890-1967)

Civic Activism:	battlefield nurse during World War I; bequeathed $250,000 to Children's Hospital, Cincinnati, OH (now, Cincinnati Children Hospital Medical Center); bequeathed $50,000 to Society of Transfiguration, Glendale, OH; bequeathed $50,000 to the Protestant Episcopal Foundation, Washington, DC; bequeathed $50,000 to Cathedral School for Girls; bequeathed $50,000 to National Cathedral, Washington, DC; bequeathed her art collection to the Cincinnati Art Museum, Cincinnati, OH; worked with missionaries in The Philippines
Address:	Oceanview Lane, Amagansett
Name of estate:	*Devon House*
Year of construction:	1909
Style of architecture:	Mediterranean Villa
Architect(s):	Tietig and Lee designed the house (for W. C. Procter)
Landscape architect(s):	
House extant: yes	
Historical notes:	

The seven-bedroom, five-bath house was built by William Cooper Procter. It was later owned by his niece Mary Elizabeth Johnston, who called it *Devon House*.

She was the daughter of William Alexander and Anna Ramsdell Johnston.

In 1967 Mary bequeathed *Devon House* and its furnishings to her niece Anne Johnston Sawyer Greene, who resided at *Devon House* with her husband John Bradley Greene II.

In 1987 Jack Dobbs McSpadden, Jr. purchased the house from Mrs. Greene and continued to call it *Devon House*.

Jones, Dr. Oswald Roberts (1896-1970)

Occupation(s):	physician - internist, St. Luke's Hospital, NYC; consulting physician, Bellevue Hospital, NYC
	educator - assistant clinical professor, College of Physicians and Surgeons, Columbia University, NYC, 1923
Civic Activism:	chairman of board, New York State Committee on Tuberculosis; president of board, St. Luke's Hospital, NYC; director, East Hampton League
Marriage(s):	1929 – Elizabeth Mulvane
Address:	Lee Avenue, East Hampton
Name of estate:	
Year of construction:	
Style of architecture:	
Architect(s):	
Landscape architect(s):	
House extant:	unconfirmed
Historical notes:	

The Blue Book of The Hamptons, 1958 lists Dr. Oswald and Mrs. Jones as residing on Lee Avenue, East Hampton. He was the son of William Samuel Jones of Waterbury, CT.

Elizabeth Mulvane Jones was the daughter of John David and Katherine F. Mulvane.

Dr. Oswald Roberts and Mrs. Elizabeth Mulvane Jones' daughter Elinor married Paul Vincent Robinson, Jr. and resided in Akron, OH. Their daughter Elizabeth married William Deming Struby, the son of Walter V. Struby of Denver, CO. Their daughter Katherine married Peter Vanderveen Struby, the son of Walter V. Struby.

By 1979 Mrs. Jones had relocated to 7 Maidstone Lane, East Hampton.

Jones, Rodney Wilcox, Sr. (1876-1984)

Occupation(s):	merchant - manager, Quinn and O'Hara, Utica, NY (ice dealers)
	industrialist - manager, W. A. Fish, Utica, NY (manufacturer of women's shoes);
	a founder and treasurer, American Knits Goods Co., Utica, NY (later, Augusta Knitting Co.);
	a founder and director, Augusta Knitting Co., Utica, NY;
	a founder, Sherborne Knitting Co.;
	a founder, Bath Knitting Co.;
	a founder, Associated Warehouse Co. (later, Augusta Knitting Corp.);
	director, Genesee Knitting Mills;
	director, Duofold Health Underwear Co.
	inventor - patents for improvements in knit underwear manufacturing
	writer - numerous articles on horticulture
Civic Activism:	treasurer, Art Alliance;
	treasurer, National Arts Club;
	director, Grand Central School of Art;
	president, Westchester County, NY, Horticultural Society, 1938-1940;
	president, National Alliance of Art and Industry;
	president, National Hospital for Speech Disorders;
	president, American Orchid Society*;
	treasurer, Eastern Long Island Yachting Association;
	governor, Devon Yacht Club, Amagansett
Marriage(s):	M/1 – 1905-1919 – Kate Hopkins Pinkney (d. 1919)
	M/2 – 1921-1984 – Charlotte Constantine
Address:	Bluff Road, Amagansett
Name of estate:	*Broadview*
Year of construction:	
Style of architecture:	
Architect(s):	
Landscape architect(s):	
House extant:	unconfirmed
Historical notes:	

Rodney Wilcox Jones, Sr. was the son of Enoch and Mary Rozilla Davis Jones of Utica, NY.

Kate Hopkins Pinkney Jones was the daughter of Edward Austin Pinkney of Georgetown, CT.

Rodney Wilcox and Kate Hopkins Pinkney Jones, Sr.'s son Wilbur married Beatrice Dorothy Milton, the daughter of Joseph Milton of Lynbrook, NY, and resided in Lumberton, NC. Their son Rodney Wilcox Jones, Jr. resided in Rye, NY.

The Blue Book of The Hamptons, 1958 lists Rodney Wilcox and Charlotte Constantine Jones [Sr.] as residing at *Broadview* on Bluff Road, Amagansett.

She was the daughter of Robert Constantine of NYC.

Rodney Wilcox and Charlotte Constantine Jones, Sr.'s daughter Eleanor married Richard Henderson, the son of Walter Henderson of Hilo, Hawaii, and resided in Hilo. Their son Curtis married Mary Van Sciver, the daughter of Russell Van Sciver, and, later, Elizabeth Grace Augustus, the daughter of Ellsworth Hunt Augustus of *Waite Hall* in Willoughby, OH.

*Jones was a collector of rare orchids from Mexico, Central and South America, the East Indies, Malaya, Siam [Thailand], and The Philippines. [*The East Hampton Star* February 12, 1942, p. 5.]

Joyner, Dr. James Craig (1893-1978)

Occupation(s):	physician
Marriage(s):	1948-1968 – Lucie Burke Alcott (d. 1968)
	- Civic Activism: director, Ladies Village Improvement Society, East Hampton; corresponding secretary, Garden Club of East Hampton
Address:	Lily Pond Lane, East Hampton
Name of estate:	
Year of construction:	
Style of architecture:	
Architect(s):	
Landscape architect(s):	
Builder:	Dayton and Dayton
House extant: unconfirmed	
Historical notes:	

The house was built by Dr. James Craig Joyner on the site of John Drew's residence. [*The East Hampton Star* November 19, 1953, p. 2, and January 24, 1957, p. 1.]

The *Social Register Summer, 1950* lists Dr. James Craig and Mrs. Lucie B. Alcott Joyner as residing on Lily Pond Lane, East Hampton.

He was the son of Patrick Henry Joyner of Princeton, NC.

Lucie Burke Alcott Joyner was the daughter of Clarence Frank and Lucie A. Burke Alcott of East Hampton. Her sister Jane married Jay Holmes, the son of Dr. Christian R. and Mrs. Bettie Fleischmann Holmes of *The Chimneys* in Sands Point, and resided at *Shady Brook Farm* in Poughquag, NY, and East Hampton. [*See* Spinzia, *Long Island's Prominent North Shore Families, vol. I* – Holmes entry.] Jane later married Dudley DeVore Roberts of East Hampton.

In February 1955 Thomas Pope purchased the Joyners' house and its contents and in April 1955 put them up for sale. [*The East Hampton Star* April 28, 1955, p. 12.]

The house was later owned by William Stanton Barbour.

By 1957 the Joyners had relocated to James Lane in East Hampton. [*The East Hampton Star* January 16, 1958, p. 1.]

Julianelli, Charles A. (1907-1962)

Occupation(s):	fashion designer – Julianelli & Co. (women's shoes)
Marriage(s):	1939-1962 – Mabel Winkel (1908-1994)
	- fashion designer - Julianelli & Co. (women's shoes)
Address:	Terbell Lane, East Hampton
Name of estate:	
Year of construction:	c. 1900
Style of architecture:	Adamesque
Architect(s):	
Landscape architect(s):	
House extant: no*	
Historical notes:	

The house, originally named *Lockdune*, was built by Williston Benedict Lockwood. It was later owned by Laurette Helen Cooney Manners, Dr. Earl R. Carlson, Paul Joseph Moranti, and, subsequently, by Julianelli.

He was the son of Onorata Julianelli of Fairview, NJ.

Mabel Winkel Julianelli was the daughter of Charles Winkel of Brooklyn. She had previously been married to Carl S. Singer of Manhattan.

Charles A. and Mabel Winkel Julianelli's daughter is a *New York Times* journalist.

After Charles' death, the house was abandoned and vandalized.

*The carriage house is extant.

Kaplan, Barton (d. 2002)

Occupation(s): merchant - antiques dealer, NYC

Marriage(s): bachelor

Address: 52 Middle Lane, East Hampton
Name of estate:
Year of construction: 2011
Style of architecture:
Architect(s):
Landscape architect(s):
House extant: yes
Historical notes:

The thirteen-room, 18,000-square-foot house was partially finished when Kaplan's nude body was found in his swimming pool. The Suffolk County Medical Examiner's office classified Kaplan's death as an accidental drowning.

Upon its completion in 2011 the house was listed for sale. The asking price was $19.5 million. It was purchased in 2011 by Canadian residential builder John Daniels for $9.25 million.

Kaplan, Jacob Merrill (1895-1987)

Occupation(s): industrialist - director, Vertientes–Camaguey Sugar Co., Cuba;
    manager, Sugar Products, NYC;
    president and general manager, Oldtime Molasses Co.,
        Havana, Cuba;
    a founder and president, Dunbar Molasses Co., NYC;
    president and director, American Dry Ice Co.;
    president and director, New Mexico Timber & Lumber Co.;
    a founder and president, National Grape Corp., Brocton, NY
        (later, Navajo Corp.);
    president, Navajo Corp.;
    president, Welch Grape Juice Co.;
    director, Endicott Johnson Corp.
capitalist - Westmanton Realty Corp.;
    president, 5th Avenue and 12th Street Corp.
financier - member, New York Stock Exchange
merchant - chairman of board, Hearn Department Stores, Inc., NYC

Civic Activism: director, Freedom House, Inc.;
director, Citizens Housing Council of New York;
president, J. M. Kaplan Fund*;
governor, Knickerbocker Yacht Club, Port Washington;
instrumental in saving Carnegie Hall, NYC;
founder, Kaplan Cooperative Fund (promoted cooperative housing for
    the elderly);
trustee and chairman of board, New School for Social Research, NYC;
benefactor, Shakespeare in the Park, NYC;
trustee, Brandeis University, Waltham, MA;
a founder, CARE (provides food and clothing worldwide);
co-founder, with Evan Frankel, Jewish Center of the Hamptons;
major benefactor, East Hampton Free Library;
major benefactor, Guild Hall, East Hampton;
major benefactor, Southampton Hospital

Marriage(s): 1925-1987 – Alice Manheim (1904-1995)
    - Civic Activism: president, American Federation of Art;
        trustee, Museum of American Folk Art

Kaplan, Jacob Merrill (cont'd)

Address: Route 114, East Hampton
Name of estate:
Year of construction: c. 1885
Style of architecture: Long Island Farmhouse
Architect(s):
Landscape architect(s):
House extant: yes
Historical notes:

In the 1950s Jacob Merrill Kaplan purchased the house of Judge Samuel Seabury.
Born in Lowell, MA, and orphaned at the age of fourteen, he was the son of David and Fanny Levin Kaplan.
Alice Manheim Kaplan was the daughter of Armin Manheim of New York.
Jacob Merrill and Alice Manheim Kaplan's daughter Elizabeth married Gonzalo Fonseca of New York and Seravezza, Italy. Their daughter Joan married C. Gerard Davidson. Their daughter Mary did not marry. Their son Richard married Winston Churchill's granddaughter Edwina Sandys.
*In 1999 the Kaplan family trust donated the Kaplan's 7,846-square-foot East Hampton house and five acres to the South Fork–Shelter Island Chapter of the Nature Conservancy to serve as its headquarters. The J. M. Kaplan Fund was used by the CIA as a conduit to finance its projects. [Frances Stoner Saunders, *The Cultural Cold War: The CIA and the World of Arts and Letters*. New York: The New Press, 1999, p. 134.]
For additional Long Island Central Intelligence Agency operatives, *see* Raymond E. Spinzia, "To Look in the Mirror and See Nothing: Long Islanders and the Office of Strategic Services and Its Successor, the Central Intelligence Agency." wwwspinzialongislandestates.com.

Karan, Donna Faske (b. 1948)

Occupation(s): fashion designer - head of Ann Klein design team;
CEO, designer, and co-founder, with her husband Stephan, Donna Karen (line of clothes)
writer - *My Journey*, 2015 (autobiography)

Civic Activism: co-founder, Urban Zen

Marriage(s): M/1 – 1976-div. 1978 – Mark Karan
 - merchant - boutique owner
M/2 – 1983-2001 – Stephan Weis (d. 2001)
 - artist - sculptor and painter
 fashion designer - co-founder, with his wife, Donna Karen (line of clothes)

Address: 48 Hedges Bank Road, East Hampton
Name of estate:
Year of construction:
Style of architecture: Modern
Architect(s):
Landscape architect(s):
House extant: yes
Historical notes:

Born Donna Ivy Faske in Forest Hills, NY, she was raised in Woodmere, NY. She is the daughter of Gabby and Helen Faske.
Mark and Donna Ivy Faske Karan's daughter Gabby married Gian Palo DeFelice and resided in East Hampton.

Kast, Marie Schultze (1876-1943)

Marriage(s):	M/1 – Walter C. W. Aufermann
	- merchant - silk
	industrialist - director, Confectioners' Machinery Co., NYC
	M/2 – 1928-1941 – Dr. Ludwig Kast (1877-1941)
	- physician
	educator - adjunct professor of medicine, New York Post-Graduate Medical School
	writer - articles in medical journals
	Civic Activism: trustee, New York Post-Graduate Medical School;
	president, Josiah Macy, Jr. Foundation
Address:	87 Davids Lane, East Hampton
Name of estate:	
Year of construction:	
Style of architecture:	Cape Cod
Architect(s):	
Landscape architect(s):	
House extant: yes	
Historical notes:	

In 1941 Mrs. Kast purchased the house from Robert Barns. [*The East Hampton Star* November 13, 1941, p. 4.]

She was the daughter of Carl H. and Louise Eirfelt Schultz of New York. The Carl H. Schultz Mineral Water Company was purportedly the country's largest manufacturer of artificial mineral water in the country.

In 1943 Walton Pearl Kingsley purchased the house from Mrs. Kast. [*The East Hampton Star* April 1, 1943, p. 5.] In 1953 he sold it to John Deere Velie. [*The East Hampton Star* June 4, 1953, p. 1.]

Keim, John Richard (1862-1932)

Occupation(s):	merchant - Keim Sales Corp. (diamond merchant)
Marriage(s):	Gladys Spalding (1886-1935)
Address:	19 Lee Avenue, East Hampton
Name of estate:	
Year of construction:	1899
Style of architecture:	Shingle
Architect(s):	Joseph Greenleaf Thorp designed the house (for F. G. Potter)
Landscape architect(s):	
Builder:	Loper Brothers
House extant: yes	
Historical notes:	

The house was built by Frederick Gaul Potter. It was later owned by Keim.

Gladys Spalding Keim was the daughter of Thomas Hunt and Frances Albertina Bates Spalding.

John Richard and Gladys Spalding Keim's son Llewellyn married Agnes Lucie Munson and, later, Marion McComb, the daughter of Guy Rutherford McComb of Pittsburgh, PA.

When Keim heard of his daughter Gladys' elopement with August S. Torres, he threatened to give Torres the beating of his life and disinherit Gladys.

Despondent over business troubles, Keim committed suicide in his Manhattan office.

In 1914 Keim sold the house to Lamon Vanderburg Harkness. [*The East Hampton Star* January 22, 1915, p. 5.] It was later owned by James Branch Briggs who called it *Beehive*; Chevy Chase; and, subsequently, Peter Gabriel Terian. In 2010 Mrs. Terian listed the house for sale. The asking price was $21 million.

Kelley, William Vallandigham, Sr. (1861-1932)

Occupation(s):	industrialist - chairman of board, Miehle Printing Press and Manufacturing Co.;
	director, Armour & Co.;
	president, American Steel Foundries;
	a founder, Simplex Railway Appliance Co.
	financer - director, Continental Illinois Trust & Savings Bank
Civic Activism:	a sponsor of Theodore and Kermit Roosevelt's expedition to eastern Asia
Marriage(s):	1894-1932 – Lillian Phelps (1870-1934)
Address:	Ocean Avenue and Pudding Hill Lane, East Hampton
Name of estate:	
Year of construction:	
Style of architecture:	Queen Anne
Architect(s):	John Custis Lawrence designed 1911 alterations (for Kelley)
Landscape architect(s):	
Builder:	Edward M. Gay, 1911 alterations
House extant: unconfirmed	
Historical notes:	

Kelley was the son of William Jackson and Susan Elton Taylor Kelley of Ohio.

Lillian Phelps Kelley was the daughter of James Orson Phelps.

William Vallandigham and Lillian Phelps Kelley, Sr.'s son Gordon married Hortense Henry, the daughter of Huntington B. Henry of Chicago, IL. Their son Russell married Daphine Field, the daughter of Stanley and Sara Carroll Brown Field. Their son William Vallandigham Kelley, Jr. was killed at the age of thirty-three in an automobile accident in Melbourne, Australia. He had been married to Marjorie Eloise O'Brien, the daughter of Thomas D. O'Brien of Chicago, IL.

The house was later owned by David Helier. In 1934 it was sold at auction to settle Helier's estate. [*The East Hampton Star* June 14, 1934, p. 5.]

Kelsey, Stephen Tomlinson, Sr. (1886-1965)

Occupation(s):	financier - partner, McDonnell and Co. (stock brokerage firm);
	president, Title Guarantee & Trust Co.
Civic Activism:	director, Maidstone Club, East Hampton
Marriage(s):	1915-1962 – Anne Louise Silver (1892-1962)
Address:	Lee and Cottage Avenues, East Hampton
Name of estate:	*Leecott*
Year of construction:	
Style of architecture:	
Architect(s):	
Landscape architect(s):	
House extant: unconfirmed	
Historical notes:	

The *Social Directory of Southampton, Long Island, 1931* lists Stephen T. and Louise Silver Kelsey [Sr.] as residing on Lee Avenue, East Hampton. The *Social Register Summer, 1932* lists *Leecott* as the name of their residence.

He was the son of Clarence Hill and Elizabeth Baldwin Kelsey of East Orange, NJ.

Anne Louise Silver Kelsey was the daughter of Edgar O. Silver of East Orange, NJ.

Stephen Tomlinson and Anne Louise Silver Kelsey, Sr.'s son Stephen Tomlinson Kelsey, Jr. married Nancy Bryce, the daughter of T. Jerrold Bryce of Manhattan, and resided in New York City. Their daughter Margaret married Hendrick W. J. Van Tuyll and resided in San Francisco, CA. Their daughter Susan married Eric Richard Hansen, the son of Curt Eric and Evine Richard Hansen of East Hampton, and resided in Darien, CT.

Kendrick, Georgia Avery (1848-1922)

Occupation(s):	educator - lady principal, Vassar College, Poughkeepsie, NY
Civic Activism:	suffragist*

Marriage(s):	1880-1889 – The Reverend James Ryland Kendrick (1821-1889)
	  - clergy - Baptist minister
	    educator - acting president, Vassar College, Poughkeepsie, NY
	    writer - *Laudamus: A Hymnal for Women's Colleges and Human Depravity*, 1853;
	        Schools, 1887

Address:	Bluff Road and Miankoma Lane, Amagansett
Name of estate:	
Year of construction:	c. 1903
Style of architecture:	Beach Cottage
Architect(s):	
Landscape architect(s):	
House extant: unconfirmed	
Historical notes:	

    The house was built by Georgia Avery Kendrick. [*The East Hampton Star* June 12, 1903.]
    She was the daughter of Solon and Susan Cook Avery of Rochester, NY.
    The Reverend James Ryland Kendrick was the son of Clark and Esther Thompson Kendrick. James had previously been married to Arabella Randle.
    *For other Long Islanders involved in the suffrage movement *see* Raymond E. Spinzia, "Winning the Franchise: Long Island Activists in the Fight for Woman's Suffrage and Their Opponents, Long Island's Anti-Suffragists." wwwspinzialongislandestates.com.
    In 1911 the house was purchased for $8,000 by Davis W. John.

Kennedy, David E. (1879-1934)

Occupation(s):	industrialist - founder and president, David E. Kennedy, Inc., Brooklyn (manufacturer of floor tiles) (later, Kentile Inc.); president, New York Cork Flooring Co., NYC (manufacturer of floor tiles)
Marriage(s):	1904-1934 – Claire O'Donnell (1884-1965) - industrialist - director, David E. Kennedy, Inc., Brooklyn
Address:	Montauk Highway, Montauk
Name of estate:	*Second House**
Year of construction:	1746
Style of architecture:	Long Island Farmhouse
Architect(s):	
Landscape architect(s):	
Builder:	
House extant: yes**	
Historical notes:	

    The house, which has been enlarged over the years, was built as a line shack for cattlemen and sheep herders. It later became a school. In c. 1900 it was purchased by Kennedy.
    He was the son of David Thomas and Caroline Suddard Dixon Kennedy.
    Claire O'Donnell Kennedy was the daughter of Everett S. and Edith O'Donnell.
    David E. and Claire O'Donnell Kennedy's daughter Carolyn married Charles Jerome Massinger, Jr. of Ocean Grove, NJ, and, later, James Tyson with whom she resided at *Old Baker House* in Amagansett. Their granddaughter Patricia Massinger (aka Jane Kennedy), who they adopted, married William C. Kuhns, Sr. and, later, Henry Preston Hoppin with whom she resided in East Hampton. Their son David O'Donnell Kennedy married Phyllis Edwards Abbe, the daughter of James Edward Abbe, Sr., and resided on Centre Island.
    In the 1960s the house, which is open to the public as a museum, was purchased by the Town of East Hampton and restored, maintained, and operated by the Montauk Historical Society.
    **Second House* is the oldest surviving structure in Montauk.
    **The porch was added by Kennedy.

Kennedy, Michael John (1937-2016)

Occupation(s):	attorney - trial and civil rights*;
	staff counsel, National Emergency Civil Liberties Committee;
	advisor to President of the United Nations General Assembly
	publisher - owner, *High Times* magazine
Marriage(s):	M/1 – Pamalee Hamilton
	M/2 – 1969-2016 – Eleanora Renee Baratelli
	- Civic Activism: president, women's committee, Central Park Conservancy, NYC;
	board member, Society of Memorial Sloan-Kettering Cancer Center, NYC
Address:	40 Georgica Association Road, East Hampton
Name of estate:	*Kilkare*
Year of construction:	c. 1877
Style of architecture:	Shingle
Architect(s):	
Landscape architect(s):	Andrew Graham, stone wall surrounding pool (for Kennedy)
Builder:	Asa Otis Jones, enlarged the house, 1901 (for Mrs. W. Edwards)

House extant: yes
Historical notes:

    The house, originally named *Kilkare*, was built by Walter Edwards, Jr. It was inherited by his son William. The house remained in the Edwards family until 1975 when it was sold to Kennedy. The Kennedys continued to call it *Kilkare*.
    He was the son of Thomas and Evelyn Forbes Kennedy.
    Eleanora Renee Baratelli Kennedy is the daughter of Guido Baratelli of Jersey City, NJ. She had previously been married to Robert Charles Bongiovanni.
    Michael John and Eleanora Renee Baratelli Kennedy's daughter Anna married Michael Safir, the son of David and Ann G. Safir.
    *Kennedy's clients included the co-founder of the National Farm Workers Association Cesar Chavez; Black Panther leader Huey Newton; LSD proponent Timothy Leary; Sicilian crime boss Gaetano Badalmenti; and "The Teflon Don," Manhattan's crime boss John Gotti, Sr. He also represented Ivana Trump in her 1991 divorce from Donald Trump, who would later become the third United States President to be impeached. Ironically, the Trumps had spent several summers in *Kilkare's* former guest house.
    In 2017 Mrs. Kennedy listed the 5,000-square-foot, seven-bedroom, seven-and-a-half-bath house for sale. The asking price was $55 million.

Kerr, Selina Alva Coe (1865-1932)

Marriage(s):	M/1 – Chauncey F. Kerr (1858-1898)
	- financier - president, Kerr and Co. (stock brokerage firm)
	M/2 – 1900-div.1902 – Charles Weaver Bailey (1861-1922)
	- merchant - president, Bailey, Banks, and Biddle, Philadelphia, PA (jewelry firm)
Address:	Fithian Lane, East Hampton
Name of estate:	*Fithian House*
Year of construction:	
Style of architecture:	
Architect(s):	
Landscape architect(s):	

House extant: unconfirmed
Nassau County Museum Collection has photographs of the estate.
Historical notes:

The *Social Directory of Southampton, Long Island, 1931* lists Mrs. Chauncey Kerr as residing on Fithian Lane, East Hampton. The *Social Register Summer, 1921* lists the name of her residence as *Fithian House*.

She was the daughter of Elmore Frank and Emma Harmstead Coe of Brooklyn. Selina's brother Elmore married Elizabeth Wright Davie, the daughter of James and Alice Davie, and resided in Hewlett Bay. [*See* Spinzia, *Long Island's Prominent Families in the Town of Hempstead* – Coe entry.]

Chauncey F. Kerr was the son of John and Jane Ann Thomas Kerr of NYC.

Chauncey F. and Selina Alva Coe Kerr's son Elmore married Marian Lyman Smyth, the daughter of Sidney Lanier Smyth of Manhattan, and resided in Mill Neck. [*See* Spinzia, *Long Island's Prominent North Shore Families, vol. I* – Kerr entry.]

Charles Weaver Bailey was the son of Joseph Trowbridge and Catherine Goddard Bailey, Jr. of Philadelphia, PA.

In the fall of 1900, prior to her marriage to Charles, Selina and Bailey were canoeing in the Adirondack Mountains when they were mistaken for a deer by a hunter. The hunter's bullet entered Bailey's back and was deflected into Selina's leg. They both recovered but Selina's leg had to be amputated. Their two-year marriage ended when Selina filed for divorce charging Charles with adultery. Charles, who claimed the other woman's affidavit was false, sued Selina's brother Elmore Holloway Coe for allegedly conspiring to alienate the affections of his wife. [*The New York Times* October 16, 1902, p. 3, and January 26, 1904, p. 1.]

Selina subsequently resumed the surname of Kerr.

Kessner, Steven (b. 1953)

Occupation(s):	capitalist - president and chairman of board, RE Group of Companies (real estate firm);
	principal, Tri Partners, LLP, Singapore;
	director, Environmental Power Corp.;
	a founder, K5 Equities (real estate investment firm)
Civic Activism:	founder, Steve's Camp (gives city children a chance to experience farm life)
Marriage(s):	1974 – Cheryl Susan Klein
Address:	31 Two Mile Harbor Road, East Hampton
Name of estate:	
Year of construction:	
Style of architecture:	Shingle
Architect(s):	Lawrence Randolph designed the house
Landscape architect(s):	

House extant: yes
Historical notes:

Kessner is the son of David Kessner of Whitestone, NY.

His real estate holdings consists of nearly sixty-buildings and over 1,200 units located mostly in the Harlem and El Barrio sections of Manhattan.

Cheryl Susan Klein Kessner is the daughter of Seymour Klein of Tappan, NY.

In 2015 the 8,500-square-foot, six-bedroom house, with six and a half bathrooms, and 2.3 acres were for sale. The asking price was $18.95 million.

Kimball, Alden (1894-1943)

Occupation(s):	merchant - coal
Civic Activism:	in 1941 Alden and his sister-in-law Louise Voorhees Kimball donated land to the East Hampton Free Library for its expansion
Marriage(s):	1920-1943 – Anne Stuart Randolph (b. 1894)
Address:	Jefferys Lane, East Hampton
Name of estate:	*Eastern View*
Year of construction:	1935
Style of architecture:	
Architect(s):	Polhemus and Coffin designed the house (for Kimball)
Landscape architect(s):	
House extant:	unconfirmed
Historical notes:	

    The house, originally named *Eastern View*, was built by Alden Kimball. [*The East Hampton Star* September 6, p. 5, and April 4, 1935, p. 5.]

    The *Social Register Summer, 1937* lists Alden and Anne S. Randolph Kimball as residing at *Eastern View* in East Hampton.

    He was the son of Charles Edmund and Maie Bennett Kimball, Sr. of East Hampton.

    Kimball committed suicide by hanging himself in the basement of his East Hampton home. [*The New York Times* April 11, 1943, p. 33.]

    Anne Stuart Randolph Kimball was the daughter of Robert Lee and Phoebe Waite Elliott Randolph of Virginia and Baltimore MD. She subsequently married Barrington E. Basil Hall of *Faygate* in Middleburg, VA. Hall's daughter Nancy, by his previous marriage, married Edward Reilly Stettinius III, the son of Edward Reilly and Virginia Gordon Wallace Stettinius, Jr. of *The Shelter* in Lattingtown. [*See* Spinzia, *Long Island's Prominent North Shore Families, vol. II –* Stettinius entry.]

    [See following Kimball entries for additional family information.]

Kimball, Charles Edmunds, Jr. (1891-1938)

Occupation(s):	attorney - member, Murray, Prentice, and Aldrich
	financier - trust officer, Chemical Bank & Trust Co., NYC
Civic Activism:	member, board of estimate, Greenwich, CT
Marriage(s):	1929-1938 – Louise Van Voorhees (1904-1977)
	- Civic Activism: Louise and her brother-in-law Alden Kimball donated land to the East Hampton Free Library for its expansion
Address:	Main Street, East Hampton
Name of estate:	*Purple House*
Year of construction:	1770s
Style of architecture:	Colonial
Architect(s):	
Landscape architect(s):	

House extant: yes
Historical notes:

The house, which was the ancestral home of the Hedges family from 1775 to 1900, may have been built by William Hedges. Everett Joshua Edwards purchased it in 1900. Edwards sold the house to Mary Breck Vaill Talmage who called it *Purple House*. [*The East Hampton Star* May 4, 1972, p. 14.] In 1925 the house was purchased by Mrs. Charles Halsted Mapes who continued to call it *Purple House*. [*The East Hampton Star* February 20, 1936, p. 5.]

The *Social Register, Summer, 1937* lists Charles E. and Louise V. Voorhees Kimball [Jr.] as residing in East Hampton. He was the son of Charles Edmunds and Maie Bennett Kimball, Sr. of East Hampton.

Louise Van Voorhees Kimball was the daughter of Dr. James Ditmars and Mrs. Louise Brown Voorhees of East Hampton. She subsequently married John Rouse Webster of Greenwich, CT.

Charles Edmunds and Louise Van Voorhees Kimball, Jr.'s daughter Louise married Oakes Ames, the son of Amyas and Evelyn I. Perkins Ames of *Linden Hall* in Laurel Hollow. [*See* Spinzia, *Long Island's Prominent North Shore Families, vol. I* – Ames entry.] Their daughter Susan married Keith Ward Wheelock, the son of Ward Wheelock of Haverford, PA, and later, ___ Sugar. Their son Charles Edmunds Kimball III married Susan Ljubica, the daughter of Leonard Land and Ruby Ducich Ljubica, and resided in Florida.
[See other Kimball entries for additional family information.]

In 1941 the Kimball family deeded the house to the East Hampton Free Library.

In 1973 it was purchased by Mrs. Adelaide de Menil Carpenter who moved the house to her estate on Further Lane. When the Carpenters decided to sell their estate, Mrs. Carpenter donated it to the Town of East Hampton which incorporated it into its town hall complex on Pantigo Road.

Kimball, Charles Edmunds, Sr. (1857-1920)

Occupation(s):	capitalist - director, Litchfield & Madison Railroad Co.;
	director, Peoria & Pekin Union Railroad;
	president, Chicago, Peoria, & St. Louis Railroad;
	owned coal mines
Marriage(s):	1887-1920 – Maie Bennett (1866-1936)
Address:	Main Street, East Hampton
Name of estate:	
Year of construction:	
Style of architecture:	
Architect(s):	
Landscape architect(s):	

House extant: unconfirmed
Historical notes:

Kimball purchased Dr. Edward Monroe Osborne, Sr.'s residence. [*The East Hampton Star* December 25, 1941, p. 4.]

Charles Edmunds Kimball, Sr. was the son of William Battey and Sarah Maria Rounds Kimball.

The *Social Register Summer, 1910* and *1920* list Maie Bennet Kimball as residing in East Hampton.

Maie subsequently married Charles Halsted Mapes with whom she resided at *Purple House* in East Hampton.

Charles Edmunds and Maie Bennett Kimball, Sr.'s son Alden married Anne Stuart Randolph and resided in East Hampton. Their son William married Nancy Maffit Bates, the daughter of Charles F. Bates of St. Louis, MO, and resided in St Louis. Their son Charles Edmunds Kimball, Jr. married Louise Van Voorhees and resided in East Hampton.
[See previous Kimball entries for additional family information.]

The house was later owned by Mrs. Marion Louise Smith Peters. [*The East Hampton Star* February 20, 1936, p. 5.]

King, Hamilton (1871-1952)

Occupation(s):	artist*
Marriage(s):	Jessica Hildreth Halsey (1877-1962) - Civic Activism: president, Garden Club of East Hampton; vice president, Ladies Village Improvement Society, East Hampton
Address:	Apaquogue Road, East Hampton
Name of estate:	*Spindrift*
Year of construction:	1921
Style of architecture:	Colonial Revival
Architect(s):	Lewis Colt Albro designed the house (for King)

Landscape architect(s):
House extant: yes
Nassau County Museum Collection has photographs of the estate.
Historical notes:

The house, originally named *Spindrift*, was built by Hamilton King by combining and enlarging two fishermen's cottages.

The *Long Island Society Register, 1929* lists Hamilton and Jessica Hildreth Halsey King as residing on Apaquogue Road, East Hampton. The *Social Register Summer, 1932* lists *Spindrift* as the name of their residence.

Jessica Hildreth Halsey was the daughter of Silas Condit and Ella Price Halsey of Manhattan. Jessica had previously been married to Arthur Jarvis Slade of East Hampton. He was the son of George Patton and Cornelia Wheeler Strong Slade.

The house is on the National Register of Historic Places as part of the Jones Road Historic District.

*King painted the mural of dunes in the music room of William Carter Dickerman, Sr.'s East Hampton residence *Dune Dee*.

King, William

Occupation(s):	shipping - captain of whaling ship *Concordia*
Civic Activism:	a founder, Maidstone Club, East Hampton
Marriage(s):	
Address:	187 Main Street, East Hampton
Name of estate:	
Year of construction:	1872
Style of architecture:	French Second Empire

Architect(s):
Landscape architect(s):
House extant: yes
Historical notes:

In 2012 the five-bedroom, six-bathroom, 3,000-square-foot house sold for $2.187 million.

Kingsley, Virginia Pulleyn (b. 1896)

Civic Activism:	*[See following entry.]*
Marriage(s):	1917-1958 – Walton Pearl Kingsley (1886-1958)
	- *[See following entry.]*
Address:	128 Egypt Lane, East Hampton
Name of estate:	
Year of construction:	
Style of architecture:	
Architect(s):	Aymar Embry designed the house (for J. C. Adams)
Landscape architect(s):	
House extant: yes	
Historical notes:	

The house was built by John Cranford Adams. [*The East Hampton Star* July 16, 1959, p. 16, and March 9, 1961, p. 8.] In 1963 it was purchased by Mrs. Kingsley. [*The East Hampton Star* November 28, 1963, p. 4.]
   [See following entry for family information.]
   In 1970 she sold it to John K. Lundberg. [*The East Hampton Star* May 28, 1970, p. 4.]

Kingsley, Walton Pearl (1886-1958)

Occupation(s):	financier - director, Citizens Central National Bank of New York;
	director, Chemical National Bank;
	vice-president, Life Insurance Company of New York;
	trustee, Union Dime Savings Bank
Civic Activism:	member, East Hampton Zoning Commission;
	member, Town East Hampton Rationing Board, 1944;
	director, East Hampton League;
	treasurer, Maidstone Club, East Hampton
Marriage(s):	1917-1958 – Virginia Pulleyn (b. 1896)
	- Civic Activism: treasurer, Garden Club of East Hampton
Address:	87 Davids Lane, East Hampton
Name of estate:	
Year of construction:	
Style of architecture:	Cape Cod
Architect(s):	
Landscape architect(s):	
House extant: yes	
Historical notes:	

In 1941 Marie Schultze Kast purchased the house from Robert Barns. [*The East Hampton Star* November 13, 1941, p. 4.] In 1943 Kingsley purchased Mrs. Kast's residence. [*The East Hampton Star* April 1, 1943, p. 5.]
   The *Social Register Summer, 1949* lists Walton P. and Virginia Pulleyn Kingsley as residing on Davids Lane, East Hampton.
   He was the son of Darwin Pearl and Mary Marilla Mitchell Kingsley, Sr. of East Hampton.
   Virginia Pulleyn Kingsley was the daughter of John Joseph Pulleyn. Her brother John married Alice Moffitt and resided in East Hampton.
   In 1953 Kingsley sold the house to John Deere Velie. [*The East Hampton Star* June 4, 1953, p. 1.]

Kiser, John William, III (1920-1985)
aka John William Kiser, Jr.

Occupation(s):	industrialist - vice-president, Phoenix Iron Co., Chicago, IL
	financier - partner, Jessup and Lamont (investment banking firm)
Marriage(s):	M/1 – 1942-1953 – Anne Milholland (1922-1953)
	M/2 – 1954 – Cynthia Smathers Healey (1926-1983)
	M/3 – 1957-div. 1964 – Margot Tier Potter
Address:	Dunemere Lane, East Hampton
Name of estate:	*The Lodge*
Year of construction:	
Style of architecture:	
Architect(s):	
Landscape architect(s):	
House extant: unconfirmed	
Historical notes:	

The *Social Register Summer, 1951* lists John W. and Anne Milholland Kiser, Jr. [III] as residing in East Hampton.

He was the son of John William Kiser and Mary Buford Peirce Kiser, Jr. of *Sunset Court / Westerly* in Southampton. [*See* Spinzia, *Long Island's Prominent Families in the Town of Southampton* – Kiser entry.]

Anne Milholland Kiser, who was killed in an automobile accident, was the daughter of James Clarke and Florence Appleton Milholland of Hewlett Harbor. [*See* Spinzia, *Long Island's Prominent Families in the Town of Hempstead* – Milholland entry.] Anne's sister Mary married C. Matthews Dick, Jr. and resided in Lake Forest, IL. Her brother Peter married Dorothy Keane, the daughter of John Redmore Keane; Kathleen Hanley; Maura Mulligan; and, subsequently, Virginia Genett.

John William and Anne Milholland Kiser, III's son Anthony resided in Manhattan.

Cynthia Smathers Healey Kiser was the daughter of Justin O'Brien and Virginia Smith Smathers Healey, Sr. of East Hampton. She had previously been married to Merrill Krech, the son of Dr. Shepard and Mrs. Mary Stevens Chapin Krech, Sr. of *Briar Patch* in East Hampton. Cynthia subsequently married C. Robert Divine, the son of James J. Devine of East Hampton.

Margo Tiers Potter Kiser was the daughter of Eliphalet Nott and Margaret Tiers Potter III of Muttontown. [*See* Spinzia, *Long Island's Prominent North Shore Families, vol. II* – Potter entry.] Margot subsequently married Robert O. Denny, the son of Chalmer Emerick Denny of Kokomo, IN, and resided in Tucson, AZ.

John William and Margot Tiers Potter Kiser III's daughter Margot resided on the West Coast.

Klein, Calvin (b. 1942)
aka Calvin Richard Klein

Occupation(s):	capitalist - a founder in 1968, with Barry Schwartz, Calvin Klein, Inc. (leases name and designs fabrics, perfumes, jewelry, eyeglasses, makeup, and home products)
Marriage(s):	M/1 – 1964-div. 1974 – Jayne Centre
	- artist - textile designer
	M/2 – 1987-div. 2006 – Kelly Rector
	- professional photographer
Address:	West End Avenue, East Hampton
Name of estate:	
Year of construction:	c. 1992
Style of architecture:	
Architect(s):	Thierry W. Despont designed the house (for Klein)
Landscape architect(s):	
House extant: yes	
Historical notes:	

In 1991 Klein purchased the Juan Terry Trippe estate and demolished the main residence to build a new home.

He is the son of Leo and Flore Stern Klein of The Bronx.

Calvin Richard and Jayne Centre Klein's daughter Marci married Scott Murphy. In 1978, at the age of eleven, she had been kidnapped. She was released nine hours later unharmed after the $100,000 ransom was paid. The Kleins' former twenty-three-year-old babysitter, her nineteen-year-old brother, and a friend were apprehended and charged for allegedly kidnapping the child. The babysitter and her brother later pled guilty. [*The New York Times* February 4, 1978, p. A11, and November 1, 1978, p. A11.]

The Kleins subsequently relocated to Southampton. [*See* Spinzia, *Long Island's Prominent Families in the Town of Southampton* – Klein entry.]

Klenk, William Clifford, Jr. (1927-2015)

Occupation(s):	financier - banker
	capitalist - financed a motion picture
Marriage(s):	Hope Bacon (1917-1983)
Address:	17 Georgica Association Road, East Hampton
Name of estate:	
Year of construction:	
Style of architecture:	Ranch
Architect(s):	
Landscape architect(s):	
House extant: unconfirmed*	
Historical notes:	

Hope Bacon Klenk was the daughter of Elliot Cowdin and Hope Norman (later, Gardner) Bacon, Sr. of Old Westbury. [*See* Spinzia, *Long Island's Prominent North Shore Families, vol. I* – Bacon and Gardner entries.] She had previously been married to Richard Nelson Ryan, Sr., the son of Clendenin James and Caroline S. O'Neil Ryan, Sr. Richard was the grandson of Thomas Fortune Ryan. His brother Clendenin James Ryan, Jr. married Jean Harder and resided in Mill Neck. [*See* Spinzia, *Long Island's Prominent North Shore Families, vol. II* – Ryan entry.]

Richard Nelson and Hope Bacon Ryan, Sr.'s daughter Alix married Roy Rainey Plum, the son of Matthias Plum of Chatham, MA. Their daughter Hope married ____ Gaynor and, later, ____ Garrett. Their son Richard Nelson, Jr. resided in East Hampton.

In 1993 Klenk sold the estate, which consisted of a main residence, two cottages, and a boathouse, to Kenneth Joseph with a life tenancy in the cottages and boathouse. Klenk remodeled the boathouse into his new residence.

*In 2014 Joseph petitioned the Town to demolish the four structures and replace them with an 8,900-square-foot house.

Klotz, Charles Arthur (1873-1946)

Occupation(s):	attorney
	industrialist – founder, Virginian Limestone Corp., Klotz, VA
Marriage(s):	1898-1946 – Laura Dolese (1877-1965)
Address:	Lee Avenue, East Hampton
Name of estate:	
Year of construction:	c. 1900
Style of architecture:	Shingle
Architect(s):	
Landscape architect(s):	
House extant: yes	

Nassau County Museum Collection has photographs of the estate.
Historical notes:

The house, originally named *T-Other House*, was built by Garret Augustus Hobart, Jr. In 1940 Klotz purchased it for $17,000. [*The New York Times* February 11, 1940, p. 147, and *The East Hampton Star* July 25, 1940, p. 1.]

He was the son of Karl and Magdalena Horton Klotz of New York.

Laura Dolese Klotz was the daughter of John and Katherine Jacobs Dolese of Chicago, IL.

Charles Arthur and Laura Dolese Klotz's daughter Dorothy married Harry Austin Pardue and resided in East Hampton. Their son Charles Dolese Klotz married Nancy Doris Cochran. One of their daughters married Edward Cooley. Another daughter married Donald L. Williams, Sr.

In 1958 Mrs. Klotz built a house on Hook Pond Lane. [*The East Hampton Star* January 16, 1958, p. 1.]

Knox, Maria Speir Reid (d. 1932)

Marriage(s): 1879-1919 – John Mason Knox, Jr. (1849-1919)
- attorney - partner, Knox and Mason
financier - director, Northern River Insurance Co.
Civic Activism: trustee, Brooklyn City Dispensary, Brooklyn, NY;
trustee, Roosevelt Hospital, NYC;
treasurer, Leake & Watts Orphan House;
vice-president, Marine and Field Club, Brooklyn, NY

Address: Georgica Road, East Hampton
Name of estate:
Year of construction:
Style of architecture:
Architect(s):
Landscape architect(s):
House extant: unconfirmed
Historical notes:

    The *Long Island Society Register, 1929* lists Maria Speir Reid Knox as residing on Georgica Road, East Hampton.
She was the daughter of Aaron L. and Maria Speir Reid of Brooklyn.
    John Mason Knox, Jr. was the son of John Mason and Maria Livingston Knox, Sr. of Manhattan.
    John Mason and Maria Speir Reid Knox, Jr.'s daughters Amy and Maria did not marry. Their son John was a youth at the time of his death.
    At the time of her death, Mrs. Knox was residing on Apaquogue Road. [*The East Hampton Star* July 1, 1932, p. 7.]

Krakoff, Reed (b. 1964)

Occupation(s):	fashion designer - senior designer, Polo Ralph Lauren (apparel firm); head of design for licensed products, Tommy Hilfiger (apparel firm); creative director, Coach, Inc. (now, Tapestry, Inc.) (apparel firm) founder, Reed Krakoff (apparel firm)
Civic Activism:	governor, Parsons School for Design, NYC
Marriage(s):	M/1 – 1993 – Amy Jedlicka (b. 1962) – attorney - Simpson, Thacher, and Bartlett M/2 – 2003 – Delphine Boyon (b. 1971) – fashion designer - accessory designer, Christian Dior, Coach, Inc., Polo Ralph Lauren, and Louis Vuitton interior decorator - founder, Pamplemousse Design, Inc.
Address:	121 Further Lane, East Hampton
Name of estate:	
Year of construction:	1917
Style of architecture:	Mediterranean
Architect(s):	Arthur C. Jackson designed the house (for G. W. Schurman) Ferguson and Shamamian, alterations (for Krakoff)
Landscape architect(s):	Charles Nassau Lowrie, Sr. (for G. W. Schurman) Perry Guillot (for Krakoff)
Builder:	Edward M. Gay
House extant: yes*	
Historical notes:	

The ten-bedroom, eleven-and-a-half-bath, 8,500-square-foot house, originally named *Beachclose*, was built by George Wellington Schurman. In 1923 he sold the house to Laura Elizabeth Young Martin who died in 1924. Lion Gardiner purchased it in 1925 and sold it in the same year to Mrs. Maude Frances Sergeant Bouvier. Mrs. Bouvier, who called the house *Lasata*, deeded it to her husband in 1935. In 1950 the house was sold to Frances May Archbold Hufty. In the early 1960s it was purchased by Joseph Ansbro Meehan. It was purchased in 2006 by Krakoff.

He is the son of Robert Leonard and Sandra Gusky Krakoff of Westport, CT.

Amy Jedlicka Krakoff is the daughter of Frank E. and Mitsuko T. Jedlicka of Danby, VT.

Reed and Amy Jedlicka Krakoff's daughter Sophie is currently a student at Tufts University.

Reed and Delphine A. Boyon Krakoff's children, Maude, Lily, and Oscar, are minors.

*The stables were demolished.

In 2016 Krakoff listed the house and 7.15 acres for sale. The asking price was $38.995 million.

[For information about Krakoff's Southampton residence, *see* Spinzia, *Long Island's Prominent Families in the Town of Southampton* – Krakoff entry.]

Krech, Dr. Shepard, Sr. (1891-1968)

Occupation(s):	physician - surgeon, Southampton Hospital
	educator - instructor of surgery, College of Physicians and Surgeons, Columbia University, NYC
	Civic Activism: member, board of managers, Southampton Hospital; president, Eastern Surgical Society; chairman of board, trustee, and treasurer, New York Academy of Medicine; trustee, New York Protestant Episcopal City Mission Society; trustee, General Theological Seminary, NYC; director, Maidstone Club, East Hampton; president, Riding Club East Hampton; governor, Century Association of New York
Marriage(s):	1916-1967 – Mary Stevens Chapin (1895-1967)
	- Civic Activism: trustee, Maternity Center Association; director, East Hampton Visiting Nurse Association, Inc.
Address:	90 Briar Patch Road, East Hampton
Name of estate:	*Briar Patch*
Year of construction:	1931-1932
Style of architecture:	Modified Colonial Revival
Architect(s):	Arthur C. Jackson designed the house (for S. Krech, Sr.)
	Peter Marino; designed guest house and alterations to main residence, 1989-1991 (for Whittle)
Landscape architect(s):	
House extant: yes	
Historical notes:	

The house, originally named *Briar Patch*, was built by Dr. Shepard Krech, Sr. on the former estate of Henry Hurlbut Abbot which was also named *Briar Patch*.

The *Social Register Summer, 1937* lists Dr. Shepard and Mrs. Mary S. Chapin Krech, Sr. as residing at *Briar Patch* in East Hampton.

He was the son of Alvin William and Caroline Shepard Krech of *Hedgerow* in Southampton. [*See* Spinzia, *Long Island's Prominent Families in the Town of Southampton* – Krech entry.]

Mary Stevens Chapin Krech was the daughter of Charles Merrill and Esther Maria Lewis Chapin of Manhattan.

Dr. Shepard and Mrs. Mary Stevens Chapin Krech, Sr.'s daughter Mary married William Brinckerhoff Jackson, who was killed during World War II. William was the son of John Day and Rose Marie Herrick Jackson of Amagansett. Mary later married Lyttleton B. P. Gould, Jr. with whom she resided in Gaithersburg, GA. Their son Alvin William Krech II married Virginia Groover Mardre, the daughter of Thomas Mardre. Their son Merrill married Cynthia Smathers Healey, the daughter of Justin O'Brien and Virginia Smith Smathers Healey, Sr. of East Hampton. Their son Shepard Krech, Jr. married Nora Potter, the daughter of Clarkson and Amy Holland Potter of Old Brookville, and resided in Easton, MD. [*See* Spinzia, *Long Island's Prominent North Shore Families, vol. II* – Potter entry.]

The house was purchased in 1989 by H. Christopher Whittle. It is listed on the National Register of Historic Places.

In 2014 Whittle listed the 10,300-square-foot, ten-bedroom, nine-and-a-half bath main residence, four-bedroom guest house, and 11.2 acres for sale. The asking price was $36 million.

Krieger, Dr. Howard P. (1918-1992)

Occupation(s):	physician - chief of neurology, Beth Israel Medical Center, NYC
	scientist - medical research, Mount Sinai Medical Center, NYC
	educator - professor, Mount Sinai School of Medicine, NYC
	writer - published over seventy articles in medical journals
Marriage(s):	Dr. Dorothy Terrace (1927-1985)
	- physician - director of endocrinology, Mount Sinai School of Medicine, NYC
	scientist - researcher in endocrinology
	educator - associate professor of medicine, Mount Sinai School of Medicine, NYC
	writer - published over 200 articles in medical journals
	Civic Activism: chair, endocrinology section, National Institutes of Health, Bethesda, MD;
	vice president, Endocrine Society, 1925-1976
Address:	Old Montauk Highway, Montauk
Name of estate:	
Year of construction:	1977
Style of architecture:	Modern
Architect(s):	Norman Jaffe designed the house (for Krieger)
Landscape architect(s)	
Builder:	David Webb
House extant: unconfirmed	
Historical notes:	

The house was built by Dr. Howard P. Krieger.

Dorothy Terrace Krieger was the daughter of Morris A. Terrace of Brooklyn. She had previously been married to ____ Marks. After her divorce from Howard, she married C. Wayne Bardin.

Drs. Howard P. and Dorothy Terrace Krieger's son Dr. James Krieger resided in San Francisco, CA. Their daughter Dr. Nancy Krieger resided in Seattle, WA.

Kuchin, Kenneth Sidney (b. 1953)

Occupation(s):	capitalist - president, Suburban Trails Bus Co., New Brunswick, NJ
Civic Activism:	trustee, Park Avenue Armory, NYC;
	trustee, New Museum Limited, NYC;
	established, Kenneth S. Kuchin Scholarship Fund, Yale University, New Haven, CT
Marriage(s):	bachelor
Address:	123 Main Street, East Hampton
Name of estate:	
Year of construction:	c. 1895
Style of architecture:	Eclectic
Architect(s):	
Landscape architect(s):	
House extant: yes	
Historical notes:	

The house was built by Edward de Rose as a guest house on his estate *Millfield*. It was later owned by Harold Jack Rosinsky who sold the house to Kuchin in 1998 for $2.16 million.

He is the son of Sidney Kuchin.

In 2015 the 8,500-square-foot house, which had been enlarged over the years, was again for sale. The asking price as $11.9 million.

In 2017 it was purchased by Robert Downey, Jr.

Kurzner, Dr. Rubin Raymond

Occupation(s):	physician - orthopedic surgeon
	restaurateur - owned restaurant in NYC
Marriage(s):	M/1 – 1951-1998 – Barbara Estelle Wolfman (1931-1998)
	- interior designer
	M/2 – 2002-2018 – Helen F. Brennan
Address:	130 Bluff Road, Amagansett
Name of estate:	
Year of construction:	1970
Style of architecture:	Modern
Architect(s):	Charles Gwathmey designed the house (for Tolan)
Landscape architect(s):	
House extant:	unconfirmed
Historical notes:	

The five-bedroom, three-bath, 3,000-square-foot house was built by Michael Tolan. It was later owned by Kurzner. Barbara Estelle Wolfman Kurzner was the daughter of Herman S. Wolfman of Woodmere, NY.

Dr. Rubin Raymond and Mrs. Barbara Estelle Wolfman Kurzner's son Wayne married Elana Gross, the daughter of Dr. David A. Gross of Jerusalem, Israel. Their son Neal married Tina Sue Rosenbaum, the daughter of Erich and Estelle Rosenbaum of Dallas, TX.

In 2017 the house was for sale. The asking price was $5.995 million.

Kuser, John Louis, Jr. (1896-1964)

Occupation(s):	industrialist - vice-president, People's Brewing Co., Trenton, NJ;
	director and vice-president, Lenox, Inc.;
	director, Atlantic Products
Marriage(s):	1922 – Olivia Sturtevant Erdmann (1894-1970)
	- Civic Activism: member, Red Cross Motor Corp during World War I;
	director, Garden Club of America
Address:	Cross Highway, Amagansett
Name of estate:	
Year of construction:	c. 1910
Style of architecture:	Mediterranean Villa
Architect(s):	Tietig and Lee designed the house (for R. Levering, Sr.)
Landscape architect(s):	
House extant:	yes
Historical notes:	

The house, originally named *Devon*, was built by Richmond Levering, Sr. In 1920 it was purchased by M. Materson. [*The East Hampton Star* October 22, 1920, p. 6.] In 1930 Kuser purchased the house from Ardis J. Reynolds. [*The East Hampton Star* October 3, 1930, p. 1.]

He was the son of John Louis and Mary Dunn Kuser, Sr. of Bordentown, NJ.

Olivia Sturtevant Erdmann Kuser was the daughter of Dr. John Frederic and Mrs. Georgiana Therese Wright Erdmann of *Coxwould* in East Hampton.

John Louis and Olivia Sturtevant Erdmann Kuser, Jr.'s son John Erdmann Kuser married Eleanor Will, the daughter of Theodore Will of Atlanta, GA, and resided in Princeton, NJ. Their son Michael married Lynda Skrebel, the daughter of Michael Skrebel of Jamesburgh, NJ.

In c. 1946 *Devon* was purchased by George Epworth Devendorf who called it *El Pasaiso*. [*The East Hampton Star* July 18, 1946, p. 2.] The house was later owned by Henry Houston Chatfield who called it *Devon*.

By 1958 the Kusers had relocated to Devon Road. *The Blue Book of The Hamptons, 1958* lists Mr. and Mrs. John L. Kuser [Jr.] as residing on Devon Road, Amagansett.

LaForest, Helen A. (1835-1914)

Occupation(s):	capitalist - built and owned several rental cottages in East Hampton; owner, The Apaquogue
Civic Activism:	bequeathed money to the Ladies Village Improvement Society, East Hampton
Marriage(s):	Edward A. LaForest (1823-1910) - merchant - San Francisco and NYC (prior to his visual disability)
Address:	72 Apaquogue Road, East Hampton
Name of estate:	*The Apaquogue*
Year of construction:	c. 1884
Style of architecture:	Federal
Architect(s):	
Landscape architect(s):	
Builder:	Edward M. Gay, 1912 addition (for Mrs. Cater)*

House extant: yes
Historical notes:

    Edward A. LaForest, who had been blind since 1865, died in his East Orange, NJ, home of injuries sustained in a fall down the stairs in his East Hampton residence. As a result of his disability, his wife Helen had attended to their financial affairs. She purchased Abraham D. Candy's East Hampton boarding house and 107-acre farm. When the boarding house was destroyed by fire, she built a new boarding house.
    Edward A. and Helen A. LaForest's daughter Minnie married W. Fowler of London, England. Their son Henry, who purchased the boarding house and the farm from his mother in 1895, named it The Apaquogue. [*The East Hampton Star* March 22, 1895, p. 5; May 17, 1895, p. 5; and June 7, 1895, p.1.]
    [See following entry for additional family information.]
    By 1889 Henry's ownership had reverted back to his mother who sold it to B. H. Van Scoy and E. H. Dayton in 1901. [*Suffolk County News* April 27, 1889, p.1, and *The East Hampton Star* October 25, 1901, p. 5.] In 1912 the house was sold to Mrs. Arthur Aymar Cater who, in 1919, sold it to Julian Southall Myrick. He used it as his summer residence which he called *Apaquogue*.
    In 2019, after one hundred years of ownership by Myrick's extended family, the 10,000-square-foot, sixteen-bedroom, seven-bath house and four acres were for sale. The asking price was $16.9 million.
    In 1893 the front porch was added. [*The East Hampton Star* November 24, 1893, p. 5.]
    In 1894 houses were built for the employees. [*The East Hampton Star* June 8, 1894, p. 5.]
    *Gay's 1912 addition consisted of the installation of seven bathrooms and a rear extension for servant's quarters. [*The East Hampton Star* March 22, 1912, p. 5.]

LaForest, Henry A.

Occupation(s):	capitalist - owner, The Apaquogue; a founder, president, and treasurer, Apaquogue Gold Mining Co., Central City, CO, and Nome, AL

Marriage(s):	Clara Belle Rilea (d. 1898)
	   - artist
	     writer

Address:	72 Apaquogue Road, East Hampton
Name of estate:	*The Apaquogue*
Year of construction:	c. 1884
Style of architecture:	Federal
Architect(s):	
Landscape architect(s):	
Builder:	Edward M. Gay, 1912 addition (for Mrs. Cater)*

House extant: yes
Historical notes:

    [See previous entry for history of the premises and additional family information.]

LaMonte, George Mason (1863-1927)

Occupation(s):	financier - president, First National Bank, Bound Brook, NJ; chairman of board, Prudential Insurance Co.; vice-chairman, Federal Reserve Bank of Philadelphia
	industrialist - president, George LaMonte & Son, NYC (manufacturer of safety paper for checks and money orders); president, National Safety Paper Co., Nutley, NJ
	journalist - commercial reporter, Bradstreet Co.
	politician - member, New Jersey Assembly, 1910; New Jersey State Commissioner of Banking and Insurance; member, Democratic National Convention, 1912
Marriage(s):	1887-1927 – Anna Isabel Vaill (1861-1956)
	- Civic Activism - charter member, board of trustees, Bound Brook Memorial Library
Address:	Cottage Avenue, East Hampton
Name of estate:	
Year of construction:	1912
Style of architecture:	Colonial Revival
Architect(s):	John Custis Lawrence designed the house (for LaMonte)
Landscape architect(s):	
Builder:	Edward M. Gay
House extant: yes	
Historical notes:	

The house was built by George Mason LaMonte. [*The East Hampton Star* August 23, 1912, p. 5.]
He was the son of George and Rebecca Thweatt LaMonte.
   Anna Isabel Vaill LaMonte was the daughter of Timothy Dwight and Isabella Mary Breck Vaill of Bound Brook, NJ. Anna's mother summered in East Hampton. Anna's sister Mary, who also resided in East Hampton, married Daniel Talmage, Jr.
   George Mason and Anna Isabel Vaill LaMonte's son George Vaill LaMonte, Sr. married Marjorie Brewster Arnold, the daughter of Francis R. and Mary Martha Parkes Samuels Arnold. Their daughter Isabel married E. Byrne Hackett, the son of John Byrne and Bridget Doheny Hacket of Ireland. Their son Archibald married Helen Craven.

LaMonte, George Mason (1863-1927)

Occupation(s):	*[See previous entry.]*
Marriage(s):	1887-1927 – Anna Isabel Vaill (1861-1956)
	- *[See previous entry.]*
Address:	Dunemere Lane, East Hampton
Name of estate:	
Year of construction:	1927
Style of architecture:	Dutch Revival
Architect(s):	John Custis Lawrence designed the house (for LaMonte)
Landscape architect(s):	
Builder:	Edward M. Gay
House extant: yes	
Historical notes:	

The twelve-room house was built by George Mason LaMonte. [*The East Hampton Star* December 10, 1926.]
[See previous entry for family information.]
   In 1928 the house was purchased by Henry Randolph Sutphen who called it *Bowling Green*. [*The East Hampton Star* April 20, 1928, p.1.]

Lang, Helmut (b. 1956)

Occupation(s):	artist
	fashion designer
	industrialist - fragrance line for men and women
Marriage(s):	
Address:	Further Lane, East Hampton
Name of estate:	
Year of construction:	1600s
Style of architecture:	Salt Box
Architect(s):	
Landscape architect(s):	David Seeler, Bayberry Nursery, Amagansett, 1999 (for Lang)
Builder:	William Simons, alterations (for Tyson)
House extant: yes	
Historical notes:	

In 1949 James Tyson moved the residence of Edward Mulford Baker from Pantigo Road to Further Lane and called it *Old Baker House*. [*The East Hampton Star* August 28, 1975, p. 30, and September 4, 1986, p. 32.] In 1991 it was purchased by Frederic Milton Seegal who renamed it *Old Simons House* in honor of Tyson's builder and caretaker. [*The East Hampton Star* July 3, 1997.] In 1999 Seegal sold the estate to Lang for $15.5 million [*The New York Post* June 24, 2002.]

Langben, Halfred Alfred (1896-1986)

Occupation(s):	shipping - president and chairman of board, Boyd, Weir, and Sewell, NYC (shipping firm)
Marriage(s):	1931-1983 – Mary Anderson Luke (1901-1983)
Address:	46 Dunemere Lane, East Hampton
Name of estate:	
Year of construction:	
Style of architecture:	
Architect(s):	
Landscape architect(s):	
House extant: unconfirmed	
Historical notes:	

The house was built by Thomas Crane. In 1945 Langben purchased the house from the Oteco Corporation. [*The East Hampton Star* November 8, 1945, p. 1.]

The Blue Book of The Hamptons, 1973 lists H. Alfred and Mary A. Luke Langben as residing at 46 Dunemere Lane, East Hampton.

He was the son of J. H. Langben of Galveston, TX.

Mary Anderson Luke Langben was the daughter of David Lincoln and Bessie Caroll Anderson Luke, Sr. of Tarrytown, NY.

Halfred Alfred and Mary Anderson Luke Langben's daughter Mary married Henry Spotswood Fenimore Cooper, the son of Dr. Henry Sage Fenimore Cooper of *Heathcote* in Cooperstown, NY, and resided in NYC. Their daughter Ann married C. Lawson Willard III, the son of C. Lawson Willard, Jr. of New Haven, CT, and resided in NYC.

Lardner, Ringgold Wilmer, Sr. (1885-1933)
aka Ring Lardner

Occupation(s):	journalist - sports columnist
	writer - *Your Know Me Al*, 1916;
	Haircut, 1925;
	Some Like Them Cold;
	The Golden Honeymoon;
	Alibi Ike;
	A Day in the Life of Conrad Green;
	June Moon (play, co-authored with George S. Kaufman);
	Bib Ballads, 1915;
	Gullible's Travels, 1917;
	Treat 'Em Rough, 1918;
	The Big Town, 1921;
	How to Write Short Stories, 1924;
	Round Up, 1929
Marriage(s):	1911-1933 – Ellis Abbott (1887-1960)
Address:	15 West End Avenue, East Hampton
Name of estate:	*Iona Dune / The Mange*
Year of construction:	1927-1928
Style of architecture:	Shingle
Architect(s):	John Custis Lawrence designed the house (for Lardner)
Landscape architect(s):	
Builder:	Edward M. Gay
House extant: yes	
Historical notes:	

The house, originally named *Iona Dune / The Mange*, was built by Ringgold Wilmer Lardner, Sr.
He was the son of Henry and Lena Phillips Lardner.
Ellis Abbott Lardner was the daughter of Frank Abbott of Goshen, IN.

Ringgold Wilmer and Ellis Abbott Lardner's son John was a sports columnist and magazine writer. Their son James was killed in the Spanish Civil War while fighting with the International Brigade. Their son David, a war correspondent, was killed in Germany during World War II. Their son Ringgold Wilmer Lardner, Jr. was a screenwriter and member of the "Hollywood Ten." He was blacklisted for refusing to answer questions of the House Un-American Activities Committee. He later went on to win Academy Awards for "Woman of the Year" (1942) and "MASH" (1970).

The house was severely damaged by the 1931 hurricane, at which time Lardner moved it further back off the dunes to its present position. His good friend and next door neighbor Grantland Rice also moved his home further back of the dunes.

[For information about the Lardners' Kings Point house *The Mange*, see Spinzia, *Long Island: A Guide to New York's Suffolk and Nassau Counties* – Ring Lardner's House—*The Mange*, Kings Point.]

In 1946 Mrs. Lardner sold the house to Joseph Durand Scheerer. It was later owned by his son William Scheerer II.
[*The East Hampton Star* March 7, 1946, p. 8.]

In 2002 the house was again renovated.

Larkin, Adrian Hoffman (1865-1942)

Occupation(s):	attorney - partner, Butler, Notman, Joline, and Mynderse; partner, Joline, Larkin, and Rathbone; partner, Larkin, Rathbone, and Perry
	capitalist - chairman of board, Virginian Railway Co.; director, Brooklyn Union Gas; a founder and director, Home Water Company of East Hampton
	industrialist - director, Sloss Sheffield Steel and Iron Co.; director, Lanston Monotype Machine Co.; director, United States Industrial Alcohol Co.
Civic Activism:	member, Home Defense League during World War I; chairman, Greater New York Draft Board during World War I; president of board, Southampton Hospital; president, Southampton Colonial Society; a founder, Suffolk Hunt Club, 1910; member, Southampton War Memorial Committee, 1923
Marriage(s):	1891-1942 – Katherine Bache Satterthwaite (1866-1960) - president, Southampton Garden Club
Address:	Woods Lane, East Hampton
Name of estate:	*Green Frog*
Year of construction:	1893
Style of architecture:	
Architect(s):	
Landscape architect(s):	
Builder:	Babcock & Grimshaw, 1893 alterations (for Larkin)
House extant: no	
Historical notes:	

In 1893 Larkin remodeled the South End School as his residence, which he called *Green Frog*. [*The East Hampton Star* September 30, 1965, p. 12.]

He was the son of Francis and Sarah Elizabeth Hobby Larkin of Ossining, NY.

Katherine Bache Satterthwaite Larkin was the daughter of James Sheafe and Jane Lawrence Buckley Satterthwaite, Sr. of East Hampton.

Adrian Hoffman and Katherine Bache Satterthwaite Larkin's son James married Vera Agnes Huntington Cravath, the daughter of Paul Drennan and Agnes Huntington Cravath of Lattingtown and Matinecock. James subsequently married Lillian Sibley, the daughter of Grisby Thomas Sibley of Birmingham, AL. [*See* Spinzia, *Long Island's Prominent North Shore Families, vol. I* – Cravath and Larkin entries.] Their daughter Sarah married Albert Palmer Loening, Sr., the son of Albert Michael and Hermine Rubino Loening and resided at *Lallinden* in Southampton. [*See* Spinzia, *Long Island's Prominent Families in the Town of Southampton* – Loening entry.] Their son Lawrence married Rosanne Roudebush and resided at *Stonybroke* in East Hampton.

[See following entry for additional family information.]

By 1900 the house was owned by Clara Cooper Stratton. [*The East Hampton Star* February 9, 1900, p. 5.] It was later owned by Miss Hedwig Monberg who, in 1954, sold the house to Garvin Brackenridge, Sr. [*The East Hampton Star* March 4, 1954, p. 2, and June 24, 1954, p. 2.]

Larkin, Rosanne Roudebush (1897-1977)

Civic Activism:	donated the Agnes R. Day Lecture Hall, East Hampton Free Library, in honor of her sister; co-chair, with her husband Lawrence, art committee, Guild Hall, East Hampton
Marriage(s):	1947-1977 – Lawrence Larkin (1904-1994) - artist professional photographer Civic Activism: co-chair, with his wife Rosanne, art committee, Guild Hall, East Hampton; member, Village of East Hampton Zoning Board
Address:	Georgica Road, East Hampton
Name of estate:	*Stonybroke*
Year of construction:	1902
Style of architecture:	Modified Salt-Box
Architect(s):	
Landscape architect(s):	
House extant: yes	
Historical notes:	

The Blue Book of The Hamptons, 1958 lists Lawrence and Rosanne Roudebush Larkin as residing on Georgica Road, East Hampton.

She was the daughter of John Heywood and Vallory Odell Roudebush who previously owned *Stonybroke*. Rosanne's sister Agnes married Reginald Satterlee Willis, Sr. of Kings Point and, later, Thomas Mills Day, Jr. with whom she resided in East Hampton. [*See* Spinzia, *Long Island's Prominent North Shore Families, vol. II* – Willis entry.]

Lawrence Larkin was the son of Adrian Hoffman and Katherine Bache Satterthwaite Larkin of *Les Alouettes* in Southampton and *Green Frog* in East Hampton. [*See* Spinzia, *Long Island's Prominent Families in the Town of Southampton* – Larkin entry.]

The Larkins did not have children.

[See previous entry for additional family information.]

Laspia, Dr. Michael R. (b. 1921)

Occupation(s):	physician - dentist
Civic Activism:	vice-president, Holy Name Society, St. Philomen Roman Catholic Church, East Hampton; Lions Club
Marriage(s):	1952 – Mary Louise Roesel (b. 1929) - Civic Activism: board president, East Hampton Free Library; president, East Hampton Garden Club; vice-president Eastern Gate Garden Club
Address:	51 Meadow Way, East Hampton
Name of estate:	
Year of construction:	1957
Style of architecture:	Contemporary
Architect(s):	
Landscape architect(s):	
Builder:	Robert Barns
House extant: yes	
Historical notes:	

The 3,500-square-foot, four-bedroom, four-bath house was built by Dr. Michael R. Laspia. [*The East Hampton Star* February 28, 1957, p. 1.]

He is the son of Frank V. and Louise Laspia of Shelter Island.

Mary Louise Roesel Laspia is the daughter of Francis E. and Irene Roesel of Sagaponack.

Laughlin, Alexander Mellon, Jr. (1952-2016)

Occupation(s):	capitalist - chief executive, Alternate Care, Garden City Park (home health care firm)
	industrialist - director, True Tamper Sports; director, National Pen
Civic Activism:	trustee, Laughlin Children's Center, Sewickley, PA;
	trustee, Laughlin Memorial Library, Ambridge, PA;
	trustee and chairman of admission committee, Maidstone Club, East Hampton
Marriage(s):	M/1 – 1983 – Veronica Penelope Whitlock (b. 1961)
	- interior designer - owner, V. W. Interiors LLC, Greenwich, CT
	auctioneer - administrative assistant, William Doyle Galleries, NYC
	educator - teacher, New York School of Interior Design, NYC
	M/2 – 1998-2016 – Mary Kate Edwards (b. 1959)
	- advertising executive - marketing director, Stamford Town Center, Stamford, CT (shopping mall)
Address:	*[unable to confirm street address]*, East Hampton
Name of estate:	
Year of construction:	
Style of architecture:	
Architect(s):	
Landscape architect(s):	
House extant: yes	
Historical notes:	

The Blue Book of The Hamptons, 1992 lists Alexander M. and Veronica P. Whitlock Laughlin, Jr. as residing in East Hampton.

He was the son of Alexander Mellon and Judith Walker Laughlin, Sr. of East Hampton.

Veronica Penelope Whitlock Laughlin is the daughter of Emmet and Gloria Welch Whitlock. [*See* Spinzia, *Long Island's Prominent Families in the Town of Hempstead* - Whitlock entry.] Veronica subsequently married Bruce Dawson Coleman, the son of Central Intelligence Agency operatives Francis I. G. and Julia Montgomery Coleman. [*See* Raymond E. Spinzia, "To Look in the Mirror and See Nothing: Long Islanders and the Office of Strategic Services and Its Successor, the Central Intelligence Agency." wwwspinzialongislandestates.com]

Alexander Mellon and Veronica Penelope Whitlock Laughlin, Jr.'s daughter Julia resides in Greenwich, CT.

Mary Kate Edwards Laughlin is the daughter of Eugene G. and Jacqueline Ough Edwards of Lincoln, NE.

[See other Laughlin entries for additional family information.]

Laughlin, Alexander Mellon, Sr. (b. 1925)

Occupation(s):	financier - vice-chairman of board, Jessup and Lamont, Inc. (stock brokerage firm);
	associate director, Tucker, Anthony and R. L. Day, NY (investment banking firm);
	investment manager, Deltec Asset Management Corp., NY
Civic Activism:	chairman of trustees, National Gallery of Art, Washington, D.C.;
	trustee, John A. Hartford Foundation, NY;
	a founder, with his wife Judith, Alexander M. and Judith W. Laughlin Family Foundation;
	trustee, Southampton Hospital;
	president and secretary, Maidstone Club, East Hampton;
	secretary, Old East Hampton (organization whose members have summered in East Hampton for at least 25 years)
Marriage(s):	1947 – Judith Walker
	- Civic Activism: vice-president, Metropolitan Opera Association
	a founder, with her husband Alexander, Alexander M. and Judith W. Laughlin Family Foundation;
	trustee, Peconic Land Trust;
	member, board of managers, East Hampton Free Library

Address: 29 Ocean Avenue, East Hampton
Name of estate:
Year of construction:
Style of architecture:
Architect(s):
Landscape architect(s):
House extant: yes
Historical notes:

In 1954 Laughlin purchased the Apaquogue Road residence of Dr. Eugene Seeley Coler. [*The East Hampton Star* June 3, 1954, p. 7.]

The *Social Register Summer, 1996* lists Alexander M. and Judith Walker Laughlin [Sr.] as residing on Ocean Avenue, East Hampton. By 1996 the Laughlins had relocated to Ocean Avenue.

He is the son of Alexander and Margaret Mellon Laughlin of Pittsburgh, PA. Margaret Mellon Laughlin subsequently married Thomas Hitchcock, Jr. and resided in Sands Point and at *Broad Hollow Farm* in Old Westbury. [*See* Spinzia, *Long Island's Prominent North Shore Families, vol. I* – Hitchcock entries.]*

Judith Walker Laughlin is the daughter of Delos and Nina Elizabeth Sebring Walker of East Hampton. Judith's sister Nina married Carroll Livingston Wainwright, Jr., the son of Carroll Livingston and Edith Catherine Gould Wainwright, Sr. of *Gullcrest* in East Hampton, and resided in East Hampton.

Alexander Mellon and Judith Walker Laughlin, Sr.'s daughter Nina married John Taylor Bottomley, the son of Dr. George T. Bottomley of *Little Boars Head* in North Hampton, NH, and resides in Rye Beach, NH. Their son Alexander Mellon Laughlin, Jr, who resides in East Hampton, married Veronica Penelope Whitlock and, later, Mary Kate Edwards. Their son David, who subsequently owned the East Hampton house, married Martha Brooke Clarke, the daughter of Charles Herbert Clarke.

*[*See* Raymond E. Spinzia. "Adultery, Drugs, Murder, Untimely Deaths, and Long Island's Prominent Families: A Tangled Web." wwwspinzialongislandestates.com for Alexander's half-brother Thomas Hitchcock II's Millbrook, NY, estate.]

[See other Laughlin entries for additional family information.]

Laughlin, David Walker (b. 1958)

Occupation(s):	financier - vice-chairman of board and director, Inverness Counsel, Inc., NYC (investment counseling firm)
Civic Activism:	director, Laughlin Memorial Library, Ambridge, PA; director, Laughlin Children's Center, Sewickley, PA; trustee, Laughlin Memorial Inc., Pittsburgh, PA; treasurer, George L. Ohrstrom, Jr. Foundation
Marriage(s):	1984 – Martha Brooke Clarke (aka Brooke Clarke) - entertainers and associated professions - associate producer, Independent News, NYC
Address:	29 Ocean Avenue, East Hampton
Name of estate:	
Year of construction:	
Style of architecture:	
Architect(s):	
Landscape architect(s):	
House extant: yes	
Historical notes:	

The house was previously owned by David's parents Alexander Mellon and Judith Walker Laughlin, Sr. Martha Brooke Clarke Laughlin in the daughter of Charles Herbert Clarke.

Lauren, Ralph (b. 1939)
aka Ralph Lifshitz

Occupation(s):	fashion designer - CEO, Ralph Lauren Corporation industrialist - manufacturer of women's and men's clothing and accessories
Civic Activism:	co-founder, Nina Hyde Center for Breast Cancer Research, Georgetown University, Washington, DC; founder Polo Ralph Lauren Foundation; founder, Ralph Lauren Center for Cancer Care and Prevention, NYC
Marriage(s):	1964 - Ricky Anne Loew–Beer (b. 1943) - writer professional photographer
Address:	Old Montauk Highway, Montauk
Name of estate:	
Year of construction:	
Style of architecture:	
Architect(s):	
Landscape architect(s):	
House extant: yes	
Historical notes:	

In 1961 Edward Franklin Albee III purchased the house for $40,000. In 2018 the Albee Foundation listed the 2,970-square-foot, four-bedroom, three-full-and-two-half-bath house and 2.8 acres for sale. The asking price was $20 million. In 2019 it was purchased by Lauren.

Born in The Bronx, he is the son of Frank and Fraydl Kotlar Lifshitz.

Ricky Ann Loew–Beer Lauren is the daughter of Rudolph and Margaret Vytouch Loew–Beer.

Ralph and Ricky Ann Loew–Beer Lauren's son David married Lauren Bush. She is the daughter of Neil and Sharon Smith Bush and the granddaughter of President George Herbert Walker Bush and First Lady Barbara Pierce Bush. Their daughter Dylan married Paul Arrouet. Their son Andrew is a motion picture producer.

Lawrence, John Custis (1867-1944)

Occupation(s):	architect
	[See architect appendix in this volume for Lawrence's commission in East Hampton.]
	capitalist - director, Hamptons Hotel Corp.
Civic Activism:	a founder and director, Munchogue Club
Marriage(s):	M/1 – Mattie Davis (1874-1893)
	M/2 – 1893-1944 – Phoebe Alice Edwards (1873-1959)
Address:	Montauk Highway, East Hampton
Name of estate:	
Year of construction:	1899
Style of architecture:	Contemporary
Architect(s):	John Custis Lawrence designed his own house
Landscape architect(s):	
House extant: yes	
Historical notes:	

The house was built by John Custis Lawrence.

Born in *First House* in Montauk, he was the son of sea-captain John Bartlett Lawrence and Mrs. Nancy Edwards Lawrence. His sister Nellie married Nathan Newton Tiffany III and resided in East Hampton.

Mattie Davis Lawrence was the daughter of Samuel T. and Adaline S. Davis.

John Custis and Mattie Davis Lawrence's son Francis married Lillian Foiren and resided in Southington, CT.

Phoebe Alice Edwards Lawrence was the daughter of John Dudley and Alice M. Edwards. She had previously been married to Isaac Lawrence.

John Custis and Phoebe Alice Edwards Lawrence's daughter Mattie married Edward Fitzgerald, the son of E. Joseph Fitzgerald of Brooklyn, and resided in East Hampton. Their daughter Irene married Samuel Howell Phillips of Westhampton and resided in Milford, CT. Their daughter Marion married Darrell Parsons and resided in East Hampton. Their son Wallace died in 1921 at the age of five.

Leaman, Alfred Valentine, Jr. (1878-1933)

Occupation(s):	capitalist - president, W. A. Leaman, NYC (importing firm)
Marriage(s):	1906-1932 – Dorothea Carter (1884-1932)
Address:	115 Apaquogue Road, East Hampton
Name of estate:	*Sunset Cottage*
Year of construction:	
Style of architecture:	Shingle
Architect(s):	
Landscape architect(s):	
House extant: yes	
Historical notes:	

The *Social Directory of Southampton, Long Island, 1931* lists Alfred V. and Dorothy Carter Leaman, Jr. as residing at *Sunset Cottage* on Apaquogue Road in East Hampton.

He was the son of Alfred Valentine and Laura Josephine Williams Leaman, Sr.

Dorothea Carter Leaman was the daughter of Henry Levis and Julia L. Phillips Carter.

Alfred Valentine and Dorothea Carter Leaman, Jr.'s son Alfred Valentine Leaman III, who resided at *Swan Cross* in East Hampton, married Eunice Putnam.

Leaman was killed in an automobile accident when his car was side-swiped on Montauk Highway.

The five-bedroom, four-bath, 4,000-square-foot house was subsequently owned by their son Alfred Valentine Leaman III and, then, by Nora Ephron.

[See following entry for additional Leaman family information.]

Leaman, Alfred Valentine, III (1906-1966)

Occupation(s):	financier - member, M. C. Bouvier and Co. (stock brokerage firm); member, Richard W. Clark (produce exchange)
Marriage(s):	1930-div. 1937 – Eunice Putnam (1907-1972)
Address:	Apaquogue Road, East Hampton
Name of estate:	*Swan Cross*
Year of construction:	
Style of architecture:	
Architect(s):	
Landscape architect(s):	
House extant: unconfirmed	
Historical notes:	

The *Social Directory of Southampton, Long Island, 1931* lists Alfred V. and Eunice Putnam Leaman as residing at *Swan Cross* in East Hampton.

He was the son of Alfred Valentine and Dorothea Carter Leaman, Jr. of *Sunset Cottage* in East Hampton.

Eunice Putnam Leaman was the daughter of Israel and Louise Carlton Putnam and an heir to the Putnam publishing fortune. She had previously been married to John Chadbourne. After her divorce from Leaman, Eunice married Harry Van Alst Brower.

After his divorce from Eunice Leaman, Alfred resided at his parent's former residence *Sunset Cottage*.

[See previous entry for additional family information.]

Le Brecht, Sheila Tucker Brown (d. 2000)

Marriage(s):	1954-div. – Robert Le Brecht - financier - vice-president, R. W. Pressprick Co. (stock brokerage firm) Civic Activism: director, Maidstone Club, East Hampton
Address:	90 Egypt Lane, East Hampton
Name of estate:	
Year of construction:	
Style of architecture:	
Architect(s):	
Landscape architect(s):	
House extant: unconfirmed	
Historical notes:	

The Blue Book of The Hamptons, 1973 lists Mrs. Sheila Tucker Brown Le Brecht as residing at 90 Egypt Lane, East Hampton.

Sheila was the daughter of David Fisher Brown. She had previously been married to John Courtland Maxwell, Jr.

Robert Le Brecht was the son of William Marston Le Brecht of Brewster, NY. Robert had previously been married to Louise Lutkins, the daughter of Clinton Stephen and Nellie Barnum Dingee Lutkins of East Hampton. After her divorce from Robert, Louise married William Doerr. Robert married Sheila Tucker Brown and, subsequently, Carol Carter Straton, the daughter of John Charles Straton.

Robert and Louise Lutkins Le Brecht's daughter Sandra married Willard H. Robb, the son of Willard F. Robb of Guilford, CT.

By 1987 Mrs. Le Brecht had relocated to 35 Meadow Way, East Hampton.

Lee, James Thomas (1877-1968)

Occupation(s):	attorney
	capitalist - president, Shelton Holding Corp. (New York City real estate)*;
	president and director, Shelton Holding Co., NYC (real estate holding firm);
	president and director, 740 Park Avenue Corp. (real estate holding firm);
	director, Winmore Realty Corp.;
	director, William Street Corp. (real estate holding firm);
	director, American Express Co.
	financier - vice-president and director, Chase National Bank;
	chairman of board and president, Central Savings Bank;
	director, Eagle Indemnity Co.;
	director, Northern Insurance Co.;
	director, Newark Fire Insurance Co.;
	director, Chase Safe Deposit Co.
Civic Activism:	trustee and vice-president, Memorial Hospital for Treatment of Cancer and Allied Diseases, NYC;
	trustee, Sloane–Kettering Cancer Center, NYC;
	director, Fifth Avenue Association;
	member, Mayor's Business Advisory Board
Marriage(s):	1903-1943 – Margaret A. Merritt (1877-1943)
	- educator - teacher
Address:	Ocean and Lee Avenues, East Hampton
Name of estate:	
Year of construction:	1889
Style of architecture:	Shingle
Architect(s):	Joseph Greenleaf Thorp designed the house (for W. B. Smith)
	John Custis Lawrence, 1916 alterations (for Eastman)
Landscape architect(s):	
House extant: yes	
Historical notes:	

The house was built by Warren G. Smith. It 1916 it was purchased by Joseph Eastman from Mrs. Smith. [*The East Hampton Star* September 15, 1916, p. 7.]

In 1937 Lee purchased Joseph Eastman's twelve-room house at auction. [*The New York Times* September 29, 1937, p. 41.] He was the son of Dr. James and Mrs. Mary Theresa Norton Lee of Manhattan.

Margaret A. Merritt Lee was the daughter of Thomas Merritt of Savannah, GA.

James Thomas and Margaret A. Merritt Lee's daughter Winifred married Franklin d'Olier, Jr. and resided in East Hampton. Their daughter Janet married John Vernou Bouvier III with whom she resided at *Rowdy Hall* and *Little House* in East Hampton. Janet later married Hugh Dudley Auchincloss and, subsequently, Bingham William Morris with whom she resided at *Pra–Qua–Les* in Southampton. [*See* Spinzia, *Long Island's Prominent Families in the Town of Southampton* – Bouvier and Morris entries.] Their daughter Marian married John J. Ryan, Jr.

*Lee conceived and executed the construction of more than two hundred buildings in Manhattan.

Lee, Thomas Haskell (b. 1944)

Occupation(s):	financer -	founder, Thomas H. Lee Partners, LP; founder, Thomas H. Lee Capital Management, LLC (hedge fund); partner, Lee Equity Partners; CEO and president, THL Investment Capital Corp.; general partner, ML – Lee Acquisition Fund; vice-president, First National Bank, Boston, MA; security analyst, Institutional research department, LE Rothschild Co.; member, national advisory board, J. P. Morgan Chase & Co.; director, First Security Services Corp.; director, Mid Cap Financial
	merchant -	chairman of board, Hills Stores Co. (department store chain)
	capitalist -	director, Warner Music Group Corp.
Civic Activism:		vice-president, Whitney Museum of American Art, NYC; director, Lincoln Center for the Performing Arts, NYC; donated $22 million to Harvard University, Cambridge, MA; trustee, Beth Israel Deaconess Medical Center; trustee, Brandeis University, Waltham, MA; trustee, Harvard University, Cambridge, MA; trustee, Museum of Fine Arts, Boston, MA; trustee, Rockefeller University Museum, NYC; trustee, Mount Sinai – NYU Medical Center, NYC; trustee, Cardoza Law School, Yeshiva University, NYC; trustee, combined Jewish Philanthropies of Greater Boston; trustee, Intrepid Museum Foundation, NYC

Marriage(s):		M/1 – 1968-div. 1995 – Barbara Ellen Fish (b. 1945)
		   - educator - teacher of French, Arlington, MA
		  social worker
		  Civic Activism:
		    founder, Barbara Lee Family Foundation;
		    chair, advisory council, Emerge Massachusetts;
		    vice-chair of trustees, Institute of Contemporary Art, Boston, MA;
		    member, collection committee, Harvard University Art Museum, Cambridge, MA;
		    member, visiting committee, Museum of Fine Art, Boston, MA;
		    trustee and founding chairman, contemporary arts program, Isabella Stewart Gardner Museum, Boston, MA;
		    funded public art projects;
		    a founder, White House Project;
		    a founder, Simmons Institute for Leadership and Change;
		    founder, Family Policy Center, The Heller School, Brandeis University, Waltham, MA;
		    founder, women's study program, Brandeis University, Waltham, MA
		M/2 – Ann Tenenbaum
		   - Civic Activism - donor, with her husband Thomas, to various charities

Lee, Thomas Haskell (cont'd)

Address: 43 East Dune Lane, East Hampton
Name of estate:
Year of construction:
Style of architecture:
Architect(s):
Landscape architect(s):
House extant: yes*
Historical notes:

    The house was previously owned by Caroline Lee Bouvier Radziwill. In 2001 Radziwill sold the house to Lee for $19 million.
    He is the son of Herbert C. Lee (formerly Leibowitz) and Mildred Schiff Lee of Belmont, MA.
    Barbara Ellen Fish Lee is the daughter of Dr. Sidney Z. Fish of West Orange, NJ.
    *Lee demolished Radziwill's house and built a new house observing the same exterior but with a new infrastructure.
    In 2013 the house sustained a fire in the basement pantry. There was extensive smoke damage in the remainder of the house.

Leith, Donald E. (1898-1983)

Occupation(s): financier - senior consultant on pension plans, New England Mutual Insurance Co.
Civic Activism: director, Maidstone Club, East Hampton;
member, admission committee, University Club, NYC

Marriage(s): M/1 – 1934-div. – Phyllis Cunningham
M/2 – 1941-1983 – Delphis Bainbridge King (1905-2003)

Address: 29 Dunemere Lane, East Hampton
Name of estate:
Year of construction: 1900
Style of architecture: Stucco Cottage
Architect(s): Grosvenor Atterbury designed the house (for B. Richards)
Landscape architect(s):
Builder: Jabez E. Van Orden
House extant: yes
Historical notes:

    The house, originally named *Clas-des-Lilas*, was built by Benjamin Richards, Jr. It was later owned by his daughter Louisa Verplanck Richards who sold it to Leith.
    He was the son of Samuel and Lillian T. Leith of NYC.
    Phyllis Cunningham Leith was the daughter of John F. Cunningham of Bloomfield, NJ.
    The Blue Book of The Hamptons, 1979 lists Donald E. and Delphis B. King Leith as residing at 29 Dunemere Lane, East Hampton.
    Delphi Bainbridge King Leith was the daughter of Robert Morgan King of *Kingsway* in Old Field. She had previously been married to Finley Bailey Krause, the son of Dr. Carl Albert Krause of Brooklyn.
    In 2004 the six-bedroom, five-and-a-half-bath house and one acre sold for $3 million.

Lembcke, George Albert (1874-1949)

Occupation(s):	capitalist - secretary, Bernut, Lembcke, & Co., NYC (creosote importing firm)
Marriage(s):	1910-div. – Molly Susannah Zoller
Address:	Apaquogue Road, East Hampton
Name of estate:	*The Chimneys*
Year of construction:	1922
Style of architecture:	
Architect(s):	
Landscape architect(s):	
House extant: unconfirmed	
Historical notes:	

The house, originally named *The Chimneys*, was built by George Albert Lembcke. [*The East Hampton Star* August 18, 1922, p. 5.]

The Directory of American Society: New York State and the Metropolitan District, 1929 lists George A. and Molly Susannah Zoller Lembcke as residing at *The Chimneys* in Easthampton [East Hampton],

He was born in Germany.

Molly Susannah Zoller Lembcke was the daughter of Charles Zoller of Manhattan.

George Albert and Molly Susannah Zoller Lembcke's daughter Molly married Baron Francesco Zezza, the son of Baron Giuseppe Zezza di Campomarino of Rome, Italy.

In 1940 the house was purchased and remodeled by John Lawrence Hutton, Sr. who called it *Peep O'Day*. [*The Brooklyn Daily Eagle* April 21, 1940, p. 20, and *The East Hampton Star* February 12, 1948, p. 1.]

In 1951 it was purchased by Robert McClellen Simonds. [*The East Hampton Star* January 3, 1952, p. 1.]

Leonard, Stephen Joseph, Sr. (1875-1949)

Occupation(s):	financier - partner, S. J. Leonard and Co. (stock brokerage firm)
	merchant - president, Arnold, Constable, & Co. (department store)
Marriage(s):	M/1 – 1906-div. – Adelaide Shanahan (1881-1964)
	M/2 – 1929 – Alma Mae Curtis (b. 1898)
Address:	Ocean Avenue, East Hampton
Name of estate:	*Waterwood*
Year of construction:	1878-1880
Style of architecture:	Stick-style
Architect(s):	James Renwick, Jr. designed the house (for F. Gallatin)
Landscape architect(s):	Charles Nassau Lowrie, Sr. (for Leonard)
House extant: no; demolished in 1930s	
Historical notes:	

The house, originally named *Breezy Lawn*, was built by Frederic Gallatin. In 1919 it was purchased by Leonard who renamed it *Waterwood*. [*The East Hampton Star* March 15, 1979, p. 22.]

The *Long Island Society Register, 1929* lists Stephen J. and Adelaide Shanahan Leonard [Sr.] as residing at *Waterwood* in East Hampton.

He was the son of Thomas and Catharine Leonard.

Adelaide Shanahan Leonard was the daughter of Flora Rice Shanahan of Brooklyn.

Stephen Joseph and Adelaide Shanahan Leonard, Sr.'s daughter Stephanie married Chauncey Bradley Ives II, the son of Harry Davis and Elsie M. Young Ives of Southampton, and resided at *Dingle Ridge Farm* in Brewster, NY. Their son Craigh married Jane C. Mellon, the daughter of Edward Purcell and Ethel Churchill Humphrey Mellon of *Villa Maria* in Southampton, and resided in Southampton. [*See* Spinzia, *Long Island's Prominent Families in the Town of Southampton* –Leonard and Mellon entries.] Their daughter Jeanne married John Barbey Lewis, the son of Roger and Ida May Barbey Lewis of East Hampton.

Alma Mae Curtis Leonard was the daughter of Harry Fitz William and Margaret Emma Hoffner Curtis of Overbrook, PA. Alma had been previously married to George Albert Huhn III.

In 1943 the Hook Pond Corporation purchased the estate's ground for development. [*The East Hampton Star* October 10, 1968, p. 16.]

LeRoy, Warner (1935-2001)

Occupation(s):	capitalist / restaurateur -
	founder and president, LeRoy Adventures (holding company for Maxwell Plum, NYC and San Francisco; Tavern on the Green, NYC; Russian Tea Room, NYC; Potomac, Washington, DC; Great Adventure Park, Jackson Township, NJ; and York Cinema)
	entertainers and associated professions -
	produced and directed Off-Broadway plays
Marriage(s):	M/1 – Genevieve *[unable to determine maiden name]* (aka Gen LeRoy)
	- model;
	writer - plays, motion pictures, cookbooks, and children's books
	M/2 – 1971-div. 1999 – Kay O'Reilly
Address:	600 Old Stone Highway, Amagansett
Name of estate:	*Southwood Court*
Year of construction:	c. 1980
Style of architecture:	Contemporary
Architect(s):	
Landscape architect(s):	
House extant: unconfirmed	
Historical notes:	

   The 12,000-square-foot house, originally named *Southwood Court*, was built by Warner LeRoy.
   He was the son of Mervyn and Doris Ruth Warner LeRoy and the grandson of Harry Warner, a founder of Warner Brothers Studios.
   Genevieve _____ LeRoy subsequently married Anthony John Walton with whom she resided in Sag Harbor.
   Warner and Kay O'Reilly LeRoy's son Maximillian died in 2005 at the age of thirty from injuries sustained in a motorcycle accident. Their daughter Jennifer married Steven Michel King and resides at *Oz Farm* in Saugerties, NY.
   Kay was awarded *Southwood Court* as part of her divorce settlement.
   In 2004 the eleven-bedroom, twelve-bath house and fifty acres were sold to Michael Minkoff and Michael Araus for $14.75 million. They subdivided the property. [*The New York Times* July 11, 2004, p. L13.]

Levering, Julia Henderson (1851-1922)

Occupation(s):	writer - *Historic Indiana*, 1909; numerous periodical articles
Civic Activism:	suffragist*
Marriage(s):	1872-1909 – John Mortimer Levering [Sr.] (1849-1909) - financier - founder, Mortimer Levering Investments (investment banking firm); president, Columbia National Bank industrialist - a founder, Indiana Oil Refining Co. Civic Activism: secretary, National Wool Growers Association; a founder and president, American Shopshire Breeders' Association, Lafayette, IN; president, Commercial Club; president, Humane Society; president, Good Roads Club; president, Home Hospital Association, Lafayette, IN; secretary and treasurer, International Live Stock Exposition, Chicago, IL; a founder, Saddle and Sirloin Club, Chicago, IL
Address:	18 Cranberry Lane, Amagansett
Name of estate:	
Year of construction:	1910
Style of architecture:	Shingle
Architect(s):	Tietig and Lee designed the house (for J. H. Levering)
Builder:	Thomas E. Babcock

House extant: yes
Historical notes:

The 4,896-square-foot, six-bedroom house was built by Richmond Levering, Sr. for his mother Julia Henderson Levering after the death of her husband.

She was the daughter of Albert and Lorana Richmond Henderson of Covington, IN.

John Mortimer Levering was the son of William Hagy and Irene Smith Levering of Philadelphia, PA.

John Mortimer and Julia Henderson Levering's son Richmond, who resided at *Devon* in Amagansett, married Laura C. Barnum and, later, Helen Jean Allen.

[See following entry for additional family information.]

In 1930 the house was purchased by Jorje Ezequiel Zalles. [*The New York Times* April 6, 1930, p. 52.] It was later owned by Richard Seymour Jackson. In 1986 it was purchased by Lucy Allison Bishopric Cookson.

In 2014 the main residence, a two-bedroom, one-bath guest house, and 5.2 acres were for sale. The asking price was $13 million. In 2015 the price was reduced to $11.8 million.

*For other Long Islanders involved in the suffrage movement *see* Raymond E. Spinzia, "Winning the Franchise: Long Island Activists in the Fight for Woman's Suffrage and Their Opponents, Long Island's Anti-Suffragists." wwwspinzialongislandestates.com.

Levering, Richmond, Sr. (1881-1920)
aka John Richmond Levering, Sr.;
John Mortimer Levering, Jr.

Occupation(s):	industrialist - president, Richmond Levering & Co. (oil drilling firm);
	a founder and president, Metropolitan Petroleum Corp., DE;
	a founder and president, Island Oil and Transport Co.;
	president, Indian Refining Co.;
	president, Arkansas Valley Gas Co.
	capitalist - a founder, Gardiner Bay Co. (real estate holding company)
Civic Activism:	chief, Secret Service Division, American Protective League of New York, during World War I*;
	founded, Amagansett Public Library;
	a founder, Devon Yacht Club, Amagansett;
	a founder, Gardiner's Bay Boat Club
Marriage(s):	M/1 – 1905-div. 1915 – Laura C. Barnum (1880-1964)
	M/2 – 1915-1920 – Helen Jean Allen (b. 1881)
Address:	Cross Highway, Amagansett
Name of estate:	*Devon*
Year of construction:	c. 1910
Style of architecture:	Mediterranean Villa
Architect(s):	Tietig and Lee designed the house (for R. Levering, Sr.)
Landscape architect(s):	
House extant: yes	
Historical notes:	

The house, originally named *Devon*, was built by Richmond Levering, Sr.

He was the son of John Mortimer and Julia Henderson Levering [Sr.] of Cincinnati, OH.

Laura C. Barnum Levering was the daughter of William Milo and Anne Theresa Phelps Barnum of New York.

Richmond and Laura C. Barnum Levering, Sr.'s son Walter, who resided in Greenwich, CT, secretly married Elizabeth Gerard, the daughter of Julian M. Gerard of Newport, RI, without the knowledge of either their parents or friends. [*The New York Times* January 11, 1933, p. 6.] Elizabeth was the niece of James Watson Gerard II, the United States Ambassador to Germany during World War I, who resided in Lloyd Harbor. [*See* Spinzia, *Long Island's Prominent North Shore Families, vol. I* – Gerard entry.]

[See previous entry for additional family information.]
  *For German sabotage activities in New York, *see* Raymond E. Spinzia, "The Involvement of Long Islanders in the Events Surrounding German Sabotage in the New York Metropolitan Area 1914-1917." wwwspinzialongislandestates.com.

In 1920 the house was purchased by M. Materson. [*The East Hampton Star* October 22, 1920, p. 6.] In 1930 it was purchased by John Louis Kuser, Jr. from Ardis J. Reynolds. [*The East Hampton Star* October 3, 1930, p. 1.] In c. 1946 it was purchased by George Epworth Devendorf who called it *El Pasaiso*. [*The East Hampton Star* July 18, 1946, p. 2.] The house was later owned by Henry Houston Chatfield who called it *Devon*.

Levi, Charles Matthew

Occupation(s):	entertainers and associated professions - motion picture director
	capitalist - co-founder, director, and general manager, Charlex, 1978 (post production firm that specializes in graphics and special effects)
	writer - *Loco Parentis* (novel); motion picture scripts
Marriage(s):	
Address:	115 De Forest Road, Montauk
Name of estate:	
Year of construction:	1883
Style of architecture:	Beach Cottage
Architect(s):	McKim, Mead & White designed the house (for Benson)
Landscape architect(s):	Frederick Law Olmsted designed the site plan (for Benson)
Builder:	George A. Eldredge & Son, 1914 alterations (for Mary Benson)
	Mead and Taft

House extant: yes
Historical notes:

The 4,000-square-foot house, originally named *Weeweecho*, was built by Arthur W. Benson. It was inherited by the Bensons' daughter Mary, who continued to call it *Weeweecho*. The house was later owned by Marion Bolton Marsh, who called it *Windway* and, then, by her daughter Penelope and son-in-law Holger Lundbergh, who called it *Bayberry*. It was purchased by Levi in 1981.

In 1995 the house sold for $700,000.

Levy–Church, Kenneth (b. 1958)
aka Kenneth Wayne Church

Occupation(s):	educator - assistant professor, Eurasian history, St Lawrence University, Canton, NY
Civic Activism:	a founder, Ken and Jeanne Levy–Church Fund to Improve Cardiovascular Access;
	a founder, with his wife Jeanne, Fair Food Foundation, Ann Arbor, MI;
	a founder, with his wife Jeanne, JEHT Foundation, NYC (promotes justice, equality, human dignity, and tolerance);
	vice-president and director, The Betty & Norman F. Levy Foundation
Marriage(s):	Jeanne Diane Levy (b. 1954)
	- entertainers and association professions -
	co-producer, with her husband Jeffery Kusama Hinte:
	"The Hawk is Dying," 2007 (motion picture);
	"The Last Winter," 2007 (motion picture)
	- Civic Activism: a founder, with her husband Kenneth, Fair Food Foundation, Ann Arbor, MI;
	a founder, with her husband Kenneth, JEHT Foundation, NYC (promotes justice, equality, human dignity, and tolerance)
	co-president and director, The Betty & Norman F. Levy Foundation
Address:	230 and 234 Old Montauk Highway, Montauk
Name of estate:	
Year of construction:	2006
Style of architecture:	Modern
Architect(s):	James Biber of Pentagram designed the compound (for Levy–Church)*
Landscape architect(s):	
House extant: yes	
Historical notes:	

The house was built by Kenneth Levy–Church.

Jeanne Diane Levy–Church is the daughter of real estate tycoon Norman F. Levy and his wife Betty Levy, who named their children and Bernard Lawrence Madoff as executors of their estate. As a result of the losses sustained in the collapse of Madoff's Ponzi scheme, both the Fair and Food Foundation and the JEHT Foundation were forced to stop making grants. Jeanne had previously been married to Jeffery Levy–Hinte (aka Jeffery Kusama Hinte).

*The main residence won the American Institute of Architecture Award.

In 2013 the 5,000-square-foot main residence and the 2,400-square-foot guest house were sold to Michael Hirtenstein for $13 million. In 2018 it was sold by Hirtenstein. The asking price was $21 million.

Lewis, Ida May Barbey (1878-1960)

Civic Activism:	board chair, YWCA's Roberts House, NYC
Marriage(s):	1899-1928 – Roger Lewis (1872-1928)
	(aka Joshua Roger Lewis)
	- attorney
Address:	Dunemere Lane, East Hampton
Name of estate:	
Year of construction:	
Style of architecture:	
Architect(s):	
Landscape architect(s):	
House extant: unconfirmed	
Historical notes:	

In 1944 Mrs. Lewis purchased the house from Mrs. Austin H. Culver. [*The East Hampton Star* November 23, 1944, p. 1.]

The Blue Book of The Hamptons, 1958 lists Mrs. Roger Lewis as residing on Dunemere Lane, East Hampton.

She was the daughter of Reading, PA, brewer John Edward Barbey and his wife Mary Ellen Garst Barbey.

Roger Lewis was the son of John E. and Sarah C. Hoff Lewis.

Roger and Ida May Barbey Lewis' daughter Anne married Edward Ritzen Perry. Their daughter Mary married Russell Hopkinson, the son of Ernest and Bessie Barnes Hopkinson, and resided in East Hampton. Their son John married Jeanne Leonard, the daughter of Stephen Joseph and Adelaide Shanahan Leonard, Sr. of East Hampton.

Lewis, Reginald F. (1942-1993)

Occupation(s):	attorney - member, Paul, Weiss, Rifkind, Wharton, and Garrison; partner, Lewis and Clarkson; partner, Murphy, Thorpe, and Lewis
	capitalist - founder, TLC Group, LP (venture capitalist firm)
	industrialist - founder, chairman, and CEO, TLC Beatrice International (formerly, Beatrice Foods)
	writer - *Why Should White Guys Have All the Fun*, 2005
Civic Activism:	founder, Reginald F. Lewis Foundation; founder, Reginald F. Lewis Museum of Maryland African American History and Culture; donated $3 million to Harvard Law School, Cambridge, MA; member, New York City's Council of Economic Advisors (Dinkins administration); director, NAACP Legal Defense Fund
Marriage(s):	1969-1993 – Loida Nicholas (b. 1942)
	- industrialist - chair and CEO, TLC Beatrice International, 1994-2000
	writer - co-author, *How to Get a Green Card*
	attorney - Immigration and Naturalization Services, 1979-1990*
	Civic Activism: founder, The Lewis College, Sorsogon City, The Philippines; member, Law Students Civil Right Research Council, 1969; a founder and board chair, National Association of Filipino American Associations, 2002-2006; a founder and board chair, Us Pinoys for Good Governance; trustee, Philippine Development Foundation; a founder, Asian American Legal Defense & Education Fund; director, National Catholic Reporter; director, Apollo Theater Foundation
Address:	off Springs – Amagansett Road, Amagansett
Name of estate:	
Year of construction:	c. 1916
Style of architecture:	Neo-Georgian
Architect(s):	Trowbridge and Livingston designed the house (for D. M. Bell)
Landscape architect(s):	
Builder:	William Crawford

House extant: no; destroyed by fire, 1991**
Historical notes:

The room twenty-one-room house, originally named *Broadview*, was located on Gardiner's Bay. It was built by Dr. Dennistoun Mildeberger Bell. It was later owned by Amagan, Inc. In 1988 Reginald F. Lewis purchased the estate from Amagan, Inc.

He was the son of Carolyn Lewis.

Born in Sorsogon, Bicol, The Philippines, Loida Nicholas Lewis is the daughter of Francisco J. Nicholas of The Philippines.

Reginald F. and Loida Nicholas Lewis' daughter Christina married Daniel Halpern, the son of Joseph and Joan Halpern of Brookline, MA. Their daughter Leslie married Gavin Rodney Sword, the son of Rodney D. and Delana Sword of Nanaimo, Canada.

*Loida, who was inducted into the Asian Hall of Fame, was the first Asian to pass the New York bar exam without having attended law school in the United States.

**Lewis owned the house at the time it was destroyed by fire.

Lilley, Alexander Neil, Sr. (1905-1976)

Occupation(s):	financier - executive, Chase Securities Corp., 1929-1933
	industrialist - executive, Sperry Flour Co., 1925-1929;
	vice-president and director, Societe des Raffineries
	de Petrole de la Gironde, Paris, France (oil firm);
	executive, Pacific Coast region, Texaco, Inc., 1933-1942;
	general manager and vice-president, Eastern Hemisphere,
	Texaco, Inc.;
	president, Texaco Canada, 1957-1963;
	president and chairman of board, Caltex Petroleum Corp.
Civic Activism:	director, Maidstone Club, East Hampton
Marriage(s):	1935-1976 – Elena Musto
Address:	Crossways, East Hampton
Name of estate:	*Crossways*
Year of construction:	1902
Style of architecture:	Shingle
Architect(s):	George A. Eldredge and John Custis Lawrence designed the house (for W. W. Benjamin, Jr.)
Landscape architect(s):	Marian Cruger Coffin designed perennial garden with privet arch, the small pool, and long grass *allee*, c. 1928 (for Mrs. W. W. Benjamin, Jr.)

House extant: yes
Historical notes:

    The house, originally named *Crossways*, was built by William Wallace Benjamin, Jr. It was later owned by his son William Wallace Benjamin III. The house was subsequently owned by Lilley.
    The Blue Book of The Hamptons, 1958, 1965, and *1973* list Alex Neil and Elena Musto Lilley as residing at *Crossways* in East Hampton.
    He was the son of Alexander Spinning and Marie Juliette Williams Lilley of California.
    Elena Musto Lilley was the daughter of Geuido Musto of San Francisco, CA. She subsequently married Robert R. Forrester, Jr. with whom she resided in Gulf Stream, FL.
    Alexander Neil and Elena Musto Lilley, Sr.'s daughter Elena died in 2004 at the age of fifty-four. Their son Alexander Neil Lilley, Jr. married Margaret Mary Turner, the daughter of Henry John Turner of New York, and resides in Carmel, CA.

Lindemann, Adam Marc (b. 1961)

Occupation(s):	capitalist - president and CEO, Mega Communications, LLC, NYC (owns and operates Spanish language radio stations in the U.S.)
	financier - president, Lindemann Commercial Capital Lending, LLC, NYC (provides financing to corporations)
	merchant - owner, Venus Over Manhattan, NYC (art gallery); president, Vision Energy (distributor of liquefied gas)
Civic Activism:	trustee, Public Art Fund
Marriage(s):	M/1 – 1989-div. 2005 – Elizabeth Ashley Graham (b. 1963)
	M/2 – 2006 – Amalia Dayan (b. 1972)
	- merchant - co-owner, Luxemburg & Dayan (art gallery)
	writer - *Collecting Contemporary*; *Collecting Design*
Address:	16 Cliff Drive, Montauk
Name of estate:	
Year of construction:	1931
Style of architecture:	Colonial Revival
Architect(s):	Rolf W. Bauhan designed the compound (for R. E. Church)
	Thierry W. Despont designed the 2007 alterations (for Drexler)
Landscape architect(s):	Miranda Brooks (for Lindemann)
House extant: yes	
Historical notes:	

The compound, which consists of a seven-bedroom main residence, four guest houses, a three-car garage, and a stable, was built by Richard E. Church. In 1971 Andy Warhol and Paul Morrissey purchased the twenty-acre estate for $225,000 from the Church family and called it *Eothen*. After a portion of the estate property was donated to the Nature Conservancy, Morrissey sold the estate to Millard S. Drexler in 2007 for $27 million. In 2015 Drexler sold the main residence, guest houses, garage, and 5.6 acres to Lindemann for $50 million. The equestrian portion of the property remained on the market.

He is the son of George and Dr. Frayda B. Lindemann, Sr.

Elizabeth Ashley Graham Lindemann is the daughter of Robert C. and Christine Denny Graham, Jr. of Greenwich, CT.

Adam Marc and Elizabeth Ashley Graham Lindemann have three daughters, Helen, Charlotte, and Frances.

Amalia Dayan Lindemann is the daughter of Assi and Aharona Melkind Dayan and the granddaughter of Israeli defense minister Moshe Dayan.

Lindemann, Adam Marc (b. 1961)

Occupation(s):	*[See previous entry.]*
Civic Activism:	*[See previous entry.]*
Marriage(s):	M/1 – 1989-div. 2005 – Elizabeth Ashley Graham (b. 1963)
	M/2 – 2006 – Amalia Dayan (b. 1972)
	- *[See previous entry.]*
Address:	406 Old Montauk Highway, Montauk
Name of estate:	
Year of construction:	2004
Style of architecture:	Shingle
Architect(s):	David Adjaye designed the house (for Lindemann)
Landscape architect(s):	
House extant: yes	
Historical notes:	

The house was built by Adam Marc Lindemann.
[See previous entry for family information.]

In 2015 Lindeman listed his 5,000-square-foot, six-bedroom, eight-and-a-half-bath house for sale. The asking price was $29.5 million.

Livingston, Ruth Helene Moller (1893-1978)

Occupation(s):	merchant - antique dealer, Main Street, East Hampton, 1948-1958
Marriage(s):	1923-1939 – Johnston Livingston II (1876-1939) (aka Johnston Livingston, Jr.)
Address:	44 Fithian Lane, East Hampton
Name of estate:	
Year of construction:	
Style of architecture:	Ranch
Architect(s):	
Landscape architect(s):	

House extant: yes
Historical notes:

The *New York Social Register, 1951* lists Ruth H. Moller Livingston as residing on Fithian Lane, East Hampton. The *Social Register, 1977* lists her address as 44 Fithian Lane, East Hampton.

She was the daughter of Charles George and Helene Moller, Jr.

Johnston Livingston II was the son of Robert Cambridge and Maria Whitney Livingston III of *Lakeside* in Islip. [*See* Spinzia, *Long Island's Prominent South Shore Families* – Livingston entry.] Johnston had previously been married to Nathalie Fellows Moss, the daughter of Cortland Dixon and Carmilla Woodward Moss, Sr., and resided in Hewlett. [*See* Spinzia, *Long Island's Prominent Families in the Town of Hempstead* – Livingston entry.] Nathalie's brother Courtland Dixon Moss, Jr. married Katharine Hazzard, the daughter of William Ayrault and Laura Abell Pelton Hazzard, Sr. of *Meadow Hall* in Lawrence, and resided in Muttontown. [*See* Spinzia, *Long Island's Prominent Families in the Town of Hempstead* – Hazzard entry – and *Long Island's Prominent North Shore Families, vol. I* – Moss entry.]

Johnston and Ruth Helene Moller Livingston II's daughter Silvie married Frank William Wall, the son of Harold M. and Helen M. K. Bond Wall of *The Taj* in Southampton. [*See* Spinzia, *Long Island's Prominent Families in the Town of Southampton* – Wall entry.]

The house was later owned by Johnston Livingston III.

Lloyds, Richard

Occupation(s):	industrialist - principal, Eico (coat manufacturing firm)
Marriage(s):	
Address:	12 Heller Lane, East Hampton
Name of estate:	
Year of construction:	1977
Style of architecture:	Modern
Architect(s):	Norman Jaffe designed the house (for Lloyds)

Landscape architect(s)
House extant: no; demolished in 2015
Historical notes:

The 4,000-square-foot, four-bedroom, four-bath house was built by Richard Lloyds.
In 2015 it sold for $4.995 million.

Lockwood, William Andrew (1874-1966)

Occupation(s):	attorney - partner, Milbank, Tweed, Hope, and Hadley; partner, Morgan, Lockwood, and L. Heureux
Civic Activism:	member, zoning board of appeals, Village of East Hampton; member, board of managers, East Hampton Free Library; secretary and president, Maidstone Club, East Hampton; member, East Hampton War Memorial committee, 1924

Marriage(s):	1903-1960 – Elizabeth Erwin Edwards (1871-1960)
	   - Civic Activism: member, advisory council, New York Botanical Garden;
	                          director, New York International Flower Show;
	                          president, Garden Club of America, 1929-1932;
	                          member, board of managers, East Hampton Free Library;
	                          a founder and president, Garden Club of East Hampton

Address: Pudding Hill Lane, East Hampton
Name of estate: *Ivy Cottage*
Year of construction:
Style of architecture:
Architect(s):
Landscape architect(s):
House extant: no
Nassau County Museum Collection has photographs of the estate.
Historical notes:

   The *Social Register Summer, 1915* lists William A. and Elizabeth Edwards Lockwood as residing at *Ivy Cottage* in East Hampton.
   He was the son of John H. and Sarah L. Bennett Lockwood of Brooklyn, NY.
   Elizabeth Erwin Edward Lockwood was the daughter of James McPherson and Elizabeth Scudder Edwards of East Hampton and Morristown, NJ.
   William Andrew and Elizabeth Erwin Edwards Lockwood's son John married Henrietta Ellery Sedgewick, the daughter of Ellery Sedgwick of Boston, MA, and resided in Bedford, NY.

Lockwood, Williston Benedict (1846-1908)

Occupation(s):	financier - partner, R. P. Flower and Co. (investment banking firm); partner, Lockwood and Co. (investment banking firm)
Marriage(s):	1869-1908 – Janet Isabel Dominick (1851-1938) - Civic Activism: president, Woman's Auxiliary of the Church Temperance Society; president, Hand-in-Hand Society of the King's Daughters*
Address:	Terbell Lane, East Hampton
Name of estate:	*Lockdune*
Year of construction:	c. 1900
Style of architecture:	Adamesque
Architect(s):	
Landscape architect(s):	
House extant: no**	
Historical notes:	

The house, originally named *Lockdune*, was built by Williston Benedict Lockwood.

He was the son of LeGrand and Anna Louisa Benedict Lockwood, Sr. of New York.

Janet Isabel Dominick Lockwood was the daughter of James William and Mary Day Wells Dominick. Janet's sister Mabel married Alfred Post Hinton and resided at *Roads Meet* in East Hampton.

*The King's Daughters or King's Girls refers to a group of an estimated 700-900 women who immigrated to New France, part of present-day Quebec, from France between 1663 and 1673. The women, most of humble birth, were sponsored by the French government under Louis XIV to provide marriage partners for the men who had settled in New France.

William Benedict and Janet Isabel Dominick Lockwood's daughter Louise married Aldred K. Warren, the son of The Reverend Edward Walpole Warren, and resided in Mamaroneck, NY. Their daughter Bertha married G. Norman Bayne.

**The carriage house is extant.

The house was later owned by Laurette Helen Cooney Manners, Paul Joseph Moranti, Dr. Earl R. Carlson, and Charles A. Julianelli.

Loeb, Daniel Seth (b. 1961)

Occupation(s):	financier - member, Warburg Pincus, 1984-1987 (private equity firm);
	risk arbitrage analyst, Lafer Equity Investors;
	vice-president, Jefferies, LLC;
	vice-president, Citigroup, 1994-1995;
	founder and CEO, Third Point, 1995 (hedge fund)
	capitalist - director of corporate development, Island Records
Civic Activism:	founder, director and president, The Daniel S. Loeb Family Third Point Foundation;
	chairman of board, Success Academy Charter School, Brooklyn, NY;
	endowed Daniel S. Loeb Scholarship, Columbia University, NYC;
	trustee, Prep for Prep (prepares underprivileged children to attend private schools);
	co-founder, Students First (education advocacy organization);
	benefactor, Alzheimer's Drug Discovery Foundation;
	co-chairman of board, Governors for Industry;
	trustee, Mount Sinai Hospital, NYC;
	trustee, Manhattan Institute;
	trustee, U. S. Olympic Committee;
	trustee, Museum of Contemporary Art, Los Angeles, CA;
	a founder, Master Play
Marriage(s):	2004 – Margaret Davidson Munzer (b. 1972)
	- Civic Activism: director, The Daniel S. Loeb Family Third Point Foundation
Address:	61 Highway Behind the Pond, East Hampton

Name of estate:
Year of construction:
Style of architecture:
Architect(s):
Landscape architect(s):
House extant: yes
Historical notes:

Daniel Seth Loeb is the son of Ronald and Clare Spark Loeb of Santa Monica, CA.
Margaret Davidson Munzer Loeb is the daughter of Stephen Ira and Patricia Eve Edelman Munzer.

Loomis, Alfred Lee, Sr. (1887-1975)

Occupation(s):	attorney -	member, Winthrop and Stimson, 1916-1920
	financier -	vice-president and partner with his brother-in-law Landon Ketchum Thorne, Sr., Bonbright and Co. (investment banking firm)*
	scientist -	director, Loomis Laboratories, Tuxedo Park, NY, 1928-1941;
		president, Loomis Institute for Scientific Research, Inc., 1928-1965;
		discovered sleep K complex brainwave
	inventor -	Long Range Navigation System;
		Aberdeen Chronograph (measures muzzle velocity);
		co-inventor, with Edmund Newton Harvey, microscopic centrifuge
	industrialist -	a founder and trustee, Rand Corporation, Santa Monica, CA (developed radar)

Civic Activism: trustee, Massachusetts General Hospital, Boston, MA;
trustee, Woods Hole Oceanographic Institute, Woods Hole, MA;
trustee, Carnegie Institute, Washington, DC;
governor, New York Hospital, NYC;
trustee, Massachusetts Institute of Technology, Cambridge, MA

Marriage(s): M/1 – 1912-div. 1945 – Elizabeth Ellen Farnsworth (d. 1975)
M/2 – 1945-1975 – Manette Seeldrayers (1908-1991)
- Civic Activism: president, Ladies Village Improvement Society, East Hampton

Address: 79 Davids Lane, East Hampton
Name of estate:
Year of construction: c. 1930
Style of architecture: Modified Colonial
Architect(s):
Landscape architect(s):
House extant: yes
Historical notes:

Alfred Lee Loomis, Sr. was the son of Henry Patterson and Julia Josephine Stimson Loomis of Tuxedo Park, NY. Alfred's sister Julia married Landon Ketchum Thorne, Sr. and resided at *Thorneham* in West Bay Shore. [*See* Spinzia, *Long Island's Prominent South Shore Families* – Thorne entry.] Alfred and Julia's first cousin, the noted statesman Henry Lewis Stimson, resided at *Highold* in West Hills, Long Island. [*See* Spinzia, *Long Island's Prominent North Shore Families, vol. II* – Stimson entry.] Alfred, Julia, and Henry's grandparents Henry Clark and Julia Maria Atterbury Stimson resided in East Hampton.

Elizabeth Ellen Farnsworth Loomis was the daughter of William Farnsworth of Boston, MA.

Alfred Lee and Elizabeth Ellen Farnsworth Loomis, Sr.'s son William married Violet Amory, the daughter of John Austin Amory of *Toy Farm* in Needham, MA. Their son Henry married Mary Paul Macleod, the daughter of Cameron Macleod of Berwyn, PA. Their son Alfred Lee Loomis, Jr. married Virginia Davis Hosmer, the daughter of Thomas Jefferson Hosmer of Cincinnati, OH, and resided in Cove Neck.

The Blue Book of The Hamptons, 1973 lists Alfred L. and Manette Seeldrayers Loomis [Sr.] as residing at 79 Davids Lane, East Hampton.

Manette was the daughter of Rodolphe William Seeldrayers. She had previously been married to Garret Augustus Hobart III, the son of Garret Augustus and Caroline Frye Briggs Hobart, Jr. of *T-Other House* in East Hampton, and resided in Tuxedo Park, NY. After Alfred's death Manette married Ronald Christie.

*Bonbright and Co. is credited with helping shape the country's electrical utility industry. It was known as one of Wall Street's "Big Six" investment banks.

The house has five bedrooms and four and a half bathrooms.

Lowe, Emma Lawrence Marshall (1909-1982)

Marriage(s):	1933-div. 1943 – William Ebbets Lowe II (1905-1963) - financier - member, Boston Insurance Co.
Address:	Palmer Terrace, Sag Harbor

Name of estate:
Year of construction:
Style of architecture:
Architect(s):
Landscape architect(s):
House extant: unconfirmed
Historical notes:

The Blue Book of The Hamptons, 1973 lists Emma L. Marshall Lowe as residing on Palmer Terrace, East Hampton [Sag Harbor].

She was the daughter of Levin Rothrock and Martha Jacob Marshall of *Hawkswood* in Hewlett Harbor and *Silver Maples* in Roslyn Harbor. Emma was a descendant of Chief Justice John Marshall. [*See* Spinzia, *Long Island's Prominent Families in the Town of Hempstead* – Marshall entry – and *Long Island's Prominent North Shore Families, vol. I* – Marshall entry.]

William Ebbets Lowe II was the son of Gerald and Cora Towne Underhill Lowe of Bethayres, PA. William subsequently married Danah Bartlett, the daughter of Dr. Daniel Bartlett of Seattle, WA, and New York. She had previously been married to Julian Hinckley, the son of Samuel Parker and Rosalie Neilson Hinckley of *Sunset Hall* in Lawrence, and resided in Lawrence. [*See* Spinzia, *Long Island's Prominent Families in the Town of Hempstead* – Hinckley entries.]

Lowenstein, Peter (b. 1934)

Occupation(s):	industrialist - founder and CEO, Renolit Corp. (plastic manufacturing and distribution firm)
Civic Activism:	trustee, Concerned Citizens of Montauk; member, Montauk Citizens Advisory Committee; president, Montauk Pilots Association; donated playground at Montauk Playhouse in memory of son Alexander
Marriage(s):	Suse Ellen ____ (b. 1944) - artist - sculptress; textile designer
Address:	11 East Lake Drive, Montauk

Name of estate
Year of construction:

Style of architecture:	Modern
Architect(s):	Chimacoff & Peterson designed the house (for Lowenstein)

Landscape architect(s):

Builder:	David Webb

House extant: yes
Historical notes:

The 1,000-square-foot-house was built by Peter Lowenstein.

Peter and Suse Ellen Lowenstein's son Alexander was killed in the 1988 terrorist bombing of Pan Am flight 103 over Lockerbie, Scotland.

Lundbergh, Holger

Occupation(s):	writer - poetry; *The Personal Vision of Ingmar Bergman*, translated from Swedish; *Great Swedish Fairy Tales*, translated from Swedish; *The Cats of Summer Island*, translated from Swedish; numerous articles in magazines journalist - free-lance; assistant manager, American–Swedish News Exchange
Marriage(s):	1934 – Penelope March (1895-1981)
Address:	115 De Forest Road, Montauk
Name of estate:	*Bayberry*
Year of construction:	1883
Style of architecture:	Beach Cottage
Architect(s):	McKim, Mead & White designed the house (for Benson)
Landscape architect(s):	Frederick Law Olmsted designed the site plan (for Benson)
Builder:	George A. Eldredge & Son, 1914 alterations (for Mary Benson) Mead and Taft

House extant: yes
Historical notes:

The 4,000-square-foot house, originally named *Weeweecho*, was built by Arthur W. Benson. The house was inherited by the Bensons' daughter Mary, who continued to call it *Weeweecho*. It was later owned by Marion Bolton Marsh, who called it *Windway*, and, then, by her daughter Penelope and son-in-law Holger Lundbergh, who called it *Bayberry*.

The Blue Book of The Hamptons, 1973 lists Holger and Penelope Marsh Lundbergh as residing at *Bayberry* in Montauk.

He is the son of the noted Swedish sculptor Teodor Lundbergh and Ellen Lundbergh–Nyblom.

Penelope Marsh Lundbergh was the daughter of Frank Ballard and Marion Bolton Marsh.

Charles Matthew Levi purchased the house in 1981.

In 1995 the house sold for $700,000.

Lutkins, Clinton Stephen (1885-1978)

Occupation(s):	industrialist - vice-president and director, Allied Chemical Corp; chairman of board, Congoleum–Nairn, Inc. (floor covering firm); director, American Type Founders Corp; director, Interlake Iron Corp.; director, Hooker Electrochemical Co.
Civic Activism:	director, Maidstone Club, East Hampton
Marriage(s):	M/1 – 1908-1928 – Nellie Barnum Dingee (1886-1928) M/2 – 1930-1958 – Gladys S. Robbins (1889-1958)
Address:	Lee Avenue, East Hampton
Name of estate:	*Hedges Row*
Year of construction:	
Style of architecture:	
Architect(s):	
Landscape architect(s):	
House extant: unconfirmed	
Historical notes:	

Clinton Stephen Lutkins was the son of Stephen H. Lutkins of Rye, NY.

Nellie Barnum Dingee Lutkins was the daughter of Charles E. Dingee of Brooklyn.

Clinton Stephen and Nellie Barnum Dingee Lutkins' daughter Louise married Robert Le Brecht, the son of William Marston Le Brecht of Hingham, MA, and NYC; Alwin Michelsen; and, subsequently, William Doerr. Their son David married Nancy Holbrook Walmsley Scott of Weston, MA, and resided in Lincoln, MA. Their son LaRue, a diplomat who served in the U. S. State Department from 1942 to 1975, married Florence Helen McGovern, the daughter of Maurice Terrence and Elizabeth Stewart McGovern. When a coup by defecting Chinese Nationalist soldiers seized Kunming as well as all of Yunan Province in 1949, LaRue was the last U. S. Consul to leave Kunming.

The *Social Register Summer, 1958* lists Clinton S. and Gladys S. Robbins Lutkins as residing at *Hedges* Row in East Hampton. *The Blue Book of The Hamptons, 1958* lists their address as Lee Avenue. East Hampton.

She was the daughter of Rowland Ames Robbins of NYC.

Lyon, Marvin Thomas (1865-1906)

Occupation(s):	attorney
Marriage(s):	1985-1906 – Frances H. Rudd
Address:	Cottage Avenue, East Hampton
Name of estate:	
Year of construction:	1899
Style of architecture:	Modified Colonial
Architect(s):	Joseph Greenleaf Thorp designed the house (for Lyon)
Landscape architect(s):	
Builder:	George A. Eldredge, 1899 house and 1899 stable
House extant: yes	
Historical notes:	

The house was built by Marvin Thomas Lyon.

He was the son of William Heath and Ellen Maria Gaylord Lyon, Sr. of Brooklyn.

Marvin Thomas and Frances H. Rudd Lyon's daughter Katherine married John Laurence Hutton, Sr. and resided at *Peep O'Day* in East Hampton. Their son William married Miriam Hagy Phipps, the daughter of A. J. Phipps of New York, and resided at *Sleep Hollow* in Plymouth Meeting, PA.

Mackay, The Reverend William R. (1845-1896)

Occupation(s):	clergy - rector, St. Peter's Protestant Episcopal Church, Pittsburgh, PA
Marriage(s):	
Address:	Cottage Avenue, East Hampton
Name of estate:	
Year of construction:	1873-1874
Style of architecture:	High Victorian Gothic
Architect(s):	Joseph Greenleaf Thorp, 1899 alterations (for Mrs. Mackay)
	George A. Eldredge, alterations
Landscape architect(s):	
House extant: unconfirmed	
Historical notes:	

By 1887 Mackay had purchased this house from the firm of Dan Talmage's Sons.
He was the stepson of The Reverend Henry Mackay of Monongahela, PA.
In 1919 George A. Eldredge purchased the house for use as a rental.

Macklowe, Harry B. (b. 1937)

Occupation(s):	advertising executive - member, Kudner Agency, NYC
	capitalist - founder and president, Macklowe Real Estate Co. (holding company)
	real estate agent - partner, Wolf & Macklowe, NYC
Marriage(s):	M/1 – 1959-div. 2019 – Linda Burg (b. 1937)
	- art curator
	Civic Activism: trustee, Guild Hall, East Hampton
	M/2 – 2019 – Patricia Landeau
	- Civic Activism: president, French Friends of the Israel Museum
Address:	78 Georgica Close Road, East Hampton
Name of estate:	
Year of construction:	1989
Style of architecture:	Modern
Architect(s):	Harry Bates with Booker and Lund Architects designed the house (for Macklowe)
Landscape architect(s):	
House extant: yes	
Historical notes:	

The house was built by Harry B. Macklowe.
Born in New Rochelle, NY, he is the son of a garment industry executive.
Harry B. and Linda Burg Marklowe's son William married Tory Burch and, later, Julie Lerner. Their daughter Elizabeth married Kent Mason Swig, the son of Melvin M. Swig.
In 2019 Macklowe listed the 8,659-square-foot, five-bedroom, seven-bath house for sale. The asking price was $21 million.

Macklowe, Harry B. (b. 1937)

Occupation(s):	*[See previous entry.]*
Marriage(s):	M/1 – 1959-div. 2019 – Linda Burg (b. 1937)
	- *[See previous entry.]*
	M/2 – 2019 – Patricia Landeau
	- *[See previous entry.]*
Address:	64 West End Road, East Hampton
Name of estate:	
Year of construction:	1987
Style of architecture:	Shingle
Architect(s):	Eugene Lawrence Futterman
	designed the house
Landscape architect(s):	

House extant: yes
Historical notes:

In 2017 Macklowe purchased the 5,500-square-foot, four-bedroom, four-and-a-half bath house and 2.7 acres for $10.6 million.

[See previous entry for family information.]

Macy, Valentine Everit, Jr. (1898-1970)

Occupation(s):	publisher - president, Westchester County Publishers, Inc. (later, Gannett Co., Inc.) (chain of local newspapers); director, Gannett Co., Inc., Rochester, NY
	capitalist - partner, WFAS radio station, White Plains, NY; president, Deed Realty Corp., NYC
	industrialist - director, Alabama Fuel & Iron Co.; director, Peerless Photo Products
Civic Activism:	president, National Information Bureau; trustee, Teachers College of Columbia University, NYC; director, East Hampton League; treasurer, Devon Yacht Club, Amagansett; member, Westchester County Park and Cross County Park Commissions
Marriage(s):	M/1 – 1925-div. 1932 – Lydia P. Bodrero (b. 1902)
	- nobility
	M/2 – 1932-1933 – Alice Emily Yates (1897-1933)
	M/3 – 1934-1969 – Harriet Ayer Seymour (1907-1969)
	- trustee, Guild Hall, East Hampton
Address:	Middle Lane, East Hampton
Name of estate:	*Longlast*
Year of construction:	
Style of architecture:	
Architect(s):	
Landscape architect(s):	

House extant: unconfirmed
Historical notes:

The *Long Island Society Register, 1929* lists Valentine E. and Lydia P. Bodrero Macy, Jr. as residing at *Wayside* in Southampton. *The Blue Book of The Hamptons, 1958* lists Valentine E. and Harriet Seymour Macy, Jr. as residing at *Longlast* on Middle Lane in East Hampton. [*See* Spinzia, *Long Island's Prominent Families in the Town of Southampton* – Macy entry.]

He was the son of Valentine Everit and Edith Wiesman Carpenter Macy, Sr. of Hewlett. [*See* Spinzia, *Long Island's Prominent Families in the Town of Hempstead* – Macy entry.] His sister Editha married Burnham Lewis. His brother Josiah married Mary C. Emerson and resided in Morristown, NJ. At the time of his death Macy was residing in East Hampton.

Lydia P. Bodrero Macy was the daughter of Allesandro and Catherine Spalding Bodrero of Pasadena, CA. In 1939 Lydia became Princess di San Faustino when she married Don Ranieri, the Fifth Prince di San Faustino. In 1957 she married Roland Livingston Redmond of *White Elephant Farm* in Oyster Bay Cove. [*See* Spinzia, *Long Island's Prominent North Shore Families, vol. II* – Redmond entry.]

Valentine Everit and Lydia P. Bodrero Macy, Jr.'s daughter Edith married Frederick Karl Schoenborn.

Alice Emily Yates Macy was the daughter of Henry Brydges and Alice Mary Bunting Yates of Montreal, Canada.

Harriet Seymour Macy was the daughter of Louis Allen and Harriet Ayer Seymour of New York. She had previously been married to George Washington Helm, Sr. of East Hampton.

Madoff, Bernard Lawrence (b. 1938)
aka Bernie Madoff

Occupation(s):	financier - founder, Bernard L. Madoff Securities, LLC, 1960 (stock brokerage advisory firm)*; non-executive chairman, NASDAQ (stock market exchange)
Civic Activism:	treasurer and chairman of board of directors, Sy Syms School of Business, Yeshiva University, NYC; trustee, New York City Center; member, executive council, Wall Street division, United Jewish Appeal of New York
Marriage(s):	1959 – Ruth Alpern (b. 1941) - Civic Activism: founder, Madoff Charitable Trust
Address:	216 Old Montauk Highway, Montauk
Name of estate:	
Year of construction:	1982
Style of architecture:	Contemporary
Architect(s):	Eugene Lawrence Futterman designed the house (for Madoff) Thierry W. Despont, 2007 alterations (for Roth)
Landscape architect(s):	
House extant: yes	
Historical notes:	

The 3,000-square-foot-house was built by Bernard Lawrence Madoff.
He is the son of Ralph and Sylvia Munter Madoff of Far Rockaway, NY.
Ruth Alpern Madoff is the daughter of Saul Alpern of Far Rockaway, NY.
Bernard Lawrence and Ruth Alpern Madoff's son Andrew married Deborah West. He later became engaged to Catherine Hooper. Their son Mark, who committed suicide in 2010 by hanging himself in his Manhattan apartment, was married to Susan Elkin and, later, Stephanie Mikesell Mack.
*In 2009 Madoff was convicted of operating a $36 billion Ponzi scheme. He was sentenced to 150 years in prison and the forfeiture of $17.179 billion in assets.
In 2009 the house was purchased by Steven Roth for $9.41 million.
In 2018 Roth listed the house for sale. The asking price was $21 million.

Maguire, Edward, Sr. (1894-1971)

Occupation(s):	financier - partner, Dickinson, Maguire, and Paul, NYC (stock brokerage firm); manager, investment department, Dominick and Dominick (investment banking firm)
Civic Activism:	member, Village of East Hampton Zoning Board of Appeals; member, board of managers, East Hampton Free Library
Marriage(s):	1930-1971 – Mary Lumpkin Todd (1904-1996)
Address:	87A Buell Lane, East Hampton
Name of estate:	*Hayloft*
Year of construction:	
Style of architecture:	Beach Cottage
Architect(s):	
Landscape architect(s):	
House extant: yes	
Historical notes:	

The Blue Book of The Hamptons, 1965 lists Edward and Mary L. Todd Maguire [Sr.] as residing at *Hayloft*, 87A Buell Lane, East Hampton.
He was the son of James Herbert and Annie Ewing Maguire of Detroit, MI.
Mary Lumpkin Todd Maguire was the daughter of Hiram C. Todd of NYC.
In 2016 the four-bedroom, three-and-a-half-bath, 1,993-square-foot house was for sale. The asking price was $3.195 million.

Maharam, Donald H., Jr. (b. 1931)

Occupation(s):	industrialist - chairman of board, Maharam Fabric Corp, 1951-2000
Civic Activism:	founder, with his wife Bonnie, Donald and Bonnie Maharam Charitable Foundation
Marriage(s):	Bonnie *[unable to determine maiden name]*
	- Civic Activism: founder, with her husband Donald, Donald and Bonnie Maharam Charitable Foundation
Address:	84 Georgica Close Road, East Hampton
Name of estate:	
Year of construction:	c. 2005
Style of architecture:	
Architect(s):	
Landscape architect(s):	
House extant: yes	
Historical notes:	

In 2004 Maharam purchased the gutted shell of Gordon Bunshaft's house *Travertine House* from Martha Stewart's daughter Alexis for $9.5 million. He demolished it and built a new residence.

He is the son of Samuel D. and Edus S. Maharam of Queens, NY.

Donald and Bonnie Maharam, Jr.'s son Michael married Uschi Weismuller of Switzerland.

Main, Charles E. (b. 1900)

Occupation(s):	capitalist - director, Missouri–Kansas Pipe Line Co.;
	director, Scurry–Rainbow, Ltd., Canada (petroleum pipeline firm);
	director, Panhandle Eastern Pipe Line Co. (petroleum pipeline firm)
	financier - president, Clark Estates Inc. (family holding firm)
	industrialist - director, Singer Manufacturing Co. (sewing machine manufacturing firm);
	director, National Distillers;
	director, Chemical Corp.
Marriage(s):	Laura Sudler (1904-1980)
	- Civic Activism: president, Valley Opera, Ridgewood, NJ; president, Ridgewood Choral, Ridgewood, NJ
Address:	Lily Pond Lane, East Hampton
Name of estate:	*Main House*
Year of construction:	
Style of architecture:	
Architect(s):	
Landscape architect(s):	
House extant: unconfirmed	
Historical notes:	

In 1950 Main purchased Leo Dewey Welch's residence and named it *Main House*. [*The East Hampton Star* October 5, 1950, p. 1.]

The Blue Book of The Hamptons, 1973 lists Charles E. and Laura Sudler Main as residing at *Main House* on Lily Pond Lane, East Hampton.

Charles E. and Laura Sudler Main's son Richard married Elise McHahon. Their son Kenneth married Nancy Chichester. Their daughter Janet married Andrew d'Elia, the son of Vincenzo and Anna M. Saggese d'Elia.

In 1974 the house was sold to Stanley Richard Jaffe. [*The East Hampton Star* March 14, 1974, p. 5.]

Mairs, Isabel Tasker Gardiner (b. 1912)
aka Isabel T. L. Gardiner Mairs;
Isabel Fairfax Gardiner Mairs

Civic Activism:	East Hampton representative, Suffolk County Tercentenary Committee;
	vice-regent, East Hampton Chapter, Daughters of the American Revolution;
	Village of East Hampton historian
Marriage(s):	1934-1959 – Olney Blanchard Mairs, Jr. (1911-1959)
	- financier - member, Fahnestock and Co. (stock brokerage firm)
Address:	48 James Lane, East Hampton
Name of estate:	*Hearthstone*
Year of construction:	c. 1696
Style of architecture:	One-and-a-half story house
Architect(s):	
Landscape architect(s):	
House extant: yes	
Historical notes:	

The house is the historic John Gardiner residence.

The Blue Book of The Hamptons, 1973 lists Isabel Gardiner Mairs as residing at 48 James Lane, East Hampton. The *Social Register, 1985* lists the name of her residence as *Hearthstone*.

She was the daughter of Winthrop and Isabel Tasher Lemmon Gardiner, Sr. of *Deurcant House* in East Hampton. Olney Blanchard Mairs, Jr. was the son of Olney Blanchard and Eva Eugenie Ward Mairs, Sr. of East Hampton.

Olney Blanchard and Isabel Tasker Gardiner Mairs, Jr.'s son Olney Blanchard Gardiner Mairs became Olney Mairs Gardiner when he was adopted by Winthrop Gardiner, Jr.

[See following entry for additional family information.]

Mairs, Olney Blanchard, Sr. (1876-1943)

Occupation(s):	attorney
Marriage(s):	1905-1943 – Eva Eugenie Ward (1878-1949)
Address:	30 Lee Avenue, East Hampton
Name of estate:	
Year of construction:	1890
Style of architecture:	Queen Anne
Architect(s):	William B. Tuthill designed the house (for Adams)
	Aymar Embury II, 1930s alterations (for Mairs)
Landscape architect(s):	
Builder:	Conrad & Shott, 1931 addition (for Mairs)
House extant: yes	
Historical notes:	

The house was built by Charles Henry Adams. It was later owned by Dr. James M. Hodson. In 1930 the house was purchased by Mairs. [*The East Hampton Star* September 12, 1930, p. 7.]

The Social Directory of Southampton, Long Island, 1931 lists Olney B. and Eva Eugenie Ward Mairs [Sr.] as residing on Lee Avenue in East Hampton.

He was the son of William Henry and Ellen A. Olney Mairs of Brooklyn. Olney's sister Ella married Walter Bartow Duryea and resided in East Hampton.

Eva Eugenie Ward Mairs was the daughter of Joseph Alexander Ward.

Olney Blanchard and Eva Eugenie Ward Mairs, Sr.'s daughter Constance married McGee Baxter, Jr. of Cleveland, OH, and, later, Carol Barnett with whom she resided in Charlottesville, VA. Their daughter Marjory married Martin P. Henry and, later, Halle Wolbarst. Their son Olney Blanchard Mairs, Jr. married Isabel Tasker Gardiner.

[See previous entry for additional family information.]

The house was for sale in 2011. The asking price was $25.75 million.

Maloney, William Raywood, Jr. (1877-1945)

Occupation(s):	attorney - partner, Daru, Vischi, and Winter; assistant district attorney, New York County
Marriage(s):	1915-1945 – Ella Gaynor McCall (b. 1888)
	- Civic Activism: president, Ladies Village Improvement Society, East Hampton; acting treasurer, Garden Club of East Hampton
Address:	Jones Road, East Hampton
Name of estate:	*Glendella*
Year of construction:	
Style of architecture:	Cottage
Architect(s):	
Landscape architect(s):	
House extant: unconfirmed	
Historical notes:	

The *Long Island Society Register, 1929* lists William R. and Ella Gaynor McCall Maloney [Jr.] as residing on Jones Road in East Hampton.

The *Social Register Summer, 1932* lists *Glendella* as the name of their residence.

He was the son of William Raywood Maloney, Sr. of Poughkeepsie, NY.

Ella Gaynor McCall Maloney was the daughter of Edward and Ella Frances Gaynor McCall of *Evsdune* in East Hampton.

William Raywood and Ella Gaynor McCall Maloney, Jr.'s son Everett married Theresa Todd Schey, the daughter of Robert Paul and Laura Washington Schey of *Lauralawn* in East Hampton. Their daughter Eleanor married Robert J. Rainieri, Sr.

In 1943 the house was purchased by Joseph Haag, Jr. [*The East Hampton Star* November 25, 1943, p. 1.]

Mann, Henry (1890-1968)

Occupation(s):	capitalist -	president and chairman of board, E. Leitz, Inc., NYC (importing and United States distribution firm for Leitz microscopes and scientific instruments and Leica cameras);
		president, Potash Import and Chemical Corp., NYC
	financier -	president, Henry Mann Securities Corp.;
		vice-president, National City Co., 1934-1940 (investment affiliate of National City Bank);
		managing director, Brown, Harriman, and Co. (investment banking firm)
	industrialist -	president, Synthetic Nitrogen Products Corp.;
		chairman of board, Opto–Metric Tools;
		comptroller, Crown Cork and Seal Co., Baltimore, 1917-1927

Civic Activism: director, American Chamber of Commerce, Berlin, Germany;
director, German American Chamber of Commerce;
director, American Chamber of Commerce in France;
director, New York Chamber of Commerce

Marriage(s): 1924-1968 – Helen Morris Grimes (1903-1993)
- Civic Activism: vice-president, American Women's Unit, War Relief, Inc., 1946

Address: Further Lane, East Hampton
Name of estate: *San Souci*
Year of construction:
Style of architecture:
Architect(s):
Landscape architect(s):
House extant: unconfirmed
Historical notes:

    Born in Germany, Henry Mann came to the United States in 1913 and became a citizen in 1920.
    The Blue Book of The Hamptons, 1958 lists Henry and Helen Morris Grimes Mann as residing at *San Souci* on Further Lane, East Hampton.
    She was the daughter of Howard Spencer and Rose Fusting Grimes.
    Henry and Helen Morris Grimes Mann's daughter Barbara remained unmarried. Their daughter Mary married Gerald R. Cummins. Their daughter Helen married John Howie Wright, Jr., the son of John Howie and Ann M. Ryan Wright, Sr. of East Hampton, and resided in East Hampton. Their son William married Mercedes Spradling and, later, Anna Maria Torv, the daughter of Jacob and Sylvia Braida Torv, and resided in Southampton. [*See* Spinzia, *Long Island's Prominent Families in the Town of Southampton* – Mann entry.] Anna had previously been married to Rupert Murdock.

Manners, Laurette Helen Cooney (1883-1946)
aka Laurette Taylor

Occupation(s):	entertainers and associated professions - stage and silent motion picture actress

Marriage(s):	M/1 – 1901-div. 1910 – Charles Alonzo Taylor (1864-1942)
	   - entertainers and associated professions - actor
	      journalist - *San Francisco Examiner*
	      writer - playwright
	M/2 – 1912-1928 – John Hartley Manners (1870-1928)
	   - writer - playwright

Address:	Terbell Lane, East Hampton
Name of estate:	
Year of construction:	c. 1900
Style of architecture:	Adamesque
Architect(s):	
Landscape architect(s):	
House extant: no*	
Historical notes:	

The house, originally named *Lockdune*, was built by Williston Benedict Lockwood. In 1926 it was purchased by Manners. [*The East Hampton Star* February 26, 1926.]

She was the daughter of James and Elizabeth Dorsey Cooney of New York City.

Charles Alonzo and Laurette Helen Cooney Taylor's son Dwight married Marigold Lockhart Langworthy and, later, Natalie Visart.

In 1931 the house was purchased by Paul Joseph Moranti. [*The East Hampton Star* July 17, 1931, p. 12.] In 1936 it was purchased by Earl R. Carlson. It was subsequently owned by Charles A. Julianelli. [*The East Hampton Star* August 27, 1936, p. 4.]

*The carriage house is extant.

Mansell, Frank Luther (1922-2010)

Occupation(s):	financier - president, Blyth and Co., NYC;
	      CEO, Paine Weber, Blyth Eastman, Dillon and Co., Inc.;
	      advisory director, Paine Webber, Inc.;
	      chairman of board, Blyth Eastman, Paine Webber, and Co.;
	capitalist - owner, Mansell Stables (thoroughbred racing stable)

Civic Activism:	trustee, Freedom Institute, NYC; trustee, University of Nebraska Foundation; trustee, Boys Club of New York; trustee, Jupiter Hospital Foundation

Marriage(s):	1957-1999 – Edmona Elmore Lyman (1929-1999)
	   - Civic Activism: director, National Council on Alcoholism and Drug Dependency;
	      founder and board chair, Freedom Institute, NYC;
	      vice-president and director, Bothin Foundation, San Francisco, CA

Address:	100 Dunemere Lane, East Hampton
Name of estate:	
Year of construction:	
Style of architecture:	Modified Neo-Federal
Architect(s):	
Landscape architect(s):	
House extant: yes	
Historical notes:	

Frank Luther Mansell was the son of George Elmer and Jessie Trembeth McDonald Mansell of Nebraska.

Edmona Elmore Lyman Mansell was the daughter of Edmunds and Genevieve Bothen Lyman of California. Edmona had previously been married to Paul A. Miller.

Frank Luther and Edmona Elmore Lyman Mansell's daughter, Devon married ____ Laycox and resides in Sherbon, MA. Their daughter, who married Colin Trippe Ambrose, was the next owner of the house. In 2010 she sold it to George Robert Stephanopoulos for $3.5 million.

In 2012 Stephanopoulos sold the house for $5.13 million.

Manson, Thomas Lincoln, III (1849-1918)

Occupation(s):	financier - president, Thomas L. Manson Co. (stock brokerage firm)
	industrialist - a founder and director, Mexican Mining and Smelting Co., Durango, Mexico
Civic Activism:	chairman, Clearing House Committee of Stock Exchange
Marriage(s):	Mary Groot (aka Mae Groot Manson) (1859-1917)
	- Civic Activism:
	suffrage* -
	suffragist lecturer;
	chair, executive committee, East Hampton chapter,
	Women's Suffrage League;
	chair, East Hampton chapter, Women's Political Union;
	member of the "Suffrage Torch" contingent
	treasurer, Ladies Village Improvement Society, East Hampton
Address:	117 Main Street, East Hampton
Name of estate:	*Millfield*
Year of construction:	c. 1799
Style of architecture:	Colonial Revival**
Architect(s):	Isaac Henry Green II designed
	1889 alterations***
	Joseph Greenleaf Thorp designed
	1905 interior and exterior alterations
Landscape architect(s):	Mary Lois Deputy Lanson (for Douglas)
House extant: yes	
Historical notes:	

    The house was built by Jeremiah Miller IV.

    **It was later owned by Edward de Rose who remodeled it, changing the architecture from Georgian to Colonial Revival, and named it *Millfield*. It was then owned by Manson and, then, by his daughter Dorothea and son-in-law Kiliaen Van Rensselaer. Both Manson and Van Rensselaer continued to call it *Millfield*. After Dorothea's death, Kiliaen relocated to *Post Cottage* in Old Westbury. [*See* Spinzia, *Long Island's Prominent North Shore Families, vol. I* – Van Rensselaer entry.]

    The *Social Register Summer, 1910* and *1915* list Thomas Lincoln and Mary Groot Manson [III] as residing at *Millfield* in East Hampton.

    He was the son of Thomas Lincoln and Elizabeth Emerson Vance Manson, Jr.

    Mary Groot Manson was the daughter of Cornelius F. and Ellen Story Groot.

    Thomas Lincoln and Mary Groot Manson III's son Thomas Lincoln Manson IV married Claire Pulleyn, the daughter of John Joseph Pulleyn. Her brother John married Alice Moffit and resided in East Hampton. Their son Vance married Mabel Dickey and resided in Santa Monica, CA.

    In 1945 the house was owned by Graham Douglas. By 1950 it was owned by Franklin M. Chace, who called it *Gone With the Wind*, and, by 1973, by Richard Vincent Hare.

    *For other Long Islanders involved in the suffrage movement *see* Raymond E. Spinzia, "Winning the Franchise: Long Island Activists in the Fight for Woman's Suffrage and Their Opponents, Long Island's Anti-Suffragists." wwwspinzialongislandestates.com.

    ***For Green's other commissions, *see* Spinzia, *Long Island's Prominent South Shore Families: Their Estates and Their Country Homes in the Towns of Babylon and Islip*.

Mapes, Maie Bennett (1866-1936)

Marriage(s):	1924-1935 – Charles Halstead Mapes (1864-1935)
	- industrialist - vice-president, Mapes Formula Peruvian Guana, Co.
Address:	Main Street, East Hampton
Name of estate:	*Purple House*
Year of construction:	1700s
Style of architecture:	Colonial
Architect(s):	
Landscape architect(s):	
House extant: yes	
Historical notes:	

The house, which was the ancestral home of the Hedges family from 1775 to 1900, may have been built by William Hedges. Everett Joshua Edwards purchased it in 1900. He sold the house to Mary Breck Vaill Talmage who called it *Purple House*. [*The East Hampton Star* May 4, 1972, p. 14.] In 1925 the house was purchased by Mrs. Charles Halsted Mapes who continued to call it *Purple House*. [*The East Hampton Star* February 20, 1936, p. 5.]

The *Long Island Society Register, 1929* lists Charles H. and Maie Bennett Kimball Mapes as residing at *Purple House* in East Hampton. The *Social Directory of Southampton, Long Island, 1931* lists the Mapes' address as Main Street.

He was the son of Charles Victor and Martha Meeker Halsted Mapes.

Maie Bennett Mapes had previously been married to Charles Edmunds Kimball, Sr. of East Hampton.

The house was later owned by Mrs. Mapes' son Charles Edmunds Kimball, Jr. who also called it *Purple House*. In 1941 the Kimball family deeded the house to the East Hampton Free Library.

In 1973 it was purchased by Mrs. Adelaide de Menil Carpenter who moved the house to her estate on Further Lane. When the Carpenters decided to sell their estate, Mrs. Carpenter donated the house to the Town of East Hampton which incorporated it into its town hall complex on Pantigo Road.

Mapes, Victor (1869-1943)
aka Sidney Sharp

Occupation(s):	entertainers and associate professions -
	producer, drama critic, stage manager, and director
	writer - numerous books and plays
	journalist - Paris correspondent, *The New York Sun*, NYC, 1892-1896
Marriage(s):	1900-1943 – Anna Louise Hoeke
Address:	Lily Pond Lane, East Hampton
Name of estate:	*Century Cottage*
Year of construction:	
Style of architecture:	
Architect(s):	
Landscape architect(s):	
Builder:	Thomas E, Babcock, 1906 addition
	(for Mrs. Vaill)
	J. O. Hopping, 1914
	(for Mrs. D. Talmage, Jr.)
	Edward M. Gay, 1916 addition
	(for Mapes)
House extant: unconfirmed	
Historical notes:	

In 1902 Isabella Mary Breck Vaill moved the house from Cottage Avenue to Lily Pond Lane and made improvements. [*The East Hampton Star* November 15, 1901, p. 5.] It was later owned by her daughter Mary Breck Vaill Talmage who, in 1914, had J. O. Hopping move the house further east on the property. [*The East Hampton Star* October 30, 1914, p. 5.] It was then owned by her son Rockwell Dwight Talmage who sold the house to Mapes in 1916.

He was the son of Charles Victor and Martha Meeker Halstead Mapes.

Anna Louise Hoeke Mapes was the daughter of William Henry and Elizabeth Hoeke of Washington, DC.

Victor and Anna Louise Hoeke Mapes' son James Jay Mapes II was a bachelor when he died in 1925 of double pneumonia.

By 1940 the Mapeses had relocated to Lily Pond Lane, East Hampton.

[See previous entry for additional family information.]

In 1948 the house became the base for the Summer School of Arts. [*The East Hampton Star* September 13, 1973, p. 8.]

Marsh, Marion Bolton (b. 1861)

Marriage(s):	1888-1918 – Frank Ballard Marsh (1860-1918)
	- merchant - partner, Lazell, Marsh, & Gardner, NYC (wholesale druggist);
	member, William McNaughton Sons, NYC (wool and fur commission firm)
	industrialist - secretary, treasurer and director, Theodore Richsecker Co., NYC (perfume manufacturing firm)
	Civic Activism: assistant secretary, treasurer, president, and director, Manufacturing Perfumers' Association
Address:	115 De Forest Road, Montauk
Name of estate:	*Windway*
Year of construction:	1883
Style of architecture:	Beach Cottage
Architect(s):	McKim, Mead, & White designed the house (for Benson)
Landscape architect(s):	Frederick Law Olmstead designed the site plan (for Benson)
Builder:	Mead & Taft
	George A. Eldredge & Son, 1914 alterations (for Mary Benson)
House extant:	yes
Historical notes:	

    The 4,000-square-foot house, originally named *Weeweecho*, was built by Arthur W. Benson. It was inherited by his daughter Mary, who did not marry. The *Brooklyn Blue Book and Long Island Society Register, 1918* lists Mary Benson as residing at *Weeweecho* in Montauk. The house was later owned by Marion Bolton Marsh who called it *Windway*.

    The *Brooklyn Blue Book and Long Island Society Register 1921* and *1929* list Marion Bolton Marsh as residing in Montauk.

    She was the daughter of William Henry and Frances Howell Hewlet Bolton of Brooklyn.

    Frank Ballard Marsh was the son of Edward Henry and Harriet Hubbard Wells Marsh of Brooklyn.

    Frank Ballard and Marion Bolton Marsh's son Morrison married Louise Heusner of Portland, OR, and resided in Manhattan. Their son Edward Henry Marsh II married Helen Hirst, the daughter of Edgar H. Hirst of Purcellville, PA, and resided in Brooklyn.

    The house was later owned by their daughter Penelope and son-in-law Holger Lundbergh.

    In 1981 the house was purchased by Charles Matthew Levi.

    In 1995 the house sold for $700,000.

Martin, Laura Elizabeth Young (d. 1924)

Marriage(s):	1903-1919 – Samuel Klump Martin, Jr. (1879-1919)
	- diplomat - secretary to United States Minister to Portugal, Charles Page Bryan, 1908-1909
	financier - member, Ware and Leland, Chicago, IL (stock brokerage firm);
	director, Monroe National Bank
	capitalist - real estate holdings
	Civic Activism: member, New York Stock Club. Chicago, IL; member, executive committee, Princeton Club of Chicago
Address:	121 Further Lane, East Hampton
Name of estate:	
Year of construction:	1917
Style of architecture:	Mediterranean
Architect(s):	Arthur C. Jackson designed the house (for G. W. Schurman)
	Ferguson & Shamanian, alterations (for Krakoff)
Landscape architect(s):	Charles Nassau Lowrie, Sr. (for G. W. Schurman)
	Perry Guillot (for Krakoff)
Builder:	Edward M. Gay
House extant: yes*	
Historical notes:	

The ten-bedroom, eleven-and-a-half-bath, 8,500-square-foot house, originally named *Beachclose*, was built by George Wellington Schurman. In 1923 Schurman sold the house to Mrs. Martin.

She was the daughter of Otto and Ann Elizabeth Murphy Young of Chicago and *Youngsland* (aka *Stone Manor*) on Lake Geneva, Walworth, WI.

Samuel Klump Martin, Jr. was the son of Samuel Klump and Hattie Ann Babcock Martin, Sr. and an heir to the S. K. Martin lumberyards' fortune.

Samuel Klump and Laura Elizabeth Young Martin, Jr.'s son John married Nancy Lee Byers, the daughter of John Frederic and Caroline Mitchell Morris Byers, Sr. of *Goodwood* in Sewickley, PA. Nancy was the niece of John Denniston and Maude Fleming Byers Lyon of *Wyomissing* in Matinecock. [*See* Spinzia, *Long Island's Prominent North Shore Families, vol. I* – Lyon entry.]

The Martin's unstable son Samuel Klump Martin III, known for adulterous and violent behavior and bouts of drunkenness, married Ziegfeld Follies performer Mary Jane Kittell (aka Jane Catherine Young) of Pittsburgh, PA, and resided at *Marwood* in Potomac, MD. When Samuel refused to pay for the upkeep of *Marwood* and faced threats from the utility company to shut off the power and the refusal of the local grocer to extend credit, Mary rented *Marwood* to President John Fitzgerald Kennedy's father Joseph Patrick Kennedy, Sr. in 1934. Kennedy renamed the estate *Hindenburg's Place* and used it as his "bachelor pad" until 1935. He again rented the estate from 1937-1938. In 1939 Mary sold it to Henry Grady Gore, the cousin of Senator Albert Arnold Gore, Sr. of Tennessee. *Marwood* was later owned by Nextel founder Chris Rogers. Mary subsequently married Seward Webb Pulitzer, the son of Ralph and Frederica Vanderbilt Webb Pulitzer, Sr. of *Kiluna Farm* in North Hills. [*See* Spinzia, *Long Island's Prominent North Shore Families, vol. II* – Pulitzer entry.]

Lion Gardiner purchased the East Hampton estate in 1925 and sold it the same year to Mrs. Maude Frances Sergeant Bouvier, who called the house *Lasata*. Mrs. Bouvier deeded it to her husband in 1935. In 1950 the house was sold to Frances May Archbold Hufty. In the early 1960s the house was purchased by Joseph Ansbro Meehan. It was purchased in 2006 by Reed and Delphine Krakoff.

In 2016 the Krakoffs listed the house and 7.15 acres for sale. The asking price was $38.995 million.

*The stables were demolished.

Marvel, Josiah Peter (1896-1959)

Occupation(s):	assistant director, Brooklyn Museum of Art; director, Museum of Fine Art, Springfield, MA
Civic Activism:	a founder and chairman, American Emergency Services, NYC; member, American Friends Service Committee*; operated Quaker Hotel in Paris during World War I; aided Margaret Sanger in establishing the first birth control clinic in NYC
Marriage(s):	1941-1959 – Elinore Jacobs
Address:	Egypt Lane, East Hampton
Name of estate:	
Year of construction:	
Style of architecture:	
Architect(s):	
Landscape architect(s):	
House extant:	unconfirmed
Historical notes:	

He was the son of Charles and Amy Johnson Marvel.

Elinore Jacobs Marvel had previously been married to Frederic R. Stettenheim.

*In 1940, as a representative of the Quaker's American Service Committee, Marvel traveled throughout Nazi-occupied France visiting prisoners of war.

Despondent over poor health, he committed suicide by taking an overdose of pills.

In 1944 Sarah J. Bush Foss purchased Marvel's residence which was known as Lorenzo Easton Woodhouse's Thorpe cottage. [*The East Hampton Star* July 5, 1929, p. 8, and November 23, 1944, p. 1.]

In 1949 the house was purchased by Fielding S. Robinson. [*The East Hampton Star* May 1, 1949, p. 5.]

Mascheroni, John

Occupation(s):	artist - president, John Mascheroni Signature Collection (furniture design firm)
Marriage(s):	1952-2016 – Sarina *[unable to determine maiden name]* (1932-2016) - artist - designer of china dinnerware
Address:	30 Egypt Lane, East Hampton
Name of estate:	
Year of construction:	1884
Style of architecture:	Long Island Farmhouse
Architect(s):	
Landscape architect(s):	
Builder:	Henry S. Roscoe
House extant:	yes
Historical notes:	

In 1884 Hannah M. Worthington purchased the house from its builder for $2,800. It passed through various members of the family until it was purchased by Mascheroni, who made it his residence from 1974-1982.

He was the son of Paul Mascheroni.

John and Sarina Mascheroni's son Mark married Eleanor Forbes Earle, the daughter of Ralph Earle II of Haverford, PA.

The house was later owned by Olivia and Catherine Pennington, who sold it to Renee Kathleen Zellweger in 2003.

In 2015 Zellweger listed the 2,000-square-foot, four-bedroom, three-bath house for sale. The asking price was $4.65 million.

Massey, Maurice Richardson, Jr. (1916-1979)

Occupation(s): -	financier -	president, People's Bond and Mortgage Co., Philadelphia, PA;
		vice-president, New York Guaranty Corp.;
		vice-president, North American Mortgage Corp.;
		vice-president, Fidelity Bond and Mortgage Co, Philadelphia, PA;
		director, Quaker City Federal Savings and Loan, Philadelphia, PA
	capitalist -	president, Boulevard Center, Philadelphia, PA (real estate holding firm);
		director, General Public Warehouse Co., Inc., Philadelphia, PA;
		president, Bartle, Emens and Massey, NYC;
		member, J. R. Massey & Son (real estate holding firm)
	politician -	underwriting supervisor, Federal Housing Administration, 1936-1942;
		Assistant Zone Commissioner, Federal Housing Administration

Civic Activism: treasurer, Philadelphia Civic Grand Opera Co.;
chairman, federal legislation committee, Mortgage Bankers Association of America;
second vice-president and secretary, Guild Hall, East Hampton;
chairman, drama committee, Guild Hall, East Hampton;
vice-chairman, music committee, Guild Hall, East Hampton;
a founder and director, Mid-Ocean Bath and Tennis Club, Bridgehampton, 1962

Marriage(s): 1946-1979 – Mary Charline Bates

Address: Egypt Lane, East Hampton
Name of estate: *Pond's Edge**
Year of construction: 1951
Style of architecture: Modified French Monsard
Architect(s): Polhemus & Coffin designed the house (for Massey)

Landscape architect(s):
House extant: unconfirmed
Historical notes:

    The house was built by Maurice Richardson Massey, Jr. [*The East Hampton Star* October 5, 1950, p. 1.]
    The Blue Book of the Hamptons, 1958 lists Mr. and Mrs. Maurice R. Massey as residing on Egypt Lane, East Hampton. He was the son of Maurice Richardson and Katherine Weis Massey Sr., of Overbrook, PA.
    Mary Charline Bates Massey had previously been married to John W. Salisbury, Sr. of Palm Beach, FL.
    John W. and Mary Charline Bates Salisbury Jr.'s son David Austin Salisbury married Suzanne Jackson, the daughter of Lionel Steward and Patricia Woolsey Jackson, Sr. of East Hampton.
    **Pond's Edge* is given as the name of Massey's residence in *The East Hampton Star*, June 17, 1954, p. 7.

Maxwell, Elliott (1889-1946)

Occupation(s): -	capitalist - president, R. Elliott Maxwell Associates (import-export firm)
	industrialist - vice-president, Carnegie–Illinois Steel Co.; vice-president, Whiting Corp., Chicago, IL (foundry and crane firm)
Marriage(s):	1941-1946 – Jean F. Whiting (b. 1891)
Address:	Lily Pond Lane, East Hampton
Name of estate:	*Pineleigh*
Year of construction:	
Style of architecture:	
Architect(s):	
Landscape architect(s):	
House extant:	unconfirmed
Historical notes:	

The *Social Register Summer, 1945* lists R. Elliott and Jean Florence Whiting as residing at *Pineleigh* on Lily Pond Lane, East Hampton.

She was the daughter of John Hill and Caroline Florence Spencer Whiting of Chicago, IL. Jean had previously been married to Jesse Spalding II with whom she resided at *Pineleigh*.

Elliot Maxwell was the son of Robert and Alice Haskell Maxwell of Pittsburgh, PA.

By 1958 Mrs. Maxwell had relocated to a guest house on Apaquogue Road.

Mayo, Miss Marie Louise (1854-1933)

Occupation(s):	restaurateur - proprietor, Maidstone Lunch Room, NYC; manager, Maidstone Inn, East Hampton
Marriage(s):	unmarried
Address:	Lily Pond Lane, East Hampton
Name of estate:	*Bonnie Dune*
Year of construction:	1920
Style of architecture:	Contemporary
Architect(s):	John Custis Lawrence designed the house (for M. L. Mayo)
Landscape architect(s):	
Builder:	Edward M. Gay
House extant:	yes
Historical notes:	

The house, originally named *Bonnie Dune*, was built by Marie Louise Mayo.

The *Social Register Summer, 1923* lists Marie L. and Emily Mayo as residing at *Bonnie Dune* in East Hampton. The *Social Register Summer, 1923* lists them as residing at *Bonnie Dune* in East Hampton.

Marie was the daughter of Sylvanus and Marie Louise Ritter Mayo.

In c. 1926 the house was purchased by John Neville Wheeler. [*The East Hampton Star* February 28, 1930, p. 7.]

In 1942 it was purchased by Consuelo Vanderbilt Warburton. [*The East Hampton Star* October 22, 1942, p. 2.]

Mayo–Smith, Richmond, Sr. (1854-1901)

Occupation(s):	educator - professor of political economy and social science, Columbia College, NYC (later, Columbia University), 1883-1901*
	writer - articles, *International Statistical Institute Bulletin*; articles, *Political Science Quarterly*; *Science and Statistics*, two volumes, 1895, 1899
Civic Activism:	vice-president, America Statistical Association, 1889-1901; founder and chairman of board, Economic Association; a founder, *Political Science Quarterly*
Marriage(s):	1884-1901 – Mabel Percy Ford (1864-1938)
Address:	67 Ocean Avenue, East Hampton
Name of estate:	
Year of construction:	c. 1871
Style of architecture:	Colonial Revival (after 1901 remodeling)
Architect(s):	
Landscape architect(s):	
Builder:	Stafford Tillinghast, 1899 alterations
	Asa Otis Jones, 1890 alterations (for Draper)

House extant: yes
Historical notes:

   The house, originally named *Sea Side Cottage*, was built by The Reverend Stephen Lyon Mershon, Sr. It was later owned by Mayo–Smith.
   He was the son of Preserved and Lucy Richards Mayo Smith of Troy, OH.
   Since there were other Smiths on the Columbia University faculty, Richmond added the prefix Mayo, his mother's maiden name, to his patronymics.
   Mabel Percy Ford was the daughter of Gordon Lester Ford of Brooklyn.
   Richmond and Mabel Percy Ford Mayo–Smith, Sr.'s daughter Lucy married Ulrich Bonnell Phillips of New Orleans, LA, and resided in New Haven, CT. Their son Worthington died in 1908 at the age of twelve. Their daughter Annabel did not marry. Their son Richmond Mayo–Smith, Jr. married Elizabeth Farrington of Minneapolis, MN, and resided in Dedham, MA.
   *At his death Mayo–Smith was considered the most eminent American scientific statistician.
   The house was later owned by Frances Haggerty Draper who called it *Duneside*.

McAlpin, Cordelia Maria Rose (1845-1927)

Marriage(s):   M/1 – Dr. Judson Gale Shackleton (1836-1883)
- physician - surgeon

M/2 – 1892-1901 – David Hunter McAlpin, Sr. (1816-1901)
- merchant - partner and later sole owner, chain of tobacco stores, NYC

industrialist - partner, John Cornish & Co., NYC (later, D. H. McAlpin Co., NYC) (tobacco products manufacturer);
founder, president and director, D. H. McAlpin Co., NYC

capitalist - New York City real estate;
proprietor, Hotel McAlpin, NYC;
director, Standard Gas and Light Co.

financier - director, Eleventh Ward Bank, NYC;
director, German–American Real Estate Title and Guarantee Co.;
a founder, director, and vice-president, Home Insurance Co.;
director, Manhattan Life Insurance Co., NYC;
director, National Bank of the Republic;
director, Rutgers Fire Insurance Co.;
director, Union Trust Co.;
director; First National Bank, Morristown, NJ

Civic Activism: trustee, Union Theological Seminary, NYC;
benefactor, Union Theological Seminary Library, NYC

Address: Dunemere Lane, East Hampton
Name of estate: *Roselea*
Year of construction: 1914
Style of architecture:
Architect(s):
Landscape architect(s):
House extant: unconfirmed
Historical notes:

The house was built by Cordelia Maria Rose McAlpin. [*The East Hampton Star* July 31, 1914, p. 14.]

The *Social Register Summer, 1923* lists Cordelia Rose McAlpin as residing at *Roselea*, Dunemere Lane, East Hampton. She was the daughter of Joseph and Frances Stanton Willet Rose of NYC.

Dr. Judson Gale and Mrs. Cordelia Maria Rose Shackleton's daughter Frances married Henry Knox and resided in East Hampton.

David Hunter McAlpin, Sr. was the son of James and Jane Hunter McAlpin. In 1845 David had married Cordelia's sister Frances Adelaide Rose. In 1873 he married Adelia Dempster Gardiner, his second wife. Adelia was the daughter of James D. Gardiner. She had previously been married to George E. Chamberlin.

David Hunter and Frances Adelaide Rose McAlpin, Sr.'s son Douglas was an infant at the time of his death in 1847. Their son David Hunter McAlpin, Jr. died in 1853 at the age of two. Their son Edwin married Annie Brandreth, the daughter of Benjamin and Virginia Graham Brandreth. Their son George married Sallie Blanche Benjamin and resided at *Dune Alpin* in East Hampton. Their son William married Mary Louise Close, the daughter of David and Harriette Close, and resided at *Camp Wyndover* in Paul Smith's, NY. Their daughter Frances married James Tolman Pyle, the son of James and Esther Abigail Whitman Pyle, and resided at *Hurstmont* in Morristown, NJ. Their son Joseph died in 1888. Their son David Hunter McAlpin, Jr. [III] married Emma Rockefeller, the daughter of William and Almira Geraldine Goodsell Rockefeller and resided at *Brooklawn Manor* in Morris Plains, NJ. Their son Charles married Sara Carter Pyle, the daughter of James and Esther Abigail Whitman Pyle, and resided at *Glen Alpin* in Morristown, NJ. Their son John died of typhoid fever at the age of twenty-three.

At the time of his death in 1901 McAlpin had amassed a fortune of seventy-four million dollars.

McAlpin, David Hunter, II (1880-1932)

Occupation(s):	capitalist - proprietor, Hotel McAlpin, NYC
	financier - partner, Taylor, Bates, and Co. (stock brokerage firm)
Marriage(s):	1905-1932 – Madeline Evans (1879-1945)
Address:	Dunemere Lane, East Hampton

Name of estate:
Year of construction:
Style of architecture:
Architect(s):
Landscape architect(s):
House extant: unconfirmed
Historical notes:

    The house was built by David Hunter McAlpin II.
    He was the son of General Edwin Augustus and Mrs. Anne Brandreth McAlpin.
    Madeline Evans McAlpin was the daughter of Benjamin Franklin and Harriet Cassard Bonbright Evans of *Dunemead* in East Hampton.
    David Hunter and Madeline Evans McAlpin's daughter Madeline married Wyant Davis Vanderpoel, Jr. of Morristown, NJ. Their son Malcolm married Helen Bendelair and resided in East Hampton.

McAlpin, George Lodowich, Sr. (1856-1922)

Occupation(s):	industrialist - treasurer and director, D. H. McAlpin & Co. (manufacturer of tobacco products)
	capitalist - proprietor, Hotel McAlpin, NYC
	financier - director, East Hampton National Bank
Civic Activism:	a founder and member, first board of governors, Devon Yacht Club, Amagansett;
	governor, Riding Club of East Hampton;
	a founder, Suffolk Hunt Club, 1910
Marriage(s):	1886-1922 – Sallie Blanche Benjamin (1863-1958)
	- Civic Activism: vice-president, Sanzorey Club, NY (philanthropic organization);
	director, East Hampton Visiting Nurse Association
Address:	Lee Avenue, East Hampton
Name of estate:	*Dune Alpin*
Year of construction:	1901
Style of architecture:	Colonial Revival
Architect(s):	George Keister designed the house (for G. L. McAlpin, Sr.)*
	John Custis Lawrence, alterations
Landscape architect(s):	
Builder:	Asa Otis Jones, house
	Frank Grimshaw, 82-foot-long-stable, 1901

House extant: no; demolished in 1950
Historical notes:

The 60 x 104-foot, four-floor, fifty-foot-high, twenty-one-room house, originally named *Dune Alpin*, was built by George Lodowich McAlpin, Sr. [*The East Hampton Star* November 2, 1900, p. 5; November 23, 1900, p. 5; November 30, 1900, p. 5; January 4, 1901, p. 5; and April 19, 1901, p. 5.]

The *Social Register Summer, 1910* lists George L. and S. Blanche Benjamin McAlpin [Sr.] as residing at *Dune Alpin* in East Hampton.

He was the son of David Hunter and Frances Adelaide Rose McAlpin, Sr.

Sallie Blanche Benjamin McAlpin was the daughter of William Wallace and Delia Ann Flint Benjamin, Sr. of Sing [Ossining], NY. Sallie's brother William Wallace Benjamin, Jr. married Florence A. Briggs and resided at *Crossroads* in East Hampton.

George Lodowich and Sallie Blanche Benjamin McAlpin, Sr.'s daughter Dorothy married Alfred Dennis Bell and resided in East Hampton. Their daughter Jeannette married A. Musgrave Hyde. Their daughter Flora, who resided in East Hampton and in Los Angeles, CA, married Charles Pierce Barton, Jr. and, later, Roy Clinton Seeley, the son of Aron Seeley of Los Angeles, CA. Their son George Lodowich McAlpin, Jr. married Elizabeth Jennison; Nancy Pierson Sands; and Eleanor Campbell Best, the former wife of Henry Arnold Peckham, Jr. of *Eastmere* in East Hampton.

While a patient in Roosevelt Hospital, their son George Lodowich McAlpin, Jr. distraught over his poor health, asked his aunt Flora G. Benjamin to bring his locked valise so that he could review some papers. He shot himself in the temple with a revolver that was secreted in the valise. [*The New York Times* January 27, 1950, p. 20.]

[See other McAlpin entries for additional family information.]

*Keister also designed McAlpin's Manhattan residence.

In 1929 the estate was purchased by William Carter Dickerman, Sr. who renamed in *Dune Dee*. [*The East Hampton Star* March 29, 1929, p. 1.] In 1949 the estate was sold by Mrs. Dickerman to Thomas S. Nichols who, in 1950, sold it to Jay Holmes. Holmes demolished it to build his new residence. [*The East Hampton Star* October 5, 1950, p. 5.]

McAlpin, Malcolm Evans (1909-1985)

Occupation(s):	capitalist -	director, All American Airways, Inc. (later, Allegheny Airline, Inc.);
		director, Allegheny Airline Inc.;
		director, Brandreth Lake Lumber Co., Long Lake, NY
	merchant -	president, Macrombie Airways, Inc., Morristown, NJ (sells airplanes);
		director, ICC Chemical Corp. (distributer of chemicals, plastics, and pharmaceuticals)
	industrialist -	director, Electric Autolite Co. (manufacturer of spark plugs);
		director, Hiller Industries, Berkeley, CA (later, Hiller aircraft) (manufacturer of helicopters);
		director, Eltra Corp. (aerospace and defense firm)
	financier -	vice-president, Fiduciary Counsel, Inc. (wealth management firm);
		vice-president, Blalack–Wells–Associates, Inc. (stock brokerage firm);
		vice-president, Talcott, McAlpin, and Davis (stock brokerage firm);
		partner, Talcott, Potter, and Co. (stock brokerage firm);
		director, Continental Mortgage and Investment Co.
	writer -	sports and dog articles for magazines;
		children's book
Civic Activism:		wing commander, New Jersey Chapter, Air Force Association;
		trustee, Peck School, Morristown, NJ
Marriage(s):		1937-1985 – Helen Bendelair (1906-1999)
Address:		Lily Pond Lane, East Hampton
Name of estate:		*Dunemead*
Year of construction:		1913
Style of architecture:		Shingle
Architect(s):		John Custis Lawrence designed the house (for Evans)
Builder:		Smith and Davis built the house
		R. S. Parsons, electrical
		S. C. Grimshaw, plumbing
		S. J. Lynch, masonry
Landscape architect(s):		
House extant: yes		
Historical notes:		

 The twelve-bedroom, four-bath house, originally named *Dunemead*, was built by Benjamin Franklin Evans. It was later owned by McAlpin.
 The *Social Register, 1946* and *1950* list Helen Bendelair McAlpin as residing at *Dunemead* in East Hampton.
 She was the daughter of Fred N. Bendelair of Joplin, MO. Helen had previously been married to Egerton Ward Boughton Leigh, the son of John Hugh Ward Boughton and Alice Mary Herrick Leigh of Great Britain.
 Malcolm Evans McAlpin was the son of David Hunter and Madeline Evans McAlpin II of East Hampton.
 Both Helen and Malcolm represented the United States in the 1936 Olympics. She was captain of United States women's ski team and, in 1968, was inducted into the United States Ski Hall of Fame (now, the United States Ski and Snowboard Hall of Fame). Malcolm was a member of the United States Olympic hockey team.
 Malcolm Evans and Helen Bendelair McAlpin's son David Heywood McAlpin married Susan Ballantine Cumming, the daughter of Peter Hood Ballantine Cumming of Rumson, NJ. Their daughter Ann married ____ Cain.
 In 2002 the house was listed for sale. The asking price was $27 million. [*The New York Times* September 15, 2002, p. E118.]

McCaffray, Walter Peck (1888-1935)

Occupation(s):	financier - founder, Walter P. McCaffray and Co. (stock brokerage firm)
Civic Activism:	governor, New York Stock Exchange, NYC
Marriage(s):	Alys Mary Curran (d. 1940) - Civic Activism: donated the estate to a religious order*
Address:	Old Montauk Highway, Montauk
Name of estate:	*Sandpiper Hill*
Year of construction:	1928
Style of architecture:	Eclectic Shingle
Architect(s):	Richard Webb designed the house (for McCaffray)
Landscape architect(s):	

House extant: no; demolished in 1973**
Historical notes:

The house, originally named *Sandpiper Hill*, was built by Walter Peck McCaffray. Walter committed suicide following the 1929 stock market crash. [Russell Drumm, *The East Hampton Star* March 20, 2009.]

He was the son of Arthur S. and Jane Peck McCaffray.

Mrs. McCaffray bequeathed the estate to the Order of the Society of Jesus to provide a home or retreat for ailing or retired Jesuits. [*The New York Times* August 1, 1940, p. 23.] The Jesuits sold the estate to Sidney Rheinstein.

**The windmill section of the house was sold to Peter Beard who moved it to another bluff in the Montauk Moorlands. It was later destroyed by fire. Other sections of the house were relocated to Old Montauk Highway in Montauk.

McCall, Clifford Hyde, Sr. (1891-1969)

Occupation(s):	writer - playwright
Civic Activism:	treasurer, Maidstone Club, East Hampton
Marriage(s):	1925 – Elvine Richard (1895-1974) - Civic Activism: president, Ladies Village Improvement Society, East Hampton
Address:	Apaquogue Road, East Hampton
Name of estate:	*Kipsveen*
Year of construction:	
Style of architecture:	
Architect(s):	
Landscape architect(s):	Nellie Beatrice Osborn Allen, c. 1927 (for C. H. McCall)

House extant: unconfirmed
Nassau County Museum Collection has photographs of the estate.
Historical notes:

The house was previously owned by Lawrence Greer. [*The East Hampton Star* December 25, 1925, p. 2.]

The *Social Register New York, 1933* lists Clifford H. and Elvine Richard McCall [Sr.] as residing in East Hampton.

He was the son of John Augustine and Mary I. Horan McCall of *Shadow Lawn* in Elberon, NJ.

Elvine Richard McCall was the daughter of Edwin Auguste and Alice Bartow Moore Richard of Manhattan. She had previously been married to Curt Eric Hansen of East Hampton. Elvine's brother Auguste married Rita Conway and resided in East Hampton.

Clifford Hyde and Elvine Richard McCall, Sr.'s son Clifford Hyde McCall, Jr. married Diane Dobbs and, later, Barbara Birkelund.

In 1951 the house was purchased by Count Leonardo Mercati. [*The East Hampton Star* November 8, 1951, p. 5.]

McCall, Edward Everett (1863-1924)

Occupation(s):	attorney - judge, First District, New York State Supreme Court, 1903-1913;
	judge, New York State Supreme Court
	financier - financial director, International Bank & Trust Co.
	industrialist - president and director, International and Vehicle Tire Co.
	politician - unsuccessful Tammany candidate for mayor of New York City
Civic Activism:	chairman, New York State Public Service Commission
Marriage(s):	1886-1924 – Ella Frances Gaynor (d. 1954)

Address: West End Avenue, East Hampton
Name of estate: *Evsdune*
Year of construction: c. 1914
Style of architecture: Shingle
Architect(s):
Landscape architect(s):
House extant: no; destroyed by fire, 1927
Nassau County Museum Collection has photographs of the estate.
Historical notes:

The house, originally named *Evsdune*, was built by Edward Everett McCall.

The *Social Register Summer, 1921* lists Edward Everett and Ella F. Gaynor McCall as residing at *Evsdune* in East Hampton.

He was the son of John and Katherine McCall of Albany, NY.

Ella Frances Gaynor McCall was the daughter of Thomas S. Gaynor of Albany, NY.

Edward Everett and Ella Frances Gaynor McCall's daughter Ella married William Raywood Maloney, Sr. and resided in East Hampton. Their daughter Constance married Herbert Hartley Ramsay, the son of William Edmund and Katherine Pennoyer Ramsay, and resided in East Hampton.

McCartney, Paul (b. 1942)
aka James Paul McCartney

Occupation(s):	entertainers and associated professions -
	a founder of the Beatles (rock and roll band);
	a founder, with his wife Linda, Wings
	composer - songwriter of popular music;
	orchestral music including "Liverpool Oratorio", 1991 and "Working Classical", 1999
	capitalist - founder, MPL (umbrella firm for his business interests)
Marriage(s):	M/1 – 1969-1998 – Linda Louise Eastman (1941-1998)
	- entertainers and associated professions -
	singer, musician;
	founder, with her husband Paul, Wings
	industrialist - founder, Linda McCartney Foods (vegetarian meals; merged into H. J. Heinz Co. in 2000, then into Hain Celestial Group in 2007)
	writer - *Linda McCartney's Sixties*;
	co-authored, with Peter Cox, *Linda McCartney's Home Cooking*, 1989;
	Linda's Kitchen and Simple and Inspiring Recipes for Meatless Meals
	Civic Activism: patron, League Against Cruel Sports
	M/2 – 2002-div. 2008 – Heather Mills (b. 1968)
	- model
	writer - co-authored, with Pamela Cockerill, *Out on a Limb*, 1995 (autobiography)
	Civic Activism: patron, Vegetarians International Voice for Animals;
	patron, Vegetarian and Vegan Foundation;
	president, Limbless Association;
	goodwill ambassador, Adopt-A-Minefield

McCartney, Paul
aka James Paul McCartney (cont'd)

M/3 – 2011 – Nancy Shevell (b. 1959)
- politician - member of board, New York Metropolitan Transportation Authority

Address: 11 Pintail Lane, Amagansett
Name of estate:
Year of construction:
Style of architecture:
Architect(s):
Landscape architect(s):
House extant: yes
Historical notes:

In 1998 Paul McCartney purchased the house.

He is the son of James and Mary Patricia Mohin McCartney of Liverpool, England.

Linda Louise Eastman was the daughter of Leopold Vail Epstein (aka Lee Eastman) and Louise Sara Linder Eastman. Linda had previously been married to Joseph Melville See. Their daughter Heather was adopted by McCartney.

Paul and Linda Louise Eastman McCartney's daughter Mary married Alistair Donald and, later, Simon Aboud. Their daughter Stella married Alasdhair Willis.

Heather Mills McCartney is the daughter of John Francis and Beatrice Mary Mills of Aldershot, Great Britain. Heather had previously been married to Alfie Karmal.

Paul and Heather Mills McCartney's daughter Beatrice was born in 2003.

Nancy Shovell McCartney is the daughter of Myron P. and Arlene Walter Shevell.

*McCartney was inducted into the Rock and Roll Hall of fame two times—as a member of the Beatles in 1988 and again in 1999 as a solo artist.

McConnell, David Hall, III (1926-1990)

Occupation(s): capitalist - an owner, New England Patriots football team; co-owner, with Robert C. Wetenhall, Colony Hotel, Palm Beach, FL

Marriage(s): M/1 – 1947-div. 1954 – Shelagh Banks Bertschmann (1927-2001)
M/2 – Darlene Joy Monroe

Address: Lee Avenue, East Hampton
Name of estate:
Year of construction: 1899
Style of architecture: Colonial Revival with Federal elements
Architect(s): Leinau and Nash designed the house (for Carson)
Landscape architect(s):
Builder: Asa Otis Jones, 1899
Asa Otis Jones, 1901 alterations (for Carson)
House extant: yes*
Historical notes:

The house was built by William Moore Carson, Sr. In 1920 it was purchased by Earle Westwood Sinclair. [*The East Hampton Star* July 30, 1920, p. 6.] In 1945 Robert Elliot McCormick purchased Sinclair's residence. [*The East Hampton Star* November 8, 1945, p. 1.] In 1946 McCormick sold the house to Walter Bartow Duryea. [*The East Hampton Star* February 20, 1947, p. 6.] It was later owned by McConnell. [*The East Hampton Star* May 20, 1965, p. 2.]

He was the son of David Hall and Marjorie Anderson McConnell, Jr.

Shelagh Banks Bertschmann McConnell was the daughter of Jean Jacques and Constance Banks Bertschmann. Shelagh subsequently married Ralph Strother Richards, Jr.

The Blue Book of The Hamptons, 1987 lists David Hall and Darlene Joy Monroe McConnell [III] as residing on Lee Avenue in East Hampton.

*In 1901 a west wing was added to the house.

McConnell, Neil Anderson (1929-1994)

Occupation(s):	financier - member, Baker, Weeks, and Co. (stock brokerage firm); president, Neil A. McConnell Securities, Inc.; partner, Pioneer Group (venture capital firm)
Civic Activism:	founder and chairman of board, Neil A. McConnell Foundation

Marriage(s):
- M/1 – 1951-div. 1958 – Katherine Ann Devine (b. 1931)
- M/2 – 1961-div. 1965 – Vanessa Mary Somers (1935-2015)
  - artist - sculptress, avande works in plastic and glass
  - writer -   co-authored with Frederick Vreeland, *Key to Rome*, 2006
  - educator -   taught at Corning Glass Museum, Corning, NY; Penland School of Crafts, Bakersville, NC; Columbia Museum of Art, Columbia, SC
- M/3 – 1968-div. – Serena Mary Churchill Russell (b. 1944)
  - Civic Activism: director, U. S. Charitable Trust
- M/4 – 1982 – Sandra Dorothea Haig
  - interior designer -   president, Sandra Merriman, Inc.
  - Civic Activism: director, Animal Rescue Foundation; director, Kips Bay Boys and Girls Club; director, Neil A. McConnell Foundation

Address: Lee Avenue, East Hampton
Name of estate:
Year of construction:
Style of architecture:
Architect(s):
Landscape architect(s):
House extant: unconfirmed
Historical notes:

The Blue Book of The Hamptons, 1958 lists Mr. and Mrs. Neil A. McConnell as residing on Lee Avenue, East Hampton.

He is the son of David Hall and Marjorie Anderson McConnell, Jr. of New York and heir to Avon Products fortune.

Catherine Ann Devine McConnell is the daughter of James J. Devine of East Hampton. She subsequently married the noted actor and World War II member of the Office of Strategic Services Sterling Hayden.

Neil Anderson and Catherine Ann Devine McConnell's son Bernard Scott co-founded, with Pat Buchanan, *The American Conservative*.

Vanessa Mary Somers McConnell is the daughter of David Somers of Kent, England. She subsequently married the United States diplomat Frederick Dalziel Vreeland, the son of Thomas Reed and Diana Dalziel Vreeland, Sr.

Serena Mary Churchill Russell is the daughter of Edwin Fairman and Lady Sarah Consuelo Spencer–Churchill Russell of Brookville and the granddaughter of Duke Richard John Spencer–Churchill and Duchess Consuelo Vanderbilt Spencer–Churchill. Sarah's grandmother Consuelo subsequently married Louis Jacques Balsan with whom she resided at *Gardenside* in Southampton and at *Old Fields* in East Norwich. Sarah's great-grandparents William Kissam and Alva Erskine Smith Vanderbilt, Sr. resided at *Idlehour* in Oakdale. [*See* Spinzia, *Long Island's Prominent Families in the Town of Southampton* and *Long Island's Prominent North Shore Families, vol. I* – Balsan entries; *Long Island's Prominent South Shore Families* – Vanderbilt entry; *Long Island's Prominent North Shore Families, vol. II* – Russell entry; and *Long Island's Prominent North Shore Families, vol. I*, and *Long Island's Prominent Families in the Town of Hempstead* – Belmont entries.] Serena had previously been married to Robert Stephen Salant, Jr. After her divorce from McConnell, Serena married Neil Roxburgh Balfour of Great Britain.

Sandra Dorothea Haig McConnell is the daughter of John H. and Theodora Jacobson Haig of Chestnut Hill, PA. Sandra had previously been married to David Woods Merriman, the son of Howard R. Merriman of Providence, RI.

McCord, David Walter (1865-1945)

Occupation(s):	industrialist - vice-president, McCord Corp., Detroit, MI (automobile radiator and electrical refrigeration accessories manufacturing firm)
Civic Activism:	secretary, Maidstone Club, East Hampton, 1918
Marriage(s):	1893-1940 – Fannie Eliza Davis (1867-1940)
Address:	Hither Lane, East Hampton
Name of estate:	*Hither House*
Year of construction:	1899
Style of architecture:	Modified Cotswold
Architect(s):	Grosvenor Atterbury designed the house (for C. C. Rice)

Landscape architect(s):
House extant: no; destroyed by fire
Nassau County Museum Collection has photographs of the estate.
Historical notes:

The house was built by Dr. Clarence C. Rice. In 1910 it was purchased by McCord who called it *Hither House*. [*The East Hampton Star* February 11, 1910, p. 5.]

The *Social Register Summer, 1910* and *1937* list David W. and Fannie E. Davis McCord as residing in East Hampton. He was the son of William B. and Mary Campbell McCord.

Fannie Eliza Davis McCord was the daughter of Oliver and Sarah E. Davis of Danville, IL.

The *Social Register Summer, 1915* lists David W. and Fannie E. Davis McCord as residing at *Hither House* in East Hampton.

David Walter and Fannie Eliza Davis McCord's daughter Dorothy married William Jackson Lippincott, the son of Jason Evans and Minnie Steward Horner Lippincott of Cincinnati, OH, and resided in East Hampton and in Oyster Bay. [*See* Spinzia, *Long Island's Prominent North Shore Families, vol. 1* – Lippincott entry.] Their daughter Janet married Francis Howell Cook, the son of Henry Francis and Lena Marianna Fahys Cook of *Clench–Warton* in North Haven, and resided in East Hampton. [*See* Spinzia, *Long Island's Prominent Families in the Town of Southampton* – Cook entry.]

In 1946 Evan Frankel purchased the estate and renovated the carriage house into his residence. He sunk a swimming pool into the former main residence's foundation and named his residence *Brigadoon*.

McCormick, Robert Elliot (1903-1969)

Occupation(s):	attorney - member, Alexander and Green, NYC;
	general counsel, Olin Mathieson Corp.;
	general counsel, International Hotel Corp.
	financier - director, Gotham Investment Corp.
	industrialist - director, U. S. Materials Corp.;
	vice president and secretary, Olin Mathieson Corp.;
	director, Consolidated Machine & Engine Co.;
	director, Kardar Canadian Oils, Ltd.;
	director, Lister–Blackstone, Inc.
Civic Activism:	president, Boys Athletic League;
	director, Vocational Foundation, Inc.;
	trustee, Eye Bank;
	trustee, Retina Foundation;
	trustee, American Foundation for the Blind;
	trustee, American Foundation for the Overseas Blind;
	a founder and president, Research to Prevent Blindness, Inc.
Marriage(s):	M/1 – 1927-1942 – Helen Roberts (1903-1942)
	M/2 – 1950-1969 – Clotilde Knapp (1908-2004)
	- real estate agent
Address:	Lee Avenue, East Hampton
Name of estate:	
Year of construction:	1899
Style of architecture:	Colonial Revival with Federal elements
Architect(s):	Leinau and Nash designed
	the house (for Carson)
Landscape architect(s):	
Builder:	Asa Otis Jones, 1899
	Asa Otis Jones, 1901 alterations
	(for Carson)

House extant: yes*
Historical notes:

The house was built by William Moore Carson, Sr. In 1920 it was purchased by Earle Westwood Sinclair. [*The East Hampton Star* July 30, 1920, p. 6.] In 1945 McCormick purchased Sinclair's residence. [*The East Hampton Star* November 8, 1945, p. 1.]

He was the son of Robert Nish and Adele Elliott McCormick.

Helen Roberts McCormick was the daughter of Dr. Dudley DeVore and Mrs. Carrie Elise Steele Roberts, Sr. of *Outabounds* in East Hampton.

Robert Elliot and Helen Roberts McCormick's son Sandford married Inex Balene Cross, the daughter of William R. Cross of Rydall. PA.

Clotilde Knapp McCormick was the daughter of Charles and Martha Marie deKersauson Knapp. Clotilde had previously been married to Charles James Miratti and Count Hans Clemens von Franken–Sierstorpff. She subsequently married General Charles Eskridge Saltzman.

*In 1901 a west wing was added to the house.

In 1946 McCormick sold the house to Walter Bartow Duryea. [*The East Hampton Star* February 20, 1947, p. 6.]

It was later owned by David Hall McConnell III. [*The East Hampton Star* May 20, 1965, p. 2.]

McKeon, Robert Brian (1954-2012)

Occupation(s):	financier - a founder and chairman of board, Wasserstein Perella Management (investment banking firm); a founder, Veritas Capital (private equity firm); director, First Boston Corporation
Civic Activism:	trustee, Fordham University, The Bronx, NY; endowed lectures at Council of Foreign Affairs; founder, Robert B. McKeon Fellowship Fund for Military Personnel, Harvard University, Cambridge, MA; chairman of board, Connecticut Health and Educational Facilities Authority
Marriage(s):	M/1 – 1977-div. – Patricia Ann Finnegan (b. 1954) - educator - assistant principal, International School of Dundee, Greenwich, CT M/2 – 2007-2012 – Clare Elizabeth Smith (b. 1974)
Address:	Further Lane, East Hampton
Name of estate	
Year of construction:	
Style of architecture:	Contemporary
Architect(s):	
Landscape architect(s):	
House extant: yes	
Historical notes:	

McKeon was the son of Donald Stillwell and Diana Brady McKeon, Sr. of New Windsor, NY. McKeon's death was ruled a suicide by asphyxia.

Patricia Ann Finnegan McKeon is the daughter of Michael Finnegan of Nanuet, NY.

Robert Brian and Patricia Ann Finnegan McKeon's daughter Jacqueline married William Stuart Shufelt, the son of Douglas G. and Elizabeth D. Shufelt of Wilmington, VT.

Clare Elizabeth Smith McKeon is the daughter of Philip Reginald and Mary Roberts Smith of Gloucestershire, England.

In 2013 the 10,000-square-foot, seven-bedroom house was purchased by Steven A. Cohen for $60 million.

McKittrick, Marjorie Holland (1891-1941)

Marriage(s):	1912-div. 1926 – Walter McKittrick (1873-1965) - merchant - vice-president, McKittrick Dry Goods Co., St. Louis, MO; vice-president and treasurer, Ely–Walker & Co., St. Louis, MO (dry goods firm); vice-president, Rice–Stix Dry Goods Co., St. Louis, MO financier - director, Mercantile–Commercial Bank and Trust Co., St. Louis, MO
Address:	New Highway, East Hampton
Name of estate:	
Year of construction:	1940
Style of architecture:	
Architect(s):	
Landscape architect(s):	
Builder:	Barns Brothers
House extant: unconfirmed	
Historical notes:	

The house was built by Marjorie Holland McKittrick. [*The Brooklyn Daily Eagle* April 21, 1940, p. 20.]

She was the daughter of George H. and Nora Wilcoxsou Holland of Carrollton, MO.

Walter McKittrick was the son of Hugh and Mary Webber Cutter McKittrick of St. Louis, MO.

Walter and Marjorie Holland McKittrick's daughter Marjorie married Frank Whittesley Berrien, the son of F. D. Berrien of Brookline, MA, and, later, Richard Bull Smith, the son of Edward Henry Leighton and Katharine Louise Hagemeyer Smith, Sr.

In 1941 the house was purchased by Mrs. Lucie Wilshire Graham. [*The East Hampton Star* October 23, 1941, p. 5.]

McLanahan, Scott (1877-1946)

Occupation(s):	attorney - partner, Austin and McLanahan (later, Austin, McLanahan, and Merritt) industrialist - director, Austrian Brentwood Furniture Co.; director, American Hide and Leather Co., Boston, MA financier - director, Lawyer's Mortgage Corp., NYC industrialist - director, Savage Arms Corp., Utica, NY; Chipman Knitting Mills, Easton, PA
Civic Activism:	secretary, Citizen's Committee of One Hundred; president, Maidstone Club, East Hampton; governor, Riding Club of East Hampton; member of board, Village of East Hampton; governor, University Club, NYC
Marriage(s):	1913-1946 – Clara Lee Ogden (1879-1964)
Address:	Huntting Lane, East Hampton
Name of estate:	*Nevermind*
Year of construction:	
Style of architecture:	1918
Architect(s):	
Landscape architect(s):	

House extant: unconfirmed
Historical notes:

The house, originally named *Nevermind*, was built by Scott McLanahan. [*The East Hampton Star* September 28, 1917, p. 5, and May 23, 1946, p. 1.]

The *Long Island Society Register, 1929* lists Scott and Clara Lee Ogden McLanahan as residing at *Nevermind* on Huntting Lane in East Hampton.

He was the son of Dr. Johnston and Mrs. Rebekah A. Austin McLanahan of Chambersburg, PA.

Clara Lee Ogden McLanahan was the daughter of Willis Lord and Ellen Louise Smith Ogden of Brooklyn. Clara's sister Elsie married Alexander Moss White, Sr. and resided at *Weymouth* in Cove Neck. [*See* Spinzia, *Long Island's Prominent North Shore Families, vol. II* – White entry.]

McSpadden, Jack Dobbs, Jr. (b. 1945)

Occupation(s):	financier - vice-president, Goldman Sachs, 1974-1992; managed director, Credit Suisse First Boston, 1992-1999; managing director, Citigroup, Inc., 1999-present
Marriage(s):	1979 – Ruth Ann Wood - interior designer Civic Activism: trustee, Junior League of New York; member, board of women managers, Babies Hospital, NYC; trustee, Eleanor Whitmore Early Childhood Center
Address:	Oceanview Lane, Amagansett
Name of estate:	*Devon House*
Year of construction:	1909
Style of architecture:	Mediterranean Villa
Architect(s):	Tietig and Lee designed the house (for W. C. Procter)

Landscape architect(s):
House extant: yes
Historical notes:

The seven-bedroom, five-bath house was built by William Cooper Procter. It was later owned by Procter's niece Mary Elizabeth Johnston, who called it *Devon House*. In 1967 she bequeathed *Devon House* and its furnishings to her niece Anne Johnston Sawyer Greene, who resided at *Devon House* with her husband John Bradley Greene II. In 1987 McSpadden purchased the house from Mrs. Greene and continued to call it *Devon House*.

He is the son of Jack Dodds McSpadden, Sr. of Birmingham, AL.

Ruth Ann Wood McSpadden is the daughter of Geoffrey Richard Wood of Edinburg, NY.

By 2008 the McSpaddens had relocated to *Swansong* in Amagansett. *The Blue Book of The Hamptons, 2008* lists Jack Dobbs and Ruth Ann Wood McSpadden, Jr. as residing at *Swansong* at 332 Bluff Road, Amagansett.

Meehan, Joseph Ansbro (1917-1972)

Occupation(s):	financier - partner, M. J. Meehan and Co. (stock brokerage firm); governor, New York State Stock Exchange; vice-president, Henderson Brothers (stock brokerage firm) industrialist - president and chairman of board, Good Humor Corp. (ice cream manufacturing firm)*
Civic Activism:	chairman, finance committee, Winchendon School, Winchendon, MA
Marriage(s):	1939-1972 – Katherine Esther Sullivan (1919-2011)
Address:	121 Further Lane, East Hampton
Name of estate:	
Year of construction:	1917
Style of architecture:	Mediterranean
Architect(s):	Arthur C. Jackson designed the house (for G. W. Schurman) Ferguson & Shamamian, alterations (for Krakoff)
Landscape architect(s):	Charles Nassau Lowrie, Sr. (for G. W. Schurman) Perry Guilott (for Krakoff)
Builder:	Edward M. Gay

House extant: yes**
Historical notes:

The ten-bedroom, eleven-and-a-half bath, 8,500-square-foot house, originally named *Beachclose*, was built by George Wellington Schurman. In 1923 Schurman sold the house to Laura Elizabeth Young Martin, who died in 1924. Lion Gardiner purchased it in 1925 and sold it to Mrs. Maude Frances Sergeant Bouvier, who called the house *Lasata*. Mrs. Bouvier deeded it to her husband in 1935. In 1950 the house was sold to Frances May Archbold Hufty. In the early 1960s the house was purchased by Meehan, who had previously resided at *Adare* in Southampton. [*See* Spinzia, *Long Island's Prominent Families in the Town of Southampton* – Meehan entry.]

He was the son of Michael J. and Elizabeth Higgins Meehan of Manhattan.

Katherine Esther Sullivan Meehan was the daughter of Dr. Raymond Peter and Mrs. Marie E. Mc Namee Sullivan, Sr. of Bay Shore. [*See* Spinzia, *Long Island's Prominent South Shore Families* – Sullivan entry.] Katherine's sister Marie did not marry. Her brother William married Jean Kay Simonson, the daughter of Henry James Simonson of Southampton. Her brother Raymond Peter Sullivan, Jr. married Catherine McDonnell, the daughter of James Francis and Anna Murray McDonnell, Sr. of *East Wickapogue Cottage* in Southampton and resided in Southampton. [*See* Spinzia, *Long Island's Prominent Families* in the Town of Southampton – Simonson and Sullivan entries.] Her brother John married Pauline Elaine Gerli, the daughter of Paolina Gerli of Manhattan, and resided at *Longford* in Ridgefield, CT.

Joseph Ansbro and Katherine Ester Sullivan Meehan's son Michael J. Meehan II married Alexandra Duer Irving, the daughter of Alexander Duer Irving II of Unionville, PA. Their daughter Marcia married Bayard George Schaeffer, the son of John George Schaeffer of Reading, PA, and resided in Southampton. [*See* Spinzia, *Long Island's Prominent Families in the Town of Southampton* – Schaeffer entry.]

*The Meehan family owned the Good Humor Corporation until 1962 when they sold the company to Thomas J. Lipton, Inc. for estate-planning purposes.

The house was purchased in 2006 by Reed and Delphine Krakoff. In 2016 the Krakoffs listed the house and 7.15 acres for sale. The asking price was $38.995 million.

**The stables were demolished.

Mercati, Count Leonardo (1901-1974)

Occupation(s):	industrialist - chairman of board, Athenian Brewery, Athens, Greece nobility

Marriage(s):	M/1 – 1934 – Lily Stathatos
	    - nobility
	M/2 – 1973-1974 – Barbara Tapper (1907-1995)
	    - nobility
	        Civic Activism: member, national council, Metropolitan
	                Opera, NYC;
	           vice-president and director, English Speaking
	                Union

Address:	Apaquogue Road, East Hampton
Name of estate:	
Year of construction:	
Style of architecture:	
Architect(s):	
Landscape architect(s):	Nellie Beatrice Osborn Allen, c.1927 (for C. H. McCall)

House extant: unconfirmed
Nassau County Museum Collection has photographs of the estate.
Historical notes:
    The house was previously owned by Lawrence Greer and Clifford Hyde McCall, Sr. [*The East Hampton Star* December 25, 1925, p. 2.] In 1951 it was purchased by Mercati. [*The East Hampton Star* November 8, 1951, p. 5.]
    He was the son of the Lord Chamberlain of Greece Count Alexander and his wife Countess Harriet Wright Mercati. Lily Stathatos Mercati was the daughter of Anthony Stathatos of Athens, Greece.
    Count Leonardo and Countess Lily Stathatos Mercati's daughter Atalanta married Constantine B. Goulandris, the son of Basil Goulandris of London, England. Their daughter Eleni married Costi Dracopulo of New York.
    Barbara Tapper Mercati had previously been married to Baron Antonio d'Almedia and Paul Felix Solomon Warburg.
    By 1958 Mercati had relocated to Georgica Road. *The Blue Book of The Hamptons, 1958* lists Count Leonardo and Countess Lily Stathatos Mercati as residing at *Meltemi* on Georgica Road in East Hampton.

Mercer, Norman J. (1916-2007)

Occupation(s):	artist - sculptor capitalist - president, Import Associates Art Ltd. industrialist - president, Englishtown Cutlery, Inc.
Civic Activism:	member, War Production Board (FDR and Truman administrations) president, East Hampton Historical Society

Marriage(s):	1971-2007 – Carol Mary Keyser (1923-2016)
	    - entertainers and associated professions - Broadway dancer
	    landscape architect - co-owner, with Lisa Verderosa,
	            The Secret

Address:	33 Ocean Avenue, East Hampton
Name of estate:	
Year of construction:	1977
Style of architecture:	Modern

Architect(s):	Robert Arthur Morton Stern designed
	    the house (for Mercer)
	Alfredo De Vido designed the 1982
	    addition of the 2,200-square-foot shop,
	    sculpture gallery, and greenhouse
	    (for Mercer)

Landscape architect(s)	Carol Keyser Mercer designed her own gardens

House extant: yes
Historical notes:
    The six-bedroom, six-bath, 7,500-square-foot house was built by Norman J. Mercer.
    Carol Keyser Mercer is the daughter of Walter G. and Beatrice Lewis Keyser. Carol had previously been married to Robert McElfresh and the noted actor William Windom.
    In 2017 the house and three acres were for sale. The asking price was $13.9 million.

Mershon, The Reverend Stephen Lyon, Sr. (1827-1874)

Occupation(s):	clergy - pastor, East Hampton Presbyterian Church, 1854-1866
	writer - *The Christian Sanctuary or, the Church of the Colony and Town of East Hampton, Long Island, NY. A. D. 1649-1861*, 1861
Marriage(s):	Mary Talmage (1828-1872)
Address:	67 Ocean Avenue, East Hampton
Name of estate:	*Sea Side Cottage*
Year of construction:	c. 1871
Style of architecture:	Colonial Revival (after 1901 remodeling)
Architect(s):	
Landscape architect(s):	
Builder:	Stafford Tillinghast, 1899 alterations (for Mayo–Smith)
	Asa Otis Jones, 1890 alterations (for Draper)

House extant: yes
Historical notes:

The house, originally named *Sea Side Cottage*, was built by The Reverend Stephen Lyon Mershon, Sr.

He was the son of William Titus and Sarah Lyon Mershon.

Mary Talmage Mershon was the daughter of David T. and Catherine Van Nest Talmage of Somerset County, NJ.

The Reverend Stephen Lyon and Mrs. Mary Talmage Mershon, Sr.'s son Stephen Lyon Mershon, Jr. married Adelaide Jane Hawkins, the daughter of John and Sarah Chichester Hawkins, and resided in Montclair, NJ. Their daughter Sarah married The Reverend Ralph Brokaw. Their daughter Emma married Gerald R. Cushman. Their son David was an infant at the time of his death. Their daughter Grace married Frederick W. Hannahs of Newark, NJ. Their son Dan resided in Manhattan. Their daughter Mary married Henry D. Ames. Their daughter Bessie was youth at the time of her death.

The house was later owned by Richmond Mayo–Smith, Sr. and, then, by Frances S. Haggerty Draper who called it *Duneside*.

Michaels, Lorne (b. 1944)
aka Lorne Lipowitz

Occupation(s):	entertainers and associated professions* -
	a creator, "Saturday Night" (later, "Saturday Night Live");
	founder, Broadway Video, 1979;
	executive producer, "Light Night", "30 Rock", "Up All Night", "The Tonight Show", and "The Tonight Show Starring Jimmy Fallon"
	actor - Canadian television
	writer - CBC radio, "Laugh-In", "The Beautiful Phyllis Diller Show"
Marriage(s):	M/1 – 1967-1980 – Rosie Shuster (b. 1950)
	- writer - "Square Pegs"; scriptwriter, "Saturday Night Live"
	entertainers and associated professions - actress
	M/2 – 1984-1987 – Susan Forrestal
	- entertainers and associated professions - television actress
	model
	M/3 – 1991 – Alice Berry
	- entertainers and associated professions - Lorne's former assistant
Address:	458 Further Lane, East Hampton
Name of estate:	
Year of construction:	
Style of architecture:	Georgian Revival
Architect(s):	
Landscape architect(s)	

House extant: yes
Historical notes:

Lorne Michaels is the son of Abraham and Florence Becker Lipowitz of Toronto, Canada.

Rosie Shuster Michaels is the daughter of Frank and Ruth Burstyn Shuster of Toronto, Canada.

*Michaels has been inducted into the Hollywood Hall of Fame and into the Canadian Hall of Fame. He was awarded the Mark Twain Prize for American Humor.

Miller, Dudley Livingston, Sr. (1921-1969)

Occupation(s):	attorney - partner, Gerdes, Montgomery, and Miller; partner, Miller, Montgomery, and Spalding
	capitalist - director, Realty and Industrial Corp.
	educator - law teaching fellow, New York University, NYC
	industrialist - director, Knapp Brothers Shoe Manufacturing Co.; director, Homes Leather Co.
Civic Activism:	mayor, Village of Laurel Hollow, 1951-1959;
	trustee, Boys Harbor, East Hampton;
	governor, Union Club, NYC;
	manager, St. Nicholas Society;
	member, National Board of Consultants, United States Small Business Administration;
	counsel, United States Committee for the United Nations, 1954-1959
Marriage(s):	M/1 – 1943-div. 1959 – Margery Gerdes (1921-2013)
	- attorney
	Civic Activism: volunteer defender, Westbury Family Court; Westbury, NY; chair, Radiology Volunteers, Huntington Hospital, Huntington, NY
	M/2 – 1962-1969 – Marilyn Morris Matthews (aka Tee)
Address:	Highway Behind the Pond, East Hampton
Name of estate:	
Year of construction:	
Style of architecture:	
Architect(s):	Robert Venturi and William Short, 1961-1962 alterations
Landscape architect(s)	
House extant: unconfirmed	
Historical notes:	

    Dudley Livingston Miller, Sr. was the son of Andrew Otterson and Gretchen MacDowell Miller, Sr. of South Orange, NJ. His brother Andrew Otterson Miller, Jr. married Jeanne Loring White, the daughter of Loring Quincy and Arlene White of Cohasset, MA, and resided at *Ducks Landing* in Laurel Hollow. [*See* Spinzia, *Long Island's Prominent North Shore Families, vol. I* – Miller entry.]

    Margery Gerdes Miller was the daughter of John and Theodora McCaren Gerdes who resided at *Brookedge* in Plandome, at *Cannonhill Point* in Laurel Hollow, and at *Pepperidge Point* in Mill Neck. [See Spinzia, *Long Island's Prominent North Shore Families, vol. I* – Gerdes entries.] Margery later married Edmund S. Twining III, Harold Leighton Fates, Sr., and, subsequently, Dr. John Sylvester Tessier.

    Dudley Livingston and Margery Gerdes Miller, Sr.'s daughter Alexandra married George Henry Howard III and resided at *Holly House* in Laurel Hollow. [*See* Spinzia, *Long Island's Prominent North Shore Families, vol. I* – Howard entry.] Their son Courtland married Gina Maria Salvatore, the daughter of James Salvatore in Palm Beach, FL. Their son Dudley Livingston Miller, Jr. resided in Greenwich, CT.

    [For information about Dudley Livingston and Margery Gerdes Miller, Sr.'s Laurel Hollow residence *Merrywitch*, *see* Spinzia, *Long Island's Prominent North Shore Families, vol. I* – Miller entry.]

    Marilyn Morris Matthews Miller was the daughter of Robert Morris and Alice Matthews of Winter Haven, FL. Marilyn had previously been married to James Earl Webb and Edward Thomas Bedford Davie, Sr., the son of Preston and Emily Harriet Bedford Davie of *The Oasis* in Salisbury. [*See* Spinzia, *Long Island's Prominent Families in the Town of Hempstead* – Davie entry.] Marilyn subsequently married cartoonist Charles Samuel Addams with whom she resided at *The Swamp* in Sagaponack. [*See* Spinzia, *Long Island's Prominent Families in the Town of Southampton* – Addams entry.]

Miller, Jeremiah, IV (1777-1839)

Occupation(s):	East Hampton's first postmaster, appointed 1816
Marriage(s):	1798-1839 – Phebe Baker (d. 1870)
Address:	117 Main Street, East Hampton
Name of estate:	
Year of construction:	c. 1799
Style of architecture:	Georgian*
Architect(s):	Isaac Henry Green II designed 1889 alterations**
	Joseph Greenleaf Thorp designed 1905 interior and exterior alterations
Landscape architect(s):	Mary Lois Deputy Lamson (for Douglas)

House extant: yes
Historical notes:

The house was built by Jeremiah Miller IV.
He was the son of Jeremiah and Mary Sanford Miller, Jr.
Phebe Baker Miller was the daughter of Thomas and Betsy Conklin Baker.
Jeremiah and Phebe Baker Miller IV's daughter Mary married Abel Conklin of Huntington. Their daughter Phebe married Felix Dominey. Their daughter Helen married Henry D. Stratton. Their daughter Joann did not marry. Their daughter Rosalie married Edward M. Baker. In 1830 their nineteen-year-old son drowned in the Indian Ocean.

*The house, which is on the National Register of Historic Places, was later owned by Edward de Rose who remodeled it, changing the architecture from Georgian to Colonial Revival, and named it *Millfield*. In c. 1885 de Rose also built a guest cottage on the property in an eclectic windmill style. In 1910 the Colonial-Revival-style house was owned by Thomas Lincoln Manson III and, then, by his daughter Dorothea and son-in-law Kilian Van Rensselaer. Both Manson and Van Rensselaer continued to call the estate *Millfield*.

In 1945 the Colonial Revival-styled house was owned by Graham Douglas. By 1950 it was owned by Franklin M. Chace who called it *Gone With the Wind*. By 1973 it was owned by Richard Vincent Hare.

**For Green's other commissions, see Spinzia, *Long Island's Prominent South Shore Families: Their Estates and Their Country Homes in the Towns of Babylon and Islip.*

Mills, Abraham (d. 1948)

Occupation(s):	
Civic Activism:	a founder and director, Maidstone Club, East Hampton
Marriage(s):	Ella W. Townsend
Address:	Ocean Avenue and Jefferys Lane, East Hampton
Name of estate:	*The Chalet*
Year of construction:	c. 1872
Style of architecture:	Italianate
Architect(s):	Charles Peter Beauchamp Jefferys designed his own house
Landscape architect(s):	

House extant: yes
Historical notes:

The house, originally named *Sommariva*, was built by Charles Peter Beauchamp Jefferys, Sr. It was inherited by the Jefferyses' daughter Marie and son-in-law Henry Lee Hobart, who moved the house about 100 yards east to its present site. The house, which is on the National Register of Historic Places, was later owned by Mills who called it *The Chalet*.

The *Social Register, August 1894* lists Abraham and Ella W. Townsend Mills as residing at *The Chalet* in East Hampton.

Ella W. Townsend Mills was the daughter of Robert Cornell and Mary Augusta Whittemore Townsend, Sr. of Manhattan. Ella's sister Mary married James Lawrence McKeever, Sr. and resided at *Red Top Farm* in Southampton. [See Spinzia, *Long Island's Prominent Families in the Town of Southampton* – McKeever entry.] Her sister Annie married Walter Bowne Lawrence, the son of John W. and Mary King Bowne Lawrence of Flushing.

Abraham and Ella W. Townsend Mills' daughter Edith married Wilson W. Drake, the son of Benjamin Drake and, later, Guy Carleton, the son of Horace Morrison Carleton. Their daughter Amy married Louis Besant Wadsworth deKoven, the son of LeRoy and Alice Besant deKoven.

The house was subsequently owned by Dr. Stuart Lessley Craig.

Milne, John Cruickshank, II (d. 1966)

Occupation(s):	interior designer - owner, John C. Milne Fabrics, NYC
Marriage(s):	1951 – Gertrude Howell Behr (1892-1979)

\
Address: 108 Egypt Lane, East Hampton
Name of estate:
Year of construction: c. 1920s
Style of architecture: Colonial Revival
Architect(s):
Landscape architect(s):
House extant:
Historical notes: yes

The Blue Book of The Hamptons, 1958, 1965, and *1973* list Mr. and Mrs. John C. Milne as residing at 108 Egypt Lane, East Hampton.

He was the son of Joseph D. and Georgia A. Milne of Fall River, MA.

Gertrude Howell Behre Milne was the daughter of Herman and Grace Howell Behr, Sr. of NYC and Brooklyn, NY. Gertrude's sister Margaret married Archibald Mudge Reid and resided in East Hampton.

Miner, Mary Louise Woodin (1891-1993)

Civic Activism:	trustee, Turtle Bay Music School, NY; member, board of managers, women's auxiliary, Union Settlement, NY
Marriage(s):	1917-div. 1926 – Charles Miner, Sr. (1894-1970) (aka Robert Charles Miner, Sr.)

Address: Drew Lane, East Hampton
Name of estate: *Mi Dune*
Year of construction:
Style of architecture:
Architect(s):
Landscape architect(s):
House extant: unconfirmed
Historical notes:

The *Long Island Society Register, 1929* lists Mrs. Mary L. Woodin Miner as residing on Drew Lane, East Hampton. The *Social Directory of Southampton, Long Island, 1931* lists her as residing at *Mi–Dune* in East Hampton.

She was the daughter of William Hartman and Annie Jessup Woodin, Sr. of *Dune House* in East Hampton.

Charles Miner, Sr. was the son of General Asher and Mrs. Hetty Lonsdale Miner of Wilkes–Barre, PA.

Charles and Mary Louise Woodin Miner, Sr.'s daughter Anne married William Hamilton Phipps, the son of Louis Eugene Phipps of Englewood, NJ, and, later, Leonard Arthur St. Philip with whom she resided on Pond View Lane in East Hampton. Their son Charles Miner, Jr. married Mae Hoffman, the daughter of Francis Henry Hoffman of Charlotte, NC, and resided in Darien, CT.

By 1950 Mrs. Miner was residing at *Dune House*.

The house was later owned by Frederick Bryant Ashplant, Sr. who sold it to Edward Durell Stone, Sr. in 1961. [*The East Hampton Star* November 23, 1944, p. 8, and May 4, 1961, p. 4.]

Miner, Mary Louise Woodin (1891-1993)

Civic Activism:	*[See previous entry.]*
Marriage(s):	1917-div. 1926 – Charles Miner, Sr. (1894-1970) (aka Robert Charles Miner, Sr.)
Address:	Lily Pond Lane, East Hampton
Name of estate:	
Year of construction:	1924
Style of architecture:	Shingle Cottage
Architect(s):	Roger Bullard designed the house (for P. A. Salembier)
	Grosvenor Atterbury, 1927 alterations (for P. A. Salembier)
Landscape architect(s):	
Builder:	Edward M. Gay
House extant: yes	
Historical notes:	

The house, originally named *Seacroft*, was built by Paul Albert Salembier. In 1943 it was purchased from Mrs. Salembier by Mary Louise Woodin Miner. [*The East Hampton Star* July 22, 1943, p. 5.]
 [See previous entry for family information.]

Mirick, Edna B. de Beixedon (1902-1988)

Civic Activism:	secretary, Orphan Asylum Society, Brooklyn, NY
Marriage(s):	1931-1954 – Harry Lawrence Mirick, Sr. (1897-1954)
	- construction program engineer, American Telephone and Telegraph Co.
Address:	Cottage Avenue, East Hampton
Name of estate:	*Tanglebrae*
Year of construction:	
Style of architecture:	
Architect(s):	
Landscape architect(s):	
House extant: unconfirmed	
Historical notes:	

 The Blue Book of The Hamptons, 1958 and 1965 list Edna B. de Beixedon Mirick as residing at *Tanglebrae* on Cottage Avenue, East Hampton.
 She was the daughter of Edward Francis Fremaux and Olive Cantoni de Beixedon who previously owned the house. Edna had previously been married to Pierre Paul Mirc of San Francisco, CA.
 Harry Mirick, Sr. was the son of John Charles Freemont and Abbie Greenwood Allen Mirick of Princeton, MA.
 Harry Lawrence and Edna B. de Beixedon Mirick, Sr.'s son Harry Lawrence Mirick, Jr. married Jean Alice Erickson and resided in Andover, MA. Their daughter Joan married Thomas White Brander, Jr. of Orange, VA.

Mitchell, Christopher (b. 1969)

Occupation(s):	publisher - vice-president and chief business officer, Condé Nast Cultural Publications which includes *Vanity Fair, The New Yorker, W, Teen Vogue*, and *Them*; vice-president, Fairchild Publications
Marriage(s):	Pilar Guzman (b. 1970)

    - publisher - senior editor, *Real Simple*;
                  editor–in-chief, *Cookie*;
                  editor-in-chief, *Martha Stewart Living*;
                  executive editor, *One*;
                  design and architecture editor, *City*;
                  editor-in-chief, *Condé Nast Traveler*
      journalist - *The New York Times;*
                  I.D;
                  Metropolis;
                  Wallpaper;
                  Marie Claire
      writer - co-author, *Time for Dinner*

Address:	62 Dunemere Lane, East Hampton*
Name of estate:	
Year of construction:	1897
Style of architecture:	Shingle
Architect(s):	Tamer Pepemehmetoglu, designed and built 2015 renovation (for Mitchell)
Landscape architect(s):	
Builder:	George A. Eldredge, 1897
House extant: yes	
Historical notes:	

    The house was previously owned by Elizabeth Clossey Nesbit who called it *Seaward*.
    *In 1907 she relocated it to the center of her property.
    In 2012 the house was for sale. The asking price was $6.5 million.
    It was purchased in 2013 by Mitchell for $4.567 million.
    Pilar Guzman Mitchell is the daughter of Claudio and Anna Maria Alberghetti Guzman.
    In 2018 the eight bedroom, six-and-a-half-bath, 8,000-square-foot house and 1.14 acres were for sale by Mitchell. The asking price was $12.5 million.

Mitchell, Ledyard, Sr. (1881-1964)
aka William Ledyard Mitchell

Occupation(s):	industrialist - president, Maxwell Motor Co. (automobile manufacturing firm); vice-president, secretary and general manager, Chrysler Corp. (automobile manufacturing firm)
Marriage(s):	1910-1964 – Sara Moulton Sherman (1888-1969)
Address:	Highway Behind the Pond, East Hampton
Name of estate:	*Dunes*
Year of construction:	
Style of architecture:	
Architect(s):	
Landscape architect(s):	
House extant: unconfirmed	
Historical notes:	

In 1940 Mitchell purchased the Sidney Webster Fish residence [*The East Hampton Star* September 12, 1940, p. 5.]

The Blue Book of The Hamptons, 1958 and 1965 list Ledyard and Sara Sherman Mitchell [Sr.] as residing at *Dunes* on Highway Behind the Pond, East Hampton.

He was the son of Richard Hannaford and Maria Lucia Lincoln Mitchell.

Sara Moulton Sherman Mitchell was the daughter of Frank Allen and Ada Louise Bacon Sherman of Des Moines, IA.

Ledyard and Sara Moulton Sherman Mitchell, Sr.'s daughter Mary married Paul Deming, Jr. and resided in Grosse Pointe Farms, MI. Their son Frank Sherman Mitchell (aka Sherman Mitchell) married Ann Buhl. Their daughter Ann married Henry M. Campbell III. Their daughter Sara married John O'Keefe and, later, James W. Walker with whom she resided in Oyster Bay. Their son Ledyard Mitchell, Jr. married Heidi Flannery and resided in Westwood, MA.

Ruth Dean Embury of *Third House* in East Hampton received the Architectural League's Gold Medal of Honor for her landscape design of the Mitchell's Detroit residence. [*The New York Times* May 27, 1932, p. 21.]

Mitchell, MacNeil (1904-1996)

Occupation(s):	attorney
	politician - member, New York State Assembly, silk stocking district, NYC - 9 years;
	member, New York State Senate - 18 years
Civic Activism:	director, Carnegie Hall, NYC;
	director, New York City Opera;
	secretary and governor, Devon Yacht Club, Amagansett;
	chairman, Junior Yacht Club, Devon Yacht Club, Amagansett
Marriage(s):	1938-1996 – Martha Katherine McGowin
	(aka Katherine McGowin)
	- Civic Activism: recording secretary, Association for the Relief of Respectable Aged, Indigent Females, NYC
Address:	Meeting House Lane and Main Street, Amagansett
Name of estate:	*Elmshade*
Year of construction:	
Style of architecture:	
Architect(s):	
Landscape architect(s):	
House extant: unconfirmed	
Historical notes:	

In 1953 Mitchell purchased the old Emery homestead.

The Blue Book of The Hamptons, 1965 and 1973 list MacNeil and Katherine Mitchell as residing at *Elmshade* at the intersection of Meeting House Lane and Main Street in Amagansett.

He was the son of George Henry and Harriet Louisa MacNeil Mitchell.

Martha Katherine McGowin Mitchell was the daughter of Willis Marion McGowin of Chapman, AL.

MacNeil and Martha Katherine McGowin Mitchell's daughter Marian married Frederick Ogden Nicholson, the son of Frederick E. Nicholson of Laguna Beach, CA, and resided in Laguna Beach. Their daughter Martha married Farhad Ettehadieh, the son of Ali Ettehadieh of Teheran, Iran. Their son Charles married Laura Ann Grossen, the daughter of Harry Grossen of Shelby, MI, and resided at *Beach Home* in Amagansett.

In 1955 Mitchell co-sponsored, with Alfred A. Lama, the Mitchell–Lama housing law which allowed private developers and non-profit organizations to receive large property tax abatements and low-interest mortgages backed by either city or state bonds.

Mnuchin, Alan Geoffrey (b. 1946)

Occupation(s):	financer - a founder, AGM Partners (merger and acquisitions firm); head of Media Group, investment banking division, Lehman Brothers, Inc.; vice-president, Goldman Sachs and Co.
Civic Activism:	director, Montefiore Medical Center, NYC; director, Children's Center, Montefiore Hospital, NYC
Marriage(s):	1995 – Kimberly Ellen Kassel (b. 1967) - public relations executive - director, public relations, Tommy Hilfiger, USA
Address:	8 Hither Lane, East Hampton
Name of estate:	
Year of construction:	2000
Style of architecture:	Shingle
Architect(s):	Francis Fleetwood designed the house (for Jeffery Colle)
Landscape architect(s)	Edmund Hollander
Builder:	Jeffery Colle
House extant: yes	
Historical notes:	

Alan Geoffrey Mnuchin purchased the 8,500-square-foot, six-bedroom house with six and a half bathrooms, from its builder Jeffery Colle for $5.35 million.
He is the son of Robert and Elaine Terner Cooper Mnuchin.
Kimberly Ellen Kassel Mnuchin is the daughter of Robert Kassel.
In 2009 the house was for sale. The asking price was $17.5 million.

Moffett, James Andrew, Jr. (1886-1953)

Occupation(s):	industrialist - junior clerk (1906) and, later, member, sales department, Vacuum Oil Co.;
	member, lubricating sales department, Standard Oil of Kentucky, 1907;
	member, sales department, Atlantic Refining Co.;
	member, sales department, Northern Pipe Line Co.;
	assistant to the president, Standard Oil of Louisiana, 1909;
	director of sales, Standard Oil of Louisiana, 1911;
	vice-president, Standard Oil of New Jersey, 1924-1933;
	vice-president, Standard Oil of California, 1934;
	chairman of board, Texas Oil Co.
	politician - member, advisory board, National Recovery Administration (FDR administration);
	administrator, Federal Housing Administration (FDR administration)
Civic Activism:	a founder and governor, Montauk Swordfish Club
Marriage(s):	M/1 – 1910-1934 – Adelaide Taft McMichael (1887-1934)
	M/2 – 1934-div. 1937 – Adelaide Kieu (1894-1981)
	M/3 – 1941-1953 – Irene Curley (1891-1965)
Address:	Lily Pond and Hedges Lanes, East Hampton
Name of estate:	*Inadune*
Year of construction:	1917
Style of architecture:	
Architect(s):	
Landscape architect(s):	
House extant: unconfirmed	
Historical notes:	

    The house was built by John LaRue Helm, Jr. In 1923 Mrs. Helm sold it to Moffett, Jr. [*The East Hampton Star* March 16, 1923, p. 5.]

    The *Social Directory of Southampton, Long Island, 1931* lists James A. and Adelaide Taft McMichael Moffett [Jr.] as residing at *Inadune* on Lily Pond Lane, East Hampton.

    He was the son of James Andrew and Kate Ingersoll Jackson Moffett, Sr. His brother George, who resided at *Les Bois* in Old Brookville, married Madeline Buchner and, later, Countess Odette Fuller Feder. [*See* Spinzia, *Long Island's Prominent North Shore Families, vol. 1* – Moffett entry.]

    Adelaide Taft McMichael Moffett was the daughter of Dr. Arkley Roger and Mrs. Amy Elizabeth Hicks McMichael of NYC. Adelaide died after falling eight stories from the bedroom window of her New York City apartment. [*The New York Times* October 27, 1934, p. 1.]

    James Andrew and Adelaide Taft McMichael Moffett, Jr.'s daughter Margaret married Jay Freeborn Carlislie, Jr., the son of Jay Freeborn and Mary Pinkerton Carlisle, Sr. of *Rosemary* in East Islip; James Gordon Douglas, Jr.; George Edward Altemus; and George J. Atwell. [*See* Spinzia, *Long Island's Prominent South Shore Families* – Carlisle entry.] In 1932, prior to Margaret's marriage to Jay, his father foiled a plot to kidnap the young couple and hold them for $30,000 ransom. [*The New York Times* November 13, 1937, p. 5.] The Moffetts' son Robert married Ruth Marian Quigley, the daughter of Frank Thomas Quigley of Cleveland, OH, and Mary Margaret Drudy. Their son Jackson married Nancy Short. Their daughter Adelaide married David Brooks, the son of Reginald Brooks of Southampton. At the age of twenty-six, David fell from the window of his fourteenth floor apartment in New York City's Mayfair House. [*The New York Times* November 16, 1936, p. 40.] Adelaide later married William Paul Buckner, Jr.; David Douglas Craven; and, subsequently, her sister Margaret's former husband James Gordon Douglas, Jr. Douglas had previously been married to Margaret Helen Phipps, the daughter of John Shaffer and Margarita Celia Grace Phipps of *Westbury House* in Old Westbury. [*See* Spinzia, *Long Island's Prominent North Shore Families, vol. II* – Phipps entry.]. Their daughter Ruth married Warren Johnson, the son of Harry T. F. Johnson of Bronxville, NY.

    Adelaide Kieu Moffett had previously been married to Joseph F. Moran of NYC.

    Irene Curley Moffett had previously been married to John R. Bodde and Franklin Laws Hutton of Bay Shore. [*See* Spinzia, *Long Island's Prominent South Shore Families* – Hutton entry.]

    In 1937 Moffett sold the house to John Lafayette Weeks. [*The East Hampton Star* January 28, 1937, p. 1.] In 1951 it was purchased by Roy Lennox Cammann. [*The East Hampton Star* May 3, 1951, p. 1.]

Monberg, Miss Hedwig (1892-1978)

Occupation(s): physiotherapist

Marriage(s):

Address: Woods Lane, East Hampton
Name of estate:
Year of construction:
Style of architecture:
Architect(s):
Landscape architect(s):
House extant: no
Historical notes:

    In 1893 Adrian Hoffman Larkin remodeled the South End School as his residence which he called *Green Frog*. [*The East Hampton Star* September 30, 1965, p. 12.] By 1900 the house was owned by Clara Cooper Stratton. [*The East Hampton Star* February 9, 1900, p. 5.] It was later owned by Monberg who, in 1954, sold the house to Garvin Brackenridge, Sr. [*The East Hampton Star* March 4, 1954, p. 2, and June 24, 1954, p. 2.]

Monell, Theodore, Jr. (b. 1911)

Occupation(s): industrialist - executive, International Nickel Co.

Marriage(s): 1937 – Suzanne Louise Warriner (b. 1915)

Address: East Lake Drive, Montauk
Name of estate:
Year of construction:
Style of architecture:
Architect(s):
Landscape architect(s):
House extant: unconfirmed
Historical notes:

    The Blue Book of The Hamptons, 1965 and 1973 list Mr. and Mrs. Theodore Monell, Jr. as residing on East Lake Drive, Montauk.
    He was the son of Theodore and Elinor Haight Monell, Sr. of Shinnecock Hills and Montauk.
    Suzanne Louise Warriner Monell was the daughter of Rŭel Chaffee and Suzanne C. Gutherz Warriner of Glen Ridge, NJ.
    [See following entry for additional family information.]

Monell, Theodore, Sr. (1875-1950)

Occupation(s):	military - colonel, American Expeditionary Forces during World War I*
Marriage(s):	c. 1910 – Elinor Haight (1879)
Address:	East Lake Drive, Montauk

Name of estate:
Year of construction:
Style of architecture:
Architect(s):
Landscape architect(s):
House extant: unconfirmed
Historical notes:

In 1942 Monell moved the house from what was to become the site of Fort Hero. [*The East Hampton Star* February 19, 1942, p. 3, and December 28, 1950, p. 1.]

He was the son of Ambrose and Jennie Hyatt Monell, Sr. and a direct descendant of Anneke Jans who settled in New Amsterdam.

Elinor Haight Monell was the daughter of Henry Jansen and Mary Lucy Church Haight and the great-granddaughter of David Henry Haight, a founder of Manhattan's St. Bartholomew Church. Elinor subsequently married E. H. Brush of NYC.

Theodore and Elinor Haight Mondell, Sr.'s daughter Elinor married Harlan Wheadon Short whose maternal ancestor was the commander of Washington's Life Guards and Governor of Virginia. Their daughter Dorothy married Paul Snow Tilden, the son of Harry Francis Tilden of Boston and Cohasset, MA, and a descendant of Sir William Tilden who settled in Cohasset in 1640. Their son Theodore Monell, Jr. subsequently owned the house.

*William Merritt Chase painted a portrait of Monell in his military uniform.

[See previous entry for additional family information.]

Montgomery, Paul (1892-1978)
aka John Paul Montgomery

Occupation(s):	artist*; publisher - vice-president and director, McGraw Hill, Inc. writer - *Adventures in Watercolor Painting*
Civic Activism:	director, Advertising Research Foundation; director, New York Heart Association; trustee, Milkin University, Decatur, IL; chairman of board, Guild Hall, East Hampton, 1961-1966; director, Amagansett Village Improvement Society
Marriage(s):	M/1 – 1925-1974 – Frances Treat (1889-1974) - interior designer M/2 – Dorothy Henron
Address:	Bluff Road, Amagansett

Name of estate:
Year of construction:
Style of architecture:
Architect(s):
Landscape architect(s):
House extant: unconfirmed
Historical notes:

In 1945 Montgomery purchased the Nelson Osborne residence. [*The East Hampton Star* November 8, 1945, p. 8.]

The Blue Book of The Hamptons, 1965 and 1973 list Mr. and Mrs. Paul Montgomery as residing on Bluff Road, Amagansett.

He is the son of John and Adelaide Montgomery of Dexter, MO.

Frances Treat Montgomery was the daughter of Edwin M. Treat of Plainfield, NJ, and St. Louis, MO.

Paul and Frances Treat Montgomery's daughter Susan married Frederick Thompson Card, the son of Raymond Card of East Hampton.

*Montgomery did not begin painting seriously until after he retired as vice-president of McGraw Hall, Inc. In 1966 he was inducted into the American Watercolor Society. [*The East Hampton Star* April 6, 1978, p. 2.]

Montgomery, Robert (1904-1981)
aka Robert Montgomery, Sr.;
Henry Montgomery, Jr.

Occupation(s):	entertainers and associated professions - actor, director, and producer
Civic Activism:	president, Screen Actors Guild
Marriage(s):	M/1 – 1928-div. 1950 – Elizabeth Bryan Allen (1904-1992) - entertainers and associated professions - Broadway actress
	M/2 – 1950-1981 – Elizabeth Grant (1909-2003)
Address:	42 Highway Behind the Pond, East Hampton
Name of estate:	*Swan Cove*
Year of construction:	c. 1903
Style of architecture:	Modified Colonial Revival
Architect(s):	
Landscape architect(s):	
House extant:	no; demolished*
Historical notes:	

    Gerald Clery and his wife Sara Sherman Wiborg Murphy remodeled the dairy barn of Sara's parents' estate *The Dunes* into their residence which they called *Swan Cove*. In 1959 Montgomery purchased the house and continued to call it *Swan Cove*.

    He was the son of Henry and Mary Weed Montgomery, Sr.

    Elizabeth Bryan Allen Montgomery was the daughter of Bryant Hunt Allen.

    Robert and Elizabeth Bryan Allen Montgomery, Sr.'s daughter Martha died in 1931 at the age of fourteen months. Their daughter Elizabeth, who was the noted actress of the television series "Bewitched," married Frederick Gallatin Cammann; actor Gig Young; producer and director of "Bewitched" William Asher; and, subsequently, Robert Foxworth. Their son Robert Montgomery, Jr. married Deborah Chase.

    Elizabeth Grant Montgomery was the daughter of James Pierce Grant of Rye, NY. She had previously been married to William Hale Harkness, the son of William Lamon and Edith Hale Harkness of Glen Cove. [*See* Spinzia, *Long Island's Prominent North Shore Families, vol. I* – Harkness entry.]

    In 1955 the guest house was built. [*The East Hampton Star* June 16, 1955, p. 12.]

    In 1973 the main residence was purchased from Montgomery by Alfred de Liagre, Jr. [*The East Hampton Star* March 1, 1973, p. 4.] Both Montgomery and de Liagre continued to call it *Swan Cove*. Because the house had a pink stucco exterior, it is sometimes referred to as *Pink House*.

    In 2009 the 3,500-square-foot, five-bedroom house was purchased by Peter Jay Solomon for $19 million. [*The East Hampton Star* April 15, 2010, p. 5.]

    *In 2010 Solomon demolished the house and built a new residence on the site. [*The East Hampton Star* December 2, 2010, p. 3.]

Moody, Sidney Clarke, Sr. (1895-1974)

Occupation(s):	industrialist - assistant general manager, Calco Chemical Co., 1943-1945; general manager and vice president, Calco Chemical Co. (later, American Cyanamid Co.); vice-president, American Cyanamid Co.
	educator - taught chemistry Williams College, Williamstown, MA, 1917
Civic Activism:	president, Synthetic Organic Chemicals Manufacturers Association; chairman, budget committee, Amagansett Village Improvement Society; president, Amagansett Village Improvement Society
Marriage(s):	1925-1974 – Frances Trent Glenn (d. 1975)
	- Civic Activism: president, Amagansett Village Improvement Society
Address:	Further Lane, Amagansett
Name of estate:	*Water's Edge*
Year of construction:	
Style of architecture:	
Architect(s):	
Landscape architect(s)	
House extant: unconfirmed	
Historical notes:	

The Blue Book of The Hamptons, 1958 lists Sidney C. and Frances Glenn Moody as residing on Further Lane, Amagansett. *The Blue Book of The Hamptons, 1965* lists *Water's Edge* as the name of their residence.

He was the son of Francis Kempton and Emma Bridges Moody.

Frances Trent Glenn Moody was the daughter of Richard M. C. and Harriet Brookes Glenn of Montclair, NJ.

Sidney Clarke and Frances Trent Glenn Moody, Sr.'s daughter Mary married John W. Bainton, the son of William Lewis Bainton of Larchmont, NY. Their daughter Patricia married Clinton Fox Ivins of Plainfield, NJ. Their son Sidney Clarke Moody, Jr. married Patricia Ivins.

At the time of their deaths the Moodys were residing on Barnes Landing.

Moore, Dr. Oliver Semon, Jr. (b. 1916)

Occupation(s):	physician - surgeon, Memorial Hospital
Marriage(s):	
Address:	Georgica Road, East Hampton
Name of estate:	
Year of construction:	
Style of architecture:	
Architect(s):	
Landscape architect(s)	
House extant: unconfirmed	
Historical notes:	

Moore had previously resided on Apaquogue Road. [*The East Hampton Star* June 3, 1954, p. 7.] By 1958 he had relocated to Georgica Road.

The Blue Book of The Hamptons, 1958, 1965, and *1973* list Dr. and Mrs. Oliver S. Moore [Jr.] as residing on Georgica Road, East Hampton.

Their daughter Leslie married Richard Scott Greathead, the son of Edward Burton Greathead of Santa Barbara, CA, and, later, Alexander Shoumatoff, the son of Nichols Shoumatoff of Bedford, NY. Their daughter Jane married Roy Goodrich Cary, the son of Vaughn Cary of East Hampton.

Moran, Thomas, Jr. (1837-1926)

Occupation(s):	artist - painter; etcher
Civic Activism:	a founder and vice-president, Maidstone Club, East Hampton
Marriage(s):	1862-1899 – Mary Nimmo (1842-1899) - artist - painter; etcher
Address:	229 Main Street, East Hampton
Name of estate:	*The Studio*
Year of construction:	1884
Style of architecture:	
Architect(s):	
Landscape architect(s):	
House extant:	yes
Historical notes:	

The house, originally named *The Studio*, was built by Thomas Moran, Jr.

Born in Bolton, Lancashire, England, he was the son of Thomas and Mary Higson Moran, Sr.

Mary Nimmo Moran was the daughter of Archibald and Mary Nimmo. She was born in Strathaven, Scotland, but immigrated to the United States as a youth with her family.

Thomas was seventeen when he immigrated to the United States with his parents and brothers. He worked in Philadelphia for two years as a wood-engraver before taking up oil painting. Under the tutelage of his brothers, who were also painters, he became an accomplished artist. In the 1860s he returned to Europe several times, visiting France, Italy, and England, where he was profoundly influenced by Turner. In 1871 he returned to the United States to accompany F. V. Hayden on an expedition to the West. Moran made several western trips during which he painted his famous *The Grand Canyon,* which measures eight feet by twelve feet, and the *Chasm of the Colorado.* Both were purchased by Congress for $10,000 and are displayed in the United States Capitol Building. His name is still linked to the West today, not only through his painting but by other lasting memorials: Mount Moran in Wyoming and Moran Point in Arizona are named in his honor. Moran was internationally acclaimed, becoming a fellow of the British Society of Painter-Etchers. John Ruskin, the famous nineteenth-century English essayist and critic, claimed that Moran was one of the best etchers in America.

Always interested in art, Mary took painting lessons and eventually became a student of the noted artist Thomas Moran, Jr., whom she married in 1862. They lived in Philadelphia, PA, for ten years before moving to Newark, NJ, Manhattan, and, ultimately, to East Hampton. Mary, known for her landscape etching, was the first woman member of the British Society of Painter-Etchers.

Thomas and Mary Nimmo Moran, Jr.'s daughter Mary married Wirt de Vivier Tassin. Their son Paul Nimmo Moran, also a noted artist, died in Los Angeles, CA.

The house, which is on the National Register of Historic Places, is currently owned by Guild Hall Museum.

Moranti, Paul Joseph (b. 1884)

Occupation(s):	engineer - assistant engineer, Empire Steel & Iron Co., 1906; superintendent of construction, Pennsylvania Railroad Tunnel, NYC, 1906-1909; general superintendent, Mount Royal Tunnel, C. N. Railroad, 1911-1912; general superintendent, C. N. Railroad Barge Canal, 1913-1917; construction engineer, Eastern Mines Development Co., 1917-1920
	capitalist - president, Moranti & Raymond (later, Paul J. Moranti, Inc.); president, Paul J. Moranti, Inc. (construction firm which built New York City subway tunnels and streets)
Marriage(s):	1923 – Marietta Dwyer
Address:	Terbell Lane, East Hampton
Name of estate:	*Lago–Del–Mare*
Year of construction:	c. 1900
Style of architecture:	Adamesque
Architect(s):	
Landscape architect(s):	
House extant: no*	

Historical notes:

The house, originally named *Lockdune*, was built by Williston Benedict Lockwood. It 1926 it was purchased by Laurette Helen Cooney Manners. In 1931 the house was purchased by Moranti.

The *Social Directory of Southampton, Long Island, 1931* lists Paul J. and Marietta Dwyer Moranti as residing at *Lago–Del–Mare* on Turbell [sic] Lane, East Hampton.

Born in Sorrento, Italy, Paul Joseph Moranti was the son of Francisco and Carmelia Spinelle Moranti.

Marietta Dwyer Moranti was the daughter of John and Elizabeth Taggart Dwyer of St. Louis, MO.

In 1936 the house was purchased by Dr. Earl R. Carlson. [*The East Hampton Star* August 27, 1936, p. 4.] It was subsequently owned by Charles A. Julianelli.

*The carriage house is extant.

Morris, Theodore Wilson, Jr. (1871-1935)

Occupation(s):	attorney - partner, Moses and Morris
Civic Activism:	treasurer, Maidstone Club, East Hampton, 1918
Marriage(s):	1898-1935 – Mary Maynadler Steele (1877-1935)
Address:	Hither Lane, East Hampton
Name of estate:	
Year of construction:	1916
Style of architecture:	Colonial Revival
Architect(s):	
Landscape architect(s)	
House extant: unconfirmed	

Historical notes:

The house was built by Theodore Wilson Morris, Jr.

The *Social Register Summer, 1915* lists Theodore W. and Mary M. Steele Morris [Jr.] as residing in East Hampton.

He was the son of Theodore Wilson and Frances Schanck Morris, Sr. of *The Vines* in Freehold, NJ. His brother McLean married Lucy E. Linderman and resided in Hewlett Neck. [*See* Spinzia, *Long Island's Prominent Families in the Town of Hempstead* – Morris entry.]

Mary Maynadler Steele Morris was the daughter of The Reverend James Nevetl and Mrs. Helen Hudson Aldrich Steele, Sr. of *Dunemere* in East Hampton.

Theodore Wilson and Mary Maynadler Steele Morris, Jr.'s son Steele married Marjorie Cannon, the daughter of Charles Augustus Cannon of Auburn, NY, and, later, Ruth Virginia Mott, the daughter of Elwood Dean and Alice G. Patterson Mott of Marion, OH. Their son Theodore Wilson Morris III married Marcia Seawall Webb, the daughter of Stuart Weston Webb of Boston, MA, and NYC, and, later, Dorothy Soden. Their son John married Katherine Herndon of Beverly Hills, CA.

In 1927 the house was purchased by Irvin Shewsbury Cobb who called it *Back Home*. [*The East Hampton Star* October 7, 1927, p. 1, and May 2, 1935, p. 5.] In 1940 Justine O'Brien Haynes purchased the house from Cobb.

Morrissey, Paul (b. 1938)

Occupation(s):	entertainers and associated professions - motion picture director (avant-garde films)
Civic Activism:	writer - *Factory Days* (autobiography)
Marriage(s):	bachelor
Address:	16 Cliff Drive, Montauk
Name of estate:	*Eothen*
Year of construction:	1931
Style of architecture:	Colonial Revival
Architect(s):	Rolf W. Bauhan designed the compound (for R. E. Church)
	Thierry W. Despont designed the 2007 alterations (for Drexler)
Landscape architect(s):	Miranda Brooks (for Lindemann)

House extant: yes
Historical notes:

The compound, which consisted of a seven-bedroom main residence, four guest houses, a three-car garage, and a stable, was built by Richard E. Church. It remained in the Church family until 1971 when it was purchased for $225,000 by Andy Warhol and Morrissey.

In 2007 he sold the estate to Millard S. Drexler (aka Mickey Drexler) for $27 million. In 2015 Drexler sold the main residence, guest house, garage, and 5.6 acres to Adam Marc Lindemann for $50 million. The equestrian portion of the property remained on the market.

Morse, Tyler (1875-1933)

Occupation(s):	attorney
Civic Activism:	a founder and member, first board of governors, Devon Yacht Club, Amagansett
Marriage(s):	1907-1916 – Allon Mae Fuller (1875-1915)
Address:	88 Lily Pond Lane, East Hampton
Name of estate:	
Year of construction:	1905
Style of architecture:	Neo-Italian Renaissance
Architect(s):	Albro and Lindeberg designed the house (for Cockcroft)
Landscape architect(s):	

House extant: no; destroyed by fire in 2008
Historical notes:

The house, originally named *Little Burlees*, was built by Edward Truesdell Cockcroft, Sr. In 1912 it was purchased by Morse. [*The East Hampton Star* August 16, 1912, p. 5.]

The *Social Directory of Southampton, Long Island, 1931* lists Tyler Morse as residing on Lily Pond Lane, East Hampton.

He was the son of Leopold and Georgiana Ray Morse of Boston, MA.

Allon Mae Fuller was the daughter of George A. Fuller. She had previously been married to Harry S. Black of *Allondale Farm* in Lloyd Harbor. [*See* Spinzia, *Long Island's Prominent North Shore Families, vol. I* – Black entry.]

The proceedings of Mrs. Morse's 1905 divorce from Black were sealed by the court. [*The New York Times* January 18, 1906, p. 16.] Her will stipulated that Black would be the trustee of her estate which was estimated at $4-6 million. Black received $250,000 in lieu of claims if she died prior to 1920. After making a few minor bequests, the balance of the estate was bequeathed to Tyler Morse and her nephew Fuller Chenery. Chenery received one-third of the estate if he lived until 1920. The balance, including *Morse Lodge* which was situated in Old Westbury, went to Tyler Morse with the stipulation that he would forfeit *Morse Lodge* to Chenery if he remarried. [*The New York Times* October 19, 1915, p. 14.]

[For information about Morse's Old Westbury estate, *see* Spinzia, *Long Island's Prominent North Shore Families, vol. I* – Morse entry.]

The house was owned from 1936 to 1994 by Franklin Woolman d'Olier, Jr. In 1994 it was purchased from d'Olier by Jonathan Everett Sandelman for $2.15 million. He owned the house when it was destroyed by fire.

Morton, Peter (b. 1947)

Occupation(s):	restaurateur - co-founder, Hard Rock Café
	capitalist - owner, Hard Rock Hotel and Casino; Las Vegas, NV
Civic Activism:	trustee, The Museum of Contemporary Art, Los Angeles, CA;
	trustee, Natural Resources Defense Council;
	trustee, Young Eisner Scholars;
	donated funds to refurbish outpatient medical plaza, University of California, Los Angeles, CA
Marriage(s):	M/1 – 1980-div. 1989 – Paulene Stone
	M/2 – 1990-div. 1997 – Tarlton Pauley (b. 1941)
	- model
Address:	57 West End Avenue, East Hampton
Name of estate:	
Year of construction:	1926
Style of architecture:	Modified Cotswold
Architect(s):	Roger Bullard designed the house (for E. S. James, Sr.)
Landscape architect(s):	Ellen Biddle Shipman, 1926 *[attributed]*
Builder:	Frank Johnson
House extant:	no; destroyed by fire in 2015*
Historical notes:	

The house, originally named *Heather Dune*, was built by Ellery Sedgwick James, Sr. It was later owned by Jack A. Rounick, who, in 1993, sold it to Dr. Gary Feldstein. In 1998 Morton purchased the house from Feldstein.

He is the son of Arnie Morton.

Paulene Stone is a British model who had previously been married to Tony Norris and to the noted actor Laurence Harvey. After her divorce from Morton, she married Mark Burns.

Peter and Tarlton Pauley Morton have two children, Mathew and Grace.

*The house was owned by Morton at the time of the fire. It started when construction workers were attempting to repair a chimney's flashing with a welding torch in forty-mile-per-hour winds.

Munroe, Dr. George E., Jr. (1851-1932)

Occupation(s):	physician, surgeon and gynecologist, Woman's Hospital
	capitalist - vice-president, East Hampton Electric Light Co.
Civic Activism:	a founder and president, Maidstone Club, East Hampton;
	president, Lawn Tennis Club, East Hampton
Marriage(s):	1881-1928 – Jessie Reynolds (d. 1928)
Address:	24 Ocean Avenue, East Hampton
Name of estate:	*Wayside*
Year of construction:	1888
Style of architecture:	Shingle with Dutch elements
Architect(s):	Isaac Henry Green II designed the house (for G. E. Munroe)*
Landscape architect(s):	
House extant:	yes
Historical notes:	

The 4,000-square-foot, five-bedroom, five-and-a-half bath, house, originally named *Wayside*, was built by Dr. George E. Munroe, Jr. on the site of the former Abraham Fithian residence. [*The East Hampton Star* March 27, 1941, p. 1.]

Munroe was born aboard the clipper ship *Mandarin* in the Indian Ocean during a voyage to China. [*The East Hampton Star* July 27, 1944, p. 3.]

Jessie Reynolds Munroe was from Burlington, VT.

Dr. George E. and Mrs. Jessie Reynolds Munroe, Jr.'s unmarried daughter Marjory inherited the house.

Additions were made to the house in 1894 and in 1950.

The house and 2.6 acres sold in 2012 for $9.999 million.

*For Green's other commissions, *see* Spinzia, *Long Island's Prominent South Shore Families: Their Estates and Their Country Homes in the Towns of Babylon and Islip*.

Murphy, Gerald Clery (1888-1964)

Occupation(s):	merchant - president, Mark Cross Co., NYC (leather goods store)
Civic Activism:	director, Fifth Avenue Association
Marriage(s):	1915-1964 – Sara Sherman Wiborg (1883-1975)
Address:	42 Highway Behind the Pond, East Hampton
Name of estate:	*Swan Cove*
Year of construction:	c. 1903
Style of architecture:	Modified Colonial Revival
Architect(s):	
Landscape architect(s):	
House extant:	no; demolished*
Historical notes:	

The Murphys remodeled the dairy barn on Sara's parents' estate *The Dunes* into their residence.

She was the daughter of Frank Bestow and Adeline Moulton Sherman Wiborg. Sara's sister Mary did not marry. Her sister Olga married Sidney Webster Fish, the son of Stuyvesant and Marian Graves Anthon Fish of Newport, RI, and resided in East Hampton and at *The Duck Pond* in Brookville. [*See* Spinzia, *Long Island's Prominent North Shore Families, vol. I* – Fish entry.]

Gerald Clery Murphy was the son of Patrick Francis and Ann Ryan Murphy of *Agawam* in Southampton. [*See* Spinzia, *Long Island's Prominent Families in the Town of Southampton* – Murphy entry.] His sister Esther married John St. Loe Strachey, Jr. and resided in London, England.

Gerald Clery and Sara Sherman Wiborg Murphy's daughter Honoria married John O. L. Shelton, the son of M. A. Shelton of *Windmill Lodge* in Eastbourne, Sussex, England, and, later, William M. Donnelly of Detroit, MI.

Mrs. Murphy denied the assertion that they were the models for the Divers in F. Scott Fitzgerald's *Tender in the Night*.

In 1955 the guest house was built. [*The East Hampton Star* June 16, 1955, p. 12.]

In 1959 the 3,500-square-foot, five-bedroom main residence was purchased by the noted actor Robert Montgomery In 1973 it was purchased from Montgomery by Alfred de Liagre, Jr. [*The East Hampton Star* March 1, 1973, p. 4.] Both Montgomery and de Liagre continued to call it *Swan Cove*. Because the house had a pink stucco exterior, it is sometimes referred to as *Pink House*.

In 2009 it was purchased by Peter Jay Solomon for $19 million. [*The East Hampton Star* April 15, 2010, p. 5.]

*In 2010 Solomon demolished the house and built a new residence on the site. [*The East Hampton Star* December 2, 2010, p. 3.]

Myrick, Julian Southall (1880-1969)

Occupation(s):	financier - general agent, Charles H. Raymond and Co. (insurance brokerage firm);
	general agent, Mutual Life Insurance Co., 1898;
	general agent, Washington Life Insurance Co., 1907-1909;
	manager and vice-president, Mutual Life Insurance Co.;
	president, Metropolitan Life Insurance Co.*
Civic Activism:	honorary president, New York State Association of Life Underwriters;
	president, New York City Underwriters Association;
	president and chairman of board, National Association of Life Underwriters;
	a founder and chairman of board, College of Life Underwriters;
	president, West Side Tennis Club, Forest Hills, NY, 1915-117;
	president, United States Lawn Tennis Association**;
	president, Maidstone Club, East Hampton
Marriage(s):	1910-1968 – Marion Susan Washburn (1885-1968)
Address:	72 Apaquogue Road, East Hampton
Name of estate:	*Apaquogue*
Year of construction:	c. 1884
Style of architecture:	Federal
Architect(s):	
Landscape architect(s)	
Builder:	Edward M. Gay, 1912 addition (for Mrs. A. A. Cater)***

House extant: yes
Historical notes:

Edward A. LaForest, who had been blind since 1865, died in his East Orange, NJ, home of injuries sustained in a fall down the stairs in his East Hampton residence. As a result of his disability, his wife Helen had attended to their financial affairs. She purchased Abraham D. Candy's East Hampton boarding house and 107-acre farm. When the boarding house was destroyed by fire, she built a new boarding house. The LaForest's son Henry, who purchased the boarding house and the farm from his mother in 1895, named it The Apaquogue. [*The East Hampton Star* March 22, 1895, p. 5; May 17, 1895, p. 5; and June 7, 1895, p.1.] By 1889 ownership had reverted back to his mother. In 1901 Helen LaForest sold it to B. H. Van Scoy and E. H. Dayton. [*Suffolk County News* April 27, 1889, p. 1, and *The East Hampton Star* October 25, 1901, p. 5.] In 1912 the house was sold to Mrs. Arthur Aymar Cater who sold it to Myrick in 1919. He used it as his summer residence which he called *Apaquogue*.

The Blue Book of The Hamptons, 1958 lists Julian S. and Marion S. Washburn Myrick as residing at *Apaquogue House* on Apaquogue Road, East Hampton. *The Blue Book of The Hamptons, 1965* lists the name of their residence as *Apaquogue*.

He was the son of Charles English and Susan Blanche Colton Myrick of Murfreesboro, NC.

Marion Susan Washburn Myrick was the daughter of William Tucker and Mary Rosenia Doughty Washburn.

Julian Southall and Marion Susan Washburn Myrick's daughter Cynthia married Charles E. Saltzman and resided in New York. Their daughter Marion married John E. MacCraken, the son of Charles E. MacCracken of Mount Vernon, NY, and resided on Orrs Island, ME. Their daughter Shirley married William H. Clyde. Their son William resided in New York.

*Myrick was inducted into the Insurance Hall of Fame, Ohio State University, Columbus, OH.

**In 1969 he was inducted into the International Tennis Hall of Fame, Newport, RI.

In 1893 the front porch was added. [*The East Hampton Star* November 24, 1893, p. 5.]

In 1894 houses were built for the employees. [*The East Hampton Star* June 8, 1894, p. 5.]

***Gay's 1912 addition consisted of the installation of seven bathrooms and a rear extension for servant's quarters. [*The East Hampton Star* March 22, 1912, p. 5.]

In 2019, after one hundred years of ownership by Myrick's extended family, the 10,000-square-foot, sixteen-bedroom, seven-bath house and four acres were for sale. The asking price was $16.9 million.

Nadel, Charles Coleman (1855-1931)

Occupation(s):	attorney - partner, Nadal, Smyth, and Carrere;
	partner, Carrere, Trafford, and Nadal;
	partner, Nadal, Jones, and Mowton
	financier - general counsel and vice-president, Fidelity Casualty Co., NYC
	capitalist - counsel and director, Macmillan Co. (publishing firm)
	industrialist - director, Wilson Aluminum Co.
Civic Activism:	a founder, Citizens' Union, 1896;
	president, Council of Confederated Good Government Clubs, NYC;
	director, Hawthorn Apartment Association
Marriage(s):	1890-1931 – Mary Taylor Warrin (d. 1943)
Address:	*[unable to determine street address]*, East Hampton
Name of estate:	
Year of construction:	
Style of architecture:	
Architect(s):	
Landscape architect(s):	
House extant:	unconfirmed
Historical notes:	

The *Social Register Summer, 1910*; the *Long Island Society Register, 1929*; and the *Social Directory of Southampton, Long Island, 1931* list Charles C. and Mary Taylor Warrin Nadal as residing in East Hampton.

He was the son of Bernard Harrison and Sarah Jane Mayse Nadal of Greencastel, IN.

Mary Taylor Warrin Nadal was the daughter of Thomas and Elizabeth W. Lord Warrin of New York City. Mary's brother Dr. Marshall Lord Warrin resided in Amagansett.

Charles Coleman and Mary Taylor Warrin Nadal's son Charles Warrin Nadal was a youth at the time of his death.

Nash, Stephen Edward (1850-1931)

Occupation(s):	attorney
	capitalist - partner, Nash, Watjen, & Bangs, Ltd. (importing firm)
Civic Activism:	treasurer, Protestant Episcopal Public School Corp.;
	senior warden, Trinity Church, NYC;
	a founder and second president, New York City Bar Association
Marriage(s):	Isabel Coggill (1850-1936)
Address:	David's Lane, East Hampton
Name of estate:	*Crossways*
Year of construction:	1929
Style of architecture:	
Architect(s):	
Landscape architect(s):	
House extant:	unconfirmed
Historical notes:	

The house, originally named *Crossways*, was built by Stephen Edward Nash. [*The Brooklyn Daily Eagle* July 14, 1929, p. 23.]

The *Long Island Society Register, 1929* lists S. Edward and Isabel Coggill Nash as residing in East Hampton.

He was the son of Stephen Payn and Catherine McLean Nash, Sr.

Isabel Coggill Nash was the daughter of Charles J. and Glorianna Muir Coggill of Brooklyn.

Stephen Edward and Isabel Coggill Nash's son Stephen Payn Nash II married Ruth Winchester Schultz, the daughter of Norman Schultz of Summit, NJ, and resided in Westhampton Beach. [*See* Spinzia, *Long Island's Prominent Families in the Town of Southampton* – Nash entry.] Their daughter Edna did not marry.

[See following entry for additional family information.]

Nash, Stephen Edward (1850-1931)

Occupation(s):	*[See previous entry.]*
Civic Activism:	*[See previous entry.]*
Marriage(s):	Isabel Coggill (1850-1936)
Address:	Huntting Lane, East Hampton
Name of estate:	
Year of construction:	1902
Style of architecture:	Shingle
Architect(s):	Thomas Nash designed the house (for S. E. Nash)
Landscape architect(s):	
Builder:	Asa Otis Jones
House extant: unconfirmed	
Historical notes:	

The house was built by Stephen Edward Nash. [*The East Hampton Star* August 22, 1902, p. 5.]
[See previous entry for family information.]

Nash, Thomas (1860-1926)

Occupation(s):	architect*
Marriage(s):	
Address:	Lee Avenue, East Hampton
Name of estate:	
Year of construction:	1900
Style of architecture:	Shingle
Architect(s):	Thomas Nash designed his own house
	Robert Arthur Morton Stern, 1961 alterations; replaced 1951 addition with east porch
Landscape architect(s):	
Builder:	Asa Otis Jones, house and 1902 stable
House extant: yes**	

Historical notes:
   The house was built by Thomas Nash.
   He was the son of Stephen Payn and Catherine McLean Nash, Sr.
   [See previous entry for additional family information.]
   *Among Nash's designs were St. Luke's Episcopal Church in East Hampton and All Saints Chapel of Trinity Episcopal Church in Manhattan.
   The house was later owned by Robert Arthur Morton Stern.
   **Alterations were made to the house in 1904, 1951, and 1969.

Nederlander, Robert Elliot, Sr. (b. 1933)

Occupation(s):	attorney - partner, Fenton, Nederlander, Tracy, and Dodge, Detroit, MI
	capitalist - president and director of family's thirty-theater conglomerate;
	general partner, New York Yankees;
	president, Nederlander Television and Film Productions
	industrialist - chairman of board and CEO, Allis-Chalmers
Civic Activism:	director, Nederlander Foundation;
	regent, University of Michigan, Ann Arbor, MI
Marriage(s):	M/1 – 1962-div. 1985 – Caren Elaine Berman
	- psychologist
	M/2 – 1988-2008 – Gladys Lenore Blum (1925-2008)
	- merchant - owner, clothing store in Palm Springs, CA
	entertainers and associated professions - radio interviewer
	capitalist - Broadway producer;
	executive producer, Nederlander Television and Film Productions
Address:	104 Georgica Close Road, East Hampton
Name of estate:	
Year of construction:	1985
Style of architecture:	
Architect(s):	
Landscape architect(s):	
Builder:	Francis E. Grimshaw, Jr.

House extant: yes
Historical notes:

Robert Elliot Nederlander, Sr. is the son of David Tobias and Sarah Applebaum Nederlander of Detroit, MI.

Caren Elaine Berman Nederlander is the daughter of Morris Berman of Detroit, MI.

Robert Elliot and Caren Elaine Berman Nederlander, Sr.'s son Eric married Nina Danielle Sklar and, later, Dr. Lindsey Kupferman. Their son Robert Elliot Nederlander, Jr. married Suzanne Beth Meirowitz.

Gladys Lenore Blum Nederlander was the daughter of Gaston Blum. She had previously been married to Fred Stryker and Milton Rackmil.

In 2017 the 5,000-square-foot, seven-bedroom, seven-bath house and two acres were for sale. The asking price was $13.5 million.

Nesbit, Elizabeth Clossey (d. 1921)

Marriage(s):	Robert Wilson Nesbit
	- merchant
Address:	62 Dunemere Lane, East Hampton*
Name of estate:	*Seaward*
Year of construction:	1897
Style of architecture:	Shingle
Architect and Builder:	Tamer Pepemehmetoglu, 2015 renovation (for Mitchell)
Landscape architect(s);	
Builder:	George A. Eldredge

House extant: yes
Historical notes:

The *Social Register Summer, 1910* lists Elizabeth Clossey Nesbit as residing at *Seaward* in East Hampton.

She was the daughter of Myles Franklin and Eliza Logan Clossey of New York.

Robert Wilson Nesbit was the son of John and Sarah Wilson Nesbit of Philadelphia, PA.

Robert Wilson and Elizabeth Clossey Nesbit's children Isabel, Jean, Louis, and Robert Cecil did not marry.

*In 1907 Mrs. Nesbit relocated the house to the center of the property.

In 2012 the house was for sale. The asking price was $6.5 million.

It was purchased in 2013 by Christopher Mitchell for $4.567 million.

In 2018 the eight-bedroom, six-and-a-half-bath, 8,000-square-foot house and 1.14 acres were for sale by Mitchell. The asking price was $12.5 million.

Newman, Angeline Ensign (1827-1909)

Civic Activism:	bequeathed funds for the establishment of a church and school in Jerusalem;
	donated $7,000 to Woman's Foreign Missionary Society
Marriage(s):	1855-1899 – John Philip Newman (1826-1899)
	- clergy - pastor, Oneida, NY, conference, 1849-1856;
	pastor, Troy, NY, conference, 1857;
	pastor, Bedford Street Methodist Episcopal Church, Troy, NY, 1858-1860;
	held pastorates in Hamilton, NY, Albany, NY, NYC, and New Orleans, LA;
	reorganized church in the South by establishing three conferences, two colleges, and a church journal, 1864-1869;
	organized and became pastor of Metropolitan ME Church, Washington, DC, 1869, 1876-1879;
	chaplin, United States Senate, 1869-1874;
	pastor, Central Church, NYC, 1879-1882;
	pastor, Madison Avenue Church, NYC. 1882-1884;
	pastor, Metropolitan Church, Washington, DC;
	elected bishop, 1888
	diplomat - inspector of United States consuls in Asia, 1874-1876 (appointed by President Grant)
	writer - *From Dan to Beersheba*; 1864;
	Babylon and Nineveh, 1875;
	Christianity Triumphant, 1884;
	Evenings with the Prophets on the Lost Empires, 1887;
	America for Americans, 1887
Address:	20 Apaquogue Road, East Hampton
Name of estate:	
Year of construction:	1901
Style of architecture:	Modified Shingle
Architect(s):	
Landscape architect(s):	
Builder:	Francis E. Grimshaw, Jr.
House extant: yes	
Historical notes:	

 The house was built by Angeline Ensign Newman.
 She was the daughter of The Reverend Datus Ensign of Mechanicville, NY.
 John Philip Newman was born in Manhattan. His father was of German descent; his mother was French. According to John, he received a message from God at the age of sixteen when a stranger accosted him on the street saying, "God wants your heart." Newman went on to account that two weeks later the same man gave him a piece of paper on which the same words were written. Within a month he joined the Methodist Episcopal Church. [*The New York Times* July 6, 1899, p. 7.] He became the spiritual advisor to President Grant and delivered the eulogy at the president's funeral. He also delivered the eulogy at the funeral of General John A. Logan and at that of Leland Stanford, Jr., the son of Senator Stanford. For the later eulogy Newman was reputed to have received a fee of $10,000. [*The New York Times* July 6, 1899, p. 7.]
 The house was later owned by James Wilde DeGraff and, subsequently, by his daughter Eleanor who married Dr. Frank Clyde Carr, Sr. Both the DeGraffs and Carrs called it *Cherridune*.
 The 7,400-square-foot house with nine bedrooms, six full bathrooms, two half bathrooms, a guest house which was originally the chauffeur's cottage, and one acre were for sale in 2014. The asking price was $6.95 million.

Newton, Francis (1872-1944)

Occupation(s):	artist
Civic Activism:	governor, East Hampton Riding Club; volunteer ambulance driver in France during World War I; a founder, Suffolk Hounds Club; chairman, art committee, Guild Hall, East Hampton; member, East Hampton War Memorial Committee, 1924
Marriage(s):	1904-1944 – Amy James (1870-1949)
Address:	Georgica Road, East Hampton
Name of estate:	*Fulling Mill Farm*
Year of construction:	1910
Style of architecture:	Colonial Revival
Architect(s):	William Welles Bosworth designed the house (for F. Newton)*
Landscape architect(s):	
Builder:	George A. Eldredge, house and 1913 studio

House extant: yes**
Historical notes:

The house, originally named *Fulling Mill Farm*, was built by Francis Newton on the former site of J. S. Corwin's farm. [*The East Hampton Star* October 1, 1909, p. 5, and March 11, 1910, p. 5.]

The *Social Register Summer, 1910* and *1915* list Frances and Amy James Newton as residing at *Fulling Mill Farm* in East Hampton.

He was the son of The Reverend Richard Heber and Mrs. Mary Elizabeth Lewis Newton, Sr. of *Dunecott* in East Hampton.

[See following entry for additional family information.]

*Bosworth utilized Grosvenor Atterbury's plans for the house design.

The house was later owned by Lucius Franklin Robinson, Jr. who continued to call it *Fulling Mill Farm*.

In 1946 John Carrington Yates purchased the art studio and relocated it to LaForest Road. [*The East Hampton Star* December 12, 1946, p. 5.]

**In 1947 a fire caused extensive damage to the house. [*The East Hampton Star* May 22, 1947, p. 5.]

The house is on the National Register of Historic Places.

Newton, The Reverend Richard Heber, Sr. (1840-1914)

Occupation(s):	clergy -	pastor, St. Paul's Church, Philadelphia, PA; pastor, Trinity Church, Springs, NY; pastor, All Soul's Church, NYC
	writer -	*The Children's Church; The Morals of Trade; Womanhood; The Right and Wrong Uses of the Bible*; The Book of the Beginning; Philistinism; Church and Creed; Social Studies; Christian Science*
Civic Activism:		director, Protestant Episcopal Congress; vice-president, Congress of Religions
Marriage(s):		1864-1913 – Mary Elizabeth Lewis (1840-1913)
Address:		West End Avenue, East Hampton
Name of estate:		*Dunecott*
Year of construction:		1889
Style of architecture:		Shingle
Architect(s):		Joseph Greenleaf Thorp *[attributed]* (for R. H. Newton)
Landscape architect(s):		
House extant: no		
Historical notes:		

The house, originally named *Dunecott*, was built by The Reverend Richard Heber Newton, Sr.

The *Social Register Summer, 1895* lists The Reverend R. Heber Newton as residing at *Dunecott* in East Hampton.

He was the son of Richard and Lydia Gretorex Newton of Philadelphia, PA.

Mary Elizabeth Lewis was the daughter of Charles S. Lewis of Philadelphia, PA.

The Reverend Richard Heber and Mrs. Mary Elizabeth Lewis Newton, Sr.'s son Francis married Amy James and resided at *Fulling Mill Farm* in East Hampton. Their daughter Elizabeth married the noted architect William Welles Bosworth, who resided at *Old Trees* in Matinecock. [*See* Spinzia, *Long Island's Prominent North Shore Families, vol. I* – Bosworth entry.] Their son Richard Heber Newton, Jr., who resided at *Box Farm* in Water Mill, married Grace Clarke, the daughter of Thomas Benedict and Fanny E. Morris Clarke, Sr. of *Lindenland* in Southampton; Mildred Gautier Rice, the daughter of William Low Rice of Cleveland, OH; and, subsequently, Blanch Uhlmann Helier, the widow of David Helier of East Hampton. [*See* Spinzia, *Long Island's Prominent Families in the Town of Southampton* – Clarke and Newton entries.]

[See previous entry for additional family information.]

*In 1883 Newton was accused of heresy for a series of sermons published in his book *The Right and Wrong Uses of the Bible*.

Nichols, Harold Willis, Jr. (1911-1985)

Occupation(s):	industrialist - chairman of board, Fox Paper Co. (paper bag manufacturing firm)
	publisher - Horseman Publishing Co.
Civic Activism:	chairman of board, Ohio Heart Association;
	president, Madeira and Indian Hill Fire Department;
	director, American Heart Association of New York City;
	director and vice-president, Queen City Club, Cincinnati, OH;
	director, Lexington Trots Breeders Association;
	trustee, The Trotting Horse Museum Hall of Fame of the Trotter (now, Harness Racing Museum and Hall of Fame);
	trustee, Stable of Memories, Lexington, KY;
	chairman of board, Grand Circuit;
	director, The Little Brown Jug Society, Delaware, OH;
	director, American Standard Breeders Association
Marriage(s):	1936-1985 – Katherine Harkness Edwards (1910-1986)
	- Civic Activism: director, The Little Brown Jug Society, Delaware, OH;
	director, American Standard Breeders Association;
	director, Lexington Trots Breeders Association, Lexington, KY;
	a founder and director, Charolais (cattle breeding association);
	director, American Shetland Sheepdog Association
Address:	10 Lee Avenue, East Hampton
Name of estate:	*Dunehurst*
Year of construction:	1898-1899
Style of architecture:	Shingle
Architect(s):	Cyrus Lazelle Warner Eidlitz designed the house (for Quackenbush)
Landscape architect(s):	
Builder:	George A. Eldredge
House extant: yes	
Historical notes:	

The house was built by Schuyler Quackenbush. It was owned by Dr. Ogden Matthias Edwards, Jr. and, subsequently, by his daughter Katherine who married Harold Willis Nichols, Jr. Both the Edwards and Nichols families called the estate *Dunehurst*.

Harold was the son of Harold Willis and Margaret Rowe Nichols, Sr. of *Crow's Nest* in East Hampton.

Harold Willis and Katherine Harkness Edwards Nichols, Jr.'s daughter Katherine married Christopher Morse Wiedenmayer, the son of Gustave Eugene Wiedenmayer of South Orange, NJ. Their daughter Margaret married George Morrison Jewett, the son of Edward Hill and Georgina Frances Morrison Jewett, Jr. of East Hampton. Their daughter Martha married Stephen Mansfield Brown, the son of John T. Brown of Whitesburg, KY. Their daughter Elizabeth married Stephen Peter O'Keefe, the son of George O'Keefe.

[See following entry for additional family information.]

In 2016, the approximately 10,000-square-foot house, with ten bedrooms and six and a half bathrooms, and 3.3 acres were for sale. The asking price was $18.95 million.

Nichols, Harold Willis, Sr. (1883-1973)

Occupation(s):	industrialist - chairman of board, Fox Paper Co. (paper mill); president, Chesapeake Pulp and Paper Co. (paper mill);
Civic Activism:	chairman of board, Cincinnati Chamber of Commerce, Cincinnati, OH; member, executive committee, Ohio Valley Improvement Association; director, River Valley Transfer Board; director, National Paperboard Association; director, American Pulp and Paper Association; president, Cincinnati Golfer's League, Cincinnati, OH; chairman of board, War Industries Board during World War I; president, Harvard Club; president, Commercial Club; governor, Devon Yacht Club, Amagansett; trustee, Guild Hall, East Hampton
Marriage(s):	1909-1973 – Margaret Rowe (1888-1973) - Civic Activism: Red Cross volunteer during World Wars I and II
Address:	Lily Pond Lane, East Hampton
Name of estate:	*Crow's Nest*
Year of construction:	
Style of architecture:	
Architect(s):	
Landscape architect(s):	
House extant: unconfirmed	
Historical notes:	

In 1944 Nichols purchased the house from Daniel Darrow. [*The East Hampton Star* November 23, 1944, p. 1]

The Blue Book of The Hamptons, 1958 lists Harold Willis and Margaret Rowe Nichols as residing at *Crow's Nest* on Lily Pond Lane, East Hampton.

He was the son of James M. and Elizabeth Marsh Nichols of Cincinnati, OH.

Margaret Rowe Nichols was the daughter of William Stanhope and Margaret Anna Richardson Rowe, Sr. of Amagansett.

Harold Willis and Margaret Rowe Nichols, Sr.'s daughter Margaret married David M. Forker, Sr. Their daughter Sarah married Charles Ruffin Hook of Cincinnati, OH, and, later, Elmore Coe Kerr, Jr., the son of Elmore Coe and Marian Lyman Smyth Kerr, Sr. of Mill Neck. [*See* Spinzia, *Long Island's Prominent North Shore Families, vol. I* – Kerr entry.] Their daughter Mary married Aertsen Parry Keasbey, Jr. of NYC. Their daughter Charlotte married Laurance Laird Davis, Sr. Their son Harold Willis Nichols, Jr. married Katherine Harkness Edwards and resided in East Hampton.

[See previous entry for additional family information.]

Noble, Francis Osborn (1895-1950)

Occupation(s):	attorney - member, law department, Union Carbide Corp.; member, law department, Carbon Corp.
Marriage(s):	1931-1950 – Camilla Leonard Edwards (1905-1990)
Address:	*[unable to determine street address]*, East Hampton
Name of estate:	*Solidago*
Year of construction:	
Style of architecture:	
Architect(s):	
Landscape architect(s):	
House extant: unconfirmed	
Historical notes:	

The *Social Register Summer, 1946* lists Francis O. and Camilla L. Edwards Noble as residing at *Solidago* in Wainscott.

He was the son of Dr. Eugene Allen and Mrs. Lillian Osborn Noble of New York.

Camilla Leonard Edwards Nobel was the daughter of William Henry Leonard and Susan Sherman White Edwards of *Kilkare* in East Hampton.

Francis Osborn and Camilla Leonard Edwards Nobel's daughter Lillian married Stephen Potter, the son of Rowland F. Potter of Buffalo, NY. Their daughter Frances married DuBois Tangier Smith, the son of Edward Henry Leighton Smith of St. James, Long Island. They were descendants of Richard "Bull" Smith, the founder of Smithtown, Long Island. Their son William married Joyce Gafke, the daughter of John W. Gafke of Madison, WI, and, later, Jennifer Sands Lowe, the daughter of James Jenkins Lowe of Bedford Hills, NY. Their son Timothy resided in Manhattan.

Noble, Mark Ainslie (1878-1950)

Occupation(s):	financier - partner, Noble and Corwin (stock brokerage firm); founder, Mark A. Noble and Co. (stock brokerage firm); a founder and president, Financial Stock Clearing Co., Inc.
	capitalist - director, The Great South Bay Realty Co., 1906; director, Hamilton Place Realty Co., NYC
Civic Activism:	president, Bank, Stock, and Unlisted Dealers Association; president, New York Security Dealers Association
Marriage(s):	Florence Hawson
Address:	Middle Lane, East Hampton
Name of estate:	
Year of construction:	1933
Style of architecture:	
Architect(s):	
Landscape architect(s):	
Builder:	Charles Rush
House extant: yes	
Historical notes:	

The house was built by Mark Ainslie Noble. [*The East Hampton Star* August 4, 1933, p. 6.]
He was the son of Thomas Satterwhite and Mary Caroline Hogan Noble, Sr.
The house was later owned by Thomas Hopper Beardsley. [*The East Hampton Star* January 24, 1946, p. 5.]

Northrop, John Burr, Sr. (1901-1964)

Occupation(s):	attorney
	financier - vice-president, Metropolitan Life Insurance Co.
	writer - co-authored, with his brother William, *The Insolence of Office*, 1932
Civic Activism:	president, East Hampton League; president, South Fork Civic Conference
Marriage(s):	1926-1964 – Virginia Osborne Cox (1902-1992)
	- real estate agent - Northrop–Lamb, East Hampton
	Civic Activism: vice-chair, Garden Club of East Hampton
Address:	87 Buell Lane, East Hampton
Name of estate:	
Year of construction:	
Style of architecture:	
Architect(s):	
Landscape architect(s):	
House extant: yes	
Historical notes:	

In 1958 Northrop purchased the house from Glock. [*The East Hampton Star* December 4, 1958, p. 1.]
The Blue Book of The Hamptons, 1965 lists John B. Northrop, Sr. as residing at 87 Buell Lane, East Hampton.
He was the son of Howard Gould and Mary DeS. Richey Northrop.
Virginia Osborne Cox Northrop was the daughter of Albert Schenck and Myrtle Baresford Osborne Cox of Short Hills, NJ. Virginia subsequently married Arthur J. Smith with whom she continued to reside at the Buell Lane residence.
John Burr and Virginia Osborne Cox Northrop, Sr.'s son John Burr Northrop, Jr. married Barbara Stewart, the daughter of Robert Giffen Stewart of New York.
While recovering from a slipped disk, John Burr Northrop, Jr., who resided in Cold Spring Harbor, passed the time by reading the transcripts of President Nixon's White House tapes. He discovered the transcripts had sections missing and notified Woodward and Bernstein, the reporters at *The Washington Post* who were investigating the Watergate affair. [*The New York Times* May 15, 1974, p. 94.] *[See Bradlee entry in this volume for another Watergate connection.]*
In 2016 the four bedroom, three-and-a-half-bath, 1,993-square-foot house and 0.43 acres were for sale. The asking price was $3.195 million.

Nouri, Edmond Joseph (1918-2012)

Occupation(s): journalist - staff writer, *New Yorker* magazine
financier - a founder, Edmund J. Nouri & Associates;
general agent, New England Mutual Life Insurance Co.,
commodities traders, U. S. Steel

Marriage(s): M/1 – Gloria Montgomery (b. 1923)
M/2 – 1971-2012 – Diana Crocker

Address: Indian Wells Highway, Amagansett
Name of estate: *Further Moor*
Year of construction:
Style of architecture:
Architect(s):
Landscape architect(s):
House extant: unconfirmed
Historical notes:

In 1962 Nouri purchased the house from Mrs. David Millar. [*The East Hampton Star* June 14, 1962, p.6.]

The Blue Book of The Hamptons, 1965 lists Edmond J. and Gloria Montgomery Nouri as residing at *Further Moor* on Indian Wells Highway in Amagansett.

Born in Baghdad, Iraq, he was the son of Joseph N. Nouri.

Gloria Montgomery Nouri is the daughter of Robert H. and Elizabeth A. Murphy Montgomery.

Edmond Joseph and Gloria Montgomery Nouri's daughter Katherine married President Eisenhower's speechwriter and aide to New York State Governor Nelson Rockefeller Emmet John Hughes. Their son Michael, who is a noted actor, married Lynn Rubin. Their son Guy, also a noted actor, married Margaret Warren and resides in Hillsdale, NY.

Diana Crocker Nouri is the daughter of William W. Crocker of San Francisco, CA. She had previously been married to John Redington.

Nugent, Dr. Paul Fordham, Sr. (1896-1989)

Occupation(s): physician - East Hampton

Marriage(s): 1923-1989 – Margaret White (1897-2003)
- assistant clinical pathologist

Address: 11 Davids Lane, East Hampton
Name of estate:
Year of construction: 1926
Style of architecture: Stucco
Architect(s): Joseph Greenleaf Thorp designed
the house (for Nugent)
Landscape architect(s):
Builder: Frank B. Smith
House extant: yes
Historical notes:

The 4,600-square-foot, five-bedroom house, with five and a half bathrooms, was built by Dr. Paul Fordham Nugent, Sr.

He was the son of Dr. John and Mrs. Helen Howell Fordham Nugent, Sr. of Southampton. [*See* Spinzia, *Long Island's Prominent Families in the Town of Southampton* – Nugent entry.]

Margaret White Nugent was the daughter of Gilbert H. and Judith Angeli White of Southampton.

Dr. Paul Fordham and Mrs. Margaret White Nugent, Sr.'s daughter Margaret married Thomas O. Conklin, the son of Otis D. Conklin of Bridgehampton, and resided in Bridgehampton. Their son Dr. Paul Fordham Nugent, Jr. married Caroline Gibson, the daughter of James Gibson, Jr., and resided in Xenia, OH.

The house was for sale in 2015. The asking price was $6.495 million.

Oakley, Ralph Lawrence (1890-1963)

Occupation(s):	financier - partner, Maynard, Oakley, and Lawrence (stock brokerage firm); governor, New York Stock Exchange
Civic Activism:	chairman, New York Stock Exchange Admission Committee; vice-chairman, New York Stock Exchange Committee on Public Relations; secretary, Maidstone Club, East Hampton
Marriage(s):	1913-1963 – Sarah Lee Perot (d. 1982)
Address:	Drew Lane, East Hampton
Name of estate:	
Year of construction:	1926
Style of architecture:	Shingle
Architect(s):	John Custis Lawrence designed the house (for Oakley)
Landscape architect(s):	
House extant: yes	
Historical notes:	

The house was built by Ralph Lawrence Oakley.

The *Social Register Summer, 1945* lists R. Lawrence and Sarah Lee Perot Oakley as residing in East Hampton.

He was the son of Ralph Oakley of Manhattan.

Sarah Lee Perot Oakley was the daughter of Edward S. and Elizabeth Lee Albertson Perot, Sr. of *Perot's Hill* in Yonkers, NY.

Ralph Lawrence and Sarah Lee Perot Oakley's daughter Audrey married George Eddison Haines, the son of Franklin Mifflin Haines of Ardsley-on-Hudson, NY, and, later, Robert de Liesseline Johnson, the son of Francis Edgar Johnson of *Ellistan* in Far Hills, NJ. Their daughter Elaine married Charles Wadsworth Howard, Jr. and, later, Karl Behr, Jr., with whom she resided in East Hampton. Their daughter Dora married A. Porter Waterman, the son of Arthur H. Waterman of Greenwich, CT.

By 1958 they had relocated to Lily Pond Lane, East Hampton.

O'Brien, W. Howard, Sr. (1874-1944)

Occupation(s):	industrialist - vice-president, American Tobacco Co. publisher - director, Ahrens Publishing Co. capitalist - director, O'Brien, Fortin, Inc., NY (construction firm); director, Hegeman Harris Co., NY (construction firm)
Marriage(s):	1904-1944 – Katherine Maus (1877-1945)
Address:	Egypt Lane, East Hampton
Name of estate:	
Year of construction:	
Style of architecture:	
Architect(s):	
Landscape architect(s):	
House extant: unconfirmed	
Historical notes:	

The *Social Directory of Southampton, Long Island, 1931* lists Mr. and Mrs. W. Howard O'Brien as residing on Egypt Lane, East Hampton.

He was the son of Martin and Elizabeth Prendergast O'Brien of Chicago, IL.

Katherine Maus O'Brien was the daughter of Frederick K. Maus of Chicago, IL.

W. Howard and Katherine Maus O'Brien, Sr.'s daughter Kathleen married Lucien Scott Neely, the son of Charles H. Neely of Bronxville, NJ. Their son W. Howard O'Brien, Jr. married Hester Ann Fisher, the daughter of Harry White Fisher.

In 1943 the house was purchased by James Wilde DeGraff. [*The East Hampton Star* August 10, 1944, p. 1.]

Ogden, Miss Clara Foster (1832-1915)

Marriage(s):	unmarried
Address:	Lily Pond Lane, East Hampton
Name of estate:	
Year of construction:	1899
Style of architecture:	Shingle
Architect(s):	George A. Eldredge designed the house (for Ogden)
Landscape architect(s):	
Builder:	George A. Eldredge
House extant: yes	
Historical notes:	

The house was built by Miss Clara Foster Ogden.
She was the daughter of David and Ann Foster Ogden of Staten Island, NY.
The previous house, which was built on Divinity Hill by The Reverend Thomas B. McLeod, was destroyed by fire in 1898.
In 1912 the house was purchased by Miss Maria S. Heuser. [*The East Hampton Star* September 13, 1912, p. 5.]

Ogden, James Lawrence, Jr. (1862-1924)

Occupation(s):	industrialist - director and secretary, A. A. Griffing Iron Co.
Marriage(s):	1900-1924 – Mary E. Jenkinson (d. 1924)
Address:	Ocean Avenue, East Hampton
Name of estate:	
Year of construction:	1892
Style of architecture:	
Architect(s):	
Landscape architect(s):	
House extant: unconfirmed	
Historical notes:	

In 1915 Lawrence purchased Thomas Benedict Clarke's residence *The Lanterns*. [*The East Hampton Star* November 2, 1944, p. 3.]
The *Social Register Summer, 1921* lists James L. and Mary E. Jenkinson Ogden [Jr.] as residing on South Beach Lane in East Hampton.
He was the son of James Lawrence and Emily Matilda Wandell Lawrence, Sr.
Mary E. Jenkinson Ogden was the daughter of George B. Jenkinson. She had previously been married to James T. Ball.
The Ogdens did not have children. They were residing in East Hampton at the time of their deaths.
By 1923 the Ogdens had relocated to South Beach Lane.

Olin, John Merrill (1892-1982)

Occupation(s):	industrialist - vice-president, Western Cartridge Co., 1918-1944 (arms manufacturing firm which merged with Winchester Repeating Arms Co. to form Olin Industries)
	president and director, Olin Industries (arms manufacturing firm which merged with Mathieson Chemical Corp. to form Olin Mathieson Chemical Corp.);
	director and chairman of board, Olin Mathieson Chemical Corp.
	inventor - held twenty-four patents for gun powder and cartridge designs
	financier - president and director, Illinois State Bank of East Alton, IL;
	director, First National Bank and Trust Co., Alton, IL;
	director, St. Louis Union Trust Co., St. Louis, MO;
	director, Banker's Trust Co., NYC
Civic Activism:	established John M. Olin Foundation;
	director, World Wildlife Fund, Washington, DC;
	director, Illinois Shooting Preservation Association;
	director, Washington University Corporation, St. Louis, MO;
	trustee, Cornell University, Ithaca, NY;
	trustee, Johns Hopkins University, Baltimore, MD;
	trustee, National Industrial Conference Board;
	trustee, Midwest Research Institute, Kansas City, MO;
	trustee, American Museum of Natural History, NYC;
	president and treasurer, Orthopedic Foundation for Animals
Marriage(s):	M/1 – 1917–div. 1935 – Adele Louise Levis (1899-1994)
	M/2 – 1940-1982 – Evelyn Brown (1905-1993)
Address:	Lily Pond Lane, East Hampton
Name of estate:	
Year of construction:	1926
Style of architecture:	Spanish Farmhouse
Architect(s):	Robert Tappan designed the house (for E. F. Warner, Jr.)

Landscape architect(s):
House extant: yes
Nassau County Museum Collection has photographs of the estate.
Historical notes:

The house, originally named *Cima Del Mundo*, was built by Eltinge Fowler Warner, Jr. In 1944 Olin purchased the house from Warner. [*The East Hampton Star* November 23, 1944, p. 1.]

He was the son of Franklin Walter and Mary Mott Moulton Olin, Sr. of Alton, IL.

Adele Louise Levis Olin was the daughter of George M. Levis of Alton, IL. She subsequently married Frank Chambles Rand.

John Merrill and Adele Louise Levis Olin's daughter Joan died in childhood. Their daughter Louise married James B. Braun and, later, David D. Walker. Their daughter Georgene married Frederick Lewis Macfarlane.

The Blue Book of The Hamptons, 1958 lists John M. and Evelyn Brown Olin as residing on Lily Pond Lane, East Hampton.

She was the daughter of Dr. John Young Brown of St. Louis, MO, and had previously been married to William Francis Niedringhaus.

The house is on the National Register of Historic Places.

Onderdonk, Dr. Thomas Williams (1860-1926)

Occupation(s):	physician - dentist
Marriage(s):	M/1 – 1893-1905 – Julia Prior (1874-1905)
	M/2 – 1919-1926 – Mary C. Belknap (1864-1944)
Address:	Lily Pond Lane, East Hampton
Name of estate:	
Year of construction:	1914-1915
Style of architecture:	Salt-Box*
Architect(s):	John Custis Lawrence designed the house (for Onderdonk)
Landscape architect(s):	
Builder:	Edward M. Gay
House extant: unconfirmed	
Historical notes:	

The house was built by Dr. Thomas Williams Onderdonk. [*The Brooklyn Daily Eagle* October 26, 1913, p. 63, and August 6, 1914, p. 5.]

He was the son of Adrian and Mary Willets Pearsall Onderdonk.

Julia Prior Onderdonk was the daughter of Thomas S. and Ida L. Prior of Roslyn, NY.

Dr. Thomas Williams and Mrs. Julia Prior Onderdonk's son Prior was twenty-three years old at the time of his death in 1917. Their daughter Marjorie married ____ Bettin.

Mary C. Belknap Onderdonk was the daughter of S. E. Belknap of NYC and Hackettstown, NJ.

Despondent over his deteriorating health, Onderdonk committed suicide in his office by inhaling nitrous oxide gas. [*The New York Times* May 12, 1926, p. 20.]

*The house was modeled after John Howard Payne's residence *Home Sweet Home*. [*The Brooklyn Daily Eagle* August 6, 1914, p. 5.]

It is on the National Register of Historic Houses.

Ordway, Samuel Gilman (1887-1942)

Occupation(s):	attorney -	partner, Butler and Mitchell;
		partner, Moore, Oppenheimer, and Peterson, 1919-1920;
		partner, Graves and Ordway, 1920-1927
	capitalist -	secretary and treasurer, Crushed Stone and Gravel Co., Saskatoon, Canada;
		treasurer, International Telephone & Telegraph Co.;
		secretary and treasurer, American Cable & Radio Corp.;
		treasurer, All American Corp.
Marriage(s):	1914-1942 – Mildred O. Wurtele (1889-1978)	
Address:	Apaquogue Road, East Hampton	
Name of estate:	*Dellwood*	
Year of construction:		
Style of architecture:		
Architect(s):		
Landscape architect(s):		
House extant: unconfirmed		
Historical notes:		

In 1940 Ordway purchased Samuel Hanson Ordway, Jr.'s residence and called it *Dellwood*. [*The East Hampton Star* April 18, 1940, p. 5.]

He was the son of Lucius Pond and Jessie Cornwell Gilman Ordway of St. Paul, MN.

Mildred O. Wurtele Ordway was the daughter of Joseph George Wurtele of Chicago, IL. She subsequently married Francis Dewey Everett, the son of Dr. Oliver Hurd and Mrs. Sarah Frances Dewey Everett of Worcester, MA.

Samuel Gilman and Mildred O. Wurtele Ordway's daughter Joan married John Griswold Livingston, Jr., the son of John Griswold and Clara M. Dudley Livingston, Sr. of Lawrence, and resided in New Canaan, CT. [*See* Spinzia, *Long Island's Prominent Families in the Town of Hempstead* – Livingston entry.] Their daughter Dorothy married Charles James Mills, the son of Edward S. Mills of NYC.

Ordway died in the bathtub of his Manhattan apartment. The cause of death was listed as alcohol poisoning. The night prior to his death Ordway was involved in an altercation with a drug addict and petty thief in the latter's hotel room. [*The New York Times* June 1, 1942, p. 15, and June 3, 1942, p. 25.]

[See other Ordway entries for additional family information.]

Ordway, Samuel Hanson, Jr. (1900-1971)

Occupation(s):	attorney -	member, Burlingham, Veeder, Master, and Fearey; partner, Spencer, Ordway, and Wierum; partner, Ordway and Wierum; council, New York City Civil Service Commission, 1933-1935
	educator -	lecturer, University of Southern California; lecturer, New York University, NYC; lecturer, American University, Washington, DC
	politician -	member, New York City Art Commission, 1937, 1940; member, New York City Civil Service Commission, 1934-1936; member, United States Civil Service Commission, 1937-1939; head of employment branch, United States Naval Department
	writer -	*The Intellect Is a Brute*, 1929; *Measurement of Effective Work of Government Employees*, 1934; *More Objective Oral Tests*, 1937; *The Conservation Handbook*, 1949; *Resources of the American Dream*, 1953; *Prosperity Beyond Tomorrow*, 1956
Civic Activism:		chairman, executive committee, Civil Service Reform Association; treasurer and president, Civil Service Reform League; treasurer, City Club, NYC; secretary, Municipal Art Society, NYC; member, Municipal Smoke Abatement Board; chairman of board, National Resources Council of America; trustee, American Conservation Association*; a founder, with his wife Anna, Anna W. and Samuel H. Ordway, Jr. Foundation, Inc.
Marriage(s):		1927-1971 – Anna Wheatland (1900-1999) - Civic Activism: vice-chair, New York Committee of the Frontier Nursing Service; member, board of managers, Jacob A. Riis Neighborhood Settlement, NY; a founder, with her husband Samuel, Anna W. and Samuel H. Ordway, Jr. Foundation, Inc.

Address: Apaquogue Road, East Hampton
Name of estate:
Year of construction:
Style of architecture:
Architect(s):
Landscape architect(s):
House extant: unconfirmed
Historical notes:

    He was the son of Samuel Hanson and Frances Hunt Throop Ordway, Sr.
    Anna Wheatland Ordway was the daughter of Richard Wheatland of Boston, MA.
    Samuel Hanson and Anna Wheatland Ordway, Jr.'s daughter Anna died in 1934 at the age of nine. Their son Stephen died in 1936 at the age of sixteen. Their son Samuel Hanson Ordway III married Penelope Joan Bronson, the daughter of Norton Bronson of Greenwich, CT. Their daughter Dr. Ellen Ordway, a noted biologist and melittologist, did not marry.
    *In recognition of his work in conservation, the Samuel H. Ordway, Jr. Memorial Preserve in Leola, South Dakota, was named for him.
    [See other Ordway entries for additional family information.]
    In 1940 the house was purchased by Samuel Gilman Ordway. [*The East Hampton Star* April 18, 1940, p. 5.]

Ordway, Samuel Hanson, Sr. (1860-1934)

Occupation(s):	attorney - partner, Stickney, Spencer, and Ordway, 1890-1903; partner, Spencer, Ordway, and Wierum; assistant district attorney, New York County, 1901; judge, New York State Supreme Court, 1917
Civic Activism:	member, committee to revise New York State tax laws, 1906; member, New York State committee to investigate securities and commodities speculation; president, New York State Civil Service Commission, 1915-1917; member, New York City Selective Serve Board, 1918; trustee, Brown University, Providence, RI; president, Civil Service Reform Association
Marriage(s):	1894-1933 – Frances Hunt Throop (1860-1933) - artist Civic Activism: director, New York Exchange for Women's Work; member, executive committee, Garden Club of East Hampton
Address:	Apaquogue Road, East Hampton
Name of estate:	*Subacawan*
Year of construction:	
Style of architecture:	
Architect(s):	
Landscape architect(s):	
House extant:	unconfirmed
Historical notes:	

The *Long Island Society Register, 1929* lists Samuel H. and Frances Hunt Throop Ordway [Sr.] as residing at *Subacawan* in East Hampton.

He was the son of Aaron Lucius and Frances Ellen Hanson Ordway of Manhattan.

Frances Hunt Throop Ordway was the daughter of Enos Thompson and Cornelia Gridley Throop II. Frances' sister Katharine married The Reverend William Montague Geer, Sr. of Oyster Bay. Her brother George married Ida Morrell Ewen and resided in Chicago, IL. Her sister Caroline married John A. Kernan of New York. Her brother Enos Thompson Throop III married Bessie Sands Tyler and resided in Brooklyn.

Samuel Hanson and Frances Hunt Throop Ordway, Sr.'s son Samuel Hanson Ordway, Jr. married Anna Wheatland, the daughter of Richard Wheatland of Boston, MA, and resided at *Rollicking Ridge* in Yorktown Heights, NY.

[See other Ordway entries for additional family information.]

Orr, Alexander Ector (1831-1914)

Occupation(s):	shipping -	partner, David Dows & Co. (shipping and importing firm)
	financier -	trustee, Brooklyn Savings Institution;
		director, Queens Insurance Company of America;
		president, New York Produce Exchange;
		director, United States Trust Co.;
		president, New York Produce Exchange Safe Deposit & Storage;
		vice-president, Mechanics National Bank;
		director, Associated Merchants Company Bond & Mortgage Co.;
		director, Continental Insurance Co.;
		director, Federal Insurance Co.;
		director, The Fidelity and Casualty Co.;
		president, New York Life Insurance Co., 1905-1907
	capitalist -	vice-president and director, Delaware & Hudson Co.;
		director, Rock Island & Pacific Railway Co.;
		director, Erie Railroad;
		director, Realty Associates
	publisher -	director, Harper & Brothers
Civic Activism:		trustee, Greenwood Cemetery, Brooklyn, NY;
		member, New York State Canal Committee, 1875;
		member, Brooklyn Civil Service Commission;
		trustee, Brooklyn Academy of Music;
		president, New York Chamber of Commerce;
		president, New York Rapid Transit Commissioners
Marriage(s):		M/1 – 1857-1872 – Juliet Buckingham Dows (1834-1872)
		M/2 – 1873-1913 – Margaret Shippen Luquer (1940-1913)
Address:		165 De Forest Road, Montauk
Name of estate:		
Year of construction:		1883
Style of architecture:		Beach Cottage
Architect(s):		McKim, Mead & White designed the house
Landscape architect(s):		Frederick Law Olmsted designed the site plan
Builder:		Mead and Taft

House extant: no; destroyed by fire, 1997*
Historical notes:

    The house is one of the Montauk Association's "Seven Sisters." It was owned by Alexander Ector Orr.
Born in Strabane, County Tyrone, Ireland, he was the son of William and Mary Moore Orr.
    Juliet Buckingham Dows Orr was the daughter of Ammie and Jane Eliza Wilbor Dows.
    Alexander Ector and Juliet Buckingham Dows Orr's daughter Jane married James Buchanan Niles. Their daughter Juliet married Albert H. Munsell. Their daughter Mary did not marry.
    Margaret Shippen Luquer Orr was the daughter of Nicholas Luquer.
    The house was later owned by James L. Darby and, then, jointly by Harrison Tweed, Alexander Ector Orr, Dr. Fessenden Nott Otis, Louis Clark, Andrew J. Thomas, and E. M. Jackson prior to being purchased in 1924 by Harrison Tweed, who named it *Tick Hall*.
    *The house was owned by Richard Alva Cavett when it was destroyed by fire in 1997. He built a contemporary version similar to the original house on the site. The new house was designed by James Hadley. In 2017 the house and twenty acres were for sale by Cavett. The asking price was $62 million.

Osborn, Jeremiah, Sr. (c. 1707-1775)

Occupation (s:

Marriage(s):					1735-1767 – Mercy Baker (c. 1705-1767)

Address:					Woods Lane, East Hampton
Name of estate:
Year of construction:				Eighteenth century
Style of architecture:				Colonial Revival
Architect(s):
Landscape architect(s):
House extant: yes
Historical notes:

   The house was originally facing Main Street. In 1906 it was moved back on the property and turned to face Woods Lane.
   Jeremiah Osborn, Sr. was the son of Joseph and Mary Hedges Osborn of East Hampton.
   Jeremiah and Mercy Baker Osborn, Sr.'s daughter Elizabeth was an infant at the time of her death in 1744. Their daughter Ester married Timothy Mulford. Their daughter Puah married William Huntting, the son of Nathaniel and Mary Hedges Huntting of East Hampton. Their son Jeremiah Osborn, Jr. married Mary Parsons and, later, Jersuha Gardiner. Their daughter Mercy married William Arthur, the son of John Arthur.

Osborne, Burnett Mulford (1856-1943)

Occupation(s):					capitalist - co-owner, with his brother William A. Osborne,
						    Osborne House, East Hampton (now, The
						    Maidstone Arms);
						owned a mill;
						owned a livery stable, East Hampton
						real estate agent - East Hampton

Marriage(s):					M/1 – 1889-1921 – Annie Phillips (1862-1921)
						M/2 – 1922-1943 – Lina Bucher (b. 1877)

Address:					Terbell Lane, East Hampton
Name of estate:
Year of construction:				1904
Style of architecture:				Shingle
Architect(s):					John Custis Lawrence designed
						   the house (for B. M. Osborne)

Landscape architect(s):
Builder:					Thomas E. Babcock, house
						Babcock and Grimshaw, 1893 addition
						   of veranda (for B. M. Osborne)*

House extant: unconfirmed
Historical notes:

   The house was built by Burnett Mulford Osborne. [*The East Hampton Star* September 20, 1929, p. 2.]
   He was the son of William Lewis Huntting and Sarah Mulford Osborne of East Hampton.
   Annie Philips Osborne was the daughter of Elizabeth Phillips of Shelter Island.
   Lina Bucher Osborne was from Zurich, Switzerland.
   The Osbornes did not have children.
   *Additions were also made to the house in 1904.

Osborne, Dr. Edward Monroe, Sr. (1842-1916)

Occupation(s):	physician - veterinarian
Marriage(s):	M/1 – Phebe Hendrickson
	M/2 – 1902-1917 – Grace Raymond White (1877-1923)
Address:	Main Street and Woods Lane, East Hampton
Name of estate:	
Year of construction:	1700s
Style of architecture:	Colonial
Architect(s):	
Landscape architect(s):	
House extant: unconfirmed	
Historical notes:	

    Edward Monroe Osborne, Sr. was the son of Charles and Harriet Eliza Cook Osborne of East Hampton. Edward's brother Joseph married Grace's sister Bessie and resided in East Hampton.

    Grace Raymond White Osborne was the daughter of William Cohu and Ada Moore Street White of Sag Harbor. Grace's brother Thaddeus, who was the United States Deputy Consul General in Shanghai, married Der Ling, who was not a princess as she claimed but rather lady-in-waiting and interpreter for the Dowager Empress Cixi from 1903 to 1905. Der Ling's father Yu Keng was Chinese Minister to Japan and France. Her mother Louise Pearson was the daughter of John Pearson, a Boston merchant stationed in Shanghai, and his Chinese wife.

    Dr. Edward Monroe and Mrs. Grace Raymond White Osborne, Sr.'s daughter Helen married Cyril Roarick; Harold Cofer; and, later, Walter Zdyb. Their son Edward Monroe Osborne, Jr. married Ethel Diffene, the daughter of Henry W. Diffene of Hawley, PA, and resided in Springs. Their son Thaddeus married Margaret Bauld and resided in East Hampton.

    The house was later owned by Charles Edmunds Kimball. It was subsequently owned by Marion Louise Smith Peters. [*The East Hampton Star* February 20, 1936, p. 5.]

Osborne, Mrs. George A.

Marriage(s):	
Address:	173 Main Street, East Hampton
Name of estate:	
Year of construction:	1903
Style of architecture:	Queen Anne
Architect(s):	George A. Eldredge designed the house (for Mrs. G. A. Osborne)
Landscape architect(s):	
Builder:	George A. Eldredge
House extant: yes	
Historical notes:	

    The six-bedroom, six-and-a-half-bathroom, 6,000-square-foot house was built by Mrs. George A. Osborne. [*The East Hampton Star* November 20, 1952, p. 9.]

    It was for sale in 2014. The asking price was $2.3 million.

Osborne, Joseph Septimus (1852-1926)

Occupation(s):	politician - East Hampton Town Clerk, 1874-1903
	capitalist - a founder, Home Water Co., East Hampton; a founder, East Hampton Electric Light Co., 1902
	merchant - a founder, East Hampton Lumber Co., 1899
	financier - a founder, Osborne Trust Co., East Hampton*; founder, Osborne Insurance and Real Estate Agency, East Hampton
Civic Activism:	member, committee appointed to reproduce first five volumes of East Hampton Town Records
Marriage(s):	M/1 – 1885-1901 – Florence Nightingale Worthington (1861-1901)
	M/2 – 1905-1926 – Bessie Moore White (1879-1958)
Address:	Main Street, East Hampton
Name of estate:	
Year of construction:	1898
Style of architecture:	Shingle
Architect(s):	Joseph Septimus Osborne designed his own house
Landscape architect(s):	
Builder:	George A. Eldredge
House extant: yes	
Historical notes:	

    The house was built by Joseph Septimus Osborne.
    He was the son of Charles and Harriet Eliza Cook Osborne of East Hampton.
    Florence Nightingale Worthington Osborne was the daughter of Benjamin Franklin and Hannah Cook Worthington.
    Joseph Septimus and Florence Nightingale Worthington Osborne's son Charles was a teenager at the time of his death. Their daughter Mary, aka Marguerite, married Stephen Lewis Ham, Sr. Their son Nelson, who later owned the house, married Eleanor Clark and, later, Alice D. Miller.
    Bessie Moore White Osborne was the daughter of William Cohu and Ada Street Moore White of Sag Harbor. Bessie subsequently married Henry G. Ham. Her sister Grace married Dr. Edward Monroe Osborne, Sr. and resided in East Hampton.
    *His bank was the first in East Hampton to permit depositors to draw checks against their deposits.

Osborne, Nelson Cook, Sr. (1888-1967)

Occupation(s):	financier - a founder, Osborne Trust Co., East Hampton*; founder, Osborne Insurance and Real Estate Agency, East Hampton
	politician - president, Village of East Hampton, 1922-1925; supervisor, Town of East Hampton, 1932-1934
	merchant - director, East Hampton Lumber Co.
	capitalist - Home Water Co., East Hampton; East Hampton Electric Light Co.
Civic Activism:	president, East Hampton Historical Society; president and Treasurer, Guild Hall, East Hampton; chairman, advisory board, East Hampton Free Library; chairman of board, East Hampton Village Zoning Board of Appeals; trustee, South End Cemetery, East Hampton
Marriage(s):	M/1 – 1921-1946 – Eleanor Clark (1897-1946)
	M/2 – 1947-1967 – Alice D. Miller (b. 1908)
Address:	Main Street, East Hampton
Name of estate:	
Year of construction:	1898
Style of architecture:	Shingle
Architect(s):	Joseph Septimus Osborne designed his own house
Landscape architect(s):	
Builder:	George A. Eldredge
House extant: yes	
Historical notes:	

The house was built by Joseph Septimus Osborne. It was subsequently owned by Nelson, the son of Joseph and his first wife Florence Nightingale Worthington Osborne.

Eleanor Clark Osborne was the daughter of C. J. Clark of Hornell, NY.

Nelson Cook and Eleanor Clark Osborne Sr.'s son Charles married Patricia Armitage, the daughter of Patrick Armitage. Their son Robert married Joan C. Day, the daughter of Bernard Day of Kingston, NJ. Their daughter Eleanor married Ilmar Carl Ratsep, the son of Rudolph Ratsep of Middle Island. Their son Nelson Cook Osborne, Jr. married Mary Jane Coy and, later, Barbara Morgan.

Alice D. Miller Osborne subsequently married Stephen Lewis Ham, Jr. of Southampton.

*The Osborne Trust Co. was the first bank in East Hampton to permit depositors to draw checks against their deposits.

Osserman, Stanley (1903-1963)

Occupation(s):	attorney
	industrialist - chairman of board, Dictograph Products, Inc.
Marriage(s):	1924-1963 – Elizabeth Tonkonogy (1904-1967)
	- real estate agent - New York City apartments
Address:	Apaquogue Road, East Hampton
Name of estate:	*The Gatehouse*
Year of construction:	
Style of architecture:	Colonial Revival
Architect(s):	
Landscape architect(s):	
House extant: unconfirmed	
Historical notes:	

In 1951 Osserman purchased Philip Ruxton's residence *Cairnhill* and renamed it *The Gatehouse*. [*The East Hampton Star* June 21, 1951, p. 6.]

He was the son of Edward and Rose Bauman Osserman of Manhattan.

Elizabeth Tonkonogy Osserman was the daughter of George Ferdin and Sylvia Zuckerman Tonkonogy of Brooklyn.

Stanley and Elizabeth Tonkonogy Osserman's daughter Wendy married Georgos Papakonstantis of Athens, Greece. Their daughter Carol married James Hugh Merritt, the son of Josiah Merritt and, later, Dr. Robert Walter of East Hampton. Their daughter Joan married Georges Du Pont, the son of Louis Du Pont of Geneva, Switzerland, and resided in St. Cloud, France.

Ossorio, Alfonso Angel (1916-1990)

Occupation(s):	artist - painter, sculptor
	merchant - a founder and director, Signa Gallery, East Hampton; director, Exhibitions House, NYC, 1956-1958
Marriage(s):	bachelor
Address:	Montauk Highway, East Hampton
Name of estate:	*The Creeks*
Year of construction:	1898-1899
Style of architecture:	Italian Villa
Architect(s):	Grosvenor Atterbury designed the house (for A. Herter)
Landscape architect(s):	Albert and Adele McGinnis Herter designed their own gardens
	Rupert Barneby designed evergreen plantings (for Ossorio)
Builder:	Frank Grimshaw

House extant: yes*
Nassau County Museum Collection has photographs of the estate.
Historical notes:

   The house, originally named *Près Choisis*, was built by Albert Herter who later renamed it *The Creeks*. After Herter's death, his son Christian sold the estate to Ossorio.
   He was the son of Miquel José and Maria Paz Yuango Ossorio of The Philippines.
   Alfonso bequeathed the estate to his longtime companion Edward F. Dragon. Both Ossorio and Dragon continued to call the estate *The Creeks*. In the 1990s Dragon sold the estate to Ronald Owen Perelman who made extensive alterations.
   The house is on the National Register of Historic Places.
   The stables were added to the estate in 1899 and a studio was added in 1912.
   *In 2018 a portion of the house was damaged by fire.

Pagel, Elinor Robertson Bronaugh (1906-2002)

Marriage(s):	1936-1971 – Alex John Pagel, Jr. (1888-1971)
	- capitalist - a founder and president, Pagel, Horton, and Co. (wood pulp and newsprint importing firm); director, Western and Maryland Railway
Civic Activism:	a "dollar-a-year-man" involved in the production of armored tanks during World War II;
	organizer, Wings for Norway (bought aircraft for Norwegian resistant forces in exile);
	president, American Wood Pulp Importers Association;
	president, American–Swedish News Exchange;
	president, Swedish Chamber of Commerce in United States;
	treasurer, John Ericsson Republican League of America

Address:	67 Woods Lane, East Hampton
Name of estate:	*Elsufral*
Year of construction:	1900
Style of architecture:	Colonial Revival
Architect(s):	
Landscape architect(s):	
House extant: yes	
Historical notes:	

    The compound consists of a 6,000-square-foot, three-story, six-bedroom main residence and a turn-of-the-century guest cottage. It was previously owned by Elinor's parents Frederick Lewis and Sue Robertson Bronaugh who also called it *Elsufral*.
    The *Social Register Summer, 1982* lists Elinor R. Bronaugh as residing at *Elsufral*, 67 Woods Lane, East Hampton.
    Alex John Pagel, Jr. was originally from Stockholm, Sweden. He had previously been married to Aleda C. Chamberlin.
    Alex John and Elinor Robertson Bronaugh Pagel, Jr.'s son Alex Bronaugh Pagel married Luisa Margharita La Viola, the daughter of Joseph La Viola of New York.
    In 2015 the 2.75-acre estate was for sale. The asking price was $4.995 million; the annual taxes were $19,169.
    The house is on the National Register of Historic Places.

Paltrow, Gwyneth Kate (b. 1972)

Occupation(s):	entertainers and associated professions -
	motion picture and television actress;
	narrator of children's books
	writer - co-author, with Mario Batali, *Spain*, 2008;
	My Father's Daughter, 2011;
	Notes From the Kitchen Table, 2011;
	It's All Good, 2013;
	The Clean Plate, 2019
Civic Activism:	ambassador, Save the Children;
	trustee, Robin Hood Foundation (established to alleviate poverty in NYC)
Marriage(s):	M/1 – 2003-div. 2016 – Christopher Anthony John Martin (b. 1977)
	- entertainers and associated professions -
	co-founder, Coldplay (band);
	songwriter;
	motion picture actor (cameos)
	Civic Activism - director, Global Citizen Festival
	M/2 – Brad Falchuk
	- entertainers and associated professions -
	co-creator, with Ryan Murphy, "Glee";
	co-creator, "Scream";
	creator, "American Horror Story";
	executive producer, "Nip/Tuck"
Address:	35 Old Montauk Highway, Amagansett
Name of estate:	
Year of construction:	
Style of architecture:	
Architect(s):	
Landscape architect(s)	
House extant: yes	
Historical notes:	

    Gwyneth Kate Paltrow is the daughter of Bruce and Blythe Danner Paltrow of Santa Monica, CA.
    Christopher Anthony John Martin is the son of Anthony and Alison Martin of Exeter, England.
    Christopher Anthony John and Gwyneth Kate Paltrow Martin's daughter Apple was born in 2004; their son Moses was born in 2006.
    Brad Falchuk had previously been married to fellow television producer Suzanne Bukinik. Brad and Suzanne Falchuk had two children.

Pardridge, Albert Jerome (1876-1947)

Occupation(s):	capitalist - president, A. J. Pardridge and Co., Chicago, IL (real estate firm);
	partner, A. J. Pardridge & Harold Bradley, Chicago, IL (real estate firm)
	merchant - executive, Marshall Field and Co., Chicago, IL (department store);
	executive, Siegel, Cooper and Co., Chicago, IL (department store);
	executive, Atkins Sons & Co., NYC;
	executive, Hillman's, Chicago, IL
Civic Activism:	member, Cook County Real Estate Board, Chicago, IL;
	member, Chicago Real Estate Board
Marriage(s):	1898-1947 – Florence Evelyn Myers (1880-1972)
Address:	Drew Lane, East Hampton
Name of estate:	*Duneside*
Year of construction:	
Style of architecture:	
Architect(s):	
Landscape architect(s):	
House extant:	unconfirmed
Historical notes:	

 The *Social Register Summer, 1937* and *1945* list Albert J. and Florence Myers Partridge as residing at *Duneside* in East Hampton.
 He was the son of Charles Wellington and Theresa Louise Marsland Pardridge of Chicago, IL. Albert's sister Evelyn married Prince Nickolas Engalitcheff, the former Russian Consul in Chicago. [*Chicago Tribune* July 28, 1944, p. 10.]
 Florence Evelyn Myers Pardridge was the daughter of Walter T. Myers of Phillipsburg, NJ.
 Albert Jerome and Florence Myers Pardridge's son John married Kathleen Haggerty, the daughter of Dr. Daniel Leo Hagerty of Trenton, NJ. Their daughter Priscilla, whose stage name was Eden Gray, married Lester Cohen.
 In 1951 the house was purchased by Harry J. Johnson. [*The East Hampton Star* February 8, 1951, p.8.]
 The Blue Book of The Hamptons, 1958 lists Florence Myers Pardridge as residing at *Swan's Way* on Ocean Avenue, East Hampton.

Parker, Cecil Carlton (1890-1970)

Occupation(s):	inventor - dish rack;
	Parker Method of Incinerating;
	hand held personal alarm
Marriage(s):	M/1 – 1931-div. – Wilhelmina Gesiena Asser (1900-1961)
	M/2 – 1952-1970 – Helen Livingston Satterlee (1903-1985)
	- merchant - owner, Old Barn Bookshop, East Hampton
Address:	146 Main Street, East Hampton
Name of estate:	*Postscript*
Year of construction:	c. 1800
Style of architecture:	
Architect(s):	
Landscape architect(s):	
House extant:	yes*
Historical notes:	

 Parker purchased the Mulford ancestral residence.
 He was the son of Cecil E. and Mary Green Parker of Hyde Park, NY.
 Wilhelmina Gesiena Asser Parker was the daughter of Hendrik Lodewijk and Catharina Margaretha Piek Asser.
 Cecil Carlton and Wilhelmina Gesiena Asser Parker's son Peter married Eleanor Alice Webster, the daughter of Bethuel M. Webster of NYC.
 The Blue Book of The Hamptons, 1958 and *1965* list C. Carlton and Helen Livingston Satterlee Parker as residing at *Postscript*, 146 Main Street, East Hampton.
 She was the daughter of Dr. Francis LeRoy and Mrs. Ebba Peterson Satterlee, Jr. of *House of Four Winds* in Montauk.
 *Alterations were made to the house in 1890 and 1970.

Parker, Roy Tilden, Jr. (b. 1914)

Occupation(s):	attorney - member, Kirlin, Campbell, Hickox, Keating, and McGrann
Marriage(s):	1938 – Louise Hurlbut
Address:	35 Huntting Lane, East Hampton
Name of estate:	
Year of construction:	1894
Style of architecture:	Queen Anne
Architect(s):	
Landscape architect(s):	
House extant: yes*	
Historical notes:	

The Blue Book of The Hamptons, 1965 and *1973* list Mr. and Mrs. Roy T. Parker as residing at 35 Huntting Lane, East Hampton.

He was the son of Roy Tilden Parker, Sr. of Pelham, NY.

Louise Hurlbut Parker was the daughter of William Nathan Hurlbut of Pelham Manor, NY.

Roy Tilden and Louise Hurlbut Parker, Jr.'s son Roy Tilden Parker III married Lynda Stucker, the daughter of Lyman M. Stucker.

*In 1980 the upstairs bedrooms and bathroom sustained damage in a fire. [*The East Hampton Star* January 24, 1980, p. 4.]

Paxton, The Reverend John Randolph, Sr. (1843-1923)

Occupation(s):	clergy - pastor, West Presbyterian Church, NYC
Marriage(s):	1870-1894 – Mary Lindsey (1851-1894)
Address:	86 Lily Pond Lane, East Hampton
Name of estate:	*Windward*
Year of construction:	1901
Style of architecture:	Neo Tudor
Architect(s):	Joseph Greenleaf Thorp designed the house (for Paxton)
Landscape architect(s):	
Builder:	George A. Eldredge
House extant: yes	
Historical notes:	

The house, originally named *Windward*, was built by The Reverend John Randolph Paxton, Sr.

He was the son of John and Elizabeth Power Wilson Paxton of Canonsburg, PA.

Mary Lindsey Paxton was the daughter of John Lindsey of Pittsburgh, PA.

The Reverend John Randolph and Mrs. Mary Lindsey Paxton, Sr.'s daughter Rebecca died at age thirteen of heart failure. Their daughter Elizabeth died in early childhood. Their son John Randolph Paxton, Jr. died at age twenty-five. Their daughter Mary, who later owned *Windward*, married Harry Leon Hamlin.

Paxton was a member of the 140th Regiment of the Pennsylvania Volunteers which was famed for repelling Pickett's charge during the Civil War Battle of Gettysburg.

In 1946 Mrs. Hamlin sold the house to Leonard Gerard Bisco. [*The East Hampton Star* February 14, 1946, p. 5.]

In 1963 it was purchased by Alvin Gibbs Fox. [*The East Hampton Star* April 23, 1964, p. 3.]

It was later owned by Carol Ann Morgan who sold it for $25.5 million in 2010.

Alterations were made to the house in 1906 and in 1926.

Peddy, John Richard (1906-1980)

Occupation(s):	attorney - Engel, Judge, and Miller, NYC
	capitalist - director, National Water Corp, NY (bottler and distributor of spring water and carbonated beverages)
Marriage(s):	Merrie Edgeworth (1907-1980)
Address:	4 Ocean Avenue, East Hampton
Name of estate:	*Pudding Hill*
Year of construction:	c. 1887
Style of architecture:	Shingle
Architect(s):	Isaac Henry Green II designed the house and the 1906 extension (for E. Herrick)*
Landscape architect(s):	
House extant: yes	
Historical notes:	

The house, originally named *Pudding Hill*, was built by Dr. Everett Herrick. It was later owned by his brother-in-law James Bishop Ford; by Ford's cousin Bennett Bishop; and, subsequently, by Peddy. Ford, Bishop, and Peddy continued to call it *Pudding Hill*.

The Blue Book of The Hamptons, 1965 and 1973 list John R. and Merrie Edgeworth Peddy as residing at *Pudding Hill* at the intersection of Ocean Avenue and Woods Lane, East Hampton.

Their son Jackson married Patricia Scheyhing, the daughter of Herman Karl Scheyhing of Darien, CT, and resided in NYC. Their daughter Barbara married John Deering Watson, the son of John C. Watson of Steubenville, OH, and resided in Crownsville, MD. Both John and Merrie Peddy died in a fire that destroyed the Watsons' home.

*For Green's other commissions, *see* Spinzia, *Long Island's Prominent South Shore Families: Their Estates and Their Country Homes in the Towns of Babylon and Islip.*

Perelman, Ronald Owen (b. 1943)

Occupation(s):	industrialist - chairman of board, Revlon, Inc. (cosmetics firm); partner, with his father, Belmont Iron Works (later, Belmont Industries);
	capitalist - chairman of board, Mac Andrews & Forbes Holdings, Inc., Wilmington, DE; chairman of board, Mac Andrews & Forbes Group, Inc., NYC; chairman of board, National Health Labs, Inc., La Jolla, CA; chairman of board, Andrews Group, Inc., NYC
	publisher - *The Independent*
Civic Activism:	president, Solomon R. Guggenheim Museum, NYC; donated $63.5 million to various charities, 2008; donated $20 million to The University of Pennsylvania in honor of his former wife Claudia, 2007; donated over $114 million to various charities, 2006; donated $100 million to Columbia University, School of Business, 2013; a founder, The Chapman Perelman Foundation
Marriage(s):	M/1 – 1965-div.1984 – Faith Golding (b. 1946) - capitalist - board chair and chief executive officer, First Sterling Corp., NYC (operates non-residential buildings)
	M/2 – 1985-div. 1994 – Claudia Lynn Cohen (1950-2007) - entertainers and associated professions - gossip reporter for television and newspapers
	M/3 – 1995-div. 1996 – Patricia Michelle Orr (b. 1954) (aka Patricia Duff) - entertainers and associated professions - producer, John McLaughlin radio show Civic Activism: founder, Show Coalition; founder, The Common Good; political and environmental activist
	M/4 – 2000-div. 2006 – Ellen Rona Barkin (b. 1954) - entertainers and associated professions - actress
	M/5 – Anna Chapman - physician - psychiatrist Civic Activism: a founder, The Chapman Perelman Foundation
Address:	Montauk Highway, East Hampton
Name of estate:	
Year of construction:	1898-1899
Style of architecture:	Italian Villa
Architect(s):	Grosvenor Atterbury designed the house (for A. Herter)
Landscape architect(s):	Albert and Adele McGinnis Herter designed their own gardens Rupert Barneby designed evergreen plantings (for Ossorio)
Builder:	Frank Grimshaw

House extant: yes*
Nassau County Museum Collection has photographs of the estate.
Historical notes:
   The house, which is on the National Register of Historic Places, was originally named *Près Choisis*. It was built by Albert Herter who later renamed it *The Creeks*. After Herter's death his son Christian sold the estate to Alfonso Angel Ossorio who bequeathed the estate to his longtime companion Edward F. Dragon. Both Ossorio and Dragon continued to call the estate *The Creeks*. In the 1990s Dragon sold the estate to Perelman.
   He is the son of Raymond G. and Ruth Caplan Perelman.
   Faith Golding Perelman subsequently married Dr. Peter J. Linden of NYC.
   Ronald Owen and Faith Golding Perelman's daughter Debra married Gideon Gil and resides in Manhattan. The Perelmans adopted three children—Steven, Josh, and Hope.

Perelman, Ronald Owen (cont'd)

Claudia Lynn Cohen Perelman was the daughter of Robert and Harriet Cohen of Englewood, NJ.

Patricia Michelle Orr is the daughter of Robert and Mary Orr. Patricia had previously been married to Thomas Zabrodsky, Daniel Duff, and Morris Mike Medavoy. In 1995 Patricia gave birth to Caleigh Sophia.

Ellen Rona Barkin Perelman is the daughter of Sol and Evelyn Rozin Barkin of The Bronx, NY. She had previously been married to Gabriel Byrne. Her brother George was formerly the editor-in-chief of *National Lampoon* and *High Times*. Ellen received an Emmy Award as Outstanding Lead Actress for her role in the 1997 film "Before Women Had Wings." For her role in "The Big Easy" in 1987 she was named the Best Foreign Actress at the Sant Jordi Awards in Barcelona, Spain.

The stables were added to the estate in 1899 and a studio was added in 1912.

*In 2018 a portion of the house was damaged by fire.

Perot, Edward Sansom, Jr. (1889-1963)

Occupation(s):	industrialist - president, Ford Instrument Co. (later, division of Sperry Rand Corp.); president, Southern Dairies, Inc.; president and director, Crocker–Wheeler Electric Manufacturing Co.; vice-president, National Conduit and Cable Co.
Marriage(s):	M/1 – 1912-1961 – Katherine Oakley (d. 1961) M/2 – Dale Beulah Winter (1893-1985) - capitalist - a founder, with Henry Kendall Duffy, Dufwin Theaters entertainers and associated professions - motion picture actress
Address:	Lily Pond Lane, East Hampton
Name of estate:	
Year of construction:	
Style of architecture:	
Architect(s):	
Landscape architect(s):	
House extant:	unconfirmed
Historical notes:	

The *Social Directory of Southampton, Long Island, 1930* lists Mr. and Mrs. Edward S. Perot, Jr. as residing on Lily Pond Lane, East Hampton.

He was the son of Edward Sansom Perot, Sr. of Yonkers, NY.

Katherine Oakley Perot was the daughter of Ralph Oakley of Manhattan.

Edward Sansom and Katherine Oakley Perot, Jr.'s daughter Sarah married Harvey Wright Branigar, Jr. of Chicago, IL. Their daughter Katherine married Andrew Cobb Blake, the son of Glenard Worthington Blake of Santa Barbara, CA, and, later, Duane S. Doolittle. Their son Edward Sansom Perot III married Mary Frances Jones, the daughter of John Frank Jones of Richmond, VA.

Dale Beulah Winter Perot was the daughter of Frank and Estelle H. Ziegler Winter. Dale had previously been married to Chicago's white slave ring figure Giacomo "Big Jim" Colosimo; Henry Kendall Duffy; and Hershel McGraw.

Peters, Marion Louise Smith (1875-1950)

Civic Activism:	chair, tree committee, Ladies Village Improvement Society, East Hampton;
	aided in restoration of *Mulford House* and *Home Sweet Home*, East Hampton
Marriage(s):	1899-1929 – William Sterling Peters (d. 1929)
	- financier - partner, Carlisle, Mellick, and Co. (stock brokerage firm)
Address:	Main Street and Woods Lane, East Hampton
Name of estate:	
Year of construction:	1700s
Style of architecture:	Colonial
Architect(s):	
Landscape architect(s):	
House extant: unconfirmed	
Historical notes:	

    Charles Edmunds Kimball, Sr. purchased the residence of Dr. Edward Monroe Osborne. It was later owned by Mrs. Peters. [*The East Hampton Star* February 20, 1936, p. 5.]
    The *Social Register Summer, 1937* lists Marion L. Smith Peters as residing in East Hampton.
    She was the daughter of William Cyrus and Louise McPhail Smith of Brooklyn.
    William Sterling Peters was the son of Hamilton Halliberton Jackson and Clementine Dixon Peters.

Peterson, Peter George (1926-2018)

Occupation(s):	statesman - Secretary of Commerce, 1972-1973 (Nixon administration)

financier - vice-president and director, Market Facts Inc., Chicago, IL;
    director, First National Bank, Chicago, IL;
    chairman of board, Lehman Brothers;
    chairman of board, Lehman Brothers, Kuhn;
    co-founder, with Steven Allan Schwartzman, The Blackstone
        Group, LP;
    chairman of board, Federal Reserve Bank, NY

industrialist - director, RCA Corp.;
    director, General Foods Corp.;
    director, Black & Decker Co.;
    director, Minnesota Mining & Manufacturing Co.;
    director and chairman of board, Bell & Howell Co.;
    director, Bell Telephone Co.;
    director, Sony Corp.;
    director, Cities Service Co.

merchant - director, Federated Department Stores

advertising executive - director of marketing services, vice-president,
        and general manager, McCann Erickson,
        Chicago, IL

capitalist - director, Rockefeller Center Properties, Inc., NYC;
    director, National Education Television

politician - assistant to U. S. President for International Economic
    Affairs, 1970-1972 (Nixon administration)

writer - *Facing Up*, 1993;
    Will America Grow Up Before It Grows Old, 1996;
    Gray Dawn, 2000;
    On Borrowed Time, 2004;
    Running on Empty, 2005;
    The Education of an American Dreamer, 2009 (autobiography)

Civic Activism: founder, The Peter G. Peterson Foundation with a donation $1 billion*;
chairman, planning committee, Citizens for Eisenhower, 1952;
co-chairman, with John Snow, Conference Board Commission on
    Public Trust and Private Enterprise;
chairman, Commission on Foundations and Private Philanthropy;
director, Public Agenda Foundation;
trustee, Blind Book Club, Purchase, NY;
trustee, Japan Society;
member, Bi-Partisan Committee on Entitlement and Tax Reform,
    1994 (Clinton administration);
trustee, Cancer Research Foundation;
trustee, Salk Institute of Biological Research;
trustee, Brookings Institute;
trustee, University of Chicago, Chicago, IL;
chairman of board, Council of Foreign Relations;
chairman of board, Institute of International Relations;
a founder, Bi-Partisan Budget Appeal;
president, The Concord Coalition;
trustee, Museum of Modern Art, NYC;
executive director, Council on International Economic Policy;
director, Nixon Presidential Library & Museum

Marriage(s): M/1 – 1948-div.1950 – Kris Krengel
M/2 – 1953-div. 1979 – Sally Hornbogen (b. 1931)
    - psychologist - counselor, New York Mental Health Center, NYC
        Civic Activism: trustee, The Dalton Schools, NYC;
            director, Women's Action Alliance;
            trustee and director, Fielding Institute, Santa
                Barbara, CA;
            member, women's board, University of
                Chicago, Chicago, IL

Peterson, Peter George (cont'd)

    M/3 – 1980-2018– Joan Ganz (aka Joan Ganz Cooney) (b. 1929)
        - entertainers and associated professions -
            producer; television**;
            director, WNET (Channel 13);
            co-founder, "Sesame Street";
            founder, "Electric Company";
            founder, "3-2-1 Contact";
            founder, Square One TV;
            founder, Children's Television Network;
            documentary producer, Channel 13 (NY PBS station WNET)
        industrialist - director, Xerox;
            director, Johnson and Johnson
        financier - director, Chase Manhattan Bank;
            director, Metropolitan Life Insurance Co.
        Civic Activism: co-founder & executive director, Joan Ganz Cooney Center, at Sesame Workshop;
            trustee, Mayo Foundation;
            member, President's Commission on Marijuana and Drug Abuse, 1971-1973;
            director, National News Council, 1973-1981;
            director, Council on Foreign Relations;
            member, President's Commission for Agenda for the 1980s, 1980-1981 (Carter administration);
            member, Carnegie Foundation National Panel on High Schools, 1980-1982;
            director, National Organization for Women;
            director, National Academy of Television Arts and Sciences;
            director, National Institute of Social Sciences;
            director, Radio and Television Society;
            director, Women in Radio and Television;
            director, Museum of Television & Radio;
            director, Columbia Presbyterian Hospital, NYC;
            member, National Child Labor Committee

Address: Drew Lane, East Hampton
Name of estate:
Year of construction:
Style of architecture:
Architect(s):
Landscape architect(s):
House extant: yes
Historical notes:

  Peter George Peterson was the son of George Peterson (aka Georgios Petropoulos) and Venet Peterson.
  Sally Hornbogen Peterson is the daughter of Dr. Daniel P. and Mrs. Katherine A. Barnes Hornbogen of Marquette, MI. Sally subsequently married Michael Carlisle.
  Peter George and Sally Hornbogen Peterson's son Michael married Meredith Loveday Maher, the daughter of Peter S. and Martha B. Maher, and, later, Tara Marie Peters, the daughter of Richard L. and Kay L. Peters of New York. Their daughter Holly married Richard Ayer Kimball, Jr. of Darien, CT. Their son David married actress Paige Matthews.
  Joan Ganz Peterson is the daughter of Sylvan Cleveland and Pauline Reddon Ganz of Phoenix, AZ. Joan had previously been married to Timothy Jeffries Cooney.
  *Peterson was one of the fifty billionaires that signed a pledge to donate at least half of their fortune to charity.
  **In 1989 Joan received the Lifetime Achievement Award and inducted into the Academy of Television Arts and Sciences Hall of Fame. In 1995 she was awarded the Presidential Medal of Freedom. In 1998 she inducted into the National Woman's Hall of Fame. In 2004 she was inducted into the Association of Educational Publishers Hall of Fame.
  The Petersons relocated to Water Mill. [*See* Spinzia, *Long Island's Prominent Families in the Town of Southampton* – Peterson entry.]
  The house was later owned by Mortimer Benjamin Zuckerman.

Phillips, Fleming Stanhope (d. 1901)

Occupation(s):	industrialist - partner, Phillips, Kunhardt, & Allen, NYC (wool textile manufacturing firm); partner, Lawrence Woolen Co., Lawrence, MA (wool textile manufacturing firms)
	merchant - dry goods
Marriage(s):	M/1 – annulled c. 1873 – Grace McGregor
	M/2 – Martha Bagg (1857-1943)
Address:	3 West End Avenue, East Hampton
Name of estate:	
Year of construction:	1897
Style of architecture:	Shingle
Architect(s):	Joseph Greenleaf Thorp designed the house (for F. S. Phillips)
	Eugene Lawrence Futterman, 1980 alterations (for Bradlee)
Landscape architect(s):	Anna Park Gilman Hill designed her own gardens, with Ruth Dean, 1914
	Victoria Fensteer, 1985- (for Bradlee)
Builder:	George A. Eldredge

House extant: yes*
Nassau County Museum Collection has photographs of the estate.
Historical notes:

The house was built by Fleming Stanhope Phillips.

Martha Bagg Phillips was the daughter of John Sherman Bagg, editor of the *Detroit Free Press*.

The court rejected the claim by Phillips' brother James Ralph Phillips that Martha had exercised undue influence over her husband due to the latter's supposed incompetence and that she had cremated his body to hide the evidence of brain disease. [*The New York Times* March 6, 1901, p. 5, and April 3, 1901.]

The Phillipses did not have children.

In 1913 the house was sold to Robert Carmer Hill, who named it *Grey Gardens*. In 1924 Hill sold the house to Phelan Beale, Sr. who continued to call it *Grey Gardens*. As part of his divorce settlement, Beale deeded the house to his wife Edith. The Beales' daughter Edith sold the house in 1979 to Benjamin Crowninshield Bradlee, Sr. Both the Beales and the Bradlees continued to call the house *Grey Gardens*.

*Alterations were made to the house c. 1972 and in 1980.

In 2017 the 6,000-square-foot, seven-bedroom, six-bath house and 1.7 acres were for sale. The asking price was $19.995 million.

The house is on the National Register of Historic Places.

Phillips, Martha Bagg (1857-1943)

Marriage(s):	Fleming Stanhope Phillips (d. 1901) - *[See previous entry.]*
Address:	75 Dunemere Lane, East Hampton
Name of estate:	
Year of construction:	1916
Style of architecture:	Colonial Revival with Dutch Colonial elements
Architect(s):	Isaac Henry Green II designed the house (for Mrs. F. S. Phillips)*
Landscape architect(s):	
Builder:	Philip Ritch

House extant: yes
Historical notes:

The house was built by Martha Bagg Phillips. [*The East Hampton Star* October 1, 1915, p. 5.]
[See previous entry for family information.]
*For Green's other commissions, *see* Spinzia, *Long Island's Prominent South Shore Families: Their Estates and Their Country Homes in the Towns of Babylon and Islip.*

Pierson, Warren Lee, Sr. (1896-1978)

Occupation(s):	attorney -	member, O'Melveny, Milliken, Tuller, and Macneil; special counsel, Reconstruction Finance Corp., Washington, DC
	capitalist -	president, American Cable and Radio Corp.; president, Commercial Cable Corp.; president, Mackay Radio Corp.; president, All American Cable and Radio, Inc.; vice-president, American Telephone and Telegraph Corp.; director and chairman of board, Trans World Airlines Corp.; director, International Telephone and Telegraph World Communications
	financier -	chairman of board, Great Western Financial Corp., Beverly Hills, CA; president, Export–Import Bank, Washington, DC; director, Investment Diversified Services; director, Great Western Savings and Loan Association; director, West Coast Savings and Loan Association
	industrialist -	director, Fruehauf Trailer Co.; director, United States Industries Inc.; director, Commercial Oil Refining Corp.
	diplomat -	rank of United States Ambassador, Tripartite Commission on German Debts, 1951-1952
Civic Activism:		financial advisor, U. S. delegation, Consultations of Ministers of General Affairs of the American Republics, Rio de Janeiro, Brazil, 1942; financial advisor, U. S. delegation, United Nations Monetary Conference, Bretton Woods, NH, 1944; financial advisor, U. S. delegation, Inter-American Conference on Problems of War and Peace, Mexico City, Mexico, 1945; member, National Emergency Council, 1934-1936; member, Inter-American Financial and Economic Advisory Committee, 1940-1945; chairman, United States Council of International Chamber of Commerce, 1951-1955
Marriage(s):		1927-1978 – Eleanor Shelton Mehnert (1903-1989)
Address:		Further Lane, East Hampton
Name of estate:		*Furthermoor*
Year of construction:		1965
Style of architecture:		
Architect(s):		
Landscape architect(s):		
House extant: unconfirmed		
Historical notes:		

   The house, originally named *Furthermoor*, was built by Warren Lee Pierson, Sr.
   The Blue Book of The Hamptons, 1965 and *1973* list Warren Lee and Eleanor Shelton Mehnert Pierson [Sr.] as residing at *Furthermoor* on Further Lane, East Hampton.
   He was the son of Louis W. and Hilda Pearson Pierson.
   Eleanor Shelton Mehnert Pierson was the daughter of Herman A. Mehnert.
   Warren Lee and Eleanor Shelton Mehnert Pierson, Sr.'s son Warren Lee Pierson, Jr. was an infant at time of his death in 1935.

Pittman, Ernest Wetmore (1889-1970)

Occupation(s):	engineer - apprentice, Niles, Bement, Pond, and Co., 1912-1914; engineer, Dillon Read and Co., 1926-1931 industrialist - president, Rathbone, Sard, and Co., 1922, 1926; director and chairman of board, Interchemical Corp.
Civic Activism:	trustee, Memorial Hospital, NYC; chief of U. S. Rubber Mission to the Soviet Union, 1942; fund chairman, Hook Pond Associates
Marriage(s):	1915-1970 – Estelle Young Romeyn (1894-1980) - Civic Activism: secretary, Garden Club of East Hampton
Address:	Terbell Lane, East Hampton
Name of estate:	
Year of construction:	
Style of architecture:	
Architect(s):	
Landscape architect(s):	
House extant: unconfirmed	
Historical notes:	

In 1946 Pittman purchased Mrs. Charles Philip Coleman's house. [*The East Hampton Star* August 21, 1947, p. 2.]

The Blue Book of The Hamptons, 1958, 1965, and *1973* list Ernest W. and Estelle Y. Romeyn Pittman as residing on Terbell Lane, East Hampton.

He was the son of Lansing Mizner and Annette Phelps Steuart Pittman of Detroit, MI.

Estelle Young Romeyn Pittman was the daughter of Charles William and Estelle Young Romeyn of Manhattan. Her sister Rosalind married William Everdell, Jr. and resided in North Hills. [*See* Spinzia, *Long Island's Prominent North Shore Families, vol. I* – Everdell and Horace Havemeyer, Jr. entries – and *Long Island's Prominent South Shore Families* – Horace Havemeyer, Jr. entry.]

Ernest Wetmore and Estelle Young Romeyn Pittman's son Steuart, who was Assistant Secretary of Defense in the Kennedy and Johnson administrations, married Antoinette Eno Pinchot, the daughter of Amos Richards Eno and Ruth Pickering Pinchot and niece of Governor Gifford Pinchot of Pennsylvania. Antoinette's sister Mary married Cord Meyer IV, the son of Cord and Katharine Blair Thaw Meyer III of *Little River Farm* in North Hampton, NH, and grandson of Cord and Cornelia M. Covert Meyer II of *The Cove* in Kings Point. [*See* Spinzia, *Long Island's Prominent North Shore Families, vol. I* – Meyer entry.] Cord Meyer IV was Chief of Covert Action Staff of the Directorate of Plans for the CIA's worldwide clandestine activities. His wife Mary was murdered in 1964 while walking along the former tow path of the Chesapeake and Ohio Canal in Georgetown, VA. [*See* Raymond E. Spinzia, "Adultery, Drugs, Murder, Untimely Deaths, and Long Island's Prominent Families: A Tangled Web." www.spinzialongislandestates.com and Judith Ader Spinzia, "Women of Long Island: Cornelia Bryce Pinchot, Feminist, Social-Activist – The Long Islander Who Became First Lady of Pennsylvania." www.spinzialongislandestates.com.] Steuart later married Barbara Milburn White, the daughter of Will Walter White. Antoinette subsequently married Benjamin Crowninshield Bradlee, Sr. of *Grey Gardens* in East Hampton. The Pittmans' daughter Estelle married Richard Inman Pearce, the son of Arthur Williams and Lucy Inman Pearce of Hewlett. [*See* Spinzia, *Long Island's Prominent Families in the Town of Hempstead* – Pearce entry.]

In 1965 the roof of the house sustained fire damage ignited by sparks from the chimney. [*The East Hampton Star* June 17, 1965, p. 3.]

Plimpton, George Ames (1927-2003)

Occupation(s):	journalist - editor-in-chief, *Paris Review*, 1953-2003;
	associate editor, *Horizon Magazine*;
	associate editor, *Harper's Magazine*
	educator - instructor, Barnard College, NYC
	writer - numerous magazine articles;
	Rabbit's Umbrella, 1956;
	Out of My League, 1961;
	Paper Lion, 1966;
	The Bogey Man, 1968;
	Mad Ducks and Bears, 1973;
	One for the Record, 1974;
	Shadow Box, 1976;
	One More July, 1976;
	Sports!, 1978;
	Sports Bestiary, 1982;
	Fireworks, 1984;
	Open Net, 1985;
	The Curious Case of Sidd Finch, 1987;
	The X-Factor, 1990;
	The Best of Plimpton, 2000;
	Shackleton, 2003;
	The Man in the Flying Lawn Chair, 2005
	(co-authored with Sarah Whitehead Dudley Plimpton)
	entertainers and associated professions -
	television host;
	actor - motion pictures and television
Civic Activism:	trustee, East Harlem Tutorial Program;
	trustee, New York Philharmonic Orchestra
Marriage(s):	M/1 – 1968-div. 1988 – Freddy Medora Espy (1942-2015)
	- artist
	interior designer
	M/2 – 1992-2003 – Sarah Whitehead Dudley (b. 1952)
	- writer - freelance;
	The Man in the Flying Lawn Chair, 2005
	(written by George Plimpton;
	edited by Sarah Whitehead Dudley Plimpton;
	and published posthumously)
Address:	Bendigo Road, Amagansett
Name of estate:	*Xanadu*
Year of construction:	
Style of architecture:	
Architect(s):	
Landscape architect(s):	
House extant: yes	
Historical notes:	

The Blue Book of The Hamptons, 1973 lists George Ames and Freddy Espy Plimpton as residing at *Xanadue* on Bendigo Road, Amagansett.

George Ames Plimpton was the son of Francis Taylor Pearsons and Pauline Ames Plimpton, Sr., who resided at *Sweet Hollow* in West Hills. [*See* Spinzia, *Long Island's Prominent North Shore Families, vol. II* – Plimpton entry.]

Freddy Medora Espy Plimpton was the daughter of Willard Richardson and Hilda S. Cole Espy.

George Ames and Freddy Medora Espy Plimpton's daughter Medora married Spencer Knight Harris, the son of Robert Harris of Alstead, NH. Their son Taylor married Lizzy Eggers.

By 1971 the Plimptons had relocated to Amagansett from Sagaponack. [*See* Spinzia, *Long Island's Prominent Families in the Town of Southampton* – Plimpton entry.]

Sarah Whitehead Dudley Plimpton is the daughter of James Chittenden and Elizabeth Claypool Dudley.

George Ames and Sarah Whitehead Dudley Plimpton had twin daughters, Laura and Olivia.

Pollock, Jackson (1912-1956)

Occupation(s): artist - abstract expressionist*

Marriage(s): 1945-1956 – Lee Krasner (1908-1984)
    (aka Lena Krasner and Lenore Krasner)
 - artist - abstract expressionist

Address: 830 Springs – Fireplace Road, East Hampton
Name of estate:
Year of construction:
Style of architecture: Long Island Farmhouse
Architect(s):
Landscape architect(s):
House extant: yes
Historical notes:

   Born in Cody, Wyoming, Jackson Pollock was the son of LeRoy and Stella May McClure Pollock. Jackson died in an automobile accident less than a mile from his house while driving under the influence of alcohol.
   *He was dubbed "Jack the Dripper" in a rather unflattering article in *The New York Times*.
   Lee Krasner Pollock was born Lena Krasner in Brooklyn, NY, to Russian Jewish immigrants.
   The Pollocks did not children.
   The house is currently owned and administered by the Stony Brook Foundation which is affiliated with Stony Brook University. Known as the Pollock–Krasner House and Study Center, it is open for tours May through October.

Pool, Mary Baldwin Schwab (1925-1997)

Marriage(s): M/1 – 1949-1963 – Henry Lawrence Pool (1917-1963)
 - educator - member, Department of Aeronautical Engineering, Princeton University, Princeton, NJ
M/2 – 1971-1988 – Philip Milledoler Brett, Jr.
 - financier - member, Stillman, Maynard, and Co. (stock brokerage firm);
 member, H. G. Wellington and Co. (stock brokerage firm)
Civic Activism: trustee, Judson Health Center, NYC; trustee, Fund for the Blind

Address: Ocean Avenue, East Hampton
Name of estate:
Year of construction:
Style of architecture:
Architect(s):
Landscape architect(s):
House extant: unconfirmed
Historical notes:

   The Blue Book of The Hamptons, 1965 lists Mary Schwab as residing on Ocean Avenue, East Hampton.
   She was the daughter of Hermann Casper and Ruth Baldwin Bliss Schwab of *Chicken Valley Farm* in Old Brookville. [*See* Spinzia, *Long Island's Prominent North Shore Families, vol. II* – Schwab entry.] Mary subsequently married Philip Milledoler Brett, Jr. with whom she resided on Ocean Avenue.
   Henry Lawrence Pool was the son of William Henry and Isabelle Donahue Pool of Warrenton, CT. Henry had previously been married to Olivia Ames Peters, the daughter of R. Dudley Peters of Milton, MA.
   Henry Lawrence and Mary Baldwin Schwab Pool's daughter Katharine married Louis Henry Schmidt III and resided in Fairfield, CT. Their son James married Kathryn Lucinda Sass, the daughter of Robert E. Sass of Sharon, PA, and resided in Sherborn, MA. Their son William Henry Pool II married Mary P. Heller and resided in Greenwich, CT.

Poor, James Harper (1862-1919)

Occupation(s):	capitalist - partner, with his father and brother, E. E. Poor, Jr. (importing firm);
	partner, Denny, Poor, & Co. (importing firm);
	partner, Poor Brothers (importing firm);
	president, J. Harper Poor & Co. (later, Amory Browne & Co.) (importing firm);
	director, Amory Browne & Co.
Civic Activism:	a founder and member, first board of governors, Devon Yacht Club, Amagansett;
	a founder, Suffolk Hunt Club, 1910
Marriage(s):	1885-1919 – Evelyn Bolton (1864-1956)
Address:	181 Main Street, East Hampton
Name of estate:	*As You Like It*
Year of construction:	
Style of architecture:	Elizabethan
Architect(s):	Joseph Greenleaf Thorp, 1910 alterations (for Poor)
	Eric Woodward, 1996 alterations (for Reiswig)
Landscape architect(s):	
House extant:	yes
Historical notes:	

In 1899 Poor purchased the former Daniel Howe/Thomas Baker residence. [*The East Hampton Star* June 2, 2005, p. 44.]

The *Social Directory of Southampton, Long Island, 1931* lists Mrs. J. Harper Poor as residing on Main Street, East Hampton. The *Social Register Summer, 1932* lists *As You Like It* as the name of her residence.

She was the daughter of Thomas J. and Evelyn Hamlin Keep Bolton.

James Harper Poor was the son of Edward Erie and Mary Wellington Lane Poor, Jr. of Manhattan.

James Harper and Evelyn Bolton Poor's daughter Evelyn married Philip Parkhurst Gardiner, the son of Asa Bird Gardiner, Sr. Their daughter Mildred married Dr. Alexander Yelverton Garnett of Washington, DC.

In 1943 the house was purchased by Robert Graham Dunn Douglas. [*The East Hampton Star* July 1, 1943, p. 1.]

In 1959 Harry Wilfred Watts purchased the house from Douglas. [*The East Hampton Star* April 16, 1959, p. 1.] In 1973 Mrs. Watts donated it to the Southampton Hospital. [*The East Hampton Star* May 25, 1973, p. 20.]

In 1996 the house was purchased by Gary D. and Rita Reiswig who remodeled it into The Baker House 1650, a bed and breakfast inn. In 2004 the Reiswigs listed it for sale. The asking price was $3.95 million.

The house was purchased by Robert and Antonella Rosen.

Potter, Dickson Bayard (1894-1985)

Occupation(s):	educator - founder, director, and headmaster, Potter School, Tucson, AZ
Civic Activism:	founder, governor, and treasurer, first board of governors, Devon Yacht Club, Amagansett; governor, Riding Club of East Hampton; director, Maidstone Club, East Hampton
Marriage(s):	1923-1985 – Sue Cunningham Bucknell (1905-1987)
Address:	14 Huntting Lane, East Hampton
Name of estate:	*Falaise Farm*
Year of construction:	1899
Style of architecture:	Shingle with Dutch Colonial Elements
Architect(s):	
Landscape architect(s):	
House extant:	yes
Historical notes:	

The Blue Book of The Hamptons, 1965 lists Dickson Bayard and Sue C. Bucknell Potter as residing at *Falaise Farm*, 14 Huntting Lane, East Hampton. They had previously resided on Further Lane.

He was the son of Eugene Clifford and Margaret Somerville Potter of *A–Y–Mor* in East Hampton.

Sue Cunningham Bucknell Potter was the daughter of Dr. Howard and Mrs. Susan Cunningham Bucknell of Atlanta, GA.

Dickson Bayard and Sue Cunningham Bucknell Potter's son Eugene Clifford Potter II married Sylvie Bryce, the granddaughter of Lloyd Stephens Bryce of *Bryce House* in Roslyn Harbor and the daughter of Peter Cooper Bryce and Angelica Schuyler Brown who resided in Brookville and at *Villa Vera* in Locust Valley. Eugene later married Ruth Saxer, the daughter of John Saxer of Lloyd Harbor. [*See* Spinzia, *Long Island's Prominent North Shore Families, vol. I* – Brown and Bryce entries.] Their daughter Susanne married Arnold Gillatt.

[See following entry for additional family information.]

In 2017 the 3,045-square-foot, five-bedroom, two-and-a-half-bath house and 0.34 acres were for sale. The asking price was $3.9 million.

Potter, Eugene Clifford (1863-1937)

Occupation(s):	capitalist - partner, with his brother Frederick, Clifford Realty Co., NYC (real estate builder and holding firm);
	partner, with his brother Frederick, Potter Brothers, Inc., NYC (real estate builder and holding firm);
	president, 373 Park Avenue Corp., NYC (real estate holding firm);
	president, Montsana Realty Co., NYC
	financier - member, advisory committee, Bank of Manhattan Trust Co.
Civic Activism:	president, Braker Memorial Home, The Bronx;
	member, board of managers, home for the Incurables;
	a founder and first treasurer, Devon Yacht Club, East Hampton;
	director, East Hampton Visiting Nurse Association;
	vice-president and treasurer, Maidstone Club, East Hampton;
	director, Fifth Avenue Association;
	director, Uptown Club;
	director, Riding Club, East Hampton;
	member, executive committee, East Hampton Associates
Marriage(s):	Margaret Somerville (d. 1936)
	- Civic Activism: board chair, Presbyterian Home for Aged Women;
	a founder, Garden Club of East Hampton
Address:	Lily Pond Lane, East Hampton
Name of estate:	*A–Y–Mor*
Year of construction:	1899
Style of architecture:	Shingle
Architect(s):	Joseph Greenleaf Thorp designed the house (for E. C. Potter)
Landscape architect(s):	
Builder:	George A. Eldredge
House extant: yes	
Historical notes:	

The eleven-bedroom house, originally named *A–Y–Mor*, was built by Eugene Clifford Potter.

The *Social Register Summer, 1932* lists E. Clifford and Margaret Sommerville Potter as residing in East Hampton.

He was the son of Joseph and Jane Shave Potter. Eugene's brother Frederick, who married Clara Von Keller, also resided in East Hampton.

Margaret Somerville Potter was the daughter of Day Somerville of Manhattan.

Eugene Clifford and Margaret Somerville Potter's son Dickson married Sue Cunningham Bucknell and resided at *Falaise Farm* in East Hampton.

[See other Potter entries for additional family information.]

The house was later owned by J. J. O'Connell and, subsequently, by Jon Bon Jovi, who bought it in 2004.

Potter, Frederick Gaul (1860-1926)

Occupation(s):	capitalist - partner, with his brother Eugene, Clifford Realty Co., NYC (real estate builder and holding firm); partner, with his brother Eugene, Potter Brothers, Inc., NYC (real estate builder and holding firm)
Civic Activism:	director, Water Mill Gun Club, Water Mill
Marriage(s):	1879-1926 – Clara Von Keller
Address:	19 Lee Avenue, East Hampton
Name of estate:	
Year of construction:	1899
Style of architecture:	Shingle
Architect(s):	Joseph Greenleaf Thorp designed the house (for F. G. Potter)
Landscape architect(s):	
Builder:	Loper Brothers
House extant: yes	
Historical notes:	

The house was built by Frederick Gaul Potter.

He was the son of Joseph and Jane Shave Potter. Frederick's brother Eugene married Margaret Somerville and resided at *A–Y–Mor* in East Hampton.

Frederick Gaul and Clara Von Keller Potter's daughter Clara married Sir Robert Henry Green–Price, the Third Baronet of *Norton Manor*, County Radnor, England. Their daughter Grace married Stuart C. Grant of London, England, and, later, Massiter Leeds. Their daughter Florence did not marry.

[See other Potter entries for additional family information.]

The house was later owned by John Richard Keim who sold it to Lamon Vanderburg Harkness in 1914. [*The East Hampton Star* January 22, 1915, p. 5.] It was later owned by James Branch Briggs, who called it *Beehive;* Chevy Chase; and subsequently, by Peter Gabriel Terian. In 2010 Mrs. Terian listed the house for sale. The asking price was $21 million.

Potter, Frederick Gaul (1860-1926)

Occupation(s):	*[See previous entry.]*
Civic Activism:	*[See previous entry.]*
Marriage(s):	1879-1926 – Clara Von Keller
Address:	1 Lily Pond Lane, East Hampton
Name of estate:	
Year of construction:	1905
Style of architecture:	Shingle
Architect(s):	Joseph Greenleaf Thorp designed the house (for F. G. Potter)
Landscape architect(s):	
Builder:	Thomas E. Babcock
House extant: yes	
Historical notes:	

The house was built by Frederick Gaul Potter.
[See previous entry for family information.]
The house was later owned by Daniel Rose.

Potter, Jeffrey Brackett (1918-2012)

Occupation(s):	capitalist - founder and president, Stony Hill Service Corp., Amagansett (construction firm);
	established Stony Hill School (horse riding);
	founder and president, East Hampton Dredge and Dock Corp.
	journalist - reporter, Columbia, SC, newspaper
	industrialist - machinist, Diesel Engine Co., OH
	writer - magazine articles;
	Men, Money and Magic: The Story of Dorothy Schiff, 1976;
	Robin Is a Bear, 1958 (children's book);
	Disaster By Oil, 1973;
	Elephant Bridge, 1960;
	To a Violent Grave: An Oral Biography of Jackson Pollock, 1985
	entertainers and associated professions -
	co-founder, with his wife Madeleine, Cape Playhouse, Dennis, MA
Civic Activism:	committee member, Opportunity Shop, Amagansett;
	director, Amagansett Village Improvement Society;
	governor, Amagansett Residents Society
Marriage(s):	M/1 – 1948-div. 1959 – Madeleine Penelope Sack (d. 1984)
	(aka Penelope Sack)
	- entertainers and associated professions -
	actress;
	co-founder, with her husband Jeffrey, Cape Playhouse, Dennis, MA
	Civic Activism: a founder and director, Hampton Animal Shelter, Inc., 1955;
	read books for Reading for the Blind, Inc.;
	advisory trustee, Guild Hall, East Hampton;
	member, art committee, Guild Hall, East Hampton;
	member, drama committee, Guild Hall, East Hampton;
	trustee, Association of American Indian Affairs, NY
	M/2 – 1963-div. – Diana Hitt (b. 1933)
	M/3 – 1981-2012 – Priscilla Bowden
	- artist
Address:	341 Town Lane, Amagansett
Name of estate:	*Stony Hill Farm*
Year of construction:	1914
Style of architecture:	Colonial Revival
Architect(s):	Edward M. Gay, 1914
	alterations (for Hamlin)
Landscape architect(s):	
Builder:	Edward M. Gay (for Hamlin)
	Jeffrey Colle (for Baldwin)

House extant: no*
Historical notes:

Nathaniel Baker's 1680s house was purchased by Samuel Schellinger who enlarged it in 1797. The house was purchased in 1913 by Harry Leon Hamlin who moved it from Main Street to what was to become his 325-acre Town Lane dairy farm *Stony Hill Farm*. [*The East Hampton Star* October 3, 1913, p. 3, and Carleton Kelsey and Lucinda Mayo, *Images of America: Amagansett* (Dover, NH: Arcadia Publishing, 1997), p. 12.] In 1949 it was purchased from Mrs. Hamlin by Potter who continued to call it *Stony Hill Farm*. [*The East Hampton Star* November 17, 1949, p. 4.]

He was the son of Joseph Wiltsie Fuller and Mary Barton Atterbury Potter.

Madeleine Penelope Sack Potter was the daughter of George D. Sack of Manhattan. She subsequently married ____ Bradford.

Jeffrey Brackett and Madeleine Penelope Sack Potter's daughter Gayle married the noted cultural and linguistic anthropologist Keith Hamilton Basso. Their son Job married artist Janet Jenning and resided in Amagansett. Their daughter Manon also resides in Amagansett.

Potter, Jeffrey Bracket (cont'd)

Diana Hitt Potter is the daughter of Robert Reynolds Hitt of Manhattan. She had previously been married to Henry Simmons Romaine, the son of Theodore Cole Romaine of Bridgehampton, NY.

Jeffrey Brackett and Diana Hitt Potter's son Robert (aka Horatio) married Elizabeth Gunn O'Connell.

Priscilla Bowden Potter is the daughter of Clifford Bowden of Glen Head, NY.

The main residence was purchased by Michael Minkoff who flipped it to Alexander Rae Baldwin III (aka Alec Baldwin) in 1996. In 2015 Baldwin substantially enlarged and remodeled the house into a contemporary style.

*Some portions of the original interior remain.

Preusse, Charles Francis (1902-1977)

Occupation(s):	attorney - partner, Whitman and Ransom; counsel, 1964 World's Fair, NY; member, Baldwin, Hutchins, and Todd; member, Chadbourne, Wallace, Park, and Whiteside; Acting Corporate Counsel, NYC, 1946-1950
	politician - New York City Administrator, 1956-1959 (Wagner administration)
Civic Activism:	trustee, Hall of Science, Flushing Meadow Park, NYC
Marriage(s):	1933-1977 – Josephine Florence (1899-1985) - interior decorator real estate agent - Previews Inc.; Douglas Gibbons; Holiday and Ives
Address:	34 Hither Lane, East Hampton
Name of estate:	
Year of construction:	
Style of architecture:	Colonial Revival
Architect(s):	
Landscape architect(s):	
House extant: yes	
Historical notes:	

In 1925 Mary Lang DeVries (aka Mary MacKinnon) purchased the house and ten acres from Thomas Robinson. [*The East Hampton Star* December 11, 1925, p. 7.] In 1930 the house was purchased from Mrs. DeVries by Chester Marts Cloud. [*The East Hampton Star* March 7, 1930, p. 5.] In 1946 Irwin Hewlett Cornell purchased it from Cloud. [*The East Hampton Star* October 3, 1946, p. 5.] In 1963 the house was purchased by Preusse. [*The East Hampton Star* May 16, 1963, p. 4.]

The Blue Book of The Hamptons, 1973 lists Charles F. and Josephine Florence Preusse as residing on Hither Lane in East Hampton. *The Blue Book of The Hamptons, 1979* lists Mrs. Preusse's address as 34 Hither Lane in East Hampton.

He was the son of William and Bridget Sheridan Preusse of NYC.

Josephine Florence Preusse was the daughter of John and Martha Courter Florence of East Orange, NJ.

Charles Francis and Josephine Florence Preusse's daughter Sandra, who resided in Boulder, CO, married George Balmforth Johnston, Jr. of Louisville, KY. Their son Charles Sheridan Preusse married Susan Kroner and resided in East Hampton.

Procter, William Cooper (1862-1934)

Occupation(s):	industrialist - president and chairman of board, Procter & Gamble Co., Cincinnati, OH; (consumer products conglomerate)
	capitalist - director, New York Central Railroad Co.; a founder, Gardiner Bay Co. (real estate holding company)
	financier - director, National City Bank of New York
Civic Activism:	president, Cincinnati Red Cross Chapter, 1914-1934;
	trustee and benefactor, Princeton University, Princeton, NJ;
	trustee, Charles P. Taft Foundation;
	member, Council of National Defense during World War I;
	chairman, Cincinnati War Chest campaign, 1918;
	chairman, Cincinnati Red Cross drives, 1917 and 1918;
	chairman, Cincinnati Community Chest drive, 1927;
	chairman, national committee, organized by Herbert Hoover, to bring about greater efficiency and economy in Community Chest and social service work, 1928;
	president, Cincinnati Institute of Fine Arts;
	a founder, Devon Yacht Club, Amagansett;
	trustee, Children's Hospital, Cincinnati, OH (now, Cincinnati Children's Hospital Medical Center)
Marriage(s):	1889-1934 – Jane Eliza Johnston (1864-1953)
Address:	Oceanview Lane, Amagansett
Name of estate:	
Year of construction:	1909
Style of architecture:	Mediterranean Villa
Architect(s):	Tietig and Lee designed the house (for W. C. Procter)
Landscape architect(s):	
House extant: yes	
Historical notes:	

The seven-bedroom, five-bath house was built by William Cooper Procter.
He was the son of William Alexander and Charlotte Elizabeth Jackson Procter of Glendale, OH.
Jane Eliza Johnston Procter was the daughter of Thomas and Mary Elizabeth Mallory Johnston of Glendale, OH.
The Procters did not have children.
The house was later owned by Procter's niece Mary Elizabeth Johnston, who called it *Devon House*. In 1967 she bequeathed *Devon House* and its furnishings to her niece Anne Johnston Sawyer Greene, who resided at *Devon House* with her husband John Bradley Greene II.
In 1987 Jack Dobbs McSpadden, Jr. purchased the house from Mrs. Greene and continued to call it *Devon House*. By 2008 the McSpaddens had relocated to *Swansong* at 332 Bluff Road, Amagansett.

Pruyn, Miss Mary Lansing (1855-1943)

Occupation(s): artist
Civic Activism: president, New York Diet Kitchen

Marriage(s): unmarried

Pruyn, Miss Neltje Knickerbocker (1858-1949)

Occupation(s): artist

Marriage(s): unmarried

Address: Jones Road, East Hampton
Name of estate:
Year of construction:
Style of architecture: Modified Long Island Farmhouse
Architect(s): Charles A. Platt designed
    the house (for Pruyns)
Landscape architect(s): Ellen Biddle Shipman, 1919
    (for Pruyns)
House extant: yes
Nassau County Museum Collection has photographs of the estate.
Historical notes:

    The house was built by the Pruyns.
    Mary Lansing and Neltje Knickerbocker Pruyn were the daughters of John Knickerbocker and Mary Catherine Lansing Pruyn.

Pulleyn, John William, Sr. (1891-1958)

Occupation(s): financier - partner, Gibbons and Co. (bond brokerage firm);
    director, M. Berardini State Bank
Civic Activism: president of board, St. Joseph's Day Nursery, NY

Marriage(s): 1920-1958 – Alice Moffitt (b. 1893)

Address: Lily Pond Lane, East Hampton
Name of estate:
Year of construction:
Style of architecture:
Architect(s):
Landscape architect(s):
House extant: unconfirmed
Historical notes:

    The *Social Directory of Southampton, Long Island, 1931* lists John W. and Alice Moffitt Pulleyn [Sr.] as residing on Lily Pond Lane, East Hampton.
    He was the son of John Joseph Pulleyn. His sister Claire married Thomas Lincoln Manson III, the son of Thomas Lincoln and Mary Groot Manson, Jr. of *Millfield* in East Hampton. His sister Virginia married Walton Pearl Kingsley and resided in East Hampton.
    Alice Moffitt Pulleyn was the daughter of Samuel Moffitt of New York.
    John William and Alice Moffitt Pulleyn, Sr.'s son John William Pulleyn, Jr., who resided in Charleston, SC, married Mary Margaret Buck, the daughter of Solon Justius Buck of Washington, DC, and, later, Laura Thompson. Their son S. Robert Pulleyn married Jeanne Phillips, the daughter of Robert C. Phillips of Milford, PA, and resided in North Haven, CT.
    In 1935 Pulleyn sold the house to Ernest H. Rice, Sr. [*The East Hampton Star* July 11, 1935, p. 1.]

Putnam, Harrington, Jr. (1906-1978)

Occupation(s):	financier - manager, American Foreign Insurance Association, Rio de Janeiro, Brazil
Civic Activism:	trustee, Bridgehampton Historical Society
Marriage(s):	M/1 – 1930-div. 1945 – Barbara Jacquelin Stout (1909-2012)
	M/2 – 1946-div. 1955 – Michelle Caroline Bouvier (1905-1987)
	- Civic Activism: president, Ladies Village Improvement Society, East Hampton; vice-president, Daughters of the Cincinnati
	M/3 – Violeta Maldonado (1921-2018)
Address:	Apaquogue Road, East Hampton
Name of estate:	*Little House**
Year of construction:	
Style of architecture:	Modified Colonial Revival
Architect(s):	
Landscape architect(s):	Victoria Fensterer designed the pergola plantings

House extant: yes
Historical notes:

Harrington Putnam, Jr. was the son of Judge Harrington and Mrs. Mildred Smythe Putnam, Sr. of Brooklyn, NY.

Barbara Jacquelin Stout Putnam was the daughter of Joseph Suydam and Ethel G. Jacquelin Stout. She subsequently married Arthur Masten Crocker, the son of George A. and Elizabeth Masten Crocker of Oyster Bay, and resided in Glen Cove.

Harrington and Barbara Jacquelin Stout Putnam, Jr.'s son Harrington Putnam III married Chauncie McKeever, the daughter of Chauncey McKeever of San Francisco, CA, and, later, Gail Wilkins with whom he resided in Charlotte, NC.

Michelle Caroline Bouvier Putnam was the daughter of John Vernou and Maude Sergeant Bouvier, Jr. of *Little House* and *Lasata* in East Hampton. Michelle had previously been married to Henry Clarkson Scott, Sr. with whom she resided in Woodmere. [*See* Spinzia, *Long Island's Prominent Families in the Town of Hempstead* – Scott entry.] Michelle's brother William married Emma Stone, who resided in Southampton. [*See* Spinzia, *Long Island's Prominent Families in the Town of Southampton* – Bouvier entry.] Her sister Edith married Phelan Beale, Sr. and resided at *Grey Gardens* in East Hampton. Her sister Maude married John Ethelbert Davis and resided in Ridgefield, CT. Her brother John Vernou Bouvier III, who resided at *Rowdy Hall* and, later, at *Little House* in East Hampton, married Janet Norton Lee.

Violeta Maldonado Putnam was the daughter of Gualbeto and Blanca Ipince Maldonado of Lima, Peru.

*Little House was also known as *Wildmoor* when it was owned by John Vernou Bouvier III.

In 1960 the house was purchased by Adolph Gottlieb who converted the garage into his art studio.

Quackenbush, Schuyler (1847-1917)

Occupation (s):	financier - partner, Edward Sweet and Co., NYC (later, Chandler Brothers and Co.) (investment banking firm)
	capitalist - treasurer, Maidstone Improvement Co., 1899; a founder and director, East Hampton Electric Light Co., 1902
Marriage(s):	1874-1917 – Harriet Frances Eidlitz (1851-1940)
Address:	10 Lee Avenue, East Hampton
Name of estate:	
Year of construction:	1898-1899
Style of architecture:	Shingle
Architect(s):	Cyrus Lazelle Warner Eidlitz designed the house (for Quackenbush)
Landscape architect(s):	
Builder:	George A. Eldredge
House extant: yes	
Historical notes:	

The house was built by Schuyler Quackenbush.

He was the son of Adonijah Schuyler and Sophia Earle Quackenbush.

Harriet Frances Eidlitz Quackenbush was the daughter of Leopold and Harriet Armanda Lazelle Warner Eidlitz. Harriet's brother Cyrus, who resided at *Overlea* in East Hampton, designed the Quackenbushs' house.

Schuyler and Harriet Frances Eidlitz Quackenbush's daughters Marguerite and Ethel both did not marry. Their daughter Grace married J. R. Charlton Armstrong. Their son Leopold resided in Oxbow, ME.

The house was later owned by Dr. Ogden Matthus Edwards, who called it *Dunehurst*, and, later, by Edwards' daughter Katherine who married Harold Willis Nichols, Jr.

In 2016, the approximately 10,000-square-foot house, with ten bedrooms and six and a half bathrooms, and 3.3 acres were for sale. The asking price was $18.95 million.

Quackenbush, Schuyler (1847-1917)

Occupation (s):	*[See previous entry.]*
Marriage(s):	1874-1917 – Harriet Frances Eidlitz (1851-1940)
Address:	Lee Avenue, East Hampton
Name of estate:	
Year of construction:	1915
Style of architecture:	Shingle
Architect(s):	John Custis Lawrence designed the house (for Quackenbush)
	John Custis Lawrence, 1929 alterations (for Barton)
Landscape architect(s):	
Builder:	Edward M. Gay
House extant: yes	
Historical notes:	

The house was built by Schuyler Quackenbush.
[See previous entry for family information.]

It was later owned by Flora Benjamin McAlpin Barton, the daughter of George Lodowich and Sallie Blanche Benjamin McAlpin, Sr. of *Dune Alpin*.

Rabbe, Richard Frederick (1912-2005)

Occupation(s):	industrialist - vice-president, Harrison Structural Steel Co., Inc.
Marriage(s):	1944-2005 – Marjorie R. Harris (1915-2005)
Address:	55 Davids Lane, East Hampton
Name of estate:	*Seafields*
Year of construction:	
Style of architecture:	Colonial Revival
Architect(s):	
Landscape architect(s):	
House extant: yes	
Historical notes:	

The Blue Book of The Hamptons, 1973 lists Richard F. and Marjorie R. Harris Rabbe as residing at *Seafields*, 55 Davids Lane, East Hampton.

He was the son of Frederick and Amelia Voege Rabbe.

Marjorie R. Harris Rabbe was the daughter of George William and Minnie Camman Harris of Manhattan.

Richard Frederick and Marjorie R. Harris Rabbe's son George married Theodora Aspegren, the daughter of John Bacon and Lois Frances Barstow Aspegren, Sr. of *Sunnymeade* in Southampton, and resided in East Hampton. [*See* Spinzia, *Long Island's Prominent Families in the Town of Southampton* – Aspegren entry.]

The 2,800-square-foot house has four bedrooms and three bathrooms.

Radziwill, Caroline Lee Bouvier (1933-2019)
aka Lee Radziwill

Occupation(s):	nobility - princess
	public relations executive - Giorgio Armani
	entertainers and associated professions - actress
	interior designer
	writer - *Happier Times*, 2003 (autobiography)
Marriage(s):	M/1 – 1953-div. 1959 – Michael Temple Canfield (1926-1969)
	- publisher - London editorial representative, Harper & Row
	M/2 – 1959-div. 1974 – Stanislaw Albrecht Radziwill (1914-1976)
	- nobility - prince
	Civic Activism: a founder, Sikorski Historical Institute, London, England;
	a founder, St. Anne's Church at Fawley Court, Henley-on-Thames, England (school)
	M/3 – 1988-div. 2001 – Herbert David Ross (1925-2001)*
	- entertainers and associated professions -
	actor;
	dance choreographer (Broadway and motion pictures);
	motion picture director**
Address:	43 East Dune Lane, East Hampton
Name of estate:	
Year of construction:	
Style of architecture:	
Architect(s):	
Landscape architect(s):	
House extant: no***	
Historical notes:	

   She was the daughter of John Vernou and Janet Norton Lee Bouvier III of *Rowdy Hall* and *Little House* in East Hampton. Janet later married Hugh Dudley Auchincloss and, subsequently, Bingham William Morris with whom she resided at *Pra-Qua-Les* in Southampton. Caroline's sister Jacqueline was married to President John Fitzgerald Kennedy and, subsequently, Aristotle Onassis. [*See* Spinzia, *Long Island's Prominent Families in the Town of Southampton* – Morris entry.]
   Michael Temple Canfield was allegedly the illegitimate son of Prince George, Duke of Kent. He was reputed to have been adopted by the American publisher Cass Canfield, Sr. [*See* Spinzia, *Long Island's Prominent North Shore Families, vol. I* – Canfield entry.] Michael subsequently married Laura Charteris, the former Countess of Dudley.
   Prince Stanislaw Albrecht Radziwill was the son of Prince Janusz Francisze and Princess Anna Lubomirska Radziwill of Szpanow, Poland. Stanislaw had previously been married to Rose de Monleon, the daughter of County Guy de Monleon, and, subsequently, to Grace Maria Kolin.
   Prince Albrecht and Princess Caroline Lee Bouvier Radziwill's son Anthony married Carole Ann DiFalco. Their daughter Anna married Ottavio Arancio.
   *Herbert David Ross is listed in *Who's Who in Entertainment, 1989-1990* as having been born in 1925, not 1927 as reported in most sources.
   **During his career as a director Ross directed twelve different actors in Oscar-nominated performances.
   After her divorce from Ross, Caroline Lee returned to the surname Radziwill.
   In 2001 Caroline Lee sold the house to Thomas Haskell Lee for $19 million.
   ***Caroline Lee demolished the house and built a new home observing the same exterior but with a new infrastructure.
   In 2013 the house sustained a fire in the basement pantry which caused extensive smoke damage in the remainder of the house.

Rahr, Stewart J. (b. 1944)

Occupation(s):	merchant - CEO and president, Kinray, Inc., Whitestone, NY (wholesale pharmaceutical distributor)
Civic Activism:	donated $10 million to the Make-A-Wish Foundation; donated fifty ambulances to United Hatzalah, Israel; donated $500,000 to North Shore Animal League America; donated $640,000 to Israel Cancer Research Fund; donated $100,000 to Salvation Army (for Hurricane Sandy relief); donated $50,000 to Russian American Jewish Experience; founder, Stewart J. Rahr Foundation; transferred ownership of *Burnt Point* to Stewart J. Rahr Foundation; donated $2 million to Muhammad Ali Parkinson Center, Phoenix, AZ
Marriage(s):	1969-div. 2013 – Carol K. Lang (b. 1947) - industrialist - co-owner, Beach to Ballroom (jewelry firm)
Address:	38 Mathew's Road, East Hampton
Name of estate:	*Burnt Point*
Year of construction:	1977
Style of architecture:	
Architect(s):	Francis Fleetwood designed the house (for Campbell)
Landscape architect(s)	
House extant:	yes

Historical notes:

The house, originally named *Burnt Point*, was built by David Campbell. In 2005 Rahr purchased the 18,000-square-foot house from Campbell for $45 million and continued to call it *Burnt Point*.

He is the son of Joseph Rahr of Far Rockaway, NY.

Stewart J. and Carol Lang Rahr's daughter Felicia married Jeffery A. Bersh.

In 2015 Rahr listed the house for sale. The asking price was $95 million.

Ramee, Joseph Russell (1882-1955)

Occupation(s):	capitalist - partner, Argulmbau & Ramee (importer of fruit and olive oil, and manufacturer of peanut butter)
Civic Activism:	vice-chairman, entertainment committee, Maidstone Club, East Hampton
Marriage(s):	1916 – Marie Virginia Hoguet (1888-1967) - Civic Activism: board chair, Cribside Social Service Committee, Babies Hospital, NYC; president, Garden Club of East Hampton
Address:	Middle Lane, East Hampton
Name of estate:	*Twinmill*
Year of construction:	1903
Style of architecture:	Eclectic
Architect(s):	George A. Eldredge and John Custis Lawrence designed the house (for Wessel, Sr.)
Landscape architect(s):	Mary Lois Deputy Lamson, c. 1941 (for Ramee)
House extant:	no; demolished except for windmill-style tower, 1980*

Historical notes:

The house, originally named *Mill Crest*, was built by Homer Augustus Wessel, Sr. It was later owned by Ramee who renamed it *Twinmill*.

The *Social Register Summer, 1932* lists Mrs. and Mrs. Joseph R. Ramee as residing at *Twinmill* on Middle Lane, East Hampton.

He was the son of Louis Charles and Rosalie Beauregard Page Ramee.

Marie Virginia Hoguet Ramee was the daughter of Robert Joseph and Marie Noel Hoguet of Long Branch, NJ.

*The plans for the original house are in the East Hampton Library.

Ramsay, Herbert Hartley (1887-1939)

Occupation(s):	attorney - partner, Rogers, Ramsay, and Hoge
Civic Activism:	president, United States Golf Association, 1931
Marriage(s):	1925-1939 – Constance McCall (1899-1975)
Address:	Apaquogue Road, East Hampton

Name of estate:
Year of construction:
Style of architecture:
Architect(s):
Landscape architect(s):
House extant: unconfirmed
Historical notes:

The *Long Island Society Register, 1929* lists N. [sic] Hartley and (McCall) Ramsay as residing on Apaquogue Road, East Hampton.

He was the son of William E. and Katherine Pennoyer Ramsay.

Constance McCall Ramsay was the daughter of Edward Everett and Ella Frances Gaynor McCall of *Evsdune* in East Hampton.

Herbert Harley and Constance McCall Ramsay's sons Hartley and Allan were bachelors.

Randell, Caroline Amelia Boardman (1856-1934)

Marriage(s):	Rufus Randell (1845-1925)
	(aka Roof the Roofer)
	- writer - *The Earth for a Dollar: or a Romance of the King of Wall Street*;
	Prettybad Rogers, 1896;
	thirty-nine articles
Address:	70 Dunemere Lane, East Hampton
Name of estate:	
Year of construction:	1905
Style of architecture:	Shingle
Architect(s):	Joseph Greenleaf Thorp designed the house (for Mrs. Randell)
Landscape architect(s):	
Builder:	Thomas E. Babcock

House extant: yes
Historical notes:

The house was built by Caroline Amelia Boardman Randell.

She was the daughter of Norman and Annie T. Williams Boardman of New York. Caroline's brother Albert, who married Georgiana Gertrude Bonner and, later, Louise Suydam Oakley, resided at *Villa Mille Fiori* and *Windswept* in Southampton. [*See* Spinzia, *Long Island's Prominent Families in the Town of Southampton* – Boardman entries.]

Rufus Randell was the son of John M. and A. D. Waller Randell of St. Louis, MO.

Rufus and Caroline Amelia Boardman Randell's son George married Gladys Newell, the daughter of William H. Newell of Lewiston, ME, and resided in Manhattan.

In 1919 the house was purchased by John Bradley Carse, Sr. who called it *End Cottage*. [*The East Hampton Star* May 20, 1971, p. 2.]

It was later owned by Norman Smith Cleaves. [*The East Hampton Star* January 5, 1934, p. 5.]

Ranieri, Salvatore Anthony

Occupation(s):	attorney - member, Hardy and Bardovich, NYC
Civic Activism:	member, East Hampton Design Review Board; trustee, Council of Peconic Land Trust
Marriage(s):	M/1 – 1977-div. – Francine Gualtier
	M/2 – 2005 – Mary Louise Gioiella
	- financier - stockbroker
	Civic Activism: trustee, Council of Peconic Land Trust
Address:	54 and 58 Highway Behind the Pond, East Hampton
Name of estate:	
Year of construction:	1972
Style of architecture:	Eclectic
Architect(s):	Hugh Hardy designed the house (for E. Spaeth)
	Hugh Hardy designed 1999 alterations to house (for Ranieri)
Landscape architect(s)	Tiziana Hardy designed house gardens (for E. Spaeth)
House extant: unconfirmed	

Historical notes:

   The 2,000-square-foot, three-bedroom, two-bath guest house was built by Eloise O'Mara Spaeth after the death of her husband Otto Lucien Spaeth, Sr. In 1999 Ranieri purchased the house and used it as a guest house for his main residence at 54 Highway Behind the Pond.

   He is the son of Nina Ranieri of Brooklyn.

   Francine Gualtier Ranieri is the daughter of Angelo and Margaret Lindini Gualtier of Pottsville, PA.

   In 2012 Ranieri sold the guest house for $25 million and his main residence for $20 million.

Rattray, Arnold Elsmere (1898-1954)

Occupation(s):	capitalist - owned travel agency, East Hampton
	journalist - East End correspondent, Manhattan and Brooklyn newspapers;
	editor, *The East Hampton Star*
	publisher - owner, *The East Hampton Star*
Civic Activism:	worked for Hoover relief in Ukraine and Germany;
	worked for Red Cross in France
Marriage(s):	1925-1954 – Jeannette Frances Edwards (1893-1974)
	- capitalist - a founder of a private kindergarten
	educator - teacher, kindergarten
	journalist - editor, *The East Hampton Star*;
	stringer and East End social correspondent for six Manhattan and three Brooklyn newspapers;
	wrote "One of Ours" column, *The East Hampton Star*;
	wrote "Looking Them Over" a weekly column, *The East Hampton Star*;
	correspondent, *Daily Bulletin*, Manila, The Philippines;
	correspondent, *China Press*
	publisher - *The East Hampton Star*
	writer - numerous books and monographs
	Civic Activism: member, board of managers, East Hampton Free Library
Address:	Edwards Lane, East Hampton
Name of estate:	
Year of construction:	
Style of architecture:	
Architect(s):	
Landscape architect(s):	
House extant:	yes
Historical notes:	

  Arnold Elsmere Rattray was the son of James Thompson and Ellen Greig Rattray of San Francisco, CA.
  Jeannette Frances Edwards Rattray was the daughter of Everett Joshua and Florence Huntting Edwards of East Hampton.
  Arnold Elsmere and Jeannette Frances Edwards Rattray's son Everett, who later owned the house, married Helen Hinda Seldon and resided in Amagansett and East Hampton. Their daughter Mary married Howard E. Kanovitz, the son of Meyer J. Kanovitz of Fall River, MA, and resides in Amagansett. Their son David married Carolyn Fisher and resided in Amagansett.
  [See following Rattray entries for additional family information.]

Rattray, David Greig (1935-1993)

Occupation(s): journalist*- editor, *Reader's Digest*
writer - *A Visit to St. Elizabeth's*, 1957;
Semiotexte;
Opening the Eyelid, 1990;
How I Became One of the Invisible, 1992

Marriage(s): 1964-1993 – Carolyn Fisher

Address: *[unable to determine street address]*, Amagansett
Name of estate:
Year of construction:
Style of architecture:
Architect(s):
Landscape architect(s):
House extant: unconfirmed
Historical notes:

David Greig Rattray was the son of Arnold Elsmere and Jeannette Frances Edwards Rattray of East Hampton.
Carolyn Fisher Rattray is the daughter of George Fisher of Staten Island, NY.
David Greig and Carolyn Fisher Rattray's daughter Mary married ____ Geis and resides in Highland Falls, NY.
*Fluent in Greek, Latin, French, German, Spanish, Italian, and Sanskript, David was a noted translator of the works of the French authors Antonin Artaud, René Crevei, and Roger Gilbert Lecomie.
[See other Rattray entries for additional family information.]

Rattray, Everett Tennant (1932-1980)

Occupation(s): journalist- editor, *The East Hampton Star*
writer - *The South Fork: Land and People of Long Island*, 1979;
The Adventure of Jeremiah Dimon, 1985 (novel)

Civic Activism: member, advisory commission, Fire Island National Seashore;
director, East Hampton Historical Society;
a founder, East Hampton Town Marine Museum, Amagansett

Marriage(s): 1960-1980 – Helen Hinda Seldon (b. 1934)
- journalist - weekly columnist, *The East Hampton Star*
publisher - president, *The East Hampton Star*;
founder and president, *Sag Harbor Herald*

Address: Cranberry Hole Road, Amagansett
Name of estate:
Year of construction: c. 1963
Style of architecture:
Architect(s):
Landscape architect(s):
House extant: unconfirmed
Historical notes:

The house was built by Everett Tennant Rattray.
He was the son of Arnold Elsmere and Jeannette Frances Edwards Rattray of East Hampton.
Helen Hinda Seldon Rattray is the daughter of Abraham H. and Yetta Seldon of Bayonne, NY. Helen subsequently married Christopher Thayer Cory, the son of David Cleveland and Constance Thayer Cory of Amagansett, with whom she resides in East Hampton.
Everett Tennant and Helen Hinda Seldon Rattray's daughter Bess married Paul Gartside, the son of Robert and Norma Gartside of Canada. Their son David married Lisa Ann Heilbrunn, the daughter of Dr. Karl and Mrs. Elaine Heilbrunn of NYC.
The Rattrays later relocated to his parents' former house at 17 Edwards Lane, East Hampton.
[See other Rattray entries for additional family information.

Rawson, Joseph, Jr. (1850-1927)

Occupation(s):	financier - vice-president and director, First National Bank of Cincinnati
	industrialist - partner, Rawson & Sons, Cincinnati, OH (pork-packing firm)
	capitalist - director, C, H, & D Railroad Co.;
	a founder, Gardiner Bay Co. (real estate holding company)
Civic Activism:	donated land for Rawson Woods Bird Preserve, Cincinnati, OH, 1923
	a founder, Devon Yacht Club, Amagansett
Marriage(s):	1876-1927 – Lucie Russell (1850-1938)
Address:	10 Cross Highway, Amagansett
Name of estate:	*Red Roof** / *Windy Dune*
Year of construction:	c. 1910
Style of architecture:	Mediterranean Villa
Architect(s):	Tietig and Lee designed the house (for J. Rawson, Jr.)
	Christopher Bickford, 1992-1994 alterations (for Cookson)
	Rick Hirt, 2003 and 2006 alterations (for Cookson)**
Landscape architect(s):	
House extant: yes	
Historical notes:	

The 7,000-square-foot house, originally named *Red Roof*, was built by Joseph Rawson, Jr.
He was the son of Joseph and Mary Whiting Richards Rawson, Sr. of Cincinnati, OH.
Lucie Russell Rawson was the daughter of John Henry Ware and Mary Smith Ryland Russell of Cincinnati, OH.
Joseph and Lucie Russell Rawson, Jr.'s daughters Bessie, Martha, and Gwendolyn did not marry. Their daughter Lucy married William R. Collins of Cincinnati, OH.
*The terra cotta roof was lost in the 1938 hurricane; the house was renamed *Windy Dune*.
**Hirt designed extensive alterations. The service wing off the dining room was replaced with a new wing; the kitchen was enlarged; and the family living space was extended into the former staff rooms.
The house was later owned by Allison Bishopric, Jr. and, then, by Allison's daughter Lucy Bishopric Cookson, both of whom continued to call it *Windy Dune*.

Raymond, Dana Merriam (1914-2003)

Occupation(s):	attorney - member, Cravath, Swaine, and Moore; partner, Brumbaugh, Graves, Donahue, and Raymond
Civic Activism:	secretary, Armstrong Memorial Research Foundation
Marriage(s):	M/1 – 1935 – Frances L. Forrester
	M/2 – 1949-2000 – Josephine Sheehan (d. 2000)
	- journalist - assistant chief of research, *Life Magazine*
	Civic Activism: trustee and secretary, Guild Hall, East Hampton; chairman, Drew Drama Committee of Guild Hall; trustee and secretary, Archive of American Art at the Smithsonian Society's Civil Support Division; trustee, Legal Aid Society Civil Support Division; trustee, Children of Bellevue Hospital, NYC; trustee, James Weldon Johnson Community Center, NYC
Address:	21 Jefferys Lane, East Hampton
Name of estate:	
Year of construction:	
Style of architecture:	
Architect(s):	
Landscape architect(s):	
House extant:	yes

Historical notes:

Raymond purchased the house in 1964 from Mrs. Chase Henchman Davis. [*The East Hampton Star* May 28, 1964, p. 4, and August 21, 2003, p. 2.]

The Blue Book of The Hamptons, 1965 and *1973* list Mr. and Mrs. Dana Raymond as residing at 21 Jefferys Lane, East Hampton.

He was the son of Charles Merriam and June Leonard Raymond.

Josephine Sheehan Raymond was the daughter of John Sheehan.

Dana Merriam and Josephine Sheehan Raymond's son Peter married Anne Keating Willcox, the daughter of John K. Willcox, and, later, Christina Morris, the daughter of Dr. John McLean Morris of Woodbridge, CT. Their daughter Catherine married Burt Prentice Flickinger III and resides in NYC.

Regan, John Nicholas, Sr. (1899-1992)

Occupation(s):	attorney - member, Sherman and Sterling; partner, Regan and Barrett, NYC; partner, Walsh and Young, NYC
	publisher - president, *Martindale–Hubbell Law Dictionary*
Marriage(s):	Kathleen Maguire (d. 1994)
Address:	Old Beach Road, East Hampton
Name of estate:	
Year of construction:	
Style of architecture:	
Architect(s):	
Landscape architect(s):	
House extant:	unconfirmed

Historical notes:

The Blue Book of The Hamptons, 1958 lists Mr. and Mrs. John N. Regan as residing in East Hampton.

He was the son of Patrick Regan of Essex Falls, NJ.

Kathleen Maguire Regan was the daughter of Hugh O'Donnell Maguire of County Fermanagh, Ireland.

John Nicholas and Kathleen Maguire Regan, Sr.'s daughter Ellen married Orin McCluskey, the son of Richard and Ellen Lehman McCluskey of Mill Neck. [*See* Spinzia, *Long Island's Prominent North Shore Families, vol. 1* – Lehman entry.] Their daughter Virginia married Luis Charles Dominguez, the son of Vincent L. Dominguez of London, England, and, later, John Bennett Coleman. Their daughter Robin did not marry. Their son Thomas married Courtney Koudacheff Armour, the daughter of Norman Armour, Jr. of New York. Their son Andrew married Mary Seton Ferer, the daughter of Dr. José Ferer of Southampton, and, later, Elizabeth Harper Detwiler, the daughter of Peter M. and Helen P. Detwiler of New York. Their son John Nicholas Regan, Jr. married Katherine Theresa Carter, the daughter of William and Nancy Deere Wiman Carter, Jr. Their daughter Joan married Owen McGivern.

Reid, Archibald Mudge (1884-1967)

Occupation(s):	financier - partner, Carlisle and Jacquelin (stock brokerage firm)
Civic Activism:	president, United States Golf Association;
	president, Professional Golfers' Association;
	director, Maidstone Club, East Hampton
Marriage(s):	1918-1967 – Margaret Howell Behr (1887-1977)
	- Civic Activism: trustee, Home for Old Men and Aged Couples, NYC;
	member, museum committee, United States Golf Association
Address:	84 Egypt Lane, East Hampton
Name of estate:	
Year of construction:	18th century
Style of architecture:	Long Island Farmhouse
Architect(s):	
Landscape architect(s):	
Builder:	George Eldredge, alterations*
House extant: yes	
Historical notes:	

    In the 1860s George Eldredge moved the house to Egypt Lane and modified it for his own residence. It was later owned by William Sumner Williams and his wife Charlotte Maria Eldredge Williams.

    In 1939 Reid purchased the house from D. W. McCord, who called it *White Cottage*. [*The East Hampton Star* August 31, 1939, p. 8.]

    The Blue Book of The Hamptons, 1958 lists Mr. and Mrs. Archibald M. Reid as residing at 84 Egypt Lane, East Hampton.

    He was the son of John Reid, Sr. of Yonkers, NY, who was known as the father of American golf.

    Margaret Howell Behr Reid was the daughter of Herman and Grace Howell Behr, Sr. of NYC and Brooklyn, NY. Margaret's sister Gertrude married John Cruickshank Milne II and resided in East Hampton.

    Archibald Mudge and Margaret Howell Behr Reid's daughter Jean married Daniel Carrington Cook, the son of Clarence P. Cook of Waterbury, CT. Their son John Reid III married Denyse Eugenie Ann Marie Van Hove, the daughter of Jacques Van Hove of Brussels, Belgium, and resided in New York.

    *Alterations were made to the house in 1876 and during the 20th century.

Reid, Wallace (1869-1957)

Occupation(s):	financier - partner, Wallace Reid and Co., NYC (insurance); director, American Insurance Co., Camden, NJ; director, Westchester Fire Insurance Co.; director, Manhattan Fire and Marine Insurance Company of New York; trustee, Franklin Savings Bank, Franklin Square, NY
Civic Activism:	chairman, Fire Patrol, New York Board of Fire Underwriters; director, Fire Insurance Association; a founder, Devon Yacht Club, Amagansett
Marriage(s):	Emma Read (d. 1941)
Address:	Further Lane, East Hampton
Name of estate:	
Year of construction:	1917
Style of architecture:	Modified Georgian Revival
Architect(s):	Arthur Truscott and John Custis Lawrence designed the house (for W. Reid)
Landscape architect(s):	
Builder:	Edward M. Gay
House extant: yes	
Historical notes:	

The house was built by Wallace Reid.

The *Social Register, 1920* lists Wallace and Emma Read Reid as residing in East Hampton.

Wallace and Emma Read Reid's daughter Margaret did not marry. Their son Hugh married Agnes McGuire and resided in Stamford, CT.

In 1945 the house was purchased by Oliver Sterling James, Sr.

Reiswig, Gary D.

Occupation(s):	city planner capitalist - proprietor, Maidstone Inn, East Hampton; proprietor, The Baker House 1650, East Hampton writer - *Living it Up in the Poor House*; several screen plays real estate agent
Civic Activism:	member, East Hampton Village Design Review Board; member, East Hampton Village Planning and Zoning Committee
Marriage(s):	Rita *[unable to determine maiden name]* - psychoanalyst
Address:	181 Main Street, East Hampton
Name of estate:	
Year of construction:	
Style of architecture:	Elizabethan
Architect(s):	Joseph Greenleaf Thorp, 1910 alternations (for Poor) Eric Woodward, 1996 alterations (for Reiswig)
Landscape architect(s):	
House extant: yes	
Historical notes:	

In 1899 James Harper Poor purchased the former Daniel Howe/Thomas Baker residence. [*The East Hampton Star* June 2, 2005, p. 44.] In 1943 the house was purchased by Robert Graham Dunn Douglas. In 1959 it was purchased by Harry Wilfred Watts from Douglas. [*The East Hampton Star* April 16, 1959, p. 1.] In 1973 Mrs. Watts donated the house to the Southampton Hospital. [*The East Hampton Star* May 25 1973, p. 20.] It 1996 it was purchased by the Reiswigs who remodeled it into The Baker House 1650, a bed and breakfast inn.

In 2000 the Reiswigs listed the house for sale. The asking price was $3.95 million.

It was purchased by Robert and Antonella Rosen.

Rentschler, George Adam, Jr. (1892-1972)

Occupation(s):	industrialist -	president, Hooven, Owens, Rentschler Co.;
		president, General Machinery Corp.;
		chairman of board, Lima–Hamilton Corp.;
		chairman of board, Baldwin–Lima Hamilton Corp.;
		director, Armour & Co;
		a founder, Southeastern Shipbuilding Corp. (constructed 83 Liberty ships during World War II);
		a founder, General Machinery Corp.;
		a founder, General Machinery Ordinance Corp.;
		a founder, American Oerlikon Co.;
		director, Barber Oil Corp.;
		director, Bendix Aviation Corp.;
		director, Hamilton Foundry & Machine Co.;
		director, Motor Wheel Corp.;
		director, Philip Carey Manufacturing Corp.;
		director, William Powell Manufacturing Co.;
		director, West Virginia Coal & Coke Co.
	capitalist -	president, Charleston Ship Repair and Dry Dock Co.;
		director, Cincinnati Suburban & Bell Telephone Co.;
		director, Cincinnati Gas & Electric Co.
	financier -	director, Fifty-Third Union Trust Co.
	shipping -	director, United States Lines

Marriage(s):   1936-1972 – Rita Rend Mitchell (1914-1994)
  - Civic Activism: trustee, Animal Medical Center;
                              trustee, Musicians Emergency Fund

Address: West End Road, East Hampton
Name of estate: *Summertime*
Year of construction: 1927
Style of architecture: Shingle
Architect(s):
Landscape architect(s):
House extant: unconfirmed
Nassau County Museum Collection has photographs of the house.
Historical notes:

The house, originally named *Bayberry,* was built by John Nelson Cole, Jr. In c. 1952 it was purchased by Rentschler. [*The East Hampton Star* January 3, 1952, p. 1.]

The Blue Book of The Hamptons, 1965 lists George A. and Rita R. Mitchell Rentschler [Jr.] as residing at *Summertime*, West End Road, East Hampton.

His brother Gordon, who married Mary S. Coolidge, resided in Old Brookville and Matinecock. [*See* Spinzia, *Long Island's Prominent North Shore Families, vol. II* – Rentschler entry.] They were the sons of George Adam and Phoebe Schwab Rentschler, Sr. of Fairfield, OH.

Rita Rend Mitchell Rentschler was the daughter of Charles Edwin Mitchell. She subsequently married Allerton Cushman, Sr.

George Adam and Rita Rend Mitchell Rentschler, Jr.'s son Charles married Suzanne Steward Snowden, the daughter of James M. Snowden of New York and Watch Hill, RI. Their son George Adam Rentschler III married Frederica Price Schlaff, the daughter of Nelson W. Schlaff of Grosse Point, MI. Their son Frederick married Pamela Abney.

The house was later owned by Charles Schuveldt Dewey, Jr. [*The East Hampton Star* April 28, 1960, p. 11.]

Reutershan, Paul V. (1892-1941)

Occupation(s): politician - Suffolk County Deputy Treasurer
Civic Activism: treasurer and director, Neighborhood Association; board member, East Hampton School District; secretary, East Hampton Fire Department

Marriage(s): 1915-1941 – Helen Boughton (1890-1951)

Address: Pantigo Road, East Hampton
Name of estate:
Year of construction: 1922
Style of architecture:
Architect(s): Joseph Greenleaf Thorp designed the house (for Reutershan)
Landscape architect(s):
Builder: Frank B. Smith
House extant: unconfirmed
Historical notes:

The house was built by Paul V. Reutershan. [*The East Hampton Star* May 5, 1922, p. 5.]
He was the son of Max William and Henrietta Hall Reutershan of East Hampton.
Helen Boughton Reutershan was the daughter of Edward Smith and Bertha Emeline Welby Boughton of East Hampton.
Paul V. and Helen Boughton Reutershan's daughter Mildred married Donald Kerr, the son of Aaron Kerr and resided in Hingham, MA.

Rheinstein, Sidney (1887-1968)

Occupation(s): financier - stockbroker; governor, New York Stock Exchange, NYC; member, nominating committee, New York Stock Exchange, NYC
writer - *Trade Whims: My Fifty Years on the New York Stock Exchange*, 1960
Civic Activism: established scholarship at Princeton University, Princeton, NJ, with a grant of $2.5 million

Marriage(s): Florence Nanry (1892-1969)

Address: Old Montauk Highway, Montauk
Name of estate:
Year of construction: 1928
Style of architecture: Eclectic Shingle
Architect(s): Richard Webb designed the house (for McCaffray)
Landscape architect(s):
House extant: no; demolished in 1973*
Historical notes:

The house, originally named *Sandpiper Hill*, was built by Walter Peck McCaffray. Mrs. McCaffray bequeathed the estate to the Order of the Society of Jesus to provide a home or retreat for ailing or retired Jesuits. [*The New York Times* August 1, 1940, p. 23.] The Jesuits sold the estate to Rheinstein.
He was the son of Ferdinand Frederick and Adele Dannenbaum Rheinstein.
Florence Nanry Rheinstein had previously been married to John Leslie Hubbard.
*The windmill section of the house was sold to Peter Beard who moved it to another bluff in the Montauk Moorlands. It was later destroyed by fire. Other sections of the house were relocated to Old Montauk Highway in Montauk.

Rice, Dr. Clarence Charles (1853-1935)

Occupation(s):	physician - nose and throat specialist*
	educator - professor diseases, New York Post Graduate Medical School and Hospital, NYC, 1916-1935
	writer - numerous articles in medical journals
Civic Activism:	director, New York Post Graduate Medical School and Hospital, NYC, 1887-1897
Marriage(s):	M/1 – div. 1915 – Jeannie Terry Durant (1863-1919)
	- artist - potter
	M/2 – 1915 – Mary Heard Masterson (b.1878)
Address:	Hither Lane, East Hampton
Name of estate:	
Year of construction:	1899
Style of architecture:	Modified Cotswold
Architect(s):	Grosvenor Atterbury designed the house (for C. C. Rice)
Landscape architect(s):	
Builder:	Jabez E. Van Orden

House extant: no; destroyed by fire**
The Nassau County Museum Collection has photographs of the estate.
Historical notes:

The house was built by Dr. Clarence Charles Rice.
He was the son of Abner and Nancy Reeves Rice of Natick, MA.
Jeannie Terry Durant Rice was the daughter of Edward Payson and Jeannie Terry Durant.
Dr. Clarence Charles and Mrs. Jeannie Terry Durant Rice's daughter Gladys married John L. Saltonstall of Boston, MA; J. Henry Billings with whom she resided in Rhinebeck, NY; and, subsequently Van Wyck Brooks. Their daughter Marjorie married William Godon Means of Boston, MA, and resided in Boston. Their son Durant married his cousin Louise Durant, the daughter of Clark Henry Durant of Hartford, CT.
*The famed operatic tenor Enrico Caruso was Rice's patient.
In 1910 the house was purchased by David Walter McCord who called it *Hither House*. [*The East Hampton Star* February 11, 1910, p. 5.]
**In 1946 Evan M. Frankel purchased the estate and renovated the carriage house into his residence. He sunk a swimming pool into the former main residence's foundation and named his residence *Brigadoon*.
Dr. Clarence Charles and Mrs. Jeannie Terry Durant Rice's granddaughter Jean Saltonstall married Benjamin Crowninshield Bradlee, Jr. of *Grey Gardens* in East Hampton.
Mary Heard Masterson Rice was the daughter of Judge James R. Masterson. She had previously been married to Sherman Goodwin Peticolas.

Rice, Ernest H., Sr. (1904-1987)

Occupation(s):	financier - chairman of board, Bondex Inc., Chicago, IL, and NY (investment banking service); chairman of board, First National Bank and Trust Co., Paterson, NJ industrialist - president, Burdell Oil Co., Dallas, TX merchant - proprietor, with his wife Charlotte, health food store, Rutland, VT
Civic Activism:	governor, Metropolitan Club, NYC
Marriage(s):	M/1 – 1927-div. 1944 – Miriam Van Winkle Coward (1909-1958) M/2 – 1944-1987 – Charlotte Virginia Coughlan - merchant - proprietor, with her husband Ernest, health food store, Rutland, VT
Address:	Lily Pond Lane, East Hampton
Name of estate:	
Year of construction:	
Style of architecture:	
Architect(s):	
Landscape architect(s):	
House extant:	unconfirmed
Historical notes:	

In 1935 Rice purchased John William Pulleyn, Sr.'s residence. [*The East Hampton Star* July 11, 1935, p. 1.]

He was the son of Elwood E. and Mary Elizabeth O'Neill Rice of Dayton, OH.

Miriam Van Winkle Coward Rice was the daughter of John Moore and Minnie Van Winkle Coward of Glen Ridge, NJ. Miriam subsequently married Arthur Newton Pierson, Jr.

Ernest H. and Miriam Van Winkle Coward Rice, Sr.'s son Ernest H. Rice, Jr. married Jeanne Vroman Borst, the daughter of Harry Vroman Borst of Amsterdam, NY.

Charlotte Virginia Coughlan Rice was the daughter of Harry Orsemus and Mary Clark Coughlan of Nutley, NJ. Charlotte had previously been married to William MacDuff Stevens.

Ernest H. and Charlotte Virginia Coughlan Rice, Sr.'s daughter Gail resided in Austin, TX.

Rice, Henry Grantland (1880-1954)
aka Grantland Rice

Occupation(s):	journalist - sports editor, *Atlanta Journal*, 1902-1904;
	sports editor, *Cleveland News*, 1905-1906;
	sports editor, *Nashville Tennessean*, 1906-1910;
	sports columnist, *New York Evening Mail*, 1911-1914;
	sports columnist, *New York Tribune* (later, *Herald Tribune*), 1914-1930;
	syndicated columnist, "The Sportlight" – in over 100 newspapers;
	editor, *American Golfer*, 1920-1936
	entertainers and associated professions -
	hosted radio program on football
	capitalist - president, Grantland Rice Sportlight, Inc. (produced series of one-reel sports films)
	writer - *The Winning Shots*, 1915;
	The Duffer's Handbook, 1926;
	Baseball Ballads, 1910;
	Songs of the Stalwart, 1917;
	Sportlights of 1923;
	Songs of the Open, 1924;
	Only the Brave, 1941 (war poems)
Civic Activism:	director, National Football Shrine and Hall of Fame;
	a founder and governor, Montauk Swordfish Club;
	director, Maidstone Club, East Hampton
Marriage(s):	1906-1954 – Katharine Hollis (d. 1966)
Address:	West End Avenue, East Hampton*
Name of estate:	
Year of construction:	1927
Style of architecture:	Modified Shingle
Architect(s):	John Custis Lawrence designed the house (for H. G. Rice)
Landscape architect(s):	
Builder:	Edward M. Gay
House extant: yes	
Historical notes:	

The house was built by Henry Grantland Rice.
He was the son of Bolling Hendon and Beulah Grantland Rice.
Katharine Hollis Rice was the daughter of Benjamin Hollis of Americus, GA.
Henry Grantland and Katharine Hollis Rice's daughter Florence married Fred Butler.
*Rice moved the house further back from the dunes to its present location after it was severely damaged by the 1931 hurricane. His good friend and neighbor Ring Lardner (Ringgold Wilmer Lardner, Sr.) also moved his house further back of the dunes to its present position.
The house was later owned by ____ Meyer.
The house is on The National Register of Historic Places.

Richard, Auguste (1890-1980)

Occupation(s):	industrialist - vice-president, Pacific Mills; partner, Lawrence & Co., NYC (textile commission firm); treasurer and general manager, Ipswich Mills, MA (hosiery manufacturer); president, Spool Cotton Co.; president and director, Crown Fastener Corp., Warren, RI; director, Clark Thread Co., Newark, NJ; director, J. & P. Coates, Inc., Pawtucket, RI financier - director, Bank of the Manhattan Co., NYC; partner, F. Eberstadt and Co. (investment banking firm)
Civic Activism:	trustee, Pomfret School, Pomfret, CT; president, Five Towns Community Chest, 1936; director, Manhattan Eye, Ear, and Throat Hospital, NYC; director, Merchants Association of New York; director, Cotton Thread Institute; director, American Management Association; director, Foundation House; chairman, Army & Navy Munitions Board, 1942; trustee, Village of Hewlett Harbor

Marriage(s):	M/1 – 1917-1961 – Hetty Lawrence Hemenway (1892-1961)
	 - writer - "Four Days" (short story)
	  Civic Activism: co-chairman, Mercy Ships for Children
	   Committee, 1940;
	   trustee, Spence–Chapin Adoption Service;
	   co-founder, Fountain House Foundation,
	    Inc. (West Side New York mental
	    rehabilitation center)
	M/2 – 1970-1980 – Rita Conway

Address:	217 Main Street, East Hampton
Name of estate:	
Year of construction:	1836
Style of architecture:	Modified Colonial Revival
Architect(s):	
Landscape architect(s):	
House extant: yes	
Historical notes:	

 The house was built by David G. Thompson. Around 1882 John Alexander Tyler purchased the house from Mrs. Thompson. It was later owned by Richard.
 The *Long Island Society Register, 1929* lists Auguste and Hetty L. Hemenway Richard as residing at *Tenant Farm* in Lawrence. The 1930 Federal Census lists the Richards at this address. [*See* Spinzia, *Long Island's Prominent Families in the Town of Hempstead* – Richard entry.]
 He was the son of Edwin Auguste and Alice Moore Richard of Manhattan. Auguste's sister Elvine married Curt Eric Hansen of East Hampton and, later, Clifford Hyde McCall, Sr. of *Kipsveen* in East Hampton.
 Hetty Lawrence Hemenway Richard was the daughter of Edward Augustus and Harriet Dexter Lawrence Hemenway of Readville, MA.
 Auguste and Hetty Lawrence Hemenway Richard's daughter Harriett married Lindsay Coates Herkness, Jr. of Meadow Brook, PA, and, resided in Lawrence. Harriett later married ____ Dawson. Their daughter Elvine married John Holmes Magruder III; Paul Scott Rankine with whom she resided in Washington, DC; and, subsequently, Rufus King. Their son Mark married Veronica Dwight and resided in East Hampton.
 By 1973 Auguste and Rita Conway Richard were also summering in East Hampton. *The Blue Book of Hamptons, 1973* lists Auguste and Rita Conway Richard as residing at 217 Main Street, East Hampton.
 [See following entry for additional family information.]
 Rita Conway had previously been married to Thomas A. Clark.
 The north addition to the house was built between 1902 and 1916.

Richard, Mark Gadd (1924-2003)

Occupation(s):	merchant - owned Buick/Pontiac dealership in East Hampton
Civic Activism:	member, East Hampton Fire Department

Marriage(s):
    M/1 –1950 – Veronica Dwight
       - Civic Activism: director, American Humane Education Society
    M/2 – 1974-div. 1981 – Mary Ella Brooks (b. 1921)
       - educator - teacher, East Hampton and Southampton Public Schools
       real estate agent - East Hampton, NY
       capitalist - founder and owner, Senior Services, Amagansett, NY
       financier - mortgage broker and consultant, Riverhead/American Savings Bank, Riverhead, NY
       politician - councilwoman, Town of East Hampton, NY, 1980-1981
       Civic Activism: treasurer, Suffolk County Inter Agency Coordinator Council, Riverhead;
         corresponding secretary, Riverhead Health Center Community Advisory Board;
         director, South Fork Community Health Initiative, Inc., East Hampton;
         member. East Hampton Town Board of Ethics;
         a founder, Suffolk Women's Political Caucus;
         co-founder, The Stony Hill Association (community activist association)
    M/3 – 1985-2003 – Catherine Kelsey

Address:	72 Egypt Lane, East Hampton
Name of estate:	
Year of construction:	
Style of architecture:	
Architect(s):	
Landscape architect(s):	
House extant: yes	
Historical notes:	

The Blue Book of The Hamptons, 1973 lists Mark G. and Veronica Dwight Richard as residing at 72 Egypt Lane, East Hampton.

He was the son of Auguste and Hetty Lawrence Hemenway Richard of Hewlett Harbor and East Hampton.

Veronica Dwight Richard was the daughter of Philip J. and Emily Thomas Dwight of Hewlett Neck. [*See* Spinzia, *Long Island's Prominent Families in the Town of Hempstead* – Dwight entry.]

Mark Gadd and Veronica Dwight Richard's son Mark Edward resided in Melrose, MA. Their son John Warren resided in Fort Meyers Beach, FL. Their son Auguste Richard II resided in San Jose, CA. Their daughter Catherine Dwight married Paul William Higgins, the son of Robert W. Higgins of Glen Rock, NJ, and resided in Greenwich, RI.

Mary Ella Brooks Richard is the daughter of James Vincent Hopkins and Mamie DeArmond Brooks. Mary had previously been married to James Hall Reutershan.

[See previous entry for additional family information.]

In 2002 the house sold for $2.34 million.

Richards, Benjamin, Jr. (1835-1917)

Occupation(s):	industrialist - secretary, Verplanck Brick Co., Fishkill-on-Hudson, NY real estate agent - NYC properties
Marriage(s):	1862-1914 – Eliza Fenno Verplanck (1838-1914) (aka Eliza Fenno Ver Planck) - Civic Activism: president, Woman's South Africa League
Address:	29 Dunemere Lane, East Hampton
Name of estate:	*Clas-des-Lilas*
Year of construction:	1900
Style of architecture:	Stuccoed Cottage
Architect(s):	Grosvenor Atterbury designed the house (for B. Richards)
Landscape architect(s):	
Builder:	Jabez E. Van Orden

House extant: yes
Historical notes:

The thirteen-room house, originally named *Clas-des-Lilas*, was built by Benjamin Richards, Jr.

The *Social Register Summer, 1910* lists Benjamin and Eliza F. Verplanck Richards [Jr.] as residing at *Clas-des-Lilas* in East Hampton.

He was the son of Benjamin and Jane H. Scott Richards, Sr.

Eliza Fenno Verplanck Richards was the daughter of William Samuel and Anna Biddle Newlin Ver Planck of Fishkill-on-Hudson, NY.

Benjamin and Eliza Fenno Verplanck Richards, Jr.'s daughter Louisa and son Gulian both did not marry. Their son Guy married Alice Reese, the daughter of W. Henry Reese of New York, and resided in Woodmere.

The house was later owned by their daughter Louisa who sold it to Donald E. Leith.

In 2004 the six-bedroom, five-and-a-half-bath house and one acre were sold for $3 million.

Richards, Richard Draper (1908-1982)
aka Richards Follett

Occupation(s):	capitalist - president, Richards and Ayer Associates, St. Croix, U. S. Virgin Islands (built and developed Estate Carlton, St. Croix, U. S. Virgin Islands – hotel and golf course complex)
Civic Activism:	trustee, St. Croix Chamber of Commerce, St. Croix, U. S. Virgin Islands; trustee, parole board, St. Croix, U. S. Virgin Islands; a founder, Pre-Columbian Museum, St. Croix, U. S. Virgin Islands
Marriage(s):	M/1 – 1933 – Constance Pierrpont Zabriskie (b. 1911) M/2 – 1947-1982 – Elizabeth Jenney (1909-2000)
Address:	81 Ocean Avenue, East Hampton
Name of estate:	*Little Too Close*
Year of construction:	1969
Style of architecture:	
Architect(s):	
Landscape architect(s):	

House extant: unconfirmed
Historical notes:

The house, originally named *Little Too Close*, was built by Richard Draper Richards. [*The East Hampton Star* June 13, 1946, p. 1, and October 23, 1969, p. 4.]

Richard Draper Richards was the son of Trustran Roberts Coffin and Marion Houghton Richards.

Constance Pierrpont Zabriskie Richards was the daughter of Frederick Conklin and Theresa Pierrpont Zabriskie of Hackensack, NJ. She subsequently married Elliot Kingman Ludington, Jr., the son of Elliot Kingman and Florence Edson Bemis Ludington, Sr., and resided in Greenwich, CT.

Richard Draper and Constance Pierrepont Zabriskie Richards' daughter Fredericka married Clarence King, Jr.

The *Social Register Summer, 1975* lists R. Draper and Betty Jenney Richards as residing at *Little Too Close* on Ocean Avenue, East Hampton.

She was the daughter of William Sherman and Nina Bevin Jenney of *Little Close* in East Hampton. Elizabeth had previously been married to Frederick Ayer II of Hewlett, Locust Valley, and Bellport. He was the son of Dr. James Cook and Mrs. May Candee Hancock Ayer of *Shadowland* in Glen Cove. [*See* Spinzia, *Long Island's Prominent Families in the Town of Hempstead* – Ayer entry – and *Long Island's Prominent North Shore Families, vol. I* – Ayer entries.]

Richey, The Reverend Alban, Sr. (1860-1934)

Occupation(s):	clergy - rector, St. Paul's Episcopal Church, Patchogue, 1886-1889; assistant rector, Trinity Chapel, NYC; rector, St. John's Episcopal Church, Wilmington, DE
	writer - *The Kenosi*
Marriage(s):	1889-1934 – Josephine Wood Potter (1864-1945)
Address:	Georgica Road, East Hampton
Name of estate:	*Rosebrae*
Year of construction:	1895
Style of architecture:	Shingle Cottage
Architect(s):	John Custis Lawrence, 1906 additions
Landscape architect(s):	
House extant:	yes

Historical notes:

The house, originally named *Rosebrae*, was built by The Reverend Alban Richey, Sr.

The Social *Register Summer, 1910* and *1915* list The Reverend Alban and Mrs. Josephine W. Potter Richey as residing at *Rosebrae* in East Hampton.

He was the son of The Reverend Thomas and Mrs. Emma Cecelia Bacot Richey, Sr., who resided on the adjacent property.

Josephine Wood Potter Richey was the daughter of Philip Justis and Margaret Elisabeth Potter.

The Reverend Alban and Mrs. Josephine Wood Potter Richey's daughter Margaret married Francis D. Buck and resided in Brooklyn. Their son Thomas Richey II married Virginia Elizabeth Shropshire, the daughter of George E. Shropshire of Yonkers, NY, and resided in Norwich, CT. Their daughter Josephine married Floyd Tomkins, Jr. of Philadelphia, PA, and resided in Washington, CT. Their daughter Alice married Henry Cranston Jones, the son of William and Isabel Barr Jones, and resided in Bronxville, NY. Their son Alban Richey, Jr. resided in Montpelier, VT.

[See following entry for additional family information.]

Richey, The Reverend Thomas, Sr. (1831-1905)

Occupation(s):	clergy - rector, St. Luke's Episcopal Church, Catskill, NY, 1854-1858; rector, Mt. Calvary Church, Baltimore, MD, 1858-1862
	educator - professor of ecclesiastical history, Seabury Hall, MN, 1869-1875; professor of ecclesiastical history, General Theological Seminary, NYC, 1869;
	writer - *Truth and Counter Truth*, 1869; *The Nicene Creed and Fillioque*, 1884; *The Parables of the Lord Jesus*, 1888
Marriage(s):	1858-1905 – Emma Cecelia Bacot (1833-1916)
Address:	Georgica Road, East Hampton
Name of estate:	
Year of construction:	1894
Style of architecture:	Shingle Cottage
Architect(s):	
Landscape architect(s):	
Builder:	Frank Grimshaw
House extant:	yes

Historical notes:

The house was built by The Reverend Thomas Richey, Sr.

He was born in Ireland.

Emma Cecelia Bacot Richey was the daughter of Peter and Mary Eugenia Cochran Bacot.

The Reverend Thomas and Mrs. Emma Cecelia Bacot Richey's daughter Emma, who did not marry, resided in Bronxville, NY. Their son Francis married Mary Elizabeth Lowe and resided in Sag Harbor. Their son Alban married Josephine Wood Potter and resided on the adjacent property.

[See previous entry for additional family information.]

The house was inherited by their daughter Josephine and son-in-law Samuel Seabury, who called it *Wyandanch Acres*.

In c. 1920 the Seaburys added a library, enlarged the kitchen, and altered the second floor. In 1979 an oriel entrance was added to the east facade.

Rifkind, Dr. Richard A (1930-2019)

Occupation(s):	physician - chairman of board, Sloan-Kettering Institute, NYC
	scientist - chief scientific officer, Sloan Kettering Institute, NYC
	educator - assistant, associate, and professor of Medicine and Human Genetics, Columbia University College of Physicians and Surgeons, NYC;
	director, Sloan Kettering Graduate School, NYC
	entertainers and associated professions -
	co-producer, with his wife Carole:
	"The Venetian Dilemma";
	"Naturally Obsessed: The Making of a Scientist"
	writer - over 250 articles in medical and scientific journals;
	Fundamentals of Hematology, 1986
Civic Activism:	director, The Winston Foundation;
	governor, New York Academy of Science;
	trustee, New York Academy of Medicine;
	trustee, New York Hall of Science;
	trustee, John Simon Guggenheim Memorial Foundation;
	established, with his wife Carole, The Richard Rifkind and Carole Lewis Rifkind 56 Faculty Support Fund
Marriage(s):	1956-2019 – Carole Lewis (1935-2019)
	- architectural historian
	writer - articles in professional journals;
	Mansions, Mills, and Main Streets, 1975;
	Main Street: The Face of Urban America, 1977;
	A Field Guide to American Architecture, 1980;
	Tourism and Communities: Process, Problems, and Solutions, 1981;
	A Field Guide to Contemporary American Architecture, 1998;
	America's Fantasy Urbanism, 1996
	entertainers and associated professions -
	co-producer, with her husband Richard:
	"The Venetian Dilemma";
	"Naturally Obsessed: The Making of a Scientist"
	Civic Activism: established, with her husband Richard, The Richard Rifkind and Carole Lewis Rifkind 56 Faculty Support Fund;
	trustee, Municipal Art Society;
	trustee, New Museum of Contemporary Art;
	trustee, East River Waterfront Conservancy
Address:	Meeting House Lane, Amagansett
Name of estate:	
Year of construction:	1973
Style of architecture:	Cape Cod
Architect(s):	
Landscape architect(s):	
House extant: yes	
Historical notes:	

In 1992 Rifkind purchased the four-bedroom house. [*The East Hampton Star* November 27, 2003, p. 70.]
He was the son of Simon Hirsch and Adele Singer Rifkind.
Carole Lewis Rifkind was the daughter of Julius Lewis of Brooklyn.
Dr. Richard A. and Mrs. Carole Lewis Rifkind's daughter Barbara married Adam M. Brandenburger, the son of Frank E. and Ennis Brandenburger.
[See following entry for additional family information.]

Rifkind, Robert Singer (b. 1936)

Occupation(s):	attorney - assistant to Solicitor General, Department of Justice, 1965-1968; partner, Cravath, Swaine and Moore, NYC
Civic Activism:	trustee, Salton School, NYC; trustee, Brandeis University, Waltham, MA; trustee, The Loomis Institute; director, Charles H. Revson Foundation; director, Jewish Theological Seminary, NYC; director, Leo Baeck Institute; director, Benjamin N. Cardozo School of Law, Yeshiva University, NYC; founder, Robert S. Rifkind Charitable Foundation; president, American Jewish Committee
Marriage(s):	1961 – Dr. Arleen Brenner (b. 1938) - physician - research associate and resident physician, Rockefeller University, NYC; physician and clinical associate, Endocrine Board, National Cancer Institute
	educator - assistant and associate professor of medicine, Cornell University Medical College, NYC; associate professor of pharmacology, Cornell University Medical College, NYC
	writer - articles in professional journals
	Civic Activism: board chair, National Environment Health Services Review Committee; chair, science counselors, United States Public Health Service Agency for Toxic Substances & Disease Registry, 1991-1995; member of board, Drug Metabolism and Disposition, 1994-1996; member of board, Toxicology and Applied Pharmacology
Address:	Georgica Pond, East Hampton
Name of estate:	
Year of construction:	1998
Style of architecture:	Modern
Architect(s):	Tod Williams, Billie Tsien Architects designed the house (for Rifkind)
Landscape architect(s):	
House extant:	yes
Historical notes:	

The house was built by Robert Singer Rifkind.
He is the son of Simon Hirsch and Adele Singer Rifkind.
Arleen Brenner Rifkind is the daughter of Michael C. and Regina Gottlieb Brenner.
Robert Singer and Arleen Brenner Rifkind's daughter Amy married Bruce David Brown, the son of Bernard and Barbara Brown of Leawood, Kansas. Their daughter Nina married Marc Harold Lerner, the son of Dr. Laurance and Mrs. Susan Lerner of NYC.
[See previous entry for additional family information.]

Robert, Stephen Kniznick (b. 1940)

Occupation(s):	financier - co-chairman of board and CEO, Faulker, Dawkins, and Sullivan, 1965-1967;
	vice-president, Oppenheimer Funds, NYC, 1968-1976;
	chief portfolio manager, Oppenheimer Funds, NYC, 1969-1976;
	general partner, Oppenheimer and Co., Inc., NYC, 1970-1982;
	director of research, Oppenheimer and Co., Inc., NYC, 1976-1978;
	president, Oppenheimer and Co., Inc., NYC 1979-1983;
	chairman of board and CEO, Oppenheimer and Co., Inc., NYC, 1983-1997;
	chairman of board and CEO, Renaissance Institutional Management, LLC, 2005-2008;
	director, Reinsurance Corp.
	CEO, Robert Capital Management, NYC
	industrialist - director, Xerox Corp.
	educator - chancellor, Brown University, Providence, RI, 1998-2007
Civic Activism:	director and chairman, finance committee, Wilwych School for Boys, Esopus, NY, 1968-1978;
	director, Joffrey Ballet, NYC, 1981- ;
	trustee, The Dalton School, 1984- ;
	overseer, Watson Institute for International Studies;
	director, United States / Middle East Project;
	director, Millennium Promise;
	member, foreign policy program leadership committee, The Brookings Institution;
	member, investment committee, Peter G. Peterson Foundation;
	trustee, Presbyterian Medical Center;
	co-founder, with his wife Pilar, Source of Hope Foundation

Robert, Stephen Kniznick (cont'd)

Marriage(s):
M/1 – 1965 – Eileen Marks Levin
- capitalist - vice-president, Halstead Property, NYC (real estate brokerage firm)

M/2 – Catherine Price

M/3 – Pilar Crespi (b. 1944)
- model;
fashion coordinator, Valentino, Rome, Italy
journalist - assistant editor, *Vogue*;
contributing editor, *Veranda*
public relations executive -
co-owner, Crespi and Mariani Associates, 1995-1999;
director of communications, Gucci, Milan, Italy
capitalist - producer, "Vlast", 2010 (a documentary on Russian politics)
entertainers and associated professions - motion picture actress
Civic Activism:
co-founder, with her husband Stephen, Source of Hope Foundation;
vice-president of board, Henry Street Settlement, NYC;
member, advisory board, Casita Maria, NYC;
member, advisory board, Peggy Guggenheim Collections, NYC

Address: 18 Lee Avenue, East Hampton

Name of estate:
Year of construction: 1899
Style of architecture: Shingle
Architect(s): Joseph Greenleaf Thorp designed the house (for Hackstaff)
Landscape architect(s):
Builder: Loper Brothers
George A. Eldredge, 1902 additions*

House extant: yes

Historical notes:

The house, originally named *Tarriawyle*, was built by Charles Ludovic Hackstaff. It was later owned by Harkness Edwards, Sr. and, subsequently, by Robert.

He is the son of Samuel Kniznick Robert of Haverhill, MA.

Eileen Marks Levin Robert is the daughter of I. Victor and Behna Marks Levin of Kings Point, NY.

Stephen Kniznick and Eileen Marks Levin Robert's daughter Tracey married Steven Eric Gordon, the son of Roy and Myra Gordon of Cambridge, MA, and resides in San Francisco, CA. Their daughter Elisabeth resides in New York.

Pilar Crespi Robert is the daughter of Count Rodolfo and Countess Consuelo Pauline O'Brien O'Connor Crespi of Italy. Pilar had previously been married to Gabriel Echavarra, the son of Julio Echavarra of Colombia.

She was inducted into the International Best-Dressed Hall of Fame.

In 2012 the 7,500-square-foot, eight-bedroom, seven-and-a-half-bath house and 1.9 acres were for sale by Robert. The asking price was $18.5 million. It was sold for $14.9 million in 2014.

*The 1902 addition on the south facade was built by Eldridge. In 1969 the front porch was enclosed.

Roberts, Dudley DeVore, Jr. (1900-2000)

Occupation(s):	financier - founder, Roberts and Co. (investment banking firm); partner, Cady, Roberts, and Co. (investment banking firm)
	capitalist founder and president, Cinerama Productions (pioneered wide-screen motion pictures)
Civic Activism:	president, Maidstone Club, East Hampton
Marriage(s):	M/1 – 1933-div. – Elizabeth Boies Belden (1911-1968)
	M/2 – 1953 – Maria Fahys Cook (1900-1983)
	M/3 – Jane Alcott (d. 1989)
	M/4 – Laura Serra (b. 1928)
Address:	Further Lane, East Hampton
Name of estate:	*Whale Off*
Year of construction:	
Style of architecture:	
Architect(s):	
Landscape architect(s):	
House extant: yes	
Historical notes:	

In 1946 Roberts purchased East Hampton's historic Dominy clock shop and cabinet shop. He relocated them to his Further Lane property where he had them joined together as a single building.

The Blue Book of The Hamptons, 1958 lists Mrs. and Mrs. Dudley Roberts as residing on Further Lane in East Hampton. He was the son of Dr. Dudley DeVore and Mrs. Carrie Elise Steele Roberts, Sr. of *Outabounds* in East Hampton.

Elizabeth Boies Belden Roberts was the daughter of James Jerome and Helen Boies Belden of *Windybrow* in Scranton, PA. Elizabeth subsequently married W. Miles Cary, Jr.

Maria Fahys Cook Roberts was the daughter of Henry Frances and Lena Mariana Fahys Cook of *Clench–Warton* in North Haven. Maria had previously been married to Howard Brush Dean, Sr., the son of Herbert Hollingshead and Marion Atwater Brush Dean of *Deanlea* in Lattingtown, and resided in Garden City. [*See* Spinzia, *Long Island's Prominent Families in the Town of Southampton* – Cook entry; *Long Island's Prominent North Shore Families, vol. I* – Dean entry; *Long Island's Prominent Families in the Town of Hempstead* – Dean entry.]

Jane Alcott Roberts was the daughter of Clarence Frank and Lucie Arrington Burke Alcott of East Hampton. Jane had previously been married to Jay Holmes of East Hampton. He was the son of Dr. Christian R. and Mrs. Bettie Fleishman Holmes of *The Chimneys* in Sands Point. [*See* Spinzia, *Long Island's Prominent North Shore Families, vol. I* – Holmes entry.]

The Blue Book of The Hamptons, 1997 lists Dudley and Laura Serra Roberts as residing at *Whale Off* on Further Lane, East Hampton.

She was the daughter of Luigi and Rosetta Garibaldi Serra of Genoa, Italy. Laura had previously been married to Aubrey Wray Fitch, Jr. and to Dr. Henry Pinkney Phyfe, Sr.

[See following entry for additional family information.]

The property was sold to Elizabeth Fondaras who sold it to Christopher H. Browne in c. 2007. Browne built a 9,000-square-foot, four-bedroom, one-story house on the property and converted the Dominy shops into a guest house. After Browne's death it was owned by Browne's partner of ten years Andrew S. Gordon. Upon Gordon's death in 2014 the estate reverted to Browne's family.

In 2014 the estate and 18 acres were purchased for $147 million by Barry Rosenstein who intends to demolish the main residence and build a new one on the site. Plans are in progress to relocate the Dominy buildings to a site in the village where they will be open to the public as a museum.

Roberts, Dr. Dudley DeVore, Sr. (1874-1940)

Occupation(s):	physician - gastroenterologist - Bellevue Hospital, NYC, 1898-1900; Brooklyn Hospital; Long Island College Dispensary; King's Park State Hospital
	writer - articles in numerous medical journals
Civic Activism:	president, Associate Physicians of Long Island; trustee, Brooklyn Parks and Playgrounds Association; director, Maidstone Club, East Hampton
Marriage(s):	1900-1940 – Carrie Elise Steele (1877-1952)
Address:	Further Lane, East Hampton
Name of estate:	*Outabounds*
Year of construction:	1901-1902
Style of architecture:	
Architect(s):	Joseph Greenleaf Thorp designed the house (for J S. Schurman, Sr.)

Landscape architect(s):
House extant: remodeled into a ranch, 1949
Historical notes:

   In 1927 Roberts purchased Jacob Gould Schurman's residence *Breezy Knowe* and renamed it *Outabounds*. [*The East Hampton Star* October 28, 1927, p. 1.]

   The *Social Directory of Southampton, Long Island, 1931* lists Dr. Dudley and Mrs. Carrie Steele Roberts [Sr.] as residing at *Outabounds* on Further Lane, East Hampton.

   He was the son of William M. and Susan Emily Whitehead Roberts of Newark, NJ.

   Carrie Elise Steele Roberts was the daughter of Sanford Henry and Carrie Elise Hinman Steele of Brooklyn.

   Dr. Dudley DeVore and Mrs. Carrie Elise Steele Roberts, Sr.'s son Henry, who resided in Ridgefield, CT, and Remsenburg, married Caroline Spahr, the daughter of Albert Hubbard Spahr of Sewickley, PA, and, later, Mary Patricia Selden, the daughter of Charles Selden of Washington, DC. [*See* Spinzia, *Long Island's Prominent Families in the Town of Southampton* – Roberts entry.] Their daughter Helen married Robert Elliott McCormick, the son of Robert Nish and Adelle Elliott McCormick, and resided in East Hampton. Their daughter Carolyn married Edson K. Green and resided in Ridgefield, CT. Their son Dudley D. Roberts, Jr. resided in East Hampton.

[See previous entry for additional family information.]

Roberts, George Hewitt, Jr. (1884-1968)

Occupation(s):	attorney - partner, Winthrop, Stimson, Putnam, and Roberts
	capitalist - vice-president and director, Thorne Looms & Co.
Civic Activism:	vice-president, Maidstone Club, East Hampton;
	governor, Riding Club of East Hampton;
	member, executive committee, East Hampton Associates
Marriage(s):	1918-1968 – Grace Lee Middleton (1892-1983)
	- Civic Activism: president, Garden Club of East Hampton
Address:	32 Middle Lane, East Hampton
Name of estate:	*Furtherfield*
Year of construction:	1930-1931
Style of architecture:	Neo-Federal
Architect(s):	Aymar Embury II designed the house
	(for G. H. Roberts, Jr.)
Landscape architect(s):	Ruth Bramley Dean, 1930
	(for G. H. Roberts, Jr.)
	Mary Lois Deputy Lamson, c. 1941
	(for G. H. Roberts, Jr.)

House extant: yes
Nassau County Museum Collection has photographs of the estate.
Historical notes:

The six-bedroom, five-bath, 8,268-square-foot house, originally named *Furtherfield*, was built by George Hewitt Roberts, Jr.

The *Social Register of Southampton, Long Island, 1931* lists George and Grace Lee Middleton Roberts [Jr.] as residing on Middle Lane, East Hampton.

He was the son of George Hewitt and Maria Pettit Roberts, Sr. of Brooklyn.

Grace Lee Middleton Roberts was the daughter of Clifford L. and Grace Graham Ball Middleton of Brooklyn.

George Hewitt and Grace Lee Middleton Roberts, Jr.'s daughter Rosamond married Donald Arthur, Jr. of Manchester, VT, and resided in Cold Spring Harbor. Their daughter Constance married Robert L. Hoguet, Jr. and resided in Manhattan.

The house was later owned by Daniel Anthony Breen, Jr.

In 2017 the house and 5.2 acres were for sale. The asking price was $29.95 million. The annual taxes were $60,378. The estate sold in 2017 for $25 million.

Roberts, Walter Scott

Occupation(s):	industrialist - president, Pennsylvania Textile Co.; Aracoma Silk Mill, Wellsboro, PA; Aracoma Drapery Fabrics, Inc.; Aracoma Textile Co., Inc.
	writer - *Silk Culture in America*, 1945
Marriage(s):	1901-div. 1925* – May Garnett
Address:	Georgica Road, East Hampton
Name of estate:	
Year of construction:	1895
Style of architecture:	Neo-Tudor
Architect(s):	Joseph Greenleaf Thorp designed the house (for Spring)
	Howard Greenley, 1915 alterations (for Roberts)
	Spencer Fullerton Weaver, Sr., 1925 alterations (for himself)
Landscape architect(s):	John Raum, 1917 (for Roberts)
	Jacob John Spoon designed the swimming pool (for Weaver)
Builder:	Philip Ritch

House extant: no**
Nassau County Museum Collection has photographs of the estate.
Historical notes:

The house, originally named *Winklehawk*, was built by Preston Brady Spring, Sr. In 1915 it was purchased by Roberts. [*The East Hampton Star* August 6, 1915, p. 5; December 13, 1918, p. 5; and June 8, 1944, p. 3.]

*May Garnett Roberts charged Walter's secretary Gertrude Warnken, with whom Walter was reputed to have fathered two children, with alienation of affections in a long and very public divorce proceeding.

The Roberts did not have children.

In 1925 the house was purchased by Spencer Fullerton Weaver, Sr. who renamed it *Spencecliff*.

In 1949 it was purchased by William Seligson who subdivided the estate's property into six building lots. [*The East Hampton Star* January, 13, 1955, p. 5, and June 16, 1955, p. 12.]

The house was subsequently owned by Adolph Green.

**In 1969 the house was destroyed by fire during a wedding at Green's estate when a caterer's gas line leaked and ignited.

Robertson, Clifford Parker, III (1923-2011)
aka Cliff Robertson

Occupation(s):	entertainers and associated professions - actor and director writer journalist

Marriage(s):	M/1 – 1957-div. 1959 – Cynthia Stone (1926-1988)
	   - entertainers and associated professions - actress
	M/2 – 1966–div. 1989 – Nedenia Marjorie Hutton (1923-2017)
	     (aka Dina Merrill)
	   - financier - director, E. F. Hutton and Co. (investment banking firm);
	     chair, compensation and benefits committee, and director, Lehman Brothers (investment banking firm)
	   capitalist - partner, Pavilion Communications (later, RKO Pictures); board vice-chair, RKO Pictures;
	   entertainers and associated professions - actress
	   industrialist - president, Amaranthe (cosmetic manufacturer)
	   Civic Activism: a founder and trustee, Eugene O'Neill Theater Center, NYC;
	     trustee, John F. Kennedy Center for the Performing Arts, Washington, DC;
	     vice-president, New York City Mission Society, NYC;
	     a founder, Juvenile Diabetes Foundation;
	     vice-chair, Republican Pro-Choice Coalition;
	     trustee, Population Resource Council;
	     trustee, Paley Center for Media, NYC;
	     director, Project Orbis (teaches eye care & surgical techniques worldwide);
	     co-founder, with husband Ted, The Story Project;
	     co-founder, with husband Ted, Hartley–Merrill International Screenwriting Award

Address:	Highway Behind the Pond, East Hampton
Name of estate:	
Year of construction:	
Style of architecture:	
Architect(s):	
Landscape architect(s):	
House extant:	unconfirmed
Historical notes:	

    Clifford Parker Robertson III was the son of Clifford Parker and Audrey Olga Willingham Robertson, Jr.
    Cynthia Stone Robertson was the daughter of John Boyd and Dorothy Drayton Stone of Peoria, IL. Cynthia had previously been married to the noted actor Jack Lemmon. After her divorce from Robertson, Cynthia married Robert McDougal III of Santa Monica, CA.
    Clifford Parker and Cynthia Stone Robertson III's daughter Stephanie married Dr. Donald Eugene Saunders III and resided in Charleston, SC.
    The Blue Book of The Hamptons, 1979 lists Cliff and Nedenia Hutton Robertson as residing on Highway Behind the Pond, East Hampton.
    She was the daughter of Edward Francis and Marjorie Merriweather Post Hutton who resided at *Hillwood* in Brookville. Nedenia had previously been married to Stanley Maddox Rumbough, Jr. of Old Brookville and East Hampton. He was the son of Stanley and Elizabeth Morse Colgate Rumbough, Sr. of *Elston Oaks* in Lloyd Harbor. [*See* Spinzia, *Long Island's Prominent North Shore Families, vol. I* – Hutton entry – and *vol. II* – Post and Rumbough entries.] After her divorce from Robertson, Nedenia married Theodore Ringwalt Hartley with whom she also resided in East Hampton.
    Clifford Parker and Nedenia Marjorie Hutton Robertson III's daughter Heather died in 2007 at the age of thirty-eight of ovarian cancer.

Robertson, Hugh James, Jr. (1899-1983)

Occupation(s):	industrialist - president, Fibre Conduit Co., Orangeburg, NJ; president, Orangeburg Manufacturing Co., Orangeburg, NJ (pipe manufacturing firm)
Civic Activism:	chairman, Charles Dickerman Memorial Cup Golf Tournament, 1943; vice-president, Maidstone Club, East Hampton
Marriage(s):	1922-1983 – Isabelle Bradley (1901-1986)
Address:	56 James Lane, East Hampton
Name of estate:	
Year of construction:	
Style of architecture:	
Architect(s):	
Landscape architect(s):	
House extant: yes	
Historical notes:	

In 1938 Robinson purchased the house. [*The East Hampton Star* November 6, 1986, p. 2.]

The Blue Book of The Hamptons, 1958, 1965, and *1973* list Mr. and Mrs. Hugh J. Robertson, Jr. as residing at 56 James Lane, East Hampton.

He was from Independence, MO.

Isabelle Bradley Robertson was the daughter of William C. and Isabelle Galloway Bradley of NYC.

Hugh James and Isabelle Bradley Robertson, Jr.'s daughter Isabelle married Edward Francis Wrenn, Jr., the son of Edward Francis Wrenn, Sr. of Charleston, SC; ____ Wasson; and, later, Charles H. Farmer, Sr. Their daughter Czara married William T. Cahill of Lawrence, MA. Their daughter Barbara married ____ Maraventano and resided in Florence, Italy.

In 1999 the house sold for $1,612,500.

Robinson, Fielding S. (d. 1967)

Occupation(s):	industrialist - general manager, Crosby Radio Co., NY; executive, Hazeltine Electronic Corp. financier - electronic consultant, Smith Barney and Co. aides-de-camp to President Wilson at the Paris Peace Conference, 1919
Civic Activism:	advisory trustee, Guild Hall, East Hampton
Marriage(s):	M/1 – 1933-div. – Evelyn Walker (1908-1972) M/2 – Mary Jane Cassidy
Address:	Egypt Lane, East Hampton
Name of estate:	
Year of construction:	
Style of architecture:	
Architect(s):	
Landscape architect(s):	
House extant: unconfirmed	
Historical notes:	

In 1944 Mrs. Martin Moore Foss, Sr. purchased Josiah Peter Marvel's Egypt Lane residence which was known as Lorenzo Easton Woodhouse's Thorp cottage. [*The East Hampton Star* July 5, 1929, p. 8, and November 23, 1944, p. 1.] In 1947 it was purchased by Robinson. [*The East Hampton Star* November 23, 1944, p. 1, and May 1, 1947, p. 5.]

He was the son of Emmett Robinson of Norfolk, VA, and a captain in the Fifth Regiment of the Marines during World War I. Fielding was awarded the Croix de Guerre and made a Chevalier of the Legion of Honor. He was also a member of the Belgian Order of Leopold.

Evelyn Walker Robinson was the daughter of Harold Walker of NYC and *Welbley Farm* in McDaniel, MD. In 1935 she married Assistant Secretary of the U. S. Treasury Lawrence Wood Robert, Jr.

The Blue Book of The Hamptons, 1958 and *1965* list Mr. and Mrs. Fielding S. Robinson as residing on Egypt Lane, East Hampton.

Robinson, Lucius Franklin, Jr. (1897-1989)

Occupation(s):	attorney - partner, Robinson, Robinson, and Cole, Hartford, CT; partner, Robinson and Cole, Hartford, CT
	capitalist - director, The Hartford Steam Boiler (inspections and insurance); director, Southern New England Telephone Co.
	financier - director, Connecticut General Life Insurance Co.; director, Mutual Insurance Co., Hartford, CT
Civic Activism:	president, Hartford County Bar Association; president, Connecticut Bar Association; vice-chairman, Hartford Redevelopment Agency
Marriage(s):	1922-1987 – Augusta James McLane (1901-1991)
	- politician - delegate at large, Connecticut Constitutional Convention, 1937
	Civic Activism:
	president, Old East Hampton (residents of twenty-five years or more in East Hampton);
	president, Women's Auxiliary, Hartford Symphony Orchestra;
	chair, Connecticut Women's Organization for National Prohibition Reform, 1929-1933;
	vice-chair, national committee, Women's Organization for National Prohibition Reform, 1930-1933;
	director, Women's Exchange;
	president, Hartford Garden Club;
	director, Gray Lodge Shelter;
	director, Union for Home Work
Address:	Georgica Road, East Hampton
Name of estate:	*Fulling Mill Farm*
Year of construction:	1910
Style of architecture:	Colonial Revival
Architect(s):	William Welles Bosworth designed the house (for F. Newton)*
Landscape architect(s):	
Builder:	George A. Eldredge, house and 1913 studio

House extant: yes**
Historical notes:

   The house, originally named *Fulling Mill Farm*, was built by Francis Newton on the former site of J. S. Corwin's farm. [*The East Hampton Star* October 1, 1909, p. 5, and March 11, 1910, p. 5.] It was later owned by Robinson who continued to call it *Fulling Mill Farm*.
   He was the son of Lucius Franklin and Eleanor L. Cooke Robinson, Sr. of Hartford, CT.
   Augusta James McLane Robinson was the daughter of Judge Allan and Mrs. Augusta James McLane, Sr. of Baltimore, MD. Her brother Allan McLane, Jr., who resided at *Homewood* in Lattingtown, married Edith Gibb Pratt, the daughter of Herbert Lee and Florence Gibb Pratt, Sr. of *The Braes* in Glen Cove; Anne King Weld, the daughter of Edward Motley and Sara Lothrop Weld of Tuxedo Park, NY; and, subsequently, Patricia Appleton. [*See* Spinzia, *Long Island's Prominent North Shore Families, vol. I* – McLane entry - and *vol. II* – Pratt entries.]
   Lucius Franklin and Augusta James McLane Robinson, Jr.'s daughter Amy married Gerald David Campbell–Harris, the son of Arthur E. Campbell–Harris of London and West Brabourne, England. Their daughter Augusta married John deKoven Alsop, the son of Joseph Wright Alsop of Avon, CT, and resided in Old Lyme, CT. Their daughter Elinor married George Shaw Green, Jr. of Dayton, OH, and resided in Philadelphia. Their daughter Anne married Alden Young Warner, Jr. of Farmington, CT, and resided in Farmington, CT.
   *Bosworth utilized Grosvenor Atterbury's plans for the house.
   **In 1947 a fire caused extensive damage to the house. [*The East Hampton Star* May 22, 1947, p. 5.]
   The house is on The National Register of Historic Places.

Rose, Daniel (b. 1929)

Occupation(s):	capitalist - vice-president, Dwelling Managers, Inc.; president and chairman of board, Rose Associates (developed, managed, and owned Manhattan residential properties)
Civic Activism:	founder, Harlem Educational Activities Fund, 1991
Marriage(s):	1956 – Joanna Semel - publisher - chairman of board, *Partisan Review* (cultural journal) Civic Activism: trustee, The Village Preservation Society, East Hampton
Address:	1 Lily Pond Lane, East Hampton
Name of estate:	
Year of construction:	1905
Style of architecture:	Shingle
Architect(s):	Joseph Greenleaf Thorp designed the house (for F. G. Potter)
Landscape architect(s):	
Builder:	Thomas E. Babcock
House extant: yes	
Historical notes:	

The house was built by Frederick Gaul Potter. It was later owned by Rose.
He is the son of Samuel Benedict and Belle Rose of Mount Vernon, NY.
Joanna Semel Rose is the daughter of Philip Ephraim Semel of Cedarhurst.
Daniel and Joanna Semel Rose's daughter Emily married James H. Marrow, the son of Jerome and Helen C. Marrow. Their son Joseph, who was head of New York City's Planning Commission in the Giuliani administration, married Wendi Rose, the daughter of Marshall Rose. Their son Gideon is the managing editor of *Foreign Affairs* magazine. Their son David, the president of Rose Tech Ventures, married Gail Ruth Gremse.

Rose, Marshall (b. 1930)

Occupation(s):	capitalist - chairman of board, Georgetown Group, Inc. (real estate development firm);
	director, One Liberty Properties, Great Neck (real estate investment trust);
	director, BRT Realty Trust
	industrialist - director, Este Lauder, Inc.
	financier - member, Longstreet Corp. (investment banking firm)
Civic Activism:	chairman of board, New York Public Library, NYC;
	director, New York University Medical Center, NYC;
	director, Lincoln Center for the Performing Arts, NYC;
	chairman of board, Lincoln Center Redevelopment Project, NYC;
	director, The City of New York's Graduate School and University Center;
	member, Bryant Park Restoration Committee, NYC;
	director, Robert Steel Foundation for Pediatric Research
Marriage(s):	M/1 – 1965-1996 – Jill Caroll Kupin (1944-1996)
	- Civic Activism: president, International Photo Center;
	volunteer social worker, Spence–Chapin Services to Families and Children
	M/2 – 2000 – Candice Bergen (b. 1946)
	- entertainers and associated professions -
	motion picture, television, and stage actress
	Vogue fashion model
	writer - *Knock Wood*, 1984 (autobiography);
	A Fine Romance, 2015 (autobiography)
Address:	1 Lily Pond Lane, East Hampton
Name of estate:	
Year of construction:	1984
Style of architecture:	Dutch Colonial Revival
Architect(s):	Jaquelin T. Robertson of Cooper, Robertson and Partners designed the house and 2004 alterations (for M. Rose)
Landscape architect(s):	
House extant: yes	
Historical notes:	

   The house was built by Marshall Rose.
   He is the son of Jack Rose of New York.
   Jill Caroll Kupin Rose was the daughter of Nathan R. Kupin of Kings Point.
   Marshall and Jill Caroll Kupin Rose's daughter Wendi married Joseph Benedict Rose, the son of Daniel and Joanna Rose and resided in East Hampton. Their son Andrew resides in Santa Monica, CA.
   Candice Bergen Rose is the daughter of Edgar and Frances Westerman Bergen of Beverly Hills, CA. Candice had previously been married to Louis Malle.
   Their daughter Chloé Malle is a fashion editor for *Vogue*.

Rosenstein, Barry (b. 1960)

Occupation(s):	financier - member, Plaza Securities Corp.;
	member, Merrill, Lynch & Co. (specialized in mergers and acquisitions);
	a founder and managing partner, Reatta Partners;
	a founder and head, Genesis Merchants Group's Investment and Banking Group;
	a founder and managing partner, Sagaponack Partners (private equity firm);
	a founder and managing partner, Jana Partners (hedge fund)
Civic Activism:	trustee, Brown University, Providence, RI;
	trustee, 92nd Street Y, NYC;
	trustee, Make the Road New York;
	trustee, United States Olympic Foundation
Marriage(s):	1986 – Lizanne Teitelbaum
Address:	60 Further Lane, East Hampton
Name of estate:	
Year of construction:	2007
Style of architecture:	Modern
Architect(s):	Andrew S. Gordon designed the house (for Browne)
Landscape architect(s)	Christopher H. Browne and Andrew S. Gordon
House extant: no	
Historical notes:	

The 9,000-square-foot, four-bedroom, one-story house with two guest suites was built by Christopher H. Browne on property he purchased from Elizabeth Fondaras. The property was previously owned by Dudley DeVore Roberts, Jr. who called it *Whale Off*. Roberts relocated the historic Dominy clock shop and cabinet shop to his property and merged them into a single building.

The estate and Brown's fortune were inherited by Browne's partner of ten years Andrew S. Gordon. Upon Gordon's death in 2014, the inheritance reverted to Browne's family. In 2015 the house was purchased by Rosenstein for $147 million.

He is the son of Herbert and Harriet Wolf Rosenstein of West Orange, NJ.

Lizanne Teitelbaum Rosenstein is the daughter of Dr. Seymour and Mrs. Lilian Ostrovsky Teitelbaum of Briarcliff Manor, NY.

Plans are in progress to relocate the Dominy buildings to a site in village where they will be open to the public.

In 2015 Rosenstein built a new 20,000-square-foot house on the site.

Rosenstein, Barry (b. 1960)

Occupation(s):	*[See previous entry.]*
Civic Activism:	*[See previous entry.]*
Marriage(s):	1986 – Lizanne Teitelbaum
Address:	27 Drew Lane, East Hampton
Name of estate:	
Year of construction:	1920
Style of architecture:	Shingle
Architect(s):	John Custis Lawrence designed the house (for F. K. Hollister)
	Richard A. Cook of CookFox Associates designed 2007 alterations (for Rosenstein)
Landscape architect(s):	Paula Hayes (for Rosenstein)
Builder:	Edward M. Gay (for F. K. Hollister)
	Bulgin & Associates, 2007 alterations (for Rosenstein)

House extant: yes
Historical notes:

The house was built by Dr. Frederick Kellogg Hollister.

In 1939 Mrs. Hollister sold it to Jesse William Sweetser, Sr. [*The East Hampton Star* June 22, 1939, pp. 1 and 5.]

In 1941 Alexander Fraser purchased the house from Sweetser and called it *Wilsheron*. [*The East Hampton Star* October 23, 1941, p. 5.]

In 1960 Frances Ann Cannon (Hersey) Dougherty purchased it from Fraser. [*The East Hampton Star* April 28, 1960, p. 11.]

In 2005 her husband Frazer Lowber Welsh Dougherty sold the house to Barry Rosenstein for $19.2 million. [*The East Hampton Star* June 23, 2005, p. 35.]

[See previous entry for family information.]

In 2017 Rosenstein listed the house for sale. The asking price was $70 million.

In 2019 the 10,425-square-foot, nine-bedroom, thirteen-bath house, a separate two-bedroom caretakers/guest cottage and 1.567 acres was again for sale. The asking price was $52.5 million.

Rosinsky, Harold Jack (1922-2009)
aka Harold Jack Rosinski

Occupation(s):	industrialist - manufacturer of paper and plastic products
	capitalist - commercial real estate developer
Marriage(s):	M/2 – 1971-2009 – Dame Claude Daste (b. 1942)
	- diplomat - member, French consulates, London and Hong Kong
	fashion designer - assistant designer, Christian Dior, Paris, France;
	assistant designer, Lanvin, NYC;
	assistant designer, Givenchy, Paris, France
	Civic Activism: a founder and board chair, International Children's Museum, Palm Beach, FL
Address:	123 Main Street, East Hampton
Name of estate:	
Year of construction:	c. 1895
Style of architecture:	Eclectic
Architect(s):	
Landscape architect(s):	

House extant: yes
Historical notes:

The house was built by Edward de Rose as a guest house on his estate, *Millfield*. It was later owned by Rosinsky.

Dame Calude Daste Rosinsky's father was the personal physician to King Hassan of Morocco.

In 1998 Kenneth Sidney Kuchin purchased the house from Rosinsky for $2.16 million. In 2015 the 8,500-square-foot house, which had been enlarged over the years, was again for sale. The asking price as $11.9 million. In 2017 it was purchased by Robert Downey, Jr.

Ross, Steven Jay (1927-1992)
aka Steven Jay Rechnitz

Occupation(s):	restaurateur - co-owner, Nick & Tony's, East Hampton
	capitalist - founder, Abbey Rent a Car (merged into Kinney Parking Co. which became Kinney National Services);
	president, Kinney National Services (a holding company which acquired Ashley–Famous (talent agency) and Warner Brothers–Seven Arts (film studio); Kinney National Services became Warner Communications);
	CEO, Warner Communications, 1969-1972 (Warner Communications merged with Time Inc. to form TimeWarner);
	CEO, TimeWarner;
	a founder, New York Cosmos, 1971 (soccer team)
	educator - founder, with his wife Courtney, Ross School, East Hampton;
	founder, with his wife Courtney, Ross Global Academy
Marriage(s):	M/1 – 1953-div. 1978 – Carol Rosenthal
	M/2 – 1979-div. 1981 – Amanda Mortimer (b. 1944)
	- capitalist - member, Bloomberg Associates (international consulting firm to help city governments improve city life)
	politician - director, City Planning, NYC; board chair, City Planning Commission, NYC, 2002-2013 (Bloomberg administration); member, New York State Development Corp.; vice-president, Planning and Design of Battery Park City Authority, NYC
	M/3 – 1982-1992 – Courtney Sale
	- educator - founder, with her husband Steven, Ross School, East Hampton; founder, with her husband Steven, Ross Global Academy
	Civic Activism: founder, Ross Institute
Address:	West End Road, East Hampton
Name of estate:	*Cody House*
Year of construction:	
Style of architecture:	Modified Shingle
Architect(s):	
Landscape architect(s):	
House extant: yes	
Historical notes:	

Steven Jay Ross was born in Brooklyn, NY. His father changed the surname to Ross.

Carol Rosenthal Ross was the daughter of Edward Rosenthal of Brooklyn.

Steven Jay and Carol Rosenthal Ross' daughter Toni married Jeffrey H. Salaway. Their son Mark is a music producer.

Amanda Mortimer Ross is the daughter of Stanley Grafton and Barbara Cushing Mortimer, Jr. and the step-daughter of William Samuel Paley of *Kiluna Farm* in North Hills. [*See* Spinzia, *Long Island's Prominent North Shore Families, vol. II –* Paley entry.] Amanda had previously been married to Shirley Carter Burden, Jr. of Water Mill. [*See* Spinzia, *Long Island's Prominent Families in the Town of Southampton* – Burden entry.] Since 1973 she has had a long-standing relationship with television personality Charlie Rose, aka Charles Peter Rose, Jr., of Bellport, NY.

In 2013 Courtney Sale Ross listed the 7,500-square-foot, six-bedroom, six-bath main residence, the estate's three-bedroom guest house and 5.5 acres for sale. The asking price was $75 million.

In 2014 it was purchased by David Lawrence Geffen.

Rosset, Barnet Lee, Jr. (1922-2012)
aka Barney Rosset

Occupation(s):	publisher - owner, Grove Press; owner, *Evergreen Review* writer - *My Life in Publishing and How I Fought Censorship*, 2016

Marriage(s):	M/1 – 1949-div. 1952 – Joan Mitchell (1925-1992)
	  - artist - abstract expressionist
	    Civic Activism: established Joan Mitchell Foundation
	M/2 – 1953-div. 1957 – Hannelore Eckert (aka Lily Eckert)
	  - sales manager, Grove Press
	M/3 – 1965-div 1979 – Cristina Agnini
	M/4 – 1980-div 1991 – Elisabeth Krug (b. 1952)
	M/5 – 2007-2012 – Astrid Myers
	  - publisher - associate publisher, *Evergreen Review*

Address:	400 Hands Creek Road, East Hampton
Name of estate:	
Year of construction:	
Style of architecture:	Eclectic
Architect(s):	
Landscape architect(s):	
House extant: yes	
Historical notes:	

  Barnet Lee Rosset, Jr. was the son of Barnet Lee and Mary Tansey Rosset, Sr. of Chicago, IL.
  Joan Mitchell Rosset was the daughter of Dr. James Herbert and Mrs. Marion Strobel Mitchell.
  Barnet Lee and Hannelore Eckert Rosset, Jr.'s son Peter resides in Cristobal de las Casas, Mexico.
  Barnet Lee and Cristina Agnini Rosset, Jr.'s daughter Tansey resides in Ann Arbor, MI. Their son Beckett resides in Manhattan.
  Barnet Lee and Elizabeth Krug Rosset, Jr.'s daughter Chantal married Charles Hyde and resides in Boston, MA.

Roth, Steven (b. 1941)

Occupation(s):	capitalist - a founder and managing partner, Interstate Properties, 1964 (shopping center firm);
	CEO and chairman of board, Vornado Realty Trust (a conglomerate with major holdings in commercial real estate, Alexander's Inc., Merchandise Mart; Charles E. Smith Commercial Realty, Toys "R" Us; J. C. Penney, and Two Guys)
	merchant - chairman and CEO, Alexander's Inc. (discount department store chain);
	director, Toys "R" Us (children's store chain);
	director, J. C. Penney (department store chain)
Civic Activism:	chairman of board, Intrepid Museum Foundation, NYC;
	trustee, New York University School of Medicine Foundation, NYC;
	trustee, Horace Mann School, NYC;
	trustee, Jewish Theological Seminary of America, NYC;
	trustee, Whitney Museum of American Art, NYC;
	overseer, Tuck School of Business, Dartmouth College, Hanover, NH:
	overseer, Dartmouth Alumni Council;
	overseer, President's Leadership Council, Dartmouth College, Hanover, NH;
	trustee and chairman, finance committee, Dartmouth College, Hanover, NH;
	chairman, National Association of Real Estate Investment Trusts;
	together with his wife Daryl, son Jordan, daughter Amanda, and son-in-law Michael, gifted $15 million to Dartmouth College for the Roth Center for Jewish Life
Marriage(s):	1969 – Daryl Adkins (b. 1944)
	- capitalist - owner, Daryl Roth Productions, NYC – produced over 70 plays on and off Broadway including 7 Pulitzer Prize productions:
	"August Osage County";
	"Proof";
	"Wit";
	"How I Learned to Drive";
	"Three Tall Women";
	"Anna in the Tropics";
	"Clybourne Park";
	owner, DR2 Theater
	entertainers and association professions -
	co-anchor, "New York Theater Review", PBS
	Civic Activism: together with his husband Steven, son Jordan, daughter Amanda, and son-in-law Michael, gifted $15 million to Dartmouth College for the Roth Center for Jewish Life;
	director, Sundance Institute;
	director, LaByrinth Theater Co.;
	director, Albert Einstein College of Medicine, The Bronx, NY;
	director, New York State Council on the Arts;
	honorary trustee, Lincoln Center Theater, NYC

Roth, Steven (cont'd)

Address: 216 Old Montauk Highway, Montauk
Name of estate:
Year of construction: 1982
Style of architecture: Contemporary
Architect(s): Eugene Lawrence Futterman designed
 the house (for Madoff)
 Thierry W. Despont, alterations
 (for Roth)
Landscape architect(s):
House extant: yes
Historical notes:

The 3,000-square-foot house was built by Bernard Lawrence Madoff. In 2009 it was purchased by Roth for $9.41 million.
 He is the son of Fred and Virginia Roth of The Bronx, NY.
 Steven and Daryl Adkins Roth's daughter Amanda married Michael Salzhauer. Their son Jordan, a bachelor, is president of Jujamcyn Theaters, which owns and operates a chain of Broadway theaters.
 Steven was named by *Barron's* as one of the World's Most Respected CEOS three years in a row.
 In 2001 Daryl was chosen as one of the 100 Most Influential Women in Business.
 In 2018 Roth listed the house for sale. The asking price was $21 million.

Roudebush, John Heywood (1871-1925)

Occupation(s): artist - sculptor*

Marriage(s): 1896-1925 – Vallory Odell (1871-1941)

Address: Georgica Road, East Hampton
Name of estate: *Stonybroke*
Year of construction: 1902
Style of architecture: Modified Salt-Box
Architect(s):
Landscape architect(s):
House extant: yes
Historical notes:

The house, originally named *Stonybroke*, was built by John Heywood Roudebush.
 The *Long Island Society Register, 1929* lists Vallory Odell Roudebush as residing at *Stonybroke* in East Hampton.
 At the age of twenty-one John took part in an expedition to explore and map the Himalayas.
 John Heywood and Vallory Odell Roudebush's daughter Roseanne, who later owned *Stonybroke*, married Lawrence Larkin, the son of Adrian Hoffman and Katherine Bache Satterwaite Larkin of *Les Alouettes* in Southampton. [*See* Spinzia, *Long Island's Prominent Families in the Town of Southampton* – Larkin entry.] Their daughter Agnes married Reginald Satterlee Willis, Sr., the son of William Henry and Adele Satterlee Willis of Flushing, NY, and resided in Kings Point. [*See* Spinzia, *Long Island's Prominent North Shore Families, vol. II* – Willis entry.] She later married Thomas Mills Day III, the son of Thomas Mills and Anna Perkins Smith Day, Jr. of Plainfield, NJ, and resided in East Hampton.
 *Roudebush won the silver medal for sculpture at the 1901 Pan-American Exposition. He was a student of Augustus Saint-Gaudens.
 The house is listed on the National Register of Historic Places.

Rounick, Jack A. (1926-2000)

Occupation(s):	industrialist - president, Maro Hosiery Co., Thomasville, NC (hosiery manufacturer and wholesaling firm); president, Rex Knitting Mills merchant - president and CEO, Spartan Industries (soft goods retailer) (merged with E. J. Korvette, discount department store chain); director and vice-president, Martin Lawrence Limited, Van Nuys, CA (chain of art galleries)
Marriage(s):	M/1 – div. – Phyllis Hartmann (1938-2010) - real estate agent M/2 – 1949 – Barbara Taylor M/3 – Lois *[unable to determine maiden name]*
Address:	57 West End Avenue, East Hampton
Name of estate:	
Year of construction:	1926
Style of architecture:	Modified Cotswold
Architect(s):	Roger Bullard designed the house (for E. S. James, Sr.)
Landscape architect(s):	Ellen Biddle Shipman, 1926 *[attributed]*
Builder:	Frank Johnson

House extant: no; destroyed by fire in 2015*

Historical notes:

   The house, originally named *Heather Dune*, was built by Ellery Sedgwick James, Sr. It was later owned by Rounick. He was the son of Max and Bessie Rounick.

   Phyllis Hartmann Rounick was the daughter of Philip and Margaret Frawley Hartmann of Riverdale, NY.

   Jack A. and Lois Rounick's son Christopher married Marianna Olszewski, the daughter of Albert Olszewski of Mount Carmel, PA.

   Lois Rounick subsequently married Andre Nasser of NY.

   In 1993 Rounick sold the house to Dr. Gary Feldstein. In 1998 Peter Morton purchased the house from Feldstein.

*The house was owned by Morton at the time of the fire. It started when construction workers were attempting to repair a chimney's flashing with a welding torch in forty-mile-per-hour winds.

Rowe, John Jay, Jr. (1918-2005)

Occupation(s):	industrialist - Procter and Gamble, Cincinnati, OH
Marriage(s):	1941-2005 – Diana Victoria Cutler (1919-2013)
Address:	36 Bendigo Road, Amagansett
Name of estate:	*Devon*
Year of construction:	1978
Style of architecture:	
Architect(s):	
Landscape architect(s):	

House extant: yes

Historical notes:

   The house was built by John Jay Rowe. [*The East Hampton Star* September 15, 2005, p. 2.]

   The Blue Book of The Hamptons, 1979 lists John Jay and Diana Cutler Rowe, Jr. as residing on Bendigo Road, Amagansett.

   He was the son of John Jay and Grace Sherlock Probasco Rowe, Sr.

   Diana Victoria Cutler Rowe was the daughter of George Chalmers and Susan Margaret Stackpole Cutler.

   John Jay and Diana Victoria Cutler Rowe, Jr.'s daughter Sandra married Francis Henry Low Beer and resided in Canada. Their daughter Susan married Vere Egerton Warburton Gaynor, the son of Dr. William Charles Thomas and Mrs. Rosamund Warburton Gaynor of *Dragon Hall* in Southampton and the grandson of Rosamund Lancaster [Warburton] Vanderbilt, of *Eagles Nest* in Centerport, and her former husband Barclay H. Warburton, Jr. of Philadelphia, PA. [*See* Spinzia, *Long Island's Prominent Families in the Town of Southampton* – Gaynor entry – and *Long Island's Prominent North Shore Families, vol. II* – Vanderbilt entry.] Their daughter Grace married Harold De Waltoff II. Their daughter Priscilla did not marry. Their son John Jay Rowe III, who later owned the house, married Susan Saunders. Their daughter Wendy died in childhood.

[See other Rowe entries for additional family information.]

Rowe, John Jay, Sr. (1885-1965)

Occupation(s):	financier - vice-president, First National Bank of Cincinnati, 1918; president, First National Bank of Cincinnati, 1929-1934; president, Fifth Third Union Trust, Cincinnati, OH, 1934-1955; chairman of board, Fifth Third Union Trust, Cincinnati, 1955-1957; director, Federal Reserve Bank of Cleveland; director, Cincinnati Equitable Insurance Co.
	industrialist - director, Baldwin–Lima–Hamilton Corp.; director, Crosley Corp.; director, West Virginia Coal & Coke Corp.; director, Globe–Wernicke Co.; director, Eagle–Picker Lead Co.; director, Procter and Gamble Co., Cincinnati, OH; director, United States Printing & Lithography Co.; director, Fox Paper Co.; director, Cincinnati Industries, Inc.
	capitalist - director, Cincinnati Gas & Electric Co.
Civic Activism:	a founder and trustee, Cincinnati Institute of Fine Arts; a found and trustee, Cincinnati Country Day School; vice-chairman of board, University of Cincinnati, Cincinnati, OH; trustee, Cincinnati Symphony Orchestra; trustee, Children's Convalescent Hospital; member, finance committee, Cincinnati Orphan Asylum; chairman, Hamilton County Chapter of the Red Cross; member, executive committee, Hamilton County Council; member, executive committee, Boy Scouts of America; president, Cincinnati Clearing House Association; member, Liberty Loan Central Committee during World War I; chairman of board Third Ohio Area War Finance Committee during World War II
Marriage(s):	1909-1965 – Grace Sherlock Probasco (1888-1975)
Address:	Ocean View Lane, Amagansett
Name of estate:	*Devon*
Year of construction:	
Style of architecture:	
Architect(s):	
Landscape architect(s):	
House extant: unconfirmed	
Historical notes:	

The Blue Book of The Hamptons, 1958 lists John Jay and Grace Probasco Rowe, Sr. as residing at *Devon* on Ocean View Lane, Amagansett.

He was the son of William Stanhope and Margaret Anna Richardson Rowe, Sr. of Amagansett.

Grace Sherlock Probasco Rowe was the daughter of Henry and Grace Sherlock Probasco of Cincinnati, OH.

John Jay and Grace Sherlock Probasco Rowe, Sr.'s daughter Grace married Charles Mathews Mackall. Their daughter Margaret married Henry Houston Chatfield, the son of William Hayden Chatfield of Cincinnati, OH, and resided in Amagansett. Their son William Stanhope Rowe III married Martha Phyllis Whitney, the daughter of George and Martha Beatrix Bacon Whitney, Sr. of *Home Acres* in Old Westbury. [*See* Spinzia, *Long Island's Prominent North Shore Families, vol. II* – Whitney entry.] Their son John Jay Rowe, Jr. married Diana Victoria Cutler and resided in Amagansett.

[See other Rowe entries for additional family information.]

Rowe, William Stanhope, Sr. (1857-1941)

Occupation(s):	financier - president, First National Bank of Cincinnati, 1902-1929; director, Federal Reserve Bank of Cleveland
	industrialist - director, Procter & Gamble Co., Cincinnati, OH; director, The Fox Paper Co.
	capitalist - a founder, Gardiner Bay Co. (real estate holding company)
Civic Activism:	member, Federal Advisory Council
	a founder, Devon Yacht Club, Amagansett
Marriage(s):	1879-1941 – Margaret Anna Richardson (1859-1942)
	- writer - *Living With Our Flowers Four Seasons of the Year*, 1932
Address:	Craneberry Hole Road, Amagansett
Name of estate:	
Year of construction:	c. 1910
Style of architecture:	Mediterranean Villa
Architect(s):	Tietig and Lee designed the house (for W. S. Rowe, Sr.)
Landscape architect(s):	
House extant: yes	
Historical notes:	

The house was built by William Stanhope Rowe, Sr.
He was the son of Stanhope Sanderson and Frances Mary Thomas Rowe of Cincinnati, OH.
Margaret Anna Richardson Rowe was the daughter of James and Mary E. Robinson Richardson of Ohio.
William Stanhope and Margaret Anna Richardson Rowe Sr.'s son William Stanhope Rowe, Jr. died in 1896 at the age of fifteen. Their son Basil died in 1906 at the age of twenty-three. Their daughter Margaret married Harold Willis Nichols, Sr., the son of James and Elizabeth March Nichols of Cincinnati, OH, and resided at *Crow's Nest* in East Hampton. Their daughter Charlotte, who resided in East Hampton, married Edward Mailler Radway, the son of John Symonds and Mary Anna Mailler Radway of Quogue. [*See* Spinzia, *Long Island's Prominent Families in the Town of Southampton* – Radway entry.] Charlotte later married Chase Henchman Davis.
Their son William Wallace Rowe, Sr. married Elizabeth Foster Woodin and resided in East Hampton. Their son John Jay Rowe, Sr. married Grace Sherlock Probasco and resided at *Devon* in Amagansett.
[See other Rowe entries for additional family information.]

Rowe, William Wallace, Sr. (1899-1978)

Occupation(s):	industrialist - president, Cincinnati Industries, Inc.;
	inventor - creping corrugated paper (6 patents)
Marriage(s):	1923-1978 – Elizabeth Foster Woodin (1901-1998)
Address:	*[unable to determine street address]*, East Hampton
Name of estate:	
Year of construction:	
Style of architecture:	
Architect(s):	
Landscape architect(s):	
House extant: unconfirmed	
Historical notes:	

The *Long Island Society Register, 1929* lists William Wallace and Elizabeth F. Wooden Rowe [Sr.] as residing in East Hampton.
He was the son of William Stanhope and Margaret Anna Richardson Rowe, Sr. of Cincinnati, OH, and Amagansett.
Elizabeth Foster Woodin Rowe was the daughter of William Hartman and Annie Jessup Woodin, Sr. of *Dune House* in East Hampton. Elizabeth's sister Mary, who married Charles Miner, Sr., the son of William P. Miner of Wilkes–Barre, PA, resided in East Hampton. Her brother William Hartman Woodin, Jr. married Carolyn Hyde.
William Wallace and Elizabeth Foster Woodin Rowe, Sr.'s son William Woodin Rowe married Eleanor Christine Dombrowski, the daughter of Alfred Francis and Janina Rojcewicz Dombrowski. Their son William Wallace Rowe II married Emmy Loraine Pollack; Marian Adeline Sanzone; and, subsequently, Jessica Campbell.
[See other Rowe entries for additional family information.]

Rubin, Samuel (1901-1978)

Occupation(s):	industrialist - founder and president, Fabergé (cosmetics firm)
Civic Activism:	founder, Samuel Rubin Foundation;
	chairman of board, American Fund for Israel Institutions;
	chairman of board, Fordham Hospital, The Bronx;
	a founder, New York University–Belleview Medical Center, NYC;
	chairman of board, American Symphony;
	founder, Institute for Policy Studies;
	founder, Academy of Music, Jerusalem, Israel;
	president, International Peace Bureau;
	president, The Hague Appeal for Peace;
	established scholarship fund for Amagansett High School students;
	established chair of anthropology, Brandeis University, Waltham, MA

Marriage(s): M/1 – div. – Vera D. *[unable to determine maiden name]* (1911-1985)
- scientist - anthropologist;
director, Research Institute for the Study of Man
Civic Activism: president, Society for Applied Anthropology;
director, American Orthopsychiatric Association
M/2 – Hazel *[unable to determine maiden name]*

Address:	Town Lane, Amagansett
Name of estate:	*Hilly Close*
Year of construction:	1953
Style of architecture:	Modern
Architect(s):	Alfred A. Scheffer designed the house (for Rubin)

Landscape architect(s):
House extant: yes
Historical notes:

    The main residence, which was originally named *Hilly Close*, was built by Samuel Rubin. He also had an 1830 windmill converted into a guest/caretakers' cottage.
    Born in Bialystok, Russia, he was the son of Julius and Lena Rubin with whom he immigrated to New York in 1905.
    Vera D. Rubin was born in Moscow, Russia.
    Samuel and Vera D. Rubin's daughter Cora married Peter Weiss, the son of Emil Weiss of NYC. Their son Reed married Jane Gregory, the daughter of Philip Henry Gregory, and resides in Manhattan.
    In 1967 Deborah Light purchased the estate from Rubin and renamed it *Quail Hill.*
    In 1989 Robert and Richard Schwagerl purchased it from Light. Robert chose to reside in the main residence while his brother Richard chose the windmill as his residence.
    In 2017 the 5,500 square-foot house, detached three-car garage, 650-square-foot guest/caretaker's cottage, and 5.3 acres were for sale. The asking prices was $7.595 million.

Rumbough, Stanley Hutton (b. 1947)

Occupation(s):	financier - director, E. F. Hutton Group, Inc. (later, E. F. Hutton America, Inc., Springfield, OH (internet financial software and services firm);
	chairman of board, E. F. Hutton America, Inc., Springfield, OH;
	chairman of board, E. F. Hutton Financial Corp, NYC (subsidiary of E. F. Hutton Group, NYC)
Civic Activism:	trustee, New York Mission Society, NYC
Marriage(s):	1987 – Leah Kathleen Jensen
	- model
Address:	Highway Behind the Pond, East Hampton
Name of estate:	
Year of construction:	
Style of architecture:	
Architect(s):	
Landscape architect(s):	
House extant: unconfirmed	
Historical notes:	

The Blue Book of The Hamptons, 1997 lists Stanley H. and Leah Kathleen Jensen Rumbough as residing on Highway Behind the Pond, East Hampton.

He is the son of Stanley Maddox and Nedenia Marjorie Hutton Rumbough, Jr. of Old Brookville and East Hampton. [*See* Spinzia, *Long Island's Prominent North Shore Families, vol. II* – Rumbough entry.]

Leah Kathleen Rumbough is the daughter of Dale Keith and Barbara Ann Basten Jensen.

Rumbough, Stanley Maddox, Jr. (1920-2017)

Occupation(s):	a founder or chief executive officer of more than forty companies
	industrialist - president, White Metal Manufacturing Co., Hoboken, NJ;
	president, Metal Container Corp.;
	co-founder, Trinidad Flour Mills;
	co-founder and director, Jamaica Flour Mills;
	president, American Totalistor, Baltimore MD;
	director, Dart Industries (conglomerate)
	capitalist - co-founder and chairman of board, Electric Engineering Ltd.;
	vice-president, Willis Air Service, Teterboro, NJ;
	director, Telemedia, Inc.;
	director, New York World's Fair Corp., 1961-1970;
	chairman of board, Wallace Clark & Co. (management consulting firm
	financier - director, ABT Family of Funds, Inc.
	statesman - assistant to Secretary of Commerce in the Eisenhower administration;
	White House special assistant in charge of executing board liaison (Eisenhower administration)
Civic Activism:	director, National Conference on Citizenship;
	trustee, Library for Presidential Papers;
	trustee, American Health Association;
	chairman of board and CEO, Palm Beach Association;
	a founder, Citizens for Eisenhower;
	director, Planned Parenthood Foundation of America;
	president, Planned Parenthood of Palm Beach area;
	chairman, United States Committee for the United Nations;
	director, Foreign Policy Association;
	director, Population Resource Center;
	trustee, Kravis Center for the Performing Arts, West Palm Beach, FL;
	a founder and director, Young Presidents Organization;
	a founder and director, Washington Tennis Patrons Foundation;
	chairman of board, Raymond J. Kunkel Foundation;
	director, United States Tennis Association Davis Cup Committee;
	trustee, International House, NYC

Rumbough, Stanley Maddox, Jr. (cont'd)

Marriage(s):	M/1 – 1946-div. 1966 – Nedenia Marjorie Hutton (1923-2017)

             (aka Dina Merrill)
- financier - director, E. F. Hutton and Co. (investment banking firm);
chair, compensation and benefits committee, and
  director, Lehman Brothers (investment banking firm)
capitalist - partner, Pavilion Communications (later, RKO Pictures);
board vice-chair, RKO Pictures;
entertainers and associated professions - actress
industrialist - president, Amaranthe (cosmetic manufacturer)
Civic Activism: a founder and trustee, Eugene O'Neill Theater Center,
  NYC;
trustee, John F. Kennedy Center for the Performing
  Arts, Washington, DC;
vice-president, New York City Mission Society, NYC;
a founder, Juvenile Diabetes Foundation;
vice-chair, Republican Pro-Choice Coalition;
trustee, Population Resource Council;
trustee, Paley Center for Media, NYC;
director, Project Orbis (teaches eye care & surgical
  techniques worldwide);
co-founder, with husband Ted, The Story Project;
co-founder, with husband Ted, Hartley–Merrill
  International Screenwriting Award

M/2 – 1967-div. 1990 – Margaretha Wagstrom
- professional photographer -
  free-lance portrait and commercial photographer

M/3 – 1990-2017 – Janne Herlow
- Civic Activism: director, Animal Rescue League, Palm Beach, FL

Address:	Highway Behind the Pond, East Hampton
Name of estate:	
Year of construction:	1960
Style of architecture:	Beach Cottage
Architect(s):	Alexander McIlvaine designed the house (for Rumbough)
Landscape architect(s):	
House extant:	yes
Historical notes:	

 The house was built by Stanley Maddox Rumbough, Jr. [*The East Hampton Star* December 4, 1958, p. 1.]

 The Blue Book of The Hamptons, 1965 lists Stanley M. and Nedenia M. Hutton Rumbough, Jr. as residing on Highway Behind the Pond, East Hampton.

 He is the son of Stanley and Elizabeth Morse Colgate Rumbough, Sr., who resided at *Elston Oaks* in Lloyd Harbor. [*See* Spinzia, *Long Island's Prominent North Shore Families, vol. II* – Rumbough entry.] His sister Elizabeth married Duncan Van Norden and resided in Manhattan.

 Nedenia Marjorie Hutton Rumbough was the daughter of Edward Francis and Marjorie Merriweather Post Hutton who resided at *Hillwood* in Brookville. [*See* Spinzia, *Long Island's Prominent North Shore Families, vol. I* – Hutton entry.] She later married the actor Cliff Robertson, who resided in Water Mill and East Hampton, and, subsequently, Theodore Ringwalt Hartley with whom she also resided in East Hampton. [*See* Spinzia, *Long Island's Prominent Families in the Town of Southampton* – Robertson entry.]

 Stanley Maddox and Nedenia Marjorie Hutton Rumbough, Jr.'s twenty-three-year-old son David drowned in a boating mishap. Their daughter Nedenia married Charles Stiffer Craig of Birmingham, MI, and, later, Jan Roosenburg. Their son Stanley Hutton Rumbough married Leah Kathleen Jensen and resides in East Hampton.

 The Blue Book of The Hamptons, 1979 lists Stanley M. and Margaretha Wagstrom Rumbough, Jr. as residing on Egypt Close, East Hampton. By 1987 they had relocated to 44 Fithian Lane, East Hampton.

 She was the daughter of Nils Erik Wagstrom of Ornskoldsvik, Sweden. Margaretha had previously been married to ____ Srybnik.

 The Blue Book of The Hamptons, 2008 lists Stanley M. and Janna [sic] Herlow Rumbough, Jr. as residing on Behind the Pond, East Hampton.

 She had previously been married to Carl E. Janson.

 [For information on the Rumboughs' Old Brookville residence, see Spinzia, *Long Island's Prominent North Shore Families, vol. II* – Rumbough entry.]

Ruxton, Philip (1866-1945)

Occupation(s):	industrialist - founder, president, and treasurer, Philip Ruxton, Inc. (later, Interchemical Corp.) (manufacturer of printing ink); director, Interchemical Corp.
	capitalist - treasurer, A. J. Sheldon Co.
Civic Activism:	president, Ink Association of America
Marriage(s):	1891-1945 – Louise Virginia DeWitt (1868-1948)
Address:	Apaquogue Road, East Hampton
Name of estate:	*Cairnhill*
Year of construction:	
Style of architecture:	Colonial Revival
Architect(s):	
Landscape architect(s):	Ellen Biddle Shipman (for Ruxton)

House extant: unconfirmed
Historical notes:

The *Social Directory of Southampton, Long Island, 1931* lists Philip and Louise DeWitt Ruxton as residing at *Cairnhill* on Apaquogue Road, East Hampton.

He was the son of William Brown and Mary Anna Howell Ruxton of Staten Island, NY, and a direct descendant of Governor Bradford, the first governor of Plymouth Colony.

Louise Virginia DeWitt Ruxton was the daughter of Thomas T. and Louise Ginnel DeWitt.

Philip and Louise Virginia DeWitt Ruxton's daughter Louise married Alexander Wallace Chauncey and resided at *Our Place* in East Hampton. Their daughter Frances married William Christian Heppenheimer, Jr. with whom she resided in Manhattan and Newport, RI, and, later, Gerald G. Philbin, the son of Judge Eugene A. Philbin.

In 1951 the house was purchased by Stanley Osserman who called it *The Gatehouse*. [*The East Hampton Star* June 21, 1951, p. 6.]

Ryan, Bruce Edgar (1916-1944)

Occupation(s):	advertising executive - president, Ruthrauff and Ryan, Inc., NYC
Marriage(s):	1938-1944 – Frances Louise Weeks
Address:	Lily Pond Lane, East Hampton
Name of estate:	
Year of construction:	
Style of architecture:	
Architect(s):	
Landscape architect(s):	

House extant: unconfirmed
Historical notes:

The *Social Register Summer, 1946* lists Frances L. Weeks Ryan as residing on Lily Pond Lane, East Hampton.

She was the daughter of John Lafayette and Margaret Louise Clarbough Weeks of East Hampton. Frances had previously been married to David Balderston Stone, the son of Robert E. Stone of Brookline, MA. After Bruce's death, she married Benjamin Carlton Betner, Jr. which whom she resided in East Hampton.

Bruce Edgar Ryan was the son of Frederick Behrens and Elizabeth Cady Ryan, Sr. of East Hampton. He was killed in 1944 when his B-17 bomber crashed.

Bruce Edgar and Frances Louise Weeks Ryan's daughter Dionne married Henry Lohmann Murray, the son of Arthur Matthew Murray of Lawrence. Their daughter Mary married Richard Wallace Smith, Jr. of East Hampton.

[See following entry for additional family information.]

Ryan, Frederick Behrens, Sr. (1883-1955)

Occupation(s):	advertising executive - a founder and chairman, Ruthrauff and Ryan, NYC*

Marriage(s):	M/1 – 1904-1954 – Elizabeth Cady (1886-1954)
	   - Civic Activism: president, Women's Metropolitan Golf Association;
	   a founder and president, Women's New Jersey Golf Association;
	   a founder and president, Women's New Jersey Squash and Racquets Association
	M/2 – 1955-1955 – Lucy Layfield (1900-1997)

Address:	Lily Pond Road, East Hampton
Name of estate:	*East of 69*
Year of construction:	1920
Style of architecture:	Modified Shingle
Architect(s):	John Custis Lawrence designed the house (for Coppell) Robert Tappin, 1928 alterations (for Coppell)
Landscape architect(s):	
Builder:	Edward M. Gay
House extant:	unconfirmed
Historical notes:	

The house, originally named *White-Cottage-By-the-Sea*, was built by Herbert Coppell. In 1933 it was purchased by Ryan who renamed it *East of 69*. [*The East Hampton Star* October 24, 1935, p. 21.]

The *Social Register Summer, 1937* lists Frederick Behrens and Elizabeth Cady Ryan [Sr.] as residing at *East of 69* in East Hampton.

He was the son of Dr. Charles Edgar and Mrs. Florence Behrens Ryan of NYC.

Elizabeth Cady Ryan was the daughter of Dr. Edward Everett Cady.

Frederick Behrens and Elizabeth Cady Ryan, Sr.'s son Quincy married Barbara Strong Baxter and resided in Short Hills, NJ. Their son Bruce married Frances Weeks and resided in East Hampton. Their son Frederick Behrens Ryan, Jr. [aka Barry and F. Barry Ryan] married Nancy Baldwin of Boston and resided in Short Hills, NJ.

Lucy Layfield Ryan was the daughter of W. D. Layfield of Columbus, GA. She had previously been married to ____ Laird.

[See previous entry for additional family information.]

*Ruthrauff and Ryan, which had six hundred and fifty employees and thirteen worldwide offices, was one of the largest advertising agencies in the world.

The house, which is listed on The National Register of Historic Places, was later owned by Elie Hirschfeld who completely renovated the house in 2002.

In 2011 it was rented to President Clinton.

In 2015 Hirschfeld listed the 10,000-square-foot, eight-bedroom, nine-full-bath and two-half-bath house for sale. The asking price was $32.5 million.

Ryan, Richard Nelson, Jr. (1946-2010)

Occupation(s):	financier - member, Carlisle and Jacqueline
Civic Activism:	bequeathed just over one million dollars to Ladies Village Improvement Society, East Hampton
Marriage(s):	
Address:	62 David's Lane, East Hampton
Name of estate:	
Year of construction:	1978
Style of architecture:	Ranch
Architect(s):	
Landscape architect(s):	
House extant: yes	
Historical notes:	

Richard Nelson Ryan, Jr. was the son of Richard Nelson and Hope Bacon Ryan, Sr. and the great-grandson of Thomas Fortune Ryan. After his father's death, Richard's mother married William Clifford Klenk and also resided in East Hampton.

Richard's grandfather Elliot Cowdin Bacon, Sr. married Hope Norman (later, Gardner) and resided in Old Westbury. [*See* Spinzia, *Long Island's Prominent North Shore Families, vol. I* – Bacon and Gardner entries.]. His sister Hope married William E. Farnell, Jr.; Kim Davis Gaynor, the son of Dr. William C. T. Gaynor of Southampton; and, later, ____ Garrett. She resided in Seattle, WA, and East Hampton. His sister Alix married Roy Rainey Plum, the son of Matthias Plum of Chatham, MA.

Salembier, Harold Paul (1908-1987)

Occupation(s):	industrialist - vice-president, Burlington Mills Ribbon Corp.; Daniel F. Sheehy Co. & Hosiery Industries merchant - president, Salembier & Co. (sales agent for mass marketing organizations)
Marriage(s):	M/1 – 1942-1969 – Mary Woodward Lathrop (d. 1969) M/2 – 1973-1987 – Anita Van Lennep Higgins (b. 1921)
Address:	Highway Behind the Pond, East Hampton
Name of estate:	*Dormie Dune*
Year of construction:	1949
Style of architecture:	
Architect(s):	
Landscape architect(s):	
House extant: unconfirmed	
Historical notes:	

The house, originally named *Dormie Dune*, was built by Harold Paul Salembier. [*The East Hampton Star* October 21, 1948, p.1, and May 26, 1949, p. 7.]

The Blue Book of The Hamptons, 1958 lists Harold P. and Mary Woodward Lathrop Salembier as residing at *Dormie Dune* on Highway Behind the Pond, East Hampton.

He was the son of Paul Albert and Florence Helen Richolson Salembier of *Seacroft* in East Hampton.

Mary Woodward Lathrop Salembier was the daughter of Kirke and Beatrice Elizabeth Proudlock Lathrop of Detroit, MI.

Harold Paul and Mary Woodward Lathrop Salembier's son Paul married Sybil Calhoun, the daughter of Joseph Clay Calhoun of New Orleans, LA. Their son Stephen married Magee Hickey, the daughter of Lawrence Hickey of New York.

Anita Van Lennep Higgins Salembier was the daughter of Charles Houchin and Claire Trumbull Van Lennep Higgins. Anita had previously been married to Charles Coe Townsend of Oyster Bay.

By 2003 she had relocated to 95 Egypt Lane, East Hampton.

[See following entry for additional family information.]

Salembier, Paul Albert (1874-1936)

Occupation(s):	capitalist - treasurer, Salembier & Villate, NYC (raw silk importers); director, United States Testing Co.
	financier - director, New Netherlands Bank of New York
Civic Activism:	member, board of admissions, New York Commodity Exchange; member, nominating committee, Maidstone Club, East Hampton
Marriage(s):	1897-1936 – Florence Helen Richolson (1875-1944)
Address:	Lily Pond Lane, East Hampton
Name of estate:	*Seacroft*
Year of construction:	1924
Style of architecture:	Shingle Cottage
Architect(s):	Roger Bullard designed the house (for P. A. Salembier)
	Grosvenor Atterbury, 1927 alterations (for P. A. Salembier)
Landscape architect(s):	
Builder:	Edward M. Gay
House extant: yes	
Historical notes:	

The house, originally named *Seacroft*, was built by Paul Albert Salembier.

The *Long Island Society Register, 1929* lists Paul A. and Floy [sic] Richolson Salembier as residing on Lily Pond Lane in East Hampton. The *Social Register Summer, 1937* lists *Seacroft* as the name of their residence.

He was the son of Richard Evrard and Marie Anne Marchal Salembier.

Florence Richolson Salembier was the daughter of Samuel L. and Marietta Mehan Richolson.

Paul Albert and Florence Richolson Salembier's daughter Florence married William Joseph Devine and resided at *Swanscot* in East Hampton. Their son Harold, who married Mary Woodward Lathrop and, later, Anita Higgins, resided at *Dormie Dune* in East Hampton.

[See previous entry for additional family information.]

In 1943 the house was purchased from Mrs. Salembier by Mrs. Charles Miner, Sr. [*The East Hampton Star* July 22, 1943, p. 5.]

Saltzman, Renny B. (1930-2000)

Occupation(s):	interior designer - founder and president, Renny B. Saltzman, Inc., NYC
Civic Activism:	benefactor, Robin Hood Foundation (established to alleviate poverty in NYC); trustee, Carlyle House, Inc.
Marriage(s):	1960-2000 – Ellin Jane Sadowsky (b. 1937)
	- journalist - fashion editor, *Glamour* magazine
	merchant - vice-president, Saks Fifth Avenue; vice-president and fashion director, R. H. Macy
Address:	20 Spaeth Lane, East Hampton
Name of estate:	
Year of construction:	1970
Style of architecture:	Modern
Architect(s):	Richard Meier designed the house (for Saltzman)
Landscape architect(s):	
House extant: yes	
Historical notes:	

The house, which is a romanticized adaptation of LaCorbusier's *Villa Savoi* in Poissy, France, was built by Renny B. Saltzman. He was the son of Jacob and Edna Saltzman of Brooklyn, NY.

Ellin Jane Sadowskly Saltzman is the daughter of David R. Sadowsky.

Renny B. and Ellin Jane Sadowsky Saltzman's daughter Elizabeth married Glenn Russell Dubin. Their son David married Elizabeth Doyle.

Sandelman, Jonathan Everett (b. 1958)

Occupation(s):	attorney
	financier - president, securities unit, Bank America Corp.; head, equity-derivatives unit, Salomon Brothers; founder and CEO, Sandelman Partners (hedge fund); president and director, NMS Services Inc.; president and director, NMS Services (Cayman) Inc.; president and director, BAC Services, Inc.; CEO, Mercer Park, LP; CEO, Main Place Funding, LLC
	capitalist - advisory board, Northern Star Mining Corp.
Civic Activism:	director, Film Society of Lincoln Center, Inc., NYC; director, Whitney Museum of American Art, NYC; a founder, Corrie and Jonathan Sandelman Foundation, NYC
Marriage(s):	1985 – Corrie Jill Mark (b. 1958)
	- Civic Activism: a founder, Corrie and Jonathan Sandleman Foundation, NYC
Address:	88 Lily Pond Lane, East Hampton
Name of estate:	
Year of construction:	1905
Style of architecture:	Neo-Italian Renaissance
Architect(s):	Albro and Lindeberg designed the house (for Cockcroft)

Landscape architect(s):
House extant: no; destroyed by fire in 2008
Historical notes:

   The house, originally named *Little Burlees*, was built by Edward Truesdell Cockcroft, Sr. In 1912 it was purchased by Tyler Morse. [*The East Hampton Star* August 16, 1912, p. 5.] [For information on Morse's Old Westbury estate, *see* Spinzia, *Long Island's Prominent North Shore Families, vol. I* – Morse entry.]
   The house was owned from 1936 to 1994 by Franklin Woolman d'Olier, Jr. In 1994 it was purchased by Sandelman for $2.15 million.
   He is the son of Robert M. and Barbara Rosenberg Sandelman of Forest Hills, NY.
   Sandelman owned the house when it was destroyed by fire.

Sanger, Henry (1823-1886)

Occupation (s):	financier - trustee, Brooklyn Trust Co.;
	trustee, Hamilton Avenue Bank, Brooklyn
	capitalist - importer
Civic Activism:	director, Academy of Music, Brooklyn
Marriage(s):	1851-1888 – Mary E. Requa (1835-1910)
Address:	De Forest Road, Montauk
Name of estate:	
Year of construction:	1883
Style of architecture:	Beach Cottage
Architect(s):	McKim, Mead & White designed the house
	Francis Fleetwood, c. 1994 alterations (for Dennis)
Landscape architect(s):	Frederic Law Olmstead designed the site plan

House extant: yes
Historical notes:

The house is one of the Montauk Association's "Seven Sisters." It was owned by Henry Sanger who called it *Moorland*.

He was the son of The Reverend Zedekiah and Mrs. Maria Kissam Sanger.

Mary E. Requa Sanger was the daughter of James and Mary Kelly Requa.

Henry and Mary E. Requa Sanger's daughter Lilian did not marry. Their son William Carey Sanger, Sr., who was Assistant Secretary of War in the McKinley and Theodore Roosevelt administrations, married Mary Ethel Cleveland Dodge, the daughter of W. E. Dodge of New York. Their daughter Mary married Frank Lyman.

The house was later owned by Carl Graham Fisher, Sr., Frank and Helen Hourtel and, then, by Thomas Dennis.

Satterlee, Dr. Francis Le Roy, Jr. (1881-1935)

Occupation (s):	physician - radiologist, Flushing Hospital, Flushing, NY;
	radiologist, Greenport Hospital, Greenport, NY
	inventor - experiments with x-Ray photographs*;
	co-inventor, with Louis Kolozsy, of a system that corrected short wave fading, cut down static, allowed radio waves to pass through steel
Marriage(s):	1901-1935 – Ebba Louise Peterson (1874-1955)
Address:	*[unable to determine street address]*, Montauk
Name of estate:	*House of Four Winds*
Year of construction:	
Style of architecture:	
Architect(s):	
Landscape architect(s):	

House extant: unconfirmed
Historical notes:

The *Long Island Society Register, 1929* lists Francis Le Roy and Ebba L. Peterson Satterlee [Jr.] as residing in Montauk. *The Brooklyn Daily Eagle* December 4, 1935, p. 15, lists the name of their residence as *House of Four Winds*.

He was the son of Dr. Francis Le Roy and Mrs. Laura Suydam Satterlee, Sr. of Manhattan. His brother Henry Suydam Satterlee, Sr., who resided in Cove Neck married Ethel Alice Whitney and, later, Cecily I. Sheldon. [*See* Spinzia, *Long Island's Prominent North Shore Families, vol. II* – Satterlee entry.]

While a junior in college Francis and Ebba, who was an orphan from Sweden, were secretly married.

Francis Le Roy and Ebba L. Peterson Satterlee, Jr.'s daughter Helen married Cecil Carlton Parker, the son of Cecil E. Parker of Hyde Park, NY, and resided at *Postscript* in East Hampton.

*Satterlee was the first American to take an x-Ray photograph. As a result of his experiments in radiology, Satterlee underwent forty-four operation for burns and the amputation of his fingers.

Satterthwaite, James Sheafe, Sr. (1840-1884)

Occupation(s):	financier - Catlin and Satterthwaite (marine insurance firm)
Marriage(s):	1865-1884 – Jane Lawrence Buckley (1846-1892)
Address:	25 Ocean Avenue, East Hampton
Name of estate:	
Year of construction:	1874
Style of architecture:	Stick-style with Chalet elements
Architect(s):	Briggs and Corman designed the house (for J. S. Satterthwaite, Sr.)
	McKim, Mead & White, 1893-1894 alterations which transformed the house into Georgian Revival style *[attributed]* (for C. G. Thompson)
	John Custis Lawrence, 1910 alterations to servants' quarters
Landscape architect(s):	
Builder:	R. V. Breece (for J. S. Satterthwaite, Sr.)
	George A. Eldredge, 1893-1894 alterations (for C. G. Thompson)

House extant: yes
Historical notes:

The house was built by James Sheafe Satterthwaite, Sr.
He was the son of Thomas Wilkinson and Ann Fisher Sheafe Satterthwaite.
Jane Lawrence Buckley Satterthwaite was the daughter of Phineas Henry and Julia Lawrence Buckley.
James Sheafe and Jane Lawrence Buckley Satterthwaite, Sr.'s daughter Katherine married Adrian Hoffman Larkin and resided at *Green Frog* in East Hampton and, later, at *Les Alouettes* in Southampton. [*See* Spinzia, *Long Island's Prominent Families in the Town of Southampton* – Larkin entry.] Their daughter Julia married Ernest Rollin Tilton. Their daughter Anne married the architect Peter William Ludvig Strom. Their son James Sheafe Satterthwaite, Jr. married Lillie Marden, the daughter of Francis Alexander Marden of Nutley, NJ, and resided in Nutley.
In 1893 the house was purchased by its second owner Charles Griswold Thompson. The Thompson family donated the house to the New York Historical Society, NYC. The house was later owned by Howard Brush Dean, Jr. [Jeannette Edwards Rattray. *History of East Hampton: Including Genealogies of Early Families.* (East Hampton, NY: East Hampton Star Press, 1953), p. 438.] By 1973 the Deans had relocated to Hook Pond Lane, East Hampton.

Scheerer, Joseph Durand, Jr. (1926-2019)

Occupation(s):	capitalist - president, Newark Milk and Cream Co.
	financier - stockbroker, Spencer Trask and Co.
Civic Activism:	volunteer, Meals on Wheels
Marriage(s):	1959-2019 – Nancy Pardue
Address:	5 Alexis Court, Amagansett
Name of estate:	
Year of construction:	
Style of architecture:	
Architect(s):	
Landscape architect(s):	

House extant: unconfirmed
Historical notes:

He was the son of Joseph Durand and Jane Bond Ingersoll Scheerer, Sr. of East Hampton.
Nancy Pardue Scheerer is the daughter of The Reverend Austin Pardue.
Joseph Durand and Nancy Pardue Scheerer, Jr.'s son Daniel married Nancy Jane Lavin, the daughter of Robert Carson Lavin.
In 2011 the house sold for $2 million.

Scheerer, Joseph Durand, Sr. (1900-1978)

Occupation(s):	capitalist - president, Alderney Dairy Co., Newark, NJ; president, Newark Milk and Cream Co.; director, Public Service Electric & Gas Co.
	financier - director, American Insurance Co.
Civic Activism:	vice-president, Treat Council of Boy Scouts of America
Marriage(s):	M/1 – 1922-1966 – Jane Bond Ingersoll (d. 1966)
	- president, Junior League of The Oranges, NJ
	M/2 – Nancy Holdsworth (d. 1988)
	- a fund raiser, Beauport Museum, Gloucester, MA
Address:	15 West End Avenue, East Hampton
Name of estate:	
Year of construction:	1927-1928
Style of architecture:	Shingle
Architect(s):	John Custis Lawrence designed the house (for Lardner)
Landscape architect(s):	
Builder:	Edward M. Gay
House extant: yes	
Historical notes:	

The house, originally named *Iona Dune / The Mange*, was built by Ringgold Wilmer Lardner, Sr. In 1946 Scheerer purchased it from Mrs. Lardner. [*The East Hampton Star* March 7, 1946, p. 8.]

He was the son of William and Louise Durand Scheerer, Sr. of Llewellyn Park, West Orange, NJ.

Jane Bond Ingersoll Scheerer was the daughter of Charles H. and Eleanor Bond Ingersoll of Llewellyn Park, West Orange, NJ. Jane's sister Anne married Gavin Brackenridge, Sr. and resided in East Hampton.

Joseph Durand and Jane Bond Ingersoll Scheerer, Sr.'s son Joseph Durand Scheerer, Jr. married Nancy Pardue and resided in Amagansett. Their son William Scheerer II, who later owned the house, married Idoline Lochrane Watts Crabbe.

The Blue Book of The Hamptons, 1976 lists Joseph D. and Nancy Holdworth Scheerer [Sr.] as residing on West End Road, East Hampton.

She was the daughter of Frederick and Jessie Margaret McCreary Holdsworth, Sr. of Brookline, MA. Nancy had previously been married to Edward Stotesbury Hutchinson, the son of Sydney E. Hutchinson of Philadelphia.

Scheerer, Paul Renner, Jr.

Occupation(s):	capitalist - real estate developer
	industrialist - director, Sag Harbor Industries, Inc. (electrical coil and inductor manufacturing firm)
	financier - a founder and director, First National Bank of East Hampton, 1964 (merged into North Fork Bank)
	Civic Activism: director, assistant treasurer and chairman of board, Southampton Hospital;
	chairman of board, Southampton Hospital Association;
	president of trustees, Hampton Day School, Bridgehampton;
	treasurer, Maidstone Club, East Hampton;
	member, Village of East Hampton Planning Board
Marriage(s):	1953 – Barbara Hopkinson
Address:	20 Windmill Lane, East Hampton
Name of estate:	
Year of construction:	1957
Style of architecture:	
Architect(s):	Alfred A. Scheffer designed the house (for P. R. Scheerer, Jr.)
Landscape architect(s):	
House extant: yes	
Historical notes:	

The house was built by Paul Renner Scheerer, Jr. [*The East Hampton Star* February 28, 1957, p. 1.]

He is the son of Paul Renner and Gladys Knight Scheerer, Sr. of Llewellyn Park, NJ.

Barbara Hopkinson Scheerer is the daughter of Russell and Mary Barbey Lewis Hopkinson of East Hampton.

Paul Renner and Barbara Hopkinson Scheerer, Jr.'s daughter Wendy married John T. Fitz Patrick, the son of John F. and Denise Fitz Patrick III of Billerica, MA.

Scheerer, William, II (1923-2008)

Occupation(s):	capitalist - Newark Milk and Cream Co.
	financier - vice-president, Fred Alger & Co., 1967-1982; investment advisor, Legg, Mason, Wood, Walker
Marriage(s):	1954-2008 – Idoline Lochrane Watts Crabbe
Address:	15 West End Avenue, East Hampton
Name of estate:	
Year of construction:	1927-1928
Style of architecture:	Shingle
Architect(s):	John Custis Lawrence designed the house (for Lardner)
Landscape architect(s):	
Builder:	Edward M. Gay
House extant: yes	
Historical notes:	

   The house, originally named *Iona Dune / The Mange*, was built by Ringgold Wilmer Lardner, Sr. In 1946 Joseph Durand Scheerer, Sr. purchased it from Mr. Lardner. [*The East Hampton Star* March 7, 1 946, p. 8.] It was later owned by Joseph's son William.
   Idoline Lochrane Watts Crabbe Scheerer is the daughter of Thomas Mackay Crabbe of Hewlett, NY.
   William and Idoline Lochrane Watts Crabbe Scheerer II's daughter Jane married Simon D. Parkes. Their daughter Idoline married Angier Biddle Duke, Jr., the son of Angier Biddle and Robine Chandler Tippett Duke, Sr. of *Wyndecote Barn* in Southampton, and resided in Stowe, VT. [*See* Spinzia, *Long Island's Prominent Families* in the Town of Southampton – Duke entry.] Their daughter Laura married James Apel Whitney.

Scheffer, Alfred A. (1894-1976)

Occupation(s):	architect - *
Civic Activism:	a founder, Amagansett East Association
Marriage(s):	1949-1976 – Theresa Trach (1915-1978)
	- Civic Activism: a founder, Amagansett East Association
Address:	10 Hampton Lane, Amagansett
Name of estate:	
Year of construction:	1950
Style of architecture:	Beach Cottage
Architect(s):	Alfred A. Scheffer designed his own residence
Landscape architect(s):	
House extant: unconfirmed; damaged by fire in 2010	
Historical notes:	

   The house was built by Alfred A. Scheffer.
   The Blue Book of The Hamptons, 1965 and *1973* list Alfred A. and Theresa Trach Scheffer as residing on Hampton Lane, Amagansett.
   Theresa Trach Scheffer was the daughter of Gregory and Anna Gula Trach of NYC.
   Alfred A. and Theresa Trach Scheffer's daughter Suzanne married Jerome J. Mangini. Their son Rodman married Claudia Nichols and resided in Plymouth, MA.
   *Scheffer designed some two hundred homes in Westchester County, Douglaston, Queens, and the Hamptons.
   The Amagansett house was owned by Jack and Linda Carrol Accardi for eighteen years prior to the 2010 fire. The Accardis added a wing with additional bedrooms.

Schey, Robert Paul (1876-1942)

Occupation(s):	industrialist - founder, Robert Schey Studio, NYC, London, and Paris (textile design firm)
Civic Activism:	chairman of board, Guild Hall, East Hampton; director, Maidstone Club, East Hampton; vice-president, Grand Jurors Association of New York County; chairman, committee for textile design, Design Restoration Bureau of the National Federation of Textiles, Inc.; director, National Horse Show
Marriage(s):	1918-1942 – Laura Washington Todd (1882-1978)
Address:	Georgica Road, East Hampton
Name of estate:	*Lauralawn*
Year of construction:	1891
Style of architecture:	Adamesque-Colonial
Architect(s):	Isaac Henry Green II designed the house (for W. A. Wheelock)* Aymar Embury II, 1929-1930 alterations transformed the house into Adamesque-Colonial style
Landscape architect(s):	
Builder:	Philip Ritch
House extant: yes	

Historical notes:

The house was built by William Almy Wheelock. It was later owned by Schey. [*The East Hampton Star* December 22, 1977, p. 26.]

The *Social Directory of Southampton, Long Island, 1931* lists Robert and Laura Schey as residing at *Lauralawn* in East Hampton. *The Blue Book of The Hamptons, 1973* lists the address for *Lauralawn* as 1362 Georgica Road, East Hampton.

He was the son of Anthony and Lina Schey of Vienna, Austria.

Laura Washington Todd Schey was the daughter of James Austin and Laura Brake Todd.

Robert Paul and Laura Washington Todd Schey's daughter Theresa married Everett McCall Maloney, the son of William Raywood and Ella Gaynor McCall Maloney, Jr. of *Glendella* in East Hampton. Their son George married Lucy Ann Redding, the daughter of Edwin Wright and Rebecca Elizabeth Billingsley Redding.

*For Green's other commissions, *see* Spinzia, *Long Island's Prominent South Shore Families: Their Estates and Their Country Homes in the Towns of Babylon and Islip.*

Schmidt, Dederick Herman (1868-1933)

Occupation(s):	financier - a founder and partner, Reitze, Stern, and Schmidt (stock brokerage firm); a founder and partner, D. H. Schmidt and Co., (stock brokerage firm)
Marriage(s):	1896-1933 – Anna Catherine Offerman (1868-1960)
Address:	Georgica Road and Burnell Lane (now, Pudding Hill Lane), East Hampton
Name of estate:	
Year of construction:	1905
Style of architecture:	
Architect(s):	James Custis Lawrence designed the house (for Hinton)
Landscape architect(s):	
Builder:	Thomas E. Babcock
House extant: unconfirmed	

Historical notes:

The eleven-bedroom, four-bath house, originally named *Roads Meet*, was built by Alfred Post Hinton at a cost of $12,000. [*The East Hampton Star* November 18, 1904, p. 5.] In 1929 Schmidt purchased the house. [*The East Hampton Star* November 8, 1929, p. 12.]

The *Social Directory of Southampton, Long Island, 1931* lists Dederick and Anna C. Offerman Schmidt as residing on Apaquogue Road [Georgica Road], East Hampton.

He was the son of Herman and Charlotte Knubel Schmidt.

Anna Catherine Offerman Schmidt was the daughter of Heinrich and Lena Maria Will Offerman of Brooklyn.

Dederick Herman and Anna Catherine Offerman Schmidt's daughter Katherine died at the age of thirteen. Their daughter Charlotte did not marry.

Schmidt, Max Eberhardt (1848-1921)*
aka Max Everhart Smith

Occupation(s):	inventor - escalator
	industrialist - president, Continuous Transit Securities Co., NYC; director, Multiple Speed and Traction Co.
	engineer - designed Eads Bridge, St. Louis, MO; designed Eads jetties at mouth of Mississippi River
Marriage(s):	1875-1921 – Mary Everhart (d. 1936)
Address:	68 Woods Lane, East Hampton
Name of estate:	
Year of construction:	1902
Style of architecture:	Shingle
Architect(s):	Isaac Henry Green II designed the house (for M. E. Schmidt)**
Landscape architect(s):	
Builder:	Breckenridge and Ashby
House extant: yes	
Historical notes:	

The house was built by Max Eberhardt Schmidt.
He was the son of Albert and Angelica Hoefer Schmidt of Berlin, Germany.
Mary Everhart Schmidt was the daughter of William and Margaret Lowrey Smith Everhart of Pennsylvania.
*In 1918 Schmidt legally anglicized his name to Max Everhart Smith. [*The New York Times* July 11, 1918, p. 20.]
Distraught over his failing eyesight, Max committed suicide with a 32-caliber revolver. He left two notes, one to his wife and the other to his son George Plumber Smith (aka Schmidt), who was a partner in the brokerage firm of Smith and Gallatin, on how he wanted his estate distributed and instructing them to tell everyone that he had died in a car accident. [*The New York Times* January 25, 1921, p. 3.]
**For Green's other commissions, *see* Spinzia, *Long Island's Prominent South Shore Families: Their Estates and Their Country Homes in the Towns of Babylon and Islip.*
The house was later owned by George Ethridge.
In 1943 it was purchased from the Riverhead Savings Bank by Mrs. John Howie Wright, Jr.
In 2009 the five-bedroom house was for sale. The asking price was $3.95 million.

Schnable, Julian (b. 1951)

Occupation(s):	artist - sculptor and plate printer
	entertainers and associated professions -
	    director, producer, musician, and scriptwriter*
	writer - *C V J: Nicknames of Maitre D's & Other Excerpts From Life*,
	    1987 (autobiography)

Marriage(s):	M/1 – 1980 – Jacquelin Beaurang (b. 1955)
	    - entertainers and associated professions - Belgian film stylist
	      fashion designer - shoe designer
	M/2 - Olatz Lopez Garmendia
	    - model
	      art curator
	      industrialist - producer of line of linens and silk nightwear
	      interior designer - Interiors by Olatz

Address:	129 De Forest Road, Montauk
Name of estate:	
Year of construction:	1883
Style of architecture:	
Architect(s):	McKim, Mead and White designed the house
Landscape architect(s):	Frederick Law Olmstead designed the site plans

House extant: yes
Historical notes:

    The house is one of the Montauk Association's "Seven Sisters." Schnabel was one of the subsequent owners. He is the son of Jack and Esta Greenberg Schnabel.
    Julian and Jacquelin Beaurang Schnabel have three children, Stella, an actress and poet; Lola, a painter and filmmaker; and Vito, an art dealer.
    Julian and Olatz Lopez Garmendia Schnabel's two sons Cy and Olmo reside in the SoHo section of Manhattan. Schnabel fathered a son, Shooter, with May Anderson.
    *Schnabel's art work can be found in the Metropolitan Museum of Art, Museum of Modern Art, NYC; the Whitney Museum of American Art, NYC; the Museum of Contemporary Art, Los Angeles, CA; Los Angeles County Museum of Art; Reina Sofia, Madrid, Spain; Tate Modern, London, England; and the Centre Georges Pompidou, Paris, France. His motion picture "The Diving Bell and the Butterfly" was nominated for four Academy Awards. "Before Night Falls", which he directed, became a vehicle for Javier Bardem's Academy Award nomination.

Schulman, Lowell M. (1926-2017)

Occupation (s):	financier - director, Empire State Federal Savings and Loan Co., White Plains, NY
	capitalist - developer of corporate office parks, Westchester County, NY; developed and owned Atlantic Golf Club, Bridgehampton
Civic Activism:	chairman, Westchester County Commission on Homeless;
	director, Metropolitan Golf Association;
	president, Old Oaks Country Club, Purchase, NY;
	member, advisory board, Professional Golf Association;
	member, museum committee, United States Golf Association
Marriage(s):	M/1 – Toni Scheckner
	M/2 – Diane [unable to confirm maiden name]
Address:	89 Lily Pond Lane, East Hampton
Name of estate:	Beechwood
Year of construction:	1912
Style of architecture:	Coxwold
Architect(s):	Albro and Lindeberg designed the house (for Erdmann)
Landscape architect(s):	Edwina Von Gal designed the gardens (for Schulman)*
Builder:	Smith and Davis
House extant: yes	
Historical notes:	

The eight-bedroom, eight-bath, 9,000-square-foot house, originally named *Coxwould*, was built by Dr. John Frederic Erdmann. It was later owned by his daughter Jane Erdmann Burton who, in 1954, sold it to Dayton Hedges. [*The East Hampton Star* August 5, 1954, p. 1.] In 1958 Hedges' son Burke Osborn Hedges purchased the house. [*The East Hampton Star* July 3, 1958, p. 4.] It was then owned by Joseph Weinstein and, subsequently, by Schulman who renamed it *Beechwood*.

He was the son of Louis A. and Rose Sadowsky Schulman of White Plains, NY.

In 2012 the house was for sale by Schulman. The asking price was $24.95 million; the annual taxes were $60,000.

*Edwina Von Gal created fifteen garden rooms which were inspired by English gardens.

Schultz, Howard Mark (b. 1953)

Occupation(s):	restaurateur - director, Pinkberry, Inc.;
	director, Potbelly Corp.;
	a founder, Il Giornal (later, Starbucks Coffee Co.);
	marketing director, Starbucks Coffee and Tea Co. (later, Starbucks Coffee Co);
	a founder, president, and CEO, Starbucks Coffee Co.
	capitalist - owner, Seattle Super-Sonics (NBA basketball team);
	director, Dream Works Animation SKG;
	director, Groupon (offers discounts);
	director, Square, Inc. (mobile payment firm)
	industrialist - vice-president, Hammarplast (Swedish drip coffee machine manufacturing firm);
	chairman of board, Neure Metrix, Inc. (produces medical devices for neurological complications of diabetes)
	financier - a founder, Maveron
	merchant - director, Drugstore.com;
	director, eBay, Inc.
	writer - co-authored, with Dori Jones Yang, *Put Your Heart Into It*, 1997;
	co-authored, with Joanne Gordon, *Onward*, 2011;
	From the Ground Up: A Journey to Reimage the Promise of America, 2019
Civic Activism:	co-founder, with his wife Sheri, Schultz Family Foundation
Marriage(s):	1982 – Sheri Kersch
	- interior decorator
	Civic Activism: co-founder, with her husband Howard, and president, Schultz Family Foundation
Address:	14 Gracie Lane, East Hampton
Name of estate:	
Year of construction:	c. 1985
Style of architecture:	Modern
Architect(s):	Charles Gwathmey designed the house (for Steinberg)
	Kang H. Chang, 2011 alterations (for Schultz)
Landscape architect(s):	
House extant: yes	
Historical notes:	

The 8,500-square-foot house was built by Robert Michael Steinberg. It was later owned by Schultz.
He is the son of Fred and Elaine Schultz of Brooklyn.
Howard Mark and Sheri Kersch Schultz's son Eliahu married Breanna Lind Hawes, the daughter of Taylor L. Hawes of Redwood, WA. Their daughter Addison married Tal Hirshberg.

Schurman, George Wellington (1867-1931)

Occupation(s):	attorney - partner, Carter, Hughes, and Dwight; partner, Hughes, Schurman, and Dwight; assistant district attorney, New York County, 1901
Civic Activism:	trustee, Brearley School, NYC; a founder and member, first board of governors, Devon Yacht Club, Amagansett
Marriage(s):	1898-1931 – Helen Isabella Munro (1875-1955)
Address:	121 Further Lane, East Hampton
Name of estate:	*Beachclose*
Year of construction:	1917
Style of architecture:	Mediterranean
Architect(s):	Arthur C. Jackson designed the house (for G. W. Schurman) Ferguson & Shamanian, alterations (for Krakoff)
Landscape architect(s):	Charles Nassau Lowrie, Sr. (for G. W. Schurman) Perry Guillot (for Krakoff)
Builder:	Edward M. Gay

House extant: yes*

Historical notes:

The ten-bedroom, eleven-and-a-half-bath, 8,500-square-foot house, originally named *Beachclose*, was built by George Wellington Schurman.

The *Social Register Summer, 1921* lists George W. and Helen I. Munro Schurman as residing at *Beachclose* in East Hampton.

He was the son of Robert and Lydia Gouldrup Schurman of Canada. George's brother Jacob, who also resided on Further Lane, married Helen Isabella Munro Schurman's sister Barbara Forrest Munro.

Barbara and Helen were the daughters of George and Catherine Forrest Munro.

George Wellington and Helen Isabella Munro Schurman's daughter Catherine married Dr. George Gavin Miller and resided in Montreal, Canada. Their daughter Beatrice married Holbrook Cushman and resided in Bedford, NY.

[See following entry for additional family information.]

In 1923 Schurman sold the house to Laura Elizabeth Young Martin, who died in 1924. Lion Gardiner purchased it in 1925 and sold it the same year to Mrs. Maude Frances Sergeant Bouvier, who called the house *Lasata*. Mrs. Bouvier deeded it to her husband in 1935. In 1950 the house was sold to Frances May Archbold Hufty. In the early 1960s the house was purchased by Joseph Ansbro Meehan. It was purchased in 2006 by Reed and Delphine Krakoff.

In 2016 the Krakoffs listed the house and 7.15 acres for sale. The asking price was $38.995 million.

*The stables were demolished.

Schurman, Jacob Gould, Sr. (1854-1942)

Occupation(s):	attorney	
	educator -	professor of English literature and metaphysics, Dalhousie College, Halifax, Nova Scotia;
		chairman, department of philosophy, Cornell University, Ithaca, NY;
		dean, Sage School of Philosophy, Cornell University, Ithaca, NY;
		president, Cornell University, Ithaca, NY, 1892-1920
	diplomat -	United States Minister to Greece and Montenegro, 1912-1913 (Wilson and Taft administrations);
		United States Minister to Japan, 1921 (Harding administration);
		United States Ambassador to Germany, 1925-1930 (Coolidge administration)
	journalist -	editor, *The Philosophical Review*, 1891-1905
	writer -	*Kantian Ethics and Ethics of Evolution*, 1881;
		Agnosticism and Religion, 1886;
		The Ethical Import of Darwinism, 1888;
		A Generation at Cornell, 1898;
		Philippine Affairs – A Retrospect and Outlook, 1902;
		The Balkan Wars 1912 and 1913, 1914;
		Why America Is At War, 1917;
		numerous articles in professional journals
Civic Activism:	president, first United States Commission to The Philippines, 1899; member, New York State Food Commission during World War I; member, Vanderlip Commission to Japan, 1920	
Marriage(s):	1884-1930 – Barbara Forrest Munro (1865-1930)	
Address:	Further Lane, East Hampton	
Name of estate:	*Breezy Knowe*	
Year of construction:	1901-1902	
Style of architecture:		
Architect(s):	Joseph Greenleaf Thorp designed the house (for J. G. Schurman) George A. Eldredge designed and built the stable, 1902 (for Schurman, Sr.)	

Landscape architect(s):
House extant: remodeled into a ranch, 1949
Historical notes:

The house, originally named *Breezy Knowe*, was built by Jacob Gould Schurman, Sr.

The *Social Register Summer, 1910* and *1915* list Jacob G. and Barbara F. Munro Schurman [Sr.] as residing at *Breezy Knowe* in East Hampton.

He was the son of Robert and Lydia Gouldrup Schurman of Canada. Jacob's brother George, who also resided on Further Lane, married Barbara Forrest Munro Schurman's sister Helen Isabella Munro.

Helen and Barbara were the daughters of George and Catherine Forrest Munro.

Jacob Gould and Barbara Forrest Munro Schurman, Sr.'s daughter Catherine married Raymond Ware. Their daughter Helen married John Magruder. Their daughter Barbara married Vladimer Petro-Pavlovsky. Their daughter Dorothy married James S. Sisk. Their son George married Kerstin Taube, the daughter of Count Henning Gustav Taube.

[See previous entry for additional family information.]

In 1927 the house was purchased by Dr. Dudley DeVore Roberts, Sr. who renamed it *Outabounds*. [*The East Hampton Star* October 28, 1927, p. 1.]

Schwab, Laurence, Sr. (1892-1951)

Occupation(s):	writer - Broadway writer and lyricist
	capitalist - partner, Schwab & Mandel (Broadway producers); theater owner
	journalist - drama critic, *The Boston Herald*
	publisher - Miami tabloid newspaper
Marriage(s):	M/1 – 1921-div. 1928 – Marie Gaspar
	- entertainers and associated professions - vaudeville actress
	M/2 – 1929-1951 – Mildred Leona Brown
	- entertainers and associated professions - actress
Address:	644 Montauk Highway, Montauk
Name of estate:	
Year of construction:	1948
Style of architecture:	Beach Cottage
Architect(s):	
Landscape architect(s):	
House extant: yes	
Historical notes:	

The 2,200-square-foot house was built by Laurence Schwab, Sr.
Laurence and Marie Gaspar Schwab, Sr.'s son Laurence Schwab, Jr. is also a noted Broadway producer.
Mildred Leona Brown Schwab was the daughter of John P. Brown of Shamokin, PA.
The house was for sale in 2015. The asking price was $8 million.

Schwarzman, Stephen Allen (b. 1947)

Occupation(s):	financier - member, Donaldson, Lufkin, and Jeanrette (investment banking firm);
	managing director, Lehman Brothers;
	co-founder, with Peter George Peterson, and CEO, The Blackstone Group, LP
	educator - adjunct professor, Yale School of Management, Yale University, New Haven, CT
Civic Activism:	chairman, board of trustee, John F. Kennedy Center for the Performing Arts, Washington, DC, 2004-2010;
	endowed $100 million to establish scholarship program, Tsinghua, China;
	funded new football stadium, Abington Senior High School;
	donated $100 million for expansion of the New York Public Library, NYC;
	donated $150 million to Yale University (for a campus center);
	donated $25 million to his public high school;
	a founder, Atlantic Golf Club, Bridgehampton, NY
Marriage(s):	M/1 – 1971-div. 1990 – Ellen Philips
	- Civic Activism: trustee, Northwestern University, Evanston, IL; trustee, Mount Sinai Medical Center, NYC; trustee, Icahn School of Medicine, Mount Sinai Medical Center, NYC; trustee, Lincoln Center Theater, NYC; founder, the Ellen Philips Schwarzman Katz Foundation
	M/2 – 1995 – Christine Mularchuk
	- attorney - member, Cowan, Liebowitz and Latman, NYC
Address:	52 Ruxton Road, East Hampton
Name of estate:	*Cove Hollow Farm*
Year of construction:	1987
Style of architecture:	Shingle
Architect(s):	
Landscape architect(s):	
Builder:	
House extant: yes	
Historical notes:	

In 1996 Allen Schwarzman purchased the 3,200-square-foot, four-bedroom, three-bath house for $2.3 million.

He is the son of Joseph and Arlene Schwarzman of Huntingdon Valley, PA.

Ellen Philips Schwarzman is the daughter of Jessie and Carol Levitan Philips of Dayton, Ohio. Ellen subsequently married Howard Carl Katz.

Stephen Allen and Ellen Philips Schwarzman's daughter Elizabeth married Andrew Curtis Right. Their son Edward married Ellen Marie Zajac.

Christine Mularchuk Schwarzman is the daughter of Peter and Peggie Mularchuk of Hicksville, NY. Christine had previously been married to Austin Chilton Hearst, the grandson of William Randolph Hearst who resided at *Saint Joan* in Sands Point. [*See* Spinzia, *Long Island's Prominent North Shore Families, vol. I* – Hearst entry.]

In 2010 Mrs. Schwarzman sold the house to Thomas Gallagher for $6.25 million.

[For information about the Schwarzmans' Water Mill residence, *see* Spinzia, *Long Island's Prominent Families in the Town of Southampton* – Schwarzman entry.]

Scull, Robert C. (1917-1986)

Occupation(s):	artist - freelance illustrator and industrial designer
	capitalist - president, Super Operating Corp. (130-taxi fleet with 400 drivers)
Civic Activism:	co-founder, Robert and Ethel Scull Foundation
Marriage(s):	M/1 – 1944-div. 1975 – Ethel Redner (1921-2001)
	- co-founder, Robert and Ethel Scull Foundation
	M/2 – Stephanie *[unable to determine maiden name]*
Address:	123 Georgica Road, East Hampton
Name of estate:	
Year of construction:	c. 1962
Style of architecture:	Modern
Architect(s):	Paul Lester Weiner designed the house (for Scull)
Landscape architect(s):	

House extant: unconfirmed

Historical notes:

    The house was built by Robert C. Scull.
    He was the son of Meyer Scull who anglicized the family's surname from Sokolnikoff.
    Ethel Redner Scull was the daughter of Benjamin Redner.
    After her divorce from Robert, Ethel instituted a ten-year litigation over their art collection which was not settled until 1985.
    In 2019 the four-bedroom, four-bath, 2140-square-foot house was for sale. The asking price was $3.895 million.

Seabury, Samuel (1873-1958)

Occupation(s):	attorney - partner, Seabury, Massey, and Lowe*;
	judge, New York State Supreme Court, 1906;
	judge, New York State Court of Appeals, 1914-1916
	writer - *Municipal Ownership and Operation of Public Utilities in New York City*, 1905;
	The Law and Practice of City Court of the City of New York, 1907;
	275 Years of East Hampton, New York, 1926;
	numerous articles in professional journals
Civic Activism:	referee, appellate division, New York State Supreme Court, 1930;
	commissioner to investigate corruption in New York County (Theodore Roosevelt administration)
	president, Maidstone Club, East Hampton;
	a founder and member, East Hampton War Memorial Committee, 1924
Marriage(s):	1900-1950 – Josephine Maud Richey (1878-1950)
	- Civic Activism: president, Garden Club of America;
	president, National Council of Club Women;
	chair, East Hampton chapter, American Red Cross during World War I;
	chair, New York Chapter of the English Speaking Union;
	president, Garden Club of East Hampton
Address:	Georgica Road, East Hampton
Name of estate:	*Wyandanch Acres*
Year of construction:	1894
Style of architecture:	Shingle Cottage
Architect(s):	
Landscape architect(s):	
Builder:	Frank Grimshaw
House extant: yes	
Historical notes:	

    The house was built by The Reverend Thomas Richey, Sr. It was later owned his daughter Josephine and son-in-law Samuel Seabury, who called it *Wyandanch Acres*.
    He was the son of William Jones and Alice Van Wyck Beare Seabury of Manhattan.
    In c. 1920 the Seaburys added a library, enlarged the kitchen, and altered the second floor. In 1979 an oriel entrance was added to the east facade.
    *Seabury's partner John Zollicoher Lowe, Jr. defended the notorious World War I German spy Franz von Rintelen.
[*See* Raymond E. Spinzia, "The Involvement of Long Islanders in the Events Surrounding German Sabotage in the New York City Metropolitan Area 1914-1917." @ spinzialongislandestates.com.]

Seaman, Joseph Husband, Sr. (1865-1948)

Occupation(s):	financier -	a founder and partner, A. Read and Co., NYC (later, Dillon, Read, and Co.) (investment banking firm);
		partner, Dillon, Read, and Co. (investment banking firm);
		partner, Shields and Co. (investment banking firm);
		a founder, Seaman and Co. (stock brokerage firm)
	capitalist -	director, Electric Railway Co.;
		director, Third Avenue Railway Co., NYC;
		director, Southern Boulevard Railway Co., NYC;
		director, Yonkers Railway, NY;
		director, Belt Line Railway Co., NYC;
		director, Kingsbridge Railway Co., NY;
		director, New York City Interborough Railway Co., NY;
		director, Westchester & Connecticut Traction Co., NY;
		director, Nichols Avenue Railways Co.;
		director, Union Railway Co., NYC
	industrialist -	director, Victor Chemical Works, Chicago, IL
Civic Activism:		governor, New York Stock Exchange, NYC, 1920-1937;
		assistant treasurer, New York Stock Exchange, NYC, 1927-1937

Marriage(s): 1913-1944 – Josephine Richardson (1873-1944)

Address: Lee Avenue, East Hampton
Name of estate: *Seamanor*
Year of construction:
Style of architecture: Colonial Revival
Architect(s):
Landscape architect(s):
House extant: unconfirmed
Historical notes:

In 1919 Seaman purchased the house from Frank Smith. [*The East Hampton Star* August 8, 1919, p. 3.]

The *Social Directory of Southampton, Long Island, 1931* lists Joseph H. and Josephine Richardson Seaman [Sr.] as residing at *Seamanor* on Lee Avenue, East Hampton.

He was the son of Samuel Hicks and Richardson Husband Seaman of Brooklyn.

Josephine Richardson Seaman was the daughter of Henry Thomas and Sophie Richardson of Manhattan. She had previously been married to Clyde Notman.

Joseph Husband and Josephine Richardson Seaman, Sr.'s son Joseph Husband Seaman, Jr. married Madeleine Cook Dixon, the daughter of Theodore P. Dixon of Sag Harbor.

Sedacca, Joseph M. (b. 1930)

Occupation(s):	artist - manager of graphic arts, American Museum of Natural History
	writer - *Feather Arts Exhibition Photographs*, 1980
Marriage(s):	bachelor
Address:	19 Northwest Landing Road, East Hampton
Name of estate:	
Year of construction:	1968
Style of architecture:	Modern
Architect(s):	Charles Gwathmey designed the house (for Sedacca)
Landscape architect(s):	
Builder:	John Caramagna
House extant: yes	
Historical notes:	

The 1,200-square-foot, three-bedroom, three-bath house was built by Joseph M. Sedacca.
In 1993 he sold it to Paul A. Amador for $245,000. In 2015 Amador listed the house for sale. The asking price was $2.495 million.
In 2019 the house was again listed for sale. The asking price was $2.395 million.

Seegal, Frederic Milton

Occupation(s):	financier - president, Lehman Brothers;
	president, Soloman Brothers;
	managing director, Shearson, Lehman, Hutton;
	president, Wasserstein and Perella Co.;
	head, New York office, Stephens Inc.;
	a founder, Seegal, Benson, Leucadia Securities, LLC
	capitalist - director, I-Beam;
	owned WEHM and WBEA (radio stations);
	director, Digital River Hollywood.com
Civic Activism:	trustee, Neuberger Museum of Art, Purchase, NY;
	trustee, Parrish Art Museum, Southampton, NY;
	trustee, New York City Center;
	trustee, Center for Public Integrity;
	chairman of board, James Beard Foundation
Marriage(s):	1986 – Robin Neimark
	- advertising executive - marketing specialist, Frederic Atkins, NY
	Civic Activism: president, Child Development Center of the Hamptons Foundation for Special Children
Address:	Further Lane, Amagansett
Name of estate:	*Old Simons House*
Year of construction:	1600s
Style of architecture:	Salt Box
Architect(s):	
Landscape architect(s):	David Seeler, Bayberry Nursery, Amagansett, 1999 (for Lang)
Builder:	William Simons, alterations (for Tyson)
House extant: unconfirmed	
Historical notes:	

In 1949 James Tyson moved the residence of Edward Mulford Baker from Pantigo Road to Further Lane and called it *Old Baker House*. [*The East Hampton Star* August 28, 1975, p. 30, and September 4, 1986, p. 32.] In 1991 it was purchased by Seegal who renamed it *Old Simons House* in honor of Tyson's builder and caretaker. [*The East Hampton* Star July 3, 1997.]
He is the son of Milton and Miriam Emden Seegal of Los Angeles, CA.
Robin Neimark Seegal is the daughter of Ira Neimark.
In 1999 Seegal sold the estate to Helmut Lang for $15.5 million. [*The New York Post* June 24, 2002.]

Seegal, Frederic Milton

Occupation(s):	*[See previous entry.]*
Civic Activism:	*[See previous entry.]*
Marriage(s):	1986 – Robin Neimark
	- *[See previous entry.]*
Address:	Terbell Lane, East Hampton
Name of estate:	
Year of construction:	1964
Style of architecture:	Modern
Architect(s):	Julian and Barbara Neski designed the house (for Chalif)
Landscape architect(s):	
Builder:	H. H. Wilde*
House extant: yes*	
Historical notes:	

The house was built by Seymour Hunt Chalif. It was later owned by Seegal.
[See previous entry for family information.]
*Extensive additions to the house have been made.

Seinfeld, Jerry (b. 1954)
aka Jerome Allen Seinfeld

Occupation(s):	entertainers and associated professions - director, comedian, actor, and producer
	writer - *Seinlanguage*, 1993; *Halloween* (children's book)
Marriage(s):	1999 – Nina Danielle Sklar (aka Jessica Sklar) (b. 1971)
	- public relations executive - Golden Books Entertainment; Tommy Hilfiger
	writer - *Deceptively Delicious*, 2007; *Double Delicious*, 2010; *The Can't Cook Book*, 2013
	Civic Activism: Baby Buggy (provided clothes and essentials to underprivileged women and children)
Address:	330 Further Lane, East Hampton
Name of estate:	
Year of construction:	
Style of architecture:	Modified Colonial Revival
Architect(s):	
Landscape architect(s):	
House extant: yes	
Historical notes:	

In 2000 Jerry Seinfeld purchased the twelve-acre estate which included a main residence, a guest house, a pool and a barn, from Billy Joel for $32 million. He demolished the main residence and built a new one.

He is the son of Kalmen and Betty Hosni Seinfeld of Massapequa, NY.

Nina Danielle Sklar Seinfeld had previously been married to Eric Nederlander, the son of Robert Elliot and Caren Elaine Berman Nederlander, Sr. of East Hampton.

The Seinfelds have three children: Sascha, born in 2000; Julian born in 2003; and Shepherd born in 2005.

Seligson William (1899-1971)

Occupation(s):	attorney
	capitalist - owner, East Hampton Hotel; owner, Halsey Garage Building, Newtown Lane, East Hampton; an owner, Monmouth Park Jockey Club
Civic Activism:	president, Young Men's Philanthropic League
Marriage(s):	Lucille Meadow
Address:	Georgica Road, East Hampton
Name of estate:	
Year of construction:	1895
Style of architecture:	Neo-Tudor
Architect(s):	Joseph Greenleaf Thorp designed the house (for Spring)
	Howard Greenley, 1915 alterations (for Roberts)
	Spencer Fullerton Weaver, Sr., 1925 alterations (for himself)
Landscape architect(s):	John Raum, 1917 (for Roberts)
	Jacob John Spoon designed the swimming pool (for Weaver)
Builder:	Philip Ritch

House extant: no; destroyed by fire, 1969*
Nassau County Museum Collection has photographs of the estate.
Historical notes:

The house, originally named *Winklehawk*, was built by Preston Brady Spring, Sr. In 1915 it was purchased by Walter Scott Roberts. [*The East Hampton Star* August 6, 1915, p. 5; December 13, 1918, p. 5; and June 8, 1944, p. 3.] In 1925 the house was purchased by Spencer Fullerton Weaver, Sr. who renamed it *Spencecliff*. In 1949 it was purchased by Seligson who subdivided the estate's property into six building lots. [*The East Hampton Star* January, 13, 1955, p. 5, and June 16, 1955, p. 12.]
The house was subsequently owned by Adolph Green.
*In 1969 the house was destroyed by fire during a wedding at Green's estate when a caterer's gas line leaked and ignited.

Semel, Terrance Steven (b. 1943)

Occupation(s):	entertainers and associated professions -
	chairman of board and co-chief executive officer, Warner Brothers;
	sales manager, CBS Cinema Center Films;
	vice-president, Warner Brothers Distribution Corp.;
	vice-president and COO, Warner Brothers
	industrialist - director, Revlon;
	director, Polo Ralph Lauren Corp.
	capitalist - chairman of board and CEO, Yahoo
Civic Activism:	co-chairman of trustees, Los Angeles County Museum of Art;
	director, Guggenheim Museum, NYC;
	donated, with his wife Jane, $25 million to UCLA for the study of
	Alzheimer's disease, mood disorders, autism, and addiction
Marriage(s):	M/1 – 1968-div. 1974 – Maryann Soloway
	M/2 – 1977 – Jane Bovingdon
	- entertainers and associated professions -
	director, Bill T. Jones / Arnie Zane Dance Co.;
	special photographer, "Falling Down", 1992 (motion picture)
	Civic Activism: donated, with her husband Terrance, $25 million
	to UCLA for the study of Alzheimer's disease,
	mood disorders, autism, and addiction
Address:	408 Further Lane, Amagansett
Name of estate:	
Year of construction:	c. 2006
Style of architecture:	
Architect(s):	Charles Gwathmey designed the
	guest house, 2008 (for Semel)
Landscape architect(s):	
House extant: yes	
Historical notes:	

  The house was built by Terrance Steven Semel. In 2005 Semel had purchased the 8.5-acre lot from Steven Allen Schwarzman for $43 million.
  He is the son of Ben and Mildred Wenig Semel of Bayside, NY.

Sewell, Robert Van Vorst (1860-1924)

Occupation(s):	artist - painter and sculptor
Marriage(s):	1888-1924 – Lydia Amanda Brewster (1859-1926)
	(aka Amanda Brewster Sewell)
	- artist
Address:	Briar Patch Road, East Hampton
Name of estate:	
Year of construction:	
Style of architecture:	
Architect(s):	
Landscape architect(s):	
House extant: no; demolished, 1930*	
Historical notes:	

  The house was built by Robert Van Vorst Sewell.
  He was the son of Robert and Sarah Brower Van Vorst Sewell.
  Lydia Amanda Brewster Sewell was the daughter of Benjamin T. and Julia Washburn Brewster.
  Robert Van Vorst and Lydia Amanda Brewster Sewell's son William married Marion Brown, the daughter of the noted artist Bolton Brown.
  *Dr. Shepard Krech, Sr.'s residence *Briar Patch* was built on the site of Sewell's house.
  [For information about Sewell's Oyster Bay Cove residence *Fleetwood, see* Spinzia, *Long Island's Prominent North Shore Families, vol. II* – Sewell entry.]

Shafran, Irving (b. 1944)

Occupation(s):	attorney - partner, Anderson, Kill, Olick, and Oshinsky
	merchant - director, Henry Schein, Inc. (distributor of health products and services)
Civic Activism:	vice-president, New York Chapter, American Academy of Matrimonial Lawyers
Marriage(s):	Judith *[unable to determine maiden name]* - publisher - book editor
Address:	Georgica Road and Crossings, East Hampton
Name of estate:	
Year of construction:	1903
Style of architecture:	Shingle
Architect(s):	John Custis Lawrence designed the house (for S. F. Johnson)
	Peter Cook designed 1992 alterations (for Shafran)
Landscape architect(s):	
Builder:	George A. Eldredge
House extant: yes	
Historical notes:	

The thirty-three-room, thirteen-bedroom, nine-bath house, originally named *Onadune*, was built by Servetus Fisher Johnson. It was later owned by his daughter Edith and son-in-law Edward de Clifford Chisholm who continued to call it *Onadune*. In 1940 the house was purchased by Dr. Frank Earl Adair who renamed it *Sherwood*. In 1992 the house was purchased by Shafran.

Judith ____ Shafran had previously been married to Jacob M. Schlein.

By 2005 the Shafrans had relocated to 43 Surfside Drive, Bridgehampton. By 2012 they relocated to another Bridgehampton residence.

Shyer, Henry (b. 1934)

Occupation(s):	industrialist - vice-chairman, Zyloware Eyeware
Civic Activism:	president, Ridgeway Country Club, White Plains, NY
Marriage(s):	Carol *[unable to determine maiden name]* (b. 1940)
Address:	40 Hedges Banks Drive, East Hampton
Name of estate:	
Year of construction:	1989
Style of architecture:	Modern
Architect(s):	Bruce Dean Nagel designed the house (for Shyer)
Landscape architect(s):	
House extant: yes	
Historical notes:	

The house was built by Henry Shyer.
He is the son of Joseph Shyer.
Henry and Carol Shyer's daughter Lori married Steven Ray Glick, the son of Stanton Glick of Boca Raton, FL.
The house was later owned by Sean Combs (aka Puff Daddy, Daddy and P. Diddly).

Simmons, Edward Emerson (1852-1931)

Occupation(s):	artist - muralist, impressionist painter*
	writer - *From Seventy to Seventy: Memories of a Painter and Yankee*
Marriage(s):	M/1 – 1883-1897 – Vesta Schallenberger (1862-1897)
	- artist
	writer - *Green Tea: A Love Story*, 1892 (novel)
	Men and Men (novel)
	M/2 – 1903-1913 – Alice Ralston Morton (1871-1913)
Address:	Briar Patch Road, East Hampton
Name of estate:	
Year of construction:	1900
Style of architecture:	Modified Salt-Box
Architect(s):	
Landscape architect(s):	
Builder:	George A. Eldredge
House extant: yes	
Historical notes:	

The combination of house and art studio was built by Edward Emerson Simmons.
He was the son of George Frederick and Mary Emerson Ripley Simmons.
Vesta Schallenberger Simmons was the daughter of Cyrus and Sarah Ball Schallenberger.
Edward Emerson and Vesta Schallenberger Simmons' son George married Georgie Swindell.
Alice Ralston Morton Simmons was the daughter of Charles Carroll and Alice Ralston–Parke Morton.
*One of Simmons' murals, entitled "Melpomene", can be seen on the first floor of the Library of Congress Thomas Jefferson Building in Washington, DC.
The house is on The National Register of Historic Places.
It was later owned by Arthur Myron Dubrow.

Simmons, Russell Wendell (b. 1957)

Occupation(s):	entertainers and associated professions -
	motion picture producer –
	"Krush Groove";
	"The Nutty Professor"
	capitalist - a founder, Def Jam Recordings;
	CEO, Rush Communications (holding company);
	founder, Hip Hop Summit Action Network
	industrialist - founder, Phat Farm (line of clothes)
	writer - *Life and Def*, 2002;
	Russell Simmons Def Poetry Jam on Broadway, 2005;
	Do You!, 2008
Civic Activism:	founder, Rush Philanthropic Organization;
	a founder and chairman of board, Foundation for Ethic Understanding;
	Good Will Ambassador, U. S. Slavery Memorial
Marriage(s):	M/1 – Samantha *[unable to determine maiden name]*
	M/2 – 1998-div. 2009 – Kimora Lee (b. 1975)
	(aka Kimora Whitlock)
	- industrialist - a founder, Baby Phat (line of clothes);
	founder, line of perfumes;
	founder, KLS (line of clothes)
	capitalist - president and creative director, JustFab (personalized shopping website)
	merchant - boutique featuring KLS clothing, Beverly Hills, CA
	entertainers and associated professions - television actress
	writer - *Fabulosity*, 2006
	Civic Activism: founder, Kimora Lee Simmons Scholarship Fund
Address:	20 Jericho Lane, East Hampton
Name of estate:	
Year of construction:	
Style of architecture:	
Architect(s):	
Landscape architect(s):	
House extant: yes	
Historical notes:	

Russell Wendell Simmons is the son of Daniel and Evelyn Penn Simmons, Sr.

Kimora Lee Simmons is the daughter of Vernon and Joanne Perkins Whitlock, Jr. Kimora subsequently married Tim Leissner.

Simon, Paul Frederic (b. 1941)

Occupation(s):	entertainers and associated professions -
	musician, actor, singer, Broadway producer*
	composer - songwriter
Civic Activism:	benefactor and co-founder, Children's Health Project;
	trustee, Berklee College of Music, Boston, MA;
	trustee and co-founder, The Children's Health Fund
Marriage(s):	M/1 – 1969-div. 1975 – Peggy Harper
	M/2 – 1983-div. 1984 – Carrie Frances Fisher (1956-2016)
	- entertainers and associated professions -
	actress (best known for her role as Princess Leia Organa
	in "Star Wars");
	screenwriter;
	playwright
	writer - *Postcard From the Edge,* 1987 (novel);
	Wishful Drinking, 2008 (autobiography);
	Surrender in the Pink, 1990 (novel);
	Delusions of Grandma, 1993 (novel);
	Hollywood Moms, 2001 (novel);
	The Best Awful There Is, 2005 (novel);
	Shockaholic, 2011;
	The Princess Dearest, 2016
	M/3 – 1993 – Edie Arlisa Brickell (b. 1966)
	- entertainers and associated professions - singer
	composer - songwriter
Address:	15 Cliff Drive, Montauk
Name of estate:	
Year of construction:	
Style of architecture:	Shingle with Victorian Elements
Architect(s):	
Landscape architect(s):	
House extant: yes	
Historical notes:	

    Paul Frederic Simon is the son of Louis and Belle Simon of Forest Hills, NY.
    Peggy Harper Simon had previously been married to Paul's manager Mort Lewis.
    Paul Frederic and Peggy Harper Simon's son Harper is a singer, songwriter, guitarist, and producer.
    Carrie Frances Fisher Simon was the daughter of Eddie and Debbie Reynolds Fisher. Carrie died on the same day as did her mother, the actress, Debbie Reynolds.
    Edie Arlisa Brickell Simon is the daughter of Paul Edward and Jean Sellers Brickell of Texas.
    Paul Frederic and Edie Arlisa Brickell Simon have three children: Adrian, Lulu, and Gabriel.
    *Simon was the recipient of twelve Grammy awards. In 1998 he was inducted into the Grammy Hall of Fame. In 2001 he was inducted into the Rock and Roll Hall of Fame as a solo artist and in 1990 as partner in Simon and Garfunkel.
    The Simones relocated to New Canaan, CT.

Simon, William Edward, Sr. (1927-2000)

Occupation (s):	statesman - Deputy Secretary, United States Department of the Treasury, 1973-1974 (Nixon administration);
	United States Secretary of the Treasury, 1974-1977 (Nixon and Ford administrations);
	first administration, Federal Energy Office (Nixon administration)
	financier - vice-president, Weeden and Co. (stock brokerage firm);
	partner, in charge of the Government and Municipal Bond departments, Salomon Brothers (stock brokerage firm);
	member, seven-man executive committee, Salomon Brothers;
	vice-chairman of board, Blyth, Eastman, Dillon;
	co-founder, Wesray Capital Corp. (among their take-overs were: Gibson Greeting Cards, Anchor Glass Co., and Simmons Mattress Co.) (leverage buyout firm);
	a founder, WSGP International (financial services and real estate firm);
	a founder, William E. Simon and Sons (investment banking firm);
	a founder, Catterton–Simon Partners (private equity firm)
	industrialist - director of more than thirty companies, including: Citibank; Xerox Corp.; Halliburton; Kraft Foods; United Technologies
	writer - *Time For Truth*, 1980;
	Reforming the Income Tax System: Studies in Tax Policy, 1981;
	Time For Action, 1982;
	A Time for Reflection: An Autobiography, 2003
Civic Activism:	established, William E. Simon Foundation;
	chairman of board, United States Olympic Foundation;
	member, United States Olympic Committee, 1981-1985;
	director, Jesse Owens Foundation;
	director, Basketball Hall of Fame;
	director; National Tennis Foundation and Hall of Fame;
	director; Amateur Boxing Foundation;
	director, Women's Sports Foundation;
	created hundreds of scholarships for underprivileged students;
	endowed chairs at Lafayette College, Easton, PA, and at Center for Strategic and International Studies, Washington, DC;
	president, John M. Olin Foundation;
	trustee, John Templeton Foundation;
	director, Heritage Foundation;
	director, Hoover Foundation;
	chairman of board, Economic Policy Board;
	chairman of board, East–West Trade Board;
	chairman of board, President's Oil Policy Committee
Marriage(s):	M/1 – 1950-1995 – Carol Ann Girard (d. 1995)
	M/2 – 1996-2000 – Tania Adams Donnelly
Address:	Windmill Lane, East Hampton
Name of estate:	
Year of construction:	1778
Style of architecture:	Colonial Cape Cod Style
Architect(s):	
Landscape architect(s):	
House extant: yes	

Simon, William Edward, Sr. (cont'd)

Historical notes:

The house, originally named *South Wind*, was previously owned by Robert Whittle Dowling. In 1951 Dowling purchased nine acres on Windmill Lane and moved a 1737 house from Amagansett, a 1751 saltbox-style house from Springs, a 1778 Cape Cod-style house from Egypt Lane in East Hampton, and an 1802 windmill from Water Mill to the site. The compound was later owned by Simon, who purchased the 4.3-acre estate, which consists of a six-bedroom main residence, a cottage, and an 1802, thirty-six-foot-tall windmill, in 1976 for a reported $541,000.

The *Social Register Summer, 1982* lists William E. and Carol Girard Simon [Sr.] as residing on Windmill Lane, East Hampton.

He was the son of Charles and Eleanor Kearns Simon, Jr. of Paterson, NJ.

William Edward and Carol Ann Girard Simon, Sr. had seven children. Their son William E. Simon, Jr. was the Republican nominee for governor of California in 2002. Their daughter Mary married Dana Streep, the son of Harry William and Mary Wolf Wilkinson Streep, Jr. of Bernardsville, NJ, and the brother of actress Meryl Streep.

In 1986 the Graduate School of Management at the University of Rochester, Rochester, NY, was renamed the William E. Simon Graduate School of Business Administration.

In 2000 Simon's heirs placed the estate on the market. The asking price was $25 million.

Simonds, Francis May, Sr. (1866-1939)

Occupation(s):	mining engineer - Piedmont Corp., North Carolina
Civic Activism:	president, Engineer Alumni Association, Columbia University, NYC

Marriage(s):	1892-div. – Edith Vernon Mann (1871-1955)
	   - artist
	     writer - poetry

Address:	Further Lane, East Hampton
Name of estate:	*Heather Hill*
Year of construction:	
Style of architecture:	
Architect(s):	
Landscape architect(s):	
House extant:	unconfirmed

Historical notes:

The *Social Register Summer, 1919* lists Francis M. and Edith V. Mann Simonds [Jr.] as residing at *Heather Hill* in East Hampton.

He was the son of Frederick William and Sophia de Luze Simonds.

Edith Vernon Mann Simonds, who later owned the house, was the daughter of Samuel Vernon and Harriet Cogswell Onderdonk Mann, Sr. of Flushing, Queens. Edith subsequently married Charles Kingsley Moses with whom she continued to reside at *Heather Hill*. Edith's brother Samuel Vernon Mann, Jr. married Helen Wagstaff Colgate and resided at *Grove Point* in Kings Point. [*See* Spinzia, *Long Island's Prominent North Shore Families, vol. 1* – Mann entry.]

Francis May and Edith Vernon Mann Simonds, Sr.'s daughter Cecile married Daniel Varney Thompson, Jr. of Boston, MA, and resided in London, England. Their daughter Edith Vernon Mann Simonds married Leopold Damrosh Mannes and, later, John Crosby–Brown Moore with whom she resided at *Marsh Hill* in Menemsha, MA. Their son Francis May Simonds, Jr. married Marion Carey Dinsmore and resided in King Point. [*See* Spinzia, *Long Island's Prominent North Shore Families, vol. II* – Simonds entry .] Their son Samuel Vernon Mann Simonds was an infant at the time of his death in 1900. Their daughter Eleanor married Marion Jackson Verdery, Jr. and, subsequently, William S. Sloan with whom she resided at *Woodcrythe* in New Canaan, CT.

In 1955 the house was owned by Henry Mann. [*The East Hampton Star* March 17, 1955, p. 6.]

Sinclair, Earle Westwood (1874-1944)

Occupation(s):	financier - a founder and cashier, State Bank of Commerce, Independence, KS, 1908; vice-president, Exchange National Bank, Tulsa, OK, 1908-1910 industrialist - president, Sinclair Consolidated Oil Corp.; president, Sinclair Refining Co.
Marriage(s):	1902-1944 – Blanche Stich (1877-1952)
Address:	Lee Avenue, East Hampton
Name of estate:	*Fairlawn*
Year of construction:	1899
Style of architecture:	Colonial Revival with Federal elements
Architect(s):	Leinau and Nash designed the house (for Carson)
Landscape architect(s):	
Builder:	Asa Otis Jones, 1899 Asa Otis Jones, 1901 alterations (for Carson)

House extant: yes*
Historical notes:

 The house was built by William Moore Carson, Sr. In 1920 it was purchased by Sinclair. [*The East Hampton Star* July 30, 1920, p. 6.]

 The *Social Directory of Southampton, Long Island, 1931* lists Mr. and Mrs. Earle W. Sinclair as residing at *Fairlawn*, Lee Avenue, East Hampton.

 He was the son of John and Phoebe Simmons Sinclair. Earle's brother Harry married Elizabeth Farrell and resided in Kings Point. [*See* Spinzia, *Long Island's Prominent North Shore Families, vol. II* – Sinclair entry.]

 The Sinclairs' attorney in the Teapot Dome Scandal, James William Zevely, also resided in East Hampton.

 Earle Westwood and Blanche Stich Sinclair's daughter Kathleen married Dr. Louis Faugeres, Jr. and resided in East Hampton. Their son John married Laura Louise James, the daughter of Ellery Sedgwick and Louise Russell Hoadley James, Sr., of *Heather Dune* in East Hampton. At the time of John's divorce in 1949 he was residing in New Hyde Park, NY.

 *In 1901 a west wing was added to the house.

 In 1945 it was purchased by Robert Elliot McCormick. [*The East Hampton Star* November 8, 1945, p. 1.]

 In 1946 McCormick sold the house to Walter Bartow Duryea. [*The East Hampton Star* February 20, 1947, p. 6.]

 It was later owned by David Hall McConnell III. [*The East Hampton Star* May 20, 1965, p. 2.]

Sinclaire, Paul (1904-1983)

Occupation(s):	industrialist - Corning Glass Works, Corning, NY
Marriage(s):	M/1 – 1930-1935 – Claire Callaway Harris (1905-1935)
	M/2 – 1936-1940 – Christine Biller (1893-1940)
	- Civic Activism: board chair, Women's National Organization for Prohibition Reform; captain, Welfare Drive, Des Moines, IA
	M/3 – 1941 – Helen Schonwolf Hunt (b. 1899)
	M/4 – Gense Brashaer (1907-1982)
Address:	Georgica Road, East Hampton
Name of estate:	*Georgica Farm*
Year of construction:	
Style of architecture:	
Architect(s):	
Landscape architect(s):	
House extant:	unconfirmed
Historical notes:	

    Paul Sinclaire was the son of William and Helen Bostwick Sinclaire, Sr. of Corning, NY.
    Claire Callaway Harris Sinclaire was the daughter of William and Viera Callaway Harris.
    Paul and Claire Callaway Harris Sinclair's daughter Ann married John Clifford Mathews.
    Christine Biller Sinclaire was the daughter of Ulrey Biller of Des Moines, IA. She had previously been married to Vernon L. Clark of Des Moines, IA.
    The Blue Book of The Hamptons, 1965 and *1973* list Paul and Helen S. Hunt Sinclaire as residing at *Georgica Farm* on Georgica Road, East Hampton.
    She was the daughter of Gustav S. Hunt of East Orange, NJ. She had previously been married to Frederick Helier of East Hampton, the son of David Helier.
    The Blue Book of The Hamptons, 1979 lists Paul and Gense Brashaer Sinclaire as residing at 81 Dunemere Lane, East Hampton.
    She was the daughter of Peter Cominges and Rida Cronly Payne Brashaer of *Pointed Firs* in Castleton-on-Hudson, NY. Gense had previously been married to Vernon Cadwallader Gordon Parry, the son of Ernest H. Parry of Sussex, England, and heir to the Simmons mattress fortune Zalmon Gilbert Simmons III of Greenwich, CT.
    In 1950 Sinclaire had an addition made to his *Georgica Farm* residence. [*The East Hampton Star* March 9, 1950, p. 7.]
    It was purchased by Martin Tepper who subdivided the estate's property. [*The East Hampton Star* November 24, 1977, p. 4.]

Singh, Vinayak

Occupation(s):	industrialist - president and managing director, Si Group (developer and manufacturer of chemical intermediates)
	financier - portfolio manager, Republic Western, 1991-1994 (insurance firm); financial analyst, U-Haul International, 1990-1991; president, International Strategy and Investment Group, 2008
Marriage(s):	
Address:	386 Further Lane, Amagansett
Name of estate:	
Year of construction:	2001
Style of architecture:	Eclectic Colonial Revival
Architect(s):	
Landscape architect(s):	
House extant:	yes
Historical notes:	

    Vinayak Singh purchased the 9,000-square-foot, five-bedroom, eight-bath house from Moreton Binn for $9.5 million.
    In 2013 Singh listed the house for sale. The asking price, which represented a $1 million loss for Singh, was $8.5 million.

Sischy, Ingrid Barbara (1952-2015)

Occupation(s):	journalist - editor, *Artforum*; editor, *The New Yorker*; editor, *Interview*; contributing editor, *Vanity Fair*
	writer - magazine articles
Marriage(s):	2015-2015 – Sandra Simms (b. 1955)
	- journalist - editor, *Vanity Fair*
Address:	*[unable to determine street address]*, Montauk
Name of estate:	
Year of construction:	1883
Style of architecture:	
Architect(s):	McKim, Mead and White designed the house
Landscape architect(s):	Frederick Law Olmstead designed the site plan
House extant: unconfirmed	
Historical notes:	

The house is one of the Montauk Association's "Seven Sisters." It was later owned by Sischy.

She was the daughter of Dr. Benjamin and Mrs. Claire Sishy of Johannesburg, South Africa, and, later, Edinburgh, Scotland.

Sandra Simms had previously been married to the publisher of *Interview*, Peter Mark Brant, Sr.

Skidmore, James Bond (1900-1977)

Occupation(s):	merchant - president, Pattison and Browns (wholesale coal firm); president, Skidmore Coal Co.
Civic Activism:	trustee and mayor, Village of East Hampton, 1967, 1972; corresponding secretary, Garden Club of East Hampton; trustee, Southampton Hospital; secretary, Maidstone Club, East Hampton
Marriage(s):	1925-1977 – Emma Pattison (1900-1978)
	- Civic Activism: corresponding secretary, Garden Club of East Hampton
Address:	35 Dunemere Lane, East Hampton
Name of estate:	*Honeysuckle Hedge*
Year of construction:	
Style of architecture:	Flemish*
Architect(s):	
Landscape architect(s):	
House extant: yes	
Historical notes:	

The house, originally named *The Ingle*, was built by Mary Newlin Verplanck Johnson. It was then owned by her unmarried daughter Edith who sold it to Skidmore in 1936. The Skidmores renamed it *Honeysuckle Hedge*. [*The East Hampton Star* March 25, 1937, p. 1.]

The Blue Book of The Hamptons, 1965 lists James B. and Emma Pattison Skidmore as residing at 35 Dunemere Lane, East Hampton.

He was the son of Lemuel and Mary Johnson Skidmore, Sr. of Short Hills, NJ.

Emma Pattison Skidmore was the daughter of Gardiner and Susie Watson Pattison of Short Hills, NJ.

James Bond and Emma Pattison Skidmore's daughter Susie married David Harris, the son of Victor and Catherine Lawrence Richardson Harris of East Hampton, and, later, Eckley B. Coxe. Their daughter Patricia married S. Staley Tregellas, Jr. of Baltimore, MD.

*In 1937 the house was remodeled by Skidmore.

Skidmore, John Drake (1830-1903)

Occupation(s):	attorney
	financier - director, Eagle Fire Co.
Marriage(s):	1861-1871 – Elizabeth Newton Wetmore (1837-1871)
Address:	Georgica Road, East Hampton
Name of estate:	
Year of construction:	1894
Style of architecture:	Shingle
Architect(s):	John Tredwell Skidmore II, original design
	Isaac Henry Green II supervised the design of the house (for J. D. Skidmore)*
Landscape architect(s):	
Builder:	Philip Ritch
House extant: yes	
Historical notes:	

 The house was built by John Drake Skidmore.
 He was the son of Samuel Tredwell and Angelina E. Drake Skidmore, Sr. of Manhattan.
 Elizabeth Newton Skidmore was the daughter of Prosper Montgomery and Lucy Ann Ogsbury Wetmore.
 John Drake and Elizabeth Newton Skidmore's son Samuel later owned the house and called it *Idlerest*.
 [See following entry for additional family information.]
 *For Green's other commissions, *see* Spinzia, *Long Island's Prominent South Shore Families: Their Estates and Their Country Homes in the Towns of Babylon and Islip.*

Skidmore, Samuel Tredwell, II (1866-1947)

Occupation(s):	architect
	financier - stockbroker
Civic Activism:	vice-president and secretary, Maidstone Club, East Hampton
Marriage(s):	1908-1947 – Judith Wilcox Dousman (1883-1951)
Address:	Georgica Road, East Hampton
Name of estate:	*Idlerest*
Year of construction:	1894
Style of architecture:	Shingle
Architect(s):	John Tredwell Skidmore II, original design
	Issac Henry Green II supervised the design of the house (for J. D. Skidmore)*
Landscape architect(s):	
Builder:	Philip Ritch
House extant: yes	
Historical notes:	

 The house was built by John Drake Skidmore. It was later owned by his son Samuel who continued to call it *Idlerest*.
 The *Social Register Summer, 1910* and *1915* list Samuel T. and Judith W. Dousman Skidmore [II] as residing at *Idlerest* in East Hampton.
 She was the daughter of Hercules Louis and Nina Linn Sturgis Dousman of Prairie du Chien, WI.
 Samuel Tredwell and Judith Wilcox Dousman Skidmore II's daughter Nina did not marry.
 [See previous entry for additional family information.]
 *For Green's other commissions, *see* Spinzia, *Long Island's Prominent South Shore Families: Their Estates and Their Country Homes in the Towns of Babylon and Islip.*

Slifka, Alan Bruce (1929-2011)

Occupation(s):	financier - analyst and partner, L. F. Rothschild and Co. (investment banking firm;
	a founder and co-chairman, Halcyon / Alan B. Slifka Management Co., NYC;
	founder, Alan B. Slifka and Co., NYC (arbitrage firm)
	capitalist - a founder and chairman of board, Big Apple Circus, NYC
Civic Activism:	trustee, Jewish Funders Network;
	trustee, Tannenbaum Center;
	trustee, Interfaith Center, NYC;
	chairman of board, New Leadership Division, Federation of Jewish Philanthropies;
	a founder, Abraham Fund (promotes peaceful co-existence between Israelis and Arabs);
	trustee, American Jewish Congress;
	trustee, Bronx House (Emanuel Campus);
	trustee, Abraham Joshua Heschel School, NYC;
	gifted $15 million to the Abraham Joshua Heschel School, NYC;
	established Joseph Slifka Center for Jewish Life, Yale University, New Haven, CT;
	co-founder, with Eugene Wiener Slifka, Alan B. Slifka Foundation;
	chairman of board, New York School for Circus Arts;
	established Slifka Program on International Coexistence, Brandeis University, Waltham, MA
Marriage(s):	M/1 – 1958 – Jacqueline Watkins (b. 1935)
	- financier - stockbroker
	Civic Activism: president, Association of Residential Boards; president, Apartment Owners Association
	M/2 – Virginia B. *[unable to determine maiden name]*
	M/3 – 2004-2011 – Riva Arilla Golan (b. 1955)
	- capitalist - director, Retvo Clinic, Los Angeles, CA (treatment of autism)
Address:	Apaquogue Road, East Hampton
Name of estate:	
Year of construction:	
Style of architecture:	Neo-Georgian
Architect(s):	
Landscape architect(s):	
House extant: yes	
Historical notes:	

   Alan Bruce Slifka was the son of Joseph and Sylvia Slifka.
   Jacqueline Watkins Slifka is the daughter of Herman Mark and Rose Levine Watkins of Merion, PA.
   Alan Bruce and Jacqueline Watkins Slifka's son Randolph married Lauren Anne Kaskel, the daughter of Howard Kaskel of New York.
   Riva Arilla Golan Slifka is the daughter of Dr. Moshe and Mrs. Haya Biderman Golan of Netanya, Israel. Riva had previously been married to Edward Ritvo.
   Shortly after Slofka's death the six-bedroom, five-bath house was put on the market. The asking price was $13.9 million.

Smith, Warren G. (1848-1910)

Occupation(s):	merchant - partner, J. W. Green & Smith, Brooklyn, NY (wholesale jewelry firm);
	founder, Warren G. Smith, Brooklyn, NY (wholesale jewelry firm)
	Civic Activism: a founder, Maidstone Club, East Hampton
Marriage(s):	1883-1910 – Jessie Talmage (d. 1937)
Address:	Ocean and Lee Avenues, East Hampton
Name of estate:	
Year of construction:	1889
Style of architecture:	Shingle
Architect(s):	Joseph Greenleaf Thorp, 1901 alterations (for W. G. Smith)
	John Custis Lawrence, 1916 alterations (for Eastman)
Landscape architect(s):	
House extant: yes	
Historical notes:	

The house was built by Warren G. Smith.

He was the son of George W. and Jane Elizabeth Smith of Brooklyn.

Jessie Talmage Smith was the daughter of The Reverend Thomas DeWitt and Mary Rebecca Halsey Avery Talmage of East Hampton.

Warren G. and Jessie Talmage Smith's daughter Hazel married Martin Sullivan Baldwin, the son of William Delavin Baldwin of Manhattan.

In 1916 the house was purchased from Mrs. Smith by Joseph Eastman. [*The East Hampton Star* September 15, 1916, p. 7.]

In 1937 the twelve-room house was sold to James Thomas Lee. [*The New York Times* September 29, 1937, p. 41.]

Snow, Violetta Pierce (1882-1972)

Marriage(s):	1914-1932 – Dr. Irving Miller Snow (1881-1932)
	- physician - pediatrician –
	Buffalo Hospital, Buffalo, NY;
	Children's Hospital, Buffalo, NY;
	City Hospital, Buffalo, NY
	educator - instructor and clinical professor of diseases, University of Buffalo, Buffalo, NY, 1889-1916
	writer - numerous medical articles
	Civic Activism: a founder, Buffalo Fresh Air Mission;
	a founder, trustee, and president, Buffalo Academy of Medicine;
	member, Erie County, NY, exemption board during World War I
Address:	Craig Lane, East Hampton
Name of estate:	*Windermere*
Year of construction:	
Style of architecture:	
Architect(s):	
Landscape architect(s):	
House extant: unconfirmed	
Historical notes:	

The *Social Register Summer, 1950* lists Violetta Pierce Snow as residing at *Windermere* in East Hampton. *The Blue Book of The Hamptons, 1958 and* 1965 list her address as Craig Lane, East Hampton.

She was the daughter of Henry Joshua and Violetta Edwards Pierce of Buffalo, NY.

Dr. Irving Miller and Mrs. Violetta Pierce Snow's daughter Julia married Francis Emmett Neagle, Jr., the son of Francis Emmett and Irene McEnteer Du Bois Neagle, Sr. of Bronxville, NY.

Solley, Dr. Fred Palmer (1867-1950)

Occupation(s):	physician - internal medicine -
	St. Luke's Hospital, NYC, 1893-1894;
	Presbyterian Hospital, NYC, 1900-1910;
	Knickerbocker Hospital, NYC, 1920-1935;
	consulting physician, Southampton Hospital, Southampton, NY, 1920-1950
	educator - instructor, College of Physicians and Surgeons, Columbia University, NYC
	writer - *Malarial Fever in New York*, 1905
Marriage(s):	1895-1944 – Mary Houston Westcott (1866-1944)
Address:	Lee Avenue, East Hampton
Name of estate:	*Tanglebrae*
Year of construction:	1910
Style of architecture:	Mediterranean
Architect(s):	Joseph Greenleaf Thorp designed the house (for Solley)
Landscape architect(s):	
House extant:	no
Historical notes:	

    The house, originally named *Tanglebrae*, was built by Dr. Fred Palmer Solley.
    The *Social Register Summer, 1915* lists Dr. Fred Palmer and Mrs. Mary H. Westcott Solley as residing at *Tanglebrae* in East Hampton.
    He was the son of John Beach and Frances Mead Hedden Solley of Newark, NJ.
    Mary Houston Westcott Solley was the daughter of Robert Folger Westcott of Manhattan.
    Dr. Fred Palmer and Mrs. Mary Houston Westcott Solley's daughter Margaret married George Marshall Durant and resided in Ridgefield, CT. Their son Frederick married Dorothy Van Heusen Bates, the daughter of Howland Capen Bates of Berlin, NH. Their son Theodore married Evangeline Shreiter, the daughter of Arthur E. Shreiter of Detroit, MI. Their son Robert married Lila Childress, the daughter of L. Wade Childress of St. Louis, MO.

Solomon, Peter Jay (b. 1939)

Occupation(s):	financier -	vice-chairman of board, director, and partner, Lehman Brothers Kuhn Loeb;
		vice-chairman of board, director, chairman of acquisition department, Shearson Lehman / American Express;
		founder and chairman of board, Peter J. Solomon (investment banking firm), 1989
	capitalist -	director, Century Communications Corp.
	merchant -	director, Associated Dry Goods (department stores);
		director, Miller–Wohl (women's apparel);
		director, Edison Brothers Stores, St. Louis, MO;
		director, Stop & Shop Companies, Boston, MA;
		director, Phillips–Van Heusen
	journalist -	financial commentator, CNNfn
	publisher -	director, Esquire Inc.;
	politician -	New York City Deputy Mayor of Economic Development (Koch administration);
		chairman, campaign finance committee (for Koch)

Marriage(s): M/1 – 1963-div. – Linda Newman (b. 1941)
M/2 – 1996 – Susan Barach (b. 1944)
 - financier - vice-president, Mercer Management Consulting

Address: 42 Highway Behind the Pond, East Hampton
Name of estate:
Year of construction: c. 1903
Style of architecture: Modified Colonial Revival
Architect(s):
Landscape architect(s):
House extant: no; demolished*
Historical notes:

   Gerald Clery and his wife Sara Sherman Wiborg Murphy remodeled the dairy barn of Sara's parents' estate *The Dunes* into their residence which they called *Swan Cove*. In 1959 the noted actor Robert Montgomery purchased the house. In 1973 it was purchased from Montgomery by Alfred de Liagre, Jr. [*The East Hampton Star* March 1, 1973, p. 4.] Both Montgomery and de Liagre continued to call it *Swan Cove*. Because the house had a pink stucco exterior, it is sometimes referred to as *Pink House*. In 2009 the 3,500-square-foot, five-bedroom house was purchased by Peter Jay Solomon for $19 million. [*The East Hampton Star* April 15, 2010, p. 5.]
   He is the son of Sidney L. Solomon of New York.
   Linda Newman Solomon is the daughter of Eric Pfeiffer and Evelyn Edison Newman of St. Louis, MO. Linda subsequently married Donald Schapiro, the son of John and Lydia Schapiro.
   Peter Jay and Linda Newman Solomon's daughter Abigail married Jason Birkestrand, the son of O. J. and Carol Barenberg Birkestrand.
   Susan Barach Solomon is the daughter of Arnold and Stephanie Barach. Susan had previously been married to ____ Rebell.
   In 1955 the guest house was built. [*The East Hampton Star*, June 16, 1955, p. 12.]
   *In 2010 Solomon demolished the house and built a new residence on the site. [*The East Hampton Star* December 2, 2010, p. 3.]

Sonnenfeld, Barry (b. 1953)

Occupation(s): educator - a founder, Northwest Woods School, Bridgehampton, NY
entertainers and associated professions -
television and motion picture director and producer

Marriage(s): 1989 – Susan L. Ringo
- educator - a founder, Northwest Woods School, Bridgehampton, NY

Address: 50 Broadview Road, Amagansett
Name of estate:
Year of construction: 1995
Style of architecture: Modified Shingle
Architect(s):
Landscape architect(s):
House extant: yes
Historical notes:

The seven-bedroom, eight-and-a-half-bath, 9,000-square-foot house was built by Barry Sonnenfeld.
He is the son of Sonny and Irene Kellerman Sonnenfeld of NYC.
Susan L. Ringo Sonnenfeld had previously been married to Elliott Erwitt.
Barry and Susan L. Ringo Sonnenfeld's daughter Chole is an actress.
The house was later owned by Roy Lance Furman who sold it to Harvey Weinstein in 2014 for $11.65 million.
In 2018 Weinstein sold the house for $10 million.

Soule, Henri Remy (1903-1966)

Occupation(s): restaurateur - president, French Pavillion Restaurant Corp., NYC
(Le Pavillion restaurant, NYC, and La Cote Basque, NYC);
The Hedges Inn, East Hampton;
president, Le Pavillion, Inc., CA;
president, Le Pavillion, Inc., FL

Marriage(s): Olga Muller

Address: 74 James Lane, East Hampton
Name of estate:
Year of construction: 1873
Style of architecture: Colonial Revival
Architect(s):
Landscape architect(s):
Builder: E. Marvin Conklin, 1935
alterations (for Mrs. Hamlin)

House extant: yes
Historical notes:

The house was built by John Daniel Hedges. In 1935 it was purchased by Mrs. Mary Elkins Paxton Hamlin who enlarged the house for use as an inn.
In 1954 Mrs. Hamlin sold the house to Soule who called it The Hedges Inn.
He was the son of Louis and Loetitia Hargous Soule of Saubrigues–Landes, France.
The house, which is on the National Register of Historic Places, is currently The Hedges Inn.

Spaeth, Eloise O'Mara (1903-1998)

Civic Activism:	director, Contemporary Gallery;
	trustee and director, Dayton Art Institute, 1938-1944;
	chair, extension services, American Federation of the Arts, 1949;
	trustee, American Federation of the Arts;
	chair, art committee, Guild Hall, East Hampton;
	trustee, Guild Hall, East Hampton;
	trustee, Archives of American Art;
	director, Friends of Whitney Museum of American Art, NYC;
	co-founder, with her husband Otto, Spaeth Foundation, 1950 (assists young artists)
Marriage(s):	1923-1966 – Otto Lucien Spaeth, Sr. (1897-1966)
	- industrialist - president, Premier Distribution Co., St. Louis, MO, 1923-1935 (manufacturers of malt extract; merged into Pabst Brewing Co.);
	president, Dayton Tool and Engineering Co., Dayton, OH, 1935-1946;
	president, Otto L. Spaeth, Inc., Dayton, OH, 1940-1942;
	chairman of board, Metal–Mold Magnesium Corp., 1952-1954
	Civic Activism: member, War Manpower Commission, Dayton, OH, 1940-1946;
	delegate, First Congress of World's Catholic Artists, Rome, Italy, 1951;
	co-founder, with his wife Eloise, Spaeth Foundation, 1950 (assists young artists);
	vice-president, Whitney Museum of American Art, NYC;
	director and president, Liturgical Arts Society;
	founder and trustee, Americans for Democratic Action
Address:	58 Highway Behind the Pond, East Hampton
Name of estate:	
Year of construction:	1972
Style of architecture:	Eclectic
Architect(s):	Hugh Hardy designed the house (for E. Spaeth)
	Hugh Hardy designed alterations, 1999 (for Ranieri)
Landscape architect(s):	Tiziana Hardy designed the gardens (for E. Spaeth)
House extant: unconfirmed	
Historical notes:	

The 2,000-square-foot, three-bedroom, two-bath house was built by Eloise O'Mara Spaeth after the death of her husband.

[See following entry for family information.]

In 1999 Salvatore Anthony Ranieri purchased the house and used it as a guest house for his main residence at 54 Highway Behind the Pond. In 2012 Ranieri sold the guest house for $25 million and his main residence for $20 million.

Spaeth, Otto Lucien, Sr. (1897-1966)

Occupation(s):	*[See previous entry.]*
Civic Activism:	*[See previous entry.]*
Marriage(s):	1923-1966 – Eloise O'Mara (1903-1998)
	- *[See previous entry.]*
Address:	Further Lane, East Hampton
Name of estate:	
Year of construction:	1955
Style of architecture:	Modified Austrian Hunting Lodge*
Architect(s):	Nelson and Chadwick designed the house (for O. Spaeth)
Landscape architect(s):	
House extant: yes	
Historical notes:	

The house was built by Otto Lucien Spaeth, Sr.
He was the son of Anton and Clara Melchiors Spaeth.
Eloise O'Mara Spaeth was the daughter of James and Alice Margaret Moroney O'Mara.

Otto Lucien and Eloise O'Mara Spaeth's daughter Marna married Gregory Hancock Doherty and resided in Tarrytown, NY. Their daughter Deborah married Francis Shakespere and resided in Greenwich, CT. Their daughter Mary Louise married Bernard Thomas Koon, Jr. and resided in St. Louis, MO. Their son Otto Lucien Spaeth, Jr. married Anna Carolina Barringer, the daughter of Thomas C. Barringer of McLean, VA, and resided in Rye, NY.

*The house is reminiscent of the Hapsburg's hunting lodge.

Spalding, Jesse, II (1888-1934)

Occupation(s):	financier - partner, Farnum, Winter, and Co. (stock brokerage firm); partner, Spalding, Tucker, and Co. (stock brokerage firm)
Civic Activism:	director, Beekman Street Hospital, NYC; president, National Catholic Converts League
Marriage(s):	1914-1934 – Jean Fredericka Whiting (b. 1891)
	- Civic Activism: director, Saint Cecilia Club, NYC
Address:	Lily Pond Lane, East Hampton
Name of estate:	*Pineleigh*
Year of construction:	c. 1890
Style of architecture:	Modified Colonial Revival
Architect(s):	
Landscape architect(s):	John Custis Lawrence, 1910 garage (for Gordon)
Builder:	Edward M. Gay, 1910 garage (for Gordon)
House extant: unconfirmed	
Historical notes:	

The house was built by Anna Mary Brown Ireland. [*The East Hampton Star* May 16, 1940, p. 2.] In 1909 it was purchased by George Breed Gordon. [*The East Hampton Star* October 8, 1909, p. 5.] In 1920 the house was purchased by Edward Elliott Jenkins from Mrs. Gordon. [*The East Hampton Star* October 1, 1920, p. 5.] In 1926 it was purchased by Spaulding. [*The East Hampton Star* November 17, 1933, p. 4.]

The *Social Directory of Southampton, Long Island, 1931* lists Jesse and Jean Whiting Spalding [II] as residing at *Pineleigh* on Lily Pond Lane, East Hampton.

He was the son of Charles F. and Elizabeth Bertrand Clarke Spalding of Chicago, IL.

Jean Fredericka Whiting Spalding was the daughter of John Hill and Caroline Florence Spencer Whiting of Chicago. Jean subsequently married Robert Elliott Maxwell, the son of Robert and Alice Haskell Maxwell of Pittsburgh, PA, and continued to reside at *Pineleigh*.

Jesse and Jean Fredericka Whiting Spalding II's daughter Jane married Allison Ripley Maxwell, Jr. of Pittsburgh, PA. Their son Jesse Spaulding III, who resided in East Hampton, married Marie Brander, the daughter of Thomas Brander of Manhattan, and, later, Elvira Fairchild, the daughter of William and Elvira Brokaw McNair Fairchild of *Northway House* in Lattingtown. [*See* Spinzia, *Long Island's Prominent North Shore Families, vol. I* – Fairchild entry.] Their son John married Elizabeth Cooper, the daughter of Ernest R. and Esther Taggart Cooper of West Newton, MA. Their daughter Joyce married George Latimer Maxwell.

Spielberg, Steven Allan (b. 1946)

Occupation(s): entertainers and associated professions -
co-founder, Dream Works Studios;
motion picture director, producer, and screenwriter*
notable films include:

"Duel", 1971;
"The Sugarland Express", 1974;
"Jaws", 1975;
"Close Encounters of the Third Kind", 1977;
"1941", 1979;
"Raiders of the Lost Ark", 1981;
"E.T, the Extra-Terrestrial", 1982;
"Poltergeist", 1982;
"Twilight Zone The Movie", 1983;
"Indiana Jones and the Temple of Doom", 1984;
"The Color Purple", 1985;
"The Goonies", 1985;
"Empire of the Sun", 1987;
"Always", 1989;
"Hook", 1991;
"Jurassic Park", 1993;
"Schindler's List", 1993;
"The Lost World: Jurassic Park", 1997;
"Armistad", 1997;
"Indiana Jones and the Kingdom of the Crystal Skull", 2008;
"Saving Private Ryan", 1998;
"Black Hawk Down", 2001;
"A. I. Artificial Intelligence", 2001;
"Minority Report", 2002;
"Catch Me If You Can", 2002;
"The Terminal", 2004;
"War of the Worlds", 2005;
"Munich", 2005;
"Super 8", 2011;
"War Horse", 2011;
"Lincoln", 2012;
"Bridge of Spies", 2015;
"The BFG", 2016

Civic Activism: trustee, American Film Institute

Marriage(s): M/1 – 1985-div. 1989 – Amy Davis Irving (b. 1953)
- entertainers and associated professions -
stage and motion picture actress
M/2 – 1991 – Kathleen Sue Nail (b. 1953)
(aka Kate Capshaw)
- entertainers and associated professions -
television and motion picture actress

Address: 110 Apaquogue Road, East Hampton
Name of estate: *Quelle Farm*
Year of construction: 1985
Style of architecture: Industrial Modern
Architect(s): Charles Gwathmey designed
the complex *Quelle Farm*
(for Spielberg)
Landscape architect(s):
House extant: yes
Historical notes:

 The *Quelle Farm* complex, which consists of a 5,000-square-foot main residence, two guest houses, and a caretaker's cottage, was built by Steven Allen Spielberg.
 He is the son of Arnold and Leah Adler Spielberg.
 Amy Davis Irving Spielberg is the daughter of Jules and Priscilla Pointer Irving of California. Amy later married Bruno Barreto and, subsequently, Kenneth Bowser, Jr.
 Kathleen Sue Nail Spielberg is the daughter of Edwin Leon and Beverly Sue Simon Nail. Kathleen was previously married to Robert Capshaw.
 *Spielberg has been nominated for seven Academy Awards and has received three Academy Awards. He is the first non-literary member to be inducted into the Science Fiction Hall of Fame.

Spring, Preston Brady, Sr. (1841-1913)

Occupation(s):	attorney - Bartlett, Wilson, and Hayden, NYC
Civic Activism:	a founder, secretary, and treasurer, Maidstone Club, East Hampton
Marriage(s):	M/1 – 1864 – Julia C. Ireland
	M/2 – 1887-1913 – Betsy Eliza Royce (1854-1928)
	- educator - teacher
Address:	Georgica Road, East Hampton
Name of estate:	*Winklehawk*
Year of construction:	1895
Style of architecture:	Neo-Tudor
Architect(s):	Joseph Greenleaf Thorp designed the house (for Spring)
	Howard Greenley, 1915 alterations (for Roberts)
	Spencer Fullerton Weaver, Sr., 1925 alterations (for himself)
Landscape architect(s):	John Raum, 1917 (for Roberts)
	Jacob John Spoon designed the swimming pool (for Weaver)
Builder:	Philip Ritch

House extant: no*
Nassau County Museum Collection has photographs of the estate.
Historical notes:

The house, originally named *Winklehawk*, was built by Preston Brady Spring, Sr.
He was the son of Edward and Elizabeth Riker Spring of Manhattan.
Julia C. Ireland Spring was the daughter of George C. Ireland, Jr. of East Hampton.
Preston Brady and Julia C. Ireland Spring, Sr.'s son Preston Brady Spring, Jr. was an infant at the time of his death in 1880.
Betsy Royce Spring was the daughter of The Reverend Moses Strong and Mrs. Martha Ann Broyles Royce.
Preston Brady and Betsy Eliza Royce Spring Sr.'s daughter Margaret married Robert Ramsey and resided in Manhattan. Their daughter Elizabeth married C. Thomas Beach, the son of S. A. Beach of Belmont, NY. Their son Royce married Harriet Deyo, the daughter of S. L. F. Deyo, and resided at *Harleigh* in Easton, MD. Their son Rodney was killed at the Battle of Argonne in World War I.
In 1915 the house was purchased by Walter Scott Roberts. [*The East Hampton Star* August 6, 1915, p. 5; December 13, 1918, p. 5; and June 8, 1944, p. 3.]
In 1925 it was purchased by Spencer Fullerton Weaver, Sr. who renamed it *Spencecliff*.
In 1949 it was purchased by William Seligson who subdivided the estate's property into six building lots. [*The East Hampton Star* January, 13, 1955, p. 5, and June 16, 1955, p. 12.]
The house was subsequently owned by Adolph Green.
*In 1969 it was destroyed by fire during a wedding at Green's estate when a caterer's gas line leaked and ignited.

Stanton, Dr. Frederick Lester (1873-1945)

Occupation(s):	physician - orthodontist
	educator - professor of preventive dentistry and research, College of Dentistry, New York University, NYC
	writer - numerous articles in medical journals
	inventor - co-inventor, with Dr. Rudolph Hanau, a device to survey human dentition
Civic Activism:	a founder and president, Alumni Society of Angle School of Orthodontia; secretary, Angle School of Orthodontia
Marriage(s):	1911-1945 – Virginia Randell (1881-1967)
Address:	Georgica Road, East Hampton
Name of estate:	
Year of construction:	c. 1915
Style of architecture:	Modified Colonial Revival
Architect(s):	John Custis Lawrence, 1928 alterations (for A. D. Bell, Sr.)
Landscape architect(s):	
House extant: yes	
Historical notes:	

The house was built by Dr. Frederick Lester Stanton.
He was the son of George and Caroline Stanton of Norwich, CT.
Dr. Frederick Lester and Mrs. Virginia Randell Stanton's daughter Caroline married Woodford Carter Rhoades, the son of Sumner Rhodes of Montclair, NJ, and resided in Montclair, NJ. Their son John married Elizabeth Alden Fish, the daughter of John D. Rockefeller, Jr.'s private secretary Harry Potter Fish.
In 1928 Alfred Dennis Bell purchased the house.

Starke, Hamilton Jackson (1899-1972)

Occupation(s):	capitalist - a founder, Citizens Realty Co., Inc. (a holding firm for commercial buildings in East Hampton)
Civic Activism:	a founder and director, East Hampton League
Marriage(s):	1931-1972 – Mildred Genevieve Meagher
Address:	Jones Road, East Hampton
Name of estate:	
Year of construction:	
Style of architecture:	
Architect(s):	
Landscape architect(s):	
House extant: unconfirmed	
Historical notes:	

The house, originally named *Westover*, was built by Mary Breck Vaill Talmage. It was later owned by her son Rockwell Dwight Talmage who, in 1936, sold the house to Starke. [*Times Union* December 20, 1936, p. 21.]
He was the son of Albert Gunther and Jennie Laura Jackson Starke.
Mildred Genevieve Meagher Starke was the daughter of Ward C. and Beulah M. Sladden Meagher of NYC. Mildred subsequently married Louis Thorton Steel of East Hampton.
In 1946 Bertha Shults Dougherty purchased the house from Starke and renamed it *Westmeath*. [*The East Hampton Star* March 28, 1946, p. 6.]

Steele, The Reverend James Nevett, Sr. (1850-1916)

Occupation(s):	clergy - vicar, Trinity Church, NYC (17 years)
	writer - *The Importance of Musical Knowledge to the Priesthood*, 1894
Civic Activism:	trustee, General Theological Seminary, NYC;
	president, General Theological Seminary Alumni Association;
	chaplain, Daughters of the American Revolution;
	a founder, Maidstone Club, East Hampton;
	director, Gardiner's Bay Boat Club
Marriage(s):	1872-1916 – Helen Hudson Aldrich (1851-1926)
Address:	Dunemere Lane, East Hampton
Name of estate:	*Dunemere*
Year of construction:	c. 1891
Style of architecture:	Shingle
Architect(s):	Joseph Greenleaf Thorp designed the house (for J. N. Steele, Sr.)
Landscape architect(s):	
House extant: unconfirmed	
Historical notes:	

The house, originally named *Dunemere*, was built by The Reverend James Nevett Steele. Sr.

The *Social Register Summer, 1905* lists The Reverend J. Nevett and Mrs. Helen H. Aldrich Steel [Sr.] as residing at *Dunemere* in East Hampton.

He was the son of Isaac Nevett and Rosa Londonia Nelson Steele. James' brother Charles, a J. P. Morgan and Co. partner, married Nannie Gordon French and resided in Old Westbury and Southampton. [*See* Spinzia, *Long Island's Prominent North Shore Families, vol. II* and *Long Island's Prominent Families in the Town of Southampton* – Steele entries.] Their maternal great-grandfather Roger Nelson served as a brigadier general in the Revolutionary War, as a member of Congress, and as a judge in Maryland. Their maternal grandfather John Nelson was a member of Congress, United States Minister to Naples, and United States Attorney General, 1843-1845.

Helen Hudson Aldrich Steele was the daughter of Herman Daggett and Elizabeth Wyman Aldrich. Helen's brother Spencer married Harriett Holly Dall and resided at *Windermere* in Bay Shore. [*See* Spinzia, *Long Island's Prominent South Shore Families* – Aldrich entry.] Her brother James married Mary Gertrude Edson and resided at *Maycroft* in North Haven. [*See* Spinzia, *Long Island's Prominent Families in the Town of Southampton* – Aldrich entry.]

The Reverend James Nevett and Mrs. Helen Hudson Aldrich Steele, Sr.'s daughter Mary married Theodore Wilson Morris, Jr. and resided in East Hampton. Their daughter Ruth married Joseph Carleton Borden, Sr. of South Orange, NJ. Their son Charles married Corrine Caucholis, the daughter of Frederick A. Caucholis of NYC. Their daughter Helen married J. Leon Morgan, the son of Edward Morgan of Philadelphia, PA. Their son Leverett married Genevieve E. Green. Their son James Nevett Steele, Jr. married Elizabeth Arnold Congdon of Providence, RI.

The house was later owned by Clarence Hopkins Hensel who, in 1928, sold it to Theodorus Bailey II. Hensel and Bailey continued to call it *Dunemere*. [*The East Hampton Star* May 17, 1929, p. 7, and June 24, 1944, p. 1.]

Steele, Louis Thorton (1911-2002)

Occupation(s):	advertising executive - chairman of executive committee, Benton and Bowles, NYC (advertising firm)
Marriage(s):	M/1 – 1941-1981 – Marjorie Blair Dalberg (d. 1981) - Civic Activism: director, Ladies Village Improvement Society, East Hampton; treasurer, East Hampton Garden Club M/2 – 1982 – Mildred Genevieve Meagher
Address:	Apaquogue Road, East Hampton
Name of estate:	*Cobwebs*
Year of construction:	
Style of architecture:	
Architect(s):	
Landscape architect(s):	
House extant:	unconfirmed
Historical notes:	

The Blue Book of The Hamptons, 1958, 1965, and *1973* list L. T. and Marjorie Blair Dalberg Steele as residing at *Cobwebs* on Apaquogue Road, East Hampton.

He was the son of Harlow Leroy Steele.

Marjorie Blair Dalberg Steele was the daughter of Melvin H. Dalberg.

Mildred Genevieve Meagher Steele was the daughter of Ward C. and Beulah M. Sladden Meagher of NYC. She had previously been married to Hamilton Jackson Starke with whom she resided in East Hampton.

By 1987 the Steeles had relocated to 5 Pondview Lane, East Hampton.

Steinberg, Robert Michael

Occupation(s):	financier - president, Reliance Group Holdings, Inc. (insurance firm)
Marriage(s):	1964 – Kathryn Joanne Newman - real estate agent
Address:	14 Gracie Lane, East Hampton
Name of estate:	
Year of construction:	c. 1985
Style of architecture:	Modern
Architect(s):	Charles Gwathmey designed the house (for Steinberg) Kang H. Chang, 2011 alterations (for Schultz)
Landscape architect(s):	
House extant:	yes
Historical notes:	

The 8,500-square-foot house was built by Robert Michael Steinberg.

He is the son of Julius and Anne Cohen Steinberg of Hewlett Bay Park, NY.

Kathryn Joanne Newman Steinberg is the daughter of Fred and Madelon Newman.

The house was later owned by Howard Mark Schultz.

Stephanopoulos, George Robert (b. 1961)

Occupation(s):	entertainers and associated professions -
	chief anchor, ABC News;
	co-anchor, "Good Morning America";
	host, "This Week";
	chief political correspondent, ABC News;
	"fill-in" anchor, "ABC World News Tonight"
	politician - Democratic Party political advisor;
	member, Michael Dukakis presidential campaign, 1988;
	"floor man" in U. S. House of Representatives for Richard Gephardt;
	member, William J. Clinton's presidential campaign, 1992;
	senior advisor on policy and campaign strategy (Clinton administration)
	writer - *All Too Human*, 1999 (memoir);
	My Life (autobiography)
Marriage(s):	2001 – Alexandra Elliot Wentworth (b. 1965)
	- entertainers and associate professions -
	comedienne;
	television and motion picture actress;
	producer;
	scriptwriter for the television series "Head Case"
Address:	100 Dunemere Lane, East Hampton
Name of estate:	
Year of construction:	
Style of architecture:	Modified Neo-Federal
Architect(s):	
Landscape architect(s):	
House extant: yes	
Historical notes:	

The 4,500-square-foot, five-bedroom, four-bath house was previously owned by Frank Luther Mansell and then by his daughter Jessica Lyman Mansell Ambrose. In 2010 Stephanopoulos purchased the house from Jessica Ambrose for $3.5 million.

He is the son of Robert and Nickolitsa Gloria Chafos Stephanopoulos.

Alexandra Elliot Wentworth Stephanopoulos is the daughter of Eric Wentworth and First Lady Nancy Reagan's White House social secretary Mabel Hobart Wentworth.

In 2012 Stephanopoulos sold the house for $5.13 million.

Sterling, Oliver James, Sr. (1906-1974)

Occupation(s):	attorney - partner, Lawler, Sterling, and Kent
	capitalist - chairman, board of directors, East Hampton Airport
Marriage(s):	M/1 – 1934-div. 1941 – Virginia Lee Roberts Boyce (1911-2006)
	M/2 – 1943-1964 – Dorothea McElhone (1913-1964)
	- Civic Activism: director, Girls Vacation Fund
	M/3 – 1965-1974 – Hazel May Mason (1907-1975)
Address:	Further Lane, East Hampton
Name of estate:	
Year of construction:	1917
Style of architecture:	Modified Georgian Revival
Architect(s):	Arthur Truscott and John Custis Lawrence designed the house (for W. Reid)
Landscape architect(s):	
Builder:	Edward M. Gay
House extant: yes	
Historical notes:	

The house was built by Wallace Reid. In 1945 it was purchased by Sterling.
He was the son of Robert Dutcher and Ruth Lancaster Hoe Sterling of NYC.
Virginia Lee Roberts Boyce Sterling was the daughter of the founder of the Boy Scouts of America William Dixon Boyce. Virginia later married Gustave A. Mueller and, subsequently, Albert William Lind.
Oliver James and Virginia Lee Roberts Boyce Sterling, Sr.'s son Oliver James Sterling, Jr. married Miriam Kotler.
The Blue Book of The Hamptons, 1958 lists Oliver J. and Dorothea McElhone Sterling [Sr.] as residing on Further Lane, East Hampton.
She was the daughter of Arthur Johnson and Jane Dierken McElhone of NYC. Dorothea had previously been married to Noel Bleecker Leggett, Jr.
The Blue Book of The Hamptons, 1973 lists Oliver J. and Hazel Mason Sterling [Sr.] as residing on Further Lane, East Hampton.
She was the daughter of Frank Sherwood and Adalian Louise Burke Mason. Hazel had previously been married to William Bertram Edmondson; ____ Pocock; and Edward L. Reed.

Stern, Henry Root, Sr. (1882-1959)

Occupation(s):	attorney - partner, Rushmore, Bisbee, and Stern; partner, Mudge, Stern, Baldwin, and Todd
	politician - permanent president, New York State Electoral College; treasurer, Nassau County and New York State Republican Party Committees
Civic Activism:	chairman, New York State Board of Social Welfare in the Dewey administration;
	member, Nassau County Emergency Work Bureau, during the Depression;
	helped draft New York State's child labor law;
	trustee, Hofstra University, Hempstead
Marriage(s):	1909-1947 – Elsie Weston Lazarus (1890-1947)
	- Civic Activism: director, Greenwich House, NY; chair, Manhasset chapter, American Red Cross; member, executive committee, Nassau County chapter, American Red Cross; vice-chairman, disaster relief committee, Nassau County; director, Nassau County Federation of Republican Women

Address: Huntting Lane, East Hampton
Name of estate:
Year of construction:
Style of architecture:
Architect(s):
Landscape architect(s):
House extant: unconfirmed
Historical notes:

The *Social Register Summer, 1915* lists Henry Root and Elsie W. Lazarus Stern [Sr.] as residing on Huntting Lane, East Hampton.

By 1924 the Sterns had relocated to North Hills. [*See* Spinzia, *Long Island's Prominent North Shore Families, vol. I* – Stern entry.]

He was the son of Simon Hunt and Sara Stern.

Elsie Weston Lazarus Stern was the daughter of Eleazar Frank and Alice Furman Lazarus.

Henry Root and Elsie Weston Lazarus Stern, Sr.'s son Henry Root Stern, Jr. married Sarah Thomas Hamlin, the daughter of Arthur Sears Hamlin of Summit, NJ.

Stern, Joel Mark (b. 1941)

Occupation(s):	financier - vice-president, Chase Manhattan Bank; president, Stern, Stewart, Putnam, and Macklis, Ltd.; chairman of board and CEO, Stern, Stewart, and Co.; director, Stern, Stewart Europe Limited (later, Stern Value Management Ltd); chairman of board and CEO, Stern Value Management Ltd.; director, Stern, Stewart India
	writer - two books; co-authored six books
	educator - visiting professor, Graduate School of Business, University of Wisconsin, Madison, WI, 1971-1973; visiting professor, University of Florida, Gainsville, FL, 1973-1974; visiting professor, University of California - Berkeley, Berkeley, CA , 1975-1976; visiting professor, Columbia University, NYC, 1976- ; visiting professor, University of Hawaii, Honolulu, HI, 1978-1980; visiting professor, University of Cape Town, Cape Town, Republic of South Africa, 1979-1982; visiting professor, University of Witwatersrand, Johannesburg, Republic of South Africa, 1982; visiting professor, Fordham University, The Bronx, NY
Civic Activism:	member, visiting committee, Graduate School of Business, Fordham University, The Bronx, NY; member, advisory committee, University of Rochester, Rochester, NY
Marriage(s):	
Address:	74 Further Lane, East Hampton
Name of estate:	
Year of construction:	1980
Style of architecture:	Modern
Architect(s):	Norman Jaffe designed the house (for Stern)
Landscape architect(s):	
House extant: unconfirmed	
Historical notes:	

The 6,000-square-foot, four-bedroom, four-and-a-half-bath house was built by Joel Mark Stern. In 2016 the house and three acres were for sale. The asking price was $17.9 million.

Stern, Leonard Norman (b. 1938)

Occupation(s):	capitalist - chairman of board and CEO, Hartz Group (manufacturer of pet supplies; real estate); chairman of board and CEO, Hartz Mountain Industries (real estate holding firm); owner, Soho Grand Hotel, NYC; owner, TriBeca Grand Hotel, NYC
	merchant - director, Rite Aid (drugstore chain)
	restaurateur - partner, Chart House Restaurant
Civic Activism:	member, New York Real Estate Board; founder and chairman of board, Homes for Homeless; donated $33 million to New York University, NYC; founder, Milk From the Heart, 2011 (provided free milk to NYC's low income families)

Marriage(s):	M/1 – 1962-div.1980 – Judith Falk
	  - psychologist
	M/2 – 1987 – Allison Maher
	  - entertainers and associated professions -
	     television producer
	   model
	   Civic Activism: trustee and board vice-chair, Wildlife Conservation Society; trustee, Central Park Zoo, NYC; established Allison Maher Stern Foundation

Address:	20 Drew Lane, East Hampton
Name of estate:	
Year of construction:	
Style of architecture:	Contemporary with French Country Elements
Architect(s):	
Landscape architect(s):	
House extant: yes	
Historical notes:	

Leonard Norman Stern is the son of Max and Hilda Lowenthal Stern.

Judith Falk Stern is the daughter of Charles and Charlotte Rothfeld Falk. Judith subsequently married Stephen M. Peck.

Leonard Norman and Judith Falk Stern's son Emanuel married Elizabeth Eagan. Their son Edward married Stephanie Beth Rein. Their daughter Andrea is a photographer.

The house, which had been uninhabited for many years and in need of refurbishing, was purchased from Stern in 1987 by Jerry Della Femina for $3.4 million. Della Femina spent an additional $6 million to remodel the house. In 2012 he sold it to David Zaslav for $24.5 million.

Stern, Robert Arthur Morton (b. 1939)

Occupation(s):	architect -	founder and senior partner, Robert A. M. Stern Architects*; partner, Stern, Hagmann Architects
	educator -	dean, Yale School of Architecture, Yale University, New Haven, CT; professor of architecture and director of Historical Preservation Program, Graduate School of Architecture, Planning and Preservation, Columbia University, NYC; director, Temple Hoyne Bell Center for the Study of American Architecture, Columbia University, NYC, 1984-1988
	writer -	*New Directions in American Architecture*, 1969, revised 1977; *George Howe: Toward a Modern American Architecture*, 1975; *Modern Classicism*, 1988; co-authored, *East Hampton's Heritage*, 1982. revised 1996; co-authored, *New York, 1900*, 1983; co-authored, *New York, 1930*, 1987; co-authored, *New York, 1960*, 1995; co-authored, *New York, 1880*, 1999; co-authored, *New York, 2000*, 2006
	capitalist -	director, The Walt Disney Co, 1992-2003
	entertainers and associated professions -	hosted "Pride of Place: Building the American Dream", 1986 (eight-part, eight-hour PBS television documentary)

Marriage(s): 1966-div. 1977 – Lynn Solinger (b. 1942)
- professional photographer - editor, Ross – Gaffney Films, NYC, 1965-1966; photographic archivist, Stern, Hagmann Architects, 1968-1977
Civic Activism: member, National Council of Environmental Defense, NYC; director, Alva B. Gimbel Foundation; member, board of advisors, National Abortion and Reproductive Rights Action League, NYC

Address: Cottage and Lee Avenues, East Hampton
Name of estate:
Year of construction: 1900
Style of architecture: Shingle
Architect(s): Thomas Nash designed his own house
Robert Arthur Morton Stern, 1961 alterations; replaced 1951 addition with east porch
Landscape architect(s):
Builder: Asa Otis Jones
House extant: yes**
Historical notes:

The house was built by Thomas Nash. [*The East Hampton Star* April 19, 1901, p. 5.] It was later owned by Robert Arthur Morton Stern.

He is the son of Sidney Stanley and Sonya Cohen Stern of Brooklyn.

Lynn Solinger Stern is the daughter of David Morris and Hope Alva Gimbal Solinger of Manhattan. Lynn subsequently married Jeremy Pollard Lang.

Robert Arthur Morton and Lynn Solinger Stern's son Nicholas married Courtney ____ and resides at 101 Cove Hollow Road, East Hampton.

*The firm of Robert A. M. Stern Architects also designs furniture, lighting, fabrics, and other decorative household items. Its recent commissions include: Federal Courthouse, Richmond, VA, 2006; Jacksonville Public Library, Jacksonville, FL, 2005; Disney Boardwalk, Orlando, FL, 1996; Norman Rockwell Museum, Stockbridge, MA, 1993; Disney Yacht Club Resort, Orlando, FL, 1990; Disney Beach Club Resort, Orlando, FL, 1990.

**Alterations were made to the house in 1904, 1951, and 1969.

Stevens, Leighton H. (1903-1969)

Occupation(s):	financier - partner, Cornwall and Stevens, NYC (insurance firm)
Marriage(s):	Anna Fay Prosser (1907-1973)
Address:	Terbell Lane, East Hampton
Name of estate:	
Year of construction:	
Style of architecture:	
Architect(s):	
Landscape architect(s):	
House extant: unconfirmed	
Historical notes:	

In 1939 Stevens purchased the William Walker Green house. *[The New York Times* May 28, 1939, p. D3.]

He was the son of George Canning and Josephine Wolfe Shinn Stevens of Quogue and West Orange, NJ. [*See* Spinzia, *Long Island's Prominent Families in the Town of Southampton* – Stevens entry.] Leighton's sister Barbara married Spencer Brainard. His sister Serena married George Wilhelm Merck, the chairman of the board of the pharmaceutical firm of Merck & Co.

Anna Fay Prosser Stevens was the daughter of Seward and Constance Barber Prosser. She had previously been married to Dan Platt Caukins of NYC, the son of Edward Caukins of Grosse Pointe, MI.

Stewart, Martha Helen Kostyra (b. 1941)

Occupation(s):	entertainers and associated professions* -
	     host, "Martha Stewart Living", 1993-2005;
	     host, "Martha", 2005-2012;
	     host, "The Martha Stewart Show";
	     host, "The Apprentice", 2005;
	     host, "The Apprentice: Martha Stewart", 2005;
	     host, "Martha Stewart's Cooking School", 2012
	 capitalist - president, CEO, and director, Martha Stewart Living Omnimedia (holding company)
	 journalist - numerous newspaper columns and magazine articles
	 writer - *Entertaining*, 1982; *Martha Stewart's Quick Cook*, 1983; *Martha Stewart's Hors D'oeuvres*, 1984; *Martha Stewart's Pies & Tarts*, 1985; *Weddings*, 1987; *The Wedding Planner*, 1988; *Martha Stewart's Quick Cook Menus*, 1988; *Martha Stewart's Christmas*, 1989; *Martha Stewart's Rules*, 2005; *Martha Stewart's Baking Handbook*, 2005; *Martha Stewart's Homekeeping Handbook*, 2006

Marriage(s):	1961-div. 1990 – Andrew Stewart (b. 1937)
	   - attorney - corporate attorney, Times–Mirror (publishing firm);
	     publisher - president, Harry N. Abrams, Inc., NYC;
	     a founder, Stewart, Tabori, Chang (publishing firm)

Address:	58 Lily Pond Lane, East Hampton
Name of estate:	
Year of construction:	1873
Style of architecture:	Shingle
Architect(s):	Joseph Greenleaf Thorp, 1893 alterations (for Talmage)
Landscape architect(s):	
Builder:	George A. Eldredge, 1893 alterations
House extant: yes	
Historical notes:	

The house was built by The Reverend Thomas De Witt Talmage. In 1990 it was purchased by Stewart.
She is the daughter of Edward and Martha Ruszkowski Kostryra of Nuttley, NJ.
Andrew Stewart is the son of George and Ethel Stewart.
Andrew and Martha Helen Kostyra Stewart's daughter Alexis married John Robert Cuti.
*In 2011 Martha was inducted into the New Jersey Hall of Fame.

Stewart, Martha Helen Kostyra (b. 1941)

Occupation(s): *[See previous entry.]*

Marriage(s): 1961-div. 1990 – Andrew Stewart (b. 1937)
- *[See previous entry.]*

Address: 84 Georgica Close Road, East Hampton
Name of estate:
Year of construction: 1963
Style of architecture: Modern
Architect(s): Gorden Bunshaft designed his own residence
Landscape architect(s):
House extant: no; demolished in 2004
Historical notes:

The 2,300-square-foot, two-bedroom house, originally named *Travertine House*, was built by Gordon Bunshaft. His widow Nina Elizabeth Wayler Bunshaft willed it to the Museum of Modern Art.

In 1995 Martha Stewart purchased the house from the museum for $3.2 million. She had architect John Pawson gut the house's interior and was preparing to renovate it when she became involved in litigation over shrubbery and a service building which she was planning to erect. Martha transferred the house's gutted shell to her daughter Alexis, who sold it to Donald H. Maharam in 2004 for $9.5 million. Maharam demolished the house and built a new residence.

Stimson, Henry Clark (1813-1894)

Occupation(s): capitalist - president, Dayton and Altoona Railroad;
president, Paterson & Hudson River Railroad;
president, Paterson & Ramapo Railroad;
president, Union of Ohio Railroad
financier - founder and senior partner, Henry C. Stimson & Sons,
NYC (stock brokerage firm)*

Marriage(s): Julia Maria Atterbury (1819-1908)

Address: Main Street and Buell Lane, East Hampton
Name of estate:
Year of construction:
Style of architecture: Victorian
Architect(s): Theodore Weston, alterations (for himself)
Landscape architect(s):
House extant: no
Historical notes:

In 1894 Stimson purchased the Reverend Samuel Buell / Timothy Hedges ancestral property and remodeled the house. He was the son of The Reverend Bowen and Mrs. Rebecca Pond Stimson of Windham, NY.

Julia Maria Atterbury Stimson was the daughter of Lewis and Catharine Boudinot Atterbury.

Henry Clark and Julia Maria Atterbury Stimson's son The Reverend Henry Albert Stimson married Alice Wheaton Bartlett, the daughter of Samuel Colcord and Mary Bacon Learned Bartlett. Their son Lewis married Candace Thurber Wheeler, the daughter of Thomas Mason and Candace Thurber Wheeler. Their son John married Edith Everett Burgess, the daughter of Harriet Proctor Burgess; Eleanor Elvira Maxson, the daughter of Schuyler Abel and Joanna Kenyon Maxson; and Mary Rose. Their son William died in 1872 at the age of eighteen. Their son Frederick married Emma Burham, the daughter of George and Anna Hemple Burham and, later, Elizabeth Harrison. Their daughter Julia married Henry Patterson Loomis. Their daughter Mary, who later owned the house did not marry. The house was then owned by Mary's sister Catherine who married Theodore Weston.

*After leaving his parent's farm in Windham, Stimson worked for a period in a locomotive shop in Paterson, NJ. His wife's inheritance enabled him to purchase a seat on the New York Stock Exchange where he gained a reputation for being cool-headed and scrupulously honest. Notable among his clients were Winston Churchill's grandfather Leonard Jerome of Brooklyn, who was known for making and losing fortunes in the market, and financiers and market manipulators Jay Gould and Commodore Vanderbilt. Stimson hated the stress of market volatility and suffered from nightmares. His worse fears were realized when he suffered severe losses in the Panic of 1873 but was able to maintain a comfortable standard of living with what money he was able to retain coupled with that of his wife's trust fund. [Godfrey Hodgson. *The Colonel: The Life and Wars of Henry Stimson 1867-1950.* New York: Alfred A. Knopf, 1990, pp. 26-27.]

The Stimson's grandson, the noted statesman Henry Lewis Stimson, resided at *Highold* in West Hills, Long Island. [*See* Spinzia, *Long Island's Prominent North Shore Families, vol. II* – Stimson entry.] Their grandson the noted inventor Alfred Lee Loomis resided in East Hampton.

The house was later purchased by the Osborne family who demolished it and donated the land to the East Hampton Free Library.

Stokes, The Reverend John Dunlap (1839-1921)

Occupation(s): clergy - pastor, First Presbyterian Church, East Hampton
writer - *The Presbyterian Church, East Hampton, Long Island*, 1887

Marriage(s): 1867-1915 – Mary Benjamin Williams (1841-1915)

Address: 54 Lee Avenue, East Hampton
Name of estate:
Year of construction: 1900
Style of architecture: Dutch Colonial Revival
Architect(s): George A. Eldredge
Landscape architect(s):
Builder: George A. Eldredge
House extant: yes
Historical notes:

The house was designed and built by George A. Eldredge. It was later owned by Stokes.
He was the son of Joseph and Ann Wallace Stokes.
Mary Benjamin Williams Stokes was the daughter of Judge James Williams.
The Reverend John Dunlap and Mrs. Mary Benjamin Williams Stokes' son Dr. John Wallace Stokes married Alice Peck Wheeler and resided in Southold. Their daughter Jean did not marry. Their daughter Mary married Dr. James Brown Griswold and resided in Morristown, NJ.
In 2013 the house sold for $7 million.

Stone, Edward Durell, Sr. (1902-1978)

Occupation(s): architect - member, Coolidge, Shepley, Bullfinch, & Abbott, Boston, MA;
member, Schultze and Weaver;
member, Associated Architects of Rockefeller Center;
independent architect*
educator - taught advanced design, New York University, NYC;
associate and full professor, Yale University, New Haven, CT
writer - *My Life Took a New and Highly Significant Turn*, 1953

Marriage(s): M/1 – 1931-div. 1954 – Orlean Vandiver (1905-1988)
 - interior decorator
M/2 – 1954-div. 1966 – Maria Eleana Torch (b. 1927)

Address: Drew Lane, East Hampton
Name of estate:
Year of construction:
Style of architecture:
Architect(s):
Landscape architect(s):
House extant: unconfirmed
Historical notes:

Frederick Bryant Ashplant purchased Mary Louise Woodin Miner's residence *Mi Dune*. [*The East Hampton Star* November 23, 1944, p. 8.] In 1961 he sold the house to Stone. [*The East Hampton Star* May 4, 1961, p. 4.]
He was the son of Benjamin Hicks and Ruth Johnson Stone of Fayetteville, Arkansas.
Orlean Vandiver Stone was the daughter of Robert Merritt Vandiver of Montgomery, AL. She subsequently married Albert Halstead and, later, Ernest Curtin and resided in NYC and in Old Lyme, CT.
Edward Durell and Orlean Vandiver Stone, Sr.'s son Edward Durell Stone, Jr. married Carolyn Ellis Ordway, the daughter of John R. and Marjorie Ellis Ordway of Montclair, NJ; Jacqueline Marty, daughter of Jemuel Gates Marty, Jr.; and, later, Helen Ecclestone.
Maria Eleana Torch Stone was the daughter of the noted architect Carl Franc Torch.
*Among Stone's numerous commissions were Radio City Music Hall, NYC; John F. Kennedy Center for the Performing Arts, Washington, DC; Museum of Modern Art, NYC; United States Embassy, New Delhi, India; and the Anson Conger Goodyear, Sr. residence, Old Westbury, NY. [*See* Spinzia, *Long Island's Prominent North Shore Families*, vol. I – Goodyear entry.]

Storey, Emma Josephine de Raismes (1852-1929)

Marriage(s): Edward Albert Storey (1842-1908)
- diplomat – vice-consul, Geneva, Switzerland
  shipping -   ship broker
  financier -   member, New York Produce Exchange

Address: Further Lane, Amagansett
Name of estate: *Homelot*
Year of construction:
Style of architecture:
Architect(s):
Landscape architect(s):
House extant: unconfirmed
Historical notes:

The *Brooklyn Blue Book and Long Island Society Register, 1918* lists Emma Josephine de Raismes Storey as residing at *Homelot* in Amagansett.

She was the daughter of Jean Francois Joseph and Martha Ella Holt de Raismes. Emma's sister Martha married Dr. Marshall Lord Warrin and resided at *Kemah* in Amagansett.

Edward Albert and Emma Josephine de Raismes Storey's son Frank married Mona Mundell and resided in Manhattan and at *Homelot*. Their son John married Phyllis Elwyn Moore, the daughter of John Bassett Moore of NYC, and resided in Mamaroneck and at *Homelot*. Their daughter Gladys married George Curtis Kip and resided in Brooklyn and at *Homelot*. Their son Richard died in 1897 at the age of eighteen.

Stratton, Clara Cooper (d. 1910)

Marriage(s): 1856-1884 – Charles Preston Stratton (1828-1884)
- attorney;
  judge -   Camden County, NJ
  politician - member, Camden City Council
  financier - director, Bridgeton National Bank
  capitalist - director, West Jersey Railroad
  shipping - director, Camden & Philadelphia Ferry Co.

Address: Woods Lane, East Hampton
Name of estate:
Year of construction:
Style of architecture:
Architect(s):
Landscape architect(s):

House extant: no
Historical notes:

In 1893 Adrian Hoffman Larkin remodeled the South End School as his residence which he called *Green Frog*. [*The East Hampton Star* September 30, 1965, p. 12.] By 1900 the house was owned by Mrs. Stratton. [*The East Hampton Star* February 9, 1900, p. 5.]

She was the daughter of Benjamin and Abigail Pride Cooper.

Charles Preston Stratton was the son of Nathan Leake and Hannah Buck Stratton.

Charles Preston and Clara Cooper Stratton's daughter Clara married Thomas Lea Perot and resided in Morristown, NJ. Their daughter Anna married Hoffman Livingston of Camden, NJ. Their son Richard married Marion Elizabeth MacGill. Their son Preston married Rose McLaughlin.

The house was later owned by Miss Hedwig Monberg who, in 1954, sold it to Garvin Brackenridge, Sr. [*The East Hampton Star* March 4, 1954, p. 2, and June 24, 1954, p. 2.]

Strong, George Arthur (1848-1926)

Occupation(s):	attorney - partner, Martin and Smith, NYC
Marriage(s):	Harriet Efner Wheelock (1854-1931)
Address:	Georgica Road, East Hampton
Name of estate:	
Year of construction:	1895
Style of architecture:	Cottage
Architect(s):	Theodore Weston designed the house (for W. A. Wheelock)
Landscape architect(s):	
Builder:	George A. Eldredge
House extant: yes	
Historical notes:	

    The house was built by William Almy Wheelock of East Hampton as a present for his daughter Harriet Efner Wheelock Strong.

    George Arthur Strong was the son of George Perrine and Malinda P. Fales Strong.

    George Arthur and Harriet Efner Wheelock Strong's daughter Harriet married Thomas Leighton McCready, Sr. Their daughter Agnes married Howard Huntington. Their daughter Helen married William Burke Belknap II.

    The house is listed on the National Register of Historic Places.

Strong, Theron George (1846-1924)

Occupation(s):	attorney
	writer - *Landmarks of a Lawyer's Lifetime*, 1914;
	Joseph H. Choate: New Englander, New Yorker, Lawyer, Ambassador, 1917
Civic Activism:	trustee, New York Presbytery;
	president, Alumni Association, University of Rochester, Rochester, NY;
	director, New York Juvenile Asylum;
	director, Legal Aid Society of New York;
	director, New York Bible Society
Marriage(s):	1878-1924 – Martha Howard Prentice (d. 1949)
	- Civic Activism: secretary, women's auxiliary, New York Botanical Garden*
Address:	Lily Pond Lane and Cottage Avenue, East Hampton
Name of estate:	*The Dolphins*
Year of construction:	1899
Style of architecture:	Shingle
Architect(s):	George A. Eldredge designed and built 1899 alterations to the house and the 1902 stable (for Strong)

Landscape architect(s):
House extant: unconfirmed
Nassau County Museums has photographs of the estate.
Historical notes:

In 1899 Theron George Strong purchased Dan Talmage's *Red Cottage*. He altered the house and renamed it *The Dolphins*. [*The East Hampton Star* January 6, 1899, p. 5, and November 23, 1944, p. 3.]

The *Brooklyn Blue Book and Long Island Society Register, 1918* and *1921* list Theron George and Martha Howard Prentice Strong as residing at *The Dolphins* in East Hampton.

He was the son of Judge Theron Rudd and Mrs. Cornelia Barnes Strong of Palmyra, NY.

Martha Howard Prentice Strong was the daughter of John H. Prentice of Brooklyn.

*She was awarded the Horticultural Medal in Bronze by the Garden Club of America.

[For information about the Strongs' Bay Shore residence, *see* Spinzia, *Long Island's Prominent South Shore Families* – Strong entry.]

Theron George and Martha Howard Prentice Strong's son Theron Roundell Strong married Maude Robbins and resided at *Asher House* in Southampton. [*See* Spinzia, *Long Island's Prominent Families in the Town of Southampton* – Strong entry.] Their daughter Martha married Harold Turner.

In 1941 Mrs. Strong sold the house to Frederick Bryant Ashplant, Sr. [*The East Hampton Star* October 9, 1941, p. 1.]

Sutphen, Henry Randolph, Jr. (1902-1970)

Occupation(s):	financier - president and chairman of board, American Savings Bank; partner, Hopkinson and Sutphen, 1936-1945 (stock brokerage firm); Chicago representative, Chemical Corn Exchange Bank of New York, 1945-1948; director, Hanover Insurance Co.; director, Fulton Insurance Co.
Civic Activism:	director, New York County Grand Jury Association; trustee, St. Luke's Hospital, NYC; trustee, Fifth Avenue Presbyterian Church, NYC; trustee, Southampton Hospital; treasurer and director, Maidstone Club, East Hampton; president, Old East Hampton (members who have summered in East Hampton for at least 25 years)
Marriage(s):	
Address:	Dunemere Lane, East Hampton
Name of estate:	*Bowling Green*
Year of construction:	1927
Style of architecture:	Dutch Colonial Revival
Architect(s):	John Custis Lawrence designed the house (for LaMonte)
Landscape architect(s):	
Builder:	Edward M. Gay
House extant: yes	
Historical notes:	

The twelve-room house was built by George Mason LaMonte. [*The East Hampton Star* December 10, 1926.] In 1928 it was purchased by Henry Randolph Sutphen, Sr. who called it *Bowling Green*. [*The East Hampton Star* April 20, 1928, p. 1.] The house was later owned by his son Henry.

The *Social Register Summer, 1969* lists Henry Randolph Sutphen [Jr.] as residing at *Bowling Green*, Box 928, East Hampton.

[See following entry for additional family information.]

Sutphen, Henry Randolph, Sr. (1875-1950)

Occupation(s):	engineer - electrical engineer
	engineer and general manager, Elco Works (later, division of Electric Boat Co.)
	industrialist - director and vice-president, Electric Boat Co. (shipbuilding firm);
	director, Wright Aeronautical Corp.;
	director, Canadair (aircraft manufacturer)
	inventor - numerous devices and appliances for electrical and gasoline boatbuilding
	financier - director, American Savings Bank, NYC
Civic Activism:	chairman of board, Pediatrics Foundation, NYC;
	president, National Association of Boat and Engine Manufacturers;
	director, Maidstone Club, East Hampton
Marriage(s):	1898-1950 – Susanna Preston Lees (d. 1956)
	- Civic Activism: secretary, YWCA's Roberta House, NYC
Address:	Dunemere Lane, East Hampton
Name of estate:	*Bowling Green*
Year of construction:	1927
Style of architecture:	Dutch Colonial Revival
Architect(s):	John Custis Lawrence designed the house (for LaMonte)
Landscape architect(s):	
Builder:	Edward M. Gay
House extant: yes	
Historical notes:	

    The twelve-room house was built by George Mason LaMonte. [*The East Hampton Star* December 10, 1926.] In 1928 it was purchased by Sutphen who called it *Bowling Green*. [*The East Hampton Star* April 20, 1928, p. 1.]
    The *Long Island Society Register, 1929* lists Henry R. and Susanna P. Lees Sutphen [Sr.] as residing in East Hampton. The *Social Directory of Southampton, Long Island, 1931* lists their address as Dunemere Lane, East Hampton. The *Social Register Summer, 1951* lists the name of the estate as *Bowling Green*.
    He was the son of The Reverend Morris Crater and Mrs. Eleanor Brush Sutphen of Morristown, NJ.
    Susanna Preston Lees Sutphen was the daughter of James Lees of NYC.
    Henry Randolph and Susanna Preston Lees Sutphen, Sr.'s son Preston married Marion Fahys Hodenpyl, the daughter of Eugene Hodenpyl, and resided at *Gawley House* in North Haven.
    The house was subsequently owned by Henry Randolph Sutphen, Jr. who continued to call it *Bowling Green*.
[See previous entry for additional family information.]

Sweetser, Jesse William, Sr. (1902-1989)

Occupation(s):	industrialist - vice-president, Glenn L. Martin Co. (later, Martin Marietta); vice-president, Martin Marietta
	capitalist - founder Sweetser Corp. (developer and marketer of wartime products for commercial use)
Civic Activism:	president and chairman of board, Metropolitan Golf Association; treasurer, United States Golf Association; director, Maidstone Club, East Hampton; chairman, golf committee, Maidstone Club, East Hampton
Marriage(s):	M/1 – 1926-1972 – Agnes Isabel Lewis (1905-1972) (aka Nan Lewis)
	M/2 – Virginia Lee
Address:	27 Drew Lane, East Hampton
Name of estate:	
Year of construction:	1920
Style of architecture:	Shingle
Architect(s):	John Custis Lawrence designed the house (for F. K. Hollister)
	Richard A. Cook of CookFox Associates designed 2007 alterations (for Rosenstein)
Landscape architect(s):	Paula Hayes (for Rosenstein)
Builder:	Edward M. Gay (for F. K. Hollister)
	Bulgin & Associates, 2007 alterations (for Rosenstein)

House extant: yes
Historical notes:

    The house was built by Dr. Frederick Kellogg Hollister. In 1939 Mrs. Hollister sold it to Sweetser. [*The East Hampton Star* June 22, 1939, pp. 1 and 5.]
    He was the son of George E. and Boone Small Sweetser of NYC and St. Louis, MO. At the age of twenty, Jesse won the U. S. Amateur Golf championship. He went on to become the first American-born player to win the British Amateur Golf championship.
    Agnes Isabel Lewis Sweetser was the daughter of Adam L. Lewis of Toronto, CA.
    Jesse William and Agnes Isabel Lewis Sweetser, Sr.'s daughter Nan married Robert Price Dodds and resided in Rancho Santa Fe, CA. Their son Jesse William Sweetser, Jr. married Nadine Harbaugh, the daughter of Philip D. Harbaugh and resided in La Mirada, CA.
    In 1941 Alexander Fraser purchased the house from Sweetser and called it *Wilsheron*. [*The East Hampton Star* October 23, 1941, p. 5.]
    In 1960 Frances Ann Cannon (Hersey) Dougherty purchased it from Fraser. [*The East Hampton Star* April 28, 1960, p. 11.]
    In 2005 her husband Frazer Lowber Welsh Dougherty sold the house to Barry Rosenstein for $19.2 million. [*The East Hampton Star* June 23, 2005, p. 35.]
    In 2017 Rosenstein listed the house for sale. The asking price was $70 million.
    In 2019 the 10,425-square-foot, nine-bedroom, thirteen-bath house, a separate two-bedroom caretakers/guest cottage and 1.567 acres was again for sale. The asking price was $52.5 million.

Talmadge, John Frelinghuysen (1873-1931)

Occupation(s):	financier - partner, George Prentiss and Co., NYC (stock brokerage firm); treasurer, Long Island Safe Deposit Co.
Civic Activism:	trustee, St. John's Hospital; trustee, Home of St. Giles, the Cripple
Marriage(s):	1903-1931 – Louise Thorne Ditmas (1882-1937)
Address:	Ocean Avenue, East Hampton
Name of estate:	*Tollemache House*
Year of construction:	
Style of architecture:	
Architect(s):	
Landscape architect(s):	
House extant: unconfirmed	
Historical notes:	

    The *Social Directory of Southampton, Long Island, 1931* lists Mr. and Mrs. John F. Talmadge as residing on Ocean Avenue, East Hampton. The *Long Island Society Register, 1929* lists the name of the estate as *Tollemache House*.
    He was the son of Samuel and Arietta Minthorn Clark Talmadge.
    Louise Thorne Ditmas Talmadge was the daughter of John and Louise Rhinelander Thorne Ditmas, Jr.
    John Frelinghuysen and Louise Thorne Ditmas Talmadge's son Samuel was a youth at the time of his death. Their daughter Gladys married Richard Scott Perkins and resided in Garden City. Their son Theodore married Elizabeth Jean Clark, the daughter of Ivor Bache and Jessie E. Gillies Clark of *Driftwood* in Amagansett, and resided in Brooklyn. Their son John married Hope Lewis, the daughter of The Reverend Tuttle and Mrs. Constance McMurtry Lewis of Brooklyn. Their daughter Louise married David S. Hirschberg and resided in Brookline, MA.

Talmage, Mary Breck Vaill (1858-1943)

Marriage(s):	1882-1918 – Daniel Talmage, Jr. (1846-1918) - merchant - partner, Dan Talmage and Sons (rice merchant) Civic Activism: president, Amherst Athletic Association
Address:	Apaquogue Road, East Hampton
Name of estate:	
Year of construction:	1914
Style of architecture:	
Architect(s):	
Landscape architect(s):	
Builder:	Edward M. Gay
House extant: unconfirmed	
Historical notes:	

    The house was built by Mary Breck Vaill Talmage. [*The Brooklyn Daily Eagle* August 30, 1914, p. 60, and *The East Hampton Star* November 23, 1914, p. 25.]
    She was the daughter of Timothy Dwight and Isabella Mary Breck Vaill of Bound Brook, NJ. Mary's mother also resided in East Hampton. Mary's sister Anna married George Mason LaMonte and resided in East Hampton.
    Daniel Talmage, Jr. was the son of Daniel and Hannah Fowler Talmage, Sr. He had previously been married to Phebe M. Terbell, the daughter of Jason Terbell of Wainscott, NY. Daniel and Phebe M. Terbell Talmage, Jr.'s daughter Cora married Henry H. Wehrhane of New York. Their daughter Laura married Francis Conklin Huyck of Albany, NY. Their son Henry was an infant at the time of his death in 1874.
    Daniel and Mary Breck Vaill Talmage, Jr.'s son Rockwell married Helen Oswald Hoggarth, the daughter of W. H. Hoggarth of Melbourne, Australia.
    [See other Talmage entries for additional family information.]

Talmage, Mary Breck Vaill (1858-1943)

Marriage(s):	1882-1918 – Daniel Talmage, Jr. (1846-1918)
	- *[See previous entry.]*
Address:	Lily Pond Lane, East Hampton
Name of estate:	*Century Cottage*
Year of construction:	
Style of architecture:	
Architect(s):	
Landscape architect(s):	
Builder:	Thomas E. Babcock, 1906 addition
	(for Mrs. Vaill)
	J. O. Hopping, 1914
	(for Mrs. D. Talmage, Jr.)
	Edward M. Gay, 1916 addition
	(for Mapes)

House extant: unconfirmed
Historical notes:

In 1902 Mrs. Isabella Mary Breck Vaill moved the house from Cottage Avenue to Lily Pond Lane and made improvements. [*The East Hampton Star* November 15, 1901, p. 5.] It was later owned by her daughter Mary Breck Vaill Talmage.

In 1914 Mary had the house moved further east on the property by J. O. Hopping. [*The East Hampton Star* October 30, 1914, p. 5.]

It was later owned by Mary's son Rockwell who, in 1916, sold it to Victor Mapes who still owned it at the time of his death in 1943. [*The East Hampton Star* June 9, 1916, p. 5, and December 16, 1943, p. 43.]

In 1948 the house became the base for the Summer School of Arts. [*The East Hampton Star* September 13, 1973, p. 8.]

Talmage, Mary Breck Vaill (1858-1943)

Marriage(s):	1882-1918 – Daniel Talmage, Jr. (1846-1918)
	- *[See first Talmage entry.]*
Address:	Jones Road, East Hampton
Name of estate:	*[unable to determine if this house is New Century Cottage or Westover]*
Year of construction:	1910
Style of architecture:	Colonial Revival
Architect(s):	Mary Breck Vaill designed the house
Landscape architect(s):	
Builder:	Edward M. Gay

House extant: yes
Historical notes:

The house was built by Mary Breck Vaill Talmage as a rental.

Talmage, Mary Breck Vaill (1858-1943)

Marriage(s): 1882-1918 – Daniel Talmage, Jr. (1846-1918)
- *[See first Talmage entry.]*

Address: Main Street, East Hampton
Name of estate: *Purple House*
Year of construction: 1770s
Style of architecture: Colonial
Architect(s):
Landscape architect(s):
House extant: yes
Historical notes:

The house, which was the ancestral home of the Hedges family from 1775 to 1900, may have been built by William Hedges. In 1900 it was purchased by Everett Joshua Edwards. Edwards sold the house to Mary Breck Vaill Talmage who called it *Purple House*. [*The East Hampton Star* May 4, 1972, p. 14.]

In 1925 the house was purchased by Mrs. Charles Halsted Mapes who continued to call it *Purple House*. [*The East Hampton Star* February 20, 1936, p. 5.]

It was later owned by Mrs. Mapes' son Charles Edmunds Kimball, Jr. who also called it *Purple House*.

In 1941 the Kimball family deeded the house to the East Hampton Free Library.

In 1973 it was purchased by Mrs. Adelaide de Menil Carpenter who moved the house to her estate on Further Lane. When the Carpenters decided to sell their estate, Mrs. Carpenter donated the house to the Town of East Hampton which incorporated it into its Town Hall complex on Pantigo Road.

Talmage, Rockwell Dwight (1883-1955)

Occupation(s): professional photographer in East Hampton

Marriage(s): 1924-1952 – Helen Oswald Hoggarth (d. 1952)

Address: Lily Pond Lane, East Hampton
Name of estate: *Century Cottage*
Year of construction:
Style of architecture:
Architect(s):
Landscape architect(s):
Builder: Thomas E. Babcock, 1906 addition
 (for Mrs. Vaill)
J. O. Hopping, 1914
 (for Mrs. D. Talmage, Jr.)
Edward M. Gay, 1916 addition
 (for Mapes)
House extant: unconfirmed
Historical notes:

In 1902 Mrs. Isabella Mary Breck Vaill moved the house from Cottage Avenue to Lily Pond Lane and made improvements. [*The East Hampton Star* November 15, 1901, p. 5.] It was later owned by her daughter Mary Breck Vaill Talmage.

In 1914 Mary had the house moved further east on the property by J. O. Hopping. [*The East Hampton Star* October 30, 1914, p. 5.]

It was later owned by Mary's son Rockwell who, in 1916, sold it to Victor Mapes who still owned at the time of his death in 1943. [*The East Hampton Star* June 9, 1916, p. 5, and December 16, 1943, p. 43.]

In 1948 the house became the base for the Summer School of Arts. [*The East Hampton Star* September 13, 1973, p. 8.]

Talmage, Rockwell Dwight (1883-1955)

Occupation(s): *[See previous entry.]*

Marriage(s): 1924-1952 – Helen Oswald Hoggarth (d. 1952)

Address: Jones Road, East Hampton
Name of estate: New *Century Cottage*
Year of construction:
Style of architecture:
Architect(s):
Landscape architect(s):
House extant: unconfirmed
Historical notes:

    The house, originally named *New Century Cottage*, was built by Mary Breck Vaill Talmage. In 1916 she sold it to her son Rockwell. [*The East Hampton Star* August 4, 1916, p. 5.]
    Helen Oswald Hoggarth Talmage was the daughter of W. H. Hoggarth of Melbourne, Australia.
    The Talmages did not have children.

Talmage, Rockwell Dwight (1883-1955)

Occupation(s): *[See previous Talmage entries.]*

Marriage(s): 1924-1952 – Helen Oswald Hoggarth (d. 1952)

Address: Jones Road, East Hampton
Name of estate: *Westover*
Year of construction:
Style of architecture:
Architect(s):
Landscape architect(s):
House extant: unconfirmed
Historical notes:

    The house, originally named *Westover*, was built by Mary Breck Vaill Talmage. It was later owned by her son Rockwell who sold it to Hamilton Jackson Starke in 1926. [*Times Union* December 20, 1936, p. 21.]
    In 1946 Bertha Shults Dougherty purchased the house from Starke and renamed it *Westmeath*. [*The East Hampton Star* March 28, 1946, p. 6.]

Talmage, The Reverend Thomas DeWitt (1832-1902)

Occupation(s):	clergy -	pastor, Second Reformed Dutch Church, Philadelphia, PA; pastor, Central Presbyterian Church, Brooklyn; pastor, First Presbyterian Church, Washington, DC
	writer -	published his lectures in journals; *Crumbs Swept Up*, 1870; *Abominations of Modern Society*, 1872; *Sermons, 1872-1875* (4 volumes); *Old Wells Dug Out*, 1874; *Sports That Kill*, 1875; *Night Sides of City Life*, 1878; *The Brooklyn Tabernacle: A Collection of 104 Sermons*, 1884; *The Marriage Ring*, 1886
journalist -		editor, *The Christian at Work*, 1873-1876; editor, *The Advance*; editor, *Frank Leslie's Sunday Magazine*
Marriage(s):		M/1 – 1856-1861 – Mary Rebecca Halsey Avery (1830-1861)
		M/2 – 1863-1895 – Susan Curtis Whittemore (1836-1895)
		M/3 – 1898-1902 – Eleanor Collier (b. 1859)
Address:		58 Lily Pond Lane, East Hampton
Name of estate:		
Year of construction:		1873
Style of architecture:		Shingle
Architect(s):		Joseph Greenleaf Thorp, 1893 alterations (for Talmage)
Landscape architect(s):		
Builder:		George A. Eldredge, 1893 alterations
House extant: yes		
Historical notes:		

The house was built by The Reverend Thomas DeWitt Talmage.

He was the son of David and Catherine Van Nest Talmage of Somerset, NJ.

Mary Rebecca Halsey Avery Talmage was the daughter of Samuel Putnam and Hannah Ann Coyne Avery, Sr. Mary drowned in Philadelphia's Schuylkill River while boating.

The Reverend Thomas DeWitt and Mrs. Mary Rebecca Halsey Avery Talmage's daughter Jessie married Warren G. Smith and resided in East Hampton.

Susan Curtis Whittemore Talmage had previously been married to Charles W. Collier.

The Reverend Thomas DeWitt and Mrs. Susan Curtis Whittemore Talmage's daughter May married Daniel Delevan Mangam and resided in Manhattan. Their son Frank married Gertrude Barlow and resided in Brooklyn. Their daughter Maude married Clarence F. Wyckoff and resided in Ithaca, NY. Their daughter Edith married Allen E. Donnan and resided in Richmond, VA.

In 1990 the house was purchased by television personality Martha Stewart.

Taylor, Irving Howland (1889-1949)

Occupation(s):	publisher - director, McGraw–Hill Publishing Co.; director, McGraw–Hill Book Co.
	capitalist - president, Merchants Chemical Co. (industrial chemical distribution firm)
	industrialist - vice-president and director, Michigan Alkali Co.; president, Merchants Chemical Co., NY
Civic Activism:	member, War Industries Board during World War I; member, Hoover Food Administration during World War I
Marriage(s):	Irene Hinman (1887-1985)
	- Civic Activism: vice-president, East Hampton Garden Club
Address:	80 Dunemere Lane, East Hampton
Name of estate:	
Year of construction:	1913
Style of architecture:	Modified Norman
Architect(s):	John Custis Lawrence designed the house (for Voorhes)
Landscape architect(s):	
Builder:	Edward M. Gay
House extant: yes	
Historical notes:	

The house was built by Dr. James Ditmars Voorhees. In 1936 the house was purchased by Valentine Britton Havens. [*The East Hampton Star* December 17, 1936, p. 5.] It was later owned by Taylor.

He was the son of Eugene M. and Ella Howland Taylor of Brooklyn.

Irving Howland and Irene Hinman Taylor's daughter Irene married James Keir Watkins, Jr. of Grosse Pointe Farms, MI.

Teetor, Charles Jessup (1923-2004)

Occupation(s):	journalist - free-lance reporter in South America
	industrialist - representative, South American section export sales, General Motors Corp.; founder and president, Nettle Creek Industries (home furnishing manufacturing firm)
	merchant - founder and president, Nettle Creek Shops
	writer - *Charlie Teetor's Hometown* (history of his family)
Civic Activism:	director, Knickerbocker Hospital, NYC
Marriage(s):	1948-2004 – Marjorie Ann Purcell (b. 1926) (aka Mickie Purcell)
Address:	Town Lane, Amagansett
Name of estate:	*Westernesse Farm*
Year of construction:	1973
Style of architecture:	
Architect(s):	Alfred A. Scheffer designed the house (for Teetor)
Landscape architect(s):	
House extant: unconfirmed	
Historical notes:	

The house, originally named *Westernesse Farm*, was built by Charles Jessup Teetor.

He was the son of Assistant Secretary of Commerce for Domestic Affairs Lothair and Mrs. Hilda Jessup Teetor.

Marjorie Ann Purcell Teetor is the daughter of William W. and Molly Anderson Purcell of Memphis, TN.

Charles Jessup and Marjorie Ann Purcell Teetor's daughter Victoria married José Miguel Reig and resides in Barcelona, Spain. Their daughter Amanda (aka Christine) married Edward LeBaron Goodwin and resides in Great Falls, VA.

In 1987 the fifteen-acre property was for sale. [*The East Hampton Star* April 30, 1987, p. 8.]

Terbell, Edward Dyer (1850-1924)

Occupation(s):	
Civic Activism:	a founder and director, Laurelton Club, Queens County, NY
Marriage(s):	1876-1921 – Elijean Stites (1853-1921)
Address:	47 Ocean Avenue, East Hampton
Name of estate:	*Maidstone Hall*
Year of construction:	1869-1870
Style of architecture:	Colonial Revival
Architect(s):	Walter E. Brady, 1901 alterations (for E. D. Terbell)*
	David Mann, 1990 alterations
Landscape architect(s):	Lear + Mahoney, 1990
Builder:	George Eldredge, 1895 alterations (for H. S. Terbell)
	Jeffery Collé, 1990

House extant: yes
Historical notes:

The house was built by Henry S. Terbell, Sr. The house was later owned by his son Edward Dyer Terbell who had the original 1869-1870 Stick-style house redesigned into a Colonial Revival style, which he named *Maidstone Hall*.

Elijean Stites Terbell was the daughter of Elijah Stites of New York.

Edward Dyer and Elijean Stites Terbell's daughter Anna did not marry.

[See following entry for additional family information.]

In 1906 Edward sold the house to Arthur Kennedy. [*The East Hampton Star* November 6, 1908, p. 5.]

In 1915 Kennedy sold it to Robert Alexander Gardiner, who, in 1915, made extensive alterations and continued to call the house *Maidstone Hall*.

*Alterations were made to the house in 1895, 1901, 1908, 1915, and in 1990.

Terbell, Henry S., Sr. (1813-1898)

Occupation (s):	financier - director, Equitable Life Assurance Society of the United States
Civic Activism:	trustee, Hospital for the Ruptured and Crippled, NYC
Marriage(s):	1843-1898 – Hannah Dyer (1820-1900)
Address:	47 Ocean Avenue, East Hampton
Name of estate:	
Year of construction:	1869-1870
Style of architecture:	Stick-style
Architect(s):	Walter E. Brady, 1901 alterations (for E. D. Terbell)*
	David Mann, 1990 alterations
Landscape architect(s):	Lear + Mahoney, 1990
Builder:	George Eldredge, 1895 alterations (for H. S. Terbell)
	Jeffery Collé, 1990

House extant: yes
Nassau County Museum Collection has photographs of the estate.
Historical notes:

The house was built by Henry S. Terbell, Sr.

He was the son of Jubal and Ruth Latham Terbell of Sag Harbor.

Hannah Dyer Terbell was the daughter of Davis and Hannah Thurber Dyer.

Henry S. and Hannah Dyer Terbell Sr.'s son Edward Dyer Terbell, who inherited the house, married Elijean Stites. Their son Henry S. Terbell, Jr. was an infant at the time of death in 1864. Their daughter Anna died in 1876 at the age of nineteen. Their daughter Emma, who resided in East Hampton and Los Angeles, married ____ Blakeman.

The house was inherited by the Terbells' son Edward Dyer Terbell. In 1901 Edward had the original 1869-1870 Stick-style house redesigned into a Colonial Revival style, which he named *Maidstone Hall*.

[See previous entry for additional family information.]

Edward sold the house to Arthur Kennedy.

In 1915 Kennedy sold it to Robert Alexander Gardiner, who, in 1915, made extensive alterations and continued to call the house *Maidstone Hall*.

*Alterations were made to the house in 1895, 1901, 1908, 1915, and in 1990.

Terian, Peter Gabriel (1944-2002)

Occupation(s):	merchant - founder, Rally Motor Co., Roslyn, NY (later, Rally Group) (luxury automobile dealership)
Civic Activism:	board member, Dakota Building, NYC
Marriage(s):	1994-2002 – Juliana Mae Curran (b. 1955) - model; merchant - president, chair of board, and CEO, Rally Motor Co., Roslyn, NY (later, Rally Group) (luxury automobile dealership)* Civic Activism: director, District 10, New York State Automobile Dealer Association; member, acquisition committee, Hirshhorn Museum and Sculpture Garden, Washington, DC; trustee, Maymount School of New York, NYC; trustee, Pratt Institute, Brooklyn; endowed Juliana Curran Terian Design Center Pavilion, Pratt Institute, Brooklyn; member, visiting committee, Metropolitan Museum of Art, NYC
Address:	19 Lee Avenue East Hampton
Name of estate:	
Year of construction:	1899
Style of architecture:	Shingle
Architect(s):	Joseph Greenleaf Thorp designed the house (for F. G. Potter)
Landscape architect(s):	
Builder:	Loper Brothers
House extant: yes	
Historical notes:	

    The 10,000-square-foot, ten-bedroom house was built by Frederick Gaul Potter. It was later owned by John Richard Keim who sold it to Lamon Vanderburg Harkness in 1914. [*The East Hampton Star* January 22, 1915, p. 5.] James Branch Briggs, who subsequently purchased the house, called it *Beehive*. It was then owned by Chevy Chase. Terian purchased the house from Chase for $10 million in 2001.
    Peter Gabriel Terian was from Paris, France.
    Juliana Mae Curran Terian is the daughter of Thomas Vincent and Frances Steven Curran of Los Angeles, CA. Juliana subsequently married motion picture producer Bruce Gilbert. He produced "On Golden Pond."
    *The Rally Group is the largest dealership owned by a women in the country.
    In 2010 Mrs. Terian placed the house on the market; the asking price was $21 million.

Terry, Dr. Arthur Hutchinson, Jr. (1884-1973)

Occupation(s):	physician - chief of medical staff, Beekman Hospital, NYC (later, Beekman–Downtown Hospital); director of surgery, Beekman–Downtown Hospital, NYC
Civic Activism:	treasurer, Hook Pond Associates; president, Conservation Club, East Hampton
Marriage(s):	1914-1973 – Marie Kelley French (1891-1977) - Civic Activism: co-chair, Curbside Social Service Committee, Babies Hospital, NYC; secretary, Garden Club of East Hampton
Address:	105 Egypt Lane, East Hampton
Name of estate:	*Causeway*
Year of construction:	
Style of architecture:	
Architect(s):	
Landscape architect(s):	
House extant: yes*	
Historical notes:	

    The *Social Directory of Southampton, Long Island, 1931* lists Dr. and Mrs. Arthur H. Terry, Jr. as residing on Egypt Lane, East Hampton. The *Social Register Summer, 1932* lists *Causeway* as the name of their residence.
    He was the son of Dr. Arthur Hutchinson and Mrs. Hannah Rosetta Tuthill Terry, Sr. of Patchogue.
    Marie Kelley French Terry was the daughter of Thomas Kelley French.
    Dr. Arthur Hutchinson and Mrs. Marie Kelley French Terry, Jr.'s son Arthur Hutchinson Terry III married Sophia Fediow of Wilkes Barre, PA.
    *In 1966 the house suffered severe damage from a fire. [*The East Hampton Star* June 2, 1966, p. 15.]

Thaw, William, III (1877-1948)

Occupation(s):
Civic Activism: a founder and commodore, Devon Yacht Club, Amagansett

Marriage(s): 1910-1948 – Gladys Virginia Bradley (1889-1956)
- merchant - proprietor, couturier shop*
Civic Activism: a founder, Unit 124, Comforts Committee,
Navy League of the United States, 1917

Address: Lily Pond Lane, East Hampton
Name of estate: *Dune Top*
Year of construction: 1915
Style of architecture:
Architect(s):
Landscape architect(s):
Builder: Edward M. Gay, house and garage

House extant: unconfirmed
Historical notes:

The house, originally named *Dune Top*, was built by William Thaw III. [*The East Hampton Star* September 11, 1914, p. 5, and November 19, 1915, p. 1.]

The *Social Directory of Southampton, Long Island, 1931* lists the Thaws as residing at *Sans Souci* on First Neck Lane, Southampton. [*See* Spinzia, *Long Island's Prominent Families in the Town of Southampton* – Thaw entry.]

He was the son of William and Elizabeth Dohrmann Thaw, Jr. of Pittsburgh, PA, and a nephew of Harry K. Thaw, who murdered the noted architect Stanford White.

Gladys Virginia Bradley Thaw was the daughter of Charles Henderson Bradley of Bridgeport, CT. Her sister Cordelia married Anthony Joseph Drexel Biddle, Sr.

Known as "Wild Will," William's drinking habits had become notorious prior to his marriage to Gladys. He was even hospitalized, in critical condition, as a result of drinking seventy brandy and sodas on a wager. At one point his mother had petitioned the court that William be declared a habitual drunkard and that she be made a guardian of his affairs but withdrew the proceedings when William promised to remain sober. Aware of William's problem, the Bradleys insisted that he had to refrain from all forms of alcoholic beverages for six months before they could consent to his marrying Gladys. [*The New York Times* February 10, 1911, p. 1; *The Los Angeles Times* February 4, 1911, p. 14, and February 11, 1911, section II, p. 1.]

William and Gladys Virginia Bradley Thaw III's daughter Virginia married Rodman Lewis Wanamaker II and resided in Southampton. Their son William Thaw IV died in 1948 at the age of twenty-seven. [*The New York Times* March 8, 1948, p. 23.]

*In 1939 Marjorie Post Close Hutton Davies loaned Mrs. Thaw $18,000 to open a couturier shop. When Mrs. Thaw refused to pay the money back, claiming it was gift, not a loan, Mrs. Davies sued for the return of the money. [*The New Yorker* February 11, 1939, p. 23.]

[For information on the Davieses' Brookville estate, *Hillwood*, *see* Spinzia, *Long Island's Prominent North Shore Families, vol. II* – Post entry.]

In 1922 the house was purchased by James William Zevely for $85,000. [*The East Hampton Star* December 1, 1922, p. 5.]

Thiele, Albert Edward, Jr. (1892-1982)

Occupation(s):	financier - partner, Guggenheim Brothers (investment banking firm) industrialist - president and director, Elgerbar Corp., Hopewell, NJ (temperature sensor manufacturing firm); chairman of board, Pacific Tin Consolidated Corp.; director, Kennecott Copper Co.; director, Barber Oil Corp.; director, Anglo Lautaro Nitrate Co.
Civic Activism:	director, Corlette Glorney Foundation; trustee, New York University, NYC; vice-president and trustee, Solomon R. Guggenheim Fund; trustee, Guggenheim Museum, NYC
Marriage(s):	1918-1977 – Alice Irene Kelly (d. 1977) - president, Jennie Clarkson Home, Valhalla, NY
Address:	Lily Pond Lane East Hampton
Name of estate:	*Taramar*
Year of construction:	
Style of architecture:	
Architect(s):	
Landscape architect(s):	
House extant:	unconfirmed
Historical notes:	

The Blue Book of The Hamptons, 1958, 1965, and *1973* list Albert E. and Alice Irene Kelly Thiele as residing at *Taramar* on Lily Pond Lane, East Hampton.

He was the son of Albert Edward and Matilda Foster Thiele, Sr. of Brooklyn.

Albert Edward and Alice Irene Kelly Thiele, Jr.'s son Roger, who inherited *Taramar*, married Karen Ely and, later, Florence Hapeman Lainhart.

[See following entry for additional family information.]

Thiele, Roger Harvey (1919-2006)

Occupation(s):	restaurateur - Howard Johnson franchises educator - professor, Westchester Community College, Valhalla, NY
Civic Activism:	president, Sportsman Pilot Association; commodore, Crossroads Yacht Club, Stuart, FL; president, New York State Restaurant Association
Marriage(s):	M/1 – 1940-div. – Karen Ely - writer - *Listen* (poetry); *Look Up! Look Up!* (poetry) M/2 – 1954-2006 – Florence Hapeman Lainhart
Address:	Lily Pond Lane, East Hampton
Name of estate:	*Taramar*
Year of construction:	
Style of architecture:	
Architect(s):	
Landscape architect(s):	
House extant:	unconfirmed
Historical notes:	

Roger Harvey Thiele was the son of Albert Edward and Alice Irene Kelly Thiele, Jr. from whom he inherited *Taramar*.
Karen Ely Thiele was the daughter of Laurence Driggs and Gladys Noggle Ely, Sr. of *Olde Trees* in East Hampton.
Roger Harvey and Karen Ely Thiele's daughter Karen married Lee Wells Eighmy III of North Tarrytown, NY, and, later, ____ McVie. Their son Christopher married Moira Ann Woolard, the daughter of Paul P. Woolard of Rockleigh, NJ.
Florence Hapeman Lainhart Thiele was the daughter of Spencer Toll and Helen Hapeman Lainhart, Sr. of West Palm Beach, FL, and Chicago, IL.
By 2008 Florence had relocated to 21 Egypt Close, in East Hampton.

[See previous entry for additional family information.]

Thomas, Andrew Jackson (1875-1965)

Occupation(s):	architect - specialized in garden apartment projects; appointed New York State Architect
Civic Activism:	member, Committee of 100 (promoted civic interest in Montauk)
Marriage(s):	Grace I. M. Stewart (d. 1938)
Address:	Flamingo Road, Montauk
Name of estate:	
Year of construction:	mid to late 1920s
Style of architecture:	Spanish Colonial Revival
Architect(s):	Andrew Jackson Thomas designed his own residence and boathouse
Landscape architect(s):	
House extant: unconfirmed	
Historical notes:	

The house was built by Andrew Jackson Thomas who also maintained a private zoo on the estate's property. [*The East Hampton Star* September 20, 1945, p. 2.].

The *Social Directory of Southampton, 1931* lists Andrew J. Thomas as residing on Flamingo Road, Montauk.

Orphaned at the age of thirteen, he, who was a self-taught architect, is credited with popularizing the garden apartment concept. [*The New York Times* July 27, 1965, p. 33.] In 1924 he designed a $7 million, six-block apartment complex in Queens, NY, for the Metropolitan Life Insurance Company. He also designed apartment complexes in Cleveland, OH, Bayonne, NJ, Long Island City, Brooklyn, and The Bronx as well as John D. Rockefeller, Jr.'s Manhattan housing project. His non-apartment commissions included the Queens Court House, the Board of Transportation Building in Brooklyn, and the Coney Island Hospital.

Grace I. M. Stewart Thomas was the daughter of George W. and Matilda B. Stewart.

The Thomases did not have children.

In 1931 the house was purchased by Dr. William Henry Walker, Jr. [*The East Hampton Star* August 28, 1931, p. 1.]

In 1936 it was purchased by Elbert McGran Jackson who made extensive alterations. [*The East Hampton Star* October 8, 1936, p. 3, and November 26, 1936, p. 3.]

Thomas, Augustus (1857-1934)

Occupation(s):	artist - illustrator - *Post-Dispatch*, St. Louis, MO; *Republic*, St. Louis, MO; *World*, NYC;
	art director - Charles Frohman, Inc.
	journalist - *Post-Dispatch*, St. Louis, MO; *Republic*, St. Louis, MO; *World*, NYC
	publisher - owner and editor, *Kansas City Mirror*, Kansas City, MO
	entertainers and associated professions - stage actor
	writer - playwright*; *The Print of My Remembrance*, 1922 (autobiography)
Civic Activism:	chairman of board, Producing Managers Association; president, National Institute of Arts and Letters, 1914-1916; president, Society of American Dramatists, 1906-1911
Marriage(s):	1890-1934 – Lisle U. Colby (1871-1949)
Address:	Briar Patch Road, East Hampton
Name of estate:	
Year of construction:	1901
Style of architecture:	Shingle
Architect(s):	
Landscape architect(s):	
Builder:	George A. Eldredge
	Thomas E. Babcock, 1905 two-story addition
House extant:	yes
Historical notes:	

The house was built by Augustus Thomas.
The *Social Register Summer, 1910* lists Augustus and Lisle Colby Thomas as residing in East Hampton.
He was the son of Dr. Elihu Baldwin and Mrs. Imogene Garrettson Thomas.
Lisle U. Colby was the daughter of John Peck Colby of St. Louis, MO. Her brother Bainbridge served as United States Secretary of State in the Woodrow Wilson administration.
Augustus and Lisle U. Colby Thomas' daughter Glory married William Elliott, Jr. and resided in East Hampton. Their son Luke, who also resided in East Hampton, married Dorothy Stuart Mahoney, the daughter of James Augustin Mahoney of Manhattan, and, later, Elizabeth Clarkson.
*Thomas was considered the dean of American playwrights.
He was residing in East Hampton at the time of his death. [*The New York Times* August 13, 1934, p. 1.]
The house is listed on the National Register of Historic Places.

Thompson, Charles Griswold (1840-1919)

Occupation(s):	financier - trustee, Life Insurance & Trust Co.
Marriage(s):	bachelor
Address:	25 Ocean Avenue, East Hampton
Name of estate:	
Year of construction:	1874
Style of architecture:	original Stick-style with Chalet elements; altered to Georgian Revival (by Thompson)
Architect(s):	Briggs and Corman designed the house (for J. S. Satterthwaite, Sr.) McKim, Mead & White, 1893-1894 alterations [attributed] (for C. G. Thompson) John Custis Lawrence, 1910 alterations to servants' quarters
Landscape architect(s):	
Builder:	R. V. Breece (for J. S. Satterthwaite, Sr.) George A. Eldredge, 1893-1894 alterations (for C. G. Thompson)

House extant: yes
Historical notes:

The house was built by James Sheafe Satterthwaite, Sr. Its second owner was Thompson who purchased the house in 1893.

He was the son of David Thompson and the grandson of John Lyon Gardiner.

The Thompson family donated the house to the New York Historical Society, NYC. The house was later owned by Howard Brush Dean, Jr. [Jeannette Edwards Rattray. *History of East Hampton: Including Genealogies of Early Families* (East Hampton, NY: East Hampton Star Press, 1953), p. 438.] By 1973 the Deans had relocated to Hook Pond Lane, East Hampton.

Thompson, Dr. Frederick Roeck (1907-1983)

Occupation(s):	physician - chief orthopedic surgeon, St. Luke's Hospital, NYC inventor - Thompson Vitalgery Hip Prosthesis educator - clinical professor of orthopedic surgery, New York Polyclinic Hospital, NYC
Civic Activism:	president, orthopedic section, American Medical Association; president, orthopedic section, Association of Bone and Joint Surgeons; vice-president, American Academy of Orthopedic Surgeons
Marriage(s):	1936-1983 – Carolyn Laura Bryan (1909-1990)
Address:	49 Toilsome Lane, East Hampton
Name of estate:	
Year of construction:	
Style of architecture:	Long Island Farmhouse
Architect(s):	
Landscape architect(s):	

House extant: yes
Historical notes:

The Blue Book of The Hamptons, 1979 lists Dr. Frederick R. and Carolyn Bryan Thompson as residing at 49 Toilsome Lane, East Hampton.

He was the son of Dr. James Edwin Thompson of Galveston, TX.

Carolyn Laura Bryan Thompson was the daughter of Guy Morrison and Florence Ella Carter Bryan.

Dr. Frederick Roeck and Mrs. Carolyn Laura Bryan Thompson's son Guy married Sallie Ann Mullins, the daughter of Lev DeWitt Mullens, Jr. Their daughter Carolyn, who resided in Houston, TX, married Gary Eugene Morrison, Jr. of Austin, TX, and, later, ____ Old. Their daughter Eleanor married Christopher C. Wragge and resided in Auckland, New Zealand.

In 2015 the 3,000-square-foot, four-bedroom, three-and-a-half-bath house sold for $1.775 million.

Thorne, Henry Sanford (1898-1959)

Occupation(s):	research engineer
	capitalist - partner, Blackbeard's Tavern, Nassau, Bahamas
Marriage(s):	M/1 – 1918-div. 1922 – Mabel M. Bacon (1898-1989)
	M/2 – 1926-div. 1927 – Helen Mitchell Havemeyer (1900-1947)
	M/3 – 1933-div. 1935 – Ruth Patterson
	M/4 – 1936-div. 1941 – Bessie Draper McKeldin (1905-1958)
	M/5 – div. 1958 – Sarah J. Bush (1895-1973)
	(aka Sally Bush)
Address:	111 Egypt Lane, East Hampton
Name of estate:	*Rowdy Hall*
Year of construction:	early-to-mid-eighteenth century
Style of architecture:	Colonial
Architect(s):	Joseph Greenleaf Thorp, 1926 alterations
	(for Mrs. Harry L. Hamlin)
Landscape architect(s):	
House extant: yes	

Historical notes:

The house was originally the Osborn family residence. It was later owned by David H. Huntting and, then, by his adopted daughter Annie who utilized it as a boarding house. In 1895, the house was moved from Main Street to Gay Lane. In 1925 it was purchased by Mrs. Mary Elkins Paxton Hamlin who moved it to Egypt Lane. [*The East Hampton Star* November 15, 1934, p. 5.] In 1953 the house was purchased from Mrs. Hamlin by Robert Barnes who made alterations and repairs to it and, in 1954, sold the house to Thorne. [*The East Hampton Star* November 26, 1953, p. 4, and June 17, 1954, p. 7.]

He was the son of Dr. Victor Corse and Mrs. Clara McCullough Thorne of Greenwich, CT.

Mabel M. Bacon Thorne was the daughter of Henry Douglas and Mabel Marks Bacon, Sr. of Bath, ME. She later married Laurent Roger Generelly and, subsequently, Franklin Russell Pope.

Henry Sanford and Mabel M. Bacon Thorne's daughter Rosalie married John Bechtel Hulburd.

Helen Mitchell Havemeyer Thorne was the daughter of John F. Havemeyer of Ardsley-on-Hudson, NY.

Ruth Patterson Thorne was the daughter of Raymond Patterson. She had previously been married to Melville W. Fuller Wallace.

Bessie Draper McKeldin Thorne was the daughter of James Reese and Bessie Draper Simmons McKeldin. She had previously been married to Howard Newell Tucker, Jr. After her divorce from Thorne, she married Morris Richard Clark.

The Blue Book of The Hamptons, 1958 lists Harry Sanford and Sarah Bush Thorne as residing at *Rowdy Hall*, Egypt Lane, East Hampton. Sarah had previously been married to ____ Bullard and Martin Moore Foss, Sr. with whom she resided in East Hampton.

In 2003 the house was listed for sale. The asking price was $2.25 million.

Thorp, Joseph Greenleaf (1862-1934)

Occupation(s):	architect
	[See Architects appendix for selected list of commissions in the Town of East Hampton.]
Civic Activism:	a founder, Maidstone Club, East Hampton;
	chairman, World War I Memorial Committee;
	director, East Hampton Historical Society
Marriage(s):	bachelor
Address:	12 Woods Lane, East Hampton
Name of estate:	
Year of construction:	1893
Style of architecture:	Neo-Tudor
Architect(s):	Joseph Greenleaf Thorp designed his own residence
Landscape architect(s):	
House extant: yes	

Historical notes:

The house was built by Joseph Greenleaf Thorp.

He was the son of George Washington and Anna Greenleaf Thorp of East Orange, NJ.

Thorp sold the house to Louis B. Bock in 1912 and moved to Florence, Italy, to be with his mother and unmarried sister Emily. [*The East Hampton Star* June 8, 1944, p. 3, and September 26, 1985, p. 35.]

The house is on the National Register of Historic Places.

Tiedeman, Irvin Bruce, Sr. (1895-1979)

Occupation(s):	financier - executive, Mutual Life Insurance Company of New York
Marriage(s):	1922 – Margaret Irene Bethel (b. 1901) (aka Irene Bethel)
Address:	27 Edwards Lane, East Hampton
Name of estate:	
Year of construction:	c. 1840
Style of architecture:	Modified Federal
Architect(s):	
Landscape architect(s):	
Builder:	George A. Eldredge, architectural details

House extant: yes*
Historical notes:

In 1940 Dr. James Manning Dunn moved the Charles Osborne house from Main Street to Edwards Lane. [*The East Hampton Star* June 20, 1940, p. 5.] In 1958 the house was purchased by Tiedeman. [*The East Hampton Star* May 1, 1958, p. 5.]

He was the son of Christopher H. and Helen Seymour Tiedeman of Brooklyn.

Margaret Irene Bethel Tiedeman was the daughter of Stella Tallman Bethel.

Irvin Bruce and Margaret Irene Bethel Tiedeman's daughter Carol married Kenneth William MacDonald, Jr. and resided in Mahwah, NJ.

*Alterations to the house were made by Dunn and Tiedeman.

Tiffany, Nathan Newton, III (1883-1969)

Occupation(s):	financer - a founder, vice-president, and secretary, Osborne Trust Co., East Hampton (later, Valley National Bank); director, Valley National Bank, East Hampton
	capitalist - secretary, treasurer, and president, East Hampton Electric Light Co.; director, Home Water Co.
	merchant - treasurer and president, Southampton Lumber and Coal Co.; director, East Hampton Lumber and Coal Co.
	politician - chairman, Suffolk County Board of Supervisors, 1916-1921
Civic Activism:	chairman, preparedness committee, 1917; treasurer and vice-chairman of board, Guild Hall, East Hampton; president, East Hampton School Board; treasurer, East Hampton Free Library; treasurer, East Hampton Historical Society
Marriage(s):	1907-1966 – Nellie May Lawrence (1883-1966)
Address:	Bridgehampton Road, East Hampton
Name of estate:	
Year of construction:	
Style of architecture:	
Architect(s):	
Landscape architect(s):	

House extant: unconfirmed
Historical notes:

Nathan Newton Tiffany III was the son of Nathan Newton and Frederica Gertrude Corwith Tiffany, Jr. of Bridgehampton.

Nellie May Lawrence Tiffany was the daughter of John Bartlett and Nancy Edwards Lawrence of Montauk. Her brother John Custis Lawrence, who married Mattie Davis and, later, Phoebe Alice Edwards, resided in East Hampton.

Nathan Newton and Nellie May Lawrence Tiffany III's daughter Helena married William Harry Lillywhite, the son of William F. H. Lillywhite of Southampton, and resided in Southampton. Their daughter Sarah married Richard F. Steele and resided in East Hampton. Their daughter Constance married Robert Elmore Nichols. Their son Nathan Newton Tiffany IV married Helen Elizabeth Crapser, the daughter of Levi Crapser, and resided in Hagerstown, MD.

Tillich, The Reverend Paul Johannes (1886-1965)

Occupation(s):	clergy - Lutheran minister
	educator - privatdozent of theology, University of Berlin, Berlin, Germany, 1919-1924;
	professor theology, Philipp University of Marburg, Marburg, Germany, 1924-1925;
	professor of theology, Dresden University of Technology, Dresden, Germany, 1925-1929;
	professor of theology, University of Leipzig, Leipzig, Germany, 1925-1929;
	professor of theology, University of Frankfurt, Frankfurt, Germany, 1929-1933;
	visiting professor, philosophy of religion, Union Theological Seminary, NYC, 1933-1934;
	visiting lecturer of Philosophy, Columbia University, NYC, 1933-1934;
	professor of philosophical theology, Union Theological Seminary, NYC, 1940-1955;
	professor, Harvard Divinity School, Cambridge, MA, 1955-1962;
	professor of theology, University of Chicago, Chicago, IL, 1962-1965
	writer - *On The Boundary*, 1936;
	The Protestant Era, 1948;
	The Shaking of the Foundation, 1948;
	Systematic Theology, 1951-1963 (3 volumes);
	The Courage to Be, 1952;
	Dynamics of Faith, 1957
Civic Activism:	a founder, Society for the Arts, Religion and Contemporary Culture
Marriage(s):	M/1 – 1914-div.1919 – Margarethe Weve (1888-1968)
	M/2 – 1924-1965 – Johanna Werner (1896-1988)
	(aka Hannah Werner)
	- writer - sexually explicit poetry
	From Time to Time, 1973 (memoir)*;
	From Place to Place: Travels with Paul Tillich, Travels Without Paul Tillich, 1976 (memoir);
	Harbor Mouse, 1978 (novel);
Address:	84 Woods Lane, East Hampton
Name of estate:	
Year of construction:	
Style of architecture:	
Architect(s):	
Landscape architect(s):	
House extant: unconfirmed	
Historical notes:	

Paul Johannes Tillich purchased the house in 1946.

Born in Starzeddel, Germany, he was the son of Johannes and Wilhelmina Mathilde Duselen Tillich. Johannes, a Lutheran pastor, rose to prominence in the hierarchy of the Evangelical Church of Prussia. Paul was close to and deeply influenced by his mother. After returning home at the end of World War I, Paul divorced Margarethe when he discovered that she had an illegitimate child while he was serving on the front lines.

Johanna Werner Tillich had previously been married to Albert Gottschow.

Paul Johannes and Johanna Werner Tillich's daughter Erdmuthe married Theodore N. Farris and resided in Manhattan. Their son Rene Stephen Tillich resided in Honolulu, HI.

*Johanna shocked the ecclesiastical community when she revealed her husband's numerous extramarital affairs in her memoir *From Time to Time*.

Tishman, Peter Valentine (1932-2017)

Occupation(s):	capitalist - president and chairman of board, Tishman Realty and Construction Company;
	president, Peter Tishman Real Estate Co.
Civic Activism:	trustee, Citymeals on Wheels;
	director, Young Men's and Young Women's Hebrew Association of Greater New York;
	governor, New York Real Estate Board
Marriage(s):	M/1 – 1956-1973 – Ellen Margery Morse (d. 1973)
	M/2 – 1974-1989 – Judith A. Rothenberg (1935-1989)
	- composer - music for motion pictures and television
	agent for commercial photographers
	M/3 – 1992-2017 – Lynn Perkins (b. 1951)
Address:	Briar Patch Road, East Hampton
Name of estate:	
Year of construction:	1980
Style of architecture:	Eclectic Shingle
Architect(s):	Eugene Lawrence Futterman designed the house (for Tishman)
Landscape architect(s):	
Builder:	Pat Trunzo
House extant: yes	
Historical notes:	

   The house was built by Peter Valentine Tishman.
   He is the son of Norman and Rita B. Valentine Tishman of Mamaroneck, NY.
   Ellen Margery Morse Tishman was the daughter of Alfred Lawrence Morse of Brookline, MA.
   Peter Valentine and Ellen Margery Morse Tishman's daughter Anita married Andrew Scott Winkler, the son of Arthur and Mimi Winkler, and resided in Pound Ridge, NY.

Todd, John Reynard, Sr. (1867-1945)

Occupation(s):	educator - teacher, Syrian Protestant College, Beirut, Lebanon
	attorney
	capitalist - partner, Iron and Todd (construction firm); a founder and president, Todd, Robertson, Todd Engineering Firm; director and chairman of executive committee, Todd & Brown, Inc. (construction firm)
Civic Activism:	trustee, Steven Institute of Technology, Hoboken, NJ; director, Maidstone Club, East Hampton; governor, Riding Club of East Hampton
Marriage(s):	1895-1945 – Alice Peck Bray (1865-1956)
Address:	54 Dunemere Lane, East Hampton
Name of estate:	
Year of construction:	1929
Style of architecture:	Shingle
Architect(s):	
Landscape architect(s):	
House extant:	yes
Historical notes:	

The house was built by John Reynard Todd, Sr. [*The East Hampton Star* September 20, 2007, p. 28.]

The *Social Directory of Southampton, Long Island, 1931* lists Mr. and Mrs. John R. Todd [Sr.] as residing on Dunemere Road, East Hampton.

He was the son of The Reverend James Doeg and Mrs. Susan Sophia Webster Todd of Johnstown, WI.

Alice Peck Bray Todd was the daughter of The Reverend William Louis and Mrs. Emily Ann Temple Bray of Oskaloosa, IA.

John Reynard and Alice Peck Bray Todd, Sr.'s daughter Frances married Myron Converse Wick, Jr. and, later, Newell C. Bolton. Their son Webster, who subsequently owned the house, married Eleanor Prentice Schley. Their son John Reynard Todd II married Frances Abbey Starr and resided in East Hampton.

Todd's firms were affiliated with the construction of the Cunard Steamship Company Building, the Equitable Trust Building, the America Woolen Building, the Ritz Towers, the Postum Building, the Hotel Barclay, and Rockefeller Center, and with the restoration of Colonial Williamsburg in Virginia.

[See following entry for additional family information.]

In 1971 the estate's laundry building was sold to Mrs. Tina S. Fredericks who moved it to Georgica Road. [*The East Hampton Star* April 15, 1971, p. 4.]

In 2008 the eight-bedroom, nine-and-a-half-bath house with an additional four-bedroom, one-bath staff wing and 0.75 acres sold for $6.325 million.

Todd, Webster Bray, Sr. (1899-1989)

Occupation(s):	capitalist - partner, Todd, Robertson, Todd Engineering Firm financier - director, Metropolitan Life Insurance Co.
Civic Activism:	director, Office of Economic Affairs Mission to North American Treaty Organization; chairman, New Jersey Republican State Committee
Marriage(s):	1933-1989 – Eleanor Prentice Schley (1911-1990) - Civic Activism: president, New Jersey Republican Finance Committee; member, New Jersey Board of Higher Education
Address:	54 Dunemere Road, East Hampton
Name of estate:	
Year of construction:	1929
Style of architecture:	Shingle
Architect(s):	
Landscape architect(s):	
House extant: yes	
Historical notes:	

The house was built by John Reynard Todd, Sr. [*The East Hampton Star* September 20, 2007, p. 28.] It was later owned by his son Webster.

Eleanor Prentice Schley Todd was the daughter of Reeve Schley.

Webster Bray and Eleanor Prentice Schley Todd's daughter Kate married Charles O. Thompson of Brookline, MA, and, later, Samuel Ferguson Beach, Jr. Their son John Reynard Todd II married Frances Abbey Starr, the daughter of Louis Starr. Their daughter Christine, who became the Governor of New Jersey, married John Russell Whitman. Their son Webster Bray Todd, Jr. married Susan Mitchell O'Keefe, the daughter of John O'Keefe of Carthage, MO.

[See previous entry for additional family and house information.

Tolan, Michael (1925-2011)
aka Seymour Tuchow

Occupation(s):	attorney entertainers and associated professions - stage, motion picture, and television actor capitalist - co-founder, American Palace Theater, NYC; co-founder, Apple Core Theater, NYC
Marriage(s):	M/1 – 1966-div. 1975 – Rosemary Forsyth (b. 1943) - entertainers and associated professions - motion picture and television actress M/2 – Carol Hume (b. 1926)
Address:	130 Bluff Road, Amagansett
Name of estate:	
Year of construction:	1970
Style of architecture:	Modern
Architect(s):	Charles Gwathmey designed the house (for Tolan)
Landscape architect(s):	
Builder:	John Caramaga
House extant: yes	
Historical notes:	

The five-bedroom, three-bath, 3,000-square-foot house was built by Michael Tolan.

He was the son of Morris and Gertrude Tuchow of Detroit, MI.

Rosemary Forsyth Tolan is the daughter of David and Rosemary Collins Forsyth. She later married Ron Waranach and, subsequently, Alan Skip Horwits.

Michael and Rosemary Forsyth Tolan's daughter Alexandra resides in Watertown, MA.

Carol Hume Tolan is the daughter of Jaquelin Holliday and Caroline Howard Hume of San Francisco, CA.

The house was later owned by Dr. Rubin Raymond Kurzner.

In 2017 the house was listed for sale. The asking price was $5,995 million.

Topping, Daniel Reid, Sr. (1912-1974)

Occupation(s):	capitalist - president and an owner, New York Yankees, 1948-1966 (baseball team);
	owner, National Football League's Brooklyn Dodgers, 1931 (later, New York Yankees football team);
	director, National Airlines Inc.;
	director, Madison Square Garden, NYC;
	director, Automatic Canteen Co. of America;
	director, Louis Sherry Inc., NYC
Marriage(s):	M/1 – 1932-div. 1935 – Theodora Boettger
	M/2 – 1937-div. 1940 – Arline Judge (1912-1974)
	- entertainers and associated professions -
	1930s and 1940s motion picture actress
	M/3 – 1940-div. 1946 – Sonja Henje (1912-1969)
	- entertainers and associated professions -
	figure skater*;
	motion picture actress;
	Ice Capades performer
	M/4 – Katherine Warburton Sutton (1915-1988)
	(aka Kay Sutton)
	- entertainers and associated professions -
	motion picture and television actress
	M/5 – 1952 – Alice Meade Lawson (b. 1927)
	M/6 – 1957-1974 – Charlotte Ann Lillard (1931-2012)
Address:	189 Marine Boulevard, East Hampton
Name of estate:	
Year of construction:	1941
Style of architecture:	Ranch
Architect(s):	
Landscape architect(s):	
House extant: yes	
Historical notes:	

    Daniel Reid Topping, Sr. was the son of Henry J. and Rhea Reid Topping of Greenwich, CT.
    Theodora Boettger was the daughter of Henry W. Boettger of Manhattan.
    Arline Judge Topping had previously been married to Wesley Ruggles. After her divorce from Topping, she married James M. Bryant, James Ramage Addams; Vincent Morgan Ryan, Henry J. Topping, George Ross III, and Edward Cooper Heard.
    Daniel Reid and Arline Judge Topping, Sr.'s, son Daniel Reid Topping, Jr. resided in Miami Shore, FL.
    Sonja Henje Topping was the daughter of Wilhelm and Selma Henie of Oslo, Norway. After her divorce from Topping, Sonja married Winthrop Gardiner, Jr. of Gardiner's Island and East Hampton, and, subsequently, Niels Ornstad.
    *She was a three-time Olympic Champion (1928, 1932, and 1936), a ten-time World Champion (1927-1936), and six-time European Champion (1931-1936). Sonja won more Olympic and World figure skating titles than did any other ladies figure skater.
    Katherine Warburton Sutton Topping had previously been married to Frederick Moulton Alger. After her divorce from Topping, she married Clifton Stokes Weaver, the son of Spencer Fullerton and Emily Maloney Stokes Weaver of *Spencecliff* in East Hampton and, subsequently, Edward Cronjager.
    Daniel Reid and Katherine Warburton Sutton Topping, Sr.'s daughter Rhea married ____ Saffer and resided in Far Hills, NJ.
    Daniel Reid and Alice Meade Lawson Topping, Sr.'s son David married Kerri Ellen Moritz, the daughter of Edwin and Helen Moritz of Sag Harbor. Their daughter Tracy resided in Manhasset.
    Charlotte Ann Lillard Topping subsequently married Rankin M. Smith, Sr.
    In 2016 the 2,600-square-foot, five-bedroom main residence, 1,000-square-foot, three-bedroom guest house, and 1.25 acres sold for $9.95 million.

Towbin, Abraham Robert (b. 1935)

Occupation(s):	financier -	associate, McKinsey and Co.;
		analyst, Goldman Sachs;
		portfolio manager, Siegler, Collery, and Co.;
		managing director, Shearson, Lehman Brothers;
		director, Arden Holdings (insurance firm);
		founder, president and chief executive officer, SAB Capital Management LP, NYC;
		vice-president, Stephens, Inc.;
		co-chairman and senior managing director, C. E. Unterberg, Towbin (investment banking firm);
		president and CEO, Russian – American Enterprise Fund;
		vice-chairman, The U. S. Russia Investment Fund;
		co-chairman of Technology, Lehman Brothers;
		vice-chairman and director, L. F., Rothschild, Unterberg, Towbin Holdings, Inc.
	capitalist -	director, National Black Network;
		director, Globecomm Systems, Inc. (satellite communications firm);
		director, Intertrust Technologies Corp. (software technology firm)
	industrialist -	director, Convergent Technologies, Inc.;
		director, Lafayette Radio Electronics;
		director, Con Vida Systems, Inc.
Civic Activism:	vice-chairman and treasurer, Film Society, Lincoln Center, NY.	
Marriage(s):	M/1 – Irene Katherine Lyons (1936-2011)*	
	- nurse;	
	artist	
	Civic Activism: funded irrigation system at *Home Sweet Home*, East Hampton	
	M/2 – Jacqueline Mary de Chollet	
	- Civic Activism: trustee, Bioversity International;	
	a founder and director, Global Foundation for Humanity;	
	a founder Veerni Project;	
	commissioner, Women's Refuge Commission	
Address:	West End Avenue, East Hampton	
Name of estate:	*The Ink Pot*	

Architect(s):
Landscape architect(s):
House extant: no**
Nassau County Museum Collection has photographs of the estate.
Historical notes:

In 1915 Edward Hull Jewett, Sr. purchased Mrs. William Stom's residence and called it *The Ink Pot*. [*The East Hampton Star* September 24, 1915, p. 5.]Towbin purchased the house in 1972 and continued to call it *The Ink Pot*.

Irene Katherine Lyons Towbin was the daughter of Harry and Rose Joyce Lyons of Brooklyn.

Abraham Robert and Irene Katherine Lyons Towbin's daughter Minna married Edward B. Pinger, Jr., the son of Edward B. and Jean Schaupp Pinger, Sr. of San Francisco, CA. Their son Bram resides in Manhattan. Their son Zachary resides in Madrid, Spain.

*When George W. Bush was re-elected President, Irene emigrated to Ireland claiming the U. S. government had become too "right-wing." Her favorite quote was from Dr. Seuss—"Don't cry because it's over. Smile because it happened."

Jacquelin Mary de Chollet Towbin was the daughter of Baron Louis de Chollet. She had previously been married to Viscount William Kenneth James Weir III, the son of Viscount James Kenneth Weir II and Dorothy Isabel Lucy Crowdy Weir.

**In 2009 Towbin sold the house for $26.5 million. The new owner allowed the East Hampton Fire Department to set fire to the house as a training exercise.

Trippe, Charles White, Sr. (1872-1920)

Occupation(s):	financier - partner, Trippe & Co (investment banking firm)
Marriage(s):	1895-1920 – Lucy Adeline Terry (1872-1947)
Address:	Dunemere Lane, East Hampton

Name of estate:
Year of construction:
Style of architecture:
Architect(s):
Landscape architect(s):
House extant: unconfirmed
Historical notes:

    The Trippes had resided in East Hampton since 1914.
    The *Social Register Summer, 1921* and *1923* list Lucy A. Terry Trippe as residing in East Hampton.
    She was the daughter of Juan T. Terry.
    Charles White Trippe was the son of Frederick and Mary Louise White Trippe.
    Charles White and Lucy Adeline Terry Trippe, Sr.'s son Charles White Trippe, Jr. died in 1899 at the age of two in a train accident. Their daughter Katharine married Sargent Bradlee, the son of Frederick Josiah Bradlee of Boston, MA, and resided in Boston. Their son Juan married Elizabeth Stettinius and resided in East Hampton.
    The former carriage house was later the residence of their granddaughter Elizabeth Stettinius Trippe De Vecchi.
    The house was later owned by the Trippes' son Juan who, in 1929, sold it to John Mingus Dodd III. Dodd called it *The Kennels*. [*The East Hampton Star* October 11, 1929, p. 1.]
    [See following entry for additional family information.]

Trippe, Juan Terry (1899-1981)

Occupation(s);	financier - member, Lee, Higginson, and Co., Boston, MA (investment banking firm); director, Metropolitan Life Insurance Co.
	industrialist - director, Chrysler Corp.
	capitalist - founder and president, Long Island Airways, Inc.; a founder and director, Colonial Air Transport, Inc.; a founder, Aviation Corporation of America (holding company for several airlines); president and general manager, Pan American Airways, Inc.; director, Waldorf Astoria Corp.
Civic Activism:	president, International Air Traffic Association; president, Maidstone Club, East Hampton
Marriage(s):	1929-1981 – Elizabeth Stettinius (1904-1983)
	- Civic Activism: trustee, Federation of Protestant Welfare Agencies; trustee, Citizens Committee for Children of New York; trustee, Child Welfare League of America; president, Ladies Village Improvement Society of East Hampton; trustee, Guild Hall, East Hampton
Address:	West End Avenue, East Hampton
Name of estate:	
Year of construction:	1891
Style of architecture:	Shingle with Dutch elements
Architect(s):	Joseph Greenleaf Thorp designed the 1894, 1896, and 1899 alterations (for Mrs. James)
Landscape architect(s):	
Builder:	George A. Eldredge, 1894, 1896, and 1899 alterations
House extant: no	
Historical notes:	

The house, originally named *Blomioff*, was built by Laura Brevoort Sedgwick prior to her marriage to Henry Amman James. It was later owned by Trippe.

He was the son of Charles White and Lucy Adeline Terry Trippe, Sr. of East Hampton.

Elizabeth Stettinius Trippe was the daughter of Edward Reilly and Judith Carrington Stettinius, Sr. of *The Shelter* in Lattingtown. [*See* Spinzia, *Long Island's Prominent North Shore Families, vol. II* – Stettinius entry.]

Juan Terry and Elizabeth Stettinius Trippe's daughter Elizabeth married William H. Duke; William Angus Douglass; Stuyvesant Wainwright II of Wainscott; and, subsequently, Robert Paolo De Vecchi with whom she resided in East Hampton. Their son Charles White Trippe II married Pamela Joan Reid, the daughter of Cornelius Joseph Reid, Sr. of *Meadow Farm* in Mill Neck, and resided in Chicago, IL. [*See* Spinzia, *Long Island's Prominent North Shore Families, vol. II* – Reid entry.] Their son John married Jane Barrett Reis, the daughter of Lincoln Reis of Rhinebeck, NY, and resided in Doylestown, PA.

[See previous entry for additional family information.]

In 1991 the house was purchased by Calvin Klein who built a new house on the site.

The house was on the National Register of Historic Places.

Tuck, Frederick W., Jr. (1901-1966)

Occupation(s):	attorney - partner, Tuck and Van Brunt, Sayville, NY
	financier - a founder, director, and counsel, Sayville Federal Savings & Loan;
	director and counsel, Oysterman's Bank & Trust Co.;
	director and counsel, First National Bank of Islip;
	director and counsel, Patchogue Mortgage Co.;
	director and counsel, Suffolk County Personal Finance Co.;
	chairman of board, Eastern Federal Savings & Loan
Civic Activism:	secretary, Sayville Yacht Club
Marriage(s):	1934-1966 – Merle Fiske
	- educator - teacher
	Civic Activism: chair, acquisitions committee, Guild Hall, East Hampton
Address:	118 Egypt Lane, East Hampton
Name of estate:	*Off-The Teeee*
Year of construction:	1957
Style of architecture:	Mediterranean
Architect(s):	
Landscape architect(s):	
Builder:	Safeway Developers Corporation
House extant: yes	
Historical notes:	

 The house, originally named *Off-The Teeee*, was built by Frederick W. Tuck, Jr. [*The East Hampton Star* February 28, 1957, p. 1.]
 The Blue Book of The Hamptons, 1973 lists Mrs. Frederick W. Tuck [Jr.] as residing at *Off-The Teeee*, 118 Egypt Lane, East Hampton.
 She was the daughter of Henry Fiske of Greenport.
 Frederick W. Tuck, Jr. was the son of Frederick W. and Julia Tuck, Sr.
 Frederick W. and Merle Fiske Tuck, Jr.'s daughter Nancy married Sylvester Belleau Gardiner, Jr. of Locust Valley. Their daughter Merle married Robert D. Clark. Their son Frederick F. Tuck married Jane Rogers.

Turner, Kathleen (b. 1954)
aka Mary Kathleen Turner

Occupation(s):	entertainers and associated professions -
	motion picture, television, and Broadway actress
	educator - taught acting classes, New York University, NYC
	writer - co-authored, with Gloria Feldt, *Send Yourself Roses*, 2008 (autobiography)
Civic Activism:	board chair, Planned Parenthood;
	trustee, American Way
Marriage(s):	1984-div. 2007 – Jay Weiss
	- capitalist - president, Little Peach Realty, Inc. (real estate developer and management firm)
Address:	318 Bluff Road, Amagansett
Name of estate:	
Year of construction:	1903
Style of architecture:	Mediterranean
Architect(s):	
Landscape architect(s):	
House extant: yes	
Historical notes:	

 The 5,000-square-foot, six-bedroom house with five and a half bathrooms, was built by The Reverend Howard Duffield. It was originally named *Dune Crest*. In 1990 it was purchased by Turner for $488,500.
 She is the daughter of Allen Richard and Patsy Magee Turner.
 *Turner won a Golden Globe Award and was nominated twice for Tony awards.
 In 2010 Turner sold the house for $3.9 million.

Tweed, Harrison (1885-1969)

Occupation(s):	attorney -	partner, Byrne and Cutcheon;
		partner, Byrne, Cutcheon, and Taylor;
		partner, Humes, Buck, Smith, and Tweed;
		partner, Murray, Prentice, and Aldrich;
		partner, Milbank, Tweed, and Hope;
		partner, Milbank, Tweed, Hadley, and McCloy
	writer -	*The Legal Aid Society – New York City 1876-1951*, 1954;
		co-authored, *Life and Testamentary Estate Planning*, 1949, revised 1959;
		wrote chapter "Other Lawyer's Life" in *Listen to Leaders in Law*, 1963;
		numerous articles in law journals
	educator -	interim president, Sarah Lawrence College, 1959-1960

Civic Activism:
president, American Law Institute, 1947-1961;
chairman of board, American Law Institute, 1962-1969;
chairman, committee on continuing legal education;
aided in drafting Uniform Commercial Code;
chairman, legal aid committee, 1939-1947;
president, Legal Aid Society of New York, 1936-1945;
president, National Legal Aid Association, 1949-1955;
director, National Legal and Defender Association;
president, Association of the Bar of the City of New York;
chairman, New York State Temporary Commission on the Courts, 1953-1958;
co-chairman, Committee for Civil Rights Under Law, 1963-1965;
director, Committee for Civil Rights Under Law, 1966-1969;
conducted experimental summer school for boys at his Montauk residence, 1928-1930;
chairman of board, Sarah Lawrence College;
overseer, Harvard University, 1950-1956;
trustee, The Cooper Union for the Advancement of Science and Art, NYC, 1940-1965;
director, Birth Control Research Bureau

Marriage(s):
M/1 – 1914-div. 1928 – Eleanor Jenckes Roelker (1889-1952)
 - writer - *Largely Fiction*, 1948 (autobiography);
   The Painter
M/2 – 1929-div. 1942 – Blanche Oelrichs (1890-1950)
     (aka Michael Strange)
 - writer - *Poems*, 1919;
   Claire de Lune, c. 1920 (play);
   Miscellaneous Poems, 1921;
   Miss Reuter Reflects (novel);
   Who Tells Me True, 1940 (autobiography);
   Resurrecting Life (poetry);
   The Dark Crown (play);
   Lord and Lady Byron (play)
  entertainers and associated professions -   actress
  Civic Activism: suffragist*
M/3 – 1942-1969 – Barbara Banning (1907-2001)
 - entertainers and associated professions -
   member, Isadora Duncan Dancers
  Civic Activism: trustee, Child Education Fund;
         trustee, Protestant Welfare Agencies;
         president, Woman's City Club;
         president and trustee, Schepp Foundation

Address: 165 De Forest Road, Montauk
Name of estate: *Tick Hall*

Tweed, Harrison (cont'd)

Year of construction: 1883
Style of architecture: Beach Cottage
Architect(s): McKim, Mead & White designed the house
Landscape architect(s): Frederick Law Olmsted designed the site plan
Builder: Mead and Taft
House extant: no; destroyed by fire, 1997**
Historical notes:

The house is one of the Montauk Association's "Seven Sisters." It was owned by Alexander Ector Orr. It was later owned by James L. Darby and, then, jointly by Tweed, Alexander Ector Orr, Dr. Fessenden Nott Otis, Louis Clark, Andrew J. Thomas, and E. M. Jackson prior to being purchased in 1924 by Tweed, who named it *Tick Hall*.

The *Social Register Summer, 1950* lists Harrison and Barbara Banning Tweed as residing at *Tick Hall* in Montauk.

He was the son of Charles Harrison and Helen Minerva Evarts Tweed of Manhattan.

Eleanor Jenckes Roelker Tweed was the daughter of William Greene and Eleanor Jenckes Roelker of East Greenwich, CT. She subsequently married Count Paul Palffy of Budmerice, Hungary.

Harrison and Eleanor Jenckes Roelker Tweed's daughter Eleanor married Nelson W. Aldrich; Vinton Lindley; John C. Stockham; and, subsequently, Herbert von Metzler. Their daughter Katharine married Archibald Bulloch Roosevelt, Jr. with whom she resided at *Turkey Lane House* in Cold Spring Harbor, and, later, Dr. Robert Blackwood Robertson. [*See* Spinzia, *Long Island's Prominent North Shore Families, vol. II* – Roosevelt entry.]

Blanche Oelrichs Tweed was the daughter of Charles May Oelrichs of Newport, RI, and a childhood friend of Eleanor. She had previously been married to Leonard Thomas, Sr. and to the actor John Barrymore.

*For other Long Islanders involved in the suffrage movement *see* Raymond E. Spinzia, "Winning the Franchise: Long Island Activists in the Fight for Woman's Suffrage and Their Opponents, Long Island's Anti-Suffragists." wwwspinzialongislandestates.com.

Barbara Banning Tweed was the daughter of Kendall and Hedwig von Briesen Banning of Manhattan. Barbara subsequently married Holland Estill.

Harrison and Barbara Banning Tweed's daughter Sandra married Broadway director Peter Hunt.

**The house was owned by Richard Alva Cavett when it was destroyed by fire in 1997. He built a contemporary version similar to the original house on the site. The new house was designed by James Hadley.

In 2017 the 7,000-square-foot, seven-bedroom, five-bath house and twenty acres were for sale by Cavett. The asking price was $62 million. The annual taxes were $50,000.

Tyler, John Alexander (1848-1883)

Occupation(s): civil engineer
United States Surveyor of Indian Lands
Inspector of Surveys, New Mexico Territory

Marriage(s): 1875-1927 – Sarah Griswold Gardiner (1848-1927)

Address: 217 Main Street, East Hampton
Name of estate:
Year of construction: c. 1836
Style of architecture: Modified Colonial Revival
Architect(s):
Landscape architect(s):
House extant: yes
Historical notes:

The house was built by David G. Thompson. Around 1882 Tyler purchased the house from Mrs. Thompson.

He was the son of President John Tyler and Mrs. Julia Gardiner Tyler.

Sarah Griswold Gardiner Tyler was the daughter of Samuel Buell and Mary Thompson Gardiner of Gardiner's Island and East Hampton.

John Alexander and Sarah Griswold Gardiner Tyler's son Samuel died in 1892 at the age of twenty. Their daughter Lilian married Alben N. Margraff of Germany.

The house was later owned by Auguste Richard.

The north addition to the house was built somewhere between 1902 and 1916.

The house is occasionally referred to as the *White House*.

Tyson, James (1906-1975)

Occupation(s):	industrialist - Kentile Inc. (manufacturers of floor tiles)
Civic Activism:	James and his wife Carolyn saved six historic buildings and moved them to their estate;
	James and his wife Carolyn were instrumental in saving *Miss Amelia's Cottage*, Amagansett, and *Second House*, Montauk
Marriage(s):	1930-1975 – Carolyn Kennedy (1905-1996)
	- artist
	writer - *Ten Years Poetry and Paintings*, 1973
	entertainers and associated professions -
	co-produced, with Robert Blaisdell:
	"By Daylight" (documentary);
	"In Dream" (documentary)
	Civic Activism:
	Carolyn and her husband James saved six historic buildings and moved them to their estate;
	Carolyn and her husband James were instrumental in saving *Miss Amelia's Cottage*, Amagansett, and *Second House*, Montauk;
	trustee, Amagansett Historical Society;
	trustee, Montauk Historical Society;
	president, Amagansett Village Improvement Society
Address:	Further Lane, Amagansett
Name of estate:	*Old Baker House*
Year of construction:	1600s
Style of architecture:	Salt Box
Architect(s):	
Landscape architect(s):	David Seeler, Bayberry Nursery, Amagansett, 1999 (for Lang)
Builder:	William Simons, alterations (for Tyson)

House extant: yes
Historical notes:

In 1949 James Tyson moved the residence of Edward Mulford Baker from Pantigo Road to Further Lane and called it *Old Baker House*. [*The East Hampton Star* August 28, 1975, p. 30, and September 4, 1986, p. 32.]

The Blue Book of The Hamptons, 1973 lists James and Carolyn Kennedy Tyson as residing at *Old Baker House* on Further Lane, Amagansett. She was the daughter of Edward E. and Claire O'Donnell Kennedy of *Second House* in Montauk. Carolyn had previously been married to Charles Jerome Massinger, Jr. of Ocean Grove, NJ. The Massingers' daughter Patricia Massinger (aka Jane Kennedy), who was adopted by Carolyn's parents, married William C. Kuhn, Sr. and, later, Henry Preston Hoppin with whom she resided in East Hampton.

James and Carolyn Kennedy Tyson's son David married Kathleen Mary Sheehan, the daughter of Daniel Sheehan of Riverdale, NY, and resided in Amagansett.

In 1991 the house was purchased by Frederic Milton Seegal who renamed it *Old Simons House* in honor of Tyson's builder and caretaker. [*The East Hampton* Star July 3, 1997.]

In 1999 Seegal sold the estate to Helmut Lang for $15.5 million. [*The New York Post* June 24, 2002.]

Tyson, Mark (1908-1967)

Occupation(s):	industrialist - sales executive, Allied Chemical; partner, Mercantile Chemical Co., NY
Marriage(s):	M/1 – 1932-div. 1938 – Amy Fownes Barnes M/2 – 1940-1967 – Rosemary Ward (1911-1967)
Address:	Lily Pond Lane, East Hampton
Name of estate:	
Year of construction:	
Style of architecture:	
Architect(s):	
Landscape architect(s):	
House extant:	unconfirmed
Historical notes:	

Mark Tyson was the son of The Reverend Stuart Lawrence Tyson.

Amy Fownes Barnes Tyson was the daughter of John and Amy Fownes Barnes, Sr. of *Four Winds* in Haverford, PA.

Mark and Amy Fownes Barnes Tyson's son John married Joanne Lee Erhart, the daughter of Charles Huntington and Joanna Bright Erhart, Sr. of Cornwall, CT. Charles Huntington Erhart had previously been married to Katherine Kent with whom he had resided in Jericho. [*See* Spinzia, *Long Island's Prominent North Shore Families, vol. I* – Erhart entry .]

Rosemary Ward Tyson was the daughter of Newell Jube and Ethel L. Conderman Ward, Sr. of East Hampton. Rosemary had previously been married to George W. Blabon II, the son of Edwin L. Blabon of Bryn Mawr, PA.

Mark and Rosemary Ward Tyson's daughter Holly married Arthur Stephen Kelly of Far Hills, NJ, and resided in Landrum, SC. Their son Anthony married Vivian Alice Thompson, the daughter of Harvey Steward Thompson of New York and Woodstock, NH, and resided in East Hampton.

In 1963 Tyson made alterations to the house. [*The East Hampton Star* September 19, 1963, p. 13.]

Vaill, Isabella Mary Breck (1835-1914)

Marriage(s):	1856-1883 – Timothy Dwight Vaill (1817-1883)
Address:	Lily Pond Lane, East Hampton
Name of estate:	*Century Cottage*
Year of construction:	
Style of architecture:	
Architect(s):	
Landscape architect(s):	
Builder:	Thomas E, Babcock, 1906 addition (for Mrs. Vaill) J. O. Hopping, 1914 (for Mrs. D. Talmage, Jr.) Edward M. Gay, 1916 addition (for Mapes)
House extant:	unconfirmed
Historical notes:	

In 1902 Isabella Mary Breck Vaill moved the house from Cottage Avenue to Lily Pond Lane and made improvements. [*The East Hampton Star* November 15, 1901, p. 5.]

Timothy Dwight Vaill was the son of The Reverend Joseph and Mrs. Ann Kirtland Vaill, Jr.

Timothy Dwight and Isabella Mary Breck Vaill's daughter Anna married George Mason LaMonte and resided in East Hampton. Their daughter Mary, who later owned the house, married Daniel Talmage, Jr., the son of Daniel and Hannah Fowler Talmage, Sr.

In 1914 Mary had J. O. Hopping move the house further east on the property. [*The East Hampton Star* October 30, 1914, p. 5.]

It was later owned by her son Rockwell Dwight Talmage.

In 1916 Rockwell sold the house to Victor Mapes who still owned it at the time of his death in 1943. [*The East Hampton Star* June 9, 1916, p. 5, and December 16, 1943, p. 43.].

In 1948 the house became the base for the Summer School of Arts. [*The East Hampton Star* September 13, 1973, p. 8.]

Van Brunt, Arthur Hoffman, Sr. (1865-1951)

Occupation(s):	attorney - partner, Joline, Larkin, and Rathbone
Civic Activism:	treasurer, Holland Society
Marriage(s):	1902-1947 – Ethel Townsend Edson (1878-1947)
Address:	61 Ocean Avenue, East Hampton
Name of estate:	*The Breezes*
Year of construction:	1907
Style of architecture:	Shingle
Architect(s):	John Custis Lawrence designed the house (for Van Brunt, Sr.)
Landscape architect(s):	
Builder:	Thomas E. Babcock
House extant: yes	
Historical notes:	

The house, originally named *The Breezes*, was built by Arthur Hoffman Van Brunt, Sr.

The *Social Register, Summer, 1921* lists Arthur Hoffman and Ethel T. Edson Van Brunt [Sr.] as residing at *The Breezes* in East Hampton.

He was the son of Charles Holmes and Amelia Chesterman Henry Van Brunt.

Ethel Edson Van Brunt was the daughter of New York City Mayor Franklin Edson.

Arthur Hoffman and Ethel T. Edson Van Brunt, Sr.'s daughter Carol married George C. Comstock, Jr. and resided in Manhattan. Their son Edson married Elizabeth Rice and resided in Manhattan. Their son Arthur Hoffman Van Brunt, Jr. married Mary Harrsen and resided in Essex Falls, NJ. Their son David married Jane Green Allen.

In 1977 alterations were made to the house.

Vanderbilt, Oliver DeGray, III (1914-2000)

Occupation(s):	industrialist - vice-president, Weir Kilby Corp., Highbridge, NJ, and Easton, PA (later, Taylor–Wharton Iron and Steel Co.) (manufacturer of manganese steel castings and high pressure gas cylinders);
	president Taylor–Wharton Iron and Steel Co., 1949-1954 (now, Harso):
	vice-president and director, Baldwin–Lima–Hamilton Corp., Philadelphia, PA, 1955-1956
	financier - chairman of board and director, Blair and Co., 1963-1970 (investment banking firm);
	founder, Vanderbilt Corporation, Philadelphia, PA (specialized in tax shelters);
	a founder and president, Capital Management Corp.;
	a founder and president, Innovest Group (venture capital firm);
	a founder, Seaboard Savings Bank, Stuart, FL
Civic Activism:	director, Home of the Merciful Savior for Crippled Children, Philadelphia, PA;
	board member, United Cerebral Palsy Association;
	director, Family Service Organization;
	director, Northeastern Y.M.C.A., Cincinnati, OH;
	director, Foundation for Medical Research, University of Pennsylvania, Philadelphia, PA
Marriage(s):	1939-2000 – Frances Montgomery Philips (1917-2000)
Address:	Buell Lane, East Hampton
Name of estate:	*Old Post Office*
Year of construction:	
Style of architecture:	
Architect(s):	
Landscape architect(s):	
House extant: unconfirmed	
Historical notes:	

 The *Long Island Society Register, 1929* lists Mr. and Mrs. O. DeGray Vanderbilt, Jr. [III] as residing on Drew Lane, East Hampton. By 1965 they had relocated to Buell Lane. *The Blue Book of The Hamptons, 1965* lists the Vanderbilts as residing at *Old Post Office* on Buell Lane in East Hampton.
 He was the son of Oliver DeGray and Madelon Weir Vanderbilt, Jr. of Manhattan and the grandson of Levi Candee and Mary Emma Weibel Weir of *The Hedges* in Lattingtown. [*See* Spinzia, *Long Island's Prominent North Shore Families, vol. II* – Weir entry.]
 Frances Montgomery Philips Vanderbilt was the daughter of William Byers and Ruth Montgomery Philips of Birmingham, AL.
 Oliver DeGray and Frances Montgomery Philips Vanderbilt III's daughter Madelon married Charles S. Peck and resided in Altadena, CA. Their son Oliver DeGray Vanderbilt IV married Katharine Spahr and resided in Molokai, HI.

Van Rensselaer, Kiliaen, III (1879-1949)

Occupation(s):	financier - partner, Thomas H. Manson and Co. (stock brokerage firm)
Civic Activism:	president, St. Nicholas Society; trustee, New York Historical Society; president, Colonial Lords of the Manor of America; trustee, Holland Society
Marriage(s):	M/1 – 1905-1927 – Dorothea Manson (1885-1927)
	M/2 – 1934-1949 – Mabel Lorraine Miller (1889-1953)
Address:	117 Main Street, East Hampton
Name of estate:	*Millfield*
Year of construction:	c. 1799
Style of architecture:	Colonial Revival*
Architect(s):	Isaac Henry Green II designed 1889 alterations**
	Joseph Greenleaf Thorp designed 1905 interior and exterior alterations
Landscape architect(s):	Mary Lois Deputy Lanson (for Douglas)

House extant: yes
Historical notes:

The house was built by Jeremiah Miller IV.
*It was later owned by Edward de Rose who remodeled it, changing the architecture from Georgian to Colonial Revival, and named it *Millfield*. It was then owned by Thomas Lincoln Manson III and, then, by his daughter Dorothea and son-in-law Kiliaen Van Rensselaer. Both Manson and Van Rensselaer continued to call it *Millfield*.

The *Social Directory of Southampton, Long Island, 1931* lists Mr. Kiliaen Van Rensselaer [III] as residing on Main Street, East Hampton. The *Long Island Society Register, 1929* lists the name of his estate as *Millfield*.

Van Rensselaer was a descendant of his colonial era namesake, he was the son of Kiliaen and Oliva Phelps Atterbury Van Rensselaer.

Kiliaen and Dorothea Manson Van Rensselaer III's daughter Barbara married John Taylor Sherman II, the son of Frederick Deming and Leslie Whitman Sherman of Greenwich, CT, and resided in Amagansett.

Mabel Lorraine Miller Van Rensselaer was the daughter of Alvah and Phebe Miller of Ossining and Brooklyn, NY. Mabel had previously been married to Kingsley Swan. In 1914 she married Robert Graves II of *Treborcliffe* in Lloyd Harbor. [*See* Spinzia, *Long Island's Prominent North Shore Families, vol. I* – Graves entry .] In 1928 Mabel married Benjamin Wood, the son of New York City Mayor Fernando Wood. After his death in 1934, she married Van Rensselaer. She then married Henry Aldrich Granary of Old Westbury.

[For information about Van Rensselaer's Old Westbury residence, *see* Spinzia, *Long Island's Prominent North Shore Families, vol. II* – Van Rensselaer entry.]

In 1945 the house was owned by Graham Douglas. By 1950 it was owned by Franklin M. Chace, who called it *Gone With the Wind*, and, by 1973, by Richard Vincent Hare.

**For Green's other commissions, *see* Spinzia, *Long Island's Prominent South Shore Families: Their Estates and Their Country Homes in the Towns of Babylon and Islip.*

Vaughan, Eliza Jennie Potter (1852-1926)

Marriage(s):	1873-1908 – Dr. Henry Wheaton Vaughan (1848-1908) - scientist - chemist - member, Haase & Vaughan (chemists); City Inspector of Milk, Providence, RI; Rhode Island State Assayer
Address:	Lee Avenue, East Hampton
Name of estate:	*Beulahside*
Year of construction:	1892
Style of architecture:	Modified Dutch Colonial Revival
Architect(s):	George A. Eldredge designed the house (for E. J. P. Vaughan)
Landscape architect(s):	
Builder:	George A. Eldredge
House extant: unconfirmed	
Historical notes:	

The house, originally named *Beulahside*, was built by Eliza Jennie Potter Vaughan, who had been estranged from her husband for over twenty years.

The *Social Register Summer, 1915* lists E. Jennie Potter Vaughan as residing at *Beulahside* in East Hampton.

She was the daughter of Joseph and Jane Potter. Eliza's brother Eugene married Margaret Somerville and resided at *A–Y–Mor* in East Hampton.

Henry Wheaton Vaughan was the son of Daniel Wheaton and Mary Elizabeth Jones Vaughan.

When Eugene Potter was questioned about Henry's suicide, he replied that his brother-in-law's death was not unexpected as he had suffered from consumption for many years and for the last five years had been a hopeless invalid. Eugene went on to say, "It is just a common death of an ordinary man. He was not a man of prominence, belonged to no big clubs in New York and had lived here little. The general public can be interested in no way in his death." [*The New York Times* July 18, 1908, p. 1.] Eugene's statement surely raised a few eyebrows at Manhattan's prestigious Metropolitan Club which listed Vaughan as one of its members.

Henry Wheaton and Eliza Jennie Potter Vaughan's son Clifford married Eleanor Lewis, the daughter of Clifford Lewis of Philadelphia, PA, and resided in East Hampton.

Velie, John Deere, II (1908-1978)

Occupation(s):	capitalist - president, Mines Corporation, Joplin, MO (mining firm)
Marriage(s):	1935-1978 – Betty Banks (1910-2002)
Address:	87 Davids Lane, East Hampton
Name of estate:	
Year of construction:	
Style of architecture:	Cape Cod
Architect(s):	
Landscape architect(s):	
House extant: yes	
Historical notes:	

In 1941 Marie Schultze Kast purchased the house from Robert Barns. [*The East Hampton Star* November 13, 1941, p. 4.] In 1943 it was purchased by Walton Pearl Kingsley from Mrs. Kast. [*The East Hampton Star* April 1, 1943, p. 5.] In 1953 he sold it to Velie. [*The East Hampton Star* June 4, 1953, p. 1.]

The Blue Book of The Hamptons, 1958 lists John Deere and Betty Banks Velie as residing at 87 Davids Lane, East Hampton.

He was the son of Thomas Ainsworth and Cordelia Estelle Combs Hoskin Velie.

Betty Banks Velie was the daughter of Lynn Stanton and Ethel P. Callaway Banks of Kansas City, MO.

Verglas, Antoine (b. 1962)

Occupation(s):	professional photographer*
	entertainers and associated professions -
	host, "Cinq sur Cinq" (French television show)
	merchant - co-founder, Calypso St. Barth
Marriage(s):	
Address:	61 and 65 Dune Lane, Amagansett
Name of estate:	
Year of construction:	
Style of architecture:	Beach Cottage
Architect(s):	
Landscape architect(s):	
House extant: yes	
Historical notes:	

*Verglas is a well-known fashion photographer who gained notoriety for his nude photographs of Melania Knavs (aka Melania Knauss). She later married Donald John Trump who would become the third President of the United States to be impeached.

In 2017 the house was listed for sale. The asking price was $12.5 million.

Volckening, Lloyd Irwin (1857-1984)

Occupation(s):	industrialist - president and vice-chairman of board, Ivers–Lee Co.
	(pharmaceutical packing firm)
	attorney
	inventor - pharmaceutical packing machine
Civic Activism:	trustee, New York Board of Trade;
	chairman of drug and chemical section, New York Board of Trade;
	established Volckening Scholarship, Phi Delta Theta
Marriage(s):	M/1 – 1924 – Rita Webster
	M/2 – 1927-1984 – Madelon Alberta Bartlett
Address:	Middle Lane, East Hampton
Name of estate:	
Year of construction:	
Style of architecture:	
Architect(s):	
Landscape architect(s):	
Builder:	Robert Barnes, 1955 guest cottage
	(for Volckening)
House extant: unconfirmed	
Historical notes:	

The Blue Book of The Hamptons, 1965 and *1973* list Mr. and Mrs. Lloyd I. Volckening as residing on Middle Lane, East Hampton.

He was the son of Gustave J. and Anna I. Volckening of Brooklyn, NY.

Rita Webster Volckening was the daughter of Howard Shimer Webster of Brooklyn, NY.

Madelon Alberta Bartlett Volckening was the daughter of Ernest John and Madelon Luna Mears Bartlett of Wolfeboro, MA.

Lloyd Irving and Madelon Alberta Bartlett Volckening's son Lloyd Edgar Volckening married Jane Harriet Metcalfe, the daughter of Robert Davis and Gladys McKennon Metcalf, and, later, Elizabeth Oat with whom he resided in Moorestown, NJ.

In 1955 the house was remodeled. [*The East Hampton Star* June 16, 1955, p. 12.]

Voorhees, Dr. James Ditmars (1869-1929)
aka Dr. James Ditmars Van Voorhees

Occupation(s):	physician - obstetrician -
	    Presbyterian Hospital, NYC, 1894-1896;
	    New York Foundling Hospital, NYC, 1896-1897;
	    Sloane Hospital for Women, NYC, 1897-1900;
	    consulting physician, Southampton Hospital
	educator - associate professor of obstetrics, College of Physicians and Surgeons, Columbia University, NYC, 1901-1905
	inventor - Voorhees bag (used in obstetrics)

Marriage(s):	1902-1929 – Louise Brown (1871-1958)
Address:	80 Dunemere Lane, East Hampton
Name of estate:	
Year of construction:	1913
Style of architecture:	Modified Norman
Architect(s):	John Custis Lawrence designed the house (for Voorhees)
Landscape architect(s):	
Builder:	Edward M. Gay
House extant:	yes
Historical notes:	

    The house was built by Dr. James Ditmars Voorhees.
    The *Social Register Summer, 1910* and *1915* list Dr. James D. and Mrs. Louise Brown Voorhees as residing in East Hampton.
    He was the son of George Emmell and Mary Gertrude Voorhees of Morristown, NJ.
    Louise Brown Voorhees was the daughter of Samuel Queen and Nancy Elizabeth Lamb Brown of *Breezy Knowl* in East Hampton.
    Dr. James Ditmars and Mrs. Louise Brown Voorhees' daughter Louise married Charles Edmunds Kimball, Jr. of East Hampton and, later, John Rouse Webster of Greenwich, CT. Their daughter Elizabeth married Donald C. Webster and resided in Greenwich, CT. Their daughter Nancy married Clarence Redington Barrett and resided in Greenwich, CT. Their son Brown married Gladis Barber, the daughter of S. Morgan Barber of *Elm Court* in Green Farms, CT, and resided in La Jolla, CA.
    In 1936 the house was purchased by Valentine Britton Havens. [*The East Hampton Star* December 17, 1936, p. 5.] It was later owned by Irving Howland Taylor.

Wainwright, Carroll Livingston, Jr. (1925-2016)

Occupation(s):	attorney - partner, Milbank, Weed, Hadley, and McCloy
	financier - director, United States Trust Corporation of New York
	educator - adjunct professor, Washington and Lee Law School
Civic Activism:	member, New York State Commission on Judicial Conduct;
	trustee, Cooper Union, NYC;
	treasurer and vice-president, New York City Bar Association;
	president, Down Town Association, 1985-1992;
	president, Maidstone Club, East Hampton, 1970-1973;
	president, Boys Club of New York;
	trustee, Southampton Hospital;
	vice-president, Old East Hampton (members who have summered in East Hampton for at least 25 years)
Marriage(s):	1948-2016 – Nina Walker
	- recording secretary - East Hampton Garden Club
Address:	57 Dunemere Lane, East Hampton

Name of estate:
Year of construction:
Style of architecture:
Architect(s):
Landscape architect(s):
House extant: unconfirmed
Historical notes:

The Blue Book of The Hamptons, 1987 lists Mr. and Mrs. Carroll L. Wainwright, Jr. as residing at 57 Dunemere Lane, East Hampton.

He was the son of Carroll Livingston and Edith Catherine Gould Wainwright, Sr. of *Gullcrest* in East Hampton.

Nina Walker Wainwright was the daughter of Delos and Nina Elizabeth Sebring Walker of East Hampton.

Carroll Livingston and Nina Walker Wainwright, Jr.'s son Mark married Mary La Branche Stockman, the daughter of Henry C. Stockman of Locust Valley, and resides in Los Gatos, CA. Their son Delos married Alice Elizabeth Baldridge, the daughter of Robert Connell Baldridge of Lawrence, and resides in East Hampton.

[See other Wainwright entries for additional family information.]

Wainwright, Carroll Livingston, Sr. (1899-1967)

Occupation(s):	artist
	financier - stockbroker
Marriage(s):	1920-div. 1932 – Edith Catherine Gould (1901-1937)
Address:	West End Avenue, East Hampton
Name of estate:	*Gullcrest*
Year of construction:	1928
Style of architecture:	Neo-Federal
Architect(s):	Penrose V. Stout designed the house (for C. L. Wainwright, Sr.)
Landscape architect(s):	John Raum designed 1928 rock, rose, and walled gardens, tennis courts and greenhouse (for C. L. Wainwright, Sr.)
Builder:	Frank Johnson

House extant: yes
Nassau County Museum Collection has photographs of the estate.
Historical notes:

The house, originally named *Gullcrest*, was built by Carroll Livingston Wainwright, Sr.
He was the son of Stuyvesant and Caroline Smith Snowden Wainwright, Sr. of Rye, NY. Caroline subsequently married Dr. Carol F. Wolff and resided at *Shadowmere* in East Hampton. Carroll's brother Loudon married Eleanor Painter Sloan, the daughter of Burrows and Eleanor Painter Sloan of *Orchard Hill* in Ardmore, PA, and resided in Hewlett Neck. [*See* Spinzia, *Long Island's Prominent Families in the Town of Hempstead* – Wainwright entry.] His brother Stuyvesant Wainwright, Jr. married Louise Flinn, the daughter of George Hamilton and Sara Louise Negley Flinn of East Hampton, and resided in Bay Shore and at *Duckwood* in Hampton Bays. [*See* Spinzia, *Long Island's Prominent Families in the Town of Southampton* and *Long Island's Prominent South Shore Families* – Wainwright entries.] Their grandfather Archibald Loudon Snowdon was the director of the United States Mint in Philadelphia, PA.

Carroll had nervous breakdowns in 1916 and in 1923. In 1931 he was committed to the Bloomingdale Hospital in White Plains, NY, for evaluation. His brothers Stuyvesant, John, and Loudon petitioned the court to declare him mentally incompetent to manage his affairs. After five hours of testimony by specialists on mental and nervous disorders, it took the jury only thirteen minutes to declare him completely competent. [*The New York Times* May 21, 1931, p. 24, and *Patchogue Advance* May 22, 1931, p. 1.]

Edith Catherine Gould Wainwright was the daughter of George Jay and Edith M. Kingdon Gould. She later married Hector Murray McNeal.

Carroll Livingston and Edith Catherine Gould Wainwright, Sr.'s daughter Caroline married Edward Townsend Shean, the son of Edward J. Shean of Syosset. Their son Stuyvesant Wainwright II, who resided in Wainscott, married Janet Isabel Parsons, the daughter of Thomas Crouse Parsons of *Parsons Farms* near Jourdanton, TX; Mary Greis Harris with whom he resided in Wainscott; Elizabeth Trippe, the daughter Juan Terry and Elizabeth Stettinius Trippe of East Hampton; and Helene Elizabeth Henning, the daughter of George Henning, the Mayor of Muttontown. Their son Carroll Livingston Wainwright, Jr. married Nina Walker and resided in East Hampton.

[See other Wainwright entries and Wolff entry for additional family information.]

Wainwright, John Howard (1896-1968)

Occupation(s):	financier - J. L. Cutter Co. (insurance brokerage firm)
Marriage(s):	M/1 – 1919 – Caroline Seymour
	M/2 – 1952-1968 – Aimee du Pont Andrews (1909-1980)
Address:	38 Dayton Lane, East Hampton
Name of estate:	
Year of construction:	
Style of architecture:	Ranch
Architect(s):	
Landscape architect(s):	
House extant: yes	
Historical notes:	

The Blue Book of The Hamptons, 1958 lists Mr. and Mrs. J. Howard Wainwright as residing at 38 Dayton Lane, East Hampton.

He was the son of Stuyvesant and Caroline Smith Snowden Wainwright of Rye, NY. Caroline, who later resided at *Shadowmere* in East Hampton, subsequently married Dr. Carol F. Wolff.

Aimee du Pont Andrews Wainwright was the daughter of James Newman Andrews of Aiken, SC. She had previously been married to Charles Morgan Howell.

By 1965 the Wainwrights had relocated to Lily Pond Lane, East Hampton.

[See Wainwright and Wolff entries for additional family information.]

The 3,200-square-foot house has four bedrooms and four bathrooms.

The Blue Book of The Hamptons, 1979 lists the Wainwrights as residing at *El Pato Feo* on Lily Pond Lane, East Hampton.

Wainwright, Stuyvesant, II (1921-2010)

Occupation(s):	attorney - partner, Abberley, Kooiman, Marcellino; and Clay; partner, Walker, Beale, Wainwright, and Wolf; partner, Battle, Fowler, Lidstone, Jaffin, Pierce, and Kheel
	politician - member, United States Congress, New York's First Congressional District, 1953-1961
	educator - taught political science, Rutgers University, New Brunswick, NJ, 1960-1961
	intelligence agent - member, OSS during World War II
	industrialist - director and general counsel, Potter Instrument Co.; president, Miltope Corp., Melville, NY
Civic Activism:	chairman, East Hampton Village Design Board; trustee, Southampton Hospital; trustee, Guild Hall, East Hampton
Marriage(s):	M/1 – 1941-div. – Janet Isabel Parsons (1920-2000)
	M/2 – 1961-div. – Mary Greis Harris
	M/3 – 1965-div.– Elizabeth Stettinius Trippe (1932-2009)
	- Civic Activism: president, Project Orbis (equipped a jetliner for eye surgery and ophthalmology); trustee, New York Association for the Blind; trustee, Institute of Visual Science; trustee, National Home Care Council; trustee, Eugene O'Neill Theater Center; trustee Outward Bound; trustee, Ackerman Institute
	M/4 – 1982 – Helene Elizabeth Henning (b. 1945)
	- industrialist - managing director, Allan Campbell, Inc. (designers and manufacturers of fabrics and wallpaper)
Address:	Wainscott Road, East Hampton
Name of estate:	*Green Oaks*
Year of construction:	
Style of architecture:	Contemporary
Architect(s):	
Landscape architect(s):	
House extant: yes	
Historical notes:	

The *Social Register Summer, 1950* lists Stuyvesant and Janet I. Parsons Wainwright [II] as residing at *Green Oaks* on Wainscott Road in East Hampton [Wainscott].

He was the son of Carroll Livingston and Edith Catherine Gould Wainwright, Sr. of *Gullcrest* in East Hampton.

Janet Isabel Parsons Wainwright was the daughter of Thomas Crouse Parsons of Jourdanton, TX.

Stuyvesant and Janet Isabel Parsons Wainwright II's daughter Janet married Charles Brandon Waring, the son of Antonio J. Waring of Savannah, GA, and, subsequently, Edmund Kirby–Smith IV. Their son Jonathan Mayhew Wainwright II married Patricia Gilcrest, the daughter of Alan and Mary Grace Harris Gilcrest of Southport, CT, and, later, Candace F. Drake. Their son Stuyvesant Wainwright III married Marcella C. Mittendorf and resides in East Hampton.

Mary Greis Harris Wainwright had previously been married to Alan Gilchrist.

Elizabeth Stettinius Trippe Wainwright was the daughter of Juan Terry and Elizabeth Stettinius Trippe of East Hampton. Elizabeth had previously been married to William H. Duke and to William A. Douglass. After her divorce from Wainwright she married Robert Paolo De Vecchi and resided in East Hampton.

Helene Elizabeth Henning Wainwright was the daughter of George Henning, the Mayor of Muttontown. She had previously been married to Edward Francis Cavanagh III, the son of Edward Francis and Nancy Miller Cavanagh, Jr. of *Naghward* in Old Brookville. [*See* Spinzia, *Long Island's Prominent North Shore Families, vol. 1* – Cavanagh entry.]

[See other Wainwright entries for additional family information.]

Wainwright, Stuyvesant, III

Occupation(s):	capitalist - member, Dayton–Halstead Real Estate, East Hampton (later, Corcoran Group)
Civic Activism:	chairman of Design Review Board, Village of East Hampton
Marriage(s):	Marcella Callery Mittendorf - educator - director, Park Avenue Christian Church Day School
Address:	16 Fithian Lane, East Hampton
Name of estate:	
Year of construction:	
Style of architecture:	Colonial Revival
Architect(s):	
Landscape architect(s):	
House extant: yes	
Historical notes:	

The *Social Register, 2002* lists Stuyvesant and Marcella C. Mittendorf Wainwright III as residing at 16 Fithian Lane, East Hampton.

He was the son of Stuyvesant and Janet Isabel Parsons Wainwright II of *Green Oaks* in Wainscott.

Marcella Callery Mittendorf Wainwright is the daughter of Joseph and Marcella Hernon Mittendorf.

Stuyvesant and Marcella Callery Mittendorf Wainwright III's daughter Marcella married Jeffrey Shepard Sohm, the son of Jacques Sohm of Scarsdale, NY.

Walker, Bayard Sr. (1915-1985)

Occupation(s):	financier - member, D'Assern and Co. (stock brokerage firm); director, Quotron Systems, Inc. (financial information service firm) capitalist - president, Long Island Co. (holding company specializing in oil and real estate)
Marriage(s):	1945-1985 – Maud Tilghman (1918-2002)
Address:	93 Lily Pond Lane, East Hampton
Name of estate:	*Normandie*
Year of construction:	
Style of architecture:	
Architect(s):	
Landscape architect(s):	
House extant: yes	
Historical notes:	

The Blue Book of The Hamptons, 1958 lists Bayard and Maud Tilghman Walker [Sr.] as residing on Lily Pond Lane, East Hampton.

He was the son of Elisha and Adele D'Orn Walker, Sr. of *Les Pommiers* in Muttontown. [*See* Spinzia, *Long Island's Prominent North Shore Families, vol. II* – Walker entry.]

Maud Tilghman Walker was the daughter of Sidell Tilghman of Madison, NJ.

Bayard and Maud Tilghman Walker Sr.'s daughter Maud married Joseph Hersey Pratt II, the son of Dr. T. Dennie Pratt of New York. Their daughter Cynthia married Piers Louis Sunderland Diacre, the son of Kenneth Diacre. Their son David married Lisa Jean Amoroso, the daughter of Eugene V. Amoroso of Houston, TX. Their daughter Cristina married Richard Paxton Burks, the son of Dr. James L. and Mrs. Mary Paxton Burks. Their daughter Leonie married Joseph Conrad Thieringer, the son of Otis P. and Lenlen Fleming Thieringer and, later, Dr. Katherine Anne O'Hanlan, the daughter of Dr. J. Treacy O'Hanlan. [*The New York Times* November 16, 2003, p. ST20.] Their son Bayard Walker, Jr. married Sue Kepford, the daughter of John and Betty Kepford of Hendersonville, NC.

The five-bedroom, five-and-a-half-bath house, guest house, and 2.8 acres sold in 2007 for $17.5 million.

In 2014 it was purchased by Scott Bommer, who sold it in 2016.

Walker, Delos (1892-1963)

Occupation(s):	merchant - vice-president, secretary, and director, R. H. Macy's Co. (department store chain)
	journalist - Scripps–McRae Newspapers, Denver, CO
Civic Activism:	vice-president, National Committee on Housing;
	president, Retail Dry Goods Association;
	member, United States Senate advisory council on Social Security;
	vice-president and director, Regional Plan Association;
	member, United States Coal Committee, 1923-1924;
	chairman of board, American Retail Federation;
	member, advisory committee, New York University School of Retailing, NYC;
	member, New York State Council of Merchants;
	trustee, Institute of Public Administration;
	director and treasurer, Maidstone Club, East Hampton;
	chairman of board, Village of East Hampton Zoning Board of Appeals;
	director, East Hampton League
Marriage(s):	1924-1963 – Nina Elizabeth Sebring (1896-1966)
	- Civic Activism: secretary, American Red Cross, Sebring Chapter, Sebring, PA
Address:	Dunemere Lane, East Hampton
Name of estate:	
Year of construction:	c. 1891
Style of architecture:	Shingle
Architect(s):	Joseph Greenleaf Thorp designed the house (for J. N. Steele, Sr.)
Landscape architect(s):	
House extant: unconfirmed	
Historical notes:	

The house, originally named *Dunemere*, was built by The Reverend James Nevett Steele. Sr. It was later owned by Clarence Hopkins Hensel who continued to call it *Dunemere*. In 1928 Hensel sold the house to Theodorus Bailey II who also continued to call it *Dunemere*. [*The East Hampton Star* May 17, 1929, p. 7.] In 1944 it was purchased by Walker. [*The East Hampton Star* November 23, 1944, p. 1.]

He was the son of Dr. Henry and Mrs. Villa McFadden Walker.

Nina Elizabeth Sebring Walker was the daughter of Frank Albert and Emma Louisa Harbison Sebring.

Delos and Nina Elizabeth Sebring Walker's daughter Judith married Alexander Mellon Laughlin, Sr., the son of Alexander and Margaret Mellon (later, Mrs. Thomas Hitchcock, Jr.) Laughlin of Pittsburgh, PA, and resided in East Hampton. [*See* Spinzia, *Long Island's Prominent North Shore Families, vol. I* – Hitchcock entry.] [For information on Alexander's half-brother Thomas Hitchcock II's Millbrook, NY, estate, see Raymond E. Spinzia. "Adultery, Drugs, Murder, Untimely Deaths, and Long Island's Prominent Families: A Tangled Web." wwwspinzialongislandestates.com.] Their daughter Nina married Carroll Livingston Wainwright, Jr., the son of Carroll Livingston and Edith Catherine Gould Wainwright, Sr. of *Gullcrest* in East Hampton, and resided in East Hampton.

By 1958 the Walkers had relocated to Lee Avenue in East Hampton.

Walker, George Gholson, Sr. (1902-1984)

Occupation(s):	capitalist - chairman of board, Electric Bond and Share Co. (engineering and management firm) (later, Ebasco Industries, Inc.)
Civic Activism:	chairman of board, Correction Association of New York; trustee, St. Luke's–Roosevelt Hospital, NYC; co-chairman of board, Commission on Resources at Harvard Medical School; director, Maidstone Club, East Hampton
Marriage(s):	M/1 – 1928-div. – Elizabeth Schroeder M/2 – 1953-1973 – Caroline Shields (1902-1973) M/3 – Emily Schniewind (1904-2002) 　- Civic Activism: trustee and board chair, The Turtle Bay Music School, NYC; corresponding secretary, East Hampton Garden Club; co-chair, resource committee, Harvard University Medical School, Cambridge, MA
Address:	Hither Lane, East Hampton
Name of estate:	
Year of construction:	
Style of architecture:	
Architect(s):	
Landscape architect(s):	
House extant: unconfirmed	
Historical notes:	

　George Gholson Walker, Sr. was the son of Norman Stuart and Minnie Affie Wiman Walker of Staten Island, NY.
　Elizabeth Schroeder Walker was the daughter of James Langdon Schroeder of Bernardsville, NJ.
　George Gholson and Elizabeth Schroeder Walker, Sr.'s daughter Diana married Stephen Benedict Carbone, the son of Frank B. Carbone of New York and, later, ____ Novelli and resided in New York. Their son George Gholson Walker, Jr. married Teresa E. Blatz, the daughter of Philip Blatz, and resided in Plymouth, ME.
　The Blue Book of The Hamptons, 1965 and *1973* list George G. and Caroline Shields Walker [Sr.] as residing on Hither Lane, East Hampton.
　Caroline Shields Walker was the daughter of Edwin W. Shields of Kansas City. She had previously been married to Philip Dickson.
　Emily Schniewind Walker was the daughter of Henry Ernest and Helen Greeff Schniewind, Jr. of *Wyndhem* and *Little Acorn* in Glen. Cove. [*See* Spinzia, *Long Island's Prominent North Shore Families, vol. II* – Schniewind entries.] Emily had previously been married to James Jackson Lee, Sr., the son of George Cabot and Madeline Jackson Lee.

Walker, Dr. John Baldwin, Sr. (1860-1942)

Occupation(s):	physician - surgeon -	assistant surgeon, General Memorial Hospital, NYC;
		visiting surgeon, Bellevue Hospital, NYC;
		visiting surgeon, Hospital for the Ruptured and Crippled, NYC;
		consulting surgeon, Manhattan State Hospital, NYC;
		inspector, New York Board of Health
	educator -	instructor of surgery, New York Polyclinic, NYC;
		professor of clinical surgery, College of Physicians and Surgeons Columbia University, NYC
	writer -	numerous articles in medical journals
Civic Activism:	president, Harvard Medical Society of New York;	
	trustee, Bard College, Annandale-on-Hudson, NY;	
	trustee, City Mission;	
	trustee, Home for Old Men and Aged Couples	
Marriage(s):	1910-1942 – Mai Elmendorf Hackstaff (1883-1967)	
Address:	Lee Avenue, East Hampton	
Name of estate:	*Tarriawyle*	
Year of construction:	1899	
Style of architecture:	Shingle	
Architect(s):	Joseph Greenleaf Thorp designed the house (for Hackstaff)	
Landscape architect(s):		
Builder	Loper Brothers	
	George A. Eldredge, 1902 alterations*	
House extant: unconfirmed		
Historical notes:		

The 7,500-square-foot, eight-bedroom, seven-and-a-half-bath house, originally called *Tarriawyle*, was built by Charles Ludovic Hackstaff.

The *Social Register Summer, 1915* lists Dr. John B. and Mai E. Hackstaff Walker [Sr.] as residing at *Tarriawyle* in East Hampton.

He was the son of The Reverend Avery Skinner and Mrs. Rosanna Baldwin Walker.

Mai Elmendorf Hackstaff Walker was the daughter of Charles Ludovic and Margaret Euphemia Hoffman Hackstaff of *Tarriawyle* in East Hampton.

Dr. John Baldwin and Mrs. Mai Elmendorf Hackstaff Walker, Sr.'s daughter Margaret married Richard C. Raymond, the son of William Raymond of Wayland, MA. Their son John Baldwin Walker, Jr. married Adele Van Anden Frank, the daughter of George S. Frank of New Canaan, CT. Their son Eugene married Mary Morris, the daughter of Robert Tuttle Morris of *Merribrooke Farm* in Stamford, CT. Their daughter Rosanne married George Roseborough Collins, the son of Harold Fisher Collins of Newton Highlands, MA.

*The 1902 alteration on the south facade was built by Eldredge. In 1969 the porch was enclosed.

The house was later owned by Stephen Kniznick Robert. In 2012 the house and 1.9 acres were for sale by Robert. The asking price was $18.5 million. It was sold for $14.9 million in 2014.

Walker, Dr. William Henry, Jr. (1879-1946)

Occupation(s):	physician - medical examiner, NYC Board of Education; medical examiner, NYS Athletic Commission
Marriage(s):	1903-1946 – May Behr
Address:	Flamingo Road, Montauk
Name of estate:	
Year of construction:	mid to late 1920s
Style of architecture:	Spanish Colonial Revival
Architect(s):	Andrew Jackson Thomas designed his own residence and boathouse
Landscape architect(s):	
House extant: unconfirmed	
Historical notes:	

The house was built by Andrew Jackson Thomas who also maintained a private zoo on the estate's property [*The East Hampton Star* September 20, 1945, p. 2.]. In 1931 the house was purchased by Walker. [*The East Hampton Star* August 28, 1931, p. 1.]

He was the son of William Henry and Ellen Ida Roon Walker, Sr. of Manhattan. His brother James John "Jimmy" Walker was the flamboyant and controversial mayor New York City. Like his brother James, William's career was beset by scandal.

In 1936 the house was purchased by Elbert McGran Jackson who made extensive alterations. [*The East Hampton Star* October 8, 1936, p. 3, and November 26, 1936, p. 3.]

Warbuton, Consuelo Vanderbilt (1903-2011)

Marriage(s):	M/1 – 1926-div. 1935 – Earl Edward Tailer Smith, Sr. (1903-1991)

- financier - a founder and partner, Paige, Smith, and Remick (investment firm);
  director, Bank of Palm Beach & Trust Co., Palm Beach, FL
- industrialist - director, United States Sugar Corp;
  director, Lionel Corp.;
  director, C. F. and I. Steel Corp.
- capitalist - director, New York Central Railroad
- diplomat - United States Ambassador to Cuba, 1957-1959
- politician - mayor, City of Miami, FL, 1971-1977;
  mayor, Palm Beach, FL
- writer - *The Fourth Floor*
- Civic Activism: member, War Production Board during World War II;
  chairman of board, Preservation Foundation, Palm Beach, FL;
  member, presidential commission on broadcasting to Cuba (Reagan administration)

M/2 – 1936-div. 1940 – Henry Gassaway Davis III (1902-1984)
- financier - member, J. P. Morgan (investment banking firm);
  member, Hayden Stone;
  member, A. Islin;
  member, Robert Winthrop & Co.

M/3 – 1941-div. 1946 – William John Warburton III (1895-1979)

M/4 – 1951-1969 – Noble Clarkson Earl, Jr. (1900-1969)
- restaurateur - president, Childs Co. (restaurant chain);
  president, D. A. Schule (restaurant chain);
  president, Howard Johnson (restaurant chain)
- financier - director, Trade Bank & Trust Co., NY
- industrialist - president, Louis Sherry (ice cream and candy firm);
  chairman of board, Doman Helicopters, Inc., Danbury, CT
- merchant - president, General Stores Corp.

Address: Lily Pond Lane, East Hampton
Name of estate:
Year of construction: 1920
Style of architecture: Contemporary
Architect(s): John Custis Lawrence designed the house (for M. L. Mayo)

Landscape architect(s):
Builder: Edward M. Gay
House extant: yes

Warburton, Consuelo Vanderbilt (cont'd)

Historical notes:

The house, originally named *Bonnie Dune*, was built by Miss Marie Louise Mayo.

In c. 1926 the house was purchased by John Neville Wheeler. [*The East Hampton Star* February 28, 1930, p. 7.] In 1942 it was purchased by Mrs. Warburton. [*The East Hampton Star* October 22, 1942, p. 2.]

She was the daughter of William Kissam and Virginia Graham Fair Vanderbilt, Jr. of *Deepdale* in Lake Success. Consuelo was named for her aunt Consuelo Vanderbilt (Spencer–Churchill, Duchess of Marlborough) Balsan, the daughter of William Kissam and Alva Erskine Smith Vanderbilt of *Idlehour* in Oakdale. [*See* Spinzia, *Long Island's Prominent North Shore Families, vol. I – Balsan entry; Long Island's Prominent North Shore Families, vol. II –* Vanderbilt entries; *Long Island's Prominent South Shore Families –* Vanderbilt entry; and *Long Island's Prominent Families in the Town of Southampton –* Balsan entry.]

Earl Edward Tailer Smith, Sr. was the son of Sidney Johnston and Fannie Bogert Tailer Carpenter Smith.

[For Earl and Consuelo's Sands Point residence *Iradell*, see Spinzia, *Long Island's Prominent North Shore Families, vol. II –* Smith entry.]

Earl Edward Tailer and Consuelo Vanderbilt Smith, Sr.'s daughter Virginia married William Landon Hutton, the son of John Laurence and Katherine Lyon Hutton, Sr. of *Peep O'Day*. She later married Edwin Marston Burke, Sr., the son of Oscar Moech and Edna Marston Burke of East Hampton, and resided in Far Hills, NJ.

Henry Gassaway Davis III was the son of John Thomas and Elizabeth Irwin Armstead Davis.

William John Warburton III was the son of William John and Josephine W. Bochman Warburton, Jr.

Ward, Newell Jube (1882- 1929)

Occupation(s):	advertising executive - vice-president, Allen Advertising Co.; secretary, Frank Seaman Co., NYC (advertising firm)
Marriage(s):	1904-1929 – Ethel L. Concerman (1879-1952) - Civic Activism: a founder, East Hampton Riding Club, East Hampton, NY
Address:	Lily Pond Lane, East Hampton
Name of estate:	
Year of construction:	1919
Style of architecture:	
Architect(s):	
Landscape architect(s):	
House extant: unconfirmed	
Historical notes:	

The house was built by Newell Jube Ward, Sr. [*The East Hampton Star* June 27, 1919, p. 5, and April 5, 1929, p. 5.]

The *Social Directory of Southampton, Long Island, 1931* lists Mrs. Newell J. Ward [Sr.] as residing on Lily Pond Lane, East Hampton.

He was the son of Edgar Bethune and Harriet Newell Ward of East Orange, NJ.

Ethel L. Concerman Ward was the daughter of Theodore H. Concerman of Philadelphia, PA.

Newell Jube and Ethel L. Concerman Ward, Sr.'s daughter Harriet was an infant at the time of her death in 1915. Their daughter Rosemary married George W. Blabon II, the son of Edwin L. Blabon of Bryn Mawr, PA, and, later, Mark Tyson with whom she resided in East Hampton. Their son Newell Jube Ward, Jr. married Bettina Belmont, the daughter of Raymond Rogers Belmont II and the granddaughter of August and Elizabeth Hamilton Morgan Belmont II of *Blemton Manor* in Hempstead, and resided at *Valley View Farm* in Middleburg, VA. [*See* Spinzia, *Long Island's Prominent Families in the Town of Hempstead –* Belmont entry.]

Ward, William L. (d. 1938)

Occupation(s):	merchant - partner, N. H. White & Co. (jewelry firm)
Civic Activism:	president, Marcus L. Ward Homestead for Respectable Bachelors and Widowers
Marriage(s):	
Address:	88 Indian Wells Highway, Amagansett
Name of estate:	*Willward Lodge*
Year of construction:	1909
Style of architecture:	Mediterranean
Architect(s):	
Landscape architect(s):	
Builder:	Frank M. Griffing
House extant: yes	
Historical notes:	

The seven-bedroom, nine-and-a-half-bath, 6,5000-square-foot house, originally named *Willward Lodge*, was built by William L. Ward.

He was the son of Aaron Ward of Newark, NJ.

William's daughters Constance and Janet, who remained unmarried, resided in East Orange, NJ.

The estate was later owned by John Day Jackson.

In 2013 the house and 2.54 acres sold for $7.5 million.

Wardle, H. Allen (1892-1973)

Occupation(s):	financier - member, Hubbard Brothers and Co. (stock brokerage firm); governor, New York Stock Exchange
	writer - *Union Club of the City of New York*, 1947
Civic Activism:	director, Maidstone Club, East Hampton
Marriage(s):	Estelle Ewing (1894-1989)
Address:	24 Jefferys Lane, East Hampton
Name of estate:	
Year of construction:	
Style of architecture:	Colonial Revival
Architect(s):	
Landscape architect(s):	
House extant: yes	
Historical notes:	

In c. 1923 Mary Talmage purchased the Dayton ancestral house and moved it to Jefferys Lane. In 1930 the house was purchased by Wardle.

The Blue Book of The Hamptons, 1965 lists H. Allen and Estelle Ewing Wardle as residing on Jefferys Lane, East Hampton.

Estelle Ewing Wardle was the daughter of Caruthers Ewing, Sr., of Memphis, TN. She had previously been married to Eugene Frederick Rowe of Cincinnati, OH, who died in 1918 of the Spanish Flu. He was the son of Casper H. Rowe

The house is listed on the National Register of Historic Places.

Warhol, Andy (1928-1987)
aka Andrew Warhola, Jr.

Occupation(s):	artist
	capitalist - produced over 60 *avant-garde* motion pictures
	publisher - a founder, *Interview*
	writer - *25 Cats Named Sam and One Blue Pussy*, 1954;
	A Novel, 1968;
	The Philosophy of Andy Warhol, 1975;
	Popism, 1980;
	Andy Warhol Diaries, 1989;
	Cats, Cats, Cats;
	Holy Cats;
	Wild Raspberries;
	A Gold Book
Civic Activism:	a founder, New York Academy of Art, 1979;
	established Andy Warhol Foundation for the Visual Arts*
Marriage(s):	bachelor
Address:	16 Cliff Drive, Montauk
Name of estate:	*Eothen*
Year of construction:	1931
Style of architecture:	Colonial Revival
Architect(s):	Rolf W. Bauhan designed the compound (for R. E. Church)
	Thierry W. Despont designed the 2007 alterations (for Drexler)
Landscape architect(s):	Miranda Brooks (for Lindemann)
House extant: yes	
Historical notes:	

    The compound, which consists of a seven-bedroom main residence, four guest houses, a three-car garage, and a stable, was built by Richard E. Church. In 1971 Warhol and Paul Morrissey purchased the twenty-acre estate for $225,000 from the Church family and called it *Eothen*.
    Warhol was the son of Andrew and Julia Zavacka Warhola, Sr. of Mikova, Slovakia, and, later, Pittsburgh, PA.
    He coined the expression, "fifteen minutes of fame."
   *The Andy Warhol Foundation for Visual Arts donated 14.3 acres of the compound to the Nature Conservancy.
    In 2007 Morrissey sold the estate to Millard S. Drexler for $27 million.
    In 2015 Drexler sold the main residence, guest house, garage, and 5.6 acres to Adam Marc Lindemann for $50 million. The equestrian portion of the property remained on the market.

Warner, Eltinge Fowler, Jr. (1885-1964)

Occupation(s):	publisher - *Arts & Decorations*, 1925-1934; Field & Stream Publishing Co., 1906-1937; Congratulations, Inc. 1937- ; a founder, Warner Publications, Inc., NYC; treasurer, Pro Distributors Publication, Inc.; Smart Set, 1914-1926; *Fishing and Vacation Year Book*, 1942
	capitalist - a founder, Town and Country Films, 1916-1918; a founder, Zane Grey Picture Group, 1918
Civic Activism:	director, Maidstone Club, East Hampton
Marriage(s):	1908-1956 – Ruth Lois Eaton (1884-1956)
Address:	Lily Pond Lane, East Hampton
Name of estate:	*Cima del Mundo*
Year of construction:	1926
Style of architecture:	Spanish Farmhouse
Architect(s):	Robert Tappan designed the house (for E. F. Warner, Jr.)

Landscape architect(s):
House extant: yes
Nassau County Museum Collection has photographs of the estate.
Historical notes:

    The house, originally named *Cima Del Mundo*, was built by Eltinge Fowler Warner, Jr.
    The *Social Register Summer, 1932* lists Eltinge F. and Ruth L. Easton Warner [Jr.] as residing at *Cima del Mundo* on Lily Pond Lane, East Hampton. They previously resided at *Dunecrest* in East Hampton.
    He was the son of Eltinge Fowler and Helen Josephine Thompson Warner, Sr. of St. Paul, MN.
    Ruth Lois Eaton Warner was the daughter of Bradley Eaton of Maine.
    Eltinge Fowler and Ruth Lois Eaton Warner, Jr.'s daughter Lois married Maynard Emerson Womar.
    In 1944 the house was sold to John Merrill Olin. [*The East Hampton Star* November 23, 1944, p. 1.]
    It is listed on the National Register of Historic Places.

Warrin, Dr. Marshall Lord (1858-1942)

Occupation(s):	physician
Marriage(s):	M/1 – Martha Jeanne de Raismes (1859-1929)
	M/2 – 1930-1942 – Alma Elizabeth Anable (1860-1956)
Address:	Indian Well Hollow Highway, Amagansett
Name of estate:	*Kemah*

Year of construction:
Style of architecture:
Architect(s):
Landscape architect(s):
House extant: unconfirmed
Historical notes:

    The Blue Book and Long Island Society Register, 1921 lists Dr. Marshall Lard [sic] and Mrs. Martha de Raismes Warrin as residing in Amagansett. The *Social Register Summer, 1919* lists the name of their estate as *Kemah*.
    He was the son of Thomas and Elizabeth W. Lord Warrin. Marshall's sister Mary married Charles Coleman Nadel and resided in East Hampton.
    Martha Jeanne de Raismes Warrin was the daughter of Jean Francois Joseph and Martha Ella Holt de Raismes. Martha's sister Emma, who married Edward Albert Storey, resided at *Homelot* in Amagansett.
    Dr. Marshall Lord and Mrs. Martha Jeanne de Raismes Warrin's daughter Martha married Hugh McCullogh Branham, the son of Dr. J. H. Branham, and resided at *Chestertown Farm* in Chestertown, MD. Their daughter Dorothy married Leonard Hatch and resided in Old Greenwich, CT. Their daughter Jocelyn married Beekman Finlay Ilsiey and resided in Schenectady, NY, and Fort Wayne, IN.
    Alma Elizabeth Anable Warrin was the daughter of Henry Sheldon and Rosanna Frick Anable.

Wasey, Louis Rice (1885-1961)

Occupation(s):	advertising executive - director and chairman of board, Erwin Wasey and Co.
	industrialist - founder, Barbasol Co.; director and vice-president, Musterole Co. (mustard ointment manufacturing firm)
	capitalist - owner, Cat Cay, Bahamas (resort)
Civic Activism:	trustee, Hobart College, Geneva, NY
Marriage(s):	1911-1961 – Rae Gager (1885-1969)
Address:	211 East Lake Drive, Montauk
Name of estate:	
Year of construction:	1929
Style of architecture:	Modified French Chateau
Architect(s):	K. B. C. Smith designed the house (for Wasey)
Landscape architect(s):	
House extant: yes	
Historical notes:	

The fourteen-room house was built by Carl Graham Fisher, Sr. It was later owned by Wasey.

The *Social Directory of Southampton, 1931* lists Mr. and Mrs. Louis R. Wasey as residing on East Lake Drive, Montauk.

She was the daughter of J. Pratt Gager of Cleveland, OH. Rae had previously been married to ____ Alexander.

Louis Rice and Rae Gager Wasey's daughter Jane married Domenico Mortellito, the son of John Mortellito of New York. Their son Gage married Elizabeth Adele Cook, the daughter of Arthur Lee Cook of Manhattan and, later, Sheila Stewart.

[See following entry for information about Wasey's East Hampton residences.]

In 1955 Marion Clay Harper, Jr. purchased the house from Wasey and converted the residence into a private club called the Captain's Marina. [*The New York Times* December 8, 1955, p. 65.] Beginning in the 1960s President Nixon was a frequent guest at the club. In 2003 the club was purchased by Double K. Management Company which refurbished the premises and operates it as the Montauk Lake Club & Marina.

Wasey, Louis Rice (1885-1961)

Occupation(s):	*[See previous entry.]*
Civic Activism:	*[See previous entry.]*
Marriage(s):	1911-1961 – Rae Gager (1885-1969)
Address:	Georgica Road, East Hampton
Name of estate:	*Vingt-et Un*
Year of construction:	
Style of architecture:	
Architect(s):	
Landscape architect(s):	
House extant: unconfirmed	
Historical notes:	

The Blue Book of The Hamptons, 1958 lists Louis R. and Rae Gager Wasey's as residing on Georgica Road, East Hampton. *The Blue Book of The Hamptons, 1965* lists the name of the residence as *Vingt-et Un*.

[See previous entry for family information.]

In 1959 the house was purchased by Harry W. Watts.

Wasey, Louis Rice (1885-1961)

Occupation(s):	*[See first Wasey entry.]*
Civic Activism:	*[See first Wasey entry.]*
Marriage(s):	1911-1961 – Rae Gager (1885-1969)
Address:	Lily Pond Lane, East Hampton
Name of estate:	
Year of construction:	1901
Style of architecture:	Shingle
Architect(s):	James Brown Lord designed the house (for Drew)
Landscape architect(s):	
Builder:	George A. Eldredge
House extant: no	
Historical notes:	

The house, originally named *Kyalami*, was built by John Drew, Jr. It was later owned by his daughter Louise Devereaux, who sold the house to Auguste Cordier in 1919. The Cordiers continued to call it *Kyalami*. [*The East Hampton Star* October 11, 1929, p. 1.] In c. 1944 the house was purchased by Wasey. [*The East Hampton Star* November 23, 1944, p. 1.]

Washburn, George (1914-2005)

Occupation(s):	financier*- manager, mutual fund department, Kidder Peabody, 1949-1953 (stock brokerage firm); partner, Paine, Webber, Jackson, and Curtis, 1963-1971 (stock brokerage firm); member, Loeb, Rhodes, and Co. (stock brokerage firm); member, Donaldson, Lufkin, and Jenrette (stock brokerage firm)
Civic Activism:	president, National Mutual Fund Managers, 1967
Marriage(s):	1947-2005 – Anne Gibson Clark (1919-2018) - entertainers and associated professions - actress
Address:	117A Main Street, East Hampton
Name of estate:	*Tree House*
Year of construction:	Colonial Revival
Style of architecture:	
Architect(s):	
Landscape architect(s):	
House extant: yes	
Historical notes:	

The Blue Book of The Hamptons, 1973 and *1987* list George and Anne Gibson Clark Washburn as residing at *Tree House*, 117A Main Street, East Hampton.
He was the son of Edgar Washburn of Forest Hills, NY.
Anne Clark Gibson Washburn was the daughter of Rensselaer Weston Clark of Brooklyn Heights.
George and Anne Gibson Clark Washburn's daughter Constance married ____Castle and resided in Lagunitos, CA. Their daughter Lynn married George Frederick Robert Hanke, Sr., the son of Ralph and Jean Flager Hanke, and resided in East Hampton.
[See other Washburn entries for additional family information.]
*Washburn pioneered the concept of mutual funds and managed the first mutual fund department on Wall Street. [*Palm Beach Daily News* January 9, 2005, p. 2.]

Washburn, Ira Hedges, Sr. (1893-1979)

Occupation(s): industrialist - executive, Devoe and Raynolds (paint manufacturing firm) (later, a division of Celanese Saugerties)

Marriage(s): 1923-1966 – Ida E. Wuertz (d. 1966)

Address: Further Lane, East Hampton
Name of estate:
Year of construction:
Style of architecture:
Architect(s):
Landscape architect(s):
House extant: unconfirmed
Historical notes:

The Blue Book of The Hamptons, 1965 lists Mr. and Mrs. Ira H. Washburn [Sr.] as residing on Further Lane, East Hampton.

He was the son of Mordecai Fowler and Margaret Knapp Hedges Washburn.

Ida E. Wuertz Washburn was the daughter of O. William Wuertz of NYC.

Ira Hedges and Ida E. Wuertz Washburn, Sr.'s daughter Jean married Richard Seymour Jackson, the son of John Day and Rose Marie Herrick Jackson of Amagansett, and resided in Amagansett. Jean later married Lawrence Irving Clarke, the son of James Clarke, and resided in East Hampton. Their son Ira Hedges Washburn, Jr. married Calista Sayre, the daughter of Caryl Henry and Marion Mershon Sayre.

[See other Washburn entries for additional family information.]

Washburn, Mary Rosenia Doughty (d. 1926)

Marriage(s): 1881-1916 – William Tucker Washburn (1841-1916)
- attorney - partner, Washburn and Oritz–Canavate, NYC
writer - *Harvard: The Story of American College Life*, 1869;
Poems (2 vols.), 1878;
The Dicer and Other Poems, 1879;
The Unknown City: A Story of New York, 1880;
Spring and Summer, or Blushing Hours, 1890 (poetry);
The Muses: Terpsichore, c. 1890-1900;
The Deuce of Hearts, 1901;
The First Stone and Other Stories, 1904

Address: Apaquogue Road, East Hampton
Name of estate:
Year of construction:
Style of architecture:
Architect(s):
Landscape architect(s):
Builder:
House extant: unconfirmed
Historical notes:

The *Social Register Summer, 1921* lists Mary R. Doughty Washburn as residing in East Hampton.

William Tucker Washburn was the son of William Rounseville and Susan Ellen Tucker Washburn.

In 1871 he had married Katherine Sedgwick (1831-1884), the daughter of Robert and Elizabeth Ellery Sedgwick. Katherine had previously been married to Joseph Valerio of Genoa, Italy.

William Tucker and Katherine Sedgwick Washburn's daughter Nathalie, a noted author, was raised by Katherine's sister Henrietta and brother-in-law Henry Dwight Sedgwick II and assumed the surname of Sedgwick. Nathalie married President Woodrow Wilson's Secretary of State Bainbridge Colby.

William Tucker and Mary Rosenia Doughty Washburn's son William married Elizabeth Clarkson, the daughter of Robert R. L. Clarkson of Tivoli-on-Hudson, NY. Their son Frank married Elizabeth's sister Pauline, also the daughter of Robert R. L. Clarkson, and resided at *Nearthebay* in Bellport. Their daughter Marion married Julian Southall Myrick, the son of Charles English and Susan Blanche Colton Myrick, and resided at *Apaquogue*. Their son Watson also resided at *Apaquogue*. Their daughter Emma (aka Lucy) married Sidney Beardsley Wood, Sr. Their grandson Sidney Beardsley Wood, Jr. married Edith Godfrey Betts, the daughter of Wyllys Rosseter and Ada Godfrey Betts of Southampton, and resided at *Mocomanto* in Southampton. [*See* Spinzia, *Long Island's Prominent Families in the Town of Southampton* – Betts and Wood entries.]

Washburn, Watson (1894-1973)

Occupation(s):	attorney - partner, Washburn and Gray; partner, Perkins, Malone, and Washburn; Assistant Attorney General, New York State
	statesman - special assistant to the United States Under Secretary of the Treasury, 1921 (Harding administration); acting secretary to New York State Governor Thomas E. Dewey
	journalist - editor and chief, Columbia Law Review, 1916
	industrialist - director, William Whitman Co., Inc. (textile manufacturing firm); director, DeBothezat Impeller Co., Inc. (industrial fan manufacturing firm); director, Helicopter Corp. (helicopter manufacturing firm)
	capitalist - director, J. W. Woods Co., Inc.; director, World Art, Inc.
	writer - co-author, *High and Low Financiers*, 1932
Civic Activism:	a founder, National Law Tennis Hall of Fame, Newport, RI; secretary, Greater New York Hoover Committee; chairman, 17th Congressional District Hoover Committee; chairman, rule and constitution committee, United States Lawn Tennis Association, 1920-1930; director, Osborne Association; director, Citizens for Freedom, Inc.: trustee, Ballot Foundation; president, Reading Reform Foundation
Marriage(s):	bachelor
Address:	Apaquogue Road, East Hampton
Name of estate:	*Apaquogue / Apaquogue House*
Year of construction:	
Style of architecture:	
Architect(s):	
Landscape architect(s):	
House extant:	unconfirmed
Historical notes:	

The *Long Island Society Register, 1929* lists Watson Washburn as residing at *Apaquogue* in East Hampton.

The son of William Tucker and Mary Rosenia Doughty Washburn. His sister Marion, who subsequently owned the house, resided at *Apaquogue / Apaquogue House*, with her husband Julian Southall Myrick.

Watson was ranked among the ten best tennis players in the country. He was a member of the Davis Cup and Olympic teams, won the United States doubles championship, won three veterans' doubles titles, one veterans' singles crown, one indoor doubles championship, and was runner-up in the Wimbledon and United States doubles championships. In 1965 he was elected to the National Lawn Tennis Hall of Fame.

[See other Washburn entries for additional family information.]

Wasserstein, Bruce Jay (1947-2009)

Occupation(s):	financier -	managing director, First Boston Corp., 1977-1988 (investment banking firm);
		president, Wasserstein and Perella Co., 1988-2000;
		executive chairman, Dresdner Kleinworth, Wasserstein, 2000-2001 (investment banking firm);
		CEO, Lazard, LLC (investment banking firm);
		founder, Wasserstein and Co. (private equity firm)
	attorney -	member, Cravath, Swaine, and Moore, NYC
	publisher -	owner, "American Lawyer Media";
		owner, "The Daily Deal";
		owner, "New York"
	writer -	co-authored, with Mark Green, *With Justice for Some*, 1970;
		Corporate Finance Law, 1978;
		Big Deal: The Battle for the Control of America's Leading Corporations, 1988;
		Big Deal: Mergers and Acquisitions in the Digital Age, 1998

Civic Activism: trustee, Dalton School, NYC;
donated $25 million to Harvard Law School, Cambridge, MA

Marriage(s):
M/1 – 1968-div. 1974 – Laura Lynelle Killin
M/2 – div. 1992 – Christine Parrott
 - psychoanalyst
M/3 – 1996-div. 2008 – Claude Becker
 - entertainers and associated professions - CBS news producer
 merchant - owner, Susie's Supper Club (frozen health meals)
 Civic Activism: member of board, WNET, PBS;
 director, Child Mind Institute;
 director, Yale Center for Dyslexia and Creativity
M/4 – 2009-2009 – Angela Chao

Address: 350 Further Lane, East Hampton
Name of estate: *Cranberry Dune*
Year of construction:
Style of architecture: Modified Shingle
Architect(s):
Landscape architect(s):
House extant: yes
Historical notes:

Bruce Jay Wasserstein was the son of Morris and Lola Wasserstein of Brooklyn, NY.
Laura Lynelle Killin Wasserstein is the daughter of Richard Clark and Clara Davis Killin of Larchmont, NY.
Christine Parrott is the daughter of Victor E. and Sarah M. Parrott of New Castle, PA. Christine subsequently married Daniel Steven Rattiner, the son of A. Alan and Jeannette B. Rattiner of Montauk.
Angela Chao Wasserstein is the daughter of Dr. James S. C. and Mrs. Ruth Mu Lan Chu Chao of Syosset. Angela's sister Elaine is married to Senator Mich McConnell of Kentucky. Elaine served as United States Secretary of Labor in the George W. Bush administration and Secretary of Transportation in the Trump administration.

Watts, Harry Wilfred (1899-1970)

Occupation(s):

Marriage(s):   M/1 – Alma Elizabeth Hulsapple (1899-1978)
                                   M/2 – Beatrice Ann Strite (1906-1991)

Address: 181 Main Street, East Hampton
Name of estate:
Year of construction:
Style of architecture: Elizabethan
Architect(s):   Joseph Greenleaf Thorp, 1910
                                   alterations (for Poor)
                              Eric Woodward, 1996
                                   alterations (for Reiswig)
Landscape architect(s):
House extant: yes
Historical notes:

    In 1899 Poor purchased the former Daniel Howe/Thomas Baker residence. [*The East Hampton Star* June 2, 2005, p. 44.] In 1943 the house was purchased by Robert Graham Dunn Douglas. [*The East Hampton Star* July 1, 1943, p. 1.]
    In 1959 Watts purchased the house from Douglas. [*The East Hampton Star* April 16, 1959, p. 1.]
    He was the son of Wilfred and Sophia Tierney Watts.
    Alma Elizabeth Hulsapple Watts was the daughter of Harry Montgomery and Louisa Burkin Hulsapple of Larchmont, NY.
    Harry Wilfred and Alma Elizabeth Hulsapple Watts' daughter Cynthia married Alton Gould Wentworth, Jr. of Seymour, CT.
    Beatrice Ann Strite Watt's father Charles Perkins Strite was the inventor of the electric pop-up toaster. She had previously been married to Dr. Eugene Rhea Chapman who, after his divorce from Beatrice, married the noted opera singer Dorothy Kirsten.
    In 1973 Beatrice donated the house to the Southampton Hospital. [*The East Hampton Star* May 25, 1973, p. 20.]
    In 1996 the house was purchased by Gary D. and Rita Reiswig who remodeled it into The Baker House 1650, a bed and breakfast inn. In 2004 the Reiswigs listed it for sale. The asking price was $3.95 million.
    It was purchased by Robert and Antonella Rosen.

Watts, Harry Wilfred (1899-1970)

Occupation(s):

Marriage(s):   M/1 – Alma Elizabeth Hulsapple (1899-1978)
                                       M/2 – Beatrice Ann Strite (1906-1991)

Address: 15 Jefferys Lane, East Hampton
Name of estate:
Year of construction: 1920
Style of architecture: Tuscan
Architect(s):
Landscape architect(s):
House extant: yes
Historical notes:

    In 1954 Watts purchased the house. [*The East Hampton Star* January 13, 1955, p. 5.]
    [See previous entry for family information.]
    In 1957 Watts sold the house to George Albert Highet. [*The East Hampton Star* March 28, 1957, p. 5.]
    In 2015 the 5,000-square-foot, five-bedroom, and five-and-a-half-bath house and 0.9 acres sold for $6.5 million.

Weaver, Spencer Fullerton, Sr. (1879-1939)

Occupation(s):	architect -	partner, Schultze & Weaver;
		designer, the new Waldorf–Astoria Hotel, NYC;
		designer, Park Lane Apartments Hotel, NYC;
		designer, the Sherry–Netherland, NYC;
		designer, Pierre Hotel, NYC;
		designer, Lexington Hotel, NYC;
		designer, Breakers Hotel, Palm Beach, FL;
		designer, Nautilus Hotel, Miami, FL;
		designer, Miami News Building, Miami, FL;
		designer, Roney Plaza Hotel, Miami Beach, FL
	capitalist -	a founder and president, Fullerton Weaver Realty Co., NY (construction firm that built Park Lane Apartments Hotel, NYC);
		owner, Park Lane Apartments Hotel, NYC;
		also owned two other apartment complexes on Park Avenue, NYC
Civic Activism:		governor, New York Real Estate Board;
		president, West Side Tennis Club, NYC
Marriage(s):		M/1 – 1903-div. 1920 – Emily Maloney Stokes (1878-1930)
		M/2 – 1929-1939 – Lillian Leacock Howell (1896-1959)
Address:		Georgica Road, East Hampton
Name of estate:		*Spencecliff*
Year of construction:		1895
Style of architecture:		Neo-Tudor
Architect(s):		Joseph Greenleaf Thorp designed the house (for Spring)
		Howard Geenley, 1915 alterations (for Roberts)
		Spencer Fullerton Weaver, Sr., 1925 alterations (for himself)
Landscape architect(s):		Jacob John Spoon designed swimming pool (for Weaver)
Builder:		Philip Ritch

House extant: no*
Nassau County Museum Collection has photographs of the estate.
Historical notes:

The house, originally named *Winklehawk*, was built by Preston Brady Spring, Sr. In 1915 it was purchased by Walter Scott Roberts. [*The East Hampton Star* August 6, 1915, p. 5; December 13, 1918, p. 5; and June 8, 1944, p. 3.] In 1925 the house was purchased by Weaver who renamed it *Spencecliff*.

He was the son of James Buchanan and Mary Hall Fullerton Weaver of Philadelphia, PA, and the great-great-grandnephew of President James Buchanan.

Emily Maloney Stokes Weaver was the daughter of James Christy and Sara Jane Stokes of Philadelphia, PA.

Spencer Fullerton and Emily Maloney Stokes Weaver, Sr.'s son Clifton's wife Katherine Warburton Sutton, aka Kay Sutton, had previously been married to Daniel Reid Topping. Sr. of East Hampton and *Fairlea* in Southampton. [*See* Spinzia, *Long Island's Prominent Families in the Town of Southampton* – Topping entry.] Their son Spencer Fullerton Weaver, Jr. married June Gibbs Mathieson and resided in Honolulu, HI.

The *Social Register Summer, 1945* lists Lillian L. Howell Weaver as residing at *Spencecliff* in East Hampton.

She was the daughter of William Frances Howell of New Orleans, LA.

In 1949 the house was purchased by William Seligson who subdivided the estate's property into six building lots. [*The East Hampton Star* January, 13, 1955, p. 5, and June 16, 1955, p. 12.]

It was subsequently owned by Adolph Green.

*In 1969 the house was destroyed by fire during a wedding at Green's estate when a caterer's gas line leaked and ignited.

Weber, Bruce (b. 1946)

Occupation(s):	professional photographer
	entertainers and associated professions -
	producer and director of motion pictures, shorts, and music videos
	fashion designer - Weberbilt (clothing line)
	publisher - co-owner, with his wife Nan, Little Bear Press
Civic Activism:	co-founder, Bruce Weber Nan Bush Foundation
Marriage(s):	Nan Bush
	- entertainers and associated professions -
	producer and agent for Bruce
	publisher - co-owner, with her husband Bruce, Little Bear Press
	Civic Activism: co-founder, Bruce Weber Nan Bush Foundation; Association House
Address:	*[unable to determine street address]*, Montauk
Name of estate:	
Year of construction:	1883
Style of architecture:	
Architect(s):	McKim, Mead, and White designed the house
Landscape architect(s):	Frederick Law Olmstead designed the site plan
House extant: yes	
Historical notes:	

The house is one of the Montauk Association's "Seven Sisters." It was later owned by Weber.

Webster, Dr. Bruce Peck (1901-1976)

Occupation(s):	physician - surgeon, New York Hospital, NYC
	journalist - medical director, Times, Inc.
	educator - associate professor of clinical medicine, Tulane University, New Orleans, LA, 1931-1932;
	associate professor of clinical medicine, Cornell Medical School, 1932-1946
Civic Activism:	director, American Social Health Association;
	president, Society of Medical Consultants to Armed Forces;
	president, American Venereal Disease Association;
	president, International Union Against Venereal Disease;
	chairman, National Commission on Venereal Disease
Marriage(s):	bachelor
Address:	Briar Patch Road, East Hampton
Name of estate:	
Year of construction:	
Style of architecture:	
Architect(s):	
Landscape architect(s):	
House extant: unconfirmed	
Historical notes:	

The Blue Book of The Hamptons, 1965 and *1973* list Dr. Bruce Webster as residing on Briar Patch Road, East Hampton.
   He was the son of Thomas Amos and Bertha Peck Webster of Canada.

Weeks, John Kirkland, Sr. (1906-1986)

Occupation(s):	financier - partner, Luke, Banks, and Weeks (stock brokerage firm)
Civic Activism:	chairman, ranking committee, Metropolitan Squash and Racquets Association
Marriage(s):	M/1 – 1926 – Geraldine Sewall Boardman (1906-1979)
	M/2 – Phoebe Cabell Sterret (1902-1976)
	M/3 – Margaret Ellen Schofield (1921-2007)
Address:	85 Lee Avenue, East Hampton
Name of estate:	
Year of construction:	
Style of architecture:	
Architect(s):	
Landscape architect(s):	
House extant: yes	
Historical notes:	

John Kirkland Weeks, Sr. was the son of John Lafayette and Margaret Louise Clarbough Weeks of East Hampton. Geraldine Sewall Boardman Weeks was the daughter of Sidney Sewall Boardman of NYC.

John Kirkland and Geraldine Sewall Boardman Weeks, Sr.'s daughter Sewall married John Cullen Weadock, the son of Bernard Weadock of Greenwich, CT, and, later, Drennen Mann with whom she resided in Cockeysville, MD. Their son A. Kirkland Weeks resided in North Augusta, GA. Their son John Kirkland Weeks, Jr. married Mary MacKinnon, the daughter of William MacKinnon of Corby, England, and resided in Bethpage, NY.

Margaret Ellen Schofield Weeks was the daughter of Henry N. and Mary A. Schofield of Washington, DC. Margaret had previously been married to Charles J. Savarese.

[See following entry for additional family information.]

In c. 1952 the house was purchased by Morgan Hatton Grace, Jr. [*The East Hampton Star* January 3, 1952, p. 1.]

Weeks, John Lafayette (1882-1951)

Occupation(s):	financier - member, Talbot J. Taylor and Co. (stock brokerage firm); a founder and partner, Luke, Banks, and Weeks (stock brokerage firm)
Marriage(s):	1902-1948 – Margaret Louise Clarbough (1883-1948)
Address:	Lily Pond and Hedges Lanes, East Hampton
Name of estate:	
Year of construction:	1917
Style of architecture:	
Architect(s):	
Landscape architect(s):	
Builder:	
House extant: unconfirmed	
Historical notes:	

The house was built by John LaRue Helm, Jr. In 1923 Mrs. Helm sold it to James Andrew Moffett, Jr. who called it *Inadune*. [*The East Hampton Star* March 16, 1923, p. 5.] In 1937 Moffett sold the house to Weeks. [*The East Hampton Star* January 28, 1937, p. 1.]

Margaret Louise Clarbough Weeks was the daughter of A. T. Clarbough of Mount Washington, MO.

John Lafayette and Margaret Louise Clarbough Weeks' daughter Margaret married William Nottingham Beebe, Sr. and resided in East Hampton. Their daughter Frances married David Balderston Stone, the son of Robert E. Stone of Brookline, MA; Bruce Edgar Ryan of East Hampton; and, later, Benjamin Carlton Betner, Jr. with whom she resided in East Hampton. Their son John Kirkland Weeks, Sr., who resided in East Hampton, married Geraldine Sewall Boardman; Phoebe Cabell Sterret; and Margaret Ellen Schofield.

[See previous entry for additional family information.]

In 1951 the house was purchased by Roy Lennox Cammann. [*The East Hampton Star* May 3, 1951, p. 1.]

Weinstein, Harvey (b. 1952)

Occupation(s):	entertainers and associated professions -
	motion picture producer and director;
	a founder, with his brother Robert, Miramax;
	a founder, Harvey & Corky Productions (produced rock concerts);
	a founder, The Weinstein Company (motion picture producing firm)
Civic Activism:	trustee, Robin Hood foundation
Marriage(s):	M/1 – 1987-div. 2004 – Eve Chilton (b. 1955)
	- entertainers and associate professions -
	assistant to Harvey Weinstein at Miramax
	M/2 – 2007-div. 2018 - Georgina Rose Chapman (b. 1976)
	- fashion designer – co-founder Marchesa
	entertainers and associated professions - actress
Address:	50 Broadview Road, Amagansett
Name of estate:	
Year of construction:	1955
Style of architecture:	Modified Shingle
Architect(s):	
Landscape architect(s):	
House extant: yes	
Historical notes:	

   The seven-bedroom, eight-and-a-half-bath, 9,000-square-foot house was built by Barry Sonnenfeld. It was later owned by Roy Lance Furman who sold the house to Weinstein for $11.65 million in 2014.
   He is the son of Max and Miriam Postel Weinstein of NYC.
   Eve Chilton Weinstein is the daughter of Thomas and Maude Chilton of Massachusetts. Eve subsequently married Sal Martirano.
   Harvey and Eve Chilton Weinstein have three children.
   Georgina Rose Chapman Weinstein is the daughter of Brian and Caroline Wonfor Chapman of England.
   Harvey and Georgina Rose Chapman Weinstein have two children.
   In 2018, beset by accusations of sexual misconduct, Weinstein sold the house for $10 million.

Weinstein, Joseph (1900-1986)

Occupation(s):	capitalist - president, Versailles Management Co. (New York real estate developer)
Civic Activism:	trustee, Goddard College, Plainfield, VT; trustee, Guild Hall, East Hampton; member, Committee of Public Justice
Marriage(s):	Bobbi K. Kaufman (d. 1989)
Address:	89 Lily Pond Lane, East Hampton
Name of estate:	
Year of construction:	1912
Style of architecture:	Coxwold
Architect(s):	Albro and Lindberg designed the house (for Erdmann)
Landscape architect(s):	Edwina Von Gal designed the gardens (for Schulman)*
Builder:	Smith and Davis

House extant: yes
Historical notes:

The eight-bedroom, eight-bath, 9,000-square-foot house, originally named *Coxwould*, was built by Dr. John Frederic Erdmann. It was later owned by his daughter Jane Erdmann Burton who, in 1954, sold it to Dayton Hedges. [*The East Hampton Star* August 5, 1954, p. 1.]. In 1958 the house was purchased by Hedges' son Burke Osborn Hedges. [*The East Hampton Star* July 3, 1958, p. 4.] In 1960 it was purchased by Weinstein. [*The East Hampton Star* November 6, 1986, p. 2.]

He was the son of Jacob and Sarah Weinstein of NYC.

Joseph and Bobbi K. Kaufman Weinstein's daughter Lois married Richard M. Sontag, the son of John Sontag of New York, and resided in Stamford, CT. Their son James, a life-long socialist, married four times. He was the founder and editor of *In These Times* which was headquartered in Chicago, IL.

The house was, subsequently, owned by Lowell M. Schulman, who renamed it *Beechwood*.

In 2012 the house was for sale by Schulman. The asking price was $24.95 million; the annual taxes were $60,000.

*Edwina Von Gal created fifteen garden rooms which were inspired by English gardens.

Welch, Leo Dewey (1898-1978)

Occupation(s):	financier - vice-president, First City Bank of New York
	industrialist - director, treasurer, and vice-president, Standard Oil of New Jersey;
	director, Compania Ontario, South America;
	director, Scudder Duo Vest, Inc.
	capitalist - director and chairman of board, Communications Satellite Corp.
Civic Activism:	chairman, National Arbitration Panel;
	president, United States Chamber of Commerce in Argentina;
	vice-chairman, United States Council of International Chamber of Commerce;
	director, Maidstone Club, East Hampton
Marriage(s):	1926-1970 – Veronica Arvilla Purviance (1902-1970)
Address:	Lily Pond Lane, East Hampton
Name of estate:	
Year of construction:	
Style of architecture:	
Architect(s):	
Landscape architect(s):	
House extant: unconfirmed	
Historical notes:	

Welch was the son of William Frederick and Mary Elizabeth Compton Welch.

Veronica Arvilla Purviance Welch was the daughter of Charles M. and Katherine Sullivan Purviance.

Leo Dewey and Veronica Arvilla Purviance Welch's daughter Gloria married Dr. Robert Brown Case, the son of W. Lyman Chase of Columbus, OH, and, later, Emmett Whitlock.

By 1958 the Welchs had relocated to Apaquogue Road. *The Blue Book of The Hamptons, 1958* lists Mr. and Mrs. Leo D. Welch as residing on Apaquogue Road, East Hampton.

In 1950 the house was purchased by Charles E. Main who called it *Main House*. [*The East Hampton Star* October 5, 1950, p. 1.]

In 1974 Stanley Richard Jaffe purchased the house from Main. [The East Hampton Star May 14, 1974, p. 5.]

Wenner, Jann Simon (b. 1946)

Occupation(s):	publisher - co-founder, with Ralph J. Gleason, *Rolling Stone**;
	owner, *Men's Journal*;
	owner, *Us Weekly*;
	owner, *Outside*;
	owner, *Family Life*;
	owner, Straight Arrow Publications
	capitalist - founder, with his wife Jane, Wenner Media (holding company)
Marriage(s):	1967-div. 2011 – Jane Schindelheim (b. 1946)
	- capitalist - founder, with her husband Jann, Wenner Media (holding company);
	vice-president, Wenner Media (holding company)
Address:	372 Montauk Highway, Montauk
Name of estate:	
Year of construction:	
Style of architecture:	Modified Cape Cod
Architect(s):	
Landscape architect(s):	

House extant: yes
Historical notes:

In 2009 Jann Simon Wenner purchased the 6,300-square-foot, eight-bedroom house, with six and a half bathrooms, and one and a half acres for $11.9 million.

He is the son of Edward Wenner, who founded Baby Formula, Inc. which later became famous as Enfamil.

Jane Schindelheim Wenner's father was a Brooklyn dentist.

Jann Simon and Jane Schindelheim Wenner's son Alexander married Emily Eisen–Berkeley, the daughter of Joseph W. and Margaret M. Eisen Berkeley of Osterville, MA. Their son Theodore is a photographer for *Rolling Stone*. Their son Edward is the head of Wenner Media's digital operations.

*Wenner was inducted into the Rock and Roll Hall of Fame.

Wessel, Homer Augustus, Sr. (1856-1934)

Occupation(s):	capitalist - president, treasurer, and general manager, Cincinnati Railway Supply Co., Cincinnati, OH
Marriage(s):	1878-1934 – Louise Meyer
Address:	Middle Lane, East Hampton
Name of estate:	*Mill Crest*
Year of construction:	1903
Style of architecture:	Eclectic
Architect(s):	George A. Eldredge and John Custis Lawrence designed the house (for Wessel, Sr.)
Landscape architect(s):	Mary Lois Deputy Lamson, c. 1941 (for Ramee)

House extant: no; demolished except for windmill-style tower, 1980*
Historical notes:

The house, originally named *Mill Crest*, was built by Homer Augustus Wessel, Sr.

The *Social Register Summer, 1915* lists Homer A. and Louise Meyer Wessel [Sr.] as residing at *Mill Crest* in East Hampton.

He was the son of Augustus and Eliza Albray Wessel of Cincinnati, OH.

Louise Meyer Wessel was the daughter of M. H. Meyer of New York City. She subsequently married Arthur Herbert Vaughn–Williams of England and Palm Springs, FL.

Homer Augustus and Louise Meyer Wessel, Sr.'s daughter Pauline married S. McL. Lawrence of New York City Their daughter Margery married John H. McCluney, Jr. of St. Louis, MO, and, later, Herbert J. Swenson with whom she resided in Tarrytown, NY. Their son Homer Augustus Wessel, Jr. resided in Cincinnati, OH.

At the time of his death Wessel was residing at *Nestle-down-in-the-Hill* in Briar Cliff Manor, NY. [*The New York Times* October 28, 1934, p. 32.]

*The original plans for *Mill Crest* are in the East Hampton Library.

The house was later owned by Joseph Russell Ramee who called it *Twinmill*. [*The East Hampton Star* August 31, 1944, p. 1.]

Weston, Catherine Boudinot Stimson (1845-1942)

Civic Activism:	a founder, Settlement House, East Hampton
Marriage(s):	Theodore Weston (1831-1919)

    - engineer - assistant engineer, New York State canal system, 1855-1857;
        assistant engineer, survey and construction, Brooklyn Water Works, 1857-1860;
        engineer in charge, New York City's sewerage and drainage, 1861-1870
    architect - Metropolitan Museum of Art, NYC;
        Equitable Life Assurance Society Building, NYC
    financier - trustee, Equitable Life Assurance Society
    writer - *Report on Works of Rome*;
        The Crayon
    Civic Activism: a founder, Metropolitan Museum of Art, NYC;
        a founder, Century Association

Address:	Main Street and Buell Lane, East Hampton
Name of estate:	*Seven Gables*
Year of construction:	
Style of architecture:	Victorian
Architect(s):	Theodore Weston, alterations (for himself)
Landscape architect(s):	
House extant:	unconfirmed
Historical notes:	

    In 1894 Henry Clark Stimson purchased Reverend Samuel Buell / Timothy Hedges ancestral property and remodeled the house. It was later owned by his daughter Miss Mary Atterbury Stimson and, then, by her sister Catherine Boudinot Stimson Weston who called it *Seven Gables*.

    The *Social Register Summer, 1915* lists the Westons as residing at *Buells Corner* in East Hampton. The *Long Island Society Register, 1929* lists Mrs. Theodore Weston as residing at *Seven Gables* in East Hampton. The *Social Directory of Southampton, Long Island, 1931* lists her address as Main Street, East Hampton.

    She was the daughter of Henry Clark and Julia Maria Atterbury Stimson of Paterson, NJ, Manhattan, and East Hampton. Catherine's ancestor Elias Boudinot was President of the Continental Congress from 1782 to 1783 and served as Director of the United States Mint from 1795 until 1805.

    Theodore Weston was the son of Frederick and Elizabeth Hart Weston of Sandy Hill, NY. Theodore had previously been married to Sarah Chauncey Winthrop who died in 1864.

    Theodore and Catherine Boudinot Stimson Weston's daughter Mary married William F. Dominick and resided at *Noailles* on Stanwich Road, Greenwich, CT.

Wheeler, John Neville (1886-1973)

Occupation(s):	journalist - reporter and sports reporter, *New York Herald*
	publisher - founder, president and director, Wheeler Syndicate, NYC (news and feature articles);
	founder and president, Bell Syndicate, NYC;
	general manager and chairman of board, North American Newspaper Alliance (news service)
	writer - ghostwriter for baseball players:
	Christy Matheson;
	Ty Cobb;
	Johnny Evers;
	John J. McGraw
	ghostwriter for evangelist Bill Sunday
Civic Activism:	donated his correspondence to Columbia University, NYC
Marriage(s):	Elizabeth Wood Thompson (1893-1985)
	- Civic Activism: established John N. Wheeler–Elizabeth Wheeler Ellison Scholarship Fund (for students of Ridgefield High School, Ridgefield, CT)
Address:	Lily Pond Lane, East Hampton
Name of estate:	
Year of construction:	1920
Style of architecture:	Contemporary
Architect(s):	John Custis Lawrence designed the house (for M. L. Mayo)
Landscape architect(s):	
Builder:	Edward M. Gay
House extant: yes	
Historical notes:	

    The house, originally named *Bonnie Dune*, was built by Marie Louise Mayo. In c. 1926 it was purchased by Wheeler. [*The East Hampton Star* February 28, 1930, p. 7.]
    He was the son of Charles W. and Kate Bell Neville Wheeler of Yonkers, NY.
    Elizabeth Wood Thompson Wheeler was the daughter of Smith and Harriet Weems Woods Thompson, Jr. of Washington, DC.
    John Neville and Elizabeth Wood Thompson Wheeler's daughter Elizabeth married William McLaren Ellison, the son of Bennett Ellison of Wassaic, NY.
    In 1942 the house was purchased by Consuelo Vanderbilt Warburton. [*The East Hampton Star* October 22, 1942, p. 2.]

Wheelock, John Hall (1886-1978)

Occupation(s):	publisher - treasurer, director and senior editor, Charles Scribner & Sons
	writer - poet* - *Verses by Two Undergraduates*, 1905; *Human Fantasy*, 1911; *Beloved Adventure*, 1912; *Love and Liberation*, 1913; *Dust and Light*, 1919; *The Black Panther*, 1922; *The Bright Doom*, 1927; *Collected Poems, 1911-1936*, 1936; *Poems Old and New*, 1956; *The Gardener and Other Poems*, 1961; *Dear Men and Women: New Poems*, 1966; *By Daylight and in Dream: New and Collected Poems, 1904-1970*, 1970; *In Love and Song Poems*, 1971; *Alan Seeger; Poet of the Foreign Legion*, 1918; *The Face of a Nation; Poetical Passages from the Writings of Thomas Wolfe*, 1939; Editor to Author *A Bibliography of Theodore Roosevelt*, 1920; *The Letters of Maxwell E. Perkins*, 1950
Civic Activism:	donated antique furniture and artwork to the East Hampton Historical Society;
	vice-president, National Institute of Arts and Letters;
	chancellor, Academy of American Poets;
	honorary consultant, Library of Congress, Washington, DC
Marriage(s):	1940-1978 – Phyllis Edwalyn de Kay (1889-1987)
	- writer
Address:	35 Georgica Road, East Hampton
Name of estate:	*Wuthering*
Year of construction:	1891
Style of architecture:	Dutch Colonial Revival
Architect(s):	Isaac Henry Green II designed the house (for W. E. Wheelock)**
	Robert Arthur Morton Stern, 1979-1980 alterations
Landscape architect(s):	
Builder:	George Eldredge. 1892 additions to rear of house
	Asa Otis Jones, 1904 additions on North end of front facade
House extant: yes	
Historical notes:	

    The house, originally named *Wuthering*, was built by William Almy Wheelock for his son Dr. William Efner Wheelock on his parents' property to form a family compound. It was inherited by W. E. Wheelock's son John.

    Phyllis Edwalyn de Kay Wheelock was the daughter of Charles and Lucy Edwalyn Coffy de Kay of *Abrigada* in East Hampton. Phyllis had previously been married to Edward Basil Bury, the son of John Bury of Cambridge, England.

    *Wheelock wrote over 1,000 poems. His *Collected Poems 1911-1936* was awarded the Golden Rose by the New England Poetry Society. His *Poems Old and New* received the Ridgely Torrence Memorial Award in 1956 and the Borestone Mountain Poetry Award in 1957. He was also the recipient of the Bollingen Prize in 1962, the Signet Society Medal in 1965, and the Poetry Society of America's Gold Medal in 1972.

    In 2016 the 4,500-square-foot, four-bedroom, three-bath house and 6.7+ acres were for sale. The asking price was $17.995 million.

    **For Green's other commissions, *see* Spinzia, *Long Island's Prominent South Shore Families: Their Estates and Their Country Homes in the Towns of Babylon and Islip.*

Wheelock, William Almy (1825-1905)

Occupation(s):	financier - president and director, Central National Bank; director, Equitable Life Assurance Society; director, Citizen's National Bank; trustee, American Surety Co.; president, State Trust Co.; president, First National Bank of New York
	capitalist - director, Gold and Stock Telegraph Co.; director, Ophthalmic and Aural Institute; director, New York, Lake Erie and Western Railway
Civic Activism:	president, Council of New York University, NYC; treasurer, New York University, NYC; director, New England Society; trustee, University of the City of New York; a founder and director, Maidstone Club, East Hampton
Marriage(s):	1850-1905 – Harriette Efner (1827-1911)
Address:	Georgica Road, East Hampton
Name of estate:	
Year of construction:	1891
Style of architecture:	Adamesque-Colonial
Architect(s):	Isaac Henry Green II designed the house (for W. A. Wheelock)*
	Aymar Embury II, 1929-1930 alterations that transformed the house into Adamesque-Colonial style
Landscape architect(s):	
Builder:	Philip Ritch
House extant: yes	
Historical notes:	

The house was built by William Almy Wheelock.
He was the son of Joseph and Amelia Ames Wheelock of Manhattan.
Harriette Efner Wheelock was the daughter of Elijah D. Efner of Buffalo, NY.
William Almy and Harriette Efner Wheelock's daughter Harriette married George Arthur Strong and resided in East Hampton. Their son William married Emily Charlotte Hall and resided at *Wuthering* in East Hampton.
[See following entry for additional family information.]
The house was later owned by Robert Paul Schey who called it *Lauralawn*. [*The East Hampton Star* December 22, 1977, p. 26.]
*For Green's other commissions, *see* Spinzia, *Long Island's Prominent South Shore Families: Their Estates and Their Country Homes in the Towns of Babylon and Islip.*

Wheelock, Dr. William Efner (1852-1926)

Occupation(s):	physician
	attorney
Marriage(s):	1885-1926 – Emily Charlotte Hall (1859-1938)
	- Civic Activism: president, Garden Club of East Hampton
Address:	35 Georgica Road, East Hampton
Name of estate:	*Wuthering*
Year of construction:	1891
Style of architecture:	Dutch Colonial Revival
Architect(s):	Isaac Henry Green II designed the house (for W. E. Wheelock)*
	Robert Arthur Morton Stern, 1979-1980 alterations
Landscape architect(s):	
Builder:	George Eldredge, 1892 additions to rear of house
	Asa Otis Jones, 1904 additions on North end of front facade

House extant: yes
Historical notes:

    The house, originally named *Wuthering*, was built by William Almy Wheelock for his son Dr. William Efner Wheelock on his parents' property to form a family compound.
    The *Social Register Summer, 1910* and *1915* list William E. and Emily C. Hall Wheelock as residing at *Wuthering* in East Hampton.
    He was the son of William Almy and Harriette Efner Wheelock.
    Emily Charlotte Hall Wheelock was the daughter of The Reverend John and Mrs. Emily Bolton Hall.
    Dr. William Efner and Mrs. Emily Charlotte Hall Wheelock's daughter Emily, who fell to her death from the eighteenth floor solarium of Manhattan's Barbizon Hotel, married H. Van Rensselear Fairfax, the son of Hamilton R. Fairfax of Merrick. [*The New York Times* August 16, 1939, p. 2.] Their son William Almy Wheelock II died in 1897 at the age of nine. Their son John, who inherited the house, married Phyllis Edwalyn de Kay.
    [See previous entry for additional family information.]
    In 2016 the 4,500-square-foot, four-bedroom, three-bath house and 6.7+ acres were for sale. The asking price was $17.995 million.
    *For Green's other commissions, *see* Spinzia, *Long Island's Prominent South Shore Families: Their Estates and Their Country Homes in the Towns of Babylon and Islip.*

Whitney, Elwood (1904-1992)

Occupation(s):	advertising executive - art director and vice-president, J. Walter Thompson; vice-president, Foote, Cone, and Belding
Civic Activism:	trustee, Southampton Hospital; a founder, Hampton Classic Horse Show

Marriage(s):	M/1 – Virginia Enfield (1909-1969)
	    - fashion designer, American Enka Corp.
	M/2 – 1973-1992 – Kate Case (1919-2004)
	    - real estate agent - Condie Lamb Agency, East Hampton
	    Civic Activism: president, Georgica Association;
	    vice-president, Ladies Village Improvement Society, East Hampton

Address:	Lee Avenue, East Hampton
Name of estate:	
Year of construction:	1955
Style of architecture:	
Architect(s):	
Landscape architect(s):	
House extant: unconfirmed	
Historical notes:	

The house, originally called *Tall Trees*, was built by Edward Reinow Fuller. [*The East Hampton Star* June 16, 1955, p. 12.]
In 1964 Whitney purchased the house. [*The East Hampton Star* May 7, 1964, p. 4.]
The Blue Book of The Hamptons, 1965 lists Elwood and Virginia Enfield Whitney as residing on Lee Avenue, East Hampton.
The Blue Book of The Hamptons, 1973 lists Elwood and Kate Case Whitney as residing on Lee Avenue.
She was the daughter of John and Kate Whiteside Case of Oklahoma. Kate had previously been married to Donald E. Barnes.

Whittemore, William John (1860-1955)

Occupation(s):	artist - water colorist, miniature painting, and portraitures*

Marriage(s):	M/1 – 1895-1911 – Alice Vaud Whitmore (1868-1911)
	    - artist
	M/2 – 1921-1955 – Charlotte Helen Simpson (1865-1955)
	    - artist

Address:	Pantigo Lane, East Hampton
Name of estate:	*Robinsfield*
Year of construction:	1900
Style of architecture:	
Architect(s):	
Landscape architect(s):	
House extant: unconfirmed	
Historical notes:	

The house was built by William John Whittemore. [*The East Hampton Star* March 30, 1950, p. 1.]
He was the son of Charles and Maria Frances Kimball Whittemore of NYC.
Alice Vaud Whitmore Whittemore was the daughter of Frederic Whitmore of NYC.
The *Long Island Society Register, 1929* lists William J. and C. Helen Simpson Whittemore as residing at *Robinsfield* in East Hampton. The *Social Directory of Southampton, Long Island, 1931* lists their address as Pantigo Lane, East Hampton.
She was the daughter of The Reverend Robert William Simpson of Birmingham, England.
The Whittemores did not have children.
*Whittemore's paintings are exhibited at several major museums. His portrait of William Stryker Gummere, Chief Justice of the Supreme Court of New Jersey, hangs in the New Jersey State House in Trenton, NJ and his portrait of the second wife of Commodore Cornelius Vanderbilt, Frank Armstrong Crawford Vanderbilt, hangs in Kirkland Hall on the campus of Vanderbilt University in Nashville, TN.

Whittle, Chris (b. 1947)
aka H. Christopher Whittle

Occupation(s):	educator - chairman of board and CEO, Whittle School and Studies; founder and president, Edison Schools (later, Edisonlearning); founder and chairman of board, Avenue: The World School (NYC private school system management firm)
	publisher - founder and chairman of board, 13-20 Corp (Nashville, TN); chairman of board, Whittle Communications
	writer - *Crash Course: Imagining a Better Future for Public Education*, 2005; chapter in *Customizing Schooling: Beyond Whole-School Reform*, 2011
Civic Activism:	president, United States Foundation for Atlantic College
Marriage(s):	1990 – Priscilla Rattazzi (b. 1956)
	- writer - *Una Famiglia*, 1982; *Best Friends*, 1989; *Luna & Lola*, 2010; *Children*, 1992; *Georgica Pond*, 2000
	professional photographer
Address:	90 Briar Patch Road, East Hampton
Name of estate:	*Briar Patch*
Year of construction:	1931-1932
Style of architecture:	Modified Colonial Revival
Architect(s):	Arthur C. Jackson designed the house (for S. Krech, Sr.)
	Peter Marino designed the 1989-1991 guest house and alterations to main residence (for Whittle)
Landscape architect(s):	
House extant: yes	
Historical notes:	

The house, originally named *Briar Patch*, was built by Dr. Shepard Krech, Sr. on the former estate of Henry Hurlbut Abbott which was also named *Briar Patch*.

In 1989 Krech's estate was purchased by Whittle.

Priscilla Rattazzi Whittle is the daughter of Count Urbano and Countess Susan Agnelli Rattazzi of Italy. Priscilla had previously been married to Alessandro Ponti, the son of Carlo and Iaia Fiastri Ponti of Italy, and Claus Moehlmann.

In 2014 Whittle listed the 10,300-square-foot, ten-bedroom main residence, with nine and a half bathrooms; the four-bedroom guest house; and 11.2 acres for sale. The asking price was $36 million.

Wiborg, Frank Bestow (1855-1930)

Occupation(s):	statesman - United States Assistant Secretary of Commerce and Labor (Taft administration)
	industrialist - vice-president, Ault & Wiborg Co., Cincinnati, OH, NYC, and Toronto, Canada (printing ink manufacturing firm)
	writer - *Travels with an Unofficial Attaché*, 1904; *A Commercial Traveler in South America*, 1905
Civic Activism:	a founder and member, first board of governors, Devon Yacht Club, Amagansett;
	a founder, Suffolk Hunt Club, 1910
Marriage(s):	1882-1917 – Adeline Moulton Sherman (1859-1917)
Address:	Oak Beach Lane, East Hampton
Name of estate:	*The Dunes*
Year of construction:	1895
Style of architecture:	Mediterranean
Architect(s):	Grosvenor Atterbury remodeled existing gambrel-roofed farm house into a 30-room house (for Wiborg)

Landscape architect(s):
House extant: no; demolished in 1941
Nassau County Museum Collection has photographs of the estate.
Historical notes:

The house, originally named *The Dunes*, was built by Frank Bestow Wiborg.
He was the son of Henry Paulinus and Susan Isidora Bestow Wiborg of Cleveland, OH.
Adeline Moulton Sherman Wiborg was the daughter of Hoyt Sherman and a niece of General Tecumseh Sherman of Civil War fame.
In 1913 Adeline was indicted in Federal District Court on two counts for smuggling. Returning to the United States from Europe, Mrs. Wiborg claimed that her twenty trunks of luggage contained only $500 worth of foreign purchases. In reality they contained $5,000 worth of foreign purchases of which $3,000 was liable to duty. Her attorney, John Barry Stanchfield of *Afterglow* in Islip, who had established a defendant's right of non-incrimination based on the Fifth Amendment to the United States Constitution in a previous case, convinced Mrs. Wiborg to plead guilty. She was fined $1,750. [*The New York Times* September 12, 1913, p. 13, and October 24, 1913, p. 6.] [*See* Spinzia, *Long Island's Prominent South Shore Families* – Stanchfield entry.]
Frank Bestow and Adeline Moulton Sherman Wiborg's unmarried daughter Mary, who wrote the 1922 play "Taboo" which starred Paul Robeson, also had a problem of undeclared items. In 1928 custom officials seized her seventeen pieces of luggage for appraisal. [*The New York Times* August 1, 1928, p. 9.] The Wiborgs' daughter Olga married Sidney Webster Fish, the son of Stuyvesant and Marian Graves Anthon Fish of Newport, RI, and resided at *Duck Pond* in Old Brookville. [*See* Spinzia, *Long Island's Prominent North Shore Families, vol. I* – Fish entry.] His father, Stuyvesant Fish, was president of the Illinois Central Railroad. Sidney's mother was the famous Newport socialite Marian Graves Anthon Fish, who was known for her bizarre formal dinner parties at which domestic pets were the guests of honor. Sidney's sister Marion married Albert Zebriskie Gray of *Orchard Farm* in Old Westbury. [*See* Spinzia, *Long Island's Prominent North Shore Families, vol. I* – Gray entry.] The Wiborgs' daughter Sara married Gerald Clery Murphy, the son of Patrick Francis and Ann Ryan Murphy of *Agawam* in Southampton, and resided at *Swan Cove* in East Hampton. [*See* Spinzia, *Long Island's Prominent Families in the Town of Southampton* – Murphy entry.]

Williams, Eugene Flewilyn, Jr. (1923-2013)

Occupation(s):	financier - chairman of board, St. Louis Trust Co., St. Louis, MO; chairman of board, Centerre Trust Co., St. Louis MO; director, Boatmen's Trust Co.
	industrialist - director, Olin Mathieson Chemical Corp.; director, Bristol–Myers Squibb; director, Emerson Electric
	capitalist - director, American Airlines; chairman of board, Pitchfork Land and Cattle Co., Texas and Oklahoma
Civic Activism:	chairman of board, St. Luke's Hospital, St. Louis, MO; director, Blue Cross Blue Shield, St. Louis, MO; director, Country Day School, St. Louis, MO; director, St. Louis Municipal Opera, St. Louis, MO; director, St. Louis University, St. Louis, MO
Marriage(s):	1947-2013 – Evelyn Nixon Niedringhaus (b. 1928)
Address:	201 Lily Pond Lane, East Hampton
Name of estate:	
Year of construction:	
Style of architecture:	Eclectic
Architect(s):	
Landscape architect(s):	
House extant: yes	
Historical notes:	

    The Blue Book of The Hamptons, 1973 lists Eugene F. and Evelyn Niedringhaus Williams, Jr. as residing on Apaquogue Road, East Hampton. By 1997 they had relocated to 201 Lily Pond Lane in East Hampton.

    He is the son of Eugene Flewilyn and Marie Wight Williams, Sr. of Ladue, MO.

    Evelyn Nixon Niedringhaus Williams was the daughter of William Francis Niedringhaus of Ohio.

    Eugene Flewilyn and Evelyn Nixon Niedringhaus Williams, Jr.'s daughter Rebecca married Count Loic de Kertanguy, the son of Count Herve de Kertanguy of Lyon, France, and, later, Thomas M. Kantor, the son of MacKinley Kantor. Their son John married Ann Lacy Ford, the daughter of Gerard William Ford of New York. Their son Eugene Flewilyn William III married Jacqueline Dorothy Russell, the daughter of Edwin Fairman and Lady Sarah Consuelo Spencer–Churchill Russell of Lattingtown, and resided at *Barn House*, 29 Jones Road, East Hampton. [*See* Spinzia, *Long Island's Prominent North Shore Families, vol. II* – Russell entry.]

    Williams was residing on Jones Road in East Hampton at the time of his death.

Wolff, Caroline Smith Snowden (1865-1960)

Marriage(s):	M/1 – Stuyvesant Wainwright
	M/2 – 1915-1934 – Dr. Carl F. Wolff (1864-1934)
	- physician - chief physician, Port Chester Hospital, Port Chester, NY
Address:	Bridgehampton Road, East Hampton
Name of estate:	*Shadowmere*
Year of construction:	
Style of architecture:	
Architect(s):	
Landscape architect(s):	
House extant: unconfirmed	
Historical notes:	

    The *Social Directory of Southampton, Long Island, 1931* lists Dr. and Mrs. Carl F. Wolff as residing on Bridgehampton Road, East Hampton. The *Social Register Summer 1932* lists the name of their residence as *Shadowmere*.

    Caroline Smith Snowden Wolff was the daughter of Archibald Loudon and Elizabeth Robinson Smith Snowden. She had previously been married to Stuyvesant Wainwright of Rye, NY. Caroline's son Loudon Snowden Wainwright, Sr. married Eleanor Painter Sloan and resided in Hewlett Neck. [*See* Spinzia, *Long Island's Prominent Families in the Town of Hempstead* – Wainwright entry.] Her son Carroll Livingston Wainwright, Sr. married Edith C. Gould and resided at *Gullcrest* in East Hampton. Her son Stuyvesant Wainwright, Jr. married Louise Flinn and resided in Bay Shore and at *Duckwood* in Hampton Bays. [*See* Spinzia, *Long Island's Prominent Families in the Town of Southampton* and *Long Island's Prominent South Shore Families* – Wainwright entries.] Her son John Howard Wainwright married Aimee Andrews and resided in East Hampton. *[See Wainwright entries in this volume for additional family information.]*

Wood, Arthur B. (1875-1930)
aka Arthur W. B. Wood

Occupation(s):	architect - partner, Wood and Whitaker (specialized in country homes and churches)
Marriage(s):	Alice Isabell Dayton (1883-1980)
Address:	162 Fairview Avenue, Montauk
Name of estate:	
Year of construction:	1928
Style of architecture:	Eclectic Dutch Farmhouse
Architect(s):	Arthur B. Wood designed his own residence
Landscape architect(s):	
House extant: yes	
Historical notes:	

The house, which has been extensively altered over the years, was built by Arthur B. Wood.

He was the son of Frederick W. Wood.

Arthur B. and Alice Isabell Dayton Wood's daughter Marghretta married Samuel A. Dathlowe and resided in Essex, CT.

The house was later owned by Lindsey Hopkins, Jr.

In 1966 it was purchased by Mary Ellen Harrington Gosman. Gosman sold the house to Marion Daily, who listed it for sale in 2018. The asking price was $1.9 million.

[For information about Wood's Garden City residence, *see* Spinzia, *Long Island's Prominent Families in the Town of Hempstead* – Wood entry.]

Wood, Howard Ogden, Jr. (1894-1964)

Occupation(s):	financier - partner, Wood, Walker, and Co. (stock brokerage firm)
Marriage(s):	1918-1957 – Caryl Hackstaff (1895-1957)
Address:	Lee Avenue, East Hampton
Name of estate:	*Tarriawyle*
Year of construction:	1899
Style of architecture:	Shingle
Architect(s):	Joseph Greenleaf Thorp designed the house (for Hackstaff)
Landscape architect(s):	
Builder:	Loper Brothers George A. Eldredge, 1902 alterations*
House extant: yes	
Historical notes:	

The 7,500-square-foot, eight-bedroom, seven-and-a-half-bath house, originally named *Tarriawyle*, was built by Charles Ludovic Hackstaff.

The *New York Summer Social Register, 1919* lists Howard Ogden and Caryl Hackstaff Wood, Jr. as residing at *Tarriawyle* in East Hampton. The *Long Island Society Register, 1929* lists the Woods as residing on Meadow Lane, Cedarhurst [Lawrence]. [*See* Spinzia, *Long Island's Prominent Families in the Town of Hempstead* – Wood entry.]

He was the son of Howard Ogden and Julia Curtis Twichell Wood, Sr. who resided in East Hampton.

Caryl Hackstaff Wood was the daughter of Charles Ludovic and Margaret Euphemia Hoffman Hackstaff of *Tarriawyle*.

Howard Ogden and Caryl Hackstaff Wood, Jr.'s daughter Caryl married Richard Livingston Davies, the son of Edward Livingston and Margaret C. Taylor Davies of Garden City, and resided in Valley Stream. Their son Howard Ogden Wood III married Sarah Jane Fraser, the daughter of George C. Fraser of Hastings-on-Hudson, NY.

[See following entry for additional family information.]

*The 1902 addition on the south facade was built by Eldredge. In 1969 the front porch was enclosed.

The house was subsequently owned by Stephen Kniznick Robert.

In 2012 the house and 1.9 acres were for sale by Robert. The asking price was $18.5 million. It was sold for $14.9 million in 2014.

Wood, Howard Ogden, Sr. (1866-1940)

Occupation(s):	attorney - partner, Wood and Hill; partner, Wood, Cooke, and Seitz
	financier - director, Brevoort Savings Bank, Brooklyn
	educator - taught law, Columbia University, NYC
Civic Activism:	president and trustee, Children's Aid Society of Brooklyn; chairman of board, Brooklyn Y.M.C.A.; president of board of trustees, Brooklyn Eye and Ear Hospital
Marriage(s):	1892-1940 – Julia Curtis Twichell (1869-1945)
Address:	Briar Patch Road, East Hampton
Name of estate:	
Year of construction:	1897
Style of architecture:	Shingle
Architect(s):	
Landscape architect(s):	
Builder:	George A. Eldredge
House extant: yes	
Historical notes:	

The house was built by Howard Ogden Wood, Sr. [*The East Hampton Star* February 22, 1945, p. 1.]

The *Long Island Society Register, 1929* lists Howard Ogden and Julia Curtis Twichell Wood [Sr.] as residing in East Hampton.

He was the son of Cornelius Delano and Helen Ogden Wood of Brooklyn.

Julia Curtis Twichell Wood was the daughter of The Reverend Joseph H. Twichell and Mrs. Harmony Cushman Twichell.

Howard Ogden and Julia Curtis Twichell Wood, Sr.'s daughter Helen married Auguste Julien Cordier, Jr. and resided in East Hampton. Their son Howard Ogden Wood, Jr. married Caryl Hackstaff and resided in Lawrence and at *Tarriawyle* in East Hampton. [*See* Spinzia, *Long Island's Prominent Families in the Town of Hempstead* – Wood entry.]

[See previous entry for additional family information.]

The house is listed on the National Register of Historic Places.

Wood, Robert Williams, Jr. (1868-1955)

Occupation(s):	scientist - research physicist, Johns Hopkins University, Baltimore, MD; pioneered development of infrared and ultraviolet photography*; consultant to Manhattan Project, 1944-1946
	writer - *How to Tell the Birds From the Flowers*, 1907 (children's book); *Animal Analogues*, 1908; *The Man Who Rocked the Earth*, 1915, co-authored with Arthur Train (science fiction); *The Moon Maker*, 1916; numerous articles on spectroscopy, phosphorescence, and diffraction
Marriage(s):	1892-1955 – Gertrude Ames (1866-1958)
Address:	Apaquogue and Jones Roads, East Hampton
Name of estate:	
Year of construction:	
Style of architecture:	Colonial
Architect(s):	
Landscape architect(s):	
House extant: unconfirmed	
Historical notes:	

In 1908 Wood purchased the Miller homestead. [*The East Hampton Star* August 1, 1955, p. 2.]

He was the son of Dr. Robert Williams and Mrs. Lucy Jane Davis Wood, Sr. of Jamaica Plains, MA.

Gertrude Ames Wood was the daughter of Pelham Warren and Augusta Wood Hooper Ames.

Robert Williams and Gertrude Ames Wood, Jr.'s daughter Elizabeth married Edward Osgood Bogert and resided in East Hampton. Their daughter Margaret Wood (aka Margot White), who resided in Lawrence, married Victor Gerald White, Sr. and, later, Arthur Ulysses Newton. [*See* Spinzia, *Long Island's Prominent Families in the Town of Hempstead* – Newton and White entries.] Their son Robert Williams Wood III, who later resided at the house with his sister Elizabeth, married Oliva Saunders, the daughter of Arthur Percy Saunders of Clinton, NY.

*Wood, a consultant on the Manhattan Project which produced the first atomic bomb, was called "The Wizard of Invisible Light." In 1938 he was awarded the Royal Society's prestigious Rumford Medal for his work in physics and optics.

Wood, Wilfrid (1897-1960)

Occupation(s):	attorney - member, Clark Dodge and Co., NYC; financier - member, Coggeshall and Hicks, 1920 (stock brokerage firm); partner, Mitchell, Hutchins, and Co., 1946 (stock brokerage firm)
Marriage(s):	M/1 – 1916-div. – Helen Price Barclay Riordan M/2 – Charlotte Miller
Address:	Egypt Lane, East Hampton
Name of estate:	
Year of construction:	c. 1725-1750
Style of architecture:	Colonial*
Architect(s):	
Landscape architect(s):	Gaines Ruger Donoho designed his own gardens
House extant: unconfirmed	
Historical notes:	

In 1891 Gaines Ruger Donohue purchased the house. [John Esten. *Hampton Gardens: 350 Years.* (New York: Rizzoli, 2008), p. 22.] In 1919 it was purchased by Frederick Childe Hassam. In 1940 Wood purchased the house. [*The New York Times* December 8, 1940, p. 221, and *The East Hampton Star* August 22, 1940, p. 1.]

He was the son of Frederic and Caroline Chessman Wood of Morristown, NJ.

Helen Price Barclay Riordan Wood was the daughter of James and Ethel L. Riordan of Manhattan. She subsequently married John Mingus Dodd III with whom she resided in East Hampton.

Wilfrid and Helen Price Barclay Riordan Wood's daughter Louise married John Haynes Porter, the son of Alfred Haynes Porter of Rumson, NJ, and, later, Blair Phillips. Their daughter Suzanne married ____ Monoghan.

The *Social Register Summer, 1945* lists Wilfrid and Charlotte Miller Wood as residing in East Hampton.

She was the daughter of Charles Miller of Summit, NJ.

Wilfrid and Charlotte Miller Wood's son Wilfrid Parnell Wood married Margaret Frances McCarthy, the daughter of John Murray McCarthy of Madison, NJ.

*The house was modified into Shingle-style architecture.

Woodhouse, Lorenzo Easton (1857-1935)

Occupation(s):	financier - president, Merchant's National Bank, Burlington, VT
Civic Activism:	purchased land and built the 1911 East Hampton Free Library;
	chairman of board and benefactor, Guild Hall and Drew Theater, East Hampton;
	director, East Hampton Visiting Nurse Association;
	director, East Hampton Historical Society;
	vice-chairman of board, Guild Hall, East Hampton
Marriage(s):	1886-1935 – Mary Leland Kennedy (1865-1961)
	- Civic Activism:
	a founder and president, Garden Club of East Hampton;
	donated Japanese garden and meadow for Nature Trail and Bird Sanctuary;
	purchased land and financed building of the East Hampton Free Library;
	helped finance construction of Guild Hall and Drew Theater, East Hampton;
	restored Clinton Academy, East Hampton, 1921;
	donated *Greycroft* to Leighton Rollins School of Acting, 1937;
	a founder and vice-president, Montauk Historical Society;
	a founder, Civic Arts Association, 1934
Address:	Huntting Lane, East Hampton
Name of estate:	*The Fens*
Year of construction:	c. 1903
Style of architecture:	Shingle
Architect(s):	Joseph Greenleaf Thorp designed the house (for L. E. Woodhouse)
	Francis Burrall Hoffman, Jr. designed the 1916 *Playhouse* (for L. E. Woodhouse)
	Richard Webb converted *The Playhouse* into a residence, 1949
Landscape architect(s):	
House extant:	no; demolished in 1949
Historical notes:	

    The house, originally named *The Fens*, was built by Lorenzo Easton Woodhouse.
    He was the son of Charles Williamson and Emma Easton Day Woodhouse of Vermont.
    Mary Leland Kennedy Woodhouse was the daughter of Frederick C. and Mary A. Kennedy.
    Lorenzo Easton and Mary Leland Kennedy Woodhouse's daughter Marjorie married Frederick William Procter of Manhattan, heir to the Procter and Gamble fortune, and, later, Carter Randolph Leidy with whom she resided in Rye, NY. Their son Charles married Dorrit Van Dusen Stevens, who successfully sued Charles' parents in 1922 for alienation of affections. She was awarded $465,000 by the court. In 1929 the thirty-five-year-old Dorrit married William Wells Brock, a twenty-five-year-old sophomore at Columbia University. [*The New York Times* November 1, 1922, p. 15; November 18, 1922, p. 12; December 8, 1922, p. 6; February 24, 1927, p. 4; and January 25, 1929, p. 3.]
    The Playhouse, which is on the National Register of Historic Places, was later owned by Daniel David Brockman.
    In 1908 an addition was made to the house. The gardener's cottage was built in 1911.

Woodhouse, Lorenzo Guernsey (1839-1903)

Occupation(s):	merchant - partner and New York buyer, Marshall Field & Co., Chicago, IL. (department store)
	financier - director, Exchange Fire Insurance Co.
Civic Activism:	director, Shelter Island Improvement Association
Marriage(s):	1866-1903 – Emma Douglas Arrowsmith (1846-1908)
Address:	63 Huntting Lane, East Hampton
Name of estate:	*Greycroft*
Year of construction:	1894
Style of architecture:	Shingle
Architect(s):	Isaac Henry Green II designed the house (for L. G. Woodhouse)*
	George A. Eldredge, designed 1897 addition
	Robert Arthur Morton Stern designed 1980-1981 alterations to the playhouse
Landscape architect(s):	
House extant:	yes
Historical notes:	

The house, originally named *Greycroft*, was built by Lorenzo Guernsey Woodhouse.

He was the son of The Reverend Charles and Mrs. Lepha Lucinda Guernsey Woodhouse.

Emma Douglas Arrowsmith Woodhouse was the daughter of Dr. I. Edgar and Mrs. Maria Craig Arrowsmith of New York. Emma subsequently married Stephen Swete Cummins with whom she resided at *Greycroft*.

Lorenzo Guernsey and Emma Douglas Arrowsmith Woodhouse's daughter Grace married Robert Barnwell Roosevelt, Jr. of *The Lilacs* in Sayville. [*See* Spinzia, *Long Island's Prominent South Shore Families* – Roosevelt entry.]

Library of Congress photographs of the estate are listed under Stephen Swete Cummins.

*For Green's other commissions, *see* Spinzia, *Long Island's Prominent South Shore Families: Their Estates and Their Country Homes in the Towns of Babylon and Islip*.

Woodin, William Hartman, Sr. (1868-1934)

Occupation(s):	statesman - United States Secretary of Treasury (Franklin Delano Roosevelt administration)
	industrialist - president, Jackson & Woodin Manufacturing Co., Berwick, PA (manufacturer of railroad freight cars) (later, American Car & Foundry Co.);
	president and director, American Car & Foundry Co.;
	director, Standard Plunger Elevator Co.;
	director, Hoyt & Woodin Manufacturing Co.;
	president and director, American Locomotive Works;
	director, Remington Arms Co.;
	director, Superheater Co.
	capitalist - director, American Car and Foundry Export Co.;
	director, Good Land Cypress Co.;
	chairman of board, Brill Corp.;
	director, Cuba Co.;
	director, Cuba Railway Co.;
	director, Compania Cubana;
	director, Consolidated Railroad of Cuba;
	director, Atlantic Mail Corp.;
	director, Fifth Avenue Corp.
	financier - director, Federal Reserve Bank of New York;
	president, American Car & Foundry Securities Corp.;
	director, Coal & Iron National Bank;
	trustee, American Surety Co.
	shipping - director, American Ship & Commerce Corp.
	composer - numerous songs and classical music
Civic Activism:	trustee, Fifth Avenue Presbyterian Church, NYC;
	New York State Fuel Administrator (Miller administration);
	chairman, finance committee, Georgia Warm Springs Foundation;
	chairman, American Tagore Association;
	treasurer, Council on Adult Education for Foreign Born;
	trustee, Lafayette College, Easton, PA;
	chairman, board of trustees, Guild Hall, East Hampton;
	a founder and president, Maidstone Club, East Hampton;
	a founder and member, first governing board, and commodore, Devon Yacht Club, Amagansett
Marriage(s):	1889-1934 – Annie Jessup (1867-1941)
Address:	Lily Pond Lane, East Hampton
Name of estate:	*Dune House*
Year of construction:	1916
Style of architecture:	Cotswold
Architect(s):	Grosvenor Atterbury *[attributed]* designed the house and 1925 gardener's cottage (for Woodin, Sr.)
Landscape architect(s):	Marian Cruger Coffin, 1927 (for Woodin, Sr.)
Builder:	Frank B. Smith
House extant: yes	
Historical notes:	

The house, originally named *Dune House*, was built by William Hartman Woodin, Sr.
He was the son of Clemuel Ricketts and Mary Louise Dickerman Woodin of Berwick, PA.
Annie Jessup Woodin was the daughter of William Hunting Jessup of Montrose, PA.
William Hartman and Annie Jessup Woodin, Sr.'s daughter Mary, who resided at *Gray Wing* in East Hampton, married Charles Miner, Sr., the son of William P. Miner of Wilkes–Barre, PA. Their daughter Elizabeth married William Wallace Rowe, Sr., the son of William Stanhope and Margaret Anna Richardson Rowe, Sr. of Amagansett, and resided in East Hampton. Their son William Hartman Woodin, Jr. married Carolyn Hyde. Their daughter Annie married Oline Frisbee Harvey, Jr. and resided in Greenwich, CT.
The estate was purchased in 1941 by Lawrence Flinn, Sr. who was killed in World War II at the Battle of the Rhine, and, then, by Donald J. Bruckman.

Woodward, Shaun Anthony (b. 1958)

Occupation(s):	statesman - Under Secretary of State, Department for Culture, Media, and Sport, Great Britain, 2006; Secretary of State for Northern Ireland, 2007-2010; Shadow Secretary of State for Northern Ireland, 2010-2011
	politician - member, British Parliament, 1997-2015; director of communication, Conservative Party
	entertainers and associated professions - researcher and producer: BBC News; "That's Life!"; "Panorama"; "Newsnight"
	writer - co-author, with Ester Rantzen, *Ben: Story of Ben Hardwick*, 1985; co-author, with Ron Lacy, *That's Life*
Marriage(s):	1987 – Camilla Davan Sainsbury (b. 1962)
Address:	33 Highway Behind the Pond, East Hampton
Name of estate:	
Year of construction:	
Style of architecture:	Colonial Revival
Architect(s):	Brian Sawyer, alterations (for Woodward)
Landscape architect(s):	
House extant:	yes
Historical notes:	

In 2005 Shaun Anthony Woodward purchased the 5,000-square-foot, six-bedroom, seven-bath house for $12 million. He is the son of Dennis George and Joan Lillian Nunn Woodward of Great Britain.

Camilla Davan Sainsbury Woodward is the daughter of The Right Honorable Sir Timothy Alan Davan Sainsbury and Susan Mary Mitchell Sainsbury.

In 2011 he listed the house for sale. The asking price was $18.5 million. It sold for $16.750 million.

Woolley, Knight (1895-1984)

Occupation(s):	financier - partner, Harriman Brothers and Co., 1927-1931 (investment banking firm); partner, Brown Brothers, Harriman, and Co., 1931-1982 (investment banking firm)
	industrialist - director, Hewitt Robbins; director, National Sugar Refining Co.; director, Air Reduction Co.; director, American Sumatra Tobacco Co.
	capitalist - director, Southern Railroad Co.
Civic Activism:	trustee, Boys Club of New York; trustee, Southampton Hospital, Southampton, NY; president, Hook Pond Associates
Marriage(s):	M/1 – 1934-1954 – Sarah Currier (d. 1954)
	M/2 – 1957-1984 – Marjorie Fleming (1894-1985)
	- Civic Activism: trustee, Clara H. Fleming Memorial Fund*
Address:	Terbell Lane, East Hampton
Name of estate:	
Year of construction:	
Style of architecture:	
Architect(s):	
Landscape architect(s):	
House extant: unconfirmed	
Historical notes:	

Knight Wooley was the son of Ulysses Grant and Helen Eaton Knight Wooley of Brooklyn.

Sarah Currier Wooley was the daughter of Guy W. Currier. She had previously been married to William Arthur Stickney and Felton Elkins.

The Blue Book of The Hamptons, 1965 and *1973* list Knight and Marjorie Fleming Woolley as residing on Terbell Lane, East Hampton.

She was the daughter of Arthur Henry and Clara Huntington Fleming. Marjorie had previously been married to Wilton Lloyd–Smith of *Kenjockety* in Lloyd Harbor. [*See* Spinzia, *Long Island's Prominent North Shore Families, vol. I* – Lloyd–Smith entry.]

Woolley did not have children.

*Marjorie served as co-trustee with her father, who established the fund which was named for Marjorie's mother. Five million dollars was donated by the fund to California Institute of Technology for its establishment. [*The New York Times* August 12, 1940, p. 15.]

Worthington, Louise Grant (d. 1919)

Marriage(s):	Henry Carver Worthington
Address:	Lily Pond Lane, East Hampton
Name of estate:	
Year of construction:	1898-1899
Style of architecture:	Neo-Tudor
Architect(s):	
Landscape architect(s):	
Builder:	Edward G. Duryea
House extant: yes	
Historical notes:	

The house was built by Louise Worthington.

Henry Carver and Louise Grant Worthington's daughter Laura did not marry.

Wright, John Howie, Jr. (1878-1962)

Occupation(s):	publisher - *Postage*
	journalist - editor, *Postage*;
	editor, *Mailbag*
	industrialist - president, Home Pattern Co. (dress pattern firm)
Marriage(s):	M/1 – 1900-div. 1922 – Anna R. H. Hill (1881-1935)
	M/2 – Anne M. Ryan (d. 1953)
Address:	Ocean Avenue and Apaquogue Road, East Hampton
Name of estate:	
Year of construction:	
Style of architecture:	
Architect(s):	
Landscape architect(s):	
House extant: yes	
Historical notes:	

John Howie Wright, Jr. was the son of John Howie and Mary Wilson Wright, Sr. of Portgleone, Ireland.

Anna R. H. Hill Wright drowned in a bathtub in Connecticut's Griswold Hotel.

John Howie and Anna R. H. Hill Wright, Sr.'s son Lyman married Adline Juroshek of Sheridan, WY.

Anne M. Ryan Wright had previously been married to ____ Griffin. Her sister Frances married James J. Devine and resided in East Hampton.

John Howie and Anne M. Ryan Wright, Sr.'s daughter Ann, who resided in East Hampton, married Matthew Andrews Baxter, Sr.; Elmore Coe Kerr, Jr., the son of Elmore Coe and Marian Lyman Smyth Kerr, Sr. of Mill Neck; and, subsequently, David R. Williams, Jr. [*See* Spinzia, *Long Island's Prominent North Shore Families, vol. I* – Kerr entry.] Their son John Howie Wright III resided in East Hampton and, later, on Shelter Island.

[See previous entry for additional family information.]

In 1943 Mrs. Wright purchased Mrs. George Ethridge's former Woods Lane residence from the Riverhead Savings Bank. [*The East Hampton Star* July 1, 1943, p. 5.]

Wright, John Howie, III (1923-1994)

Occupation(s):	industrialist - vice-president, New York Pattern Co. (dress pattern firm);
	publisher - King Features (division of Hearst Publications)
	capitalist - co-founder, with Richard Edwards, Shelter Island–Montauk Airways, Inc.
Marriage(s):	M/1 – 1949-div. – Helen Louise Mann
	M/2 – Betsy *[unable to determine maiden name]*
Address:	Lily Pond Lane, East Hampton
Name of estate:	
Year of construction:	
Style of architecture:	
Architect(s):	
Landscape architect(s):	
House extant: unconfirmed	
Historical notes:	

John Howie Wright III was the son of John Howie and Anne M. Ryan Wright, Jr. of East Hampton.

Helen Louise Mann Wright was the daughter of Henry and Helen Morris Grimes Mann of *San Souci* in East Hampton.

John Howie and Helen Louise Mann Wright III's daughter Helen (aka Cecilia) married Matthew Baird Hobbs, the son of Franklin Warren Hobbs of Chestnut Hill, MA, and resides in Cambridge, MA. Their son Christopher resides in NYC. Their daughter Cindy married ____ Jones and resides in Collins, CO.

Their son John Howie Wright IV married Joy D. Plummer, the daughter of Howard A. Plummer.

By 1956 Wright had relocated to Shelter Island.

[See following entry for additional family information.]

Yates, James Saville (1902-1971)

Occupation(s);	journalist - art edition, *Saturday Evening Post*; art editor, *Holiday* magazine; art director, Curtis Publishing Co., Philadelphia, PA
	advertising executive - vice-president, Lennen & Mitchell; vice-president, William Esty & Co.; art director, Walter Thompson Co.; creative assistant to president, Buchanan & Co.; a founder and vice-president, Beach, Yates, & Mattoon; vice-president for art, Leo Burnett Co., Inc.
Marriage(s):	Clara Louise Campbell (1913-1989)
Address:	Georgica and Apaquogue Roads, East Hampton
Name of estate:	
Year of construction:	1949
Style of architecture:	
Architect(s):	Polhemus & Coffin designed the house and guest house (for J. S. Yates)
Landscape architect(s):	
Builder:	E. H. Howell
House extant:	no
Historical notes:	

The house was built by James Saville Yates.

He was the son of James Henry and Mary Adeline Reed Yates.

Clara Louise Campbell Yates was the daughter of Joseph K. Campbell of Ambler, PA. She had previously been married to Harold Grove Knight, Jr. with whom she had resided in Ambler, PA.

At the time of his death, Yates was residing on Davison Street in Sag Harbor.

Yates, John Carrington (1883-1951)

Occupation(s);	entertainers and associated professions -
	     member, Nat Goodwin Co. (stage actors)
	 capitalist - real estate manager for William Vincent Astor
	     (aka Vincent Astor)*

Civic Activism:	a founder and secretary, East Hampton Chapter, United World Federalist

Marriage(s):	M/1 – 1912-div. 1926 – Helen A Schley (d. 1975)
	 M/2 – 1937-div. 1942 – Frances Wise
	 M/3 – 1943-1951 – Linda L. Lindeberg (1915-1973)
	     - artist - abstract
	         interior designer - decorated New York City's mayor's
	             residence, *Gracie Mansion*,
	             during the La Guardia administration

Address:	LaForest Road, East Hampton
Name of estate:	
Year of construction:	
Style of architecture:	
Architect(s):	
Landscape architect(s):	
House extant: no	
Historical notes:	

    In 1946 Yates purchased Francis Newton's art studio and relocated it to LaForest Road. [*The East Hampton Star* December 12. 1946, p. 5.]
    He was the son of Walter Yates of Stockport, England.
    Helen A. Schley Yates was the daughter of Dr. Fayette Schley. She subsequently married Curtenius Gillette, Sr., the son of Dr. Walter Roberts and Mrs. Anne T. Gillette of NYC.
    John Carrington and Helen A. Schley Yates's daughter Helen married Howard Boulton, Jr., the son of Howard and Grace Russell Jones Boulton, Sr. of Hewlett Bay Park, NY. [*See* Spinzia, *Long Island's Prominent Families in the Town of Hempstead* – Boulton entry.] Helen later married Mario G. Fernandez and Henry Kilburn Riggs.
    Frances Wise Yates was the daughter of James Vincent Wise of Newark, NJ.
    Linda L. Lindeberg Yates was the daughter of the noted architect Harrie Thomas Lindeberg and his wife Lucia E. Hull Lindeberg of *West Gate Lodge* in Matinecock. Linda subsequently married the noted artist Giorgio Cavallon with whom she resided in Manhattan. [*See* Spinzia, *Long Island's Prominent North Shore Families, vol. I* – Lindeberg entry]
    *[For information about William Vincent Astor's Sands Point estate *Cloverly Manor*, see Spinzia, *Long Island's Prominent North Shore Families, vol. I* – Astor entry.]

Zalles, Jorje Ezequiel, Sr. (1872-1954)
aka Jorge Ezequiel Zalles, Sr.

Occupation(s):	attorney	
	capitalist -	secretary, Bolivian Railway Co.
	diplomat -	secretary, Bolivian Legation, London, 1900-1903;
		secretary and *charge d'affairs*, Bolivian Legation, Washington, DC, 1903-1905
	financier -	chairman of board, Banco de la Nacion Bolivia, 1911-1920;
		financial advisor, Bolivian delegation to the United Nations, 1953;
		financial advisor, Bolivian Embassy, Washington, DC
	shipping -	vice-president, W. R. Grace & Co.
Civic Activism:	governor, Devon Yacht Club	

Marriage(s): M/1 – 1900-1951 – Arcadia Calderon (1879-1951)
 - Civic Activism: member, Women's Voluntary Services during World War II
 M/2 – Rose ____

Address: 18 Cranberry Lane, Amagansett
Name of estate:
Year of construction: 1910
Style of architecture: Shingle
Architect(s): Tietig and Lee designed the house (for J. H. Levering)
House extant: yes
Builder: Thomas E. Babcock
Historical notes:

The 4,896-square-foot, six-bedroom house was built by Richmond Levering, Sr. for his mother Julia Henderson Levering after the death of her husband. In 1930 Zalles purchased the house. [*The New York Times* April 6, 1930, p. 52.]

He was the son of Ezequiel and Balbina Soto Zalles of Bolivia.

Arcadia Calderon Zalles was the daughter of Bolivian Minister to the United States Ignacio Calderon.

Jorje Ezequiel and Arcadia Calderon Zalles, Sr.'s daughter Leonor married Emile C. Freeland of Manhattan and New Orleans, LA. Their daughter Martha married Francis John Pettee of Manhattan. Their daughter Maria, who was the founder and director for twenty years of the East Harlem Recreation Center in Manhattan, did not marry. Their son Robert married Maria Esperanza Santivanez, the daughter of Luis Santivanez of La Paz, Bolivia, and resided in La Paz, Bolivia. Their son Reginald resided in Boston, MA. Their son John resided in La Paz, Bolivia. In 1927 their son George Ezequiel Zalles, Jr. died at the age of twenty-six. [*The New York Times* February 21, 1927, p. 17.]

The house was later owned by Richard Seymour Jackson. In 1986 it was purchased by Lucy Allison Bishopric Cookson.

The main residence, a two-bedroom, one-bath guest house, and 5.2 acres were for sale in 2014. The asking price was $13 million. In 2015 the price was reduced to $11.8 million.

Zamichow, Bernard (1917-1980)

Occupation(s):	advertising executive - chairman of board, Lambert Agency

Marriage(s):	1954-1980 – Nadine Cherner (1926-2013)
	   - landscape architect
	       writer - free lance

Address:	32 Ocean Avenue, East Hampton
Name of estate:	
Year of construction:	1889
Style of architecture:	Shingle
Architect(s):	
Landscape architect(s):	
Builder:	James L'Hommedieu
House extant: yes	
Historical notes:	

The twelve-bedroom, eight-and-a-half-bath, 8,000-square-foot house, originally named *Clifford-by-the-Sea*, was built by Robert Southgate Bowne. It was later owned by Zamichow. [*The East Hampton Star* March 22, 1979, p. 22.]

He was the son of Joseph and Rebecca Zamichow of New York.

Nadine Cerner Zamichow was the daughter of Joseph and Ruth Cherner of Washington, DC. Nadine subsequently married James B. Liberman.

Zaslav, David M. (b. 1960)

Occupation(s):	attorney - member, Le Boeuf, Lamb, Leiby, and MacRae capitalist - president, CEO, and director, Discovery Communications Holding LLC; president, Discovery Communications, Inc.; president, cable and domestic television, NBC; president, NBC Universal Media, LLC; president, NBC domestic television distribution; director, Grupo Televisa, SAB; director, Univision Communications, Inc.; director, Respond TV; director, Sirius Radio educator - adjunct professor, Fordham University, The Bronx, NY
Civic Activism:	director, National Cable and Television Association; director, The Cable Center for Communications; director, Skills for America's Future; director, USC Shoah Foundation; trustee, Mount Sinai Medical Center; director, The Advertising Council; trustee, Paley Center for Media, NYC; trustee, State University of New York at Binghamton, Binghamton, NY; trustee, Boston University, Boston, MA
Marriage(s):	1987 – Pamela Eisnger
Address:	20 Drew Lane, East Hampton
Name of estate:	
Year of construction:	
Style of architecture:	Contemporary with French Elements
Architect(s):	
Landscape architect(s):	
House extant: yes	
Historical notes:	

The house, which had been uninhabited for many years and in need of refurbishing, was previously owned by Leonard Stern. In 1987 he sold it to Jerry Della Femina for $3.4 million. Della Femina spend an additional $6 million remodeling the house. In 2012 Zaslav purchased the house from Della Femina for $24.5 million.

Born in Brooklyn, he married his high school sweetheart.

The Zaslovs have three children.

Zellweger, Renee Kathleen (b. 1969)

Occupation(s):	entertainers and associated professions - motion picture actress*
	restaurateur - co-owner, Blue Parrot
Civic Activism:	member, Swiss government's HIV prevention campaign, 2005;
	benefactor, The Great Initiative (supports gender equality)
Marriage(s):	2005-annulled 2005 – Kenneth Arnold Chesney (b. 1968)
	- entertainers and associated professions -
	country music singer and composer**;
	motion picture producer, "The Boys of Fall"
Address:	30 Egypt Lane, East Hampton
Name of estate:	
Year of construction:	1884
Style of architecture:	Long Island Farmhouse
Architect(s):	
Landscape architect(s):	
Builder:	Henry S. Roscoe
House extant: yes	
Historical notes:	

In 1884 Hannah M. Worthington purchased the house from its builder for $2,800. It passed through various members of the family until it was purchased by John Mascheroni who made it his residence from 1974 to 1982. It was later owned by Olivia and Catherine Pennington, who sold the house to Zellweger for $2.15 million in 2003.

She is the daughter of Emil Erich and Kjelifrid Irene Andreassen Zellweger of Texas.

*Renee has won an Academy Award, a BAFTA Award, three Golden Globe Awards, and three Screen Actors Guild Awards.

Kenneth Arnold Chesney is the son of David and Karen Chandler Chesney of Corryton, Tennessee.

**Kenneth has won six awards from the Country Music Association.

In 2015 Zellweger listed the 2,000-square-foot, four-bedroom, three-bath house for sale. The asking price was $4.65 million.

Zevely, James William, Sr. (1861-1927)

Occupation(s):	attorney - partner, Zevely, Givens, and Stoutz*
	politician - secretary, Missouri State Labor Bureau;
	Missouri State Librarian
Marriage(s):	1908-1927 – Jane Clay (b. 1862)
Address:	Lily Pond Lane, East Hampton
Name of estate:	
Year of construction:	1915
Style of architecture:	
Architect(s):	
Landscape architect(s):	
Builder:	Edward M. Gay, house and garage
House extant: unconfirmed	
Historical notes:	

The house, originally named *Dune Top*, was built by William Thaw III. [*The East Hampton Star* September 11, 1914, p. 5, and November 19, 1915, p. 1.] In 1922 it was purchased by Zevely for $85,000. [*The East Hampton Star* December 1, 1922, p. 5.]

The Social Directory of Southampton, Long Island, 1931 lists Mrs. James W. Zevely [Sr.] as residing on Lily Pond Lane, East Hampton.

She was from Mexico, MO.

James William Zevely, Sr. was the son of Thaddeus and Mary Ann Miller Zevely of Linn, MO.

James William and Jane Clay Zevely, Sr.'s daughter Jane married Lloyd Hilton Smith of *Linden* in Southampton and, later, Alfred Sherman Foote, the son of Arthur E. Foote of Englewood, NJ, with whom she resided in Bedford Village, NY. [*See* Spinzia, *Long Island's Prominent Families in the Town of Southampton* – Smith entry.]

*Zevely was the attorney for Sinclair Consolidated Oil Corporation and the personal attorney of Henry Ford Sinclair, Sr. of Kings Point. Sinclair named his famous race horse *Zev* after Zevely. [*See* Spinzia, *Long Island's Prominent North Shore Families, vol. II* – Sinclair entry – and Sinclair entry, this volume.]

Zuckerman, Mortimer Benjamin (b. 1937)

Occupation(s):	capitalist - co-founder, executive chairman, and CEO, Boston Properties (real estate investment trust); vice-president and chief financial officer, Cabot, Cabot and Forbes (real estate firm)
	advertising executive - director, Snyder Communications (later, Havas Advertising)
	publisher - owner, *New York Daily News*, NYC; owner and editor-in-chief, *U. S. News and World Report*; owner and chairman of board, *The Atlantic Monthly*; owner, *Fast Company*; owner, *New York Post*, NYC
	educator - associate professor, Harvard Business School, Cambridge, MA; member of faculty, Yale University, New Haven, CT
	journalist - columnist, *U. S. News and World Report*; columnist, *New York Daily News*, NYC
	entertainers and associated professions - television commentator; producer, "The McLaughlin Group"; producer, "Charlie Rose"
Civic Activism:	chairman, Conference of Presidents of Major American Jewish Organizations;
	member, Honorary Delegation to Jerusalem, 2008;
	trustee, New York University, NYC;
	trustee, Aspen Institute;
	trustee, Memorial Sloan–Kettering Cancer Center, NYC;
	trustee, Hole in the Wall Gang Fund;
	trustee, Center for Communications;
	member, J. P. Morgan's National Advisory Board;
	president, board of trustees, Dana Farber Cancer Institute, Boston, MA
Marriage(s):	1996-div. 2001 – Maria Prather (b. 1956) - art historian and curator
Address:	Drew Lane, East Hampton
Name of estate:	
Year of construction:	
Style of architecture:	Eclectic
Architect(s):	
Landscape architect(s):	
House extant: yes	
Historical notes:	

Mortimer Benjamin Zuckerman purchased the house from Peter George Peterson.
He is the son of Abraham and Esther Zuckerman of Canada.
Maria Prather Zuckerman is the daughter of John and Jane Prather of Salina, Kansas. Maria subsequently married Jonathan D. Schiller and resides in the East Hampton hamlet of Three Mile Harbor.

APPENDICES

Table of Contents for Appendices

Architects	651
Civic Activism	670
Estate Names	681
Landscape Architects	691
Maiden Names	697
Occupations	733
Rehabilitative Secondary Uses of Surviving Estate Houses	754
Statesmen and Diplomats Who Resided in East Hampton	755
Village Locations of Estates	758
Biographical Sources Consulted	768
Maps Consulted for Estate Locations	769
About the Authors	770

Architects

See the surname entry to ascertain if more than one architect was involved in designing the various buildings on an estate. This list reflects their Town of East Hampton commissions and includes the original and subsequent owners of the estates. When the owner who contracted with the architect is known, it is indicated by an asterisk.

David Adjaye

    * Lindemann, Adam Marc   Montauk

Albro and Lindeberg

Burton, Jane Erdman	*Coxwould*	East Hampton
* Cockcroft, Edward Truesdell	*Little Burlees*	East Hampton
d'Olier, Franklin Woolman, Jr.		East Hampton
* Erdmann, Dr. John Frederic	*Coxwould*	East Hampton
Hedges, Burke Osborn		East Hampton
Hedges, Dayton aka William Dayton Hedges		East Hampton
* Hollister, Dr. Frederick Kellogg		East Hampton
Morse, Tyler		East Hampton
Sandelman, Jonathan Everett		East Hampton
Schulmann, Lowell M.	*Beechwood*	East Hampton
Weinstein, Joseph		East Hampton

Lewis Colt Albro

    * King, Hamilton   *Spindrift*   East Hampton

James Lawrence Aspinwall

    * Aspinwall, James Lawrence   East Hampton

Grosvenor Atterbury

Brockman, Donald J.	(house and 1925 gardener's cottage are attributed)	East Hampton
Dragon, Edward F. [*see* Ossorio entry]	*The Creeks*	East Hampton
Flinn, Lawrence, Sr.	*Sea Song* (house and 1925 gardener's cottage are attributed)	East Hampton
* Herter, Albert	*Près Choisis / The Creeks*	East Hampton
Leith, Donald E.		East Hampton
McCord, David Walter	*Hither House*	East Hampton
Miner, Mary Louise Woodin	(1927 alterations)	East Hampton
Ossorio, Alfonso Angel	*The Creeks*	East Hampton
Perelman, Ronald Owen		East Hampton
* Rice, Dr. Clarence Charles		East Hampton
* Richards, Benjamin, Jr.	*Clas-des-Lilas*	East Hampton
Richards, Louisa Verplanck [*see* B. Richards, Jr. entry]		East Hampton
* Salembier, Paul Albert	*Seacroft* (1927 alterations)	East Hampton
* Wilborg, Frank Bestow	*The Dunes*	East Hampton

Architects

Grosvenor Atterbury (cont'd)

    * Woodin, William Hartman, Sr.   (house and 1925 gardener's cottage are attributed)   East Hampton

Harry Bates with Booker and Lund Architects

    * Macklowe, Harry B.   East Hampton

Boris Baranovich

    * Browne, Christopher H.   *Chateau Amorois*   East Hampton

Rolf W. Bauhan

    * Church, Richard E.   Montauk

    Drexler, Millard S.   Montauk
      aka Mickey Drexler

    Lindemann, Adam Marc   Montauk

    Morrissey, Paul   *Eothen*   Montauk

    Warhol, Andy   *Eothen*   Montauk
      aka Andrew Warhola, Jr.

James Biber

    Hirtenstein, Michael   Montauk

    Levy–Church, Kenneth   Montauk
      aka Kenneth Wayne Church

Christopher Bickford

    Bishopric, Allison, Jr.   *Windy Dune* (1992-1994 alterations)   Amagansett

    * Cookson, Lucy Bishopric   *Windy Dune* (1992-1994 alterations)   Amagansett

    Rawson, Joseph, Jr.   *Red Roof* (1992-1994 alterations)   Amagansett

William Welles Bosworth

    * Newton, Francis   *Fulling Mill Farm* (utilized Grosvenor Atterbury's plans)   East Hampton

    Robinson, Lucius Franklin, Jr.   *Fulling Mill Farm* (utilized Grosvenor Atterbury's plans)   East Hampton

Walter E. Brady

    Gardiner, Robert Alexander   *Maidstone Hall* (1901 alterations)   East Hampton

    Kennedy, Arthur   (1901 alterations)   East Hampton
      [*see* Terbell entry]

    * Terbell, Edward Dyer   *Maidstone Hall* (1901 alterations)   East Hampton

    Terbell, Henry S., Sr.   (1901 alterations)   East Hampton

Briggs and Corman

    Dean, Howard Brush, Jr.   East Hampton

    * Satterthwaite, James Sheafe, Sr.   East Hampton

    Thompson, Charles Griswold   East Hampton

G. Piers Brookfield

    * Shepherd, Myrtle Abby Leach   East Hampton

Architects

Roger Bullard

    Feldstein, Dr. Gary   East Hampton

  * James, Ellery Sedgwick, Sr.   *Heather Dune*   East Hampton
      aka William Ellery Sedgwick James, Sr.

    Miner, Mary Louise Woodin   East Hampton

    Morton, Peter   East Hampton

    Rounick, Jack A.   East Hampton

  * Salembier, Paul Albert   *Seacroft*   East Hampton

Gordon Bunshaft

  * Bunshaft, Gordon   *Travertine House*   East Hampton

    Maharam, Donald H.   East Hampton

    Stewart, Martha Helen Kostyra   East Hampton

Chimacoff and Peterson

  * Lowenstein, Peter   Montauk

Craig Claiborne

  * Claiborne, Craig   East Hampton

Kang H. Chang

  * Schultz, Howard Mark   (2011 alterations)   East Hampton

    Steinberg, Robert Michael   (2001 alterations)   East Hampton

Peter Cook

    Adair, Frank Earl   *Sherwood* (1992 alterations)   East Hampton

    Chisholm, Edward de Clifford   *Onadune* (1992 alterations)   East Hampton

    Johnson, Servetus Fisher   *Onadune* (1992 alterations)   East Hampton

  * Shafran, Irving   (1992 alterations)   East Hampton

Richard A. Cook (CookFox Associates)

    Dougherty, Frances Ann Cannon (Hersey)   East Hampton

    Fraser, Alexander   *Wilsheron*   East Hampton

    Hollister, Dr. Frederick Kellogg   East Hampton

  * Rosenstein, Barry   East Hampton

    Sweetser, Jesse William, Sr.   East Hampton

Thierry W. Despont

    Church, Richard E.   (2007 alterations)   Montauk

  * Drexler, Millard S.   (2007 alterations)   Montauk
      aka Mickey Drexler

  * Klein, Calvin   East Hampton
      aka Calvin Richard Klein

    Lindemann, Adam Marc   (2007 alterations)   Montauk

    Madoff, Bernard Lawrence   (2007 alterations)   Montauk

    Morrissey, Paul   (2007 alterations)   Montauk

  * Roth, Steven   (2007 alterations)   Montauk

Architects

Thierry W. Despont (cont'd)

Warhol, Andy aka Andrew Warhola, Jr.	(2007 alterations)	Montauk

Alfredo De Vido

* Mercer, Norman J.	(1982 addition of 2,200-square-foot shop, sculpture gallery, and greenhouse)	East Hampton

Cyrus Lazelle Warner Eidlitz

Edwards, Dr. Ogden Matthias	*Dunehurst*	East Hampton
* Eidlitz, Cyrus Lazelle Warner	*Overlea*	East Hampton
Gerli, Anne Woodin Harvey	*Maya*	East Hampton
Gram, Carl William, Jr.	*Maya*	East Hampton
Nichols, Harold Willis, Jr.	*Dunehurst*	East Hampton
* Quackenbush, Schuyler		East Hampton

George A. Eldredge

Ashplant, Frederick Bryant, Sr.	*The Dolphins* (1899 alterations and 1902 stables)	East Hampton
Cummins, Edward Swete	*Greycroft* (1897 alterations)	East Hampton
* Dunbar, Arthur T.		East Hampton
Heuser, Miss Maria S. [*see* C. F. Ogden entry]		East Hampton
* Ogden, Miss Clara Foster		East Hampton
* Osborne, Mrs. George A.		East Hampton
Ramee, Joseph Russell	*Twinmill*	East Hampton
Stokes, The Reverend John Dunlap		East Hampton
* Strong, Theron George	*The Dolphins* (1899 alterations and 1902 stables)	East Hampton
* Vaughan, Eliza Jennie Potter	*Beulahside*	East Hampton
* Woodhouse, Lorenzo Guernsey	*Greycroft* (1897 addition)	East Hampton

George A. Eldredge and John Custis Lawrence

* Benjamin, William Wallace, Jr.	*Crossways*	East Hampton
Benjamin, William Wallace, III	*Crossways*	East Hampton
Lilley, Alexander Neil, Sr.	*Crossways*	East Hampton
* Wessel, Homer Augustus, Sr.	*Mill Crest*	East Hampton

Aymar Embury II

* Adams, Charles Henry	(1930s alterations)	East Hampton
* Adams, John Cranford		East Hampton
Bell, Emily Carrington Trowbridge		East Hampton
Breen, Daniel Anthony, Jr.	*Furtherfield*	East Hampton
* Chauncey, Alexander Wallace	*Our Place*	East Hampton
* Embury, Aymar, II	*Third House* (1929 alterations)	East Hampton
Hodson, Dr. James M. [*see* Adams entry]	(1930s alterations)	East Hampton

Architects

Aymar Embury II (cont'd)

* Homans, Marion Bennett		East Hampton
Kingsley, Virginia Pulleyn		East Hampton
Lundberg, John K. [*see* Adams entry]		East Hampton
* Mairs, Olney Blanchard, Sr.	(1930s alterations)	East Hampton
Miller, Isaac W.	(1929 alterations)	East Hampton
* Roberts, George Hewitt, Jr.	*Furtherfield*	East Hampton
Schey, Robert Paul	*Lauralawn*	East Hampton
Shepherd, Myrtle Abby Leach	(1948 alterations)	East Hampton
Wheelock, William Amy	(1929-1930 alterations)	East Hampton

Ferguson and Shamamian

Bouvier, John Vernou, Jr.	*Lasata* (c. 2007 alterations)	East Hampton
Bouvier, Maude Frances Sergeant	*Lasata* (c. 2007 alterations)	East Hampton
Gardiner, Lion	(c. 2007 alterations)	East Hampton
Hufty, Frances May Archbold	(c. 2007 alterations)	East Hampton
* Krakoff, Reed	(c. 2007 alterations)	East Hampton
Lundberg, John K. [*see* Adams entry]		East Hampton
Martin, Laura Elizabeth Young	(c. 2007 alterations)	East Hampton
Meehan, Joseph Ansbro	(c. 2007 alterations)	East Hampton
Schurman, George Wellington	*Beachclose* (c. 2007 alterations)	East Hampton

Francis Fleetwood

Andrews, William Loring	(1992 alterations)	Montauk
* Campbell, David	*Burnt Point*	East Hampton
* Colle, Jeffery		East Hampton
* Dennis, Thomas	(c. 1994 alterations)	Montauk
* Donovan, Roberta Gosman	(1992 alterations)	Montauk
Fisher, Carl Graham, Sr.	(c. 1994 alterations)	Montauk
* Fleetwood, Francis		Amagansett
Mnuchin, Alan Geoffrey		East Hampton
Rahr, Stewart J.	*Burnt Point*	East Hampton
Sanger, Henry	(c. 1994 alterations)	Montauk
Sanger, Lilian	*Moorland* (c. 1994 alterations)	Montauk
Upright, Frederick	(1992 alterations)	Montauk
Vogel, George [*see* Andrews entry]	(1992 alterations)	Montauk
Wagner, Miss H. Corinne [*see* Andrews entry]	(1992 alterations)	Montauk

Architects

Eugene Lawrence Futterman

	Beale, Phelan, Sr.	*Grey Gardens* (1980 alterations)	East Hampton
*	Bradlee, Benjamin Crowninshield, Sr.	*Grey Gardens* (1980 alterations)	East Hampton
	Hill, Robert Carmer	*Grey Gardens* (1980 alterations)	East Hampton
	Macklowe, Harry B.		East Hampton
*	Madoff, Bernard Lawrence aka Bernie Madoff		Montauk
	Phillips, Fleming Stanhope	(1980 alterations)	East Hampton
	Roth, Steven		Montauk
*	Tishman, Peter Valentine		East Hampton

Edward M. Gay

	Baldwin, Alexander Rae, III aka Alec Baldwin	(1914 alterations)	Amagansett
*	Hamlin, Harry Leon	*Stony Hill Farm* (1914 alterations)	Amagansett
	Potter, Jeffrey Brackett	*Stony Hill Farm* (1914 alterations)	Amagansett

Andrew S. Gordon

*	Browne, Christopher H.		East Hampton
	Rosenstein, Barry		East Hampton

Isaac Henry Green II

	Bishop, Bennett	*Pudding Hill* (designed house and 1906 extension)	East Hampton
	Chace, Franklin M.	*Gone With the Wind* (1889 alterations)	East Hampton
	Cummins, Stephen Swete	*Greycroft*	East Hampton
	Dayton, E. T. [see Huntting entry]		East Hampton
	de Rose, Edward	*Millfield* (1889 alterations)	East Hampton
	Douglas, Graham	(1889 alterations)	East Hampton
	Ethridge, George		East Hampton
	Ford, James Bishop	*Pudding Hill* (designed house and 1906 extension)	East Hampton
	Friedman, Marvin Ross		East Hampton
	Hare, Richard Vincent	(1889 alterations)	East Hampton
*	Herrick, Dr. Everett	*Pudding Hill* (designed house and 1906 extension)	East Hampton
	Huntting, Annie		East Hampton
	Manson, Thomas Lincoln, III	*Millfield* (1889 alterations)	East Hampton
	Miller, Jeremiah, IV	(1889 alterations)	East Hampton
*	Munroe, Dr. George E., Jr.	*Wayside*	East Hampton
	Munroe, Marjory	*Wayside*	East Hampton

Architects

Isaac Henry Green II (cont'd)

Peddy, John Richard	*Pudding Hill* (designed house and 1906 extension)	East Hampton
* Phillips, Martha Bagg		East Hampton
Schey, Robert Paul	*Lauralawn*	East Hampton
* Schmidt, Max Eberhardt aka Max Everhart Smith		East Hampton
* Skidmore, John Drake	(supervised design)	East Hampton
Skidmore, Samuel Tredwell, II	*Idlerest* (supervised design)	East Hampton
Van Rensselaer, Kilian	*Millfield* (1889 alterations)	East Hampton
Wheelock, John Hall	*Wuthering*	East Hampton
* Wheelock, William Almy		East Hampton
* Wheelock, Dr. William Efner	*Wuthering*	East Hampton
* Woodhouse, Lorenzo Guernsey	*Greycroft*	East Hampton

Howard Greenley

Green, Adolph	(1915 alterations)	East Hampton
* Roberts, Walter Scott	(1915 alterations)	East Hampton
Seligson, William	(1915 alterations)	East Hampton
Spring, Preston Brady, Sr.	(1915 alterations)	East Hampton
Weaver, Spencer Fullerton, Sr.	*Spencecliff* (1915 alterations)	East Hampton

Frank Greenwald

* Garten, Jeffery E.	*The Barn*	East Hampton

Jordan Lee Gruzen

* Gruzen, Jordan Lee		Amagansett

Charles Gwathmey

Amador, Paul A.		East Hampton
* Bronfman, Edgar Miles	(1990 alterations)	Amagansett
* Cogan, Marshall Stuart		East Hampton
* Cohn, Maurice J.		Amagansett
Cullman, Joseph Frederick, III		East Hampton
* de Menil, Francois aka Francois Conrad Thomas de Menil	*Toad Hall*	Amagansett
Fuhrman, Gary L.		East Hampton
Gagosian, Lawrence Gilbert		Amagansett
* Gwathmey, Charles	(2001 alterations)	Amagansett
* Gwathmey, Robert, Jr.	(house and art studio)	Amagansett
* Haupt, Melville I.		Amagansett
Kurzner, Dr. Rubin Raymond		Amagansett
Schultz, Howard Mark		East Hampton
* Sedacca, Joseph M.		East Hampton
* Semel, Terrance Steven	(2008 guest house)	Amagansett

Architects

Charles Gwathmey (cont'd)

* Spielberg, Steven Allan	*Quella Farm*	East Hampton
* Steinberg, Robert Michael		East Hampton
* Tolan, Michael aka Seymour Tuchow		Amagansett

James Hadley

* Cavett, Richard Alva	(designed second DeForest Road house)	Montauk

Hugh Hardy

* Spaeth, Eloise O'Mara		East Hampton
* Ranieri, Salvatore Anthony	(1999 guest house alterations)	East Hampton

Michael Robert Haverland

* Haverland, Michael Robert		East Hampton

Hewitt and Bottomley

* Bartlett, Edward Everett, Jr.	*Furtherlane*	Amagansett

Rick Hirt

Bishopric, Allison, Jr.	*Windy Dune* (2003 and 2006 alterations)	Amagansett
* Cookson, Lucy Bishopric	*Windy Dune* (2003 and 2006 alterations)	Amagansett
Rawson, Joseph, Jr.	*Red Roof* (2003 and 2006 alterations)	Amagansett

Francis Burrall Hoffman, Jr.

Brockman, Daniel David	(1917 playhouse)	East Hampton
* Woodhouse, Lorenzo Easton	(1917 playhouse)	East Hampton

Hart Howerton

* Baron, Ronald Stephen		East Hampton

Arthur C. Jackson

Bouvier, John Vernou, Jr.	*Lasata*	East Hampton
Bouvier, Maude Frances Sergeant	*Lasata*	East Hampton
Gardiner, Lion		East Hampton
Hufty, Frances May Archbold		East Hampton
Krakoff, Reed		East Hampton
* Krech, Dr. Shepard, Sr.	*Briar Patch*	East Hampton
Martin, Laura Elizabeth Young		East Hampton
Meehan, Joseph Ansbro		East Hampton
* Schurman, George Wellington	*Beachclose*	East Hampton
Whittle, Chris aka H. Christopher Whittle	*Briar Patch*	East Hampton

Norman Jaffe

Altachul, Arthur Goodhart, Jr.		East Hampton
* Becker, Harold		East Hampton
* Cohen, Peter Anthony		East Hampton
* Gruss, Martin David		East Hampton

Architects

Norman Jaffe (cont'd)

* Hamilton Chico aka Foreststorn Hamilton		East Hampton
* Hillman, Murray		East Hampton
* Krieger, Dr. Howard P.		Montauk
* Lloyds, Richard		East Hampton
* Stern, Joel Mark		East Hampton

Charles Peter Beauchamp Jefferys, Sr.

Craig, Dr. Stuart Lessley		East Hampton
Hobart, Henry Lee	*Sommariva*	East Hampton
* Jefferys, Charles Peter Beauchamp, Sr.	*Sommariva*	East Hampton
Mills, Abraham	*The Chalet*	East Hampton

Helen Louise Kendrick Johnson

* Johnson, Rossiter	*Thalatta Cottage*	Amagansett

George Keister

Dickerman, William Carter, Sr.	*Dune Dee*	East Hampton
* McAlpin, George Lodowich, Sr.	*Dune Alpin*	East Hampton
Nichols, Thomas S. [*see* McAlpin entry]		East Hampton

L. Bancel LaFarge

* Bishop, Dr. Louis Faugeres, Jr.	*Holiday*	East Hampton
Gianis, Socrates George, Sr.		East Hampton

John Custis Lawrence

Adair, Dr. Frank Earl	*Sherwood*	East Hampton
Alexander, Edward, Sr.	*Sterling–Haven*	East Hampton
* Avery, Edward Strong		East Hampton
Baker, John T., Jr.		East Hampton
* Baker, John T., Sr.		East Hampton
* Barton, Flora Benjamin McAlpin	(1929 alterations)	East Hampton
Chisholm, Edward de Clifford	*Onadune*	East Hampton
* Cody, Frederick	*Fairways*	East Hampton
* Coppell, Herbert	*White-Cottage-By-the-Sea*	East Hampton
Davies, Francis Herbert	*Tidelands* (1910 alterations)	East Hampton
Dean, Howard Brush, Jr.	(1910 alterations to servants' quarters)	East Hampton
Dickerman, William Carter, Sr.	*Dune Dee* (alterations)	East Hampton
Dougherty, Frances Ann Cannon (Hersey)		East Hampton
* Eastman, Joseph	(1916 alterations)	East Hampton
* Edwards, James McPherson		East Hampton
* Evans, Benjamin Franklin	*Dunemead*	East Hampton
Fraser, Alexander		East Hampton
Havens, Valentine Britton		East Hampton

Architects

John Custis Lawrence (cont'd)

Helier, David	(1911 alterations)	East Hampton
Heyman, Stephen J.	*Dunemead*	East Hampton
Hinton, Alfred Post	*Roads Meet*	East Hampton
Hirschfeld, Elie		East Hampton
* Hollister, Dr. Frederick Kellogg	[his second house]	East Hampton
* Gordon, George Breed	(1910 garage)	East Hampton
Gowen, George W., II		East Hampton
Helier, David	(1911 alterations)	East Hampton
* Helm, John E.		East Hampton
Ireland, Anna Mary Brown	(1910 garage)	East Hampton
Jenkins, Edward Everett	(1910 garage)	East Hampton
* Johnson, Servetus Fisher	*Onadune*	East Hampton
* Kelley, William Vallandigham, Sr.	(1911 alterations)	East Hampton
* LaMonte, George Mason		East Hampton
* Lardner, Ringgold Wilmer, Sr. aka Ring Lardner	*Iona Dune / The Mange*	East Hampton
* Lawrence, John Custis		East Hampton
Lee, James Thomas	(1916 alterations)	East Hampton
* Mayo, Miss Marie Louise	*Bonnie Dune*	East Hampton
McAlpin, George Lodowich, Sr.	*Dune Alpin*	East Hampton
McAlpin, Malcolm Evans	*Dunemead* (alterations)	East Hampton
Nichols, Thomas S. [see McAlpin entry]	(alterations)	East Hampton
* Oakley, Ralph Lawrence		East Hampton
* Onderdonk, Dr. Thomas Williams		East Hampton
* Osborne, Burnett Mulford		East Hampton
* Quackenbush, Schuyler		East Hampton
Ramee, Joseph Russell	*Twinmill*	East Hampton
* Rice, Henry Grantland aka Grantland Rice		East Hampton
* Richy, The Reverend Alban, Sr.	*Rosebrae*	East Hampton
Rosenstein, Barry		East Hampton
Ryan, Frederick Behrens	*East of 69*	East Hampton
Satterthwaite, James Sheafe, Sr.	(1910 alterations to servants' quarters)	East Hampton
Scheerer, Joseph Durand, Sr.		East Hampton
Scheerer, William, II		East Hampton
Schmidt, Dederick Herman		East Hampton
Shafran, Irving		East Hampton
Smith, Warren G.	(1910 alterations)	East Hampton
Spalding, Jesse, II	*Pineleigh* (1910 garage)	East Hampton
Stanton, Dr. Frederick Lester		East Hampton

Architects

John Custis Lawrence (cont'd)

Sutphen, Henry Randolph, Jr.	*Bowling Green*	East Hampton
Sutphen, Henry Randolph, Sr.	*Bowling Green*	East Hampton
Sweetser, Jesse William, Sr.		East Hampton
Taylor, Irving Howland		East Hampton
Thompson, Charles Griswold	(1910 alterations to servants' quarters)	East Hampton
Thorpe, H. C.	(1910 alterations)	East Hampton
* Van Brunt, Dr. Arthur Hoffman, Sr.	*The Breezes*	East Hampton
* Voorhees, Dr. James Ditmars aka Dr. James Ditmars Van Voorhees		East Hampton
Warburton, Consuelo Vanderbilt		East Hampton
Wheeler, John Neville		East Hampton

Leinau and Nash

* Carson, William Moore, Sr.		East Hampton
Duryea, Walter Bartow		East Hampton
McConnell, David Hall, III		East Hampton
McCormick, Robert Elliot		East Hampton
Sinclair, Earle Westwood	*Fairlawn*	East Hampton

Harrie Thomas Lindeberg

* Alcott, Clarence Frank		East Hampton

James Brown Lord

Cordier, Auguste Julien, Jr.	*Kyalami*	East Hampton
* Drew, John, Jr.	*Kyalami*	East Hampton
Wasey, Louis Rice		East Hampton

David Mann

Gardiner, Robert Alexander	*Maidstone Hall* (1990 alterations)	East Hampton
Kennedy, Arthur [*see* Terbell entry]	(1990 alterations)	East Hampton
Terbell, Edward Dyer	(1990 alterations)	East Hampton
Terbell, Henry S., Sr.	*Maidstone Hall* (1990 alterations)	East Hampton

Peter Marino

Krech, Dr. Shepard, Sr.	*Briar Patch* (guest house and 1989-1991 alterations to main residence)	East Hampton
Whittle, Chris aka H. Christopher Whittle	*Briar Patch* (guest house and 1989-1991 alterations to main residence)	East Hampton

Alexander McIlvaine

* Rumbough, Stanley Maddox, Jr.		East Hampton

McKim, Mead and White

Adams, Grant		Montauk
Agnew, Dr. Cornelius Rea, Sr.		Montauk
Andrews, William Loring		Montauk

Architects

McKim, Mead and White (cont'd)

* Benson, Arthur W.	*Weeweecho*	Montauk
Benson, Mary	*Weeweecho*	Montauk
Biggs, Florence		Montauk
Brisbane, Arthur		Montauk
Cavett, Richard Alva aka Dick Cavett	[owned two houses in Montauk]	Montauk
Darby, James L.		Montauk
Dean, Howard Brush, Jr.	(1893-1894 alterations are attributed)	East Hampton
de Forest, Henry Grant		Montauk
Dennis, Thomas		Montauk
Donovan, Roberta Gosman		Montauk
DuVal, Guy	*Awepesha*	Montauk
Eastman, Erik		Montauk
Fisher, Carl Graham, Sr.	[owned two houses in Montauk]	Montauk
Goddard, Sidney		Montauk
Hourtel, Frank		Montauk
Hoyt, Alfred Miller		Montauk
Levi, Charles Matthew		Montauk
Lundbergh, Holga	*Bayberry*	Montauk
Marsh, Marion Bolton	*Windway*	Montauk
Miller, L. W.		Montauk
Orr, Alexander Ector		Montauk
Sanger, Henry		Montauk
Sanger, Lilian	*Moorland*	Montauk
Satterthwaite, James Sheafe, Sr.	(1893-1894 alterations are attributed)	East Hampton
Schnabel, Julian		Montauk
Sischy, Ingrid Barbara		Montauk
Smith, Dr. Dewey		Montauk
Smith, Hazanne		Montauk
* Thompson, Charles Griswold	(1893-1894 alterations are attributed)	East Hampton
Tweed, Harrison	*Tick Hall*	Montauk
Upright, Frederick		Montauk
Vogel, George [see Andrews entry]		Montauk
Wagner, Miss H. Corinne [see Andrews entry]		Montauk
Weber, Bruce		Montauk

Richard Meier

* Hoffman, David Lehman, Sr.		East Hampton
* Saltzman, Renny B.		East Hampton

Architects

Bruce Dean Nagel
    Combs, Sean John   East Hampton
        aka Puff Daddy, Diddy, and P. Diddy
    * Shyer, Henry   East Hampton

Thomas Nash
    * Nash, Stephen Edward   East Hampton
    * Nash, Thomas   East Hampton
    Stern, Robert Arthur Morton   East Hampton

Nelson and Chadwick
    * Spaeth, Otto Lucien, Sr.   East Hampton

Julian and Barbara Neski
    * Chalif, Seymour Hunt   East Hampton
    Seegal, Frederic Milton   East Hampton

Frank Eaton Newton
    * Appleton, Robert Wilmarth   *Nid de Papillion*   East Hampton
    Johnson, James Loring   *Nid de Papillion*   East Hampton

Joseph Septimus Osborne
    * Osborne, Joseph Septimus   East Hampton
    Osborne, Nelson Cook, Sr.   East Hampton

Peabody, Wilson, and Brown
    * Brown, Lathrop   *The Windmill*   Montauk

Tamer Pepemehmetoglu
    * Mitchell, Christopher   (2015 renovation)   East Hampton
    Nesbit, Elizabeth Clossey   *Seaward*   East Hampton
                                                  (2015 renovation)

Charles A. Platt
    * Pruyn, Miss Mary Lansing   East Hampton
    * Pruyn, Miss Neltje Knickerbocker   East Hampton

Polhemus and Coffin
    * Jenney, William Sherman   *Little Close*   East Hampton
    * Kimball, Alden   *Eastern View*   East Hampton
    * Massey, Maurice Richardson, Jr.   *Pond's Edge*   East Hampton
    * Yates, James Saville   East Hampton

Lawrence Randolph
    Kessner, Steven   East Hampton

James Renwick, Jr.
    * Gallatin, Frederic   *Breezy Lawn*   East Hampton
    Leonard, Stephen Joseph, Sr.   *Waterwood*   East Hampton

Ritzema and Perry
    * Cook, Harry   *Holly Hall*   East Hampton
    * Hopkinson, Russell   East Hampton

Architects

Jaquelen T. Robertson

    * Rose, Marshall   East Hampton

Brian Sawyer

    * Woodward, Shaun Anthony   (alterations)   East Hampton

Alfred A. Scheffer

    Accardi, Jack   Amagansett
        [*see* Scheffer entry]

    Light, Deborah   *Quail Hill*   Amagansett

    * Rubin, Samuel   *Hilly Close*   Amagansett

    * Scheerer, Paul Renner, Jr.   East Hampton

    * Scheffer, Alfred A.   Amagansett

    Schwagerl, Richard   Amagansett

    Schwagerl, Robert   Amagansett

    * Teetor, Charles Jessup   *Westernesse Farm*   Amagansett

Mott B. Schmidt

    * Ford, William Clay, Sr.   *Dunemere*   East Hampton

Samuel Tredwell Skidmore II

    * Skidmore, John Drake   East Hampton

    Skidmore, Samuel Tredwell, II   *Idlerest*   East Hampton

K. B. C. Smith

    Harper, Marion Clay, Jr.   Montauk

    Wasey, Louis Rice   Montauk

Stamberg Alferiat + Associates

    * Hoffman, Anita Vogel   (1997 alterations)   East Hampton

Frederick Stelle

    Avedon, Richard   (2009 alterations)   Montauk

Robert Arthur Morton Stern

    Cummins, Edward Swete   *Greycroft*   East Hampton
        (1980-1981 alterations to playhouse)

    * Mercer, Norman J.   East Hampton

    Nash, Thomas   (1961 alterations)   East Hampton

    * Stern, Robert Arthur Morton   (1961 alterations)   East Hampton

    Wheelock, John Hall   *Wuthering*   East Hampton
        (1979-1980 alterations)

    Wheelock, Dr. William Efner   *Wuthering*   East Hampton
        (1979-1980 alterations)

    Woodhouse, Lorenzo Guernsey   *Greycroft*   East Hampton
        (1980-1981 alterations to playhouse)

Penrose V. Stout

    * Wainwright, Carroll Livingston, Sr.   *Gullcrest*   East Hampton

William Strom

    * Beardsley, Samuel Arthur, Sr.   East Hampton

Mary Breck Vaill Talmage

    * Talmage, Mary Breck Vaill   East Hampton

Architects

Robert Tappan

    Bennett, Russell Conwell   East Hampton

  * Campbell, Nathaniel Adams, Sr.   *Camelot*   East Hampton

  * Coppell, Herbert   *White-Cottage-By-the-Sea*   East Hampton
                                                   (1928 alterations)

    Hirschfeld, Elie   (1928 alterations)   East Hampton

    Olin, John Merrill   East Hampton

    Ryan, Frederick Behrens, Sr.   *East of 69*   East Hampton

    Stokes, Lydia   East Hampton
       [*see* Campbell entry]

  * Warner, Eltinge Fowler, Jr.   *Cima Del Mundo*   East Hampton

Andrew Jackson Thomas

    Jackson, Elbert McGran   Montauk

  * Thomas, Andrew Jackson   Montauk

    Walker, Dr. William Henry, Jr.   Montauk

Joseph Greenleaf Thorp

    Bailey, Dr. Thedorus, II   *Dunemere*   East Hampton

    Barnes, Robert   *Rowdy Hall*   East Hampton
                                             (1926 alterations)

    Beale, Edith   *Grey Gardens*   East Hampton

    Beale, Phelan, Sr.   *Grey Gardens*   East Hampton

    Bellas, Alfred Constantine   East Hampton

    Beumont, Perry H.   East Hampton

    Bisco, Leonard Gerard   East Hampton

    Bock, Louis B.   East Hampton
       [*see* Thorp entry]

    Bon Jovi, Jon   East Hampton
       aka John Francis Bongiovi, Jr.

    Borden, Lewis Mercer, Sr.   *Seaholme*   East Hampton

    Bradlee, Benjamin Crowninshield, Sr.   *Grey Gardens*   East Hampton

  * Bradley, Andrew Coyle   East Hampton

    Briggs, James Branch   *Beehive*   East Hampton

    Callan, Erin M.   East Hampton

  * Cammann, George Philip, Jr.   *Seaholme*   East Hampton

    Carse, John Bradley   *End Cottage*   East Hampton

    Chace, Franklin M.   *Gone With the Wind*   East Hampton
                                          (1905 interior and exterior alterations)

    Chase, Chevy   East Hampton
       aka Cornelius Crane Chase

    Cleaves, Norman Smith   East Hampton

  * Davies, Francis Herbert   *Tidelands*   East Hampton

    de Rose, Edward   *Millfield*   East Hampton
                                      (1905 interior and exterior alterations)

    Douglas, Graham   (1905 interior and exterior alterations)   East Hampton

Architects

Joseph Greenleaf Thorp (cont'd)

Douglas, Robert Graham Dunn aka Robert Graham Dunn Douglass		East Hampton
Eastman, Joseph		East Hampton
Edwards, Harkness, Sr.		East Hampton
Eldredge, George A.	(1899 alterations)	East Hampton
Fiore, Christopher J. [*see* Beaumont entry]		East Hampton
Flannery, John [*see* Beaumont entry]		East Hampton
Fox, Alvin Gibbs		East Hampton
Green, Adolph		East Hampton
* Hackstaff, Charles Ludovic	*Tarriawyle*	East Hampton
* Hamlin, Mary Elkin Paxton	*Rowdy Hall* (1926 alterations)	East Hampton
Hamlin, Mary Elkin Paxton	*Windward*	East Hampton
Hammond, John Carnahan	*Aunt Phoebe's* (1926 alterations)	East Hampton
* Hammond, Percy	*Aunt Phoebe's* (1926 alterations)	East Hampton
* Hand, John White		East Hampton
Hare, Richard Vincent	(1905 interior and exterior alterations)	East Hampton
Harkness, Lamon Vanderburg		East Hampton
Hensel, Clarence Hopkins	*Dunemere*	East Hampton
Heyman, Stephen J.		East Hampton
Hill, Robert Carmer	*Grey Gardens*	East Hampton
Huntting, Annie	*Rowdy Hall* (1926 alterations)	East Hampton
* James, Laura Brevoort Sedgwick	*Blomioff* (designed house and 1894, 1896, and 1899 alterations)	East Hampton
* Johnson, Servetus Fisher	(designed two houses for Johnson, both in East Hampton)	East Hampton
Keim, John Richard		East Hampton
Klein, Calvin	(designed house and 1894, 1896, and 1899 alterations)	East Hampton
Lachman, Judith		East Hampton
Lee, James Thomas		East Hampton
* Lyon, Marvin Thomas		East Hampton
* Mackay, Mrs. William R.	(1899 alterations)	East Hampton
Manson, Thomas Lincoln, III	*Millfield* (1905 interior and exterior alterations)	East Hampton
Miller, Jeremiah, IV	(1905 interior and exterior alterations)	East Hampton
Morgan, Carol Ann [*see* Paxton entry]		East Hampton
* Newton, The Rev. Richard Heber, Sr.	*Dunecott*	East Hampton
* Nugent, Dr. Paul Fordham, Sr.		East Hampton

Architects

Joseph Greenleaf Thorp (cont'd)

	O'Connell, J. J. [*see* Potter entry]		East Hampton
*	Paxton, John Randolph, Sr.	*Windward*	East Hampton
*	Phillips, Fleming Stanhope		East Hampton
*	Poor, James Harper	*As You Like It* (1910 alterations)	East Hampton
*	Potter, Eugene Clifford	*A-Y-Mor*	East Hampton
*	Potter, Frederick Gaul	(designed two houses for Potter, both in East Hampton)	East Hampton
*	Randell, Caroline Amelia Boardman		East Hampton
*	Reiswig, Gary D.	(1910 alterations)	East Hampton
*	Reutershan, Paul V.		East Hampton
	Robert, Stephen Kniznick		East Hampton
	Roberts, Dr. Dudley DeVore, Sr.	*Outabounds*	East Hampton
	Roberts, Walter Scott		East Hampton
	Rose, Daniel		East Hampton
*	Schurman, Jacob Gould, Sr.	*Breezy Knowe*	East Hampton
	Seligson, William		East Hampton
*	Smith, Warren G.	(1901 alterations)	East Hampton
*	Solley, Dr. Fred Palmer	*Tanglebrae*	East Hampton
*	Spring, Preston Brady, Sr.	*Winklehawk*	East Hampton
*	Steele, The Rev. James Nevitt, Sr.	*Dunemere*	East Hampton
	Stewart, Martha Helen Kostyra	(1893 alterations)	East Hampton
*	Talmage, The Reverend Thomas DeWitt	(1893 alterations)	East Hampton
	Terian, Juliana Mae Curran		East Hampton
	Terian, Peter Gabriel		East Hampton
	Thompson, Michael P. [*see* Beaumont entry]		East Hampton
	Thorne, Henry Sanford	*Rowdy Hall* (1926 alterations)	East Hampton
*	Thorp, Joseph Greenleaf		East Hampton
	Thorpe, H. C.		East Hampton
	Trippe, Juan Terry	(designed house and 1894, 1896, and 1899 alterations)	East Hampton
	Van Rensselaer, Kiliaen, III	*Millfield* (1905 interior and exterior alterations)	East Hampton
	Walker, Delos		East Hampton
	Walker, Dr. John Baldwin, Sr.	*Tarriawyle*	East Hampton
	Watts, Harry Winfield		East Hampton
	Weaver, Spencer Fullerton, Sr.	*Spencecliff*	East Hampton
	Wood, Howard Ogden, Jr.	*Tarriawyle*	East Hampton
*	Woodhouse, Lorenzo Easton	*The Fens*	East Hampton

Architects

Tietig and Lee

Bishopric, Allison, Jr.	*Windy Dune*	Amagansett
Chatfield, Henry Houston	*Devon*	Amagansett
Cookson, Lucy Allison Bishopric	*Windy Dune*	Amagansett
Devendorf, George Epworth	*El Paraiso*	Amagansett
Greene, Anne Johnston Sawyer	*Devon House*	Amagansett
Jackson, Richard Seymour		Amagansett
Johnston, Mary Elizabeth	*Devon House*	Amagansett
Kuser, John Louis, Jr.		Amagansett
* Levering, Julia Henderson	(1910)	Amagansett

* Levering, Richmond, Sr.
   aka John Richmond Levering, Sr.;
   John Mortimer Levering, Jr.
	Devon	Amagansett

Materson, M. [*see* Levering entry]		Amagansett
McSpadden, Jack Dobbs, Jr.	*Devon House*	Amagansett
* Procter, William Cooper		Amagansett
* Rawson, Joseph, Jr.	*Red Roof*	Amagansett
Reynolds, Ardis J. [*see* Levering entry]		Amagansett
* Rowe, William Stanhope, Sr.		Amagansett
Zalles, Jorje Ezequiel, Sr. aka Jorge Ezequiel Zalles, Sr.		Amagansett

Trowbridge and Livingston

* Bell, Dr. Dennistoun Mildeberger	*Broadview*	Amagansett
Lewis, Reginald F.		Amagansett

Arthur Truscott and John Custis Lawrence

* Reid, Wallace		East Hampton
Sterling, Oliver James, Sr.		East Hampton

William B. Tuthill

* Adams, Charles Henry		East Hampton
Hodson, Dr. James M. [*see* Adams entry]		East Hampton
Mairs, Olney Blanchard, Sr.		East Hampton

Robert Venturi and William Short

Miller, Dudley Livingston, Sr.	(1961-1962 alterations)	East Hampton

Walker and Gillette

Aubert, Marion Eugenia Bragg	*Star Acres*	Montauk
* Bragg, Caleb Smith		Montauk

Spencer Fullerton Weaver, Sr.

Green, Adolph	(1925 alterations)	East Hampton
Roberts, Walter Scott	(1925 alterations)	East Hampton
Seligson, William	(1925 alterations)	East Hampton
Spring, Preston Brady, Sr.	*Winklehawk*	East Hampton

Architects

Spencer Fullerton Weaver, Sr. (cont'd)

    * Weaver, Spencer Fullerton, Sr.   *Spencecliff*   East Hampton
                                            (1925 alterations)

Richard Webb

    Brockman, Daniel David   (1949 conversion of playhouse into a residence)   East Hampton

    * McCaffray, Walter Peck   *Sandpiper Hill*   Montauk

    Rheinstein, Sidney   Montauk

    Walker, John Baldwin, Sr.   *Tarriawyle*   East Hampton

    Wood, Howard Ogden, Jr.   *Tarriawyle*   East Hampton

    Woodhouse, Lorenzo Easton   (1949 conversion of playhouse into a residence)   East Hampton

Paul Lester Weiner

    * Scull, Robert C.   East Hampton

Theodore Weston

    Stimson, Henry Clark   (alterations)   East Hampton

    Strong, George Arthur   East Hampton

    * Weston, Theodore   *Seven Gables* (alterations)   East Hampton

Tod Williams Billie Tsien Architects

    * Rifkind, Robert Singer   East Hampton

Arthur B. Wood (aka Arthur W. B. Wood)

    Akin, Robert Macomber, Jr.   *Hilltop House*   Montauk

    Daily, Marion   Montauk
       [*see* Wood entry]

    * Fisher, Carl Graham, Sr.   Montauk

    Gosman, Mary Ellen Harrington   Montauk

    Hopkins, Lindsey, Jr.   Montauk

    * Wood, Arthur B.   Montauk
       aka Arthur W. B. Wood

Eric Woodward

    Douglas, Robert Graham Dunn   East Hampton
       aka Robert Graham Dunn Douglass

    Poor, James Harper   *As You Like It*   East Hampton

    * Reiswig, Gary D.   (1996 alterations)   East Hampton

Wyeth and King

    Gardiner, Robert David Lion   East Hampton

    * Gardiner, Miss Sarah Diodati   East Hampton

Civic Activism

See the surname entry to ascertain specific civic activism information.

Abbe, Kathryn McLaughlin
Abbott, Florence Louise Call
Abbott, Henry Hurlbut
Adair, Dr. Frank Earl
Adair, Marion Hopkinson
Adams, Charles Henry
Adams, John Cranford
Agnew, Dr. Cornelius Rea, Sr.
Agnew, Mary Nash
Akin, Robert Macomber, Jr.
Albee, Edward Franklin, III
Alcott, Clarence Frank
Aldrich, Malcolm Pratt, Sr.
Alker, Ernestine Josephine Sierck
Altachul, Arthur Goodhard, Jr.
Ammon, Robert Theodore
   aka Ted Ammon
Anderson, Helen Natalie Johnson
Andrews, Jane Elizabeth Crane
Andrews, William Loring
Appleton, Robert Wilmarth
Ashplant, Frederick Bryant, Sr.
Aspinwall, James Lawrence
Aubert, Marion Eugenia Bragg
Backus, Harriet Ivins
Bacon, Clarence Everett, Jr.
Bailey, Alice Van Benschoten Foss
Baker, Lawrence Adams, Sr.
Baldwin, Alexander Rae, III
   aka Alec Baldwin
Barbour, Martha Buckham Benedict
Baron, Ronald Stephen
Bartholomew, Frederick A.
   [*see* M. A. L. Shepherd entry]
Bartlett, Edward Everett, Jr.
Baxter, Ann Wright
Baxter, George White
Beale, Phelan, Sr.
Beard, Cheryl Rae Tiegs

Beard, Lillian H. Osborn
Beardsley, Samuel Arthur, Sr.
Beardsley, Thomas Hopper
Beaumont, Perry H.
Beckers, Annadel Kelly
Beckers, William Kurt
Bell, Alfred Dennis, Sr.
Bell, George Newell
Bellas, Alfred Constantine
Bellas, Kathryn Mazzo
   aka Kay Mazzo
Benjamin, Candace Catlin Woodruff
Benjamin, Florence Almira Briggs
Benson, Arthur W.
Bernstein, Carl
   [*see* Ephron entry]
Bianchi, Gladys Wickes
Binn, Marisol Fernandes
Binn, Moreton
   aka Moreton Binstock
Bishop, Kathleen Sinclair
Bishop, Dr. Louis Faugeres, Jr.
Bishop, Dr. Louis Faugeres, Sr.
Bishopric, Marjorie Lee Collins
Blackburn, Wilmuth Earle
Blair, Edith Draper
Bogert, Edward Osgood
Bon Jovi, Jon
   aka John Francis Bongiovi, Jr.
Bonner, Frederic
Borden, Marie Jaeckel
Bouvier, Janet Norton Lee
Bouvier, John Vernou, Jr.
Bowne, Robert Southgate
Bracken, James W.
Brackenridge, Anne Ingersoll
Bradlee, Benjamin Crowninshield, Sr.
Bradlee, Sally Quinn
   aka Sally Quinn
Bragg, Caleb Smith

Civic Activism

Breen, Margaret Patricia McCloskey

Breinin, Dr. Goodwin Milton

Brett, Mary Baldwin Schwab

Brett, Philip Milledoler, Jr.

Breyer, Joanne Braatz

Brisbane, Arthur

Brockman, Elizabeth

Bronfman, Clarissa Alcock

Bronfman, Edgar Miles, Jr.

Brown, Helen Chamblet Hooper

Brown, Philip Wilson Tate, Sr.

Brown, Winifred Lee d'Olier

Browne, Christoper H.

Brockman, Daniel David

Buddenhagen, Kathleen Ingrid Burns

Bunshaft, Gordon

Bunshaft, Nina Elizabeth Wayler

Burchell, Henry J., Jr.

Burke, Oscar Moech

Burns, Ingrid Lily Froblich

Burns, Thomas Robert

Burton, Jane Erdmann

Butler, Howard Russell, Sr.

Calicchio, John

Campbell, Elizabeth Warne Detwiller

Campbell, Nathaniel Adams, Sr.

Carlson, Dr. Earl R.

Carpenter, Louise Adelaide
   aka Adelaide de Menil

Carpenter, Edmund Snow

Carr, Eleanor Maitland DeGraff

Carse, Caroline Louise Doerr

Carse, Donald Rede, Sr.

Carse, John Bradley, Sr.

Carson, Jean Maclay Williams

Carson, William Moore, Sr.

Cater, Arthur Aymar

Chace, Jeanetta Chalmers Jameson

Chalif, Rona Miriam Stern
   aka Ronnie Chalif

Chanos, Amy

Chanos, James Steven

Chapman, Benjamin Gains, Jr.

Chapman, Lucile Campbell

Chase, Ethelyn Atha

Chase, Jayni Ann

Chauncey, Alexander Wallace

Chauncey, Louise Ginnel Ruxton

Church, Richard Newton Loomis

Clark, Evans

Clark, Ivor Bache, Sr.

Clarke, Thomas Benedict, Sr.

Clements, Hurin Martin

Cloud, Chester Marts

Cobb, Henry Ives, Sr.

Cogan, Marshall Stuart

Cogan, Maureen Nancy Abramson

Cohen, Brooke Goodman

Cohen, Steven A.

Cohn, Marilyn B.

Cohn, Maurice J.

Cole, John Nelson, Jr.

Coleman, Charles Philip

Coleman, Helen Douglas Rulison

Combs, Sean John
   aka Puff Daddy, Diddy, and P. Diddy

Conway, Dorothea Brandes

Conway, Edmund Virgil, II

Conway, Edmund Virgil, III

Conway, Elaine Wingate

Cook, Harry

Cook, Leila Harkness Edwards

Cordier, Auguste Julien, Jr.

Cornell, Adelaide Pendergast

Cornell, Irwin Hewlett

Cory, David Cleveland

Couric, Katie
   aka Katherine Anne Couric

Craig, Dr. Stuart Lessley

Crane, Thomas

Cullman, Joan Paley

Cullman, Joseph Fredrick, III

Culver, Austin H.

Cummins, Stephen Swete

Civic Activism

Cummins, Virginia P. Kent
Cushman, Edith Marie Macon
Davis, Vernon Mansfield
Day, Agnes Roudebush
Dean, Howard Brush, Jr.
de Forest, Henry Grant
de Forest, Julia Mary Weekes
DeGraff, James Wilde
de Kay, Charles
de Kay, Margaret McClure
de Kay, Ormonde, Sr.
de Liagre, Mary Rogers
 aka Mary Howard
de Menil, Francois
 aka Francois Conrad Thomas de Menil
de Menil, Susan Kadin Silver
De Niro, Grace Hightower
De Niro, Robert, Jr.
De Palma, Gale Anne Hurd
De Palma, Nancy Allen
de Rose, Edward
Deutsch, Donny
 aka Donald Jay Deutsch
De Vecchi, Elizabeth Stettinius Trippe
De Vecchi, Robert Paolo
Devendorf, Alfred Ervin
Devereaux, Louise Drew
DeVries, Mary Lang
 aka Mary MacKinnon
Dewey, Catherine Harriet Kresge
Dewey, Charles Schuveldt, Jr.
Dewey, Marjory Sawyer Goodman
Dickerman, Alice Carter
Dickerman, William Carter, Sr.
Dodge, Washington, Jr.
D'Olier, Franklin Woolman, Jr.
Donovan, Roberta Gosman
Dougherty, Bertha Shults
Dougherty, Eleanor Sage
Dougherty, Frances Ann Cannon
Dowdney, Louis Purcell
Dowling, Alice Bevier Hall
Dowling, Robert Whittle

Downey, Robert, Jr.
Drew, John, Jr.
Drexler, Millard S.
 aka Mickey Drexler
Drexler, Peggy F.
Dubow, Arthur Myron
Duffield, The Reverend Howard
Duke, Anthony Drexel, Sr.
Duke, Diane M. Douglas
Duke, Elizabeth Ordway
Duke, Maria De Lourdes Alcebo
DuVal, Florence Fairbanks
DuVal, Guy
Edwards, Harkness, Sr.
Edwards, James Cook, Sr.
Edwards, Dr. Ogden Matthias, Jr.
Edwards, Sally Ann Matson
Edwards, Walter, Jr.
Eidlitz, Cyrus Lazelle Warner
Eldredge, George A.
Eldredge, Mary
Ely, Harriet Jackson
Ely, John Ingraham
Embury, Aymar, II
Eno, Alfred Joseph
Eno, Eva Walling
Entenmann, Charles, Sr.
Entenmann, Nancy Lee Drake
Entenmann, Robert William, Sr.
Erdmann, Dr. John Frederic
Ethridge, George
Ethridge, Julia Dinsmore Flandrau
Evans, James Hurlburt
Farrington, Selwyn Kip, Jr.
Finkbeiner, Dr. John A.
Fleming, Caroline M. Pelgram
Fleming, Matthew Corry, Sr.
Flinn, Lawrence, Jr.
Flinn, Marion de Vlaming
Flinn, Stephanie Hanes Strubling
Ford, James Bishop
Ford, Martha Parke Firestone

Civic Activism

Franey, Elizabeth Chardenet

Frankel, Evan M.

Fraser, Alexander

Fraser, Patricia Dodd

Fraser, Ronald Goodall

Fuhrman, Dorian Flynn

Fuhrman, Gary L.

Fuller, Edward Reinow

Furman, Frieda Anne Bueler

Furman, Roy Lance

Gagosian, Lawrence Gilbert

Gallatin, James

Gardiner, Nancy Deere Wiman

Gardiner, Robert David Lion

Gardiner Sonja Henje

Gardiner, Winthrop, Jr.

Garten, Ina Rosenberg

Garten, Jeffery E.

Garvin, John S., Sr.
[see E. C. T. Bell entry]

Geary, John White, III
aka John White Geary, Jr.

Geffen, David Lawrence

Gerli, Anne Woodin Harvey

Gleason, Carlisle Joyslin

Gleason, Ellen L. Fifield

Goelet, Robert Guestier

Gordon, George Breed

Gordon, Mary Edwards Boorum

Gossler, Philip Green, Jr.

Gottlieb, Adolph

Gottlieb, Ester Dick

Gowen, George W., II

Gowen, Marcia Fennelly

Gram, Ann Woodin Harvey

Gram, Carl William, Jr.

Green, Elizabeth Reitell

Green, Phyllis Newman
aka Phyllis Newman

Greene, Anne Johnston Sawyer

Greer, Lawrence

Gribetz, Lester

Gruen, Robert L.

Gruss, Audrey M. Butvay

Gruss, Martin David

Gruzen, Barnet Sumner

Gruzen, Jordan Lee

Gunster, Harriet Ruth Harris

Gunster, Joseph Frederick

Gwathmey, Charles

Gwathmey, Robert, Jr.

Hackstaff, Charles Ludovic

Hackstaff, Margaret Euphemia Hoffman

Hall, Christine Collings

Halsted, Hedi Klaschke

Hamlin, Harry Leon

Hamlin, Mary Elkins Paxton

Hand, John White

Hand, Mary Coolidge

Hanke, George Frederick Roberts, Sr.

Hansen, Evine Richard

Hare, Richard Vincent

Harris, Catherine Lawrence Richardson

Harris, William Victor
aka Victor Harris

Hartley, Nedenia Marjorie Hutton
aka Dina Merrill

Hartley, Theodore Ringwalt

Hassam, Frederick Childe
aka Childe Hassam

Haupt, Melville I.

Havens, Nellie F. Laycock

Hayden, William Martin, Sr.

Haynes, Evelyn Green

Hedges, Burke Osborn

Hedges, Caroline Isabella Homan

Hedges, Dayton
aka William Dayton Hedges

Hedges, Henry Denison

Helm, John La Rue, Jr.

Helmuth, Isabel Spaulding Lockman

Hendrix, Eugenia M. Terry
aka Gena Terry

Heppenheimer, William Christian, III

Herrick, Anson Boulton, Sr.

Herrick, Dr. Everett

Civic Activism

Herrick, Harriet Ford
Herrick, Ruth May Burdett
Herter, Adel McGinnis
Heyman, Barbara G.
Heyman, Stephen J.
Hill, Robert Carmer
Hinton, Alfred Post
Hinton, Dr. James William
Hinton, Jannett Williams Lord
Hirschfeld, Elie
Hirschfeld, Maricia Riklis
Hirschfeld, Dr. Sarah J. Schlesinger
Hirschfeld, Dr. Susan T. Aronson
Hirtenstein, Michael
Hiss, Alger
Hiss, Priscilla Harriet Fansler
Hobart, Garret Augustus, Jr.
Hobart, Henry Lee
Hobart, Marie Elizabeth Jefferys
Hollister, Dr. Frederick Kellogg
Hollister, Harriet May Shelton
Holmes, Jay
Hopkins, Alison Low Turnbull
Hopkins, John Appleton Haven, Sr.
Hopkins, Lindsey, Jr.
Hopkinson, Mary Barbey Lewis
Hopkinson, Russell
Howell, Frederica Gilchrist
Howell, John White, Sr.
Hufty, Frances May Archbold
Hufty, Mann Randolph Page
   aka Page Hufty
Hutton, John Laurence, Sr.
Hutton, Virginia Consuelo Smith
Hutton, William Langdon
Ichan, Carl Celian
Icahn, Gail Golden
Jackson, John Day
Jackson, Lionel Stewart, Sr.
Jackson, Patricia Hope Johnstone
Jackson, Richard Seymour
Jackson, Rose Marie Herrick

Jaffe, Melinda Jill Marciano
Jaffe, Stanley Richard
James, Ellery Sedgewick, Sr.
   aka William Ellery Sedgewick James, Sr.
James, Henry Amman
James, Laura Brevoort Sedgwick
James, Louise Russell Hoadley
Jefferys, Charles Peter Beauchamp, Sr.
Jefferys, Harry Leapold
Jenney, Nina George Bevan
Jewett, Edward Hull, Sr.
Jewett, Maude Sherwood
   aka Maude Sherwood
Joel, Billy
   aka William Martin Joel
Joel, Katie Lee
   aka Kathleen Rebekah Lee
Johnson, Miss Edith
Johnson, Eleanora Renee Baratelli
Johnson, Frederick, Sr.
   [see DeVries entry]
Johnson, Gretchen Ann Wittenborn
Johnson, James Loring
Johnson, Rossiter
Johnston, Mary Elizabeth
Jones, Dr. Oswald Roberts
Jones, Rodney Wilcox, Sr.
Joyner, Lucie Burke Alcott
Kaplan, Alice Manheim
Kaplan, Jacob Merrill
Karan, Donna Ivy Faske
Kast, Dr. Ludwig
Kelley, William Vallandigham, Sr.
Kelsey, Stephen Tomlinson, Sr.
Kerr, Elmore Coe, Jr.
   [see Baxter entry]
Kessner, Steven
Kimball, Alden
Kimball, Charles Edmunds, Jr.
Kimball, Louise Van Voorhees
King, Jessica Hildreth Halsey
King, William
Kingsley, Virginia Pulleyn
Kingsley, Walton Pearl

Knox, John Mason, Jr.

Krakoff, Reed

Krech, Mary Stevens Chapin

Krech, Dr. Shepard, Sr.

Krieger, Dr. Dorothy Terrace

Kuchin, Kenneth Sidney

Kuser, John Louis, Jr.

Kuser, Olivia Sturtevant Erdmann

LaForest, Helen A.

LaMonte, Anna Isabel Vaill

Larkin, Adrian Hoffman

Larkin, Katherine Bache Satterthwaite

Larkin, Lawrence

Larkin, Roseanne Roudebush

Laspia, Mary Louise Roesel

Laspia, Dr. Michael R.

Laughlin, Alexander Mellon, Jr.

Laughlin, Alexander Mellon, Sr.

Laughlin, David Walker

Laughlin, Judith Walker

Lauren, Ralph
 aka Ralph Lifshitz

Le Brecht, Robert

Lee, Ann Tenenbaum

Lee, Barbara Ellen Fish

Lee, James Thomas

Lee, Thomas Haskell

Leith, Donald E.

Levering, John Mortimer [Sr.]

Levering, Richmond, Sr.
 aka John Richmond Levering, Sr.;
 John Mortimer Levering, Jr.

Levy–Church, Jeanne Diane

Levy–Church, Kenneth
 aka Kenneth Wayne Church

Lewis, Ida May Barbey

Lewis, Loida Nicholas

Lewis, Reginald F.

Lilley, Alexander Neil, Sr.

Lindemann, Adam Marc

Lockwood, Elizabeth Erwin Edwards

Lockwood, Janet Isabel Dominick

Lockwood, William Andrew

Loeb, Daniel Seth

Loeb, Margaret Davidson Munzer

Loomis, Alfred Lee, Sr.

Loomis, Manette Seeldrayers

Lowenstein, Peter

Lutkins, Clinton Stephen

Macklowe, Linda Burg

Macklowe, Patricia Landeau

Macy, Harriet Ayer Seymour

Macy, Valentine Everit, Jr.

Madoff, Bernard Lawrence
 aka Bernie Madoff

Madoff, Ruth Alpern

Maguire, Edward, Sr.

Maharam, Bonnie

Maharam, Donald, Jr.

Main, Laura Sudler

Mairs, Isabel Tasker Gardiner
 aka Isabel T. L. Gardiner Mairs;
 Isabel Fairfax Gardiner Mairs

Maloney, Ella Gaynor McCall

Mann, Helen Morris Grimes

Mann, Henry

Mansell, Edmona Lyman

Mansell, Frank Luther

Manson, Thomas Lincoln, III

Marsh, Frank Ballard

Martin, Christopher Anthony John
 [see Paltrow]

Martin, Samuel Klump, Jr.

Marvel, Josiah Peter

Massey, Maurice Richardson, Jr.

Mayo–Smith, Richmond, Sr.

McAlpin, David Hunter, Sr.

McAlpin, George Lodowich, Sr.

McAlpin, Malcolm Evans

McAlpin, Sally Blanche Benjamin

McCaffray, Alys Mary Curran

McCaffray, Walter Peck

McCall, Clifford Hyde, Sr.

McCall, Edward Everett

McCall, Elvine Richard

McCartney, Heather Mills

Civic Activism

McCartney, Linda Louise Eastman
McConnell, Neil Anderson
McConnell, Sandra Dorothea Haig
McConnell, Serena Mary Churchill Russell
McCord, David Walter
McCormick, Robert Elliot
McKeon, Robert Brian
McLanahan, Scott
McSpadden, Ruth Ann Wood
Meehan, Joseph Ansbro
Mercati, Barbara Tapper
Mercer, Norman J.
Miller, Margery Gerdes
Miller, Dudley Livingston, Sr.
Mills, Abraham
Miner, Mary Louise Woodin
Mirick, Edna B. de Beixedon
Mitchell, MacNeil
Mitchell, Martha Katherine McGowin
   aka Katherine McGowin
Mnuchin, Alan Geoffrey
Moffett, James Andrew, Jr.
Moody, Frances Trent Glen
Moody, Sidney Clarke, Sr.
Montgomery, Paul
   aka John Paul Montgomery
Montgomery, Robert
   aka Henry Montgomery, Jr.;
   Robert Montgomery, Sr.
Moran, Thomas, Jr.
Morris, Theodore Wilson, Jr.
Morse, Tyler
Morton, Peter
Munroe, Dr. George E., Jr.
Murphy, Gerald Clery
Myrick, Julian Southall
Nadal, Charles Coleman
Nash, Stephen Edward
Nederlander, Robert Elliot, Sr.
Newman, Angeline Ensign
Newton, Amy James
Newton, Francis
Newton, The Reverend Richard Heber, Sr.

Nichols, Harold Willis, Jr.
Nichols, Harold Willis, Sr.
Nichols, Katherine Harkness Edwards
Nichols, Margaret Rowe
Nobel, Mark Ainslie
Northrop, John Burr, Sr.
Northrup, Virginia Osborne Cox
Oakley, Ralph Lawrence
Olin, John Merrill
Ordway, Anna Wheatland
Ordway, Frances Hunt Throop
Ordway, Samuel Hanson, Jr.
Ordway, Samuel Hanson, Sr.
Orr, Alexander Ector
Osborne, Joseph Septimus
Osborne, Nelson Cook, Sr.
Pagel, Alex John, Jr.
Paltrow, Gwyneth Kate
Pardridge, Albert Jerome
Perelman, Patricia Michelle Orr
   aka Patricia Duff
Perelman, Ronald Owen
Peters, Marion Louise Smith
Peterson, Joan Ganz
   aka Joan Ganz Cooney
Peterson, Peter George
Peterson, Sally Hornbogen
Pierson, Warren Lee, Sr.
Pittman, Estelle Young Romeyn
Pittman, Ernest Wetmore
Plimpton, George Ames
Poor, James Harper
Potter, Dickson Bayard
Potter, Eugene Clifford
Potter, Frederick Gaul
Potter, Jeffrey Brackett
Potter, Madeleine Penelope Sack
   aka Penelope Sack
Potter, Margaret Somerville
Preusee, Charles Francis
Procter, William Cooper
Pulleyn, John William, Sr.
Putnam, Harrington, Jr.

Civic Activism

Putnam, Michelle Caroline Bouvier
Radziwill, Stanislaw Albrecht
Rahr, Stewart J.
Ramee, Joseph Russell
Ramee, Marie Virginia Hoguet
Ramsay, Herbert Hartley
Ranieri, Mary Louise Gioiella
Ranieri, Salvatore Anthony
Rattray, Arnold Elsmere
Rattray, Everett Tennant
Rattray, Jeannette Frances Edwards
Rawson, Joseph, Jr.
Raymond, Dana Merriam
Raymond, Josephine Sheehan
Reid, Archibald Mudge
Reid, Margaret Howell Behr
Reid, Wallace
Reiswig, Gary D.
Rentschler, Rita Rend Mitchell
Reutersham, Paul V.
Rheinstein, Sidney
Rice, Dr. Clarence Charles
Rice, Ernest H., Sr.
Rice, Henry Grantland
   aka Grantland Rice
Richard, Auguste
Richard, Hetty Lawrence Hemenway
Richard, Mark Gadd
Richard, Mary Ella Brooks
Richard, Veronica Dwight
Richards, Eliza Fenno Verplanck
Richards, Richard Draper
   aka Richards Follett
Rifkind, Dr. Arleen Brenner
Rifkind, Carole Lewis
Rifkind, Dr. Richard A.
Rifkind, Robert Singer
Robert, Pilar Crespi
Robert, Stephen Kniznick
Roberts, Dudley DeVore, Jr.
Roberts, Dr. Dudley DeVore, Sr.
Roberts, George Hewitt, Jr.

Roberts, Grace Lee Middleton
Robertson, Hugh James, Jr.
Robertson, Nedenia Marjorie Hutton
   aka Dina Merrill
Robinson, Augusta James McLane
Robinson, Lucius Franklin, Jr.
Rose, Daniel
Rose, Jill Caroll Kupin
Rose, Joanna Semel
Rose, Marshall
Rosenstein, Barry
Rosinsky, Claude Daste
Ross, Courtney Sale
Rosset, Joan Mitchell
   aka Joan Mitchell
Roth, Daryl Adkins
Roth, Steven
Rowe, John Jay, Sr.
Rowe, William Stanhope, Sr.
Rubin, Samuel
Rubin, Vera D,
Rumbough, Janne Herlow
Rumbough, Nedenia Marjorie Hutton
   aka Dina Merrill
Rumbough, Stanley Hutton
Rumbough, Stanley Maddox, Jr.
Ruxton, Philip
Ryan, Richard Nelson, Jr.
Salembier, Paul Albert
Saltzman, Renny B.
Sandleman, Corrie
Sandelman, Jonathan Everett
Sanger, Henry
Scheerer, Jane Bond Ingersoll
Scheerer, Joseph Durand, Jr.
Scheerer, Joseph Durand, Sr.
Scheerer, Nancy Holdsworth
Scheerer, Paul Renner, Jr.
Scheffer, Alfred A.
Scheffer, Theresa Trach
Schey, Robert Paul
Schulman, Lowell M.
Schultz, Howard Mark

Civic Activism

Schultz, Sheri Kerach
Schurman, George Wellington
Schurman, Jacob Gould, Sr.
Schwarzman, Ellen Philips
Schwarzman, Stephen Allen
Scull, Ethel Redner
Scull, Robert C.
Seabury, Josephine Maud Richey
Seabury, Samuel
Seaman, Joseph Husband, Sr.
Seegal, Frederic Milton
Seegal, Robin Neimark
Seinfeld, Nina Danielle Sklar
    aka Jessica Sklar
Seligson, William
Semel, Jane Bovingdon
Semel, Terrance Steven
Shafran, Irving
Shepherd, James Gardner
Shyer, Henry
Simmons, Kimora Lee
    aka Kimora Whitlock
Simmons, Russell Wendell
Simon, Paul Frederic
Simon, William Edward, Sr.
Simonds, Francis May, Sr.
Sinclaire, Christine Biller
Skidmore, Emma Pattison
Skidmore, James Bond
Skidmore, Samuel Tredwell, II
Slifka, Alan Bruce
Slifka, Jacqueline Watkins
Smith, Earl Edward Tailer, Sr.
    [*see* Warburton entry]
Smith, Warren G.
Snow, Dr. Irving Miller
Spaeth, Eloise O'Mara
Spaeth, Otto Lucien, Sr.
Spalding, Jean Fredericka Whiting
Spalding, Jesse, II
Spielberg, Steven Allan
Spring, Preston B.
Stanton, Dr. Frederick Lester

Starke, Hamilton Jackson
Steele, The Reverend James Nevett, Sr.
Steele, Marjorie Blair Dalberg
Sterling, Dorothea McElhone
Stern, Allison Maher
Stern, Elsie Weston Lazarus
Stern, Henry Root, Sr.
Stern, Joel Mark
Stern, Leonard Norman
Stern, Lynn Solinger
Strong, Martha Howard Prentice
Strong, Theron George
Sutphen, Henry Randolph, Jr.
Sutphen, Henry Randolph, Sr.
Sutphen, Susanna Lees
Sweetser, Jesse William
Talmadge, John Frelinghuysen
Talmage, Daniel, Jr.
Taylor, Irene Hinman
Taylor, Irving Howland
Teetor, Charles Jessup
Terbell, Edward Dyer
Terbell, Henry S., Sr.
Terian, Julianna Mae Curran
Terian, Peter Gabriel
Terry, Dr. Arthur Hutchinson, Jr.
Terry, Marie Kelley French
Thaw, Gladys Virginia Bradley
Thaw, William, III
Thiele, Albert Edward, Jr.
Thiele, Alice Irene Kelly
Thiele, Roger Henry
Thomas, Andrew Jackson
Thomas, Augustus
Thompson, Dr. Frederick Roeck
Thorp, Joseph Greenleaf
Tiffany, Nathan Newton, III
Tillich, The Reverend Paul Johannes
Tishman, Peter Valentine
Todd, Eleanor Prentice Schley
Todd, John Reynard, Sr.
Todd, Webster Bray, Sr.

Civic Activism

Topping, Sonja Henje
Towbin, Abraham Robert
Towbin, Irene Katherine Lyons
Towbin, Jacqueline Mary de Chollet
Trippe, Elizabeth Stettinius
Trippe, Juan Terry
Tuck, Frederick W., Jr.
Tuck, Merle Fiske
Tufo, Peter Francis
   [see Goelet entry]
Turner, Kathleen
   aka Mary Kathleen Turner
Tweed, Barbara Banning
Tweed, Harrison
Tyson, Carolyn Kennedy
Tyson, James
Van Brunt, Arthur Hoffman, Sr.
Vanderbilt, Oliver DeGray, III
Van Rensselaer, Kiliaen, III
Volckening, Lloyd Irwin
Wainwright, Elizabeth Stettinius Trippe
Wainwright, Nina Walker
Wainwright, Stuyvesant, II
Wainwright, Stuyvesant, III
Walker, Caroline Shields
Walker, Delos
Walker, Emily Schniewind
Walker, Dr. John Baldwin, Sr.
Walker, John Gholson, Sr.
Walker, Nina Elizabeth Sebring
Ward, Ethel L. Conderman
Ward, William L.
Wardle, H. Allen
Warhol, Andy
   aka Andrew Warhola, Jr.
Warner, Eltinge Fowler, Jr.
Wasey, Louis Rice
Washburn, George
Washburn, Watson

Wasserstein, Bruce Jay
Wasserstein, Claude Becker
Weaver, Spencer Fullerton, Sr.
Weber, Bruce
Weber, Nan Bush
Webster, Dr. Bruce Peck
Weeks, John Kirkland, Sr.
Weinstein, Harvey
Weinstein, Joseph
Welch, Leo Dewey
Weston, Catherine Boudinot Stimson
Weston, Theodore
Wheeler, John Neville
Wheeler, Elizabeth Wood Thompson
Wheelock, Emily Charlotte Hall
Wheelock, John Hall
Wheelock, William Almy
Whitney, Elwood
Whitney, Kate Case
Whittle, Priscilla Rattazzi
Wiborg, Frank Bestow
Williams, Eugene Flewilyn, Jr.
Williams, John Pattison, Sr.
   [see A. J. S. Greene entry]
Wood, Howard Ogden, Sr.
Woodhouse, Lorenzo Easton
Woodhouse, Mary Leland Kennedy
Woodin, William Hartman, Sr.
Woolley, Knight
Woolley, Marjorie Fleming
Yates, Linda L. Lindeberg
Zalles, Arcardia Calderon
Zalles, Jorje Ezequel, Sr.
   aka Jorge Ezequel Zalles, Sr.
Zaslav, David M.
Zellweger, Renee Kathleen
Zuckerman, Mortimer Benjamin

Civic Activism

Anti – Suffragists:

    Backus, Harriet Ivins Davis

    Johnson, Helen Louise Kendrick

Suffragists:

    Abbott, Florence Louise Call

    Baxter, George White

    Brisbane, Arthur

    Cobb, Irvin Shewsbury

    Eno, Eva Walling

    Fleming, Caroline M. Pelegram

    Hopkins, Alison Low Turnbull

    Hopkins, John Appleton Haven, Sr.

    Kendrick, Georgia Avery

    Levering, Julia Henderson

    Manson, Mary Groot
      aka Mae Groot Manson

    Tweed, Blanch Oelrichs
      aka Michael Strange

Brook Russell Astor,

chairman of the Astor Foundation and wife of William Vincent Astor,

quipped on the concept of *nobless oblige*:

"Money is like manure, it should be spread around.

Estate Names

When the owner who contracted with the architect is known, it is indicated by an asterisk. Multiple owners are listed in chronological order of ownership, not alphabetically by surname. Ownership of estates is listed only for those that used that particular estate name. See the surname entry to ascertain names used by other owners of the same estate.

Abbey Cottage	* Abbe, James Edward, Jr.	Montauk
Abrigada	* de Kay, Charles	East Hampton
Adana	Hyde, Frank Dana	East Hampton
Apaquogue	Myrick, Julian Southhall	East Hampton
Apaquogue House	Cater, Louise Bowers	East Hampton
The Apaquogue	LaForest, Helen A. LaForest, Henry A.	East Hampton
As You Like It	Poor, James Harper	East Hampton
Aunt Phoebe's	Hammond, John Carnahan Hammond, Percy	East Hampton
Avery Place	Lee, James Thomas	East Hampton
Awepesha	DuVal, Guy	Montauk
A–Y–Mor	* Potter, Eugene Clifford	East Hampton
Back Home	Cobb, Irvin Shewsbury	East Hampton
Baker's Acres	Baker, Lawrence Adams, Sr.	East Hampton
Bayberry	* Cole, John Nelson, Jr.	East Hampton
Bayberry	Lundbergh, Holger	Montauk
Bay Bush	* Butler, Howard Russell, Sr.	East Hampton
Beachclose	* Schurman, George Wellington	East Hampton
Beechwood	Schulman, Lowell M.	East Hampton
Beehive	Briggs, James Branch	East Hampton
Beaulahside	* Vaughan, Eliza Jennie Potter	East Hampton
Bishopgate	Bishop, Dr. Louis Faugeres, Sr.	East Hampton
Blomioff	* James, Laura Brevoort Sedgwick	East Hampton
Bonnie Dune	* Mayo, Marie Louise	East Hampton
Bowling Green	Sutphen, Henry Randolph, Sr. Sutphen, Henry Randolph, Jr.	East Hampton
The Breezes	* Van Brunt, Arthur Hoffman, Sr.	East Hampton
Breezy Knowe	* Schurman, Jacob Gould, Sr.	East Hampton
Breezy Lawn	* Gallatin, Frederic	East Hampton
The following three entries are on different streets:		
Briar Patch	* Abbott, Henry Hurlbut	East Hampton
Briar Patch	Collins, William Bradley Isham, Sr. aka Bradley Isham Collins	East Hampton
Briar Patch	* Krech, Dr. Shepard, Sr. Whittle, Chris aka H. Christopher Whittle	East Hampton

Estate Names

Brigadoon	* Frankel, Evan M.	East Hampton
The following two entries are different houses:		
Broadview	* Bell, Dr. Dennistoun Mildeberger	Amagansett
Broadview	Jones, Rodney Wilcox, Sr.	Amagansett
Bruton Braes	De Koven, Louis Besant Wadsworth	East Hampton
Burnt Point	* Campbell, David	East Hampton
	Rahr, Stewart J.	
Cairnhill	Ruxton, Philip	East Hampton
Camelot	* Campbell, Nathaniel Adams, Sr.	East Hampton
Captain's House	Hattersley, Lelia Marie Chopin	East Hampton
Causeway	Terry, Dr. Arthur Hutchinson, Jr.	East Hampton
Century Cottage	Vaill, Isabella Mary Breck	East Hampton
	Talmage, Mary Breck Vaill	
	Talmage, Rockwell Dwight	
	Mapes, Victor	
	aka Sidney Sharp	
The Chalet	Mills, Abraham	East Hampton
Chateau Amorois	* Browne, Christopher H.	East Hampton
Cherokee Cottage	Baxter, George White	East Hampton
Cherridune	DeGraff, James Wilde	East Hampton
	Carr, Eleanor Maitland DeGraff	
The Chimneys	* Lembcke, George Albert	East Hampton
Cima Del Mundo	* Warner Eltinge Fowler, Jr.	East Hampton
Clas-des-Lilas	* Richards, Benjamin, Jr.	East Hampton
Clifford-by-the Sea	* Bowne, Robert Southgate	East Hampton
Clover Cottage	Brown, Anthony Coates	East Hampton
Cobwebs	Steele, Louis Thorton	East Hampton
Cody House	Ross, Steven, Jay	East Hampton
	aka Steven Jay Rechnitz	
Cove Hollow Farm	Schwarzman, Stephen Allen	East Hampton
	Gallagher, Thomas	
Coxwould	* Erdmann, Dr. John Frederic	East Hampton
	Burton, Jane Erdmann	
Cranberry Bog	Chase, Edward Tinsley	East Hampton
Cranberry Dune	Wasserstein, Bruce Jay	Amagansett
The Creeks	* Herter, Albert	East Hampton
	Ossorio, Alfonso Angel	
	Dragon, Edward F.	
Crestmere	Butler, William Allen, III	East Hampton
The following two entries are different houses:		
Crossways	* Benjamin, William Wallace, Jr.	East Hampton
	Benjamin, William Wallace, III	
	Lilley, Alexander Neil, Sr.	
Crossways	* Nash, Stephen Edward	East Hampton
Crowland	Godwin, Courtlandt	East Hampton
Crow's Nest	Nichols, Harold Willis, Sr.	East Hampton
Dellwood	Ordway, Samuel Gilman	East Hampton

Estate Names

Deurcant House	Gardiner, Winthrop, Sr.	East Hampton

The following two entries are different houses:

Devon	* Levering, Richmond, Sr.
	   aka John Richmond Levering, Sr.;
	   John Mortimer Levering, Jr.
	Materson, M.
	   [*see* Levering entry]
	Chatfield, Henry Houston
		Amagansett

Devon	* Rowe, John Jay, Sr.	Amagansett
Devon House	Johnston, Mary Elizabeth Greene, Anne Johnston Sawyer McSpadden, Jack Dobbs, Jr.	Amagansett
The Dolphins	Strong, Theron George Ashplant, Frederick Bryant, Sr.	East Hampton
Dormie Dune	Salembier, Harold Paul	East Hampton
Driftwood	Clark, Ivor Bache, Sr.	Amagansett
Dune Alpin	* McAlpin, George Lodowich, Sr.	East Hampton
Dunecott	* Newton, The Reverend Richard Heber, Sr.	East Hampton
Dune Crest	* Duffield, The Reverend Howard	Amagansett
Dune Dee	Dickerman, William Carter, Sr.	East Hampton
Duneden	* Jefferys, Harry Leapold	East Hampton
Dune Gate	Bacon, Clarence Everett, Jr.	East Hampton
Dune Home	Harris, William Victor aka Victor Harris	East Hampton
Dune House	* Woodin, William Hartman, Sr.	East Hampton
Dunehurst	Edwards, Dr. Ogden Matthias, Jr. Nichols, Harold Willis, Jr.	East Hampton
Dunemead	* Evans, Benjamin Franklin McAlpin, Malcolm Evans	East Hampton

The following two entries are different houses:

Dunemere	* Steele, The Reverend James Nevett, Sr. Hensel, Clarence Hopkins Bailey, Dr. Theodorus, II	East Hampton
Dunemere	Ford, William Clay, Sr.	East Hampton
Dune Pasture	Bates, Jerome Elliott	East Hampton
Dunes	Mitchell, Ledyard, Sr. aka William Ledyard Mitchell	East Hampton
The Dunes	* Wiborg, Frank Bestow	East Hampton
Duneside	Pardridge, Albert Jerome	East Hampton
Dune Top	* Thaw, William, III	East Hampton
Dunfour	Carr, Eleanor Maitland DeGraff	East Hampton
Dunside	Draper, Frances S. Haggerty	East Hampton
Eastern View	Kimball, Alden	East Hampton
East of 69	Ryan, Frederick Behrens, Sr.	East Hampton
Elmshade	Mitchell, MacNeil	Amagansett

Estate Names

The following two entries are different houses:

El Paraiso	Devendorf, Alfred Ervin	East Hampton
El Paraiso	Devendorf, George Epworth	Amagansett
El Pato Feo	Wainwright, John Howard	East Hampton
Elsufral	Bronaugh, Frederick Lewis Pagel, Elinor Robertson Bronaugh	East Hampton
End Cottage	Carse, John Bradley, Sr.	East Hampton
End of the Lane	Green, William Walker	East Hampton
Eothen	Morrissey, Paul Warhol, Andy aka Andrew Warhola, Jr.	Montauk
Es Moli	Hare, Richard V.	Amagansett
Evsdune	* McCall, Edward Everett	East Hampton
Fairlawn	Sinclair, Earle Westwood	East Hampton
Fairways	* Cody, Frederick	East Hampton
Falaise Farm	Potter, Dickson Bayard	East Hampton
The Fens	* Woodhouse, Lorenzo Easton	East Hampton
Finning Out	Farrington, Selwyn Kip, Jr.	East Hampton
Fithian House	Kerr, Selina Alva Coe	East Hampton
Foxall	* Hinton, Dr. James William	East Hampton
Fulling Mill Farm	* Newton, Francis Robinson, Lucius Franklin, Jr.	East Hampton
Furtherfield	* Roberts, George Hewitt, Jr. Breen, Daniel Anthony, Jr.	East Hampton
Furtherlane	* Bartlett, Edward Everett, Jr.	Amagansett
Further Moor	Nori, Edmond Joseph	Amagansett
Furthermoor	* Pierson, Warren Lee, Sr.	East Hampton
The Gatehouse	Osserman, Stanley	East Hampton
Gay Cottage	Burchell, Henry J., Jr.	East Hampton
Georgica Cove	Burns, Thomas Robert	East Hampton
Glendella	Maloney, William Raywood, Jr.	East Hampton
Gone With the Wind	Chace, Franklin M.	East Hampton
The Green Flag	Fleming, Henry Stuart	East Hampton
Green Frog	* Larkin, Adrian Hoffman	East Hampton
Green Oaks	Wainwright, Stuyvesant, II	East Hampton
Greycroft	* Woodhouse, Lorenzo Guernsey Cummins, Stephen Swete	East Hampton
Grey Gardens	Hill, Robert Carmer Beale, Phelan, Sr. Beale, Edith Ewing Bouvier Bradlee, Benjamin Crowninshield	East Hampton
Greyshingles	Gleason, Carlisle Joyslin	East Hampton
Gullcrest	* Wainwright, Carroll Livingston, Sr.	East Hampton

Estate Names

The following two entries are different houses:

Half-a-Gale	*	Hayden, William Martin, Sr.	Amagansett
Half-a-Gale	*	Davis, Vernon Mansfield	Amagansett
Harbor House		Duke, Anthony Drexel, Sr.	East Hampton
Hayloft		Maguire, Edward, Sr.	East Hampton
Hearthstone		Mairs, Isabel Tasker Gardiner aka Isabel Fairfax Gardiner Mairs; Isabel T. L. Gardiner Mairs	East Hampton
Heather Dune	*	James, Ellery Sedgwick, Sr. aka William Ellery Sedgwick James, Sr.	East Hampton
Heather Hill		Simonds, Francis May, Sr.	East Hampton
Hedges Row		Lutkins, Clinton Stephen	East Hampton
Hell–Gate		Ely, John Ingraham	Amagansett
Hill Cottage		Gardiner, Winthrop, Jr.	East Hampton
Hilltop House	*	Fisher, Carl Graham, Sr. Akin, Robert Macomber, Jr.	Montauk
Hilly Close	*	Rubin, Samuel	Amagansett
Hither House		McCord, David Walter	East Hampton
Holiday	*	Bishop, Dr. Louis Faugeres, Jr.	East Hampton
Holly Hall	*	Cook, Harry	East Hampton
Homelot		Storey, Emma Josephine de Raismes	Amagansett
Home Sweet Home		Buek, Gustav H. aka Gustavus H. Buek	East Hampton
Honeysuckle Hedge		Skidmore, James Bond	East Hampton
House of Four Winds		Satterlee, Dr. Francis Le Roy, Jr.	Montauk
Idlerest		Skidmore, Samuel Tredwell, II	East Hampton
Inadune		Moffet, James Andrew, Jr.	East Hampton
The Ingle	*	Johnson, Mary Newlin Verplanck Johnson, Miss Edith	East Hampton
The Ink Pot		Jewett, Edward Hull, Sr.	East Hampton
Iona Dune / The Mange	*	Lardner, Ringgold Wilmer, Sr. aka Ring Lardner	East Hampton
Ironsides		Dodge, Washington, Jr.	Amagansett
Ivy Cottage		Lockwood, William Andrew	East Hampton
Kemah		Warren, Dr. Marshall Lord	Amagansett
The Kennels		Dodd, John Mingus, III	East Hampton
Kilkare	*	Edwards, Walter, Jr. Edwards, William Henry Leonard Kennedy, Michael John	East Hampton
Kipsveen		McCall, Clifford Hyde, Sr.	East Hampton
Kumonin		Helmuth, Dr. William Tod, Jr.	East Hampton
Kyalami	*	Drew, John, Jr. Cordier, Julien, Jr.	East Hampton
Lago–Del–Mare		Moranti, Paul Joseph	East Hampton
The Lanterns		Clarke, Thomas Benedict, Sr.	East Hampton

Estate Names

Lasata	Bouvier, Maude Frances Sergeant Bouvier, John Vernou, Jr.	East Hampton
Lauralawn	Schey, Robert Paul	East Hampton
Leecott	Kelsey, Stephen Tomlinson, Sr.	East Hampton
Little Burlees	* Cockcroft, Edward Truesdell	East Hampton
Little Close	* Jenney, William Sherman	East Hampton
Little House	Bouvier, John Vernou, Jr.	East Hampton
Little Too Close	* Richards, Richard Draper aka Richards Follett	East Hampton
Lockdune	* Lockwood, William Benedict	East Hampton
The Lodge	Kiser, John William, III aka John William Kiser, Jr.	East Hampton
Longlast	Macy, Valentine Everit, Jr.	East Hampton
Maidstone Hall	Terbell, Edward Dyer Gardiner, Robert Alexander	East Hampton East Hampton
Main House	Main, Charles E.	East Hampton
Manor House	* Gardiner, Sarah Diodati Gardiner, Robert David Lion Creel, Alexandra Diodati Gardiner Goelet, Alexandra Gardiner Creel	Gardiner's Island
Maya	Gram, Carl William, Jr. Gerli, David Anne Woodin Harvey	East Hampton
Mayfair House	Darrow, Daniel	East Hampton
Meltemi	Mercati, Count Leonardo	East Hampton
MiDune	Miner, Mary Louise Woodin	East Hampton
The Mill Cottage	Gardiner, Winthrop, Jr.	East Hampton
Mill Crest	* Wessel, Homer Augustus, Sr.	East Hampton
Millfield	* de Rose, Edward Manson, Thomas Lincoln, III Van Rensselaer, Kiliaen, III	East Hampton East Hampton
Moorland	Sanger, Lilian	Montauk
Nevermind	* McLanahan, Scott	East Hampton
New Century Cottage	* Talmage, Mary Breck Vaill Talmage, Rockwell Dwight	East Hampton
Nid de Papillion	* Appleton, Robert Wilmarth Johnson, James Loring	East Hampton
Normandie	Walker, Bayard, Sr.	East Hampton
*Off-the-*Teeee	* Tuck, Frederick W., Jr.	East Hampton
Old Baker House	Tyson, James	Amagansett
Old Post Office	Vanderbilt, Oliver DeGray, III	East Hampton
Old Simmons House	Seegal, Frederic Milton	Amagansett
Olde Trees	Ely, Laurence Driggs, Sr.	East Hampton
Onadune	* Johnson, Servetus Fisher Chisholm, Edward de Clifford	East Hampton
Our Place	* Chauncey, Alexander Wallace	East Hampton
Outabounds	Roberts, Dr. Dudley DeVore, Sr.	East Hampton

Estate Names

Over Hook	Flinn, Lawrence, Jr.	East Hampton
Overlea	* Eidlitz, Cyrus Lazelle Warner	East Hampton
The following two entries are different houses:		
Peep O'Day	Hutton, John Laurence, Sr.	East Hampton
Peep O'Day	Hutton, William Langdon	East Hampton
Pineleigh	Spalding, Jesse, II Spalding, Jesse, III Maxwell, Elliott	East Hampton
The Playhouse	* Woodhouse, Lorenzo Easton Brockman, Daniel David	East Hampton
Pond House	Bonner, Marie Louise Clifford	East Hampton
Pond's Edge	* Massey, Maurice Richardson, Jr.	East Hampton
Pondside	Aldrich, Malcolm Pratt, Sr.	East Hampton
Postscript	Parker, Cecil Carlton	East Hampton
Près Choisis / The Creeks	* Herter, Albert Caruso, Enrico [rented house]	East Hampton
Prim Close	Cloud, Chester Marts	East Hampton
Pudding Hill	* Herrick, Dr. Everett Ford, James Bishop Bishop, Bennett Peddy, John Richard	East Hampton
Purple House	Talmage, Mary Breck Vaill Mapes, Maie Bennett Kimball, Charles Edmunds, Jr.	East Hampton
Quail Hill	Light, Deborah [*see* Rubin entry]	Amagansett
Quelle Farm	* Spielberg, Steven Allan	East Hampton
The Rainbow	* Gallatin, James	East Hampton
Red Roof	* Rawson, Joseph, Jr.	Amagansett
Roads Meet	* Hinton, Alfred Post	East Hampton
Robinsfield	Whittemore, William John	East Hampton
Rosebrae	* Richey, The Reverend Alban, Sr.	East Hampton
Roselea	* McAlpin, Cordelia Maria Rose	East Hampton
Rowdy Hall	Huntting, Annie Hamlin, Mrs. Harry Leon Bouvier, John Vernou, III [rented house] Barnes, Robert Thorne, Henry Sanford	East Hampton
Sandpiper Hill	* McCaffray, Walter Peck	Montauk
Sandylands	Howell, John White, Sr.	Amagansett
San Souci	Mann, Henry	East Hampton
Sea Bluff	* Cory, David Cleveland	Amagansett
Seacroft	* Salembier, Paul Albert	East Hampton
Seafields	Rabbe, Richard Frederick	East Hampton
Seaholme	* Cammann, George Philip, Jr. Borden, Lewis Mercer, Sr.	East Hampton
Seamanor	Seaman, Joseph Husband, Sr.	East Hampton

Estate Names

Sea Side Cottage	* Mershon, The Reverend Stephen Lyon, Sr.	East Hampton
Sea Song	Flinn, Lawrence, Sr.	East Hampton
Sea Spray	* Homans, Eugene Vanderpool	East Hampton
Seaward	Nesbit, Elizabeth	East Hampton
Second Dune	Finkbeiner, Dr. John A.	East Hampton
Second House	Kennedy, David E.	Montauk
Seven Gables	Weston, Catherine Boudinot Stimson	East Hampton
Shadowmere	Wolff, Caroline Smith Snowden	East Hampton
Sherwood	Adair, Dr. Frank Earl	East Hampton
Solidago	Noble, Francis Osborn	East Hampton
Sommariva	* Jefferys, Charles Peter Beauchamp, Sr. Hobart, Marie Elizabeth Jefferys	East Hampton
South Wind	Dowling, Robert Whittle	East Hampton
Southwood Court	* LeRoy, Warner	Amagansett
Spencecliff	Weaver, Spencer Fullerton, Sr.	East Hampton
Spindrift	* King, Hamilton	East Hampton
Star Acres	Aubert, Marion Eugenia	Montauk
Sterling–Haven	Alexander, Edward Renick, Sr.	East Hampton
Stonybroke	Roudebush, John Heywood Larkin, Rosanne Roudebush	East Hampton
Stony Hill Farm	* Hamlin, Harry Leon Potter, Jeffrey Bracket	Amagansett
The Studio	* Moran, Thomas, Jr.	East Hampton
Subacawan	Ordway, Samuel Hanson, Sr.	East Hampton
Summertime	Rentschler, George Adam, Jr.	East Hampton
Sunset Cottage	Leaman, Alfred Valentine, Jr. Leaman, Alfred Valentine, III	East Hampton

Swan Cove	* Murphy, Gerald Clery
	Montgomery, Robert
	  aka Henry Montgomery, Jr.;
	  Robert Montgomery, Sr.
	de Liagre, Alfred, Jr.
	  aka Alfred Gustav Entienne de Liagre, Jr.
		East Hampton

Swan Cross	Leaman, Alfred Valentine, III	East Hampton
Tall Trees	Fuller, Edward Reinow	East Hampton
The following two entries are different houses:		
Tanglebrae	Mirick, Edna B. de Beixedon	East Hampton
Tanglebrae	* Solley, Dr. Fred Palmer	East Hampton
Taramar	Thiele, Albert Edward, Jr. Thiele, Roger Harvey	East Hampton
Tarriawyle	* Hackstaff, Charles Ludovic Walker, Dr. John Baldwin, Sr. Wood, Howard Ogden, Jr.	East Hampton
Ten Elms	Gunster, Joseph Frederick	East Hampton
Thalatta Cottage	* Johnson, Rossiter	Amagansett
Third House	Embury, Aymar, II	East Hampton

Estate Names

Tick Hall	Tweed, Harrison	Montauk
Tidelands	* Davies, Francis Herbert	East Hampton
Toad Hall	* de Menil, Francois 　　aka Francois Conrad Thomas de Menil	Amagansett
Tollemache House	Talmadge, John Frelinghuysen	East Hampton
T'Other House	* Hobart, Garret Augustus, Jr.	East Hampton
Tranquility	Backus, Henry Clinton	East Hampton
Travertine House	* Bunshaft, Gordon	East Hampton
Tree House	Washburn, George	East Hampton
Twinmill	Ramee, Joseph Russell	East Hampton
Under the Willows	Donoho, Gaines Ruger 　　aka Ruger Donoho	East Hampton
Up-the-Hill	Anderson, Edward Ewen	East Hampton
Vingt-et-Un	Wasey, Louis Rice	East Hampton
Water's Edge	Moody, Sidney Charles, Sr.	Amagansett
Waterwood	Leonard, Stephen Joseph, Sr.	East Hampton
Wayside	* Munroe, Dr. George E., Jr. Munroe, Marjory	East Hampton
Weeweecho	* Benson, Arthur W.	Montauk
Westernesse Farm	* Teetor, Charles Jessup	Amagansett
Westmeath	Dougherty, Bertha	East Hampton
Westover	* Talmage, Mary Breck Vaill Talmage, Rockwell Dwight	East Hampton
West Side Story	Blackburn, Wilmuth	East Hampton
Whale Off	Roberts, Dudley DeVore, Jr.	East Hampton
White-Cottage-By-the-Sea	* Coppell, Herbert	East Hampton
The White Elephant	Boots, Dr. Ralph Henderson, Sr.	East Hampton
The following two entries are different houses:		
White House	Gardiner, David Lion, Sr. Gardiner, David Lion, Jr. Gardiner, Miss Sarah Diodati	East Hampton
White House	* Gardiner, Miss Sarah Diodati Gardiner, Robert David Lion	East Hampton
Wildmoor	Bouvier, John Vernou, III	East Hampton
Willow Bend	Donoho, Gaines Ruger 　　aka Ruger Donoho Hassam, Frederick Childe 　　aka Childe Hassam	East Hampton
Willward Lodge	* Ward, William L.	Amagansett
Wilsheron	Fraser, Alexander	East Hampton
Windermere	Snow, Violetta Pierce	East Hampton
The Windmill	* Brown, Lathrop	Montauk
Windrow	Coler, Dr. Eugene Seeley	East Hampton

Estate Names

The following two entries are different houses:

Windward		* Paxton, The Reverend John Randolph, Sr. Hamlin, Mary Elkins Paxton	East Hampton
Windward		Francisco, Donald W., Sr. aka Don Francisco	Amagansett
Windway		Marsh, Marion Bolton	Montauk
Windy Dune		Bishopric, Allison, Jr. Cookson, Lucy Allison Bishopric	Amagansett
Winklehawk		* Spring, Preston Brady, Sr.	East Hampton
Wuthering		* Wheelock, Dr. William Efner Wheelock, John Hall	East Hampton
Wyandanch Acres		Seabury, Samuel	East Hampton
Yondermere		Greer, The Reverend David Hummell	East Hampton
Zanadu		Plimpton, George Ames	Amagansett

Hereditary Titles

Macy, Princess Lydia P. Bodrero

Mercati, Countess Barbara Tapper

Mercati, Countess Lily Stathatos

Mercati, Count Leonardo

Radziwill, Princess Caroline Lee Bouvier
aka Lee Radziwill

Radziwill, Prince Stanislaw Albrect

Landscape Architects

When the date of landscaping is known, it has been included in brackets. Since, in some instances, more than one landscape architect worked on an estate and, in some rare instances, the architect who designed the house also designed the estate's grounds, the surname entry should be consulted to determine if anyone else was involved in designing the estate grounds. When the estate owner who contracted for landscaping is known, it is indicated by an asterisk. Original and subsequent estate owners are included in the list.

Nellie Beatrice Osborn Allen

Greer, Lawrence		East Hampton
* McCall, Clifford Hyde, Sr.	*Kipsveen*	East Hampton
Mercati, Leonardo		East Hampton

Rupert Barneby

Dragon, Edward F. [see Ossorio entry]	*The Creeks* (designed evergreen plantings)	East Hampton
Herter, Albert	*Près Choisis / The Creeks* (designed evergreen plantings)	East Hampton
* Ossorio, Alfonso Angel	*The Creeks* (designed evergreen plantings	East Hampton
Perelman, Ronald Owen	(designed evergreen plantings)	East Hampton

Miranda Brooks

Church, Richard E.		Montauk
Drexler, Millard S. aka Mickey Drexler		Montauk
* Lindemann, Adam Marc		Montauk
Morrissey, Paul	*Eothen*	Montauk
Warhol, Andy aka Andrew Warhola, Jr.	*Eothen*	Montauk

Christopher H. Browne

* Browne, Christopher H.	*Chateau Amoris*	East Hampton
Rosenstein, Barry		East Hampton

Christopher H. Browne and Andrew S. Gordon

* Browne, Christopher H.		East Hampton

Marian Cruger Coffin

* Benjamin, Florence Almira Briggs	*Crossways* (designed perennial garden with privet arch, a small pool, and long grass *allee*, c. 1928)	East Hampton
* Benjamin, William Wallace, Jr.	*Crossways* (designed perennial garden with privet arch, a small pool, and long grass *allee*, c. 1928)	East Hampton
Benjamin, William Wallace, III	*Crossways* (designed perennial garden with privet arch, a small pool, and long grass *allee*, c. 1928)	East Hampton
Bruckman, Donald J.	(1927)	East Hampton
Flinn, Lawrence, Sr.	*Sea Song* (1927)	East Hampton
Lilley, Alexander Neil Sr.	*Crossways* (designed perennial garden with privet arch, a small pool, and long grass allee, c. 1928)	East Hampton

Landscape Architects

Marian Cruger Coffin (cont'd)

*	Woodin, William Hartman, Sr.	*Dune House* (1927)	East Hampton

Clara Couric

*	Couric, Katie aka Katherine Anne Couric		East Hampton

Ruth Bramley Dean

	Breen, Daniel Anthony, Jr.	*Furtherfield*	East Hampton
*	Embury, Aymar, II	*Third House*	East Hampton
*	Roberts, George Hewitt, Jr.	*Furtherfield*	East Hampton

Ruth Bramley Dean with **Anna Park Gilman Hill**

	Beale, Edith	*Grey Gardens*	East Hampton
	Beale, Phelan	*Grey Gardens*	East Hampton
	Bradlee, Benjamin Crowninshield, Sr.	*Grey Gardens*	East Hampton
*	Hill, Robert Carmer	*Grey Gardens*	East Hampton
	Phillips, Fleming Stanhope		East Hampton

Gaines Ruger Donoho (aka Ruger Donoho)

	Hassam, Frederick Childe aka Childe Hassam	*Willow Bend / Under the Willows*	East Hampton
*	Donoho, Gaines Ruger aka Ruger Donoho	*Willow Bend / Under the Willows*	East Hampton
	Stoddard, Mrs. Lillian M. [*see* Donoho entry]		East Hampton
	Strong, James W. [*see* Donoho entry]		East Hampton
	Wood, Wilfred		East Hampton

Victoria Fensterer

	Beale, Edith	*Grey Gardens*	East Hampton
	Beale, Phelan	*Grey Gardens*	East Hampton
	Bouvier, John Vernou, Jr.	*Little House* (pergola plantings)	East Hampton
*	Bradlee, Benjamin Crowninshield, Sr.	*Grey Gardens*	East Hampton
	Gottlieb, Adolph	(pergola plantings)	East Hampton
	Hill, Robert Carmer	*Grey Gardens*	East Hampton
	Phillips, Fleming Stanhope		East Hampton

Andrew Graham

	Edwards, Walter, Jr.	*Kilkare* (pool complex)	East Hampton
	Edwards, William Henry Leonard	*Kilkare* (pool complex)	East Hampton
*	Kennedy, Michael John	*Kilkare* (pool complex)	East Hampton

Perry Guillot

	Bouvier, John Vernou, Jr.	*Lasata*	East Hampton
	Bouvier, Maude Frances Sergeant	*Lasata*	East Hampton

Landscape Architects

Perry Guillot (cont'd)

    Gardiner, Lion   East Hampton

    Hufty, Frances May Archbold   East Hampton

*   Krakoff, Reed   East Hampton

    Martin, Laura Elizabeth Young   East Hampton

    Meehan, Joseph Ansbro   East Hampton

    Schurman, George Wellington   *Beachclose*   East Hampton

Tiziana Hardy

*   Spaeth, Eloise O'Mara   (gardens)   East Hampton

    Ranieri, Salvatore Anthony   (guest house gardens)

Paula Hayes

    Dougherty, Frances Cannon   East Hampton

    Fraser, Alexander   *Wilsheron*   East Hampton

    Hollister, Dr. Frederick Kellogg   East Hampton

*   Rosenstein, Barry   East Hampton

    Sweetser, Jesse William, Sr.   East Hampton

Albert and Adele McGinnis Herter

    Dragon, Edward F.   *The Creeks*   East Hampton
    [*see* Ossorio entry]

*   Herter, Albert   *Près Choisis / The Creeks*   East Hampton

    Ossorio, Alfonso Angel   *The Creeks*   East Hampton

    Perelman, Ronald Owen   East Hampton

Edmund Hollander

    Mnuchin, Alan Geoffrey   East Hampton

Mary Lois Deputy Lamson

    Breen, Daniel Anthony, Jr.   *Furtherfield*   East Hampton
        (c. 1941)

    Chace, Franklin M.   *Gone With the Wind*   East Hampton

    de Rose, Edward   *Millfield*   East Hampton

*   Douglas, Graham   *Millfield*   East Hampton

    Hare, Richard Vincent   East Hampton

    Manson, Thomas Lincoln, III   *Millfield*   East Hampton

    Miller, Jeremiah, IV   East Hampton

*   Ramee, Joseph Russell   *Twinmill*   East Hampton
        (c. 1941)

*   Roberts, George Hewitt, Jr.   *Furtherfield*   East Hampton
        (c. 1941)

    Van Rensselaer, Kiliaen   *Millfield*   East Hampton

    Wessel, Homer Augustus, Sr.   *Mill Crest*   East Hampton

Lear + Mahoney

    Gardiner, Robert Alexander   *Maidstone Hall*   East Hampton
        (1990)

    Gossler, Philip Green, Jr.   East Hampton

Landscape Architects

Lear + Mahoney (cont'd)

	Kennedy, Arthur	(1990)	East Hampton
	[see Terbell entry]		
	Terbell, Edward Dyer	*Maidstone Hall* (1990)	East Hampton
	Terbell, Henry S., Sr.	(1990)	East Hampton

Charles Nassau Lowrie, Sr.

	Bouvier, John Vernou, Jr.	*Lasata*	East Hampton
	Bouvier, Maude Frances Sergeant	*Lasata*	East Hampton
	Gallatin, Frederic	*Breezy Lawn*	East Hampton
	Gardiner, Lion		East Hampton
	Hufty, Frances May Archbold		East Hampton
	Krakoff, Reed		East Hampton
*	Leonard, Stephen Joseph, Sr.	*Waterwood*	East Hampton
	Martin, Laura Elizabeth Young		East Hampton
	Meehan, Joseph Ansbro		East Hampton
*	Schurman, George Wellington	*Beachclose*	East Hampton

Carol Keyser Mercer

*	Mercer, Norman J.		East Hampton

Frederick Law Olmsted

	Adams, Grant	(designed site plan)	Montauk
	Agnew, Dr. Cornelius Rea, Sr.	(designed site plan)	Montauk
	Andrews, William Loring	(designed site plan)	Montauk
	Aubert, Marion Eugenia Bragg	*Star Acres* (1929-1930)	Montauk
*	Benson, Arthur W.	*Weeweecho* (designed site plan)	Montauk
	Benson, Mary	*Weeweecho* (designed site plan)	Montauk
	Biggs, Florence	(designed site plan)	Montauk
	Bragg, Caleb Smith	(1929-1930)	Montauk
	Brisbane, Arthur	(designed site plan)	Montauk
	Cavett, Richard Alva aka Dick Cavett	(designed site plan)	Montauk
	[Cavett owned two houses in Montauk; both site plans were designed by Olmstead.]		
	Darby, James L.	(designed site plan)	Montauk
	de Forest, Henry Grant	(designed site plan)	Montauk
	Dennis, Frank	(designed site plan)	Montauk
	Donovan, Con	(designed site plan)	Montauk
	DuVal, Guy	*Awepesha* (designed site plan)	Montauk
	Eastman, Erik	(designed site plan)	Montauk
	Fisher, Carl Graham, Sr.	(designed site plan)	Montauk
	Goddard, Sidney	(designed site plan)	Montauk

Landscape Architects

Frederick Law Olmsted (cont'd)

Hourtel, Frank	(designed site plan)	Montauk
Hoyt, Alfred Miller	(designed site plan)	Montauk
Levi, Charles Matthew	(designed site plan)	Montauk
Lundberg, Holga	*Bayberry* (designed site plan)	Montauk
Marsh, Marion Bolton	*Windway* (designed site plan)	Montauk
Miller, L. W.	(designed site plan)	Montauk
Orr, Alexander Ector	(designed site plan)	Montauk
Sanger, Henry	(designed site plan)	Montauk
Sanger, Lilian	(designed site plan)	Montauk
Schnabel, Julian	(designed site plan)	Montauk
Sischy, Ingrid Barbara	(designed site plan)	Montauk
Smith, Dr. Dewey	(designed site plan)	Montauk
Smith, Hazanne	(designed site plan)	Montauk
Tweed, Harrison	*Tick Hall* (designed site plan)	Montauk
Upright, Frederick	(designed site plan)	Montauk
Vogel, George [*see* Andrews entry]	(designed site plan)	Montauk
Wagner, Miss H. Corinne [*see* Andrews entry]	(designed site plan)	Montauk
Weber, Bruce	(designed site plan)	Montauk

John Raum

Green, Adolph	(1917)	East Hampton
* Roberts, Walter Scott	(1917)	East Hampton
Seligson, William	(1917)	East Hampton
Spring, Preston Brady, Sr.	*Winklehawk* (1917)	East Hampton
* Wainwright, Carroll Livingston, Sr.	*Gullcrest* (designed rock, rose, and walled gardens, tennis courts, and greenhouse)	East Hampton
Weaver, Spence Fullerston, Sr.	*Spencecliff* (1917)	East Hampton

David Seeler

* Lang, Helmut	(1999)	Amagansett
Seegal, Frederic Milton	(1999)	Amagansett
Tyson, James	(1999)	Amagansett

Ellen Biddle Shipman

Fieldstein, Gary	(1926) [attributed]	East Hampton
* James, Ellery Sedgwick, Sr. aka William Ellery Sedgwick James, Sr.	*Heather Dune* [attributed]	East Hampton
Morton, Peter	(1926) [attributed]	East Hampton

Landscape Architects

Ellen Biddle Shipman (cont'd)

* Pruyn, Miss Mary Lansing		East Hampton
* Pruyn, Miss Neltje Knickerbocker		East Hampton
Rounick, Jack A.	(1926) *[attributed]*	East Hampton
* Ruxton, Philip	*Cairnhill*	East Hampton

Jacob John Spoon

Green, Adolph	(swimming pool)	East Hampton
Roberts, Walter Scott	(swimming pool)	East Hampton
Seligson, William	(swimming pool)	East Hampton
Spring, Preston Brady, Sr.	*Winklehawk* (swimming pool)	East Hampton
* Weaver, Spencer Fullerton, Sr.	*Spencecliff* (swimming pool)	East Hampton

Edwina Von Gal

Burton, Jane Erdmann	*Coxwould*	East Hampton
Erdmann, Dr. John Frederic	*Coxwould*	East Hampton
Hedges, Burke Osborn		East Hampton
Hedges, Dayton aka William Dayton Hedges		East Hampton
* Schulman, Lowell M.	*Beechwood*	East Hampton
Weinstein, Joseph		East Hampton

Maiden Names

The following list of maiden names of women associated with Town of East Hampton estates was compiled from various biographical sources, social registers, and newspaper obituaries. It should be noted that women occasionally gave surnames from previous marriages to editors, without designating them as such. If there were multiple marriages, husbands are listed in chronological order. Please note that the women included in this list were either the homeowners or spouses of homeowners. Women of subsequent generations are not included unless they assumed ownership of the house.

Abbott, Diahnne Eugenia aka Diahnne Dea	*married*	**De Niro**, Robert, Jr.
Abbott, Ellis		**Lardner**, Ringgold Wilmer, Sr. aka Ring Lardner
Abramson, Maureen Nancy		**Cogan**, Marshall Stuart
Ackley, Emily Matilda		**Donoho**, Gaines Ruger aka Ruger Donoho
Adams, Ida Robinson		**Gallatin**, James Nicholson **Anderson**, Francis Baldwin
Adkin, Daryl		**Roth**, Steven
Agnini, Cristina		**Rosset**, Barnet Lee, Jr. aka Barney Rosset
Alcebo, Maria De Lourdes		**Longaray**, ____ **Duke**, Anthony Drexel, Sr.
Alcock, Clarissa		**Bronfman**, Edgar Miles, Jr.
Alcott, Jane		**Holmes**, Jay **Roberts**, Dudley DeVore, Jr.
Alcott, Lucie Burke		**Joyner**, Dr. James Craig
Aldrich, Helen Hudson		**Steele**, The Reverend James Nevett, Sr.
Allen, Elizabeth Bryan		**Montgomery**, Robert aka Henry Montgomery, Jr.; Robert Montgomery, Sr.
Allen, Helen Jean		**Levering**, Richmond, Sr. aka John Richmond Levering, Sr.; John Mortimer Levering, Jr.
Allen, Nancy		**De Valma**, Brian Russell **Shoemaker**, Craig **Bailey**, Randy
Alpern, Ruth		**Madoff**, Bernard Lawrence aka Bernie Madoff
Ames, Gertrude		**Wood**, Robert Williams, Jr.
Anable, Alma Elizabeth		**Warrin**, Dr. Marshall Lord
Andrews, Aimee du Pont		**Howell**, Charles Morgan **Wainwright**, John Howard
Andrews, Jennie Morgan		**Shepherd**, James Gardner
Antman, Marion E.		**Bishop**, Bennett
Appleton, Florence		**Milholland**, James Clarke **Dodd**, John Mingus, III
Archbold, Frances May		**Hufty**, Mann Randolph Page aka Page Hufty
Armstrong, Edith		**Beardsley**, Thomas Hopper

Maiden Names

Aronson, Susan T.   **Hirschfeld**, Elie

Arrowsmith, Emma Douglas   **Woodhouse**, Lorenzo Guernsey
    Cummins, Edward Swete

Ashurst, Camilla   **Haag**, Joseph, Jr.

Asser, Wilhelmina Gesiena   **Parker**, Cecil Carlton

Atha, Ethelyn   **Chase**, Edward Tinsley

Atterbury, Julia Marie   **Stimson**, Henry Clark

Auchincloss, Josephine Lee   **Betner**, Benjamin Carlton, Jr.
    Nicholas, Harry Ingersoll, III

Auchincloss, Rosamund Saltonstall   **Burton**, James Lee, Jr.
    Betner, Benjamin Carlton, Jr.
    Plowden–Wardlaw, Thomas Campbell

Ault, Hildegard   **Buchner**, Ashby Wallingford, III
    Helm, George Washington, Sr.
    Tjeder, Rolf

Aurora, Alice   **Dunn**, Dr. James Manning

Avery, Georgia   **Kendrick**, The Reverend James Ryland

Avery, Mary Rebecca Halsey   **Talmage**, The Reverend Thomas DeWitt

Bacon, Hope   **Ryan**, Richard Nelson, Sr.
    Klenk, William Clifford, Jr.

Bacon, Mabel M.   **Thorne**, Henry Sanford
    Generelly, Laurent Roger
    Pope, Franklin Russell

Bacot, Emma Cecelia   **Richey**, The Reverend Thomas, Sr.

Bagg, Martha   **Phillips**, Fleming Stanhope

Bailey, Eunice   **Oakes**, William Pitt, II
    Gardiner, Robert David Lion

Baker, Josephine   **Drew**, John, Jr.

Baker, Laura Spencer   **Cobb**, Irvin Shewsbury

Baker, Mercy   **Osborn**, Jeremiah, Sr.

Baker, Viola A.   **Tilden**, John Newell, Sr.
    Cockcroft, Edward Truesdell

Banks, Betty   **Verlie**, John Deere, II

Banning, Barbara   **Tweed**, Harrison
    Estill, Holland

Barach, Susan   **Rebell**, ____
    Solomon, Peter Jay

Baratelli, Eleanora Renee   **Bonjovanni**, Robert Charles
    Kenney, Michael John

Barbey, Ida May   **Lewis**, Roger
       aka Joshua Roger Lewis

Barkin, Ellen Rona   **Byrne**, Gabriel
    Perelman, Ronald Owen

Barnes, Amy Fownes   **Tyson**, Mark

Barnes, Eliza Whitmore   **Bates**, Jerome Elliott

Maiden Names

Barnum, Laura C.

Bartlett, Madelon Alberta

Basinger, Kimila Ann
   aka Kim Basinger

Bates, Mary Charline

Bayer, Mary L.

Beaurang, Jacquelin

Becker, Claude

Beckwick, Bethany Ann

Begg, Frances Balfour

Behr, Gertrude Howell

Behr, Margaret Howell

Behr, May

Belden, Elizabeth Boies

Belknap, Mary C.

Bendelair, Helen

Benedict, Martha Buckham

Benjamin, Dorothy Park

Benjamin, Sallie Blanche

Bennett, Dorothy Elizabeth

Bennett, Maie

Bennett, Marion

Bergen, Candice

Berman, Caren Elaine

Bernard, Judy

Berry, Alice

Bertram, LoRaine

Bertschmann, Shelagh Banks

Bethel, Margaret Irene
   aka Irene Bethel

Bevan, Nina George

Levering, Richmond, Sr.
   aka John Richmond Levering, Sr.;
   John Mortimer Levering, Jr.

Volckening, Lloyd Irwin

Snyder–Britton, Ron
Baldwin, Alexander Rae, III
   aka Alec Baldwin

Salisbury, John W., Sr.
Massey, Maurice Richardson, Jr.

Entenmann, Robert William, Sr.

Schnabel, Julian

Wasserstein, Bruce Jay

Gardiner, Winthrop, Jr.
Nobel, Dana Gibson
Clark, Alfred Corning, II

Ashplant, Frederick Bryant, Sr.

Milne, John Cruickshank, II

Reid, Archibald Muge

Walker, Dr. William Henry, Jr.

Roberts, Dudley DeVore, Jr.
Cary, W. Miles, Jr.

Onderdonk, Dr. Thomas Williams

Leigh, Egerton Ward Boughton
McAlpin, Malcolm Evans

Barbour, William Stanton

Caruso, Enrico
Ingram, Ernest, A.
Holder, Dr. Charles Adams

McAlpin, George Lodowich, Sr.

Church, Richard Newton Loomis
Kaminski, Maximillian F.

Kimball, Charles Edmunds, Sr.
Mapes, Charles Halsted

Homans, Eugene Vanderpool

Malle, Louis
Rose, Marshall

Nederlander, Robert Elliot, Sr.

Baron, Ronald Stephen

Michaels, Lorne
   aka Lorne Lipowitz

Evans, James Hulburt

McConnell, David Hall, III
Richards, Ralph Strothers, Jr.

Tiedeman, Irvin Bruce, Sr.

Jenney, William Sherman

Maiden Names

Biller, Christine   **Clark**, Vernon L.
    Sinclaire, Paul

Bingham, Mabel   **Hess**, Harry Bellas

Birchett, Altana   **Garni**, Adolph
    aka Adolf Garni

Bishopric, Lucy Allison   **Bolch**, Carl Edward, Jr.
    Sprunger, Jean–Charles
    Cookson, Steven D.

Blum, Gladys Lenore   **Stryker**, Fred
    Rackmil, Milton
    Nederlander, Robert Elliot, Sr.

Boardman, Caroline Amelia   **Randell**, Rufus
    aka Roof the Roofer

Boardman, Geraldine Sewall   **Weeks**, John Kirkland, Sr.

Bochman, Ester Jean   **Bogert**, Edward Osgood

Bodrero, Lydia P.   **Macy**, Valentine Everit, Jr.
    Ranieri, Prince Don di San Faustino
    Redmond, Roland Livingston

Boettger, Theodora   **Topping**, Daniel Reid, Sr.

Bolton, Evelyn   **Poor**, James Harper

Bolton, Marion   **Marsh**, Frank Ballard

Bonbright, Harriet Cassard   **Evans**, Benjamin Franklin

Boorum, Mary Edwards   **Gordon**, George Breed

Bound, Josephine   **Embury**, Aymar, II
    Millett, Richard Caldwell

Bouvier, Caroline Lee   **Canfield**, Michael Temple
  aka Lee Bouvier   **Radziwill**, Stanislaw Albrecht
    Ross, Herbert David

Bouvier, Edith Ewing   **Beale**, Phelan, Sr.

Bouvier, Michelle Caroline   **Scott**, Henry Clarkson, Sr.
    Putnam, Harrington, Jr.

Bovingdon, Jane   **Semel**, Terrance Steven

Bowden, Priscilla   **Potter**, Jeffrey Brackett

Bowers, Louise   **Cater**, Arthur Aymar

Boyce, Virginia Lee Roberts   **Sterling**, Oliver James, Sr.
    Mueller, Gustave A.
    Lind, Albert William

Boyon, Delphine A.   **Krakoff**, Reed

Braatz, Joanne   **Breyer**, Henry William, III

Bradley, Gladys Virginia   **Thaw**, William, III

Bradley, Isabelle   **Robertson**, Hugh James, Jr.

Bragg, Marion Eugenia   **Laws**, Harry Langdon, III
    Aubert, Ludvig Caesar Martin, II

Brandes, Dorothea   **Conway**, Edmund Virgil, II

Brashaer, Gense   **Parry**, Vernon Cadwallerader Gordon
    Simmons, Zalmon Gilbert, III
    Sinclaire, Paul

Maiden Names

Bray, Alice Peck	**Todd**, John Reynard, Sr.
Breck, Isabella Mary	**Vaill**, Timothy Dwight
Breckinridge, Isabella Goodrich	**Dubow**, Arthur Myron
Brennan, Helen F.	**Kurzner**, Dr. Rubin Raymond
Brenner, Dr. Arleen	**Rifkind**, Robert Singer
Brewer, Sherry	**Bronfman**, Edgar Miles, Jr.
Brewster, Lydia Amanda aka Amanda Brewster	**Sewell**, Robert Van Vorst
Brickell, Edie Arlisa	**Simon**, Paul Frederic
Briggs, Caroline Frye	**Hobart**, Garret Augustus, Jr.
Briggs, Florence Almira	**Benjamin**, William Wallace, Jr.
Brinkley, Christie	**Allaux**, Jean–Francois **Joel**, Billy aka William Martin Joel **Taubman**, Richard **Cook**, Peter Halsey
Brof, Ethel Bernstein	**Gruzen**, Barnet Sumner
Brooks, Mary Ella	**Reutersham**, James Hall **Richard**, Mark Gadd
Brown, Anna Mary	**Ireland**, George, Jr.
Brown, Evelyn	**Niedringhaus**, William Francis **Olin**, John Merrill
Brown, Georgia	**Hedges**, Burke Osborn
Brown, Helen	**Hale**, Herbert Dudley, Sr. **Dodge**, Washington, Jr.
Brown, Louise	**Voorhees**, Dr. James Ditmars aka Dr. James Ditmars Van Voorhees
Brown, Mildred Leona	**Schwab**, Laurence, Sr.
Brown, Sheila Tucker	**Maxwell**, John Courtland, Jr. **Le Brecht**, Robert
Browning, Cathalene Parker aka Cathalene Crane	**Widdoes**, ____ **Chase**, Edward Tingsley **Cederquist**, John
Bryan, Carolyn Laura	**Thompson**, Dr. Frederick Roeck
Bucher, Lina	**Osborne**, Burnett Mulford
Bucknell, Sue Cunningham	**Potter**, Dickson Bayard
Buffington, Ella Fisher	**Aldrich**, Malcolm Pratt, Sr.
Buhler, Edith Louise	**Fennelly**, Leo C.
Bumiller, Elizabeth F.	**Clarke**, E. Thurston **Beard**, Jeremiah Robinson, Jr. **Johnstone**, Vanderburgh
Burdett, Ruth Mary	**Herrick**, Anson Boulton, Sr.
Burg, Linda	**Macklowe**, Harry B.
Burke, Lucie A.	**Alcott**, Clarence Frank

Maiden Names

Burns, Kathleen Ingrid

Bush, Nan

Bush, Sarah
   aka Sally Bush

Butvay, Audrey M.

Cady, Elizabeth

Calderon, Arcadia

Call, Florence Louise

Callan, Erin M.

Callaway, Jencie
   aka Jencie Callaway–John

Campbell, Clara Louise

Campbell, Elizabeth Detwiller

Campbell, Lucile

Cannon, Frances Ann

Carlin, Jacquelin Jean

Carnahan, Florence

Carnochan, Mary Morris

Carter, Alice

Carter, Dorothea

Cary, Jacqueline

Cary, Phoebe

Case, Kate

Cassidy, Mary Jane

Centre, Jayne

Chao, Angela

Chapin, Mary Stevens

Chapman, Anna

Chardenet, Elizabeth

Chefetz, Harriet

Cherner, Nadine

Chisholm, Sarah H.
   aka Chise Farrington

Bartle, Thomas Preston, Jr.
Buddenhagen, Frederick Leonard

Weber, Bruce

Bullard, ____
Foss, Martin Moore, Sr.
Thorne, Henry Sanford

Nach, Dr. Ralph J.
Gruss, Martin David

Ryan, Frederick Behrens, Sr.

Zalles, Jorje Ezequiel, Sr.
   aka Jorge Ezequiel Zalles, Sr.

Abbott, Henry Hurlbut

Thompson, Michael P.
Montella, Anthony

John, Davis W.

Yates, James Saville

Blackburn, Wilmuth Earle

Chapman, Benjamin Gaines, Jr.

Hersey, John
Dougherty, Frazer Lowber Welsh

Chase, Chevy
   aka Cornelius Crane Chase
Canon, Peter Bryan
Jorden, Terrence Paul
   aka Terry Melcher

Hammond, Percy

Aspinwall, James Lawrence

Dickerman, William Carter, Sr.

Leaman, Alfred Valentine, Jr.

Holmes, Jay

Brisbane, Arthur

Barnes, Donald E.
Whitney, Elwood

Robinson, Felding S.

Klein, Calvin
   aka Calvin Richard Klein

Wasserstein, Bruce Jay

Krech, Dr. Shephard, Sr.

Perelman, Ronald Owen

Franey, Pierre

Hillman, Murray
Arnold, Henri

Zamichow, Bernard
Liberman, James B.

Farrington, Selwyn Kip, Jr.

Maiden Names

Chopin, Lelia Marie   **Hattersley**, Frederick Robert

Clarbough, Margaret   **Weeks**, John Lafayette

Clark, Eleanor   **Osborne**, Nelson Cook, Sr.

Clarke, Anne Gibson   **Washburn**, George

Clarke, Catherine Fowler   **Whitmarsh**, Karl Russell
                                             Carse, Donald Rede
                                             Bint, A. A.

Clarke, Martha Brooke   **Laughlin**, David Walker
    aka Brooke Clarke

Clay, Jane   **Zevely**, James William, Sr.

Clement, Tamara Victoria   **Gianis**, Socrates George, Sr.

Clifford, Marie Louise   **Bonner**, Frederic

Clossey, Elizabeth   **Nesbit**, Robert Wilson

Coe, Dorothy   **Embury**, Aymar, II

Coe, Selina Alva   **Kerr**, Chauncy F.
                          Bailey, Charles Weaver

Coffey, Lucy Edwalyn   **de Kay**, Charles

Coggill, Isabel   **Nash**, Stephen Edward

Cohen, Claudia Lynn   **Perelman**, Ronald Owen

Colby, Lisle U.   **Thomas**, Augustus

Coleman, Judith Crittenden   **Adams**, Charles Henry

Coler, Helen Danforth   **Jackson**, Richard Seymour
                             Seiferheld, David F.
                             Muensterberger, Werner

Collier, Eleanor   **Talmage**, The Reverend Thomas DeWitt

Collier, Margaret Eleanor   **Fisher**, Carl Graham, Sr.
                               Lyon, Howard W.

Collings, Christine   **Hall**, William Claiborne

Collins, Marjorie Lee   **Bishopric**, Allison, Jr.

Collyer, Harriet   **Eastman**, Joseph

Conde, Naomi Clele   **Cammann**, Roy Lennox

Conderman, Ethel L   **Ward**, Newell Jube, Sr.

Constantine, Charlotte   **Jones**, Rodney Wilcox, Sr.

Conway, Rita   **Clark**, Thomas A.
                Richard, Auguste

Cook, Maria Fahys   **Dean**, Howard Brush, Sr.
                    Roberts, Dudley DeVore, Jr.

Cooney, Laurette Helen   **Taylor**, Charles Alonzo
                             Manners, John Hartley

Cooper, Clara   **Stratton**, Charles Preston

Cory, Pauline Munroe   **Gallatin**, James Nicholson
                        Ullman, Joseph Stevens
                        Dansey, Sir Claude Edward Marjoribanks

Coughlan, Charlotte Virginia   **Stevens**, William MacDuff
                                   Rice, Ernest H., Sr.

Maiden Names

Couric, Katie
    aka Katherine Anne Couric

Coward, Miriam Van Winkle

Cox, Virginia Osborne

Crabbe, Idoline Lochrane Watts

Crane, Ida E.

Crane, Jane Elizabeth

Creel, Alexandra Gardiner

Crespi, Pilar

Crocker, Diana

Croll, Selina Schroeder
    aka Tina Croll

Crouch, Dorothy

Cunningham, Phyllis

Curley, Irene

Curran, Alys Mary

Curran, Juliana Mae

Currier, Sarah

Curtis, Alma Mae

Cushing, Mary Olivia Cochran

Cutler, Diana Victoria

Dalberg, Marjorie Blair

Dale, Michelle

Damson, Betty Ann

Darrow, Emma

Daste, Claude

Davis, Fannie Eliza

Davis, Harriet Ivins

Davis, Katharine

Davis, Mattie

Monahan, John Paul, III
Molner, John P.

Rice, Ernest H., Sr.
Pierson, Arthur Newton, Jr.

Northrop, John Burr, Sr.
Smith, Arthur J.

Scheerer, William, II

Benjamin, Park, III
    aka Park Benjamin, Jr.

Andrews, William Loring

Tufo, Peter Francis
Goelet, Robert Guestier

Echavarra, Gabriel
Robert, Stephen Kniznick

Redington, John
Nori, Edmond Joseph

Bellas, Albert Constantine

Harris, Joseph
Ashplant, Frederick Bryant, Sr.

Leith, Donald E.

Bodde, John R.
Hutton, Franklin Laws
Moffett, James Andrew, Jr.

McCaffray, Walter Peck

Terian, Peter Gabriel
Gilbert, Bruce

Stickney, William Arthur
Elkins, Felton
Woolley, Knight

Huhn, George Albert, III
Leonard, Stephen Joseph, Sr.

Beard, Peter Hill
Coleman, James Julian, Jr.

Rowe, John Jay, Jr.

Steele, Louis Thorton

Gerli, David Charles, Sr.

Steel, Robert, Sr.
Gwathney, Charles

Dodd, Charles Goodhue
Burnett, Eugene Rodney

Rosinsky, Harold Jack
    aka Harold Jack Rosinski

McCord, David Walter

Backus, Henry Clinton

Bracken, James W.

Lawrence, John Custis

Maiden Names

Dawson, Elisabeth Hill

Day, Randee Elaine

Dayan, Amalia

Dayton, Alice Isabell

Dean, Ruth Bramley

de Baume, Germaine Adelaide

De Bache, Maritza

de Beixedon, Edna B.

de Chollet, Jacqueline Mary

DeGraff, Eleanor Maitland

de Kay, Phyllis Edwalyn

Denton, Elizabeth

de Menil, Louise Adelaide
 aka Adelaide de Menil

de Raimes, Emma Josephine

de Raimes, Martha Jeanne

de Saussure, Mary Peronneau

Detwiller, Elizabeth Warne

Deutsch, Karen Mae

de Vlaming, Marion

Devine, Katherine Ann

DeWitt, Louise Virginia

Dick, Esther

Diller, Ramona Elsie

Dimon, Katharine

Dingee, Nellie Barnum

Ditmas, Louise Thorne

Doane, Kathleen Maude

Dodd, Helen Marr

Dodd, Patricia

Doerr, Caroline Louise

Dolan, Frances A.

Dolese, Laura

Gallatin, James

Ammon, Robert Theodore
 aka Ted Ammon
Grogos, George Morganakis

Lindemann, Adam Marc

Wood, Arthur B.
 aka Arthur W. B. Wood

Embury, Aymar, II

Christie, Arthur Read
Gossler, Philip Green, Jr.
Benjamin, Henry Rogers, Sr.
Cromwell, James H. R.

Hedges, Burke Osborn

Mirc, Pierre Paul
Mirick, Harry Lawrence, Sr.

Weir, Viscount Kenneth James, III
Towbin, Abraham Robert

Carr, Dr. Frank Clyde, Sr.

Bury, Edward Basil
Wheelock, John Hall

Akin, Robert Macomber, Jr.

Carpenter, Edmund Snow

Storey, Edward Albert

Warrin, Dr. Marshall Lord

Craig, Dr. Stuart Lessley

Campbell, Nathaniel Adams, Sr.

Cohen, Peter Anthony

Flinn, Lawrence, Sr.
Tuohy, Thomas F., Jr.

McConnell, Neil Anderson
Hayden, Sterling

Ruxton, Philip

Gottlieb, Adolph

Bacon, Clarence Everett, Jr.

Hamlin, Harry Leon

Lutkins, Clinton Stephen

Talmadge, John Frelinghuysen

Hassam, Frederick Childe
 aka Childe Hassam

Cole, John Nelson, Jr.

Fraser, Ronald Goodall

Carse, Donald Rede, Sr.

Bell, Dr. Dennistoun Mildeberger

Klotz, Charles Arthur

Maiden Names

d'Olier, Winfred Lee — **Brown,** Anthony Coates
Dominick, Janet Isabel — **Lockwood,** Williston Benedict
Dominick, Mabel — **Hinton,** Alfred Post
Donaldson, Dorothy — **Snell,** Lawrence Woodsworth, Jr.
    Gossler, Philip Green, Jr.
Donnelly, Tania Adams — **Simon,** William Edward, Sr.
Doughty, Mary Rosenia — **Washburn,** William Tucker
Douglas, Adelaide Louise — **Austin,** William Gage
Douglas, Diane M. — **Duke,** Anthony Drexel, Sr.
    Goodrich, Hunter, Jr.
    Lamborn, George D. F.
Dourman, Judith Wilcox — **Skidmore,** Samuel Tredwell, II
Dows, Juliet Buckingham — **Orr,** Alexander Ector
Dowden, Isabelle — **Johnson,** Malcolm Perry
    Hiss, Alger
Drake, Mary Cortland — **Howell,** John White, Sr.
Drake, Nancy Lee — **Entenmann,** Charles, Sr.
Draper, Edith — **Blair,** Montgomery, II
Draper, Jessie — **Bowne,** Robert Southgate
Drew, Louise — **Devereaux,** Jack
Du Croz, Dorothy Patience — **May,** Patrick William
    Young, Roland
    Benjamin, William Wallace, III
Dudley, Jennie T. — **Eidlitz,** Cyrus Lazelle Warner
Dudley, Sarah Whitehead — **Plimpton,** George Ames
Durant, Jeannie Terry — **Rice,** Dr. Clarence Charles
Durham, Dorothy D. — **Beale,** Phelan, Sr.
Dwight, Veronica — **Richard,** Mark Gadd
Dwyer, Marietta — **Moranti,** Paul Joseph
Dyer, Hannah — **Terbell,** Henry S., Sr.
    aka Henry S. Tarbell
Eastman, Linda Louise — **See,** Joseph Melville
    McCartney, Paul
        aka James Paul McCartney
Eaton, Ruth Lois — **Warner,** Eltinge Fowler, Jr.
Eckert, Hannelore — **Rosset,** Barnet Lee, Jr.
    aka Lily Eckert —   aka Barney Rosset
Edgeworth, Merri — **Peddy,** John Richard
Edson, Ethel Townsend — **Van Brunt,** Arthur Hoffman, Sr.
Edwards, Camilla Leonard — **Nobel,** Francis Osborn
Edwards, Elizabeth Erwin — **Lockwood,** William Andrew
Edwards, Jeannette Frances — **Rattray,** Arnold Elsmere
Edwards, Katharine Irene — **Bennett,** Russell Conwell, Sr.
Edwards, Katherine Harkness — **Nichols,** Harold Willis, Jr.

Maiden Names

Edwards, Lela Harkness   **Cook**, Harry
                                     Closson, A. Burton

Edwards, Mary Kate   **Laughlin**, Alexander Mellon, Jr.

Edwards, Phoebe Alice   **Lawrence**, Isaac
                                     Lawrence, John Custis

Efner, Harriette   **Wheelock**, William Almy

Eidlitz, Harriet Frances   **Quackenbush**, Schuyler

Eisinger, Pamela   **Zaslav**, David M.

Ely, Karen   **Thiele**, Roger Harvey

Emerson, Margaret Genevieve   **Dowdney**, Louis Purcell

Enfield, Virginia   **Whitney**, Elwood

Ensign, Angeline   **Newman**, The Reverend John Philip

Epes, Virginia Millan   **Harper**, Marion, Clay, Jr.
                                     Jennings, Lewis B.

Ephron, Nora   **Greenberg**, Dan
                                     Bernstein, Carl
                                     Pileggi, Nicholas, Jr.

Erdmann, Jane   **Burton**, William Lafayette
                                     Gonzalez, Francisco Aurelio
                                     Whitney, Morgan

Erdmann, Olivia Sturtevant   **Kuser**, John Louis, Jr.

Espy, Freddy M.   **Plimpton**, George Ames

Evans, Madeline   **McAlpin**, David Hunter, II

Everhart, Mary   **Schmidt**, Max Eberhardt
                                     aka Max Everhart Smith

Ewing, Estelle   **Rowe**, Eugene Frederick
                                     Wardele, H. Allen

Fagan, Madeline   **DeVoe**, Raymond Forsyth, Sr.

Fairbanks, Florence   **DuVal**, Guy

Falconer, Deborah   **Downey**, Robert, Jr.

Falk, Judith   **Stern**, Leonard Norman
                                     Peck, Stephen M.

Fansler, Priscilla Harriet   **Hobson**, Francis Thayer
                                     Hiss, Alger

Farnsworth, Elizabeth Ellen   **Loomis**, Alfred Lee, Sr.

Faske, Donna Ivy   **Karan**, Mark
                                     Weiss, Stephan

Feit, Valerie   **Harper**, Marion Clay, Jr.

Fennelly, Marcia Ann   **Gowen**, George W., II

Ferguson, Lee   **Gruzen**, Jordan Lee

Fernandes, Marisol   **Binn**, Moreton
                                     aka Moreton Binstock

Fifield, Ellen L.   **Gleason**, Carlislie Joyslin

Finke, Patricia   **Cohen**, Steven A.

Finnegan, Patricia Ann   **McKeon**, Robert Brian

Maiden Names

Firestone, Martha Parke
Fish, Barbara Ellen
Fisher, Carrie Frances
Fiske, Merle
Flandrau, Julia Dinsmore
Fleming, Marjorie

Florence, Josephine
Flynn, Dorian
Foos, Alice Van Benschoten
Ford, Harriet
Ford, Mabel Percy
Forrestal, Susan

Forrester, Frances L.
Forsyth, Rosemary

Foss, Esther

Fox, Susan
Franklin, Evelyn
French, Marie
Fried, Elaine Marie Catherine
Froblich, Ingrid Lily
Fuller, Allon Mae

Gager, Rae

Gaither, Imogen
Gallatin, Jean Buchanan
Ganz, Joan
   aka Joan Ganz Cooney
Garcia, Alexandra
Gardiner, Adelia Dempster

Gardiner, Alexandra Diodati
Gardiner, Isabel Tasker
   aka Isabel T. L. Gardiner;
   Isabel Fairfax Gardiner
Gardiner, Miss Sarah Diodati
Gardiner, Sarah Griswold

Ford, William Clay, Sr.
Lee, Thomas Haskell
Simon, Paul Frederic
Tuck, Frederick W., Jr.
Ethridge, George
Lloyd–Smith, Wilton
Woolley, Knight
Preusse, Charles Frances
Fuhrman, Gary L.
Bailey, Dr. Theodorus, II
Herrick, Dr. Everett
Mayo–Smith, Richmond, Sr.
Michaels, Lorne
   aka Lorne Lipowitz
Waranach, Ron
Horwits, Alan Skip
Raymond, Dana Merriam
Tolan, Michael
   aka Seymour Tuchow
Waranach, Ron
Horwits, Alan Skip
Moore, George Gordon
Roark, Aiden
Fish, Sidney Webster
Deveraux, John Drew
Avedon, Richard
Terry, Dr. Arthur H., Jr.
de Kooning, Willem
Burns, Thomas Robert
Black, Harry S.
Morse, Tyler
Alexander, ____
Wasey, Louis Rice
Aldrich, Spencer Wyman
Cammann, George Philip, Jr.
Cooney, Timothy Jefferies
Peterson, Peter George
Cohen, Steven A.
Chamberlin, George E.
McAlpin, David Hunter, Sr.
Creel, James Randall, Jr.
Mairs, Olney Blanchard, Jr.

Tyler, John Alexander

Maiden Names

Garmendia, Olatz Lopez — **Schnabel**, Julian
Garnett, May — **Roberts**, Walter Scott
Gaspar, Marie — **Schwab**, Laurence, Sr.
Gaynor, Ella Frances — **McCall**, Edward Everett
Greenleaf, Katharine Nash — **Duffield**, Howard
Geer, Helen Danforth — **Coler**, Dr. Eugene Seeley
Goodwin, Harold

Gerdes, Margery — **Miller**, Dudley Livingston, Sr.
Twining, Edmund S.
Fates, Harold Leighton, Sr.
Tessier, Dr. John Sylvester

Gerry, Amy Goelet — **Gallatin**, Frederic
Getman, Sarah Frances — **Plumb**, Ralph Hudson
Finbeiner, Dr. John A.

Gilchrist, Frederica Burckle — **Howell**, John White, Sr.
Gilfillan, Rebecca Janet — **Avery**, Edward Strong
Gillies, Jessie E. — **Clark**, Ivor Bache, Sr.
Gilman, Anna Park — **Hill**, Robert Carmer
Gioiella, Mary Louise — **Ranieri**, Salvatore Anthony
Girard, Carol Ann — **Simon**, William Edward, Sr.
Glenn, Frances Trent — **Moody**, Sidney Clarke, Sr.
Golan, Riva Arilla — **Ritvo**, Edward
Slifka, Alan Bruce

Golden, Gail — **Ichan**, Carl Celian
Golding, Faith — **Perelman**, Ronald Owen
Linden, Peter J.

Goodman, Brooke — **Cohen**, Peter Anthony
Goodman, Joan Ellen — **Jaffe**, Stanley Richard
Goodman, Marjorie Sawyer — **Dewey**, Charles Schuveldt, Jr.
Graff, Robert D.

Gosman, Roberta — **Donovan**, Cornelius Peter, Jr.
aka Con Donovan

Gould, Edith Catherine — **Wainwright**, Carroll Livingston, Sr.
McNeal, Hector Murray

Gould, Josephine — **Betts**, Hobart Dominick, Sr.
Gradinger, Rita — **Haupt**, Melville I.
Mayer, ____

Graham, Elizabeth Ashley — **Lindemann**, Adam Marc
Graham, Dr. Fiona Margaret — **Idriss**, Jarvard S.
Citron, Casper Henry

Grant, Elizabeth — **Harkness**, William Hale
Montgomery, Robert
aka Henry Montgomery, Jr.;
Robert Montgomery, Sr.

Grant, Louise — **Worthington**, Henry Carver

Maiden Names

Green, Evelyn

Greenberg, Joan Ellen

Greenleaf, Katharine Nash

Gregorio, Darnell
aka Darnell Gregorio–De Palma

Grimes, Helen Morris

Grimm, Evelyn

Groot, Mary
aka Mae Groot Manson

Gruner, Charlotte Dater

Gualtier, Francine

Guzman, Pilar

Hackstaff, Caryl

Hackstaff, Mai Elemendorf

Haddock, Anne Elizabeth

Haggerty, Frances S.

Haig, Sandra Dorothea

Haight, Elinor

Hale, Christina

Hall, Alice Bevier

Hall, Emily Charlotte

Halsey, Jessica Hildreth

Hamilton, Pamalee

Harkness, Lela

Harper, Peggy

Harrington, Mary Ellen

Harris, Claire Callaway

Harris, Harriet Ruth

Harris, Judith C.

Harris, Marjorie R.

Harris, Mary Greis

Hartmann, Phyllis

Harvey, Anne Woodin

Hamm, Fred John
Haynes, Justin O'Brien, Sr.

Gruzen, Jordan Lee
Levinson, Monroe
aka Mon Levinson

Duffield, The Reverend Howard

Holland, Keith
De Palma, Brian Russell
Baldi, Edoardo

Mann, Henry

Jenkins, Edward Elliott

Manson, Thomas Lincoln, III

Bishop, Dr. Louis Faugeres, Sr.

Ranieri, Salvatore Anthony

Mitchell, Christopher

Wood, Howard Ogden, Jr.

Walker, Dr. John Baldwin, Sr.

Hare, Richard Vincent

Draper, Simeon, Jr.

Merriman, David Woods
McConnell, Neil Anderson

Monell, Theodore, Sr.
Brush, E. H.

Hirtenstein, Michael

Bartle, William A., Jr.
Dowling, Robert Whittle

Wheelock, Dr. William Efner

Slade, Arthur Jarvis
King, Hamilton

Kennedy, Michael John

Edwards, Dr. Ogden Matthias, Jr.

Lewis, Mort
Simon, Paul Frederic

Gosman, Robert H.

Sinclaire, Paul

Work, Horace Hutchins, Sr.
Gunster, Joseph Frederick

Douglas, Paul
Geddes, Gerald Maxwell

Rabbe, Richard Frederick

Gilchrist, Alan
Wainwright, Stuyvesant, II

Rounick, Jack A.

Gram, Carl William, Jr.
Gerli, David Charles, Sr.

Maiden Names

Havemeyer, Helen Mitchell   **Thorne**, Henry Sanford
Hawson, Florence   **Noble**, Mark Ainslie
Hays, Virginia   **Butler**, Howard Russell, Sr.
Healey, Cynthia Smathers   **Krech**, Merrill
    Kiser, John William, III
      aka John William Kiser, Jr.

Hedge, Sara Woodbury Sylvester   **Godwin**, Courtlandt
Heins, Clara   **Cornell**, William Frank
Hemenway, Hetty Lawrence   **Richard**, Auguste
Henderson, Jane   **Deveraux**, John Drew
Henderson, Julia   **Levering**, John Mortimer [Sr.]
Hendrickson, Phebe   **Osborne**, Dr. Edward Monroe, Sr.
Henje, Sonja   **Topping**, Daniel Reid, Sr.
    Gardiner, Winthrop, Jr.
    Ornstad, Niels

Henning, Helene Elizabeth   **Cavanagh**, Edward Francis, III
    Wainwright, Stuyvesant, II

Henron, Dorothy   **Montgomery**, Paul
      aka John Paul Montgomery

Herlow, Janne   **Janson**, Carl E.
    Rumbough, Stanley Maddox, Jr.

Herrick, Rose Marie   **Jackson**, John Day
Hewitt, Suzanne   **Chase**, Chevy
      aka Cornelius Crane Chase

Higgins, Anita Van Lennep   **Townsend**, Charles Coe
    Salembier, Harold Paul

Hightower, Grace   **De Niro**, Robert, Jr.
Hilger, Cicely Mary   **Cameron**, Walter Scott
    Burke, Oscar Moech

Hill, Anna R. H.   **Wright**, John Howie, Jr.
Hill, Christine   **Bartlett**, Edward Everett, Jr.
Hinman, Irene   **Taylor**, Irving Howland
Hitt, Diana   **Romaine**, Henry Simmons
    Potter, Jeffrey Brackett

Hoadley, Louise Russell   **James**, Ellery Sedgwick, Sr.
      aka William Ellery Sedgwick James, Sr.
    Wright, Richardson

Hoban, Elise Alexandrine   **Alexander**, Edward Renick, Sr.
Hoeke, Anna Louise   **Mapes**, Victor
      aka Sidney Sharp

Hoffman, Margaret Euphemia   **Hackstaff**, Charles Ludovic
Hoggarth, Helen Oswald   **Talmage**, Rockwell Dwight
Hoguet, Marie Virginia   **Ramee**, Joseph Russell
Holdsworth, Nancy   **Hutchinson**, Edward Stotesbury
    Scheerer, Joseph Durand, Sr.

Holland, Marjorie   **McKittrick**, Walter

Maiden Names

Hollis, Katharine — **Rice**, Henry Grantland
    aka Grantland Rice

Holmes, Helen Burt — **Streit**, Samuel F.
Bell, Alfred Dennis, Sr.

Homan, Caroline Isabella — **Hedges**, John Daniel

Hook, Rosalie Dean — **Gwathmey**, Robert, Jr.

Hooper, Helen Chamblet — **Brown**, Lathrop

Hopkinson, Barbara — **Scheerer**, Paul Renner, Jr.

Hopkinson, Marion — **Brooks**, Ernest
Adair, Dr. Frank Earl

Hopper, Elizabeth Ann — **Beardsley**, Samuel Arthur, Sr.

Hornbogen, Sally — **Peterson**, Peter George
Carlisle, Michael

Horsman, Mary — **Appleton**, Robert Wilmarth
Swain, Spencer
La Mont, Murray Herbert

Howard, Rose — **Jewett**, Edward Hull, Sr.

Howell, Lillian Leacock — **Weaver**, Spencer Fullerton, Sr.

Howes, Ellen Osborn — **Hedges**, Henry Denison

Hubbard, Helen Kent — **Dodge**, Washington, Jr.
Ferrara, Peter Joseph

Huidekoper, Page Caroline — **Dougherty**, Frazer Lowber Welsh
Wilson, Thomas W., Jr.

Hulsapple, Alma Elizabeth — **Watts**, Harry Wilfred

Hume, Carol — **Tolan**, Michael
    aka Seymour Tuchow

Hunt, Helen Schonwolf — **Helier**, Frederick
Sinclaire, Paul

Hurd, Gale Anne — **Cameron**, James
De Palma, Brian Russell
Hensleigh, Jonathan

Hurlbut, Louise — **Parker**, Roy Tilden, Jr.

Hurley, Dorothea — **Bon Jovi**, Jon
    aka John Francis Bongiove, Jr.

Hutton, Nedenia Marjorie
    aka Dina Merrill — **Rumbough**, Stanley Maddox, Jr.
Robertson, Clifford Parker, III
    aka Cliff Robertson
Hartley, Theodore Ringwalt

Ingersoll, Anne — **Brackenridge**, Gavin, Sr.

Ingersoll, Jane Bond — **Scheerer**, Joseph Durand, Sr.

Ireland, Julia C. — **Spring**, Preston Brady, Sr.

Irving, Amy Davis — **Spielberg**, Steven Allan
Barreto, Bruno
Bowser, Kenneth, Jr.

Jackson, Harriet — **Ely**, John Ingraham

Jacobs, Elinore — **Stettenheim**, Frederic R.
Marvel, Josiah Peter

Maiden Names

Jaeckel, Marie — **Borden**, Lewis Mercer, Sr.
James, Amy — **Newton**, Francis
Jameson, Jeanetta Chalmers — **Chace**, Franklin M.
Jarcho, Alice — **Gallagher**, Thomas
Jebreal, Rula — **Rivalta**, Davide
    Altschul, Arthur Goodhart, Jr.

Jedlicka, Amy — **Krakoff**, Reed
Jefferys, Marie Elizabeth — **Hobart**, Henry Lee
Jenkinson, Mary E. — **Ball**, James T.
    Ogden, James Lawrence, Jr.

Jenney, Elizabeth — **Ayer**, Frederick, II
    Richards, Richard Draper
        aka Richards Follett

Jensen, Leah Kathleen — **Rumbough**, Stanley Hutton
Jessup, Annie — **Woodin**, William Hartman, Sr.
Johnson, Edith Seymour — **Chisholm**, Edward de Clifford
Johnson, Helen Natalie — **Anderson**, Edward Ewen
Johnson, Martha Frances — **Harkness**, Lamon Vanderburg
Johnston, Jane Eliza — **Procter**, William Cooper
Johnston, Mary Catherine — **Head**, Benjamin Thomas
    Evans, James Hurlburt

Johnstone, Patricia Hope — **McAuliffe**, Edward Timothy, Sr.
    Jackson, Lionel Stewart, Sr.

Jones, Ruth Arven — **Cornell**, Irwin Hewlett
Jordan, Katharine Semple — **Peavey**, George Wright
    Appleton, Robert Wilmarth

Josloff, Stacy — **Deutsch**, Donny
    aka Donald Jay Deutsch

Judge, Arline — **Ruggles**, Wesley
    Topping, Daniel Reid, Sr.
    Bryant, James M.
    Addams, James Ramage
    Ryan, Vincent Morgan
    Topping, Henry J.
    Ross, George, III
    Heard, Edward Cooper

Karan, Gabby — **DeFelice**, Gian Palo
Kassel, Kimberly Ellen — **Mnuchin**, Alan Geoffrey
Kaufman, Bobbi K. — **Weinstein**, Joseph
Keith, Caroline Augusta — **Greer**, The Reverend David Hummel
Kelly, Alice Irene — **Thiele**, Albert Edward, Jr.
Kelly, Annadel — **Beckers**, William Kurt
Kelly, Helen Margaret — **Gould**, Frank Jay
    Thomas, Ralph Hill
    Vlora, Noureddin
    Burke, Oscar Moech

Kelsey, Catherine — **Richard**, Mark Gadd

Maiden Names

Kendrick, Helen Louise   **Johnson**, Rossiter

Kennedy, Carolyn   **Tyson**, James

Kennedy, Jane   **Kuhns**, William C., Sr.
  aka Patricia Massinger   **Hoppin**, Henry Preston

Kennedy, Mary Leland   **Woodhouse**, Lorenzo Easton

Kent, Virginia P.   **Magee**, Louis
    Cummins, Stephen Swete

Kerr, Jean Adelaide   **Finbeiner**, Dr. John A.
    Watson, John E.

Kersch, Sheri   **Schultz**, Howard Mark

Keys, Mary Agnes   **Johnson**, Rossiter

Keyser, Carol Mary   **McElfresh**, Robert
    Windom, William
    Mercer, Norman J.

Khanum, Nejama   **Beard**, Peter Hill

Kieu, Adelaide   **Moran**, Joseph F.
    Moffet, James Andrew, Jr.

Killin, Laura Lynelle   **Wasserstein**, Bruce Jay

King, Delphis Bainbridge   **Krause**, Finley Bailey
    Leith, Donald E.

Kingsley, Lois   **Boots**, Dr. Ralph Henderson, Sr.

Kip, Elizabeth C.   **Von Dehn**, Hyatt
    Geddes, Gerald Maxwell

Kirchwey, Frederika   **Clark**, Evans
  aka Freda Kirchwey

Kitchen, Louise Richmond   **Mygatt**, Henry Daniels
    Havens, Valentine Britton

Klaschke, Hedi   **Halsted**, Dr. Harbeck

Klein, Cheryl Susan   **Kessner**, Steven

Klemm, Marie Celeste   **Jefferys**, Harry Leapold

Knapp, Clotilde   **Miratti**, Charles James
    von Francken–Sierstorpff, Count Hans Clemens
    McCormick, Robert Elliott
    Saltzman, Charles Eskridge

Kneip, Jacqueline   **Wieland**, Robert
    Gerli, David Charles, Sr.
    Legget, David Graham, III

Kohlsaat, Louise   **Laws**, Harry Langdon, III

Kopelman, Rose–Helen   **Breinin**, Dr. Goodwin Milton

Kostyra, Martha Helen   **Stewart**, Andrew

Krasner, Lee   **Pollock**, Jackson
  aka Lena Krasner;
  Lenore Krasner

Krengel, Kris   **Peterson**, Peter George

Kresge, Catherine Harriet   **Wijki**, Baron Carl Carlson
    Murphy, Charles B. G.
    Dewey, Charles Schuveldt

Maiden Names

Krug, Elisabeth

Kupin, Jill Carroll

Labourel, Claire Sylvie

LaGaye, Generosa Rand

Laing, Elizabeth M.

Lainhart, Florence Hapeman

Lancaster, Barbara Jean
   aka Bonnie Devendorf

Landeau, Patricia

Lander, Florence

Lane, Ruth R.

Lang, Carol R.

Lange, Mary

Lathrop, Mary Woodward

Lawrence, Dorothy Quincy

Lawrence, Jane

Lawrence, Nellie May

Lawson, Alice Meade

Laycock, Nellie F.

Layfield, Lucy

Lazarus, Elsie Weston

Leach, Myrtle Abby

Leary, Alice

Lee, Janet Norton

Lee, Katie
   aka Kathleen Rebekah Lee

Lee, Kimora
   aka Kimora Whitlock

Lee, Margaret Winifred

Lee, Virginia

Lees, Susanna Preston

Lehman, Susan

Rosset, Barnet Lee, Jr.
   aka Barney Rosset

Rose, Marshall

Ayer, Frederick, III

Ammon, Robert Theodore
Pelosia, Daniel

Foss, Martin Moore, Sr.
Proctor, Frederick
Tim, Louis DeJonge
Williams, John J., Sr.

Thiele, Roger Harvey

Devendorf, Alfred Ervin

Macklowe, Harry B.

Darrow, Daniel

Robinson, ____
Cleaves, Norman Smith

Rahr, Stewart J.

MacKinnon, Archibald Angus
DeVries, John T.
Johnson, Frederick, Sr.

Salembier, Harold Paul

Fitch, George Hopper
Cushman, Blinn Sill, Jr.

Satterthwaite, James Sheafe, Sr.

Tiffany, Nathan Newton, III

Topping, Daniel Reid, Sr.

Havens, Valentine Britton

Laird, ____
Ryan, Frederick Behrens, Sr.

Stern, Henry Root, Sr.

Bartholomew, Frederick A.
McKinley, Andrew Barrett
Shepherd, James Gardner

Foss, Martin Moore, Sr.
St. John, Ralph Woodford

Bouvier, John Vernou, III
Auchincloss, Hugh Dudley, Jr.
Morris, Bingham Willing

Joel, Billy
   aka William Martin Joel

Simmons, Russell Wendell
Leissner, Tim

d'Olier, Franklin Woolman, Jr.

Sweetser, Jesse William

Sutphen, Henry Randolph, Sr.

Cullman, Joseph Fredrick, III

Maiden Names

Lemmon, Isabel Tasher — **Gardiner**, Winthrop, Sr.
Leonard, Camilla Davis — **Edwards**, Walter, Jr.
Lester, Edith Hallock — **Cleaves**, Norman Smith
Levin, Eileen Marks — **Robert**, Stephen Kniznick
Levin, Susan Nicole — **Downey**, Robert, Jr.
Levis, Adele Louise — **Olin**, John Merrill
    Rand, Frank Chambles

Levy, Jeanne Diane — **Levy–Church**, Kenneth
    aka Kenneth Wayne Church
  Levy–Hinte, Jeffery
    aka Jeffery Kusama Hinte

Lewis, Agnes Isabel — **Sweetser**, Jesse William
  aka Nan Lewis

Lewis, Carole — **Rifkind**, Dr. Richard A.
Lewis, Mary Barbey — **Hopkinson**, Russell
Lewis, Mary Elizabeth — **Newton**, The Reverend Richard Heber, Sr.
Licht, Judith Carol — **Wolsk**, Eugene V.
  Della Femina, Jerry
    aka Gennaro Tomas Della Femina

Lillard, Charlotte Ann — **Topping**, Daniel Reid, Sr.
  Smith, Rankin M., Sr.

Lindsey, Mary — **Paxton**, The Reverend John Randolph, Sr.
Little, Constance M. — **Francisco**, Donald W., Sr.
  aka Don Francisco

Lindeberg, Linda L. — **Yates**, John Carrington
  Cavallon, Giorgio

Livingston, Camilla Woodward — **McVikar**, Donald
  Erwin, Daniel Peart, Jr.

Livingston, Miriam — **Gruen**, Robert L
Lobell, Harriet — **Davis**, Vernon Mansfield
Loew–Beer, Ricky Anne — **Lauren**, Ralph
  aka Ralph Lifshitz

Loftus, Agnes C. — **Bell**, Dr. Dennistoun Mildeberger
Loftus, Nora — **Gardiner**, Robert Alexander
Lockman, Isabel Spaulding — **Helmuth**, Dr. William Tod, Jr.
Lord, Jannett Williams — **Tucker**, William Ashton
  Hinton, Dr. James William

Lord, Pauline Estelle — **Deveraux**, John Drew
Loveland, Florence Lee — **Clark**, Ivor Bache, Sr.
  Barron, Lawrence Edward
  Griswold, Harry Herbert

Luke, Jayni Ann — **Chase**, Chevy
  aka Cornelius Crane Chase

Luke, Mary Anderson — **Langben**, Halfred Alfred
Luquer, Margaret Shippen — **Orr**, Alexander Ector
Lutkins, Louise — **Le Brecht**, Robert
  Doerr, William

Maiden Names

Lyman, Edmona

Lynch, Caroline Dodd

Lyon, Katherine

Lyons, Irene Katherine

MacInnes, Helen Clark
aka Helen MacInnes

MacLachlan, Juliana

Maclay, Laura Grace

Macon, Edith Marie

Maguire, Kathleen

Maher, Allison

Mairs, Ella Louise

Maitland, Andree Belden

Maldonado, Violeta

Manheim, Alice

Mann, Edith Vernon

Mann, Helen Louise

Mansell, Jessica Lyman

Manson, Dorothea

Mapp, Katherine Seymour

March, Penelope

Marciano, Melinda Jill

Margolin, Emily

Mark, Corrie Jill

Marks, Jane Ann

Marshall, Charlotte

Marshall, Emma Lawrence

Marston, Helen Edna

Martin, Mary Vincent

Mason, Hazel May

Massinger, Patricia
aka Jane Kennedy

Materson, Mary Heard

Mathers, Nattie

Matson, Sally Ann

Miller, Paul A.
Mansell, Frank Luther

Brackenridge, Gavin, Jr.

Hutton, John Laurence, Sr.

Towbin, Abraham Robert

Highet, Gilbert Albert

Gardiner, David Lion, Sr.

Dana, Robert Bingham

Cushman, Blinn Sill, Jr.
Blakeley, ____

Regan, John Nicholas, Sr.

Stern, Leonard Norman

Duryea, Walter Bartow

Dean, Howard Bush, Jr.

Putnam, Harrington, Jr.

Kaplan, Jacob Merrill

Simonds, Francis May, Sr.
Moses, Charles Kingsley

Wright, John Howie, III

Briner, William Drew
Ambrose, Colin Trippe

Van Rensselaer, Kiliaen, III

Havens, Valentine Britton

Lundbergh, Holger

Jaffe, Stanley Richard

Gwathmey, Charles

Sandelman, Jonathan Everett

Benson, Arthur W.

Hammond, John Carnahan

Lowe, William Ebbets, II

Burke, Oscar Moech
Beekman, Robert Livingston

Hanke, George Frederick Robert, Sr.

Edmondson, William Bertram
Pocock, ____
Reed, Edward L.
Sterling, Oliver James, Sr.

Kuhns, William, Sr.
Hoppin, Harry Preston

Peticolas, Sherman Goodwin
Rice, Dr. Clarence Charles

Shepherd, James Gardner

Edwards, James Cook, Sr.

Maiden Names

Matthews, Marilyn Morris   **Webb**, James Earle
                                                               Davie, Edward Thomas Bedford
                                                               Miller, Dudley Livingston, Sr.
                                                               Addams, Charles Samuel

Maurice, Charlotte   **Morris**, Charles
                                                               Hammond, John Carahan

Maus, Katherine   **O'Brien**, W. Howard, Sr.

Mayes, Cordella   **Bell**, Dr. James Finley

Mayo, Miss Marie Louise

Mazzo, Kathryn   **Bellas**, Alfred Constantine
   aka Kay Mazzo

McAlpin, Dorothy   **Bell**, Alfred Dennis, Sr.

McAlpin, Flora Benjamin   **Barton**, Charles Pierce, Jr.
                                                                Seeley, Roy Clinton

McCall, Constance   **Ramsay**, Herbert Hartley

McCall, Ella Gaynor   **Maloney**, William Raywood, Sr.

McClellan, Virginia   **Tuttle**, Guertin
                                                Bartlett, Edward Everett, Jr.

McCloskey, Margaret Patricia   **Breen**, Daniel Anthony, Jr.

McClure, Margaret   **de Kay**, Ormonde, Sr.

McCord, Janet   **Cook**, Francis Howell

McCormick, Mary Elizabeth   **Hedges**, Dayton
                                                        aka William Dayton

McDonnell, Mary Kathryn   **Brackenridge**, Gavin, Jr.

McElhone, Dorothea   **Leggert**, Noel Bleeker, Jr.
                                              Sterling, Oliver James, Sr.

McGeoy, Caroline Nye   **Cavett**, Richard Alva
   aka Carrie Nye   aka Dick Cavett

McGhee, Margaret White   **Baxter**, George White

McGinnis, Adele   **Herter**, Albert

McGowen, Martha Katherine   **Mitchell**, MacNeil
   aka Katherine McGowen

McGrann, Esther   **Coy**, James Joseph, Jr.

McGregor, Grace   **Phillips**, Fleming Stanhope

McKeldin, Bessie Draper   **Tucker**, Howard Newell, Jr.
                                                Thorne, Henry Sanford
                                                Clark, Morris Richard

McLane, Augusta James   **Robinson**, Lucius Franklin, Jr.

McLaughlin, Kathryn   **Abbe**, James Edward, Jr.

McLerie, Allyn Ann   **Green**, Adolph
                                              Gaynes, George
                                                  aka George Jongejans

McMichael, Adelaide Taft   **Moffet**, James Andrew, Jr.

Meadow, Lucille   **Seligson**, William

Meagher, Mildred Genevieve   **Starke**, Hamilton Jackson
                                                Steele, Louis Thorton

Maiden Names

Mehnert, Eleanor Shelton   **Pierson**, Warren Lee, Sr.
Merritt, Margaret A.   **Lee**, James Thomas
Merryman, Margaret Austin   **Bogert**, George Henry
Meyer, Louise   **Wessel**, Homer Augustus, Sr.
    Vaughn–Williams, Herbert

Middleton, Grace Lee   **Roberts**, George Hewitt, Jr.
Milholland, Anne   **Kiser**, John William, III
       aka John William Kiser, Jr.

Miller, Alice D.   **Osborne**, Nelson Cook, Sr.
    Ham, Stephen Lewis, Sr.

Miller, Aralene Paul   **Brown**, Philip Wilson Tate, Sr.
Miller, Charlotte   **Wood**, Wilfrid
Miller, Elizabeth   **Jefferys**, Charles Peter Beauchamp. Sr.
Miller, Mabel Lorraine   **Swan**, Kingsley
    Graves, Robert, II
    Wood, Benjamin
    Van Rensselaer, Kiliaen, III

Milliken, Carrie Thompson   **DeGraff**, James Wilde
Mills, Amy Hawxhurst   **DeKoven**, Louis Besant Wadsworth
Mills, Heather   **Karmal**, Alfie
    McCartney, Paul
       aka James Paul McCartney

Mitchell, Joan   **Rosset**, Barnet Lee, Jr.
       aka Barney Rosset

Mitchell, Rita Rend   **Rentschler**, George Adam, Jr.
    Cushman, Allerton, Sr.

Mittendorf, Marcella Callery   **Wainwright**, Stuyvesant, III
Mixsell, Mallory   **Kerr**, Elmore Coe, Jr.
    Minton, Robert

Moffitt, Alice   **Pulleyn**, John William, Sr.
Moller, Ruth Helene   **Livingston**, Johnston, II
       aka Johnston Livingston, Jr.

Moncure, Vivienne Randolph   **Butler**, William Allen, III
Monroe, Darlene Joy   **McConnell**, David Hall, III
Montgomery, Gloria   **Nori**, Edmond Joseph
Moore, Mary   **Erwin**, Daniel Peart, Jr.
Moore, Virginia C.   **Briggs**, James Branch
Morris, Fanny Eugenia   **Clarke**, Thomas Benedict, Sr.
Morrison, Georgina Frances   **Jewett**, Edward Hull, Jr.
    Krueger, William C.

Morrison, Lily Clapp   **Clements**, Hurin Martin
Morse, Ellen Margery   **Tishman**, Peter Valentine
Mortimer, Amanda   **Burton**, Shirley Carter, Jr.
    Ross, Steven Jay
       aka Steven Jay Rechthal

Morton, Alice Ralston   **Simmons**, Edward Emerson

Maiden Names

Mueller, Helen E.
Mularchuk, Christine

Muller, Olga
Mulvane, Elizabeth
Munro, Barbara Forrest
Munro, Helen I.
Munzer, Margaret Davidson
Murray, Alice deBois
Musto, Elena

Myers, Astrid

Myers, Florence Evelyn
Myers, Georgie Estelle

Nail, Kathleen Sue
  aka Kate Capshaw
Nanry, Florence

Nash, Mary
Negley, Clara Louise
Neher, Elizabeth

Neimark, Robin
Newman, Kathryn Joanne
Newman, Linda

Newman, Phyllis
Nicholas, Loida
Nichols, Sarah
Nicoll, Mary Goodall
Niedringhaus, Evelyn Nixon
Nimmo, Mary
Noggle, Gladys Ione
Nowell, Dorcas Marie
  aka Doe Avedon;
  Betty Harper
Oakes, Georgiana
Oakley, Katherine
O'Connell, Nancy Louise

Odell, Vallory

Hardy, Charles J., Jr.
Hearst, Austin Chilton
Schwarzman, Stephen Allen
Soule, Henri Remy
Jones, Dr. Oswald Roberts
Schurman, Jacob Gould, Sr.
Schurman, George Wellington
Loeb, Daniel Seth
Adams, John Cranford
Lilley, Alexander Neil, Sr.
Forrester, Robert R., Jr.
Rosset, Barnet Lee, Jr.
  aka Barney Rosset
Pardridge, Albert Jerome
Church, Samuel Christy
Coppell, Herbert
Capshaw, Robert
Spielberg, Steven Allan
Hubbard, John Leslie
Rheinstein, Sidney
Agnew, Dr. Cornelius Rea, Sr.
Flinn, George Hamilton, Sr.
Copp, Gordon Miles
Gardiner, Winthrop, Jr.
Seegal, Frederic Milton
Steinberg, Robert Michael
Solomon, Peter Jay
Schapiro, Donald
Green, Adolph
Lewis, Reginald F.
Kerr, Elmore Coe, Jr.
Fraser, Alexander
Williams, Eugene Flewilyn, Jr.
Moran, Thomas, Sr.
Ely, Laurence Driggs, Sr.
Avedon, Richard
Matthews, Donald
Siegel, Donald
Greer, Lawrence
Perot, Edward Sansom, Jr.
Fox, Alvin Gibbs
Williams, Francis Bryan, Jr.
Gordon, Alan
Smith, Warren
Roundbush, John Haywood

Maiden Names

Odengarden, Thelma Jacobsen — **Fleming**, Henry Stuart
O'Donnell, Claire — **Kennedy**, David E.
Oehler, Audrey Joan — **Conway**, Edmund Virgil, III
Oelrichs, Blanche — **Thomas**, Leonard, Sr.
    Barrymore, John
    Tweed, Harrison

Offerman, Anna Catherine — **Schmidt**, Dederick Herman
Ogden, Miss Clara F.
Ogden, Clara Lee — **McLanahan**, Scott
Ohmer, Mary Carol — **Collins**, William Bradley Isham, Sr.
    aka Bradley Isham Collins

O'Mara, Eloise — **Spaeth**, Otto Lucien, Sr.
Ordway, Elizabeth — **Duke**, Anthony Drexel, Sr.
    Dunn, John Richard

O'Reilly, Kay — **LeRoy**, Warner
Orr, Patricia Michelle — **Zabrodsky**, Thomas
    aka Patricia Duff — **Duff**, Daniel
    Medavoy, Morris Mike
    Perelman, Ronald Owen

Osborn, Lillian H. — **Beard**, Jeremiah Robinson, Jr.
Page, Betsy — **Gaynor**, Norman Jay, Sr.
    Cordier, Auguste Julien, Jr.

Paleari, Candida — **Burchell**, Henry J., Jr.
Paley, Joan — **Straus**, Barnard Sachs
    Cullman, Joseph Frederick, III

Paltrow, Gwyneth Kate — **Martin**, Christopher Anthony John
    Falchuk, Brad

Pardue, Nancy — **Scheerer**, Joseph Durand, Jr.
Parker, Sarah Jessica — **Broderick**, Matthew
Parrott, Christine — **Wasserstein**, Bruce Jay
    Rattiner, Daniel Steven

Parsons, Janet Isabel — **Wainwright**, Stuyvesant, II
Patterson, Ruth — **Wallace**, Melville W. Fuller
    Thorne, Henry Sanford

Pattison, Emma — **Skidmore**, James Bond
Pauley, Tarlton — **Norris**, Tony
    Harvey, Laurence
    Morton, Peter
    Burns, Mark

Paxton, Mary Elkins — **Hamlin**, Harry Leon
Peabody, Eva — **Bacon**, Clarence Everett, Jr.
Pelgram, Caroline M. — **Fleming**, Henry Stuart
Pendergast, Adelaide — **Durant**, Lawrence T.
    Cornell, Irwin Hewlett

Perkins, Lynn — **Tishman**, Peter Valentine
Perot, Sarah Lee — **Oakley**, Ralph Lawrence

Maiden Names

Perry, Dorothy   **Bell**, Alfred Dennis, Sr.
     Hammond, Leonard C.

Peters, Frances Sarah   **Holmes**, Jay
     Cushing, Harry Cook, III

Peters, Oliva Ames   **Pool**, Henry Lawrence

Peterson, Ebba Louise   **Satterlee**, Dr. Francis Le Roy, Jr.

Phelps, Lillian   **Kelley**, William Vallandigham, Sr.

Philips, Ellen   **Schwarzman**, Stephen Allen
     Katz, Howard Carl

Philips, Frances Montgomery   **Vanderbilt**, Oliver DeGray, III

Phillips, Anne   **Osborne**, Burnet Mulford

Pierce, Violetta   **Snow**, Dr. Irving Miller

Pinchot, Antoinette Eno   **Pittman**, Steuart Lansing, II
     Bradlee, Benjamin Crowninshield, Sr.

Pine, Alice   **Garver**, Chauncey B.
     Hutton, John Laurence, Sr.

Pinkey, Kate Hopkins   **Jones**, Rodney Wilcox, Sr.

Platt, Elizabeth   **Adams**, Charles Henry

Poppiti, Evelyn   **Coy**, James Joseph, III

Porter, Sophia Seymour   **Fraser**, Ronald Goodall

Potter, Eliza Jennie   **Vaughan**, Dr. Henry Wheaton

Potter, Josephine Wood   **Richey**, The Reverend Alban, Sr.

Potter, Margot Tier   **Kiser**, John William, III
     aka John William Kiser, Jr.
     Denny, Robert O.

Prather, Marian   **Zuckerman**, Mortimer Benjamin
     Schiller, Jonathan D.

Prentice, Martha Howard   **Strong**, Theron George

Price, Catherine   **Robert**, Stephen Kniznick

Prior, Julia   **Onderdonk**, Dr. Thomas Williams

Probasco, Grace Sherlock   **Rowe**, John Jay, Sr.

Prosser, Anna Fay   **Caukins**, Dan Platt
     Stevens, Leighton H.

Pruyn, Miss Mary Lansing

Pruyn, Miss Neltje Knickerbocker

Pulleyn, Virginia   **Kingsley**, Walton Pearl

Purcell, Marjorie Ann   **Teetor**, Charles Jessup
     aka Mickie Purcell

Purviance, Veronica Arvilla   **Welch**, Leo Dewey

Putnam, Eunice   **Chadbourne**, John
     Leaman, Alfred Valentine, III
     Brower, Harry Van Alst

Quinn, Sally   **Bradlee**, Benjamin Crowninshield, Sr.

Rabinowitz, Dorothy   **Bisco**, Leonard Gerard

Randell, Virginia   **Stanton**, Dr. Frederick Lester

Maiden Names

Randolph, Anne Stuart | **Kimball**, Alden
Hall, Barrington E. Basil

Rattazzi, Priscilla | **Ponti**, Alessandro
Moehlmann, Claus
Whittle, Chris
   aka H. Christopher Whittle

Read, Emma | **Reid**, Wallace

Reber, Audrey A. | **Williams**, ____
Dowling, Robert Whittle

Rector, Kelly | **Klein**, Calvin
   aka Calvin Richard Klein

Redner, Ethel | **Scull**, Robert C.

Reese, Rosina Elizabeth | **Hoyt**, Alfred Miller

Reid, Maria Speir | **Knox**, John Mason, Jr.

Reitell, Elizabeth | **Hammond**, John
Green, Adolph
Smith, Eldon

Requa, Mary E. | **Sanger**, Henry

Reynolds, Jessie | **Munroe**, Dr. George E., Jr.

Richard, Evine | **Hansen**, Curt Eric
McCall, Clifford Hyde, Sr.

Richardson, Catherine Lawrence | **Harris**, William Victor
   aka Victor Harris

Richardson, Josephine | **Notman**, Clyde
Seaman, Joseph Husband, Sr.

Richardson, Margaret Anna | **Rowe**, William Stanhope, Sr.

Richey, Josephine Maud | **Seabury**, Samuel

Richolson, Florence | **Salembier**, Paul Albert

Riklis, Marcia | **Kletter**, Benjamin
Hirschfeld, Elie

Rilea, Clara Belle | **LaForest**, Henry A.

Rine, Celia Beatrice | **Smith**, Harry
Shepherd, James Gardner

Ringo, Susan L. | **Erwitt**, Elliott
Sonnenfeld, Barry

Riordan, Helen Price Barclay | **Wood**, Wilfrid
Dodd, John Mingus, III

Ritzer, Marguerite | **Dunn**, Dr. James Manning

Robbins, Gladys S. | **Lutkins**, Clinton Stephen

Robbins, Sarah Elizabeth | **Bishopric**, Allison, Jr.
Minor, William Ernst, Jr.

Roberts, Helen | **McCormick**, Robert Elliott

Robertson, Ethel Finch | **Dowling**, Robert Whittle

Roderick, Alexis | **Joel**, Billy
   aka William Martin Joel

Roelker, Eleanor Jenckes | **Tweed**, Harrison
Palffy, Count Paul

Maiden Names

Rogers, Martha

Rogers, Mary
  aka Mary Howard

Rokenbaugh, Cornelia Scott

Romeyn, Estelle Young

Rose, Constance

Rose, Cordelia Maria

Rose, Frances Adelaide

Rosenberg, Ina

Rosenthal, Carol

Rothenberg, Judith A.

Roudebush, Agnes

Roudebush, Rosanne

Rowe, Charlotte Frances

Rowe, Margaret

Rowe, Margaret Anna Tince

Roy, Camilla L.

Royce, Betsey Eliza

Rudd, Frances H.

Rulison, Helen Douglas

Russ, Marjorie

Russell, Lucie

Russell, Serena Mary Churchill

Rutgers, Alice Noel

Ruxton, Louise Ginnel

Ryan, Anne M.

Ryan, Mary Frances

Sack, Madeleine Penelope
  aka Penelope Sack

Sadowsky, Ellin Jane

Sage, Eleanor

Sainsbury, Camilla Davan

Sale, Courtney

Cavett, Richard Alva
  aka Dick Cavett

de Liagre, Alfred, Jr.
  aka Alfred Gustav Etienne de Liagre, Jr.

Davies, Francis Herbert

Pittman, Ernest Wetmore

Hamilton, Gordon C.

Shackleton, Dr. Judson Gale
McAlpin, David Hunter, Sr.

McAlpin, David Hunter, Sr.

Garten, Jeffery E.

Ross, Steven Jay
  aka Jay Rechnitz

Tichman, Peter Valentine

Willis, Reginald Satterlee
Day, Thomas Mills, Jr.

Larkin, Lawrence

Radiway, Edward Miller
Davis, Chase Henchman

Nichols, Harold Willis, Sr.

Chatfield, Henry Houston

Jewett, Edward Hull, Jr.

Spring, Preston Brady, Sr.

Lyon, Marvin Thomas

Coleman, Charles Philip

Baker, Lawrence Adams, Sr.

Rawson, Joseph, Jr.

Salant, Robert Stephen
McConnell, Neil Anderson
Balfour, Neil Roxburgh

Duke, Anthony Drexel, Sr.
Dodge, Marshall Jewell, Jr.
Philbin, Gerald G.

Chauncey, Alexander Wallace

Griffin, ____
Wright, John Howie, Jr.

Devine, James Joseph

Potter, Jeffrey Brackett
Bradford, ____

Saltzman, Renny B.

Howard, ____
Dougherty, Frazer Lowber Welsh

Woodward, Shaun Anthony

Ross, Steven Jay
  aka Steven Jay Rechnitz

Maiden Names

Saltonstall, Jean   **Bradlee**, Benjamin Crowninshield, Sr.
    Hausserman, Oscar William, Jr.

Sands, Emmeline Dore   **Heppenheimer**, William Christian, III

Satterlee, Helen Livingston   **Parker**, Cecil Carlton

Satterthwaite, Katherine Bache   **Larkin**, Adrian Hoffman

Sawyer, Anne Johnston   **Williams**, John Pattison, Sr.
    Greene, John Bradley, II

Schabbehar, Jane E.   **Embury**, Aymar, II
    Benepe, Robert Steiner

Schallenberger, Vesta   **Simmons**, Edward Emerson

Scheckner, Toni   **Schulman**, Lowell M.

Schindelheim, Jane   **Wenner**, Jann Simon

Schlesier, Edna   **Fuller**, Edward Reinow
    Prosser, Stuart A.

Schlesinger, Sarah J.   **Hirschfeld**, Eli

Schley, Eleanor Prentice   **Todd**, Webster Bray, Sr.

Schley, Helen A.   **Yates**, John Carrington
    Gillette, Curtenius, Sr.

Schnakenberg, Anna Katherine   **Bartlett**, Edward Everett, Jr.

Schneider, Ilse   **Carlson**, Dr. Earl R.

Schniewind, Emily   **Lee**, James Jackson, Sr.
    Walker, George Gholson, Sr.

Schofield, Margaret Ellen   **Savarese**, Charles J.
    Weeks, John Kirkland, Sr.

Schroeder, Elizabeth   **Walker**, George Gholson, Sr.

Schultze, Marie   **Aufermann**, Walter C. W.
    Kast, Dr. Ludwig

Schuster, Rosie   **Michaels**, Lorne
      aka Lorne Lipowitz

Schwab, Mary Baldwin   **Pool**, Henry Lawrence
    Brett, Philip Milledoler, Jr.

Schwartz, Penny   **Binn**, Moreton
      aka Moreton Binstock

Scott, Linda Gilbert   **Flinn**, Lawrence, Jr.
   aka Linda Scott   **Pitts**, Richard

Scoville, Grace Kellogg   **Bishop**, Bennett

Scudder, Elizabeth Erwin   **Edwards**, James McPherson

Sebring, Nina   **Walker**, Delos

Sedgwick, Katherine   **Valerio**, Joseph
    Washburn, William Tucker

Sedgwick, Laura Brevoort   **James**, Henry Amman

Seeldrayers, Manette   **Hobart**, Garret Augustus, III
    Loomis, Alfred Lee, Sr.
    Christie, Ronald

Seldon, Helen Hinda   **Rattray**, Everett Tennant
    Cory, Christopher Thayer

Maiden Names

Semel, Joanna   **Rose**, Daniel

Sergeant, Maude Frances   **Bouvier**, John Vernou, Jr.

Serra, Laura   **Fitch**, Aubrey Wray, Jr.
                                                       Phyfe, Dr. Henry Pinkney, Sr.
                                                       Roberts, Dudley DeVore, Jr.

Seymour, Caroline   **Wainright**, John Howard

Seymour, Harriet Ayer   **Helm**, George Washington, Sr.
                                                       Macy, Valentine Everit, Jr.

Seymour, Sara L.   **Johnson**, Servetus Fisher

Shanahan, Adelaide   **Leonard**, Stephen Joseph, Sr.

Shattuck, Barbara J.   **Kohn**, Arthur Eugene
                                                     Dubow, Arthur Myron

Shay, Mildred Helen   **Murphy**, Thomas Francis
                                                    Gardiner, Winthrop, Jr.
                                                    Steel, Geoffrey

Sheehan, Josephine   **Raymond**, Dana Merriam

Shelton, Harriet May   **Hollister**, Dr. Frederick Kellogg

Sherman, Adeline Moulton   **Wiborg**, Frank Bestow

Sherman, Sara Moulton   **Mitchell**, Ledyard, Sr.
                                                     aka William Ledyard Mitchell

Sherwood, Maude   **Jewett**, Edward Hull, Sr.

Shevell, Nancy   **McCartney**, Paul
                                                aka James Paul McCartney

Shields, Caroline   **Dickson**, Philip
                                                Walker, George Gholson, Sr.

Shropshire, Mattie–King   **Massock**, Richard G.
                                                  Hardy, Charles J., Jr.

Shults, Bertha   **Dougherty**, Russell Keresey

Shuster, Rosie   **Michaels**, Lorne
                                      aka Lorne Lipowitz

Silleck, Helen Ruppert   **Holleran**, Frank Joseph

Silver, Anne Louise   **Kelsey**, Stephen Tomlinson, Sr.

Silver, Susan Kadin   **de Menil**, Francois
                                         aka Francois Conrad Thomas de Menil

Simpkins, Natalie   **Gianis**, Socrates George, Sr.
                                          Workum, Robert Hamill

Simms, Sandra   **Brant**, Peter M.
                                 Sischy, Ingrid Barbara

Simpson, Charlotte Helen   **Whittemore**, William John

Simrod, Sheila Natasha   **Friedman**, Marvin Ross

Sims, Bessie   **Miller**, ____
   aka Billie Sims   **Gerli**, David Charles, Sr.

Sinclair, Kathleen   **Bishop**, Dr. Louis Faugeres, Jr.

Sklar, Nina Danielle   **Nederlander**, Eric
   aka Jessica Sklar   **Seinfeld**, Jerry
                                                   aka Jerome Allen Seinfeld

Sloan, Florence Lincoln   **De Vecchi**, Robert Paolo

Maiden Names

Smathers, Virginia Smith — **Healey**, Giles Greville
Haynes, Justine O'Brien, Sr.

Smith, Clare Elizabeth — **McKeon**, Robert Brian

Smith, Dorothy — **Hopkins**, Lindsey, Jr.

Smith, Emma Martin — **Cobb**, Henry Ives, Sr.

Smith, Marion Louise — **Peters**, William Sterling

Smith, Virginia Consuelo — **Hutton**, William Langdon
Burke, Edwin Marston, Sr.

Snowden, Caroline Smith — **Wainwright**, Stuyvesant
Wolff, Dr. Carl F.

Solinger, Lynn — **Stern**, Robert Arthur Morton
Lang, Jeremy Pollard

Soloway, Maryann — **Semel**, Terrance Steven

Somers, Vanessa Mary — **McConnell**, Neil Anderson
Vreeland, Frederick

Somerville, Margaret — **Potter**, Eugene Clifford

Spalding, Gladys — **Keim**, John Richard

Spinetti, Adelina — **Devendorf**, George Epworth

Stathatos, Lily — **Mercati**, Count Leonardo

Stedman, Lucille — **Cody**, Frederick

Steele, Carrie Elise — **Roberts**, Dr. Dudley DeVore, Sr.

Steele, Mary Maynadler — **Morris**, Theodore Wilson, Jr.

Stern, Gertrude — **Greene**, John Bradley, II

Stern, Rona Miriam
  aka Ronnie Chalif — **Chalif**, Seymour Hunt

Sterret, Phoebe Cabell — **Weeks**, John Kirkland, Sr.

Stettinius, Elizabeth — **Trippe**, Juan Terry

Stewart, Grace I. M. — **Thomas**, Andrew Jackson

Stimson, Catherine Boudinot — **Weston**, Theodore

Stitch, Blanche — **Sinclair**, Earl Westwood

Stites, Elijean — **Terbell**, Edward Dyer

Stokes, Emily Maloney — **Weaver**, Spencer Fullerton, Sr.

Stone, Cynthia — **Lemmon**, Jack
Robertson, Clifford Parker, III
  aka Cliff Robertson
McDougal, Robert, III

Stone, Hilda Elizabeth — **Hopkins**, John Appleton Haven, Sr.

Stone, Marguerite — **Cameron**, William
Inman, John Hamilton, Jr.
Burke, Oscar Moech

Stone, Paulene — **Norris**, Tony
Harvey, Laurence
Morton, Peter
Burns, Mark

Stout, Barbara Jacquelin — **Putnam**, Harrington, Jr.
Crocker, Arthur Masten

Maiden Names

Straton, Carol Carter
Strite, Beatrice Ann

Strubling, Stephanie Hanes
Stuart, Mary
Sudler, Laura
Sullivan, Katherine Esther
Sutton, Katherine Warburton
   aka Kay Sutton

Suydam, Emilia Wickham
Suydam, Mary Bedell

Swanstrom, Ruth Lilly Margareta
Talmage, Jessie
Talmage, Mary
Tapper, Barbara

Taylor, Barbara
Teitelbaum, Lizanne
Tenenbaum, Ann
Terbell, Emma Augusta
Terrace, Dr. Dorothy

Terry, Eugenia M.
   aka Gena Terry
Terry, Isabelle Amelia
Terry, Lucy Adeline
Thayer, Constance
Thayer, Jessica R.
Thomas, Ada Evelyn

Thomas, Glory
Thomas, Hilaria

Thompson, Elizabeth Wood
Throop, Frances Hunt
Tiegs, Cheryl Rae

Tilghman, Maud
Tobler, Adele

Le Brecht, Robert
Chapman, Dr. Eugene Rhea
Watts, Harry Wilfred

Flinn, Lawrence, Jr.
Finkbeiner, Dr. John A.
Main, Charles E.
Meehan, Joseph Ansbro
Alger, Frederick Moulton
Topping, Daniel Reid, Sr.
Weaver, Clifton Stokes
Cronjager, Edward

Davis, George Samler
Edwards, Harkness, Sr.
Jenney, Sherman

Aubert, Ludvig Caesar Martin, II
Smith, Warren G.
Mershon, The Reverend Stephen Lyon, Sr.
d'Almedia, Baron Antonio
Warburg, Paul Felix Solomon
Mercati, Count Leonardo

Rounick, Jack A.
Rosenstein, Barry
Lee, Thomas Haskell
Blakeman, ____
Marks, ____
Krieger, Dr. Howard P.
Bardin, C. Wayne

Hendrix, Clifford Rathbone, Sr.

Culver, Austin H.
Trippe, Charles White, Sr.
Cory, David Cleveland
Green, William Walker
Mayfield, Reuben Newton
Hyde, Frank Dana

Elliott, William, Jr.
Baldwin, Alexander Rae, III
   aka Alec Baldwin

Wheeler, John Neville
Ordway, Samuel Hanson, Sr.
Dragoti, Stanley John
Peck, Anthony
Stryker, Rod

Walker, Bayard, Sr.
Judd, Frank Henry, Jr.
Hone, Harold

Maiden Names

Todd, Laura Washington — **Schey**, Robert Paul
Todd, Mary Lumpkin — **Maguire**, Edward, Sr.
Tonkonogy, Elizabeth — **Osserman**, Stanley
Torch, Maria Eleana — **Stone**, Edward Durell, Sr.
Tousley, Louise — **Beardsley**, Thomas Hopper
    Vernon, Paul E.

Townsend, Ella W. — **Mills**, Abraham
Trach, Theresa — **Scheffer**, Alfred A.
Treat, Francis — **Montgomery**, Paul
    aka John Paul Montgomery

Trejbal, Liba — **Icahn**, Carl Celian
Trippe, Elizabeth Stettinius — **Duke**, William H.
    Douglass, William Angus
    Wainwright, Stuyvesant, III
    De Vecchi, Robert Paolo

Trowbridge, Emily Carrington — **Gallatin**, Frederick, II
    Garvin, John S., Sr.
    Bell, George Newell

Twichell, Julia Curtis — **Wood**, Howard Ogden, Sr.
Turk, Lillian B. — **MacKewan**, ____
    Aldrich, Spencer Wyman

Turnbull, Alison Low — **Hopkins**, John Appleton Haven, Sr.
Turner, Kathleen — **Weiss**, Jay
    aka Mary Kathleen Turner

Turner, Stephanie — **Fleetwood**, Francis
Uhlmann, Blanche — **Helier**, David
    Newton, Richard Heber, Jr.

Vaill, Anna Isabel — **LaMonte**, George Mason
Vaill, Mary Breck — **Talmage**, Daniel, Jr.
Valentine, Hannah Louse — **Buek**, Gustav H.
    aka Gustavus H. Buek

Vanderbilt, Consuelo — **Smith**, Earl Edward Tailer, Sr.
    Davis, Henry Gassaway, III
    Warburton, William John, III
    Earl, Noble Clarkson, Jr.

Vandiver, Orlean — **Stone**, Edward Durell, Sr.
    Halstead, Albert
    Curtin, Ernest

Van Rensselaer, Barbara — **Sherman**, John Taylor, II
Van Voorhees, Louise — **Kimball**, Charles Edmunds, Jr.
    Webster, John Rouse

Varnum, Julia Mathilda — **de Rose**, Edward
Varnum, Susan Graham — **de Rose**, Edward
Verplanck, Eliza Fenno — **Richards**, Benjamin, Jr.
    aka Eliza Fenno Ver Planck

Verplanck, Mary Newlin — **Johnson**, Samuel William
Vogel, Anita — **Hoffman**, David Lehman, Sr.

Maiden Names

Volck, Roma Virginia
   aka Doris Dudley

Wagstrom, Margaretha

Walker, Evelyn

Walker, Judith

Walker, Nina

Walling, Eva

Walpole–Moore, Lillian Valerie Ella

Walther, May Christine

Ward, Eva Eugenie

Ward, Rosemary

Warrin, Mary Taylor

Warriner, Suzanne Louise

Washburn, Jean Wuertz

Washburn, Lynn S.

Washburn, Marion Susan

Washington, Lucy Amelia

Watkins, Jacqueline

Watts, Jane

Watts, Natalie O.

Wayler, Nina Elizabeth

Weber, Elizabeth

Webster, Rita

Weekes, Julia Mary

Weeks, Frances Louise

Weeks, Margaret Louise

Weinman, Frances

Welby, Bertha Emeline

Weld, Elizabeth Minot

Wentworth, Alexandra Elliot

Werner, Johanna
   aka Hannah Werner

Westcott, Mary Houston

Erwin, Daniel Peart, Jr.
Franklin, Gordon P.
Jenkins, Jack

Srybnik, ____
Rumbough, Stanley Maddox, Jr.

Robinson, Fielding S.
Robert, Lawrence Wood, Jr.

Laughlin, Alexander Mellon, Sr.

Wainwright, Carroll Livingston, Jr.

Eno, Alfred Joseph

Beardsley, Samuel Arthur, Sr.

Cloud, Chester Mart

Mairs, Olney Blanchard, Sr.

Blabon, George W.
Tyson, Mark

Nadal, Charles Coleman

Monell, Theodore, Jr.

Jackson, Richard Seymour
Clarke, Lawrence Irving

Hanke, George Frederick Robert, Sr.

Myrick, Julian Southall

Helm, John LaRue, Jr.

Slifka, Alan Bruce

Fisher, Carl Graham, Sr.
Johnson, Robert

Grace, Morgan Hatton, Jr.

Bunschaft, Gordon

Small, Jon
Joel, Billy
   aka William Martin Joel

Volckening, Lloyd Irwin

de Forest, Henry Grant

Stone, David Balderston
Ryan, Bruce Edgar
Betner, Benjamin Carlton, Jr.

Beebe, William Nottingham, Sr.

Latimer, William Carroll
Gardiner, Winthrop, Jr.
Luro, Horatio A.

Boughton, Edward Smith

Brett, Philip Milledoler, Jr.
Haskel, Joseph Farrell

Stephanopoulos, George Robert

Gottschow, Albert
Tillich, The Reverend Paul Johannes

Solley, Dr. Fred Palmer

Maiden Names

Wetmore, Elizabeth Newton — **Skidmore**, John Drake
Weve, Margarete — **Tillich**, The Reverend Paul Johannes
Wheatland, Anna — **Ordway**, Samuel Hanson, Jr.
Wheeler, Ellen Rose — **Hoffman**, David Lehman, Sr.
Wheelock, Harriet Efner — **Strong**, George Arthur
White, Bessie Moore — **Osborne**, Joseph Septimus
 Ham, Henry G.
White, Grace Raymond — **Osborne**, Dr. Edward Monroe, Sr.
White, Margaret — **Nugent**, Dr. Paul Fordham, Sr.
White, Susan Sherman — **Edwards**, William Henry Leonard
Whiting, Jean Fredericka — **Spalding**, Jessie, II
 Maxwell, Robert Elliott
Whitlock, Veronica Penelope — **Laughlin**, Alexander Mellon, Jr.
 Coleman, Bruce Dawson
Whitmore, Alice Vaud — **Whittemore**, William John
Whittemore, Susan Curtis — **Collier**, Charles W.
 Talmage, The Reverend Thomas DeWitt
Wiborg, Olga — **Fish**, Sidney Webster
Wiborg, Sara Sherman — **Murphy**, Gerald Clery
Wilckes, Gladys — **Bianchi**, Albert William
 Marvin, Arthur B.
Wilde, Dorothy — **Moon**, Earl Joseph
 Adair, Dr. Frank Earl
Williams, Anna Reed — **Carse**, John Bradley, Sr.
Williams, Dorothy — **Dwyer**, ____
 DeVoe, Raymond Forsyth, Sr.
Williams, Jean Maclay — **Carson**, William Moore, Sr.
Williams, Mary Benjamin — **Stokes**, The Reverend John Dunlap
Wilshire, Lucie — **Graham**, James Leonard, Sr.
Wilson, Angeline — **Fleming**, Matthew Corry, Sr.
Wiman, Nancy Deere — **Carter**, Arthur William, Jr.
 Wakeman, William Thomson
 Gardiner, Winthrop, Jr.
Wingate, Elaine — **Conway**, Edmund Virgil, III
Winkel, Mabel — **Singer**, Carl S.
 Julianelli, Charles A.
Winter, Dale Beulah — **Colosimo**, Giacomo
 Duffy, Henry Kendall
 McGraw, Hershel
 Perot, Edward Sansom, Jr.
Winthrop, Sarah Chauncey — **Weston**, Theodore
Wise, Frances — **Yates**, John Carrington
Wister, Elizabeth English — **Geary**, John White, III
 aka John White, Jr.
Wittenborn, Gretchen Ann — **Snow**, Sabin Tucker
 Johnson, James Loring

Maiden Names

Wolfman, Barbara Estelle — **Kurzner**, Dr. Rubin Raymond
Wood, Elizabeth — **Bogert**, Edward Osgood
Wood, Helen Ogden — **Cordier**, Auguste Julien, Jr.
Wood, Ruth Ann — **McSpadden**, Jack Dobbs, Jr.
Woodin, Elizabeth Foster — **Rowe**, William Wallace, Sr.
Woodin, Mary Louise — **Miner**, Charles, Sr.
    aka Robert Charles Miner, Sr.

Woodruff, Candace Catlin — **Benjamin**, William Wallace, III
Woolsey, Patricia — **Jackson**, Lionel Stewart, Sr.
Worthington, Florence Nightingale — **Osborne**, Joseph Septimus
Wren, Genevieve — **Gerli**, David Charles, Sr.
    Ham, Frederick

Wright, Anne — **Baxter**, Matthew Andrews, Sr.
    Kerr, Elmore Coe, Jr.
    Williams, David R., Jr.

Wright, Constance Cabell — **Jackson**, Elbert McGran
Wright, Georgianna Therese — **Erdmann**, Dr. John Frederic
Wuertz, Ida E. — **Washburn**, Ira Hedges, Sr.
Wurtele, Mildred O. — **Ordway**, Samuel Gilman
    Everett, Francis Dewey

Yates, Alice Emily — **Macy**, Valentine Everit, Jr.
Young, Laura Elizabeth — **Martin**, Samuel Klump, Jr.
Young, Sue H. — **Bradley**, Andrew Coyle
Zabriskie, Anne Louise — **Citron**, Casper Henry
    Noble, John Harmon

Zabriskie, Constance Pierrpont — **Richards**, Richard Draper
    aka Richard Follett
    Ludington, Elliot Kingman, Jr.

Zellweger, Renee Kathleen — **Chesney**, Kenneth Arnold
Zoller, Molly Susannah — **Lembcke**, George Albert

Occupations

See the surname entry to ascertain if an individual is listed under several occupational headings.

ADVERTISING EXECUTIVES

Ambrose, Colin Trippe
Breen, Daniel Anthony, Jr.
Briggs, James Branch
Cavett, Martha Rogers
Cody, Frederick
Cory, David Cleveland
Della Femina, Jerry
   aka Gennaro Tomas Della Femina
Deutsch, Donny
   aka Donald Jay Deutsch
Devine, James Joseph
Ethridge, George
Francisco, Donald, Sr.
   aka Don Francisco
Fraser, Ronald Goodall
Fuhrman, Dorian Flynn
Fuller, Edward Reinow
Gruss, Audrey M. Butvay
Hamilton, Gordon C.
Harper, Marion Clay, Jr.
Laughlin, Mary Kate Edwards
Macklowe, Harry B.
Peterson, Peter George
Ryan, Bruce Edgar
Ryan, Fredrick Behrens, Sr.
Seegal, Robin Neimark
Steele, Louis Thorton
Ward, Newell Jube, Sr.
Wasey, Louis Rice
Whitney, Elwood
Yates, James Saville
Zamichow, Bernard
Zuckerman, Mortimer Benjamin

APPRAISERS

Dean, Andree Belden Maitland

ARCHITECTS

Bunshaft, Gordon
Cobb, Henry Ives, Sr.
de Menil, Francois
   aka Francois Conrad Thomas de Menil
Eidlitz, Cyrus Lazelle Warner
Embury, Aymar, II
Fleetwood, Francis
Gruen, Robert L.
Gruzen, Barnet Sumner
Gruzen, Jordan Lee
Gwathmey, Charles
Haverland, Michael Robert
Lawrence, John Custis
Nash, Thomas
Scheffer, Alfred A.
Skidmore, Samuel Tredwell, II

Stern, Robert Arthur Morton
Stone, Edward Durell, Sr.
Thorp, Joseph Greenleaf
Thomas, Andrew Jackson
Weaver, Spencer Fullerton, Sr.
Weston, Theodore
Wood, Arthur B.
   aka Arthur W. B. Wood

ARTISTS

Bogert, George Henry
Breinin, Rose–Helen Kopelman
Butler, Howard Russell, Sr.
Chalif, Rona Miriam Stern
   aka Ronnie Chalif
Cookson, Lucy Allison Bishopric
de Kooning, Elaine Marie Catherine Fried
de Kooning, Willem
DeVries, John T.
DeVries, Mary Lange
   aka Mary MacKinnon
Donoho, Gaines Ruger
   aka Ruger Donoho
Dougherty, Frazer Lowber Welsh
Flinn, Linda Gilbert Scott
   aka Linda Scott
Flinn, Stephanie Hanes Strubling
Gianis, Tamar Victoria Clement
Gottlieb, Adolph
Gwathmey, Robert, Jr.
Gwathmey, Rosalie Dean Hook
Hassam, Frederick Childe
   aka Childe Hassam
Herter, Albert
Herter, Adele McGinnis
Jackson, Elbert McGran
Jewett, Maude Sherwood
   aka Maude Sherwood
Joel, Christie Brinkley
   aka Christie Brinkley
Johnson, James Loring
King, Hamilton
Klein, Jayne Centre
LaForest, Clara Belle Rilea
Lang, Helmut
Larkin, Lawrence
Lowenstein, Suse Ellen
MacKinnon, Archibald Angus
   [see DeVries entry]
Mascheroni, John
Mascheroni, Sarina
McConnell, Vanessa Mary Somers
Mercer, Norman J.
Montgomery, Paul
   aka John Paul Montgomery
Moran, Mary Nimmo
Moran, Thomas, Jr.

Occupations

ARTISTS (cont'd)

Newton, Francis
Ordway, Frances Hunt Throop
Ossorio, Alfonso Angel
Plimpton, Freddy Medora Espy
Pollock, Jackson
Pollock, Lee
   aka Lena Kranser;
   Lee Krasner;
   Lenora Krasne
Potter, Priscilla Bowden
   aka Priscilla Bowden
Pruyn, Miss Mary Lansing
Pruyn, Miss Neltje Knickerbocker
Rice, Jeannie Terry Durant
Rosset, Joan Mitchell
   aka Joan Mitchell
Roundebush, John Heywood
Schnabel, Julian
Scull, Robert C.
Sedacca, Joseph M.
Sewell, Lydia Amanda Brewster
   aka Amanda Brewster Sewell
Sewell, Robert Van Vorst
Simmons, Edward Emerson
Simmons, Vesta Schallenberger
Sprunger, Charles–Jean
   [*see* Cookson entry]
Thomas, Augustus
Towbin, Irene Katherine Lyons
Tyson, Carolyn Kennedy
Wainwright, Carroll Livingston, Sr.
Warhol, Andy
   aka Andrew Warhola, Jr.
Weiss, Stephan
   [*see* D. Karan entry]
Whittemore, Alice Vaud Whitmore
Whittemore, Charlotte Helen Simpson
Whittemore, William John
Yates, Linda L. Lindeberg

ATTORNEYS

Abbott, Henry Hurlbut
Adams, Charles Henry
Alexander, Edward Renick, Sr.
Ammon, Robert Theodore
   aka Ted Ammon
Avery, Edward Strong
Ayer, Claire Labourel
Backus, Henry Clinton
Baker, Lawrence Adams, Sr.
Baron, Ronald Stephen
Beale, Phelan, Sr.
Beardsley, Samuel Arthur, Sr.
Beardsley, Thomas Hopper
Bell, George Newell
Bellas, Alfred Constantine
Benjamin, Park, III
   aka Park Benjamin, Jr.
Bisco, Leonard Gerard
Blair, Montgomery
Bolch, Carl Edward, Jr.
Bouvier, John Vernou, Jr.
Bradley, Andrew Coyle
Brockman, Daniel David
Butler, Howard Russell, Sr.
Callan, Erin M.
Chalif, Seymour Hunt
Chatfield, Henry Houston
Chauncey, Alexander Wallace
Clark, Evans
Conway, Edmund Virgil, III
Coppell, Herbert
Coy, James Joseph, III
Creel, James Randall, Jr.
Davis, Vernon Mansfield
de Forest, Henry Grant
Devendorf, Alfred Ervin
Dubow, Arthur Myron
Edwards, James Cook, Sr.
Edwards, Walter, Jr.
Edwards, William Henry Leonard
Ely, John Ingraham
Eno, Eva Walling
Evans, James Hulburt
Fennelly, Leo C.
Fish, Sidney Webster
Fleming, Matthew Corry, Sr.
Friedman, Marvin Ross
Furman, Roy Lance
Gallatin, Frederic
Gardiner, David Lion, Sr.
Gleason, Carlisle Joyslin
Gordon, George Breed
Gowen, George W., II
Green, William Walker
Greer, Lawrence
Gunster, Joseph Frederick
Hanke, George Frederick Robert, Sr.
Hardy, Charles J., Jr.
Havens, Valentine Britton
Helm, George Washington, Sr.
Hirschfeld, Elie
Hiss, Alger
James, Henry Amman
Jenney, William Sherman
Kennedy, Michael John
Kimball, Charles Edmunds, Jr.
Klotz, Charles Arthur
Knox, John Mason, Jr.
Krakoff, Amy Jedlicka
Larkin, Adrian Hoffman
Lee, James Thomas
Lewis, Loida Nicholas
Lewis, Reginald F.
Lewis, Roger
   aka Joshua Roger Lewis
Lockwood, William Andrew
Loomis, Alfred Lee, Sr.
Lyon, Marvin Thomas
Mairs, Olney Blanchard, Sr.

Occupations

ATTORNEYS (cont'd)

Maloney, William Raywood, Sr.
McCall, Edward Everett
McCormick, Robert Elliot
McLanahan, Scott
Miller, Dudley Livingston, Sr.
Miller, Margery Gerdes
Mitchell, MacNeil
Monahan, John Paul, III
   [*see* K. Couric entry]
Morris, Theodore Wilson, Jr.
Morse, Tyler
Nadal, Charles Coleman
Nash, Stephen Edward
Nederlander, Robert Elliot, Sr.
Noble, Francis Osborn
Northrop, John Burr, Sr.
Ordway, Samuel Gilman
Ordway, Samuel Hanson, Jr.
Ordway, Samuel Hanson, Sr.
Osserman, Stanley
Parker, Roy Tilden, Jr.
Peddy, John Richard
Pierson, Warren Lee, Sr.
Preusse, Charles Frances
Ramsay, Herbert Hartley
Ranieri, Salvatore Anthony
Raymond, Dana Merriam
Regan, John Nicholas, Sr.
Rifkind, Robert Singer
Roberts, George Hewitt, Jr.
Robinson, Lucius Franklin, Jr.
Sandelman, Jonathan Everett
Schurman, George Wellington
Schurman, Jacob Gould, Sr.
Schwarzman, Christine Mularchuk
Seabury, Samuel
Seligson, William
Shafran, Irving
Skidmore, John Drake
Spring, Preston Brady, Sr.
Sterling, Oliver James, Sr.
Stern, Henry Root, Sr.
Stewart, Andrew
Stratton, Charles Preston
Strong, George Arthur
Strong, Theron George
Todd, John Reynard, Sr.
Tolan, Michael
   aka Seymour Tuchow
Tuck, Frederick W., Jr.
Tufo, Peter Francis
   [*see* Goelet entry]
Tweed, Harrison
Van Brunt, Arthur Hoffman, Sr.
Volckening, Lloyd Irwin
Wainright, Carroll Livingston, Jr.
Wainwright, Stuyvesant, II
Washburn, Watson
Washburn, William Tucker
Wasserstein, Bruce Jay

Wheelock, Dr. William Efner
Wood, Howard Ogden, Sr.
Wood, Wilfred
Zalles, Jorje Ezequiel, Sr.
   aka Jorge Ezequiel Zalles, Sr.
Zaslav, David M.
Zevely, James William, Sr.

AUCTIONEERS:

Draper, Simeon, Jr.
Laughlin, Veronica Penelope Whitlock

CAPITALISTS

Aldrich, Malcolm Pratt, Sr.
Altschul, Arthur Goodhart, Jr.
Anderson, Helen Natalie Johnson
Appleton, Robert Wilmarth
Bacon, Clarence Everett, Jr.
Bailey, Dr. Theodorus, II
Baldwin, Alexander Rae, III
   aka Alec Baldwin
Baldwin, Hilaria Thomas
Baldwin, Kimila Ann Basinger
   aka Kim Basinger
Barbour, William Stanton
Bartholomew, Frederick A.
   [*see* M. A. L. Shepherd entry]
Baxter, George White
Beard, Jeremiah Robinson, Jr.
Beardsley, Samuel Arthur, Sr.
Beardsley, Thomas Hopper
Benjamin, William Wallace, III
Benson, Arthur W.
Binn, Marisol Fernandes
Binn, Moreton
   aka Moreton Binstock
Bishop, Bennett
Bon Jovi, Jon
   aka John Frances Bongiovi, Jr.
Borden, Lewis Mercer, Sr.
Brackenridge, Gavin, Jr.
Bragg, Caleb Smith
Brisbane, Arthur
Bronfman, Edgar Miles, Jr.
Brown, Samuel Queen
Burchell, Henry J., Jr.
Butler, Howard Russell, Sr.
Calicchio, John
Cammann, George Philip, Jr.
Campbell, Nathaniel Adams, Sr.
Carson, William Moore, Sr.
Cater, Louise Bowers
Chace, Franklin M.
Chalif, Seymour Hunt
Chauncey, Alexander Wallace
Clark, Evans
Clark, Ivor Bache, Sr.

CAPITALISTS (cont'd)

Cleaves, Norman Smith
Clements, Hurin Martin
Cobb, Henry Ives, Sr.
Cohen, Steven A.
Coleman, Charles Philip
Conway, Edmund Virgil, III
Cory, David Cleveland
Culver, Austin H.
Cushman, Blinn Sill, Jr.
Dana, Robert Bingham
Darrow, Daniel
Day, Thomas Mills, Jr.
de Forest, Henry Grant
de Menil, Francois
    aka Francois Conrad Thomas de Menil
De Niro, Robert, Jr.
de Rose, Edward
Devendorf, Alfred Ervin
Devendorf, George Epworth
Devereaux, Jack
DeVoe, Raymond Forsyth, Sr.
Dewey, Marjorie Sawyer Goodman
Dickerman, William Carter, Sr.
Dougherty, Frazer Lowber Welsh
Dowdney, Louis Purcell
Dowling, Robert Whittle
Dubow, Arthur Myron
Duke, Anthony Drexel, Sr.
DuVal, Guy
Eastman, Joseph
Edwards, James McPherson
Edwards, Harkness, Sr.
Eldredge, George A.
Ely, Laurence Driggs, Sr.
Eno, Eva Walling
Entenmann, Robert William, Sr.
Evans, James Hurlburt
Fisher, Carl Graham, Sr.
Fleming, Henry Stuart
Fleming, Matthew Corry, Sr.
Flinn, George Hamilton, Sr.
Flinn, Lawrence, Jr.
Ford, Martha Parke Firestone
Ford, William Clay, Sr.
Franey, Elizabeth Chardenet
Frankel, Evan M.
Gallager, Thomas
Gardiner, Robert David Lion
Gardiner, Winthrop, Jr.
Garni, Adolph
    aka Adolpf Garni
Garten, Jeffery E.
Geary, John White, III
    aka John White Greary, Jr.
Geffen, David Lawrence
Gleason, Carlisle Joyslin
Goelet, Robert Guestier
Greer, Lawrence
Haag, Joseph, Jr.
Hamlin, Harry Leon

Hanke, George Frederick Robert, Sr.
Hanke, Lynn S. Washburn
Harkness, Lamon Vanderburg
Hartley, Nedena Marjorie Hutton
    aka Dina Merrill
Hartley, Thedore Ringwalt
Hedges, Burke Osborn
Hedges, Dayton
    aka William Dayton Hedges
Helmuth, Dr. William Tod, Jr.
Hensel, Clarence Hopkins
Heppenheimer, William Christian, III
Herrick, Dr. Everitt
Hinton, Alfred Post
Hirschfeld, Elie
Hirschfeld, Marcia Riklis
Hirtenstein, Michael
Hobart, Henry Lee
Hopkins, Lindsey, Jr.
Hoyt, Alfred Miller
Hufty, Mann Randolph Page
    aka Page Hufty
Huntting, Annie
Hyde, Frank Dana
Icahn, Carl Celian
Icahn, Gail Golden
James, Ellery Sedgwick, Sr.
    aka William Ellery Sedgwick James, Sr.
Jenney, William Sherman
Johnson, Frederick, Sr.
    [see DeVries entry]
Johnson, Servetus Fisher
Kaplan, Jacob Merrill
Kessner, Steven
Kimball, Charles Edmunds, Sr.
Klein, Calvin
    aka Calvin Richard Klein
Klenk, William Clifford, Jr.
Kuchin, Kenneth Sidney
LaForest, Helen A.
LaForest, Henry A.
Larkin, Adrian Hoffman
Laughlin, Alexander Mellon, Jr.
Lawrence, John Custis
Laws, Harry Langdon, III
    [see Aubert entry]
Leaman, Alfred Valentine, Jr.
Lee, James Thomas
Lee, Thomas Haskell
Lembcke, George Albert
LeRoy, Warner
Levering, Richmond, Sr.
    aka Richmond Levering, Sr.;
    John Mortimer Levering, Jr.
Levi, Charles Matthew
Lewis, Reginald F.
Lindemann, Adam Marc
Loeb, Daniel Seth
Macklowe, Harry B.
Macy, Valentine Everit, Jr.
Main, Charles E.

Occupations

CAPITALISTS (cont'd)

Mann, Henry
Mansell, Frank Luther
Martin, Samuel Klump, Jr.
Massey, Maurice Richardson, Jr.
Maxwell, Elliot
McAlpin, David Hunter, II
McAlpin, David Hunter, Sr.
McAlpin, George Lodowich, Sr.
McAlpin, Malcolm Evans
McCartney, Paul
   aka James Paul McCartney
McConnell, David Hall, III
McKinley, Andrew Barrett
   [see M. A. L. Shepherd entry]
Mercer, Norman J.
Miller, Dudley Livingston
Moranti, Paul Joseph
Morton, Peter
Munroe, Dr. George E., Jr.
Nadal, Charles Coleman
Nash, Stephen Edward
Nederlander, Gladys Lenore Blum
Nederlander, Robert Elliot, Sr.
Noble, Mark Ainslie
O'Brien, W. Howard, Sr.
Ordway, Samuel Gilman
Orr, Alexander Ector
Osborne, Burnett Mulford
Osborne, Joseph Septimus
Osborne, Nelson Cook, Sr.
Pagel, Alex John, Jr.
Pardridge, Albert Jerome
Peddy, John Richard
Perelman, Faith Golding
Perelman, Ronald Owen
Perot, Dale Beulah Winter
Peterson, Peter George
Pierson, Warren Lee, Sr.
Poor, James Harper
Potter, Eugene Clifford
Potter, Frederick Gaul
Potter, Jeffrey Brackett
Procter, William Cooper
Quackenbush, Schuyler
Radway, Edward Mailer
   [see Davis entry]
Ramee, Joseph Russell
Rattray, Arnold Elsmere
Rattray, Jeannette Frances Edward
Rawson, Joseph, Jr.
Reiswig, Gary D.
Rentschler, George Adam, Jr.
Rice, Henry Grantland
   aka Grantland Rice
Richard, Mary Ella Brooks
Richards, Richard Draper
   aka Richards Follett
Robert, Eileen Levin
Robert, Pilar Crespi
Roberts, Dudley DeVore, Jr.

Roberts, George Hewitt, Jr.
Robertson, Nedenia Marjorie Hutton
   aka Dina Merrill
Robinson, Lucius Franklin, Jr.
Rose, Daniel
Rose, Marshall
Rosinsky, Harold Jack
   aka Harold Jack Rosinski
Ross, Amanda Mortimer
Ross, Steven Jay
   aka Steven Jay Rechnitz
Roth, Daryl Adkin
Roth, Steven
Rowe, John Jay, Sr.
Rowe, William Stanhope, Sr.
Rumbough, Nedenia Marjorie Hutton
   aka Dina Merrill
Rumbough, Stanley Maddox, Jr.
Ruxton, Philip
Salembier, Paul Albert
Sandelman, Jonathan Everett
Sanger, Henry
Scheerer, Joseph Durand, Jr.
Scheerer, Joseph Durand, Sr.
Scheerer, Paul Renner, Jr.
Scheerer, William, II
Schulman, Lowell M.
Schultz, Howard Mark
Schwab, Laurence, Sr.
Scull, Robert C.
Seaman, Joseph Husband
Seegal, Frederic Milton
Seeley, Roy Clinton
   [see Barton entry]
Seligson, William
Semel, Terrance Steven
Shepherd, James Gardner
Simmons, Kimora Lee
   aka Kimora Whitlock
Simmons, Russell Wendell
Slifka, Alan Bruce
Slifka, Riva Arilla Golan
Smith, Earl Edward Tailer, Sr.
   [see Warburton entry]
Solomon, Peter Jay
Starke, Hamilton Jackson
Sterling, Oliver James, Sr.
Stern, Leonard Norman
Stern, Robert Arthur Morton
Stewart, Martha Helen Kostyra
Stimson, Henry Clark
Stratton, Charles Preston
Sweetser, Jesse William
Taylor, Irving Howland
Thorne, Henry Sanford
Tiffany, Nathan Newton, III
Tishman, Peter Valentine
Todd, John Reynard, Sr.
Todd, Webster Bray, Sr.
Tolan, Michael
   aka Seymour Tuchow

CAPITALISTS (cont'd)

Topping, Daniel Reid, Sr.
Towbin, Abraham Robert
Trippe, Juan Terry
Velie, John Deere, II
Wainwright, Stuyvesant, III
Walker, Bayard, Sr.
Walker, George Gholson, Sr.
Warhol, Andy
  aka Andrew Warhola, Jr.
Warner, Eltinge Fowler, Jr.
Wasey, Louis Rice
Washburn, Watson
Weaver, Spencer Fullerton, Sr.
Weinstein, Joseph
Weiss, Jay
  [see K. Turner entry]
Welch, Leo Dewey
Wenner, Jane Schindelheim
Wenner, Jann Simon
Wessel, Homer Augustus, Sr.
Wheelock, William Almy
Williams, David R., Jr.
  [see Baxter entry]
Williams, Eugene Flewilyn, Jr.
Williams, John Pattison, Sr.
  [see A J. S. Greene entry]
Woodin, William Hartman, Sr.
Woolley, Knight
Wright, John Howie, III
Yates, John Carrington
Zalles, Jorje Ezequiel, Sr.
  aka Jorge Ezequiel Zalles, Sr.
Zaslav, David M.
Zuckerman, Mortimer Benjamin

CLERGY

Duffield, The Reverend Howard
Greer, The Reverend David Hummell
Kendrick, The Reverend James Ryland
Mackay, The Reverend William R.
Mershon, The Reverend Stephen Lyon, Sr.
Newman, The Reverend John Philip
Newton, The Reverend Richard Heber, Sr.
Paxton, The Reverend John Randolph, Sr.
Richey, The Reverend Alban, Sr.
Richey, The Reverend Thomas, Sr.
Steele, The Reverend James Nevett, Sr.
Stokes, The Reverend John Dunlap
Talmage, The Reverend Thomas DeWitt
Tillich, The Reverend Paul Johannes

COMPOSERS

Bon Jovi, Jon
  aka John Francis Bongiovi, Jr.
Bronfman, Edgar Miles, Jr.
Hamilton, Chico
  aka Foreststorn Hamilton

Harris, William Victor
  aka Victor Harris
Joel, Billy
  aka William Martin Joel
McCartney, Paul
  aka James Paul McCartney
Simon, Edie Alisa Brickell
Simon, Paul Frederic
Tishman, Judith A. Rothenberg
Woodin, William Hartman, Sr.

DIPLOMATS

Aubert, Ludvig Caesar Martin, II
Bragg, Caleb Smith
de Kay, Charles
Hiss, Alger
Martin, Samuel Klump, Jr.
Newman, The Reverend John Philip
Pierson, Warren Lee, Sr.
Rosinsky, Claude Daste
Schurman, Jacob Gould, Sr.
Smith, Earl Edward Tailer, Sr.
  [see Warburton entry]
Storey, Edward Albert
Tufo, Peter Francis
  [see Goelet entry]
Zalles, Jorje Ezequiel, Sr.
  aka Jorge Ezequiel Zalles, Sr.

EDUCATORS

Abbe, James Edward, Jr.
Adair, Dr. Frank Earl
Adams, John Cranford
Agnew, Dr. Cornelius Rea, Sr.
Bailey, Dr. Theodorus, II
Beaumont, Perry H.
Becker, Susan E.
Bon Jovi, Dorothea Hurley
Bradley, Andrew Coyle
Breinin, Dr. Goodwin Milton
Browne, Christopher H.
Burchell, Henry J., Jr.
Butler, Howard Russell, Sr.
Carpenter, Edmund Snow
Cavett, Martha Rogers
Chanos, James Steven
Chase, Edward Tinsley
Clark, Evans
Clarke, Thomas Benedict, Sr.
Cody, Frederick
Cookson, Lucy Allison Bishopric
Cushman, Edith Marie Macon
Davis, George Samler
Davis, Vernon Mansfield
de Kooning, Willem
Devine, James Joseph

Occupations

EDUCATORS (cont'd)

DeVries, Mary Lange
   aka Mary MacKinnon
Drexler, Peggy F.
Dunn, Dr. James Manning
Dunn Marguerite Ritzer
Edwards, Dr. Ogden Matthias, Jr.
Erdmann, Dr. John Frederic
Flinn, Lawrence, Sr.
Francisco, Donald W., Sr.
   aka Don Francisco
Furman, Frieda Anne Bueler
Garten, Jeffery E.
Gianis, Socrates George, Sr.
Gottlieb, Esther Dick
Gowen, George W., II
Gwathmey, Charles
Gwathmey, Robert, Jr.
Halsted, Dr. Harbeck
Hamilton, Chico
   aka Foreststorn Hamilton
Hand, Mary Coolidge
Havens, Valentine Britton
Haverland, Michael Robert
Hayden, Rose Mill Betts
Helmuth, Dr. William Tod, Jr.
Herter, Albert
Highet, Gilbert Albert
Hillman, Murray
Hinton, Dr. James William
Hirschfeld, Dr. Susan T. Aronson
Hiss, Priscilla Harriet Fansler
Hollister, Dr. Frederick Kellogg
Jones, Dr. Oswald Roberts
Kast, Dr. Ludwig
Kendrick, Georgia Avery
Kendrick, The Reverend James Ryland
Krech, Dr. Shepard, Sr.
Krieger, Dr. Dorothy Terrace
Krieger, Dr. Howard P.
Laughlin, Veronica Penelope Whitlock
Lee, Barbara Ellen Fish
Levy–Church, Kenneth
   aka Kenneth Wayne Church
Mayo–Smith, Richmond, Sr.
McConnell, Vanessa Mary Somers
McKeon, Patricia A. Finnegan
Miller, Dudley Livingston, Sr.
Moody, Sidney Clarke, Sr.
Ordway, Samuel Hanson, Jr.
Plimpton, George Ames
Pool, Henry Lawrence
Potter, Dickson Bayard
Rattray, Jeannette Frances Edwards
Rice, Dr. Clarence Charles
Richard, Mary Ella Brooks
Richey, The Reverend Thomas, Sr.
Rifkind, Dr. Arleen Brenner
Rifkind, Dr. Richard A.
Robert, Stephen Kniznick
Ross, Courtney Sale
Ross, Steven Jay
   aka Steven Jay Rechnitz
Schurman, Jacob Gould, Sr.
Schwarzman, Stephen Allen
Snow, Dr. Irving Miller
Solley, Dr. Fred Palmer
Sonnenfeld, Barry
Sonnenfeld, Susan L. Ringo
Spring, Betsey Eliza Royce
Stanton, Dr. Frederick Lester
Stern, Joel Mark
Stern, Robert Arthur Morton
Stone, Edward Durell, Sr.
Thiele, Roger Harvey
Thompson, Dr. Frederick Roeck
Tillich, The Reverend Paul Johannes
Todd, John Reynard, Sr.
Tuck, Merle Fiske
Turner, Kathleen
   aka Mary Kathleen Turner
Tweed, Harrison
Voorhees, Dr. James Ditmars
   aka Dr. James Ditmars Van Voorhees
Wainwright, Carroll Livingston, Jr.
Wainwright, Marcella Callery Mittendorf
Wainwright, Stuyvesant, II
Walker, Dr. John Baldwin, Sr.
Webster, Dr. Bruce Peck
Whittle, Chris
   aka H. Christopher Whittle
Wood, Howard Ogden, Sr.
Zaslav, David M.
Zuckerman, Mortimer Benjamin

ENTERTAINERS AND ASSOCIATED PROFESSIONS

Adair, Marion Hopkinson
Ambrose, Jessica Lyman Mansell
Avedon, Dorcas Marie
   aka Doe Avedon;
   Betty Harper
Baldwin, Alexander Rae, III
   aka Alec Baldwin
Baldwin, Kimila Ann Basinger
   aka Kim Basinger
Becker, Harold
Becker, Susan E.
Bellas, Kathryn Mazzo
   aka Kay Mazzo
Bellas, Selina Schroeder Croll
   aka Tina Croll
Binn, Penny Schwartz
Bon Jovi, Jon
   aka John Francis Bongiovi, Jr.
Bradlee, Sally Quinn
   aka Sally Quinn
Broderick, Matthew
Broderick, Sarah Jessica Parker
   aka Sarah Jessica Parker
Bronfman, Sherry Brewer
Bunshaft, Nina Elizabeth Wayler

ENTERTAINERS AND ASSOCIATED PROFESSIONS (cont'd)

Caruso, Enrico
Cavett, Caroline Nye McGeoy
   aka Carrie Nye
Cavett, Richard Alva
   aka Dick Cavett
Chase, Cathalene Parker Browning
   aka Cathalene Crane
Chase, Chevy
   aka Cornelius Crain Chase
Chase, Ethelyn Atha
Chase, Jacquelin Jean Carlin
Cheaney, Kenneth Arnold
   [see Zellweger entry]
Citron, Casper Henry
Combs, Sean John
   aka Puff Daddy, Diddy, and P. Diddy
Couric, Katie
   aka Katherine Ann Couric
Coy, James Joseph, Jr.
de Kay, Lucy Edwalyn Coffey
Della Femina, Judith Carol Licht
de Liagre, Alfred, Jr.
   aka Alfred Gustav Etienne de Liagre, Jr.
de Liagre, Mary Rogers
   aka Mary Howard
de Menil, Francois
   aka Francois Conrad Thomas de Menil
de Menil, Susan Kadin Silver
De Niro, Diahnne Eugenia Abbott
   aka Diahnne Dea
De Niro, Grace Hightower
De Niro, Robert, Jr.
De Palma, Brian Russell
De Palma, Darnell Gregorio
   aka Darnell Gregorio–De Palma
De Palma, Gale Anne Hurd
De Palma, Nancy Allen
Deutsch, Donny
   aka Donald Jay Deutsch
Devereaux, Jack
Devereaux, Jane Henderson
Devereaux, John Drew
Devereaux, Louise Drew
Dougherty, Frances Ann Cannon
Downey, Deborah Falconer
Downey, Robert, Jr.
Downey, Susan Nicole Levin
Drew, John, Jr.
Ephron, Nora
Erwin, Roma Virginia Volck
   aka Doris Dudley
Falchuk, Brad
   [see Paltrow entry]
Farrington, Selwyn Kip, Jr.
Franey, Pierre
Furman, Roy Lance
Gardiner, Mildred Helen Shay
Gardiner, Nancy Deere Wiman
Gardiner, Sonja Henje

Garten, Ina Rosenberg
Geffen, David Lawrence
Gerli, Jacqueline Kneip
Grace, Natalie O. Watts
Green, Adolph
Green, Allyn Ann McLerie
Green, Elizabeth Reitell
Green, Phyllis Newman
   aka Phyllis Newman
Gruzen, Ethel Bernstein Brof
Gruzen, Lee Ferguson
Hamilton, Chico
   aka Foreststorn Hamilton
Harris, William Victor
   aka Victor Harris
Hartley, Nedenia Marjorie Hutton
   aka Dina Merrill
Hartley, Theodore Ringwalt
Highet, Gilbert Albert
Hoffman, Ellen Rose Wheeler
Icahn, Liba Trejbal
Jaffe, Stanley Richard
Joel, Billy
   aka William Martin Joel
Joel, Christie Brinkley
   aka Christie Brinkley
Joel, Elizabeth Weber
Joel, Katie Lee
   aka Kathleen Rebekah Lee
John, Jencie Callaway
   aka Jencie Callaway–John
Laughlin, Martha Brooke Clarke
   aka Brooke Clarke
LeRoy, Warner
Levi, Charles Matthew
Levy–Church, Jeanne Levy
Manners, Laurette Helen Cooney
   aka Laurette Taylor
Mapes, Victor
   aka Sidney Sharp
Martin, Christopher Anthony John
   [see Paltrow entry]
McCartney, Linda Louise Eastman
McCartney, Paul
   aka James Paul McCartney
Mercer, Carol Keyser
Michaels, Alice Berry
Michaels, Lorne
   aka Lorne Lipowitz
Michaels, Rosie Schuster
Michaels, Susan Forrestal
Montgomery, Elizabeth Bryan Allan
Montgomery, Robert
   aka Henry Montgomery, Jr.;
   Robert Montgomery, Sr.
Morrissey, Paul
Nederlander, Gladys Lenore Blum
Paltrow, Gwyneth Kate
Perelman, Claudia Lynn Cohen
Perelman, Ellen Rona Barkin

Occupations

ENTERTAINERS AND ASSOCIATED PROFESSIONS (cont'd)

Perelman, Patricia Michelle Orr
   aka Patricia Duff
Perot, Dale Beulah Winters
Peterson, Joan Ganz
   aka Joan Ganz Cooney
Pilleggi, Nicholas, Jr.
   [see Ephron entry]
Potter, Jeffrey Brackett
Potter, Madeleine Penelope Sack
   aka Penelope Sack
Radziwill, Caroline Lee Bouvier
   aka Lee Radziwill
Rice, Henry Grantland
   aka Grantland Rice
Rifkind, Carole Lewis
Rifkind, Dr. Richard A.
Robert, Pilar Crespi
Robertson, Clifford Parker, III
   aka Cliff Robertson
Robertson, Cynthia Stone
Robertson, Nedenia Marjorie Hutton
   aka Dina Merrill
Rose, Candice Bergen
   aka Candice Bergen
Ross, Herbert David
   [see Radziwill entry]
Roth, Daryl Adkins
Rumbough, Nedenia Marjorie Hutton
   aka Dina Merrill
Schnabel, Jacquelin Beaurang
Schnabel, Julian
Schwab, Marie Gaspar
Schwab, Mildred Leona Brown
Seinfeld, Jerry
   aka Jerome Allen Seinfeld
Semel, Jane Bovingdon
Semel, Terrance Steven
Simmons, Kimora Lee
   aka Kimora Whitlock
Simmons, Russell Wendell
Simon, Carrie Frances Fisher
   aka Carrie Fisher
Simon, Edie Arlisa Bricknell
Simon, Paul Frederic
Sonnenfeld, Barry
Spielberg, Kathleen Sue Nail
   aka Kate Capshaw
Spielberg, Steven Allan
Stephanopoulas, Alexandra Elliot Wentworth
Stephanopoulos, George Robert
Stern, Allison Maher
Stern, Robert Arthur Morton
Stewart, Martha Helen Kostyra
Taylor, Charles Alonzo
   [see Manners entry]
Thomas, Augustus
Tolan, Michael
   aka Seymour Tuchow
Tolan, Rosemary Forsyth

Topping, Arline Judge
Topping, Katherine Warburton
   aka Kay Sutton
Topping, Sonja Henje
Tufo, Peter Francis
   [see Goelet entry]
Turner, Kathleen
   aka Mary Kathleen Turner
Tweed, Barbara Banning
Tweed. Blanche Oelrichs
Tyson, Carolyn Kennedy
Verglas, Antoine
Washburn, Ann Gibson Clark
Wasserstein, Claude Becker
Weber, Bruce
Weber, Nan Bush
Weinstein, Eve Chilton
Weinstein, Georgina Rose Chapman
Weinstein, Harvey
Woodward, Shaun Anthony
Yates, John Carrington
Zellweger, Renee Kathleen
Zuckerman, Mortimer Benjamin

FASHION DESIGNERS

Beard, Cheryl Rae Tiegs
Friedman, Sheila Natasha
Julianelli, Charles A.
Julianelli, Mabel Winkel
Karan, Donna Ivy Faske
Krakoff, Delphine A. Boyon
Krakoff, Reed
Lauren, Ralph
   aka Ralph Lifshitz
Robert, Pilar Crespi
Rosinsky, Claude Daste
Schnabel, Jacquelin
Weber, Bruce
Weinstein, Georgina Rose Chapman
Weiss, Stephan
   [see D. Karan]
Whitney, Virginia Enfield

FINANCIERS

Adams, Charles Henry
Alcott, Clarence Frank
Aldrich, Malcolm Pratt, Sr.
Aldrich, Spencer Wyman
Alker, Edward Paul
Altschul, Arthur Goodhart, Jr.
Amador, Paul A.
Ammon, Randee E. Day
Ammon, Robert Theodore
   aka Ted Ammon
Anderson, Edward Ewen
Andrews, William Loring
Ashplant, Frederick Bryant, Sr.
Austin, William Gage
Avery, Edward Strong

Occupations

FINANCIERS (cont'd)

Bacon, Clarence Everett, Jr.
Baron, Ronald Stephen
Bartlett, Edward Everett, Jr.
Beardsley, Samuel Arthur, Sr.
Beardsley, Thomas Hopper
Beaumont, Perry H.
Beckers, William Kurt
Beebe, William Nottingham, Sr.
Bellas, Alfred Constantine
Benson, Arthur W.
Bianchi, Albert William
Blackburn, Wilmuth Earle
Bouvier, John Vernou, Jr.
Bouvier, John Vernou, III
Bowne, Robert Southgate
Bracken, James W.
Brackenridge, Gavin, Jr.
Brackenridge, Gavin, Sr.
Breen, Daniel Anthony, Jr.
Brett, Philip Milledoler, Jr.
   [see Pool entry]
Brown, Anthony Coats
Brown, Lathrop
Brown, Philip Wilson Tate, Sr.
Browne, Christopher H.
Buddenhagen, Frederick Leonard
Burnett, Eugene Rodney
Burton, William Lafayette, II
Callan, Erin M.
Campbell, David
Campbell, Nathaniel Adams, Sr.
Chanos, James Steven
Chapman, Benjamin Gains, Jr.
Chauncey, Alexander Wallace
Chisholm, Edward de Clifford
Clark, Ivor Bache, Sr.
Cloud, Chester Marts
Cogan, Marshall Stuart
Cohen, Peter Anthony
Cohen, Steven A.
Cohn, Maurice J.
Cole, John Nelson, Jr.
Conway, Edmund Virgil, II
Conway, Edmund Virgil, III
Cook, Harry
Coppell, Herbert
Cory, David Cleveland
Coy, James Joseph, III
Culver, Austin H.
Cummins, Stephen Swete
Davies, Francis Herbert
Davis, Henry Gassaway, III
   [see Warburton entry]
Dean, Howard Brush, Jr.
de Kay, Ormonde, Sr.
De Koven, Louis Besant Wadsworth
Della Femina, Barbara
Devendorf, George Epworth
Devine, James Joseph
DeVoe, Raymond Forsyth, Sr.

Dewey, Charles Schuveldt, Jr.
Dickerman, William Carter, Sr.
Dodd, John Mingus, III
Dodge, Washington, Jr.
Dowling, Robert Whittle
Draper, Simeon, Jr.
Dubow, Arthur Myron
Duke, Anthony Drexel, Sr.
DuVal, Guy
Earl, Noble Clarkson, Jr.
   [see Warburton entry]
Eastman, Joseph
Edwards, James Cook, Sr.
Edwards, Dr. Ogden Matthias, Jr.
Eldredge, George A.
Elliott, William, Jr.
Eno, Alfred Joseph
Entenmann, Robert William, Sr.
Ethridge, George
Evans, Benjamin Franklin
Evans, James Hurlburt
Farrington, Selwyn Kip, Jr.
Flinn, Lawrence, Jr.
Flinn, Lawrence, Sr.
Fraser, Alexander
Fuhrman, Gary L.
Furman, Roy Lance
Gallagher, Alice Jarcho
Gallatin, Frederick, II
   [see E. C. T Bell entry]
Gallatin, James Nicholson
Gardiner, Robert David Lion
Garten, Jeffery E.
Garvin, John S.
   [see E. C. T. Bell entry]
Geddes, Gerald Maxwell
Gianis, Socrates George, Sr.
Gleason, Carlisle Joyslin
Goelet, Robert Guestier
Gowen, George W., II
Grace, Morgan Hatton, Jr.
Greene, Anne Johnston Sawyer
Greene, John Bradley, II
Gruss, Martin David
Hamilton, Helen
Hammond, John Carnahan
Hanke, George Frederick Robert, Sr.
Hartley, Nedenia Marjorie Hutton
   aka Dina Merrill
Hartley, Theodore Ringwalt
Hattersley, Frederick Robert
Haynes, Justin O'Brien, Sr.
Hedges, John Daniel
Hensel, Clarence Hopkins
Helm, John LaRue, Jr.
Hendrix, Clifford Rathbone, Sr.
Heppenheimer, William Christian, III
Herrick, Anson Boulton, Sr.
Hill, Robert Carmer
Hobart, Garret Augustus, Jr.
Holleran, Frank Joseph
Homans, Eugene Vanderpool

FINANCIERS (cont'd)

Hopkins, John Appleton Haven, Sr.
Hopkins, Lindsey, Jr.
Hoyt, Alfred Miller
Hufty, Mann Randolph Page
   aka Page Hufty
Icahn, Carl Celian
Icahn, Gail Golden
Jackson, John Day
Jackson, Lionel Stewart, Sr.
James, Ellery Sedgwick, Sr.
   aka William Ellery Sedgwick James, Sr.
Jefferys, Harry Leapold
Jenkins, Edward Elliott
Jewett, Edward Hull, Jr.
Jewett, Edward Hull, Sr.
Joel, Alexis Roderick
Johnson, Servetus Fisher
Kaplan, Jacob Merrill
Kelley, William Vallandigham
Kelsey, Stephen Tomlinson, Sr.
Kerr, Chauncey F.
Kerr, Elmore Coe, Jr.
   [see Baxter entry]
Kimball, Charles Edmunds, Jr.
Kingsley, Walton Pearl
Kiser, John William, III
   aka John William Kiser, Jr.
Klenk, William Clifford, Jr.
Knox, John Mason, Jr.
LaMonte, George Mason
Laughlin, Alexander Mellon, Sr.
Laughlin, David Walker
Leaman, Alfred Valentine, III
Le Brecht, Robert
Lee, James Thomas
Lee, Thomas Haskell
Leith, Donald E.
Leonard, Stephen Joseph, Sr.
Levering, John Mortimer [Sr.]
Lilley, Alexander Neil, Sr.
Lindemann, Adam Marc
Lockwood, Williston Benedict
Loeb, Daniel Seth
Loomis, Alfred Lee, Sr.
Lowe, William Ebbets, II
Madoff, Bernard Lawrence
   aka Bernie Madoff
Maguire, Edward, Sr.
Main, Charles E.
Mairs, Olney Blanchard, Jr.
Mann, Henry
Mansell, Frank Luther
Manston, Thomas Lincoln, III
Martin, Samuel Klump, Jr.
Massey, Maurice Richardson, Jr.
McAlpin, David Hunter, II
McAlpin, David Hunter, Sr.
McAlpin, George Lodowich, Sr.
McAlpin, Malcolm Evans
McCaffray, Walter Peck

McCall, Edward Everett
McConnell, Neil Anderson
McCormick, Robert Elliott
McKeon, Robert Brian
McKittrick, Walter
McLanahan, Scott
McSpadden, Jack Dobbs, Jr.
Meehan, Joseph Ansbro
Mnuchin, Alan Geoffrey
Molner, John P.
   [see K. Couric entry]
Myrick, Julian Southall
Nadal, Charles Coleman
Noble, Mark Ainslie
Nori, Edmond Joseph
Northrop, John Burr, Sr.
Oakley, Ralph Lawrence
Olin, John Merrill
Orr, Alexander Ector
Osborne, Joseph Septimus
Osborne, Nelson Cook, Sr.
Peters, William Sterling
Peterson, Joan Ganz
   aka Joan Ganz Cooney
Peterson, Peter George
Pierson, Warren Lee, Sr.
Potter, Eugene Clifford
Procter, William Cooper
Pulleyn, John William, Sr.
Putnam, Harrington, Jr.
Quackenbush, Schuyler
Ranieri, Mary Louise Gioiella
Rawson, Joseph, Jr.
Reid, Archibald Mudge
Reid, Wallace
Rentschler, George Adam, Jr.
Rheinstein, Sidney
Rice, Ernest H., Sr.
Richard, Auguste
Richard, Mary Ella Brooks
Robert, Stephen Kniznick
Roberts, Dudley DeVore, Jr.
Robertson, Nedenia Marjorie Hutton
   aka Dina Merrill
Robinson, Lucius Franklin, Jr.
Rose, Marshall
Rosenstein, Barry
Rowe, John Jay, Sr.
Rowe, William Stanhope, Sr.
Rumbough, Nedenia Marjorie Hutton
   aka Dina Merrill
Rumbough, Stanley Hutton
Rumbough, Stanley Maddox, Jr.
Ryan, Richard Nelson, Jr.
Salembier, Paul Albert
Sandelman, Jonathan Everett
Sanger, Henry
Satterthwaite, James Sheafe
Scheerer, Joseph Durand, Jr.
Scheerer, Joseph Durand, Sr.
Scheerer, Paul Renner, Jr.

Occupations

FINANCIERS (cont'd)

Scheerer, William, II
Schmidt, Dederick Herman
Schulman, Lowell M.
Schultz, Howard Mark
Schwarzman, Stephen Allan
Seaman, Joseph Husband, Sr.
Seegal, Frederic Milton
Shepherd, James Gardner
Sherman, John Taylor, II
Simon, William Edward, Sr.
Sinclair, Earle Westwood
Singh, Vinayak
Skidmore, John Drake
Skidmore, Samuel Tredwell, II
Slikfa, Alan Bruce
Slikfa, Jacqueline Watkins
Smith, Earl Edward Tailer, Sr.
   [*see* Warburton entry]
Solomon, Peter Jay
Solomon, Susan Barach
Spalding, Jesse, II
Steinberg, Robert Michael
Stern, Joel Mark
Stevens, Leighton H.
Stimson, Henry Clark
Storey, Edward Albert
Stratton, Charles Preston
Sutphen, Henry Randolph, Jr.
Sutphen, Henry Randolph, Sr.
Talmadge, John Frelinghuysen
Terbell, Henry S., Sr.
Thiele, Albert Edward, Jr.
Thompson, Charles Griswold
Tiedeman, Irvin Bruce, Sr.
Tiffany, Nathan Newton, III
Todd, Webster Bray, Sr.
Towbin, Abraham Robert
Trippe, Charles White, Sr.
Trippe, Juan Terry
Tuck, Frederick W., Jr.
Tufo, Peter Francis
   [*see* Goelet entry]
Vanderbilt, Oliver DeGray, III
Van Rensselaer, Kiliaen, III
Wainwright, Carroll Stuyvesant, Jr.
Wainwright, Carroll Stuyvesant, Sr.
Wainwright, John Howard
Walker, Bayard, Sr.
Wardle, H. Allen
Washburn, George
Wasserstein, Bruce Jay
Weeks, John Kirkland, Sr.
Weeks, John Lafayette
Welch, Leo Dewey
Weston, Theodore
Wheelock, William Almy
Williams, Eugene Flewilyn, Jr.
Wood, Howard Ogden, Jr.
Wood, Howard Ogden, Sr.
Wood, Wilfrid

Woodhouse, Lorenzo Easton
Woodhouse, Lorenzo Guernsey
Woodin, William Hartman, Sr.
Woolley, Knight
Zalles, Jorje Ezequiel, Sr.
   aka Jorge Ezequiel Zalles, Sr.

INDUSTRIALISTS

Adams, Charles Henry
Akin, Robert Macomber, Jr.
Alker, Edward Paul
Altschul, Arthur Goodhart, Jr.
Aufermann, Walter C. W.
   [*see* Kast entry]
Austin, William Gage
Bacon, Charles Everett, Jr.
Baxter, Matthew Andrews, Sr.
Beckers, William Kurt
Bennett, Russell Conwell, Sr.
Betner, Benjamin Carlton, Jr.
Betts, Hobart Dominick, Sr.
Bishopric, Allison, Jr.
Borden, Lewis Mercer, Sr.
Bragg, Caleb Smith
Breyer, Henry William, III
Broderick, Sarah Jessica Parker
   aka Sarah Jessica Parker
Bronfman, Edgar Miles, Jr.
Buek, Gustav H.
   aka Gustavus H. Buek
Burke, Oscar Moech
Cammann, Roy Lennox
Campbell, Nathaniel Adams, Sr.
Carse, Donald Rede, Sr.
Carse, John Bradley, Sr.
Caruso, Dorothy Park Benjamin
Chalif, Seymour Hunt
Chauncey, Alexander Wallace
Church, Richard Newton Loomis
Clarke, Thomas Benedict, Sr.
Cloud, Chester Marts
Cogan, Marshall Stuart
Cohen, Peter Anthony
Cole, John Nelson, Jr.
Coleman, Charles Philip
Combs, Sean
   aka Puff Daddy, Diddy, and P. Diddy
Cook, Francis Howell
Cook, Harry
Coppell, Herbert
Cordier, Auguste Julien, Jr.
Cornell, Irwin Hewlett
Cornell, William Frank
Coy, James Joseph, III
Crane, Thomas
Cullman, Joseph Frederick, III
Cummins, Stephen Swete
Davis, Chase Henchman
Dickerman, William Carter, Sr.

Occupations

INDUSTRIALISTS (cont'd)
d'Olier, Franklin Woolman, Jr.
DeVoe, Raymond Forsyth, Sr.
Dougherty, Russell Keresey
Drexler, Millard S.
   aka Mickey Drexler
Earl, Noble Clarkson, Jr.
   [see Warburton entry]
Edwards, James McPherson
Ely, Laurence Driggs, Sr.
Entenmann, Charles, Sr.
Entenmann, Robert William, Sr.
Evans, James Hurlburt
Fisher, Carl Graham, Sr.
Fleming, Henry Stuart
Fleming, Matthew Corry, Sr.
Ford, James Bishop
Ford, William Clay, Sr.
Francisco, Donald W., Sr.
   aka Don Francisco
Fraser, Alexander
Fuhrman, Gary L.
Fuller, Edward Reinow
Garni, Adolph
   aka Adolf Garni
Garten, Jeffery E.
Geary, John White, III
   aka John White Greary, Jr.
Gerli, David Charles, Sr.
Gleason, Carlisle Joyslin
Gordon, George Breed
Graham, James Leonard, Sr.
Gram, Carl William, Jr.
Gribetz, Lester
Gruss, Audrey M. Butvay
Gwathmey, Bette-Ann Damson
Haag, Joseph, Jr.
Hall, William Claiborne
Hansen, Curt Eric
Hardy, Charles J., Jr.
Harkness, Lamon Vanderberg
Hartley, Nedenia Marjorie Hutton
   aka Dina Merrill
Haupt, Melville I.
Havens, Valentine Britton
Haynes, Justin O'Brien, Sr.
Hedges, Burke Osborn
Hedges, Dayton
   aka William Dayton Hedges
Helier, David
Heppenheimer, William Christian, III
Herter, Albert
Heyman, Stephen J.
Hill, Robert Carmer
Hillman, Murray
Hirschfeld, Dr. Sarah J. Schlesinger
Hobart, Henry Lee
Holmes, Jay
Hopkinson, Russell
Hufty, Mann Randolph Page
   aka Page Hufty

Hutton, John Laurence, Sr.
Hutton, William Langdon
Icahn, Carl Celian
Jackson, Elbert McGean
Joel, Billy
   aka William Martin Joel
Joel, Christie Brinkley
   aka Christie Brinkley
John, Davis W.
Johnson, Samuel William
Jones, Rodney Wilcox, Sr.
Kaplan, Jacob Merrill
Kelley, William Vallandigham, Sr.
Kennedy, Clair O'Donnell
Kennedy, David E.
Kiser, John William, III
   aka John William Kiser, Jr.
Klotz, Charles Arthur
Kuser, John Louis, Jr.
LaMonte, George Mason
Lang, Helmut
Larkin, Adrian Hoffman
Laughlin, Alexander Mellon, Jr.
Lauren, Ralph
   aka Ralph Lifshitz
Levering, John Mortimer [Sr.]
Levering, Richmond, Sr.
   aka John Richmond Levering, Sr.;
   John Mortimer Levering, Jr.
Lewis, Loida Nicholas
Lewis, Reginald F.
Lilley, Alexander Neil, Sr.
Lloyds, Richard
Loomis, Alfred Lee, Sr.
Lowenstein, Peter
Lutkins, Clinton Stephen
Macy, Valentine Everit, Jr.
Maharam, Donald, Jr.
Main, Charles E.
Mann, Henry
Manson, Thomas Lincoln, III
Mapes, Charles Halsted
Marsh, Frank Ballard
Maxwell, Elliott
McAlpin, David Hunter, Sr.
McAlpin, George Lodowich, Sr.
McAlpin, Malcolm Evans
McCall, Edward Everett
McCartney, Linda Louise Eastman
McCord, David Walter
McCormick, Robert Elliott
McLanahan, Scott
Meehan, Joseph Ansbro
Mercati, Leonardo
Mercer, Norman J.
Miller, Dudley Livingston, Sr.
Mitchell, Ledyard, Sr.
   aka William Ledyard Mitchell
Moffett, James Andrew, Jr.
Monell, Theodore, Jr.
Moody, Sidney Clarke, Sr.

Occupations

INDUSTRIALISTS (cont'd)

Nadal, Charles Coleman
Nederlander, Robert Elliot, Sr.
Nichols, Harold Willis, Jr.
Nichols, Harold Willis, Sr.
O'Brien, W. Howard, Sr.
Ogden, James Lawrence, Jr.
Olin, John Merrill
Osserman, Stanley
Perelman, Ronald Owen
Perot, Edward Sansom, Jr.
Peterson, Joan Ganz
   aka Joan Ganz Cooney
Peterson, Peter George
Phillips, Fleming Stanhope
Pierson, Warren Lee, Sr.
Pittman, Ernest Wetmore
Potter, Jeffrey Brackett
Procter, William Cooper
Rabbe, Richard Frederick
Rahr, Carol K. Lang
Rawson, Joseph, Jr.
Rentschler, George Adam, Jr.
Rice, Ernest H., Sr.
Richard, Auguste
Richards, Benjamin, Jr.
Robert, Stephen Kniznick
Roberts, Walter Scott
Robertson, Hugh James, Jr.
Robertson, Nedenia Marjorie Hutton
   aka Dina Merrill
Robinson, Felding S.
Rose, Marshall
Rosinsky, Harold Jack
   aka Harold Jack Rosinski
Rounick, Jack A.
Rowe, John Jay, Jr.
Rowe, John Jay, Sr.
Rowe, William Stanhope, Sr.
Rowe, William Wallace, Sr.
Rubin, Samuel
Rumbough, Nedenia Marjorie Hutton
   aka Dina Merrill
Rumbough, Stanley Maddox, Jr.
Ruxton, Philip
Salembier, Harold Paul
Scheerer, Paul Renner, Jr.
Schey, Robert Paul
Schmidt, Max Eberhardt
   aka Max Everhart Smith
Schnabel, Olatz Lopez Garmendia
Schultz, Howard Mark
Seaman, Joseph Husband
Semel, Terrance Steven
Shyer, Henry
Simmons, Kimora Lee
   aka Kimora Whitlock
Simmons, Russell Wendell
Simon, William Edward, Sr.
Sinclair, Earl Westwood
Sinclaire, Paul

Singh, Vinayak
Smith, Earl Edward Tailer, Sr.
   [*see* Warburton entry]
Spaeth, Otto Lucien, Sr.
Sutphen, Henry Randolph, Sr.
Sweetser, Jesse William
Taylor, Irving Howland
Teetor, Charles Jessup
Thiele, Albert Edward, Jr.
Towbin, Abraham Robert
Trippe, Juan Terry
Tyson, James
Tyson, Mark
Vanderbilt, Oliver DeGray, III
Volckening, Lloyd Irwin
Wainwright, Elizabeth Henning
Wainwright, Stuyvesant, II
Wasey, Louis Rice
Washburn, Ira Hedges, Sr.
Washburn, Watson
Welch, Leo Dewey
Wiborg, Frank Bestow
Williams, Eugene Flewilyn, Jr.
Woodin, William Hartman, Sr.
Woolley, Knight
Wright, John Howie, Jr.
Wright, John Howie, III

INTELLIGENCE AGENTS

Bradlee, Benjamin Crowninshield, Sr.
Coy, James Joseph, Jr.
Dewey, Charles Schuveldt, Jr.
Gardiner, Robert David Lion
Highet, Gilbert Albert
Wainwright, Stuyvesant, II

INTERIOR DESIGNERS

Cockcroft, Edward Truesdell
Cole, Helen Marr Dodd
Dewey, Marjorie Sawyer Goodman
Dougherty, Eleanor Sage
Hare, Richard Vincent
Krakoff, Delphine A. Boyon
Kurzner, Barbara Estelle Wolfman
Laughlin, Veronica Penelope Whitlock
McConnell, Sandra Dorothea Haig
McSpadden, Ruth Ann Wood
Milne, John Cruickshank, II
Montgomery, Francis Treat
Plimpton, Freddy Medora Espy
Preusse, Josephine Florence
Radziwill, Caroline Lee Bouvier
   aka Lee Radziwill
Saltzman, Renny B.
Schnabel, Olatz Lopez Garmendia
Schultz, Sheri Kersch
Stone, Orlean Vandiver
Yates, Linda L. Lindeberg

Occupations

INVENTORS

Beaumont, Perry H.
Bragg, Caleb Smith
Howell, John White, Sr.
Jones, Rodney Wilcox, Sr.
Loomis, Alfred Lee, Sr.
Olin, John Merrill
Parker, Cecil Carlton
Rowe, William Wallace, Sr.
Satterlee, Dr. Francis Le Roy, Jr.
Schmidt, Max Eberhardt
   aka Max Everhart Smith
Stanton, Dr. Frederick Lester
Sutphen, Henry Randolph, Sr.
Thompson, Dr. Frederick Roeck
Volckening, Lloyd Irwin
Voorhees, Dr. James Ditmars
   aka Dr. James Ditmars Van Voorhees

JOURNALISTS

Altschul, Rula Jebreal
Baldwin, Alexander Rae, III
   aka Alec Baldwin
Baldwin, Hilaria Lynn Thomas
Benjamin, Park, III
   aka Park Benjamin, Jr.
Bernstein, Carl
   [*see* Ephron entry]
Boughton, Edward Smith
Bradlee, Benjamin Crowninshield, Sr.
Bradlee, Sally Quinn
   aka Sally Quinn
Brisbane, Arthur
Citron, Casper Henry
Claiborne, Craig
Clark, Evans
Clark, Frederika Kirchwey
   aka Freda Kirchwey Clark
Cobb, Irvin Shewsbury
Cory, Christopher Thayer
Couric, Katie
   aka Katherine Anne Couric
de Kay, Charles
de Kooning, Elaine Marie Catherine Fried
Della Femina, Judith Carol Licht
Devereaux, Pauline Estelle
Dodge, Washington, Jr.
Dougherty, Page Caroline Huidekoper
Ephron, Nora
Ethridge, George
Farrington, Sarah H. Chisholm
   aka Chise Farrington
Farrington, Selwyn Kip, Jr.
Franey, Pierre
Garten, Ina Rosenberg
Garten, Jeffery E.
Gwathmey, Rosalie Dean Hook
Hamilton, Gordon C.
Hammond, Percy
Haynes, Evelyn Green

Highet, Gilbert Albert
Hiss, Priscilla Harriet Fansler
Jackson, John Day
Jackson, Richard Seymour
Joel, Katie Lee
   aka Kathleen Rebekah Lee
Johnson, Rossiter
LaMonte, George Mason
Lardner, Ringgold Wilmer, Sr.
   aka Ring Lardner
Lundbergh, Holger
Mapes, Victor
   aka Sidney Sharp
Mitchell, Pilar Guzman
   aka Pilar Guzman
Nouri, Edmond Joseph
Plimpton, George Ames
Potter, Jeffrey Brackett
Rattray, Arnold Elsmere
Rattray, David Greig
Rattray, Everett Tennant
Rattray, Helen Hinda Seldon
Rattray, Jeannette Frances Edwards
Raymond, Josephine Sheehan
Rice, Henry Grantland
   aka Grantland Rice
Robert, Pilar Crespi
Robertson, Clifford Parker, III
   aka Cliff Robertson
Saltzman, Ellen Jane Sadowsky
Schurman, Jacob Gould, Sr.
Schwab, Laurence, Sr.
Sischy, Ingrid Barbara
Sischy, Sandra Simms
Solomon, Peter Jay
Stewart, Martha Helen Kostyra
Talmage, The Reverend Thomas DeWitt
Taylor, Charles Alonzo
   [*see* Manners entry]
Teetor, Charles Jessup
Thomas, Augustus
Walker, Delos
Washburn, Watson
Webster, Dr. Bruce Peck
Wheeler, John Neville
Wright, John Howie, III
Yates, James Saville
Zuckerman, Mortimer Benjamin

LANDSCAPE ARCHITECTS

Embury, Ruth Bramley Dean
Herter, Albert
Mercer, Carol Keyser
Zamichow, Nadine Cherner

MERCHANTS

Abbe, James Edward, Jr.
Aufermann, Walter C. W.
   [*see* Kast entry]

MERCHANTS (cont'd)

Bailey, Charles Weaver
   [see Kerr entry]
Bates, Jerome Elliott
Borden, Lewis Mercer, Sr.
Calicchio, Millicent E.
   aka Lee Calicchio
Cater, Arthur Aymar
Clarke, Thomas Benedict, Sr.
Cleaves, Norman Smith
Cockcroft, Edward Truesdell
Cogan, Marshall Stuart
Cookson, Lucy Allison Bishopric
Cummins, Stephen Swete
Darrow, Daniel
DeGraff, James Wilde
Dowling, Robert Whittle
Drexler, Millard S.
   aka Mickey Drexler
Duryea, Walter Bartow
Earl, Noble Clarkson, Jr.
   [see Warburton entry]
Smith, Earl Edward Tailer, Sr.
   [see Warburton entry]
Fisher, Carl Graham, Sr.
Friedman, Marvin Ross
Fuhrman, Gary L.
Gagosian, Lawrence Gilbert
Gallatin, James Nicholson
Garten, Ina Rosenberg
Garten, Jeffery E.
Garvin, John S., Sr.
   [see E. C. T. Bell entry]
Godwin, Courtlandt
Gosman, Robert H.
Gribetz, Lester
Gruss, Agneta
Hand, John White
Hedges, Henry Denison
Helm, John LaRue, Jr.
Hess, Harry Bellas
Hiss, Alger
Hobart, Henry Lee
Hopkins, Alison Low Turnbull
Icahn, Carl Celian
Jackson, Helen Danforth Coler
Joel, Billy
   aka William Martin Joel
Jones, Rodney Wilcox, Sr.
Kaplan, Barton
Kaplan, Jacob Merrill
Karan, Mark
Keim, John Richard
Kerr, Elmore Coe, Jr.
   [see Baxter entry]
Kimball, Alden
Lee, Thomas Haskell
Leonard, Stephen Joseph, Sr.
Lindemann, Adam Marc
Lindemann, Amalia Dayan
Livingston, Ruth Helene Moller

Marsh, Frank Ballard
McAlpin, David Hunter, Sr.
McAlpin, Malcolm Evans
McKittrick, Walter
Murphy, Gerald Clery
Nederlander, Gladys Lenore Blum
Nesbit, Robert Wilson
Osborne, Joseph Septimus
Osborne, Nelson Cook, Sr.
Ossorio, Alfonso Angel
Pardridge, Albert Jerome
Parker, Helen Livingston Satterlee
Peterson, Peter George
Phillips, Fleming Stanhope
Rahr, Stewart J.
Rice, Charlotte Virginia Coughlan
Rice, Ernest H., Sr.
Richard, Mark Gadd
Roth, Steven
Rounick, Jack A.
Salembier, Harold Paul
Saltzman, Ellin Jan Sadowsky
Schultz, Howard Mark
Shafran, Irving
Simmons, Kimora Lee
   aka Kimora Whitlock
Skidmore, James Bond
Smith, Warren G.
Solomon, Peter Jay
Stern, Leonard Norman
Talmage, Daniel, Jr.
Teetor, Charles Jessup
Terian, Juliana Mae Curran
Terian, Peter Gabriel
Thaw, Gladys Virginia Bradley
Tiffany, Nathan Newton, III
Verglas, Antoine
Walker, Delos
Ward, William L.
Wasserstein, Claude Becker
Woodhouse, Lorenzo Guernsey

MILITARY

Monell, Theodore, Sr.

PHYSICIANS

Adair, Dr. Frank Earl
Agnew, Dr. Cornelius Rea, Sr.
Bailey, Dr. Theodorus, II
Bell, Dr. Dennistoun Mildeberger
Bell, Dr. James Finley
Bishop, Dr. Louis Faugeres, Jr.
Bishop, Dr. Louis Faugeres, Sr.
Boots, Dr. Ralph Henderson, Sr.
Breinin, Dr. Goodwin Milton
Carlson, Dr. Earl R.
Carr, Dr. Frank Clyde, Sr.
Coler, Dr. Eugene Seeley

Occupations

PHYSICIANS (cont'd)

Craig, Dr. Stuart Lessley
Dunn, Dr. James Manning
Edwards, Dr. Ogden Matthias, Jr.
Erdmann, Dr. John Frederic
Finbeiner, Dr. John A.
Halsted, Dr. Harbeck
Helmuth, Dr. William Tod, Jr.
Herrick, Dr. Everett
Hinton, Dr. James William
Hirschfeld, Dr. Sarah J. Schlesinger
Hirschfeld, Dr. Susan T. Aronson
Hodson, Dr. James M.
 [*see* Adams entry]
Hollister, Dr. Frederick Kellogg
Jones, Dr. Oswald Roberts
Joyner, Dr. James Craig
Kast, Dr. Ludwig
Krech, Dr. Shepard, Sr.
Krieger, Dr. Dorothy Terrace
Krieger, Dr. Howard P.
Kurzner, Dr. Rubin Raymond
Laspia, Dr. Michael R.
Moore, Dr. Oliver Semon, Jr.
Munroe, Dr. George E., Jr.
Nugent, Dr. Paul Fordham, Sr.
Onderdonk, Dr. Thomas Williams
Osborne, Dr. Edward Monroe, Sr.
Rice, Dr. Clarence Charles
Rifkind, Dr. Arleen Brenner
Rifkind, Dr. Richard A.
Roberts, Dr. Dudley DeVore, Sr.
Satterlee, Dr. Francis Le Roy, Jr.
Shackleton, Dr. Judson Gale
 [*see* C. M. R. McAlpin]
Snow, Dr. Irving Miller
Solley, Dr. Fred Palmer
Stanton, Dr. Frederick Lester
Terry, Dr. Arthur Hutchinson, Jr.
Thompson, Dr. Fredrick Roeck
Voorhees, Dr. James Ditmars
 aka Dr. James Ditmars Van Voorhees
Walker, Dr. John Baldwin, Sr.
Walker, Dr. William Henry, Jr.
Warrin, Dr. Marshall Lord
Webster, Dr. Bruce Peck
Wheelock, Dr. William Efner
Wolff, Dr. Carl F.

POLITICIANS

Adams, Charles Henry
Barton, Charles Pierce, Jr.
Baxter, George White
Bell, Alfred Dennis, Sr.
Brown, Lathrop
Conway, Edmund Virgil, III
Conway, Elaine Wingate
Davis, Vernon Mansfield
Devendorf, Alfred Ervin
Draper, Simeon, Jr.
Gardiner, David Lion, Sr.
Hedges, Dayton
 aka William Dayton Hedges
LaMonte, George Mason
Massey, Maurice Richardson, Jr.
McCall, Edward Everett
McCartney, Nancy Shevell
Mitchell, MacNeil
Moffett, James Andrew, Jr.
Ordway, Samuel Hanson, Jr.
Osborne, Joseph Septimus
Osborne, Nelson Cook, Sr.
Peterson, Peter George
Preusse, Charles Francis
Reutershan, Paul V.
Richard, Mary Ella Brooks
Ross, Amanda Mortimer
Smith, Earl Edward Tailer, Sr.
 [*see* Warburton entry]
Solomon, Peter Jay
Stephanopoulos, George Robert
Stern, Henry Root, Sr.
Stratton, Charles Preston
Tiffany, Nathan Newton, III
Wainwright, Stuyvesant, II
Woodward, Shaun Anthony
Zevely, James William, Sr.

PROFESSIONAL PHOTOGRAPERS

Abbe, James Edward, Jr.
Abbe, Kathryn McLaughlin
Avedon, Richard
Ayer, Frederick, III
Beard, Peter Hill
Becker, Harold
Gwathmey, Rosalie Hook
Klein, Kelly Rector
Larkin, Lawrence
Lauren, Ricky Anne Loew–Beer
Rumbough, Margaretha Wagstrom
Stern, Lynn Solinger
Talmage, Rockwell Dwight
Verglas, Antoine
Weber, Bruce
Whittle, Priscilla Rattazzi

PUBLIC RELATIONS EXECUTIVES

Cory, Christopher Thayer
Della Femina, Barbara
Dodge, Washington, Jr.
Gowen, Marcia A. Fennelly
Hillman, Murray
Mnuchin, Kimberly Ellen Kassel
Radziwill, Caroline Lee Bouvier
 aka Lee Radziwill
Robert, Pilar Crespi
Seinfeld, Nina Daniel Sklar
 aka Jessica Sklar

Occupations

PUBLISHERS

Ammon, Robert Theodore
   aka Ted Ammon
Benjamin, Park, III
   aka Park Benjamin, Jr.
Bonner, Frederic
Boughton, Bertha Emeline Welby
Boughton, Edward Smith
Brackenridge, Gavin, Jr.
Bradlee, Benjamin Crowninshield, Sr.
Brisbane, Arthur
Brown, Lathrop
Buek, Gustav H.
   aka Gustavus H. Buek
Burns, Thomas Robert
Canfield, Michael Temple
   [see Radziwill entry]
Chase, Edward Tinsley
Clark, Frederika Kirchwey
   aka Freda Kirchwey
Cogan, Marshall Stuart
Cogan, Maureen Nancy Abramson
Cummins, Virginia P. Kent
Della Femina, Jerry
   aka Gennaro Tomas Della Femina
Devereaux, Pauline Estelle
Devine, James Joseph
Dodge, Washington, Jr.
Donovan, Cornelius Peter, Jr.
   aka Con Donovan
Farrington, Selwyn Kip, Jr.
Foss, Martin Moore, Sr.
Franey, Pierre
Hammond, John Carnahan
Hardy, Charles J., Jr.
Hoffman, Anita Vogel
Jackson, John Day
Jackson, Lionel Stewart, Sr.
Jackson, Richard Seymour
Kennedy, Michael John
Macy, Valentine Everit, Jr.
Mitchell, Christopher
Mitchell, Pilar Guzman
   aka Pilar Guzman
Montgomery, Paul
   aka John Paul Montgomery
Nichols, Harold Wills, Jr.
O'Brien, W. Howard, Sr.
Orr, Alexander Ector
Perelman, Ronald Owen
Rattray, Arnold Elsmere
Rattray, Helen Hinda Seldon
Rattray, Jeannette Frances Edwards
Regan, John Nicholas, Sr.
Rose, Joanna Semel
Rosset, Astrid Myers
Rosset, Barnet Lee, Jr.
   aka Barney Rosset
Schwab, Laurence, Sr.
Shafran, Judith
Solomon, Peter Jay
Stewart, Andrew
Taylor, Irving Howland
Thomas, Augustus
Warhol, Andy
   aka Andrew Warhola, Jr.
Warner, Eltinge Fowler, Jr.
Wasserstein, Bruce Jay
Weber, Bruce
Weber, Nan Bush
Wenner, Jann Simon
Wheeler, John Neville
Wheelock, John Hall
Whittle, Chris
   aka H. Christopher Whittle
Wright, John Howie, Jr.
Wright, John Howie, III
Zuckerman, Mortimer Benjamin

REAL ESTATE AGENTS

Brown, Lathrop
Devendorf, Barbara Jean
   aka Bonnie Devendorf
Eno, Alfred Joseph
Haupt, Rita Gradinger
Hoffman, David Lehman, Sr.
Macklowe, Harry B.
McCormick, Clotilde Knapp
Osborne, Burnett Mulford
Osserman, Elizabeth Tonkonogy
Northrop, Virginia Osborne Cox
Preusse, Josephine Florence
Reiswig, Gary D.
Richard, Mary Ella Brooks
Richards, Benjamin, Jr.
Rounick, Phyllis Hartmann
Steinberg, Kathryn Joanne Newman
Whitney, Kate Case

RESTAURATEURS

Ambrose, Colin Trippe
Bon Jovi, Dorothea Hurley
Bon Jovi, Jon
   aka John Francis Bongiovi, Jr.
Combs, Sean John
   aka Puff Daddy, Diddy, and P. Diddy
Cogan, Marshall Stuart
DeFelice, Gabby
DeFelice, Gian Palo
Della Femina, Jerry
   aka Gennaro Tomas Della Femina
De Niro, Robert, Jr.
De Palma, Darnell Gregorio
   aka Darnell Gregorio–De Palma
Donovan, Roberta Gosman
Duke, Diane M. Douglas
Earl, Noble Clarkson, Jr.
   [see Warburton entry]
Franey, Pierre
Gosman, Mary Ellen Harrington

Occupations

RESTAURATEURS (cont'd)

Gosman, Robert H.
Hamlin, Mary Elkins Paxton
Kurzner, Dr. Rubin Raymond
LeRoy, Warner
Mayo, Miss Marie Louise
Morton, Peter
Ross, Steven Jay
   aka Steven Jay Rechnitz
Stern, Leonard Norman
Schultz, Howard Mark
Soule, Henri Remy
Thiele, Roger Harvey
Zellweger, Renee Kathleen

SCIENTISTS

Carpenter, Edmund Snow
Fox, Alvin Gibbs
Hirschfeld, Dr. Sarah J. Schlesinger
Krieger, Dr. Dorothy Terrace
Krieger, Dr. Howard P.
Loomis, Alfred Lee, Sr.
Rifkind, Dr. Richard A.
Rubin, Vera D.
Wood, Robert Williams, Jr.

SHIPPING

Ammon, Randee E.
Calicchio, John
Garni, Adolph
   aka Adolf Garni
King, William
Langben, Halfred Alfred
Orr, Alexander Ector
Rentschler, George Adam, Jr.
Storey, Edward Albert
Stratton, Charles Preston
Woodin, William Hartman, Sr.
Zalles, Jorje Ezequiel, Sr.
   aka Jorge Ezequiel Zalles, Sr.

STATESMEN

Aldrich, Malcolm Pratt, Sr.
Dewey, Charles Schuveldt, Jr.
Garten, Jeffery E.
Hedges, Burke Osborn
Hiss, Alger
Peterson, Peter George
Rumbough, Stanley Maddox, Jr.
Simon, William Edward, Sr.
Washburn, Watson
Wiborg, Frank Bestow
Woodin, William Hartman, Sr.
Woodward, Shaun Anthony

SUFFRAGISTS

see Civic Activism –
   Anti-Suffragists and Suffragists

WRITERS

Abbe, Kathryn McLaughlin
Abbott, Florence Louise Call
Adair, Dr. Frank Earl
Adams, John Cranford
Agnew, Dr. Cornelius Rea, Sr.
Albee, Edward Franklin, III
Altschul, Rula Jebreal
Andrews, William Loring
Avedon, Richard
Baldwin, Alexander Rae, III
   aka Alec Baldwin
Barton, Charles Pierce, Jr.
Beard, Peter Hill
Beaumont, Perry H.
Benjamin, Park, III
   aka Park Benjamin, Jr.
Bernstein Carl
   [*see* Ephron entry]
Bishop, Dr. Louis Faugeres, Jr.
Bishop, Dr. Louis Faugeres, Sr.
Bradlee, Benjamin Crowninshield, Sr.
Bradlee, Sally Quinn
   aka Sally Quinn
Breinin, Dr. Goodman Milton
Brisbane, Arthur
Browne, Christopher H.
Buddenhagen, Frederick Leonard
Butler, Howard Russell, Sr.
Carlson, Dr. Earl R.
Carpenter, Edmund Snow
Caruso, Dorothy Park Benjamin
Cavett, Martha Rogers
Cavett, Richard Alva
   aka Dick Cavett
Chase, Chevy
   aka Cornelius Crane Chase
Chase, Jayni Ann Luke
Citron, Casper Henry
Claiborne, Craig
Clark, Evans
Clarke, Thomas Benedict, Sr.
Cobb, Irvin Shewsbury
Cory, Christopher Thayer
Couric, Katie
   aka Katherine Anne Couric
Cullman, Joseph Fredrick, III
Cummins, Virginia P. Kent
Cushman, Edith Marie Macon
de Kay, Charles
de Kay, Lucy Edwalyn Coffey
Della Femina, Jerry
   aka Gennaro Tomas Della Femina
de Menil, Susan Kadin Silver
De Palma, Brian Russell
De Palma, Gale Anne Hurd

Occupations

WRITERS (cont'd)

Deutsch, Donny
   aka Donald Jay Deutsch
Drexler, Peggy F.
Dickerman, William Carter, Sr.
Dougherty, Page Caroline Huidekoper
Duke, Anthony Drexel, Sr.
Embury, Aymar, II
Embury, Ruth Bramley Dean
Ephron, Nora
Farrington, Sarah H. Chisholm
   aka Chise Farrington
Farrington, Selwyn Kip, Jr.
Franey, Pierre
Gardiner, David Lion, Sr.
Gardiner, Miss Sarah Diodati
Garten, Ina Rosenberg
Garten, Jeffery E.
Gowen, George W., II
Green, Elizabeth Reitell
Greenberg, Dan
   [*see* Ephron entry]
Greer, The Reverend David Hummell
Gruzen, Lee Ferguson
Gwathmey, Emily Margolin
Hammon, John Carahan
Hammond, Percy
Highet, Gilbert Albert
Highet, Helen Clark MacInnes
   aka Helen MacInnes
Hill, Anna Park Gilman
Hinton, Dr. James William
Hirschfeld, Dr. Sarah J. Schlesinger
Hiss, Alger
Hiss, Isabelle Dowden
Hobart, Marie Elizabeth Jefferys
Hollister, Dr. Frederick Kellogg
Howell, John White, Sr.
Jefferys, Elizabeth Miller
Joel, Christie Brinkley
   aka Christie Brinkley
Joel, Katie Lee
   aka Kathleen Rebekah Lee
Johnson, Helen Louis Kendrick
Johnson, Rossiter
Jones, Rodney Wilcox, Sr.
Karan, Donna Ivy Faske
Kast, Dr. Ludwig
Kendrick, The Reverend James Ryland
Krieger, Dr. Dorothy Terrace
Krieger, Dr. Howard P.
LaForest, Clara Belle Rilea
Lardner, Ringgold Wilmer, Sr.
   aka Ring Lardner
Lauren, Ricky Anne Loew–Beer
LeRoy, Genevieve
   aka Gen LeRoy
Levering, Julia Henderson
Levi, Charles Matthew
Lewis, Loida Nicholas
Lewis, Reginald F.

Lindemann, Amalia Dayan
Lundbergh, Holger
Manners, John Hartley
Mapes, Victor
   aka Sidney Sharp
Mayo–Smith, Richmond, Sr.
McAlpin, Malcolm Evans
McCall, Clifford Hyde, Sr.
McCartney, Heather Mills
McCartney, Linda Louise Eastman
McConnell, Vanessa Mary Somers
Mershon, The Reverend Stephen Lyon, Sr.
Michaels, Lorne
   aka Lorne Lipowitz
Michaels, Rosie Shuster
Mitchell, Pilar Guzman
   aka Pilar Guzman
Montgomery Paul
   aka John Paul Montgomery
Morrissey, Paul
Newman, The Reverend John Philip
Newton, The Reverend Richard Heber, Sr.
Northrop, John Burr, Sr.
Ordway, Samuel Hanson, Jr.
Paltrow, Gwyneth Kate
Peterson, Peter George
Pileggi, Nicholas, Jr.
   [*see* Ephron entry]
Plimpton, George Ames
Plimpton, Sarah Whitehead Dudley
Potter, Jeffrey Brackett
Radziwill, Caroline Lee Bouvier
   aka Lee Radziwill
Randell, Rufus
   aka Roof the Roofer
Rattray, David Greig
Rattray, Everett Tennant
Rattray, Jeannette Frances Edwards
Reiswig, Gary D.
Rheinstein, Sidney
Rice, Dr. Clarence Charles
Rice, Henry Grantland
   aka Grantland Rice
Richard, Hetty Lawrence Hemenway
Richey, The Reverend Alban, Sr.
Richey, The Reverend Thomas, Sr.
Rifkind, Dr. Arleen Brenner
Rifkind, Carole Lewis
Rifkind, Dr. Richard A.
Roberts, Dr. Dudley DeVore, Sr.
Roberts, Walter Scott
Robertson, Clifford Parker, III
   aka Cliff Robertson
Rose, Candice Bergen
   aka Candice Bergen
Rosset, Barnet Lee, Jr.
   aka Barney Rosset
Rowe, Margaret Anna Richardson
Schnabel, Julian
Schultz, Howard Mark
Schurman, Jacob Gould, Sr.

Occupations

WRITERS (cont'd)

Schwab, Laurence, Sr.
Seabury, Samuel
Sedacca, Joseph M.
Seinfeld, Jerry
   aka Jerome Allen Seinfeld
Seinfeld, Nina Danielle Sklar
   aka Jessica Sklar
Simmons, Edward Emerson
Simmons, Kimora Lee
   aka Simmons Whitlock
Simmons, Russell Wendell
Simmons, Vesta Schallenberger
Simon, Carrie Frances Fisher
   aka Carrie Fisher
Simon, William Edward, Sr.
Sischy, Ingrid Barbara
Smith, Earl Edward Tailer, Sr.
   [*see* Warburton entry]
Snow, Dr. Irving Miller
Solley, Dr. Fred Palmer
Stanton, Dr. Frederick Lester
Steele, The Reverend James Nevett, Sr.
Stephanopoulos, George Robert
Stern, Joel Mark
Stern, Robert Arthur Morton
Stewart, Martha Helen Kostyra
Stokes, The Reverend John Dunlap
Stone, Edward Durell, Sr.
Strong, Theron George
Talmage, The Reverend Thomas DeWitt
Taylor, Charles Alonzo
   [*see* Manners entry]
Teetor, Charles Jessup
Thiele, Karen Ely

Thomas, Augustus
Tillich, Johanna Werner
   aka Hannah Werner
Tillich, The Reverend Paul Johannes
Turner, Kathleen
   aka Mary Kathleen Turner
Tweed. Blanche Oelrichs
Tweed, Eleanor Jenckes Roelker
Tweed, Harrison
Tyson, Carolyn Kennedy
Walker, Dr. John Baldwin, Sr.
Wardle, H. Allen
Warhol, Andy
   aka Andrew Warhola, Jr.
Washburn, Watson
Washburn, William Tucker
Wasserstein, Bruce Jay
Weston, Theodore
Wheeler, John Neville
Wheelock, John Hall
Wheelock, Phyllis Edwalyn de Kay
Whittle, Chris
   aka H. Christopher Whittle
Whittle, Priscilla Rattazzi
Wiborg, Frank Bestow
Wood, Robert Williams, Jr.
Woodward, Shaun Anthony
Zamichow, Nadine Cherner

Rehabilitative Uses

Non-residential rehabilitative secondary uses of surviving estate houses listed are current as of 2020. Estates are identified by the original owner. For subsequent estate owners, see surname entry.

Amagansett Historical Society	Mary Amelia Schellinger house 129 Main Street, Amagansett
The Baker House, 1650	James Harper Poor house 181 Main Street, East Hampton
East Hampton Historical Society	Jonathan Osborn house 101 Main Street, East Hampton
East Hampton Village Hall	Lyman Beecher house 86 Main Street, East Hampton
East Hampton Village Municipal Office	Isaac Osborne house 88 Newton Lane, East Hampton
The Hedges Inn	John Hedges house 74 James Lane, East Hampton
Home Sweet Home Museum	John Howard Payne house 14 James Lane, East Hampton
The Huntting Inn	Reverend Nathaniel Huntting house 94 Main Street, East Hampton
Jewish Center of the Hamptons	George Philip Cammann house 44 Woods Lane, East Hampton
Ladies Village Improvement Society	Abraham Gardiner house 95 Main Street, East Hampton
Ladies Village Improvement Society Thrift and Book Shops	Lawrence Adams Baker, Sr. house, *Baker's Acres* 95 Main Street, East Hampton
Maidstone Arms Inn	William Lewis Huntting Osborne house 207 Main Street, East Hampton
The Mill House Inn	William D. Parsons house 31 North Main Street, East Hampton
Montauk Yacht Club Resort and Marina	Caleb Smith Bragg house Star Island Road, Montauk
Mulford Farm Museum	John Mulford house 10 James Lane, East Hampton
The Nature Conservancy, South Fork – Shelter Island Chapter	Samuel Seabury property Route 114, East Hampton
The 1770 House Restaurant and Inn	Jonathan Dayton house 143 Main Street, East Hampton
Second House	David E. Kennedy house Montauk Highway, Montauk
Pollock – Krasner House and Study Center	Jackson Pollack house 830 Springs–Fireplace Road, East Hampton
Montauk Lake Club & Marina	Louis Rice Wasey house 211 East Lake Drive, Montauk
Thomas & Mary Nimmo Moran Studio	Thomas Moran, Jr. house, *The Studio* 229 Main Street, East Hampton

Statesmen and Diplomats

Listed are only those statesmen and diplomats who resided in the Town of East Hampton.

Statesmen

Department of the Treasury

   Secretaries of the Treasury –

   Simon, William Edward, Sr., 1974-1977 (Nixon and Ford administrations)
      East Hampton

   Woodin, William Hartman, Sr. (Franklin Delano Roosevelt administration)
      Dune House, East Hampton

   Under Secretaries, Deputy Secretaries, and Assistant Secretaries of the Treasury –

   Simon, William Edward, Sr.
      – Deputy Secretary of Treasury, 1973-1974 (Nixon administration)
      East Hampton

Department of Commerce and Labor

   Secretaries of Commerce –

   Peterson, Peter George, 1972-1973 (Nixon administration)
      East Hampton

   Under Secretaries and Assistant Secretaries of Commerce and Labor –

   Garten, Jeffery E.
      – Under Secretary of Commerce for International Trade
        (Clinton administration)
      East Hampton

   Wiborg, Frank Bestow
      – Assistant Secretary of Commerce and Labor (Taft administration)
      The Dunes, East Hampton

also -   **Woodward**, Shaun Anthony
      – Secretary of State for Northern Ireland, 2007-2010
      – Shadow Secretary of State for Northern Ireland, 2010-2012
      – Under Secretary of State, Department for Culture, Media, and Sport, 2006
      East Hampton

Diplomats

Aubert, Ludvig Caesar Martin, II
      – Norwegian Consul General, Montreal, Canada, 1921
      – Norwegian Envoy Extraordinary and Minister Plenipotentiary to Japan, 1932
   Star Acres, Montauk

Bragg, Caleb Smith
      – attaché, United States Embassy, Paris, France, 1914 (Wilson administration)
      Montauk

Statesmen and Diplomats

Diplomats (cont'd)

de Kay, Charles
– Consul-General, Berlin, Germany, 1894-1897 (Cleveland administration)
Abrigada, East Hampton

Hedges, Burke Osborn
– Cuban Ambassador to Brazil, 1958-1959
East Hampton

Newman, John Philip
– inspector of United States consuls in Asia, 1874-1876 (Grant administration)
East Hampton

Pierson, Warren Lee
– rank of United States ambassador, Tripartite Commission on German Debts, 1951-1952
East Hampton, *Furthermoor*

Rosinsky, Claude Daste
– member, French consulates, London and Hong Kong
East Hampton

Schurman, Jacob Gould, Sr.
– Minister to Greece and Montenegro, 1912-1913 (Taft administration)
– Minister to Japan, 1921 (Harding administration)
– Ambassador to Germany, 1925-1930 (Coolidge administration)
Breezy Knowe, East Hampton

Smith, Earl Edward Tailer, Sr. [*see* Warburton entry]
– United States Ambassador to Cuba, 1957-1959
East Hampton

Zalles, Jorje Ezequiel, Sr.
– secretary and *charge d'affairs*, Bolivian Legation, Washington, DC, 1903-1905
Amagansett

Advisors and Personal Secretaries

Aldrich, Malcolm Pratt, Sr.
– special assistant to Secretary of the Navy for Air, 1942-1945
(Franklin Delano Roosevelt and Truman administrations)
Pondside, East Hampton

Brown, Lathrop
– special assistant to Secretary of the Interior Franklin Knight Lane, 1917-1918
– secretary, President Woodrow Wilson's Industrial Conference, 1919
The Windmill, Montauk
Land of Clover, St. James
Southampton

Dewey, Charles Schuveldt, Jr.
– secretary to Assistant Secretary of Treasury Charles Schuveldt, Sr., 1924-1927
(Coolidge administration)
East Hampton

Statesmen and Diplomats

Advisors and Personal Secretaries (cont'd)

Hiss, Alger
- advisor, Yalta Conference
- assistant to Secretary of State Edward Reilly Stettinus, Jr.
- assistant to Director of Far Eastern Affairs
- special assistant to director, Office of Special Political Affairs
- Executive Secretary, Dumbarton Oaks Conference
- Director, Office of Special Political Affairs
- Secretary-General, United Nations Conference on International Organizations

East Hampton

Martin, Samuel Klump, Jr.
- secretary to United States Minister to Portugal Charles Page Bryan, 1908-1909

East Hampton

Rumbough, Stanley Maddox, Jr.
- assistant to Secretary of Commerce (Eisenhower administration)
- White House Special Assistant in charge of executive board liaison
  (Eisenhower administration)

East Hampton

Washburn, Watson
- special assistant to Under-Secretary of the Treasury, 1921 (Harding administration)

Apaquogue, East Hampton

Zalles, Jorje Ezequiel, Sr.
- secretary, Bolivian Legation, London, 1900-1903

Amagansett

Villlages

The village references used in this compilation are the current (2020) village or hamlet boundaries and should not be confused with zip code designations. When the owner who contracted for the original construction of the house is known, it is indicated by an asterisk.

AMAGANSETT

    Accardi, Jack
        [see Scheffer entry]
    Austin, William Gage
    Baldwin, Alexander Rae, III
        (aka Alec Baldwin)
* Bartlett, Edward Everett, Jr., *Furtherlane*
* Bell, Dr. Dennistoun Mildeberger, *Broadview*
    Binn, Moreton
        (aka Moreton Binstock)
    Bishopric, Allison, Jr., *Windy Dune*
    Broderick, Matthew
    Bronfman, Edgar Miles, Jr.
    Chatfield, Henry Houston, *Devon*
    Clark, Ivor Bache, Sr., *Driftwood*
* Cohn, Maurice J.
    Cookson, Lucy Allison Bishopric, *Windy Dune*
        [Cookson owned three houses in Amagansett.]
* Cory, David Cleveland, *Sea Bluff*
    Dana, Robert Bingham
* Davis, George Samler
    Davis, Mary Schiefflin Samler
* Davis, Vernon Mansfield, *Half-a-Gale*
* de Menil, Francois
        (aka Francois Conrad Thomas de Menil), *Toad Hall*
    Devendorf, George Epworth, *El Paraiso*
    Dodge, Washington, Jr., *Ironsides*
* Duffield, The Reverend Howard, *Dune Crest*
    Ely, John Ingraham, *Hell-Gate*
    Farrell, John J.
        [see Sherman entry]
* Fleetwood, Francis
    Francisco, Donald W., Sr.
        (aka Don Francisco), *Windward*
    Furman, Roy Lance
    Gagosian, Laurence Gilbert
    Greene, Anne Johnston Sawyer, *Devon House*
    Gribetz, Lester
    Gruzen, Barnet Sumner
    Gruzen, Jordan Lee
    Gwathmey, Charles
* Gwathmey, Robert, Jr.
* Hamlin, Harry Leon, *Stony Hill Farm*
    Hare, Richard V., *Es Moli*
* Haupt, Melville I.
* Hayden, William Martin, Sr., *Half-a-Gale*
    Herrick, Anson Boulton, Sr.
    Hiss, Alger
    Howell, John White, Sr., *Sandylands*
    Jackson, John Day
    Jackson, Richard Seymour
    John, Davis W.
* Johnson, Rossiter, *Thalatta Cottage*

    Johnston, Mary Elizabeth, *Devon House*
    Jones, Rodney Wilcox, Sr., *Broadview*
    Kendrick, Georgia Avery
    Kurzer, Dr. Rubin Raymond
    Kuser, John Louis, Jr.
    Lang, Helmut
* LeRoy, Warner, *Southwood Court*
* Levering, Julia Henderson
* Levering, Richmond, Sr.
        (aka John Richmond Levering, Sr. and John Mortimer Lervering, Jr.), *Devon*
    Lewis, Reginald F.
    Light, Deborah, *Quail Hill*
        [see Rubin entry]
    Materson, M.
        [see Levering entry]
    McCartney, Paul
        (aka James Paul McCartney)
    McSpadden, Jack Dobbs, Jr., *Devon House*
    Millar, Mrs. David
        [see Nouri entry]
    Mitchell, MacNeil, *Elmshade*
    Montgomery, Paul
        (aka John Paul Montgomery)
    Moody, Sidney Clarke, Sr., *Water's Edge*
    Nouri, Edmond Joseph, *Further Moor*
    Osborne, Nelson
        [see Montgomery entry]
    Paltrow, Gwyneth, Kate
    Plimpton, George Ames, *Xanadu*
    Potter, Jeffrey Brackett, *Stony Hill Farm*
* Procter, William Cooper
    Rattray, David Greig
    Rattray, Everett Tennant
* Rawson, Joseph, Jr., *Red Roof*
    Rifkind, Dr. Richard A.
* Rowe, John Jay, Jr.
    Rowe, John Jay, Sr., *Devon*
* Rowe, William Stanhope, Sr.
* Rubin, Samuel, *Hilly Close*
    Scheerer, Joseph Durand, Jr.
* Scheffer, Alfred A.
    Schwagerl, Richard
        [see Rubin entry]
    Schwagerl, Robert
        [see Rubin entry]
    Seegal, Frederic Milton, *Old Simmons House*
* Semel, Terrance Steven
    Sherman, John Taylor, II
    Singh, Vinayak
* Sonnefeld, Barry
    Storey, Emma Josehine de Raismes, *Homelot*
    Teetor, Charles Jessup, *Westernesse Farm*
* Tolan, Michael
        (aka Seymour Tuchow)

AMAGANSETT (cont'd)

Turner, Kathleen
 (aka Mary Kathleen Turner)
Tyson, James, *Old Baker House*
Verglas, Antoine
* Ward, William L., *Willward Lodge*
Warrin, Dr. Marshall Lord, *Kemah*
Wasserstein, Bruce Jay, *Cranberry Dune*
Weinstein, Harvey
Zalles, Jorje Ezequiel, Sr.
 (aka Jorge Ezequiel Zalles, Sr.)

EAST HAMPTON

* Abbott, Henry Hurlbut, *Briar Patch*
Adair, Dr. Frank Earl, *Sherwood*
* Adams, Charles Henry
* Adams, John Cranford
* Alcott, Clarence Frank
Alexander, Edward Renick, Sr., *Sterling–Haven*
Aldrich, Malcolm Pratt, Sr., *Pondside*
Aldrich, Spencer Wyman
Alker, Ernestine Josephine Sierck
Altschul, Arthur Goodhart, Jr.
Amador, Paul A.
Ambrose, Jessica Lyman Mansell
Ammon, Robert Theodore
 (aka Ted Ammon)
Anderson, Edward Ewen, *Up-the-Hill*
* Appleton, Robert Wilmarth, *Nid de Papillon*
Ashplant, Frederick Bryant, Sr., *The Dolphins*
* Aspinwall, James Lawrence
* Avery, Edward Strong
Ayer, Frederick, III
Backus, Henry Clinton, *Tranquility*
Bacon, Clarence Everett, Jr., *Dune Gate*
Bailey, Dr. Theodorus, II, *Dunemere*
Baker, John T., Jr.
* Baker, John T., Sr.
Baker, Lawrence Adams, Sr., *Baker's Acres*
Barbery, Ida May
 [*see* Culver entry]
Barbour, William Stanton
* Baron, Ronald Stephen
Barton, Flora Benjamin McAlpin
Bates, Jerome Elliott, *Dune Pasture*
Baxter, Ann Wright
Baxter, George White, *Cherokee Cottage*
Beale, Phelan, Sr., *Grey Gardens*
Beard, Jeremiah Robinson, Jr.
* Beardsley, Samuel Arthur, Sr.
Beardsley, Thomas Hooper
Beaumont, Perry H.
* Becker, Harold
Beckers, William Kurt
Beebe, William Notthingham, Sr.
Bell, Alfred Dennis, Sr.
Bell, Emily Carrington Trowbridge
* Bell, Dr. James Finley
Bellas, Alfred Constantine

Benjamin, Park, III
 (aka Park Benjamin, Jr.)
* Benjamin, William Wallace, Jr., *Crossways*
Benjamin, William Wallace, III, *Crossways*
Bennett, Russell Conwell, Sr.
Betner, Benjamin Carlton, Jr.
Betts, Hobart Dominick, Sr.
Bianchi, Albert William
Bisco, Leonard Gerard
Bishop, Bennett, *Pudding Hill*
* Bishop, Dr. Louis Faugeres, Jr., *Holiday*
Bishop, Dr. Louis Faugeres, Sr., *Bishopgate*
Blackburn, Wilmuth Earle, *West Side Story*
Blair, Montgomery, II
Blakeman, Emma August Terbell
Bock, Louis B.
 [*see* Thorp entry]
Bogert, Edward Osgood
Bogert, George Henry
Bon Jovi, Jon
 (aka John Francis Bongiovi, Jr.)
Bonner, Marie Louise Clifford, *Pond House*
Boots, Dr. Ralph Henderson, Sr.,
 The White Elephant
Borden, Lewis Mercer, Sr., *Seaholme*
Boughton, Edward Smith
Bouvier, John Vernou, Jr., *Little House*
Bouvier, John Vernou, Jr., *Lasata*
Bouvier, John Vernou, III, *Rowdy Hall*
Bouvier, Maude Frances Sergeant, *Lasata*
* Bowne, Robert Southgate, *Clifford-by-the-Sea*
Bracken, James W.
Brackenridge, Gavin, Jr.
Brackenridge, Gavin, Sr.
Bradlee, Benjamin Crowninshield, Sr.,
 Grey Gardens
* Bradley, Andrew Coyle
Breen, Daniel Anthony, Jr., *Furtherfield*
Breinin, Dr. Goodwin Milton
Brett, Philip Milledoler, Jr.
Breyer, Henry William, III
Briggs, James Branch, *Beehive*
Brockman, Daniel David, *The Playhouse*
Bronaugh, Frederick Lewis, *Elsufral*
Brown, Anthony Coates, *Clover Cottage*
Brown, Philip Wilson Tate, Sr.
* Browne, Christopher H., *Chateau Amorois*
 [Browne built two houses in the Village of East Hampton.]
Bruckman, Donald J.
Buckwalter, Florence F.
 [*see* Chase entry]
Buddenhagen, Frederick Leonard
Buek, Gustav H.
 (aka Gustavus H. Buek), *Home Sweet Home*
* Bunshaft, Gordon, *Travertine House*
Burchell, Henry J., Jr., *Gay Cottage*
Burke, Oscar Moech
Burnett, Eugene Rodney
Burns, Thomas Robert
Burton, Jane Erdman, *Coxwould*
* Butler, Howard Russell, Sr., *Bay Bush*

Villages

EAST HAMPTON (cont'd)

    Butler, William Allen, III, *Crestmere*
    Callan, Erin M.
    Calicchio, John
*   Cammann, George Philip, Jr., *Seaholme*
    Cammann, Roy Lennox
*   Campbell, David, *Burnt Point*
    Campbell, Nathaniel Adams, Jr.
*   Campbell, Nathaniel Adams, Sr., *Camelot*
    Candy, Abraham D.
        [*see* LaForest entry]
    Carlson, Dr. Earl R.
    Carpenter, Louise Adelaide de Menil
        (aka Adelaide de Menil)
    Carr, Eleanor Maitland DeGraff,
        Cherridune and Dunfour [Carr owned two houses in the Village of East Hampton.]
    Carse, Donald Rede, Sr.
    Carse, John Bradley, Sr., *End Cottage*
*   Carson, William Moore, Sr.
    Caruso, Enrico, *Près Choisis / The Creeks*
    Cater, Louise Bowers, *Apaquogue House*
    Chace, Franklin M., *Gone With the Wind*
    Chalif, Seymour Hunt
    Chanos, James Steven
    Chapman, Benjamin Gaines
    Chase, Chevy
        (aka Cornelius Crane Chase)
    Chase, Edward Tinsley, *Cranberry Bog*
*   Chauncey, Alexander Wallace, *Our Place*
    Chisholm, Edward de Clifford, *Onadune*
    Citron, Casper Henry
    Claiborne, Craig
    Clark, Evans
    Clarke, Thomas Benedict, Sr., *The Lanterns*
    Cleaves, Norman Smith
    Clements, Hurin Martin
    Cloud, Chester Marts, *Prim Close*
    Cobb, Henry Ives, Sr.
    Cobb, Irvin Shewsbury, *Back Home*
*   Cockcroft, Edward Truesdell, *Little Burlees*
*   Cody, Frederick, *Fairways*
*   Cogan, Marshall Stuart
*   Cohen, Peter Anthony
    Cohen, Steven A. [Cohen owned two houses in the Village of East Hampton]
*   Cole, John Nelson, Jr., *Bayberry*
    Coleman, Helen Douglas Rulison
    Coler, Dr. Eugene Seeley, *Windrow*
    Collins, William Bradley Isham, Sr.
        (aka Bradley Isham Collins), *Briar Patch*
    Combs, Sean John
        (aka Puff Daddy, Diddy, and P. Diddy)
    Cook, Francis Howell
*   Cook, Harry, *Holly Hall*
    Cookson, Lucy Allison Bishopric
*   Coppell, Herbert, *White-Cottage-By-the-Sea*
    Cordier, Auguste Julien, Jr., *Kyalami*
    Cornell, Irwin Hewlett
    Cornell, William Frank
    Cory, Helen Hinda Seldon

    Couric, Katie
        (aka Katherine Anne Couric)
    Coy, James Joseph, Jr.
    Coy, James Joseph, III
    Craig, Dr. Stuart Lessley
*   Crane, Thomas
    Creel, Alexandra Diodate Gardiner,
        Manor House
    Cullman, Joseph Fredrick, III
*   Culver, Austin H.
    Cummins, Stephen Swete, *Greycroft*
    Cushman, Blinn Sill, Jr.
    Daniels, John
        [*see* Kaplan entry]
    Darrow, Daniel, *Mayfair House*
*   Davies, Francis Herbert, *Tidelands*
    Davis, Charlotte Frances Rowe
    Day, Thomas Mills, Jr.
    Dayton, E. T.
        [*see* A. Huntting entry]
*   DeFelice, Gian Palo
*   Dean, Howard Brush, Jr.
    DeGraff, James Wilde, *Cherridune*
*   de Kay, Charles, *Abrigada*
    de Kay, Ormonde, Sr.
    de Kooning, Willem
    De Koven, Louis Besant Wadsworth,
        Bruton Braes
    de Liagre, Alfred, Jr., *Swan Cove*
        (aka Alfred Gustav Etienne de Liagre, Jr.)
    Della Femina, Jerry
        (aka Gennaro Tomas Della Femina)
    De Palma, Brian Russell
*   de Rose, Edward, *Millfield*
    Deutsch, Donny
        (aka Donald Jay Deutsch)
    De Vecchi, Robert Paolo
    Devendorf, Alfred Ervin, *El Paraiso*
*   Devereaux, Jack
    Devereaux, John Drew
*   Devine, William J., *Swanscot*
    DeVoe, Raymond Forsyth, Sr.
    DeVries, Mary Lange
        (aka Mary MacKinnon)
    Dewey, Charles Schuveldt, Jr.
    Dickerman, William Carter, Sr., *Dune Dee*
    Dimon, Michael
        [*see* Gardiner entry]
    Dodd, John Mingus, III, *The Kennels*
    d'Olier, Franklin Woolman, Jr.
    Donoho, Gaines Ruger
        (aka Ruger Donoho),
        Willow Bend / Under the Willows
    Donovan, Roberta Gosman
    Dougherty, Bertha Shults, *Westmeath*
    Dougherty, Frazer Lowber Welsh
    Douglas, Graham
    Douglas, Robert Graham Dunn
        (aka Robert Graham Dunn Douglass)
    Dowdney, Louis Purcell
    Dowling, Robert Whittle, *South Wind*
    Downey, Robert, Jr.

Villages

EAST HAMPTON (cont'd)
    Dragon, Edward F.
        [*see* Ossorio entry]
    Draper, Frances S. Haggerty, *Duneside*
* Drew, John, Jr., *Kyalami*
    Dubow, Arthur Myron
    Duke, Anthony Drexel, Sr., *Harbor House*
* Dunbar, Arthur T.
    Dunn, Dr. James Manning
    Duryea, Walter Bartow
    Eastman, Joseph
    Edwards, Everett Joshua
        [*see* Talmage entry]
    Edwards, Harkness, Sr.
    Edwards, James Cook, Sr.
* Edwards, James McPherson
    Edwards, Dr. Ogden Matthias, Jr., *Dunehurst*
    Edwards, Walter, Jr., *Kilkare*
    Edwards, William Henry Leonard, *Kilkare*
* Eidlitz, Cyrus Lazelle Warner, *Overlea*
    Eldredge, George
    Eldredge, George A. [Eldredge owned two houses in the Village of East Hampton.]
    Elliott, William, Jr.
    Ely, John Ingraham, *Hell-Gate*
    Ely, Laurence Driggs, Sr., *Olde Trees*
    Embury, Aymar, II, *Third House*
    Eno, Alfred Joseph
    Ephron, Nora
* Erdmann, Dr. John Frederic, *Coxwould*
    Erwin, Daniel Peart, Jr.
    Ethridge, George
* Evans, Benjamin Franklin, *Dunemead*
* Evans, James Hurlburt
    Farrington, Selwyn Kip, Jr., *Finning Out*
    Feldstein, Dr. Gary
    Fennelly, Leo C.
    Finkbeiner, Dr. John A., *Second Dune*
    Fiore, Christopher J.
        [*see* Beaumont entry]
    Fish, Sidney Webster
* Flannery, John
        [*see* Beaumont entry]
    Fleming, Henry Stuart, *The Green Flag*
    Fleming, Matthew Corry, Sr.
    Flinn, George Hamilton, Sr.
    Flinn, Lawrence, Jr., *Over Hook* [Flinn owned three houses in the Village of East Hampton.]
    Flinn, Lawrence, Sr., *Sea Song*
    Ford, James Bishop, *Pudding Hill*
    Ford, William Clay, Sr., *Dunemere*
    Fox, Alvin Gibbs
    Franey, Pierre
* Frankel, Evan M., *Brigadoon*
    Fraser, Alexander, *Wilsheron*
    Fraser, Ronald Goodall
    Friedman, Marvin Ross
* Fuhrman, Gary L. [Fuhrman owned two houses in the Village of East Hampton.]
    Fuller, Edward Reinow, *Tall Trees*
    Gallagher, Thomas, *Cove Hollow Farm*
* Gallatin, Frederic, *Breezy Lawn*

* Gallatin, James, *The Rainbow*
* Gallatin, James Nicholson
    Gardiner, David Lion, Jr., *White House*
        [*see* D. L. Gardiner, Sr. entry]
    Gardiner, David Lion, Sr., *White House*
    Gardiner, Olney Mairs
        [*see* W. Gardiner entry]
    Gardiner, Robert Alexander, *Maidstone Hall*
    Gardiner, Robert David Lion, *Manor House*
        [Gardiner owned two houses in East Hampton; one on Gardiner's Island and the other in the village.]
* Gardiner, Miss Sarah Diodati, *White House*
        [Gardiner owned two houses in East Hampton; one on Gardiner's Island and the other in the village.]
    Gardiner, Winthrop, Jr.,
        The Mill Cottage/Hill Cottage/Mill Cottage
    Gardiner, Winthrop, Sr., *Deurcant House*
    Garten, Jeffery E.
    Geary, John White, III
        (aka John White Geary, Jr.)
    Geddes, Gerald Maxwell
    Geffen, David Lawrence
    Gerli, Anne Woodin Harvey, *Maya*
    Gianis, Socrates George, Sr.
    Gilmartin, ____
        [*see* Coleman entry]
    Gleason, Carlisle Joyslin, *Greyshingles*
    Godwin, Courtlandt, *Crowland*
    Goelet, Alexandra Gardiner Creel,
        Manor House
    Gordon, ____
        [*see* Hamlin entry]
    Gordon, George Breed
    Gordon, Martin
        [*see* Gallatin entry]
    Gossler, Philip Green, Jr.
    Gottlieb, Adolph
    Gowen, George W., II
    Grace, Morgan Hatton, Jr.
    Graham, Lucie Wilshire
    Gram, Carl William, Jr., *Maya*
    Green, Adolph
    Green, William Walker, *End of the Lane*
    Greer, The Reverend David Hummell,
        Yondermere
    Greer, Lawrence
    Gruen, Robert L.
* Gruss, Martin David
    Gunster, Joseph Frederick, *Ten Elms*
* Hackstaff, Charles Ludovic, *Tarriawyle*
    Haag, Joseph, Jr.
    Hall, William Claiborne
    Halsey, Frank
        [*see* Kimball entry]
    Halsted, Dr. Harbeck
    Hamlin, Mary Elkins Paxton, *Windward*
        [Hamlin owned several houses in the Village of East Hampton.]
* Hamilton, Chico
        (aka Foreststorn Hamilton)
    Hamilton, Gordon C.
    Hammond, John Carnahan, *Aunt Phoebe's*
    Hammond, Percy, *Aunt Phoebe's*

Villages

EAST HAMPTON (cont'd)

* Hand, John White
  Hanke, George Frederick Robert, Sr.
  Hansen, Curt Eric
  Hardy, Charles J., Jr.
  Hare, Richard Vincent
  Harkness, Lamon Vanderburg
  Harris, William Victor (aka Victor Harris),
    Dune Home
  Hartley, Theodore Ringwalt
  Hassam, Frederick Childe
    (aka Childe Hassam), *Willow Bend*
  Hattersley, Lelia Marie Chopin,
    Captain's House
  Havens, Valentine Britton
* Haverland, Michael Robert
  Haynes, Justin O'Brien, Sr.
  Hedges, Burke Osborn
  Hedges, Dayton
    (aka William Dayton Hedges)
  Hedges, Henry Denison
  Hedges, James M.
    [*see* Gruen entry]
  Hedges, John Daniel
  Hedges, William
    [*see* Mapes entry]
  Helier, David
  Helm, George Washington, Sr.
  Helm, John E.
  Helm, John LaRue, Jr.
  Helmuth, Dr. William Tod, Jr., *Kumonin*
  Hendrix, Clifford Rathbone, Sr.
  Hensel, Clarence Hopkins, *Dunemere*
  Heppenheimer, William Christian, III
* Herrick, Dr. Everett, *Pudding Hill*
* Herter, Albert, *Près Choisis / The Creeks*
  Hess, Harry Bellas
  Heuser, Miss Maria S.
    [*see* C. F. Ogden entry]
  Heyman, Stephen J.
  Highet, Gilbert Albert
  Hill, Robert Carmer, *Grey Gardens*
* Hillman, Murray
* Hinton, Alfred Post, *Roads Meet*
* Hinton, James William, *Foxall*
  Hirschfeld, Elie
* Hobart, Garret Augustus, Jr., *T-Other House*
  Hobart, Henry Lee, *Sommariva*
  Hodson, Dr. James M.
    [*see* Adams entry]
* Hoffman, David Lehman, Sr.
  Holleran, Frank Joseph
* Hollister, Dr. Frederick Kellogg
    [Hollister owned three house in the
    Village of East Hampton.]
* Holmes, Jay
* Homans, Eugene Vanderpool, *Sea Spray*
* Homans, Marion Bennett
  Hopkins, John Appleton Haven, Sr.
* Hopkinson, Russell
  Hoppin, Henry Preston

  Hufty, Frances May Archbold
  Huntting, Annie
  Hutton, John Laurence, Sr., *Peep O'Day*
  Hutton, William Langdon, *Peep O'Day*
  Hyde, Frank Dana, *Adana*
  Icahn, Carl Celian
* Ireland, Anna Mary Brown
  Jackson, Lionel Stewart, Sr.
  Jaffe, Stanley Richard
* James, Ellery Sedgwick, Sr.
    (aka William Ellery Sedgwick James, Sr.),
    Heather Dune
* James, Laura Brevort Sedgwick, *Blomioff*
* Jefferys, Charles Peter Beauchamp, Sr.,
    Sommariva
* Jefferys, Harry Leapold, *Duneden*
  Jenkins, Edward Elliot
* Jenney, William Sherman, *Little Close*
  Jewett, Edward Hull, Jr.
  Jewett, Edward Hull, Sr., *The Ink Pot*
* Joel, Billy
    (aka William Martin Joel)
  Johnson, Miss Edith [Johnson owned two houses
    in the Village of East Hampton.]
  Johnson, Harry J.
    [*see* Pardridge entry]
  Johnson, James Loring, *Nid de Papillion*
* Johnson, Mary Newlin Verplanck, *The Ingle*
* Johnson, Servetus Fisher, *Onadune*
    [Johnson owned three houses in the Village of
    East Hampton.]
  Jones, Dr. Oswald Roberts
  Joyner, Dr. James Craig
  Julianelli, Charles A.
* Kaplan, Barton
  Kaplan, Jacob Merrill
  Karan, Donna Ivy Faske
  Kast, Marie Schultze
  Keim, John Richard
  Kelley, William Vallandigham, Sr.
  Kelsey, Stephen Tomlinson, Sr., *Leecott*
  Kennedy, Arthur
    [*see* Terbell entry]
  Kennedy, Michael John, *Kilkare*
  Kerr, Selina Alva Coe, *Fithian House*
  Kessner, Steven
  Kimball, Alden, *Eastern View*
  Kimball, Charles Edmunds, Jr., *Purple House*
  Kimball, Charles Edmunds, Sr.
* King, Hamilton, *Spindrift*
  King, William
  Kingsley, Virginia Pulleyn
  Kingsley, Walton Pearl
  Kiser, John William, III
    (aka John William Kiser, Jr.), *The Lodge*
* Klein, Calvin
    (aka Calvin Richard Klein)
  Klenk, William Clifford, Jr.
  Klotz, Charles Arthur
  Krakoff, Reed
* Krech, Dr. Shepard, Sr., *Briar Patch*
  Knox, Maria Speir Reid

Villages

EAST HAMPTON (cont'd)
  Kuchin, Kenneth Sidney
  Lachman, Judith
    [*see* Bradley entry]
* LaForest, Helen A., *The Apaquogue*
  LaForest, Henry A., *The Apaquogue*
* LaMonte, George Mason [LaMonte built several houses in the Village of East Hampton.]
  Langben, Halfred Alfred
* Lardner, Ringgold Wilmer, Sr.
    (aka Ring Lardner),
    Iona Dune / The Mange
* Larkin, Adrian Hoffman, *Green Frog*
  Larkin, Rosanne Roudebush, *Stonybroke*
* Laspia, Dr. Michael R.
  Laughlin, Alexander Mellon, Jr.
  Laughlin, Alexander Mellon, Sr.
  Laughlin, David Walker
* Lawrence, John Custis
  Leaman, Alfred Valentine, Jr., *Sunset Cottage*
  Leaman, Alfred Valentine, III,
    Swan Cross and *Sunset Cottage*
  Le Brecht, Shelia Tucker Brown
  Lee, James Thomas, *Avery Place*
* Lee, Thomas Haskell
  Leith, Donald E.
* Lembcke, George Albert, *The Chimneys*
  Leonard, Stephen Joseph, Sr., *Waterwood*
  Lewis, Ida May Barbey
  Lilley, Alexander Neil, Sr., *Crossways*
  Livingston, Ruth Helene Moller
* Lloyds, Richard
  Lockwood, William Andrew, *Ivy Cottage*
* Lockwood, Williston Benedict, *Lockdune*
  Loeb, Daniel Seth
  Lundberg, John K.
    [*see* Adams entry]
  Loomis, Alfred Lee, Sr.
  Lutkins, Clinton Stephen, *Hedges Row*
* Lyon, Marvin Thomas
  Mackay, The Reverend William R.
  MacKinnon, Mary
    [*see* Cloud entry]
* Macklowe, Harry B. [Macklowe owned two houses in the Village of East Hampton.]
  Macy, Valentine Everit, Jr., *Longlast*
  Maharam, Donald H.
  Maguire, Edward, Sr., *Hayloft*
  Main, Charles E., *Main House*
  Mairs, Isabel Tasker Gardiner;
    (aka Isabel Fairfax Gardiner Mairs;
    Isabel T. L. Gardiner Mairs), *Hearthstone*
  Mairs, Olney Blanchard, Sr.
  Maloney, William Raywood, Sr., *Glendella*
  Mann, Henry, *San Souci*
  Manners, Laurette Helen Cooney
    (aka Laurette Taylor)
  Mansell, Frank Luther
  Manson, Thomas Lincoln, III, *Millfield*
  Mapes, Maie Bennett, *Purple House*

  Mapes, Victor, *Century Cottage*
    (aka Sidney Sharp)
  Martin, Laura Elizabeth Young
  Marvel, Josiah Peter
  Mascheroni, John
* Massey, Maurice Richardson, Jr., *Pond's Edge*
  Materson, M.
    [*see* Levering entry]
  Maxwell, Elliott, *Pineleigh*
  Mayo, Miss Marie Louise, *Bonnie Dune*
  Mayo–Smith, Richmond, Sr.
* McAlpin, Cordelia Maria Rose, *Roselea*
  McAlpin, David Hunter, II
* McAlpin, George Lodowich, Sr., *Dune Alpin*
  McAlpin, Malcolm Evans, *Dunemead*
  McCall, Clifford Hyde, Sr., *Kipsveen*
* McCall, Edward Everett, *Evsdune*
  McConnell, David Hall, III
  McConnell, Neil Anderson
  McCord, David Walter, *Hither House*
  McCormick, Robert Elliott
  McKeon, Robert Brian
* McKittrick, Marjorie Holland
* McLanahan, Scott, *Nevermind*
    [*see* Sinclair entry]
  Meehan, Joseph Ansbro
  Mercati, Count Leonardo, *Meltemi*
  Mercer, Norman J.
* Mershon, The Reverend Stephen Lyon, Sr.,
    Sea Side Cottage
  Michaels, Lorne
    (aka Lorne Lipowitz)
  Miller, Dudley Livingston, Sr.
  Mills, Abraham, *The Chalet*
  Milne, John Cruickshank, II
  Miner, Mary Louise Woodin, *Mi Dune*
    [Miner owned two house in the Village of East Hampton.
  Mirick, Edna B de Beixedon, *Tanglebrae*
  Mitchell, Christopher
  Mitchell, Ledyard, Sr.
    (aka William Ledyard Mitchell), *Dunes*
  Mnuchin, Alan Geoffrey
  Moffett, James Andrew, Jr., *Inadune*
  Monberg, Miss Hedwig
  Montgomery, Robert
    (aka Henry Montgomery, Jr.;
    Robert Montgomery, Sr.), *Swan Cove*
  Moore, Dr. Oliver Semon, Jr.
* Moran, Thomas, Jr., *The Studio*
  Moranti, Paul Joseph, *Lago–Del–Mare*
  Morgan Carol Ann
    [*see* Paxton entry]
  Morris, Theodore Wilson, Jr.
  Morse, Tyler
  Morton, Peter
* Munroe, Dr. George E., Jr., *Wayside*
  Munroe, Marjory, *Wayside*
* Murphy, Gerald Clery, *Swan Cove*
  Myrick, Julian Southall,
    Apaquogue/Apaquogue House
  Nadal, Charles Coleman

EAST HAMPTON (cont'd)

* * Nash, Stephen Edward, *Crossways*
  [Nash built two houses in East Hampton]
* * Nash, Thomas
* Nederlander, Robert Elliot, Sr.
* Nesbit, Elizabeth Clossey, *Seaward*
* * Newton, Francis, *Fulling Mill Farm*
* * Newman, Angeline Ensign
* * Newton, The Reverend Richard Heber, Sr., *Dunecott*
* Nichols, Harold Willis, Jr., *Crows Nest*
* Nichols, Harold Wills, Jr., *Dunehurst*
* Noble, Francis Osborn, *Solidago*
* * Noble, Mark Ainslie
* Northrop, John Burr, Sr.
* * Nugent, Dr. Paul Fordham, Sr.
* * Oakley, Ralph Lawrence
* O'Brien, W. Howard, Sr.
* O'Connell, J. J.
  [*see* Potter entry]
* Ogden, James Lawrence, Jr.
* * Ogden, Miss Clara Foster
* Olin, John Merrill
* * Onderdonk, Dr. Thomas Williams
* Ordway, Samuel Gilman, *Dellwood*
* Ordway, Samuel Hanson, Jr.
* Ordway, Samuel Hanson, Sr., *Subacawan*
* Osborn, Jeremiah, Sr.
* * Osborne, Burnett Mulford
* Osborne, Dr. Edward Monroe, Sr.
* * Osborne, Mrs. George A.
* * Osborne, Joseph Septimus
* Osborne, Nelson Cook, Sr.
* Osserman, Stanley, *The Gatehouse*
* Ossorio, Alfonso Angel, *The Creeks*
* Pagel, Elinor Robertson Bronaugh, *Elsufral*
* Pardridge, Albert Jerome, *Duneside*
* Parker, Cecil Carlton, *Postscript*
* Parker, Roy Tilden, Jr.
* * Paxton, The Reverend John Randolph, Sr., *Windward*
* Peddy, John Richard, *Pudding Hill*
* Perelman, Ronald Owen
* Perot, Edward Sansom, Jr.
* Peters, Marion Louise Smith
* Peterson, Peter George
* * Phillips, Fleming Stanhope
* * Phillips, Martha Bagg
* * Pierson, Warren Lee, Sr., *Furthermoor*
* Pittman, Ernest Wetmore
* Pollock, Jackson
* Pool, Mary Baldwin Schwab
* Poor, James Harper, *As You Like It*
* Pope, Thomas
  [*see* Joyner entry]
* Potter, Dickson Bayard, *Falaise Farm*
* * Potter, Eugene Clifford, *A–Y–Mor*
* * Potter, Frederick Gaul [Potter owned two houses in the Village of East Hampton.]
* Preusse, Charles Francis
* * Pruyn, Miss Mary Lansing

* * Pruyn, Miss Neltje Knickerbocker
* Pulleyn, John William, Sr.
* Putnam, Harrington, Jr.
* * Quackenbush, Schuyler [Quackenbush owned two houses in the Village of East Hampton.]
* Rabbe, Richard Frederick, *Seafields*
* Radziwill, Caroline Lee Bouvier
  (aka Lee Radziwill)
* Rahr, Stewart J.
* Ramee, Joseph Russell, *Twinmill*
* Ramsay, Herbert Hartley
* * Randell, Caroline Amelia Boardman
* Ranieri, Salvatore Anthony
* Rattray, Arnold Elsmere
* Rattray, Everett Tennant
* Raymond, Dana Merriam
* Regan, John Nicholas, Sr.
* Reid, Archibald Mudge
* * Reid, Wallace
* Reiswig, Gary D.
* Rentschler, George Adam, Jr., *Summertime*
* * Reutershan, Paul V.
* Reynolds, Ardis J.
  [*see* Levering entry]
* * Rice, Dr. Clarence Charles
* Rice, Ernest H., Sr.
* * Rice, Henry Grantland
  (aka Grantland Rice)
* Richard, Auguste
* Richard, Mark Gadd
* * Richards, Benjamin, Jr., *Clas-des-Lilas*
* Richards, Miss Louisa Verplanck
  [*see* B. Richards, Jr. entry]
* * Richards, Richard Draper
  (aka Richards Follett), *Little Too Close*
* * Richey, The Reverend Alban, Sr., *Rosebrae*
* * Richey, The Reverend Thomas, Sr.
* * Rifkind, Robert Sanger
* Roarick, Helen Osborne
  [*see* Maloney entry]
* Robert, Stephen Kniznick
* Roberts, Dudley DeVore, Jr., *Whale Off*
* Roberts, Dr. Dudley DeVore, Sr., *Outabounds*
* Roberts, George Hewitt, Jr., *Furtherfield*
* Roberts, Walter Scott
* Robertson, Clifford Parker, III
  (aka Cliff Robertson)
* Robertson, Hugh James, Jr.
* Robinson, Felding S.
* Robinson, Lucius Franklin, Jr., *Fulling Mill Farm*
* Robinson, Thomas
  [*see* DeVries entry]
* Rose, Daniel
* * Rose, Marshall
* Rosen, Robert
  [*see* Poor entry]
* Rosenstein, Barry
* Rosinsky, Harold Jack
  (aka Harold Jack Rosinski)
* Ross, Steven Jay
  (aka Steven Jay Rechnitz), *Cody House*

Villages

EAST HAMPTON (cont'd)

Rosset, Barnet Lee, Jr.
   (aka Barney Rosset)
Roudebush, John Heywood, *Stonybroke*
Rounick, Jack A.
Rowe, William Wallace, Sr.
Rumbough, Stanley Hutton
* Rumbough, Stanley Maddox, Jr.
Ruxton, Philip, *Cairnhill*
Ryan, Bruce Edgar
Ryan, Frederick Behrens, Sr., *East of 69*
Ryan, Richard Nelson, Jr.
Salembier, Harold Paul, *Dormie Dune*
* Salembier, Paul Albert, *Seacroft*
* Saltzman, Renny B.
Sandelman, Jonathan Everett
* Satterthwaite, James Sheafe, Sr.
Scheerer, Joseph Durand, Sr.
* Scheerer, Paul Renner, Jr.
Schey, Robert Paul, *Lauralawn*
Schmidt, Dederick Herman
* Schmidt, Max Eberhardt
   (aka Max Everhart Smith)
Schulman, Lowell M., *Beechwood*
Schultz, Howard Mark
* Schurman, George Wellington, *Beachclose*
* Schurman, Jacob Gould, Sr., *Breezy Knowe*
Schwarzman, Stephen Allen
* Scull, Robert C.
Seabury, Samuel, *Wyandanch Acres*
Seaman, Joseph Husband, Sr., *Seamanor*
* Sedacca, Joseph M.
Seegal, Frederic Milton
* Seinfeld, Jerry
   (aka Jerome Allen Seinfeld)
Seligson, William
* Sewell, Robert Van Vorst
Shafran, Irving
Shepherd, James Gardner
* Shepherd, Myrtle Abby Leach
* Shyer, Henry
Simmons, Edward Emerson
Simmons, Russell Wendell
Simon, William Edward, Sr.
Simonds, Francis May, *Heather Hill*
Simonds, Robert McClellen
   [*see* Lembcke entry]
Sinclair, Earl Westwood, *Fairlawn*
Sinclaire, Paul, *Georgica Farm*
Skidmore, James Bond, *Honeysuckle Hedge*
* Skidmore, John Drake
Skidmore, Samuel Tredwell, II, *Idlerest*
Slifka, Alan Bruce
Smith, Frank
   [*see* Seaman entry]
Smith, Warren G.
Snow, Violetta Pierce, *Windermere*
* Solley, Dr. Fred Palmer, *Tanglebrae*
* Solomon, Peter Jay
Soule, Henri Remy
* Spaeth, Otto Lucien, Sr.

* Spaeth, Eloise O'Mara
Spalding, Jesse, II, *Pineleigh*
* Spielberg, Steven Allan, *Quelle Farm*
* Spring, Preston Brady, Sr., *Winklehawk*
Stanton, Arthur
   [*see* Gunster entry]
* Stanton, Dr. Frederick Lester
* Steele, The Reverend James Nevett, Sr.,
   Dunemere
Steele, Louis Thorton, *Cobwebs*
* Steinberg, Robert Michael
Stephanopoulos, George Robert
Sterling, Oliver James, Sr.
Stern, Henry Root, Sr.
* Stern, Joel Mark
Stern, Leonard Norman
Stern, Robert Arthur Morton
Stewart, Martha Helen Kostyra [Stewart owned
   two houses in the Village of East Hampton.]
Stevens, Leighton H.
Stimson, Henry Clark
Stoddard, Mrs. Lillian M.
   [*see* Donoho entry]
Stokes, The Reverend John Dunlap
Stokes, Lydia
   [*see* Campbell entry]
Stone, Edward Durell, Sr.
Stone, Miss Emma
   [*see* Butler entry]
Stratton, Clara Cooper
Strong, George Arthur
Strong, Mrs. James M., Jr.
   [*see* Donoho entry]
Strong, Theron George, *The Dolphins*
Sutphen, Henry Randolph, Jr., *Bowling Green*
Sutphen, Henry Randolph, Sr., *Bowling Green*
Sweetser, Jesse William
Talmadge, John Frelinghuysen,
   Tollemache House
Talmage, Mary Breck Vaill, *Century Cottage*
* Talmage, Mary Breck Vaill, *New Century Cottage*
* Talmage, Mary Breck Vaill, *Westover*
Talmage, Mary Breck Vaill, *Purple House*
Talmage, Rockwell Dwight, *Century Cottage*
Talmage, Rockwell Dwight, *New Century Cottage*
Talmage, Rockwell Dwight, *Westover*
* Talmage, The Reverend Thomas DeWitt
Taylor, Harriet
Taylor, Irving Howland
Terbell, Edward Dyer, *Maidstone Hall*
* Terbell, Henry S., Sr.
Terian, Julianna Mae Curran
Terian, Peter Gabriel
Terry, Dr. Arthur Hutchinson, Jr., *Causeway*
* Thaw, William, III, *Dune Top*
Thiele, Albert Edward, Jr., *Taramar*
Thiele, Roger Harvey, *Taramar*
* Thomas, Augustus
Thompson, Charles Griswold
Thompson, Dr. Frederick Roeck
Thompson, Michael P.
   [*see* Beaumont entry]

Villages

EAST HAMPTON (cont'd)

    Thorne, Henry Sanford, *Rowdy Hall*
* Thorp, Joseph Greenleaf
    Tiedeman, Irvin Bruce, Sr.
    Tiffany, Nathan Newton, III
    Tillich, The Reverend Paul Johannes
* Tishman, Peter Valentine
    Tobin, Abraham Robert
        [*see* Jewett entry]
    Todd, John Reynard, Sr.
    Todd, Webster Bray, Sr.
    Topping, Daniel Reid, Sr.
    Trippe, Charles White, Sr.
    Trippe, Juan Terry
* Tuck, Frederick W., Jr., *Off-the-Teeee*
    Tyler, John Alexander
    Tyson, Mark
    Vaill, Isabella Mary Breck, *Century Cottage*
* Van Brunt, Arthur Hoffman, Sr., *The Breezes*
    Vanderbilt, Oliver DeGray, III, *Old Post Office*
    Van Rensselaer, Kiliaen, III, *Millfield*
* Vaughan, Eliza Jennie Potter, *Beulahside*
    Velie, John Deere, II
    Volckening, Lloyd Irwin
* Voorhees, Dr. James Ditmars
        (aka Dr. James Ditmars Van Voorhees)
    Wainwright, Carroll Livingston, Jr.
* Wainwright, Carroll Livingston, Sr., *Gullcrest*
    Wainwright, John Howard
    Wainwright, Stuyvesant, II, *Green Oaks*
    Wainwright, Stuyvesant, III
    Walker, Bayard, Sr., *Normandie*
    Walker, Delos
    Walker, George Gholson, Sr.
    Walker, Dr. John Baldwin, Sr., *Tarriawyle*
    Warburton, Consuelo Vanderbilt
* Ward, Newell Jube, Sr.
    Wardle, H. Allen
    Warner, Eltinge Fowler, Jr., *Cima Del Mundo*
    Wasey, Louis Rice, *Vingt-et-Un*
    Washburn, George
    Washburn, Ira Hedges, Sr.
    Washburn, Mary Rosenia,
        Apaquoge/Apaquogue House
    Washburn, Watson,
        Apaquoge/Apaquogue House
    Watts, Harry Wildred
    Weaver, Spencer Fullerton, Sr., *Spencecliff*
    Webster, Dr. Bruce Peck
    Weeks, John Kirkland, Sr.
    Weeks, John Lafayette
    Weinstein, Joseph
    Welch, Leo Dewey
* Wessel, Homer Augustus, Sr., *Mill Crest*
    Weston, Catherine Boudinot Stimson,
        Seven Gables
    Wheeler, John Neville
    Wheelock, John Hall, *Wuthering*
* Wheelock, William Almy
* Wheelock, Dr. William Efner, *Wuthering*
    Whitney, Elwood

    Whittemore, William John, *Robinsfield*
    Whittle, Chris
        (aka H. Christopher Whittle), *Briar Patch*
* Wilborg, Frank Bestow, *The Dunes*
    Williams, Eugene Flewilyn, Jr.
    Wolff, Caroline Smith Snowden, *Shadowmere*
    Wood, Howard Ogden, Sr.
    Wood, Howard Ogden, Jr., *Tarriawyle*
    Wood, Robert Williams, Jr.
    Wood, Wilfrid
* Woodhouse, Lorenzo Easton, *The Fens*
* Woodhouse, Lorenzo Guernsey, *Greycroft*
* Woodin, William Hartman, Sr., *Dune House*
    Woodward, Shaun Anthony
    Woolley, Knight
* Worthington, Louise Grant
    Wright, John Howie, Jr.
    Wright, John Howie, III
* Yates, James Saville
    Yates, John Carrington
    Zamichow, Bernard
    Zaslav, David M.
    Zellweger, Renee Kathleen
    Zevely, James William, Sr.
    Zuckerman, Mortimer Benjamin

MONTAUK

* Abbe, James Edward, Jr., *Abbey Cottage*
    Agnew, Dr. Cornelius Rea, Sr.
    Akin, Robert Macomber, Jr., *Hilltop House*
    Albee, Edward Franklin, III
    Alfis, M. V.
        [*see* Garni entry]
    Andrews, William Loring
    Aubert, Marion Eugenia Bragg, *Star Acres*
* Avedon, Richard
    Beard, Peter Hill
* Benson, Arthur W., *Weeweecho*
    Benson, Mary, *Weeweecho*
        [*see* A. Benson entry]
    Biggs, Florence
        [*see* Hoyt entry]
* Bragg, Caleb Smith
    Brisbane, Arthur
* Brown, Lathrop, *The Windmill*
    Cavett, Richard Alva
        (aka Dick Cavett)
        [Cavett owns two houses in Montauk.]
* Church, Richard E.
* Church, Richard Newton Loomis
    Conway, Edmund Virgil, II
    Conway, Edmund Virgil, III
    Daily, Marion
        [*see* Wood entry]
    de Forest, Henry Grant
    De Niro, Robert, Jr.
    Drexler, Millard S.
        (aka Mickey Drexler)
    DuVal, Guy, *Awepesha*
    Entenmann, Charles, Sr.
    Entenmann, Robert William, Sr.

Villages

MONTAUK (cont'd)

* Fisher, Carl Graham, Sr.
  [Fisher owned two houses in Montauk.]
  Garni, Adolph
    (aka Adolf Garni)
  Goddard, Sidney
    [*see* Hoyt entry]
  Gosman, Mary Ellen Harrington
  Harper, Marion Clay, Jr.
  Hirtenstein, Michael
  Hone, Harold
  Hopkins, Lindsey, Jr.
  Hoyt, Alfred Miller
  Jackson, Elbert McGran
  Kennedy, David E., *Second House*
* Krieger, Dr. Howard P.
  Lauren, Ralph
    (aka Ralph Lifshitz)
  Levi, Charles Matthew
* Levy–Church, Kenneth
    (aka Kenneth Wayne Church)
  Lindemann, Adam Marc
    [Lindemann owned two houses in Montauk.]
* Lowenstein, Peter
  Lundbergh, Holger, *Bayberry*
* Madoff, Bernard Lawrence
    (aka Bernie Madoff)
  Marsh, Marion Bolton, *Windway*
* McCaffray, Walter Peck, *Sandpiper Hill*
  Monell, Theodore, Jr.
  Monell, Theodore, Sr.
  Morrisey, Paul, *Eothen*
  Orr, Alexander Ector
  Rheinstein, Sidney
  Roth, Steven
  Sanger, Henry
  Sanger, Lilian, *Moorland*
  Satterlee, Dr. Francis Le Roy, Jr.,
    House of Four Winds
  Schnabel, Julian
* Schwab Laurence, Sr.
  Simon, Paul Frederic
  Sischy, Ingrid Barbara
  Smith, Dr. Dewey
    [*see* Hoyt entry]
* Thomas, Andrew Jackson
  Tweed, Harrison, *Tick Hall*
  Vogel, George
    [*see* Andrews entry]
  Wagner, Corienne
    [*see* Andrews entry]
  Walker, Dr. William Henry, Jr.
  Warhol, Andy
    (aka Andrew Warhola, Jr.), *Eothen*
  Wasey, Louis Rice
  Weber, Bruce
  Wenner, Jann Simon
* Wood, Arthur B.
    (aka Arthur W. B. Wood)

SAG HARBOR

Lowe, Emma Lawrence Marshall

Biographical Sources Consulted

Biographical Dictionaries Master Index 1975–1976. Detroit: Gale Research Co., 1975.

Biography and Genealogy Master Index 1981–1985. Detroit: Gale Research Co., 1985.

Biography and Genealogy Master Index 1986–1990. Detroit: Gale Research Co., 1990.

Biography and Genealogy Master Index 1991–1995. Detroit: Gale Research Co., 1995.

Brooklyn Daily Eagle Online 1841-1902, Internet.

Current Biography Yearbook. New York: The H. W. Wilson Co. [selected volumes]

Dow Jones News Internet Retrieval.

The Eagle and Brooklyn: The Record of the Progress of the Brooklyn Daily Eagle. 2 vols. Brooklyn, NY: The Brooklyn Eagle, 1893.

Levy, Felice, ed. *Obituaries on File.* New York: Facts on File, 1979.

Lexis Nexis Academic Universe, Internet.

Malone, Dumas, ed. *Dictionary of American Biography.* New York: Charles Scribner's Sons, 1935.

The National Cyclopaedia of American Biography. Clifton, NJ: James T. White & Co., 1984.

Newsday Internet Retrieval.

New York State's Prominent and Progressive Men. 2 vols. New York: New York Tribune, 1900.

The New York Times Index. New York: The New York Times. [annual obituaries from 1979–1997]

The New York Times Obituaries Index, vol. 1, 1858–1968. New York: The New York Times, 1970.

The New York Times Obituaries Index, vol. 2, 1969–1978. New York: The New York Times, 1980.

Prominent Families of New York. New York: The Historical Co., 1898.

Standard and Poor's Register of Corporations, Directors and Executives. Charlottesville, VA: Standard and Poors, Inc. [selected volumes]

Who's Who in America. Chicago: Marquis Who's Who, Inc. [selected volumes]

Who's Who in Finance and Industry. Chicago: Marquis Who's Who, Inc. [selected volumes]

Who's Who in New York. New York: Lewis Historical Publishing Co. [selected volumes]

Who's Who in New York City and State. New York: L. R. Hamersly Co., 1904–1960 [selected volumes]

Who's Who in the East. Chicago: Marquis Who's Who, Inc. [selected volumes]

Who's Who of American Women. Chicago: Marquis Who's Who, Inc. [selected volumes]

Who Was Who in America with World Notables. New Providence, NJ: Marquis Who's Who, Inc. [selected volumes]

Maps Consulted

Atlas of a Part of Suffolk County, Long Island, New York: South Side – Ocean Shore. Brooklyn: E. Belcher Hyde, Inc., 1916.

Dolph's Street, Road and Land Ownership Map of Suffolk County. New York: Dolph & Stewart, 1929.

Eastern Suffolk County New York Street Map. Maspeth, NY: Hagstrom Map Co., Inc., 2006.

Pease and Elliman Real Estate Map, c. 1930s.

Suffolk County, Long Island. Brooklyn: E. Belcher Hyde, Inc., 1902.

About the Authors

Judith and Raymond Spinzia are former Long Island residents, now residing in central Pennsylvania. Their first book, *Long Island: A Guide to New York's Suffolk and Nassau Counties* (New York: Hippocrene Books, 1988; 1991 revised; 2008 revised), is a standard reference book which has been used as a textbook for teaching Long Island history and can be found in almost all public libraries and schools on Long Island.

The Spinzias write and speak, jointly and separately, on a variety of Long Island-related subjects including the North and South Shore estates, Tiffany stained-glass windows, and the Vanderbilts of Long Island. On several occasions their lectures have been chosen by the former radio station of *The New York Times*, WQXR, as the cultural event of the day in the New York Metropolitan area. Additionally, they have been featured on local television and radio programs and in articles published by *The New York Times, Newsday*, and other regional newspapers.

The Spinzias served as Long Island history consultants for a local cable television channel that, in an effort to encourage local interest, aired material from their guidebook twice daily. They also were consultants for a Japanese television network for a documentary on Louis Comfort Tiffany and contributed material to the Arts and Entertainment Network's "Biography" series for its presentations on the Vanderbilt and Tiffany families.

Their six-volume documentation of Long Island's estate era presently includes:
Long Island's Prominent North Shore Families: Their Estates and Their Country Homes. 2 volumes, revised 2019.
Long Island's Prominent South Shore Families: Their Estates and Their Country Homes in the Towns of Babylon and Islip, 2007.
Long Island's Prominent Families in the Town of Hempstead: Their Estates and Their Country Homes, 2010.
Long Island's Prominent Families in the Town of Southampton: Their Estates and Their Country Homes, 2010.
Long Island's Prominent Families in the Town of East Hampton: Their Estates and Their Country Homes, 2020.

The following articles by the Spinzias can be downloaded at **spinzialongislandestates.com**:

Spinzia, Judith Ader.
"Artistry In Glass: Louis Comfort Tiffany's Legacy In Nassau County." *The Nassau County Historical Society Journal,* 1991:8-17.
"Artistry In Glass: The Undisputed Master, Our Oyster Bay Neighbor." *The Freeholder* 2 (Winter 1998):3-5; and 2 (Spring 1998):3-5, 24.
"Louis Comfort Tiffany: A Bibliography Relevant to the Man, His Work, and His Oyster Bay, Long Island, Home." 2010
"Women of Long Island: Clare Boothe Luce (1903-1987), The Long Island Connection" *The Freeholder* 2 (Summer 2009):3-5; 17-10.
"Women of Long Island: Cornelia Bryce Pinchot, Feminist, Social-Activist – The Long Islander Who Became First Lady of Pennsylvania." 2010
"Women of Long Island: Mary Elizabeth Jones; Rosalie Gardiner Jones." *The Freeholder* 11 (Spring 2007):2-7.
"Women of Long Island: Mary Williamson Averell Harriman; her daughter Mary Harriman Rumsey." *The Freeholder*, 12 (Spring 2008):8-9, 16-20.

Spinzia, Raymond E.
"Adultery, Drugs, Murder, Untimely Deaths, and Long Island's Prominent Families: A Tangled Web." 2011
"Elliott Roosevelt, Sr. – A Spiral Into Darkness" *The Freeholder* 12 (Fall 2007):3-7, 15-17.
"In Her Wake: The Story of Alva Smith Vanderbilt." *The Long Island Historical Journal* 6 (Fall 1993):96-105.
"The Involvement of Long Islanders in the Events Surrounding German Sabotage in the New York Metropolitan Area 1914-1917." 2019
"Long Island Statesmen and Diplomats." revised 2020
"Michael Straight and the Cambridge Spy Ring." *The Freeholder* 5 (Winter 2001): 3-5.
"Socialite Spies: The Grandchildren of Henry Baldwin Hyde, Sr." *East Islip Historical Society Newsletter* 16 (March 2008):1, 3.
"Society Chameleons: Long Island's Gentlemen Spies." *The Nassau County Historical Society Journal* 55 (2000):27-38.
"Sumner Welles: Brilliance and Tragedy." *The Freeholder* 9 (Winter 2005):8-9, 22.
"Those Other Roosevelts: The Fortescues." *The Freeholder* 11 (Summer 2006):8-9, 16-22.
"To Look in the Mirror and See Nothing: Long Islanders and the Office of Strategic Services and Its Successor, the Central Intelligence Agency." revised December 2017
"Winning the Franchise: Long Island Activists in the Fight for Woman's Suffrage and Their Opponents, Long Island's Anti-Suffragists." 2018

Spinzia, Raymond E. and Judith A. Spinzia.
"*Gatsby:* Myths and Realities of Long Island's North Shore Gold Coast." *The Nassau County Historical Society Journal* 52 (1997):16–26.

www.ingramcontent.com/pod-product-compliance
Lightning Source LLC
Chambersburg PA
CBHW080717300426
44114CB00019B/2407